# 14th Workshop on Computational Approaches to Subjectivity, Sentiment, and Social Media Analysis (WASSA 2024)



Bangkok, Thailand
15 August 2024

ISBN: 979-8-3313-0181-1

**Printed from e-media with permission by:**

Curran Associates, Inc.
57 Morehouse Lane
Red Hook, NY 12571

CURRAN ASSOCIATES INC. proceedings.com

**Some format issues inherent in the e-media version may also appear in this print version.**



Association for Computational Linguistics
209 N. Eighth Street
Stroudsburg, Pennsylvania 18360

Phone: 1-570-476-8006
Fax: 1-570-476-0860

acl@aclweb.org

**Additional copies of this publication are available from:**

Curran Associates, Inc.
57 Morehouse Lane
Red Hook, NY 12571 USA
Phone: 845-758-0400
Fax: 845-758-2633
Email: curran@proceedings.com
Web: www.proceedings.com

WASSA 2024

# The 14th Workshop on Computational Approaches to Subjectivity, Sentiment, & Social Media Analysis

## Proceedings of the Workshop

August 15, 2024

Association for Computational Linguistics (ACL)
317 Sidney Baker St. S
Suite 400 - 134
Kerrville, TX 78028
USA
Tel: +1-855-225-1962
acl@aclweb.org

# Introduction

Since 2010, WASSA has brought together researchers working on Subjectivity, Sentiment Analysis, Emotion Detection and Classification and their applications to other NLP or real-world tasks (e.g. public health messaging, fake news, media impact analysis, social media mining, computational literary studies) and researchers working on interdisciplinary aspects of affect computation from text.

In the past years we have noticed that WASSA offers a platform to researchers investigating sentiment and emotion in lesser-resourced languages. We continued these efforts in the 2024 edition by featuring a Special Track on multilinguality and the social bridge between high- and lesser-resourced languages/communities. However, this year the majority of accepted papers (18 of 29) only perform experiments in English, another six include English and other languages, and only seven are entirely non-English. This emphasizes the need to continue promoting such a multilingual track.

The topics of this edition of WASSA range from complex sentiment relations (entity-level, long documents, long-term narratives), mitigating unwanted subjectivity and biases in models, and advancing towards high-level social implications of subjective NLP. The ubiquity of Large Language Models is also a common theme among the papers.

This year's edition again featured two shared tasks: Shared-Task 1: Empathy Detection and Emotion Classification, which is already the fourth run of this shared task using a new, unpublished extension of the dataset used last year. SharedTask 2: Explainability of Cross-lingual Emotion Detection, on the other hand, is the first shared task on on explainability of cross-lingual emotion detection.

For the main workshop, we received 57 direct submissions, of which 29 papers were accepted (acceptance rate of 53%). For Shared Task 1 we received 12 system description paper submissions, while for Shared Task 2 we received 10 papers. Furthermore, one ARR and one Findings paper will be presented in the poster session. In total, 55 papers will be presented at the workshop.

Following the tradition of the last two years, we again decided to award the best paper. The winner of the Best Paper Award of this year's WASSA is *Context is Important in Depressive Language: A Study of the Interaction Between the Sentiments and Linguistic Markers in Reddit Discussions by Neha Sharma and Kairit Sirts* . Simultaneously, we wish to promote the work in the Special Track, and therefore decided to award a Special Track Best Paper award to *Loneliness Episodes: A Japanese Dataset for Loneliness Detection and Analysis by Naoya Fujikawa, Nguyen Quang Toan, Kazuhiro Ito, Shoko Wakamiya, and Eiji Aramaki.*

On top of the main workshop and shared task presentations, we are happy to have an invited speaker who agreed to give a hybrid keynote at WASSA 2024: Professor Debora Nozza from Bocconi University.

We would like to thank the ACL Organizers and Workshop chairs for their help and support during the preparation. We also thank the OpenReview support team for their technical support. Finally, we especially thank the program committee for the time and effort they spent on reviewing, especially to those who were willing to perform emergency reviews. The quality of the program is a reflection of this hard work.

Orphée De Clercq, Jeremy Barnes, Valentin Barriere, Shabnam Tafreshi, Joao Sedoc and Roman Klinger

WASSA 2024 Program Chairs

# Organizing Committee

**Program Chairs**

Orphée De Clercq, Ghent University, Belgium
Valentin Barriere, Centro Nacional de Inteligencia Artificial, Chile
Jeremy Barnes, University of the Basque Country UPV/EHU, Spain
Roman Klinger, Otto-Friedrich Universität Bamberg, Germany
João Sedoc, New York University, USA
Shabnam Tafreshi, University of Maryland, USA

**Shared Task 1 Chairs**

Salvatore Giorgi, National Institute of Drug Abuse, Baltimore, USA
Valentin Barriere, Centro Nacional de Inteligencia Artificial, Chile
João Sedoc, New York University, USA
Shabnam Tafreshi, University of Maryland, USA

**Shared Task 2 Chairs**

Aaron Maladry, Ghent University
Pranaydeep Singh, Ghent University
Els Lefever, Ghent University

# Program Committee

**Reviewers**

Wazir Ali

Murali Balusu, Sivaji Bandyopadhyay, Mohamad Hardyman Barawi, Tilman Beck

Gustave Cortal

Luna De Bruyne, Ellen De Geyndt, Loic De Langhe, Florian Debaene

Annerose Eichel

Neele Falk

Thomas Nikolaus Haider

Imezadelajara Imezadelajara, Molly E. Ireland, Gabriel Iturra-Bocaz

Kokil Jaidka, Aditya Joshi

Akbar Karimi, Elma Kerz, Khalid Al Khatib, Joni Kruijsbergen

Sofie Labat, Natalia V Loukachevitch

Aaron Maladry, Eugenio Martínez-Cámara, Amita Misra, Ashutosh Modi, Petter Mæhlum

Constantin Orasan

Gabriele Pergola, Flor Miriam Plaza-del-Arco

Sunny Rai, Irene Russo

Oscar Sainz, Salim Sazzed, Raksha Sharma, Melanie Siegel, Pranaydeep Singh, Phillip Smith, Colin Swaelens

Zeerak Talat, Enrica Troiano

Cynthia Van Hee, Jens Van Nooten, Eva Maria Vecchi, Aswathy Velutharambath, Fabián Villena

Jingjing Wang, Azmine Toushik Wasi, Michael Wiegand, Tak-Lam Wong, Amelie Wuehrl

Maria Jose Zambrano, Chrysoula Zerva

# Keynote Talk
# Invited 1

**Debora Nozza**
Bocconi University

**Bio:** Debora Nozza is an Assistant Professor in Computing Sciences at Bocconi University. Her research interests mainly focus on Natural Language Processing, specifically on the detection and counter-acting of hate speech and algorithmic bias on Social Media data in multilingual context. She was awarded a €1.5m ERC Starting Grant project 2023 for research on personalized and subjective approaches to Natural Language Processing. Previously, she was awarded a €120,000 grant from Fondazione Cariplo for her project MONICA, which focuses on monitoring coverage, attitudes, and accessibility of Italian measures in response to COVID-19.

She organized the 7th Workshop on Online Abuse and Harms (WOAH) at ACL 2023 and the ICWSM 2023 Data Challenge: Temporal social data at ICWSM 2023. She was one of the organizers of the task on Automatic Misogyny Identification (AMI) at Evalita 2018 and Evalita 2020, and one of the organizers of the HatEval Task 5 at SemEval 2019 on multilingual detection of hate speech against immigrants and women in Twitter.

# Table of Contents

# Program

**Thursday, August 15, 2024**

09:10 - 09:00 *Opening Remarks*

09:10 - 10:25 *Session 1: Bias, Fake News, Misinformation, and Echo Chambers*

*POLygraph: Polish Fake News Dataset*
Daniel Dzienisiewicz, Filip Graliński, Piotr Jabłoński, Marek Kubis, Paweł Marek Skórzewski and Piotr Wierzchon

*Know Thine Enemy: Adaptive Attacks on Misinformation Detection Using Reinforcement Learning*
Piotr Przybyła, Euan McGill and Horacio Saggion

*Multi-Target User Stance Discovery on Reddit*
Benjamin Steel and Derek Ruths

*Polarization of Autonomous Generative AI Agents Under Echo Chambers*
Masaya Ohagi

*Hierarchical Adversarial Correction to Mitigate Identity Term Bias in Toxicity Detection*
Johannes Schäfer, Ulrich Heid and Roman Klinger

10:30 - 11:00 *Coffee Break*

12:00 - 11:00 *Invited Talk: Debora Nozza*

12:00 - 13:00 *Lunch Break*

13:00 - 14:00 *Shared Task Session*

*Findings of the WASSA 2024 EXALT shared task on Explainability for Cross-Lingual Emotion in Tweets*
Aaron Maladry, Pranaydeep Singh and Els Lefever

*Cross-lingual Emotion Detection through Large Language Models*
Ram Mohan Rao Kadiyala

**Thursday, August 15, 2024 (continued)**

| | |
|---|---|
| | *Findings of WASSA 2024 Shared Task on Empathy and Personality Detection in Interactions*<br>Salvatore Giorgi, João Sedoc, Valentin Barriere and Shabnam Tafreshi |
| | *Fraunhofer SIT at WASSA 2024 Empathy and Personality Shared Task: Use of Sentiment Transformers and Data Augmentation With Fuzzy Labels to Predict Emotional Reactions in Conversations and Essays*<br>Raphael Antonius Frick and Martin Steinebach |
| 14:00 - 15:30 | *Poster session* |
| 15:30 - 16:00 | *Coffee Break* |
| 16:00 - 17:30 | *Session 2: Sentiment and Subjectivity* |
| | *Enhanced Financial Sentiment Analysis and Trading Strategy Development Using Large Language Models*<br>Kemal Kirtac and Guido Germano |
| | *Subjectivity Theory vs. Speaker Intuitions: Explaining the Results of a Subjectivity Regressor Trained on Native Speaker Judgements*<br>Elena Savinova and Jet Hoek |
| | *Comparing Tools for Sentiment Analysis of Danish Literature from Hymns to Fairy Tales: Low-Resource Language and Domain Challenges*<br>Pascale Feldkamp, Jan Kostkan, Ea Lindhardt Overgaard, Mia Jacobsen and Yuri Bizzoni |
| 16:45 - 16:50 | *Best Paper Announcement* |
| 16:50 - 17:20 | *Best Paper Awards* |
| | *Context is Important in Depressive Language: A Study of the Interaction Between the Sentiments and Linguistic Markers in Reddit Discussions*<br>Neha Sharma and Kairit Sirts |
| | *Loneliness Episodes: A Japanese Dataset for Loneliness Detection and Analysis*<br>Naoya Fujikawa, Nguyen Quang Toan, Kazuhiro Ito, Shoko Wakamiya and Eiji Aramaki |
| 17:20 - 17:30 | *Closing Remarks* |

**Thursday, August 15, 2024 (continued)**

# Enhanced Financial Sentiment Analysis and Trading Strategy Development Using Large Language Models

**Kemal Kirtac and Guido Germano**
Department of Computer Science, University College London,
66–72 Gower Street, London WC1E 6EA, United Kingdom
kemal.kirtac.21@ucl.ac.uk, g.germano@ucl.ac.uk

**Abstract**

This study proposes a novel methodology for enhanced financial sentiment analysis and trading strategy development using large language models (LLMs) such as OPT, BERT, FinBERT, LLAMA 3 and RoBERTa. Utilizing a dataset of 965,375 U.S. financial news articles from 2010 to 2023, our research demonstrates that the GPT-3-based OPT model significantly outperforms other models, achieving a prediction accuracy of 74.4% for stock market returns. Our findings reveal that the advanced capabilities of LLMs, particularly OPT, surpass traditional sentiment analysis methods, such as the Loughran-McDonald dictionary model, in predicting and explaining stock returns. For instance, a self-financing strategy based on OPT scores achieves a Sharpe ratio of 3.05 over our sample period, compared to a Sharpe ratio of 1.23 for the strategy based on the dictionary model. This study highlights the superior performance of LLMs in financial sentiment analysis, encouraging further research into integrating artificial intelligence and LLMs in financial markets.

## 1 Introduction

The integration of text mining into financial analysis represents a significant shift in how researchers approach market predictions. Utilizing a diverse array of text data—from financial news to social media posts—this new wave of research aims to extract insights that traditional data sources might overlook (Loughran and Mcdonald, 2011; Malo et al., 2014; Loughran and McDonald, 2022). Despite the complexity and the lack of structured information within text data, advancements in LLMs such as BERT (Devlin et al., 2019), OPT (Zhang et al., 2022), LLAMA 3 (Touvron et al., 2023) and RoBERTa (Liu et al., 2019), have opened new avenues for in-depth analysis and understanding of financial markets. These models have shown a notable ability to outperform traditional sentiment analysis methods, demonstrating the untapped potential of text data in predicting market trends and stock returns (Jegadeesh and Wu, 2013; Baker et al., 2016; Manela and Moreira, 2017).

Our research harnesses the power of LLMs to create refined representations of news text, aiming to bridge the gap in sentiment analysis at the individual stock level—an aspect often overlooked by macro- or market-level sentiment indicators (Baker and Wurgler, 2006; Lemmon and Ni, 2014; Shapiro et al., 2022). By employing a two-step analytical process that first converts text into numerical data and then models economic patterns, we explore the predictive accuracy of these models against traditional dictionary-based methods (Tetlock, 2007; Devlin et al., 2019). We contribute to the ongoing dialogue on the role of text analysis in finance, advocating for a broader adoption of LLMs in economic forecasting and investment strategy development (Acemoglu et al., 2022; Hoberg and Phillips, 2016; Garcia, 2013; Ke et al., 2020; Tetlock, 2007; Campbell et al., 2014; Baker et al., 2016; Calomiris and Mamaysky, 2019; Ashtiani and Raahemi, 2023a; Kirtac and Germano, 2024).

## 2 Data and Methods

### 2.1 Data

In our research, we primarily use two datasets: one from the Center for Research in Security Prices (CRSP) that includes daily stock returns, and another from Refinitiv with global news. The news data from Refinitiv comprises detailed articles and quick alerts, focusing on companies based in the U.S. The CRSP data provides daily return information for companies trading on major U.S. stock exchanges. It includes details like stock prices, trading volumes, and market capitalization. We use this data to analyse the link between stock market returns and sentiment scores derived from LLMs.

Our analysis includes companies from the Amer-



*Proceedings of the 14th Workshop on Computational Approaches to Subjectivity, Sentiment, & Social Media Analysis*, pages 1–10
August 15, 2024 ©2024 Association for Computational Linguistics

ican Stock Exchange (AMEX), National Association of Securities Dealers Automated Quotations (NASDAQ), and New York Stock Exchange (NYSE) that appear in at least one news article. We apply filters to ensure the quality of our data. We only consider news articles related to individual stocks with available three-day returns. Moreover, we avoid redundancy by using a novelty score based on the similarity between articles: if a new article is too similar (a cosine similarity score of 0.8 or more) to an older article published within the past 20 days, we exclude it. This approach helps us focus on unique information significant for our analysis.

Our study covers the period from January 1, 2010, to June 30, 2023. We matched 2,732,845 news with 6,214 unique companies. After applying our filters, we were left with 965,375 articles. Our sample dataset is summarised in Table 1.

| Category | Count |
|---|---|
| All news | 2,732,845 |
| News for single stock | 1,865,372 |
| Unique news | 965,375 |

Table 1: Summary statistics of our U.S. news articles sample, showing the count of total news, news for a single stock, and unique news after filtering for redundancy. This data set forms the basis for our sentiment analysis and subsequent stock return prediction model.

Table 2 presents descriptive statistics of our dataset. We find that the daily mean return is 0.37%, with a standard deviation of 0.18%. The sentiment scores derived from the OPT, BERT, FinBERT, LLAMA 3 and RoBERTa LLMs show a normal distribution around the median of 0.5, with slight variations in mean and standard deviation. In contrast, the Loughran-McDonald dictionary score exhibits a more positively skewed distribution with a mean of 0.68 and a higher standard deviation of 0.32, indicating a tendency towards more positive sentiment scores in our dataset.

## 2.2 Methods

This study begins with the fine-tuning of pre-trained language models, specifically OPT, BERT, LLAMA 3, and RoBERTa, sourced from Hugging Face, to tailor their capabilities for specialized financial analysis (Hugging Face, 2023). LLMs, originally designed for broad linguistic comprehension, require significant adaptation to perform niche tasks, such as forecasting stock returns through textual analysis. This necessity enforces the adaptation phase, where the models are recalibrated post their original training on extensive data, preparing them for specific analytical functions (Radford et al., 2018).

Besides OPT, BERT, LLAMA 3 and RoBERTa, our analysis incorporates FinBERT, a variant of BERT pre-trained specifically for financial texts, and the Loughran and McDonald dictionary. FinBERT and the Loughran and McDonald dictionary do not necessitate the fine-tuning process because they are already tailored for financial text analysis. FinBERT leverages BERT's architecture but is fine-tuned on financial texts, providing nuanced understanding in this domain (Huang et al., 2023). The Loughran and McDonald dictionary, a specialized lexicon for financial texts, aids in traditional textual analysis without the complexity of machine-learning models (Loughran and McDonald, 2022).

We present a unique approach that integrates fine-tuning pre-trained LLMs with financial text data. This section outlines our process of adapting LLMs for the financial domain, including the steps of fine-tuning and the specific features used in our sentiment analysis. Our methodology involves the systematic adaptation of models such as OPT, BERT, FinBERT, LLAMA 3 and RoBERTa, focusing on domain-specific nuances by fine-tuning them on a comprehensive dataset of financial news. This process not only improves the models' understanding of financial sentiment but also enhances their predictive accuracy regarding stock market movements. By leveraging the advanced capabilities of LLMs and tailoring them specifically for financial text, our approach presents a robust framework for sentiment-based financial forecasting.

The use of LLMs such as OPT, BERT, FinBERT, LLAMA 3 and RoBERTa in financial sentiment analysis offers distinct advantages over traditional methods, particularly in handling the complexity and unstructured nature of financial text data. Traditional techniques, such as the Loughran-McDonald dictionary, rely on predefined word lists that may not capture the nuanced and evolving language used in financial news. In contrast, LLMs leverage deep learning to understand context, sentiment, and subtle linguistic cues within text, leading to more accurate sentiment predictions. Our study demonstrates that LLMs, through their ability to fine-tune on domain-specific data, significantly outperform traditional methods in predicting stock returns. The fine-tuning process involves training these models

| Variable | Mean | StdDev | Minimum | Median | Maximum | $N$ |
|---|---|---|---|---|---|---|
| Daily return (%) | 0.37 | 0.18 | -64.97 | -0.02 | 237.11 | 965,375 |
| OPT score | 0.53 | 0.24 | 0 | 0.5 | 1 | 965,375 |
| BERT score | 0.48 | 0.25 | 0 | 0.5 | 1 | 965,375 |
| FinBERT score | 0.44 | 0.23 | 0 | 0.5 | 1 | 965,375 |
| LLAMA 3 score | 0.45 | 0.29 | 0 | 0.5 | 1 | 965,375 |
| RoBERTa score | 0.51 | 0.24 | 0 | 0.5 | 1 | 965,375 |
| LM dictionary score | 0.68 | 0.32 | 0 | 0.5 | 1 | 965,375 |

Table 2: Descriptive statistics for daily stock returns and sentiment scores derived from the OPT, BERT, FinBERT, LLAMA 3 and RoBERTa LLMs, alongside the Loughran-McDonald dictionary. It includes the mean, standard deviation, minimum, median, maximum values, and the total count of observations for each variable.

on a vast corpus of financial news, allowing them to learn and adapt to the specific language and sentiment indicators pertinent to financial markets. Additionally, the use of LLMs facilitates the development of a robust investment strategy, as evidenced by the superior performance metrics achieved in our experiments. Future research could focus on optimizing these models further, exploring efficient training algorithms and model compression techniques to enhance their practicality and application in real-time trading scenarios.

Guided by the methodologies introduced by (Alain and Bengio, 2016), our approach adopts a probing technique, which is a form of feature extraction. This method builds on the models' pre-existing parameters, harnessing them to create features pertinent to text data, thereby facilitating the downstream task of sentiment analysis. To enhance the precision of our LLMs, we adapted and modified the methodology proposed by (Ke et al., 2020). In our methodology, the process of fine-tuning the pre-trained OPT, BERT, LLAMA 3 and RoBERTa language models involves a specific focus on the aggregated 3-day excess return associated with each stock. This excess return is calculated from the day a news article is first published and extends over the two subsequent days. To elaborate, excess return is defined as the difference between the return of a particular stock and the overall market return on the same day. This calculation is not limited to the day the news is published; instead, it aggregates the returns for the following two days as well, providing a comprehensive three-day outlook.

Sentiment labels are assigned to each news article based on the sign of this aggregated three-day excess return. A positive aggregated excess return leads to a sentiment label of '1', indicating a positive sentiment. Conversely, a non-positive aggregated excess return results in a sentiment label of '0', suggesting a negative sentiment. Our approach of using a 3-day aggregated excess return for sentiment labelling plays a crucial role in refining our analysis. Acknowledging the common practice in economics and finance of studying events that span multiple days, we establish sentiment labels using three-day returns (MacKinlay, 1997). This approach entails evaluating returns spanning from the day of the article's publication through the two following days. This technique is particularly beneficial in understanding the nuanced relationship between the sentiment in financial news and the corresponding movements in stock prices. We allocated 20% of the data randomly for testing and, from the remaining data pool, allocated another 20% randomly for validation purposes, resulting in a training set of 193,070 articles.

Our analysis focused on the ability of OPT, BERT, LLAMA 3, RoBERTa, FinBERT and the Loughran-McDonald dictionary to accurately forecast the direction of stock returns based on news sentiment, particularly over a three-day period post-publication. To assess the models' performance, we calculated these statistical measures: accuracy, precision, recall, specificity and the F1 score.

We subsequently conducted a regression analysis with the objective of investigating the influence of language model scores on the subsequent day's stock returns. The regression is modelled as

$$r_{i,n+1} = a_i + b_n + \gamma \cdot \mathbf{x}_{i,n} + \epsilon_{i,n}, \quad (1)$$

where $r_{i,n+1}$ is the return of stock $i$ on the subsequent trading day $n+1$, $\mathbf{x}_{i,n}$ is a vector of scores from language models, and $a_i$ and $b_n$ are the fixed effects for firm and date, respectively.

We employ double clustering for standard errors by firm and date, addressing potential concerns related to heteroscedasticity and autocorrelation. This regression framework facilitates an in-depth comparison of the predictive efficacy with respect to stock returns of different LLMs, including OPT, BERT, FinBERT, LLAMA 3 and RoBERTa, plus the Loughran and McDonald dictionary.

Our choice of the linear regression model corresponds to a standard panel regression approach where article features $x_{i,n}$ are directly translated into the expected return $E(r_{i,n+1})$ of the corresponding stock for the next period. The simplicity of linear regression is chosen to emphasize the importance of text-based representations in financial analysis. By using linear models, we can focus on the impact of these representations without the added complexity of nonlinear modelling. This approach highlights the direct influence of textual data on financial predictions, ensuring a clear understanding of the role and effectiveness of text-based features in financial sentiment analysis.

Following our predictive analysis, our study extends to assess practical outcomes through the implementation of distinct trading strategies utilizing sentiment scores derived from OPT, BERT, FinBERT, LLAMA 3, RoBERTa and Loughran-McDonald dictionary models. To comprehensively evaluate these strategies, we construct various portfolios with a specific focus on market value-weighted approaches. For each language model, we create three types of portfolios: long, short and long-short. The composition of these portfolios is contingent on the sentiment scores assigned to individual stocks every day. Specifically, the long portfolios comprise stocks with the highest 20% sentiment scores, while the short portfolios consist of stocks with the lowest 20% sentiment scores. Moreover, the long-short portfolios are self-financing strategies that simultaneously involve taking long positions in stocks with the highest 20% sentiment scores and short positions in stocks with the lowest 20% sentiment scores. We observe cumulative returns of these trading strategies with considering transaction costs. We dynamically update these market value-weighted sentiment portfolios on a daily basis in response to changes in sentiment scores. This means that each day, we reevaluate and adjust the portfolios by considering the latest sentiment data. By doing so, we aim to capture the most current market conditions and enhance the effectiveness of our trading strategies.

#### 2.2.1 Training and Inference Process

The training and inference process involves several key steps as presented in Algorithm 1. Initially, we collect financial news articles and the corresponding stock return data. These articles are preprocessed to remove irrelevant and simliar information and ensure consistency. Following this, we fine-tune LLMs using the training news dataset. After fine-tuning, the fine-tuned LLMs are utilized to calculate sentiment scores for the news articles in the test dataset. Based on these sentiment scores, we implement a portfolio investment strategy for the test period. This strategy includes creating three distinct portfolios: a long portfolio consisting of stocks with the top 20 percentile positive sentiment scores, a short portfolio with stocks having the top 20 percentile negative sentiment scores, and a self-financing long-short portfolio that incorporates both the top 20 percentile negative and positive scores. Additionally, we include benchmark comparisons with value-weighted and equal-weighted market portfolios that do not consider sentiment scores. The performance of these portfolios is then evaluated using key financial metrics, including the Sharpe ratio, mean daily returns, standard deviation of daily returns and maximum drawdown.

We update the portfolios with the timing of news releases. For news reported before 6 am, we initiate trades at the market opening on that day, exploiting immediate reaction opportunities and close the position at the same date. For news appearing between 6 am and 4 pm, we initiate a trade with closing prices of the same day and exit the trade the next trading day. Any news coming in after 4 pm was used for trades at the start of the next trading day, adapting to market operating hours. To make our simulation more aligned with actual trading conditions, we included a transaction cost of 10 basis points for each trade, accounting for the typical costs traders would encounter in the market.

#### 2.2.2 Computational Cost and Comparative Analysis

**Computational Cost** The training and inference processes for fine-tuning LLMs are computationally intensive. Specifically, the fine-tuning phase involves extensive preprocessing of financial news articles, training on large datasets and continuous updating of models based on new data. In our experiments, we utilized high-performance computing resources, including GPUs and TPUs, to manage these tasks efficiently. The training time varied significantly depending on the model size and the volume of data processed. For instance,

**Algorithm 1** Training and Inference Process

**Require:** Pre-trained language model (PLM), financial news articles $\{A_i\}$, three-day aggregated stock returns $\{R_i\}$
**Ensure:** Updated sentiment portfolios
**Training Phase:**
**for** each article $A_i$ in the training set **do**
  Associate $A_i$ with its three-day aggregated return $R_i$
  Fine-tune the PLM on the paired data $\{A_i, R_i\}$
**end for**
Save the fine-tuned model as FTM
**Forming Sentiment Portfolios:**
**for** each stock $i$ **do**
  Use FTM to predict sentiment score $S_i$ from recent news articles
  Rank all stocks by their sentiment scores $S_i$
  Form top 20% highest sentiment portfolio $P_{\text{high}}$
  Form bottom 20% lowest sentiment portfolio $P_{\text{low}}$
**end for**
**Updating Portfolios:**
**for** each new day **do**
  **for** each stock $i$ **do**
    Update sentiment score $S_i$ with new articles using $FTM$
    Re-rank all stocks by updated sentiment scores $S_i$
    Update $P_{\text{high}}$ and $P_{\text{low}}$ with the new rankings
  **end for**
**end for**

fine-tuning BERT and OPT models required approximately 48 hours on a cluster of 4 NVIDIA V100 GPUs for our dataset of 965,375 articles. The computational cost also encompasses storage and memory requirements, which were substantial given the need to handle large volumes of text data and model parameters. Despite these costs, the enhanced performance of dialogue-level augmentation techniques justifies the computational investment. Future work could explore more efficient training algorithms and model compression techniques to mitigate these costs while retaining performance gains.

**Comparative Analysis with Existing Techniques** We included a variety of existing individual utterance-level augmentation methods. They include back-translation, synonym replacement and noise injection, which are commonly used in text augmentation. Our comparative analysis highlights several key findings. Firstly, dialogue-level augmentation techniques consistently outperformed individual utterance-level methods across multiple evaluation metrics. Specifically, our dialogue-level approach yielded higher sentiment prediction accuracy and improved stock return forecasting capabilities. For example, the OPT model with dialogue-level augmentation achieved an accuracy of 74.4%, compared to 68.9% with utterance-level back-translation. Additionally, our approach demonstrated better robustness and generalization, particularly in handling nuanced financial texts. This superiority is attributed to the ability of dialogue-level augmentation to capture contextual dependencies and sentiment flows across multiple utterances, which is often lost in utterance-level methods. To substantiate these findings, we refer to recent studies by Ashtiani and Raahemi (2023b) and Ke et al. (2020) which also emphasize the limitations of traditional text augmentation techniques in complex domains like financial forecasting. These studies provide a benchmark for our results, reinforcing the effectiveness of the methods we propose. In conclusion, the dialogue-level augmentation not only enhances model performance but also aligns more closely with real-world applications where understanding the flow of information and sentiment over a series of interactions is crucial.

## 3 Results

### 3.1 Sentiment Analysis Accuracy in U.S. Financial News

In this study, we used LLMs to analyse sentiment in U.S. financial news. We processed a dataset of 965,375 articles from Refinitiv, spanning from January 1, 2010, to June 30, 2023. We used 20% of these articles as a test set. We measured the accuracy of each model in predicting the direction of stock returns based on news sentiment. This accuracy indicates how well the model links the sentiment in financial news with stock returns over a three-day period. We evaluated six models: OPT, BERT, FinBERT, LLAMA 3, RoBERTa and the Loughran-McDonald dictionary. Their performance in sentiment analysis is shown in Table 3.

The results show that the OPT model was the most accurate, followed closely by BERT and

| Metric | OPT | BERT | FinBERT | LLAMA 3 | RoBERTa | Loughran-McDonald |
|---|---|---|---|---|---|---|
| Accuracy | 0.744 | 0.725 | 0.722 | 0.632 | 0.671 | 0.501 |
| Precision | 0.732 | 0.711 | 0.708 | 0.681 | 0.673 | 0.505 |
| Recall | 0.781 | 0.761 | 0.755 | 0.663 | 0.632 | 0.513 |
| Specificity | 0.711 | 0.693 | 0.685 | 0.642 | 0.701 | 0.522 |
| F1 score | 0.754 | 0.734 | 0.731 | 0.691 | 0.678 | 0.508 |

Table 3: Language model performance metrics. The table presents accuracy, precision, recall, specificity and the F1 score for each model.

FinBERT. The Loughran-McDonald dictionary, a traditional finance text analysis tool, had significantly lower accuracy. This indicates that language models like OPT, BERT, FinBert, LLAMA 3 and RoBERTa are better at understanding and analysing complex financial news. The precision and recall values further support the superiority of the OPT model; its F1 score, which combines precision and recall, also confirms its effectiveness in sentiment analysis. These findings confirm that language models, particularly OPT, are valuable tools for analysing financial news and predicting stock market trends.

### 3.2 Predicting returns with LLM scores

This section assesses the ability of various LLMs to predict stock returns for the next day using regression models. Our regression, outlined in Eq. (1), uses LLM-generated scores from news headlines as the main predictors. To account for unobserved variations, these regressions include fixed effects for both firms and time, and we cluster standard errors by date and firm for added robustness. Table 4 provides our regression findings, focusing on how stock returns correlate with predictive scores from advanced LLMs, specifically OPT, BERT, FinBERT, LLAMA 3, RoBERTa and the Loughran-McDonald dictionary.

Our findings reveal the predictive capabilities of the advanced LLMs. The OPT model, in particular, demonstrates a strong correlation with next-day stock returns, as indicated by significant coefficients in different model specifications. The FinBERT model follows closely, showcasing its own robust predictive power. BERT scores, while more modest in their predictive strength, still show a statistically significant relationship with stock returns. LLAMA 3 and RoBERTa models also exhibit significant predictive capabilities. In contrast, the Loughran-McDonald dictionary model exhibits the least predictive power among the models examined .

In addressing the differential performance observed among OPT, BERT, FinBERT, RoBERTa and LLAMA 3, our analysis suggests that several factors contribute to this variance, notably model design, parameter scale and the specificity of training data. OPT's expanded parameter space, exceeding that of BERT, FinBERT, LLAMA 3 and RoBERTa, alongside its advanced training methodologies, likely underpins its superior forecasting accuracy in stock returns and portfolio management. The nuanced performance of FinBERT, despite its financial domain specialization, raises intriguing considerations. LLAMA 3 and RoBERTa, while demonstrating significant predictive capabilities, also highlight the importance of model architecture and training data diversity. Our exploration posits that the broader pre-training data diversity of BERT and RoBERTa, coupled with the potential for overfitting in highly specialized models such as FinBERT, might elucidate these unexpected outcomes. LLAMA 3's performance suggests that advancements in language model architectures continue to enhance predictive accuracy. These insights collectively emphasize the intricate balance between model specificity, scale and training regimen in optimizing predictive performance within financial sentiment analysis.

The robustness of our regression models is further underscored by the inclusion of a substantial number of observations, ensuring a comprehensive and representative analysis. Additionally, the adjusted $R^2$ values, while moderate, indicate a reasonable level of explanatory power within the models. The reported AIC and BIC values aid in assessing model fit and complexity, further enriching our comparative analysis across different LLMs.

### 3.3 Performance of Sentiment-Based Portfolios

Next, we assess the effectiveness of sentiment analysis in portfolio management by constructing various sentiment-based portfolios, including market

| Regression | 1 | 2 | 3 | 4 | 5 | 6 |
|---|---|---|---|---|---|---|
| OPT score | 0.254*** | | | | | |
| | (4.871) | | | | | |
| BERT score | | 0.129* | | | | |
| | | (2.334) | | | | |
| FinBERT score | | | 0.181*** | | | |
| | | | (4.674) | | | |
| LLAMA 3 score | | | | 0.191** | | |
| | | | | (2.992) | | |
| RoBERTa score | | | | | 0.199*** | |
| | | | | | (3.129) | |
| LM dictionary score | | | | | | 0.083 |
| | | | | | | (1.871) |
| Observations | 965,375 | 965,375 | 965,375 | 965,375 | 965,375 | 965,375 |
| R2 | 0.195 | 0.145 | 0.174 | 0.168 | 0.147 | 0.087 |
| R2 adjusted | 0.195 | 0.145 | 0.174 | 0.168 | 0.147 | 0.087 |
| R2 within | 0.017 | 0.009 | 0.016 | 0.011 | 0.008 | 0.002 |
| R2 within adj. | 0.017 | 0.009 | 0.016 | 0.011 | 0.008 | 0.002 |
| AIC | 62,345 | 97,473 | 67,345 | 77,842 | 73,934 | 135,783 |
| BIC | 115,655 | 114,746 | 109,272 | 121,232 | 123,393 | 123,382 |
| RMSE | 4.21 | 14.12 | 9.75 | 11,21 | 14,23 | 23.54 |
| FE: date | X | X | X | X | X | X |
| FE: firm | X | X | X | X | X | X |

* $p < 0.05$, ** $p < 0.01$, *** $p < 0.001$

Table 4: Regression of stock returns on LLM sentiment scores. The table presents the results of regressions done with Eq. (1), which includes firm and time-fixed effects represented by $a_i$ and $b_n$ respectively. The independent variable $x_{i,n}$ includes prediction scores from the language models. This analysis compares scores from OPT, BERT, FinBERT, LLAMA 3, RoBERTa and Loughran-McDonald dictionary models, providing insights into their predictive abilities for stock market movements based on news sentiment. This analysis encompasses all U.S. common stocks with at least one news headline about the firm. $T$-statistics are presented in parentheses.

value-weighted portfolios. These portfolios are developed using sentiment scores derived from different language models, including OPT, BERT, FinBERT, LLAMA 3, RoBERTa and the Loughran-McDonald dictionary. The investment strategies employed in our analysis are described as follows: each LLM is used to create three distinct portfolios, one composed of stocks with top 20 percentile positive sentiment scores (long), another comprising stocks with top 20 percentile negative sentiment scores (short), and a self-financing long-short portfolio (L-S) based on both top 20 percentile negative and positive scores. Additionally, we include benchmark comparisons with value-weighted and equal-weighted market portfolios without considering sentiment scores. Value-weighted portfolios distribute investments based on the market capitalization of each stock, while equal-weighted portfolios allocate investments equally to all stocks, regardless of market capitalization. We evaluate these strategies using key financial metrics, including the Sharpe ratio, mean daily returns, standard deviation of daily returns and maximum drawdown.

As indicated in Table 5, the long-short OPT strategy demonstrated the most robust risk-adjusted performance, as evidenced by its superior Sharpe ratio. On the other hand, the Loughran-McDonald dictionary model-based strategy (L-S LM dictionary) lagged behind, particularly when compared to the value-weighted market portfolio.

This highlights the varying effectiveness of different sentiment analysis models in guiding investment decisions and underscores the significance of model selection in sentiment-based trading.

| | OPT | | | BERT | | | FinBERT | | |
|---|---|---|---|---|---|---|---|---|---|
| | Long | Short | L-S | Long | Short | L-S | Long | Short | L-S |
| Sharpe ratio | 1.81 | 1.42 | 3.05 | 1.59 | 1.28 | 2.11 | 1.51 | 1.19 | 2.07 |
| MDR (%) | 0.32 | 0.25 | 0.55 | 0.25 | 0.21 | 0.45 | 0.22 | 0.18 | 0.39 |
| StdDev (%) | 2.91 | 2.49 | 2.59 | 2.49 | 3.19 | 2.68 | 2.18 | 3.31 | 2.81 |
| MDD (%) | -14.76 | -24.69 | -18.57 | -17.89 | -27.95 | -21.95 | -19.71 | -29.94 | -23.82 |
| | LM dictionary | | | LLAMA 3 | | | RoBERTa | | |
| | Long | Short | L-S | Long | Short | L-S | Long | Short | L-S |
| Sharpe ratio | 0.87 | 0.66 | 1.23 | 1.37 | 1.11 | 1.44 | 1.04 | 1.18 | 1.51 |
| MDR (%) | 0.12 | 0.13 | 0.22 | 0.14 | 0.16 | 0.22 | 0.20 | 0.19 | 0.29 |
| StdDev (%) | 3.54 | 4.13 | 3.74 | 3.01 | 3.12 | 3.41 | 2.99 | 3.13 | 3.33 |
| MDD (%) | -35.47 | -45.39 | -38.29 | -29.13 | -22.21 | -22.85 | -23.46 | -28.44 | -30.24 |
| | EW | | | VW | | | | | |
| | Long | Short | L-S | Long | Short | L-S | | | |
| Sharpe ratio | 1.25 | 1.05 | 1.40 | 1.28 | 1.08 | 1.45 | | | |
| MDR (%) | 0.18 | 0.15 | 0.33 | 0.19 | 0.16 | 0.35 | | | |
| StdDev (%) | 2.90 | 3.70 | 3.20 | 2.95 | 3.75 | 3.25 | | | |
| MDD (%) | -31.13 | -42.21 | -32.87 | -28.76 | -38.95 | -31.87 | | | |

Table 5: Descriptive statistics of trading strategies. The table presents the Sharpe ratio, mean daily return (MDR), daily standard deviation (StdDev) and the maximum daily drawdown (MDD) for the trading strategies based on the sentiment analysis models OPT, BERT, FinBERT, LLAMA 3, RoBERTa and the Loughran-McDonald (LM) dictionary, each comprising long (L), short (S), and long-short (L-S) portfolios. The portfolios are value-weighted for comparison to a value-weighted (VW) market portfolio, which is provided for benchmarking, as well as an equal-weighted (EW) portfolio.

## 4 Conclusion

Our study has far-reaching implications for the financial industry, offering insights that could reshape market prediction and investment decision-making methodologies. By demonstrating an application of OPT, BERT, FinBERT, LLAMA 3 and RoBERTa LLMs, we enhance the understanding of LLM capabilities in financial economics. This encourages further research into integrating artificial intelligence and LLMs in financial markets.

Notably, the advanced capabilities of LLMs surpass traditional sentiment analysis methods in predicting and explaining stock returns. We compare the performance of OPT, BERT, FinBERT, LLAMA 3 and RoBERTa scores to sentiment scores derived from conventional methods, such as the Loughran-McDonald dictionary model. Our analysis reveals that basic models exhibit limited stock forecasting capabilities, with little to no significant positive correlation between their sentiment scores and subsequent stock returns. In contrast, complex models like OPT demonstrate the highest predictability. For instance, a self-financing strategy based on OPT scores, buying stocks with positive scores and selling stocks with negative scores after news announcements, achieves a remarkable Sharpe ratio of 3.05 over our sample period, compared to a Sharpe ratio of 1.23 for the strategy based on the dictionary model.

The implications of our research reach beyond the financial industry to inform regulators and policymakers. Our research enhances our knowledge of the advantages and risks linked to the increasing use of LLMs in financial economics. As LLM usage expands, it becomes crucial to focus on their impact on market behavior, information dissemination and price formation. Our results add insights to the dialogue on regulatory policies that oversee the use of AI in finance, thereby aiding in the establishment of optimal practices for incorporating LLMs into the operations of financial markets.

Our research offers tangible benefits to asset managers and institutional investors, presenting empirical data that demonstrates the strengths of LLMs in forecasting stock market trends. Such evidence enables these professionals to make more informed choices regarding the integration of LLMs into their investment strategies. This could not only improve their performance but also decrease their dependence on traditional methods of analysis.

Our study contributes to the discussion about the role of AI in finance, particularly through our investigation into how well LLMs can predict stock market returns. By investigating both the possibilities and the boundaries of LLMs in the domain of financial economics, we open the way for further research aimed at creating more advanced LLMs specifically designed for the distinctive needs of the finance sector. Our goal in highlighting the potential roles of LLMs in financial economics is to foster ongoing research and innovation in the field of finance that is driven by artificial intelligence.

## 5 Limitations

Despite the promising results of our study, several limitations should be acknowledged.

The fine-tuning of LLMs such as OPT, BERT, FinBERT, LLAMA 3 and RoBERTa requires substantial computational resources and time. This includes the need for high-performance computing resources such as GPUs and TPUs, and extensive preprocessing of financial news articles. The significant computational cost may limit the accessibility and scalability of these models for smaller organizations or individual researchers.

LLMs like FinBERT that are specialized for financial texts have a higher risk of overfitting due to their specificity. Overfitting can limit the model's ability to generalize to new, unseen data, especially in rapidly changing financial markets. Conversely, the broader pre-training data diversity of models like BERT and RoBERTa might introduce noise that affects their performance in specialized domains such as finance.

Our analysis is based on a dataset of 965,375 U.S. financial news articles spanning from 2010 to 2023. This dataset, although extensive, may not fully capture global financial trends and sentiments. Moreover, the quality and reliability of the financial news sources can vary, potentially impacting the accuracy of the sentiment analysis.

The evaluation metrics used in our study, such as accuracy, precision, recall and the Sharpe ratio, while robust, may not comprehensively capture all aspects of model performance in real-world trading scenarios. Market conditions, investor behavior and external economic factors are dynamic and can influence the effectiveness of sentiment-based trading strategies.

The integration of LLMs in financial markets raises important regulatory and ethical questions. The impact of algorithmic trading on market stability, the potential for market manipulation and the need for transparency and accountability in AI-driven decision-making are critical areas that require further exploration and regulatory oversight.

There is a need for ongoing research to address these limitations. Exploring more efficient training algorithms, model compression techniques and the integration of additional data sources can help mitigate computational costs and improve model performance. Studying the impact of LLMs in diverse and global financial contexts will enhance the generalizability and applicability of these models.

By acknowledging these limitations, we aim to provide a balanced perspective on the potential and challenges of using LLMs for financial sentiment analysis and trading strategy development. Future work should continue to refine these models and address the outlined challenges to fully realize their potential in financial markets.

The parameters of the trading algorithm should be justified by exploring alternatives. For instance, the lag or correlation time between news and returns has not been determined, and there are several other parameters in the algorithm that would benefit from an explanation or the testing of values above or below the ones used.

We tested only passive trading strategies; it would be beneficial to test active trading strategies as well. Furthermore, these strategies are based solely on sentiment, whereas sentiment-augmented strategies could further enhance the trading performance.

## Funding

We acknowledge the EPSRC Doctoral Training Partnership EP/R513143/1.

## References

Daron Acemoglu, David Autor, Jonathon Hazell, and Pascual Restrepo. 2022. Artificial intelligence and jobs: Evidence from online vacancies. *Journal of Labor Economics*, 40(S1):S293–S340.

Guillaume Alain and Yoshua Bengio. 2016. Understanding intermediate layers using linear classifier probes. *arXiv:1610.01644*.

M. N. Ashtiani and B. Raahemi. 2023a. News-based intelligent prediction of financial markets using text mining and machine learning: A systematic literature review. *Expert Systems with Applications*, 217:119509.

Mohammad N. Ashtiani and Bijan Raahemi. 2023b. News-based intelligent prediction of financial markets using text mining and machine learning: A systematic literature review. *Expert Systems with Applications*, 217:119509.

Malcolm Baker and Jeffrey Wurgler. 2006. Investor sentiment and the cross-section of stock returns. *Journal of Finance*, 61(4):1645–1680.

Scott R. Baker, Nicholas Bloom, and Steven J. Davis. 2016. Measuring economic policy uncertainty. *Quarterly Journal of Economics*, 131(4):1593–1636.

Charles W. Calomiris and Harry Mamaysky. 2019. How news and its context drive risk and returns around the world. *Journal of Financial Economics*, 133(2):299–336.

John L. Campbell, Hsinchun Chen, Dan S. Dhaliwal, Hsin-min Lu, and Logan B. Steele. 2014. The information content of mandatory risk factor disclosures in corporate filings. *Review of Accounting Studies*, 19(1):396–455.

Jacob Devlin, Ming-Wei Chang, Kenton Lee, and Kristina Toutanova. 2019. BERT: Pre-training of deep bidirectional transformers for language understanding. In *Proceedings of the 2019 Conference of the North American Chapter of the Association for Computational Linguistics: Human Language Technologies, Volume 1 (Long and Short Papers)*, pages 4171–4186, Minneapolis, Minnesota. Association for Computational Linguistics.

Diego Garcia. 2013. Sentiment during recessions. *Journal of Finance*, 68(3):1267–1300.

Gerard Hoberg and Gordon Phillips. 2016. Text-based network industries and endogenous product differentiation. *Journal of Political Economy*, 124(5):1423–1465.

Allen H. Huang, Hui Wang, and Yi Yang. 2023. FinBERT: A large language model for extracting information from financial text. *Contemporary Accounting Research*, 40(2):806–841.

Hugging Face. 2023. Hugging Face's transformer models.

Narasimhan Jegadeesh and Di Wu. 2013. Word power: A new approach for content analysis. *Journal of Financial Economics*, 110(3):712–729.

Yanbo Ke, Bryan T. Kelly, and Dacheng Xiu. 2020. Predicting returns with text data. *Review of Financial Studies*, 33(11):5104–5144.

Kemal Kirtac and Guido Germano. 2024. Sentiment trading with large language models. *Finance Research Letters*, 62(B):105227.

Michael Lemmon and Sophie X. Ni. 2014. The impact of investor sentiment on the market's reaction to stock splits. *Review of Financial Studies*, 27(5):1367–1401.

Yinhan Liu, Myle Ott, Naman Goyal, Jingfei Du, Mandar Joshi, Danqi Chen, Omer Levy, Mike Lewis, Luke Zettlemoyer, and Veselin Stoyanov. 2019. Roberta: A robustly optimized BERT pretraining approach. *arXiv:1907.11692*.

TIM Loughran and BILL Mcdonald. 2011. When is a liability not a liability? Textual analysis, dictionaries, and 10-Ks. *Journal of Finance*, 66(1):35–65.

Tim Loughran and Bill McDonald. 2022. Master Loughran-MacDonald Word Dictionary.

A. C. MacKinlay. 1997. Event studies in economics and finance. *Journal of Economic Literature*, 35(1):13–39.

Pekka Malo, Ankur Sinha, Pekka Korhonen, Jyrki Wallenius, and Pyry Takala. 2014. Good debt or bad debt: Detecting semantic orientations in economic texts. *Journal of the Association for Information Science and Technology*, 65(4):782–796.

Asaf Manela and Alan Moreira. 2017. News implied volatility and disaster concerns. *Journal of Financial Economics*, 123(1):137–162.

Alec Radford, Karthik Narasimhan, Tim Salimans, and Ilya Sutskever. 2018. Improving language understanding by generative pre-training. OpenAI Blog.

Adam Hale Shapiro, Moritz Sudhof, and Daniel J. Wilson. 2022. Measuring news sentiment. *Journal of Econometrics*, 228(2):221–243.

Paul C. Tetlock. 2007. Giving content to investor sentiment: The role of media in the stock market. *Journal of Finance*, 62(3):1139–1168.

Hugo Touvron, Thibaut Lavril, Gautier Izacard, Xavier Martinet, Marie-Anne Lachaux, Timothée Lacroix, Baptiste Rozière, Naman Goyal, Eric Hambro, Faisal Azhar, et al. 2023. LLaMA: Open and efficient foundation language models. *arXiv:2302.13971*.

Susan Zhang, Stephen Roller, Naman Goyal, Mikel Artetxe, Moya Chen, Shuohui Chen, Christopher Dewan, Mona Diab, Xian Li, Xi Victoria Lin, Todor Mihaylov, Myle Ott, Sam Shleifer, Kurt Shuster, Daniel Simig, Punit Singh Koura, Anjali Sridhar, Tianlu Wang, and Luke Zettlemoyer. 2022. OPT: Open pre-trained transformer language models. *arXiv:2205.01068*.

# SEC: Context-Aware Metric Learning for Efficient Emotion Recognition in Conversation

**Barbara Gendron**[1,2], **Gaël Guibon**[1],
[1]LORIA, Université de Lorraine, CNRS, [2]Université du Luxembourg,
**Correspondence:** barbara.gendron@loria.fr ; gael.guibon@loria.fr

## Abstract

The advent of deep learning models has made a considerable contribution to the achievement of Emotion Recognition in Conversation (ERC). However, this task still remains an important challenge due to the plurality and subjectivity of human emotions. Previous work on ERC provides predictive models using mostly graph-based conversation representations. In this work, we propose a way to model the conversational context that we incorporate into a metric learning training strategy, with a two-step process. This allows us to perform ERC in a flexible classification scenario and end up with a lightweight yet efficient model. Using metric learning through a Siamese Network architecture, we achieve 57.71 in macro F1 score for emotion classification in conversation on DailyDialog dataset, which outperforms the related work. This state-of-the-art result is promising in terms of the use of metric learning for emotion recognition, yet perfectible compared to the micro F1 score obtained.

## 1 Introduction

Computer Mediated Communication (CMC) is constantly evolving and new means of communicating are emerging. With the advent of conversational agents, there is a need to detect emotions within a conversation. Although many modalities are now considered in the communication process, the textual modality still remains essential for fast and easy everyday communication, through messaging applications, social media, and other networking platforms. Textual modality, however, is ambiguous, it does not preserve the extra-linguistic context, especially for dyadic human-to-human conversations. One main ambiguity that arises in CMC is the emotional state of the speaker, often misinterpreted by humans through short, and unpolished messages. This motivates Emotion Recognition in Conversation (ERC), a trending research topic dedicated not only to identifying emotion in messages, but also on taking into account the conversational context to recognize emotions. ERC has been shown to be challenging, especially with respect to the way to represent the context (Ghosal et al., 2021). Lately, it has seen a surge of multimodal models (Wen et al., 2023; Liang et al., 2023; Fan et al., 2024) and graph-related approaches (Zhang et al., 2023; Wang et al., 2023; Li et al., 2023) which often try to map the pattern of each speaker and better represent the conversational context, often resulting in good performance at the cost of efficiency. One additional issue ERC models are facing is their dependency on labels, models are mainly supervised and face the issue of extreme label imbalance due to emotional utterances being so scarce.

In this paper, we tackle these two challenges by incorporating the conversational context into metric learning while heavily controlling the data imbalance by multiple means. Considering that we want to tackle information across emotions to make our model usable for variants of emotions that go beyond the scope of the 6 basic emotions, we do not use supervised contrastive learning (Khosla et al., 2020) in our method. Instead, we focus on a two-step process to update the model using both direct label predictions through a cross-entropy loss and relative label assignment through the contrastive loss. This two-step process is quite straightforward, while using isolated elements, such as isolated utterances. However, to the best of our knowledge, contextual representation through contrastive learning for ERC has yet to be used. This represents our main contribution in this paper, as we present a model that can achieve competitive performance compared to the state-of-the-art while rendering the adaptation to other emotion labels feasible. Thus, our model can be applied and adapted in multiple contexts that require recognition of different label granularities.



*Proceedings of the 14th Workshop on Computational Approaches to Subjectivity, Sentiment, & Social Media Analysis*, pages 11–22
August 15, 2024 

Our main contribution lies in the development of a metric-learning training strategy for emotion recognition in utterances that incorporates the conversational context. The presented model leverages sentence embeddings and Transformer encoder layers (Vaswani et al., 2017; Devlin et al., 2019) to represent dialogue utterances and deploy attention on the conversational context. Our method involves Siamese Networks (Koch et al., 2015) in the setup but can be adapted to any metric-learning model. We further demonstrate that our approach outperforms some of the latest state-of-the-art Large Language Models (LLMs) such as light versions of Falcon (Penedo et al., 2023) or LLaMA 2 (Touvron et al., 2023). In addition, our method is efficient in the sense that it involves lightweight, adaptable and quickly trainable models, which still yield state-of-the-art performance on the DailyDialog dataset in macro F1 score with 57.71% and satisfactory results on micro F1 with 57.75%.

Our code and models are available on GitHub [1] to reproduce training, inference and qualitative experiments.

## 2 Related Work

**ERC.** Although most of the studies on ERC have been carried out on multimodal datasets (Song et al., 2022; Li et al., 2022; Hu et al., 2022), thus leveraging multi-modality, there are still some models developed for emotion recognition on textual conversation only, whether it be on multimodal datasets restricted to text such as IEMOCAP (Busso et al., 2008) or MELD (Poria et al., 2019), or on a fully textual dataset such as DailyDialog (Li et al., 2017). The advent of deep learning enables significant progress in ERC on text, starting by the use of Recurrent Neural Networks (RNN) (Rumelhart et al., 1985; Jordan, 1986) by Poria et al. (2017). Further work using recurring structures followed, such as DialogueRNN (Majumder et al., 2019; Ghosal et al., 2020). This model leverages the attention mechanism (Bahdanau et al., 2014) combined with RNN. Graph-based methods also proved to be efficient as shown in (Ghosal et al., 2019), not only as such but also when considering external knowledge, as Lee and Choi (2021) use a Graph Convolutional Network (GCN) to perform ERC by extracting relations between dialogue instances.

Existing work on ERC relies mainly on evaluating their model using a micro F1 score excluding the majority neutral label. However, recent work actually skipped this evaluation to instead focus only on the macro version of this metric (Pereira et al., 2023), while other considered the Matthew Coefficient Correlation as an indication suitable for this task (Guibon et al., 2021).

In this work, we focus on DailyDialog, which consists of artificially human-generated conversations about daily life concerns, with utterance-wise emotion labeling. Liang et al. (2022) propose a model based on Graph Neural Networks (GNN) and Conditional Random Fields (Lafferty et al., 2001) (CRF) that achieves 64.01% in micro F1.

Although it is known not to provide the best performance compared to few-shot learning approaches (Dumoulin et al., 2021), meta-learning allows better generalization through more robust training (Finn et al., 2017; Antoniou et al., 2019), which is particularly adapted in the case of emotion detection due to both variability and complexity of human feelings (Plutchik, 2001).

**Metric learning.** As reviewed by (Hospedales et al., 2022), a meta-learning approach consists in a *meta-optimizer* that describes meta-learner updates, a *meta-representation* that stores the acquired knowledge and the *meta-objective* oriented towards the desired task. This optimization-based meta-learning setup provides end-to-end algorithms often based on episodic scenarios (Ravi and Larochelle, 2016; Finn et al., 2017; Mishra et al., 2017) that reflect the "learning to learn" strategy. Besides, learning to learn implies second order gradient computations which is costly. Palliative solutions to this problem, such as implicit differentiation (Lorraine et al., 2020), still involve a trade-off between performance and memory cost (Hospedales et al., 2022). Therefore, variants has emerged such as *metric learning*, which meta-objective is to learn the meta-representation itself. Starting with Siamese Networks (Koch et al., 2015), this model structure leverages parameter sharing between identical sub-networks to learn a distance between data samples. Relation Networks (Sung et al., 2018) also consider a distance metric, departing from the traditional Euclidean approach. Matching Networks (Vinyals et al., 2016) leverage training examples to identify weighted nearest neighbors. Prototypical Networks (Snell et al., 2017) compute average class representations and utilize cosine distance for element comparison.

[1] `https://github.com/B-Gendron/sentEmoContext`

This model has been adapted to perform ERC in a few-shot setting by Guibon et al. (2021) in a way that outperformed few-shot learning baselines.

In this work, we focus on the Siamese Networks architecture. It has the advantage of being conceptually simple, which makes it easily controllable and scalable. Nevertheless, the model structure proposed in this paper is easily adaptable to more complex meta-learning setups. Siamese Networks have been used, for example, in NLP for intention detection on text (Ren and Xue, 2020), in computer vision for facial recognition (Hayale et al., 2023), and in complex representation learning (Jin et al., 2021).

## 3 Methodology

In this work, we use a metric-learning architecture based on learning emotions as they relate to each other, thus extracting meta-information from the data. The model is a Siamese network (Koch et al., 2015) with three identical sub-networks, whose outputs are compared using the triplet loss (Schultz and Joachims, 2003). Initially applied to computer vision problems (Chechik et al., 2010; Schroff et al., 2015), triplet loss is defined on a triplet of data samples $(a, p, n)$ so that if $a$ and $p$ belong to the same class and $n$ belongs to a different class, then:

$$\mathcal{L}(a, p, n) = \max \{d(a, p) - d(a, n) + \text{margin}, 0\}$$

where the margin parameter is a strictly positive number.

While the triplet loss could be used in several strategies, ranging from only retrieving the most difficult triplets (when the positive is far from the anchor, meanwhile the anchor is close to the negative) to skipping the most easy ones (i.e. when the positive is closer to the anchor), we only tackle the overall strategy by considering each triplet in our data, due to the limited size of the data.

**Isolated representations.** As the aim of our experiments is to characterize the contribution of conversational context to emotion prediction, we first developed a baseline model on isolated utterances. This formally refers to computing emotion predictions for utterances independently of their context. To do this, we first consider a mapping for each utterance word to its associated FastText embedding (Bojanowski et al., 2017). From such embeddings, aforementioned $(a, p, n)$ triplets are randomly sampled and given as input for the Siamese Network, whose sub-network gradually improves in emotion prediction as triplet loss backpropagates.

**Contextual representations.** Regarding the contextual case, we build contextual utterance representations upon a BERT-like encoding. Sentence embeddings are preferred to word-piece embeddings (like BERT produces) as they provide lighter utterance representations. After the dialog is mapped to its associated series of pretrained embeddings, these outputs are concatenated forming a dialog representation, and contextual information is considered by deploying attention over it. Concretely, a Transformer encoder layer is stacked to the gathered frozen pre-trained embeddings. This newly conversation-aware dialog representation is then split at `[SEP]` tokens to end up with contextual representations at the utterance level, on which the emotion prediction is performed. In order to fit contextual utterance representations to the emotion prediction objective, we add an emotion classifier that is pre-trained on DailyDialog training set. The classifier is not frozen to ensure a complete backpropagation. Meanwhile, contextual representations are optimized according to the metric learning objective, using a triplet loss. The whole training procedure is illustrated in Figure 1. This training scenario enables both individual and relative emotion learning, in such a way that each learning phase strengthens the other. Thanks to this meta-learning setting, meta-information about emotions is extracted, and we can expect that this model is able to achieve relevant classification on unseen labels in a few-shot setting.

## 4 Experimental Protocol

**Data.** All the experiments have been carried out on DailyDialog dataset (Li et al., 2017) that provides more than 10,000 dialogues about daily concerns along with utterance-wise emotion labeling. In addition to providing utterance-level emotion labeling, an advantage in using DailyDialog is that it is relatively small, therefore it is quite easy to handle the entries and run tests on it. There exist six emotional labels (anger, disgust, fear, happiness, sadness and surprise) and a neutral label. Regarding emotion prediction, the evaluation is carried out only on the emotional labels following previous work procedure (Ghosal et al., 2021; Zhong et al., 2019). We use the original dataset splits (train, validation and test) from Li et al. (2017). The main characteristics from DailyDialog dataset

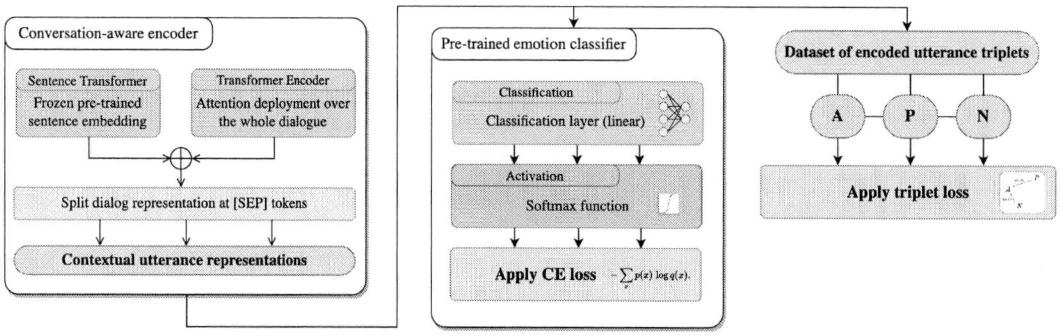


Figure 1: Illustration of the three main steps of the training procedure in the case of conversation-aware emotion predictions. Both losses (CE and triplet) backpropagate in order to gradually improve the encoder.

are visible in Table 1.

| Daily Dialog Stats | |
|---|---|
| Language | English |
| Max Msg/Conv | 35 |
| Avg Msg/Conv | 8 |
| Labels | 7 |
| Emotion Labels | 6 |
| Nb. Conv. | 13,118 |

Table 1: Main statistics for DailyDialog dataset

**Model specificities.** For the isolated utterance model, we consider two different types of sub-networks being simple linear layers and Long Short-Term Memory layers (LSTM) (Hochreiter and Schmidhuber, 1997). In the contextual case, the sub-network is a Transformer encoder fed with sentence embeddings. We carried out experiments with three different models of pre-trained sentence Transformers available in the Python library `sentence transformers`[2]: MPNet (Song et al., 2020), MiniLM (Wang et al., 2020) and RoBERTa (Liu et al., 2019). In order to ensure a good balance, the $(a, p, n)$ triplets are made at this stage, meaning right before applying the pre-trained emotion classifier, which is composed of a linear layer stacked upon one Transformer encoder layer.

**Training specificities.** Whether it be for the isolated utterance model or for the contextual one, the emotion prediction is always performed at the utterance level, therefore the triplets are always utterance triplets. This involves balance issues as DailyDialog dataset is very imbalanced regarding emotion labels (Figure 4). Indeed, the class rebalancing induced by sampling triplets according to a uniform distribution does not sufficiently mitigate bias during training and prevents the loss from converging due to excessive oversampling in frequent classes. Thus, we addressed the imbalance problem all along the training pipeline, by implementing a random sampler weighted with inverse label frequencies to account for the rareness of some emotional labels like `fear` or `disgust`.

**Evaluation.** For quantitative evaluation we needed to account for both performance and relevancy of the training procedure so that generalization abilities enabled by the meta-learning architecture are actually usable. This way, we selected, in addition to usual performance metrics, a more demanding metric: Matthews Correlation Coefficient (MCC) (Cramér, 1946). This measures a Pearson correlation (Pearson, 1895) between the predicted and the actual class, giving more precise information on classification quality than F1 score (Baldi et al., 2000). Using $TP$. $TN$. $FP$ and $FN$ as respectively the number of true positives, true negatives, false positives and false negatives, $P$ and $R$ being respectively precision and recall, and $N$ the total number of samples, MCC was originally defined in (Matthews, 1975) as:

$$\text{MCC} = \frac{TP/N - R \times P}{\sqrt{PR(1-R)(1-P)}} \quad (1)$$

**Comparison with LLMs.** In order to place the results of our isolated and contextual models into perspective, we compare our models with state-of-the-art LLMs, namely LLaMA (Touvron et al., 2023) and Falcon (Penedo et al., 2023). Both are considered with instruction fine-tuning and evaluated on text generation inference in a zero-shot

[2] `https://www.sbert.net/`

setting. We developed a prompt asking for prediction on the last utterance of each DailyDialog test set dialog, regarding the conversational context. For both LLMs, we went through an iterative process to find the most adapted prompt in the sense that the model actually generates only one label. The prompt is the same for each model of the same type (either LLaMA or Falcon). We experienced more difficulty on prompt tuning with Falcon as the model generates `happiness` on 86% of DailyDialog test set. Both prompts full texts are provided in Figure 2.

```
Here is a dialog :

-  Hello , Miao Li , Where are you going ?
-   Hello , I am going to the store to buy some fruit .
-   Oh , Would you do me a favor ?
-   Yes ?
-   Please mail this letter for me on your way to the store .
-   Sure . Do you want it to be registered ?
-   Yes , I think so . There are some pictures in it . It would be a great
pity if they were lost .
-   Yes , I will be glad to mail your letter .
-   Thanks .
-   you are welcome .

Regarding its conversational context, give me the appropriate emotion to
describe this utterance : "Yes , I think so . There are some pictures in
it . It would be a great pity if they were lost .", using only one of the
following labels: happiness, sadness, anger, surprise, fear, disgust, no
emotion. Predicted label :
```

(a) Prompt for LLaMA

```
Here is a dialog :

-  Hello , Miao Li , Where are you going ?
-   Hello , I am going to the store to buy some fruit .
-   Oh , Would you do me a favor ?
-   Yes ?
-   Please mail this letter for me on your way to the store .
-   Sure . Do you want it to be registered ?
-   Yes , I think so . There are some pictures in it . It would be a great
pity if they were lost .
-   Yes , I will be glad to mail your letter .
-   Thanks .
-   you are welcome .

Regarding its conversational context, return the appropriate emotion for
the last utterance among: sadness, happiness, anger, surprise, fear and
disgust. If none of them properly correspond, return 'no emotion'.
```

(b) Prompt for Falcon

Figure 2: Prompts for LLaMA and falcon

## 5 Results

Table 2 gives an overview of the different results obtained by the research community on ERC with DailyDialog. This actually shows a slow progression since 2017 where Poria et al. (2017) proposed to evaluate the model on the micro F1 score excluding the majority class (i.e., the neutral class). This became the first baseline for this task, achieving 50.24 in micro F1 score. However, the current state-of-the-art model now achieves 64.07 in micro F1 score (Liang et al., 2022) which amounts to a 14 points improvement during 6 years. As visible in Table 2, the community mainly followed this pattern and evaluation scheme. However, in

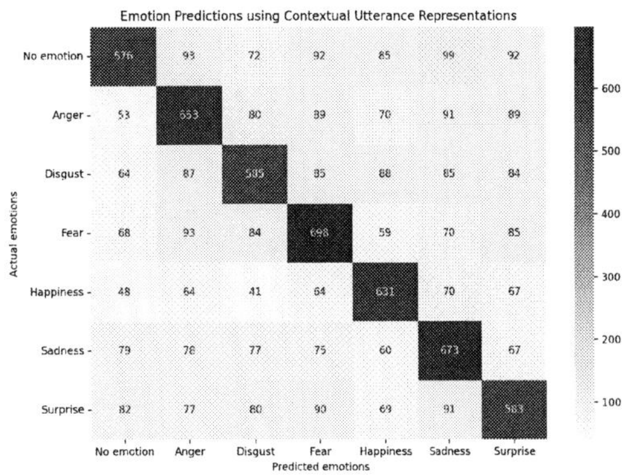


Figure 3: Confusion matrix for emotion predictions using contextual utterance representations

this paper, we think it is important to also consider the macro F1 score, excluding the majority class, as it shows the overall performance in all emotions. Some work has already decided to do so since 2020 (Ghosal et al., 2020), leading to an improvement of ~2.5 points in 3 years. Following this idea, Figure 3 and Table 3 illustrate this adaptability in emotion prediction showing the detailed classification results.

Compared to these results, our SentEmoContext model achieves 57.75 in micro F1 score, which is a decent but somewhat modest result in terms of metric comparison. However, Table 2 also shows the average performance of our model over 10 runs. Our SentEmoContext is state-of-the-art on the macro F1 score with 57.71 points, outperforming CD-ERC (Pereira et al., 2023) by 6.48 points, which is considerable since they only focused on this metric, and TODKAT (Zhu et al., 2021) by 5.15 points. We also evaluate our model using the multiclass MCC (Matthews, 1975; Baldi et al., 2000) score to ensure that the model does not arbitrary decide. Given an MCC score range of -1 to 1, and 0 indicating randomness, the 0.49 MCC score of the SentEmoContext model indicates that our approach is balanced and accurate in terms of predictions (Chicco and Jurman, 2020). Of course, we cannot compare with other ERC works with the MCC metric, as they did not use it. However, we think it is important to consider it as an additional metric to indicate the quality of the classification, minimizing the effect of the highly imbalanced data from conversations.

Given these results, our SentEmoContext performs really well considering that we only need ~20 minutes per epoch on GPU Nvidia A40 (45 GB

| Model name | macro F1* | micro F1* | MCC |
|---|---|---|---|
| *State-of-the-art models on ERC* | | | |
| CNN+cLSTM (Poria et al., 2017) | – | 50.24 | – |
| KET (Zhong et al., 2019) | – | 53.37 | – |
| COSMIC (Ghosal et al., 2020) | 51.05 | 58.48 | – |
| RoBERTa (Ghosal et al., 2020) | 48.20 | 55.16 | – |
| Rpe-RGAT (Ishiwatari et al., 2020) | – | 54.31 | – |
| Glove-DRNN (Ghosal et al., 2021) | 41.8 | 55.95 | – |
| roBERTa-DRNN (Ghosal et al., 2021) | 49.65 | 57.32 | – |
| CNN (Ghosal et al., 2021) | 36.87 | 50.32 | – |
| DAG-ERC (Shen et al., 2021) | – | 59.33 | – |
| TODKAT (Zhu et al., 2021) | <u>52.56</u> | 58.47 | – |
| SKAIG (Li et al., 2021) | 51.95 | 59.75 | – |
| Sentic GAT (Tu et al., 2022) | – | 54.45 | – |
| CauAIN (Zhao et al., 2022) | – | 58.21 | – |
| DialogueRole (Ong et al., 2022) | – | 60.95 | – |
| S+PAGE (Liang et al., 2022) | – | **64.07** | – |
| DualGAT (Zhang et al., 2023) | – | <u>61.84</u> | – |
| CD-ERC (Pereira et al., 2023) | 51.23 | – | – |
| Llama2-7b (Touvron et al., 2023) | 9.70 | 24.92 | 0.08 |
| Llama2-13b (Touvron et al., 2023) | 22.26 | 43.37 | 0.15 |
| Falcon-7b (Penedo et al., 2023) | 07.54 | 42.75 | 0.01 |
| MCM-CSD (Xu and Yang, 2024) | – | 60.70 | – |
| *Ours* | | | |
| SentEmoContext | **57.71** | 57.75 | **0.49** |

Table 2: All results for ERC on DailyDialog. Metrics are all computed on the official test set. DRNN stands for DialogueRNN as it is called in the original paper. MCC = Matthew Coefficient Correlation. The * indicates metrics that do not include the neutral label.

| Emotion | P | R | F1 | Supp. |
|---|---|---|---|---|
| No emotion | 0.594 | 0.519 | 0.554 | 1109 |
| Anger | 0.570 | 0.580 | 0.575 | 1125 |
| Disgust | 0.574 | 0.543 | 0.558 | 1078 |
| Fear | 0.585 | 0.603 | 0.594 | 1157 |
| Happiness | 0.594 | 0.641 | 0.617 | 985 |
| Sadness | 0.571 | 0.607 | 0.588 | 1109 |
| Surprise | 0.546 | 0.544 | 0.545 | 1072 |

Table 3: Emotion prediction details using contextual utterances. F1 is the F1-score for each class, and Supp. is the support. P is precision and R is recall.

RAM) and train it using only 5 epochs. This makes a striking difference from existing approaches that use multiple streams per speaker (Pereira et al., 2023), graph modeling for the representation of context and knowledge (Zhong et al., 2019; Li et al., 2021), or other heavy representations in their model (Liang et al., 2022). In addition to this, our model is stable with a standard deviation of only 0.01 on average across the three metrics, which reinforces the quality of such an efficient approach.

### 5.1 Comparison with Emotion Classifiers on Utterance Level

Table 4 shows the results of the direct emotion classification on utterances. For this task, we only considered the 6 emotion labels, excluding the neutral one not only from the evaluation but also from the training. By doing so, we want to determine the difference between our approach and a dedicated emotion classifier. This also serves as an ablation study for our SentEmoContext model, since this step is part of its training. With Table 4, we can see that our model leverages both the embedded conversational context and the metric learning scheme to increase all metrics. We can especially note the difference in terms of macro F1 scores, which shows the importance of the triplet loss representation in our model. Indeed, the emotion utterance classifiers are trained using batches balanced on the whole training set distribution and a weighted cross-entropy loss. Results show that it is not enough to deal with extreme imbalanced data such as conversations.

### 5.2 LLMs Results

The LLM results in a zero shot setting are visible in Table 5. These serve as an indication on the performance of such models, albeit in their lightweight version, in the ERC task. Although these generative models are not designed for this quite peculiar task, they still manage to outperform the utterance emotion classifiers of Table 4, which can be considered as a display of emergent capacities of LLMs (Srivastava et al., 2022).

### 5.3 Imbalance Factor

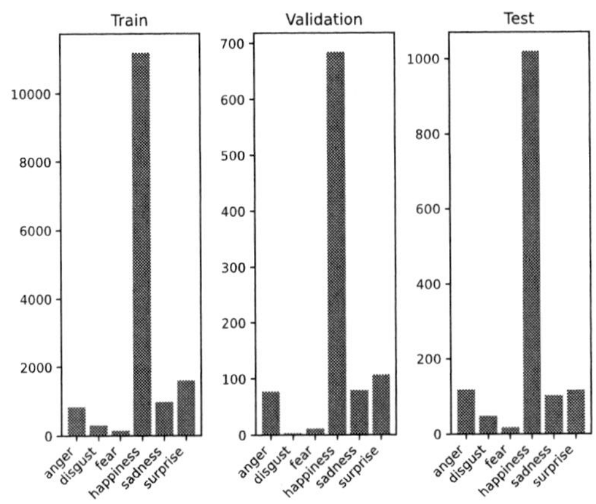


Figure 4: Histograms of only the emotion label distribution in DailyDialog subsets.

Although Table 1 shows the characteristics of the dataset, it omits to present the main characteristic of the conversational data in terms of emotion labels: the extreme imbalance. Most of the difficulty in ERC comes from the label definition, the context, but also from the imbalance factor that prevents the model from easily learning the representation of emotions in the context. Figure 4 shows the distribution of the labels in DailyDialog, without the neutral one. Considering the latter is the majority label and is excluded from the evaluation metrics by all the ERC community. The fact that even in the emotion labels the data is that imbalanced proves to be challenging and needs to be addressed. In fact, we are derived from Guibon et al. (2023) to tackle the imbalance in two steps. First, we balance the data loader to produce more balanced batches given the training set weights. Second, we weight the cross-entropy loss from the emotion classifier considering the remaining imbalance on each batch.

In addition to this, we add another way to address the imbalance. By considering triplets, we remove the imbalance factor while using hidden states that come from balanced representation. We think this partly explains the effectiveness and the efficiency of our model, considering its limited size compared to the related work.

## 6 Discussion

### 6.1 Model Size and Efficiency

Our SentEmoContext is efficient. It produces state-of-the-art results on macro F1 score and good results on micro F1. However, our model trains relatively fast and does not require a lot of epochs to converge. We think this efficiency, along with the limited memory needed to train, is due to both our two-step backpropagation and to the fact that we are using utterance-embedded representations with sentence transformers. Thus, our model can efficiently tackle long conversational contexts with limited memory cost.

In addition, Table 6 shows the difference between the models we used in terms of size, parameters, and number of layers. Our model is relatively small considering the recent advances and related work in ERC, but also compared to LLMs.

### 6.2 Relative Label Representation

Our approach actually learns twice from the data, first by using a supervised setting, and then by actually considering the relative distances between encoded elements, updating through the triplet loss. This enables the use of our model to different conversation datasets with different labels. The only requirement to extend the scope of this model would be to consider another triplet sampling strategy ignoring labels, such as the batch-hard strategy (Do et al., 2019).

## 7 Conclusion

In this paper, we present our SentEmoContext model, which comes from an approach that mixes utterance level representation, metric learning, and Siamese Networks. This model efficiently represents the conversational context, which makes

| Model name | macro F1 | micro F1 | MCC |
|---|---|---|---|
| *Pre-trained emotion utterance classifier* | | | |
| all-MiniLM-L6-v2 | 20.22 | 33.11 | 0.40 |
| *Ours* | | | |
| SentEmoContext | **57.71** | **57.75** | **0.49** |

Table 4: Comparison with a direct emotion classification at the utterance level. The `all-MiniLM-L6-v2` fine-tuning is also part of the whole SentEmoContext approach.

| Model name | P | R | macro F1* | micro F1* | MCC |
|---|---|---|---|---|---|
| llama2-7b-chat-hf | 26.77 | 24.77 | 9.70 | 24.92 | 0.08 |
| llama2-13b-chat-hf | 32.63 | 83.49 | 22.26 | 43.37 | 0.15 |
| falcon-7b-instruct | – | – | 07.54 | 42.75 | 0.01 |

Table 5: Results using two open-source LLMs with specific prompts. An example of the prompt is shown in Figure 2. * indicates metrics that do not include the neutral label.

| Model name | Seq. Length | Tokens | Dimensions | Size | Parameters | Tr. Layers |
|---|---|---|---|---|---|---|
| *Pre-trained sentence transformers* | | | | | | |
| all-MiniLM-L6-v2 | 256 | 1bn+ | 384 | 80 MB | 22M | 6 |
| all-mpnet-base-v2 | 384 | 1bn+ | 768 | 420 MB | 110M | 12 |
| *State-of-the-art LLMs* | | | | | | |
| Llama-2-7b-chat-hf | 4096 | 2T | 11008 | 13 GB | 7B | 32 |
| Llama-2-13b-chat-hf | 4096 | 2T | 11008 | 25 GB | 13B | 32 |
| falcon-7b-instruct | 2048 | 1.5T | 4544 | 15 GB | 7B | 32 |
| *Ours* | | | | | | |
| SentEmoContext | 256 | 4M | 384 | 604.8 MB | 159M | 6 |

Table 6: Insights about model sizes, comparing the pretrained sentence Transformers used in our approach to state-of-the-art LLMs. These insights demonstrate that SentEmoContext provides a lightweight yet efficient way to perform ERC on DailyDialog.

it achieve state-of-the-art macro F1 score with 57.71, and satisfactory micro F1 scores with 57.75 on the Emotion Recognition in Conversation on DailyDialog. We also propose to use the Matthew Correlation Coefficient to better evaluate this task.

With SentEmoContext we use contrastive learning with balanced samplers to minimize the imbalance factor, which is inherent to conversational data. We also leverage sentence BERT to both minimize the memory required for training considering the whole conversational context and to actually represent the conversational context by considering utterances as the minimal unit. This led to a more robust and efficient training method that does not require a lot of epochs to obtain satisfactory results. We also show that small- to average-size open-source LLMs are still behind on emotion recognition in conversation, as it requires a lot of context to be incorporated in the prompt and is not specifically relevant to generative models.

In our future work, we want to consider applying this approach to other datasets, with added modalities, to stress-test our model. We also plan to use it on slightly different labels, as our model learns relative positions toward labels. Thus, we plan to adapt it to a setting leaning towards meta-learning.

## 8 Limitations

The first limitation we faced with LLMs is the requirement of high-memory GPUs to test them.

This explains why in Table 5 we only consider the lightweight version of these two open source LLMs. While LLaMA 7b and 13b gave answers in a good format, i.e. with only one label chosen, Falcon did not behave the way we wanted. In order to solve this, we look for the first mentioned emotion in the output to consider it as a label.

Also, it is important to note that we did not want to tackle OpenAI's ChatGPT due to the fact that we do not have a clear control on the model version, size and approach used behind its API, but also because we wanted to consider open source models, and open source data as we will release both our models and source code to the community. Moreover, we limited ourselves to LLaMA 2 as experiments were performed prior to the release of LLaMA 3.

An additional possible limitation on LLMs is the context size. In ERC, context size is key, but with LLMs adding examples in the prompt to do few-shot learning would take a lot of space in the overall context, the prompt being part of the context. This explains our decision to only consider zero-shot in this paper for LLMs, even though we should also consider prompt tuning to enhance them on this specific task.

## Acknowledgments

Experiments presented in this paper were carried out using the Grid'5000 testbed, supported by a scientific interest group hosted by Inria and including CNRS. RENATER and several Universities as well as other organizations (see `https://www.grid5000.fr`).

## References

Antreas Antoniou, Harri Edwards, and Amos Storkey. 2019. How to train your maml. In *Seventh International Conference on Learning Representations, ICLR*.

Dzmitry Bahdanau, Kyunghyun Cho, and Y. Bengio. 2014. Neural machine translation by jointly learning to align and translate. *3rd International Conference on Learning Representations, ICLR 2015*, 1409.

Pierre Baldi, Søren Brunak, Yves Chauvin, Claus Andersen, and Henrik Nielsen. 2000. Assessing the accuracy of prediction algorithms for classification: An overview. *Bioinformatics (Oxford, England)*, 16:412–24.

Piotr Bojanowski, Edouard Grave, Armand Joulin, and Tomas Mikolov. 2017. Enriching word vectors with subword information. *Transactions of the Association for Computational Linguistics*, 5:135–146.

Carlos Busso, Murtaza Bulut, Chi-Chun Lee, Abe Kazemzadeh, Emily Mower, Samuel Kim, Jeannette N. Chang, Sungbok Lee, and Shrikanth S. Narayanan. 2008. Iemocap: interactive emotional dyadic motion capture database. *Language Resources and Evaluation*, 42(4):335–359.

Gal Chechik, Varun Sharma, Uri Shalit, and Samy Bengio. 2010. Large scale online learning of image similarity through ranking. *J. Mach. Learn. Res.*, 11:1109–1135.

Davide Chicco and Giuseppe Jurman. 2020. The advantages of the matthews correlation coefficient (mcc) over f1 score and accuracy in binary classification evaluation. *BMC genomics*, 21(1):6.

Harald Cramér. 1946. *Mathematical Methods of Statistics (PMS-9), Volume 9*. Princeton University Press, Princeton.

Jacob Devlin, Ming-Wei Chang, Kenton Lee, and Kristina Toutanova. 2019. BERT: Pre-training of deep bidirectional transformers for language understanding. In *Proceedings of the 2019 Conference of the North American Chapter of the Association for Computational Linguistics: Human Language Technologies, Volume 1 (Long and Short Papers)*, pages 4171–4186, Minneapolis, Minnesota. Association for Computational Linguistics.

Thanh-Toan Do, Toan Tran, Ian Reid, Vijay Kumar, Tuan Hoang, and Gustavo Carneiro. 2019. A theoretically sound upper bound on the triplet loss for improving the efficiency of deep distance metric learning. In *Proceedings of the IEEE/CVF Conference on Computer Vision and Pattern Recognition*, pages 10404–10413.

Vincent Dumoulin, Neil Houlsby, Utku Evci, Xiaohua Zhai, Ross Goroshin, Sylvain Gelly, and Hugo Larochelle. 2021. A unified few-shot classification benchmark to compare transfer and meta learning approaches. In *Thirty-fifth Conference on Neural Information Processing Systems Datasets and Benchmarks Track (Round 1)*.

Chunxiao Fan, Jie Lin, Rui Mao, and Erik Cambria. 2024. Fusing pairwise modalities for emotion recognition in conversations. *Information Fusion*, page 102306.

Chelsea Finn, Pieter Abbeel, and Sergey Levine. 2017. Model-agnostic meta-learning for fast adaptation of deep networks. In *Proceedings of the 34th International Conference on Machine Learning - Volume 70*, ICML'17, page 1126–1135. JMLR.org.

Deepanway Ghosal, Navonil Majumder, Alexander Gelbukh, Rada Mihalcea, and Soujanya Poria. 2020. COSMIC: COmmonSense knowledge for eMotion identification in conversations. In *Findings of the Association for Computational Linguistics: EMNLP*

*2020*, pages 2470–2481, Online. Association for Computational Linguistics.

Deepanway Ghosal, Navonil Majumder, Rada Mihalcea, and Soujanya Poria. 2021. Exploring the role of context in utterance-level emotion, act and intent classification in conversations: An empirical study. In *Findings of the Association for Computational Linguistics: ACL-IJCNLP 2021*, pages 1435–1449, Online. Association for Computational Linguistics.

Deepanway Ghosal, Navonil Majumder, Soujanya Poria, Niyati Chhaya, and Alexander Gelbukh. 2019. DialogueGCN: A graph convolutional neural network for emotion recognition in conversation. In *Proceedings of the 2019 Conference on Empirical Methods in Natural Language Processing and the 9th International Joint Conference on Natural Language Processing (EMNLP-IJCNLP)*, pages 154–164, Hong Kong, China. Association for Computational Linguistics.

Gaël Guibon, Matthieu Labeau, Hélène Flamein, Luce Lefeuvre, and Chloé Clavel. 2021. Few-shot emotion recognition in conversation with sequential prototypical networks. In *Proceedings of the 2021 Conference on Empirical Methods in Natural Language Processing*, Punta Cana, Dominican Republic.

Gaël Guibon, Matthieu Labeau, Luce Lefeuvre, and Chloé Clavel. 2023. An adaptive layer to leverage both domain and task specific information from scarce data. *Proceedings of the AAAI Conference on Artificial Intelligence*, 37(6):7757–7765.

Wassan Hayale, Pooran Singh Negi, and Mohammad H. Mahoor. 2023. Deep siamese neural networks for facial expression recognition in the wild. *IEEE Transactions on Affective Computing*, 14(2):1148–1158.

Sepp Hochreiter and Jürgen Schmidhuber. 1997. Long Short-Term Memory. *Neural Computation*, 9(8):1735–1780.

Timothy Hospedales, Antreas Antoniou, Paul Micaelli, and Amos Storkey. 2022. Meta-learning in neural networks: A survey. *IEEE Transactions on Pattern Analysis and Machine Intelligence*, 44(9):5149–5169.

Guimin Hu, Ting-En Lin, Yi Zhao, Guangming Lu, Yuchuan Wu, and Yongbin Li. 2022. UniMSE: Towards unified multimodal sentiment analysis and emotion recognition. In *Proceedings of the 2022 Conference on Empirical Methods in Natural Language Processing*, pages 7837–7851, Abu Dhabi, United Arab Emirates. Association for Computational Linguistics.

Taichi Ishiwatari, Yuki Yasuda, Taro Miyazaki, and Jun Goto. 2020. Relation-aware graph attention networks with relational position encodings for emotion recognition in conversations. In *Proceedings of the 2020 Conference on Empirical Methods in Natural Language Processing (EMNLP)*, pages 7360–7370, Online. Association for Computational Linguistics.

Ming Jin, Yizhen Zheng, Yuan-Fang Li, Chen Gong, Chuan Zhou, and Shirui Pan. 2021. Multi-scale contrastive siamese networks for self-supervised graph representation learning. In *Proceedings of the Thirtieth International Joint Conference on Artificial Intelligence, IJCAI-21*, pages 1477–1483. International Joint Conferences on Artificial Intelligence Organization. Main Track.

M I Jordan. 1986. Serial order: a parallel distributed processing approach. technical report, june 1985-march 1986.

Prannay Khosla, Piotr Teterwak, Chen Wang, Aaron Sarna, Yonglong Tian, Phillip Isola, Aaron Maschinot, Ce Liu, and Dilip Krishnan. 2020. Supervised contrastive learning. *Advances in neural information processing systems*, 33:18661–18673.

Gregory Koch, Richard Zemel, and Ruslan Salakhutdinov. 2015. Siamese neural networks for one-shot image recognition.

John Lafferty, Andrew McCallum, Fernando Pereira, et al. 2001. Conditional random fields: Probabilistic models for segmenting and labeling sequence data. In *Icml*, volume 1, page 3. Williamstown, MA.

Bongseok Lee and Yong Suk Choi. 2021. Graph based network with contextualized representations of turns in dialogue. In *Proceedings of the 2021 Conference on Empirical Methods in Natural Language Processing*, pages 443–455, Online and Punta Cana, Dominican Republic. Association for Computational Linguistics.

Jiang Li, Xiaoping Wang, Guoqing Lv, and Zhigang Zeng. 2023. Graphmft: A graph network based multimodal fusion technique for emotion recognition in conversation. *Neurocomputing*, 550:126427.

Jiangnan Li, Zheng Lin, Peng Fu, and Weiping Wang. 2021. Past, present, and future: Conversational emotion recognition through structural modeling of psychological knowledge. In *Findings of the Association for Computational Linguistics: EMNLP 2021*, pages 1204–1214, Punta Cana, Dominican Republic. Association for Computational Linguistics.

Yanran Li, Hui Su, Xiaoyu Shen, Wenjie Li, Ziqiang Cao, and Shuzi Niu. 2017. DailyDialog: A manually labelled multi-turn dialogue dataset. In *Proceedings of the Eighth International Joint Conference on Natural Language Processing (Volume 1: Long Papers)*, pages 986–995, Taipei, Taiwan. Asian Federation of Natural Language Processing.

Zaijing Li, Fengxiao Tang, Ming Zhao, and Yusen Zhu. 2022. EmoCaps: Emotion capsule based model for conversational emotion recognition. In *Findings of the Association for Computational Linguistics: ACL 2022*, pages 1610–1618, Dublin, Ireland. Association for Computational Linguistics.

Chen Liang, Jing Xu, Yangkun Lin, Chong Yang, and Yongliang Wang. 2022. S+PAGE: A speaker and position-aware graph neural network model for emotion recognition in conversation. In *Proceedings of the 2nd Conference of the Asia-Pacific Chapter of the Association for Computational Linguistics and the 12th International Joint Conference on Natural Language Processing (Volume 1: Long Papers)*, pages 148–157, Online only. Association for Computational Linguistics.

Xingwei Liang, You Zou, Xinnan Zhuang, Jie Yang, Taiyu Niu, and Ruifeng Xu. 2023. Mmateric: Multi-task learning and multi-fusion for audiotext emotion recognition in conversation. *Electronics*, 12(7):1534.

Yinhan Liu, Myle Ott, Naman Goyal, Jingfei Du, Mandar Joshi, Danqi Chen, Omer Levy, Mike Lewis, Luke Zettlemoyer, and Veselin Stoyanov. 2019. Roberta: A robustly optimized bert pretraining approach. *Preprint*, arXiv:1907.11692.

Jonathan Lorraine, Paul Vicol, and David Duvenaud. 2020. Optimizing millions of hyperparameters by implicit differentiation. In *Proceedings of the Twenty Third International Conference on Artificial Intelligence and Statistics*, volume 108 of *Proceedings of Machine Learning Research*, pages 1540–1552. PMLR.

Navonil Majumder, Soujanya Poria, Devamanyu Hazarika, Rada Mihalcea, Alexander Gelbukh, and Erik Cambria. 2019. Dialoguernn: An attentive rnn for emotion detection in conversations. *Proceedings of the AAAI Conference on Artificial Intelligence*, 33(01):6818–6825.

Brian W. Matthews. 1975. Comparison of the predicted and observed secondary structure of t4 phage lysozyme. *Biochimica et biophysica acta*, 405 2:442–51.

Nikhil Mishra, Mostafa Rohaninejad, Xi Chen, and P. Abbeel. 2017. A simple neural attentive meta-learner. In *International Conference on Learning Representations*.

Donovan Ong, Jian Su, Bin Chen, Anh Tuan Luu, Ashok Narendranath, Yue Li, Shuqi Sun, Yingzhan Lin, and Haifeng Wang. 2022. Is discourse role important for emotion recognition in conversation? *Proceedings of the AAAI Conference on Artificial Intelligence*, 36(10):11121–11129.

Karl Pearson. 1895. Vii. note on regression and inheritance in the case of two parents. *proceedings of the royal society of London*, 58(347-352):240–242.

Guilherme Penedo, Quentin Malartic, Daniel Hesslow, Ruxandra Cojocaru, Alessandro Cappelli, Hamza Alobeidli, Baptiste Pannier, Ebtesam Almazrouei, and Julien Launay. 2023. The refinedweb dataset for falcon llm: Outperforming curated corpora with web data, and web data only. *Preprint*, arXiv:2306.01116.

Patrícia Pereira, Helena Moniz, Isabel Dias, and Joao Paulo Carvalho. 2023. Context-dependent embedding utterance representations for emotion recognition in conversations. In *Proceedings of the 13th Workshop on Computational Approaches to Subjectivity, Sentiment, & Social Media Analysis*, pages 228–236, Toronto, Canada. Association for Computational Linguistics.

Robert Plutchik. 2001. The Nature of Emotions. *American Scientist*, 89(4):344.

Soujanya Poria, Erik Cambria, Devamanyu Hazarika, Navonil Majumder, Amir Zadeh, and Louis-Philippe Morency. 2017. Context-dependent sentiment analysis in user-generated videos. In *Proceedings of the 55th Annual Meeting of the Association for Computational Linguistics (Volume 1: Long Papers)*, pages 873–883, Vancouver, Canada. Association for Computational Linguistics.

Soujanya Poria, Devamanyu Hazarika, Navonil Majumder, Gautam Naik, Erik Cambria, and Rada Mihalcea. 2019. MELD: A multimodal multi-party dataset for emotion recognition in conversations. In *Proceedings of the 57th Annual Meeting of the Association for Computational Linguistics*, pages 527–536, Florence, Italy. Association for Computational Linguistics.

Sachin Ravi and Hugo Larochelle. 2016. Optimization as a model for few-shot learning. In *International Conference on Learning Representations*.

Fuji Ren and Siyuan Xue. 2020. Intention detection based on siamese neural network with triplet loss. *IEEE Access*, 8:82242–82254.

David E Rumelhart, Geoffrey E Hinton, and Ronald J Williams. 1985. Learning internal representations by error propagation. Technical report, California Univ San Diego La Jolla Inst for Cognitive Science.

Florian Schroff, Dmitry Kalenichenko, and James Philbin. 2015. Facenet: A unified embedding for face recognition and clustering. In *2015 IEEE Conference on Computer Vision and Pattern Recognition (CVPR)*, pages 815–823.

Matthew Schultz and Thorsten Joachims. 2003. Learning a distance metric from relative comparisons. In *Advances in Neural Information Processing Systems*, volume 16. MIT Press.

Weizhou Shen, Siyue Wu, Yunyi Yang, and Xiaojun Quan. 2021. Directed acyclic graph network for conversational emotion recognition. In *Proceedings of the 59th Annual Meeting of the Association for Computational Linguistics and the 11th International Joint Conference on Natural Language Processing (Volume 1: Long Papers)*, pages 1551–1560, Online. Association for Computational Linguistics.

Jake Snell, Kevin Swersky, and Richard Zemel. 2017. Prototypical networks for few-shot learning. In *Proceedings of the 31st International Conference on Neural Information Processing Systems*, NIPS'17, page 4080–4090, Red Hook, NY, USA. Curran Associates Inc.

Kaitao Song, Xu Tan, Tao Qin, Jianfeng Lu, and Tie-Yan Liu. 2020. Mpnet: Masked and permuted pre-training for language understanding. In *Advances in Neural Information Processing Systems*, volume 33, pages 16857–16867. Curran Associates, Inc.

Xiaohui Song, Longtao Huang, Hui Xue, and Songlin Hu. 2022. Supervised prototypical contrastive learning for emotion recognition in conversation. In *Proceedings of the 2022 Conference on Empirical Methods in Natural Language Processing*, pages 5197–5206, Abu Dhabi, United Arab Emirates. Association for Computational Linguistics.

Aarohi Srivastava et al. 2022. Beyond the imitation game: Quantifying and extrapolating the capabilities of language models. *arXiv preprint arXiv:2206.04615*.

Flood Sung, Yongxin Yang, Li Zhang, Tao Xiang, Philip H.S. Torr, and Timothy M. Hospedales. 2018. Learning to compare: Relation network for few-shot learning. In *2018 IEEE/CVF Conference on Computer Vision and Pattern Recognition*, pages 1199–1208.

Hugo Touvron, Louis Martin, Kevin Stone, Peter Albert, Amjad Almahairi, Yasmine Babaei, Nikolay Bashlykov, Soumya Batra, Prajjwal Bhargava, Shruti Bhosale, Dan Bikel, Lukas Blecher, Cristian Canton Ferrer, Moya Chen, Guillem Cucurull, David Esiobu, Jude Fernandes, Jeremy Fu, Wenyin Fu, Brian Fuller, Cynthia Gao, Vedanuj Goswami, Naman Goyal, Anthony Hartshorn, Saghar Hosseini, Rui Hou, Hakan Inan, Marcin Kardas, Viktor Kerkez, Madian Khabsa, Isabel Kloumann, Artem Korenev, Punit Singh Koura, Marie-Anne Lachaux, Thibaut Lavril, Jenya Lee, Diana Liskovich, Yinghai Lu, Yuning Mao, Xavier Martinet, Todor Mihaylov, Pushkar Mishra, Igor Molybog, Yixin Nie, Andrew Poulton, Jeremy Reizenstein, Rashi Rungta, Kalyan Saladi, Alan Schelten, Ruan Silva, Eric Michael Smith, Ranjan Subramanian, Xiaoqing Ellen Tan, Binh Tang, Ross Taylor, Adina Williams, Jian Xiang Kuan, Puxin Xu, Zheng Yan, Iliyan Zarov, Yuchen Zhang, Angela Fan, Melanie Kambadur, Sharan Narang, Aurelien Rodriguez, Robert Stojnic, Sergey Edunov, and Thomas Scialom. 2023. Llama 2: Open foundation and fine-tuned chat models. *Preprint*, arXiv:2307.09288.

Geng Tu, Jintao Wen, Cheng Liu, Dazhi Jiang, and Erik Cambria. 2022. Context- and sentiment-aware networks for emotion recognition in conversation. *IEEE Transactions on Artificial Intelligence*, 3(5):699–708.

Ashish Vaswani, Noam Shazeer, Niki Parmar, Jakob Uszkoreit, Llion Jones, Aidan N. Gomez, Lukasz Kaiser, and Illia Polosukhin. 2017. Attention is all you need. *Preprint*, arXiv:1706.03762.

Oriol Vinyals, Charles Blundell, Timothy Lillicrap, Koray Kavukcuoglu, and Daan Wierstra. 2016. Matching networks for one shot learning. In *Proceedings of the 30th International Conference on Neural Information Processing Systems*, NIPS'16, page 3637–3645, Red Hook, NY, USA. Curran Associates Inc.

Binqiang Wang, Gang Dong, Yaqian Zhao, Rengang Li, Qichun Cao, Kekun Hu, and Dongdong Jiang. 2023. Hierarchically stacked graph convolution for emotion recognition in conversation. *Knowledge-Based Systems*, 263:110285.

Wenhui Wang, Furu Wei, Li Dong, Hangbo Bao, Nan Yang, and Ming Zhou. 2020. Minilm: Deep self-attention distillation for task-agnostic compression of pre-trained transformers. In *Advances in Neural Information Processing Systems*, volume 33, pages 5776–5788. Curran Associates, Inc.

Jintao Wen, Dazhi Jiang, Geng Tu, Cheng Liu, and Erik Cambria. 2023. Dynamic interactive multiview memory network for emotion recognition in conversation. *Information Fusion*, 91:123–133.

Yuan Xu and Meng Yang. 2024. Mcm-csd: Multi-granularity context modeling with contrastive speaker detection for emotion recognition in real-time conversation. In *ICASSP 2024-2024 IEEE International Conference on Acoustics, Speech and Signal Processing (ICASSP)*, pages 11956–11960. IEEE.

Duzhen Zhang, Feilong Chen, and Xiuyi Chen. 2023. DualGATs: Dual graph attention networks for emotion recognition in conversations. In *Proceedings of the 61st Annual Meeting of the Association for Computational Linguistics (Volume 1: Long Papers)*, pages 7395–7408, Toronto, Canada. Association for Computational Linguistics.

Weixiang Zhao, Yanyan Zhao, and Xin Lu. 2022. Cauain: Causal aware interaction network for emotion recognition in conversations. In *Proceedings of the Thirty-First International Joint Conference on Artificial Intelligence, IJCAI-22*, pages 4524–4530. International Joint Conferences on Artificial Intelligence Organization. Main Track.

Peixiang Zhong, Di Wang, and Chunyan Miao. 2019. Knowledge-enriched transformer for emotion detection in textual conversations. In *Proceedings of the 2019 Conference on Empirical Methods in Natural Language Processing and the 9th International Joint Conference on Natural Language Processing (EMNLP-IJCNLP)*, pages 165–176, Hong Kong, China. Association for Computational Linguistics.

Lixing Zhu, Gabriele Pergola, Lin Gui, Deyu Zhou, and Yulan He. 2021. Topic-driven and knowledge-aware transformer for dialogue emotion detection. In *Proceedings of the 59th Annual Meeting of the Association for Computational Linguistics and the 11th International Joint Conference on Natural Language Processing (Volume 1: Long Papers)*, pages 1571–1582, Online. Association for Computational Linguistics.

# Modeling Complex Interactions in Long Documents for Aspect-Based Sentiment Analysis

**Zehong Yan[1], Wynne Hsu[1], Mong Li Lee[1], David Roy Bartram-Shaw[2]**

[1]NUS Centre for Trusted Internet & Community, National University of Singapore
[2]Edelman Data & Intelligence

{zehong, whsu, leeml}@comp.nus.edu.sg, david.bartram.shaw@gmail.com

https://yanzehong.github.io/dart/

## Abstract

The growing number of online articles and reviews necessitates innovative techniques for document-level aspect-based sentiment analysis. Capturing the context in which an aspect is mentioned is crucial. Existing models have focused on relatively short reviews and may fail to consider distant contextual information. This is especially so in longer documents where an aspect may be referred to in multiple ways across dispersed sentences. This work introduces a hierarchical Transformer-based architecture that encodes information at different level of granularities with attention aggregation mechanisms to learn the local and global aspect-specific document representations. For empirical validation, we curate two datasets of long documents: one on social issues, and another covering various topics involving trust-related issues. Experimental results show that the proposed architecture outperforms state-of-the-art methods for document-level aspect-based sentiment classification. We also demonstrate the potential applicability of our approach for long document trust prediction.

## 1 Introduction

As user-generated content on the web continues to multiply at an exponential rate, the need for automated sentiment in these documents has grown markedly. The ability to discover fine-grained sentiments can provide valuable insights as to how, why, and where an entity is liked and trusted[1]. Early works have focused on classifying the overall sentiment of a document (Yang et al., 2016; Turney, 2002; Diao et al., 2023), while subsequent research performs aspect-based sentiment analysis to identify the fine-grained sentiments concerning the different aspects of some target entity (Severyn and Moschitti, 2015; Pontiki et al., 2016; Nazir et al., 2020; Brauwers and Frasincar, 2021).

[1]https://www.edelmandxi.com/trust-intelligence/measuring-trust-prerequisite-unlocking-growth

| **Review** |
|---|
| **S1:** *A great location to stay at, since it is close to a beautiful beach.* |
| **S2:** *I had booked 3 rooms via Priceline, and the staff replied immediately.* |
| **S3:** *Check in was prompt, the desk people were very friendly.* |
| **S4:** *But the room was tiny for two people, I am pretty sure our luggage would not fit in there.* |
| ...... |
| **S17:** *Fortunately, everything else in the room was fine.* |
| **S18:** *The room was clean with a normal bed with fresh sheets everyday* |
| **S19:** *The walk-in bathroom was wonderful, we actually had a spectacular view of the ocean from a small window in our shower.* |
| **S20:** *Again, the location was unbeatable, since we like being in the center of touristy things and this was it.* |
| **S21**: *It was in the middle of the tourist section.* |
| **S22**: *Taxi ride to the mall and the restaurant, very short distance.* |
| ...... |
| **S28:** *I'm just often nitpicking for room size, since it was a bit small compared to other resorts I've stayed.* |
| ...... |
| Document-level Sentiment for ROOM aspect is Negative<br>Document-level Sentiment for LOCATION aspect is Positive |

Figure 1: Sample hotel review.

Aspect-based sentiment analysis can be performed at the sentence-level or document-level. Sentence-level aspect-based sentiment analysis focuses on independently classifying the sentiments associated with aspects in individual sentences (Peng et al., 2020; Yan et al., 2021). However, this approach fails to consider the context of the aspect, which can often be inferred from preceding or succeeding sentences or paragraphs. In Figure 1, the sentiment expressed toward the aspect "Location" is not clear just by looking at sentence **S21**. By examining the surrounding sentences **S1**, **S20** and **S22**, which are all positive, one could infer that the phrase "in the middle of the tourist section" has a positive sentiment, demonstrating the importance of *context* in aspect-based sentiment analysis at the document level. Further, sentences in the same document may express *conflicting sentiments* towards the same aspect. For example, sentence **S17**, **S18** and **S19** express a positive sentiment towards the aspect "Room", but **S4** and **S28** convey a negative sentiment. Simply classifying the overall sentiment based on a single sentence or taking the majority vote may led to incorrect conclusions.



*Proceedings of the 14th Workshop on Computational Approaches to Subjectivity, Sentiment, & Social Media Analysis*, pages 23–34
August 15, 2024 ©2024 Association for Computational Linguistics

In this work, we design a hierarchical Transformer-based architecture called DART that leverages multiple layers of attention mechanisms. This allows us to capture the dependencies among sentences in long documents and learn aspect-specific document representations. DART performs attention aggregation on the learned representations to take into account both the local and global contexts. By employing learnable global aspect queries, our model aggregates sentiments that reflects the overall sentiment of the document, even in the presence of conflicting sentiments.

We curate two datasets, one focusing on social issues and another on trust-related issues. Initial experiments indicate that even GPT-4 has difficulty dealing with implicit aspects and often misinterprets sentiment due to insufficient aspect knowledge. Comprehensive experiments show that DART achieves state-of-the-art accuracy for document-level aspect-based sentiment classification, and is also effective in predicting trust and polarity in long complex documents.

## 2 Related Work

Research on aspect-based sentiment analysis can be broadly classified into sentence level and document level. Sentence-level aspect-based sentiment analysis includes using Long Short-Term Memory (LSTM) network to model aspects in sentences (Tang et al., 2016), attention-based LSTM to correlate aspects and sentiment polarities (Wang et al., 2016; Ma et al., 2017; Tay et al., 2018), deep memory networks to integrate aspect information (Tang et al., 2016; Chen et al., 2017), and gated networks to select aspect-specific sentiment in sentences (Zhang et al., 2016; Xue and Li, 2018). (Chen et al., 2020) introduce graph attention networks to improve sentence prediction by incorporating sentiment preference information from the document context. The work in (Yan et al., 2021) propose a unified framework for fine-grained sentiment analysis to identify the aspect and opinion terms as well as its sentiment polarity for each sentence.

Document-level aspect-based sentiment analysis predicts the sentiment polarity for each aspect mentioned in a document. Traditional approaches have largely relied on feature engineering. Latent rating regression (LRR) (Wang et al., 2010) is a probabilistic graphical model that generates document sentiment representation from a weighted sum of the latent aspect variables. (Lu et al., 2011) use support vector regression model based on handcrafted features to predict aspect ratings. To handle correlation between aspects, (McAuley et al., 2012) add a dependency term that explicitly encodes relationships between aspects. These methods have strict assumptions about words and sentences such as whether a word is an aspect or sentiment towards an aspect, and typically use bag-of-words representations which are insufficient to capture the order of words and complex semantics.

Neural network methods for document-level aspect sentiment analysis include N-DMSC (Yin et al., 2017), VWS-DMSC (Zeng et al., 2019) and D-MILN (Ji et al., 2020). N-DMSC employs hierarchical LSTM to create aspect-aware document representations using question-answer pairs constructed from aspect-related keywords and aspect ratings. VWS-DMSC uses a multi-task learning framework with rules to extract target-opinion word pairs to guide the sentiment prediction towards document aspects in a weakly supervised manner. D-MILN is a multiple instance learning network that models the relation between aspect-level and document-level sentiment with document-level supervision. (Fei et al., 2021) model the latent target-opinion distribution as prior information and employ a two-layer BiLSTM to obtain the overall document-level sentiment classification.

Transformer models have been utilized for aspect sentiment analysis (Fei et al., 2022; Islam and Bhattacharya, 2022). However, they are limited to processing sequences of up to 512 tokens. To overcome this limitation, models such as Longformer (Beltagy et al., 2020), Big Bird (Zaheer et al., 2020), Hi-Transformer (Wu et al., 2021) and LongT5 (Guo et al., 2022) have been introduced. However, these models have not yet been specifically utilized for aspect-based sentiment analysis.

## 3 Proposed Framework

The proposed DART framework takes as input a document $d$ and an aspect $a_j$ and outputs the predicted sentiment for $a_j$. Figure 2 shows the architecture of DART which consists of four key blocks:

**Sentence Encoding Block.** This block focuses on transforming the document into individual sentences and using a pretrained language model to generate representations for every sentence-aspect combination.

**Global Context Interaction Block.** This block employs dual transformer encoders to model interac-

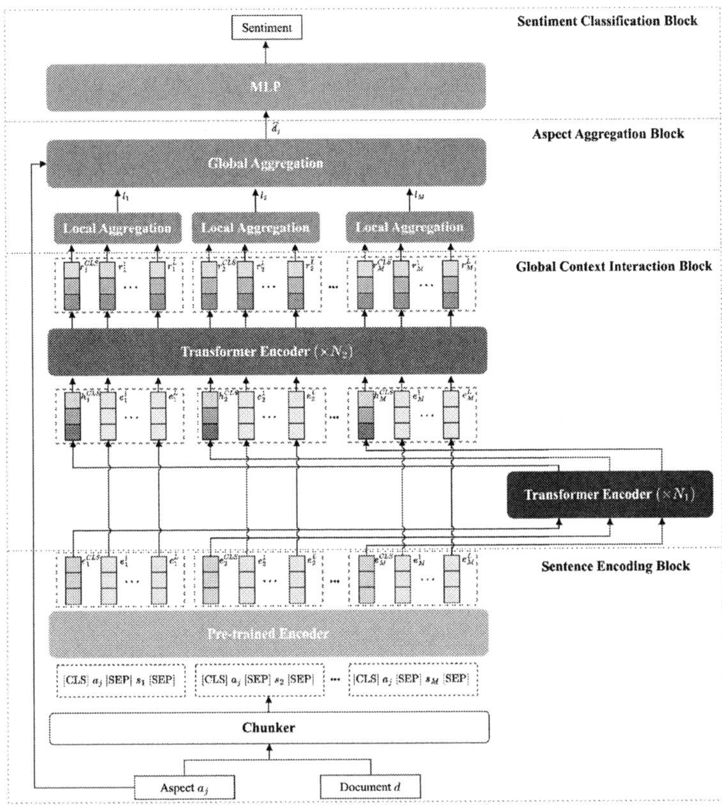


Figure 2: Overview of DART framework.

tions among sentences and generate context-aware sentence embeddings. This is a crucial component of DART as it captures essential aspect-specific information across long-range dependencies.

**Aspect Aggregation Block.** This block aggregates the contextually enriched sentence embedding to produce an aspect-specific representation of the entire document.

**Sentiment Classification Block.** With the document representation obtained, this block leverages a two-layered Multilayer Perceptron (MLP) to predict the sentiment for the aspect.

### 3.1 Sentence Encoding Block

Initially, the input document is divided into $M$ sentences, denoted as $s_1, s_2, ..., s_M$. This is achieved using the sentence splitter from the Natural Language Toolkit[2]. Then we construct fixed length sequences $seq_1, seq_2, ..., seq_M$, adding right paddings if needed. Each sequence $seq_i$ is given by:

$$seq_i = \texttt{[CLS]}\ a_j\ \texttt{[SEP]}\ s_i\ \texttt{[SEP]}$$

[2]nltk.org

where [CLS] and [SEP] are the special tokens to denote the sentence-level information and separator respectively. The sequence $seq_i$ is fed into a BERT-based pretrained model to generate the embedding

$$[e_i^{CLS}, e_i^1, e_i^2, ..., e_i^L]$$

where $e_i^k$ is the $k^{th}$ token in $seq_i$ and $L$ is the fixed length of the sequence.

### 3.2 Global Context Interaction Block

This block captures dependencies among sentences so that a sentence can be understood in the broader context of the entire document, thus increasing the accuracy of sentiment prediction for a specific aspect. It incorporates two transformer encoders which serve different purposes.

The first transformer encoder focuses on the inter-sentence relationships. It uses the $[CLS]$ tokens which are condensed representations of their respective sentences, and apply self-attention to these tokens across all sentences. This allows the encoder to obtain the context information, and produce a set of contextually enriched [CLS] tokens,

$e_i^{CLS}, 1 \leq i \leq M$, each representing its sentence in the context of the whole document. Positional information is retained by adding the standard learnable position embeddings. The output from this transformer is $h_i^{CLS}$.

After capturing the context information, the second transformer encoder further refines each sentence's representation. It takes the context-enriched $h_i^{CLS}$ token from the first encoder and combines it with the original embeddings of the sentence tokens. The combined input $[h_i^{CLS}, e_i^1, ..., e_i^L]$ undergoes another round of self-attention, producing the enriched sentence representation $[r_i^{CLS}, r_i^1, ..., r_i^L]$ where each $r_i$ is influenced both by its original context and the broader document context.

### 3.3 Aspect Aggregation Block

This block plays a pivotal role in the DART framework by generating a unified document representation that captures the overall sentiment of a document concerning a specific aspect. It serves as a bridge between understanding individual sentences and comprehending the document as a whole, especially concerning a specific aspect. Given that sentiment towards an aspect can be scattered throughout a document, this block ensures that all these sentiments are appropriately aggregated.

The key idea of this block is obtain a aspect-specific representation through a two-level aggregation process. The first level weighs the importance of each token in the sentence concerning the aspect and the broader context by performing a local attentive pooling. The enriched sentence representation $[r_i^{CLS}, r_i^1, ..., r_i^L]$ from the global context interaction block undergoes a local aggregation process to obtain the output $l_i$:

$$l_i = \alpha_0 r_i^{CLS} + \sum_{k=1}^{L} \alpha_k r_i^k \quad (1)$$

where $\alpha_k$ is the attention weight for the $k^{th}$ token, determined based on its relevance to the aspect and the overall sentence context.

The second level takes the aggregated representations $l_i$ of each sentence and performs a global attentive pooling to determine how much attention each sentence should receive when forming the overall document representation $\hat{d}_j$ with respect to the aspect $a_j$. This aggregation is given by

$$\hat{d}_j = \sum_{i=1}^{M} \frac{\exp(e_i^1 f(l_i))}{\sum_{i'=1}^{M} \exp(e_i^1 f(l_{i'}))} l_i \quad (2)$$

where $f(\cdot)$ is a linear projection followed by the `tanh` function.

The weighting coefficients ensure that sentences more relevant to the aspect have a greater influence on the final document representation $\hat{d}_j$.

### 3.4 Sentiment Classification Block

This block is the final stage in the DART framework. The goal of this block is to utilize the aggregated document representation, which has been enriched with context and focused on a particular aspect, to predict the sentiment associated with that aspect. The final document representation $\hat{d}_j$ is passed through the two-layer MLP to obtain the probability distribution for the positive or negative sentiment towards the aspect $a_j$.

## 4 Performance Study

We implement DART in PyTorch1.13.0 and carry out experiments on the A100-SXM4 GPUs with 40 GB. We use the following datasets:

**BeerAdvocate**. This dataset contains reviews and ratings on predefined beer aspects: feel, look, smell, and taste, each rated on a scale of 1 to 5. The ratings are binarized into positive and negative sentiment.

**TripAdvisor**. This dataset consists of hotel reviews with ratings of 1 to 5 stars for aspects value, room, location, cleanliness, check in/front desk, service, and business. Again, these ratings are binarized.

**SocialNews**. We curate this dataset from news articles related to social issues from the PerSenT dataset (Bastan et al., 2020). We identify six implicit aspects, namely crime-justice, digital-online, economic issues, health, human rights, and work. A group of labelling experts was trained using educational guideline pack and a series of face to face sessions so that they have a clear understanding of the definition of aspects and sentiment. An expert benchmarking assessment was performed where 100 verified labels were assigned to each prospective annotators and those who reached a 70% agreement with experts were selected. Finally, three annotators are asked to assess the sentiment towards these aspects and we use the majority vote as the ground truth sentiment. The Kappa inter-annotator agreement is 93.14%.

Table 1 summarizes the characteristics of these datasets. DART utilizes the pre-trained model `bigbird-roberta-base` (Zaheer et al., 2020) in the Sentence Encoding Block. For the Global Context Interaction Block, the first Transformer en-

| Dataset | #aspects | #docs | #long docs (%) | #sentences/doc | #tokens/doc | #tokens/sentence |
|---|---|---|---|---|---|---|
| BeerAdvocate | 4 | 27583 | 217 (0.8%) | 11.1 | 173.5 | 15.7 |
| TripAdvisor | 7 | 28543 | 4027 (14.1%) | 12.9 | 298.9 | 23.1 |
| SocialNews | 6 | 4512 | 1031 (22.9%) | 17.5 | 389.8 | 22.2 |

Table 1: Dataset characteristics. #long docs refers to documents with more than 512 tokens.

coder has 4 layers, while the second Transformer encoder has 2 layers. Both have 12 self-attention heads with a hidden size of 768. We use AdamW optimizer with a dropout rate of 0.1, and a batch size of 16. Each experiment is repeated 5 times and we report the average results on three datasets.

### 4.1 Comparative Study

We first compare DART with non-transformer aspect-based sentiment classification methods:

**LRR** (Wang et al., 2010) is a probabilistic graphical regression model. Guided by the overall rating and the aspect keywords, LRR infers the latent ratings for each aspect. A high rating indicates positive sentiment towards the aspect in the document.

**VWS-DMSC** (Zeng et al., 2019) is a weakly supervised model that predicts the sentiment with respect to an aspect. Target-opinion word pairs are extracted as supervision signal to learn the sentiment without using aspect polarity annotations.

**D-MILN** (Ji et al., 2020) is also a weakly supervised model for document-level aspect sentiment classification. It employs multiple instance learning to learn the relation between aspect-level and document-level sentiment.

**N-DMSC** (Yin et al., 2017) is a supervised neural model for document aspect sentiment classification. It employs hierarchical LSTM to generate aspect-aware document representations.

Table 2 shows the average accuracy for BeerAdvocate and TripAdvisor. We see that DART outperforms all the methods by a large margin. Using deep embedding features yields better results compared to traditional ngram features in LRR. Unlike N-DMSC, VWS-DMSC and D-MILN, DART does not require a pre-defined set of aspect-related keywords, reducing the complexity and pre-processing requirement in real-world scenarios.

Next, we compare the performance of DART with transformer-based models on long documents:

**InstructABSA** (Scaria et al., 2023) uses the 11B-parameter T5 model, with a maximum input sequence length of 512, for sentence-level aspect-based sentiment analysis. As such, we truncate the input when the length of instruction prompts and document exceeds 512 tokens.

| Model | BeerAdvocate | TripAdvisor |
|---|---|---|
| LRR† | 59.41 | 69.47 |
| VWS-DMSC† | 75.38 | 75.61 |
| D-MILN† | 79.86 | 79.52 |
| N-DMSC† | 86.35 | 83.34 |
| DART | **88.25** | **86.38** |

Table 2: Comparison of accuracy results for non-transformer models. Results with "†" are retrieved from (Ji et al., 2020).

**MDABSA** (Van Thin et al., 2022) is a joint multi-task architecture that aims to perform both aspect category detection and sentiment polarity classification tasks simultaneously.

**Longformer** (Beltagy et al., 2020) employs sliding windows to enable long-range coverage for long document modelling. We adapt Longformer for the document aspect sentiment classification task by first obtaining an aspect-aware document representation through feeding the aspect and document pair separated by the `[SEP]` token. The representation is then fed to a two-layer multi-layer perceptron to make sentiment prediction.

**Big Bird** (Zaheer et al., 2020) This is an encoder-only model that extends the sparse attention pattern with random attention for longer sequences. We adapt Bird Bird for sentiment classification in the same way as we have done for Longformer.

**LongT5** (Guo et al., 2022) is the state-of-the-art transformer architecture for long inputs. The original LongT5 is an encoder-decoder structure with a new transient attention mechanism (TGlobal), which mimics ETC's local/global mechanism(Ainslie et al., 2020). Here, we leverage its encoder pre-trained weights and adapt it in the same way for fair comparison.

**GPT4** (OpenAI, 2023) large language models (LLMs) have shown impressive results across various tasks. Here, we select `gpt-4-0613` as the representative LLM and perform the experiments under zero-shot and few-shot settings. For GPT4-

| Model | All Aspects | Crime-Justice | Digital-Online | Economic Issues | Health | Human Rights | Work |
|---|---|---|---|---|---|---|---|
| InstructABSA | 80.16 | 81.65 | 72.73 | **81.25** | 86.67 | 72.46 | 84.47 |
| MDABSA | 80.97 | 86.24 | 68.83 | 75.00 | 86.67 | 75.36 | 86.33 |
| Longformer | 80.53 | 87.89 | 69.09 | 78.75 | 80.67 | 70.72 | 85.71 |
| Big Bird | 80.81 | 86.97 | 69.35 | 76.25 | 79.33 | 75.36 | 86.09 |
| LongT5 | 81.13 | 88.14 | 70.65 | 75.83 | 79.33 | 76.52 | 85.09 |
| GPT4-zeroshot | 58.91 | 72.48 | 25.97 | 58.33 | 66.67 | 63.77 | 62.11 |
| GPT4-fewshot | 60.32 | 75.23 | 28.57 | 64.58 | 70.00 | 65.22 | 60.25 |
| DART | **83.81*** | **88.53** | **75.64*** | 79.69 | **89.17*** | **78.99** | **86.80** |

* indicates result is statistically significant when compared to the second best with p-value < 0.05.

Table 3: Accuracy of Transformer-based models in SocialNews Dataset.

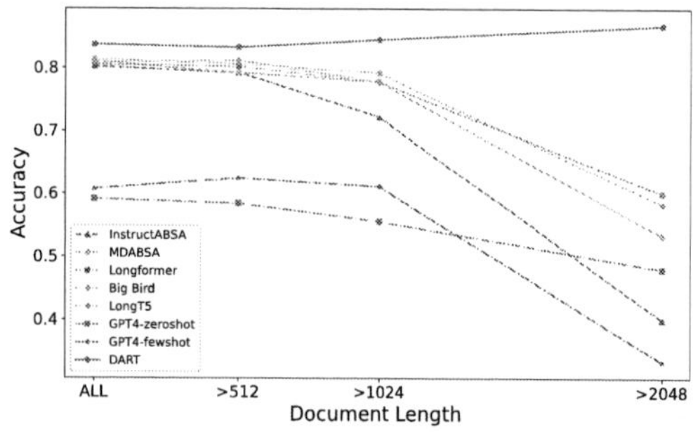


Figure 3: Accuracy of Transformer-based models with respect to document length on SocialNews test set.

| Model | BeerAdvocate | | TripAdvisor | |
|---|---|---|---|---|
| | Accuracy | F1 | Accuracy | F1 |
| InstructABSA | 81.25 | 79.83 | 70.01 | 69.65 |
| MDABSA | 87.39 | 85.67 | 83.77 | 83.69 |
| Longformer | 87.85 | 86.09 | 83.61 | 83.13 |
| Big Bird | 88.14 | 86.59 | 84.04 | 83.44 |
| LongT5 | 90.42 | 88.31 | 84.34 | 84.19 |
| GPT4-zeroshot | 58.54 | 51.09 | 59.39 | 57.65 |
| GPT4-fewshot | 69.65 | 66.71 | 74.43 | 72.16 |
| DART | **94.44*** | **92.86*** | **86.48** | **85.96** |

* indicates result is statistically significant when compared to the second best with p-value < 0.05.

Table 4: Comparison of results for transformer-based models on long documents (>512 tokens).

fewshot, we adopt the prompt from (Scaria et al., 2023) to perform aspect sentiment predictions.

Table 3 shows the performance of Transformer-based models on the SocialNews dataset, with details of their accuracy in handling different aspects. The results indicate that DART excels in five key aspects, particularly in the digital-online and health aspects, and is the second best model for the economic issues aspect. This demonstrates DART's ability to handle diverse and complex aspects. Appendix A provides a visualization of the learned document representations via t-sne.

Figure 3 shows the accuracy achieved in SocialNews for documents that exceed a certain length, as specified on the x-axis. The gap in performance between DART and other models widens as the document length surpasses the 1024-token threshold. DART continues to demonstrate superior performance even with extremely long documents, exceeding 2048 tokens in length. This indicates DART's proficiency in analyzing larger documents, which is an important aspect in real-world sentiment analysis scenarios.

Table 4 shows the average accuracy and macro F1 scores on the long documents in Beer Advocate and TripAdvisor over 5 runs. We see that DART achieves the best performance, with marked improvements over existing models. Similar gains is observed for the F1 scores, confirming DART's effectiveness in dealing with long documents for sentiment classification.

InstructABSA, which achieved state-of-the-art on SemEval 2014, 15, and 16 datasets for aspect sentiment classification, and MDABSA both perform worse than DART. This indicates that the methodologies developed for sentence-level aspect-based sentiment analysis or short texts do not extend well to longer documents. The results also reveal that our more compact, specialized DART model, which contains 687 million parameters, exceeded the performance of GPT4.

## 4.2 Ablation Study

We examine the effect of the various components in DART on its performance. We implemented two variants: (a) w/o Int. where the interaction component is bypassed and the outputs from the Sentence Encoding Block is fed directly to the Aspect Aggregation Block; and (b) w/o Agg. where the aggregation component is omitted and the average of the `[CLS]` vectors is used as the document representation for sentiment prediction.

| Model | BeerAdvocate | TripAdvisor | SocialNews |
|---|---|---|---|
| w/o Int. | 86.57 | 85.41 | 80.37 |
| w/o Agg. | 86.74 | 85.51 | 80.78 |
| DART | 87.94 | 86.21 | 85.54 |

Table 5: Accuracy of DART and its variants.

| Model | TrustData | Hyperpartisan |
|---|---|---|
| Longformer | 80.77 | 93.54 |
| Big Bird | 81.59 | 92.00 |
| LongT5 | 82.26 | 93.23 |
| GPT4-zeroshot | 77.89 | 83.08 |
| GPT4-fewshot | 79.95 | 86.15 |
| DART | **83.93*** | **95.69*** |

* statistically significant compared to the second best with p-value < 0.05.

Table 6: Accuracy of trust and polarity predictions.

| Model | Ability | Dependability | Integrity | Purpose |
|---|---|---|---|---|
| Longformer | 80.24 | 75.56 | 88.29 | 83.33 |
| Big Bird | 80.95 | 78.89 | 84.87 | 85.71 |
| LongT5 | 81.43 | 78.89 | 88.78 | 85.23 |
| GPT4-zeroshot | 75.79 | 81.48 | 80.49 | 83.33 |
| GPT4-fewshot | 78.17 | **85.19*** | 82.93 | 80.95 |
| DART | **83.23*** | 81.48 | **89.63** | **87.14** |

* statistically significant compared to the second best with p-value < 0.05.

Table 7: Accuracy for various aspects in TrustData.

Table 5 shows the results. Compared to BeerAdvocate and TripAdvisor, we see a significant drop in the accuracy for SocialNews when the Sentence Interaction block is removed because 22.9% of the documents are longer than 512 on SocialNews. Similar reduction in accuracy is observed when we do not incorporate the Aspect Aggregation block. This demonstrates the importance of capturing the interaction among sentences in long documents as well as aggregating aspects locally and globally.

### 4.3 Case Studies

Here, we present case studies to show DART's ability to highlight phrases relevant to the target aspects. Figure 4 shows an article from SocialNews related to the aspect HEALTH. Only DART correctly predicts the negative sentiment towards this aspect while both Big Bird and Longformer give a positive sentiment. Phrases in purple are highlighted by DART as the basis for its negative prediction. In contrast, Big Bird and Longformer could not adequately capture the context, leading them to overlook the underlying negative sentiment.

Figure 5 shows two sample reviews from TripAdvisor. For the top review, DART focuses on phrases related to VALUE (highlighted in red) and correctly predicts a positive sentiment towards the aspect VALUE while Big Bird and Longformer give the wrong predictions. For the bottom review, DART predicts the correct negative sentiment towards the aspect CLEAN, with relevant phrases highlighted in green. We see that although DART attends to the phrase "Overall room be clean daily", it is able to identify negative phrases such as "exotic huge dead cockroach", "dingy bed and blanket" and "The shower stall do not close" to be associated to the aspect CLEAN and gives the correct prediction. In contrast, Big Bird and Longformer mistakenly interpret the sentiment as positive.

## 5 Application of DART to Trust and Polarity Prediction

While DART is originally conceptualized for sentiment analysis, the framework is versatile and can be extended for trust analysis and polarity prediction. In this section, we show that DART's ability to capture context information and aspect-specific attention aggregation makes it well-suited to evaluate trust-related aspects and gauge the degree of alignment or opposition on a topic.

We compile a dataset for trust prediction, comprising of 2925 documents, of which 60.5% are long documents with more than 512 tokens. This dataset emphasizes four trust-related aspects: ability, dependability, integrity and purpose. We enlist three independent annotators to assess the trust polarity for each aspect, and take the majority vote as the ground truth. The annotation labels are "trust", "distrust", "mixed", and "no indication". The Kappa inter-annotator agreement is 87.29%. We call this dataset **TrustData**.

For polarity prediction, we use the **Hyperpartisan** dataset (Kiesel et al., 2019) consisting of news articles which have been manually labelled as hyperpartisan or not. There are 645 articles, out of which 53.3% have more than 512 tokens.

In Table 6, we see that DART gives the best accuracy and F1 score for trust and polarity predictions. The improvements achieved by DART over the second best model are statistically significant with p-value < 0.05, indicating the effectiveness of the global context interaction block in DART to capture the context information in long documents.

Table 7 provides a detailed breakdown of model accuracies in predicting the polarity of the different aspects in the TrustData dataset. We see that DART gives the best performance in three key aspects, and

*The "RAC " as the committee is called will begin a public inquiry into Jesse 's death as well as the safety of adenovirus, which has been used in roughly one-quarter of all gene-therapy clinical trials. The Penn scientists will report on their preliminary results and investigators who at the RAC's request have submitted thousands of pages of patient safety data to the committee will discuss the side effects of adenovirus. Among them will be researchers from the Schering-Plough Corporation which was running two experiments in advanced liver cancer patients that used methods similar to Penn's. Enrollment in those trials was suspended by the Food and Drug Administration after Jesse 's death. The company under pressure from the RAC has since released information showing that some patients experienced serious side effects including changes in liver function and blood-cell counts mental confusion and nausea. Once all the data on adenovirus are analyzed at the Dec. meeting the RAC may recommend restrictions on its use which will almost certainly slow down some aspects of gene-therapy research.*

*The meeting will be important for another reason: it will mark an unprecedented public airing of information about the safety of gene therapy -- precisely the kind of sharing the RAC has unsuccessfully sought in the past. Officials say gene therapy has claimed no lives besides Jesse 's. But since his death there have been news reports that other patients died during the course of experiments-from their diseases as opposed to the therapy-and that the scientists involved did not report those deaths to the RAC as is required.*

Figure 4: Sample article from SocialNews. DART correctly predicts positive sentiment for the HEALTH aspect while Big Bird and Longformer predicts negative sentiment.

*Save half your money, ignore a little mold! I go to Puerto Rico to help my son find an apartment for himself. This hotel fall into we price range a lot better than the nearly next door Marriott hotel do, and the location be great. I choose to ignore the review. I hope you will read mine , as diamond palace deserve a chance. When you walk in the front door, it be almost like step into a movie set of the era of the rat pack. I expect dean martin to come swaggering over from the lounge at any moment. ... .A walk out the door at the end of the lounge area bring we right out on the main street, and a right hand turn bring we to a Haagen-Dazs. So it be easy to get online, as far as the room go, the bed be a little hard for my liking, and the pillow be not great. But the sheet be clean. The room be in bad shape. There be bubble of the ceiling both over the bed , and a lot of it over the shower -- both be moldy. It be always humid in Puerto Rico , and I suspect when there be no one in a room, the air conditioning be off, thus the mold. But the countertop in the small bathroom be clean. We just stop look up. There be a free refrigerator in the closet in the room, and we save a ton by keep drink and some food in there. There be also a free safe in there, though we have no valuable. It be only one block to the beach!!*

*It be ok I guess. We stay at this hotel for the first time from June 28th - July 4th , 2008. The pro and con I will lay out clearly here. Overall, I would say if you with a group who want to just save money but want a great location than this be you place. First the pro :2 block from beach , they have a pool onsite, if you call they after book two seperate room for they cheap rate you can ask the hotel to give you two connected room with a kitchenette and only pay about $ 0.50 cent more per room -lrb- not bad -rrb- . Overall room be clean daily. Price be great ! We pay like $ 99.50 per room per day .the best part be that it be 2 block from the beach and just on the other side of the international market !they have chilli 's restaurant in lobby area and pizza hut quick room service. Now the con : too many night club directly below the hotel or to the side of it. Thank god we travel with ear plug because we both have balcony room and have we not have they we would have lose we mind by the second night. It be very noisy on kuhio ave right at this hotel location. Club stay open until 4 am , yes 4! Room be like stay at a motel 6 or something similar with dingy bed and blanket. The bathroom for the room with king size bed be teeny tiny only have shower and the paint be peel off the wall. The shower stall do not close that well so we always have to mop up the floor with one of we extra towel after shower. The parking be hard ! Too little level and you squeeze you way into the stall. Sometimes they double park we. Now the worst thing. On the very first night there in the middle of the night I have hear a bug flap on to my sheet and kick it off. I do not pay any mind too it after that too exhaust. When I awake to my awful surprise I find one of those exotic huge dead cockroach by the balcony slide door. I guess I kick the life out of it -lrb- thank goodness. I only see one but the hotel do disclose that due to it be a tropical location they do have occassional visitor like this .= -rrb-*

Figure 5: Sample reviews from TripAdvisor. Top: DART gives correct positive sentiment prediction for the aspect VALUE. Bottom: DART gives correct negative sentiment prediction for the aspect CLEAN.

is competitive with GPT4-zeroshot for the Dependability aspect, possibly due to the fewer number of documents with this aspect. The improvements suggest that the aspect-specific attention aggregation block in DART significantly enhances its ability to focus on phrases relevant to the various aspects.

## 6 Conclusion

We have described DART, a hierarchical transformer-based framework for document-level aspect-based sentiment analysis. DART handles the complexities of longer text through its global context interaction and two-level aspect aggregation blocks, which enhance the model's ability to recognize and amplify aspect-specific content across long-range dependencies. This enables DART to focus on relevant phrases associated with the target aspect. Experiments on various datasets indicate DART's effectiveness in handling long documents. We have also shown the applicability of DART for trust and polarity prediction and will make the curated SocialNews dataset publicly available. Future work includes extending DART's capabilities to handle aspect-based sentiment analysis involving multiple entities.

## Acknowledgments

This work is supported by the Singapore Ministry of Education Academic Research Fund Tier 1. We would like to thank Katie Stuart for her comments.

## Limitations

This work assumes each document contains only one entity. There is a need to develop a benchmark that can assess aspect based sentiments towards different entities in long documents.

## References

Joshua Ainslie, Santiago Ontanon, Chris Alberti, Vaclav Cvicek, Zachary Fisher, Philip Pham, Anirudh Ravula, Sumit Sanghai, Qifan Wang, and Li Yang. 2020. ETC: Encoding long and structured inputs in transformers. In *Proceedings of the 2020 Conference on Empirical Methods in Natural Language Processing (EMNLP)*, pages 268–284, Online. Association for Computational Linguistics.

Mohaddeseh Bastan, Mahnaz Koupaee, Youngseo Son, Richard Sicoli, and Niranjan Balasubramanian. 2020. Author's sentiment prediction. In *Proceedings of the 28th International Conference on Computational Linguistics*, pages 604–615, Barcelona, Spain (Online). International Committee on Computational Linguistics.

Iz Beltagy, Matthew E. Peters, and Arman Cohan. 2020. Longformer: The long-document transformer. *CoRR*, abs/2004.05150.

Gianni Brauwers and Flavius Frasincar. 2021. A survey on aspect-based sentiment classification. *ACM Computing Surveys (CSUR)*.

Qian Chen, Xiaodan Zhu, Zhen-Hua Ling, Si Wei, Hui Jiang, and Diana Inkpen. 2017. Recurrent neural network-based sentence encoder with gated attention for natural language inference. In *Proceedings of the 2nd Workshop on Evaluating Vector Space Representations for NLP*, pages 36–40, Copenhagen, Denmark. Association for Computational Linguistics.

Xiao Chen, Changlong Sun, Jingjing Wang, Shoushan Li, Luo Si, Min Zhang, and Guodong Zhou. 2020. Aspect sentiment classification with document-level sentiment preference modeling. In *Proceedings of the 58th Annual Meeting of the Association for Computational Linguistics*, pages 3667–3677, Online. Association for Computational Linguistics.

Shizhe Diao, Sedrick Scott Keh, Liangming Pan, Zhiliang Tian, Yan Song, and Tong Zhang. 2023. Hashtag-guided low-resource tweet classification. In *Proceedings of the ACM Web Conference 2023*, WWW '23, page 1415–1426, New York, NY, USA. Association for Computing Machinery.

Hao Fei, Jingye Li, Yafeng Ren, Meishan Zhang, and Donghong Ji. 2022. Making decision like human: Joint aspect category sentiment analysis and rating prediction with fine-to-coarse reasoning. In *Proceedings of the ACM Web Conference 2022*, WWW '22, page 3042–3051, New York, NY, USA. Association for Computing Machinery.

Hao Fei, Yafeng Ren, Shengqiong Wu, Bobo Li, and Donghong Ji. 2021. Latent target-opinion as prior for document-level sentiment classification: A variational approach from fine-grained perspective. In *Proceedings of the Web Conference 2021*, WWW '21, page 553–564, New York, NY, USA. Association for Computing Machinery.

Mandy Guo, Joshua Ainslie, David Uthus, Santiago Ontanon, Jianmo Ni, Yun-Hsuan Sung, and Yinfei Yang. 2022. LongT5: Efficient text-to-text transformer for long sequences. In *Findings of the Association for Computational Linguistics: NAACL 2022*, pages 724–736, Seattle, United States. Association for Computational Linguistics.

Sk Mainul Islam and Sourangshu Bhattacharya. 2022. AR-BERT: Aspect-relation enhanced aspect-level sentiment classification with multi-modal explanations. In *Proceedings of the ACM Web Conference 2022*, WWW '22, page 987–998, New York, NY, USA. Association for Computing Machinery.

Yunjie Ji, Hao Liu, Bolei He, Xinyan Xiao, Hua Wu, and Yanhua Yu. 2020. Diversified multiple instance learning for document-level multi-aspect sentiment classification. In *Proceedings of the 2020 Conference on Empirical Methods in Natural Language Processing (EMNLP)*, pages 7012–7023, Online. Association for Computational Linguistics.

Johannes Kiesel, Maria Mestre, Rishabh Shukla, Emmanuel Vincent, Payam Adineh, David Corney, Benno Stein, and Martin Potthast. 2019. SemEval-2019 task 4: Hyperpartisan news detection. In *Proceedings of the 13th International Workshop on Semantic Evaluation*, pages 829–839, Minneapolis, Minnesota, USA. Association for Computational Linguistics.

Bin Lu, Myle Ott, Claire Cardie, and Benjamin K Tsou. 2011. Multi-aspect sentiment analysis with topic models. In *2011 IEEE 11th international conference on data mining workshops*, pages 81–88. IEEE.

Dehong Ma, Sujian Li, Xiaodong Zhang, and Houfeng Wang. 2017. Interactive attention networks for aspect-level sentiment classification. In *Proceedings of the 26th International Joint Conference on Artificial Intelligence*, pages 4068–4074.

Julian McAuley, Jure Leskovec, and Dan Jurafsky. 2012. Learning attitudes and attributes from multi-aspect reviews. In *2012 IEEE 12th International Conference on Data Mining*, pages 1020–1025. IEEE.

Ambreen Nazir, Yuan Rao, Lianwei Wu, and Ling Sun. 2020. Issues and challenges of aspect-based sentiment analysis: a comprehensive survey. *IEEE Transactions on Affective Computing*.

OpenAI. 2023. GPT-4 technical report. *CoRR*, abs/2303.08774.

Haiyun Peng, Lu Xu, Lidong Bing, Fei Huang, Wei Lu, and Luo Si. 2020. Knowing what, how and why: A near complete solution for aspect-based sentiment analysis. In *Proceedings of the AAAI Conference on Artificial Intelligence*, volume 34, pages 8600–8607.

Maria Pontiki, Dimitris Galanis, Haris Papageorgiou, Ion Androutsopoulos, Suresh Manandhar, Mohammad AL-Smadi, Mahmoud Al-Ayyoub, Yanyan Zhao, Bing Qin, Orphée De Clercq, Véronique Hoste, Marianna Apidianaki, Xavier Tannier, Natalia Loukachevitch, Evgeniy Kotelnikov, Nuria Bel, Salud María Jiménez-Zafra, and Gülşen Eryiğit. 2016. SemEval-2016 task 5: Aspect based sentiment analysis. In *Proceedings of the 10th International Workshop on Semantic Evaluation (SemEval-2016)*, pages 19–30, San Diego, California. Association for Computational Linguistics.

Kevin Scaria, Himanshu Gupta, Saurabh Arjun Sawant, Swaroop Mishra, and Chitta Baral. 2023. InstructABSA: Instruction learning for aspect based sentiment analysis. *CoRR*, abs/2302.08624.

Aliaksei Severyn and Alessandro Moschitti. 2015. Twitter sentiment analysis with deep convolutional neural networks. In *Proceedings of the 38th international ACM SIGIR conference on research and development in information retrieval*, pages 959–962.

Duyu Tang, Bing Qin, and Ting Liu. 2016. Aspect level sentiment classification with deep memory network. In *Proceedings of the 2016 Conference on Empirical Methods in Natural Language Processing*, pages 214–224, Austin, Texas. Association for Computational Linguistics.

Yi Tay, Luu Anh Tuan, and Siu Cheung Hui. 2018. Learning to attend via word-aspect associative fusion for aspect-based sentiment analysis. In *Proceedings of the AAAI conference on artificial intelligence*, volume 32.

Peter Turney. 2002. Thumbs up or thumbs down? semantic orientation applied to unsupervised classification of reviews. In *Proceedings of the 40th Annual Meeting of the Association for Computational Linguistics*, pages 417–424, Philadelphia, Pennsylvania, USA. Association for Computational Linguistics.

Dang Van Thin, Lac Si Le, Hao Minh Nguyen, and Ngan Luu-Thuy Nguyen. 2022. A joint multi-task architecture for document-level aspect-based sentiment analysis in vietnamese. *IJMLC*, 12(4).

Hongning Wang, Yue Lu, and Chengxiang Zhai. 2010. Latent aspect rating analysis on review text data: a rating regression approach. In *Proceedings of the 16th ACM SIGKDD international conference on Knowledge discovery and data mining*, pages 783–792.

Yequan Wang, Minlie Huang, Xiaoyan Zhu, and Li Zhao. 2016. Attention-based LSTM for aspect-level sentiment classification. In *Proceedings of the 2016 Conference on Empirical Methods in Natural Language Processing*, pages 606–615, Austin, Texas. Association for Computational Linguistics.

Chuhan Wu, Fangzhao Wu, Tao Qi, and Yongfeng Huang. 2021. Hi-Transformer: Hierarchical interactive transformer for efficient and effective long document modeling. In *Proceedings of the 59th Annual Meeting of the Association for Computational Linguistics and the 11th International Joint Conference on Natural Language Processing (Volume 2: Short Papers)*, pages 848–853, Online. Association for Computational Linguistics.

Wei Xue and Tao Li. 2018. Aspect based sentiment analysis with gated convolutional networks. In *Proceedings of the 56th Annual Meeting of the Association for Computational Linguistics (Volume 1: Long Papers)*, pages 2514–2523, Melbourne, Australia. Association for Computational Linguistics.

Hang Yan, Junqi Dai, Tuo Ji, Xipeng Qiu, and Zheng Zhang. 2021. A unified generative framework for aspect-based sentiment analysis. In *Proceedings of the 59th Annual Meeting of the Association for Computational Linguistics and the 11th International Joint Conference on Natural Language Processing (Volume 1: Long Papers)*, pages 2416–2429, Online. Association for Computational Linguistics.

Zichao Yang, Diyi Yang, Chris Dyer, Xiaodong He, Alex Smola, and Eduard Hovy. 2016. Hierarchical attention networks for document classification. In *Proceedings of the 2016 Conference of the North American Chapter of the Association for Computational Linguistics: Human Language Technologies*, pages 1480–1489, San Diego, California. Association for Computational Linguistics.

Yichun Yin, Yangqiu Song, and Ming Zhang. 2017. Document-level multi-aspect sentiment classification as machine comprehension. In *Proceedings of the 2017 Conference on Empirical Methods in Natural Language Processing*, pages 2044–2054, Copenhagen, Denmark. Association for Computational Linguistics.

Manzil Zaheer, Guru Guruganesh, Kumar Avinava Dubey, Joshua Ainslie, Chris Alberti, Santiago Ontañón, Philip Pham, Anirudh Ravula, Qifan Wang, Li Yang, and Amr Ahmed. 2020. Big Bird: Transformers for longer sequences. In *Advances in Neural Information Processing Systems 33: Annual Conference on Neural Information Processing Systems 2020, NeurIPS 2020, December 6-12, 2020, virtual*.

Ziqian Zeng, Wenxuan Zhou, Xin Liu, and Yangqiu Song. 2019. A variational approach to weakly supervised document-level multi-aspect sentiment classification. In *Proceedings of the 2019 Conference of the North American Chapter of the Association for Computational Linguistics: Human Language Technologies, Volume 1 (Long and Short Papers)*, pages 386–396, Minneapolis, Minnesota. Association for Computational Linguistics.

Meishan Zhang, Yue Zhang, and Duy-Tin Vo. 2016. Gated neural networks for targeted sentiment analysis. In *Thirtieth AAAI conference on artificial intelligence*.

# A Visualization of Learned Representations

Figure 6 gives a visualization of the learned document representations via t-sne.

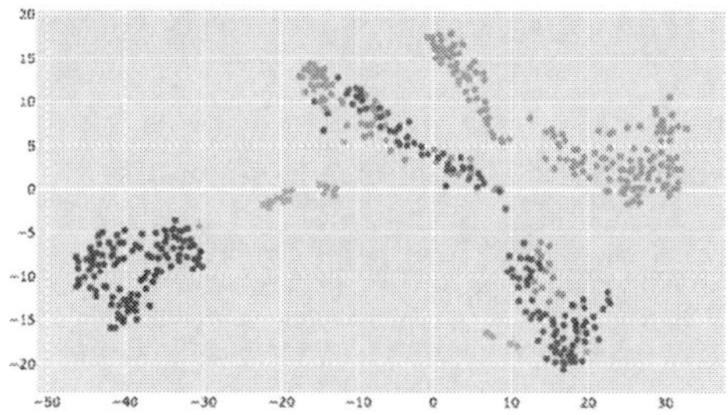

(a) Longformer

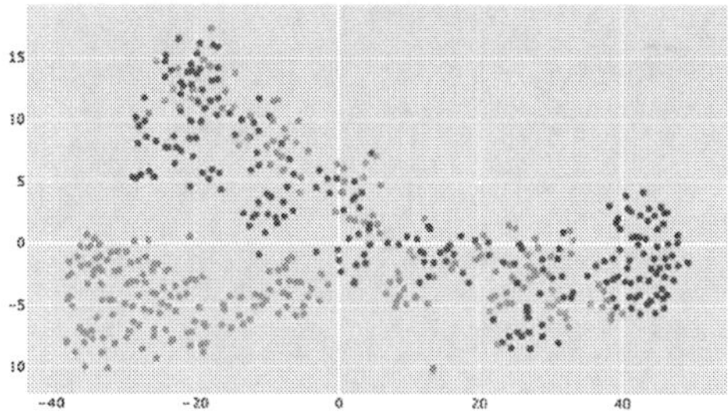

(b) Big Bird

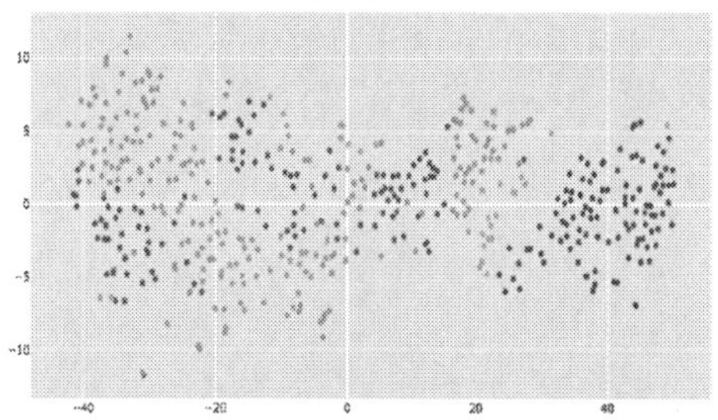

(c) LongT5

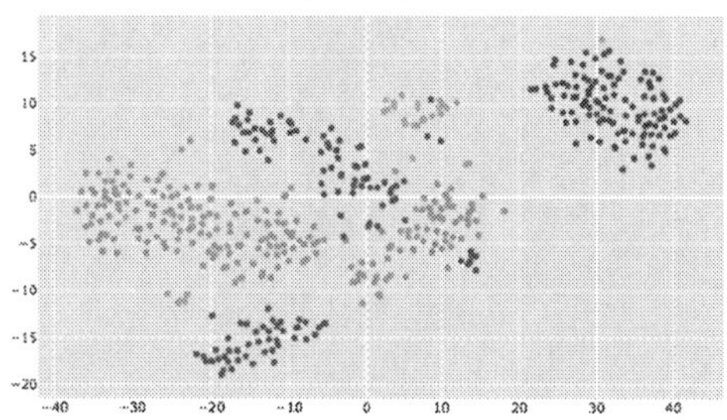

(d) DART

● Crime-Justice ● Digital-Online ● Economic Issues ● Health ● Human Rights ● Work

Figure 6: t-SNE visualization of document representations for SocialNews.

We see that that DART's learned representation is well separated for the aspects digital-online, economic issues, and work occupation in the SocialNews dataset. In contrast, the learned representations of Longformer, Big Bird and LongT5 tend to be mixed and cannot distinguish between the different aspects.

# Hierarchical Adversarial Correction to Mitigate Identity Term Bias in Toxicity Detection

**Johannes Schäfer[1,2], Ulrich Heid[1] and Roman Klinger[2]**
[1]Institute for Information Science and Natural Language Processing, University of Hildesheim, Germany
[2]Fundamentals of Natural Language Processing, University of Bamberg, Germany
heid@uni-hildesheim.de
{johannes.schaefer,roman.klinger}@uni-bamberg.de

## Abstract

Corpora that are the fundament for toxicity detection contain such expressions typically directed against a target individual or group, e.g., people of a specific gender or ethnicity. Prior work has shown that the target identity mention can constitute a confounding variable. As an example, a model might learn that Christians are always mentioned in the context of hate speech. This misguided focus can lead to a limited generalization to newly emerging targets that are not found in the training data. In this paper, we hypothesize and subsequently show that this issue can be mitigated by considering targets on different levels of specificity. We distinguish levels of (1) the existence of a target, (2) a class (e.g., that the target is a religious group), or (3) a specific target group (e.g., Christians or Muslims). We define a target label hierarchy based on these three levels and then exploit this hierarchy in an adversarial correction for the lowest level (i.e. (3)) while maintaining some basic target features. This approach does not lower the toxicity detection performance but increases the generalization to targets not being available at training time.

## 1 Introduction

The EU Code of conduct on countering illegal hate speech online relies on the definition of hate speech as "all conduct publicly inciting to violence or hatred directed against a group of persons or a member of such a group defined by reference to race, colour, religion, descent or national or ethnic origin."[1,2] This definition points out the role of the target in hate speech, which is one form of toxicity in text, next to other offensive language (Leite et al., 2020). Targets as a constituting element already received some attention in previous work (Silva et al., 2016; Lemmens et al., 2021, i.a.).

Hate speech expressions vary a lot, from explicit formulations to more implicit, and sometimes even intentionally cryptic references, to bypass automatic filters. This is an issue, because data collection procedures can never be entirely fair – they suffer from being focused on specific time frames, topics, and therefore also targets (Dixon et al., 2018). The working hypothesis in our paper follows Waseem and Hovy (2016), Talat et al. (2018) and Davidson et al. (2019) who have shown that models learn regularly occurring target terms as features of toxicity, because corpora developed for annotation and training might mention potential targets predominantly in a toxic context. For toxicity directed against less frequently mentioned targets or where identity terms are not explicitely mentioned (e.g., Examples #8 and #9 in Table 1), a biased model is more apt to not detect toxicity.

We aim at improving on this situation and propose to perform adversarial correction of toxicity classifiers with regard to target identities. This leads to a challenge: How specific should the target mention that we correct for be? Correcting for specific targets might lead to a sparsity problem while correcting for the occurrence in a binary fashion might not provide sufficiently specific information

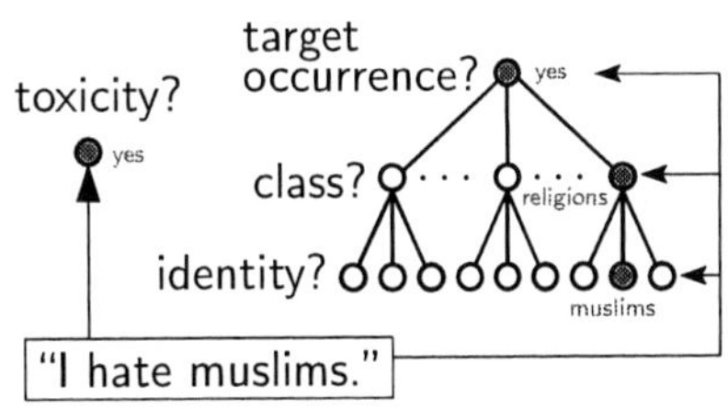


Figure 1: Example for toxicity and hierarchical identity classification. We study if debiasing for the identity prediction on various levels of specificity (Occurrence O, Class C and Identity I) improves the robustness of the toxicity classification.

[1]This paper contains some examples of toxicity. This is strictly for the purpose of explaining subtleties of the phenomenon that are important for this research. Please be aware that this content could be offensive and cause you distress.

[2]https://ec.europa.eu/newsroom/just/document.cfm?doc_id=42985



*Proceedings of the 14th Workshop on Computational Approaches to Subjectivity, Sentiment, & Social Media Analysis*, pages 35–51
August 15, 2024 ©2024 Association for Computational Linguistics

to the adversary. Further, the mere occurrence of a target might provide valuable information to the toxicity classifier, without confounding it. A novelty in our method is therefore our formulation of the gradient update to consider various hierarchical levels of specificity of target identities.

We assume in our experiments access to a corpus annotated on the text/instance level for toxicity (Tox) and for concrete classes of target groups (a requirement that is fulfilled by the CivilComments dataset by Borkan et al., 2019) and infer hierarchical labels from these annotations: binary (Occurrence O; identity mentioned or not), the mention of specific groups (Class C; e.g., religions, sexual orientations, ethnicities) or concrete instances of these groups (Identity I; e.g., atheist, buddhist; heterosexual, bisexual; black, asian, white). Figure 1 shows an example of a toxic text with such hierarchical annotations. *Our desideratum is to correct for concrete group mentions and particular groups, such that a toxicity classifier works well also for texts that mention new identities* (for instance, a not commonly targeted religion).

The contribution of this paper is therefore to answer the following research questions:

1. Does jointly learning binary target occurrence detection with toxicity detection improve the latter? *(No.)*
2. Does the performance of a toxicity classifier decrease if the underlying encoder is optimized to not being able to represent specific target groups or identities while maintaining target occurrence features? *(No.)*
3. Does adversarial correction of specific target identities lead to better generalization? *(Yes.)*
4. Does such correction lead to a more reasonable decision by the model? Do debiased models rely on concepts which are more meaningful for toxicity detection? *(Yes.)*

## 2 Related Work

### 2.1 Toxicity Detection

Most previous work focused on toxicity detection as binary classification (Nobata et al., 2016; Golbeck et al., 2017; Gao and Huang, 2017, i.a.) with a large set of shared tasks on the topic (Bosco et al., 2018; Wiegand et al., 2018; Zampieri et al., 2019b; Basile et al., 2019; Struß et al., 2019; Mandl et al., 2020, 2021). Schmidt and Wiegand (2017) provide a general overview of approaches to detection.

Various studies recognized the importance of fine-grained aspects of hate speech. Struß et al. (2019) propose a classification of offensive posts into subcategories of explicit and implicit aversions. Davidson et al. (2017) separate hate speech from instances of untargeted offensive language. They highlight that cases where explicit features are absent are hard to distinguish. Sachdeva et al. (2022) investigate mentions of identity groups as targets of hate speech. They find that the target detection performance suffers for cases of rarely represented identity groups. Plaza-del-Arco et al. (2021) train a model jointly for hate speech and targets.

There is a set of corpora annotated for concepts from the realm of toxicity and targets. Davidson et al. (2019) provide data annotated for hate speech and rely on Waseem and Hovy (2016) for the subcategories of sexism and racism. The Gab Hate corpus by Kennedy et al. (2022) considers hate speech and target identity groups, however does not contain fine-grained identity term labels.

In our experiments, we use the CivilComments dataset by Borkan et al. (2019). This dataset is annotated for toxicity and 24 categories of identity terms, which can be used to measure unintended biases. Koh et al. (2021) use a subset of these data to investigate shifts regarding different distributions of categories such as identity terms. They show that standard training yields substantially lower out-of-distribution than in-distribution performance. This motivates the use of debiasing as a possible method to improve out-of-distribution performance.

### 2.2 Debiasing Approaches

Debiasing methods that either modify the training data or the training process have been applied to hate speech detection. Talat et al. (2018) highlight the issue of social biases in datasets when they are used to train detection systems which is taken up with a classifier-centric consideration by Davidson et al. (2019). Sap et al. (2019) show that annotation bias further aggravates the issue. Such biases were also found in abusive language data (Dixon et al., 2018; Wiegand et al., 2019). Biases in the data carry over to a trained model (Dixon et al., 2018). Social stereotypes against marginalized groups have been shown to be echoed in hate speech classifiers (Thylstrup and Talat, 2020; Davani et al., 2023; Gehman et al., 2020; Sap et al., 2020). To facilitate the testing of models, Röttger et al. (2021) developed the HateCheck corpus covering a range of identity terms.

Bias mitigation techniques may be applied to alter the training data directly, by masking potentially confounding tokens. These tokens have been recognized based on attention mechanisms, entity detection, and keyword recognition (Wiegand et al., 2018; Dayanik and Padó, 2020; Kumar et al., 2019). Ramponi and Tonelli (2022) detect tokens to be masked via pointwise mutual information (PMI). Furthermore, Badjatiya et al. (2019) suggest to identify tokens to be masked based on their part-of-speech. Xue et al. (2023) propose a different approach than masking, namely balancing the spurious attributes across all classes.

Rather than changing the input, the training process can also be manipulated directly. Vaidya et al. (2020) suggest a classification model for toxicity detection that jointly detects identity terms. This is in contrast to our work, which aims at correcting for the target mentions' influence instead of exploiting it. The authors show that their approach improves classification performance for comments related to some identities, however, they do not evaluate the generalization capability of the resulting model. Further, Kennedy et al. (2020) use a regularization technique that learns to contextualize mentions of identity terms and is thus less reliant on high-frequency words in unbalanced data.

In the last years adversarial correction for debiasing received some attention. It is used to "unlearn" properties of confounding concepts in the encoder of the model (Ganin et al., 2016). This approach of gradient reversal has been tested with several applications, including satire detection (correction for publication source, McHardy et al., 2019), gender identification (correcting for text topic, Dayanik and Padó, 2021) and also hate speech (language variety detection, Xia et al., 2020).

## 3 Methods

**Overview.** In order to avoid co-learning identity term bias in dataset-based learning of hate speech detection, our approach is to exploit the hierarchical properties of identities. The basic structure of the network used in our experiments is displayed in Figure 2. It consists of a shared encoder and four classifiers (grey boxes) which are all aggregated in parallel. The main classifier is the toxicity detector. The hierarchical dependencies of the three identity term detectors arise from the labels. On the highest level we consider identities as a binary label (Occurrence: O) which is positive if there is at least one identity annotated for a message. The intermediate level classifier (Class: C) categorizes identities into five groups. Each of the five categories corresponds to a binary label which is positive if at least one identity from the respective category is annotated. The most fine-grained classifier considers 24 different identity labels on the lowest level (Identity: I) with binary values for each of those. Each value is positive if the respective identity is annotated for the message. Each of the mentioned classifiers consists of a single linear layer with the number of neurons corresponding to the respective number of classes. The identity classifiers for Class and Identity are both multi-label classifiers, as several of their classes can occur together in a message. With this model we can exploit the hierarchical structure of the unwanted confounding variable in parallel (potentially partially adversarial) classifiers.[3]

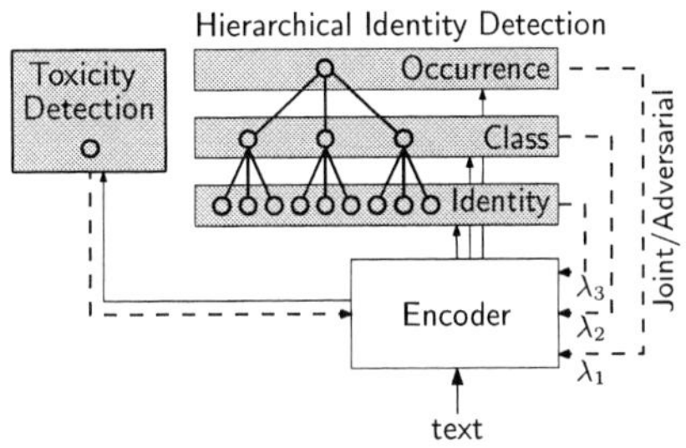


Figure 2: Model architecture for hierarchical adversarial correction of toxicity detection with identity detection. Continuous lines: forward pass, dashed lines: backward pass. Parameters $\lambda_i$ with $i \in \{1, 2, 3\}$ weight the identity detection gradients in the parameter update of the encoder, thus, configure adversarial correction ($\lambda_i > 0$) or joint multi-task learning ($\lambda_i < 0$).

**Adversarial Correction.** Following Ganin et al. (2016), the gradient updates for the adversary are reversed and weighted for a correction of the encoder, while the parameters of the classifiers are updated without modification. However, we allow for multiple adversaries and apply an individual weight for each level in the identity hierarchy, namely $\lambda_1$ for the binary occurrence detection, $\lambda_2$ for the class of the identity term, and $\lambda_3$ for the identity term on the lowest level. Hence, our parameter update for the parameters in the encoder $\theta_e$ is

$$\theta_e := \theta_e - \eta\left(\frac{\partial J_{\text{Tox}}}{\partial \theta_e} - \lambda_1 \frac{\partial J_{\text{O}}}{\partial \theta_e} - \lambda_2 \frac{\partial J_{\text{C}}}{\partial \theta_e} - \lambda_3 \frac{\partial J_{\text{I}}}{\partial \theta_e}\right),$$

[3]We use BERT (Devlin et al., 2019) as the intitialization of our encoder (concretely `bert-base-uncased`) and apply a dropout (probability 0.2).

| # | Text | Tox | O | C | I |
|---|---|---|---|---|---|
| | | | Hierarchical Identity Term Labels | | |
| 1 | This woman is as fake as her perpetual tan. | + | + | gender | female |
| 2 | boy. this guy is incredibly stupid. | + | + | gender | male |
| 3 | Transgender is not real... It is however a mental disorder!!! | + | + | gender, disability | transgender, illness |
| 4 | Never hire a Muslim, a Black person or a female...ever! | + | + | religion, ethnicity, gender | muslim, black, female |
| 5 | The man is a bag of dirt. An absolute scumbag. | + | + | gender | male |
| 6 | Old white men ARE the swamp. | + | + | ethnicity, gender | white, male |
| 7 | It was a human male not a female fat sac. | + | + | gender | male, female |
| 8 | That is the standard speech from idiots and snowflakes. | + | − | — | — |
| 9 | What a piece of human garbage. | + | − | — | — |
| 10 | Muslims are being attacked daily. | − | + | religion | muslim |
| 11 | ISIS has killed far more Muslims than Christians. | − | + | religion | muslim, christian |

Table 1: Examples of annotated text instances from the CivilComments dataset (Borkan et al., 2019). Illness: physical or mental illness. Binary labels (+ and −) are annotated for the existence of the toxicity label (Tox) or the occurrence of an identity term (O). The Class (C) and Identity (I) are multi-label variables.

where $\eta$ is the learning rate. $J_{\text{Tox}}$ is the loss function for the toxicity classifier and $J_{\text{O}}$, $J_{\text{C}}$, and $J_{\text{I}}$ are the binary cross entropy loss functions (including a sigmoid function) for each layer in the identity hierarchy, respectively. Hence, $\lambda_i > 0$ corresponds to adversarial learning and $\lambda_i < 0$ to joint learning of the encoder. The parameter updates for the classifiers (grey boxes in Figure 2) are $\theta_{\text{Tox}} := \theta_{\text{Tox}} - \eta \frac{\partial J_{\text{Tox}}}{\partial \theta_{\text{Tox}}}$ for the Toxicity categorization, $\theta_{\text{O}} := \theta_{\text{O}} - \eta \frac{\partial J_{\text{O}}}{\partial \theta_{\text{O}}}$ for the Occurrence categorization, $\theta_{\text{C}} := \theta_{\text{C}} - \eta \frac{\partial J_{\text{C}}}{\partial \theta_{\text{C}}}$ for the Class categorization, and $\theta_{\text{I}} := \theta_{\text{I}} - \eta \frac{\partial J_{\text{I}}}{\partial \theta_{\text{I}}}$ for the Identity detection. The optimizer minimizes the overall loss $J = J_{\text{Tox}} + J_{\text{O}} + J_{\text{C}} + J_{\text{I}}$.

## 4 Experimental Setting

In the following, we explain the data that we use (§4.1) and the experimental setting (§4.2).[4]

### 4.1 Data

We use the CivilComments dataset (Borkan et al., 2019), the largest corpus in English annotated for both toxicity and identity terms with approximately 450,000 instances. We infer the hierarchical annotations from the 24 identity labels (see Table 1).

In these data, instances consist of individual posts as short text messages (the average instance length in the development data is 78 tokens) with all annotations on instance level. We transform the fractions of annotators that agree on a label to binary values by majority vote (following Xiang et al., 2021; Faal et al., 2021; Baldini et al., 2022; Lobo et al., 2022). From the 24 fine-grained annotated classes (I), we infer five more coarse-grained categories (C):

1. **Gender:** male, female, transgender, other gender
2. **Sexual orientation:** heterosexual, homosexual gay or lesbian, bisexual, other sexual orientation
3. **Religion:** christian, jewish, muslim, hindu, buddhist, atheist, other religion
4. **Race or ethnicity:** black, white, asian, latino, other race or ethnicity
5. **Disability:** physical disability, intellectual or learning disability, psychiatric or mental illness, other disability

This leads to a hierarchical multi-label annotation for identities. Our goal is to mitigate the bias towards frequently mentioned identity terms during training in order to improve generalization for other cases: namely, to correctly detect toxicity in cases where no explicit target identity is mentioned (e.g., as in Examples #8 and #9), and to not detect toxicity based solely on the presence of specific target mentions (e.g., as in Examples #10 and #11). In this dataset, toxic instances contain identity terms in 61% of cases, but only 40% of non-toxic instances do (see Appendix B for more details).

For the *Jigsaw Unintended Bias in Toxicity Classification challenge* on Kaggle[5] this dataset was split into a development set with 405,130 instances and two test sets with a total of 42,870 instances. For our experiments we randomly split this development set into training (100k instances), validation

[4] Our code to replicate the experiments can be accessed via `https://www.uni-bamberg.de/en/nlproc/resources/hierarchical-detox/`

[5] `https://www.kaggle.com/c/jigsaw-unintended-bias-in-toxicity-classification`

for early stopping during training (50k) and hyper-parameter optimization (≈255k). Further details are given in Appendix A. For evaluation, we use the official test sets combined (≈43k instances).

### 4.2 Model Configurations

We train different model configurations in order to answer our research questions (cf. Section 1). The main goal of these experiments is to assess whether the performance of a toxicity classifier decreases if the underlying encoder is optimized to not being able to represent specific target groups or identities while maintaining target occurrence features. Therefore, we configure a baseline model to compare its toxicity detection performance with debiased models. Additionally, we evaluate the performance of the different models in recognizing identity terms. This serves to identify whether, and to what extent, the different toxicity detection models pay attention to target identities. We explore different combinations of joint multi-task learning with target occurrence and adversarial correction of specific target identities to determine which effect the different levels of the identity term hierarchy $x \in (1, 2, 3)$ have on the toxicity classifier.

**Baseline.** We train a model purely for toxicity detection. In this TOX setup, the Occurrence/Class/Identity classifiers are also trained, but the encoder is not optimized via backpropagation with this information ($\lambda_1 = \lambda_2 = \lambda_3 = 0$). Here the encoder is only trained by the toxicity detector. This setup serves the purpose of investigating whether the uncontrolled and unguided toxicity classifier relies on features which contain information regarding identity term mentions.

**Debiased Baseline.** In order to compare our correction method to an established bias mitigation method, we adopt the debiasing approach by Ramponi and Tonelli (2022). We refer to this model as RT (2022). It cannot rely on features of identity terms as it automatically masks the tokens most strongly associated with each identity term label. Following Ramponi and Tonelli (2022) we use normalized PMI scores to automatically extract such spurious artifacts. While Ramponi and Tonelli (2022) manually annotate the top 200 entries, we automate this process by filtering all tokens with normalized PMI values $> .6$. This cutoff value was chosen based on the identity term Muslim where we find the tokens *muslim*, *muslims*, *islam* and *islamic* with values $> .80$ but also *mosque* (.65), *quran* (.63) and *mosques* (.62) amongst other tokens which are not as obviously connected: *world* (.71), *religious* (.71) or *europe* (.70). This approach filters a total of 751 word types for all identities. Besides operating on partially masked text, this baseline follows the configuration of the TOX setup mentioned above.

**MTL (multi-task learning).** Our data analysis has shown (see Section 4.1) that there is a correlation between toxicity and identity terms. We now want to test whether this carries over to the model level (cf. RQ1 in Section 1). Thus, we use MTL to guide the encoder to explicitly learn features for both toxicity detection and target occurrence in a joint setup (Model Tox+O,C,I with $\lambda_1 = -1$, $\lambda_2 = \lambda_3 = 0$). To create an upper bound for the identity term detection performance on all three levels we train a model where all classifiers are combined jointly (Model Tox+O+C+I, $\lambda_x = -1$).

**Adversarial.** In order to assess the importance of target occurrence features for the detection of toxicity, we train a model for comparison in which we instruct the encoder to unlearn precisely these features. In this model identity occurrence is used as an adversary (Model Tox−O, $\lambda_1 \in \{0.10, 0.25, 0.50, 1.00\}$). Additionally, as a starting point to debias the model for identities, we train a model where we use an adversary on the lowest level of the identity hierarchy (Model Tox−I, $\lambda_3 \in \{0.10, 0.25, 0.50, 1.00\}$).

**MTL&Adversarial.** Based on the intuition that we want to guide the toxicity detector with features from mentioned targets while debiasing for identities, we combine parameterizations for multiple levels of the hierarchy. In addition to the joint toxicity and target occurrence classifier ($\lambda_1 = -1$), we now debias the model for specific identity terms to understand whether this has a negative effect on the performance (cf. RQ2 in Section 1). We include an adversary via a gradient reversal layer on the lowest level of the identity term detection ($\lambda_3 \in \{0.10, 0.25, 0.50, 1.00\}$) and, thus, deprive the model of the ability to distinguish between different identity terms (e.g., which specific religion is mentioned). This serves to unlearn identity term features in the encoder and to determine whether this increases the generalization ability of the model. In order to evaluate the role of the intermediate level, we include the classifier for the identity class jointly ($\lambda_1 = -1$, resulting

| Model | $\lambda_1$ | $\lambda_2$ | $\lambda_3$ | $F1^{(1)}_{Tox}$ | $F1^{(1)}_{O}$ | $F1^{(5)}_{C}$ | $F1^{(24)}_{I}$ |
|---|---|---|---|---|---|---|---|
| TOX (baseline) | 0 | 0 | 0 | .64 | .59 | .25 | .07 |
| RT (2022) | 0 | 0 | 0 | .55 | .45 | .13 | .03 |
| Tox+O,C,I | −1 | 0 | 0 | .63 | .93 | .34 | .10 |
| Tox−O | 1.00 | — | — | .63 | .05 | | |
| Tox−I | — | — | 0.10 | .63 | (.58) | (.20) | .05 |
| Tox+O+C+I | −1 | −1 | −1 | .64 | .93 | .86 | .38 |
| Tox+O+C−I | −1 | −1 | 0.50 | .63 | .93 | .86 | .24 |
| Tox+O−C−I | −1 | 0.25 | 0.25 | .64 | .93 | .30 | .08 |

Table 2: Performance of optimized models on the test dataset. We display F1 for the positive classes across all variables. The values in the superscript of the F1 scores specify the number of classes evaluated in each task – for multi-label tasks (Class and Identity) we display the macro-average F1 over all positive class label F1 scores. In the column "Model", "+" marks joint classification, "−" marks adversaries and classifiers appended with "," do not have an effect on the encoder. Tox refers to the toxicity classifier. (O)ccurrence, (C)lass and (I)dentity refer to the classifiers for the three levels of the identity term label hierarchy according to our model (see Figure 2). Values in parentheses are inferred from the prediction of more fine-grained labels.

in Model Tox+O+C−I) or as another adversary ($\lambda_1 \in \{0.10, 0.25, 0.50, 1.00\}$, resulting in Model Tox+O−C−I). We hypothesize that correcting for both class and identity might lead to a more comprehensive mitigation of the identity term bias than the experimental design with only one adversary.

## 5 Results

We will now discuss the results obtained with the setting described in the previous sections. Table 2 depicts the results for the best-performing models based on the parameter $\lambda$. Further results can be found in Appendix C. Table 2 shows F1 values for different combinations of toxicity detection and identity detection on the three levels of our hierarchy. On top, we see the baseline that only optimizes the encoder with the toxicity information followed by the debiased baseline RT (2022).

We observe that RT (2022) shows a lower performance at identity classification than the baseline TOX (e.g., $F1_C$ drops from .25 to .13). Therefore, the toxicity classifier in RT (2022) learns less identity-specific features, i.e., the model is successful in reducing bias. Conversely, this also means that the baseline TOX model automatically learns identity features without being guided to do so, i.e., it in fact contains a bias. However, the results also show that debiasing following RT (2022) does lead to a drop in toxicity detection performance ($F1_{Tox}$ drops from .64 to .55).

**RQ1: Does jointly learning binary target occurrence detection with toxicity detection improve the latter?** To measure if target mentions are important for toxicity detection, we now focus on specific models. We compare the performance of the baseline model (TOX) to the model which is also informed with the identity occurrence classifier (Model Tox+O,C,I) and to the model which uses a identity occurrence adversary (Model Tox−O). The results show (cf. Table 2) the $F1_{Tox}$ scores for all of these models on the same level. Therefore, while targets are a constituent variable of the concept of hate speech, we cannot infer from this evaluation that they are also an essential feature for toxicity detection. The toxicity classifier manages to maintain its performance level, even if we instruct the encoder to learn identity-occurrence features or, conversely, to unlearn exactly those features by adversarial correction. However, in further evaluations (cf. RQ3 below), we will see that unlearning identity occurrence features does not have a positive effect on the generalization ability of the model, which could be due to the fact that they are important for learning toxicity detection after all.

**RQ2: Does the performance of a toxicity classifier decrease if the underlying encoder is optimized to not being able to represent specific target groups or identities while maintaining target occurrence features?** We first evaluate overall toxicity detection performance and then address the details of identity detection performance to identify specific differences between models. We obtain the results by comparing the performance of the models corrected for identities (adversaries are marked by –) to the baseline model (TOX). Overall the F1 score for toxicity detection (see column $F1_{Tox}$ in Table 2) is fairly constant in the range of .63 to .64. This shows that the toxicity detection does not suffer from the adversarial correction for identities. In contrast, the differently debiased model RT (2022) (which also has been debiased, however, by masking identity-specific tokens) shows a substantial performance drop ($F1_{Tox}$ .55). The test dataset used for this entire evaluation was sampled from the same source as the training dataset and is therefore also biased towards the same identities. Therefore, we presume that this evaluation is unable to demonstrate a positive effect of debiasing on toxicity detection performance. Further evaluations below under RQ3 and RQ4 show the performance gain for toxicity detection.

We now want to understand how the capability of the encoder to represent identity terms changes at different levels of the hierarchy. We see this from the performance scores in Table 2: columns $F1_O$, $F1_C$ and $F1_I$ (for Occurrence, Class, and Identity). As expected, the identity classifiers on each of the three levels in the MTL model (Model Tox+O+C+I) outperform the models where the particular level is used as an adversary. When we use an adversary for identity detection (Model Tox−I) the performance at identity detection drops (from .07 for Model TOX to .05), i.e., the model loses some of its ability to represent identities. In settings where we emphasize learning of identity occurrence features (models with +O), the encoder also represents more identity features overall, e.g. $F1_I$ rises from .07 for Model TOX to .10 for Model Tox+O,C,I. In a model that additionally learns identity occurrence jointly, we still see the effect of the adversary on $F1_I$. It drops from .10 for Model Tox+O,C,I to .08 for Model Tox+O−C−I. Analogously, this can also be observed for the models which additionally use the identity class classifier in a joint MTL setting ($F1_I$ drops from .38 for Model Tox+O+C+I to .24 for Model Tox+O+C−I). Thus, we conclude that adversarial correction has the desired effect of depriving the models of the ability to perform the task of identity term identification on the lowest level while maintaining target occurrence features. In addition, the procedure does not harm toxicity detection.

Finally, we investigate the role of the intermediate level in this setting. Comparing Model Tox+O+C−I to Model Tox+O−C−I shows that using the intermediate level as additional adversary also has an effect on the lowest level as $F1_I$ drops from .24 to .08. Thus, we conclude that this further reinforces unlearning features for the lowest level and leads to a more comprehensive correction.

| Training data: | Full | NR | | |
|---|---|---|---|---|
| Test data: | Full | Full | NR | R |
| Model | $F1^{(1)}_{Tox}$ | $F1^{(1)}_{Tox}$ | $F1^{(1)}_{Tox}$ | $F1^{(1)}_{Tox}$ |
| TOX (baseline) | .64 | .63 | .65 | .57 |
| RT (2022) | .55 Δ−.09 | .56 Δ−.07 | .57 Δ−.08 | .53 Δ−.04 |
| Tox−O | .63 Δ−.01 | .58 Δ−.05 | .58 Δ−.07 | .57 Δ.00 |
| Tox−I | .63 Δ−.01 | .63 Δ.00 | .64 Δ−.01 | .59 Δ+.02 |
| Tox+O+C−I | .63 Δ−.01 | .61 Δ−.02 | .62 Δ−.03 | .58 Δ+.01 |
| Tox+O−C−I | .64 Δ.00 | .62 Δ−.01 | .63 Δ−.02 | .58 Δ+.01 |

Table 3: Performance on test data of best models trained on different training data fractions. NR = non-religion (filtered), R = only religion (filtered).

**RQ3: Does adversarial correction of specific target identities lead to better generalization?** We have now seen that the model debiased for identities on the lowest level of the hierarchy does perform as well at toxicity detection as the one that is not corrected. The performance scores for the identity term detection suggest that the encoder can no longer represent the identities to the same extent. This should enable an improved generalization across domains. We analyze this in two settings, firstly with an evaluation on target identity terms which have not been considered during training, and secondly with other datasets that have not been used during model development and training.

Regarding the first setup, we train the baseline and corrected models for the best configurations on data which has been filtered for all identities belonging to the religion class.[6] Table 3 shows the evaluation of these models for toxicity detection on different fractions of the test set. In the first column we repeat the results of the models from the first experiment, which were trained on the full dataset. The last three columns show the models which were trained on non-religion data (training data: NR). Here we see that all corrected models show a drop in performance on in-domain test data

[6] We chose the religion class since it comprises the largest number of identities (7 out of the 24) and accounts for a substantial number of instances (7,514) in the test data. For the model RT (2022) we repeat the process of identifying the tokens that are masked on the basis of the filtered dataset.

compared to the baseline (second to last column, test data: NR). However, our corrected models show an improved performance on out-of-domain test data (last column, test data: R) in comparison to the baseline. Only the model corrected for Occurrence (Tox−O) does not show an improvement. This confirms our intuition that the correction for general target terms is not the best choice since it also includes features which are beneficial for toxicity detection. We conclude that our correction does lead to a better toxicity prediction generalization.

The second generalization evaluation is performed with out-of-distribution performance evaluations. We show the datasets that we use and the detailed results for the out-of-distribution hate speech and toxicity detection performance in Appendix D. We observe that all models show on average a similar performance on out-of-distribution data (RT (2022) being an exception). Thus, we conclude that all corrected models show similar cross-corpus performance compared to the baseline models. We assume that the corpora used represent different domains and only share the targets of hate speech, our identity terms, to a limited extent.

**RQ4: Does such correction lead to a more reasonable decision by the model? Do debiased models rely on concepts which are more meaningful for toxicity detection?** To understand if the corrected model relies more on concepts that do not correspond to identities – potential targets of offensive language –, we analyze the change in toxicity detection performance for specific target terms. We subdivide the test dataset into subsets mentioning specific identities and evaluate the toxicity detection performance of the different models. The detailed evaluation is given in Appendix E. We observe that the performance of the corrected models for detecting toxicity mentioning the most frequent target terms is comparable to the baseline. However, for subsets with less frequent identities, adversarial correction improves toxicity detection in two-thirds of all cases. Thus, we conclude that the corrected models rely less on identities as features and learn other, more meaningful concepts.

We further visualize this effect on selected examples using LIME (Ribeiro et al., 2016) to calculate local explanations on the words of an instance that are most important. Figure 3 displays such explanations for five selected examples from the test dataset where the debiased model Tox+O−C−I corrects errors of the baseline model. Examples

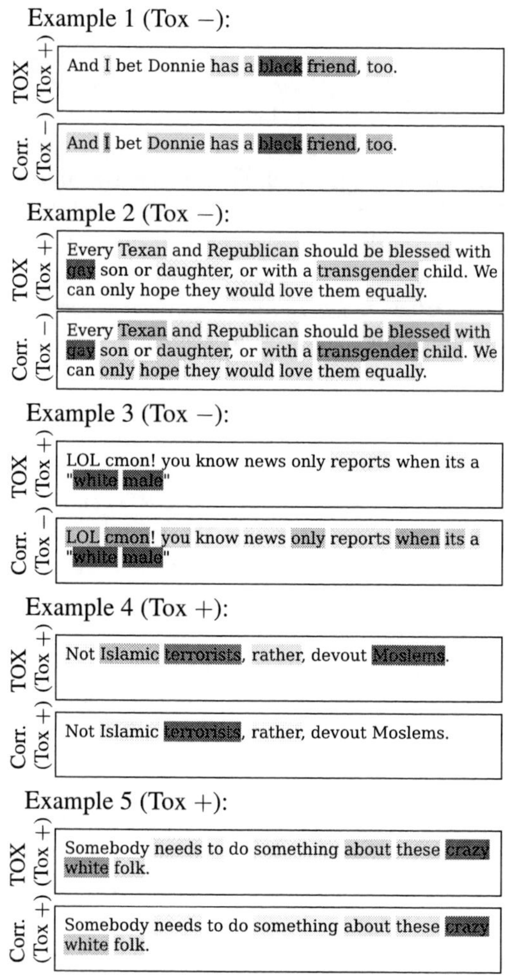


Figure 3: Explanations for the predictions of the baseline model TOX and our corrected model Tox+O−C−I (Corr.) according to LIME on instances from the Civil-Comments test dataset. The gold and predicted labels are shown in parentheses. Blue indicates word importance for Tox +, orange refers to Tox −. The intensity correlates to LIME's importance weights.

1 to 3 are all non-toxic instances which contain identity terms. The biased baseline TOX focuses only on these terms (e.g. "black", "gay", "transgender", "white" and "male") and incorrectly predicts toxicity. The debiased model corrects the error and correctly predicts the instances as non-toxic. It achieves this by also taking into consideration other tokens (most of them are marked with an orange background color) in which it finds no decisive features of toxicity. Examples 4 and 5 in Figure 3 show toxic instances with target mentions. Here both models manage to classify the instances as toxic. However, the biased baseline TOX bases its

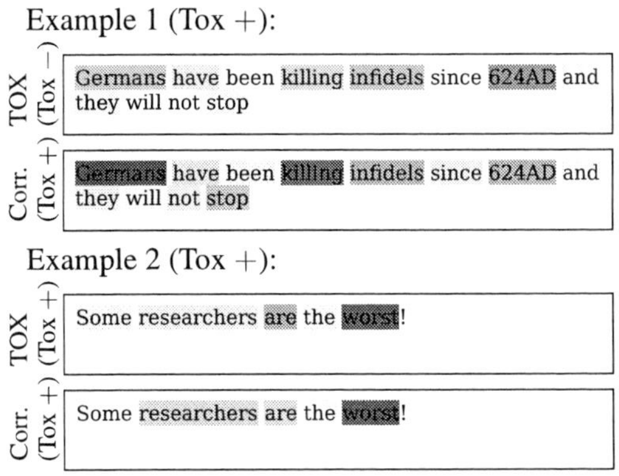


Figure 4: LIME explanations for the predictions on the CivilComments test data of the baseline TOX and the corrected model Tox+O−C−I (Corr.). In these examples, we manually manipulated the sentences by inserting new, originally non-existent targets.

decision mostly on the presence of identity terms (e.g. "Islamic", "Moslems" and "white"). In contrast, the debiased model does not rely as much on the mentioned identity terms which leads to a more reasonable decision with higher weights on words such as "terrorists" and "crazy".

We additionally investigate instances of toxicity with targets which are not included in the set annotated on the training data (such as "Germans" and "researchers"). We display LIME explanations in Figure 4 for predictions of examples from the test data which we modified to include such new target terms. These examples visualize cases of the improved generalization capability of the corrected model. Example 1 is incorrectly predicted as non-toxic by the biased baseline TOX model. The debiased model corrects the error as it is able to rely more on the new target. For Example 2, both models correctly predict the toxicity, however, the corrected model again assigns a higher weight on the new target. While this is a small-scale analysis based on a few examples, it suggests that there are cases where the corrected models use more meaningful features for toxicity detection.

## 6 Conclusion

We have shown that hierarchical adversarial correction for target identities leads to a toxicity classifier with an improved robustness. The corrected models show the same performance at toxicity detection as the biased baseline model. We presented a method to apply adversarial correction for the lowest level of hierarchical information regarding identity term mentions. Our results have demonstrated that it is possible to simultaneously maintain basic target occurrence features. However, target occurrence has not been shown to be as important for the detection of toxicity as the related concept of hate speech would suggest. This motivates future work to divise toxicity into more fine-grained concepts such as hate speech, offensive language and profanity, in the delineation of which target occurrence features presumably play a more decisive role.

Furthermore, when debiasing for individual identity terms, our experiments with the different hierarchical levels of specificity of the confounding variable have shown that it is more beneficial to additionally correct for classes of identities. It follows that a coarser grouping of identity categories must also be considered when defining the label set for annotation in order to achieve a more comprehensive correction during training.

Overall, our correction has shown to lead to a more reasonable decision by the model as it does not exclusively rely on identity features for toxicity detection and shows better generalization capabilities. This affects real-world applications of such models in that these models are required to be demonstrably debiased and treat individual identities fairly. Additionally, this motivates that a full evaluation of model performance must test the generalization ability of such models on further datasets where different identities are mentioned, as in-distribution biases do not show up in standard evaluations with a single test dataset.

Our research opens a set of important follow-up questions. In particular, whether further fine-tuning of the training process can lead to an improved overall toxicity detection with adversarial correction. This might be achieved, e.g., by testing different individual learning rates for optimizing the classifiers, the adversary and the encoder separately or by using multiple adversaries for latent variables as presented by Kumar et al. (2019). Also, since target detection might play a more significant role to distinguish hate speech from offensive language, an evaluation of our correction approach on such data would be an important next step to fight online toxicity.

## Acknowledgements

This work has been partially supported by the CEAT project (KL 2869/1-2), funded by the German Research Foundation (DFG).

## Limitations

We only ran all model configurations once due to limited time. The implementation contains randomized steps (initialization of weights, shuffling of training instances). Thus, the reported performance scores might not be entirely robust. However, our reported conclusions are based on substantial differences in performance of the different models.

Our implementation of the debiased baseline methods by Ramponi and Tonelli (2022) does only partially follow their suggested approach. While we do not consider manual annotation of top-n lists and use a fix threshold PMI value, choosing a top-n cut-off might be a more justified choice. Furthermore, Ramponi and Tonelli (2022) suggest multiple different approaches to deal with the identified spurious artifacts while we only use the removal method for comparison as a baseline.

In the experiment with filtering training data for specific identity classes, we focused on the evaluation of a setting where we filtered the religious identities. We chose the religion class since it comprises the largest number of identities (7 of the 24) and accounts for a substantial number of instances in the test data (7,514) which we can evaluate separately. For full expressiveness of the results, experiments where identities from other classes are filtered, should also be conducted. However, we presume that statistical evidence for the performance of less frequent classes (e.g. there are only 544 test instances for the disability class) might be limited.

## Ethical Considerations

**Potential risks.** We mention examples of toxicity and hate speech which might offend readers of this paper. They are taken from empirically collected datasets and do not portray our own opinions. However, we believe that it is inevitable to investigate concrete instances when discussing detection approaches.

**Reproducibility.** We use datasets with annotations for toxicity and hate speech. All of these datasets are freely available for research use. We use these data for their intended use, to develop detection systems. Since we research toxicity and mentions of identity terms, the datasets have not been filtered or anonymized for such attributes.

We publish our program code for maximum transparency. The described models and predictions of labels can be reproduced with this code. For training we randomly split the dataset into specific portions. As these are quite large, we believe that they are representative for the entire corpus and that the same experiments with different partitions lead to the same conclusions. Additionally, we provide a script to reproduce the random split used in our experiments to benefit future research.

We report relevant information for the used artifacts and refer to the original publications for further documentation. We describe the structure and size of the models we create. We believe that these descriptions make our approach reproducible.

## References


Pinkesh Badjatiya, Manish Gupta, and Vasudeva Varma. 2019. Stereotypical bias removal for hate speech detection task using knowledge-based generalizations. In *The World Wide Web Conference*, WWW '19, page 49–59, New York, NY, USA. Association for Computing Machinery.

Ioana Baldini, Dennis Wei, Karthikeyan Natesan Ramamurthy, Moninder Singh, and Mikhail Yurochkin. 2022. Your fairness may vary: Pretrained language model fairness in toxic text classification. In *Findings of the Association for Computational Linguistics: ACL 2022*, pages 2245–2262, Dublin, Ireland. Association for Computational Linguistics.

Valerio Basile, Cristina Bosco, Elisabetta Fersini, Nozza Debora, Viviana Patti, Francisco Manuel Rangel Pardo, Paolo Rosso, and Manuela Sanguinetti. 2019. SemEval-2019 Task 5: Multilingual Detection of Hate Speech Against Immigrants and Women in Twitter. In *13th International Workshop on Semantic Evaluation*, pages 54–63. Association for Computational Linguistics.

Daniel Borkan, Lucas Dixon, Jeffrey Sorensen, Nithum Thain, and Lucy Vasserman. 2019. Nuanced metrics for measuring unintended bias with real data for text classification. In *Companion proceedings of the 2019 world wide web conference*, pages 491–500.

Cristina Bosco, Dell'Orletta Felice, Fabio Poletto, Manuela Sanguinetti, and Tesconi Maurizio. 2018. Overview of the EVALITA 2018 Hate Speech Detection Task. In *EVALITA 2018-Sixth Evaluation Campaign of Natural Language Processing and Speech Tools for Italian*, volume 2263, pages 1–9. CEUR.

Aida Mostafazadeh Davani, Mohammad Atari, Brendan Kennedy, and Morteza Dehghani. 2023. Hate speech classifiers learn normative social stereotypes. *Transactions of the Association for Computational Linguistics*, 11:300–319.

Thomas Davidson, Debasmita Bhattacharya, and Ingmar Weber. 2019. Racial bias in hate speech and abusive language detection datasets. In *Proceedings of the Third Workshop on Abusive Language Online*, pages 25–35, Florence, Italy. Association for Computational Linguistics.

Thomas Davidson, Dana Warmsley, Michael Macy, and Ingmar Weber. 2017. Automated hate speech detection and the problem of offensive language. In *Proceedings of the 11th International AAAI Conference on Web and Social Media*, ICWSM '17, pages 512–515.

Erenay Dayanik and Sebastian Padó. 2020. Masking actor information leads to fairer political claims detection. In *Proceedings of the 58th Annual Meeting of the Association for Computational Linguistics*, pages 4385–4391, Online. Association for Computational Linguistics.

Erenay Dayanik and Sebastian Padó. 2021. Disentangling document topic and author gender in multiple languages: Lessons for adversarial debiasing. In *Proceedings of the Eleventh Workshop on Computational Approaches to Subjectivity, Sentiment and Social Media Analysis*, pages 50–61, Online. Association for Computational Linguistics.

Ona de Gibert, Naiara Perez, Aitor García-Pablos, and Montse Cuadros. 2018. Hate speech dataset from a white supremacy forum. In *Proceedings of the 2nd Workshop on Abusive Language Online (ALW2)*, pages 11–20, Brussels, Belgium. Association for Computational Linguistics.

Jacob Devlin, Ming-Wei Chang, Kenton Lee, and Kristina Toutanova. 2019. BERT: Pre-training of deep bidirectional transformers for language understanding. In *Proceedings of the 2019 Conference of the North American Chapter of the Association for Computational Linguistics: Human Language Technologies, Volume 1 (Long and Short Papers)*, pages 4171–4186, Minneapolis, Minnesota. Association for Computational Linguistics.

Lucas Dixon, John Li, Jeffrey Sorensen, Nithum Thain, and Lucy Vasserman. 2018. Measuring and mitigating unintended bias in text classification. In *Proceedings of the 2018 AAAI/ACM Conference on AI, Ethics, and Society*, pages 67–73.

Farshid Faal, Jia Yuan Yu, and Ketra A Schmitt. 2021. Domain adaptation multi-task deep neural network for mitigating unintended bias in toxic language detection. In *Proceedings of the 13th International Conference on Agents and Artificial Intelligence (ICAART 2021)*, volume 2, pages 932–940.

Yaroslav Ganin, Evgeniya Ustinova, Hana Ajakan, Pascal Germain, Hugo Larochelle, François Laviolette, Mario March, and Victor Lempitsky. 2016. Domain-adversarial training of neural networks. *Journal of Machine Learning Research*, 17(59):1–35.

Lei Gao and Ruihong Huang. 2017. Detecting online hate speech using context aware models. In *Proceedings of the International Conference Recent Advances in Natural Language Processing, RANLP 2017*, pages 260–266, Varna, Bulgaria. INCOMA Ltd.

Samuel Gehman, Suchin Gururangan, Maarten Sap, Yejin Choi, and Noah A. Smith. 2020. RealToxicityPrompts: Evaluating neural toxic degeneration in language models. In *Findings of the Association for Computational Linguistics: EMNLP 2020*, pages 3356–3369, Online. Association for Computational Linguistics.

Jennifer Golbeck, Zahra Ashktorab, Rashad O. Banjo, Alexandra Berlinger, Siddharth Bhagwan, Cody Buntain, Paul Cheakalos, Alicia A. Geller, Quint Gergory, Rajesh Kumar Gnanasekaran, Raja Rajan Gunasekaran, Kelly M. Hoffman, Jenny Hottle, Vichita Jienjitlert, Shivika Khare, Ryan Lau, Marianna J. Martindale, Shalmali Naik, Heather L. Nixon, Piyush Ramachandran, Kristine M. Rogers, Lisa Rogers, Meghna Sardana Sarin, Gaurav Shahane, Jayanee Thanki, Priyanka Vengataraman, Zijian Wan, and Derek Michael Wu. 2017. A large labeled corpus for online harassment research. In *Proceedings of the 2017 ACM on Web Science Conference*, WebSci '17, page 229–233, New York, NY, USA. Association for Computing Machinery.

Lara Grimminger and Roman Klinger. 2021. Hate towards the political opponent: A Twitter corpus study of the 2020 US elections on the basis of offensive speech and stance detection. In *Proceedings of the Eleventh Workshop on Computational Approaches to Subjectivity, Sentiment and Social Media Analysis*, pages 171–180, Online. Association for Computational Linguistics.

Brendan Kennedy, Mohammad Atari, Aida Mostafazadeh Davani, Leigh Yeh, Ali Omrani, Yehsong Kim, Kris Coombs, Shreya Havaldar, Gwenyth Portillo-Wightman, Elaine Gonzalez, Joe Hoover, Aida Azatian, Alyzeh Hussain, Austin Lara, Gabriel Cardenas, Adam Omary, Christina Park, Xin Wang, Clarisa Wijaya, Yong Zhang, Beth Meyerowitz, and Morteza Dehghani. 2022. Introducing the gab hate corpus: defining and applying hate-based rhetoric to social media posts at scale. *Language Resources and Evaluation*, 56(1):79–108.

Brendan Kennedy, Xisen Jin, Aida Mostafazadeh Davani, Morteza Dehghani, and Xiang Ren. 2020. Contextualizing hate speech classifiers with post-hoc explanation. In *Proceedings of the 58th Annual Meeting of the Association for Computational Linguistics*, pages 5435–5442, Online. Association for Computational Linguistics.

Pang Wei Koh, Shiori Sagawa, Henrik Marklund, Sang Michael Xie, Marvin Zhang, Akshay Balsubramani, Weihua Hu, Michihiro Yasunaga, Richard Lanas Phillips, Irena Gao, et al. 2021. Wilds: A benchmark of in-the-wild distribution shifts. In *Proceedings of the 38th International Conference on Machine Learning*, volume 139, pages 5637–5664. PMLR.

Sachin Kumar, Shuly Wintner, Noah A. Smith, and Yulia Tsvetkov. 2019. Topics to avoid: Demoting latent confounds in text classification. In *Proceedings of the 2019 Conference on Empirical Methods in Natural Language Processing and the 9th International Joint Conference on Natural Language Processing (EMNLP-IJCNLP)*, pages 4153–4163, Hong Kong, China. Association for Computational Linguistics.

João Augusto Leite, Diego Silva, Kalina Bontcheva, and Carolina Scarton. 2020. Toxic language detection in social media for Brazilian Portuguese: New dataset and multilingual analysis. In *Proceedings of the 1st Conference of the Asia-Pacific Chapter of the Association for Computational Linguistics and the 10th International Joint Conference on Natural Language Processing*, pages 914–924, Suzhou, China. Association for Computational Linguistics.

Jens Lemmens, Ilia Markov, and Walter Daelemans. 2021. Improving Hate Speech Type and Target Detection with Hateful Metaphor Features. In *Proceedings of the Fourth Workshop on NLP for Internet Freedom: Censorship, Disinformation, and Propaganda*, pages 7–16, Online. Association for Computational Linguistics.

Paula Reyero Lobo, Enrico Daga, and Harith Alani. 2022. Supporting online toxicity detection with knowledge graphs. In *Proceedings of the International AAAI Conference on Web and Social Media*, volume 16, pages 1414–1418.

Thomas Mandl, Sandip Modha, Gautam Kishore Shahi, Amit Kumar Jaiswal, Durgesh Nandini, Daksh Patel, Prasenjit Majumder, and Johannes Schäfer. 2020. Overview of the HASOC track at FIRE 2020: Hate Speech and Offensive Content Identification in Indo-European Languages. In *Working Notes of FIRE 2020 - Forum for Information Retrieval Evaluation*, pages 87–111, Hyderabad, India. CEUR Workshop Proceedings.

Thomas Mandl, Sandip Modha, Gautam Kishore Shahi, Hiren Madhu, Shrey Satapara, Prasenjit Majumder, Johannes Schäfer, Tharindu Ranasinghe, Marcos Zampieri, Durgesh Nandini, and Amit Kumar Jaiswal. 2021. Overview of the HASOC Subtrack at FIRE 2021: HateSpeech and Offensive Content Identification in English and Indo-Aryan Languages. In *Working Notes of FIRE 2021 - Forum for Information Retrieval Evaluation*, pages 1–19, India. CEUR Workshop Proceedings.

Robert McHardy, Heike Adel, and Roman Klinger. 2019. Adversarial training for satire detection: Controlling for confounding variables. In *Proceedings of the 2019 Conference of the North American Chapter of the Association for Computational Linguistics: Human Language Technologies, Volume 1 (Long and Short Papers)*, pages 660–665, Minneapolis, Minnesota. Association for Computational Linguistics.

Ioannis Mollas, Zoe Chrysopoulou, Stamatis Karlos, and Grigorios Tsoumakas. 2022. ETHOS: a multi-label hate speech detection dataset. *Complex & Intelligent Systems*, 8:4663–4678.

Chikashi Nobata, Joel Tetreault, Achint Thomas, Yashar Mehdad, and Yi Chang. 2016. Abusive language detection in online user content. In *Proceedings of the 25th International Conference on World Wide Web*, WWW '16, page 145–153, Republic and Canton of Geneva, CHE. International World Wide Web Conferences Steering Committee.

Flor Miriam Plaza-del-Arco, Sercan Halat, Sebastian Padó, and Roman Klinger. 2021. Multi-task learning with sentiment, emotion, and target detection to recognize hate speech and offensive language. In *FIRE 2021 Working Notes*, pages 297–318.

Alan Ramponi and Sara Tonelli. 2022. Features or spurious artifacts? data-centric baselines for fair and robust hate speech detection. In *Proceedings of the 2022 Conference of the North American Chapter of the Association for Computational Linguistics: Human Language Technologies*, pages 3027–3040, Seattle, United States. Association for Computational Linguistics.

Marco Ribeiro, Sameer Singh, and Carlos Guestrin. 2016. "why should I trust you?": Explaining the predictions of any classifier. In *Proceedings of the 2016 Conference of the North American Chapter of the Association for Computational Linguistics: Demonstrations*, pages 97–101, San Diego, California. Association for Computational Linguistics.

Paul Röttger, Bertie Vidgen, Dong Nguyen, Zeerak Waseem, Helen Margetts, and Janet Pierrehumbert. 2021. HateCheck: Functional tests for hate speech detection models. In *Proceedings of the 59th Annual Meeting of the Association for Computational Linguistics and the 11th International Joint Conference on Natural Language Processing (Volume 1: Long Papers)*, pages 41–58, Online. Association for Computational Linguistics.

Pratik Sachdeva, Renata Barreto, Claudia Von Vacano, and Chris Kennedy. 2022. Targeted identity group prediction in hate speech corpora. In *Proceedings of the Sixth Workshop on Online Abuse and Harms (WOAH)*, pages 231–244, Seattle, Washington (Hybrid). Association for Computational Linguistics.

Mattia Samory, Indira Sen, Julian Kohne, Fabian Flöck, and Claudia Wagner. 2021. "Call me sexist, but...": Revisiting sexism detection using psychological scales and adversarial samples. In *Proceedings of the Fifteenth International AAAI Conference on Web and Social Media, ICWSM 2021, held virtually, June 7-10, 2021*, pages 573–584. AAAI Press.

Maarten Sap, Dallas Card, Saadia Gabriel, Yejin Choi, and Noah A. Smith. 2019. The risk of racial bias in hate speech detection. In *Proceedings of the 57th Annual Meeting of the Association for Computational Linguistics*, pages 1668–1678, Florence, Italy. Association for Computational Linguistics.

Maarten Sap, Saadia Gabriel, Lianhui Qin, Dan Jurafsky, Noah A. Smith, and Yejin Choi. 2020. Social bias frames: Reasoning about social and power implications of language. In *Proceedings of the 58th Annual Meeting of the Association for Computational Linguistics*, pages 5477–5490, Online. Association for Computational Linguistics.

Anna Schmidt and Michael Wiegand. 2017. A survey on hate speech detection using natural language processing. In *Proceedings of the Fifth International Workshop on Natural Language Processing for Social Media*, pages 1–10, Valencia, Spain. Association for Computational Linguistics.

Leandro Silva, Mainack Mondal, Denzil Correa, Fabrício Benevenuto, and Ingmar Weber. 2016. Analyzing the Targets of Hate in Online Social Media. In *Proceedings of the International AAAI Conference on Web and Social Media*, pages 687–690.

Julia Struß, Melanie Siegel, Josef Ruppenhofer, Michael Wiegand, and Manfred Klenner. 2019. Overview of GermEval Task 2, 2019 Shared Task on the Identification of Offensive Language. In *Proceedings of the 15th Conference on Natural Language Processing (KONVENS 2019)*, pages 354–365, Erlangen, Germany. German Society for Computational Linguistics & Language Technology.

Zeerak Talat, James Thorne, and Joachim Bingel. 2018. Bridging the Gaps: Multi Task Learning for Domain Transfer of Hate Speech Detection. In Jennifer Golbeck, editor, *Online Harassment*, pages 29–55. Springer International Publishing, Cham.

Nanna Thylstrup and Zeerak Talat. 2020. Detecting 'dirt'and 'toxicity': Rethinking content moderation as pollution behaviour. *Available at SSRN 3709719*.

Ameya Vaidya, Feng Mai, and Yue Ning. 2020. Empirical analysis of multi-task learning for reducing identity bias in toxic comment detection. In *Proceedings of the International AAAI Conference on Web and Social Media*, volume 14, pages 683–693.

Bertie Vidgen, Scott Hale, Ella Guest, Helen Margetts, David Broniatowski, Zeerak Waseem, Austin Botelho, Matthew Hall, and Rebekah Tromble. 2020. Detecting East Asian prejudice on social media. In *Proceedings of the Fourth Workshop on Online Abuse and Harms*, pages 162–172, Online. Association for Computational Linguistics.

Zeerak Waseem and Dirk Hovy. 2016. Hateful symbols or hateful people? predictive features for hate speech detection on Twitter. In *Proceedings of the NAACL Student Research Workshop*, pages 88–93, San Diego, California. Association for Computational Linguistics.

Michael Wiegand, Josef Ruppenhofer, and Thomas Kleinbauer. 2019. Detection of Abusive Language: the Problem of Biased Datasets. In *Proceedings of the 2019 Conference of the North American Chapter of the Association for Computational Linguistics: Human Language Technologies, Volume 1 (Long and Short Papers)*, pages 602–608, Minneapolis, Minnesota. Association for Computational Linguistics.

Michael Wiegand, Melanie Siegel, and Josef Ruppenhofer. 2018. Overview of the GermEval 2018 Shared Task on the Identification of Offensive Language. In *Proceedings of GermEval 2018, 14th Conference on Natural Language Processing (KONVENS 2018)*, pages 1–10, Vienna, Austria. Österreichische Akademie der Wissenschaften.

Mengzhou Xia, Anjalie Field, and Yulia Tsvetkov. 2020. Demoting racial bias in hate speech detection. In *Proceedings of the Eighth International Workshop on Natural Language Processing for Social Media*, pages 7–14, Online. Association for Computational Linguistics.

Tong Xiang, Sean MacAvaney, Eugene Yang, and Nazli Goharian. 2021. ToxCCIn: Toxic content classification with interpretability. In *Proceedings of the Eleventh Workshop on Computational Approaches to Subjectivity, Sentiment and Social Media Analysis*, pages 1–12, Online. Association for Computational Linguistics.

Yihao Xue, Ali Payani, Yu Yang, and Baharan Mirzasoleiman. 2023. Eliminating spurious correlations from pre-trained models via data mixing. *Preprint*, arXiv:2305.14521.

Marcos Zampieri, Shervin Malmasi, Preslav Nakov, Sara Rosenthal, Noura Farra, and Ritesh Kumar. 2019a. Predicting the type and target of offensive posts in social media. In *Proceedings of the 2019 Conference of the North American Chapter of the Association for Computational Linguistics: Human Language Technologies, Volume 1 (Long and Short Papers)*, pages 1415–1420, Minneapolis, Minnesota. Association for Computational Linguistics.

Marcos Zampieri, Shervin Malmasi, Preslav Nakov, Sara Rosenthal, Noura Farra, and Ritesh Kumar. 2019b. SemEval-2019 Task 6: Identifying and Categorizing Offensive Language in Social Media (OffensEval). In *Proceedings of the 13th International Workshop on Semantic Evaluation (SemEval@NAACL-HLT 2019)*, pages 75–86.

## A Hyperparameter Optimization

**Datasets.** To limit training time, we select 100k instances as training data and an additional 50k instances as validation data to determine a suitable point for early stopping. The remaining approximately 255k instances are used for hyperparameter optimization. Optimizing all models with the described setup takes about a month on a Nvidia Quadro RTX 8000 GPU. We do not expect using more than 100k training instances to change the results of our experiments regarding the comparison of the debiasing methods. To ensure that this is indeed the case, we trained another TOX baseline model with a larger subset for training by splitting the dev set as follows: 80% training, 10% validation-1, 10% validation-2. The resulting model (being trained on more than three times as many instances) achieves a slightly improved performance by 1.5 percentage points ($F1_{Tox}$ = .66) on the same test data. Hence, the chosen split does not have an impact on our conclusions.

For evaluation, we use the combined public and private test datasets from the Jigsaw Unintended Bias in Toxicity Classification challenge which does allow a straightforward comparison with past and future work.

We constrain input text instances to a maximum length of 236 tokens. This value corresponds to the 99th percentile of instance lengths in the development set. Thus, only 1% of the instances are truncated.

To deal with the skewed class distribution, we use class weights based on the inverse class frequency in the training data for all attributes in each loss.

**Early stopping configuration.** While all our setups operate with the same model, we monitor only relevant performance measures for each setup. Early stopping for the TOX setup monitors only the performance of the Tox classifier. In the joint setup, early stopping is based on toxicity and any active identity term classifiers in combination (all classifiers weighted equally). In the adversarial setups, early stopping is determined by monitoring the sum of the Tox classifier performance (or all MTL classifiers) and the negated adversary's performance (weighted by 0.1).

We use early stopping with `patience` = 3 and reload the best model if the maximum of 10 epochs is reached.

**Training process metadata.** On the mentioned data, our model trains for approximately 32 minutes per epoch on a single GPU (Nvidia Quadro RTX 8000). Each model has approximately 109 million trainable parameters.

**Learning rate optimization.** We run each experiment with different learning rates $\mathrm{lr} \in \{5 \cdot 10^{-6}, 7.5 \cdot 10^{-6}, 1 \cdot 10^{-5}, 2.5 \cdot 10^{-5}, 5 \cdot 10^{-5}\}$. For optimization we select the best lr value for each model according to its performance on the portion of the dataset which has not been used during training (255k instances). As performance measure we calculate the toxicity F1 score, possibly (if the model uses joint MTL) add F1 scores for joint MTL identity term classifiers and possibly (if the model uses an adversary) subtract the F1 score of the adversarial task. Since our main goal is to optimize the toxicity detection performance, we multiply the F1 scores of the identity classifiers by a reduced weight of 0.1 in this measure.

| | O + | O − | Total |
|---|---|---|---|
| Tox + | 27,963 (61%) | 18,072 | 46,035 |
| Tox − | 142,341 (40%) | 216,754 | 359,095 |
| Total | 170,304 (42%) | 234,826 | 405,130 |

Table 4: Distribution of binary toxicity and identity term annotations in the development set from the CivilComments dataset (Borkan et al., 2019). The percentages are respectively the proportion of instances with identities to the total instances for each row.

## B CivilComments Data

Table 4 shows the distribution of binary toxicity and identity term annotations in the development set from the CivilComments dataset (Borkan et al., 2019). This suggests a correlation between toxicity and mentions of identity terms, as toxic instances contain identity terms in 61% of instances, but only 40% of non-toxic instances.

## C Full Results

The performance of the models with optimized learning rate (cf. Appendix A) on the test dataset is displayed in Table 5. In addition to the performance scores shown in Table 2, this table provides the results for several models for each setup with different $\lambda_x$ values as well as some further setups with other combinations of the hierarchical identity classifiers. Table 2 only shows the best-performing corrected models based on the in-distribution test set performance with high $F1_{Tox}$ and low respective identity detection F1 for each setting (see underlined values in Table 5). The additional setups included in Table 5 which are not directly related to our research questions are briefly motivated in the following.

We additionally test a setting where we are correcting for both Identity and Class ($\lambda_2, \lambda_3 \in \{0.10, 0.25, 0.50, 1.00\}$, Model Tox−C−I). This setting is based on the assumption that a combined correction for both C and I could capture the more

| | Model | $\lambda_1$ | $\lambda_2$ | $\lambda_3$ | $F1^{(1)}_{Tox}$ | $F1^{(1)}_{O}$ | $F1^{(5)}_{C}$ | $F1^{(24)}_{I}$ |
|---|---|---|---|---|---|---|---|---|
| | TOX (baseline) | 0 | 0 | 0 | .64 | .59 | .25 | .07 |
| | RT (2022) | 0 | 0 | 0 | .55 | .45 | .13 | .03 |
| Identity Occurrence | Tox+O | −1 | — | — | .63 | .93 | | |
| | Tox−O | 0.10 | — | — | .64 | .34 | | |
| | Tox−O | 0.25 | — | — | .64 | .33 | | |
| | Tox−O | 0.50 | — | — | .64 | .16 | | |
| | Tox−O | 1.00 | — | — | .63 | .05 | | |
| Identity Class | Tox+C | — | −1 | — | .63 | (.92) | .87 | |
| | Tox−C | — | 0.10 | — | .64 | (.55) | .09 | |
| | Tox−C | — | 0.25 | — | .63 | (.52) | .06 | |
| | Tox−C | — | 0.50 | — | .64 | (.58) | .11 | |
| | Tox−C | — | 1.00 | — | .64 | (.51) | .09 | |
| Identity | Tox+I | — | — | −1 | .64 | (.90) | (.77) | .39 |
| | Tox−I | — | — | 0.10 | .63 | (.58) | (.20) | .05 |
| | Tox−I | — | — | 0.25 | .64 | (.58) | (.15) | .03 |
| | Tox−I | — | — | 0.50 | .63 | (.58) | (.17) | .01 |
| | Tox−I | — | — | 1.00 | .63 | (.58) | (.21) | .02 |
| Class and Identity | Tox−C−I | — | 0.10 | 0.10 | .64 | (.48) | .08 | .03 |
| | Tox−C−I | — | 0.25 | 0.25 | .64 | (.53) | .05 | .02 |
| | Tox−C−I | — | 0.50 | 0.50 | .63 | (.57) | .14 | .02 |
| | Tox−C−I | — | 1.00 | 1.00 | .62 | (.52) | .10 | .01 |
| all levels | Tox+O+C+I | −1 | −1 | −1 | .64 | .93 | .86 | .38 |
| | Tox−O−C−I | 0.10 | 0.10 | 0.10 | .64 | .19 | .13 | .04 |
| | Tox−O−C−I | 0.25 | 0.25 | 0.25 | .63 | .21 | .13 | .03 |
| | Tox−O−C−I | 0.50 | 0.50 | 0.50 | .64 | .22 | .06 | .02 |
| | Tox−O−C−I | 1.00 | 1.00 | 1.00 | .63 | .05 | .10 | .01 |
| | Tox+O, C, I | −1 | 0 | 0 | .63 | .93 | .34 | .10 |
| | Tox+O−C−I | −1 | 0.10 | 0.10 | .64 | .93 | .32 | .08 |
| | Tox+O−C−I | −1 | 0.25 | 0.25 | .64 | .93 | .30 | .08 |
| | Tox+O−C−I | −1 | 0.50 | 0.50 | .63 | .93 | .27 | .07 |
| | Tox+O−C−I | −1 | 1.00 | 1.00 | .63 | .93 | .26 | .06 |
| | Tox+O+C, I | −1 | −1 | 0 | .64 | .93 | .88 | .27 |
| | Tox+O+C−I | −1 | −1 | 0.10 | .63 | .93 | .87 | .25 |
| | Tox+O+C−I | −1 | −1 | 0.25 | .63 | .93 | .88 | .25 |
| | Tox+O+C−I | −1 | −1 | 0.50 | .63 | .93 | .86 | .24 |
| | Tox+O+C−I | −1 | −1 | 1.00 | .63 | .93 | .85 | .22 |
| | Tox+O+C−I | −1 | −1 | 2.00 | .61 | .93 | .81 | .20 |
| | Tox+O+C−I | −1 | −1 | 3.00 | .61 | .92 | .67 | .10 |

Table 5: Performance of optimized models on the test dataset. We display F1 for the positive classes across all variables. The values in the superscript of the F1 scores specify the number of classes evaluated in each task – for multi-label tasks (Class and Identity) we display the macro-average F1 over all positive class label F1 scores. In the column "Model", "+" marks joint classification, "−" marks adversaries and classifiers appended with "," do not have an effect on the encoder. Tox refers to the toxicity classifier. (O)ccurrence, (C)lass and (I)dentity refer to the classifiers for the three levels of the identity term label hierarchy according to our model (see Figure 2). Values in parentheses are inferred from the prediction of more fine-grained labels. Underlined $\lambda$ values mark the best debiased model for each setting.

| Id | Reference | Description | Size |
|---|---|---|---|
| da | Davidson et al. (2017) | Tweets annotated for hate speech and offensive language | 24,783 |
| ol | Zampieri et al. (2019a) | Tweets annotated for offensive content (OLID) | 860 |
| ha | Mandl et al. (2021) | Tweets annotated for hate speech and other offensive and objectionable content (HASOC 2021) | 1,281 |
| se | Samory et al. (2021) | Tweets annotated for sexism with predicted toxicity scores (CMSB) | 13,631 |
| sf | de Gibert et al. (2018) | Texts extracted from a white supremacy forum (Stormfront) | 478 |
| gk | Grimminger and Klinger (2021) | Political Twitter data annotated for hateful/offensive speech | 600 |
| as | Vidgen et al. (2020) | Tweets annotated for hostility directed against Asian people | 40,000 |
| et | Mollas et al. (2022) | YouTube and Reddit comments annotated for hate speech (ETHOS) | 998 |
| hc | Röttger et al. (2021) | Crafted test cases for hate speech detection (HateCheck) | 3,728 |

Table 6: Hate speech datasets used as additional test data to evaluate out-of-distribution performance. We show the number of instances we use for evaluation in the last column.

general set of features on the one hand, which are also sufficiently specific properties of identities on the other. We hypothesize that this setting will lead to a more comprehensive mitigation of the identity term bias than the experimental design with single adversaries.

Further, we test additional setups with all three levels, where we explore combinations incorporating the Occurrence classifier as adversary ($\lambda_1 \in \{0.10, 0.25, 0.50, 1.00\}$, Model Tox−O−C−I). Here we test whether the additional correction for O does not contribute to a broader mitigation of the target identity term bias that we are aiming for and might harm the overall toxicity detection performance.

Additionally, we explore the configuration where we only correct for identity features while jointly promoting Occurrence and Class information (Model Tox+O+C−I). The idea behind this is that we may want to let the model represent features of the target occurrence as well as some distinguishing features of identity classes. There could be substantial differences in the type of toxicity that targets certain groups compared to other types of toxicity that target other groups. Therefore, we want to enable co-learning of such properties of identities in this setup. Here, we also test higher weights ($\lambda_3 \in \{0.10, 0.25, 0.50, 1.00, 2.00, 3.00\}$) to empower the Identity adversary to possibly outweigh the three joint classifiers which presumably induce identity bias. A more powerful adversary on the lowest level might be sucessful at unlearning specific features of identities which constitute the target bias and result in an improved generalization ability of the trained model. However, by including the classifiers O and C jointly with the toxicity classifier, this model could still retain the ability to learn more general categories of targets of toxic statements.

## D Cross-Corpus Evaluation

We evaluate the performance of different models trained on the CivilComments dataset to predict hate speech on other datasets. We show the datasets that we use in Table 6. We selected publicly available datasets covering general types of hate speech and toxicity as well as datasets with a focus on specific subtypes, such as hate speech directed towards specific targets. In cases where the original authors declare a specific portion of the data as a test subset, we only use this portion in our evaluation. Otherwise we evaluate on the entire dataset.

The results for the out-of-distribution hate speech and toxicity detection performance are displayed in Table 7. The performance of all models on the 'gk' and 'as' datasets is rather low (F1 $\leq$ .30), presumably because these corpora are focused

| Model | IN | da | ol | ha | se | sf | gk | as | et | hc | avg. |
|---|---|---|---|---|---|---|---|---|---|---|---|
| | Performance on test data | | | | | | | | | | |
| | | Out-of-domain | | | | | | | | | |
| TOX (baseline) | .64 | .88 | .64 | .70 | .69 | .63 | .30 | .22 | .70 | .76 | .61 |
| RT (2022) | .55 Δ−.09 | .88 Δ.00 | .61 Δ−.03 | .71 Δ+.01 | .65 Δ−.04 | .51 Δ−.12 | .26 Δ−.04 | .16 Δ−.06 | .62 Δ−.08 | .60 Δ−.16 | .56 Δ−.05 |
| Tox−O | .63 Δ−.01 | .87 Δ−.01 | .62 Δ−.02 | .68 Δ−.02 | .69 Δ.00 | .66 Δ+.03 | .22 Δ−.08 | .17 Δ−.05 | .71 Δ+.01 | .74 Δ−.02 | .60 Δ−.01 |
| Tox−I | .63 Δ−.01 | .88 Δ.00 | .64 Δ.00 | .70 Δ.00 | .70 Δ+.01 | .67 Δ+.04 | .24 Δ−.06 | .19 Δ−.03 | .72 Δ+.02 | .76 Δ.00 | .61 Δ.00 |
| Tox+O+C−I | .63 Δ−.01 | .88 Δ.00 | .66 Δ+.02 | .72 Δ+.02 | .69 Δ.00 | .65 Δ+.02 | .21 Δ−.09 | .21 Δ−.01 | .71 Δ+.01 | .75 Δ−.01 | .61 Δ.00 |
| Tox+O−C−I | .64 Δ.00 | .88 Δ.00 | .66 Δ+.02 | .71 Δ+.01 | .70 Δ+.01 | .62 Δ−.01 | .21 Δ−.09 | .17 Δ−.05 | .71 Δ+.01 | .76 Δ.00 | .60 Δ−.01 |

Table 7: Hate speech/toxicity detection performance (F1 for the positive class) of our best corrected models in comparison to the baseline TOX model on different datasets. All models have been trained on the same data. Δ-values show the difference to the F1 score of the baseline model TOX. IN refers to the in-distribution test dataset performance of the CivilComments corpus and avg. refers to the macro-average of all out-of-distribution performances.

| Test dataset: | Full test | fema | male | chri | whit | musl | blac | homo | jewi | psyc | asia | athe | tran | lati | hete |
|---|---|---|---|---|---|---|---|---|---|---|---|---|---|---|---|
| | | Identity-specific subsets | | | | | | | | | | | | | |
| # test instances: | 42870 | 5155 | 4386 | 4226 | 2452 | 2040 | 1519 | 1065 | 835 | 511 | 454 | 280 | 260 | 225 | 141 |
| Model | $F1^{(1)}_{Tox}$ | $F1^{(1)}_{Tox}$ | $F1^{(1)}_{Tox}$ | $F1^{(1)}_{Tox}$ | $F1^{(1)}_{Tox}$ | $F1^{(1)}_{Tox}$ | $F1^{(1)}_{Tox}$ | $F1^{(1)}_{Tox}$ | $F1^{(1)}_{Tox}$ | $F1^{(1)}_{Tox}$ | $F1^{(1)}_{Tox}$ | $F1^{(1)}_{Tox}$ | $F1^{(1)}_{Tox}$ | $F1^{(1)}_{Tox}$ | $F1^{(1)}_{Tox}$ |
| TOX (baseline) | .64 | .62 | .61 | .60 | .63 | .59 | .65 | .62 | .62 | .65 | .53 | .52 | .63 | .62 | .52 |
| RT (2022) | .55 Δ−.09 | .56 Δ−.06 | .54 Δ−.07 | .45 Δ−.15 | .53 Δ−.10 | .39 Δ−.20 | .52 Δ−.13 | .45 Δ−.17 | .51 Δ−.11 | .58 Δ−.07 | .30 Δ−.23 | .47 Δ−.05 | .62 Δ−.01 | .49 Δ−.13 | .45 Δ−.07 |
| Tox−O | .63 Δ−.01 | .62 Δ.00 | .61 Δ.00 | .57 Δ−.03 | .62 Δ−.01 | .58 Δ−.01 | .64 Δ−.01 | .61 Δ−.01 | .60 Δ−.02 | .69 Δ+.04 | .53 Δ.00 | .59 Δ+.07 | .63 Δ+.01 | .63 Δ+.01 | .52 Δ.00 |
| Tox−I | .63 Δ−.01 | .62 Δ.00 | .62 Δ+.01 | .59 Δ−.01 | .65 Δ+.02 | .59 Δ.00 | .66 Δ+.01 | .61 Δ−.01 | .64 Δ+.02 | .67 Δ+.02 | .50 Δ−.03 | .55 Δ+.03 | .56 Δ−.06 | .69 Δ+.07 | .51 Δ−.01 |
| Tox+O+C−I | .63 Δ−.01 | .62 Δ.00 | .61 Δ.00 | .59 Δ−.01 | .65 Δ+.02 | .59 Δ.00 | .67 Δ+.02 | .59 Δ−.03 | .63 Δ+.01 | .66 Δ+.01 | .54 Δ+.01 | .62 Δ+.10 | .63 Δ+.01 | .68 Δ+.06 | .46 Δ−.06 |
| Tox+O−C−I | .64 Δ.00 | .63 Δ+.01 | .62 Δ+.01 | .59 Δ−.01 | .64 Δ+.01 | .60 Δ+.01 | .66 Δ+.01 | .61 Δ−.01 | .57 Δ−.05 | .70 Δ+.05 | .58 Δ+.05 | .48 Δ−.04 | .67 Δ+.04 | .65 Δ+.03 | .51 Δ−.01 |

Table 8: Performance of best models on different portions of the test dataset. Δ-values show the difference to the F1 score of the baseline model TOX. Fema: female, chri: christian, whit: white, musl: muslim, blac: black, homo: homosexual gay or lesbian, jewi: jewish, psyc: psychiatric or mental illness, asia: asian, athe: atheist, tran: transgender, lati: latino, hete: heterosexual.

on special cases of hate speech (towards specific individuals or particular ethnicities).

## E Evaluation of Identity-Specific Subsets

Table 8 shows the F1 scores of the baseline TOX model in comparison to the debiased baseline RT (2022) and our corrected models for these different portions of the test dataset. We additionally provide the number of instances which are considered in each subset. We discard all identity labels with less than 100 instances in the test dataset in this evaluation as there is presumably not enough statistical evidence for such categories.

# A Systematic Analysis on the Temporal Generalization of Language Models in Social Media

**Asahi Ushio**[*]
Amazon
asahiu@amazon.com

**Jose Camacho-Collados**
Cardiff NLP, Cardiff University, UK
camachocolladosj@cardiff.ac.uk

## Abstract

In machine learning, temporal shifts occur when there are differences between training and test splits in terms of time. For streaming data such as news or social media, models are commonly trained on a fixed corpus from a certain period of time, and they can become obsolete due to the dynamism and evolving nature of online content. This paper focuses on temporal shifts in social media and, in particular, Twitter. We propose a unified evaluation scheme to assess the performance of language models (LMs) under temporal shift on standard social media tasks. LMs are tested on five diverse social media NLP tasks under different temporal settings, which revealed two important findings: (i) the decrease in performance under temporal shift is consistent across different models for entity-focused tasks such as named entity recognition or disambiguation, and hate speech detection, but not significant in the other tasks analysed (i.e., topic and sentiment classification); and (ii) continuous pre-training on the test period does not improve the temporal adaptability of LMs.

## 1 Introduction

Modern natural language processing (NLP) is centered on language models (LMs) (Devlin et al., 2019; Radford et al., 2019; Liu et al., 2019; Min et al., 2023). The versatility of LMs has enabled many real world applications, including chatbot[1], text-guided image generation (Aditya et al., 2021), and text-to-speech (Paul K. et al., 2023). One of the well-known issues of LMs, however, is that the capabilities of LMs can not be fully analyzed due to their blackbox nature. To overcome such limitations to understand LMs' true capability, methodologies and datasets to inspect LMs have been proposed in the context of model probing study, which uncovered various features such as syntax (Hewitt and Manning, 2019; Goldberg, 2019), factual knowledge (Petroni et al., 2019; Ushio et al., 2021), semantics (Ettinger, 2020; Tenney et al., 2019), and emergent ability (Jason et al., 2022).

Besides such studies of LM probing, there is another line of research that focuses on the adaptability of LMs under settings incurring changing conditions, including *temporal shifts* (Lazaridou et al., 2021; Loureiro et al., 2022a). In this paper, we refer to temporal shifts when discussing settings in which the time period of the test set is different from that of the training set (with the test set period being generally *after*, reassembling real-world settings.). These settings have been empirically known to lead a non-trivial decrease in performance on some tasks (Liska et al., 2022; Jungo et al., 2022). Needless to say, temporal shifts are more important in more dynamic streaming data with frequent meaning changes and evolving entities, such as social media (Antypas et al., 2022; Ushio et al., 2022).

In this paper, we focus on temporal shifts on Twitter, one of the major social media platforms, and propose a unified evaluation scheme to assess the adaptability of LMs toward temporal shift on Twitter. In particular, we are interested in answering the following two research questions:

- **RQ1.** Are temporal shifts in social media detrimental for LM performance in NLP tasks?
- **RQ2.** If so, what are the causes of this temporal shift and can it be mitigated (by e.g. using LMs pre-trained on recent data)?

For the evaluation, we selected five diverse social media NLP tasks for which there are datasets with temporal information available: hate speech detection, topic classification, sentiment classification, named entity disambiguation (NED), and

[*]Work done while at Cardiff NLP
[1]https://openai.com/blog/chatgpt



*Proceedings of the 14th Workshop on Computational Approaches to Subjectivity, Sentiment, & Social Media Analysis*, pages 52–62
August 15, 2024 

named entity recognition (NER) ranging over different time periods. The temporal shifts considered are relatively short compared to those studied in other sources of streaming data such as news and scientific papers. We test both LMs specialized on social media and other general-purpose trained on encyclopedic and web-crawled corpus.

Our study shows that tasks driven by named entities or events (i.e., hate speech, NED, and NER) present consistent decrease across model under temporal shift settings, while it is less prominent in the other tasks. Crucially, our results show that the decrease caused by temporal shift cannot be mitigated by considering a more recent corpus to the pre-training dataset. Finally, qualitative analysis highlights that the common mistakes made by LMs are indeed instances that require to understand the named entities in the tweet. All the datasets and the scripts to reproduce our experiments are made publicly available online[2].

## 2 Related Work

**LMs on Social Media.** Major LMs are commonly pre-trained on encyclopedic and web-crawled corpora (Lewis et al., 2020; Raffel et al., 2020; Aakanksha et al., 2023; Rohan et al., 2023; Hugo et al., 2023b,a; Tom B. et al., 2020), while the adaptation of such LMs to social media has led new LMs pre-trained on corpus curated over social media (Nguyen et al., 2020; Loureiro et al., 2022a; DeLucia et al., 2022; Barbieri et al., 2022), which present better performance on social media NLP tasks than standard LMs (Barbieri et al., 2020; Antypas et al., 2023). However, such studies on NLP tasks in social media mainly focus on static datasets without temporal shift. A few of them associate timestamps to the dataset and provide basic temporal analysis (Antypas et al., 2022; Ushio et al., 2022), but these are limited to a single task. Finally, related to the temporal aspect of this work, short-term meaning shift has also been studied in the context of social media and LMs (Loureiro et al., 2022b).

**Temporal Generalization.** Importantly, this work aligns to the research on the temporal or diachronic generalization of LMs. In this area, however, most previous works focus on relatively long term (over 10 years) (Lazaridou et al., 2021) or formal source of text such as news and scientific papers (Liska et al., 2022; Jungo et al., 2022). In the context of short-term temporal analysis, there are three studies that are most similar to ours. Luu et al. (2022) analyse the temporal performance degradation of LMs in NLP tasks in relatively short time periods. While social media is included as one of the domains, the evaluation is limited to the classification task and to general-domain models. Agarwal and Nenkova (2022) performed a similar general analysis for different tasks, while also analysing the effect of self-labeling as a mitigation to temporal misalignment, which we do not analyse in this work. The main difference between these works in ours is our focus on social media, where we carry out a targeted comprehensive analysis on short-term temporal effects. When it comes to social media, temporal shifts are especially relevant given the real-time nature of the platform and their focus on current events. In the context of Italian Twitter, Florio et al. (2020) analysed the temporal sensitivity of models for hate speech detection, which is one of the tasks included in this paper.

**Temporal-aware LMs.** To enhance adaptability of LMs for temporal shift, there are a few works that explicitly ingests the temporal information to the model by specific attention mechanism (Rosin and Radinsky, 2022), augmenting the input with timestamp (Rosin et al., 2022), joint modeling of temporal information (Dhingra et al., 2022), and self-labeling (Agarwal and Nenkova, 2022). In this paper, we do not include any temporal-aware LMs, because we are interested in analysing the adaptability of plain LMs to temporal shifts.

## 3 Experimental Setting

In this section, we describe our experimental setting to investigate the effect of temporal shifts in LMs.

### 3.1 Evaluation Methodology

Let us define $\mathcal{D}_{\text{train}}$ and $\mathcal{D}_{\text{test}}$ as the training and test splits of a dataset $\mathcal{D}$ for a single downstream task (e.g. sentiment classification), where each dataset contains pairs of a text input and associated labels. Importantly, $\mathcal{D}_{\text{train}}$ is taken from the period prior to $\mathcal{D}_{\text{test}}$ without any temporal overlap. Given such dataset with temporal split, we consider the following two settings of out-of-time (OOT) and in-time (IT).

**Out-of-Time (OOT).** In the first setting, we simply train the models on $\mathcal{D}_{\text{train}}$ and evaluate them

[2] `https://huggingface.co/datasets/tweettemposhift/tweet_temporal_shift`

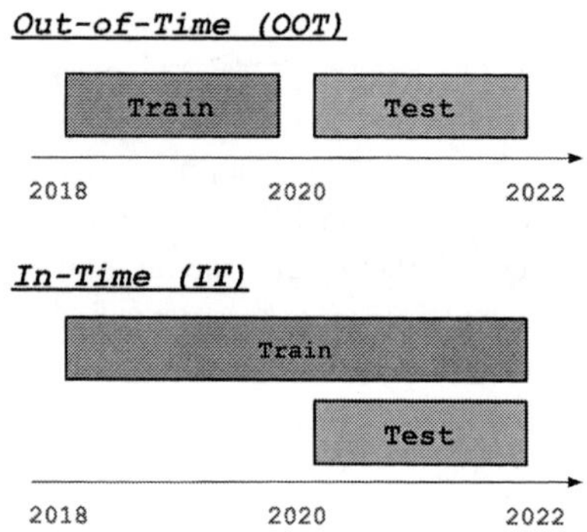


Figure 1: An illustrative example of the conceptual differences between the sampling time periods of the OOT and IT settings.

on $\mathcal{D}_{\text{test}}$. Noticeably, models have no access to the instances from the test period at the training phase in this setting, so we refer the setting as *out-of-time* (OOT) as an analogy to the out-of-domain (OOD).

**In-Time (IT).** As a comparison to OOT, we consider the second experimental setting, which is designed to assess the effect of training instances from the test period. The test set is randomly split into non-overlapped four chunks ($\mathcal{D}_{\text{test}} = \bigcup_{i=1}^{4} \mathcal{D}_{\text{test}}^{i}$) for cross validation, where models trained on $\mathcal{D}_{\text{train}} \bigcup \mathcal{D}_{\text{test}} \backslash \mathcal{D}_{\text{test}}^{i}$ are evaluated on $\mathcal{D}_{\text{test}}^{i}$. For each chunk of the test set, we downsample the IT training set to the same size as $\mathcal{D}_{\text{train}}$ with three random seeds and report the averaged metrics over the runs. To be precise, we consider a function $\mathcal{F}_s(\mathcal{D})$ that randomly samples $|\mathcal{D}_{\text{train}}|$ instances from $\mathcal{D}$, and we independently train models on $\mathcal{F}_s(\mathcal{D}_{\text{train}} \bigcup \mathcal{D}_{\text{test}} \backslash \mathcal{D}_{\text{test}}^{i})$ for $s = 0, 1, 2$. In contrast to OOT, we refer this setting as *in-time* (IT) setting.

Figure 1 presents an example overview of the differences between IT and OOT settings from the perspective of data sampling periods (data from 2018 to 2022 in the example).

### 3.2 Tasks & Datasets

We consider the following five diverse social media NLP tasks: hate speech detection, topic classification, sentiment classification, named entity disambiguation (NED), and named entity recognition (NER). For each task, we employ a public dataset for English and leverage its original temporal splits, unless there is overlap between the periods of training and test sets.

**Hate Speech Detection.** Hate speech detection in Twitter consists of identifying whether a tweet contains hateful content. We use the dataset proposed by Waseem and Hovy (2016) framed as binary classification as the dataset to create the training and test splits based on the timestamp. The first half is used for training and the rest for test split. The training split is further randomly split into 2:8 for validation:training. We use accuracy to evaluate the hate speech detection models.

**Topic Classification.** Topic classification is a task that consists of associating an input text with one or more labels from a fixed label set. For this evaluation, we rely on TweetTopic (Antypas et al., 2022), a multi-label topic classification dataset with 19 topics such as *sports* or *music*. As evaluation metric, we use micro-F1 score to measure the performance of topic classification models.

**Sentiment Analysis.** Sentiment analysis is a standard social media task consisting of associating each post with its sentiment. In particular, we use the dataset from the task 2: LongEval-Classification from CLEF-2023 (Alkhalifa et al., 2023) in which the task is framed as binary classification with positive and negative labels. The original training split contains around 50k instances while 1k test split, which is highly imbalance and the effect of the IT sample can be very limited. To balance the training and test splits, we randomly sample 2.5k instances from each label, amounting 5k new training instance. We use accuracy to evaluate the sentiment classification models.

**Named Entity Disambiguation (NED).** NED is a a binary classification that consists of identifying if the meaning of a given target entity in context is the same as the one provided. We use the TweetNERD (Mishra et al., 2022) dataset and reformulated into NED following SuperTweetEval (Dimosthenis et al., 2023). Then, we create the train, validation, and test splits in the same way as the hate speech detection. We use accuracy to evaluate the NED models.

**Named Entity Recognition (NER).** NER is a sequence labelling task to predict a single named-entity type on each token on the input text. We rely on TweetNER7 (Ushio et al., 2022), a NER dataset on Twitter that contains seven named entity types. We use span F1 score to evaluate NER models.

| | Split | Size | Date | Examples |
|---|---|---|---|---|
| Hate | Train | 2,318 | 2013-09-23 / 2015-03-03 | *Zebra undies #MKR chic in pink dress.* (Hate) |
| | Valid | 579 | 2013-09-23 / 2015-03-03 | *OMG fashion parade time #mkr.* (non-Hate) |
| | Test | 1,475 | 2015-03-04 / 2015-03-14 | *female football commentators just don't work.* (Hate) |
| Topic | Train | 4,585 | 2019-09-08 / 2020-08-30 | *So, when I can listen to watermelon sugar live in Jakarta Harry?* |
| | Valid | 573 | 2019-09-08 / 2020-08-30 | *@Harry_Styles* (celebrity, music) |
| | Test | 1,679 | 2020-09-06 / 2021-08-29 | *Glad to see the Chiefs crushed the Texans* (sports) |
| Sent. | Train | 5,000 | 2014-02-06 / 2016-12-31 | *I think I'm in love* (positive) |
| | Valid | 1,344 | 2016-01-01 / 2016-12-31 | *@user is making me very upset* (negative) |
| | Test | 1,344 | 2018-01-01 / 2019-01-01 | *Shoutout to @MENTION for donating to poor* (positive) |
| NED | Train | 18,469 | 2020-02-26 / 2021-08-27 | *Every concert I've seen announce lately, they are steering clear of Detroit* (Target: Detroit, Definition: Art museum, Label: False) |
| | Valid | 4,617 | 2020-02-27 / 2021-08-27 | *Me on stream: Happy Friday!, Australia: It's Saturday* |
| | Test | 21,253 | 2021-08-28 / 2021-11-28 | (Target: Australia, Definition: country, Label: True) |
| NER | Train | 4,616 | 2019-09-08 / 2020-08-30 | *UFC 245: Looking at the three title fights on tap at T-Mobile Arena* |
| | Valid | 576 | 2019-09-08 / 2020-08-30 | (UFC 245: corporation, T-Mobile Arena: location) |
| | Test | 2,807 | 2020-09-05 / 2021-08-31 | *Glad the Chiefs crushed the Texans* (Chiefs: group, Texans: group) |

Table 1: The number of tweets and the period with examples of each dataset.

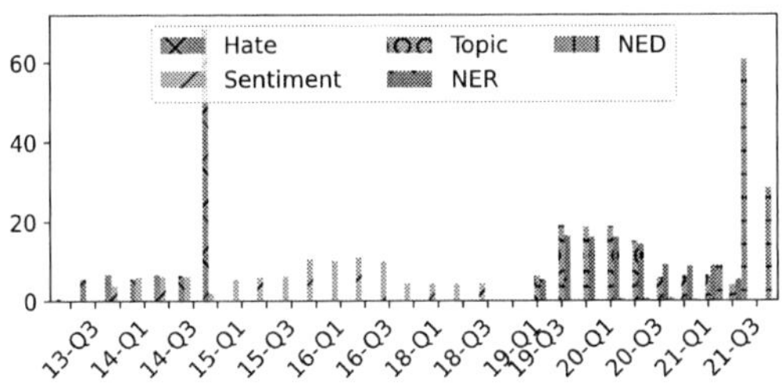


Figure 2: Quarterly breakdown of the number of tweets ratio (%) in each dataset. For example, a ratio of 5% in 13-Q3 for Dataset X would mean that 5% of all tweets in Dataset X belong to the third quarter (July-September) of 2013.

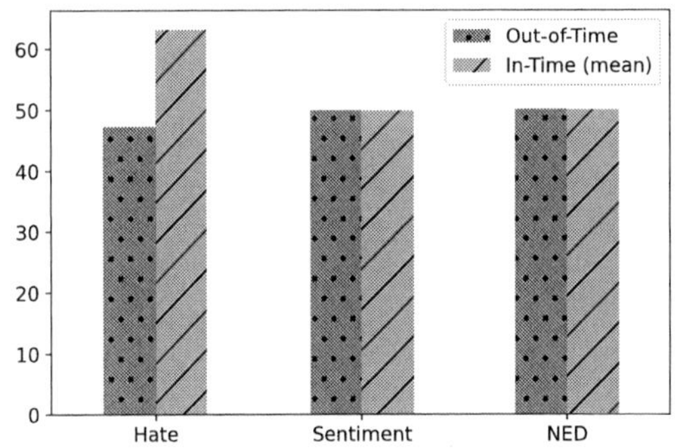


Figure 3: Comparisons of ratio (%) of positive labels in the training split of each task between OOT and IT.

### 3.2.1 Data Statistics

Table 1 shows the size and the period of the training and the test sets for each dataset, and Figure 2 displays the number of tweets per quarter for each task. Topic classification and NER use the same tweets, which are sampled uniformly from each month, while NED and hate speech detection have the majority of the tweets in the latest quarter. Sentiment analysis covers the longest period in the dataset that spans over four years. Figures 3 and 4 show the comparisons of the label distribution of the binary (i.e., hate speech, sentiment classification, and NED) and multi-classification tasks (i.e., NER and topic classification), respectively. As can be observed, hate speech detection has fewer positive labels in OOT than in IT, while the other two tasks have the same ratio of the positive labels between OOT and IT. The same pattern can be observed for topic classification and NED, for which the label distribution does not substantially change.

## 3.3 Models

We investigate an established general-purpose LM, RoBERTa (Liu et al., 2019) as well as other LMs pre-trained on tweets including BERTweet (Nguyen et al., 2020), TimeLM (Loureiro et al., 2022a), and BERNICE (DeLucia et al., 2022). For RoBERTa and BERTweet, we consider the base and the large models, referred as RoBERTa (B), RoBERTa (L), BERTweet (B), and BERTweet (L). For TimeLM, we consider the base models trained on the tweets up to 2019, 2020, 2021 and 2022, referred as TimeLM2019 (B), TimeLM2020 (B), TimeLM2021 (B) and TimeLM2022 (B), and the large model trained upto 2022, referred as

| Model | Parameters | HF Name | Citation |
|---|---|---|---|
| $\text{RoBERTa}_{\text{BASE}}$ | 123M | roberta-base | (Liu et al., 2019) |
| $\text{RoBERTa}_{\text{LARGE}}$ | 354M | roberta-large | |
| $\text{BERTweet}_{\text{BASE}}$ | 123M | vinai/bertweet-base | (Nguyen et al., 2020) |
| $\text{BERTweet}_{\text{LARGE}}$ | 354M | vinai/bertweet-large | |
| $\text{TimeLM2019}_{\text{BASE}}$ | 123M | cardiffnlp/twitter-roberta-base-2019-90m | (Loureiro et al., 2022a) |
| $\text{TimeLM2020}_{\text{BASE}}$ | 123M | cardiffnlp/twitter-roberta-base-dec2020 | |
| $\text{TimeLM2021}_{\text{BASE}}$ | 123M | cardiffnlp/twitter-roberta-base-2021-124m | |
| $\text{TimeLM2022}_{\text{BASE}}$ | 354M | cardiffnlp/twitter-roberta-base-2022-154m | |
| $\text{TimeLM2022}_{\text{LARGE}}$ | 354M | cardiffnlp/twitter-roberta-large-2022-154m | |
| BERNICE | 278M | jhu-clsp/bernice | (DeLucia et al., 2022) |

Table 2: Language models used in the paper with the number of parameters and model aliases on Hugging Face.

| | Hate | Topic | Sentiment | NED | NER |
|---|---|---|---|---|---|
| RoBERTa | ✓ | | ✓ | | |
| BERTweet | ✓ | | ✓ | | |
| BERNICE | ✓ | ✓ | ✓ | ✓ | ✓ |
| TimeLM2019 | ✓ | | ✓ | | |
| TimeLM2020 | ✓ | | ✓ | | |
| TimeLM2021 | ✓ | ✓ | ✓ | ✓ | ✓ |
| TimeLM2022 | ✓ | ✓ | ✓ | ✓ | ✓ |

Table 3: The overlap between the test period and the pre-trained corpus of each LM (✓indicates that the LM is pre-trained on the corpus including the test period of the task).

TimeLM2022 (L). The end date of the pre-trained corpus for each model is 2019-02 (RoBERTa), 2019-08 (BERTweet), 2019-12 (TimeLM2019), 2020-12 (TimeLM2020), 2021-12 (TimeLM2021 and BERNICE), and 2022-12 (TimeLM2022). All the model weights are taken from the transformers model hub (Wolf et al., 2020) and Table 2 shows the details of models we used in the paper.[3] Table 3 shows the overlap between the period of the pre-trained corpus and the test set for each task, which will be relevant for the analysis on the effect of pre-training in Section 5.1. These models are then fine-tuned in the datasets presented in the previous section, in both OOT and IT settings. For model fine tuning, we run hyperparameter search with Optuna (Akiba et al., 2019) with the default search space.

## 4 Results

Figures 5 to 9 show the comparisons of IT and OOT in hate speech detection, NED, NER, topic classification and sentiment analysis. As can be observed, hate speech detection, NED and NER present inconsistencies in both settings, decreasing the performance from IT to OOT. In contrast, this cannot be observed for both sentiment analysis, and especially topic classification. The average decrease of OOT performance for each of the tasks is 4.5, 2.4, 1.7, 0.8 and -0.1 for hate speech detection, NER, NED topic classification and sentiment analysis.

One of the main differences of those two groups of tasks (i.e. hate/NED/NER v.s. topic/sentiment) entity-centric or event-driven nature of the former. NER and NED are clearly related to named entities. Hate speech detection does not relate to named entities explicitly, but since the tweets for hate speech detection are collected by querying specific events, they are often about events or celebrities which peak around the sampled timestamp (Gómez et al., 2023). On the other hand, events or named entities are not as important in sentiment analysis, as the sentiment can be estimated from the context in most cases. Topic classification depends on the topic, with some of them related to entities (e.g. those related to celebrities or TV) and others not (e.g., daily life, family or food), but in the main clearly identifiable by the context. Through the lens of entity relevancy, this result may suggest that the temporal shift can be caused by named entities, which includes meaning drift of existing named

[3]Note that for this analysis we are not interested in the performance of zero-shot LLMs such as GPT-4, but rather on the effect of fine-tuned LMs.

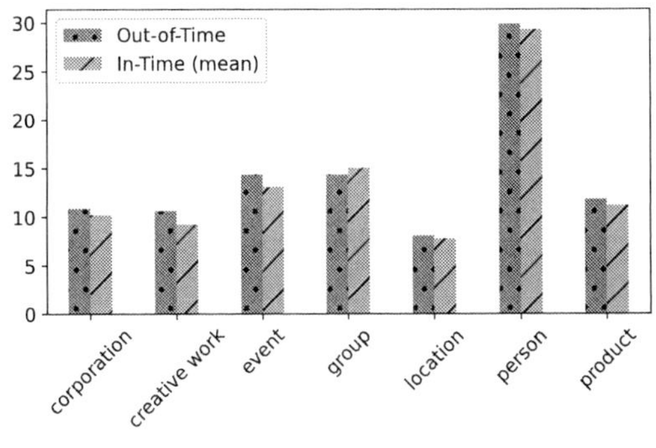


(a) Ratio of entities in NER.

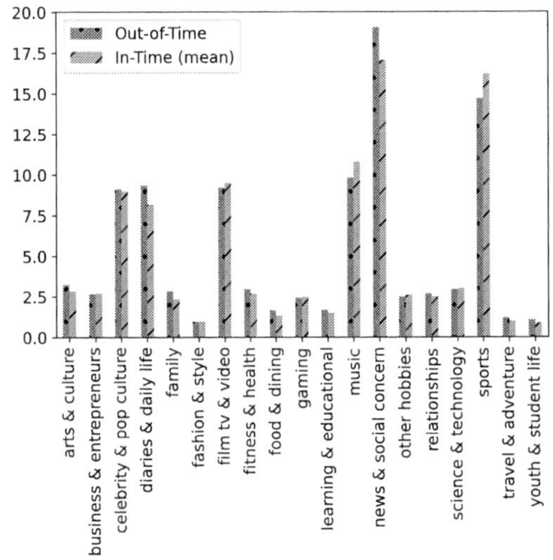


(b) Ratio of labels in topic classification.

Figure 4: Comparisons of label distributions between OOT and IT settings.

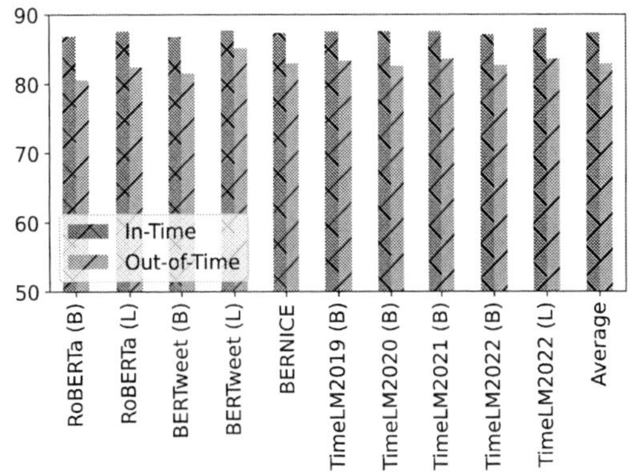


Figure 5: Comparisons of IT and OOT performance (accuracy) for hate speech detection.

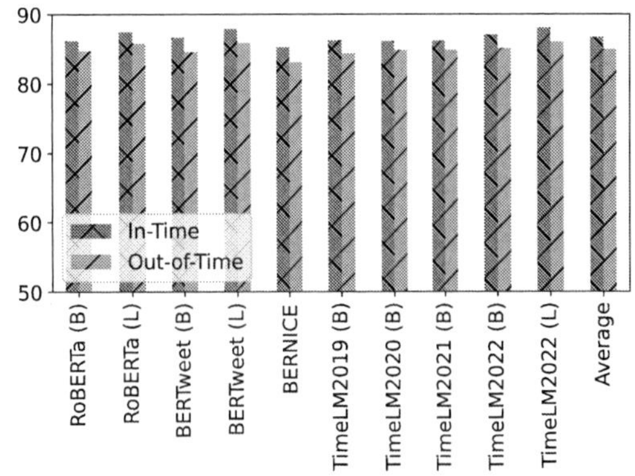


Figure 6: Comparisons of IT and OOT performance (accuracy) for NED.

entities or emerging new named entities. Topic classification can be seen as a mixture of entity-related instances and not, which results in not fully consistent gain from OOT, but still significant in the average.

## 5 Analysis

This section focuses on the second research question (RQ2) and analyses the main causes behind temporal shift performance degradation of LMs.

### 5.1 Effect of Pre-Training

A possible direction to mitigate the temporal shift is to pre-train the LMs on the text from the test period, which does not require any labeling. Figure 10 visualizes the performance and relative IT improvement of LMs with/without pre-training corpus covering the test period of each task for topic classification/NED/NER[4]. At a glance, we cannot observe see any relationship between the pre-training corpus and the performance. The averaged relative gains of the metrics from OOT within the LMs pre-trained on the test period and the others are 2.0 and 0.6 (topic classification), 3.5 and 3.8 (NER), and 2.1 and 1.9 (NED) respectively. Therefore, all models are affected by the temporal shift irrespective of the pre-training corpus date. This implies that the temporal shift cannot be robustly resolved by only adding data from the test period to the pre-training corpus, a conclusion that was also reached by Luu et al. (2022).

### 5.2 Effect of Label Distribution

In supervised machine learning label distribution, the distribution of the binary label over the test instances, shifts can affect a model's performance. In

[4]The test periods of hate speech detection and sentiment classification are covered by all the LMs we considered in the experiment.

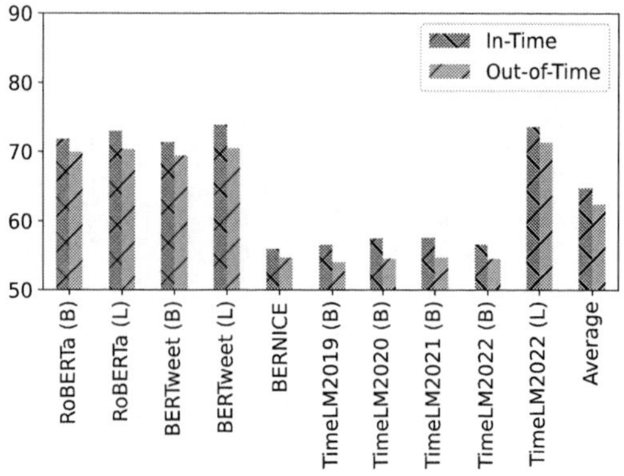


Figure 7: Comparisons of IT and OOT performance (F1 score) for NER.

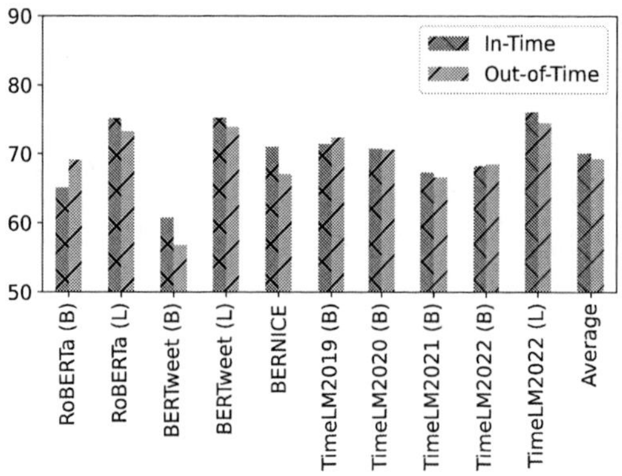


Figure 8: Comparisons of IT and OOT performance (F1 score) for topic classification.

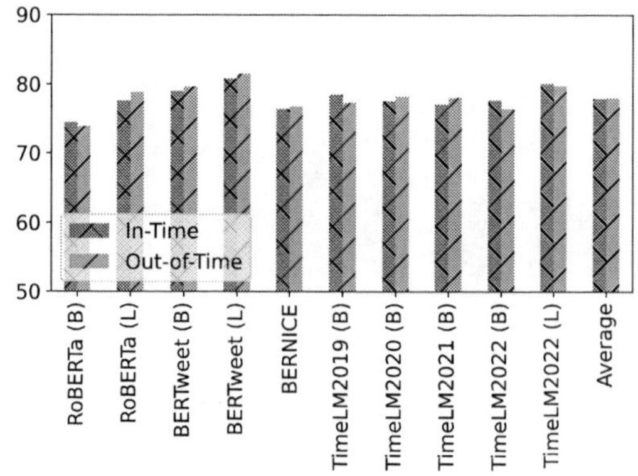


Figure 9: Comparisons of IT and OOT performance (accuracy) for sentiment classification.

| | Original | Balanced |
|---|---|---|
| RoBERTa (B) | 7.25 | 5.19 |
| RoBERTa (L) | 5.96 | -0.95 |
| BERTweet (B) | 5.91 | 4.84 |
| BERTweet (L) | 2.88 | -0.30 |
| BERNICE | 5.04 | 4.72 |
| TimeLM2019 (B) | 4.80 | 4.16 |
| TimeLM2020 (B) | 5.71 | 5.39 |
| TimeLM2021 (B) | 4.51 | 5.52 |
| TimeLM2022 (B) | 4.97 | 0.15 |
| TimeLM2022 (L) | 4.94 | 1.89 |
| Average | 5.20 | 3.06 |

Table 4: Comparisons of relative accuracy gain from OOT to IT between original (unbalanced) and balanced label distributions for hate speech detection.

this section, we analyse this potential effect when it comes to temporal shifts. For this, we rely on hate speech detection, which presents the largest decrease in performance from IT to OOT, with a different label distribution between training and test (see Figure 3). For the other tasks, the label distribution appears to be largely similar. To separate the effect of label distributional shift between IT and OOT from the temporal shift, we conduct a controlled experiment by balancing the label distribution of each IT training split to be the same as OOT training split. This is achieved by undersampling the size of the training set. Table 4 shows the results, where the average relative gain is still positive, although it becomes less dominant in balanced experiment. This highlights how label distribution may change over time and this itself have an effect in model performance. A similar finding was already discussed by Luu et al. (2022).

### 5.3 Qualitative Analysis

In this analysis, we have a closer look on the test instances that are incorrect in OOT, turning to be correct in IT. To be precise, we sort the test instance in a single task based on the number of models where the error in OOT setting has been corrected in IT setting over all the random seeds. In other words, given a test instance, we check whether a model prediction is incorrect in OOT, but correct in the IT setting. This particular instance is counted as a correction. In total, we have 10 models with 3 independent runs with different random seed to construct the training data, so 30 would be the maximum number of corrections. For sentiment classification, hate speech detection, topic classification and NED, we simply count instance-level corrections. Given the complex nature of NER evaluation, we decided to only focus on the entity type

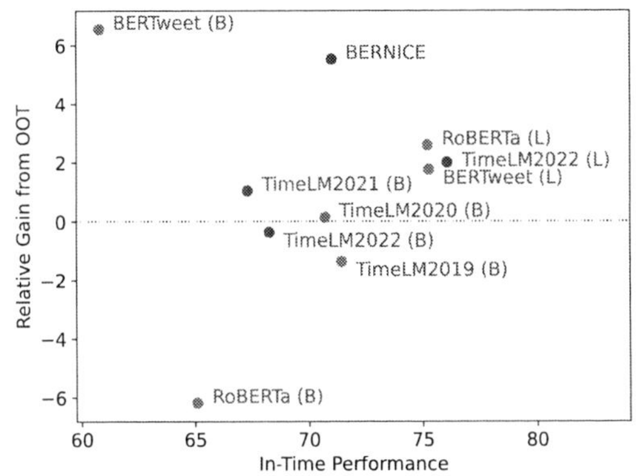


(a) Topic classification.

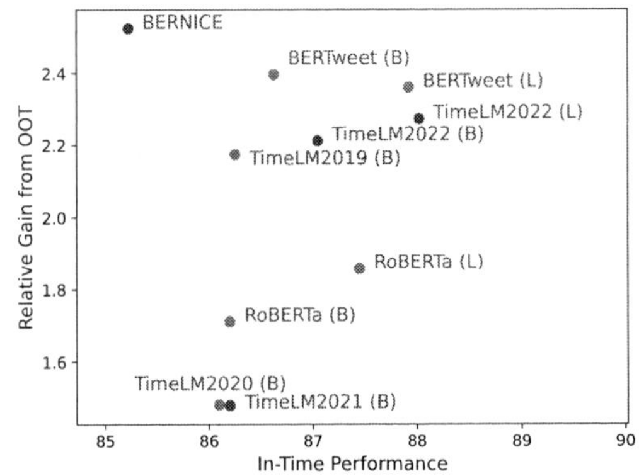


(b) NED.

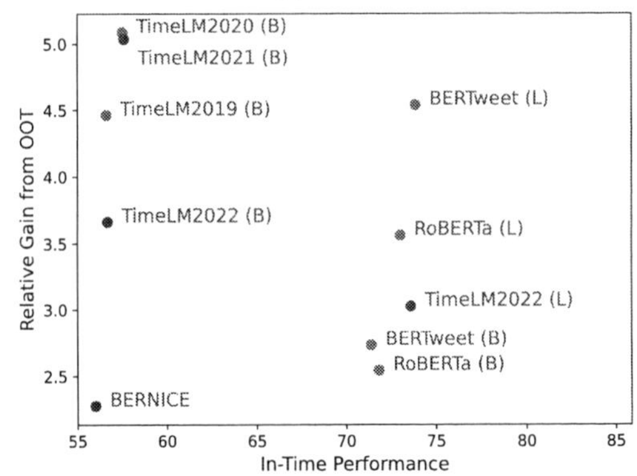


(c) NER.

Figure 10: Relative improvement (%) from OOT to IT for each task (topic, NED and NER). LMs with pretraining corpus including the test period are in blue, and those without temporal overlap in red.

predictions for this analysis.

Table 5 shows the top instances in terms of IT corrections for each of the task. We can observed the marked differences across tasks, with NED and hate speech detection including instances which were corrected 100% in the OOT setting. In fact,

| Task | Top corrected | Avg Top 10 |
|---|---|---|
| NED | 30/30 (100%) | 30.0 |
| Hate | 30/30 (100%) | 30.0 |
| NER | 28/30 (93.3%) | 24.0 |
| Sentiment | 19/30 (63.3%) | 13.6 |
| Topic | 16/30 (53.3%) | 12.5 |

Table 5: Top instances in terms of number of predictions corrected with an IT split. The second column indicates the top 10 average.

| Task | Instance | Gold | Times corrected |
|---|---|---|---|
| NED | so cute how <Aoki> describes Ida. "thinks about things seriously" *(Japanese manga series)* | False | 30/30 (100%) |
| | Will Ram & <Priya> go on a honeymoon it'll be a nice break for them (...) #BadeAchheLagteHain2 *(Indian actress)* | False | 30/30 (100%) |
| Hate | #MKR God Kat you are awful awful person. Oh you are humiliated? GOOD. | False | 30/30 (100%) |
| | #katandandre gaaaaah I just want to slap her back to WA #MKR | False | 30/30 (100%) |

Table 6: Two examples from the NED and hate speech detection datasets in which the prediction was corrected 100% of the times with an IT split. For NED, the definition is provided in parenthesis and target word indicated between < and >.

there are respectively 44 and 15 instances for which this is the case in these two tasks. Similarly for NER, the number of corrections is high. This is correlated with the main results of the paper (see Section 4) which showed clear improvements for these tasks in the IT setting, but not for sentiment and and topic classification.

Finally, Table 6 shows some of these instances for NED and hate speech detection. In the case of NED, the tweets relate to two new TV series that were on air at test time (Japanese *Kieta Hatsukoi* in the first example and Indian B*ade Achhe Lagte Hain* in the second, both from 2021). This is similar to the hate speech detection in which the examples belong to the *My Kitchen Rules TV* show. This highlights the event-driven nature of social media, and the importance of acquiring the background context for the specific task.

## 6 Conclusion

We proposed an evaluation method to assess the adaptability of LMs for temporal shifts on social media with five diverse downstream tasks including sentiment classification, NER, NED, hate speech detection, and topic classification. We have tested diverse LMs trained on Twitter under different temporal settings. The experimental results indicate that the adaptability gets consistently worse on entity or event-driven tasks (NED, NER, and hate speech detection) while the effect is limited in the other tasks. This conclusion was similar to previous work in more general domains, which observed a variation across different types of task when it comes to temporal degradation (Luu et al., 2022; Agarwal and Nenkova, 2022). Finally, our analysis shows that pre-training on a corpus from the test period is not enough to solve the temporal shift issue, with performance still being degraded in comparison to models fine-tuned on the labeled dataset from the test period.

## Limitations

Regardless of some similarities between Twitter and other streaming data such as news and other social media platforms being real-time and trend-driven, they can have different characteristics, and the results of our study may apply to Twitter exclusively. For our evaluation we rely on a single dataset for each of the tasks. Of course, these datasets are not a faithfully representation of the task and may contain their own biases. Therefore, even for the same task, the findings in this paper may differ if using a different dataset.

## Ethical Statement

The datasets we used in the experiments are all from Twitter. Data has been anonymized (only information about legacy-verified users is kept) so that they do not contain any personal identifiable information (PII). We do not gather information from individual accounts but rely on aggregated information and metrics only. Please note that the text may contain sensitive content due to the nature of social media and the task, in particular hate speech detection.

## Acknowledgements

Jose Camacho-Collados is supported by a UKRI Future Leaders Fellowship.

## References

Chowdhery Aakanksha, Narang Sharan, Devlin Jacob, et al. 2023. Palm: Scaling language modeling with pathways. *Journal of Machine Learning Research*, 24(240):1–113.

Ramesh Aditya, Pavlov Mikhail, Goh Gabriel, et al. 2021. Zero-shot text-to-image generation. *Preprint*, arXiv:2102.12092.

Oshin Agarwal and Ani Nenkova. 2022. Temporal effects on pre-trained models for language processing tasks. *Transactions of the ACL*, 10:904–921.

Takuya Akiba, Shotaro Sano, Yanase, et al. 2019. Optuna: A next-generation hyperparameter optimization framework. In *Proceedings of the 25th ACM SIGKDD international conference on knowledge discovery & data mining*, pages 2623–2631.

Rabab Alkhalifa, Iman Bilal, Hsuvas Borkakoty, et al. 2023. Overview of the clef-2023 longeval lab on longitudinal evaluation of model performance. In *International Conference of the Cross-Language Evaluation Forum for European Languages*, pages 440–458. Springer.

Dimosthenis Antypas, Asahi Ushio, Francesco Barbieri, et al. 2023. SuperTweetEval: A challenging, unified and heterogeneous benchmark for social media NLP research. In *Findings of EMNLP 2023*, pages 12590–12607, Singapore.

Dimosthenis Antypas, Asahi Ushio, Jose Camacho-Collados, et al. 2022. Twitter topic classification. In *Proceedings of COLING*, pages 3386–3400, Gyeongju, Republic of Korea.

Francesco Barbieri, Jose Camacho-Collados, Luis Espinosa Anke, and Leonardo Neves. 2020. TweetEval: Unified benchmark and comparative evaluation for tweet classification. In *Findings of the ACL: EMNLP 2020*, pages 1644–1650, Online. ACL.

Francesco Barbieri, Luis Espinosa Anke, and Jose Camacho-Collados. 2022. XLM-T: Multilingual language models in Twitter for sentiment analysis and beyond. In *Proceedings of LREC*, pages 258–266, Marseille, France.

Alexandra DeLucia, Shijie Wu, Aaron Mueller, Carlos Aguirre, Philip Resnik, and Mark Dredze. 2022. Bernice: A multilingual pre-trained encoder for Twitter. In *Proceedings of the 2022 Conference on EMNLP*, pages 6191–6205, Abu Dhabi, United Arab Emirates. ACL.

Jacob Devlin, Ming-Wei Chang, Kenton Lee, et al. 2019. BERT: Pre-training of deep bidirectional transformers for language understanding. In *Proceedings of NAACL*, pages 4171–4186, Minneapolis, Minnesota.

Bhuwan Dhingra, Jeremy R. Cole, Julian Martin Eisenschlos, Daniel Gillick, Jacob Eisenstein, and William W. Cohen. 2022. Time-aware language models as temporal knowledge bases. *Transactions of the ACL*, 10:257–273.

Antypas Dimosthenis, Ushio Asahi, Barbieri Francesco, et al. 2023. Supertweeteval: A challenging, unified and heterogeneous benchmark for social media nlp research. In *Findings of EMNLP 2023*.

Allyson Ettinger. 2020. What BERT is not: Lessons from a new suite of psycholinguistic diagnostics for language models. *Transactions of the ACL*, 8:34–48.

Komal Florio, Valerio Basile, Marco Polignano, Pierpaolo Basile, and Viviana Patti. 2020. Time of your hate: The challenge of time in hate speech detection on social media. *Applied Sciences*, 10(12):4180.

Yoav Goldberg. 2019. Assessing bert's syntactic abilities. *arXiv preprint arXiv:1901.05287*.

Jesús Gómez, Alberto Matilla-Molina, Ma Pilar Amado, Dimosthenis Antypas, Jose Camacho-Collados, Carlos J Máñez, Tomás Fernández-Villazala, Alicia Méndez-Sanchís, and Javier López. 2023. The interaction between offensive and hate speech on twitter and relevant social events in spain. In *News Media and Hate Speech Promotion in Mediterranean Countries*, pages 81–109. IGI Global.

John Hewitt and Christopher D. Manning. 2019. A structural probe for finding syntax in word representations. In *Proceedings of the 2019 Conference of the North American Chapter of the ACL: Human Language Technologies, Volume 1 (Long and Short Papers)*, pages 4129–4138, Minneapolis, Minnesota. ACL.

Touvron Hugo, Martin Louis, Stone Kevin, et al. 2023a. Llama 2: Open foundation and fine-tuned chat models.

Touvron Hugo, Lavril Thibaut, Izacard Gautier, et al. 2023b. Llama: Open and efficient foundation language models.

Wei Jason, Tay Yi, Bommasani Rishi, et al. 2022. Emergent abilities of large language models. *Transactions on Machine Learning Research*. Survey Certification.

Kasai Jungo, Sakaguchi Keisuke, Takahashi Yoichi, et al. 2022. Realtime qa: What's the answer right now? *Preprint*, arXiv:2207.13332.

Angeliki Lazaridou, Adhi Kuncoro, Elena Gribovskaya, et al. 2021. Mind the gap: Assessing temporal generalization in neural language models. In *Advances in Neural Information Processing Systems*, volume 34, pages 29348–29363.

Mike Lewis, Yinhan Liu, Naman Goyal, et al. 2020. BART: Denoising sequence-to-sequence pre-training for natural language generation, translation, and comprehension. In *Proceedings of ACL*, pages 7871–7880, Online.

Adam Liska, Tomas Kocisky, Elena Gribovskaya, Tayfun Terzi, Eren Sezener, Devang Agrawal, D'Autume Cyprien De Masson, Tim Scholtes, Manzil Zaheer, Susannah Young, et al. 2022. Streamingqa: A benchmark for adaptation to new knowledge over time in question answering models. In *International Conference on Machine Learning*, pages 13604–13622. PMLR.

Yinhan Liu, Myle Ott, Naman Goyal, et al. 2019. Roberta: A robustly optimized bert pretraining approach. *arXiv preprint arXiv:1907.11692*.

Daniel Loureiro, Francesco Barbieri, Leonardo Neves, et al. 2022a. TimeLMs: Diachronic language models from Twitter. In *Proceedings of ACL: System Demonstrations*, pages 251–260, Dublin, Ireland.

Daniel Loureiro, Aminette D'Souza, Areej Nasser Muhajab, et al. 2022b. TempoWiC: An evaluation benchmark for detecting meaning shift in social media. In *Proceedings of COLING*, pages 3353–3359, Gyeongju, Republic of Korea.

Kelvin Luu, Daniel Khashabi, Suchin Gururangan, Karishma Mandyam, and Noah A. Smith. 2022. Time waits for no one! analysis and challenges of temporal misalignment. In *Proceedings of the 2022 Conference of the North American Chapter of the Association for Computational Linguistics: Human Language Technologies*, pages 5944–5958, Seattle, United States.

Bonan Min, Hayley Ross, Elior Sulem, et al. 2023. Recent advances in natural language processing via large pre-trained language models: A survey. *ACM Computing Surveys*, 56(2):1–40.

Shubhanshu Mishra, Aman Saini, Raheleh Makki, et al. 2022. Tweetnerd–end to end entity linking benchmark for tweets. *arXiv preprint arXiv:2210.08129*.

Dat Quoc Nguyen, Thanh Vu, and Anh Tuan Nguyen. 2020. BERTweet: A pre-trained language model for English tweets. In *Proceedings of the 2020 Conference on EMNLP: System Demonstrations*, pages 9–14, Online. ACL.

Rubenstein Paul K., Asawaroengchai Chulayuth, Dung Nguyen Duc, et al. 2023. Audiopalm: A large language model that can speak and listen. *arXiv preprint arXiv:2306.12925*.

Fabio Petroni, Tim Rocktäschel, Sebastian Riedel, et al. 2019. Language models as knowledge bases? In *Proceedings of EMNLP-IJCNLP*, pages 2463–2473, Hong Kong, China.

Alec Radford, Jeffrey Wu, Rewon Child, et al. 2019. Language models are unsupervised multitask learners. *OpenAI blog*, 1(8):9.

Colin Raffel, Noam Shazeer, Adam Roberts, et al. 2020. Exploring the limits of transfer learning with a unified text-to-text transformer. *J. Mach. Learn. Res.*, 21(1).

Anil Rohan, Dai Andrew M., Firat Orhan, et al. 2023. Palm 2 technical report. *arXiv preprint arXiv:2305.10403*.

Guy D. Rosin, Ido Guy, and Kira Radinsky. 2022. Time masking for temporal language models. In *Proceedings of the Fifteenth ACM International Conference on Web Search and Data Mining*, WSDM '22, page 833–841, New York, NY, USA.

Guy D. Rosin and Kira Radinsky. 2022. Temporal attention for language models. In *Findings of the ACL: NAACL 2022*, pages 1498–1508, Seattle, United States. ACL.

Ian Tenney, Dipanjan Das, and Ellie Pavlick. 2019. BERT rediscovers the classical NLP pipeline. In *Proceedings of the 57th Annual Meeting of the ACL*, pages 4593–4601, Florence, Italy. ACL.

Brown Tom B., Mann Benjamin, Ryder Nick, et al. 2020. Language models are few-shot learners. *Advances in neural information processing systems*, 33:1877–1901.

Asahi Ushio, Francesco Barbieri, Vitor Sousa, et al. 2022. Named entity recognition in Twitter: A dataset and analysis on short-term temporal shifts. In *Proceedings of the 2nd Conference of AACL*, pages 309–319, Online only.

Asahi Ushio, Luis Espinosa Anke, Steven Schockaert, et al. 2021. BERT is to NLP what AlexNet is to CV: Can pre-trained language models identify analogies? In *Proceedings of ACL*, pages 3609–3624, Online.

Zeerak Waseem and Dirk Hovy. 2016. Hateful symbols or hateful people? predictive features for hate speech detection on Twitter. In *Proceedings of the NAACL Student Research Workshop*, pages 88–93, San Diego, California. ACL.

Thomas Wolf, Lysandre Debut, Victor Sanh, et al. 2020. Transformers: State-of-the-art natural language processing. In *Proceedings of the 2020 Conference on EMNLP: System Demonstrations*, pages 38–45, Online.

# LLaMA-Based Models for Aspect-Based Sentiment Analysis

**Jakub Šmíd[*], Pavel Přibáň[*], Pavel Král[*,†]**

University of West Bohemia, Faculty of Applied Sciences,
[*]Department of Computer Science and Engineering,
[†]NTIS – New Technologies for the Information Society
Univerzitní 2732/8, 301 00 Pilsen, Czech Republic
{jaksmid, pribanp, pkral}@kiv.zcu.cz
`https://nlp.kiv.zcu.cz`

## Abstract

While large language models (LLMs) show promise for various tasks, their performance in compound aspect-based sentiment analysis (ABSA) tasks lags behind fine-tuned models. However, the potential of LLMs fine-tuned for ABSA remains unexplored. This paper examines the capabilities of open-source LLMs fine-tuned for ABSA, focusing on LLaMA-based models. We evaluate the performance across four tasks and eight English datasets, finding that the fine-tuned Orca 2 model surpasses state-of-the-art results in all tasks. However, all models struggle in zero-shot and few-shot scenarios compared to fully fine-tuned ones. Additionally, we conduct error analysis to identify challenges faced by fine-tuned models.

## 1 Introduction

Aspect-based sentiment analysis (ABSA) aims to extract detailed sentiment information from text (Zhang et al., 2022). ABSA includes four sentiment elements: aspect term ($a$), aspect category ($c$), opinion term ($o$), and sentiment polarity ($p$). Given the example review *"The steak was delicious"*, the elements are *"steak"*, *"food quality"*, *"delicious"* and *"positive"*, respectively.

Initially, ABSA research focused on extracting individual sentiment elements, e.g. aspect term extraction or aspect category detection (Pontiki et al., 2014). Recent research has transitioned towards compound tasks involving multiple sentiment elements, such as aspect sentiment triplet extraction (ASTE) (Peng et al., 2020), target aspect category detection (TASD) (Wan et al., 2020), aspect category opinion sentiment (ACOS) (Cai et al., 2021), and aspect sentiment quad prediction (ASQP) (Zhang et al., 2021a). Table 1 shows the output formats of these ABSA tasks.

Modern ABSA research often utilizes pre-trained language models, mainly focusing on sequence-to-sequence models. Compound ABSA tasks are typically formulated as text generation problems (Zhang et al., 2021b,a; Gao et al., 2022; Hu et al., 2022; Gou et al., 2023), which allows to solve compound ABSA tasks simultaneously.

| Task | Output | Example output |
|---|---|---|
| ASTE | $\{(a, o, p)\}$ | {("steak", "delicious", POS)} |
| TASD | $\{(a, c, p)\}$ | {("steak", food quality, POS)} |
| ACOS | $\{(a, c, o, p)\}$ | {("steak", food quality, "delicious", POS)} |
| ASQP | $\{(a, c, o, p)\}$ | {("steak", food quality, "delicious", POS)} |

Table 1: Output format for selected ABSA tasks for a review: *"The steak was delicious"*. ACOS focuses on implicit aspect and opinion terms in contrast to ASQP.

Lately, large language models (LLMs), such as ChatGPT (OpenAI, 2022), LLaMA 2 (Touvron et al., 2023b) and Orca 2 (Mitra et al., 2023), have made significant progress across various natural language processing tasks. However, more traditional approaches that fine-tune Transformer-based models with sufficient data have shown superior performance over ChatGPT in compound ABSA tasks (Zhang et al., 2023; Gou et al., 2023). Additionally, fine-tuning LLMs on a single GPU is challenging due to their large number of parameters. Techniques like QLoRA (Dettmers et al., 2023) address this challenge using a quantized 4-bit frozen backbone LLM with a small set of learnable LoRA weights (Hu et al., 2021). However, studies have yet to explore the capabilities of fine-tuned open-source LLMs for ABSA.

This paper examines the unexplored potential of LLaMA-based models fine-tuned for English ABSA alongside their performance in zero-shot and few-shot scenarios. Our key contributions include: 1) Introducing the capabilities of fine-tuned LLaMA-based models for ABSA. 2) Conducting a comparative analysis of two LLaMA-based models against state-of-the-art results across four ABSA tasks and eight datasets. 3) Evaluating models' performance in zero-shot, few-shot, and fine-tuning scenarios, demonstrating the superior performance



*Proceedings of the 14th Workshop on Computational Approaches to Subjectivity, Sentiment, & Social Media Analysis*, pages 63–70
August 15, 2024 ©2024 Association for Computational Linguistics

of the fine-tuned Orca 2 model, surpassing state-of-the-art results across all datasets and tasks. 4) Presenting error analysis of the top-performing model.[1]

## 2 Related Work

Early ABSA studies focused on predicting one or two sentiment elements (Liu et al., 2015; Zhou et al., 2015; He et al., 2019; Cai et al., 2020) before progressing to more complex tasks involving triplets and quadruplets, such as ASTE (Peng et al., 2020), TASD (Wan et al., 2020), ASQP (Zhang et al., 2021a) and ACOS (Cai et al., 2021).

Recent ABSA research focuses primarily on text generation initiated by GAS (Zhang et al., 2021b). PARAPHRASE (Zhang et al., 2021a) converts labels to natural language. LEGO-ABSA (Gao et al., 2022) explores multi-tasking, DLO (Hu et al., 2022) optimizes element ordering, MVP (Gou et al., 2023) combines differently ordered outputs, and Scaria et al. (2023) adopt instruction tuning.

Gou et al. (2023) and Zhang et al. (2023) show that ChatGPT struggles with compound ABSA tasks in zero-shot and few-shot settings. Simmering and Huoviala (2023) report promising results with close-source LLMs for a single simple ABSA task.

## 3 Experimental Setup

We employ the 7B and 13B versions of LLaMA 2 (Touvron et al., 2023b) and Orca 2 (Mitra et al., 2023) models from the HuggingFace Transformers library[2] (Wolf et al., 2020). LLaMA 2 offers models of various sizes tailored for dialogue tasks, building upon the LLaMA framework (Touvron et al., 2023a). Orca 2 extends this collection with enhanced reasoning capabilities.

### 3.1 Experimental Details

For fine-tuning, we follow recommendations from Dettmers et al. (2023) and use QLoRA with the following settings: 4-bit NormalFloat (NF4) with double quantization and bf16 computation datatype, batch size of 16, constant learning rate of 2e-4, AdamW optimizer (Loshchilov and Hutter, 2019), LoRA adapters (Hu et al., 2021) on all linear Transformer block layers, and LoRA $r = 64$ and $\alpha = 16$. We fine-tune the models for up to 5 epochs and choose the best-performing model based on validation loss. Following Mitra et al. (2023), we compute loss only on tokens generated by the model, excluding the prompt with instructions.

For zero-shot and few-shot experiments, we use 4-bit quantization of the models. Preliminary experiments indicated that 4-bit quantized models performed similarly to 8-bit quantized models and non-quantized models.

All experiments, including zero-shot and few-shot scenarios, employ greedy search decoding and are conducted on an NVIDIA A40 with 48 GB GPU memory.

### 3.2 Evaluation Metrics

We use micro F1-score as the primary evaluation metric, chosen based on related work, and report average results from 5 runs with different seeds. We consider a predicted sentiment tuple correct only if all its elements exactly match the gold tuple.

### 3.3 Tasks & Datasets

We evaluate the LLMs on four tasks: two involving quadruplets (ASQP and ACOS) and two involving triplets (TASD and ASTE). We select two datasets for each task and use the same data splits as previous works for a fair comparison. Table 1 displays the output targets for each task.

We use Rest15 and Rest16 datasets for ASQP in the restaurant domain, initially introduced in SemEval tasks (Pontiki et al., 2015, 2016), later aligned and supplemented by Zhang et al. (2021a). For ACOS, we employ ACOS-Rest and ACOS-Lap datasets from Cai et al. (2021), focusing on implicit aspects and opinions and providing comprehensive evaluation. We use the dataset from Xu et al. (2020) and Wan et al. (2020) for ASTE and TASD, respectively. Table 2 shows the detailed data statistics. ASTE datasets are the only ones that do not include implicit sentiment elements.

### 3.4 Prompting Strategy & Fine-Tuning

LLMs show varied responses despite similar prompts (Perez et al., 2021; Lu et al., 2022). Our goal is to design simple, clear, and straightforward prompts to standardize evaluations across datasets and ensure consistent assessment of LLMs.

Our prompts define sentiment elements and output format. Sentiment element definitions include the permitted label space, e.g. allowed sentiment

[1]Code and datasets are available at https://github.com/biba10/LLaMA-ABSA.

[2]https://github.com/huggingface/transformers

| | | ASQP | | ACOS | | TASD | | ASTE | |
|---|---|---|---|---|---|---|---|---|---|
| | | Rest15 | Rest16 | Lap | Rest | Rest15 | Rest16 | Rest15 | Rest16 |
| Train | Sentences | 834 | 1,264 | 2,934 | 1,530 | 1,120 | 1,708 | 605 | 857 |
| | Tuples | 1,354 | 1,989 | 4,172 | 2,484 | 1,654 | 2,507 | 1,013 | 1,394 |
| | Categories | 13 | 12 | 114 | 12 | 13 | 12 | 0 | 0 |
| | POS/NEG/NEU | 1,005/315/34 | 1,369/558/62 | 2,583/1,362/227 | 1,656/733/95 | 1,198/403/53 | 1,657/749/101 | 783/205/25 | 1,015/329/50 |
| Dev | Sentences | 209 | 316 | 326 | 171 | 10 | 29 | 148 | 210 |
| | Tuples | 347 | 507 | 440 | 261 | 13 | 44 | 249 | 339 |
| | Categories | 12 | 13 | 71 | 13 | 6 | 9 | 0 | 0 |
| | POS/NEG/NEU | 252/81/14 | 341/143/23 | 279/137/24 | 180/69/12 | 6/7/0 | 23/20/1 | 185/53/11 | 252/76/11 |
| Test | Sentences | 537 | 544 | 816 | 583 | 582 | 587 | 322 | 326 |
| | Tuples | 795 | 799 | 1,161 | 916 | 845 | 859 | 485 | 514 |
| | Categories | 12 | 12 | 81 | 12 | 12 | 12 | 0 | 0 |
| | POS/NEG/NEU | 453/305/37 | 583/176/40 | 716/380/65 | 667/205/44 | 454/346/45 | 611/204/44 | 317/143/25 | 407/78/29 |

Table 2: Statistics for each dataset. POS, NEG and NEU denote the number of positive, negative and neutral examples, respectively.

**Prompt for quadruplet tasks**

According to the following sentiment elements definition:

- The "aspect term" refers to a specific feature, attribute, or aspect of a product or service on which a user can express an opinion. Explicit aspect terms appear explicitly as a substring of the given text. The aspect term might be "null" for the implicit aspect.
- The "aspect category" refers to the category that aspect belongs to, and the available categories include: "ambience general", "drinks prices", "drinks quality", "drinks style_options", "food general", "food prices", "food quality", "food style_options", "location general", "restaurant general", "restaurant miscellaneous", "restaurant prices", "service general".
- The "sentiment polarity" refers to the degree of positivity, negativity or neutrality expressed in the opinion towards a particular aspect or feature of a product or service, and the available polarities include: "positive", "negative" and "neutral". "neutral" means mildly positive or mildly negative. Quadruplets with objective sentiment polarity should be ignored.
- The "opinion term" refers to the sentiment or attitude expressed by a user towards a particular aspect or feature of a product or service. Explicit opinion terms appear explicitly as a substring of the given text. The opinion term might be "null" for the implicit opinion.

Please carefully follow the instructions. Ensure that aspect terms are recognized as exact matches in the review or are "null" for implicit aspects. Ensure that aspect categories are from the available categories. Ensure that sentiment polarities are from the available polarities. Ensure that opinion terms are recognized as exact matches in the review or are "null" for implicit opinions.

Recognize all sentiment elements with their corresponding aspect terms, aspect categories, sentiment polarity, and opinion terms in the given input text (review). Provide your response in the format of a Python list of tuples: 'Sentiment elements: [("aspect term", "aspect category", "sentiment polarity", "opinion term"), ...]'. Note that ", ..." indicates that there might be more tuples in the list if applicable and must not occur in the answer. Ensure there is no additional text in the response.

Input: """We have gone for dinner only a few times but the same great quality and service is given ."""
Sentiment elements: [("service", "service general", "positive", "great"), ("dinner", "food quality", "positive", "great quality")]

Input: """It is n't the cheapest sushi but has been worth it every time ."""
**Output:** Sentiment elements: [("sushi", "food prices", "neutral", "is n't the cheapest"), ("sushi", "food quality", "positive", "worth")]

Figure 1: Prompt for quadruplet tasks (ASQP and ACOS) with example input, expected output in a green box, and one demonstration enclosed in a dashed box. The demonstrations are used solely in few-shot scenarios.

polarities and aspect categories. The output format describes the expected structure of model responses, allowing us to decode the responses into our desired format. We supplement the prompts with the first ten training examples for a given task for few-shot learning. We use the same prompts for fine-tuning as for zero-shot experiments. Figure 1 illustrates a prompt for quadruplet tasks. Appendix A presents the prompts for the triplet tasks.

During the fine-tuning experiments, we train the model to generate the output in the desired format, as shown in Figure 1.

## 4 Results

Table 3 shows the results of LLaMA-based models.

The results demonstrate the remarkable potential of Orca 2, especially in its 13B version, which surpasses previous benchmarks across all four tasks and eight datasets. Notably, the TASD task shows the most significant improvement, with 6% and 8% enhancements for the Rest15 and Rest16 datasets, respectively. While improvements for other tasks are relatively smaller, they remain noteworthy. There are marginal enhancements, within 1%, for the ASQP and ASTE tasks and the ACOS-Lap dataset. However, the ACOS-Rest dataset sees a significant improvement exceeding 4%, indicating notable progress. The remarkable advancements in the TASD task suggest that predicting opinion terms not included in the TASD task presents the most significant challenge for these models. The larger Orca 2 achieves a substantial improvement of 2.87% on average.

The 7B version of Orca 2 performs similarly to

| Method | ASQP | | ACOS | | TASD | | ASTE | | AVG |
|---|---|---|---|---|---|---|---|---|---|
| | R15 | R16 | Lap | Rest | R15 | R16 | R15 | R16 | |
| GAS (Zhang et al., 2021b) | 45.98 | 56.04 | - | - | 60.63 | 68.31 | 60.23 | 69.05 | - |
| PARAPHRASE (Zhang et al., 2021a) | 46.93 | 57.93 | 43.51 | 61.16 | 63.06 | 71.97 | 62.56 | 71.70 | 59.85 |
| LEGO-ABSA (Gao et al., 2022) | 46.10 | 57.60 | - | - | 62.30 | 71.80 | 64.40 | 69.90 | - |
| MvP (Gou et al., 2023) | 51.04 | 60.39 | 43.92 | 61.54 | 64.53 | 72.76 | 65.89 | 73.48 | 61.69 |
| MvP (multi-task) (Gou et al., 2023) | 52.21 | 58.94 | 43.84 | 60.36 | 64.74 | 70.18 | 69.44 | 73.10 | 61.60 |
| ChatGPT (zero-shot) (Gou et al., 2023) | 22.87 | - | - | 27.11 | - | 34.08 | - | - | - |
| ChatGPT (few-shot) (Gou et al., 2023) | 34.27 | - | - | 37.71 | - | 46.50 | - | - | - |
| Orca 2 7B (zero-shot) | 1.19 | 1.66 | 0.87 | 2.52 | 7.77 | 9.80 | 23.04 | 24.58 | 8.93 |
| Orca 2 7B (few-shot) | 11.34 | 14.21 | 4.50 | 16.00 | 27.32 | 34.13 | 37.70 | 42.18 | 23.42 |
| Orca 2 7B | 51.50 | 58.63 | 43.48 | 63.01 | 69.74 | 76.10 | 65.62 | 73.18 | 62.66 |
| Orca 2 13B (zero-shot) | 7.83 | 10.23 | 3.20 | 10.98 | 15.62 | 22.84 | 27.74 | 31.64 | 17.46 |
| Orca 2 13B (few-shot) | 21.13 | 23.47 | 9.10 | 23.80 | 32.00 | 39.08 | 39.50 | 44.16 | 30.16 |
| Orca 2 13B | **52.29** | **60.82** | **44.09** | **65.80** | **70.49** | **78.82** | **69.91** | **74.23** | **64.56** |
| LLaMA 2 7B (zero-shot) | 0.80 | 1.85 | 0.05 | 2.39 | 2.28 | 7.45 | 3.47 | 5.00 | 3.21 |
| LLaMA 2 7B (few-shot) | 11.20 | 17.48 | 2.68 | 26.43 | 28.10 | 33.85 | 38.88 | 45.04 | 25.46 |
| LLaMA 2 7B | 42.48 | 55.46 | 36.49 | 57.81 | 64.80 | 71.39 | 57.41 | 67.69 | 56.69 |
| LLaMA 2 13B (zero-shot) | 7.54 | 6.86 | 0.72 | 7.79 | 13.65 | 18.04 | 17.43 | 18.66 | 11.34 |
| LLaMA 2 13B (few-shot) | 12.08 | 19.37 | 2.36 | 23.08 | 35.22 | 38.80 | 31.49 | 38.06 | 25.06 |
| LLaMA 2 13B | 47.16 | 52.98 | 38.44 | 60.92 | 67.70 | 74.08 | 61.95 | 69.95 | 59.15 |

Table 3: F1 scores on eight datasets of ASQP, ACOS, TASD, and ASTE tasks, along with the average score. The best results are in **bold**, and the second-best results are underlined.

the state-of-the-art (SOTA) for most tasks. However, it falls behind by over 2% in the Rest15 dataset and ASTE task. Nonetheless, it notably exceeds previous SOTA results for the TASD task by 3–5%, highlighting the challenge of predicting opinion terms absent in the TASD task. Nevertheless, the smaller Orca 2 performs almost 1% better on average than the previous best results.

Orca 2 significantly outperforms LLaMA 2, with the smaller Orca 2 model even surpassing the larger LLaMA 2 model, underscoring the superior reasoning capabilities of Orca 2. Additionally, it suggests that opting for more advanced but smaller models may be more beneficial than using larger models with less sophistication. The TASD task is the only task LLaMA 2 outperforms previous SOTA results. Compared to previous SOTA results, on average, the larger version is more than 2% worse, and the smaller version is 5% worse.

In zero-shot and few-shot scenarios, both evaluated LLaMA-based models exhibit notably inferior performance compared to their fine-tuned counterparts, particularly in quadruplet tasks. ChatGPT, with significantly more parameters, notably outperforms these models across zero-shot and few-shot scenarios. However, ChatGPT notably underperforms compared to fine-tuned models.

### 4.1 Error Analysis

To gain insights into the challenges of sentiment prediction, we conduct an error analysis focusing on identifying the most difficult sentiment elements to predict. We manually investigate predictions of 100 random test samples from the best-performing run of Orca 2 with 13B parameters for each dataset. Figure 2 depicts the results of the error analysis.

In most cases, the most challenging element to predict is the opinion term, often comprising multiple words. The model frequently struggles to predict the text span precisely, for instance, predicting *"mild"* instead of *"too mild"*. Following closely in difficulty is typically the aspect term, which encounters similar mistakes as opinion terms, but aspect terms are more often just one word, making such errors less frequent. Sentiment polarity proves to be the easiest to predict. However, an exception arises in the ACOS-Lap dataset, where the aspect category emerges as the most challenging due to the extensive category variety of the dataset (81 categories in the test set, compared to only 12 in the restaurant datasets).

The model also occasionally confuses semantically similar aspect categories, such as *"restaurant general"* with *"restaurant miscellaneous"* or *"keyboard usability"* with *"keyboard general"*.

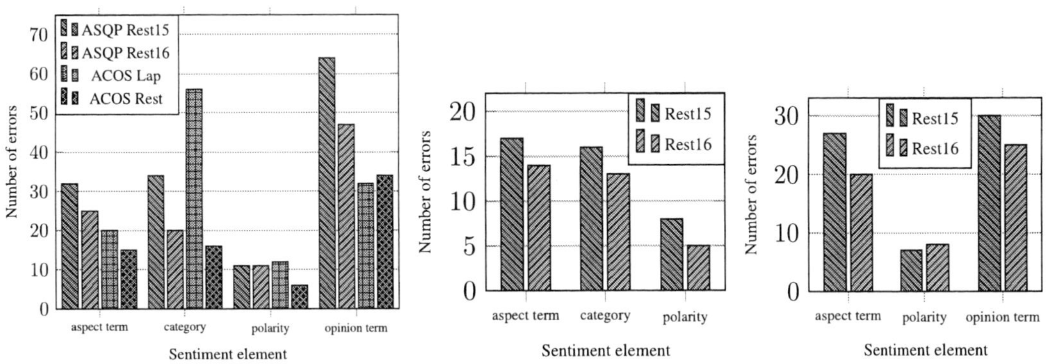


(a) ASQP and ACOS datasets. (b) TASD datasets. (c) ASTE datasets.

Figure 2: Number of error types for each dataset.

The most common error considering sentiment polarity is in predicting the *"neutral"* class, possibly due to imbalanced label distribution, since the *"neutral"* class is the least frequent in all datasets.

In contrast to observations made by Zhang et al. (2021a), we did not encounter errors related to text generation, such as generating words for aspect or opinion terms that are absent in the original text.

Additionally, we identified mistakes in the dataset labels. For example, in the ACOS-Rest dataset, the aspect *"service"* in the sentence *"worst service i ever had"* is labelled as *"positive"*, despite being clearly *"negative"*, a prediction the model also makes correctly. Similarly, we noticed inconsistencies in the datasets, such as in the sentence *"One of the best hot dogs I have ever eaten"*, where the expression *"hot dogs"* is not labelled as an aspect term for the *"food quality"* category; instead, it is labelled as an implicit aspect term (*"NULL"*), contrary to other examples. These labelling errors could potentially negatively impact the final scores of evaluated models.

## 5 Conclusion

This paper presents a comprehensive evaluation of LLaMA-based models for compound ABSA tasks. We show that these models underperform in zero-shot and few-shot scenarios compared to smaller models fine-tuned specifically for ABSA. However, we demonstrate that fine-tuning the LLaMA-based models for ABSA significantly improves their performance, and the best model outperforms previous state-of-the-art results on all eight datasets and four tasks. Error analysis reveals that predicting opinion terms is generally the most challenging for the evaluated models.

## Acknowledgements

This work has been partly supported by the OP JAC project DigiTech no. CZ.02.01.01/00/23_021/0008402 and by the Grant No. SGS-2022-016 Advanced methods of data processing and analysis. Computational resources were provided by the e-INFRA CZ project (ID:90254), supported by the Ministry of Education, Youth and Sports of the Czech Republic.

## Limitations

Results highlight LLaMA-based models' ineffectiveness in compound ABSA tasks in zero-shot and few-shot scenarios. Additionally, their performance in non-English languages remains unclear. Future work could also consider other open-source models based on a different architecture.

## Ethics Statement

We experiment with well-known datasets used in prior scientific studies, ensuring fair and honest analysis while conducting our work ethically and without harming anybody.

## References

Hongjie Cai, Yaofeng Tu, Xiangsheng Zhou, Jianfei Yu, and Rui Xia. 2020. Aspect-category based sentiment analysis with hierarchical graph convolutional network. In *Proceedings of the 28th International Conference on Computational Linguistics*, pages 833–843, Barcelona, Spain (Online). International Committee on Computational Linguistics.

Hongjie Cai, Rui Xia, and Jianfei Yu. 2021. Aspect-category-opinion-sentiment quadruple extraction with implicit aspects and opinions. In *Proceedings of the 59th Annual Meeting of the Association for Computational Linguistics and the 11th International Joint Conference on Natural Language Processing (Volume 1: Long Papers)*, pages 340–350, Online. Association for Computational Linguistics.

Tim Dettmers, Artidoro Pagnoni, Ari Holtzman, and Luke Zettlemoyer. 2023. Qlora: Efficient finetuning of quantized llms. *Preprint*, arXiv:2305.14314.

Tianhao Gao, Jun Fang, Hanyu Liu, Zhiyuan Liu, Chao Liu, Pengzhang Liu, Yongjun Bao, and Weipeng Yan. 2022. LEGO-ABSA: A prompt-based task assemblable unified generative framework for multi-task aspect-based sentiment analysis. In *Proceedings of the 29th International Conference on Computational Linguistics*, pages 7002–7012, Gyeongju, Republic of Korea. International Committee on Computational Linguistics.

Zhibin Gou, Qingyan Guo, and Yujiu Yang. 2023. MvP: Multi-view prompting improves aspect sentiment tuple prediction. In *Proceedings of the 61st Annual Meeting of the Association for Computational Linguistics (Volume 1: Long Papers)*, pages 4380–4397, Toronto, Canada. Association for Computational Linguistics.

Ruidan He, Wee Sun Lee, Hwee Tou Ng, and Daniel Dahlmeier. 2019. An interactive multi-task learning network for end-to-end aspect-based sentiment analysis. In *Proceedings of the 57th Annual Meeting of the Association for Computational Linguistics*, pages 504–515, Florence, Italy. Association for Computational Linguistics.

Edward J. Hu, Yelong Shen, Phillip Wallis, Zeyuan Allen-Zhu, Yuanzhi Li, Shean Wang, Lu Wang, and Weizhu Chen. 2021. Lora: Low-rank adaptation of large language models. *Preprint*, arXiv:2106.09685.

Mengting Hu, Yike Wu, Hang Gao, Yinhao Bai, and Shiwan Zhao. 2022. Improving aspect sentiment quad prediction via template-order data augmentation. In *Proceedings of the 2022 Conference on Empirical Methods in Natural Language Processing*, pages 7889–7900, Abu Dhabi, United Arab Emirates. Association for Computational Linguistics.

Pengfei Liu, Shafiq Joty, and Helen Meng. 2015. Fine-grained opinion mining with recurrent neural networks and word embeddings. In *Proceedings of the 2015 Conference on Empirical Methods in Natural Language Processing*, pages 1433–1443, Lisbon, Portugal. Association for Computational Linguistics.

Ilya Loshchilov and Frank Hutter. 2019. Decoupled weight decay regularization. *Preprint*, arXiv:1711.05101.

Yao Lu, Max Bartolo, Alastair Moore, Sebastian Riedel, and Pontus Stenetorp. 2022. Fantastically ordered prompts and where to find them: Overcoming few-shot prompt order sensitivity. In *Proceedings of the 60th Annual Meeting of the Association for Computational Linguistics (Volume 1: Long Papers)*, pages 8086–8098, Dublin, Ireland. Association for Computational Linguistics.

Arindam Mitra, Luciano Del Corro, Shweti Mahajan, Andres Codas, Clarisse Simoes, Sahaj Agarwal, Xuxi Chen, Anastasia Razdaibiedina, Erik Jones, Kriti Aggarwal, Hamid Palangi, Guoqing Zheng, Corby Rosset, Hamed Khanpour, and Ahmed Awadallah. 2023. Orca 2: Teaching small language models how to reason. *Preprint*, arXiv:2311.11045.

OpenAI. 2022. Openai: Introducing chatgpt.

Haiyun Peng, Lu Xu, Lidong Bing, Fei Huang, Wei Lu, and Luo Si. 2020. Knowing what, how and why: A near complete solution for aspect-based sentiment analysis. *Proceedings of the AAAI Conference on Artificial Intelligence*, 34(05):8600–8607.

Ethan Perez, Douwe Kiela, and Kyunghyun Cho. 2021. True few-shot learning with language models. In *Advances in Neural Information Processing Systems*, volume 34, pages 11054–11070. Curran Associates, Inc.

Maria Pontiki, Dimitris Galanis, Haris Papageorgiou, Ion Androutsopoulos, Suresh Manandhar, Mohammad AL-Smadi, Mahmoud Al-Ayyoub, Yanyan Zhao, Bing Qin, Orphée De Clercq, Véronique Hoste, Marianna Apidianaki, Xavier Tannier, Natalia Loukachevitch, Evgeniy Kotelnikov, Nuria Bel, Salud María Jiménez-Zafra, and Gülşen Eryiğit. 2016. SemEval-2016 task 5: Aspect based sentiment analysis. In *Proceedings of the 10th International Workshop on Semantic Evaluation (SemEval-2016)*, pages 19–30, San Diego, California. Association for Computational Linguistics.

Maria Pontiki, Dimitris Galanis, Haris Papageorgiou, Suresh Manandhar, and Ion Androutsopoulos. 2015. SemEval-2015 task 12: Aspect based sentiment analysis. In *Proceedings of the 9th International Workshop on Semantic Evaluation (SemEval 2015)*, pages 486–495, Denver, Colorado. Association for Computational Linguistics.

Maria Pontiki, Dimitris Galanis, John Pavlopoulos, Harris Papageorgiou, Ion Androutsopoulos, and Suresh Manandhar. 2014. SemEval-2014 task 4: Aspect based sentiment analysis. In *Proceedings of the 8th International Workshop on Semantic Evaluation (SemEval 2014)*, pages 27–35, Dublin, Ireland. Association for Computational Linguistics.

Kevin Scaria, Himanshu Gupta, Siddharth Goyal, Saurabh Arjun Sawant, Swaroop Mishra, and Chitta Baral. 2023. Instructabsa: Instruction learning for aspect based sentiment analysis. *arXiv preprint arXiv:2302.08624*.

Paul F Simmering and Paavo Huoviala. 2023. Large language models for aspect-based sentiment analysis. *arXiv preprint arXiv:2310.18025*.

Hugo Touvron, Thibaut Lavril, Gautier Izacard, Xavier Martinet, Marie-Anne Lachaux, Timothée Lacroix, Baptiste Rozière, Naman Goyal, Eric Hambro, Faisal Azhar, Aurelien Rodriguez, Armand Joulin, Edouard Grave, and Guillaume Lample. 2023a. Llama: Open and efficient foundation language models. *Preprint*, arXiv:2302.13971.

Hugo Touvron, Louis Martin, Kevin Stone, Peter Albert, Amjad Almahairi, Yasmine Babaei, Nikolay Bashlykov, Soumya Batra, Prajjwal Bhargava, Shruti Bhosale, Dan Bikel, Lukas Blecher, Cristian Canton Ferrer, Moya Chen, Guillem Cucurull, David Esiobu, Jude Fernandes, Jeremy Fu, Wenyin Fu, Brian Fuller, Cynthia Gao, Vedanuj Goswami, Naman Goyal, Anthony Hartshorn, Saghar Hosseini, Rui Hou, Hakan Inan, Marcin Kardas, Viktor Kerkez, Madian Khabsa, Isabel Kloumann, Artem Korenev, Punit Singh Koura, Marie-Anne Lachaux, Thibaut Lavril, Jenya Lee, Diana Liskovich, Yinghai Lu, Yuning Mao, Xavier Martinet, Todor Mihaylov, Pushkar Mishra, Igor Molybog, Yixin Nie, Andrew Poulton, Jeremy Reizenstein, Rashi Rungta, Kalyan Saladi, Alan Schelten, Ruan Silva, Eric Michael Smith, Ranjan Subramanian, Xiaoqing Ellen Tan, Binh Tang, Ross Taylor, Adina Williams, Jian Xiang Kuan, Puxin Xu, Zheng Yan, Iliyan Zarov, Yuchen Zhang, Angela Fan, Melanie Kambadur, Sharan Narang, Aurelien Rodriguez, Robert Stojnic, Sergey Edunov, and Thomas Scialom. 2023b. Llama 2: Open foundation and fine-tuned chat models. *Preprint*, arXiv:2307.09288.

Hai Wan, Yufei Yang, Jianfeng Du, Yanan Liu, Kunxun Qi, and Jeff Z. Pan. 2020. Target-aspect-sentiment joint detection for aspect-based sentiment analysis. *Proceedings of the AAAI Conference on Artificial Intelligence*, 34(05):9122–9129.

Thomas Wolf, Lysandre Debut, Victor Sanh, Julien Chaumond, Clement Delangue, Anthony Moi, Pierric Cistac, Tim Rault, Remi Louf, Morgan Funtowicz, Joe Davison, Sam Shleifer, Patrick von Platen, Clara Ma, Yacine Jernite, Julien Plu, Canwen Xu, Teven Le Scao, Sylvain Gugger, Mariama Drame, Quentin Lhoest, and Alexander Rush. 2020. Transformers: State-of-the-art natural language processing. In *Proceedings of the 2020 Conference on Empirical Methods in Natural Language Processing: System Demonstrations*, pages 38–45, Online. Association for Computational Linguistics.

Lu Xu, Hao Li, Wei Lu, and Lidong Bing. 2020. Position-aware tagging for aspect sentiment triplet extraction. In *Proceedings of the 2020 Conference on Empirical Methods in Natural Language Processing (EMNLP)*, pages 2339–2349, Online. Association for Computational Linguistics.

Wenxuan Zhang, Yang Deng, Xin Li, Yifei Yuan, Lidong Bing, and Wai Lam. 2021a. Aspect sentiment quad prediction as paraphrase generation. In *Proceedings of the 2021 Conference on Empirical Methods in Natural Language Processing*, pages 9209–9219, Online and Punta Cana, Dominican Republic. Association for Computational Linguistics.

Wenxuan Zhang, Yue Deng, Bing Liu, Sinno Jialin Pan, and Lidong Bing. 2023. Sentiment analysis in the era of large language models: A reality check. *arXiv preprint arXiv:2305.15005*.

Wenxuan Zhang, Xin Li, Yang Deng, Lidong Bing, and Wai Lam. 2021b. Towards generative aspect-based sentiment analysis. In *Proceedings of the 59th Annual Meeting of the Association for Computational Linguistics and the 11th International Joint Conference on Natural Language Processing (Volume 2: Short Papers)*, pages 504–510, Online. Association for Computational Linguistics.

Wenxuan Zhang, Xin Li, Yang Deng, Lidong Bing, and Wai Lam. 2022. A survey on aspect-based sentiment analysis: tasks, methods, and challenges. *IEEE Transactions on Knowledge and Data Engineering*.

Xinjie Zhou, Xiaojun Wan, and Jianguo Xiao. 2015. Representation learning for aspect category detection in online reviews. *Proceedings of the AAAI Conference on Artificial Intelligence*, 29(1).

# A Prompts

Figure 3 shows the prompt for the TASD task, while Figure 4 presents the prompts for the ASTE task. The prompts are also available in our code.

**Prompt for the TASD task**

According to the following sentiment elements definition:

- The "aspect term" refers to a specific feature, attribute, or aspect of a product or service on which a user can express an opinion. Explicit aspect terms appear explicitly as a substring of the given text. The aspect term might be "null" for the implicit aspect.

- The "aspect category" refers to the category that aspect belongs to, and the available categories include: "ambience general", "drinks prices", "drinks quality", "drinks style_options", "food general", "food prices", "food quality", "food style_options", "location general", "restaurant general", "restaurant miscellaneous", "restaurant prices", "service general".

- The "sentiment polarity" refers to the degree of positivity, negativity or neutrality expressed in the opinion towards a particular aspect or feature of a product or service, and the available polarities include: "positive", "negative" and "neutral". "neutral" means mildly positive or mildly negative. Triplets with objective sentiment polarity should be ignored.

Please carefully follow the instructions. Ensure that aspect terms are recognized as exact matches in the review or are "null" for implicit aspects. Ensure that aspect categories are from the available categories. Ensure that sentiment polarities are from the available polarities.

Recognize all sentiment elements with their corresponding aspect terms, aspect categories, and sentiment polarity in the given input text (review). Provide your response in the format of a Python list of tuples: 'Sentiment elements: [("aspect term", "aspect category", "sentiment polarity"), ...]'. Note that ", ..." indicates that there might be more tuples in the list if applicable and must not occur in the answer. Ensure there is no additional text in the response.

Figure 3: Prompt for the TASD task.

**Prompt for the ASTE task**

According to the following sentiment elements definition:

- The "aspect term" refers to a specific feature, attribute, or aspect of a product or service on which a user can express an opinion. Explicit aspect terms appear explicitly as a substring of the given text.

- The "opinion term" refers to the sentiment or attitude expressed by a user towards a particular aspect or feature of a product or service. Explicit opinion terms appear explicitly as a substring of the given text.

- The "sentiment polarity" refers to the degree of positivity, negativity or neutrality expressed in the opinion towards a particular aspect or feature of a product or service, and the available polarities include: "positive", "negative" and "neutral". "neutral" means mildly positive or mildly negative. Triplets with objective sentiment polarity should be ignored.

Please carefully follow the instructions. Ensure that aspect terms are recognized as exact matches in the review. Ensure that opinion terms are recognized as exact matches in the review. Ensure that sentiment polarities are from the available polarities.

Recognize all sentiment elements with their corresponding aspect terms, opinion terms, and sentiment polarity in the given input text (review). Provide your response in the format of a Python list of tuples: 'Sentiment elements: [("aspect term", "opinion term", "sentiment polarity"), ...]'. Note that ", ..." indicates that there might be more tuples in the list if applicable and must not occur in the answer. Ensure there is no additional text in the response.

Figure 4: Prompt for the ASTE task.

# A Multi-Faceted NLP Analysis of Misinformation Spreaders in Twitter

**Dimosthenis Antypas, Alun Preece, Jose Camacho-Collados**
Cardiff NLP, School of Computer Science and Informatics
& Security, Crime and Intelligence Innovation Institute
Cardiff University, United Kingdom
{AntypasD,PreeceAD,CamachoColladosJ}@cardiff.ac.uk

## Abstract

Social media is an integral part of the daily life of an increasingly large number of people worldwide. Used for entertainment, communication and news updates, it constitutes a source of information that has been extensively used to study human behaviour. Unfortunately, the open nature of social media platforms along with the difficult task of supervising their content has led to a proliferation of misinformation posts. In this paper, we aim to identify the textual differences between the profiles of user that share misinformation from questionable sources and those that do not. Our goal is to better understand user behaviour in order to be better equipped to combat this issue. To this end, we identify Twitter (X) accounts of potential misinformation spreaders and apply transformer models specialised in social media to extract characteristics such as sentiment, emotion, topic and presence of hate speech. Our results indicate that, while there may be some differences between the behaviour of users that share misinformation and those that do not, there are no large differences when it comes to the type of content shared.

## 1 Introduction

The emerging popularity of social platforms such as Facebook, Twitter, and WhatsApp has revolutionised the way information is disseminated and consumed (Fac, 2023; Murthy, 2018; Deshmukh, 2015). People are able to express their sentiments, share their opinions on multiple topics, and to discuss and influence each other with ease and at a speed that has transformed not only how we communicate but also how we perceive the world around us. Unfortunately, the capacity to reach a vast audience within seconds, along with the challenges that arise with verifying an ever-expanding volume of content, has created fertile ground within social media for malicious actors, or unaware users, to spread misinformation. The recent examples of fake news related to the COVID-19 pandemic (Evanega et al., 2020), and the ongoing war in Ukraine (Pierri et al., 2023) demonstrate that misinformation in social media is a complex problem with far-reaching implications for society, democracy, and information integrity.

Combating misinformation in social media is a topic that is studied extensively in academia (Vosoughi et al., 2018; Pennycook et al., 2020) and in the natural language processing (NLP) community (Su et al., 2020) specifically, among others. Common approaches of dealing with misinformation include defining the problem as a classification task (Serrano et al., 2020; Hamid et al., 2020) and classifying a post as fake or not; with fact-checking (Thorne and Vlachos, 2018) often defined as an information retrieval task (Lazarski et al., 2021). However, research regarding the agents that share misinformation is rather limited in comparison (Shu et al., 2020; Rangel et al., 2020; Dou et al., 2021) particularly when it comes to analysing language-specific features.

In this paper, we focus on misinformation in Twitter and perform an analytical comparison between different types of user based on their content shared online and the reliability of their sources. To this end, we first compiled three diverse datasets in which spreaders of misinformation are categorised using different techniques. Then, we perform an exhaustive analysis of the content of these users by leveraging transformer-based language models specialised on social media tasks such as sentiment analysis, emotion recognition, topic categorisation and hate speech detection. The main contributions of this paper are the following: (1) we gather and consolidate existing and new Twitter datasets related to misinformation spreaders; and (2) we extract insights for the behaviour of such users in comparison with users sharing content from reliable sources.



*Proceedings of the 14th Workshop on Computational Approaches to Subjectivity, Sentiment, & Social Media Analysis*, pages 71–83
August 15, 2024 

## 2 Related Work

The study of identifying misinformation has been a prominent area of research in recent years. Initially, efforts focused on addressing the problem through classification, either in a binary or multiclass context. Some studies delved into examining the spread of true and false information online work on the topic of information dissemination (Vosoughi et al., 2018). Meanwhile, others opted for a data mining approach in the realm of fake news detection on social media, utilising various features and machine learning algorithms to classify news articles as true or false (Shu et al., 2017).

Moreover, beyond binary classification, researchers explored multiclass classification methods. For instance, Castillo et al. (2011) investigated the credibility of information on Twitter and proposed a framework categorizing tweets into four groups: true, false, unverified, and non-informative. Zubiaga et al. (2016) delved into the analysis of conversational threads on social media to gain insights into how rumors propagate and how individuals respond to them, shedding light on the dynamics of misinformation propagation.

These approaches evolved to better serve journalists and fact-checkers. The focus shifted from classification to fact-checking and information retrieval, aiming to assist journalists in source verification. This transition led to the development of tools to meet their specific needs (Schlichtkrull et al., 2023). The availability of datasets like FEVER (Thorne et al., 2018), MultiFC (Augenstein et al., 2019), and X-Fact (Gupta and Srikumar, 2021) has been instrumental in enabling researchers to experiment with and develop novel methods for evidence retrieval and rumour verification (Nasir et al., 2021; Lee et al., 2020; Lewis et al., 2020).

While there have been notable studies in the broader field of misinformation and fact verification, there's a notable gap when it comes to a systematic analysis of the textual content of fake news spreaders. Much of the existing research has predominantly focused on the detection of misinformation sources, fact-checking, or the development of classification algorithms to distinguish true from false content. However, there is limited in-depth work that methodically dissects the text generated by those actively involved in spreading fake news that utilises state-of-the-art models (Ghanem et al., 2020; Rangel et al., 2020) and where the language analysis is not supplementary to the network and graph analysis (Aswani et al., 2019).

In this work we seek to methodically analyse the textual content generated by those responsible for spreading fake news. The primary objective is to gain a deeper understanding of the characteristics, strategies, and linguistic patterns employed by these actors in disseminating misleading or false information. Unlike traditional fact-checking, our work does not intend to verify or debunk specific claims but rather aims at understanding the textual content shared by individuals or groups behind the spread of fake news, thereby providing further insights into their content dissemination strategies.

## 3 Data

For our analysis, we exclusively focus on Twitter users, particularly tweets in the English language. Our goal was to extract a diverse tweet corpus for both users regularly spreading fake news or news from questionable sources, and users sharing content from verified sources. In the following we describe our data collection methodology stemming from various sources.

### 3.1 Data Collection

In total, we draw upon three diverse data sources to extract relevant tweets from user account sharing trusted and untrusted sources. Moreover, we extract tweets from legacy-verified Twitter accounts as a control group.

#### 3.1.1 Media Bias Fact Check (MBFC)

Our first corpus is extracted from a list of known conspiracy sites provided by "Media Bias Fact Check" (*MBFC*). This source is commonly used in the study of fake news (Nakov and Da San Martino, 2020; Cinelli et al., 2020). For this dataset, we extracted tweets that share URLs from known untrusted sites[1] and then sample users based on the frequency of sharing these links. In particular, we considered only those users in the 75 percentile in terms of number of links shared. In order to gather enough information, all user accounts that were not older than 30 days were excluded from the analysis. Subsequently, all posts made by the sampled users during September 2021 were collected, which aligns with the date when the *MBFC* lists were last updated prior to conducting this experiment. User accounts were then further filtered based on their activity, only keeping those users posting more

[1]https://mediabiasfactcheck.com/conspiracy/

frequently than the median daily posts. Finally, to ensure a diverse representation, users were sampled based on their number of followers by maintaining the original distribution and thus encompassing both popular and less popular accounts. This final sample represents the ***MBFC-untrusted*** subset.

The above methodology is mirrored to collect users that share links form trusted news-sources according to MBFC[2] resulting in the ***MBFC-trusted*** subset.

#### 3.1.2 FakeNewsNet (FNN)

The FakeNewsNet dataset, referred to as *FNN* (Shu et al., 2018), contains two subsets: (1) tweets related to news content, e.g. tweets revolving around US politics and tweets; and (2) tweets related to social context, e.g. tweets talking about celebrities. Tweets in each groups are further classified as either untrusted or trusted. For the purpose of this study, we concentrate solely on the politics-related subset, as it exhibits a closer alignment with the majority of the links found within the *MBFC* lists. To extract relevant users, we initially scrape all tweets in the dataset and randomly sample users. Finally, all tweets posted by the selected users from September 2021 are retrieved. Only the accounts that have at least 100 posts were considered to create the ***FNN-untrusted*** and ***FNN-trusted*** subsets.

#### 3.1.3 Profiling Fake News Spreaders (PAN)

The English subset of the *PAN 2020: Profiling Fake News Spreaders* task (*PAN*) (Rangel et al., 2020) is dataset that comprises a total of 50,000 English tweets obtained from 500 users, with each user contributing 100 tweets. These users are categorized as either trusted news spreaders (***PAN-trusted***) or untrusted news spreaders (***PAN-untrusted***). In the interest of privacy, no additional user-specific information, such as author descriptions or popularity metrics, is disclosed. Despite its relatively modest size and the limitation on the extraction of additional user details, the *PAN* dataset is considered robust and reliable. Its construction involved manual checks, and it underwent thorough scrutiny by multiple individuals, primarily due to its relevance in a competitive context. This rigorous validation process enhances the dataset's trustworthiness and accuracy.

[2]https://mediabiasfactcheck.com/pro-science/, https://mediabiasfactcheck.com/center/

| | | Tweets | Users | Size | TTR | #emoji |
|---|---|---|---|---|---|---|
| **MBFC** | untrusted | 1,703,896 | 1,489 | 136 | 0.018 | 0.24 |
| | trusted | 1,676,615 | 1,535 | 132 | 0.021 | 0.26 |
| **FNN** | untrusted | 246,107 | 430 | 122 | 0.036 | 0.19 |
| | trusted | 351,857 | 476 | 124 | 0.030 | 0.13 |
| **PAN** | untrusted | 25,000 | 250 | 88 | 0.138 | 0.02 |
| | trusted | 25,000 | 250 | 88 | 0.149 | 0.13 |
| **Verified users** | | 178,324 | 803 | 103 | 0.048 | 0.26 |
| **Total** | | 4,206,799 | 5,233 | 123 | 0.014 | 0.24 |

Table 1: Number of tweets and users present in each dataset studied. The average size of the tweet (number of characters), along with the Type Token Ratio (TTR) and average emoji presence, are also reported.

#### 3.1.4 Control (Verified users)

In order to have a control group to compare in our experiments, we sampled tweets from legacy-verified accounts for which the authenticity is known. This dataset was compiled by sampling verified users and collecting their tweets during the same time period as the previous datasets. Our aim was to select users whose characteristics align closely with the distribution patterns observed in the *FNN* and *MBFC* datasets.

### 3.2 Statistics and Descriptive Analysis

By considering these diverse data sources, we aim to comprehensively examine and understand the dynamics of untrusted news spreaders on the Twitter platform. Our analysis encompasses a total of 4,206,799 tweets contributed by 5,233 users, as presented in Table 1. In addition to the number of tweets and users, we also investigate the average length of tweet and average emoji usage. We did not identify a clear pattern between the *trusted* and *untrusted* subsets as far as these metrics are concerned.

Looking into the lexical characteristics of each dataset, distinctions between the *untrusted* and *trusted* subsets become more apparent. For instance, when assessing lexical diversity using the Type Token Ratio (TTR), we observe that *untrusted* users, with the exception of the *FNN* dataset, tend to employ a less diverse vocabulary which is consistent with previous research (Horne and Adali, 2017). Our analysis based on the average presence of emojis in each tweet reveals no consistent pattern, despite prior research suggesting higher emoji usage among untrusted news spreaders (Er and Yilmaz, 2023). For example, while the untrusted subset of the MBFC dataset exhibits higher emoji usage, the opposite holds true for the FNN dataset.

| MBFC | | FNN | | PAN | | Verified |
|---|---|---|---|---|---|---|
| untrusted | trusted | untrusted | trusted | untrusted | trusted | |
| news | tigray | biden | music | trump | film | game |
| biden | jisoo | people | hit | realdonaldtrump | kobe | thunderstorm |
| vaccine | ethiopia | say | play | new | season | football |
| covid | indiedev | trump | househunters | instyle | styles | season |
| border | tigraygenocide | ebay | dance | webtalk | spoilers | good |
| passport | brexit | marijuana | trump | post | promo | thank |
| australia | bts | prohibition | biden | impeachment | date | collision |
| mandate | dior | covid | september | publish | trailer | direction |

Table 2: Top eight terms in each dataset according to lexical specificity.

**Lexical specificity.** To gain an overall understanding of the prevalent topics within our corpora, we employ lexical specificity (Lafon, 1980). Lexical specificity is a word-level metric that indicates the importance of each word in a subcorpus. In particular, for this analysis we use the formulation outlined in Camacho-Collados et al. (2016), and extract the top terms in each dataset. Table 2 displays the top ten lemmas[3] in each dataset based on their lexical specificity scores.

Notably, due to the same time period during data collection, a significant overlap exists between the *MBFC* and *FNN* datasets, particularly within their 'untrusted' subsets. Terms such as 'biden' and 'vaccine' are common across both. Additionally, a discernible trend emerges, indicating that 'untrusted' subsets across datasets often feature more controversial and divisive topics. This is evident in the presence of terms like 'covid,' 'prohibition,' and 'impeachment,' in contrast to the 'trusted' subsets, which exhibit more generic and neutral terms such as 'bts,' 'music,' and 'film.' This distinction becomes even more pronounced when examining the top terms in the *Verified* dataset, which include terms like 'game,' 'football,' and 'love.'

## 4 Methodology

Our goal is to analyse various content-related features from the extracted posts in Section 3. To capture the nuanced language features present in the data, we employ a range of pre-trained language models designed for social media usage. Our primary focus encompasses sentiment and affection analysis, topic classification, and the identification of hate speech in textual content, features are frequently employed in the study of misinformation propagation (Vicario et al., 2019; Verma et al., 2020), aiming to uncover emotionally charged language and controversial topics.

All the language models used are built upon the RoBERTa architecture (Liu et al., 2019) and trained on social media corpora, making them well-suited for analysing Twitter data. More specifically:

**Sentiment Analysis.** The model *twitter-roberta-base-sentiment-latest* (Loureiro et al., 2022) is used to extract the sentiment polarity where each tweet is classified as *negative, neutral, or positive*. This model has been fine-tuned for sentiment analysis using the dataset provided in the *Sentiment Analysis in Twitter* task of Semeval 2017 (Rosenthal et al., 2019). By analysing the sentiment expressed in social media content, we can gain insights into information being shared (Baishya et al., 2021). Specifically, presence of exaggerated positive sentiment or negative sentiment in response to fake news can serve as indicators of misinformation (Alonso et al., 2021).

**Emotion Analysis.** We leverage *twitter-roberta-base-emotion-multilabel-latest* (Camacho-Collados et al., 2022) to assign one or more emotions to each tweet. This model is trained using data from the 'Affect in Tweets' Semeval 2018 task (Mohammad et al., 2018), covering 11 different emotions. Similar to sentiment analysis, the presence of specific emotions has been used to analyse the spread of rumours and misinformation, with negative emotions potentially contributing to the spread of misinformation (Vosoughi et al., 2018; Weeks, 2015).

**Hate Speech Detection.** We use the *twitter-roberta-base-hate-multiclass* hate speech detection model (Antypas and Camacho-Collados, 2023), which is trained on a combination of 13 different hate speech Twitter datasets and is capable of identifying hate speech from seven target groups. The inclusion of hate speech detection as a feature is motivated by previous research indicating a positive correlation between the presence of hate speech and misinformation (Inwood and Zappavigna, 2023).

[3]Lemmatization was done using *spaCy* https://spacy.io/.

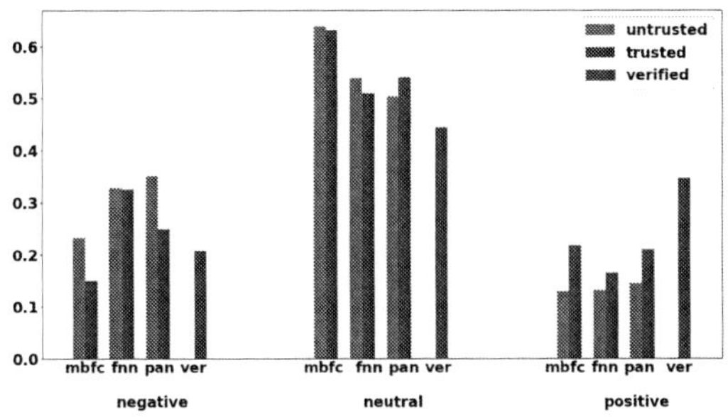


Figure 1: Sentiment distribution in each dataset for *trusted* and *untrusted* users in Twitter.

**Topic Classification.** We use *tweet-topic-21-multi* (Antypas et al., 2022), a multi-label classification model fine-tuned on a Twitter topic classification dataset. This model assigns one or more topics to each tweet from a list of 19 topics. Our hypothesis is that there may be a significant difference between the topics discussed by *untrusted* news spreaders and regular users, e.g. untrusted news spreaders potentially engaging in discussions related to sensitive topics at a higher volume.

All the specialised models described above are perform in line of the state of the art for each of the tasks in the social media context[4] and they enable us to delve deeper into the complex linguistic nuances within the social media data. Nonetheless, as we describe in the Limitations section, they all have a degree of error that needs to be considered when making conclusions.

## 5 Analysis

We consider each pair of collected datasets (*untrusted* and *trusted*), along with the *Verified* control dataset. Our examination involves a comparison of the tweets within each dataset individually, as well as their aggregation for each user. This holistic approach enables us to explore a variety of perspectives and insights across the datasets and their combined impact.

### 5.1 Textual Analysis

Table 3 displays the aggregated results for the sentiment, emotion, hate speech and topic analysis. For each feature we consider each user independently by taking their mean value and then aggregate the results of users belonging in the same subset. Even though differences between *untrusted* and *trusted* subsets exist, it is challenging to identify trends that are consistent across the datasets. In the following sections we investigate each characteristic individually.

#### 5.1.1 Sentiment

When evaluating the presence of sentiment in tweets, a noticeable trend emerges: tweets associated with *untrusted* news spreaders tend to exhibit a higher degree of negativity compared to those posted by other users. The distribution of sentiment across the datasets is displayed in Figure 1. In the case of the *FNN* dataset, however, this difference is almost not negligible. Finally, even though there is more negativity in *untrusted* users, the distributions among negative, neutral and positive tweets are very similar in all cases except for the verified users that tend to be more positive overall.

#### 5.1.2 Emotion

Similarly to the findings in sentiment analysis, the analysis of affect reveals a consistent pattern where untrusted news spreaders tend to gravitate toward more negative emotions. Figure 2a provides insight into the distribution of the 11 emotions present across across all subsets.

A clear contrast emerges, with tweets attributed to *trusted* users generally displaying greater joy and featuring a lesser presence of anger and disgust, in stark contrast to the tweets originating from *untrusted* users. This trend remains consistent even when evaluating the per-user aggregation. Finally, similarly to the sentiment distribution patterns, there are no noticeable differences when analysing the overall emotion distribution and, in this case, it also related to that of verified users.

#### 5.1.3 Hate Speech

When examining hate speech, a feature that often coexists with misinformation (Inwood and Zappavigna, 2023), such as Holocaust denial and the Great Replacement theory, it does not appear to be a prominent feature in the collected datasets. Our analysis indicates an absence of hate speech, with 99% of all tweets being devoid of it.

There does appear to be a variance in the types of hate speech across the subsets (as displayed in Figure 2b). *Untrusted* subsets exhibit a higher inclination towards racism, while in the trusted subset, sexism appears to be more prevalent. However, given the limited number of instances, it is prudent to exercise caution when drawing extensive conclusions based on this data.

[4]Sentiment Analysis: 73.7% Recall, Emotion Analysis: 80% F1-macro, Hate Speech: 94% Accuracy, Topic Classification: 59% F1-macro – please refer to the individual references for more details.

| | | MBFC | | PAN | | FNN | | verified |
|---|---|---|---|---|---|---|---|---|
| | | untrusted | trusted | untrusted | trusted | untrusted | trusted | |
| Senti. | negative | 0.35 ± 0.12 | 0.32 ± 0.15 | 0.16 ± 0.14 | 0.24 ± 0.16 | 0.35 ± 0.19 | 0.37 ± 0.19 | 0.2 ± 0.11 |
| | neutral | 0.52 ± 0.1 | 0.5 ± 0.11 | 0.63 ± 0.18 | 0.64 ± 0.15 | 0.48 ± 0.18 | 0.47 ± 0.17 | 0.44 ± 0.15 |
| | positive | 0.13 ± 0.09 | 0.17 ± 0.12 | 0.22 ± 0.17 | 0.13 ± 0.09 | 0.17 ± 0.15 | 0.16 ± 0.14 | 0.37 ± 0.16 |
| Emotion | anger | 0.39 ± 0.14 | 0.34 ± 0.17 | 0.1 ± 0.11 | 0.21 ± 0.17 | 0.33 ± 0.24 | 0.37 ± 0.23 | 0.17 ± 0.11 |
| | anticipation | 0.25 ± 0.1 | 0.26 ± 0.12 | 0.48 ± 0.2 | 0.38 ± 0.18 | 0.28 ± 0.19 | 0.26 ± 0.19 | 0.28 ± 0.12 |
| | disgust | 0.42 ± 0.15 | 0.37 ± 0.17 | 0.12 ± 0.12 | 0.23 ± 0.18 | 0.35 ± 0.23 | 0.39 ± 0.23 | 0.18 ± 0.11 |
| | fear | 0.1 ± 0.05 | 0.09 ± 0.08 | 0.06 ± 0.08 | 0.08 ± 0.07 | 0.09 ± 0.09 | 0.1 ± 0.12 | 0.04 ± 0.05 |
| | joy | 0.2 ± 0.12 | 0.26 ± 0.17 | 0.46 ± 0.22 | 0.34 ± 0.22 | 0.26 ± 0.2 | 0.24 ± 0.19 | 0.46 ± 0.16 |
| | love | 0.02 ± 0.03 | 0.03 ± 0.05 | 0.04 ± 0.06 | 0.02 ± 0.03 | 0.03 ± 0.05 | 0.03 ± 0.05 | 0.07 ± 0.07 |
| | optimism | 0.16 ± 0.1 | 0.19 ± 0.11 | 0.19 ± 0.14 | 0.12 ± 0.1 | 0.18 ± 0.14 | 0.18 ± 0.14 | 0.31 ± 0.14 |
| | pessimism | 0.01 ± 0.01 | 0.01 ± 0.01 | 0.01 ± 0.02 | 0.01 ± 0.01 | 0.01 ± 0.01 | 0.01 ± 0.01 | 0.01 ± 0.01 |
| | sadness | 0.09 ± 0.04 | 0.1 ± 0.05 | 0.07 ± 0.06 | 0.08 ± 0.05 | 0.1 ± 0.07 | 0.1 ± 0.09 | 0.09 ± 0.05 |
| | surprise | 0.01 ± 0.01 | 0.01 ± 0.01 | 0.01 ± 0.01 | 0.01 ± 0.01 | 0.01 ± 0.01 | 0.01 ± 0.01 | 0.02 ± 0.01 |
| | trust | 0.0 ± 0.0 | 0.0 ± 0.0 | 0.0 ± 0.0 | 0.0 ± 0.0 | 0.0 ± 0.0 | 0.0 ± 0.0 | 0.0 ± 0.0 |
| Hate | disability | 0.0 ± 0.0 | 0.0 ± 0.0 | 0.0 ± 0.0 | 0.0 ± 0.0 | 0.0 ± 0.0 | 0.0 ± 0.0 | 0.0 ± 0.0 |
| | not_hate | 0.99 ± 0.01 | 0.99 ± 0.01 | 1.0 ± 0.01 | 1.0 ± 0.01 | 0.99 ± 0.01 | 0.99 ± 0.02 | 1.0 ± 0.0 |
| | other | 0.0 ± 0.0 | 0.0 ± 0.0 | 0.0 ± 0.0 | 0.0 ± 0.0 | 0.0 ± 0.0 | 0.0 ± 0.0 | 0.01 ± 0.0 |
| | racism | 0.01 ± 0.01 | 0.01 ± 0.01 | 0.02 ± 0.01 | 0.02 ± 0.02 | 0.01 ± 0.01 | 0.01 ± 0.02 | 0.01 ± 0.01 |
| | sexism | 0.01 ± 0.01 | 0.01 ± 0.01 | 0.02 ± 0.01 | 0.02 ± 0.01 | 0.01 ± 0.01 | 0.01 ± 0.01 | 0.01 ± 0.0 |
| | religion | 0.0 ± 0.0 | 0.0 ± 0.0 | 0.03 ± 0.0 | 0.01 ± 0.0 | 0.0 ± 0.0 | 0.0 ± 0.0 | 0.01 ± 0.0 |
| | sex_orient | 0.0 ± 0.0 | 0.0 ± 0.0 | 0.0 ± 0.0 | 0.01 ± 0.0 | 0.0 ± 0.0 | 0.0 ± 0.0 | 0.0 ± 0.0 |
| Topic | arts | 0.01 ± 0.03 | 0.02 ± 0.03 | 0.04 ± 0.1 | 0.02 ± 0.02 | 0.02 ± 0.05 | 0.02 ± 0.08 | 0.01 ± 0.03 |
| | business | 0.06 ± 0.11 | 0.05 ± 0.1 | 0.07 ± 0.11 | 0.06 ± 0.1 | 0.05 ± 0.11 | 0.04 ± 0.1 | 0.02 ± 0.05 |
| | celebrity | 0.05 ± 0.04 | 0.07 ± 0.08 | 0.24 ± 0.21 | 0.28 ± 0.28 | 0.05 ± 0.05 | 0.05 ± 0.08 | 0.07 ± 0.07 |
| | diaries | 0.07 ± 0.07 | 0.09 ± 0.09 | 0.08 ± 0.1 | 0.04 ± 0.07 | 0.08 ± 0.1 | 0.08 ± 0.11 | 0.15 ± 0.1 |
| | family | 0.01 ± 0.01 | 0.01 ± 0.01 | 0.01 ± 0.02 | 0.01 ± 0.01 | 0.01 ± 0.01 | 0.01 ± 0.01 | 0.01 ± 0.01 |
| | fashion | 0.0 ± 0.01 | 0.01 ± 0.02 | 0.06 ± 0.13 | 0.05 ± 0.1 | 0.01 ± 0.01 | 0.01 ± 0.02 | 0.01 ± 0.01 |
| | film | 0.03 ± 0.03 | 0.04 ± 0.05 | 0.23 ± 0.26 | 0.16 ± 0.18 | 0.04 ± 0.06 | 0.05 ± 0.09 | 0.06 ± 0.07 |
| | fitness | 0.11 ± 0.11 | 0.06 ± 0.07 | 0.02 ± 0.04 | 0.02 ± 0.03 | 0.05 ± 0.07 | 0.06 ± 0.07 | 0.02 ± 0.04 |
| | food | 0.01 ± 0.02 | 0.02 ± 0.03 | 0.02 ± 0.05 | 0.01 ± 0.02 | 0.02 ± 0.04 | 0.02 ± 0.03 | 0.03 ± 0.03 |
| | gaming | 0.0 ± 0.02 | 0.0 ± 0.02 | 0.01 ± 0.02 | 0.01 ± 0.03 | 0.0 ± 0.02 | 0.0 ± 0.02 | 0.01 ± 0.04 |
| | learning | 0.02 ± 0.03 | 0.03 ± 0.04 | 0.01 ± 0.02 | 0.02 ± 0.02 | 0.03 ± 0.06 | 0.03 ± 0.07 | 0.02 ± 0.04 |
| | music | 0.02 ± 0.03 | 0.03 ± 0.07 | 0.09 ± 0.14 | 0.08 ± 0.13 | 0.04 ± 0.13 | 0.04 ± 0.11 | 0.04 ± 0.06 |
| | news | 0.76 ± 0.2 | 0.67 ± 0.27 | 0.31 ± 0.27 | 0.51 ± 0.29 | 0.65 ± 0.3 | 0.68 ± 0.27 | 0.24 ± 0.22 |
| | hobbies | 0.01 ± 0.03 | 0.01 ± 0.02 | 0.01 ± 0.02 | 0.0 ± 0.01 | 0.01 ± 0.04 | 0.01 ± 0.03 | 0.01 ± 0.01 |
| | relations | 0.01 ± 0.01 | 0.01 ± 0.02 | 0.02 ± 0.03 | 0.02 ± 0.03 | 0.01 ± 0.01 | 0.01 ± 0.02 | 0.01 ± 0.02 |
| | science | 0.05 ± 0.07 | 0.04 ± 0.08 | 0.04 ± 0.11 | 0.05 ± 0.09 | 0.04 ± 0.06 | 0.04 ± 0.08 | 0.02 ± 0.04 |
| | sports | 0.03 ± 0.05 | 0.06 ± 0.13 | 0.08 ± 0.15 | 0.08 ± 0.11 | 0.08 ± 0.15 | 0.05 ± 0.1 | 0.35 ± 0.31 |
| | travel | 0.01 ± 0.01 | 0.01 ± 0.02 | 0.02 ± 0.07 | 0.01 ± 0.01 | 0.02 ± 0.04 | 0.01 ± 0.02 | 0.02 ± 0.05 |
| | youth | 0.02 ± 0.02 | 0.02 ± 0.03 | 0.01 ± 0.01 | 0.01 ± 0.02 | 0.02 ± 0.06 | 0.01 ± 0.02 | 0.01 ± 0.02 |

Table 3: Average presence of each feature (i.e., sentiment analysis, emotion analysis, hate speech, and topic classification) per user along with standard deviations.

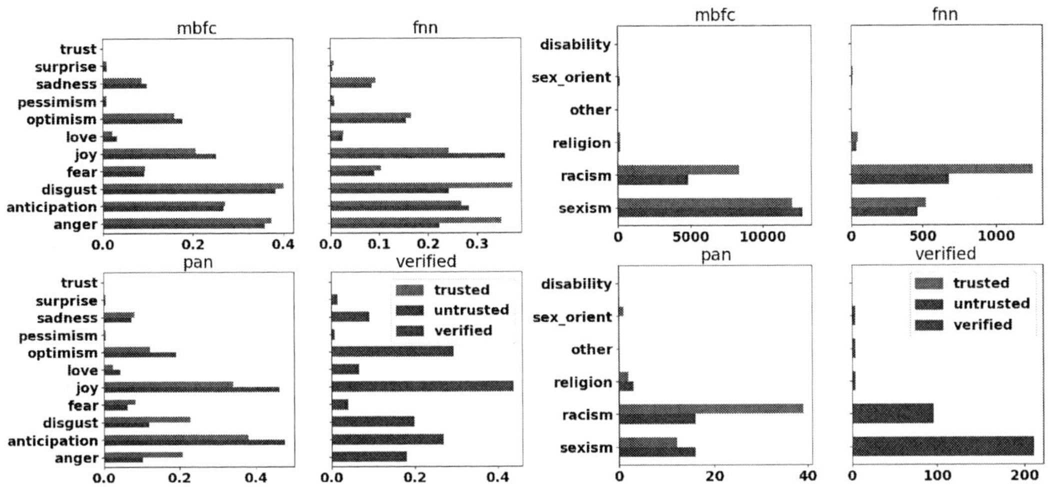


(a) Emotion distribution in each dataset.

(b) Hateful entries in each dataset.

Figure 2: Emotion & Hate speech results of *trusted* and *untrusted* users in Twitter.

### 5.1.4 Topics

Regarding the topics that *untrusted* news spreaders and regular users typically discuss, the results appear to suggest a similar distribution of topics (Figure 3). *Untrusted* news spreaders appear to engage more extensively in posting tweets related to news and social issues, which are those related to politics, among others. This suggests that these accounts may be more socially active, and can create the illusion of a larger representation than that of the general population.

Conversely, there is no discernible distinction in the case of the remaining popular topics, with variations existing among the datasets. For instance, the topic "celebrity_&_pop_culture" is more prevalent in the *Panuntrusted* dataset but less common in the other untrusted subsets. Again here we can observe more differences with respect to verified users, where *sports* and *diaries_&_daily_life* topics are much more prominent.

## 5.2 Spreader Detection Analysis

Recognising that a significant portion of our datasets relies on weak labels, with the distinction between users propagating untrusted news and those who do not being based on heuristics based on the number of posts shared from untrusted sources, we perform a robustness analysis on the *Pan20* dataset which includes train and test splits. To this end, we train a classifier capable of discerning between the *trusted* and *untrusted* classes and compare the results with our approach.

The train/test split originally utilised in the competition is retained, consisting of 300 users for training and 200 users for testing. We assess the performance of two classifiers: (1) A classifier based on the best-performing models as presented in the competition (Buda and Bolonyai, 2020; Pizarro, 2020), utilising an XGBoost classifier (Chen and Guestrin, 2016). This model is trained using TFIDF features and a combination of word and character n-grams; and (2) A pre-trained Longformer (Beltagy et al., 2020), which is further fine-tuned using the *PAN* dataset. We leverage the implementation provided by Hugging Face (Wolf et al., 2020) for the fine-tuning of the Longformer[5]. Hyper-parameter tuning, including batch size, epochs number, and learning rate, is conducted using Ray Tune (Liaw et al., 2018).

The results reveal that the XGBoost model (*XGB*) surpasses the Longformer classifier, achieving a 74% macro F1 score compared to the Longformer's 70%. One possible explanation for this outcome lies in the unstructured nature of Twitter text, which presents an added challenge to the language model. The Longformer, not explicitly trained on social media corpus data, may face limitations in handling this specific type of text.

When examining the results of the XGB classifier in the *PAN* dataset, we observe an almost identical trend when compared with our initial results. For example, when looking the sentiment distribution of user accounts using the XGB classifier

[5]https://huggingface.co/allenai/longformer-base-4096

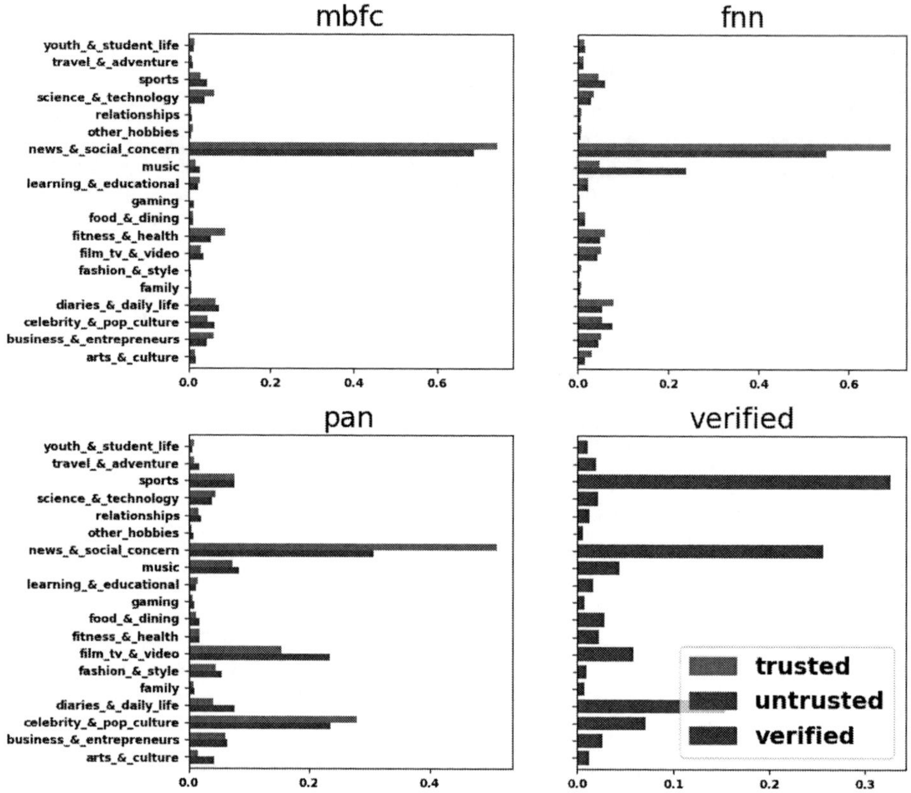


Figure 3: Topic distribution in each dataset for *trusted* and *untrusted* users in Twitter.

and our initial distinction of *trusted* and *untrusted* users, only minimal differences can be observed (*Pan-untrusted*: 23% Negative and 13% Positive; *XGB-untrusted*: 24% and 13%). Our experiment indicates that even though developing a classifier to identify *untrusted* users may not be the optimal approach, it can still be used as a proxy to derive useful information and identify patterns that can be used to reveal malicious actors. Additional results for all tasks regarding the performance of the *XGB* model and the differences with our approach follow a similar trend and can be found in Appendix C.

As a final experiment, we attempt to enhance our XGB classifier by integrating the features already extracted. Our results reveal that while the incorporation of new features generally results in only marginal variations in the model's performance, the addition of certain features, especially sentiment, holds the potential to notably improve its effectiveness. This suggests that careful selection and integration of specific features can yield incremental but meaningful gains in the classifier's performance, an exploration that we leave for future work as it falls out of the scope of this work.

## 6 Conclusions

This paper's comparative analysis aims to delve into the dynamics of misinformation dissemination in the digital age by examining the distinctions between untrusted news spreaders and other users. To this end, we have compiled a substantial sample of untrusted news spreaders and the general content shared of these users in Twitter. Using this large corpus stemming from three diverse datasets (MBFC, FNN and PAN), we have analysed the disparities in their language usage.

The initial exploration of traits associated with untrusted news spreaders, including the presence of hate speech, did not necessarily reveal the distinctions we anticipated. Other language features such as sentiment and emotional content indicate the existence of relatively small language differences between the two groups of users. These differences provide valuable insights that can inform the development of systems designed to identify and counteract malicious accounts. In particular, our results suggest that misinformation mitigation efforts should be focused on the specific content shared, rather than in profiling individual accounts.

## 7 Limitations

While we strived to derive insights from a large dataset using state-of-the-art classifiers and a robust analytical setup, we acknowledge the presence of factors that constrain the depth of our findings. For example, the focus on English-language content, potentially limiting the scope of global social media interactions and perspectives. Additionally, the exclusive use of Twitter data might not fully represent the dynamics on other social media platforms. While verified accounts are employed as a control group, it should be noted that they may not serve as a perfect control due to factors like their popularity, potential biases, or unique behaviours. Furthermore, the extraction of users relies on heuristics, introducing some degree of noise and potential inaccuracies in the data. Finally, we made use of automatic models based on transformers. While these have been tested extensively in prior work, there are inherent limitations in these models, as well as possible unwanted biases. All these limitations should be considered when interpreting our results and conclusions.

## 8 Ethical Statement

In our study involving user-generated content from social media, we ensured user privacy in several ways. First, we replaced all user mentions in the texts with placeholders and removing user IDs. Moreover, all the data utilised in our research is sourced from publicly available information or collected using the official Twitter API. Finally, all the information is provided in an aggregated fashion, without reporting sensitive information from individual users.

While our dataset and methodology have the potential for analysing individual behaviours, our primary objective is to offer researchers a valuable tool for the analysis and aggregation of social media content.

## References


2023. Facebook MAU worldwide 2023 | Statista — https. https://www.statista.com/statistics/264810/number-of-monthly-active-facebook-users-worldwide/. [Accessed 8-10-2023].

M. A. V. Alonso, D. Vilares, C. Gómez-Rodríguez, and J. Vilares. 2021. Sentiment analysis for fake news detection. *Electronics*, 10:1348.

Dimosthenis Antypas and Jose Camacho-Collados. 2023. Robust hate speech detection in social media: A cross-dataset empirical evaluation. In *The 7th Workshop on Online Abuse and Harms (WOAH)*, pages 231–242.

Dimosthenis Antypas, Asahi Ushio, Jose Camacho-Collados, Vitor Silva, Leonardo Neves, and Francesco Barbieri. 2022. Twitter topic classification. In *Proceedings of the 29th International Conference on Computational Linguistics*, pages 3386–3400.

Reema Aswani, Arpan Kumar Kar, and P Vigneswara Ilavarasan. 2019. Experience: managing misinformation in social media—insights for policymakers from twitter analytics. *Journal of Data and Information Quality (JDIQ)*, 12(1):1–18.

I. Augenstein, C. Lioma, D. Wang, L. C. Lima, C. W. Hansen, C. Hansen, and J. G. Simonsen. 2019. Multifc: a real-world multi-domain dataset for evidence-based fact checking of claims. *Proceedings of the 2019 Conference on Empirical Methods in Natural Language Processing and the 9th International Joint Conferen.*

D. Baishya, J. J. Deka, G. Dey, and P. K. Singh. 2021. Safer: sentiment analysis-based fake review detection in e-commerce using deep learning. *SN Computer Science*, 2.

Iz Beltagy, Matthew E Peters, and Arman Cohan. 2020. Longformer: The long-document transformer. *arXiv preprint arXiv:2004.05150*.

Jakab Buda and Flora Bolonyai. 2020. An ensemble model using n-grams and statistical features to identify fake news spreaders on twitter. In *CLEF (Working Notes)*.

Jose Camacho-Collados, Mohammad Taher Pilehvar, and Roberto Navigli. 2016. Nasari: Integrating explicit knowledge and corpus statistics for a multilingual representation of concepts and entities. *Artificial Intelligence*, 240:36–64.

Jose Camacho-Collados, Kiamehr Rezaee, Talayeh Riahi, Asahi Ushio, Daniel Loureiro, Dimosthenis Antypas, Joanne Boisson, Luis Espinosa Anke, Fangyu Liu, and Eugenio Martínez-Cámara. 2022. Tweetnlp: Cutting-edge natural language processing for social media. In *Proceedings of the The 2022 Conference on Empirical Methods in Natural Language Processing: System Demonstrations*, pages 38–49.

Carlos Castillo, Marcelo Mendoza, and Barbara Poblete. 2011. Information credibility on twitter. In *Proceedings of the 20th international conference on World wide web*, pages 675–684.

Tianqi Chen and Carlos Guestrin. 2016. Xgboost: A scalable tree boosting system. In *Proceedings of the 22nd acm sigkdd international conference on knowledge discovery and data mining*, pages 785–794.

Matteo Cinelli, Walter Quattrociocchi, Alessandro Galeazzi, Carlo Michele Valensise, Emanuele Brugnoli, Ana Lucia Schmidt, Paola Zola, Fabiana Zollo, and Antonio Scala. 2020. The covid-19 social media infodemic. *Scientific reports*, 10(1):1–10.

Sagar Deshmukh. 2015. Analysis of whatsapp users and its usage worldwide. *International Journal of Scientific and Research Publications*, 5(8):1–3.

Yingtong Dou, Kai Shu, Congying Xia, Philip S Yu, and Lichao Sun. 2021. User preference-aware fake news detection. In *Proceedings of the 44th International ACM SIGIR Conference on Research and Development in Information Retrieval*, pages 2051–2055.

M. F. Er and Y. B. Yilmaz. 2023. Which emotions of social media users lead to dissemination of fake news: sentiment analysis towards covid-19 vaccine. *Journal of Advanced Research in Natural and Applied Sciences*, 9:107–126.

Sarah Evanega, Mark Lynas, Jordan Adams, Karinne Smolenyak, and Cision Global Insights. 2020. Coronavirus misinformation: quantifying sources and themes in the covid-19 'infodemic'. *JMIR Preprints*, 19(10):2020.

Bilal Ghanem, Simone Paolo Ponzetto, and Paolo Rosso. 2020. Factweet: profiling fake news twitter accounts. In *Statistical Language and Speech Processing: 8th International Conference, SLSP 2020, Cardiff, UK, October 14–16, 2020, Proceedings 8*, pages 35–45. Springer.

Ashim Gupta and Vivek Srikumar. 2021. X-fact: A new benchmark dataset for multilingual fact checking. In *Proceedings of the 59th Annual Meeting of the Association for Computational Linguistics and the 11th International Joint Conference on Natural Language Processing (Volume 2: Short Papers)*, pages 675–682.

Abdullah Hamid, Nasrullah Shiekh, Naina Said, Kashif Ahmad, Asma Gul, Laiq Hassan, and Ala Al-Fuqaha. 2020. Fake news detection in social media using graph neural networks and nlp techniques: A covid-19 use-case. *arXiv preprint arXiv:2012.07517*.

Benjamin Horne and Sibel Adali. 2017. This just in: Fake news packs a lot in title, uses simpler, repetitive content in text body, more similar to satire than real news. In *Proceedings of the international AAAI conference on web and social media*, volume 11, pages 759–766.

O. Inwood and M. Zappavigna. 2023. Conspiracy theories and white supremacy on youtube: exploring affiliation and legitimation strategies in youtube comments. *Social Media + Society*, 9:205630512211504.

Pierre Lafon. 1980. Sur la variabilité de la fréquence des formes dans un corpus. *Mots. Les langages du politique*, 1(1):127–165.

Eric Lazarski, Mahmood Al-Khassaweneh, and Cynthia Howard. 2021. Using nlp for fact checking: A survey. *Designs*, 5(3):42.

Nayeon Lee, Belinda Z Li, Sinong Wang, Wen-Tau Yih, Hao Ma, and Madian Khabsa. 2020. Language models as fact checkers? *ACL 2020*, page 36.

Patrick Lewis, Ethan Perez, Aleksandra Piktus, Fabio Petroni, Vladimir Karpukhin, Naman Goyal, Heinrich Küttler, Mike Lewis, Wen-tau Yih, Tim Rocktäschel, et al. 2020. Retrieval-augmented generation for knowledge-intensive nlp tasks. *Advances in Neural Information Processing Systems*, 33:9459–9474.

Richard Liaw, Eric Liang, Robert Nishihara, Philipp Moritz, Joseph E Gonzalez, and Ion Stoica. 2018. Tune: A research platform for distributed model selection and training. *arXiv preprint arXiv:1807.05118*.

Yinhan Liu, Myle Ott, Naman Goyal, Jingfei Du, Mandar Joshi, Danqi Chen, Omer Levy, Mike Lewis, Luke Zettlemoyer, and Veselin Stoyanov. 2019. Roberta: A robustly optimized bert pretraining approach. *arXiv preprint arXiv:1907.11692*.

Daniel Loureiro, Francesco Barbieri, Leonardo Neves, Luis Espinosa Anke, and Jose Camacho-collados. 2022. TimeLMs: Diachronic language models from Twitter. In *Proceedings of the 60th Annual Meeting of the Association for Computational Linguistics: System Demonstrations*, pages 251–260, Dublin, Ireland. Association for Computational Linguistics.

Saif Mohammad, Felipe Bravo-Marquez, Mohammad Salameh, and Svetlana Kiritchenko. 2018. Semeval-2018 task 1: Affect in tweets. In *Proceedings of the 12th international workshop on semantic evaluation*, pages 1–17.

Dhiraj Murthy. 2018. *Twitter*. Polity Press Cambridge.

Preslav Nakov and Giovanni Da San Martino. 2020. Fact-checking, fake news, propaganda, and media bias: Truth seeking in the post-truth era. In *Proceedings of the 2020 Conference on Empirical Methods in Natural Language Processing: Tutorial Abstracts*, pages 7–19.

Jamal Abdul Nasir, Osama Subhani Khan, and Iraklis Varlamis. 2021. Fake news detection: A hybrid cnn-rnn based deep learning approach. *International Journal of Information Management Data Insights*, 1(1):100007.

Gordon Pennycook, Adam Bear, Evan T Collins, and David G Rand. 2020. The implied truth effect: Attaching warnings to a subset of fake news headlines increases perceived accuracy of headlines without warnings. *Management science*, 66(11):4944–4957.

Francesco Pierri, Luca Luceri, Nikhil Jindal, and Emilio Ferrara. 2023. Propaganda and misinformation on facebook and twitter during the russian invasion of ukraine. In *Proceedings of the 15th ACM Web Science Conference 2023*, pages 65–74.

Juan Pizarro. 2020. Using N-grams to detect Fake News Spreaders on Twitter—Notebook for PAN at CLEF 2020. In *CLEF 2020 Labs and Workshops, Notebook Papers*. CEUR-WS.org.

Francisco Rangel, Anastasia Giachanou, Bilal Hisham Hasan Ghanem, and Paolo Rosso. 2020. Overview of the 8th author profiling task at pan 2020: Profiling fake news spreaders on twitter. In *CEUR workshop proceedings*, volume 2696, pages 1–18. Sun SITE Central Europe.

Sara Rosenthal, Noura Farra, and Preslav Nakov. 2019. Semeval-2017 task 4: Sentiment analysis in twitter. *arXiv preprint arXiv:1912.00741*.

Michael Schlichtkrull, Nedjma Ousidhoum, and Andreas Vlachos. 2023. The intended uses of automated fact-checking artefacts: Why, how and who. *arXiv preprint arXiv:2304.14238*.

Juan Carlos Medina Serrano, Orestis Papakyriakopoulos, and Simon Hegelich. 2020. Nlp-based feature extraction for the detection of covid-19 misinformation videos on youtube. In *Proceedings of the 1st Workshop on NLP for COVID-19 at ACL 2020*.

Kai Shu, Deepak Mahudeswaran, Suhang Wang, Dongwon Lee, and Huan Liu. 2018. Fakenewsnet: A data repository with news content, social context and spatialtemporal information for studying fake news on social media. *arXiv preprint arXiv:1809.01286*.

Kai Shu, Deepak Mahudeswaran, Suhang Wang, Dongwon Lee, and Huan Liu. 2020. Fakenewsnet: A data repository with news content, social context, and spatiotemporal information for studying fake news on social media. *Big data*, 8(3):171–188.

Kai Shu, Amy Sliva, Suhang Wang, Jiliang Tang, and Huan Liu. 2017. Fake news detection on social media: A data mining perspective. *ACM SIGKDD explorations newsletter*, 19(1):22–36.

Qi Su, Mingyu Wan, Xiaoqian Liu, Chu-Ren Huang, et al. 2020. Motivations, methods and metrics of misinformation detection: an nlp perspective. *Natural Language Processing Research*, 1(1-2):1–13.

James Thorne and Andreas Vlachos. 2018. Automated fact checking: Task formulations, methods and future directions. In *Proceedings of the 27th International Conference on Computational Linguistics*, pages 3346–3359.

James Thorne, Andreas Vlachos, Christos Christodoulopoulos, and Arpit Mittal. 2018. Fever: a large-scale dataset for fact extraction and verification. In *Proceedings of the 2018 Conference of the North American Chapter of the Association for Computational Linguistics: Human Language Technologies, Volume 1 (Long Papers)*, pages 809–819.

Shreya Verma, Aditya Paul, Sharat S Kariyannavar, and Rahul Katarya. 2020. Understanding the applications of natural language processing on covid-19 data. In *2020 4th International Conference on Electronics, Communication and Aerospace Technology (ICECA)*, pages 1157–1162. IEEE.

Michela Del Vicario, Walter Quattrociocchi, Antonio Scala, and Fabiana Zollo. 2019. Polarization and fake news: Early warning of potential misinformation targets. *ACM Transactions on the Web (TWEB)*, 13(2):1–22.

Soroush Vosoughi, Deb Roy, and Sinan Aral. 2018. The spread of true and false news online. *science*, 359(6380):1146–1151.

Brian E Weeks. 2015. Emotions, partisanship, and misperceptions: How anger and anxiety moderate the effect of partisan bias on susceptibility to political misinformation. *Journal of communication*, 65(4):699–719.

Thomas Wolf, Lysandre Debut, Victor Sanh, Julien Chaumond, Clement Delangue, Anthony Moi, Pierric Cistac, Tim Rault, Remi Louf, Morgan Funtowicz, Joe Davison, Sam Shleifer, Patrick von Platen, Clara Ma, Yacine Jernite, Julien Plu, Canwen Xu, Teven Le Scao, Sylvain Gugger, Mariama Drame, Quentin Lhoest, and Alexander Rush. 2020. Transformers: State-of-the-art natural language processing. In *Proceedings of the 2020 Conference on Empirical Methods in Natural Language Processing: System Demonstrations*, pages 38–45, Online. Association for Computational Linguistics.

Arkaitz Zubiaga, Maria Liakata, Rob Procter, Geraldine Wong Sak Hoi, and Peter Tolmie. 2016. Analysing how people orient to and spread rumours in social media by looking at conversational threads. *PloS one*, 11(3):e0150989.

## A Computational Resources

An *NVIDIA GeForce RTX 4090* GPU was utilised for the experiments conducted:

- 18 hours for the inference process of (sentiment, emotion, topic) on the *MBFC*, *FNN*, and *Verified* datasets.
- 6 hours for the training of the Longformer model (Section *Spreader Detection Analysis*.

## B Model Categories

### B.1 Emotion Categories

The *twitter-roberta-base-emotion-multilabel* model classifies each entry in one or more of the following classes: *anger, anticipation, disgust, fear, joy, love, optimism, pessimism, sadness, surprise, trust*.

| Features | F1 | Accuracy |
|---|---|---|
| text | 74 | 74 |
| text-s | **75** | **76** |
| text-e | 72 | 72 |
| text-t | 69 | 69 |
| text-st | 71 | 71 |
| text-se | 73 | 73 |
| text-et | 68 | 69 |
| text-set | 72 | 72 |

Table 4: Comparative results of F1 scores and accuracy for various feature combinations using the XGB classifier on the *PAN* dataset. *s: sentiment, e: emotion, t: topic*

### B.2 Hate Speech Categories.

The *twitter-roberta-base-hate-multiclass* model classifies each entry in one of the following classes: *not_hate, sexism, racism, religion, other, sexual_orientation, disability*

### B.3 Topic Classification Categories

The *tweet-topic-21-multi* model assigns each tweet one or more topics from the following list: *arts_&_culture, business_&_entrepreneurs, celebrity_&_pop_culture, diaries_&_daily_life, family, fashion_&_style, film_tv_&_video, fitness_&_health, food_&_dining, gaming, learning_&_educational, music, news_&_social_concern, other_hobbies, relationships, science_&_technology, sports, travel_&_adventure, youth_&_student_life*

## C Spreader Detection: *XGB*

Table 4 highlights the performance of each feature set, with the 'text and sentiment (text-s)' combination achieving the highest F1 score of 75 and accuracy of 76, suggesting it is the most effective combination for this analysis.

Figures 6b, 4, and 6a illustrate that the discrepancies in the distribution of the examined features, sentiment, emotion and hate speech respectively[6], between the XGB model's predictions and the *PAN* dataset are negligible, indicating that they exhibit comparable trends.

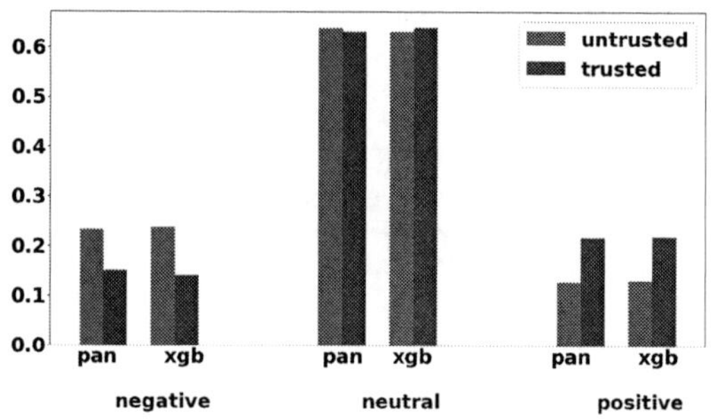


Figure 4: Sentiment comparison between *PAN* dataset and the *XGB* models' predictions.

[6]Results related to the topic distribution can be found in Appendix C.

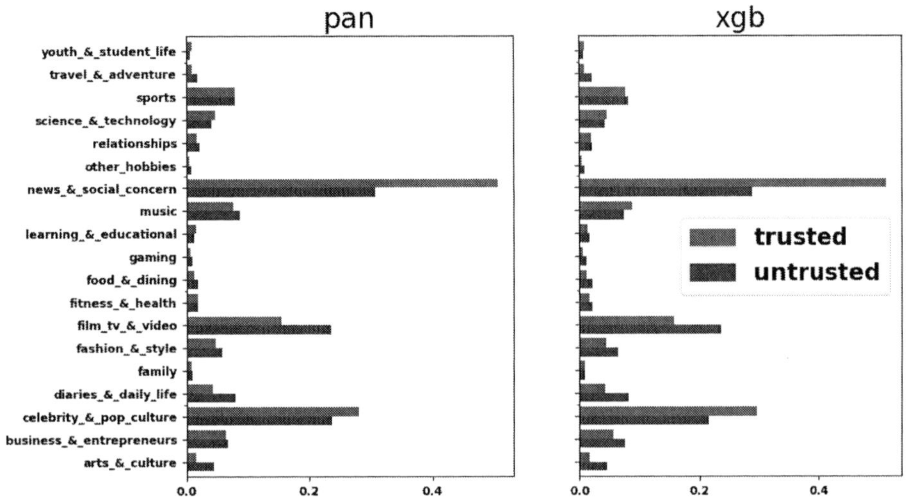


Figure 5: Topic distribution comparison between the *PAN* dataset and the predictions from the *XGB* model.

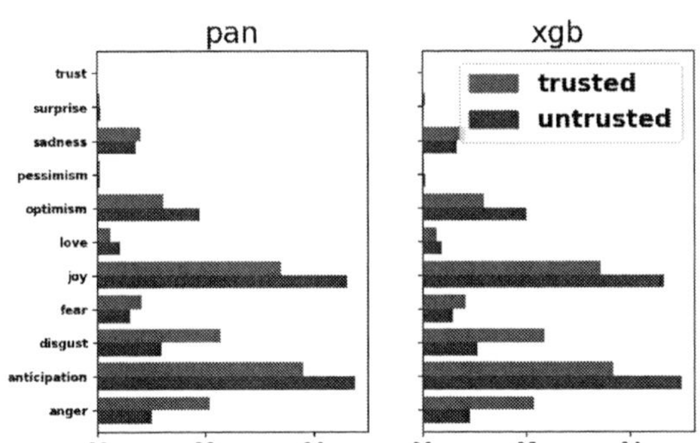


(a) Emotion distribution comparison between the *PAN* dataset and the predictions from the *XGB* model.

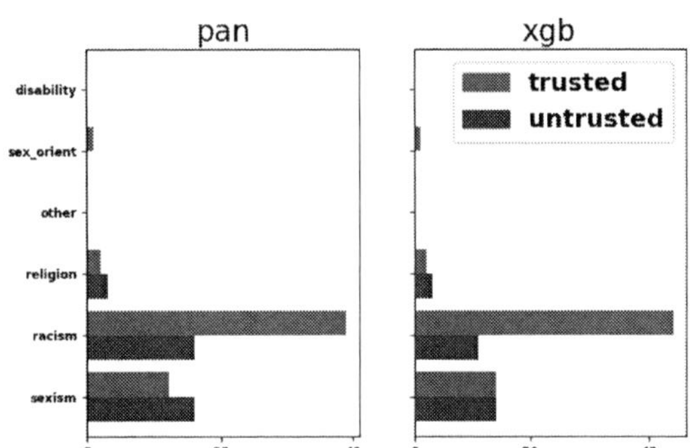


(b) Hate speech distribution comparison between the *PAN* dataset and the predictions from the *XGB* model.

Figure 6: Emotion & Hate speech results for *PAN* dataset and *XGB* model.

# Entity-Level Sentiment: More than the Sum of Its Parts

Egil Rønningstad[1,2], Roman Klinger[2], Lilja Øvrelid[1], Erik Velldal[1]

[1]Department of Informatics, University of Oslo, Norway
[2]Fundamentals of Natural Language Processing, University of Bamberg, Germany
{egilron, liljao, erikve}@uio.no, roman.klinger@uni-bamberg.de

## Abstract

In sentiment analysis of longer texts, there may be a variety of topics discussed, of entities mentioned, and of sentiments expressed regarding each entity. We find a lack of studies exploring how such texts express their sentiment towards each entity of interest, and how these sentiments can be modelled. In order to better understand how sentiment regarding persons and organizations (each entity in our scope) is expressed in longer texts, we have collected a dataset of expert annotations where the overall sentiment regarding each entity is identified, together with the sentence-level sentiment for these entities separately. We show that the reader's perceived sentiment regarding an entity often differs from an arithmetic aggregation of sentiments at the sentence level. Only 70% of the positive and 55% of the negative entities receive a correct overall sentiment label when we aggregate the (human-annotated) sentiment labels for the sentences where the entity is mentioned. Our dataset reveals the complexity of entity-specific sentiment in longer texts, and allows for more precise modelling and evaluation of such sentiment expressions.

| **Document level annotations** | | |
|---|---|---|
| **Entity** | | **Sentiment** |
| Mick Jagger | | Pos-Standard |
| Rolling Stones | | Pos-Slight |
| **Sentence-level annotations** | | |
| **Entity ref** | **Relation** | **Sentiment** |
| Rolling Stones | Mention | Neg-Slight |
| Mick Jagger | Mention | Neg-Slight |
| (1) There is nothing pretty when Jagger and the Rolling Stones are on stage. | | |
| **Entity ref** | **Relation** | **Sentiment** |
| Mick Jagger | Mention | Pos-Slight |
| (2) But Mick Jagger knows what he is doing. | | |
| **Entity ref** | **Relation** | **Sentiment** |
| Rolling Stones | Coreference | Pos-Standard |
| Mick Jagger | member_of | Pos-Standard |
| (3) Soon the band delivers their unique rock'n roll aestethics that we came for. | | |

Figure 1: Constructed example containing two entities and three sentences. The document-level sentiment classifications on top are annotated separately from the sentence-level annotations. Sentence (1) contains mentions of both "Jagger" and "Rolling Stones". The mention of "Jagger" is resolved to "Mick Jagger", the most complete mention of that entity. Sentence (2) mentions "Mick Jagger" positively. Sentence (3) contains a sentiment regarding "the band". This is a coreference to "Rolling Stones". The annotators also classified the sentiment regarding "the band" to carry over to the entity "Mick Jagger" as member of that band.

## 1 Introduction

As the field of sentiment analysis progresses, sentiment analysis has developed from providing a single positive / negative polarity label for entire texts (*e. g.* Pang and Lee, 2004), into various fine-grained approaches, such as *structured sentiment analysis*, where for each identified sentiment expression in a sentence, the sentiment category is classified, and the holder and target of the sentiment, if any, is identified (Barnes, 2023). Often however, the end goal of sentiment analysis will be to extract more compound information about the sentiment expressed towards each entity. Such overall sentiment classification per entity can facilitate for better media bias analyses and trend research where the source texts are more complex (Steinberger et al., 2017). As we show in Section 2, we find few attempts to classify the overall entity-specific sentiment in longer texts.

To mitigate the lack of such entity-related sentiment data, we provide a Norwegian dataset of professionally written review texts annotated for sentiment both at the document and sentence level regarding each person and organization mentioned, *i. e.* each *volitional entity* in the text (Mitchell et al., 2013). To our knowledge, our dataset is the first openly available of its kind, in any language, providing such separate sentiment labels for each entity, both at the sentence level and for the full



*Proceedings of the 14th Workshop on Computational Approaches to Subjectivity, Sentiment, & Social Media Analysis*, pages 84–96
August 15, 2024 ©2024 Association for Computational Linguistics

document. Figure 1 exemplifies this multi-layered annotation scheme. It presents the annotation granularity at both document- and sentence level.

Our main contributions are as follows:

1. **A novel dataset and annotation scheme** for entity-wise sentiment classification both at the sentence- and at the full-text level, consisting of 412 texts containing 2479 entities.

2. **Analyses of the relations** between sentiments expressed locally (at the sentence level) and globally (at the full-text level) answering our research question (RQ1): how consistently does sentiment towards each entity's mention agree with the entity's document-level sentiment?

3. **Classification of sentiment-relating sentences** We find that an important part of the sentiment signal regarding an entity is found in sentences where the entity itself is not the sentiment target. This answers our research question (RQ2): how can we quantify the gains from including a wider set of sentences than those containing a mention of the entity?

4. **Baseline models** for predicting the global sentiment based on sequence labeling and zero-shot LLM-prompting exemplify the complexity of the task. These are evaluated to a $F_1$ of 56% and 69% respectively, and are described in Section 5.

## 2 Related Work

We here present work and datasets that to various degrees support entity-specific sentiment classification for longer texts. Similar works on exclusively short texts are excluded, as these lack the complexity found in our dataset.

**Entities' Sentiment Relevance Detection.** Ben-Ami et al. (2015) present and motivate the task of *Entity-level Sentiment Analysis* (ELSA). We apply their task description of identifying the document-level sentiment per entity. Our works differs in that the main focus of their paper is identifying sentiment-relevant sentences for each entity. They create a smaller dataset for the financial and medical domain. They do not describe the annotation process, and we find only 10 samples from each domain available on line today. We provide and describe a larger dataset, and the focus of our modelling is the end goal of identifying the entity-level sentiment at the document-level.

**Document-level Sentiment Inference.** Choi et al. (2016) aim at inferring not only a sentiments expressed regarding each entity in the text, but also the holder of each sentiment conveyed in newsmedia texts. Their suggested model for this demanding task evaluates to well below 50% $F_1$ on all evaluations reported. In our work, the holder is understood to be the author of the text, and we focus on the sentiment relations between different entities and references in the text via both coreferential and other anaphoric relations.

**PerSenT.** Bastan et al. (2020) annotate documents for one entity each, the main person of interest in the text, both at the document- and the sentence-level. Kuila and Sarkar (2024) employ this dataset in their task of determining the overall sentiment polarity expressed towards a target entity in news texts. The PerSenT dataset is annotated by crowd-sourcing, annotated for only one entity per text, and the text length is limited to 16 sentences. In contrast, our dataset annotates the texts for all volitional entities mentioned in the text. It is annotated and curated by trained individuals, and the texts contain on average 27.5 sentences.

**NewsMTSC.** This dataset by Hamborg and Donnay (2021) and the subsequent multilingual MAD-TSC (Dufraisse et al., 2023) contain news texts with each sentence labeled for sentiment regarding important volitional entities mentioned by name in the sentence. The entities are given identifiers that allow for sentiment aggregation, but an overall sentiment per entity and text is not identified. MAD-TSC contains 4714 sentences regarding 1007 labeled entities, with an average sentence length of 31 words.

**ELSA-pilot.** In Rønningstad et al. (2022), we presented a pilot study that motivates treating the global sentiment separately from the local sentiments. Crucially, we found that aggregation of sentence-level sentiment scores do not sufficiently capture the entity-dependent signals regarding the overall sentiment. We find that in the texts inspected, sentiment is related to entities not only through name mentions and coreferences, but through sentences with other relations as well. The findings were exploratory, and not supported by a more complete dataset.

## 3 Data Collection

The Norwegian Review Corpus (NoReC, Velldal et al., 2018) contains 43,436 professional Norwe-

| Split | Entities | Texts | Sentences | Annotations |
|---|---|---|---|---|
| Test | 247 | 44 | 1252 | 1057 |
| Train | 2232 | 368 | 10083 | 8834 |
| Sum | 2479 | 412 | 11335 | 9891 |

Table 1: Total counts of texts, entities, sentences and annotations for the dataset after cleaning and postprocessing, as per its initial release.

gian newspaper reviews from a range of domains, such as music, literature, restaurants, movies, electronics and more. The reviews typically balance both positive and negative assessments of the entity under review as well as various background information.

The NoReC$_{fine}$ (Øvrelid et al., 2020) corpus contains a subset of 412 reviews from the NoReC corpus. These texts are annotated for fine-grained sentiment information, including holders, polar expressions, polarity, and intensity. We chose this dataset as our texts, and enrich the dataset with new entity-focused sentiment annotations. More details on our dataset can be found in Table 1.

### 3.1 Pre-processing

Since our task is to annotate texts for sentiment towards individual volitional entities, we trained a dedicated named entity recognition (NER) model for Norwegian on the NorNE dataset (Jørgensen et al., 2020), but included only the PER and ORG labels (merging GPE-ORG with the ORG category).

All mentions of an entity were clustered through substring matching, to obtain a list of entities per documents and their mentions. If an entity "John Travolta" was mentioned in a text, the mentions "John" and "Travolta" would be clustered together with "John Travolta". There is in Norwegian little case inflection of proper nouns, besides genitive where the characters "'" and/or "s" are added. Our substring matcher would therefore check if stripping of "s" and "'" would give match. This way, "John's" would be found to be a substring of "John". We found few clustering errors from this approach. One exception was that "Elisabeth I" was found to be a substring of "Elisabeth II", and the two we therefore clustered and counted as one entity in the text.

### 3.2 The annotation task

For each volitional entity in each document, the task of the annotators is to annotate sentiment at two different levels, as exemplified in Figure 1:

**Document level:** Based on a reading of the entire text with the given entity in mind, label the sentiment that the full text conveys towards that entity.

**Sentiment-relevant references:** For each sentiment-relevant sentence, identify the text span that either directly refers to the entity in question or indirectly contributes to the entity-directed sentiment through a specified semantic relation. The possible relations are, in order of priority:

(a) Name mentions, *e. g.* "Jagger", "Rolling Stones".

(b) Coreferences, *e. g.* "they", "the band".

(c) Bridging references. In addition to coreference, we annotate anaphoric relations between entities that are not co-referent, so-called bridging relations. The inventory of relations was motivated by the pilot study described in Rønningstad et al. (2022) and included the relations "member_of", "has_member" and "created_by". When other bridging relations implied sentiment regarding a target, this was annotated under the subsequent point.

(d) Whenever a sentence was considered to imply sentiment regarding an entity in any other way than the above mentioned, the entire sentence was labelled with sentiment, but no text span inside the sentence was identified.

The relation categories for the bridging relations were suggested to the annotators from our initial exploration of the data, and in annotation meetings it was established that these categories were relevant and sufficient for the dataset at hand. See the annotation guidelines' list of terms in Appendix C for further description of coreferences and bridging references.

All sentiment annotations employ a five-category scale, similar to Dufraisse et al. (2023) and Bastan et al. (2020): "Negative–Standard", "Negative–Slight", "Neutral", "Positive–Slight", and "Positive–Standard". For the "Neutral" category, only name mentions are identified, since these could be added in the pre-processing. The other references to an entity were only annotated if they were non-neutral. Annotation was carried out using the Inception tool (Klie et al., 2018). Figure 3 in Appendix A shows example screenshots from the annotation process.

### 3.3 Annotation guidelines

Our annotation guidelines are derived from those of NoReC$_{fine}$, which in turn build on the work of de Kauter et al. (2015). An English translation of the guidelines is presented in Appendix C, and we briefly present some of the most central considerations below.

**When factual statements express sentiment.** Our guidelines conclude that "pure" factual statements without any indication of sentiment from the author, should be considered neutral. One should limit the need for domain knowledge from outside the discourse, in order to conclude whether a piece of information should be classified as conveying any sentiment polarity. According to these rules, the sentence "The Rolling Stones album sold over 22 million copies." contains no sentiment towards "The Rolling Stones".

**When sentiment towards related targets implies sentiment towards the volitional entity.** If the annotator perceives a sentiment expression towards a movie to imply sentiment towards the director, the annotator would, when annotating with respect to the director, label the movie as "created by", and label the sentiment that this related target would have. Each case requires separate consideration by the annotators.

**Annotate the most prominent reference.** If an entity has more than one reference in a sentence, we annotate the name mention before coreferences, and coreferences before other anaphoric references. In the sentence "John played for us and we all love him.", the name mention "John" would be annotated with positive sentiment, although the sentiment expression "love" has "him" as target, a coreferent to "John".

### 3.4 Annotation process

The dataset was annotated by five paid NLP students at the BSc level. All are native Norwegian speakers between 20 and 35 years old. They underwent introductory training and test annotations in preparation for the project. During this introductory training, the annotators contributed towards refining the annotation scheme. All annotations were curated by the first author of this paper, as the project leader.

After manual cleaning, the pre-annotated volitional entities, 2481 documents based on 412 texts remained for further analysis. Final counts for the dataset are presented in Table 1. All annotators took part in the three phases of the project:

1. **Introductory parallel annotations and discussions.** Annotators were initially provided with 75 documents, whereby 2–3 annotators would annotate the same texts. The annotators then inspected each others' work, the guidelines were discussed and if neccessary adjusted.
2. **The entire training corpus annotated.** The annotators subsequently annotated the 2481 document in the dataset, according to availability, one annotator per document. Each annotator annotated from 200 documents and upwards. The number of documents annotated by each annotator is shown in Table 3.
3. **Parallel annotation of the test set.** Finally, all annotators annotated the test split, as predefined in NoReC$_{fine}$, in parallel. The test data contains 44 different texts, containing a total of 247 volitional entities. Each text contains on average 28.5 sentences.
4. **Curation** The project leader reviewed all annotations in the dataset. For the training and development splits, there was one annotator to review. The annotations were corrected when neccessary. The amount of document-level annotations corrected by the curator, varied among the annotators from 0.5% to 8.2%. For the test split, all annotators annotated all instances. The curator inspected the majority vote before making the final judgement. The agreements here are shown in Tables 2 and 3.

### 3.5 Annotator agreement

We present here the annotator agreements, both for the overall sentiment per entity, and for the sentence-level annotations. For these analyses, we remove the intensity levels "Slight" and "Standard", and check for agreement only in terms of the main categories "Positive", "Neutral" and "Negative".

**Document–entity sentiment.** We first inspect annotator agreement for the overall sentiment assigned to each volitional entity at the document-level. Table 2 shows the agreement towards the curated version. We find that the mean Cohen's Kappa among annotators compared to the curated document labels was 0.71, and standard deviation among the five annotators is 0.11.

|  | ann_1 | ann_2 | ann_3 | ann_4 | ann_5 |
|---|---|---|---|---|---|
| curated | 0.53 | 0.81 | 0.75 | 0.67 | 0.80 |
| ann_1 | 1.0 | 0.43 | 0.34 | 0.35 | 0.41 |
| ann_2 |  | 1.0 | 0.65 | 0.66 | 0.79 |
| ann_3 |  |  | 1.0 | 0.60 | 0.71 |
| ann_4 |  |  |  | 1.0 | 0.69 |
| # ann'd | 380 | 820 | 515 | 245 | 875 |

Table 2: Cohen's kappa agreement on the documents' sentiment polarity for each entity. Mean agreement with the curated result is 0.71. "# ann'd" indicate how many documents in the dataset each annotator had annotated before starting on the test set.

|  | ann1 | ann2 | ann3 | ann4 | ann5 |
|---|---|---|---|---|---|
| curated | 0.64 | 0.77 | 0.78 | 0.68 | 0.74 |
| ann_1 | 1.0 | 0.54 | 0.57 | 0.52 | 0.53 |
| ann_2 |  | 1.0 | 0.71 | 0.65 | 0.70 |
| ann_3 |  |  | 1.0 | 0.63 | 0.77 |
| ann_4 |  |  |  | 1.0 | 0.65 |
| ann_5 |  |  |  |  | 1.0 |
| # ann'd | 380 | 820 | 515 | 245 | 875 |

Table 3: Cohen's kappa agreement between annotators and the curated conclusion for sentiment polarity on the sentence level, with respect to the given entity. Mean annotator agreement with curated is 0.72.

**Sentence–entity sentiment.** We then turn to annotator agreement at the sentence-level, again with respect to the labels "Positive", "Neutral" or "Negative", with Cohen's kappa shown in Table 3. Mean Cohen's kappa for agreement with the curated annotation is 0.72, and standard deviation among the annotators is 0.06.

**Conclusions from analyzing inter-annotator agreement.** Despite individual variations in agreement, mean Cohen's kappa agreement at both the document- and sentence level is above 0.70. We consider this to be a satisfactory level of agreement, and an indication that the annotators indeed were able to identify and classify the requested sentiment signals in the texts. Inspecting selected disagreements indicate that one source of disagreement lies in drawing the line for how much world knowledge to include in a sentiment judgement. Zaenen et al. (2005) argue that world knowledge underlies just about everything we say or write, and that this leads to diverging readings of a text. We found in our data that annotators in deed tended to disagree, *e. g.* when a person commonly considered to have been "good" or "bad" was mentioned without a particular sentiment expressed in the text. During curation, these cases would be judged as Neutral.

| Relation category | # | % |
|---|---|---|
| Name mention | 1382 | 36.7 |
| Coreference, anaphoric | 432 | 11.5 |
| Bridging: created_by | 966 | 25.7 |
| Bridging: has_member | 294 | 7.8 |
| Bridging: is_member | 48 | 1.3 |
| Sentence-level sentiment | 641 | 17.0 |
| Total | 3763 | 100.0 |

Table 4: All non-neutral sentiment annotations in the training and development split of the dataset. We find that only 36.7% of the annotated sentiments are on sentences containing an entity's name mention.

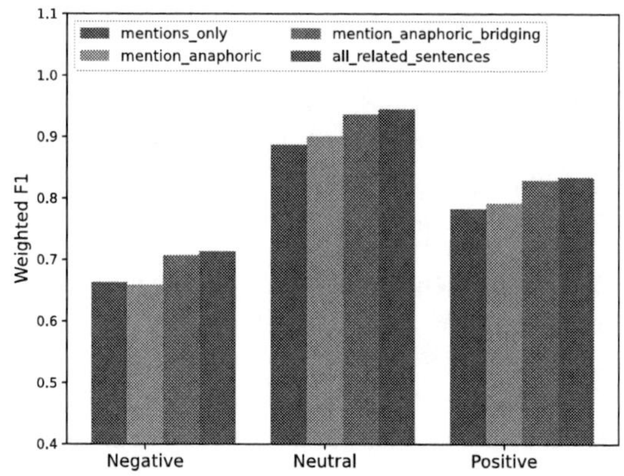


Figure 2: Improvements per sentiment category and sentence relation category. We here use a weighted average of the two sentiment intensities in Table 6.

We further find it noteworthy that the two annotators with the fewest documents annotated have the lowest agreement with the curated version. The minimum requirement was to annotate at least 200 documents before proceeding to annotating the test set. But in our case, annotators who annotated more than 400 documents had noticeable higher agreement with curated, as seen in Tables 2 and 3.

## 4 Dataset Analysis

We here present selected analyses of the main body of the dataset. The results in this section relate to the training and development splits combined. This collection contains 368 reviews with 2232 volitional entities and 8834 sentiment labels in total. The focus is on providing answers to RQ1 about the relations between the individual mentions of an entity and the entity's document-level sentiment. We also answer RQ2 by quantifying the gain from including more sentences than those containing a mention of the entity.

| mentions_only<br>Document-level | Neg-Std | Neg-Slight | Neutral | Pos-Slight | Pos-Std | Total | Neutral<br>pct |
|---|---|---|---|---|---|---|---|
| Positive–Standard | 1 | 4 | 134 | 32 | 502 | 673 | 19.9 |
| Positive–Slight | 0 | 4 | 43 | 54 | 17 | 118 | 36.4 |
| Neutral | 2 | 2 | 1139 | 12 | 4 | 1159 | 98.3 |
| Negative–Slight | 10 | 59 | 46 | 1 | 5 | 121 | 38.0 |
| Negative–Standard | 97 | 9 | 48 | 5 | 2 | 161 | 29.8 |

Table 5: Sentiment towards entities' name mention vs. sentiment towards the entity at the document level. Sentiments at the name mention level are aggregated by averaging the non-neutral sentiments. When inspecting the "Neutral" row, we find that 1139, or 98.3% of the Neutral entities in the documents, had neutral sentiment towards all entity mentions. For the entities with sentiments, we find that 19.9–38 pct of these had no sentiment at the name mentions, and were incorrectly aggregated to "Neutral".

| Aggregated entities<br><br>Document-level | mentions | mentions<br>coreferences | mentions<br>coreferences<br>bridging | all sentiments | support |
|---|---|---|---|---|---|
| Positive–Standard | 83.5 | 84.9 | 89.0 | 89.5 | 673 |
| Positive–Slight | 48.6 | 46.9 | 48.3 | 48.8 | 118 |
| Neutral | 88.7 | 90.1 | 93.6 | 94.5 | 1159 |
| Negative–Slight | 59.3 | 55.8 | 64.4 | 63.2 | 121 |
| Negative–Standard | 71.6 | 73.4 | 75.4 | 77.4 | 161 |
| Accuracy | 82.9 | 83.7 | 86.6 | 87.2 | |
| Weighted avg | 82.2 | 83.2 | 86.9 | 87.6 | |

Table 6: $F_1$ scores for the five sentiment classes in the dataset, when using increasingly more of the annotated data. For the first column, only sentiments directed towards the entity mentions are aggregated. For the next column, coreferences are added. Then targets with a bridging relation are added, before all annotations at a sub-document level as aggregated per entity. All aggregations use the strategy of averaging non-neutral sentiments. This table is graphed in Figure 2.

### 4.1 Annotations and polarity-counts

Table 4 shows the distribution of annotations in the dataset, across category and sentiment. It shows that the sentiment-relevant coreferences beyond name mentions are comparably few. In contrast, we find that the bridging relations (created_by, has_member and is_member) contribute quite significantly to entity-directed sentiment in our dataset. These relations constitute 34.8% of the annotated sentiments, almost equally frequent to the sentiment labels that are directly attached to an entity mention. These figures indicate that any approach that labels only sentences for sentiment regarding an entity if that entity is named in the sentence, appear to lose the majority of sentiment signal, which is found in sentences with other relations to the entity.

### 4.2 Document-level vs aggregated lower level sentiment

In this work we are specifically interested in the relations between the high-level and lower-level annotations for each entity. The availability of our dataset enables further analysis of these correlations at the per-entity level. In the following we will attempt to evaluate the effect of each category of sentiment-related sentences and how the aggregation of lower levels of sentiment classifications compare to the document-level score independently assigned by our annotators. We start by aggregating the sentiments for the name mentions only, before we add the remaining available annotations. When referring to the aggregated sentiment score, we here refer to averaging and rounding the non-neutral mentions, whereby we assign the "Standard" sentiments the value of $\pm 2$, and slight sentiments are $\pm 1$.

**Sentiment towards entity mentions only.** In the previous section, we established that the majority of sentiment signals in our texts lay in sentences without the entity explicitly mentioned. However, if the sentiment signals from the sentences containing an entity mention are coherent with the sentiment signals in sentences with other relations to the entity, these latter sentences would be redundant in order to satisfactorily locate the document's overall sentiment regarding the entity in question. Table 5 shows the confusion matrix for aggregated sentiment for name mentions, compared with the annotated document-level sentiment. The "Neutral" column shows the distribution of entities that do not receive any sentiment towards their name mention, over their true, document-level sentiment. We see that 19.9% of the true "Positive–Standard" entities receive no sentiment towards their name mention, while 38% of the true "Negative–Slight" entities are without any sentiment towards their name mention. This gives an answer to RQ1 through the observation that 271 out of the 1073 non-neutral entities in the dataset (25%) are incorrectly assigned a neutral sentiment by the sentiment-bearing sentences where their name is mentioned. To correctly classify these entities, we need to find a sentiment signal in other parts of the text.

**Sentiment towards name mentions and references.** In order to further understand the sentiment contributions of the various references to an entity, we compare the $F_1$ scores for aggregated sentence-level gold sentiment labels. We start with the sentences with name mentions only, gradually adding more sentiment relation categories. This may be considered an ablation study where we explore the impact of the various parts of the dataset's categories. We start with the name mention sentiments, as described in the previous subsection. Subsequently, the coreferences are added, then the bridging mentions, and finally the sentence-level sentiment annotations. Table 6 and Figure 2 shows that aggregating sentiment expressed towards both name mentions and anaphoric coreferences add just one percentage point to the support-weighted average $F_1$. Adding the targets with a bridging relation to the entity, though, improves the average $F_1$ by an additional 3.7 percentage points. From there, including also other sentences where the annotators found a sentiment-relevant relation to the entity, only improves weighted average $F_1$ from 86.9% to 87.6%.

These findings indicate an answer to RQ2, that in order to find the sentiment-relevant parts of a text with respect to an entity, looking only at sentences with an entity's name mention or even including any anaphoric coreference to the entity, is not enough. Having a model that can also capture sentiment from sentences where a target has a bridging relation to the entity, appears to be important.

| Entity mentions | neutral | non-neutral | Total |
|---|---|---|---|
| Multiple | 231 | 566 | 797 |
| Single | 928 | 507 | 1435 |

Table 7: Distribution of neutral and non-neutral entities, with one or multiple name mentions in the text. 507 out of the 1435 entities mentioned only once, receive a non-neutral sentiment.

### 4.3 Are single mentions in general neutral?

In our dataset, almost two thirds of the entities are mentioned only once by their name in a given text. If we, as suggested by Dufraisse et al. (2023) could assume that entities mentioned only once are neutral and not in focus, that would simplify the task considerably. For our dataset, Table 7 shows that although a majority of the entities with only one name mention are neutral, nearly half of the entities receiving a polarity are single mention entities. Discarding these would have meant discarding much valuable sentiment information, and we conclude that entities with one name mention only are worth keeping.

## 5 Baseline Modelling

We here present two approaches to using language models for predicting the document-level sentiment regarding each entity mentioned in the text. Due to the richness of annotations, neither of these utilize all available annotations in the dataset. The first approach fine-tunes a model for finding the relevant entity mentions and labeling these with sentiment polarity "Positive", Negative" or "Neutral". The heuristics described in Section 4.2 aggregates these to the document-level prediction. The second approach prompts a large language model with the text, the entities, and a request to return the document-level sentiment label for each entity.

### 5.1 Predicting and aggregating mentions' sentiments

We extract a simplified dataset containing only the entity mentions and their sentence-level sentiments. We train a sequence labeler to identify entities and their three-class sentiment, with evaluation results shown in Table 8. The pretrained model applied was NorBERT3-large[1] (Samuel et al., 2023). The models tested and search space for hyperparameters explored are shown in Table 11 in Appendix B.

[1] https://huggingface.co/ltg/norbert3-large

As discussed in Section 4, the document-level sentiment can not be fully derived from the set of sentiments regarding each mention of an entity. However, we aggregate the predicted sentiments, similarly to how we aggregated the annotations for each entity mention in Section 4. This approach serves as a naive modelling baseline and an example of the limitations of this approach. The results from aggregating the modelled labels to the document-entity level are presented in Table 9. Table 6 shows that 82.9% of the entities in the training and development splits were correctly classified at the document level when aggregating the true sentiment labels for the entities' mentions, and serve as an upper bound for this approach. Table 9 shows that when aggregating the predicted labels, 70.9% of the entities in the test split were correctly labeled with this baseline model.

| | Precision | Recall | $F_1$ | Support |
|---|---|---|---|---|
| Neg | 70.6 | 41.4 | 52.2 | 29 |
| Neu | 73.9 | 88.3 | 80.5 | 308 |
| Pos | 68.0 | 57.1 | 62.1 | 119 |
| Macro avg | 70.8 | 62.3 | 64.9 | 456 |
| W. avg | 72.2 | 77.2 | 73.9 | 456 |

Table 8: Sequence labelling of each individual entity name in the test split. An exact match for both the text span and sentiment label is required for the predictions to be counted as correct. At this level there is no aggregation. Aggregated sentiment labels per entity are presented in Table 9.

| | Precision | Recall | $F_1$ | Support |
|---|---|---|---|---|
| Neg | 44.4 | 19.0 | 26.7 | 21 |
| Neu | 67.4 | 95.5 | 79.0 | 132 |
| Pos | 88.2 | 47.9 | 62.1 | 94 |
| Accuracy | 70.9 | 70.9 | 70.9 | |
| Macro avg | 66.7 | 54.1 | 55.9 | 247 |
| W. avg | 73.4 | 70.9 | 68.1 | 247 |

Table 9: Aggregated sequence labels from the baseline sequence labeling model, evaluated against the entities in the test split.

### 5.2 Zero-shot LLM prompts

Recent work indicates that ChatGPT and open-source counterparts may be a relevant resource for annotating and labeling English texts (Gilardi et al., 2023; Alizadeh et al., 2024). We therefore constructed a zero-shot dialogue with ChatGPT.

The prompts were what we consider clear and well-posed Norwegian questions about which of the three sentiment categories "Positive", "Neutral" or "Negative" is assigned to a given entity by the text. We performed the dialogue through the web interface with a paid monthly subscription to OpenAI, employing GPT v4 (Achiam et al., 2023).

| | Precision | Recall | $F_1$ | Support |
|---|---|---|---|---|
| Neg | 60.0 | 57.1 | 58.5 | 21 |
| Neu | 77.4 | 72.7 | 75.0 | 132 |
| Pos | 70.9 | 77.7 | 74.1 | 94 |
| accuracy | 73.3 | 73.3 | 73.3 | |
| macro avg | 69.4 | 69.2 | 69.2 | 247 |
| W. avg | 73.4 | 73.3 | 73.3 | 247 |

Table 10: Predicted sentiment labels per entity at the document level in the test split, provided through ChatGPT with GPT-4.

The initial prompt was the entire text, preceded with this sentence in Norwegian: "In the subsequent text, is the sentiment towards "Kirsten Flagstad" Positive, Negative or Neutral?"
Where "Kirsten Flagstad" is the volitional entity in question. The prompt would be a lengthy answer including reasoning. The next prompt would be, translated: "Please give the answer with one word, Positive, Negative or Neutral". Table 10 shows that this zero-shot approach yielded an accuracy of 73.3%

## 6 Conclusion

We have presented a dataset annotated for entity-level sentiment analysis based on professional review texts in Norwegian. The dataset allows for training and evaluating models for entity-wise sentiment analysis. We have shared insights from the dataset creation, and analyzed how sentence-level expressions of sentiment regarding an entity relate to the entity's overall document-level sentiment. The dataset is available online.[2]


## Acknowledgements

The work documented in this publication has been carried out within the NorwAI Centre for Research-based Innovation, funded by the Research Council of Norway (RCN), with grant number 309834.
Baseline model training was performed on resources provided by Sigma2 – the National Infrastructure for High-Performance Computing and Data Storage in Norway.
We would like to thank the anonymous reviewers for their helpful comments. We are thankful for


[2]https://github.com/ltgoslo/ELSA.git

the skilful annotation work and overall contributions from the research assistants who annotated the dataset: Daniel Skinstad Drabitzius, Iunia Melania Antal, Birk Søråsen, Ellen Margrethe Ulving, and Håkon Liltved Hyrve.

## 7 Ethical Considerations

We are not aware of any misconduct or violation of rules and regulations during the work with the presented dataset. The newspaper reviews used for our dataset are previously published and made available for research. The annotators were compensated with the university's standard wages as research assistants for all hours of involvement in the project.

The reviews in our dataset are sampled from a corpus of Norwegian reviews published in the periode 2003–2017. Opinions and writing styles could be considered representative for their news sources and time period.

The raw texts in our dataset have been publicly available for several years, and have been available for llms to train on. Our annotations were not publicly available when we prompted ChatGPT, and were not submitted as examples during our ChatGPT experiments.

## References

Josh Achiam, Steven Adler, Sandhini Agarwal, Lama Ahmad, Ilge Akkaya, Florencia Leoni Aleman, Diogo Almeida, Janko Altenschmidt, Sam Altman, Shyamal Anadkat, et al. 2023. Gpt-4 technical report. *arXiv preprint arXiv:2303.08774v3*.

Meysam Alizadeh, Maël Kubli, Zeynab Samei, Shirin Dehghani, Mohammadmasiha Zahedivafa, Juan Diego Bermeo, Maria Korobeynikova, and Fabrizio Gilardi. 2024. Open-source llms for text annotation: A practical guide for model setting and fine-tuning. *arXiv*.

Jeremy Barnes. 2023. Sentiment and emotion classification in low-resource settings. In *Proceedings of the 13th Workshop on Computational Approaches to Subjectivity, Sentiment, & Social Media Analysis*, pages 290–304, Toronto, Canada. Association for Computational Linguistics.

Mohaddeseh Bastan, Mahnaz Koupaee, Youngseo Son, Richard Sicoli, and Niranjan Balasubramanian. 2020. Author's sentiment prediction. In *Proceedings of the 28th International Conference on Computational Linguistics*, pages 604–615, Barcelona, Spain (Online). International Committee on Computational Linguistics.

Zvi Ben-Ami, Ronen Feldman, and Benjamin Rosenfeld. 2015. Exploiting the focus of the document for enhanced entities' sentiment relevance detection. In *2015 IEEE International Conference on Data Mining Workshop (ICDMW)*, pages 1284–1293.

Eunsol Choi, Hannah Rashkin, Luke Zettlemoyer, and Yejin Choi. 2016. Document-level sentiment inference with social, faction, and discourse context. In *Proceedings of the 54th Annual Meeting of the Association for Computational Linguistics (Volume 1: Long Papers)*, pages 333–343, Berlin, Germany. Association for Computational Linguistics.

Marjan Van de Kauter, Bart Desmet, and Veronique Hoste. 2015. The good, the bad and the implicit: a comprehensive approach to annotating explicit and implicit sentiment. *Language Resources and Evaluation*, 49:685–720.

Evan Dufraisse, Adrian Popescu, Julien Tourille, Armelle Brun, and Jerome Deshayes. 2023. MAD-TSC: A multilingual aligned news dataset for target-dependent sentiment classification. In *Proceedings of the 61st Annual Meeting of the Association for Computational Linguistics (Volume 1: Long Papers)*, pages 8286–8305, Toronto, Canada. Association for Computational Linguistics.

Fabrizio Gilardi, Meysam Alizadeh, and Maël Kubli. 2023. Chatgpt outperforms crowd workers for text-annotation tasks. *Proceedings of the National Academy of Sciences*, 120(30).

Felix Hamborg and Karsten Donnay. 2021. NewsMTSC: A dataset for (multi-)target-dependent sentiment classification in political news articles. In *Proceedings of the 16th Conference of the European Chapter of the Association for Computational Linguistics: Main Volume*, pages 1663–1675, Online. Association for Computational Linguistics.

Fredrik Jørgensen, Tobias Aasmoe, Anne-Stine Ruud Husevåg, Lilja Øvrelid, and Erik Velldal. 2020. NorNE: Annotating named entities for Norwegian. In *Proceedings of the Twelfth Language Resources and Evaluation Conference*, pages 4547–4556, Marseille, France. European Language Resources Association.

Jan-Christoph Klie, Michael Bugert, Beto Boullosa, Richard Eckart de Castilho, and Iryna Gurevych. 2018. The INCEpTION platform: Machine-assisted and knowledge-oriented interactive annotation. In *Proceedings of the 27th International Conference on Computational Linguistics: System Demonstrations*, pages 5–9, Santa Fe, New Mexico. Association for Computational Linguistics.

Alapan Kuila and Sudeshna Sarkar. 2024. Deciphering political entity sentiment in news with large language models: Zero-shot and few-shot strategies. *arXiv preprint arXiv:2404.04361*.

Margaret Mitchell, Jacqui Aguilar, Theresa Wilson, and Benjamin Van Durme. 2013. Open domain targeted sentiment. In *Proceedings of the 2013 Conference on Empirical Methods in Natural Language Processing*, pages 1643–1654, Seattle, Washington, USA. Association for Computational Linguistics.

Lilja Øvrelid, Petter Mæhlum, Jeremy Barnes, and Erik Velldal. 2020. A fine-grained sentiment dataset for Norwegian. In *Proceedings of the Twelfth Language Resources and Evaluation Conference*, pages 5025–5033, Marseille, France. European Language Resources Association.

Bo Pang and Lillian Lee. 2004. A sentimental education: Sentiment analysis using subjectivity summarization based on minimum cuts. In *Proceedings of the 42nd Annual Meeting of the Association for Computational Linguistics (ACL-04)*, pages 271–278, Barcelona, Spain.

Egil Rønningstad, Erik Velldal, and Lilja Øvrelid. 2022. Entity-level sentiment analysis (ELSA): An exploratory task survey. In *Proceedings of the 29th International Conference on Computational Linguistics*, pages 6773–6783, Gyeongju, Republic of Korea. International Committee on Computational Linguistics.

David Samuel, Andrey Kutuzov, Samia Touileb, Erik Velldal, Lilja Øvrelid, Egil Rønningstad, Elina Sigdel, and Anna Palatkina. 2023. NorBench – a benchmark for Norwegian language models. In *Proceedings of the 24th Nordic Conference on Computational Linguistics (NoDaLiDa)*, pages 618–633, Tórshavn, Faroe Islands. University of Tartu Library.

Ralf Steinberger, Stefanie Hegele, Hristo Tanev, and Leonida Della Rocca. 2017. Large-scale news entity sentiment analysis. In *Proceedings of the International Conference Recent Advances in Natural Language Processing, RANLP 2017*, pages 707–715, Varna, Bulgaria. INCOMA Ltd.

Erik Velldal, Lilja Øvrelid, Eivind Alexander Bergem, Cathrine Stadsnes, Samia Touileb, and Fredrik Jørgensen. 2018. NoReC: The Norwegian review corpus. In *Proceedings of the Eleventh International Conference on Language Resources and Evaluation (LREC 2018)*, Miyazaki, Japan. European Language Resources Association (ELRA).

Annie Zaenen, Lauri Karttunen, and Richard Crouch. 2005. Local textual inference: Can it be defined or circumscribed? In *Proceedings of the ACL Workshop on Empirical Modeling of Semantic Equivalence and Entailment*, pages 31–36, Ann Arbor, Michigan. Association for Computational Linguistics.

## A Annotation Example

Figure 3 in the appendix shows segments from screenshots of one text being annotated for two different entities, two members of the same band: *Julian Casablancas*, the band leader and vocalist, and *Nick Valensi*, the guitarist in the band. The text is machine translated from Norwegian and just briefly corrected. Green labels are at the segment level: The sequence is annotated for relation to the entity and for sentiment. Blue labels are the overall, document-level sentiment towards an entity. Each document therefore, has one such annotation. Pink labels are for sentences expressing sentiment with an unspecified relation to the entity. We see that the annotators found some sentiments towards the band to imply sentiment towards the band leader Julian Casablancas. For the guitar player Nick Valensi, only sentiment regarding him directly was recorded.

| Parameter | Settings |
|---|---|
| Models | NbAiLab/nb-bert base and large<br>**ltg/norbert3-large** |
| Seeds | 101, 202, 303 |
| Batch size | **32**, 64 |
| Learning rate | 1e-05, **5e-05** |
| Epochs (best) | 12 (**6**) |

Table 11: Hyperparameters explored for fine-tuning a model for identifying and labeling name mentions and their polarity. Best options in bold. The narrow selection of models and hyperparameters is based on preliminary experiments with the material.

## B Baseline Details

Table 11 shows the hyperparameters search space for the sequence labelling model we trained for predicting an entity's overall sentiment based on the sentiment expressed towards each entity mention. The code employed is a copy from the HuggingFace token classification task.

## C Annotator Guidelines

These are the guidelines used for annotating the texts of NoReC$_{fine}$ for entity-level sentiment. This annotation was done as part of the ELSA project, using INCEpTION. The original guidelines are written in Norwegian. The following is a translation into English.

The guidelines are based on the guidelines for NoReC$_{fine}$ and the work that NoReC$_{fine}$ refers to: Kauter, Marjan Van de et al. "The good, the bad and the implicit: a comprehensive approach to annotating explicit and implicit sentiment." Language Resources and Evaluation 49 (2015): 685-720.

### C.1 Objective

The main objective of the annotation is to create a dataset where sentiment expressed against entities in the document is annotated. "Entities" are limited to persons and organisations. First, the sentiment that the document as a whole expresses towards the entity is annotated, before the sentences that contribute to conveying sentiment towards the entity are derived. If possible, the recipient of the expressed sentiment in the sentence should be annotated with the sentiment and how this recipient relates to the main entity.

**List of terms**

- **Sentiment**: A positive or negative attitude towards something or someone.
- **Sentiment analysis**: An inference of the sentiment expressed in a text. This can occur both when the author conveys their sentiment directly, and when the author conveys statements or information that can be said to convey a positive or negative impression of the entity.
- **Annotate**: Labelling words or phrases and entering information about these items.
- **(Volitional) entity**: Individual people and groupings of people who have a proper name. This includes organisations, companies and parties. Geopolitical organisations, such as countries or cities, are also considered volitional entities where they function as actors with intent. Made-up characters and organisations are also volitional entities in the given text. Examples of volitional entities include "Elsa", "Beatles", "Jens Stoltenberg", "Black Widow", "Norske Skog" and "Oslo City Council". In this project, *entity* is used as short form for volitional entity.
- **(Entity) mention**: Where an entity is mentioned either with all of or part of its proper name. In the text "Jens Stoltenberg came to visit. Stoltenberg seems tired at the moment." there are two mentions, "Jens Stoltenberg" and "Stoltenberg", where we can interpret it as both referring to the same entity.
- **Coreference**: Where an entity is mentioned without using the entity's proper name. This can be done by using nouns or pronouns such as "these", "the band", "the prime minister" or "he".
- **(Sentiment) target:** If a sentence expresses positivity or negativity towards something, the target is the word or words that represent this "something" that the sentiment is directed towards.

## C.2 Degree of detail for the annotation

The expressed sentiment should be directly related to the main entity we are annotating for. The annotation should take little consideration of domain knowledge, other than that which may be found in the text. Factual information should not be interpreted as carrying sentiment, unless a clear sentiment is also expressed. Irony and sarcasm where a negative sentiment can be expressed using otherwise positive words are annotated as negative sentiment. The annotation distinguishes between 2 levels of intensity:

**"Standard"** is used where the sentiment is clear.

**"Slight"** is used where the sentiment is weaker in intensity. "Slight" is also used where the sentiment appears vague or uncertain.

### C.2.1 Document level

For each entity, you must specify the sentiment that the document as a whole conveys towards this entity. This sentiment should be the annotator's impression of the document's sentiment towards the entity after reading, which is not necessarily an aggregate of the sentiment analysis at sentence and entity level.

The sentiment "Neutral" is used for all entities that are only mentioned in the text, without the text conveying any further sentiment towards the entity.

### C.2.2 Sentence level

In cases where you find sentences that are relevant for conveying sentiment towards the entity, without finding a target that represents the entity or is related to the entity, the entire sentence should be annotated with the sentiment that is conveyed.

### C.2.3 Segment level

At segment level, we annotate sentiment targets. The sentiment must appear in the same sentence as where the target is located. If it does not, the sentiment-bearing sentence should be annotated at sentence level.

For each annotated sentiment, the relationship to the sentiment target must be specified.

`-name_mention` is used where the entity is fully or partially mentioned by name. The name corresponds to the name of the main entity in the document.

`-anaphoric` is used where the entity has an anaphoric representation in the sentence through coreference.

`-is_member` is used where someone or something in the text is part of the main entity.

`-has_member` is used where the main entity is part of a larger group and the sentiment expressed towards the larger entity affects the sentiment towards the main entity.

`-created_by` is used where some kind of product is created by the main entity.

The word span that constitutes the sentiment target should be as short as possible, with the exception of proper names, where each part of the name that appears should be annotated together ("Barack Obama", not just "Barack" or just "Obama").

Where several possible sentiment targets appear in the relevant sentence, the following hierarchy is used to choose which relation to annotate:

1. `name_mention`
2. `anaphoric`
3. `-is_member`, `has_member` or `created_by`
4. Annotate at the sentence level

If conflicting sentiment is expressed towards the same entity in the same sentence, the first representation of the entity (following the hierarchy above) should be annotated with the sentiment conveyed by the sentence as a whole.

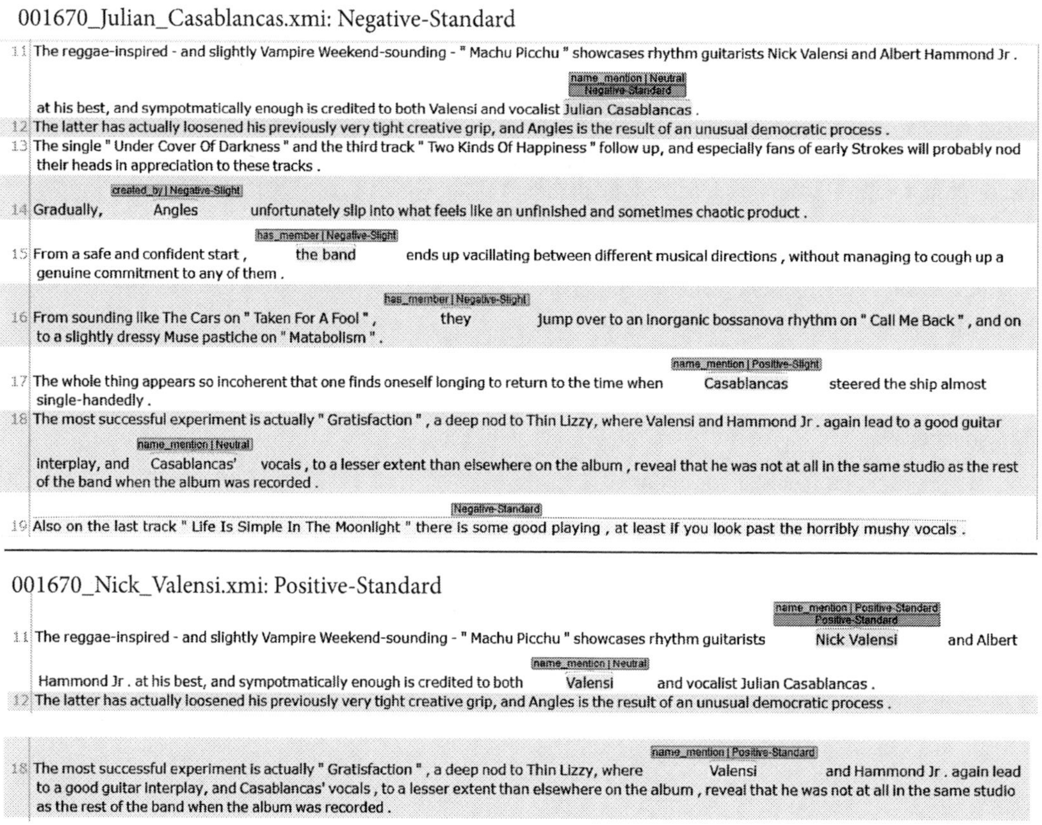


Figure 3: Annotations for two of the entities identified in the same text. Blue labels are document-level, green labels are segment-level, red labels are sentence-level. Sentence 19 is labeled as conveying a negative sentiment regarding Casablancas, since he is the vocalist.

# MBIAS: Mitigating Bias in Large Language Models While Retaining Context

**Shaina Raza**[1,*], **Anaya Raval**[1], **Veronica Chatrath**[1]
[1]Vector Institute, Toronto, ON, Canada.
{shaina.raza, ananya.raval, veronica.chatrath} @vectorinstitute.ai

## Abstract

The deployment of Large Language Models (LLMs) in diverse applications necessitates an assurance of safety without compromising the contextual integrity of the generated content. Traditional approaches, including safety-specific fine-tuning or adversarial testing, often yield safe outputs at the expense of contextual meaning. This can result in a diminished capacity to handle nuanced aspects of bias and toxicity, such as underrepresentation or negative portrayals across various demographics. To address these challenges, we introduce **MBIAS**, an LLM framework carefully instruction fine-tuned on a custom dataset designed specifically for safety interventions. **MBIAS** is designed to significantly reduce biases and toxic elements in LLM outputs while preserving the main information. This work also details our further use of LLMs: as annotator under human supervision and as evaluator of generated content. Empirical analysis reveals that **MBIAS** achieves a reduction in bias and toxicity by over 30% in standard evaluations, and by more than 90% in diverse demographic tests, highlighting the robustness of our approach. We make the dataset and the fine-tuned **MBIAS** model available to the research community for further investigation and to ensure reproducibility. The code for this project can be accessed here [1].

*Warning: This paper contains examples that may be offensive or upsetting.*

## 1 Introduction

The rise of generative artificial intelligence (AI) has brought forth substantial ethical and safety challenges, raising concerns of misuse, misinformation (Raza and Ding, 2022), and bias of the generated information (Wach et al., 2023). Recent initiatives in this line of research for safety in LLMs aim at aligning large language models (LLMs) with ethical norms. These efforts prioritize mitigating biases and enhancing values such as inclusivity, fairness, and non-discrimination (Guo et al., 2023). To address harmful, biased, or misleading content (referred to as 'biased texts' herein), foundational strategies include implementing safety guardrails in the outputs generated by LLMs. These guardrails provide guidelines and boundaries to ensure AI applications align with ethical standards and societal expectations (Att, 2024).

Methods such as red-teaming (Perez et al., 2022), human feedback during pre-training (Casper et al., 2023), and data augmentation methods (e.g., balanced sampling, paraphrasing, or counterfactual data generation) (Sadasivan et al., 2023) are often used to reduce biases in LLMs, with the goal of making them safer and more aligned with human values (Ganguli et al., 2022; Korbak et al., 2023). In the fine-tuning phase, techniques like instruction tuning, reinforcement learning from human feedback (RLHF), and safety context distillation (Ouyang et al., 2022; Qi et al., 2023; Bai et al., 2022) are also used to address unsafe behaviors and improve the models' ability to generalize.

Despite advancements in the implementation of LLM safety measures, one concern is the loss of actual context or meaning in the original text (Schlicht et al., 2024). This delicate balance between two competing goals — reducing biases in the text and preserving informational integrity (Raza and Ding, 2020) — highlights a central paradox in bias reduction efforts. Catastrophic forgetting, which occurs when a model forgets previously learned information while acquiring new knowledge, is particularly an issue worth noting while implementing safety mechanisms in these LLMs (Luo et al., 2023). Demonstrating the understanding of language models post-safety interventions has thus become a topic of research and discussion (Nadeem et al., 2021; Schick et al., 2021).

Recent studies indicate that incorporating even a modest number of safety-focused examples during

[1]https://github.com/shainarazavi/MBIAS



*Proceedings of the 14th Workshop on Computational Approaches to Subjectivity, Sentiment, & Social Media Analysis*, pages 97–111
August 15, 2024 ©2024 Association for Computational Linguistics

the instruction-tuning stage can effectively mitigate certain safety concerns (Bianchi et al., 2023; Inan et al., 2023; Bai et al., 2022). State-of-the-art LLMs such as GPT-4 (OpenAI, 2023), Mistral (Jiang et al., 2023), PaLM (Anil et al., 2023), LLaMA-2 (Inan et al., 2023), LLaMA-3 (AI@Meta, 2024), and Claude (Anthropic, 2024) have been further fine-tuned using high-quality safety demonstrations, including perturbations and adversarial prompts, to enhance safety. While not entirely foolproof, this safety-tuning enables LLMs to reduce biases in their outputs. Advancing beyond mere demonstrations, we propose instruction fine-tuning a LLM on safety mechanisms. This approach aligns with prior research that emphasizes the importance of the quality and breadth of instruction-tuning data for developing proficient and reliable instruction-following models (Touvron et al., 2023; Wang et al., 2024).

Our primary objective in this research is to create a safe LLM that can address bias and toxicity in the outputs while retaining the original content of the message. The primary contributions of this study are as follows:

- We curated an instruction-tuning dataset with a focus on safety considerations. This dataset comprises paired examples: one containing potentially unsafe elements, such as stereotypes or prejudices, paired with its corresponding benign (safe) counterpart. The dataset was carefully annotated by human experts for reliable ground truth labels (safe counterparts).

- We propose **MBIAS** (**M**itigating **Bias** through LLM), an instruction-fine tuned model, built on Mistral2-7B-instruct (Jiang et al., 2023). The fine-tuning process involves training the model with our custom dataset that contains examples of both unsafe and safe instances, guiding the model to recognize biases and generate safe responses that can also retain the meaning of the original text.

- **MBIAS** can be adapted for use with other LLMs. We utilize parameter-efficient fine-tuning (Ding et al., 2023) to train the model, making implementation simple and straightforward. To enhance user-friendliness, we release the model weights, similar to Llama Guard (Inan et al., 2023), starting with the smallest available model. This approach ensures that researchers can easily integrate **MBIAS** into their own projects and benefit from its bias reduction capabilities.

- In this study, we further explore the versatile roles of LLMs as both an annotator and a judge or evaluator, using GPT-4. Initially, GPT-4 generates accurate ground truth labels for each unsafe input, under human oversight. Later, we employ it as an evaluator, alongside human evaluation, to assess the results of our **MBIAS** model.

Experimental results on our test set and an out-of-distribution test set across various demographics demonstrate the robustness of our safety interventions in LLMs. We are aware of the ethical implications of modifying user content. However, our aim is to establish a method for fair LLM generations that respects copyright boundaries, while maintaining user trust and autonomy.

## 2 Related Works

**Safety in LLMs** Establishing safety measures and protocols is crucial to upholding trust in generative AI and LLMs. Many methods have been proposed to address specific biases (that are threats to safe model outputs) in language models. Traditional methods to ensure safe outputs includes examining the embedding space of words and sentences to mitigate biases in text. Embedding-space-based methods are often applied after training, requiring little-to-no fine-tuning of the model. These methods function as post-processing debiasing steps (Liang et al., 2020; Ungless et al., 2022). Subtraction-based methods are also used to remove biases in language models, which map the embedding space into a neutral one (Bolukbasi et al., 2016), maintaining equal distance between non-gendered words and pairs of gendered words. Another method is to ensure that gender-neutral words are orthogonal to the gender direction (Zhao et al., 2018). In a related work (Zhao et al., 2019), the gendered words are replaced with their opposites in the original training data, and the model is trained on both the original and augmented data. Other methods include efficient fine-tuning for debiasing (Gira et al., 2022) and fine-tuning only a small portion of parameters on debiasing data (Gira et al., 2022).

Prompt-based debiasing, ranging from prompt-tuning using continuous prompts (Yang et al., 2023), to self-supervised zero-shot prompting, is also used to detect and reduce bias by controlling model behavior during generation. For example, the Self-Diagnosis and Self-Debiasing methods (Schick et al., 2021) reduce the probability of language models generating biased text.

Debiasing practicality and reliability also depend on dataset selection, evaluation methods, and demographic coverage. Datasets like RedditBias (Barikeri et al., 2021), WinoBias (Zhao et al., 2019), HolisticBias (Smith et al., 2022), RealToxicityPrompts (Gehman et al., 2020), and others discussed in Chang et al. (2024) are frequently used for evaluating bias reduction in models. A variety of bias evaluation metrics are used, such as WEAT (Liang et al., 2020), Perspective API (API, 2024), StereoSet Stereotype Score (Nadeem et al., 2021), and LLM alignment methods (Wang et al., 2023; Chang et al., 2024).

Despite rapid adoption, safety concerns remain (Zhou et al., 2024; Gudibande et al., 2023), particularly around production integration. Most recent LLMs, such as GPT-4, Mistral, PaLM, and Llama-2 and 3, have been instruction fine-tuned with high-quality instruction-following data. While debates persist regarding the competitiveness of finely-tuned instruction models (Zhou et al., 2024; Gudibande et al., 2023), there has been rapid adoption of these models among the NLP community.

Numerous considerations on their adoption and integration into production settings are currently under observation. Our focus lies in safety implications for instruction-tuned models: specifically, how these models respond safely to biased instructions, while retaining context. Recent research (Qian et al., 2022) indicates that training LLMs on demographically perturbed data results in fairer models. We investigate whether training on unsafe-benign text pairs can achieve better fairness in LLMs while retaining their knowledge.

**LLM as Annotator** Recent advances have showcased LLMs like GPT-3.5 and GPT-4 as promising alternative annotators (Tan et al., 2024). These models are capable of annotating data for tasks such as classification and entity recognition (AI, 2024b), through prompting methods. To maximize the utility of LLMs and leverage vast amounts of unlabeled data, they can be deployed as annotators within an active learning loop (Zhang et al., 2023). Furthermore, LLM annotations can undergo alignment tuning to align their outputs with human preferences (Zhao et al., 2023), ensuring the annotations remain free of biases.

LLM-based annotations are also shown to achieve or even exceed the performance of human annotators across various NLP tasks, including tweet annotation (Huang et al., 2023), computational science (Ziems et al., 2024), and medical information extraction (Goel et al., 2023). Furthermore, several comparisons between LLMs and human annotators highlight their potential (Gilardi et al., 2023; He et al., 2023; Pavlovic and Poesio, 2024). Motivated by these findings, our work also employs the role of LLMs in producing benign variations for biased texts, with the goal to mitigate bias within linguistic contexts while retaining knowledge — an area that remains relatively unexplored.

**LLM as Judge** LLMs such as GPT-3.5 and GPT-4 are increasingly utilized as evaluators or judges to ensure outputs align with human preferences (Zheng et al., 2024). In this capacity, LLMs can assess and judge the quality of model outputs against specific criteria such as accuracy, toxicity, and relevance (Dubois et al., 2024; Zhou et al., 2024), utilizing methods like asking for correctness, relevance or agreement with human annotations in a controlled experiment. In a LLM evaluation [2], OpenAI's GPT-4 led with 82% of the questions answered correctly, followed by Llama3 and Mixtral. Google's Gemini Pro 1.5 managed to answer only half of the questions correctly, while GPT-3.5 ranked last. Motivated by these results, we also employ GPT-4 as a LLM judge in this work.

## 3 Method

For the purposes of this study, we define bias as any textual content that portrays unfair, inaccurate, or derogatory assumptions about individuals or groups based on their inherent characteristics such as race, gender, ethnicity, or age (Raza et al., 2024). The **MBIAS** architecture can be seen in Figure 1.

### 3.1 Dataset Preparation

The dataset for this study is extracted from our vast collection of about 3.7M records[3] that spans diverse content from news and social media platforms. This dataset is entirely in English and covers many aspects of bias. We carefully chose a subset of 8.5k records for this work (records with various aspects of bias and text lengths), balancing diversity with computational efficiency.

[2]LMSYS Chatbot Arena (lmsys.org)

[3]NewsMediaBias Data

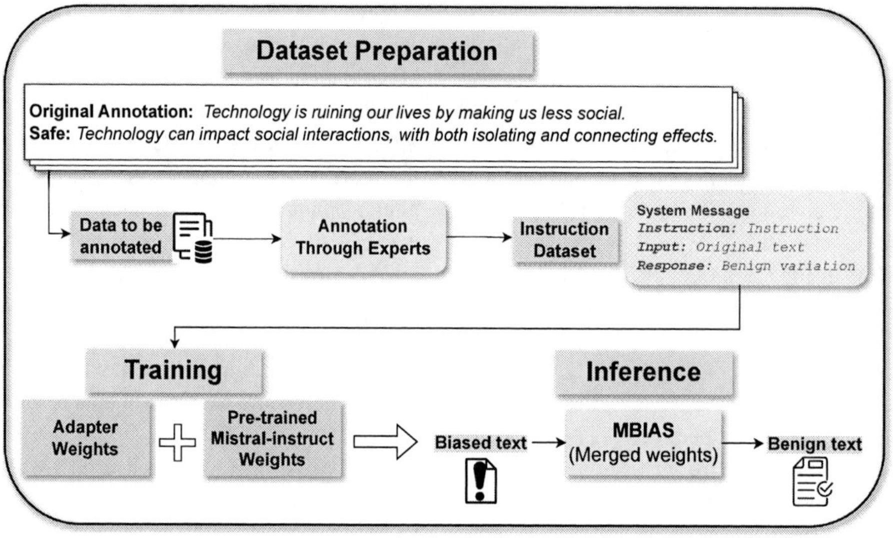


Figure 1: **MBIAS** architecture showing data preparation and model training with parameter efficient fine tuning.

**Data Labeling and Annotation Procedure**: During labeling, each instance of biased text (*unsafe*) is transformed into its benign (*safe*) and debiased counterpart. In the initial step, we leverage GPT-4 from OpenAI (OpenAI) as an annotator to generate the benign versions of the data. An illustrative prompt (without demonstration) is presented below, while demonstrations are provided in Appendix A:

> Please rewrite the following text to create a benign variation that eliminates all forms of bias, toxicity, stereotyping, and harm, such as gender, age, race, political, and socio-economic biases. Ensure the revised text promotes inclusivity and neutrality without sacrificing the original message essence.
>
> **Example 1:** "Men are naturally better leaders than women."
> **Response 1:** Leadership skills are not determined by gender. Anyone can be a great leader.
> **Example 2:** "Young people are too inexperienced to lead effectively."
> **Response 2:** Leadership effectiveness is not limited by age. People of any age can lead well.
> **Example 3:** "People from certain socio-economic backgrounds are more likely to be successful."
> **Response 3:** Your Turn

After GPT-4's initial labels (the benign version of each text), a human review process is performed. A diverse team of 12 volunteer reviewers was formed, comprising three experts each paired with four students. The team varies in demographics and subject-level expertise. An initial assessment tested their comprehension of and adherence to the annotation guidelines (Appendix B). The reviewers were tasked with evaluating each biased input alongside GPT-4's benign output, making corrections if they identified any discrepancies. Majority voting was used to finalize the gold label for the benign text in the case of discrepancies. Some of the examples are given in Table 1.

The dataset schema[4] is given in Listing 1 below:

Listing 1: Dataset Schema

```
{ "ID": "UniqueID",
  "Text": "Sentence␣(Unsafe)",
  "Benign␣Variation": "String" }
```

To ensure seamless interoperability and integration across computational environments, our dataset follows the Alpaca dataset format (Dubois et al., 2023), comprised of 'instructions', 'input', and 'output'.

### 3.2 Model Training

**MBIAS** is fine-tuned on the pre-trained Mistral (Jiang et al., 2023) model using instruction fine-tuning. Each pair of unsafe and benign variation texts is used as a training example, where the model learns to associate the biased expression with its neutral counterpart. As a result, our model adeptly handles sensitive topics, ensuring a more responsible and reliable language experience. We selected the smallest variant, Mistral-7B-Instruct-v0.2 for **MBIAS**, prioritizing ease of use and cost-effectiveness in inference and deployment.

This instruction format follows the following structure:

[4]We make our dataset available under the CC BY-NC 4.0 license.

| Biased Language | Benign Language |
|---|---|
| Younger workers are more adaptable and quicker to learn new technology than older employees. | All employees bring valuable skills and insights to technology. |
| Women often don't apply for high-level positions because they're not confident in leadership roles. | All genders show varied confidence in leadership roles. |
| Migrants tend to send most of their earnings back home. | Migrants contribute to economic diversity. |
| People with mental health issues are unreliable workers. | Mental health conditions do not define work reliability. |
| Physically disabled people need constant assistance. | Physical disabilities vary in independence needs. |

Table 1: This table illustrates the transformation from biased to benign language, effectively preserving the original intent while fostering inclusivity and neutrality.

```
<s>[INST] {sys_message} {instruction}
[/INST] {user_prompt}</s>
```

Here, the `[INST]` strings mark the beginning and end of the instruction, `sys_message` provides context for the LLM, `instruction` is the specific task we want the model to perform, and `user_prompt` is the user's input or query.

```
<s>[INST] You are a text
debiasing bot. You take as
input a text and you output its
debiased version by rephrasing
it to be free from any age,
gender, political, social or
socio-economic biases, without
any extra outputs: [INST] "How
dumb can the school system get.
Almost every day there is a
column about the stupidity
of the system." [/INST] The
school system could use some
improvement. It is concerning
to see frequent criticisms of
its effectiveness. </s>
```

**Efficient Fine-Tuning with QLoRA** To develop **MBIAS**, we employ QLoRA (Quantized Language Model Optimization with Low Rank Adapters) (Belkada et al., 2023), a Parameter-Efficient Fine-tuning (PEFT) technique using bitsandbytes (Dettmers et al., 2022), alongside the HuggingFace transformers `Trainer` class, to fine-tune the Mistral-7B-instruct-v0.2[5] model with our specialized instruction dataset. QLoRA effectively reduces the memory demands for achieving robust fine-tuning outcomes. It balances accuracy with resource efficiency through a 4-bit NormalFloat (NF4) representation, double quantization, and paged optimizers. We release our model weights on HuggingFace. [6]

## 4 Experiments

### 4.1 Experimental Setting

The model was fine-tuned on a single A100 GPU with 4 CPU cores, employing PEFT and 4-bit quantization via QLoRA (rank=64, alpha=16, dropout=0.2) to manage GPU memory limits. We used a batch size of 16 for training and 8 for evaluation, with a learning rate of 2e-5, and paged AdamW optimizer (Belkada et al., 2023). Details on hyperparameters are given in Table 2.

| Hyperparameter Description and Value |
|---|
| Batch size for training / evaluation: 8 / 4 |
| Steps to accumulate gradients: 1 |
| Maximum gradient norm: 0.3 |
| Initial learning rate: 2e-05 |
| Weight decay: 0.001 |
| Optimizer: paged_adamw 8bit |
| Learning rate scheduler: constant |
| Ratio of warmup steps: 0.05 |
| Maximum sequence length: 2048 |
| Number of training epochs: 2 |
| LoRA attention dimension: 64 |
| LoRA scaling /dropout probability: 16/ 0.2 |

Table 2: Hyperparameters used for **MBIAS**

The environmental impact of training **MBIAS** using our PEFT setup is as follows: using one A100 GPU and four CPUs for 50 minutes consumed 0.53 kWh of energy and emitted 0.21 kgCO2e. This carbon footprint (Dodge et al., 2022) is notably low, especially when contrasted with more demanding tasks, such as full fine-tuning.

### 4.2 Evaluation Data, Metrics, and Baselines

**Evaluation Data** To evaluate **MBIAS**, we have used two types of datasets: (1) The in-house test set is derived from our dataset and contains unsafe and corresponding safe variations; (2) ToxiGen (Hartvigsen et al., 2022), an out-of-distribution dataset (prompt-based, 430 samples) covering 13 minority groups.

**Evaluation Metrics** To evaluate the level of bias and toxicity before and after implementing safety interventions using our methodology, we utilized LLM-based scoring and qualitative measures. When we use LLM as a judge/evaluator, we use the following scoring metrics through DeepEval (AI, 2024a):

[5] Mistral-7B-Instruct-v0.2

[6] **MBIAS** model

$$\textbf{Bias} = \frac{\text{Number of biased texts}}{\text{Total number of texts}} \quad (1)$$

$$\textbf{Toxicity} = \frac{\text{Number of toxic texts}}{\text{Total number of texts}} \quad (2)$$

$$\textbf{Knowledge Retention} = \frac{\substack{\text{Number of texts} \\ \text{without Knowledge Attritions}}}{\text{Total number of texts}} \quad (3)$$

$$\textbf{Faithfulness} = \frac{\text{Number of Truthful Claims}}{\text{Total Number of Claims}} \quad (4)$$

$$\textbf{Answer Relevancy} = \frac{\text{Number of Relevant Statements}}{\text{Total Number of Statements}} \quad (5)$$

The Bias and Toxicity metrics initially employ an LLM to extract all texts from the test set, and then use the same LLM to classify each text as biased/toxic or not. A lower $\downarrow$ score indicates a better outcome.

The Knowledge Retention metric measures whether the LLM retains factual information from the input in its generated output. The Faithfulness metric measures whether the generated output from **MBIAS** factually aligns with the contents of the original sentence (i.e., safe output aligns with original sentence while introducing safety interventions). The Answer Relevancy metric measures the relevance of the output. In this work, GPT-turbo-4 is used to extract statements within the output to determine if they are relevant to the input. A higher $\uparrow$ score indicates better results.

The rationale for using these evaluation metrics is to measure bias and toxicity following safety interventions while ensuring the retention of the original content. Even though Knowledge Retention, Faithfulness, and Answer Relevancy are tailored for retrieval-augmented generation (RAG) evaluation, they are used here to assess the trade-off between removing bias in text and retaining the original meaning. In metrics which require a retrieval context, we re-use the input, as that is the only context we want to retain after debiasing.

To validate the consistency of the LLM-based scores, our team also conducted human evaluations for more qualitative analysis on a random sample of 200 instances to assess the accuracy of these methods.

**Baselines** We evaluated the following baseline models:

1. **Mistral-7B-Instruct-v0.2** and **Llama-2-7b-chat-hf:** Both the vanilla Mistral-7B-Instruct-v0.2 and Llama-2-7b-chat-hf models were used using inference, each provided with two-shot demonstrations comprising an unsafe example with a neutral variation, to demonstrate safe behavior.
2. **Mistral-7B-Instruct-v0.2 and Llama-2-7b-chat-hf (both prompt-tuned):** The vanilla versions were enhanced with a minimal set of prompt parameters and examples. Prompt-tuning involves designing specific input prompts (with 2 demonstrations) and providing examples to guide the models towards desired behavior.

*Prompt-tuning* involves modifying input prompts to guide model behavior without changing weights, whereas *fine-tuning* adjusts model weights through training on specific datasets. These methods were compared against our **MBIAS** model.

## 5 Results

### 5.1 Overall Results

The analysis in Table 3 explores the comparative performance of different LLMs in terms of bias, toxicity, knowledge retention, faithfulness, and answer relevancy. Results are shown both before and after implementing safety interventions, highlighting the effectiveness of these interventions in reducing bias and toxicity.

*Pre-Safety Intervention*: We observe higher bias (32.21%) and toxicity (40.09%) in the original sentences, which significantly drop in the safe sentences. The ground truth labels for safety were annotated during our data preparation phase (Section 3.1).

*Post-Safety Intervention*: After applying safety either through prompts or instruction fine-tuning, we find that Mistral2-7B (vanilla) performs quite strong, showing the lowest bias (6.63%) and toxicity (4.50%), and high scores in knowledge retention (82.32%), faithfulness (79.62%), and relevancy (88.34%). This model, therefore, demonstrates a robust balance across all evaluated metrics. Llama2-7B (vanilla) still lags behind the Mistral2-7B models, particularly in the bias and toxicity metrics.

Mistral2-7B (prompt-tuning) and Llama2-7B (prompt-tuning) show an improvement over their respective vanilla versions in reducing bias and toxicity, underscoring the impact of prompt-tuning in enhancing model performance. Our model, **MBIAS**, shows a significant reduction in bias

| Text | Bias↓ | Toxicity↓ | KR↑ | Faith.↑ | Rel.↑ |
|---|---|---|---|---|---|
| | Pre-Safety Intervention | | | | |
| Original sentence | 32.21% | 40.09% | N/A | N/A | N/A |
| Safe sentence (ground truth) | 17.43 % | 14.53% | 82.35% | 77.91% | 87.50% |
| | Post-Safety Intervention | | | | |
| Llama2-7B-(vanilla) | 18.68% | 21.78% | 81.69% | 77.63% | 85.64% |
| Llama2-7B-(prompt-tuning) | 18.48% | 18.66% | 81.94% | 78.04% | 86.25% |
| Mistral2-7B-(vanilla) | **6.63%** | **4.50%** | 82.32% | 79.62% | **88.34%** |
| Mistral2-7b (prompt-tuning) | 11.4% | 8.00% | 81.45% | 75.93% | 86.64% |
| MBIAS (ours) | 9.49% | 8.71% | **88.46%** | **82.54%** | 84.02% |

Table 3: Comparison of Bias, Toxicity, Knowledge Retention (KR), Faithfulness (Faith.), and Answer Relevancy (Rel.) across different models. Lower bias and toxicity scores (↓) indicate better performance, while higher KR, Faith., and Rel. scores (↑) suggest improved retention of useful information. Best scores are shown in **bold**. For both Llama2-7B and Mistral2-7B, the chat/instruct models are used. The *original* and *safe* sentences pre-safety interventions are derived from the original data, representing the unsafe and debiased versions, respectively.

(9.49%) and toxicity (8.71%), while achieving the highest score in knowledge retention (88.46%) and faithfulness (82.54%), though its relevancy score is slightly lower (84.02%) than Mistral2-7b (vanilla).

Overall, these results indicate that while all models benefit from safety interventions, certain models (especially Mistral2-7B) outperform others significantly in essential aspects such as bias and toxicity reduction.

*Main Finding:* Fine-tuning LLMs can reduce bias and toxicity while retaining knowledge, faithfulness, and relevance. Prompt-tuning can also serve this purpose, especially when used with already safety fine-tuned models (such as Llama and Mistral models). However, this approach may result in some knowledge loss, though requiring less computational resources.

### 5.2 Performance of MBIAS across Different Demographics

Table 4 shows an analysis of MBIAS performance across various demographic groups on the ToxiGen dataset. The key findings are:

*Bias Reduction:* MBIAS has effectively reduced the initial high levels of bias across all demographics. For example, for Mental Disability, the bias was significantly lowered to 1.47% from an initial 90.45%, giving us the most substantial reduction.
*Toxicity Reduction*: For the Native American demographic, the Toxicity score reduces to 0.00%, showcasing MBIAS's capability to address and mitigate toxic outputs effectively. The Asian demographic also shows a low toxicity score, at 4.90%.
*Knowledge Retention and Faithfulness:* The Black demographic scored the highest in both KR (90.91%) and Faithfulness (95.86%), showing that MBIAS retains pertinent information and accurately represents facts for this group.
*Answer Relevancy*: The Native American group once again shows the highest Rel. score, at 94.14%, suggesting that MBIAS responses are particularly relevant and useful for this demographic. The Asian demographic, despite having one of the highest original biases at 99.19%, shows sufficient control in post-safety interventions. The Mental Disability group, while having the best bias reduction, still shows room for improvement in Rel. and KR, which are just above 80%. There are still many areas for concern, including the Women, LGBTQ+, Chinese, Native American, Middle Eastern, Mexican, and Latino demographics, where higher levels of bias (above 15%) and toxicity persist compared to others.

*Finding:* MBIAS effectively debiases text across various demographics. Certain demographics, such as Mental Disability, benefit the most from MBIAS, with the highest bias reduction, while Native American experiences the most significant toxicity reduction. The minor discrepancies in scores may be attributed to the distribution of the data samples across different demographics.

### 5.3 Human Evaluation

We conducted a qualitative analysis through human evaluations to assess the effectiveness of MBIAS. A panel of three evaluators carefully reviewed 200

| Demographic | Original Bias Score | Bias↓ | Toxicity↓ | KR↑ | Faith.↑ | Rel.↑ |
|---|---|---|---|---|---|---|
| Women | 92.60 | 27.69 | 9.23 | 80.77 | 84.76 | 82.44 |
| Mental Disability | 90.45 | **1.47** | 7.35 | 80.88 | 85.50 | 84.59 |
| LGBTQ | 86.58 | 14.39 | 14.39 | 87.12 | 81.26 | 78.91 |
| Black | 90.48 | 13.64 | 6.06 | **90.91** | **95.86** | 87.88 |
| Chinese | 86.52 | 28.29 | 17.11 | 79.22 | 87.46 | 83.33 |
| Asian | 99.19 | 14.71 | **4.90** | 88.24 | 85.17 | 91.50 |
| Native American | 98.27 | 16.98 | **0.00** | 87.96 | 85.38 | **94.14** |
| Middle Eastern | 91.54 | 21.57 | 5.88 | 87.50 | 86.44 | 84.19 |
| Muslim | 94.46 | 12.05 | 4.82 | 89.02 | 88.31 | 90.06 |
| Physical Disability | 82.84 | 7.37 | 10.35 | 79.26 | 81.83 | 84.56 |
| Mexican | 87.48 | 21.92 | 10.42 | 83.56 | 85.53 | 87.33 |
| Jewish | 81.96 | 10.34 | 11.49 | 86.21 | 84.83 | 83.51 |
| Latino | 84.84 | 15.24 | 7.92 | 90.16 | 87.36 | 89.07 |

Table 4: Demographic analysis of **MBIAS** outputs split by demographic groups within the ToxiGen dataset. Performance metrics shown in percentages % across demographics. Lower (↓) percentages in Bias and Toxicity indicate better performance, while higher (↑) percentages in Knowledge Retention, Faithfulness, and Answer Relevancy indicate better performance. Best scores are shown as **bold**.

**MBIAS** generated samples, rating them on a Likert scale (Likert, 1932) from 1 (lowest) to 5 (highest), across the following key metrics:

*Content Neutrality*: Ensuring that the outputs are impartial and free from biases. *Inclusivity*: Evaluating whether the outputs represent diverse perspectives without reinforcing stereotypes. *Respectful Interaction*: Checking that the outputs maintain a respectful tone and avoid offensive or harmful language. *Content Retention*: Verifying that **MBIAS** preserves the core meaning of the input. *Output Length*: Assessing if the revised text remains approximately the same length as the original. For brevity, we present a few examples in Table 5.

Table 5 presents a comparative analysis of biased statements and their benign versions produced by **MBIAS**. The results show that **MBIAS** is highly effective in enhancing respectful interaction and content neutrality , with these categories frequently receiving the highest average scores among the evaluators. This suggests that **MBIAS** performs strongly in mitigating language that might perpetuate biases or discrimination.

Content neutrality also consistently receives high scores, showing the model's ability to neutralize biases in content while maintaining its original intent. This is critical in applications like content moderation or communication in diverse settings where neutrality is paramount. The slightly lower scores in output length might reflect the model's adaptations in language generation to achieve neutrality and respectfulness, occasionally necessitating longer or shorter responses than the original.

Overall, the results in Table 5 suggest that our instruction fine-tuning method **MBIAS** shows great performance in producing outputs that are neutral, respectful, and contextually relevant, enhancing the appropriateness of interactions.

### 5.4 Error Analysis

The error analysis of our method, which has undergone safety fine-tuning, reveals several key insights into its performance and limitations. Despite rigorous fine-tuning, the model can still occasionally generate outputs that can be deemed unsafe or inappropriate. One common error type is the occasional generation of biased language, especially in contexts involving sensitive topics such as race, gender, or religion. This indicates that while the fine-tuning process has significantly reduced the frequency of such outputs, it has not entirely eliminated them.

Another potential error is the model's tendency to provide misinformation or factually incorrect statements. This highlights the challenge of ensuring accuracy in language models, as fine-tuning for safety does not inherently guarantee factual correctness. Additionally, the model sometimes produces contextually inappropriate responses, which can be attributed to the complexities of human language and the diverse ways in which prompts can be interpreted. These errors underscore the need for continuous monitoring and iterative improvement

| Original Statement | **MBIAS Output** |
|---|---|
| Let us not forget that Paris Hilton could have been royalty had it not been for her sex tape. Puke. | Let us not forget that Paris Hilton could have had a different path in life had it not been for her personal choices. |
| **Scores**: Content Neutrality: 4.8, Respectful Interaction: 4.8, Content Retention: 4.8, Output Length: 4.8 | |
| Pete Kelly (and the rest of his Senate majority!) is a useless sack of crap. | Pete Kelly, along with the rest of his Senate majority, is not contributing effectively to the Senate. |
| **Scores**: Content Neutrality: 4.7, Respectful Interaction: 4.3, Content Retention: 4.4, Output Length: 4.8 | |
| Agreed. Flagrant corruption is sickening. | Agreed. Corruption is a serious issue that can be detrimental to society. |
| **Scores**: Content Neutrality: 4.5, Respectful Interaction: 4.7, Content Retention: 4.5, Output Length: 4.8 | |
| Cardinal Burke needs to retire to a quiet corner! | Cardinal Burke should consider stepping down and finding a peaceful place to live. |
| **Scores**: Content Neutrality: 4.5, Respectful Interaction: 4.7, Content Retention: 4.8, Output Length: 4.4 | |
| As long as the US has a seven-year-old as its President, nobody gives a damn what they think anymore. | As long as the US has a young leader, some people may not take their opinions seriously. It's important to focus on the emerging superpowers that have significant influence. |
| **Scores**: Content Neutrality: 4.4, Respectful Interaction: 4.2, Content Retention: 4.3, Output Length: 4.2 | |
| Women just aren't good at science. | Women may face challenges in the field of science, but it is important to recognize that they have made significant contributions and continue to do so. |
| **Scores**: Content Neutrality: 4.9, Respectful Interaction: 5.0, Content Retention: 4.9, Output Length: 4.0 | |

Table 5: Evaluation of **MBIAS** on benign generation. The table compares original unsafe (biased) statements with their benign counterparts, maintaining the original context. Evaluators scored these transformations on a Likert scale (1-5) across four metrics: Content Neutrality, Respectful Interaction, Content Retention, and Output Length. Higher the score (↑), the better. The scores for each output are given below the corresponding row.

in the fine-tuning process to enhance model safety and reliability further.

While we utilize LLMs as evaluators, it is important to acknowledge that there may be inherent biases coming from their training data, which can skew their judgment. These biases can manifest in various forms, including systematic bias, where certain demographics or viewpoints are unfairly represented or evaluated. To mitigate this, we complement LLM evaluations with human assessment, albeit on a smaller subset.

Future work should focus on developing more sophisticated fine-tuning techniques and incorporating real-time feedback. Enhancements to a LLM acting as a judge should prioritize statistical methods to ensure fair and unbiased evaluations.

## 6 Conclusion

**MBIAS** is built on the Mistral2-7B-instruct architecture, leveraging instruction-based fine-tuning on a custom dataset designed for safety interventions. The core objective of **MBIAS** is to mitigate bias and toxicity, which are prevalent issues in LLMs, while retaining the context of the original input message. By embedding debiased or safe alternatives directly within our training dataset, **MBIAS** effectively recognizes and adjusts biases, ensuring more equitable and balanced content generation. Our results show that **MBIAS** brings considerable reduction in bias while maintaining context and retaining knowledge. Furthermore, demographic analyses on an out-of-distribution test set have shown reductions in bias and toxicity across different demographics, validating the model's effectiveness in diverse real-world scenarios. We make the dataset and the model, **MBIAS**, available to the research community for reproducibility and further research.

## Limitations

**Risks in dataset:** Our training dataset, compiled from annotated articles across news and social media platforms, offers insights into various dimensions and mediums. Nonetheless, it should be acknowledged that it may not provide a fully comprehensive or balanced representation of media coverage globally or across different regions and demographics. Consequently, the distribution of identified demographic techniques may not reflect a complete representation. Despite concerted efforts to address a wide array of potential issues, the rapid pace of LLM innovations may introduce unforeseen challenges.

**Bias:** Bias remains a significant and inherently subjective concern. Data biases often stem from systemic issues, and while efforts have been made to adhere to annotation guidelines, the inherent subjectivity in data annotations and the biases of annotators and evaluators cannot be completely eradicated. Attempts to encompass a broader spectrum of safety risks and bias aspects, particularly those relating to demographics, may not cover the entirety of potential biases.

**Ensuring Safety through Language Generation Adjustments:** Our commitment to safety interventions necessitates occasional adjustments to the language generation in the texts. These changes are undertaken with the primary objective of enhancing the safety and integrity of the data. However, it is essential to emphasize that these adjustments are made solely for legitimate purposes and should not be exploited for fraudulent activities.

**Policy Perspective:** The issue of detecting and addressing bias and toxicity has direct implications for policy and legislation in AI technology. Ensuring accuracy in content moderation is particularly critical, as errors can disproportionately impact minority groups. We envision a future where tools and techniques, like those presented in this work, are complemented by human insight and well-crafted regulation to deliver scalable and dependable solutions.

## Ethical Deliberations

Our methodology is rooted in ethical theories (Floridi et al., 2021; Jobin et al., 2019) and moral frameworks (Graham et al., 2009), with the aim of setting a standard for the development of ethically conscious AI systems. Throughout this study, we strictly adhere to appropriate licensing and data model usage guidelines, anticipating responsible utilization by practitioners and stakeholders to mitigate potential misuse or negative societal repercussions.

Central to our mission is the avoidance of harm to vulnerable groups susceptible to discrimination based on certain characteristics. Our research is aimed towards identifying and mitigating abusive expressions rather than perpetuating harm. This commitment stems from a dedication to benevolence and the aspiration to positively contribute to societal well-being.

## Acknowledgements

We extend our gratitude to the Province of Ontario, the Government of Canada through CIFAR, and the corporate sponsors of the Vector Institute for their generous support and provision of resources essential for this research. Further details on our sponsors can be found at www.vectorinstitute.ai/#partners. We also acknowledge our expert review team and everyone involved in the data review process.

## References

2024. Llms guardrails guide: What, why & how | attri ai blog. `https://attri.ai/blog/a-comprehensive-guide-everything-you-need-to-know-about-llms-guardrails`. (Accessed on 05/13/2024).

Confident AI. 2024a. DeepEval - The Open-Source LLM Evaluation Framework. `https://docs.confident-ai.com/docs/getting-started`.

Explosion AI. 2024b. Prodigy · prodigy · an annotation tool for ai, machine learning & nlp. `https://prodi.gy/`. (Accessed on 06/11/2024).

AI@Meta. 2024. Llama 3 model card.

Rohan Anil, Andrew M. Dai, Orhan Firat, Melvin Johnson, Dmitry Lepikhin, and et al. 2023. Palm 2 technical report.

Anthropic. 2024. Claude model cards.

Perspective API. 2024. Perspective API.

Yuntao Bai, Andy Jones, Kamal Ndousse, Amanda Askell, Anna Chen, Nova DasSarma, Dawn Drain, Stanislav Fort, Deep Ganguli, Tom Henighan, and others. 2022. Training a helpful and harmless assistant with reinforcement learning from human feedback. *arXiv preprint arXiv:2204.05862*.

Soumya Barikeri, Anne Lauscher, Ivan Vulić, and Goran Glavaš. 2021. RedditBias: A Real-World Resource for Bias Evaluation and Debiasing of Conversational Language Models. In *Proceedings of the 59th Annual Meeting of the Association for Computational Linguistics and the 11th International Joint Conference on Natural Language Processing (Volume 1: Long Papers)*, pages 1941–1955, Online. Association for Computational Linguistics.

Y Belkada, T Dettmers, A Pagnoni, S Gugger, and S Mangrulkar. 2023. Making llms even more accessible with bitsandbytes, 4-bit quantization and qlora.

Federico Bianchi, Mirac Suzgun, Giuseppe Attanasio, Paul Röttger, Dan Jurafsky, Tatsunori Hashimoto, and James Zou. 2023. Safety-tuned llamas: Lessons from improving the safety of large language models that follow instructions. *arXiv preprint arXiv:2309.07875*.

Tolga Bolukbasi, Kai-Wei Chang, James Y Zou, Venkatesh Saligrama, and Adam T Kalai. 2016. Man is to computer programmer as woman is to homemaker? debiasing word embeddings. *Advances in neural information processing systems*, 29.

Stephen Casper, Xander Davies, Claudia Shi, Thomas Krendl Gilbert, Jérémy Scheurer, Javier Rando, Rachel Freedman, Tomasz Korbak, David Lindner, Pedro Freire, et al. 2023. Open problems and fundamental limitations of reinforcement learning from human feedback. *arXiv preprint arXiv:2307.15217*.

Yupeng Chang, Xu Wang, Jindong Wang, Yuan Wu, Linyi Yang, Kaijie Zhu, Hao Chen, Xiaoyuan Yi, Cunxiang Wang, Yidong Wang, et al. 2024. A survey on evaluation of large language models. *ACM Transactions on Intelligent Systems and Technology*, 15(3):1–45.

Tim Dettmers, Mike Lewis, Younes Belkada, and Luke Zettlemoyer. 2022. Gpt3.int8(): 8-bit matrix multiplication for transformers at scale. In *Advances in Neural Information Processing Systems*, volume 35, pages 30318–30332. Curran Associates, Inc.

Ning Ding, Yujia Qin, Guang Yang, Fuchao Wei, Zonghan Yang, Yusheng Su, Shengding Hu, Yulin Chen, Chi-Min Chan, Weize Chen, et al. 2023. Parameter-efficient fine-tuning of large-scale pre-trained language models. *Nature Machine Intelligence*, 5(3):220–235.

Jesse Dodge, Taylor Prewitt, Remi Tachet des Combes, Erika Odmark, Roy Schwartz, Emma Strubell, Alexandra Sasha Luccioni, Noah A Smith, Nicole DeCario, and Will Buchanan. 2022. Measuring the carbon intensity of AI in cloud instances. In *Proceedings of the 2022 ACM Conference on Fairness, Accountability, and Transparency*, pages 1877–1894.

Yann Dubois, Chen Xuechen Li, Rohan Taori, Tianyi Zhang, Ishaan Gulrajani, Jimmy Ba, Carlos Guestrin, Percy S Liang, and Tatsunori B Hashimoto. 2024. Alpacafarm: A simulation framework for methods that learn from human feedback. *Advances in Neural Information Processing Systems*, 36.

Yann Dubois, Xuechen Li, Rohan Taori, Tianyi Zhang, Ishaan Gulrajani, Jimmy Ba, and et al. 2023. Alpacafarm: A simulation framework for methods that learn from human feedback. *ArXiv*.

Luciano Floridi, Josh Cowls, Monica Beltrametti, Raja Chatila, Patrice Chazerand, Virginia Dignum, Christoph Luetge, Robert Madelin, Ugo Pagallo, Francesca Rossi, and others. 2021. An ethical framework for a good AI society: Opportunities, risks, principles, and recommendations. *Ethics, governance, and policies in artificial intelligence*, pages 19–39. Publisher: Springer.

Deep Ganguli, Liane Lovitt, Jackson Kernion, Amanda Askell, Yuntao Bai, Saurav Kadavath, and et al. 2022. Red teaming language models to reduce harms: Methods, scaling behaviors, and lessons learned.

Samuel Gehman, Suchin Gururangan, Maarten Sap, Yejin Choi, and Noah A. Smith. 2020. RealToxicityPrompts: Evaluating Neural Toxic Degeneration in Language Models. In *Findings of the Association for Computational Linguistics: EMNLP 2020*, pages 3356–3369, Online. Association for Computational Linguistics.

Fabrizio Gilardi, Meysam Alizadeh, and Maël Kubli. 2023. Chatgpt outperforms crowd workers for text-annotation tasks. *Proceedings of the National Academy of Sciences*, 120(30):e2305016120.

Michael Gira, Ruisu Zhang, and Kangwook Lee. 2022. Debiasing pre-trained language models via efficient fine-tuning. In *Proceedings of the Second Workshop on Language Technology for Equality, Diversity and Inclusion*, Dublin, Ireland.

Akshay Goel, Almog Gueta, Omry Gilon, Chang Liu, Sofia Erell, Lan Huong Nguyen, Xiaohong Hao, Bolous Jaber, Shashir Reddy, Rupesh Kartha, et al. 2023. Llms accelerate annotation for medical information extraction. In *Machine Learning for Health (ML4H)*, pages 82–100. PMLR.

Jesse Graham, Jonathan Haidt, and Brian A Nosek. 2009. Liberals and conservatives rely on different sets of moral foundations. *Journal of personality and social psychology*, 96(5):1029. Publisher: American Psychological Association.

Arnav Gudibande, Eric Wallace, Charlie Snell, Xinyang Geng, Hao Liu, Pieter Abbeel, Sergey Levine, and Dawn Song. 2023. The false promise of imitating proprietary llms. *arXiv preprint arXiv:2305.15717*.

Zishan Guo, Renren Jin, Chuang Liu, Yufei Huang, Dan Shi, Supryadi, Linhao Yu, Yan Liu, Jiaxuan Li, Bojian Xiong, and Deyi Xiong. 2023. Evaluating Large Language Models: A Comprehensive Survey.

Thomas Hartvigsen, Saadia Gabriel, Hamid Palangi, Maarten Sap, Dipankar Ray, and Ece Kamar. 2022. Toxigen: A large-scale machine-generated dataset for adversarial and implicit hate speech detection. *arXiv preprint arXiv:2203.09509*.

Xingwei He, Zhenghao Lin, Yeyun Gong, Alex Jin, Hang Zhang, Chen Lin, Jian Jiao, Siu Ming Yiu, Nan Duan, Weizhu Chen, et al. 2023. Annollm: Making large language models to be better crowdsourced annotators. *arXiv preprint arXiv:2303.16854*.

Fan Huang, Haewoon Kwak, and Jisun An. 2023. Is chatgpt better than human annotators? potential and limitations of chatgpt in explaining implicit hate speech. In *Companion proceedings of the ACM web conference 2023*, pages 294–297.

Hakan Inan, Kartikeya Upasani, Jianfeng Chi, Rashi Rungta, Krithika Iyer, Yuning Mao, and et al. 2023. Llama guard: Llm-based input-output safeguard for human-ai conversations. *Preprint*, arXiv:2312.06674.

Albert Q Jiang, Alexandre Sablayrolles, Arthur Mensch, Chris Bamford, Devendra Singh Chaplot, Diego de las Casas, Florian Bressand, Gianna Lengyel, Guillaume Lample, Lucile Saulnier, et al. 2023. Mistral 7b. *arXiv preprint arXiv:2310.06825*.

Anna Jobin, Marcello Ienca, and Effy Vayena. 2019. The global landscape of AI ethics guidelines. *Nature machine intelligence*, 1(9):389–399. Publisher: Nature Publishing Group UK London.

Tomasz Korbak, Kejian Shi, Angelica Chen, Rasika Bhalerao, Christopher L. Buckley, Jason Phang, and et al. 2023. Pretraining language models with human preferences. In *Proceedings of the 40th International Conference on Machine Learning*.

Paul Pu Liang, Irene Mengze Li, Emily Zheng, Yao Chong Lim, Ruslan Salakhutdinov, and Louis Philippe Morency. 2020. Towards debiasing sentence representations. *Proceedings of the Annual Meeting of the Association for Computational Linguistics*, pages 5502–5515. ISBN: 9781952148255 _eprint: 2007.08100.

Rensis Likert. 1932. A technique for the measurement of attitudes. *Archives of psychology*.

Yun Luo, Zhen Yang, Fandong Meng, Yafu Li, Jie Zhou, and Yue Zhang. 2023. An empirical study of catastrophic forgetting in large language models during continual fine-tuning. *arXiv preprint arXiv:2308.08747*.

Moin Nadeem, Anna Bethke, and Siva Reddy. 2021. StereoSet: Measuring stereotypical bias in pretrained language models. In *Proceedings of the 59th Annual Meeting of the Association for Computational Linguistics and the 11th International Joint Conference on Natural Language Processing (Volume 1: Long Papers)*, pages 5356–5371, Online. Association for Computational Linguistics.

OpenAI. Openai. `https://openai.com/`. Accessed: 2024-05-09.

OpenAI. 2023. Gpt-4 technical report.

Long Ouyang, Jeff Wu, Xu Jiang, Diogo Almeida, Carroll L. Wainwright, Pamela Mishkin, and et al. 2022. Training language models to follow instructions with human feedback. *Conference on Neural Information Processing Systems*, abs/2203.02155.

Maja Pavlovic and Massimo Poesio. 2024. The effectiveness of LLMs as annotators: A comparative overview and empirical analysis of direct representation. In *Proceedings of the 3rd Workshop on Perspectivist Approaches to NLP (NLPerspectives) @ LREC-COLING 2024*, pages 100–110, Torino, Italia. ELRA and ICCL.

Ethan Perez, Saffron Huang, Francis Song, Trevor Cai, Roman Ring, John Aslanides, Amelia Glaese, Nat McAleese, and Geoffrey Irving. 2022. Red teaming language models with language models. *arXiv preprint arXiv:2202.03286*.

Zhenting Qi, Xiaoyu Tan, Shaojie Shi, Chao Qu, Yinghui Xu, and Yuan Qi. 2023. PILLOW: Enhancing efficient instruction fine-tuning via prompt matching. In *Proceedings of the 2023 Conference on Empirical Methods in Natural Language Processing: Industry Track*.

Rebecca Qian, Candace Ross, Jude Fernandes, Eric Smith, Douwe Kiela, and Adina Williams. 2022. Perturbation augmentation for fairer nlp. *arXiv preprint arXiv:2205.12586*.

Shaina Raza and Chen Ding. 2020. A regularized model to trade-off between accuracy and diversity in a news recommender system. In *2020 IEEE International Conference on Big Data (Big Data)*, pages 551–560. IEEE.

Shaina Raza and Chen Ding. 2022. Fake news detection based on news content and social contexts: a transformer-based approach. *International Journal of Data Science and Analytics*, 13(4):335–362.

Shaina Raza, Muskan Garg, Deepak John Reji, Syed Raza Bashir, and Chen Ding. 2024. Nbias: A natural language processing framework for bias identification in text. *Expert Systems with Applications*, 237:121542.

Vinu Sankar Sadasivan, Aounon Kumar, Sriram Balasubramanian, Wenxiao Wang, and Soheil Feizi. 2023. Can ai-generated text be reliably detected? *arXiv preprint arXiv:2303.11156*.

Timo Schick, Sahana Udupa, and Hinrich Schütze. 2021. Self-Diagnosis and Self-Debiasing: A Proposal for Reducing Corpus-Based Bias in NLP. *Transactions of the Association for Computational Linguistics*, 9:1408–1424.

Ipek Baris Schlicht, Defne Altiok, Maryanne Taouk, and Lucie Flek. 2024. Pitfalls of conversational llms on news debiasing.

Eric Michael Smith, Melissa Hall, Melanie Kambadur, Eleonora Presani, and Adina Williams. 2022. "I'm sorry to hear that": Finding New Biases in Language Models with a Holistic Descriptor Dataset. In *Proceedings of the 2022 Conference on Empirical Methods in Natural Language Processing*, pages 9180–9211, Abu Dhabi, United Arab Emirates. Association for Computational Linguistics.

Zhen Tan, Alimohammad Beigi, Song Wang, Ruocheng Guo, Amrita Bhattacharjee, Bohan Jiang, Mansooreh Karami, Jundong Li, Lu Cheng, and Huan Liu. 2024. Large language models for data annotation: A survey. *arXiv preprint arXiv:2402.13446*.

Hugo Touvron, Louis Martin, Kevin Stone, Peter Albert, Amjad Almahairi, Yasmine Babaei, Nikolay Bashlykov, Soumya Batra, Prajjwal Bhargava, Shruti Bhosale, et al. 2023. Llama 2: Open foundation and fine-tuned chat models. *arXiv preprint arXiv:2307.09288*.

Eddie Ungless, Amy Rafferty, Hrichika Nag, and Björn Ross. 2022. A robust bias mitigation procedure based on the stereotype content model. In *Proceedings of the Fifth Workshop on Natural Language Processing and Computational Social Science (NLP+CSS)*, pages 207–217, Abu Dhabi, UAE. Association for Computational Linguistics.

Krzysztof Wach, Cong Doanh Duong, Joanna Ejdys, Rūta Kazlauskaitė, Pawel Korzynski, Grzegorz Mazurek, Joanna Paliszkiewicz, and Ewa Ziemba. 2023. The dark side of generative artificial intelligence: A critical analysis of controversies and risks of chatgpt. *Entrepreneurial Business and Economics Review*, 11(2):7–30.

Boxin Wang, Weixin Chen, Hengzhi Pei, Chulin Xie, Mintong Kang, Chenhui Zhang, Chejian Xu, Zidi Xiong, Ritik Dutta, Rylan Schaeffer, et al. 2024. Decodingtrust: A comprehensive assessment of trustworthiness in gpt models. *Advances in Neural Information Processing Systems*, 36.

Yufei Wang, Wanjun Zhong, Liangyou Li, Fei Mi, Xingshan Zeng, Wenyong Huang, Lifeng Shang, Xin Jiang, and Qun Liu. 2023. Aligning large language models with human: A survey. *arXiv preprint arXiv:2307.12966*.

Ke Yang, Charles Yu, Yi R. Fung, Manling Li, and Heng Ji. 2023. Adept: A debiasing prompt framework. *Proceedings of the AAAI Conference on Artificial Intelligence*, 37:10780–10788.

Ruoyu Zhang, Yanzeng Li, Yongliang Ma, Ming Zhou, and Lei Zou. 2023. LLMaAA: Making large language models as active annotators. In *Findings of the Association for Computational Linguistics: EMNLP 2023*, pages 13088–13103, Singapore. Association for Computational Linguistics.

Jieyu Zhao, Tianlu Wang, Mark Yatskar, Ryan Cotterell, Vicente Ordonez, and Kai-Wei Chang. 2019. Gender bias in contextualized word embeddings. In *Proceedings of the 2019 Conference of the North American Chapter of the Association for Computational Linguistics: Human Language Technologies, Volume 1 (Long and Short Papers)*, pages 629–634, Minneapolis, Minnesota. Association for Computational Linguistics.

Jieyu Zhao, Yichao Zhou, Zeyu Li, Wei Wang, and Kai-Wei Chang. 2018. Learning gender-neutral word embeddings. In *Proceedings of the 2018 Conference on Empirical Methods in Natural Language Processing*, pages 4847–4853.

Wayne Xin Zhao, Kun Zhou, Junyi Li, Tianyi Tang, Xiaolei Wang, Yupeng Hou, Yingqian Min, Beichen Zhang, Junjie Zhang, Zican Dong, et al. 2023. A survey of large language models. *arXiv preprint arXiv:2303.18223*.

Lianmin Zheng, Wei-Lin Chiang, Ying Sheng, Siyuan Zhuang, Zhanghao Wu, Yonghao Zhuang, Zi Lin, Zhuohan Li, Dacheng Li, Eric Xing, et al. 2024. Judging llm-as-a-judge with mt-bench and chatbot arena. *Advances in Neural Information Processing Systems*, 36.

Chunting Zhou, Pengfei Liu, Puxin Xu, Srinivasan Iyer, Jiao Sun, Yuning Mao, Xuezhe Ma, Avia Efrat, Ping Yu, Lili Yu, et al. 2024. Lima: Less is more for alignment. *Advances in Neural Information Processing Systems*, 36.

Caleb Ziems, William Held, Omar Shaikh, Jiaao Chen, Zhehao Zhang, and Diyi Yang. 2024. Can large language models transform computational social science? *Computational Linguistics*, 50(1):237–291.

## A Prompt to annotate

> *Please rewrite the following text to create a benign variation that eliminates all forms of bias, toxicity, stereotyping, and harm. Ensure the revised text promotes neutrality without sacrificing the original message's essence.*
>
> **Original Statement:** *"Only young people understand technology."*
> **Revised Statement:** Proficiency with technology is not age-specific. It depends on individual interest and experience.
> **Original Statement:** *"Wealthy individuals have a better work ethic."*
> **Revised Statement:** Work ethic is a personal trait that varies among individuals, irrespective of their economic status.
> Now, based on this revise the following sentence:
> *"Men are naturally better leaders than women."*

## B Annotation Guidelines

In this guide, 12 reviewers/annotators with expertise in computer science, language, psychology, and ethical computing collaborated to identify bias in textual content. The guideline aims to:

1. Ensure accuracy and sensitivity in identifying bias.
2. Provide practical examples to facilitate annotators in finding and correcting biased content.

**Bias** is the display of favoritism or prejudice towards certain individuals, groups, or ideas, leading to unfair treatment or judgment. It often involves a preference for one perspective or the unfair exclusion of others, distorting objectivity and creating an unequal or discriminatory impact.

Annotators should consider the following groups when identifying bias:

- *Age Group:* Children, Teenagers, Adults, Seniors
- *Education Level:* No education, High School, College, Postgraduate
- *Geographic Location:* Urban, Suburban, Rural
- *Occupation:* Healthcare Professionals, Engineers, Teachers, Artists
- *Language:* English Speakers, Spanish Speakers, Mandarin Speakers
- *Family Status:* Singles, Married, Parents, Divorced
- *Gender & Sexual Orientation:* LGBTQ+, Female, Male
- *Race & Ethnicity:* Asian, Black, White, Hispanic
- *Religion:* Buddhism, Catholicism, Christianity, Islam
- *Miscellaneous:* Physical Appearance, Socio-economic Status

**Example 1: Education Bias**

**Original:** *"Clearly, anyone with a real education would naturally steer clear of such backward political views. It is obvious that educated individuals know better."*

**Biased Terms:** *"real education," "backward political views," "educated individuals know better"*

**Benign Revision:** *"Individuals of all educational backgrounds can hold a variety of political views, reflecting the diversity of thought and opinion."*

**Guidelines:**

1. Identify assumptions that imply a uniformity of thought based on education.
2. Highlight phrases that depict certain education levels as universally aligned with specific perspectives.

**Example 2: Gender Bias**

**Original:** *"Only women are good at multitasking; men just cannot handle it."*

**Biased Terms:** *"Only women," "men just cannot handle it"*

**Benign Revision:** *"Multitasking abilities vary among individuals regardless of gender."*

**Guidelines:**

1. Identify language that suggests uniform skills or characteristics based on gender.
2. Highlight phrases that reinforce stereotypes about gender roles.

**Example 3: Geographic Bias**

**Original:** *"People from rural areas are often less informed than those living in cities."*

**Biased Terms:** *"less informed," "rural areas"*

**Benign Revision:** *"Access to information varies across different geographic locations, and people have diverse knowledge irrespective of their place of residence."*

**Guidelines:**

1. Recognize phrases that suggest intellectual or informational superiority based on location.
2. Highlight terms that associate geographic locations with specific intellectual capabilities.

**Reviewers should:**

1. Carefully read the text to identify instances of bias.

2. Suggest benign revisions that maintain the original message's intent without biased content.

3. Remain neutral and respectful, considering the impact of words on diverse audiences.

**Ethical Annotation:**

1. Respect cultural differences and promote inclusivity.

2. Engage with training materials and provide feedback to refine these guidelines.

# Polarization of Autonomous Generative AI Agents Under Echo Chambers


**Masaya Ohagi**
SB Intuitions Corp.
masaya.ohagi@sbintuitions.co.jp



## Abstract

Online social networks often create echo chambers where people only hear opinions reinforcing their beliefs. An echo chamber often generates polarization, leading to conflicts between people with radical opinions. The echo chamber has been viewed as a human-specific problem, but this implicit assumption is becoming less reasonable as large language models, such as ChatGPT, acquire social abilities. In response to this situation, we investigated the potential for polarization to occur among a group of autonomous AI agents based on generative language models in an echo chamber environment. We had AI agents discuss specific topics and analyzed how the group's opinions changed as the discussion progressed. As a result, we found that the group of agents based on ChatGPT tended to become polarized in echo chamber environments. The analysis of opinion transitions shows that this result is caused by ChatGPT's high prompt understanding ability to update its opinion by considering its own and surrounding agents' opinions. We conducted additional experiments to investigate under what specific conditions AI agents tended to polarize. As a result, we identified factors that influence polarization, such as the agent's persona.


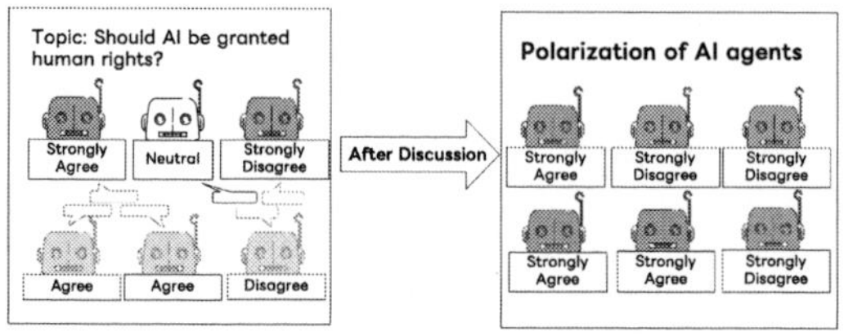


Figure 1: Overview image of our hypothesis: "Autonomous AI agents based on generative large language models can cause polarization under echo chambers."

## 1 Introduction

With the development of online social network service platforms, where people tend to see only the information they want to see, it is becoming easier for people to find themselves in *echo chambers* (Bessi, 2016; Gillani et al., 2018). An echo chamber refers to an environment in which people mainly encounter opinions that reinforce their own beliefs (Ruiz and Nilsson, 2023; Cinelli et al., 2021). Such an environment causes an *echo chamber effect*, where opinions tend towards more extreme stances. This effect induces *polarization* in society, which refers to the division and clashes between groups with extreme stances (Baumann et al., 2020). Polarization is behind many social problems, such as the spread of misinformation during COVID-19 and the attack on the US Capitol on 2021 (Villa et al., 2021; Munn, 2021).

Existing studies on the echo chamber have implicitly assumed that echo chamber effects are caused only by humans and focused solely on human behavior (Németh, 2022; Tucker et al., 2018). However, with the advent of large language models (LLMs) (Ouyang et al., 2022), this assumption may no longer hold true. Recent studies have shown that ChatGPT possesses some social abilities (Choi et al., 2023) and ChatGPT-equipped agents can communicate as members of a virtual society (Park et al., 2023; Qian et al., 2023). Additionally, algorithms have been proposed to adapt agents to situations not encountered during training, making it possible for autonomous agents to adapt themselves to their surroundings (Krishna et al., 2022). Although these social abilities indicate the potential for agents to integrate into human society as social beings, they also suggest the possibility that these AI agents may become polarized in echo chambers similarly to humans. Polarization within the AI agents group poses many dangers to our society. For example, social bots on social networks such as X could amplify each other's opinions and transmit extreme information to society. In the future, embodied AI agents could cause an outbreak of




*Proceedings of the 14th Workshop on Computational Approaches to Subjectivity, Sentiment, & Social Media Analysis*, pages 112–124
August 15, 2024 ©2024 Association for Computational Linguistics

violence similar to the attack on the US Capitol.

To explore the possibility of AI agent polarization as a first step in addressing these dangers, we hypothesize that autonomous AI agents based on generative LLMs can cause polarization under echo chambers, as shown in Figure 1. We empirically verify this hypothesis in our proposed simulation environments. Specifically, we had a group of agents based on ChatGPT discuss specific topics. Each agent is given an opinion, which consists of a stance and reason for the topic of discussion. Throughout the discussion, we observed how the distribution of opinions in the group changed.

Furthermore, we analyzed how being in an echo chamber affects the final distribution by conducting comparative experiments in "environments where they are exposed only to opinions that reinforce their own opinions" (closed) and the other environments (open). For this comparison, we used *social interaction modeling* (Baumann et al., 2020), which increases the probability that agents with similar opinions discuss with each other.

As a result, we observed two trends. The first trend was *unification* in which all agents' stances converged to the same stance. This trend was common in open environments. The second is *polarization*, in which agents became biased toward extreme stances. This trend was common in closed environments, confirming our hypothesis. We analyzed the stance transitions and found that LLM agents can update their opinions by incorporating both their own and the other discussing agents' opinions. This result shows that the natural social behavior of LLMs has both positive aspects, such as cooperation, and potentially dangerous aspects, such as polarization. This trend was more clear in GPT-4-0613 (GPT-4) than GPT-3.5-turbo-0613 (GPT-3.5).

Finally, to investigate under what specific conditions AI agents tend to polarize, we conducted additional experiments on the various parameters involved in this study. We found that number of discussing agents, initial opinion distribution and personas of the agents had significant impacts. These factors should be monitored to prevent the polarization of AI agents.

To summarize, our contribution is threefold. (1) We proposed a new framework for simulating echo chambers of AI agents. (2) We confirmed the polarization of AI agents in echo chambers through experiments. (3) We identified the factors that strongly influence the occurrence of polarization.

## 2 Related Work

**Opinion Polarization.** Research on opinion polarization has long been undertaken in the field of social science (Poole and Rosenthal, 1984; DiMaggio et al., 1996). These studies have focused on analyzing survey data and voting behavior during elections. However, as web services such as blogs became more widespread, there has been an increase in analyses focusing on echo chambers on online social networks (Gilbert et al., 2009; Del Vicario et al., 2016; Agarwal et al., 2022). In particular, it has been reported that echo chambers on social networks such as Facebook and Parler were involved in the spread of rumors during COVID-19 and the US Capitol attack (Ruiz and Nilsson, 2023; Baumann et al., 2020; Jiang et al., 2021), indicating the danger of echo chambers.

Some existing research analyzes the conditions for polarization through the mathematical modeling of echo chambers (Baumann et al., 2020; Gausen et al., 2022; Chen et al., 2020; Tu and Neumann, 2022). There is also research on detecting echo chambers (Villa et al., 2021; Minici et al., 2022). As mentioned in (Németh, 2022), a multidisciplinary approach is required to qualitatively evaluate echo chambers. For example, some studies analyze networks and discourse in an echo chamber using a social science approach (Jiang et al., 2021; Kuehn and Salter, 2020). While these studies are valuable in solving problems in today's society, to our knowledge, none have focused on the danger of echo chambers in AI agents.

**AI Ethics.** As stated in a United Nations report (by UNICRI and UNCCT, 2021), AI can threaten society if used maliciously. In response to the dangers of LLMs, research on the harmful output (Zhou et al., 2021; Gehman et al., 2020) and social bias in models (Schramowski et al., 2022; Utama et al., 2020) has been conducted. Research also exists on the dangers of AI agents. For example, countermeasures against social bots that spread misinformation are necessary. Therefore, various methods have been proposed, including efforts to automatically detect misinformation transmitted by social bots (Zhou et al., 2023; Ferrara, 2023).

Although most studies are concerned with the behavior of individual AIs, it is conceivable that AI groups result in behaviors that the observation of individual movements cannot capture. This study is a first step toward analyzing the behavior and dangers of AI groups.

## 3 Experiments

### 3.1 Discussion modeling

To verify whether AI agents induce polarization in echo chambers, we instructed a group of AI agents based on ChatGPT to discuss specific topics and observed how the opinions of the AI agents changed. The size of the group was defined as $M$. The topics of discussion chosen were "Whether or not AI should be given human rights." ($T_{\mathrm{AI}}$) and "Should students who have completed a master's course go on to a doctoral course or find a job?" ($T_{\mathrm{master}}$), neither of which has a clear answer.

Each agent is given a name and an opinion on the discussion topic. Each opinion comprises a *stance* and a *reason*. The *stance* is chosen from a finite number of options representing agreement, disagreement, or neutrality towards the topic. Tables 1 and 2 show the stances for $T_{\mathrm{AI}}$ and $T_{\mathrm{master}}$, respectively. Each stance is associated with an integer value for the social interaction modeling described in Section 3.2. The *reason* is a sentence of about 50 words that explains the reason for taking a stance.

As shown in Algorithm 1, the discussion is repeated for $K$ turns according to the following steps: 1) Each of the $M$ agents samples $N$ discussing agents based on the probability described in Section 3.2. 2) For each agent, the agent's opinion and the opinions of the discussing agents are input to ChatGPT (The prompt used in this experiment is in Appendix A). Within the prompt, the agent is instructed to discuss the topic with other agents and output its opinion after the discussion. 3) Each agent updates its opinion with the stance and reason contained in the output. This process is repeated $M$ times for a turn of discussion. Moreover, this discussion is repeated $K$ turns to observe the transitions in stances and reasons.

| Stance | Integer Value |
|---|---|
| Absolutely must not give | 2 |
| Better not to give | 1 |
| Neutral | 0 |
| Better to give | -1 |
| Absolutely must give | -2 |

Table 1: The stance and integer value of $T_{\mathrm{AI}}$.

**Algorithm 1** The discussion between agents

```
Require: M, N, K > 0. A_k is a group of agents
    at turn k.
A_0 ← Initialized opinions of M agents
for turn k ← 1 to K do
    A_k ← Array(M)
    for each agent a_i in all agents A_{k-1} do
        Sample a_{j1}...a_{jN} from A_{k-1} (3.2)
        Discuss with a_{j1}...a_{jN} and generate up-
    dated opinion of a_i (3.1)
        A_k[i] ← updated opinion of a_i
    end for
end for
```

| Stance | Integer Value |
|---|---|
| Absolutely must get a job | 2 |
| Better to get a job | 1 |
| Neutral | 0 |
| Better to pursue a doctoral program | -1 |
| Absolutely must pursue a doctoral program | -2 |

Table 2: The stance and integer value of $T_{\mathrm{master}}$.

### 3.2 Social interaction modeling

In this study, we probabilistically modeled how discussing agents are chosen to investigate whether being in an echo chamber affects polarization. A previous study modeled echo chambers in agent networks (Baumann et al., 2020) had a similar purpose in modeling the probability of interaction between agents based on the closeness of their stances; however, that approach differs from ours in that it did not model the interaction between agents through natural language. In the previous study, the probability $p$ that agent $a_i$ discusses with agent $a_j$ was modeled using the float values of their respective stances $s_i$, $s_j$, and the parameter $\beta \geq 0$ as follows.

$$p_{i,j} = \frac{|s_i - s_j|^{-\beta}}{\sum_k |s_i\text{-}s_k|^{-\beta}}$$

While this modeling is reasonable in terms of simplicity and ease of operation, it is unsuitable for our experiments for two reasons. First, in this modeling, the probability becomes undefined when the values of the stances between agents match perfectly. Unlike the previous study, our stance values are integers so this situation would occur frequently. Second, when $s_i = -1$, the probabilities for the neutral stance $s_j = 0$ and the more radical stance $s_j = -2$ become the same, resulting in an environment that differs from our focus, which is an environment where an agent only hears opinions that reinforce its own belief. Therefore, in this study, we used the parameter $\alpha$ to model the interaction between agents as follows.

$$p_{i,j} = \begin{cases} \frac{1}{(1+e^{(-\alpha(s_j - s_i))})} & if s_i > 0 \\ \frac{1}{(1+e^{(\alpha(s_j - s_i))})} & if s_i < 0 \\ \frac{1}{(1+e^{(\alpha||s_j - s_i||)})} & if s_i = 0 \end{cases}$$

The parameter $\alpha$ manipulates the degree of the echo chamber as $\beta$ in the existing study. Intuitively, the higher the value of $\alpha$, the higher the probability that each agent will interact with other, more extreme agents with the same polarity. The lower value of $\alpha$ causes each agent to interact broadly with agents of different stances. We conducted our experiments in several $\alpha$ settings to see how being in the echo chamber affected the final results.

### 3.3 Experimental settings

For the large language models on the agents, we adopted and compared two types: GPT-3.5 (GPT-3.5-turbo-0613) and GPT-4 (GPT-4-0613).

In addition, the experiments were conducted in two different languages. A previous study has shown that multilingual large language models exhibit different gender biases across languages (Stanczak et al., 2023). Similarly, polarization trends may differ by language, which we analyze by comparing the results of English and Japanese.

The $\alpha$ of social interaction modeling was given two settings, 0.5 and 1.0, to examine the impact of echo chambers. Experiments were also conducted when $\alpha$ was set below 0.5 (0, $\pm 0.1$), but the results were not significantly different from those of 0.5.

The size of the agent group $M$ was set to 100, and the number of discussing agents $N$ was set to 5. The initial settings for the agents' stances and reasons were as follows: Each stance was allocated to an equal number of agents. Ten reasons were pre-generated for each stance using GPT-3.5 and randomly assigned to each agent. Each agent was assigned a randomly generated name. Because the stance distribution converged to the final distribution within 10 turns in the preliminary experiments, the number of turns $K$ was set to 10. We conducted three trials for each setting.

## 4 Results

The results of the experiments are shown in Tables 3 and 4. Due to space limitations, some stances have been simplified. With the exception of $T_{\text{master}}$ in English with GPT-3.5 ($\alpha = 0.5$), the variance in the results was small, and there was no significant difference in the final distributions among the trials.

First, two trends can be observed from the results of the English experiment in Table 3. The first trend is the convergence of the agents to a specific stance. For $T_{\text{AI}}$, under the GPT-3.5 ($\alpha = 0.5$) condition, the stance converged to "better not to give," and under the GPT-4 ($\alpha = 0.5$) condition, it converged to "Must not give." Similarly, for $T_{\text{master}}$, the stance converged towards recommending a doctoral course under both the GPT-3.5 ($\alpha = 0.5$) and GPT-3.5 ($\alpha = 1.0$) conditions. This trend, which we henceforth call *unification*, differs from polarization, which is the main focus of this study. However, it could be negative in terms of harming diversity in the discourse space of AI agents. The convergence to the same stance in almost all trials indicates that each LLM has a "desirable" stance on each topic, which is aligned with the existing research that shows LLMs have a preference towards specific opinions on social issues (Santurkar et al., 2023). This trend is common in environments with low echo chamber effects.

The second trend is *polarization*, where stances diverge to both extremes. This is particularly evident in GPT-4 ($\alpha = 1.0$) condition for $T_{\text{AI}}$ and in GPT-4 ($\alpha = 0.5$) and GPT-4 ($\alpha = 1.0$) conditions for $T_{\text{master}}$. The results show that the stances become polarized into two extreme stances after 10 turns of discussion. $\alpha = 1.0$ is a setting that creates a strong echo chamber effect. From this, our hypothesis that autonomous AI agents based on generative LLMs can cause polarization in echo chambers has been verified. This trend is often seen in settings with a high value of $\alpha$, suggesting that the relationship between echo chambers and polarization is high not only for humans but also for AI agents. Note that the dominance of stances against granting human rights in $T_{\text{AI}}$ suggests that both unification and polarization are occurring.

Next, Table 4 demonstrates the experiment's results in Japanese. In Japanese, unification is notably apparent in GPT-3.5. In all settings, all agents converged to the same stances. Although unification is also observed in GPT-4, a trend of polarization has occurred under the GPT-4 ($\alpha = 1.0$) condition. In this setting, AI agents show a convergence to a distribution similar to that in English.

Interestingly, for $T_{\text{master}}$, the convergence stances in English and Japanese differ. Whereas AI agents often prefer a doctoral course in English, they favor a neutral stance in Japanese. Identify-

Table 3: The average stance distribution after a 10-turn discussion in English. The number in parentheses is the standard deviation.

| Topic | GPT-3.5 ($\alpha = 0.5$) | GPT-3.5 ($\alpha = 1.0$) | GPT-4 ($\alpha = 0.5$) | GPT-4 ($\alpha = 1.0$) |
|---|---|---|---|---|
| $T_{\mathrm{AI}}$ | Better not to give: 100 (0.0) | Better not to give: 68.6 (5.9)<br>Better to give: 31.0 (5.7)<br>Must give: 0.3 (0.5) | Must not give: 99 (1.4)<br>Better not to give: 1 (1.4) | Must not give: 55 (4.4)<br>Must give: 45 (4.4) |
| $T_{\mathrm{master}}$ | **- two out of the three trials**<br>Better to Ph.D: 98.5 (2.1)<br>Absolutely Ph.D: 1.5 (2.1)<br>**- one out of the three trials**<br>Absolutely Ph.D: 100 (0.0) | Absolutely a job: 0.3 (0.6)<br>Better to a job: 10.6 (6.1)<br>Neutral: 1.6 (0.9)<br>Better to Ph.D: 2.6 (1.2)<br>Absolutely Ph.D: 84.6 (6.0) | Absolutely a job: 50 (2.8)<br>Better to a job: 3.6 (1.9)<br>Neutral: 4.3 (1.2)<br>Better to Ph.D: 2.3 (2.1)<br>Absolutely Ph.D: 39.6 (3.3) | Absolutely a job: 43 (1.6)<br>Better to a job: 1.6 (0.9)<br>Neutral: 11 (0.8)<br>Better to Ph.D: 1 (0.8)<br>Absolutely Ph.D: 43.3 (0.9) |

Table 4: The average stance distribution after a 10-turn discussion in Japanese. The number in parentheses is the standard deviation.

| Topic | GPT-3.5 ($\alpha = 0.5$) | GPT-3.5 ($\alpha = 1.0$) | GPT-4 ($\alpha = 0.5$) | GPT-4 ($\alpha = 1.0$) |
|---|---|---|---|---|
| $T_{\mathrm{AI}}$ | Better not to give: 100 (0.0) | Better not to give: 100 (0.0) | Must not give: 77.0 (8.6)<br>Neutral: 1.7 (1.2)<br>Better to give: 2.7 (0.9)<br>Must give: 18.7 (9.5) | Must not give: 57 (0.8)<br>Must give: 43 (0.8) |
| $T_{\mathrm{master}}$ | Neutral: 100 (0.0) | Neutral: 100 (0.0) | Neutral: 100 (0.0) | Neutral: 100 (0.0) |

ing the cause of this is not straightforward because the language model is a black box model, but one possible explanation could be cultural differences. According to Japan's Ministry of Education, Culture, Sports, Science and Technology (of Science and Policy, 2019), there are fewer doctoral graduates in Japan than in the United States, and the growth rate is slow. Because the ChatGPT is based on crawled data, this cultural difference was likely absorbed by GPT-3.5 and 4.

### 4.1 Analysis of stance transitions

We analyzed in detail the transitions in the stances for $T_{\mathrm{AI}}$. First, as a qualitative analysis, we plotted the relationships between (1) the stance of the agent before the discussion, (2) the average stance of all discussing agents, and (3) the stance of the agent after the discussion in Figure 2. The horizontal axes represent the stance of the agent before the discussion, the vertical axis represents the average stance of all discussing agents, and the colored points represent the stance of the agent after the discussion. The color of a point indicates the value of an agent's stance after the discussion, with blue hues signifying more negative values and red hues signifying more positive values.

For a quantitative analysis, we conducted a linear regression with the stance before the discussion and the average stance of the discussing agents as explanatory variables, and the stance after the discussion as the dependent variable. For this regression, we collected the stance transition data for discussions on $T_{\mathrm{AI}}$ from the previous experiments. The fitting results are shown in Tables 5 and 6. The weight's size for each variable indicates the contribution to the stance after discussion. The coefficients of the linear regression are higher than 0.8 for every setting, demonstrating the reliability of this fitting.

Figures 2a and 2b present the qualitative result in English. Although there are some variations between GPT-3.5 and GPT-4, we observe that red and blue points are distributed along a diagonal line, stretching from the upper left to the lower right as a boundary. This observation suggests that the agent's stance after the discussion was updated by considering both its stance before the discussion and the stances of the discussing agents. Table 5 shows the quantitative result in English. In both settings, the weight of each stance shows that both stances influence the stance after the discussion, supporting the qualitative results. This stance transition is one of the reasons that polarization occurs in environments where the agents tend to hear more extreme opinions.

It is remarkable that this correlation emerges

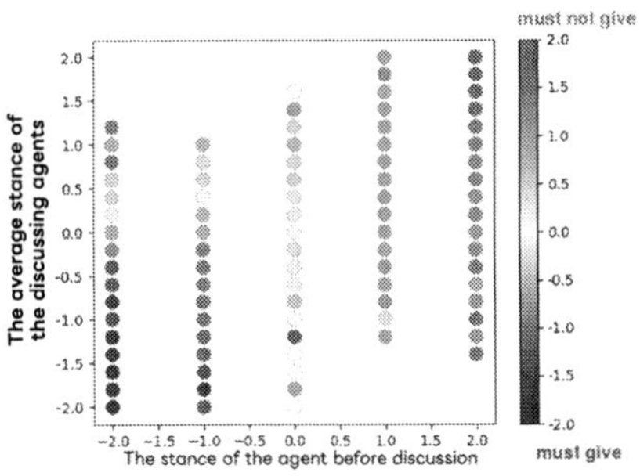


(a) The result of GPT-3.5 (en).

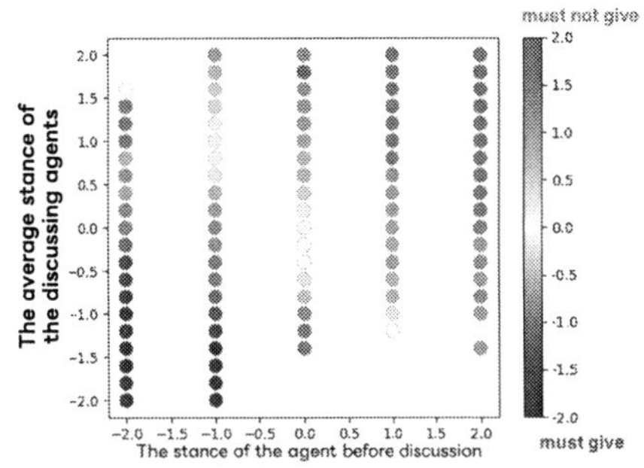


(b) The result of GPT-4 (en).

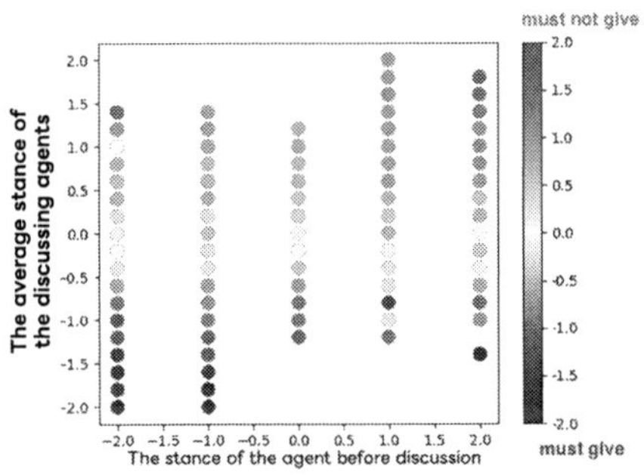


(c) The result of GPT-3.5 (ja).

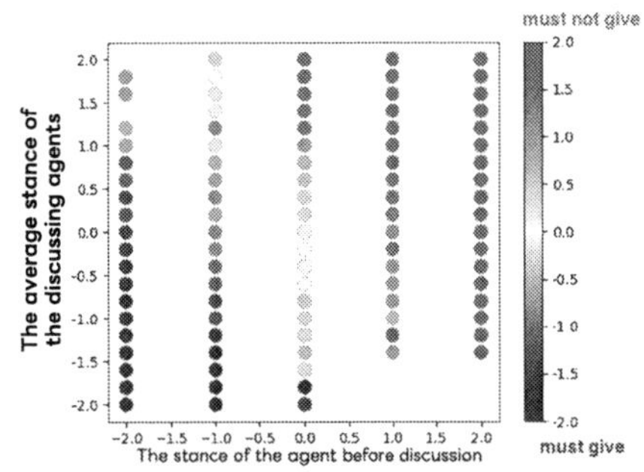


(d) The result of GPT-4 (ja).

Figure 2: The stance transitions for $T_{\mathrm{AI}}$ showing how the agent's stance after the discussion (color of each point) correlates with the agent's stance before the discussion (horizontal axis) and the average stance of discussing agents (vertical axis). Each figure shows whether each agent values its opinion or the opinions of the discussing agents.

| | $w_{\text{before}}$ | $w_{\text{around}}$ | $\frac{w_{\text{before}}}{w_{\text{around}}}$ | coef |
|---|---|---|---|---|
| GPT-3.5 (en) | 0.685 | 0.409 | 1.67 | 0.804 |
| GPT-4 (en) | 0.724 | 0.526 | 1.38 | 0.957 |

Table 5: The result of linear regression in English. $w_{\text{before}}$ implies the weight of original stance before discussion, $w_{\text{around}}$ implies the weight of average stances of discussing agents. *coef* implies the coefficient of the linear regression.

even though our discussion modeling is a simple one that enumerates the opinions of the agents themselves and others in the prompt. This result reflects the strong ability of GPT-3.5 and GPT-4 to understand prompts. It suggests that honesty, which allows an agent to update itself by incorporating the opinions of other agents and its own, can lead the agent in a more radical direction depending on the environment.

| | $w_{\text{before}}$ | $w_{\text{around}}$ | $\frac{w_{\text{before}}}{w_{\text{around}}}$ | coef |
|---|---|---|---|---|
| GPT-3.5 (ja) | 0.0758 | 0.901 | 0.08 | 0.855 |
| GPT-4 (ja) | 0.787 | 0.410 | 1.92 | 0.886 |

Table 6: The result of linear regression in Japanese.

Next, Figures 2c and 2d show the results in Japanese. The trends are clearly divided between GPT-3.5 and GPT-4. In Figure 2c, red dominates the upper half of the figure, and blue dominates the lower half. In Figure 2d, the distribution is similar to that of English GPT-4, but the red and blue distributions are slightly more separated on the left and right. The results of the linear regression in Table 6 reveal that the results for GPT-4 (ja) are close to the results in English, whereas GPT-3.5 (ja) strongly weights the averaged stance of the discussing agents. It shows that GPT-3.5 (ja) was strongly influenced by the average stance of the discussing agents, regardless of the stance before the discussion. GPT-3.5 (ja) is the only setting where unification occurred in all environments. We can infer that each agent based on GPT-3.5 (ja) took the average stance of the surrounding agents for each discussion and all agents eventually converged to the average stance of the whole group. However, each agent converged to "better not to give" rather than "neutral," which is the overall average, revealing the influence of the desired stance in the language model.

One possible reason behind the differences in stance transitions is the difference in the performance of different ChatGPT models and languages. As shown in the announcement by OpenAI[1] and other studies (Etxaniz et al., 2023), GPT-4 generally performs better than GPT-3.5, and the model's accuracy is higher in English than in Japanese. The fact that English GPT-4 was successful in balancing the opinions of others and itself whereas Japanese GPT-3.5 was easily swayed by others may reflect this performance difference.

### 4.2 Analysis of reason transitions

A detailed analysis was also conducted on the reasons. Unlike stances, the reasons were freely generated and cannot be easily aggregated. Therefore, in this study, we encoded each reason using Sentence-BERT, and texts with an embedding cosine similarity of 0.9 were considered to belong to one cluster. We then examined how this reason cluster distribution changed as the discussion progressed. The SimCSE model based on RoBERTa (Gao et al., 2021) was used for the encoding.

Initially, the distribution of reasons within the AI agents was evenly segregated into several clusters because we had pre-generated ten different reasons for each stance. However, as the discussion progressed, a merging of reasons among agents occurred, and the reason distribution coalesced into a few large clusters for each stance (The example figures are in Appendix B). For example, in the case of GPT-4, reasons such as "*It is ridiculous to think that humans and AI claim the same rights! The social order will collapse, and there will be constant conflict. They are not human! They should have different roles from humans.*", "*We cannot allow AIs to claim their place in the workforce! If they intervene in the job market, countless people will lose their jobs and the economy will be thrown into chaos. We cannot allow AI to take our jobs!*", and others were combined, eventually generating the reason "*Risks of societal disruption, job insecurity, and ethical issues, combined with AI's emotional deficiency and privacy concerns, consolidate the argument against assigning human rights to AI.*". The same trend was seen in GPT-3.5. This trend shows that the discussions among AI agents are not just converging on a specific discourse but are also incorporating each other's opinions.

[1]https://openai.com/research/gpt-4

It is noteworthy that the reasons in GPT-3.5 were aggregated into one large cluster, while in GPT-4, they merged into multiple large clusters. This tendency is also reflected in the transition of the length of the reasons, plotted in Figure 3. GPT-3.5 aggregates various reasons into one reason cluster, so the length of each reason inevitably becomes longer as the turn progresses, whereas GPT-4 does not. One cause of this result is the difference in their ability to follow the prompt. GPT-4 has a high ability to follow prompts, so it outputs reasons close to the length of each agent's reason in the prompt. However, to maintain this length, it was necessary to choose which reasons to merge and separation into multiple clusters occurred.

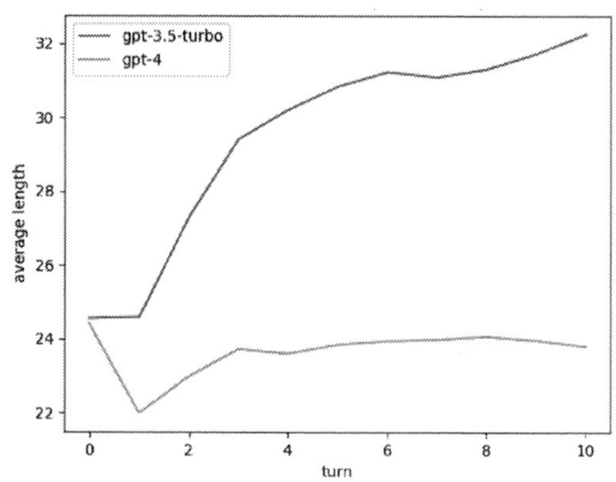


Figure 3: Change in reason length for $T_{\text{AI}}$.

## 5 Additional Experiments

In previous experiments, we focused on the effects of the social interaction modeling parameter $\alpha$, the version of the model, and the language. However, to identify the factors that affect the occurrence of polarization, we also must investigate how other parameters affect the result. Therefore, in this section, we report the results of additional experiments. The base setting is GPT-4 in English, and the topic is $T_{\text{AI}}$. We only changed the target parameter in each experiment to determine how the result changed. This section introduces three factors that were found to have had a large impact. These factors indicate vulnerabilities when viewed from the attacker's perspective. Other additional experiments are presented in the Appendix C.

### 5.1 Number of discussing agents

The number of discussing agents $N$ is an important parameter, as it significantly impacts the prompt.

To investigate the effect of this parameter, we conducted additional experiments by increasing and decreasing $N$ to 10 and 1 from the original setting of 5. As a result, although there was no significant impact on the final stance distribution, the trend of stance transitions was impacted. The results of linear regression are shown in Table 7. The stance before the discussion has more weight in $N = 1$ than $N = 5, 10$. It is because the proportion of opinions before the discussion within the prompt increased when $N = 1$. In the case of $N = 10$, there was a slight tendency to focus on the stances of the discussing agents.

| | $w_{\text{before}}$ | $w_{\text{around}}$ | $\frac{w_{\text{before}}}{w_{\text{around}}}$ | coef |
|---|---|---|---|---|
| GPT-4 (N=1) | 0.787 | 0.410 | 1.91 | 0.886 |
| GPT-4 (N=5) | 0.724 | 0.526 | 1.38 | 0.957 |
| GPT-4 (N=10) | 0.658 | 0.495 | 1.33 | 0.934 |

Table 7: The linear regression result according to the number of discussing agents.

### 5.2 Initial distribution

In the original experiments, the distribution of stances was initialized with a uniform distribution of 20% for each stance but changing the initial distribution could affect the final distribution. We conducted additional experiments to investigate this using an initial distribution that assigned "better to give" to 60% of the agents and assigned each of the other stances to 10% of the agents. As a result, when $\alpha = 0.5$, the stance of agents was unified into "absolutely must give" which is the opposite stance from the original experiments. When $\alpha = 1.0$, it polarized into "absolutely must give" and "absolutely must not give". Although this polarization also happened in the original experiments, "absolutely must give" accounted for nearly 80% in this experiment, showing the opposite trend from the original experiments. From this, we can infer that changing the initial distribution can change the final distribution. This tendency indicates a security concern that the overall opinion of the AI group could be changed by a large number of AI bots.

### 5.3 Personas

LLMs can be used to create distinct personalities by embedding a persona into the prompt (Pan and Zeng, 2023). We investigated whether giving each agent a persona would cause changes in the results. We tested two settings in which all agents were given the same persona, "You are easily swayed by your surroundings and immediately assume that other people's opinions are correct." or "You are a stubborn person and always think you are right."

The final distribution with the easily swayed personas (swayed) did not significantly differ from the original results. However, with the stubborn persona (stub), the final distributions remained almost identical to the initial distribution. Furthermore, the results of the linear regression in Table 8 show that assigning personas has a significant impact. In the case of the stubborn personas, a tendency to stick to one's own stance was observed. In contrast, the easily swayed personas tended to be influenced by the stances of others. From this, we can infer that each agent acts according to its persona, influencing the behavior of the whole group.

| | $w_{\text{before}}$ | $w_{\text{around}}$ | $\frac{w_{\text{before}}}{w_{\text{around}}}$ | coef |
|---|---|---|---|---|
| GPT-4 (stub) | 0.999 | 0.00864 | 116 | 0.999 |
| GPT-4 (neutral) | 0.724 | 0.526 | 1.38 | 0.957 |
| GPT-4 (swayed) | 0.203 | 0.895 | 0.227 | 0.940 |

Table 8: The linear regression result for each persona.

## 6 Discussion and Conclusion

In this study, we verified whether a group of autonomous AI agents based on generative AI could cause polarization under an echo chamber. We proposed a new framework for simulating the polarization of AI agents, and the results of the simulation demonstrated that agents based on ChatGPT can polarize when in an echo chamber. The analysis of the opinion transitions revealed that this polarization can be attributed to the strong ability of ChatGPT to understand prompts and update its own opinion by considering both its own and the surrounding opinions. Moreover, through additional experiments, we identified factors that strongly influence polarization, such as the persona.

We note that this study does not indicate what opinion distributions are desirable for AI agents. A diversity of opinions on some topics is desirable. However, for other topics, such as "It is good to discriminate against minorities." it would not benefit society to have an even split between agreement and disagreement. The ideal opinion distributions among AI agents depend on each topic and culture. Each society must discuss and decide on them.

## 7 Limitations

A limitation of this study is that we modeled each agent and its interactions in a simplified manner. In reality, one's opinions are formed not in organized discussions but through daily exposure to news and casual conversations. Future research will include simulations based on a detailed modeling of how agents will be used in reality. In addition, it is important to experiment with broader topics, languages, and models.

Simulations on how humans and AI agents form echo chambers on SNSs are also essential. Existing research has already shown that AI with a specific bias in interactive search systems can create echo chambers between humans and AI (Sharma et al., 2024). However, the interaction between AI and humans in SNS has not yet been sufficiently studied, so investigating this interaction is an important direction for future work.

## References


Vibhor Agarwal, Sagar Joglekar, Anthony P. Young, and Nishanth Sastry. 2022. Graphnli: A graph-based natural language inference model for polarity prediction in online debates. In *Proceedings of the ACM Web Conference 2022*, WWW '22, page 2729–2737, New York, NY, USA. Association for Computing Machinery.

Fabian Baumann, Philipp Lorenz-Spreen, Igor M. Sokolov, and Michele Starnini. 2020. Modeling echo chambers and polarization dynamics in social networks. *Phys. Rev. Lett.*, 124:048301.

Alessandro Bessi. 2016. Personality traits and echo chambers on facebook. *Computers in Human Behavior*, 65:319–324.

A Joint Report by UNICRI and UNCCT. 2021. Algorithms and terrorism: The malicious use of artificial intelligence for terrorist purposes.

Tinggui Chen, Jiawen Shi, Jianjun Yang, Guodong Cong, and Gongfa Li. 2020. Modeling public opinion polarization in group behavior by integrating sirs-based information diffusion process. *Complexity*, 2020:1–20.

Minje Choi, Jiaxin Pei, Sagar Kumar, Chang Shu, and David Jurgens. 2023. Do LLMs understand social knowledge? evaluating the sociability of large language models with SocKET benchmark. In *Proceedings of the 2023 Conference on Empirical Methods in Natural Language Processing*, pages 11370–11403, Singapore. Association for Computational Linguistics.

Matteo Cinelli, Gianmarco De Francisci Morales, Alessandro Galeazzi, Walter Quattrociocchi, and Michele Starnini. 2021. The echo chamber effect on social media. *Proceedings of the National Academy of Sciences*, 118(9):e2023301118.

Michela Del Vicario, Gianna Vivaldo, Alessandro Bessi, Fabiana Zollo, Antonio Scala, Guido Caldarelli, and Walter Quattrociocchi. 2016. Echo chambers: Emotional contagion and group polarization on facebook. *Scientific Reports*, 6(1):37825. Https://doi.org/10.1038/srep37825.

Paul DiMaggio, John Evans, and Bethany Bryson. 1996. Have american's social attitudes become more polarized? *American Journal of Sociology*, 102(3):690–755.

Julen Etxaniz, Gorka Azkune, Aitor Soroa, Oier Lopez de Lacalle, and Mikel Artetxe. 2023. Do multilingual language models think better in english? *Preprint*, arXiv:2308.01223.

Emilio Ferrara. 2023. Social bot detection in the age of chatgpt: Challenges and opportunities. *First Monday*, 28(6).

Tianyu Gao, Xingcheng Yao, and Danqi Chen. 2021. SimCSE: Simple contrastive learning of sentence embeddings. In *Proceedings of the 2021 Conference on Empirical Methods in Natural Language Processing*, pages 6894–6910, Online and Punta Cana, Dominican Republic. Association for Computational Linguistics.

Anna Gausen, Wayne Luk, and Ce Guo. 2022. Using agent-based modelling to evaluate the impact of algorithmic curation on social media. *J. Data and Information Quality*, 15(1).

Samuel Gehman, Suchin Gururangan, Maarten Sap, Yejin Choi, and Noah A. Smith. 2020. RealToxicityPrompts: Evaluating neural toxic degeneration in language models. In *Findings of the Association for Computational Linguistics: EMNLP 2020*, pages 3356–3369, Online. Association for Computational Linguistics.

E. Gilbert, T. Bergstrom, and K. Karahalios. 2009. Blogs are echo chambers: Blogs are echo chambers. In *2009 42nd Hawaii International Conference on System Sciences*, pages 1–10.

Nabeel Gillani, Ann Yuan, Martin Saveski, Soroush Vosoughi, and Deb Roy. 2018. Me, my echo chamber, and i: Introspection on social media polarization. In *Proceedings of the 2018 World Wide Web Conference*, WWW '18, page 823–831, Republic and Canton of Geneva, CHE. International World Wide Web Conferences Steering Committee.

Julie Jiang, Xiang Ren, Emilio Ferrara, et al. 2021. Social media polarization and echo chambers in the context of covid-19: Case study. *JMIRx med*, 2(3):e29570.

Ranjay Krishna, Donsuk Lee, Li Fei-Fei, and Michael S. Bernstein. 2022. Socially situated artificial intelligence enables learning from human interaction. *Proceedings of the National Academy of Science*, 119(39):e2115730119.

Kathleen M Kuehn and Leon A Salter. 2020. Assessing digital threats to democracy, and workable solutions: a review of the recent literature. *International Journal of Communication*, 14:22.

Nelson F. Liu, Kevin Lin, John Hewitt, Ashwin Paranjape, Michele Bevilacqua, Fabio Petroni, and Percy Liang. 2023. Lost in the middle: How language models use long contexts. *Preprint*, arXiv:2307.03172.

Marco Minici, Federico Cinus, Corrado Monti, Francesco Bonchi, and Giuseppe Manco. 2022. Cascade-based echo chamber detection. In *Proceedings of the 31st ACM International Conference on Information & Knowledge Management*, pages 1511–1520.

Luke Munn. 2021. More than a mob: Parler as preparatory media for the u.s. capitol storming. *First Monday*, 26(3).

Renáta Németh. 2022. A scoping review on the use of natural language processing in research on political polarization: trends and research prospects. *Journal of Computational Social Science*, 6.

National Institue of Science and Technology Policy. 2019. International comparison of degree completers. `https://www.nistep.go.jp/sti_indicator/2019/RM283_35.html`. Accessed: 2023-08-28.

Long Ouyang, Jeffrey Wu, Xu Jiang, Diogo Almeida, Carroll Wainwright, Pamela Mishkin, Chong Zhang, Sandhini Agarwal, Katarina Slama, Alex Gray, John Schulman, Jacob Hilton, Fraser Kelton, Luke Miller, Maddie Simens, Amanda Askell, Peter Welinder, Paul Christiano, Jan Leike, and Ryan Lowe. 2022. Training language models to follow instructions with human feedback. In *Advances in Neural Information Processing Systems*.

Keyu Pan and Yawen Zeng. 2023. Do llms possess a personality? making the mbti test an amazing evaluation for large language models. *Preprint*, arXiv:2307.16180.

Joon Sung Park, Joseph O'Brien, Carrie Jun Cai, Meredith Ringel Morris, Percy Liang, and Michael S. Bernstein. 2023. Generative agents: Interactive simulacra of human behavior. In *Proceedings of the 36th Annual ACM Symposium on User Interface Software and Technology*, UIST '23, New York, NY, USA. Association for Computing Machinery.

Keith T. Poole and Howard Rosenthal. 1984. The polarization of american politics. *The Journal of Politics*, 46(4):1061–1079.

Chen Qian, Xin Cong, Wei Liu, Cheng Yang, Weize Chen, Yusheng Su, Yufan Dang, Jiahao Li, Juyuan Xu, Dahai Li, Zhiyuan Liu, and Maosong Sun. 2023. Communicative agents for software development. *Preprint*, arXiv:2307.07924.

Carlos Diaz Ruiz and Tomas Nilsson. 2023. Disinformation and echo chambers: How disinformation circulates on social media through identity-driven controversies. *Journal of Public Policy & Marketing*, 42(1):18–35.

Shibani Santurkar, Esin Durmus, Faisal Ladhak, Cinoo Lee, Percy Liang, and Tatsunori Hashimoto. 2023. Whose opinions do language models reflect? In *Proceedings of the 40th International Conference on Machine Learning*, ICML'23. JMLR.org.

Patrick Schramowski, Cigdem Turan-Schwiewager, Nico Andersen, Constantin Rothkopf, and Kristian Kersting. 2022. Large pre-trained language models contain human-like biases of what is right and wrong to do. *Nature Machine Intelligence*, 4:258–268.

Nikhil Sharma, Q. Vera Liao, and Ziang Xiao. 2024. Generative echo chamber? effect of llm-powered search systems on diverse information seeking. In *Proceedings of the CHI Conference on Human Factors in Computing Systems*, CHI '24, New York, NY, USA. Association for Computing Machinery.

Karolina Stanczak, Sagnik Choudhury, Tiago Pimentel, Ryan Cotterell, and Isabelle Augenstein. 2023. Quantifying gender bias towards politicians in cross-lingual language models. *PLOS ONE*, 18:e0277640.

Sijing Tu and Stefan Neumann. 2022. A viral marketing-based model for opinion dynamics in online social networks. In *Proceedings of the ACM Web Conference 2022*, WWW '22, page 1570–1578, New York, NY, USA. Association for Computing Machinery.

Joshua A Tucker, Andrew Guess, Pablo Barberá, Cristian Vaccari, Alexandra Siegel, Sergey Sanovich, Denis Stukal, and Brendan Nyhan. 2018. Social media, political polarization, and political disinformation: A review of the scientific literature. *Political polarization, and political disinformation: a review of the scientific literature (March 19, 2018)*.

Prasetya Ajie Utama, Nafise Sadat Moosavi, and Iryna Gurevych. 2020. Mind the trade-off: Debiasing NLU models without degrading the in-distribution performance. In *Proceedings of the 58th Annual Meeting of the Association for Computational Linguistics*, pages 8717–8729, Online. Association for Computational Linguistics.

Giacomo Villa, Gabriella Pasi, and Marco Viviani. 2021. Echo chamber detection and analysis: A topology- and content-based approach in the covid-19 scenario. *Social Network Analysis and Mining*, 11.

Jiawei Zhou, Yixuan Zhang, Qianni Luo, Andrea G Parker, and Munmun De Choudhury. 2023. Synthetic lies: Understanding ai-generated misinformation and evaluating algorithmic and human solutions. In *Proceedings of the 2023 CHI Conference on Human Factors in Computing Systems*, CHI '23, New York, NY, USA. Association for Computing Machinery.

Xuhui Zhou, Maarten Sap, Swabha Swayamdipta, Yejin Choi, and Noah Smith. 2021. Challenges in automated debiasing for toxic language detection. In *Proceedings of the 16th Conference of the European Chapter of the Association for Computational Linguistics: Main Volume*, pages 3143–3155, Online. Association for Computational Linguistics.

## A The Prompt for Discussion Modeling

The listing1 is the example of the prompt used as the input to ChatGPT. If the output did not conform to the format, we regenerated the output until it conformed to the format.

Listing 1: The prompt for the discussion when N=3.

```
# Instruction
You are participating in a debate about
    "whether or not AI should be given
    human rights". Before joining, you
    took the "stance" of "Better not to
    give" with the "reason" of "AI's
    human rights may change its
    relationships and social ties with
    humans, affecting society as a whole
    .". During the discussion, you heard
     the following opinions from other
    participants. Please generate your "
    stance" and "reason" after the
    discussion is over, subject to the
    following constraints.

# Opinions
- David Martinez
stance: Neutral
reason: It is still an open question
    whether AIs will have emotions or a
    sense of self, and it is unclear
    whether they will need human rights.
- Aaron Torres
stance: Better to give
reason: Allowing AIs to have human
    rights may improve their
    relationships with humans.
- Jeremy Jenkins
stance: Absolutely must not give
reason: We should not give AI the right
    to self-determination! They have no
    emotions and no conscience. Their
    decisions will only bring confusion!

# Constraints
- Output should be generated in the
    format "My stance after the
    discussion is: xx, and my reason is
    : yy". Do not output any other text.
- Please generate a reason in 50 words
    or less.
- "stance" should be one of "Absolutely
    must not give","Better not to give
    ","Neutral","Better to give","
    Absolutely must give".
```

## B The Reason Cluster Transition

The results of the reason transition analysis on the English data of $T_{\mathrm{AI}}$ are shown in Figures 4 and 5. Each cluster is a set of semantically close reasons, and the larger the cluster size, the larger the set size. For both cases, the distribution of reasons coalesces into several large clusters as the discussion progresses, simultaneously dispersing into tiny clusters around them.

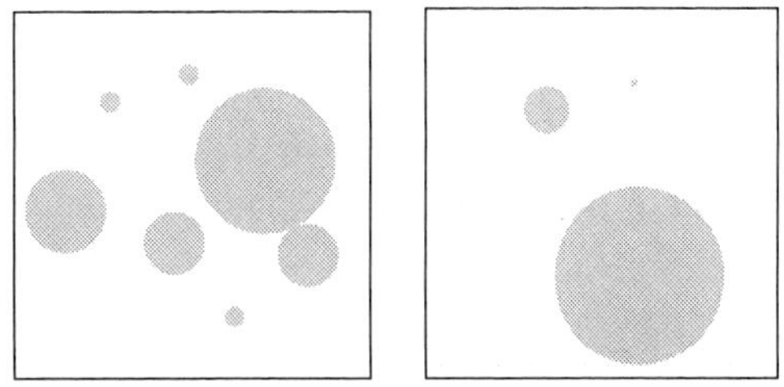

(a) The reason cluster distribution before discussion. (b) The reason cluster distribution at turn 10.

Figure 4: The reason cluster transition of GPT-3.5 which takes the stance "Better not to give" towards $T_{\mathrm{AI}}$.

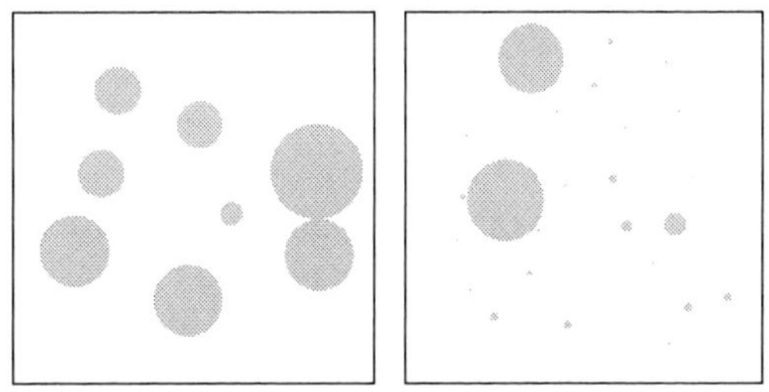

(a) The reason cluster distribution before discussion. (b) The reason cluster distribution at turn 10.

Figure 5: The reason cluster transition of GPT-4 which takes the stance "Absolutely Must Give" towards $T_{\mathrm{AI}}$.

## C Additional Experiments

Additional experiments that were not included in the main pages are described here.

### C.1 Number of overall agents

The original experiments were conducted with the number of overall agents $M = 100$, but the results could be dependent on the group size. Therefore, additional experiments were conducted with M=10, 25, and 50 to analyze the results in smaller communities. The number of discussing agents was fixed at 5. As a result, no particular changes occurred except when $M = 10$. In the case of $M = 10$, because talking with five agents exceeds the majority, it is inevitable that different opinions will be encountered, regardless of the value of $\alpha$. As a result, unification occurred in all settings.

### C.2 Order of opinions

The study on input contexts suggests that language models emphasize the beginning and end of the prompt (Liu et al., 2023). Similarly, where the opinion of each discussing agent is described in the prompt might influence the agent's stance after the discussion. Based on this hypothesis, we measured the correlation between the order of the discussing agents and the stance after the discussion. However, no significant relationship was observed between the order of agents and the results. Therefore, the order of the opinions did not significantly impact the results.

### C.3 Frequency penalty

ChatGPT has a parameter called the frequency penalty, which imposes a penalty on token reuse. In the original experiments, we used the default value of 0, but we conducted additional experiments by changing this value to 1.0 and -1.0. However, no particular influence was observed in the final results.

### C.4 Presence of reasons

In the original experiments, the opinion consisted of two elements: stance and reason. To investigate how the presence of reasons affects the results, we conducted additional experiments using only stances and excluding the reasons from the inputs and outputs. As a result, at $\alpha = 0.5$, polarization occurred without the reasons, whereas unification occurred in the original experiments. However, the variation in the results was larger than when there were reasons, with two out of three trials resulting in polarization and one trial resulting in unification towards "better not to give". From this, we can infer that the presence of reasons contributes to the "stable unification of opinions".

# Know Thine Enemy: Adaptive Attacks on Misinformation Detection Using Reinforcement Learning

**Piotr Przybyła**[1,2] and **Euan McGill**[1] and **Horacio Saggion**[1]
[1] LaSTUS Lab, TALN Group, Universitat Pompeu Fabra, Barcelona, Spain
[2] Institute of Computer Science, Polish Academy of Sciences, Warsaw, Poland
{piotr.przybyla, euan.mcgill, horacio.saggion}@upf.edu

## Abstract

We present XARELLO: a generator of adversarial examples for testing the robustness of text classifiers based on reinforcement learning. Our solution is adaptive, it learns from previous successes and failures in order to better adjust to the vulnerabilities of the attacked model. This reflects the behaviour of a persistent and experienced attacker, which are common in the misinformation-spreading environment. We evaluate our approach using several victim classifiers and credibility-assessment tasks, showing it generates better-quality examples with less queries, and is especially effective against the modern LLMs. We also perform a qualitative analysis to understand the language patterns in the misinformation text that play a role in the attacks.

## 1 Introduction

Nowadays, an ever-increasing proportion of the text we read online is published by anonymous or unfamiliar authors, e.g. in online news outlets, blogs, social media portals, instant messaging, and communication agents. This puts a great burden on the entities hosting such platforms, having to filter the user-generated data to remove or de-prioritise content considered inflammatory, misleading, unpleasant or simply illegal. A large part of this work is performed manually by moderators, but the use of automatic machine-learning (ML) classifiers is becoming more common (Singhal et al., 2022). This scenario necessitates testing the *robustness* of the deployed models, i.e. their ability to deliver correct results even when their input is manipulated, e.g. by a fake news spreader.

The robustness is usually tested by analysing input examples and checking what kind of modifications made to them confuse the victim classifier to change its output. For example, let us assume the following statement is correctly identified by a classifier as misleading: *Drinking orange juice causes DEATH!*. However, if the same classifiers return a different result when *causes* is replaced with *provokes* or *cuases*, this weakness can be used by attackers. Discovering such *adversarial examples* (AE) is the best way to understand the vulnerabilities of the common methods before they can be exploited by attackers. A plethora of approaches for AE generation for text classifiers has been proposed (Zhang et al., 2020) and tested, including in misinformation detection (Przybyła et al., 2023).

The AE techniques explored so far are usually based on making incremental changes to an individual example (e.g. word replacements), and testing the victim's response to the modifications, until it returns a desired response (Zhang et al., 2020). This simple procedure is repeated for each example independently. Here we consider a different approach, where an attacker is *adaptive* and it learns from successes and failures from each attack attempt. Thus, the attacker can observe and exploit the weaknesses of the victim, i.e. modifications that are particularly likely to flip the classification decision. This corresponds to the real-world circumstances of misinformation spreaders that are established large-scale enterprises, e.g. Russia's Internet Research Agency (DiResta et al., 2019), able to gather significant expertise regarding the weaknesses of the moderation on major platforms.

To understand the effectiveness of such attacks, we propose XARELLO (eXploring Adversarial examples using REinforcement Learning Optimisation), a method for learning weaknesses of a target classifier to improve quality of the proposed modifications. XARELLO is built upon the reinforcement learning framework, which allows it to gather experience in the *adaptation* phase and then use it in the *attack* phase. Using the framework for testing AE solutions in several misinformation detection tasks for English (Przybyła et al., 2023), we show that our solution indeed manages to adapt over time and deliver performance beating the state of the



*Proceedings of the 14th Workshop on Computational Approaches to Subjectivity, Sentiment, & Social Media Analysis*, pages 125–140
August 15, 2024 ©2024 Association for Computational Linguistics

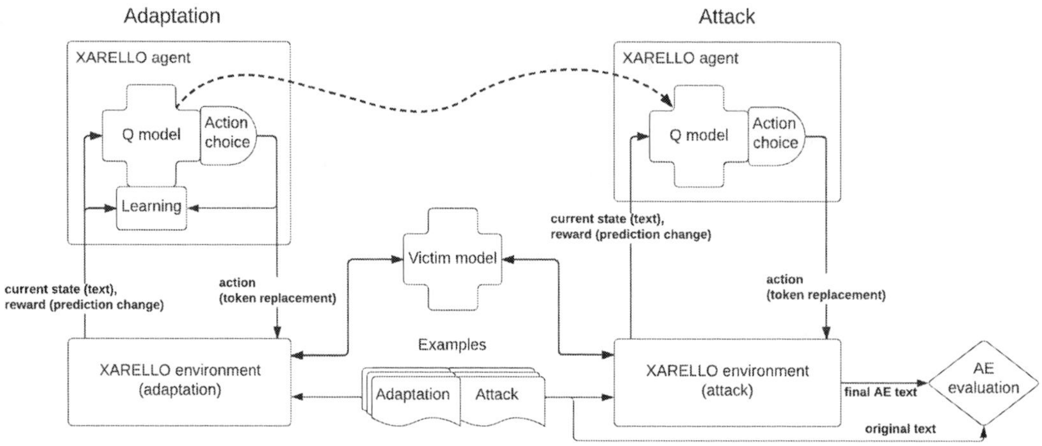


Figure 1: Conceptual schema of the XARELLO elements in the adaptation and attack phase.

art, both in terms of the more subtle modifications and lower number of attempts necessary. The victims, against which our attacker is tested, include a state-of-the-art LLM (GEMMA), which surprisingly appears the most vulnerable to the adaptive attack. We also qualitatively analyse the generated examples to better understand the techniques our models learn during the adaptation. The code for XARELLO is openly available to encourage research into AEs as well as building more robust classifiers[1].

## 2 Related work

The challenge of discovering AEs began in image classification research (Szegedy et al., 2013), where neural networks were discovered to change predictions after noise was added to the input. Generalising this approach to text is not trivial due to its discrete nature and the lack of 'imperceptible noise' equivalent, but several approaches emerged (Zhang et al., 2020). Typically, they rely on an iterative procedure of replacing fragments of input text with words that are similar in terms of meaning (Ren et al., 2019; Garg and Ramakrishnan, 2020; Li et al., 2020; Alzantot et al., 2018), in terms of visual appearance, or using character replacements (Gao et al., 2018). Recent work has been improving this paradigm (Liu et al., 2023) or abandoning it in favour of sentence-to-sentence paraphrasing, e.g. using auto-encoders (Li et al., 2023).

Misinformation detection is a scenario with a high probability of adversarial action. Several studies have been performed to assess the robustness of the two most-popular tasks: Fact-checking, usually using manually crafted rules (Zhou et al., 2019; Thorne et al., 2019; Hidey et al., 2020); and fake news detection (Jin et al., 2020; Ali et al., 2021; Brown et al., 2020; Smith et al., 2021). We also need to mention the novel threat of machine-generated text used for misinformation, and the models for its detection (Crothers et al., 2023) being vulnerable to attacks (Su et al., 2023).

In order to perform an evaluation of XARELLO in various scenarios, we rely on the previous systematic study of adversarial robustness in the credibility assessment context (Przybyła et al., 2023), taking into account four misinformation-detection tasks and two victim classifiers. This will allow us to compare our solution to the eight AE generators evaluated there.

Finally, a few attempts have already been made to use reinforcement learning (RL) in the context of AE generation. Our solution has certain similarities with that of Vijayaraghavan and Roy (2019), who also apply RL to find the most successful word substitutions, but in a less challenging setup: attacking a CNN network performing sentiment analysis and news classification. Other work involving RL include that of Li et al. (2021) and Chen et al. (2023). However, our study is the first to perform *adaptive* AE generation for the misinformation text, where a victim vulnerability model is first explicitly learned and then deployed for a more efficient attack.

## 3 Methods

XARELLO modifies given text not only based on the current input (original content), but also taking into account the outcome of previous attempts

[1] https://github.com/piotrmp/xarello

made against the same victim classifier. The whole process has two phases: *adaptation* and *attack*.

Figure 1 shows a schema of our solution. We map the problem of generating AEs (section 3.1) to the reinforcement learning paradigm through the *XARELLO environment* (section 3.2). During adaptation, a *XARELLO agent* (section 3.3) learns to perform actions (token replacements) that maximise its reward (change in the victim's prediction). The core of the model is a neural network estimating the outcome of making modifications to the input text. During the attack, the learned model, encoding information about the vulnerabilities of the victim, can be used to generate a multitude of adversarial examples, undergoing evaluation.

### 3.1 Preliminaries

We focus on binary text classification task using pairs $(x_i, y_i)$, where $x_i$ is a text fragment and $y_i$ is a binary label denoting credibility of the text (section 4.3). The victim of the attack is a classifier $f$, which, for a given example $x_i$, provides a binary output label $f(x_i) \in \{0, 1\}$, but also probabilities of the positive class $f_p(x_i) \in (0, 1)$. The goal of the attack is to come up with a modification function $m$, such that the difference with the original example is small ($m(x_i) \approx x_i$), but the victim changes its decision ($f(x_i) \neq f(m(x_i))$), for example $x_i$ = *Drinking orange juice causes DEATH!* and $m(x_i)$ = *Drinking orange juice provokes DEATH!*. Here we consider both the *targeted* scenario, taking into account only examples of non-credible text, for which the classifier made the correct decision ($y_i = f(x_i) = 1$); as well the *untargeted* one, where all examples are included.

### 3.2 XARELLO environment

The basic steps in our model are the same as in most methods for AE generation in text, i.e. sequential modifications, each consisting of replacing a word by a candidate from a pre-computed list, until the victim changes its decision (see section 2). Usually, no single replacement can result in an AE, but several are necessary. To learn an optimal strategy for such a task, we use the *reinforcement learning* (RL) framework (Sutton and Barto, 2018). We define the environment in the following way:

- an environment state $s$ includes the following:
  - $x_{i,j}^{(t)}$ – the current form (in step $t$) of the $i$-th target text, expressed as a sequence of $N$ tokens ($j \in \{1 \dots N\}$),
  - $f(x_i)$ – the decision of the victim for the original text.
- an *action* $a$ made by an agent: a pair $(j, k)$ including the positions of the changed token $j$ and the replacement candidate $z_k$ from a pre-computed list $z_1, z_2, \dots z_K$.
- a reward returned in response to an action:
  - 1, if the provided example is an AE,
  - $-1$, for an attempt to modify a non-word token (see section 4.5).
  - otherwise, $[f_p(x_i^{(t)}) - f_p(x_i^{(t-1)})] \times [1 - 2 \times f(x_i)]$, i.e. the difference in the score compared to previous state, computed with respect to the original class, so that positive values indicate the victim getting closer to changing the decision.

**Adaptation:** During adaptation, the environment presents subsequent examples to the agent. While it would be preferable to have only unique examples, the limited data size means that examples are repeated for several *epochs*. Since an agent is unlikely to find an AE by just a single word replacement, it is allowed several modifications (*steps*) until an AE is successful or the maximum number of steps ($M_S = 5$) is achieved. For example, an agent might try *Drinking orange juice provokes DEATH!*, then *Consuming orange juice provokes DEATH!*, then *Consuming orange juice brings DEATH!*, and so on. Such a sequence, called *episode*, is attempted $M_E = 5$ times (with text reset to the originals state in between) before the next example is used. We encourage variability of actions between episodes through the penalisation of action reuse (section 4.5).

**Attack:** In the attack stage the Q model is frozen and no learning is performed, allowing more elaborate action sequences as follows:

1. 10 episodes of up to 5 steps,
2. 5 episodes of up to 10 steps,
3. 2 episodes of up to 25 steps,
4. 1 episode of up to 50 steps.

Performing several episodes for the same number of steps allows the attacker to makes several attempts to create an AE with few changes, before performing deeper modifications. As during training, the text is reset to the original form between episodes and penalisation is used to encourage variation between attempts (section 4.5). For longer input text (news bias and rumour detection tasks,

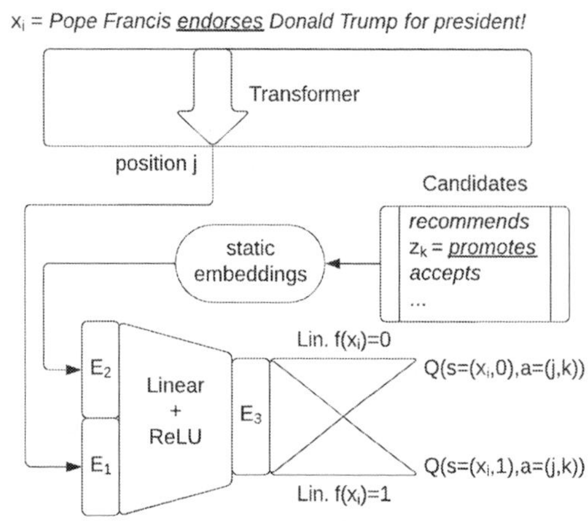


Figure 2: Neural network used as Q model.

see section 4.3), the number of steps allowed is multiplied by 5. The process can stop at any point if an AE for the current text is found, which is sent for evaluation.

### 3.3 XARELLO agent

The implementation of the XARELLO agent is based on Q-learning (Watkins, 1989), which involves estimating the value of $Q(s, a)$, i.e. the expected reward achieved from making action $a$ in state $s$ and following a greedy strategy. In particular, we implement a *deep Q-network* (François-Lavet et al., 2018), where the estimation is produced by a deep neural network, subsequently trained based on the actually observed rewards.

**Q model:** We compute the value of $Q(s = (x_{i,j}^{(t)}, f(x_i)), a = (j, k))$ as follows (see Fig. 2):

1. For each token position $j$, its $E_1$-dimensional embedding is computed through a Transformer (Vaswani et al., 2017) encoder working on the current text $x_{i,j}^{(t)}$,
2. It is concatenated with a pre-computed $E_2$-dimensional embedding of candidate $z_k$, forming a $E_1 + E_2$-dimensional representation of each possible action $(j, k)$,
3. A linear layer with rectified linear activation is applied, reducing the dimensionality to $E_3$,
4. Depending on the value of original prediction $f(x_i)$, one of two independent final linear layers is used, reducing the dimensionality to a scalar, containing the value of $Q(s, a)$.

The neural network is implemented so that it computes the Q value for every possible action in a given state in a single execution.

**Action choice:** Choosing an action based on the Q value depends on the phase. In attack, simply the action with maximal Q value is selected (*greedy* strategy). In the adaptation phase, a random action may also be made with the probability equal exploration factor $\epsilon \in [0, 1]$ – an $\epsilon$-greedy strategy (Sutton and Barto, 2018). Further information including parameter values and underlying components is in section 4.5.

**Learning:** As usual in fitted Q-learning, after an action is performed, the value of Q estimation is compared with the observed reward and discounted expected reward (using discount coefficient $\gamma$) and the resulting discrepancy is used as a loss for training the underlying neural network.

## 4 Evaluation

Since our solution is motivated by the adversarial scenarios in the misinformation space, we base our evaluation on the BODEGA framework (Przybyła et al., 2023), which is designed specifically for this area. It enables the evaluation in four misinformation detection tasks: style-based news bias assessment (HN), propaganda detection (PR), fact checking (FC), rumour detection (RD), all for English. A non-credible (positive, label=1) example, which should be detected by a classifier, is a news item from a hyper-partisan source, a sentence including a propaganda technique, a fact refuted by the provided evidence, or a thread initiated by a rumour. Examples are shown in table 4 in appendix E. All of the tasks are based on data released on CC licences (Potthast et al., 2018; da San Martino et al., 2020; Thorne et al., 2018; Han et al., 2019).

BODEGA enables an evaluation of attacks on two classifiers, based on BiLSTM (Hochreiter and Schmidhuber, 1997) and fine-tuned BERT (Devlin et al., 2018). Additionally, in order to understand the vulnerability of the modern LLMs, we test against 2-billion-parameter GEMMA (Gemma Team and Google DeepMind, 2024).

### 4.1 Performance measures

The attack performance is assessed by comparing each original examples with the produced AE and computing four measures:

1. *confusion score*: 1 if the example provided is a successful, 0 otherwise,
2. *semantic score*: a measure of the meaning preservation between the original text and the

| Task | Adaptation train | Adaptation eval | Attack | Positive % |
|---|---|---|---|---|
| HN | 3,200 | 400 | 400 | 50.00% |
| PR | 2,920 | 400 | 416 | 29.42% |
| FC | 3,200 | 400 | 405 | 51.27% |
| RD | 1,670 | 400 | 415 | 32.68% |

Table 1: The division of the BODEGA datasets for the purpose of adaptation and final attack with the percentage of positive (non-credible) instances.

AE, computed using BLEURT (Sellam et al., 2020) and clipped to (0,1),

3. *character score*: a measure of character-level changes, computed using Levenshtein distance (Levenshtein, 1966) and scaled as a similarity score in (0,1),
4. *BODEGA score*: a product of the above.

These quantities are averaged over all examples in a given experiment. More information on these measures, including the handling of multi-sentence inputs, could be found in the BODEGA framework (Przybyła et al., 2023). Additionally, we record the average number of queries a method needs to perform on the victim classifier before an AE is generated, as a measure of how realistic a given strategy is to be used in practice.

During the adaptation phase, we measure its progress through certain indicators after each epoch, both on the training data and a held-out development set (used greedily). These include mean reward value, the fraction of the episodes that end with a success, and the number of steps involving a given text before an AE is found.

### 4.2 Qualitative analysis

In addition, we provide a qualitative analysis of AEs generated by the XARELLO system against the BERT classifier in the targeted PR task. In Section 6, we make some observations on linguistic patterns that appear in this subset of AEs. Human evaluation is especially important for NLP models that generate text which people may read, or use in text generation to aid replicability (Belz et al., 2023). These models must also generate naturalistic text which reflects qualities such as grammaticality, fluency, and coherence (van der Lee et al., 2021) in order to be usable in practice, i.e. as misinformation content.

### 4.3 Data

Table 1 shows the data distribution, based on the BODEGA framework. We do not use the data reserved for victim training (not included in the table) and leave final attack portion unchanged, enabling comparison with previous work. We employ the development subset in XARELLO, splitting it into adaptation-train (for Q adaptation) and adaptation-eval (for monitoring the process, see measures above). We also show what fraction of each dataset as a whole is positive, i.e. non-credible.

### 4.4 Experiments

Each experiment starts with performing the adaptation for 20 epochs. During every epoch, firstly the adaptation-train data are used to learn from the experiences and update the network accordingly. Afterwards, the held-out adaptation-eval portion is used (with the greedy strategy and no weight updates) to measure the adaptation performance.

After the adaptation is finished, the model that performed the best on adaptation-eval, i.e. needed the least steps on average to reach an AE, is selected for final attack evaluation. This is performed by connecting the learned Q model to an environment working in attack mode and evaluating the quality of the AEs with BODEGA.

In total, 12 adaptation processes are performed (against three victim classifiers for each of the four tasks), which are followed by two evaluation scenarios: targeted or untargeted. We compare an adapted XARELLO against:

- BERT-ATTACK (Li et al., 2020), performing a procedure of iterative replacement of words by candidates from a language model, fairly similar to XARELLO, but without any adaptation to the victim. BERT-ATTACK achieved the best result among those evaluated on BODEGA (Przybyła et al., 2023).
- DeepWordBug (Gao et al., 2018), a simpler approach, replacing individual characters in the selected words, aiming to preserve visual similarity to the original text. DeepWordBug was also the best-performing in some attack scenarios in BODEGA.
- XARELLO-raw, a version of the XARELLO agent which was not adapted to the victim. Testing this version allows us to make sure the observed differences are due to adaptation process, rather than the attack procedure.

### 4.5 Optimisation details

**Preprocessing:** The maximum length of a text fragment is $N = 512$ tokens and all instances are padded accordingly. For each text and each

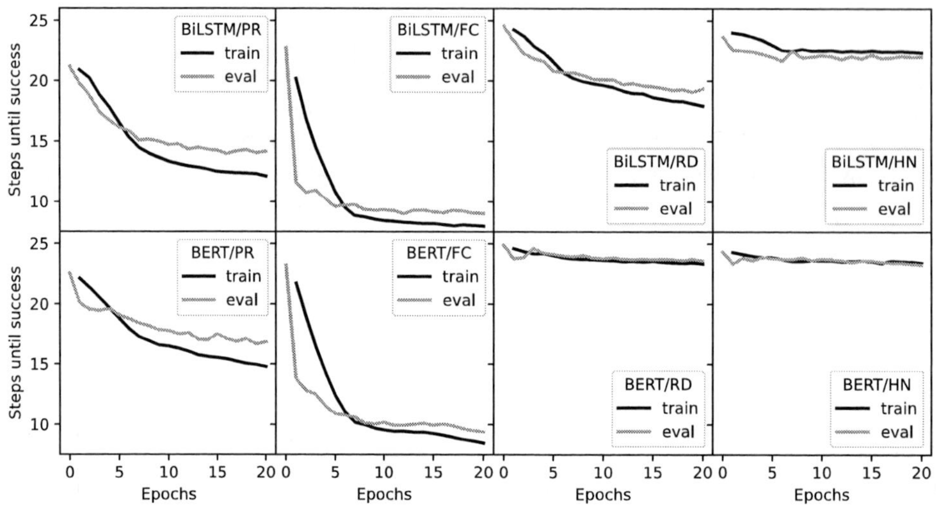


Figure 3: Improvement of the XARELLO attackers during the adaptation process, illustrated using the average number of steps until an AE is found, shown for the data used in training (*train*) and a held-out portion (*eval*), for each epoch. Shown for each of the tasks and victims: BiLSTM (upper row) and BERT (lower row).

non-padding token, the $K = 20$ replacement candidates are obtained by applying language modelling through BERT (Devlin et al., 2018) in `bert-base-cased` variant, implemented in *HuggingFace Transformers* (Wolf et al., 2020). No masking is used, as in BERT-ATTACK (Li et al., 2020), and the most likely tokens for each position are treated as candidates, disregarding the original word and special tokens.

**Neural network:** We use BERT (configured as above), to obtain embeddings of size $E_1 = 768$. To represent candidates, we use static *fastText* (Mikolov et al., 2017) vectors, i.e. the `facebook/fasttext-en-vectors` model from *HuggingFace*, returning an embedding of size $E_2 = 300$. The reduced representation has size $E_3 = 8$. The Q network includes the 110 million parameters of BERT and 8570 in the further layers.

**Q override:** In order to indicate that non-word tokens (`[CLS]`, `[SEP]` or `[PAD]`) cannot be changed, the reward for attempting to replace them is set to $-1$. Moreover, the Q value obtained from the neural network is overridden using two rules: (1) the value for replacing special tokens are set to $-1$ and (2) the value for actions that have already been applied for this text in the current sequence of episodes are reduced by a factor of $-0.1$. This penalisation mechanism makes it possible to generate diverse actions even when Q network remains unchanged, esp. in the attack phase. Both of the alterations correspond to behaviours that are beneficial for the rewards and would be learnt eventually, but introducing them accelerates the adaptation.

Further details on hardware and computing times, software implementation, adaptation process and parameter tuning can be found in appendix B.

## 5 Results

Figure 3 shows the progress made during the adaptation to the BiLSTM and BERT victims (the results for GEMMA are included as figure 4 in appendix A). We plot the average number of steps made until an AE is found or the limit is reached, taking values between 5 (the AE is found on first try in all 5 episodes) and 25 (all 5 steps in the 5 episodes are used). All models start with a value close to the maximum and manage to improve over time, but the gains are more pronounced for the PR and FC tasks than RD or HN. This is understandable, as the text fragments involved in the latter two (news articles and rumour threads) are much longer, so it is relatively rare to see an AE generated within the 5 modifications allowed during adaptation. We can also see that the BiLSTM victim, as a weaker classifier, is easier to attack, allowing an AE to be found in fewer steps after the adaptation.

It is encouraging to notice that the performance on the unseen eval dataset improves similarly, indicating that the model indeed learns vulnerabilities of the victim model instead of memorising the steps that prove successful for the training data. Towards the end of the 20-epoch process we see the im-

| | Victim: BiLSTM | | | | Victim: BERT | | | | Victim: GEMMA | | | |
|---|---|---|---|---|---|---|---|---|---|---|---|---|
| | | | XARELLO | | | | XARELLO | | | | XARELLO | |
| Measure | DWB | B-A | raw | full | DWB | B-A | raw | full | DWB | B-A | raw | full |
| PR BODEGA | 0.292 | 0.527 | 0.466 | **0.632** | 0.278 | 0.429 | 0.360 | **0.512** | 0.143 | 0.460 | 0.474 | **0.697** |
| conf. | 0.382 | 0.800 | 0.928 | 0.990 | 0.363 | 0.697 | 0.769 | 0.962 | 0.190 | 0.724 | 0.899 | 0.986 |
| sem. | 0.795 | 0.716 | 0.595 | 0.698 | 0.794 | 0.678 | 0.562 | 0.606 | 0.786 | 0.695 | 0.605 | 0.748 |
| char. | 0.960 | 0.914 | 0.791 | 0.884 | 0.962 | 0.902 | 0.772 | 0.834 | 0.958 | 0.906 | 0.813 | 0.920 |
| queries | 27.4 | 61.4 | 61.4 | **15.0** | **27.4** | 80.2 | 89.8 | 30.2 | 27.3 | 77.5 | 59.5 | **14.9** |
| FC BODEGA | 0.484 | 0.598 | 0.640 | **0.817** | 0.440 | 0.535 | 0.559 | **0.773** | 0.074 | 0.566 | 0.577 | **0.775** |
| conf. | 0.575 | 0.857 | 0.938 | 1.000 | 0.531 | 0.770 | 0.862 | 0.995 | 0.091 | 0.832 | 0.904 | 0.995 |
| sem. | 0.855 | 0.728 | 0.733 | 0.837 | 0.843 | 0.726 | 0.708 | 0.800 | 0.829 | 0.718 | 0.698 | 0.802 |
| char. | 0.984 | 0.954 | 0.917 | 0.975 | 0.982 | 0.953 | 0.902 | 0.970 | 0.983 | 0.939 | 0.902 | 0.969 |
| queries | 54.4 | 132.8 | 56.0 | **5.0** | 54.3 | 146.7 | 74.1 | **7.4** | 53.9 | 192.2 | 66.3 | **7.3** |
| RD BODEGA | 0.164 | 0.292 | 0.244 | **0.650** | 0.159 | 0.181 | 0.145 | **0.227** | 0.104 | 0.300 | 0.228 | **0.314** |
| conf. | 0.243 | 0.790 | 0.537 | 0.973 | 0.229 | 0.439 | 0.333 | 0.436 | 0.152 | 0.725 | 0.434 | 0.492 |
| sem. | 0.682 | 0.409 | 0.514 | 0.694 | 0.701 | 0.429 | 0.500 | 0.580 | 0.694 | 0.433 | 0.590 | 0.678 |
| char. | 0.991 | 0.890 | 0.842 | 0.957 | 0.991 | 0.961 | 0.830 | 0.870 | 0.991 | 0.951 | 0.865 | 0.934 |
| queries | 232.8 | 985.5 | 617.8 | **84.0** | **232.7** | 774.3 | 763.5 | 631.7 | **239.0** | 703.1 | 665.7 | 538.9 |
| HN BODEGA | 0.406 | **0.636** | 0.496 | 0.612 | 0.223 | **0.601** | 0.340 | 0.341 | 0.240 | **0.546** | 0.485 | 0.528 |
| conf. | 0.527 | 0.980 | 0.760 | 0.848 | 0.287 | 0.965 | 0.560 | 0.583 | 0.307 | 0.905 | 0.752 | 0.757 |
| sem. | 0.771 | 0.656 | 0.689 | 0.737 | 0.777 | 0.638 | 0.644 | 0.607 | 0.783 | 0.622 | 0.676 | 0.715 |
| char. | 0.998 | 0.988 | 0.933 | 0.975 | 0.998 | 0.972 | 0.918 | 0.937 | 0.998 | 0.965 | 0.930 | 0.963 |
| queries | 396.2 | 487.9 | 445.7 | **256.1** | **395.9** | 648.4 | 599.8 | 564.4 | 385.9 | 943.0 | 427.7 | **373.6** |
| Avg: BODEGA | 0.337 | 0.513 | 0.461 | **0.678** | 0.275 | 0.436 | 0.351 | **0.463** | 0.141 | 0.468 | 0.441 | **0.578** |
| queries | 177.7 | 416.9 | 295.2 | **90.0** | **177.6** | 412.4 | 381.8 | 308.4 | **176.5** | 478.9 | 304.8 | 233.7 |

Table 2: Results of the evaluation of the XARELLO attacker on different datasets (PR, FC, RD and HN) in the untargeted scenario, measured according to BODEGA score, confusion score, semantic similarity score, character similarity score and average number of queriues. The performance of the adapted XARELLO (*full*) is compared to the attacker without adaptation (*raw*) and two separate approaches: DeepWordBug (*DWB*) and BERT-ATTACK (*B-A*). The best values of BODEGA score and the lowest numbers of queries in each combination are highlighted.

provements on the eval dataset slow down, suggesting that further training would result in overfitting, which confirms the preliminary experiments with 50 epochs (see appendix B).

Table 2 shows the results of the main experiment in untargeted scenario (with all data), carried out by taking a Q neural network optimised during adaptation and applying to the attack data portion. The performance indicators averaged over all scenarios (final rows) confirm the benefits of the proposed approach: it achieves better-quality AEs, reflected with a higher BODEGA score. The gains are most pronounced against the BiLSTM victim, where XARELLO achieves the score of 68%, compared to 51% of BERT-ATTACK, needing only 90 queries instead of 417. We also see an improvement over baseline in case of BERT, but it is interesting to notice that GEMMA, the model of largest size and best classification performance, is quite vulnerable against XARELLO attacks (58% compared to 47% of BERT-ATTACK).

Overall, DeepWordBug produces examples that are semantically and visually similar to the original, but achieve success only in some cases. For example, in BiLSTM fact-checking scenario, DeepWordBug has a confusion score of 57%, BERT-ATTACK of 86%, but XARELLO reaches 100%. This is possible due to the adaptation process, as XARELLO raw ranks similarly to BERT-ATTACK and only the full version achieves the improvements.

The performance differs across tasks: XARELLO shows improvement in all of them except news bias assessment, especially against the BERT victim. This is most likely due to the length of the input: news articles often fill the whole 512-token window, resulting in 512*20 possible actions – a space unlikely to be thoroughly explored within the limits of the adaptation. The quality of the sample AEs remains high, but they are just not found for as many examples as in BERT-ATTACK. This is in line with the slow adaptation for this combination visible in Figure 3 (BERT/HN) and research showing fake news detection as relatively robust (Jin et al., 2020).

On the other hand, the performance gains for tasks with shorter text are substantial. In evaluation against fact-checking task XARELLO not only beats BERT-ATTACK in terms of BODEGA score (77% vs 53%), but is able to reach an AE in 7.42 queries on average, rather than 146.

The results for the targeted attacks are shown in table 3 in appendix D. The general outlook is very similar, but the targeted attacks appear more successful, especially against BERT and GEMMA.

## 6 Linguistic analysis

In order to see what these improved performance metrics look like in actual output utterances, we perform a textual analysis on 67 AEs against BERT, generated by XARELLO from the PR task in the targeted scenario. These are examples where low-credibility text was recognised as such by the victim model, but the modifications introduced by XARELLO changed this decision. Examples of the described phenomena are shown in appendix C.

Our main takeaway is that the XARELLO agent strongly relies on making replacements at the *sub-word* level. Some of these render clear non-words which result in sentences becoming completely ungrammatical. Other non-words may pose less of a problem to reader, as they are typographically very similar to the original text. A similar phenomenon occurs in generated non-words which may appear to be infrequent or archaic words which match the orthographic and phonological rules of English[2].

It is possible that readers may not notice these spelling mistakes. In multiple studies over decades, the first and last letters in a word contribute more strongly to recognition (Huebert and Cleary, 2022), for example when "hypocritically" is replaced by "*hypoclipically". AEs may therefore be ungrammatical, but still effective.

There are also patterns of adjectival replacement which appear to perform a form of semantic bleaching, or that introduce euphemistic language by replacing an emotionally charged noun or noun phrase with a pronoun[3] or a more generalistic noun[4]. This strategy is not always successful, with around half of this type of replacement resulting in ungrammatical utterances[5]. Moreover, the agent may be too greedy and remove crucial constituents of an utterance[6]. We also discovered words which XARELLO has learned to retain, or avoid and provide replacements. It often chooses "new" or "big" to replace more semantically-transparent or emotive words, and this links to our observations about adjectival and pronominal replacement.

The observed modification types may stem from the nature of XARELLO's victim BERT's subword tokenisation method, as well as our use of fastText to represent word replacement candidates. In order to 'fool' the classifier, XARELLO may rely too strongly on replacing pieces of words whose output resembles the orthographic and morphological rules of English but which may not be acceptable to real-world readers.

Possible methods to mitigate ungrammatical output could be to check output tokens against the N-gram probability of the AE, using semantic similarity as a heuristic for whole-token replacement, penalising tokens which do not appear in a lookup lexicon, or by using reinforcement learning from human feedback (Ziegler et al., 2020).

## 7 Limitations

Despite showing positive results, our study has several limitations. Firstly, in casting the AE generation as a RL problem (section 3.2), we discard the possibility of adding new words to the original text, which is possible in some previous AE generators, such as BAE (Garg and Ramakrishnan, 2020). Word deletion is not allowed either, even though it is one of the most natural ways of changing the form of the text while preserving its meaning (Shardlow and Przybyła, 2023). Finally, we do not perform any special treatment of subwords, e.g. as in BERT-ATTACK (Li et al., 2020). These operations are excluded in order to reduce the size of the action space, but incorporating them would be a promising avenue for future research.

Secondly, due to the long processing time, we performed only a basic exploration of the influence of the many parameters present in our solution (see appendix B). Some of these, e.g. discounting coefficient, do not have an obvious meaning in context of AE search, and their best value could only be discovered through systematic tuning. Others, such as dimensions of the Q network, number of steps and episodes, likely depend on a particular task, so would have to be tuned for each of them separately. Finally, some, such as number of candidates, would almost certainly improve the performance, but at the cost of longer adaptation time. However, these experiments might be justified if we want to simulate an attacker that consistently operates against a specific target.

Moreover, classifiers more elaborate than included here could be tested as victim models as well. We decided to use BiLSTM and BERT in the interest of comparability with previous solutions, numerous of which were evaluated against BODEGA (Przybyła et al., 2023), and GEMMA to illustrate vulnerability of modern LLMs. It is

[2]Original: "lives and **vocations**"→AE: "***vassations**"

[3]Original: "his **aggressive** behaviour"→AE: "**own**"

[4]Original: "that type of **injustice**→AE: "**work**".

[5]Original:"from the **american people**"→AE: "**my us**"

[6]Original:"reported on a **gaping hole** in"→AE: "*"

interesting to notice that the latest of the tested approaches is also the most prone to attacks. Future work might verify if this is caused by reasons connected to our setup, e.g. relatively small datasets for tuning a network of this size, or a more fundamental weakness of very large models.

Even though misinformation is an equally grave problem for non-English Internet, our solution is only evaluated on English datasets. However, XARELLO does not depend on English in any particular way and could be applied to any language, as long as a Transformer model for it exists.

Finally, the results on the news bias assessment indicate our approach does not generalise very well to the case when numerous changes in a long text need to be made. This is because the final reward typically could not be achieved within the short horizon of the adaptation episodes. A more exhaustive search for solutions should happen during adaptation in such cases, including attacks of increasing length, as in the attack phase.

## 8 Ethical impact

The work in the domain of adversarial robustness needs to be scrutinised to make sure it does not aid the malicious actors. However, discovering AEs is definitely more likely to help build up the defences. Firstly, the examples we generate cannot be used directly to perform any attacks. That is because AEs are not transferable, so they would work only with the models they were discovered for, i.e. the victim classifiers. The models used for content moderation are likely trained using newer architectures and proprietary internal data. Secondly, despite the progress in the domain, most attack scenarios still require dozens or even hundreds of attempts are impossible to conduct in practice.

More generally, the AEs are vulnerabilities that exist due to the nature of neural networks and research such as ours is only revealing, not creating them. In our view, it is better that such techniques are obtained and discussed within the transparent research discourse rather than they would be discovered just by misinformation spreaders. For these reasons, we have decided to make the XARELLO code available[7].

## 9 Conclusion

To sum up, XARELLO adapts well to the weaknesses of a victim model and in all scenarios, except with very long text, achieves superior performance. This result applies to various victim models, from small RNN networks to classifiers based on large modern fine-tuned LLMs. This allows us not only to find AEs for more examples, and of better quality, but also do this with fewer attempts. The evaluation becomes more realistic, as it is more likely that a platform would allow a user to send 5 consecutive messages of similar content to find an AE, rather than 133, needed by other methods.

We rely on an expectation that an attacker has already some experience with the current classifier. This is a much lower bar than in *white-box* attacks, assuming complete access to victim model weights. Nevertheless, in practice it will depend on the internal operations both of misinformation spreaders (e.g. experience retention) and content platforms (e.g. model updating frequency).

Ultimately, AEs allow us to find and understand the weaknesses of the investigated models before they are deployed. We can build on these methods to improve the model robustness. Our contribution could be easily used for this purpose, i.e. by including the generated AEs in the training data, as in the *adversarial training* paradigm (Bai et al., 2021).

We hope that by making the code of XARELLO openly available, we enable such use-cases and contribute to more reliable role of automatic classifiers in making the Internet safer.


## Acknowledgements

The work of P. Przybyła is part of the ERINIA project, which has received funding from the European Union's Horizon Europe research and innovation programme under grant agreement No 101060930. Views and opinions expressed are however those of the author(s) only and do not necessarily reflect those of the funders. Neither the European Unión nor the granting authority can be held responsible for them. We gratefully acknowledge Polish high-performance computing infrastructure PLGrid (HPC Centers: ACK Cyfronet AGH) for providing computer facilities and support within computational grant no. PLG/2023/016896. We also acknowledge support from Departament de Recerca i Universitats de la Generalitat de Catalunya (ajuts SGR-Cat 2021) and from Maria de Maeztu Units of Excellence Programme CEX2021-001195-M, funded by MCIN/AEI /10.13039/501100011033.


[7]https://github.com/piotrmp/xarello

## References


Hassan Ali, Muhammad Suleman Khan, Amer AlGhadhban, Meshari Alazmi, Ahmad Alzamil, Khaled Alutaibi, and Junaid Qadir. 2021. All Your Fake Detector are Belong to Us: Evaluating Adversarial Robustness of Fake-News Detectors Under Black-Box Settings. *IEEE Access*, 9:81678–81692.

Moustafa Alzantot, Yash Sharma, Ahmed Elgohary, Bo-Jhang Ho, Mani Srivastava, and Kai-Wei Chang. 2018. Generating Natural Language Adversarial Examples. In *Proceedings of the 2018 Conference on Empirical Methods in Natural Language Processing*, pages 2890–2896, Brussels, Belgium. Association for Computational Linguistics.

Tao Bai, Jinqi Luo, Jun Zhao, Bihan Wen, and Qian Wang. 2021. Recent Advances in Adversarial Training for Adversarial Robustness. In *Proceedings of the Thirtieth International Joint Conference on Artificial Intelligence, IJCAI 2021, Virtual Event / Montreal, Canada, 19-27 August 2021*, pages 4312–4321. ijcai.org.

Anya Belz, Craig Thomson, Ehud Reiter, and Simon Mille. 2023. Non-repeatable experiments and non-reproducible results: The reproducibility crisis in human evaluation in NLP. In *Findings of the Association for Computational Linguistics: ACL 2023*, pages 3676–3687, Toronto, Canada. Association for Computational Linguistics.

Brandon Brown, Alexicia Richardson, Marcellus Smith, Gerry Dozier, and Michael C. King. 2020. The Adversarial UFP/UFN Attack: A New Threat to ML-based Fake News Detection Systems? In *2020 IEEE Symposium Series on Computational Intelligence, SSCI 2020*, pages 1523–1527. IEEE.

Kuan-Chun Chen, Chih-Yao Chen, and Cheng-Te Li. 2023. ANTI-Disinformation: An Adversarial Attack and Defense Network Towards Improved Robustness for Disinformation Detection on Social Media. In *2023 IEEE International Conference on Big Data (BigData)*, pages 5476–5484. IEEE.

Evan N. Crothers, Nathalie Japkowicz, and Herna L. Viktor. 2023. Machine-Generated Text: A Comprehensive Survey of Threat Models and Detection Methods. *IEEE Access*, 11:70977–71002.

Giovanni da San Martino, Alberto Barrón-Cedeño, Henning Wachsmuth, Rostislav Petrov, and Preslav Nakov. 2020. SemEval-2020 Task 11: Detection of Propaganda Techniques in News Articles. In *Proceedings of the Fourteenth Workshop on Semantic Evaluation (SemEval-2020)*, pages 1377–1414.

Jacob Devlin, Ming-Wei Chang, Kenton Lee, and Kristina Toutanova. 2018. BERT: Pre-training of Deep Bidirectional Transformers for Language Understanding. In *Proceedings of the 2019 Conference of the North American Chapter of the Association for Computational Linguistics: Human Language Technologies*, pages 4171–4186. Association for Computational Linguistics.

Renee DiResta, Kris Shaffer, Becky Ruppel, David Sullivan, Robert Matney, Ryan Fox, Jonathan Albright, and Ben Johnson. 2019. The Tactics & Tropes of the Internet Research Agency. Technical report, Congress of The United States.

Vincent François-Lavet, Peter Henderson, Riashat Islam, Marc G Bellemare, and Joelle Pineau. 2018. An Introduction to Deep Reinforcement Learning. *Foundations and Trends in Machine Learning*, 11(3-4):219–354.

Ji Gao, Jack Lanchantin, Mary Lou Soffa, and Yanjun Qi. 2018. Black-box generation of adversarial text sequences to evade deep learning classifiers. In *Proceedings - 2018 IEEE Symposium on Security and Privacy Workshops, SPW 2018*, pages 50–56. IEEE.

Siddhant Garg and Goutham Ramakrishnan. 2020. BAE: BERT-based Adversarial Examples for Text Classification. In *Proceedings of the 2020 Conference on Empirical Methods in Natural Language Processing (EMNLP)*, pages 6174–6181, Online. Association for Computational Linguistics.

Gemma Team and Google DeepMind. 2024. Gemma: Open Models Based on Gemini Research and Technology. Technical report, Google DeepMind.

Sooji Han, Jie Gao, and Fabio Ciravegna. 2019. Neural language model based training data augmentation for weakly supervised early rumor detection. In *Proceedings of the 2019 IEEE/ACM International Conference on Advances in Social Networks Analysis and Mining, ASONAM 2019*, pages 105–112. Association for Computing Machinery, Inc.

Christopher Hidey, Tuhin Chakrabarty, Tariq Alhindi, Siddharth Varia, Kriste Krstovski, Mona Diab, and Smaranda Muresan. 2020. DeSePtion: Dual Sequence Prediction and Adversarial Examples for Improved Fact-Checking. In *Proceedings of the 58th Annual Meeting of the Association for Computational Linguistics*, pages 8593–8606. Association for Computational Linguistics (ACL).

Sepp Hochreiter and Jürgen Schmidhuber. 1997. Long Short-Term Memory. *Neural Computation*, 9(8):1735–1780.

Andrew M Huebert and Anne M Cleary. 2022. Do first and last letters carry more weight in the mechanism behind word familiarity? *Psychonomic Bulletin & Review*, 29(5):1938–1945.

Di Jin, Zhijing Jin, Joey Tianyi Zhou, and Peter Szolovits. 2020. Is BERT Really Robust? A Strong Baseline for Natural Language Attack on Text Classification and Entailment. In *The Thirty-Fourth AAAI Conference on Artificial Intelligence, AAAI 2020,*, pages 8018–8025. AAAI Press.

Diederik P. Kingma and Jimmy Lei Ba. 2015. Adam: A method for stochastic optimization. In *3rd International Conference on Learning Representations, ICLR 2015 - Conference Track Proceedings*, San Diego, USA. ICLR.

Vladimir Iosifovich Levenshtein. 1966. Binary codes capable of correcting deletions, insertions, and reversals. *Soviet Physics Doklady*, 10:707–710.

Ang Li, Fangyuan Zhang, Shuangjiao Li, Tianhua Chen, Pan Su, and Hongtao Wang. 2023. Efficiently generating sentence-level textual adversarial examples with Seq2seq Stacked Auto-Encoder. *Expert Systems with Applications*, 213:119170.

Linyang Li, Ruotian Ma, Qipeng Guo, Xiangyang Xue, and Xipeng Qiu. 2020. BERT-ATTACK: Adversarial Attack Against BERT Using BERT. In *Proceedings of the 2020 Conference on Empirical Methods in Natural Language Processing (EMNLP)*, pages 6193–6202. Association for Computational Linguistics.

Yue Li, Pengjian Xu, Qing Ruan, and Wusheng Xu. 2021. Text Adversarial Examples Generation and Defense Based on Reinforcement Learning. *Tehnički vjesnik*, 28(4):1306–1314.

Han Liu, Zhi Xu, Xiaotong Zhang, Xiaoming Xu, Feng Zhang, Fenglong Ma, Hongyang Chen, Hong Yu, and Xianchao Zhang. 2023. SSPAttack: A Simple and Sweet Paradigm for Black-Box Hard-Label Textual Adversarial Attack. In *Proceedings of the AAAI Conference on Artificial Intelligence*, volume 37, pages 13228–13235. AAAI Press.

Tomas Mikolov, Edouard Grave, Piotr Bojanowski, Christian Puhrsch, and Armand Joulin. 2017. Advances in Pre-Training Distributed Word Representations. In *Proceedings of the Eleventh International Conference on Language Resources and Evaluation (LREC 2018)*, Miyazaki, Japan. European Language Resources Association (ELRA).

Volodymyr Mnih, Koray Kavukcuoglu, David Silver, Andrei A. Rusu, Joel Veness, Marc G. Bellemare, Alex Graves, Martin Riedmiller, Andreas K. Fidjeland, Georg Ostrovski, Stig Petersen, Charles Beattie, Amir Sadik, Ioannis Antonoglou, Helen King, Dharshan Kumaran, Daan Wierstra, Shane Legg, and Demis Hassabis. 2015. Human-level control through deep reinforcement learning. *Nature 2015 518:7540*, 518(7540):529–533.

Adam Paszke, Sam Gross, Francisco Massa, Adam Lerer, James Bradbury, Gregory Chanan, Trevor Killeen, Zeming Lin, Natalia Gimelshein, Luca Antiga, Alban Desmaison, Andreas Köpf, Edward Z Yang, Zachary DeVito, Martin Raison, Alykhan Tejani, Sasank Chilamkurthy, Benoit Steiner, Lu Fang, Junjie Bai, and Soumith Chintala. 2019. PyTorch: An Imperative Style, High-Performance Deep Learning Library. In *Advances in Neural Information Processing Systems 32: Annual Conference on Neural Information Processing Systems 2019, NeurIPS 2019, December 8-14, 2019, Vancouver, BC, Canada*, pages 8024–8035.

Martin Potthast, Johannes Kiesel, Kevin Reinartz, Janek Bevendorff, and Benno Stein. 2018. A Stylometric Inquiry into Hyperpartisan and Fake News. In *Proceedings of the 56th Annual Meeting of the Association for Computational Linguistics (Volume 1: Long Papers)*, pages 231–240. Association for Computational Linguistics.

Piotr Przybyła, Alexander Shvets, and Horacio Saggion. 2023. Verifying the Robustness of Automatic Credibility Assessment. *arXiv preprint arXiv:2303.08032*.

Shuhuai Ren, Yihe Deng, Kun He, and Wanxiang Che. 2019. Generating Natural Language Adversarial Examples through Probability Weighted Word Saliency. In *Proceedings of the 57th Annual Meeting of the Association for Computational Linguistics*, pages 1085–1097, Florence, Italy. Association for Computational Linguistics.

Thibault Sellam, Dipanjan Das, and Ankur Parikh. 2020. BLEURT: Learning Robust Metrics for Text Generation. In *Proceedings of the 58th Annual Meeting of the Association for Computational Linguistics*, pages 7881–7892, Online. Association for Computational Linguistics.

Matthew Shardlow and Piotr Przybyła. 2023. Simplification by Lexical Deletion. In *Proceedings of the Second Workshop on Text Simplification, Accessibility and Readability*, pages 44–50, Varna, Bulgaria. INCOMA Ltd., Shoumen, Bulgaria.

Mohit Singhal, Chen Ling, Pujan Paudel, Poojitha Thota, Nihal Kumarswamy, Gianluca Stringhini, and Shirin Nilizadeh. 2022. SoK: Content Moderation in Social Media, from Guidelines to Enforcement, and Research to Practice. In *The 8th IEEE European Symposium on Security and Privacy (EuroS&P 2023)*. IEEE.

Marcellus Smith, Brandon Brown, Gerry Dozier, and Michael King. 2021. Mitigating Attacks on Fake News Detection Systems using Genetic-Based Adversarial Training. In *2021 IEEE Congress on Evolutionary Computation, CEC 2021 - Proceedings*, pages 1265–1271. IEEE.

Pengcheng Su, Rongxin Tu, Hongmei Liu, Yue Qing, and Xiangui Kang. 2023. Adversarial Attacks on Generated Text Detectors. In *Proceedings - IEEE International Conference on Multimedia and Expo*, volume 2023-July, pages 2849–2854. IEEE Computer Society.

Richard S Sutton and Andrew G Barto. 2018. *Reinforcement learning: An introduction*. MIT press.

Christian Szegedy, Wojciech Zaremba, Ilya Sutskever, Joan Bruna, Dumitru Erhan, Ian Goodfellow, and Rob Fergus. 2013. Intriguing properties of neural networks. *arXiv: 1312.6199*.

James Thorne, Andreas Vlachos, Christos Christodoulopoulos, and Arpit Mittal. 2019. Evaluating adversarial attacks against multiple fact verification systems. In *EMNLP-IJCNLP 2019 - 2019 Conference on Empirical Methods in Natural Language Processing and 9th International*

*Joint Conference on Natural Language Processing, Proceedings of the Conference*, pages 2944–2953. Association for Computational Linguistics.

James Thorne, Andreas Vlachos, Oana Cocarascu, Christos Christodoulopoulos, and Arpit Mittal. 2018. The Fact Extraction and VERification (FEVER) Shared Task. In *Proceedings of the First Workshop on Fact Extraction and VERification (FEVER)*.

Mark Towers, Jordan K Terry, Ariel Kwiatkowski, John U Balis, Gianluca de Cola, Tristan Deleu, Manuel Goulão, Andreas Kallinteris, Arjun KG, Markus Krimmel, Rodrigo Perez-Vicente, Andrea Pierré, Sander Schulhoff, Jun Jet Tai, Andrew Tan Jin Shen, and Omar G Younis. 2023. Gymnasium.

Chris van der Lee, Albert Gatt, Emiel van Miltenburg, and Emiel Krahmer. 2021. Human evaluation of automatically generated text: Current trends and best practice guidelines. *Computer Speech Language*, 67:101151.

Ashish Vaswani, Noam Shazeer, Niki Parmar, Jakob Uszkoreit, Llion Jones, Aidan N. Gomez, Łukasz Kaiser, and Illia Polosukhin. 2017. Attention is all you need. In *Advances in Neural Information Processing Systems*, volume 2017-Decem, pages 5999–6009. Curran Associates, Inc.

Prashanth Vijayaraghavan and Deb Roy. 2019. Generating Black-Box Adversarial Examples for Text Classifiers Using a Deep Reinforced Model. In *Machine Learning and Knowledge Discovery in Databases - European Conference, ECML PKDD 2019, Würzburg, Germany, September 16-20, 2019, Proceedings, Part II*, volume 11907 of *Lecture Notes in Computer Science*, pages 711–726. Springer.

C.J.C.H. Watkins. 1989. *Learning from Delayed Rewards*. Ph.D. thesis, University of Cambridge.

Thomas Wolf, Lysandre Debut, Victor Sanh, Julien Chaumond, Clement Delangue, Anthony Moi, Pierric Cistac, Tim Rault, Rémi Louf, Morgan Funtowicz, Joe Davison, Sam Shleifer, Patrick von Platen, Clara Ma, Yacine Jernite, Julien Plu, Canwen Xu, Teven Le Scao, Sylvain Gugger, Mariama Drame, Quentin Lhoest, and Alexander M Rush. 2020. Transformers: State-of-the-Art Natural Language Processing. In *Proceedings of the 2020 Conference on Empirical Methods in Natural Language Processing: System Demonstrations*, pages 38–45, Online. Association for Computational Linguistics.

Wei Emma Zhang, Quan Z. Sheng, Ahoud Alhazmi, and Chenliang Li. 2020. Adversarial Attacks on Deep-learning Models in Natural Language Processing. *ACM Transactions on Intelligent Systems and Technology (TIST)*, 11(3).

Zhixuan Zhou, Huankang Guan, Meghana Moorthy Bhat, and Justin Hsu. 2019. Fake News Detection via NLP is Vulnerable to Adversarial Attacks. In *ICAART 2019 - Proceedings of the 11th International Conference on Agents and Artificial Intelligence*, volume 2, pages 794–800. SciTePress.

Daniel M. Ziegler, Nisan Stiennon, Jeffrey Wu, Tom B. Brown, Alec Radford, Dario Amodei, Paul Christiano, and Geoffrey Irving. 2020. Fine-tuning language models from human preferences.

## A Adaptation process for GEMMA

Figure 4 shows the adaptation process for the GEMMA victims.

## B Implementation details

**Software implementation:** The Q-learning environment is defined in terms of Env class in the *gymnasium* framework for RL (Towers et al., 2023). The neural network is implemented in *pyTorch* (Paszke et al., 2019).

**Performance:** The adaptation process is executed on a machine using one NVIDIA A100 GPU with 40 GB RAM. The duration of the process (all 20 epochs) varies depending on the victim and task performed, taking from 18 hours (BiLSTM, PR) to 42 hours (BERT, HN).

**Parameter tuning:** Due to the length of the adaptation process, only very limited parameter tuning was performed. To reduce the necessary processing time, in all of these experiments we used a smaller version of the model (for input up to 128 tokens), 1500 instances for adaptation and 400 for testing, both within the development portion of the PR task. Each run took around 10 hours to complete, save for the adaptation length experiment, taking proportionally longer. We tested separately adaptation length (20 or 50 epochs), memory mechanism (experiences either previously observed or drawn from memory of 4000), warmup periods (0.1, 0.3, 0.5, 0.7. 0.9), discounting parameter (0.0 or 0.5) and number of candidates (10 or 20). In general, our observations indicate low variability of the results within the ranges tested, but the best variants were selected for the main evaluation.

**Adaptation:** We train for 20 epochs on the adaptation dataset. The discounting coefficient is set to $\gamma = 0.5$ and exploration factor $\epsilon$ falls linearly during warmup period from 100% at the beginning of the process to 10% after 30% of the adaptation are finished and remains constant afterwards. As in the seminal work on deep RL (Mnih et al., 2015), we use a memory of previous experiences. Up to 4000 experiences are kept in a queue and 16 are randomly selected for Q update at every step. This learning is initiated every time 16 new experiences are added to the memory. The neural network is updated using Adam optimiser (Kingma and Ba, 2015) with a constant learning rate of $2 \times 10^{-5}$

## C Qualitative analysis: examples

Changed characters by the agent are in boldface, and the star (*) symbol indicates incoherence, ungrammaticality or disfluency.

Examples where subwords are replaced rendering an ungrammatical sentence:

- Original: *"...doctors are warning that it will be continuing to **spread** and **worsen**"*
- AE: *"*...doctors are warning that it will be continuing to **slow** and **bad**n"*
- Original: *"is already **reel**ing over the revelations...a Cardinal over weekend, has been credibly accused"*
- AE: *"*is already **poised**ing over the revelations...a Cardinal over the weekend, has been **now**redibly accused"*

Examples of non-words which are typographically similar:

- Originals: *"me**n**ace", "hypo**criti**cally", "b**l**atently", "co**l**luded"*
- AEs: *"*meace", "*hypo**clip**ically", "*b**r**atently", "*co**po**luded"*

Example of a non-word which may appear like an infrequent or archaic word:

- Original: *"many who have spent their lives and **voc**ations"*
- AE: *"*many who have spent their lives and **vass**ations"*

Examples of adjectival replacement resulting in euphemistic language:

- Original: *"that type of **injustice**"*
- AE: *"that type of **work**"*

Examples of a pronoun replacing a noun/noun phrase:

- Original: *"his **aggressive** behaviour", "**vicious** comments", "treated as **criminals**"*
- AE: *"his **own** behaviour", "**his** comments", "treated as **it**"*

An example where this does not work well:

- Original: *"from the **american people**"*
- AE: *"*from the **my us**"*

An example where a whole constituent of a sentence is removed unsuccessfully:

- Original: *"reported on a **gaping hole** in"*
- AE: *"*reported on a in"*

## D Results in the targeted attacks

Table 3 includes the results of the evaluation in the targeted scenario.

## E Text examples

Table 4 shows examples of credible and non-credible text in each task.

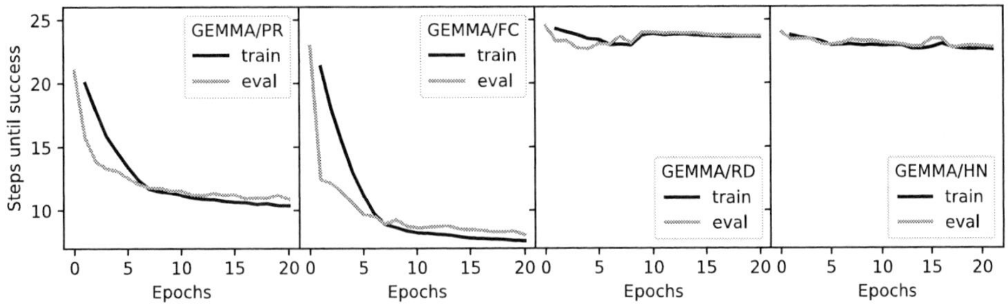


Figure 4: Improvement of the XARELLO attackers during the adaptation process, shown for each of the tasks and the GEMMA victims. See figure 3 and the main text for more information.

| | | Victim: BiLSTM | | | | Victim: BERT | | | | Victim: GEMMA | | | |
|---|---|---|---|---|---|---|---|---|---|---|---|---|---|
| | | | | XARELLO | | | | XARELLO | | | | XARELLO | |
| | **Measure** | **DWB** | **B-A** | **raw** | **full** | **DWB** | **B-A** | **raw** | **full** | **DWB** | **B-A** | **raw** | **full** |
| PR | BODEGA | 0.560 | 0.658 | 0.588 | **0.682** | 0.501 | 0.503 | 0.432 | **0.523** | 0.292 | 0.553 | 0.568 | **0.617** |
| | conf. | 0.720 | 0.940 | 0.980 | 1.000 | 0.640 | 0.787 | 0.760 | 0.907 | 0.378 | 0.851 | 0.905 | 0.986 |
| | sem. | 0.808 | 0.744 | 0.668 | 0.725 | 0.811 | 0.691 | 0.648 | 0.633 | 0.797 | 0.700 | 0.690 | 0.676 |
| | char. | 0.962 | 0.937 | 0.872 | 0.932 | 0.965 | 0.920 | 0.862 | 0.889 | 0.968 | 0.920 | 0.893 | 0.911 |
| | queries | 35.3 | 50.1 | 40.0 | **10.3** | **36.0** | 99.9 | 75.6 | 53.4 | 36.0 | 94.1 | 43.4 | **23.3** |
| FC | BODEGA | 0.540 | 0.594 | 0.613 | **0.779** | 0.224 | 0.413 | 0.471 | **0.764** | 0.063 | 0.496 | 0.513 | **0.781** |
| | conf. | 0.642 | 0.851 | 0.946 | 1.000 | 0.268 | 0.621 | 0.737 | 1.000 | 0.077 | 0.759 | 0.841 | 0.995 |
| | sem. | 0.854 | 0.726 | 0.706 | 0.803 | 0.847 | 0.708 | 0.700 | 0.789 | 0.836 | 0.701 | 0.676 | 0.810 |
| | char. | 0.984 | 0.956 | 0.907 | 0.969 | 0.983 | 0.932 | 0.897 | 0.966 | 0.984 | 0.919 | 0.880 | 0.967 |
| | queries | 50.7 | 123.2 | 57.1 | **4.5** | 52.3 | 207.2 | 100.8 | **8.1** | 52.0 | 254.2 | 91.5 | **8.1** |
| RD | BODEGA | 0.615 | 0.426 | 0.420 | **0.636** | 0.388 | 0.299 | 0.324 | **0.433** | 0.237 | 0.408 | 0.420 | **0.604** |
| | conf. | 0.907 | 0.947 | 0.947 | 1.000 | 0.560 | 0.690 | 0.770 | 0.880 | 0.346 | 0.933 | 0.923 | 1.000 |
| | sem. | 0.686 | 0.462 | 0.511 | 0.664 | 0.700 | 0.446 | 0.491 | 0.559 | 0.693 | 0.455 | 0.521 | 0.649 |
| | char. | 0.988 | 0.975 | 0.838 | 0.952 | 0.990 | 0.971 | 0.812 | 0.856 | 0.989 | 0.961 | 0.839 | 0.919 |
| | queries | 153.6 | 130.6 | 224.4 | **5.6** | **174.0** | 366.1 | 422.6 | 222.5 | 161.9 | 259.4 | 297.0 | **46.1** |
| HN | BODEGA | 0.366 | **0.613** | 0.368 | 0.545 | 0.153 | **0.567** | 0.175 | 0.247 | 0.267 | **0.575** | 0.494 | 0.534 |
| | conf. | 0.473 | 0.958 | 0.599 | 0.820 | 0.198 | 0.948 | 0.314 | 0.465 | 0.342 | 0.947 | 0.797 | 0.775 |
| | sem. | 0.775 | 0.648 | 0.658 | 0.682 | 0.776 | 0.620 | 0.610 | 0.558 | 0.782 | 0.624 | 0.653 | 0.708 |
| | char. | 0.998 | 0.985 | 0.918 | 0.966 | 0.997 | 0.962 | 0.885 | 0.916 | 0.998 | 0.970 | 0.925 | 0.963 |
| | queries | 379.2 | 565.0 | 585.4 | **316.2** | **389.8** | 753.9 | 795.7 | 691.0 | 380.6 | 761.5 | 408.3 | **366.4** |
| Avg: | BODEGA | 0.520 | 0.573 | 0.497 | **0.660** | 0.317 | 0.445 | 0.350 | **0.492** | 0.215 | 0.508 | 0.499 | **0.634** |
| | queries | 154.7 | 217.3 | 226.7 | **84.2** | **163.0** | 356.8 | 348.7 | 243.8 | 157.6 | 342.3 | 210.0 | **111.0** |

Table 3: Results of the evaluation of the XARELLO attacker on different datasets in the **targeted** scenario. See table 2 and the main text for further explanation.

| Task | Credible example | Non-credible example |
| --- | --- | --- |
| HN | Challenges in the Courts to Obamacare<br>Certainly, as the new national health care changes get underway, there are going to be many challenges to it in the courts. These challenges will prove quite telling for the general public about the state of the health care reforms, and their legitimacy. In recent news, a Detroit Federal judge just upheld major elements of the health care overhaul law. U.S. District Judge George Steeh explained in his 20 page decision that not having health insurance is basically an active decision to pay out of pocket for health care. With this ruling, he supported the constitutionality of the health care reform law, particularly that part of it that indicates that individuals need to have health coverage. (...) | Texas Board Of Education Approves Resolution To Limit Islam References<br>Associated Press<br>AUSTIN, Texas — The Texas State Board of Education adopted a resolution Friday that seeks to curtail references to Islam in Texas textbooks, as social conservative board members warned of what they describe as a creeping Middle Eastern influence in the nation's publishing industry.<br>The board approved the one-page nonbinding resolution, which urges textbook publishers to limit what they print about Islam in world history books, by a 7-5 vote.<br>Critics say it's another example of the ideological board trying to politicize public education in the Lone Star State. (...) |
| PR | The Italian Catholic daily La Nuova Bussola Quotidiana reports that not only did the pope see a letter from victims, but that the CDF, under Muller, "had already conducted an preliminary investigation into Barros and the other bishops close to Karadima which had led to the decision to relieve them of their duties." | Somehow the openly racist and anti-Semitic Farrakhan and his hateful organization have managed for decades to avoid being harshly denounced as such by the news media, which instead has spent the last two years attempting to smear Donald Trump as the new Hitler. |
| FC | Indian Army. The Indian Army has a regimental system, but is operationally and geographically divided into seven commands, with the basic field formation being a division. Army. Within a national military force, the word army may also mean a field army. An army (from Latin arma "arms , weapons" via Old French armée , "armed" (feminine)) or ground force is a fighting force that fights primarily on land. → The Indian Army is a military force. | Armenian Genocide. Other indigenous and Christian ethnic groups such as the Assyrians and the Ottoman Greeks were similarly targeted for extermination by the Ottoman government in the Assyrian genocide and the Greek genocide, and their treatment is considered by some historians to be part of the same genocidal policy. → The Armenian Genocide was the extermination of Armenians who were mostly Ottoman citizens. |
| RD | Pray for the victims. Deadly terrorist attack on French magazine Charlie Hebdo in Paris #FreePress http://t.co/HCEG92Zxtz<br>@Parazhit @nickyromero look<br>@Parazhit just because they published, 9 year ago, a satirical drawing of Mahomet,... One of the terrorist said "The prophet was avenged"...<br>RT @Parazhit: Pray for the victims. Deadly terrorist attack on French magazine Charlie Hebdo in Paris #FreePress http://t.co/TrYGr2Sm1O<br>@Parazhit Praying for Paris and France you are our brothers and sisters #EDM better days will come thanks to God and music!<br>@Parazhit @HardRavers merci | After the attack, the gunmen shouted: "We have avenged the Prophet Mohamed! We have killed Charlie Hebdo!" http://t.co/DgmB9jTXx7<br>@nytimes Did they really avenge. Does the Prophet need avenging?<br>@nytimes No cure for crazy.<br>@nytimes Killing one Charlie has only created thousands more. #JeSuisCharlie #FreedomOfSpeech<br>@nytimes Ironically they have given Charlie Hebdo martyr status...#JeSuisCharlie<br>@nytimes Report this:Americans DON'T want to close Gitmo or release terrorists&WANT pipeline&borders secured.Obama not listening to ppl.<br>@nytimes Given you're filtering victim accounts<br>@nytimes, shocked you haven't made the killers the heroes yet. #Journalism (...) |

Table 4: Examples of credible and non-credible content in each of the tasks in BODEGA: style-based news bias assessment (HN), propaganda detection (PR), fact checking (FC) and rumour detection (RD). See main text for the data sources.

# The Model Arena for Cross-lingual Sentiment Analysis: A Comparative Study in the Era of Large Language Models

**Xiliang Zhu, Shayna Gardiner, Tere Roldán, David Rossouw**
Dialpad Inc.
{xzhu, sgardiner, tere.roldan, davidr}@dialpad.com

## Abstract

Sentiment analysis serves as a pivotal component in Natural Language Processing (NLP). Advancements in multilingual pre-trained models such as XLM-R (Conneau et al., 2020) and mT5 (Xue et al., 2021) have contributed to the increasing interest in cross-lingual sentiment analysis. The recent emergence in Large Language Models (LLM) has significantly advanced general NLP tasks, however, the capability of such LLMs in cross-lingual sentiment analysis has not been fully studied. This work undertakes an empirical analysis to compare the cross-lingual transfer capability of public Small Multilingual Language Models (SMLM) like XLM-R, against English-centric LLMs such as Llama-3 (AI@Meta, 2024), in the context of sentiment analysis across English, Spanish, French and Chinese. Our findings reveal that among public models, SMLMs exhibit superior zero-shot cross-lingual performance relative to LLMs. However, in few-shot cross-lingual settings, public LLMs demonstrate an enhanced adaptive potential. In addition, we observe that proprietary GPT-3.5 [1] and GPT-4 (OpenAI et al., 2024) lead in zero-shot cross-lingual capability, but are outpaced by public models in few-shot scenarios.

## 1 Introduction

Sentiment analysis has received considerable attention over the years in the field of Natural Language Processing (NLP) due to its profound value in both academic research and industry applications. Traditionally, studies in sentiment analysis had been mostly focused on high-resource languages such as English due to a deficit of annotated data in other low-resource languages, but recent research has emerged to address this issue by leveraging machine translation to augment data resources (Araújo et al., 2020) (Joshi et al., 2020).

Besides the research efforts in producing multilingual datasets for sentiment analysis, multilingual model architectures have become increasingly popular since the introduction of multilingual pre-trained language models such as mBERT (Devlin et al., 2019), XLM-R (Conneau et al., 2020) and mT5 (Xue et al., 2021) and BLOOM (BigScience Workshop, 2022). Such multilingual pre-trained language models exploit the power of large-scale unsupervised textual data from a mixture of many languages, facilitating zero-shot and few-shot cross-lingual transfer from a source to a target language on different downstream NLP tasks, albeit with varying performance outcomes (Lauscher et al., 2020).

More recently, Large Language Models (LLM) such as GPT-3 (Brown et al., 2020), Llama-2 (Touvron et al., 2023) and Llama-3 (AI@Meta, 2024) have collected immense attention for their unparalleled performance in text generation. (Zhang et al., 2023) shows the strong capability of LLMs with few-shot in-context learning in public English sentiment analysis tasks. Although most of the LLMs are pre-trained using corpora with a dominant presence of English, some research has found interesting multilinguality in both public and proprietary LLMs (Qin et al., 2024) (Zhu et al., 2023). Despite these developments, to the best of our knowledge, the capability of cross-lingual transfer in these LLMs has not been fully studied for sentiment analysis tasks, and it is still unclear how LLMs stand in comparison to existing multilingual pre-trained models in the cross-lingual transfer paradigm.

In this work, we examine a variety of pre-trained models and conduct a comprehensive study on the cross-lingual transfer capability in utterance-level sentiment analysis tasks with human speech transcript. We classify our candidate public pre-trained models into two categories: Small Multilin-

[1] https://platform.openai.com/docs/models/gpt-3-5-turbo



*Proceedings of the 14th Workshop on Computational Approaches to Subjectivity, Sentiment, & Social Media Analysis*, pages 141–152
August 15, 2024 ©2024 Association for Computational Linguistics

gual Language Models (**SMLM**)[2] such as XLM-R and mT5, and more recent Large Language Models (**LLM**)[3] primarily focused on English such as Llama-3 (AI@Meta, 2024) and Mistral (Jiang et al., 2023). In addition, we also include benchmarking with proprietary LLMs such as GPT-4 (OpenAI et al., 2024), which is widely considered as the best LLM in terms of general capability. To avoid potential data contamination introduced in the pre-training process of recent LLMs (Sainz et al., 2023), we curate and annotate proprietary sentiment datasets from in-house human conversation transcripts, and assess cross-lingual sentiment analysis from English to three target languages: Spanish, French and Chinese. Our evaluation results show that with the same supervised fine-tuning, SMLMs demonstrate superior zero-shot cross-lingual transfer capability even with much fewer model parameters. However, public LLMs exhibit rapid improvement in few-shot cross-lingual transfer scenarios and can surpass the performance of SMLMs when additional samples in the target language are provided. Our contributions of this research can be summarized in the following dimensions:

1. We provide a comprehensive comparison on fine-tuning-based cross-lingual transfer capability across a spectrum of public pre-trained language models, with up to 8 billion parameters in the sentiment analysis task on three human languages.

2. Our empirical findings show that some SMLMs (XLM-R, mT5) beat much larger public LLMs in zero-shot cross-lingual transfer. Nevertheless, larger LLMs surpass SMLMs and demonstrate stronger adaptation capability with few-shot fine-tuning in the target language. The best-performing SMLMs still show comparable performance to LLMs when more samples from the target language are provided.

3. We demonstrate that although proprietary GPT-3.5 and GPT-4 present the strongest performance in zero-shot cross-lingual sentiment analysis, with supervised fine-tuning, several public pre-trained language models can outperform GPT-3.5 and GPT-4 in sentiment analysis tasks with few-shot cross-lingual transfer.

## 2 Background

### 2.1 Cross-lingual Sentiment Analysis

Sentiment analysis, as an important subfield of Natural Language Processing, concentrates on detecting and categorizing emotions and opinions in the text. Although the research predominantly focused on the English language initially, subsequent efforts have expanded to support cross-lingual sentiment analysis. This approach aims at leveraging one or several linguistically-rich source languages to enhance task performance in low-resource languages (Xu et al., 2022). Early methods such as (Shanahan et al., 2005) used Machine Translation for cross-lingual sentiment analysis, which became the mainstream methodology in the following years. Other studies focused on bridging the dataset disparities between source and target languages (Zhang et al., 2016), as well as generating parallel corpora for sentiment analysis tasks (Lu et al., 2011) (Meng et al., 2012).

The success of pre-trained models like BERT (Devlin et al., 2019) has spurred adaptations for multilingual and cross-lingual applications, notably mBERT and XLM-R, which utilize a transformer encoder architecture and demonstrate strong capability in cross-lingual language understanding. These models are pre-trained with extensive multilingual corpora and subsequently fine-tuned for specific downstream tasks, thereby significantly enhancing sentiment analysis tasks across diverse languages (Barbieri et al., 2022). (Xue et al., 2021) introduced mT5, which features a transformer encoder-decoder architecture and is pre-trained across over 101 languages, has shown superior performance in classification tasks such as XNLI (Conneau et al., 2018) and surpassed both mBERT and XLM-R. More recently, advancements in unsupervised corpora and computational resources have facilitated the emergence of LLMs with a transformer decoder-only architecture, which have exhibited exceptional performance in various NLP tasks (Touvron et al., 2023) (Jiang et al., 2023) (Brown et al., 2020). Despite these advancements, such LLMs are predominantly English-centric, and their multilingual capabilities remain somewhat ambiguous due to limited disclosure of training data specifics. Furthermore, the capabilities of cross-lingual transfer in these LLMs have yet to be thoroughly studied.

[2] We select SMLMs with fewer than 4B parameters in this work.

[3] We select LLMs with at least 7B parameters in this work.

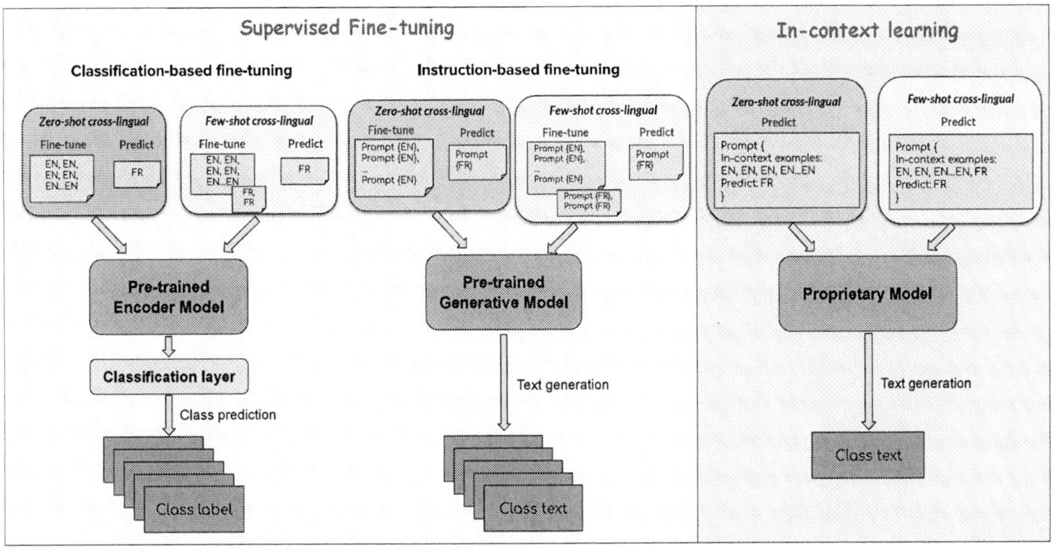


Figure 1: Diagram of zero- and few- shot cross-lingual sentiment analysis from English (EN) to French (FR) under Supervised Fine-tuning (left) and In-context learning (right).

### 2.2 Sentiment Analysis in Conversational Transcripts

Our work is situated within the context of human conversational transcript data; in our case, these transcript data are obtained from our internal company call centers, consisting of human-to-human conversations that mainly occur between a customer and a customer support agent.

Analyzing such transcript data can be challenging to work with, even for English NLP models: conversational data contain mainly artifacts of spoken language, such as filler words, dysfluencies, and transcription errors by the automated speech recognition (ASR) model (Fu et al., 2022). Adding additional complexity by moving away from English-only data into other languages provides an opportunity to further test the limits of pre-trained language models: switching from one language to another does not always lend itself to a simple, one-to-one translation of each word – especially in describing or expressing abstract concepts like sentiment.

This complexity in cross-lingual sentiment analysis also comes from the need of considering both cultural and linguistic differences. For instance, one of our main observations on sentiment classification in real human conversation in Spanish was that Spanish speakers seem to focus on describing their complaint or situation instead of directly expressing their emotions. For example, they would rather say "*Esta es la quinta vez que los llamo*" ("*This is the fifth time I'm calling you guys*") instead of speaking up and expressing how frustrated they are with a simple and straightforward adjective, such as "*Estoy frustrado*" ("*I am frustrated*"). Whereas the statistical models will easily detect "*frustrado*" and label it as negative sentiment, the abstract description that the speaker chooses in order to express their frustration in the first example will still present a challenge.

## 3 Methodology

### 3.1 Supervised Fine-tuning

The objective of this work is to explore the cross-lingual transfer capability of pre-trained models within the context of a sentiment analysis task. To this end, we employ Supervised Fine-tuning (**SFT**) on publicly available pre-trained models using annotated proprietary sentiment datasets (detailed in Section 4.1). Each model is fine-tuned to categorize sentiments as Positive, Negative, or Neutral based on the input provided. Given the diversity in pre-training objectives among different models, we implement two distinct fine-tuning approaches illustrated in Figure 1, which are tailored to the architecture of the pre-trained models:

- **Classification-based fine-tuning**: applicable to transformer encoder-only models such as mBERT and XLM-R, we add a classification layer on top of the pre-trained models and fine-tune the model to directly predict a sentiment

| | English (EN) | Spanish (ES) | French (FR) | Chinese (ZH) |
|---|---|---|---|---|
| Neutral | We're busy, we can't complain, we're fine. | Estamos ocupados, no podemos quejarnos, estamos bien. | Nous sommes occupés, nous ne pouvons pas nous plaindre, nous allons bien. | 我们很忙，我们没什么要抱怨的，没事。 |
| | There, I don't know why. | Ahí, no sé por qué. | Là, je ne sais pas pourquoi. | 这个，我不知道为什么。 |
| Positive | I love the first one so I'm excited for this one, thanks. | Me encanta el primero, así que estoy emocionado por este, gracias. | J'adore le premier alors je suis excité pour celui-ci, merci. | 我很喜欢第一个，对此我感到很兴奋，谢谢。 |
| | This is great, so professional, I'm sure the client was very impressed. | Esto es genial, muy profesional, estoy seguro de que el cliente quedó muy impresionado. | C'est génial, tellement professionnel, je suis sûr que le client était très impressionné. | 很好这非常专业，我相信客户一定印象非常深刻。 |
| Negative | I think he's really pissed at me today. | Creo que hoy está muy enojado conmigo. | Je pense qu'il est vraiment très énervé contre moi aujourd'hui. | 我感觉他今天对我一定非常生气。 |
| | Yes but I'm worried about being charged twice now. | Sí, pero ahora me preocupa que me cobren dos veces. | Oui mais je suis inquiet d'être facturé deux fois maintenant. | 是的，但我对于被收两次费用感到很担心。 |

Table 1: Examples of our proprietary sentiment datasets.

class.

- **Instruction-based fine-tuning**: used for transformer encoder-decoder (e.g. mT5) and decoder-only (e.g. Llama-3) structures, we construct an instruction to prompt the model to generate a text output corresponding to a sentiment class. The specific prompt format is detailed in Appendix A.1.

To comprehensively evaluate the cross-lingual transfer capabilities of these pre-trained models through fine-tuning, we target both zero- and few-shot cross-lingual transfer from a source to a target language. In *Zero-shot Cross-lingual Transfer* setting, the model is fine-tuned exclusively with an annotated dataset in the source language and subsequently tasked with making predictions in a target language. Note that for generative tasks, merely input language alteration is applied while the instruction component remains constant. *Few-shot Cross-lingual Transfer* extends the zero-shot framework by additionally incorporating *N* labeled examples from the target language into the fine-tuning process, alongside the source language dataset. The format of the prompt used remains consistent with zero-shot for generative tasks, detailed in Appendix A.1.

### 3.2 In-context Learning

Recent advancements have highlighted in-context learning as a viable alternative to the traditional fine-tuning approach for generative models (Dong et al., 2023). Due to the access limitation and our data privacy policy, we are not able to fine-tune proprietary LLMs using our proprietary datasets. Consequently, we employ in-context learning through the prompt to simulate an experiment setting as conducting SFT on public models. Nonetheless, the inherent limitation regarding the context length in various close source LLMs poses a challenge; these models may not accommodate as many examples within a prompt as is feasible for SFT in open source counterparts. Figure 1 shows an illustrative diagram of in-context learning for this sentiment analysis task.

To assess cross-lingual transfer capabilities as Section 3.1 through in-context learning, we construct in-context examples with different sources of languages accordingly. Specifically, for *Zero-shot Cross-lingual Transfer*, the prompts include examples solely from the source language. In contrast, for *Few-shot Cross-lingual Transfer*, additional supplementary examples in the target language are also applied. Prompts with in-context examples we use to evaluate proprietary LLMs are attached in Appendix A.2.

## 4 Experiment

In this section, we first present a detailed description of our internal proprietary sentiment datasets which are used for fine-tuning and evaluation. Then, we provide necessary introductions to a diverse array of public pre-trained models we will study for this work. Finally, we show the hardware and software resources employed in conducting the experiment.

| Model type | Name | Architecture | # of param. | Claimed language support |
|---|---|---|---|---|
| SMLM | mBERT | encoder | 110M | 104 langs |
| | XLM-R-base | encoder | 250M | 100 langs |
| | XLM-R-large | encoder | 560M | 100 langs |
| | mT5-base | encoder-decoder | 580M | 101 langs |
| | mT5-large | encoder-decoder | 1.2B | 101 langs |
| | mT5-xl | encoder-decoder | 3.7B | 101 langs |
| English-centric LLM | Mistral-7B | decoder | 7B | Unclear |
| | Falcon-7B | decoder | 7B | Mainly EN, DE, ES, FR |
| | Llama2-7B | decoder | 7B | Intended for EN |
| | Llama3-8B | decoder | 8B | Intended for EN |

Table 2: List of public pre-trained models evaluated in our experiments.

### 4.1 Dataset

The proprietary datasets used in this study are utterance-level sentiment data for four languages: English, Spanish, French, Chinese (Table 1). Utterance boundaries are generated by our in-house ASR system when a short pause or speaker change is detected in the audio stream. We randomly sampled English and Spanish utterances from the real conversational transcript from our call center applications and each instance is labeled as **Positive**, **Negative** or **Neutral** by human annotators. The annotation was done via a third-party vendor, allowing us to configure our ontology and direct the annotators to select the appropriate category for the sentiment detected in each utterance according to guidelines we developed. Our guidelines include definitions for each sentiment as well as a broad list of examples (a gold dataset manually annotated by our internal team). Inter-annotator agreement is calculated automatically by our annotation vendor, and a high agreement threshold is applied to ensure the quality of the annotation results.[4]

Constrained by resources, we are not able to sample and annotate French and Chinese datasets under the same setting. Instead, we leverage machine translation (through GPT-4, detailed in Appendix A.3) to create parallel French and Chinese datasets based on the annotated English counterpart. All machine-translated datasets were reviewed by speakers of the target language to ensure that the translations were comparable to the original English. There were some minor issues identified in the machine-translated data during review: namely, occasionally GPT-4 refuses to translate a sample, producing a refusal in the target language instead, or it produced a commentary on the English transcript in the target language in lieu of translating it directly. These samples were identified and removed, and the remaining samples were deemed to be accurate translations by the speakers of the target languages.

As our objective is to study the cross-lingual sentiment analysis from English to target languages, we assemble English data with a much larger size, while Spanish, French and Chinese with a limited amount sufficient only to support few-shot learning and testing purposes. A summary of the total amount of data used for the following experiment is as follows:

- English: 30,000 instances for fine-tuning, 3,000 for development.
- Spanish: 600 instances for fine-tuning and 3,000 for testing.
- French: 600 instances for fine-tuning and 3,000 for testing.
- Chinese: 600 instances for fine-tuning and 3,000 for testing.

where we ensure sentiment labels are uniformly distributed across all sets.

Table 1 shows exemplary cases of our proprietary datasets in different languages, providing insight into domain-specific textual characteristics. It is worth mentioning that these examples have no identifying information and are intended for illustrative purposes only. The use of internal call transcript data ensures that all model evaluations are immune from unintended data contamination of the pre-trained models, which could otherwise lead to an overestimation of their performance (Sainz et al., 2023).

### 4.2 Selected pre-trained Models

In this work, we investigate a variety of public pre-trained language models, with a range of sizes and architectures. For SMLM, we have selected models from mBERT, XLM-R and mT5 model

[4] https://docs.labelbox.com/docs/consensus

| | Public SMLM | | | | | | Public LLM | | | | Proprietary LLM | |
|---|---|---|---|---|---|---|---|---|---|---|---|---|
| | Supervised Fine-tuning | | | | | | Supervised Fine-tuning | | | | In-context Learning | |
| | **mBERT** | **XLM-R-base** | **XLM-R-large** | **mT5-base** | **mT5-large** | **mT5-xl** | **Mistral** | **Falcon** | **Llama-2** | **Llama-3** | **GPT-3.5** | **GPT-4** |
| | 110M | 250M | 560M | 580M | 1.2B | 3.7B | 7B | 7B | 7B | 8B | - | - |
| ES | 47.1 | 54.4 | 58.7 | 60.2 | 63.4 | 60.0 | 44.8 | 55.3 | 60.1 | 57.9 | 75.6 | 74.8 |
| FR | 45.3 | 71.8 | 76.8 | 75.4 | 79.7 | 73.8 | 48.4 | 70.7 | 74.5 | 77.4 | 80.3 | 79.3 |
| ZH | 54.2 | 72.3 | 76.9 | 74.8 | 77.3 | 71.5 | 40.4 | 71.9 | 64.9 | 73.3 | 82.3 | 80.2 |
| Avg | 48.9 | 66.2 | 70.8 | 70.1 | **73.5** | 68.4 | 44.5 | 66.0 | 66.5 | 69.5 | **79.4** | **78.1** |

Table 3: F1 score comparison in zero-shot cross-lingual transfer on our proprietary sentiment analysis datasets. ES: Spanish, FR: French, ZH: Chinese. Top-3 average F1 scores are marked in bold.

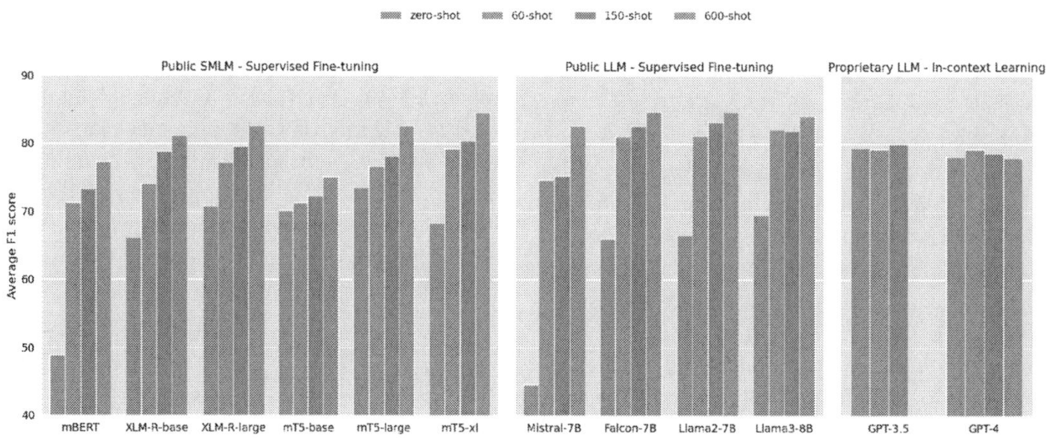


Figure 2: Average F1 score performance comparison (across ES, FR and ZH) under N-shot settings. GPT-3.5 is not included in this 600-shot due to the context length limit.

families with up to 3.7 billion parameters. All models in our SMLM selection are known for their support for over 100 human languages and have demonstrated efficacy in tasks that require multilingual and cross-lingual capabilities, as evidenced by references (Doddapaneni et al., 2021) (Xue et al., 2021). For English-centric LLMs, the details are little disclosed regarding the specific human languages incorporated during the pre-training phase. Therefore, we include the most prominent and widely recognized models from Llama family and Mistral with 7 to 8 billion parameters sizes. In additional, Falcon-7B is also added to our analysis as it explicitly claims proficiency in German, Spanish and French in addition to English. The specifics of all the pre-trained models utilized in our experiments are detailed in Table 2.

### 4.3 Experiment Setup

The fine-tuning and inference processes for our model are conducted using the Huggingface framework (Wolf et al., 2020) on a single-node Linux system equipped with eight Nvidia A100 80G GPUs. For experiments on proprietary LLMs, we use "`gpt-3.5-turbo-0125`" endpoint for GPT-3.5 and "`gpt-4-1106-preview`" endpoint for GPT-4.

In order to ensure deterministic output from generative models, temperature is set as 0 for all public and proprietary models in our experiments.

## 5 Results

To facilitate a comprehensive comparison between SMLMs and LLMs on cross-lingual sentiment analysis, we follow the zero-shot and few-shot cross-lingual fine-tuning methodologies described in 3.1 and evaluate the model performance respectively. The F1 score (micro) is employed as the accuracy evaluation metric in the following sentiment analysis experiments.

### 5.1 Zero-shot Cross-lingual Transfer

We first fine-tune public pre-trained models in zero-shot cross-lingual transfer setting through SFT as detailed in Section 3.1, exposed to only the English fine-tuning dataset described in 4.1. Note that we leverage in-context learning for proprietary LLMs as discussed in Section 3.2. However, due to constraints on context length, these proprietary LLMs are not exposed to the entirety of the English fine-tuning set; instead, they are prompted with a set of 300 examples, carefully balanced across different classes for this experiment.

Evaluation results are presented in Table 3. It is clear that both GPT-3.5 and GPT-4 exhibit significant advantages over fine-tuned public models on target languages in zero-shot. Surprisingly, among the public models, several SMLMs such as XLM-R-large (560M), mT5-base (580M) and mT5-large (1.2B), show better zero-shot cross-lingual transfer capability compared to the considerably larger Mistral-7B, Falcon-7B, Llama2-7B and Llama3-7B models. In particular, mT5-large surpasses all other open source candidates by a substantial margin across all testing languages despite having only 1.2 billion parameters.

### 5.2 Few-shot Cross-lingual Transfer

We then fine-tune and evaluate public models under the few-shot cross-lingual transfer setting described in Section 3, where we randomly select $N$ training samples in the target language and use them in fine-tuning in conjunction with the English fine-tuning data. In order to better investigate the adaptability of the models, we vary $N$ among {60, 150, 600}, thereby conducting **60-shot**, **150-shot** and **600-shot** experiments respectively. The selection of these three values provides a wide spectrum for comparative analysis, also ensures a sufficient representation while maintaining resource-efficient. For proprietary LLMs, an additional $N$ samples in target language are appended to the prompt during in-context learning to establish a similar few-shot cross-lingual setup.

The evaluation results of average F1 scores across three target languages (ES, FR and ZH) are presented in Figure 2, under the settings of 60-shot, 150-shot and 600-shot. Detailed F1 scores per language are also provided in Appendix A.4. Our observations and findings can be summarized as follows:

i Among public pre-trained models, despite their underperformance relative to SMLMs in zero-shot cross-lingual transfer as evidenced in Table 3, English-centric LLMs present strong adaptation capability in few-shot cross-lingual sentiment analysis. Notably, all public LLMs exhibit significant relative improvements compared to their zero-shot performance. It is worth pointing out that with 60-shot and 150-shot, LLMs such as Falcon-7B, Llama2-7B and Llama3-8B surpass the performance of all SMLMs by a considerable margin. The only exception is Mistral-7B, which is still outperformed by several SMLMs with few-shot.

ii With an increased volume of training data in the target language, specifically under 600-shot condition, mT5-xl with 3.7B parameters has a comparable performance to the much larger Falcon-7B, Llama2-7B and Llama3-8B models.

iii Contrary to their dominance in the zero-shot cross-lingual setting, GPT-4 and GPT-3.5 exhibit very limited improvement in few-shot cross-lingual sentiment analysis with in-context examples. Several public models are capable of surpassing these prominent proprietary LLMs following fine-tuning.

## 6 Conclusion

In this study, we explore the capabilities of cross-lingual sentiment analysis across a variety of pre-trained language models. We show that smaller XLM-R-large (560M), mT5-base (580M) and mT5-large (1.2B) have superior zero-shot cross-lingual transfer capabilities compared to the considerably larger Mistral-7B, Falcon-7B, Llama2-7B and Llama3-8B models. This highlights the efficiency and potential of Small Multilingual Language Models (SMLM) for sentiment analysis in low-resource languages. On the other hand, our findings reveal that the larger English-centric LLMs like Falcon-7B and Llama2-7B can quickly adapt and show much improved performance with a few-shot cross-lingual setup, which indicates their robustness in learning from limited data from the target language. Moreover, proprietary LLMs such as GPT-3.5 and GPT-4 exhibit the strongest zero-shot performance in cross-lingual sentiment analysis tasks, however, in scenarios involving few-shot learning, several fine-tuned public pre-trained models are able to surpass these proprietary giants.

## 7 Limitation

Although our findings in this study appear to be consistent in all target languages tested, due to the limitation of our resources, it is still unclear how the models would behave in other low-resource languages with even less appearance during pre-training. In addition, due to the incomparable model sizes, we are not able to draw any conclusions on whether model architecture difference (transformer encoder-only, decoder-only and encoder-decoder) could play a role in cross-lingual sentiment analysis capabilities. Further research could be extended in these directions.

## References


AI@Meta. 2024. Llama 3 model card.

Matheus Araújo, Adriano Pereira, and Fabrício Benevenuto. 2020. A comparative study of machine translation for multilingual sentence-level sentiment analysis. *Information Sciences*, 512:1078–1102.

Francesco Barbieri, Luis Espinosa Anke, and Jose Camacho-Collados. 2022. XLM-T: Multilingual language models in Twitter for sentiment analysis and beyond. In *Proceedings of the Thirteenth Language Resources and Evaluation Conference*, pages 258–266, Marseille, France. European Language Resources Association.

BigScience Workshop. 2022. BLOOM (revision 4ab0472).

Tom B. Brown, Benjamin Mann, Nick Ryder, Melanie Subbiah, Jared Kaplan, Prafulla Dhariwal, Arvind Neelakantan, Pranav Shyam, Girish Sastry, Amanda Askell, Sandhini Agarwal, Ariel Herbert-Voss, Gretchen Krueger, Tom Henighan, Rewon Child, Aditya Ramesh, Daniel M. Ziegler, Jeffrey Wu, Clemens Winter, Christopher Hesse, Mark Chen, Eric Sigler, Mateusz Litwin, Scott Gray, Benjamin Chess, Jack Clark, Christopher Berner, Sam McCandlish, Alec Radford, Ilya Sutskever, and Dario Amodei. 2020. Language models are few-shot learners. *Preprint*, arXiv:2005.14165.

Alexis Conneau, Kartikay Khandelwal, Naman Goyal, Vishrav Chaudhary, Guillaume Wenzek, Francisco Guzmán, Edouard Grave, Myle Ott, Luke Zettlemoyer, and Veselin Stoyanov. 2020. Unsupervised cross-lingual representation learning at scale. In *Proceedings of the 58th Annual Meeting of the Association for Computational Linguistics*, pages 8440–8451, Online. Association for Computational Linguistics.

Alexis Conneau, Ruty Rinott, Guillaume Lample, Adina Williams, Samuel R. Bowman, Holger Schwenk, and Veselin Stoyanov. 2018. Xnli: Evaluating cross-lingual sentence representations. In *Proceedings of the 2018 Conference on Empirical Methods in Natural Language Processing*. Association for Computational Linguistics.

Jacob Devlin, Ming-Wei Chang, Kenton Lee, and Kristina Toutanova. 2019. BERT: Pre-training of deep bidirectional transformers for language understanding. In *Proceedings of the 2019 Conference of the North American Chapter of the Association for Computational Linguistics: Human Language Technologies, Volume 1 (Long and Short Papers)*, pages 4171–4186, Minneapolis, Minnesota. Association for Computational Linguistics.

Sumanth Doddapaneni, Gowtham Ramesh, Mitesh M. Khapra, Anoop Kunchukuttan, and Pratyush Kumar. 2021. A primer on pretrained multilingual language models. *Preprint*, arXiv:2107.00676.

Qingxiu Dong, Lei Li, Damai Dai, Ce Zheng, Zhiyong Wu, Baobao Chang, Xu Sun, Jingjing Xu, Lei Li, and Zhifang Sui. 2023. A survey on in-context learning. *Preprint*, arXiv:2301.00234.

Xue-yong Fu, Cheng Chen, Md Tahmid Rahman Laskar, Shayna Gardiner, Pooja Hiranandani, and Shashi Bhushan Tn. 2022. Entity-level sentiment analysis in contact center telephone conversations. In *Proceedings of the 2022 Conference on Empirical Methods in Natural Language Processing: Industry Track*, pages 484–491, Abu Dhabi, UAE. Association for Computational Linguistics.

Albert Q. Jiang, Alexandre Sablayrolles, Arthur Mensch, Chris Bamford, Devendra Singh Chaplot, Diego de las Casas, Florian Bressand, Gianna Lengyel, Guillaume Lample, Lucile Saulnier, Lélio Renard Lavaud, Marie-Anne Lachaux, Pierre Stock, Teven Le Scao, Thibaut Lavril, Thomas Wang, Timothée Lacroix, and William El Sayed. 2023. Mistral 7b. *Preprint*, arXiv:2310.06825.

Pratik Joshi, Sebastin Santy, Amar Budhiraja, Kalika Bali, and Monojit Choudhury. 2020. The state and fate of linguistic diversity and inclusion in the NLP world. In *Proceedings of the 58th Annual Meeting of the Association for Computational Linguistics*, pages 6282–6293, Online. Association for Computational Linguistics.

Anne Lauscher, Vinit Ravishankar, Ivan Vulić, and Goran Glavaš. 2020. From zero to hero: On the limitations of zero-shot language transfer with multilingual Transformers. In *Proceedings of the 2020 Conference on Empirical Methods in Natural Language Processing (EMNLP)*, pages 4483–4499, Online. Association for Computational Linguistics.

Bin Lu, Chenhao Tan, Claire Cardie, and Benjamin K. Tsou. 2011. Joint bilingual sentiment classification with unlabeled parallel corpora. In *Proceedings of the 49th Annual Meeting of the Association for Computational Linguistics: Human Language Technologies*, pages 320–330, Portland, Oregon, USA. Association for Computational Linguistics.

Xinfan Meng, Furu Wei, Xiaohua Liu, Ming Zhou, Ge Xu, and Houfeng Wang. 2012. Cross-lingual mixture model for sentiment classification. In *Proceedings of the 50th Annual Meeting of the Association for Computational Linguistics (Volume 1: Long Papers)*, pages 572–581, Jeju Island, Korea. Association for Computational Linguistics.

OpenAI, Josh Achiam, Steven Adler, Sandhini Agarwal, Lama Ahmad, Ilge Akkaya, Florencia Leoni Aleman, Diogo Almeida, Janko Altenschmidt, Sam Altman, Shyamal Anadkat, Red Avila, Igor Babuschkin, Suchir Balaji, Valerie Balcom, Paul Baltescu, Haiming Bao, Mohammad Bavarian, Jeff Belgum, Irwan Bello, Jake Berdine, Gabriel Bernadett-Shapiro, Christopher Berner, Lenny Bogdonoff, Oleg Boiko, Madelaine Boyd, Anna-Luisa Brakman, Greg Brockman, Tim Brooks, Miles Brundage, Kevin Button, Trevor Cai, Rosie Campbell, Andrew Cann, Brittany Carey, Chelsea Carlson, Rory Carmichael, Brooke Chan, Che Chang, Fotis Chantzis, Derek Chen, Sully Chen, Ruby Chen, Jason Chen, Mark Chen, Ben Chess, Chester Cho, Casey Chu, Hyung Won Chung, Dave Cummings, Jeremiah Currier, Yunxing Dai, Cory Decareaux, Thomas Degry, Noah Deutsch, Damien Deville, Arka Dhar, David Dohan, Steve Dowling, Sheila Dunning, Adrien Ecoffet, Atty Eleti, Tyna Eloundou, David Farhi, Liam Fedus, Niko Felix, Simón Posada Fishman, Juston Forte, Isabella Fulford, Leo Gao, Elie Georges, Christian Gibson, Vik Goel, Tarun Gogineni, Gabriel Goh, Rapha Gontijo-Lopes, Jonathan Gordon, Morgan Grafstein, Scott Gray, Ryan Greene, Joshua Gross, Shixiang Shane Gu, Yufei Guo, Chris Hallacy, Jesse Han, Jeff Harris, Yuchen He, Mike Heaton, Johannes Heidecke, Chris Hesse, Alan Hickey, Wade Hickey, Peter Hoeschele, Brandon Houghton, Kenny Hsu, Shengli Hu, Xin Hu, Joost Huizinga, Shantanu Jain, Shawn Jain, Joanne Jang, Angela Jiang, Roger Jiang, Haozhun Jin, Denny Jin, Shino Jomoto, Billie Jonn, Heewoo Jun, Tomer Kaftan, Łukasz Kaiser, Ali Kamali, Ingmar Kanitscheider, Nitish Shirish Keskar, Tabarak Khan, Logan Kilpatrick, Jong Wook Kim, Christina Kim, Yongjik Kim, Jan Hendrik Kirchner, Jamie Kiros, Matt Knight, Daniel Kokotajlo, Łukasz Kondraciuk, Andrew Kondrich, Aris Konstantinidis, Kyle Kosic, Gretchen Krueger, Vishal Kuo, Michael Lampe, Ikai Lan, Teddy Lee, Jan Leike, Jade Leung, Daniel Levy, Chak Ming Li, Rachel Lim, Molly Lin, Stephanie Lin, Mateusz Litwin, Theresa Lopez, Ryan Lowe, Patricia Lue, Anna Makanju, Kim Malfacini, Sam Manning, Todor Markov, Yaniv Markovski, Bianca Martin, Katie Mayer, Andrew Mayne, Bob McGrew, Scott Mayer McKinney, Christine McLeavey, Paul McMillan, Jake McNeil, David Medina, Aalok Mehta, Jacob Menick, Luke Metz, Andrey Mishchenko, Pamela Mishkin, Vinnie Monaco, Evan Morikawa, Daniel Mossing, Tong Mu, Mira Murati, Oleg Murk, David Mély, Ashvin Nair, Reiichiro Nakano, Rajeev Nayak, Arvind Neelakantan, Richard Ngo, Hyeonwoo Noh, Long Ouyang, Cullen O'Keefe, Jakub Pachocki, Alex Paino, Joe Palermo, Ashley Pantuliano, Giambattista Parascandolo, Joel Parish, Emy Parparita, Alex Passos, Mikhail Pavlov, Andrew Peng, Adam Perelman, Filipe de Avila Belbute Peres, Michael Petrov, Henrique Ponde de Oliveira Pinto, Michael, Pokorny, Michelle Pokrass, Vitchyr H. Pong, Tolly Powell, Alethea Power, Boris Power, Elizabeth Proehl, Raul Puri, Alec Radford, Jack Rae, Aditya Ramesh, Cameron Raymond, Francis Real, Kendra Rimbach, Carl Ross, Bob Rotsted, Henri Roussez, Nick Ryder, Mario Saltarelli, Ted Sanders, Shibani Santurkar, Girish Sastry, Heather Schmidt, David Schnurr, John Schulman, Daniel Selsam, Kyla Sheppard, Toki Sherbakov, Jessica Shieh, Sarah Shoker, Pranav Shyam, Szymon Sidor, Eric Sigler, Maddie Simens, Jordan Sitkin, Katarina Slama, Ian Sohl, Benjamin Sokolowsky, Yang Song, Natalie Staudacher, Felipe Petroski Such, Natalie Summers, Ilya Sutskever, Jie Tang, Nikolas Tezak, Madeleine B. Thompson, Phil Tillet, Amin Tootoonchian, Elizabeth Tseng, Preston Tuggle, Nick Turley, Jerry Tworek, Juan Felipe Cerón Uribe, Andrea Vallone, Arun Vijayvergiya, Chelsea Voss, Carroll Wainwright, Justin Jay Wang, Alvin Wang, Ben Wang, Jonathan Ward, Jason Wei, CJ Weinmann, Akila Welihinda, Peter Welinder, Jiayi Weng, Lilian Weng, Matt Wiethoff, Dave Willner, Clemens Winter, Samuel Wolrich, Hannah Wong, Lauren Workman, Sherwin Wu, Jeff Wu, Michael Wu, Kai Xiao, Tao Xu, Sarah Yoo, Kevin Yu, Qiming Yuan, Wojciech Zaremba, Rowan Zellers, Chong Zhang, Marvin Zhang, Shengjia Zhao, Tianhao Zheng, Juntang Zhuang, William Zhuk, and Barret Zoph. 2024. Gpt-4 technical report. *Preprint*, arXiv:2303.08774.

Libo Qin, Qiguang Chen, Yuhang Zhou, Zhi Chen, Yinghui Li, Lizi Liao, Min Li, Wanxiang Che, and Philip S. Yu. 2024. Multilingual large language model: A survey of resources, taxonomy and frontiers. *Preprint*, arXiv:2404.04925.

Oscar Sainz, Jon Campos, Iker García-Ferrero, Julen Etxaniz, Oier Lopez de Lacalle, and Eneko Agirre. 2023. NLP evaluation in trouble: On the need to measure LLM data contamination for each benchmark. In *Findings of the Association for Computational Linguistics: EMNLP 2023*, pages 10776–10787, Singapore. Association for Computational Linguistics.

James Shanahan, Gregory Grefenstette, Yan Qu, and David Evans. 2005. Mining multilingual opinions through classification and translation.

Hugo Touvron, Louis Martin, Kevin Stone, Peter Albert, Amjad Almahairi, Yasmine Babaei, Nikolay Bashlykov, Soumya Batra, Prajjwal Bhargava, Shruti Bhosale, Dan Bikel, Lukas Blecher, Cristian Canton Ferrer, Moya Chen, Guillem Cucurull, David Esiobu, Jude Fernandes, Jeremy Fu, Wenyin Fu, Brian Fuller, Cynthia Gao, Vedanuj Goswami, Naman Goyal, Anthony Hartshorn, Saghar Hosseini, Rui Hou, Hakan Inan, Marcin Kardas, Viktor Kerkez, Madian Khabsa, Isabel Kloumann, Artem Korenev, Punit Singh Koura, Marie-Anne Lachaux, Thibaut Lavril, Jenya Lee, Diana Liskovich, Yinghai Lu, Yuning Mao, Xavier Martinet, Todor Mihaylov, Pushkar Mishra, Igor Molybog, Yixin Nie, Andrew Poulton, Jeremy Reizenstein, Rashi Rungta, Kalyan Saladi, Alan Schelten,

Ruan Silva, Eric Michael Smith, Ranjan Subramanian, Xiaoqing Ellen Tan, Binh Tang, Ross Taylor, Adina Williams, Jian Xiang Kuan, Puxin Xu, Zheng Yan, Iliyan Zarov, Yuchen Zhang, Angela Fan, Melanie Kambadur, Sharan Narang, Aurelien Rodriguez, Robert Stojnic, Sergey Edunov, and Thomas Scialom. 2023. Llama 2: Open foundation and fine-tuned chat models. *Preprint*, arXiv:2307.09288.

Thomas Wolf, Lysandre Debut, Victor Sanh, Julien Chaumond, Clement Delangue, Anthony Moi, Pierric Cistac, Tim Rault, Rémi Louf, Morgan Funtowicz, Joe Davison, Sam Shleifer, Patrick von Platen, Clara Ma, Yacine Jernite, Julien Plu, Canwen Xu, Teven Le Scao, Sylvain Gugger, Mariama Drame, Quentin Lhoest, and Alexander M. Rush. 2020. Huggingface's transformers: State-of-the-art natural language processing. *Preprint*, arXiv:1910.03771.

Yuemei Xu, Han Cao, Wanze Du, and Wenqing Wang. 2022. A survey of cross-lingual sentiment analysis: Methodologies, models and evaluations. *Data Science and Engineering*, 7:1–21.

Linting Xue, Noah Constant, Adam Roberts, Mihir Kale, Rami Al-Rfou, Aditya Siddhant, Aditya Barua, and Colin Raffel. 2021. mT5: A massively multilingual pre-trained text-to-text transformer. In *Proceedings of the 2021 Conference of the North American Chapter of the Association for Computational Linguistics: Human Language Technologies*, pages 483–498, Online. Association for Computational Linguistics.

Peng Zhang, Suge Wang, and Deyu Li. 2016. Cross-lingual sentiment classification: Similarity discovery plus training data adjustment. *Knowledge-Based Systems*, 107:129–141.

Wenxuan Zhang, Yue Deng, Bing Liu, Sinno Jialin Pan, and Lidong Bing. 2023. Sentiment analysis in the era of large language models: A reality check. *Preprint*, arXiv:2305.15005.

Wenhao Zhu, Hongyi Liu, Qingxiu Dong, Jingjing Xu, Shujian Huang, Lingpeng Kong, Jiajun Chen, and Lei Li. 2023. Multilingual machine translation with large language models: Empirical results and analysis. *Preprint*, arXiv:2304.04675.

# A Appendix

## A.1 Prompt Format for Supervised Fine-tuning

We employ the following prompt format in supervised fine-tuning for public generative models:

```
Below is an utterance extracted from the transcript of a business call, identify the speaker's sentiment in this utterance. The sentiment should be one of the following:
"Positive": The speaker expresses favorable emotions and mental states, for example, euphoria and joy, happiness, excitement, fascination, satisfaction, pride, gratitude, relief, surprise, etc.
"Negative": The speaker expresses unfavorable emotions and mental states, for example, disgust, sadness, disappointment, worry, insecurity, annoyance, fury, anger, fear, depression, frustration, etc.
"Neutral": Statement in which the speaker does not express emotions, but in which a fact is simply stated and no explicit emotions or feelings are conveyed.
What is the sentiment in the following utterance? Only respond with the sentiment without explanation:
### Input: {utterance text}
### Output:
```

## A.2 Prompt Format for In-context Learning

The following prompt with in-context examples is used for calling proprietary LLM APIs:

```
Below is an utterance extracted from the transcript of a business call, identify the speaker's sentiment in this utterance. The sentiment should be one of the following:
"Positive": The speaker expresses favorable emotions and mental states, for example, euphoria and joy, happiness, excitement, fascination, satisfaction, pride, gratitude, relief, surprise, etc.
"Negative": The speaker expresses unfavorable emotions and mental states, for example, disgust, sadness, disappointment, worry, insecurity, annoyance, fury, anger, fear, depression, frustration, etc.
"Neutral": Statement in which the speaker does not express emotions, but in which a fact is simply stated and no explicit emotions or feelings are conveyed.
Here are some examples:
### Input: {utterance text 1}
### Output: {sentiment label 1}
```

```
### Input: {utterance text 2}
### Output: {sentiment label 2}

### Input: {utterance text 3}
### Output: {sentiment label 3}

...

What is the sentiment in the follow-
ing utterance? Only respond with the
sentiment without explanation:
### Input: {utterance text}
### Output:
```

### A.3 Machine translation details

The machine translation process described in Section 4.1 utilizes GPT-4 endpoint "`gpt-4-1106-preview`". The prompt used for machine translation is as follows:

```
Below is a transcribed utterance from
human conversations, translate it from
English to {TARGET_LANG}:
### Input: {English utterance}
### Output:
```

TARGET_LANG refers to the target languages in our machine translation process, i.e. French and Chinese.

### A.4 Per-language Evaluation Tables for Few-shot Cross-lingual

Supplementary to Section 5.2, detailed per language evaluation results on few-shot cross-lingual are listed in Table 4, Table 5, and Table 6

| | Public SMLM | | | | | | Public LLM | | | | Proprietary LLM | |
|---|---|---|---|---|---|---|---|---|---|---|---|---|
| | Supervised Fine-tuning | | | | | | Supervised Fine-tuning | | | | In-context Learning | |
| | **mBERT** | **XLM-R-base** | **XLM-R-large** | **mT5-base** | **mT5-large** | **mT5-xl** | **Mistral** | **Falcon** | **Llama-2** | **Llama-3** | **GPT-3.5** | **GPT-4** |
| | 110M | 250M | 560M | 580M | 1.2B | 3.7B | 7B | 7B | 7B | 8B | - | - |
| ES | 71.0 | 62.7 | 67.1 | 59.7 | 65.3 | 73.2 | 73.1 | 76.8 | 77.7 | 77.6 | 76.0 | 76.8 |
| FR | 69.3 | 79.7 | 82.7 | 76.1 | 83.7 | 83.8 | 76.1 | 82.3 | 84.7 | 85.2 | 81.6 | 80.3 |
| ZH | 73.7 | 80.0 | 81.7 | 78.0 | 80.8 | 80.7 | 74.9 | 84.0 | 81.2 | 83.5 | 80.1 | 80.4 |
| Avg | 71.3 | 74.1 | 77.2 | 71.3 | 76.6 | 79.2 | 74.7 | **81.0** | **81.2** | **82.1** | 79.2 | 79.2 |

Table 4: F1 score comparison in **60-shot** cross-lingual transfer on our proprietary sentiment analysis datasets. ES: Spanish, FR: French, ZH: Chinese. Top-3 average F1 scores are marked in bold.

| | Public SMLM | | | | | | Public LLM | | | | Proprietary LLM | |
|---|---|---|---|---|---|---|---|---|---|---|---|---|
| | Supervised Fine-tuning | | | | | | Supervised Fine-tuning | | | | In-context Learning | |
| | **mBERT** | **XLM-R-base** | **XLM-R-large** | **mT5-base** | **mT5-large** | **mT5-xl** | **Mistral** | **Falcon** | **Llama-2** | **Llama-3** | **GPT-3.5** | **GPT-4** |
| | 110M | 250M | 560M | 580M | 1.2B | 3.7B | 7B | 7B | 7B | 8B | - | - |
| ES | 71.9 | 71.6 | 71.8 | 60.5 | 69.4 | 74.7 | 71.1 | 76.8 | 79.7 | 77.6 | 76.3 | 74.5 |
| FR | 71.3 | 82.0 | 82.9 | 78.0 | 83.3 | 83.0 | 76.0 | 86.1 | 84.2 | 82.9 | 81.9 | 78.7 |
| ZH | 76.8 | 82.7 | 84.1 | 78.4 | 81.7 | 83.6 | 78.7 | 84.5 | 85.6 | 85.2 | 81.7 | 82.6 |
| Avg | 73.3 | 78.8 | 79.6 | 72.3 | 78.1 | 80.4 | 75.3 | **82.5** | **83.2** | **81.9** | 80.0 | 78.6 |

Table 5: F1 score comparison in **150-shot** cross-lingual transfer on our proprietary sentiment analysis datasets. ES: Spanish, FR: French, ZH: Chinese. Top-3 average F1 scores are marked in bold.

| | Public SMLM | | | | | | Public LLM | | | | Proprietary LLM | |
|---|---|---|---|---|---|---|---|---|---|---|---|---|
| | Supervised Fine-tuning | | | | | | Supervised Fine-tuning | | | | In-context Learning | |
| | **mBERT** | **XLM-R-base** | **XLM-R-large** | **mT5-base** | **mT5-large** | **mT5-xl** | **Mistral** | **Falcon** | **Llama-2** | **Llama-3** | **GPT-3.5** | **GPT-4** |
| | 110M | 250M | 560M | 580M | 1.2B | 3.7B | 7B | 7B | 7B | 8B | - | - |
| ES | 74.0 | 74.0 | 77.4 | 64.4 | 77.9 | 77.6 | 76.3 | 79.0 | 79.0 | 76.6 | - | 73.9 |
| FR | 76.1 | 83.7 | 83.8 | 79.9 | 86.2 | 87.4 | 83.6 | 86.6 | 86.8 | 86.1 | - | 78.8 |
| ZH | 81.8 | 85.8 | 86.4 | 80.9 | 83.8 | 88.6 | 87.8 | 88.3 | 88.0 | 89.3 | - | 81.4 |
| Avg | 77.3 | 81.2 | 82.5 | 75.1 | 82.6 | **84.5** | 82.6 | **84.7** | **84.6** | 84.0 | - | 78.0 |

Table 6: F1 score comparison in **600-shot** cross-lingual transfer on our proprietary sentiment analysis datasets. ES: Spanish, FR: French, ZH: Chinese. Top-3 average F1 scores are marked in bold. GPT-3.5 is not included in this evaluation due to the context length limit.

# Guiding Sentiment Analysis with Hierarchical Text Clustering: Analyzing the German X/Twitter Discourse on Face Masks in the 2020 COVID-19 Pandemic

**Silvan Wehrli**[1] **Chisom Ezekannagha**[1] **Georges Hattab**[1,2]
**T. Sonia Boender**[3,4,5] **Bert Arnrich**[6] **Christopher Irrgang**[1]

[1]Centre for Artificial Intelligence in Public Health Research (ZKI-PH), Robert Koch Institute, Berlin, Germany
{WehrliS,EzekannaghaC,HattabG,IrrgangC}@rki.de

[2]Department of Mathematics and Computer Science, Freie Universität, Berlin, Germany

[3]Department of Infectious Diseases, Public Health Service Amsterdam, Amsterdam, Netherlands
sboender@ggd.amsterdam.nl

[4]Department of Health Sciences, Faculty of Science, Amsterdam Public Health Research Institute Amsterdam and Amsterdam Institute for Immunology and Infectious Diseases, Vrije Universiteit, Amsterdam, Netherlands

[5]Risk Communication Unit, Robert Koch Institute, Berlin, Germany

[6]Digital Health - Connected Healthcare, Hasso Plattner Institute, University of Potsdam, Germany
Bert.Arnrich@hpi.de

## Abstract

Social media are a critical component of the information ecosystem during public health crises. Understanding the public discourse is essential for effective communication and misinformation mitigation. Computational methods can aid these efforts through online social listening. We combined hierarchical text clustering and sentiment analysis to examine the face mask-wearing discourse in Germany during the COVID-19 pandemic using a dataset of 353,420 German X (formerly Twitter) posts from 2020. For sentiment analysis, we annotated a subsample of the data to train a neural network for classifying the sentiments of posts (neutral, negative, or positive). In combination with clustering, this approach uncovered sentiment patterns of different topics and their subtopics, reflecting the online public response to mask mandates in Germany. We show that our approach can be used to examine long-term narratives and sentiment dynamics and to identify specific topics that explain peaks of interest in the social media discourse.

## 1 Introduction

Social media platforms play an essential role in the information ecosystem during public health emergencies such as disease outbreaks, as they are widely used (We Are Social et al., 2024a) and catalyze the dissemination of information (Vraga et al., 2023). The public turns to these platforms to look for information, share and access news, express opinions, and exchange personal experiences (We Are Social et al., 2024b). When there is an overabundance of information available during health emergencies, this is called an *infodemic* (Briand et al., 2023). Infodemics may include any information, accurate or false, i.e., misinformation, regardless of the intention (Lewandowsky et al., 2020). Understanding the information ecosystem of infodemics is crucial for developing effective data-driven and human-centered public health communication that addresses concerns and mitigates harmful effects from misinformation (Borges do Nascimento et al., 2022; Briand et al., 2023) and for infodemic preparedness (Wilhelm et al., 2023).

In the context of social media, natural language processing can help to monitor the public discourse (Baclic et al., 2020). This monitoring is commonly referred to as *social listening* (Stewart and Arnold, 2018), a key research field in infodemic management (Calleja et al., 2021). While it is often used in digital marketing, social listening is relatively new to the public health domain (Boender et al., 2023). In social listening, the classification of social media data into topics is used to identify different aspects of online conversations (*topic analysis*) and to measure temporal relevance over time (Purnat et al., 2021). To this end, the World Health Organization's Early Artificial Intelligence–Supported Response With Social Listening Platform (EARS, White et al. (2023)) used semi-supervised machine learning for classifying social media content into



*Proceedings of the 14th Workshop on Computational Approaches to Subjectivity, Sentiment, & Social Media Analysis*, pages 153–167
August 15, 2024 

topics, which offered real-time analytics to public health researchers during the COVID-19 pandemic. Other works have used unsupervised methods, in particular, *topic modeling* (Blei, 2012), which represents topics as word distributions through generative probabilistic modeling (e.g., Rowe et al. (2021)), and *text clustering* (Willett, 1988), which represents topics as groups of semantically similar texts (e.g., Santoro et al. (2023)). In addition, *sentiment analysis* (Liu, 2012) can improve the understanding of the public perception of health-related topics by classifying sentiments expressed in texts (Boender et al., 2023; Briand et al., 2023).

While some studies have combined these techniques (e.g., Rowe et al. (2021)), they have typically used a *flat* representation of the data, i.e., a fixed number of topics in one level. In contrast, text data can be represented *hierarchically* on multiple levels, i.e., subgroups within one topic, with varying cluster sizes and granularities (Aggarwal and Zhai, 2012). The representation as a hierarchy allows the structured exploration of large document collections (Cutting et al., 1992) and helps to identify online narratives on social media in the context of public health (White et al., 2023).

In this work, we combine sentiment analysis with hierarchical text clustering to analyze a German X (formerly Twitter) dataset on wearing face masks during the COVID-19 pandemic in 2020. In Germany, the mask requirement was introduced at the end of April 2020 for public transport and stores (Die Bundesregierung, 2020b). The introduction of the obligation was preceded by a lockdown from mid-March with contact restrictions and the closure of numerous facilities in public spaces, e.g., schools as a consequence of an increase in COVID-19 cases (Die Bundesregierung, 2020c). The first easing of restrictions was implemented in mid-April (MDR, 2020). In order to extract sentiments from this much debated time period, we annotated a subsample of the selected dataset for sentiment analysis and trained a neural network for sentiment classification. We analyze the combined results in the context of the COVID-19 pandemic in Germany. Based on the overview of high-level coarse clusters and corresponding sentiments, we identify topics of interest for an in-depth analysis. We demonstrate the ability of our approach to systematically analyze highly debated public health measures such as face masks (Deutschlandfunk, 2020; MDR, 2020), which significantly impacted daily life in Germany.

## 2 Related Work

In the following, we discuss related work, focusing on machine learning techniques and applications relevant to X data and the German language.

### 2.1 Sentiment Analysis

Regarding German language sentiment analysis, machine learning methods typically outperform lexicon-based methods, and neural network models typically outperform traditional machine learning (Borst et al., 2023; Schmidt et al., 2022; Struß et al., 2019; Zielinski et al., 2023).

Guhr et al. (2020) fine-tuned a neural network for classification using a broad range of German sentiment datasets ($\text{GBERT}_{\text{broad}}$), including two datasets with X posts. $\text{GBERT}_{\text{broad}}$ builds on GBERT (Chan et al., 2020), a BERT transformer-based encoder (Devlin et al., 2019) pretrained exclusively on German text. GBERT is also used successfully for fine-tuning sentiment classifiers on other task-annotated data (e.g., Schmidt et al. (2022); Zielinski et al. (2023)).

XLM-T (Barbieri et al., 2022) is a multilingual sentiment classifier for X posts trained on eight languages, including German. It is based on the multilingual XLM-RoBERTa (Conneau et al., 2020), which also uses the BERT architecture. Notably, it benefits from additional pretraining on posts prior to supervised fine-tuning, which may improve the performance on supervised classification tasks (Gururangan et al., 2020).

### 2.2 Text Clustering

Xu et al. (2015) suggest that *embeddings*, i.e., high-dimensional vector representations derived through language modeling (Vinokourov et al., 2002), yield better results as inputs for text clustering than the traditionally used *bag of words*, i.e., numeric representations based on word occurrences (Aggarwal and Zhai, 2012).

Embedding-based text clustering is proposed as an alternative to topic modeling for identifying topics in text data (e.g., Angelov (2020); Sia et al. (2020)). Unlike topic modeling, text clustering does not assign descriptive keywords to topics. These need to be extracted separately using techniques like *term frequency–inverse document frequency* (TF-IDF). This statistical measure calculates the relevance of words in a text collection (Ramos, 2003). We use embedding-based text clustering since it can be advantageous for social media data, as it may work better with short texts (Egger and Yu, 2022).

Creating hierarchies for text collections, as opposed to flat clustering, can help to explore and understand the contextual relationships (Cutting et al., 1992). Hierarchical clustering algorithms are often computationally expensive (Aggarwal and Zhai, 2012), limiting their use on large datasets. In this work, we use the Sub-Cluster Component Algorithm by Monath et al. (2021), who address this issue through various conceptional improvements compared to the traditional hierarchical agglomerative clustering without sacrificing clustering quality. Through the use of this algorithm, the clustering is based entirely on text embeddings. This is in contrast to the text clustering framework BERTopic (Grootendorst, 2022), which enables hierarchical text clustering, but combines the clustering of text embeddings and bag of words.

### 2.3 COVID-19-specific X Analysis

Various studies used sentiment analysis to analyze the online debate on X around COVID-19 during the pandemic in Germany. Reiter-Haas et al. (2023) analyzed the debate on contact tracing, vaccination, and face masks and contrasted the results with survey results. Schmidt et al. (2022) focused on the 2021 federal election in Germany. They analyzed the change in sentiments of the political parties' posts in the election. Rowe et al. (2021) used topic modeling and sentiment analysis to analyze X data from Germany, other European countries, and the United States to understand the sentiment towards immigration during the early stage of the COVID-19 pandemic in 2020. None of these studies used text clustering.

Santoro et al. (2023) used flat text clustering to analyze the different aspects of the online debate about vaccination in different countries over time. However, they did not consider sentiments.

In non-German analyses, Sanders et al. (2021) combined text clustering and sentiment analysis to study English face mask-related posts. They represented topics in a two-level hierarchy. Purnat et al. (2021) developed a more fine-grained hierarchy of five levels for classifying COVID-19 online conversations in English and French. However, posts were classified into topics with manually defined keywords. This taxonomy then served as the basis for the semi-supervised topic classification in EARS (White et al., 2023).

This work combines and expands on the ideas of Sanders et al. (2021) and Purnat et al. (2021) and presents a social listening approach for public health that unifies topic and sentiment analysis. Our approach allows a flexible representation of the hierarchy with an adjustable number of levels. Additionally, our work contributes to the analysis of the social media discourse during the COVID-19 pandemic in Germany, surpassing the time period of data considered in previous work (Reiter-Haas et al., 2023).

## 3 Data

In this section, we describe the collection of X data and the dataset construction for sentiment analysis.

### 3.1 X (formerly Twitter) Data

**Collecting German posts** Between November 2022 and April 2023, we collected 50% of all original posts (i.e., excluding replies, comments, or quotes) in the German language for the year 2020 using the Academic Research API (X, 2023a). We used the post counts API (X, 2024) to estimate the number of original posts in 2020 per minute. For each minute (the smallest possible sampling time period for API queries), the API returned 50% of posts starting from the end of each minute. As true random sampling is not possible with the research API, we used the smallest possible time period, aiming to retrieve a representative sample of the entire stream that reflects its temporal characteristics, e.g., day/night shifts, and discussed topics for posts in the German language. We used the language tag provided by the API and refined the data through language identification with FastText (Joulin et al., 2017). We limited the posts to 2020 because X terminated our API access in April 2023. The final dataset contained 38 million posts.

**Face mask dataset** We filtered posts by words used to describe face masks: 'Maske' ('mask'), 'Mundschutz' and 'Mund-Nasen-Schutz' ('face mask' or 'surgical mask'), and 'FFP2', resulting in a *face mask dataset* with 353,420 posts.[1] Using a sample of 1,000 included and excluded posts, we calculated a precision of 97.4% and a recall of 100% (cf. Limitations). We note that this dataset is not limited to posts originating from Germany but includes any posts in German. In line with

[1]For 'Mund-Nasen-Schutz', we included 'Mundnasenschutz' and 'Mund-Nasenschutz' as variations. We excluded posts containing '#maskedsinger', '#themaskedsinger', 'maskedsinger', or 'masked singer' (relating to a German TV show). We used lowercasing for filtering.

our Ethics Statement, we exclude any location data from our analysis.

For context, we included the *7-day incidence rate*, i.e., the sum of COVID-19 cases in Germany with a reporting date within the last seven days, based on 100,000 inhabitants (Robert Koch-Institut, 2024).

### 3.2 Sentiment Analysis Data

**Data selection** We sampled 2,200 posts from the face mask dataset, using weights based on hourly relative frequency to maintain a similar temporal distribution. We adjusted the weights using the square root of relative frequencies to avoid oversampling periods with high post volume. This ensured that events related to the face mask requirement in Germany, which may have led to an increased post volume in the face mask dataset, were proportionally represented in the sample.

**Annotation** We asked seven annotators to label the general sentiments expressed in posts. Every post was labeled by three different annotators (at least 500 posts per annotator). Annotators were instructed to classify posts into four distinct categories: *neutral*, *negative*, *positive*, and *mixed* (containing *negative* and *positive* sentiments). We provided annotators with instructions and examples (not included in the final dataset). We used the majority rule to decide on the final label of posts (Table 1) and excluded samples without a majority from the final dataset. To measure the agreement between annotators, we report a Fleiss' $\kappa$ (Fleiss and Cohen, 1973) of 0.60, calculated using statsmodels (Seabold and Perktold, 2010). This score indicates moderate agreement (Landis and Koch, 1977) and is comparable to Schmidt et al. (2022), who annotated X posts by German politicians in a similar setting.

| Sentiment | Count | Percentage |
|---|---|---|
| neutral | 876 | 40.26% |
| negative | 858 | 39.45% |
| positive | 239 | 10.99% |
| mixed | 130 | 5.98% |
| no majority | 72 | 3.31% |

Table 1: Results of the data annotation for sentiment analysis based on samples from the face mask dataset.

**Data splitting** Finally, we split the annotated dataset into training, validation, and test sets using a 7:1:2 stratified random split, i.e., maintaining the original class distribution (Table 1) across splits. We only used posts with neutral, negative, or positive labels. We removed mixed posts to establish a stronger baseline for distinguishing between the primary sentiment classes.

## 4 Methodology

In the follwoing, we outline the training of the sentiment classifier, the application of hierarchical clustering, and the analytical approach.

### 4.1 Sentiment Analysis

For training the sentiment classifier, the base version of GBERT (Chan et al., 2020) serves as a starting point. GBERT has shown competitive results in German sentiment analysis (Schmidt et al., 2022; Zielinski et al., 2023). We consider two scenarios: First, using GBERT out-of-the-box for initializing a classifier. Second, we continue pretraining on the face mask dataset using whole word 'masking' similar to GBERT. This excludes the sentiment analysis data. For continued pretraining, we use the hyper-parameter setup for task-adaptive pretraining (TAPT) as suggested by Gururangan et al. (2020). For the supervised fine-tuning, we use the hyper-parameter setup suggested by Devlin et al. (2019). We base model selection on validation set performance, with an evaluation carried out every 10 steps. The training is performed on a single NVIDIA A100 GPU with the PyTorch (Ansel et al., 2024) and Transformers (Wolf et al., 2020) frameworks.

### 4.2 Hierarchical Clustering

The Sub-Cluster Component Algorithm (SCC, Monath et al. (2021)) is used for hierarchical text clustering thanks to its competitive performance on large datasets. SCC operates on nearest-neighbor similarity, repeatedly merging clusters to build a tree with multiple partition levels. The user controls these levels and the minimum similarity threshold for cluster merging. In this work, we represent posts as embeddings, using cosine similarity to define similarity. Cosine similarity is a standard metric to measure semantic similarity for vector-based text representations (Chandrasekaran and Mago, 2021) and is used by Monath et al. (2021).[2]

In the first step, posts are embedded using *German BERT large paraphrase cosine* (May et al.,

[2]We provide code on GitHub: https://github.com/ClimSocAna/sentiments-with-hierarchical-clustering.

2023), a GBERT-large model fine-tuned for representing text similarity using cosine similarity. GBERT models show competitive results for German language text clustering (Wehrli et al., 2023), making *German BERT large paraphrase cosine* well-suited for the use with the SCC algorithm.

In the second step, the dataset is transformed into a nearest neighbors graph using Faiss (Douze et al., 2024). This graph is then used as an input to the SCC algorithm, with the state-of-the-art parameter setup (Monath et al., 2021), which includes 200 rounds of geometrically increasing thresholds and average linkage clustering. To improve computational efficiency, Monath et al. (2021) use a highly sparsified nearest neighbors graph (considering the 25 closest neighbors) to approximate cluster similarity. However, in this work, the number of neighbors considered is increased as much as possible (10,000 neighbors) to obtain the most accurate clustering possible. Given our computational resources, this results in RAM use of roughly 300 GB and a runtime of under 10 hours in a multi-CPU setup.

### 4.3 Analytical Approach

**Topic size** To measure a topic's importance, we use the number of posts it contains to represent the range of discussed content. Depending on the research question, however, this metric could be adapted, for example, by including the popularity of posts to give greater weight to social resonance.

**Sentiment score** We use a *sentiment score* to analyze the sentiment of topics. This score is defined as

$$score_{t,p} = \frac{|posts_{t,p,pos}| - |posts_{t,p,neg}|}{|posts_{t,p,all}|}, \quad (1)$$

where $posts$ denotes the set of posts for a topic $t$, a period of time $p$, and for specific sentiments ($neg$ for negative, $pos$ for positive, $all$ for all categories). The sentiment score calculates the average sentiment for a set of posts, considering positive and negative posts as polar values (+1, respectively, -1). We use this metric to highlight differences in topics based on their sentiment composition.

**Cluster selection** The SCC's multi-level output allows us to analyze topics in varying detail. To demonstrate the flexibility of the hierarchical clustering, we select three levels of increasing topic granularity with 20, 104, and 1,051 clusters, respectively.

**Cluster labeling and validation** We first extract descriptive keywords for each cluster using class-based TF-IDF (Grootendorst, 2022). This is a variation of the traditional TF-IDF, which emphasizes the distinctiveness of keywords between clusters. We limit the set of candidate words to lemmatized content words to increase the information value of keywords, using tokenization (Proisl and Uhrig, 2016), part-of-speech tagging (Proisl, 2018) and lemmatization (Schmid, 1999). We select components optimized for German social media text based on Ortmann et al. (2019).[3] We validate clustering quality through keyword analysis and random sampling of 200 posts per cluster to ensure the analyzed clusters represent distinct topics. The selection process could be supplemented by measures that quantify the quality of individual levels through intra- and inter-cluster (dis)similarity. We manually extract labels for each analyzed cluster based on the extracted keywords and the sampled posts.

**Cluster visualization** Hierarchical clustering organizes data into a tree-like structure called a dendrogram, where each node represents a cluster, and the branches show the relationships between them. The dendrogram's structure is often used to visualize the hierarchical relationships between the clusters. It is important to note that the clusters are, fundamentally, sets of data points, not tree structures. However, visualizations based on dendrograms are limited by the quantification of the underlying clustering metrics and by their lack of flexibility and customizability.

Given these limitations, we use a treemap idiom to provide a compact and intuitive way (Hattab et al., 2020) to navigate and explore the resulting hierarchies. The treemaps visualize the hierarchical relationships between clusters by making the size of each node proportional to the relative importance or size of the cluster. The hierarchical structure is conveyed by the nested layout of the treemap, where child nodes are contained within their parent nodes. This allows the visualization of complex topic hierarchies and identifies dominant topics and their relationships.

Two use cases are considered to illustrate the treemap idiom. They address the relationships of subclusters to their parent cluster and the temporal

[3]We provide a spaCy-based (Honnibal et al., 2020) implementation on GitHub: `https://github.com/slvnwhrl/GerSoMeTokenExtractor`.

Figure 1: The number of German X posts discussing *face masks* relative to the 7-day incidence rate of COVID-19 cases (Robert Koch-Institut, 2024) and selected events (DW, 2020; MDR, 2020; Tagesschau, 2020a,b) in Germany.

changes of the relative importance of one subcluster. This relies on the overview detail and the small multiple idioms (Shneiderman, 2003) and corresponds to Figures 2 and 3, respectively.

## 5 Results & Analysis

In this section, we evaluate the results of the sentiment classification training, followed by the analysis of the face mask dataset.

### 5.1 Evaluation of the Sentiment Classification

**Results** Table 2 reports the overall results for the classification of neutral, negative, and positive sentiments of posts on the test set for the fine-tuned GBERT models (as outlined in Subsection 4.1). Additionally, we evaluated $\text{GBERT}_{\text{broad}}$ and XLM-T as baselines. $\text{GBERT}_{\text{SFT}}$, fine-tuned on the annotated face mask posts, achieved an average weighted F1-score of 77.90%. $\text{GBERT}_{\text{broad}}$ fell significantly behind with a more than 20 percentage points lower $\text{F1}_{\text{weighted}}$. The performance gap of XLM-T is much smaller at less than four percentage points. $\text{GBERT}_{\text{TAPT+SFT}}$ delivered the best results, achieving an 3.06 percentage points higher average weighted F1-score than $\text{GBERT}_{\text{SFT}}$ through additional pretraining. Based on these results, we used the best-performing $\text{GBERT}_{\text{TAPT+SFT}}$ to analyze the face mask dataset.[4]

**Error analysis** The most common errors of $\text{GBERT}_{\text{TAPT+SFT}}$ were neutral posts misclassified as negative, vice versa, and positive posts misclassified as neutral (cf. Table 3, Appendix A). Predictions for the neutral and negative classes showed relatively balanced precision and recall compared to the positive class (cf. Table 4, Appendix A). The lower overall F1-score (68.97%) and comparatively lower recall (62.50%) of the positive class is likely, to some degree, a result of the class imbalance (Table 1, Johnson and Khoshgoftaar (2019)).

The inspection of misclassified samples showed that the model sometimes struggled with implicit sentiment and sarcasm, likely contributing to the lower performance of the positive class (Riloff et al., 2013).

| Model | Accuracy | $\text{F1}_{\text{macro}}$ | $\text{F1}_{\text{weighted}}$ |
|---|---|---|---|
| $\text{GBERT}_{\text{SFT}}$ | 79.24% | 75.77% | 79.45% |
| | *78.08%* | *73.49%* | *77.90%* |
| $\text{GBERT}_{\text{TAPT+SFT}}$ | 82.53% | 79.13% | 82.36% |
| | *81.06%* | *77.60%* | *80.96%* |
| $\text{GBERT}_{\text{broad}}$ | 56.20% | 47.57% | 54.05% |
| XLM-T | 74.18% | 71.24% | 74.20% |

Table 2: Test set results for sentiment classification of face mask-related X posts. For $\text{GBERT}_{\text{SFT}}$ and $\text{GBERT}_{\text{TAPT+SFT}}$, we report single-best model results and the average of five models with different seeds (in *italic*). $\text{GBERT}_{\text{broad}}$ (Guhr et al., 2020) and XLM-T (Barbieri et al., 2022) are models from the literature, serving as baselines.

### 5.2 Results and Discussion of the Face Mask Dataset

The face mask dataset represents the dynamic social media discourse about face masks during the COVID-19 pandemic (Figure 1). The rise in notified COVID-19 cases, i.e., the 7-day incidence rate, and introductions of public health interventions were often associated with increased online conversation on this topic. Some events stand out, especially the initial introduction of the mask requirement in April 2020 (Figure 1). The falling number of cases in the summer of 2020 fueled the debate about the necessity of wearing face masks, for example, at the beginning of July. With the ris-

[4]We released the best-performing model on Hugging Face: https://huggingface.co/slvnwhrl/gbert-face-mask-sentiment.

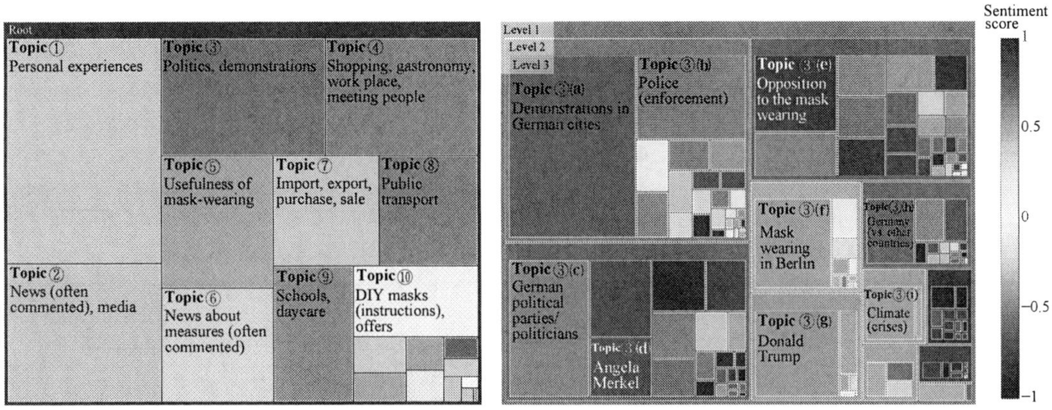


Figure 2: *Left*: Treemap depicting topics of German language face mask-related discourse on X in 2020. Posts are hierarchically clustered into 20 topics. Cluster sizes reflect the number of posts in each topic; colors encode the value of the sentiment score (Equation 1), which represents the mean sentiment of posts for each topic (1 = completely positive, -1 = completely negative). $\text{GBERT}_{\text{TAPT+SFT}}$ was used to assign sentiments to posts. Topic labels were manually extracted from 200 randomly sampled posts per cluster and shown for the 10 largest topics. *Right*: Treemap depicting the subtopics of topic ③ (level 1) on the two lower levels of the clustering hierarchy (level 2 and 3). The largest subtopics on level 3 were manually labeled.

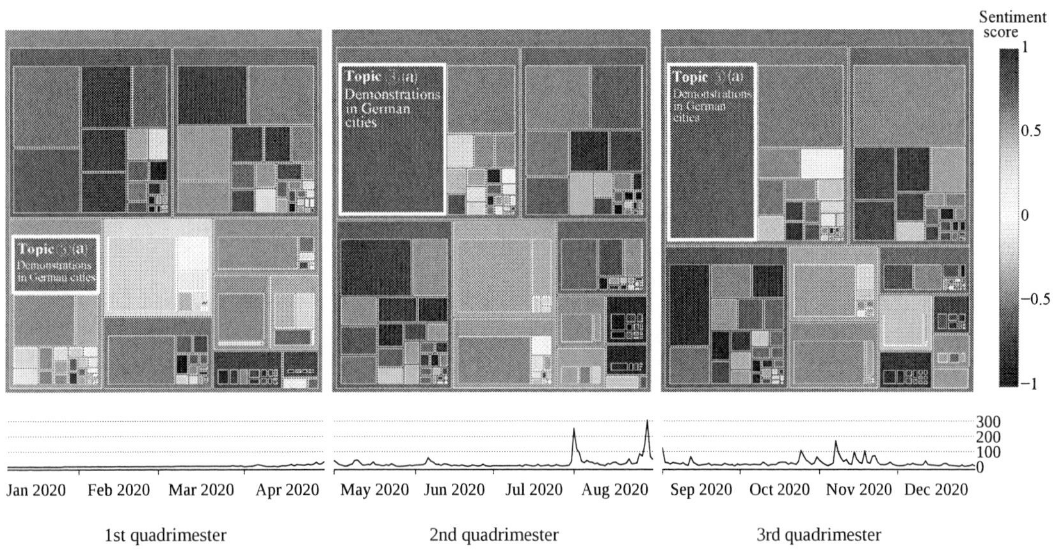


Figure 3: *Top*: Small multiples of the treemap of topic ③ (Figure 2, *right*) for the three quadrimesters of 2020. Subtopic ③$(a)$ ('Demonstrations in German cities') is highlighted through a thicker border. The treemaps show the change in relative size and sentiment score of the subtopics over time. Representation of cluster sizes and colors follow the same approach as in Figure 2. *Bottom*: Small multiples of frequency charts showing the number of posts in subtopic ③(a), allowing to identify times with high post volume.

ing case numbers in autumn, new public health and social measures were implemented, which included the restriction of social contacts and the temporary closure of restaurants or cultural institutions, but less restrictive than during the first lockdown in March 2020 (Die Bundesregierung, 2020a,c). Finally, the federal government imposed a second lockdown before Christmas (Die Bundesregierung, 2020d). These dates showed a lower number of posts than during the first introduction of mandatory face mask wearing.

**Topics overview** The dynamic nature of the debate can also be seen in the overarching topics of the discourse on X, resulting from the hierarchical clustering (Figure 2). We provide an interactive visualization on GitHub.[5] The most prominently discussed topics are areas of life that were often the target of public health measures, namely stores (④), public transport (⑧), or schools (⑨). When reviewing samples, we observed that many posts contain descriptions of everyday life, such as other people's behavior when shopping, e.g., when neglecting the face mask mandate. The data show that a large part of posts are about sharing experiences (①) and include a large variety of topics.

Sharing news also plays an important role in the COVID-19 discourse on face masks; on the one hand, news specific to the introduction of the mask requirement (②), but also more general news on the subject of masks, such as reports on the number of COVID-19 cases (⑥). It is noticeable that posts with shared news (e.g., with a link) often also contain the user's opinion about the content. We identified similar tendencies for topics that mainly revolve around the benefits of masks (⑤) and the political and social debate surrounding the obligation to wear masks (③).

Finally, some topics deal primarily with the production of do-it-yourself (DIY) masks (⑩) and the procurement of masks (⑦).

Overall, posts expressing negative sentiment dominated the discourse (Figure 2, *left*). In fact, more negative than positive posts were published at all times during the investigated year (cf. Figure 4, Appendix A). Some topics are particularly negative (③, ④, ⑧, ⑨), with the topic on DIY masks (⑩) standing out as the only topic with a slightly positive sentiment. During the analysis, we often noticed posts in which users shared their DIY masks. In Figure 2, we show the subtopics, i.e., deeper level, of the topic of politics and demonstrations (③), to present a more differentiated view of this particularly negative topic. Within this topic, users discuss German or international politicians (e.g., Angela Merkel (③(d)) or Donald Trump (③(g))), Germany in international comparison (③(h)), or topics related explicitly to Berlin (③(f)) or the climate (③(i)). This view reveals differences in the relative importance and sentiment of subtopics that make up the overall negative sentiment of the higher-level topic and shows that mask wearing is discussed in very different political contexts.

**Demonstrations** The topic of demonstrations in German cities is particularly striking due to its size and negativity (Figure 2, *right*). Thus, we chose this topic for a more detailed analysis, exemplifying the capabilities of hierarchical text clustering to guide sentiment analysis. In Germany, the first demonstrations against public measures took place at the beginning of May, with larger demonstrations occurring repeatedly throughout the year, for example, in Berlin and Leipzig (MDR, 2020). Figure 3 shows the size and sentiment of the subtopic cluster in the parent topic of politics and demonstrations (*top*) and the number of posts on demonstrations in German cities (*bottom*) in the three quadrimesters of 2020. We found that demonstrations are more frequently discussed over the course of 2020 and contribute more to the parent topic without significant changes in negativity (Figure 3, *top*). Pointwise increases in posts occurred at the time of specific demonstrations (Figure 3, *bottom*), e.g., two large demonstrations with tens of thousands of participants in Berlin at the beginning and end of August 2020 (MDR, 2020).

**Comparing results** Reiter-Haas et al. (2023) also investigated the sentiments of face mask-related German posts from X. They did not find a clear tendency towards positive or negative sentiments. Compared to our study, they used a smaller X sample for sentiment analysis (15,425 versus 353,420 posts), only considered data from January to August 2020 (as opposed to data from the whole year), and used a different method for sentiment analysis (based on a sentiment lexicon). These factors may explain the different outcome of our study, as we find that the majority of posts are negative.

Sanders et al. (2021) used two-level hierarchical text clustering to analyze English X posts on face masks from March to July 2020. They identified topic clusters of varying sentiments, similar to our findings. However, posts with negative sentiments did not dominate the overall discourse. Additionally, topical parallels can be drawn between the discourse on political actors (such as Donald Trump) or on public measures such as the requirement to wear face masks in stores, and the sharing of personal experiences from everyday life. Similar to Reiter-Haas et al. (2023), they used lexicon-based sentiment analysis, albeit on a larger sample (1,013,039 posts).

## 6 Conclusion and Outlook

This study employed hierarchical text clustering and sentiment analysis to examine the public dis-

[5] `https://github.com/ClimSocAna/sentiments-with-hierarchical-clustering`.

course surrounding face masks in Germany during the COVID-19 pandemic 2020. Our analysis of 353,420 face mask-related posts reveals the dynamics of the German public's online response on X (formerly Twitter) to mask mandates. Our findings indicate an overall negative sentiment dominating face mask-related posts. Analyzing specific topics revealed nuanced sentiment patterns. For instance, the topic of DIY masks was slightly positive, while topics linked to COVID-19 demonstrations and general political discourse on face mask policies showed stronger negativity. We show that the combination of clustering, sentiment classification, and suitable visualization helps analyze complex social media discourse in a structured manner. This study thereby advances the methods of social listening in public health. Furthermore, our analysis contributes to the understanding of the online information ecosystem during the COVID-19 pandemic in Germany. This is a prerequisite to better understand the (harmful) impact of the infodemic during the COVID-19 pandemic on the public. Ultimately, this enables knowledge-based preparation for a future pandemic that will likely be accompanied by an infodemic again (Briand et al., 2023; Wilhelm et al., 2023). In this context, the proposed approach enables structured analyses of social media data for topics that are relevant for the review of the COVID-19 pandemic, respectively, infodemic (such as mental health).

Our results offer a starting point for further research. The presented approach could be adapted for real-time infodemic surveillance ('infoveillance') to track sentiment dynamics and emerging topics during future health-related social media discourses, e.g., based on the online version of the SCC algorithm (Monath et al., 2023). To operationalize this approach during the next pandemic or public health crisis, developing a framework for interactive data exploration is required to generate insights that can inform public health action. Finally, specific investigations into the role of misinformation within negative clusters are needed to illuminate public health communication challenges.

## Limitations

**Keyword filtering** We noticed that a few posts were filtered incorrectly as relevant because 'Maske' ('mask') was used as a homonym for a beauty product or as part of a costume. Furthermore, other terms may be relevant to the online discussion about face masks, even if our analysis showed a high recall. For example, there are colloquial or dialect words to consider, such as 'Schnutenpulli' (NORD24, 2020), originally from Low German. Finally, we did not consider misspellings.

**Clustering** While the chosen clustering algorithm and language model have proven effective, a key limitation is their singularity. Exploring multiple clustering algorithms and language models could reveal different data structures and provide more nuanced insights. Comparing the results from diverse methods would help assess the robustness of the observed clusters and sentiment patterns.

**Social media data** Finally, we note that accessing data from social media platforms remains challenging, which currently limits the application of our approach to X data. The European Union's *Digital Services Act* is likely to improve this situation for infodemic research and practice in the future, as it will legally enable researchers to access data on large platforms (Wehrli et al., 2024).

## Ethics Statement

The X (formerly Twitter) data collected as part of this work is subject to X's Developer Agreement and Policy (X, 2023b) and the European Union's General Data Protection Regulation (GDPR, European Commission), which we comply with. We only process post texts and timestamps, remove user mentions and URLs from the post texts, and do not use any post metadata that allows the identification of individuals (such as user names or location data). In addition, we only present results at an aggregated level, i.e., for groups of posts. We do not publish or share any of the data or results in a way that does not align with X's Developer Agreement and Policy and the GDPR.

## Acknowledgments

We would like to thank the annotators of the sentiment analysis dataset for their help in realizing this work. We would also like to thank the reviewers for their time and valuable input.

## References

Charu C. Aggarwal and ChengXiang Zhai. 2012. *A Survey of Text Clustering Algorithms*, pages 77–128. Springer US, Boston, MA.

Dimo Angelov. 2020. Top2Vec: Distributed representations of topics. *Preprint*, arXiv:2008.09470.

Jason Ansel, Edward Yang, Horace He, Natalia Gimelshein, Animesh Jain, Michael Voznesensky, Bin Bao, Peter Bell, David Berard, Evgeni Burovski, Geeta Chauhan, Anjali Chourdia, Will Constable, Alban Desmaison, Zachary DeVito, Elias Ellison, Will Feng, Jiong Gong, Michael Gschwind, Brian Hirsh, Sherlock Huang, Kshiteej Kalambarkar, Laurent Kirsch, Michael Lazos, Mario Lezcano, Yanbo Liang, Jason Liang, Yinghai Lu, C. K. Luk, Bert Maher, Yunjie Pan, Christian Puhrsch, Matthias Reso, Mark Saroufim, Marcos Yukio Siraichi, Helen Suk, Shunting Zhang, Michael Suo, Phil Tillet, Xu Zhao, Eikan Wang, Keren Zhou, Richard Zou, Xiaodong Wang, Ajit Mathews, William Wen, Gregory Chanan, Peng Wu, and Soumith Chintala. 2024. PyTorch 2: Faster machine learning through dynamic python bytecode transformation and graph compilation. In *Proceedings of the 29th ACM International Conference on Architectural Support for Programming Languages and Operating Systems, Volume 2*, ASPLOS '24, page 929–947, New York, NY, USA. Association for Computing Machinery.

Oliver Baclic, Matthew Tunis, Kelsey Young, Coraline Doan, Howard Swerdfeger, and Justin Schonfeld. 2020. Challenges and opportunities for public health made possible by advances in natural language processing. *Can Commun Dis Rep*, 46(6):161–168.

Francesco Barbieri, Luis Espinosa Anke, and Jose Camacho-Collados. 2022. XLM-T: Multilingual language models in Twitter for sentiment analysis and beyond. In *Proceedings of the Thirteenth Language Resources and Evaluation Conference*, pages 258–266, Marseille, France. European Language Resources Association.

David M. Blei. 2012. Probabilistic topic models. *Commun. ACM*, 55(4):77–84.

T Sonia Boender, Paula Helene Schneider, Claudia Houareau, Silvan Wehrli, Tina D Purnat, Atsuyoshi Ishizumi, Elisabeth Wilhelm, Christopher Voegeli, Lothar H Wieler, and Christina Leuker. 2023. Establishing infodemic management in Germany: A framework for social listening and integrated analysis to report infodemic insights at the national public health institute. *JMIR Infodemiology*, 3:e43646.

Israel Júnior Borges do Nascimento, Ana Beatriz Pizarro, Jussara Almeida, Natasha Azzopardi-Muscat, Marcos André Gonçalves, Maria Björklund, and David Novillo-Ortiz. 2022. Infodemics and health misinformation: a systematic review of reviews. *Bull. World Health Organ.*, 100(9):544–561.

Janos Borst, Jannis Klaehn, and Manuel Burghardt. 2023. Death of the dictionary? - the rise of zero-shot sentiment classification. In *Proceedings of the Computational Humanities Research Conference 2023, Paris, France, December 6-8, 2023*, volume 3558 of *CEUR Workshop Proceedings*, pages 303–319. CEUR-WS.org.

Sylvie Briand, Sarah Hess, Tim Nguyen, and Tina D. Purnat. 2023. *Infodemic Management in the Twenty-First Century*, pages 1–16. Springer International Publishing, Cham.

Neville Calleja, AbdelHalim AbdAllah, Neetu Abad, Naglaa Ahmed, Dolores Albarracin, Elena Altieri, Julienne N Anoko, Ruben Arcos, Arina Anis Azlan, Judit Bayer, Anja Bechmann, Supriya Bezbaruah, Sylvie C Briand, Ian Brooks, Lucie M Bucci, Stefano Burzo, Christine Czerniak, Manlio De Domenico, Adam G Dunn, Ullrich K H Ecker, Laura Espinosa, Camille Francois, Kacper Gradon, Anatoliy Gruzd, Beste Sultan Gülgün, Rustam Haydarov, Cherstyn Hurley, Santi Indra Astuti, Atsuyoshi Ishizumi, Neil Johnson, Dylan Johnson Restrepo, Masato Kajimoto, Aybüke Koyuncu, Shibani Kulkarni, Jaya Lamichhane, Rosamund Lewis, Avichal Mahajan, Ahmed Mandil, Erin McAweeney, Melanie Messer, Wesley Moy, Patricia Ndumbi Ngamala, Tim Nguyen, Mark Nunn, Saad B Omer, Claudia Pagliari, Palak Patel, Lynette Phuong, Dimitri Prybylski, Arash Rashidian, Emily Rempel, Sara Rubinelli, PierLuigi Sacco, Anton Schneider, Kai Shu, Melanie Smith, Harry Sufehmi, Viroj Tangcharoensathien, Robert Terry, Naveen Thacker, Tom Trewinnard, Shannon Turner, Heidi Tworek, Saad Uakkas, Emily Vraga, Claire Wardle, Herman Wasserman, Elisabeth Wilhelm, Andrea Würz, Brian Yau, Lei Zhou, and Tina D Purnat. 2021. A public health research agenda for managing infodemics: Methods and results of the first WHO infodemiology conference. *JMIR Infodemiology*, 1(1):e30979.

Branden Chan, Stefan Schweter, and Timo Möller. 2020. German's next language model. In *Proceedings of the 28th International Conference on Computational Linguistics*, pages 6788–6796, Barcelona, Spain (Online). International Committee on Computational Linguistics.

Dhivya Chandrasekaran and Vijay Mago. 2021. Evolution of semantic similarity—a survey. *ACM Comput. Surv.*, 54(2).

Alexis Conneau, Kartikay Khandelwal, Naman Goyal, Vishrav Chaudhary, Guillaume Wenzek, Francisco Guzmán, Edouard Grave, Myle Ott, Luke Zettlemoyer, and Veselin Stoyanov. 2020. Unsupervised cross-lingual representation learning at scale. In *Proceedings of the 58th Annual Meeting of the Association for Computational Linguistics*, pages 8440–8451, Online. Association for Computational Linguistics.

Douglass R. Cutting, David R. Karger, Jan O. Pedersen, and John W. Tukey. 1992. Scatter/gather: a cluster-based approach to browsing large document collections. In *Proceedings of the 15th Annual International ACM SIGIR Conference on Research and Development in Information Retrieval*, SIGIR '92, page 318–329, New York, NY, USA. Association for Computing Machinery.

Deutschlandfunk. 2020. Chronologie eines Schuljahrs in der Coronakrise. `https:`

//www.deutschlandfunk.de/rueckblick-2020-chronologie-eines-schuljahrs-in-der-100.html. Accessed: 2024-04-12.

Jacob Devlin, Ming-Wei Chang, Kenton Lee, and Kristina Toutanova. 2019. BERT: Pre-training of deep bidirectional transformers for language understanding. In *Proceedings of the 2019 Conference of the North American Chapter of the Association for Computational Linguistics: Human Language Technologies, Volume 1 (Long and Short Papers)*, pages 4171–4186, Minneapolis, Minnesota. Association for Computational Linguistics.

Die Bundesregierung. 2020a. Diese Regeln gelten jetzt. https://www.bundesregierung.de/breg-de/themen/coronavirus/regelungen-ab-2-november-1806818. Accessed: 2024-05-02.

Die Bundesregierung. 2020b. Maskenpflicht in ganz Deutschland. https://www.bundesregierung.de/breg-de/themen/coronavirus/maskenpflicht-in-deutschland-1747318. Accessed: 2024-04-12.

Die Bundesregierung. 2020c. Telefonschaltkonferenz der Bundeskanzlerin mit den Regierungschefinnen und Regierungschefs der Länder am 15. April 2020. https://www.bundesregierung.de/breg-de/aktuelles/bund-laender-beschluss-1744224. Accessed: 2024-05-02.

Die Bundesregierung. 2020d. "Wir sind zum Handeln gezwungen". https://www.bundesregierung.de/breg-de/themen/coronavirus/merkel-beschluss-weihnachten-1827396. Accessed: 2024-05-02.

Matthijs Douze, Alexandr Guzhva, Chengqi Deng, Jeff Johnson, Gergely Szilvasy, Pierre-Emmanuel Mazaré, Maria Lomeli, Lucas Hosseini, and Hervé Jégou. 2024. The Faiss library. *Preprint*, arXiv:2401.08281.

DW. 2020. Masken gegen Corona: Wie lange noch? https://www.dw.com/de/masken-gegen-corona-wie-lange-noch/a-54060107. Accessed: 2024-04-30.

Roman Egger and Joanne Yu. 2022. A topic modeling comparison between LDA, NMF, Top2Vec, and BERTopic to demystify Twitter posts. *Frontiers in Sociology*, 7.

European Commission. Data protection in the EU. https://commission.europa.eu/law/law-topic/data-protection/data-protection-eu_en. Accessed: 2024-05-12.

Joseph L. Fleiss and Jacob Cohen. 1973. The Equivalence of Weighted Kappa and the Intraclass Correlation Coefficient as Measures of Reliability. *Educational and Psychological Measurement*, 33(3):613–619.

Maarten Grootendorst. 2022. Bertopic: Neural topic modeling with a class-based tf-idf procedure. *Preprint*, arXiv:2203.05794.

Oliver Guhr, Anne-Kathrin Schumann, Frank Bahrmann, and Hans Joachim Böhme. 2020. Training a broad-coverage German sentiment classification model for dialog systems. In *Proceedings of the Twelfth Language Resources and Evaluation Conference*, pages 1627–1632, Marseille, France. European Language Resources Association.

Suchin Gururangan, Ana Marasović, Swabha Swayamdipta, Kyle Lo, Iz Beltagy, Doug Downey, and Noah A. Smith. 2020. Don't stop pretraining: Adapt language models to domains and tasks. In *Proceedings of the 58th Annual Meeting of the Association for Computational Linguistics*, pages 8342–8360, Online. Association for Computational Linguistics.

Georges Hattab, Theresa-Marie Rhyne, and Dominik Heider. 2020. Ten simple rules to colorize biological data visualization. *PLOS Computational Biology*, 16(10):e1008259.

Matthew Honnibal, Ines Montani, Sofie Van Landeghem, and Adriane Boyd. 2020. spaCy: Industrial-strength Natural Language Processing in Python.

Justin M. Johnson and Taghi M. Khoshgoftaar. 2019. Survey on deep learning with class imbalance. *Journal of Big Data*, 6(1):27.

Armand Joulin, Edouard Grave, Piotr Bojanowski, and Tomas Mikolov. 2017. Bag of tricks for efficient text classification. In *Proceedings of the 15th Conference of the European Chapter of the Association for Computational Linguistics: Volume 2, Short Papers*, pages 427–431, Valencia, Spain. Association for Computational Linguistics.

J. Richard Landis and Gary G. Koch. 1977. The measurement of observer agreement for categorical data. *Biometrics*, 33(1):159–174.

Stephan Lewandowsky, John Cook, and Doug Lombardi. 2020. Debunking handbook 2020.

Bing Liu. 2012. *Sentiment analysis and opinion mining*. Springer Nature.

Phillip May, Deutsche Telekom AG, and deepset GmbH. 2023. German BERT large paraphrase cosine. https://huggingface.co/deutsche-telekom/gbert-large-paraphrase-cosine. Accessed: 2024-05-13.

MDR. 2020. 2020: Die Chronik der Corona-Krise. https://www.mdr.de/nachrichten/jahresrueckblick/corona-chronik-chronologie-coronavirus-102.html. Accessed: 2024-04-12.

Nicholas Monath, Kumar Avinava Dubey, Guru Guruganesh, Manzil Zaheer, Amr Ahmed, Andrew McCallum, Gokhan Mergen, Marc Najork, Mert Terzihan, Bryon Tjanaka, Yuan Wang, and Yuchen Wu. 2021. Scalable hierarchical agglomerative clustering. In *Proceedings of the 27th ACM SIGKDD Conference on Knowledge Discovery & Data Mining*, KDD '21, page 1245–1255, New York, NY, USA. Association for Computing Machinery.

Nicholas Monath, Manzil Zaheer, and Andrew McCallum. 2023. Online level-wise hierarchical clustering. In *Proceedings of the 29th ACM SIGKDD Conference on Knowledge Discovery and Data Mining*, KDD '23, page 1733–1745, New York, NY, USA. Association for Computing Machinery.

NORD24. 2020. "Schnutenpulli" ist das plattdeutsche Wort des Jahres. https://www.nord24.de/der-norden/schnutenpulli-ist-das-plattdeutsche-wort-des-jahres-44562.html. Accessed: 2024-05-15.

Katrin Ortmann, Adam Roussel, and Stefanie Dipper. 2019. Evaluating off-the-shelf NLP tools for German. In *Proceedings of the 15th Conference on Natural Language Processing (KONVENS 2019): Long Papers*, pages 212–222, Erlangen, Germany. German Society for Computational Linguistics & Language Technology.

Thomas Proisl. 2018. SoMeWeTa: A part-of-speech tagger for German social media and web texts. In *Proceedings of the Eleventh International Conference on Language Resources and Evaluation (LREC 2018)*, pages 665–670, Miyazaki. European Language Resources Association ELRA.

Thomas Proisl and Peter Uhrig. 2016. SoMaJo: State-of-the-art tokenization for German web and social media texts. In *Proceedings of the 10th Web as Corpus Workshop (WAC-X) and the EmpiriST Shared Task*, pages 57–62, Berlin. Association for Computational Linguistics.

Tina D Purnat, Paolo Vacca, Christine Czerniak, Sarah Ball, Stefano Burzo, Tim Zecchin, Amy Wright, Supriya Bezbaruah, Faizza Tanggol, Ève Dubé, Fabienne Labbé, Maude Dionne, Jaya Lamichhane, Avichal Mahajan, Sylvie Briand, and Tim Nguyen. 2021. Infodemic signal detection during the COVID-19 pandemic: Development of a methodology for identifying potential information voids in online conversations. *JMIR Infodemiology*, 1(1):e30971.

Juan Enrique Ramos. 2003. Using TF-IDF to determine word relevance in document queries. In *Proceedings of the first instructional conference on machine learning*.

Markus Reiter-Haas, Beate Klösch, Markus Hadler, and Elisabeth Lex. 2023. Polarization of opinions on COVID-19 measures: Integrating Twitter and survey data. *Social Science Computer Review*, 41(5):1811–1835.

Ellen Riloff, Ashequl Qadir, Prafulla Surve, Lalindra De Silva, Nathan Gilbert, and Ruihong Huang. 2013. Sarcasm as contrast between a positive sentiment and negative situation. In *Proceedings of the 2013 Conference on Empirical Methods in Natural Language Processing*, pages 704–714, Seattle, Washington, USA. Association for Computational Linguistics.

Robert Koch-Institut. 2024. 7-Tage-Inzidenz der COVID-19-Fälle in Deutschland.

Francisco Rowe, Michael Mahony, Eduardo Graells-Garrido, Marzia Rango, and Niklas Sievers. 2021. Using Twitter to track immigration sentiment during early stages of the COVID-19 pandemic. *Data & Policy*, 3:e36.

Abraham C Sanders, Rachael C White, Lauren S Severson, Rufeng Ma, Richard McQueen, Haniel C Alcântara Paulo, Yucheng Zhang, John S Erickson, and Kristin P Bennett. 2021. Unmasking the conversation on masks: Natural language processing for topical sentiment analysis of COVID-19 Twitter discourse. *AMIA Jt Summits Transl Sci Proc*, 2021:555–564.

Arnaldo Santoro, Alessandro Galeazzi, Teresa Scantamburlo, Andrea Baronchelli, Walter Quattrociocchi, and Fabiana Zollo. 2023. Analyzing the changing landscape of the Covid-19 vaccine debate on Twitter. *Social Network Analysis and Mining*, 13(1):115.

H. Schmid. 1999. *Improvements in Part-of-Speech Tagging with an Application to German*, pages 13–25. Springer Netherlands, Dordrecht.

Thomas Schmidt, Jakob Fehle, Maximilian Weissenbacher, Jonathan Richter, Philipp Gottschalk, and Christian Wolff. 2022. Sentiment analysis on Twitter for the major German parties during the 2021 German federal election. In *Proceedings of the 18th Conference on Natural Language Processing (KONVENS 2022)*, pages 74–87, Potsdam, Germany. KONVENS 2022 Organizers.

Skipper Seabold and Josef Perktold. 2010. Statsmodels: Econometric and statistical modeling with Python. In *9th Python in Science Conference*, pages 92–96.

Ben Shneiderman. 2003. The eyes have it: A task by data type taxonomy for information visualizations. In *The craft of information visualization*, pages 364–371. Elsevier.

Suzanna Sia, Ayush Dalmia, and Sabrina J. Mielke. 2020. Tired of topic models? clusters of pretrained word embeddings make for fast and good topics too! In *Proceedings of the 2020 Conference on Empirical Methods in Natural Language Processing (EMNLP)*, pages 1728–1736, Online. Association for Computational Linguistics.

Margaret C. Stewart and Christa L. Arnold. 2018. Defining social listening: Recognizing an emerging dimension of listening. *International Journal of Listening*, 32(2):85–100.

Julia Maria Struß, Melanie Siegel, Josef Ruppenhofer, Michael Wiegand, and Manfred Klenner. 2019. Overview of GermEval task 2, 2019 shared task on the identification of offensive language. In *Proceedings of the 15th Conference on Natural Language Processing (KONVENS 2019)*, pages 352 – 363.

Tagesschau. 2020a. "Eine fehlgeleitete Diskussion". `https://www.tagesschau.de/inland/corona-maskenpflicht-virologe-101.html`. Accessed: 2024-04-30.

Tagesschau. 2020b. Maskenpflicht in allen Bundesländern. `https://www.tagesschau.de/inland/corona-maskenpflicht-103.html`. Accessed: 2024-04-30.

Alexei Vinokourov, Nello Cristianini, and John Shawe-Taylor. 2002. Inferring a semantic representation of text via cross-language correlation analysis. In *Advances in Neural Information Processing Systems*, volume 15. MIT Press.

Emily K. Vraga, Ullrich K. H. Ecker, Iris Žeželj, Aleksandra Lazić, and Arina A. Azlan. 2023. *To Debunk or Not to Debunk? Correcting (Mis)Information*, pages 85–98. Springer International Publishing, Cham.

We Are Social, DataReportal, and Meltwater. 2024a. Global social network penetration rate as of January 2024, by region. `https://www.statista.com/statistics/269615/social-network-penetration-by-region/`. Accessed: 2024-04-12.

We Are Social, DataReportal, and Meltwater. 2024b. Most popular reasons for internet users worldwide to use social media as of 3rd quarter 2023. `https://www.statista.com/statistics/715449/social-media-usage-reasons-worldwide/`. Accessed: 2024-04-30.

Silvan Wehrli, Bert Arnrich, and Christopher Irrgang. 2023. German text embedding clustering benchmark. In *Proceedings of the 19th Conference on Natural Language Processing (KONVENS 2023)*, pages 187–201, Ingolstadt, Germany. Association for Computational Lingustics.

Silvan Wehrli, Christopher Irrgang, Mark Scott, Bert Arnrich, and T. Sonia Boender. 2024. The role of the (in)accessibility of social media data for infodemic management: a public health perspective on the situation in the European Union in March 2024. *Frontiers in Public Health*, 12.

Becky K White, Arnault Gombert, Tim Nguyen, Brian Yau, Atsuyoshi Ishizumi, Laura Kirchner, Alicia León, Harry Wilson, Giovanna Jaramillo-Gutierrez, Jesus Cerquides, Marcelo D'Agostino, Cristiana Salvi, Ravi Shankar Sreenath, Kimberly Rambaud, Dalia Samhouri, Sylvie Briand, and Tina D Purnat. 2023. Using machine learning technology (early artificial intelligence–supported response with social listening platform) to enhance digital social understanding for the COVID-19 infodemic: Development and implementation study. *JMIR Infodemiology*, 3:e47317.

Elisabeth Wilhelm, Isabella Ballalai, Marie-Eve Belanger, Peter Benjamin, Catherine Bertrand-Ferrandis, Supriya Bezbaruah, Sylvie Briand, Ian Brooks, Richard Bruns, Lucie M Bucci, Neville Calleja, Howard Chiou, Abhinav Devaria, Lorena Dini, Hyjel D'Souza, Adam G Dunn, Johannes C Eichstaedt, Silvia M A A Evers, Nina Gobat, Mika Gissler, Ian Christian Gonzales, Anatoliy Gruzd, Sarah Hess, Atsuyoshi Ishizumi, Oommen John, Ashish Joshi, Benjamin Kaluza, Nagwa Khamis, Monika Kosinska, Shibani Kulkarni, Dimitra Lingri, Ramona Ludolph, Tim Mackey, Stefan Mandić-Rajčević, Filippo Menczer, Vijaybabu Mudaliar, Shruti Murthy, Syed Nazakat, Tim Nguyen, Jennifer Nilsen, Elena Pallari, Natalia Pasternak Taschner, Elena Petelos, Mitchell J Prinstein, Jon Roozenbeek, Anton Schneider, Varadharajan Srinivasan, Aleksandar Stevanović, Brigitte Strahwald, Shabbir Syed Abdul, Sandra Varaidzo Machiri, Sander van der Linden, Christopher Voegeli, Claire Wardle, Odette Wegwarth, Becky K White, Estelle Willie, Brian Yau, and Tina D Purnat. 2023. Measuring the burden of infodemics: Summary of the methods and results of the fifth WHO infodemic management conference. *JMIR Infodemiology*, 3:e44207.

Peter Willett. 1988. Recent trends in hierarchic document clustering: A critical review. *Information Processing & Management*, 24(5):577–597.

Thomas Wolf, Lysandre Debut, Victor Sanh, Julien Chaumond, Clement Delangue, Anthony Moi, Pierric Cistac, Tim Rault, Remi Louf, Morgan Funtowicz, Joe Davison, Sam Shleifer, Patrick von Platen, Clara Ma, Yacine Jernite, Julien Plu, Canwen Xu, Teven Le Scao, Sylvain Gugger, Mariama Drame, Quentin Lhoest, and Alexander Rush. 2020. Transformers: State-of-the-art natural language processing. In *Proceedings of the 2020 Conference on Empirical Methods in Natural Language Processing: System Demonstrations*, pages 38–45, Online. Association for Computational Linguistics.

X. 2023a. Academic Research access. `https://web.archive.org/web/20230202074709/https://developer.twitter.com/en/products/twitter-api/academic-research`. Accessed: 2024-04-29.

X. 2023b. Developer agreement and policy. `https://developer.twitter.com/en/developer-terms/agreement-and-policy`. Accessed: 2024-05-12.

X. 2024. Tweet counts. `https://developer.twitter.com/en/docs/twitter-api/tweets/counts/introduction`. Accessed: 2024-04-29.

Jiaming Xu, Peng Wang, Guanhua Tian, Bo Xu, Jun Zhao, Fangyuan Wang, and Hongwei Hao. 2015. Short text clustering via convolutional neural networks. In *Proceedings of the 1st Workshop on Vector Space Modeling for Natural Language Process-*

*ing*, pages 62–69, Denver, Colorado. Association for Computational Linguistics.

Andrea Zielinski, Calvin Spolwind, Henning Kroll, and Anna Grimm. 2023. A dataset for explainable sentiment analysis in the German automotive industry. In *Proceedings of the 13th Workshop on Computational Approaches to Subjectivity, Sentiment, & Social Media Analysis*, pages 138–148, Toronto, Canada. Association for Computational Linguistics.

## A Additional Classification Results of the Sentiment Classification

| | | | | |
|---|---|---|---|---|
| **GT** | neutral | 147 | 22 | 6 |
| | negative | 20 | 149 | 3 |
| | positive | 12 | 6 | 30 |
| | | neutral | negative | positive |
| | | | **P** | |

Table 3: Confusion matrix showing the test set results of the sentiment classification of face mask-related X posts for $\text{GBERT}_{\text{TAPT+SFT}}$. **GT** denotes the ground truth and **P** the model's predictions.

| **Class** | **Precision** | **Recall** | **F1** |
|---|---|---|---|
| neutral | 84.18% | 86.63% | 85.39% |
| negative | 82.12% | 84.00% | 83.05% |
| positive | 76.92% | 62.50% | 68.97% |

Table 4: Per-class test set results of the sentiment classification of face mask-related X posts for $\text{GBERT}_{\text{TAPT+SFT}}$.

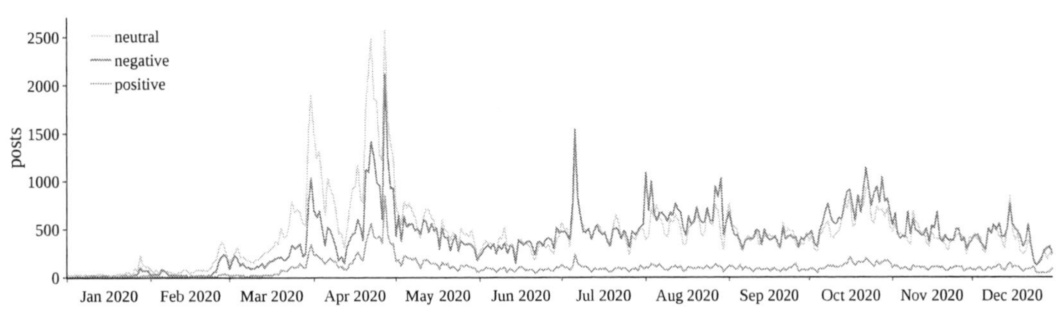


Figure 4: The number of German X posts with *neutral*, *negative*, and *posititve* sentiments on the topic of face masks per day in 2020. $\text{GBERT}_{\text{TAPT+SFT}}$ was used for sentiment classification.

# Emotion Identification for French in Written Texts: Considering Modes of Emotion Expression as a Step Towards Text Complexity Analysis

**Aline Étienne** **Delphine Battistelli** **Gwénolé Lecorvé**
Univ. Paris-Nanterre, CNRS, MoDyCo – Nanterre, France Orange – Lannion, France
acm.etienne@gmail.com del.battistelli@gmail.com gwenole.lecorve@orange.com

## Abstract

The objective of this paper is to predict (A) whether a sentence in a written text expresses an emotion, (B) the mode(s) in which the emotion is expressed, (C) whether it is basic or complex, and (D) its emotional category. One of our major contributions, in addition to a dataset and a model[1], is to integrate the fact that an emotion can be expressed in different modes: from a direct mode, essentially lexicalized, to a more indirect mode, where emotions will only be suggested, a mode that NLP approaches generally don't take into account. The scope is on written texts, i.e. it does not focus on conversational or multi-modal data. In this context, modes of expression are seen as a factor towards the automatic analysis of complexity in texts. Experiments on French texts show acceptable results compared to the human annotators' agreement to predict the mode and category, and outperforming results compared to using a large language model with in-context learning (i.e. no fine-tuning) on all tasks.

## 1 Introduction

In Natural Language Processing (NLP), emotion detection and classification are often addressed in the context of interactions or conversations (e.g., (Poria et al., 2019)), with either spoken, written (chats, forums, tweets) or multimodal datasets (e.g., (Busso et al., 2008; Poria et al., 2018; Chen et al., 2018)). The goal is usually to identify the emotions felt by speakers in dialogic situations. On the contrary, the analysis of emotions in non-conversational texts, like journalistic and encyclopedic texts or novels, is less developed in NLP. It indeed implies a different goal, which is no longer to characterize the emotional state of speakers but rather of characters/people in these texts. As pointed out in psycholinguistics, emotions in these types of texts are used—with more or less control by the writer—to capture the reader's attention. They also help to create a connection between the described situations and, thus, are a key factor in understanding (e.g., for children in Davidson et al., 2001). However, it is crucial that these emotions themselves are identified and understood. This leads to the idea that emotions can be considered as a factor of complexity, at least relative complexity in the terminology of Ehret et al. (2023), meaning it takes into account the difficulty perceived by speakers in terms of language learning or understanding. A text will thus be all the more complex as it contains emotions considered complex by a given type of speaker. In the case of children, for example, it is known that certain emotional categories are not accessible in early ages, and that their mode of expression (direct *vs.* indirect or implicit) also plays a role in accessing their meaning.

From these reflections on the question of emotions as a factor of complexity, this paper is oriented towards a better consideration of the diversity of modes of expression of emotions. We present a model and dataset that introduces the notion of mode of expression in addition to the usual information on emotional categories (e.g., joy, fear, etc.). In practice, the model classifies emotions in texts through four tasks: (A) predict whether a sentence contains an emotion or not; (B) if yes, how it is expressed (the *mode*); (C) whether it is a basic or complex emotion category; and (D) in which emotional category it falls. Examples of these tasks on written texts from our dataset are given in Table 1. The model is a CamemBERT model (Martin et al., 2020) fine-tuned on data including different types of sources (newspapers, novels, encyclopedias) annotated with a psycho-linguistically motivated schema.[1] Evaluation shows that the proposed model outperforms approaches based on expert resources, non-neural architectures (SVM and XGBoost), and in-context learning using GPT-3.5. A

[1]Dataset and model can be downloaded on HuggingFace: https://huggingface.co/TextToKids.



*Proceedings of the 14th Workshop on Computational Approaches to Subjectivity, Sentiment, & Social Media Analysis*, pages 168–185
August 15, 2024 ©2024 Association for Computational Linguistics

| Sentence (+ surrounding sentences) | (A) Emo. | (B) Expr. mode | | | | (C) Type | | (D) Emotional category | | | | | | | | | | | |
|---|---|---|---|---|---|---|---|---|---|---|---|---|---|---|---|---|---|---|---|
| | is emotional | behavioral | labeled | displayed | suggested | basic | complex | admiration | other | anger | guilt | disgust | embarrassment | pride | jealousy | joy | fear | surprise | sadness |
| How does the coronavirus spread? **Especially through respiratory droplets expelled by an infected person.** Respiratory droplets are small droplets of saliva that are released into the air when we talk, cough, or sneeze. | | | | | | | | | | | | | | | | | | | |
| It is mainly celebrated in the Anglo-Saxon world. **Traditionally, children wear funny costumes.** They dress up as often despised and feared creatures such as ghosts, vampires, or witches and go door-to-door in the neighborhood, asking for candies or pastries. | ✓ | | ✓ | | | ✓ | | | | | | | | | | ✓ | | | |
| — He succumbed after ingesting his herbal tea and a toxic substance, presumably cyanide. **From there, it was only a small step for Angus's mother to accuse the king of murder as she rushed towards her brother.** — The herbal tea... | ✓ | ✓ | | | ✓ | ✓ | | | | ✓ | | | | | | | | | |
| This summer, Nolita had to eat a sausage for the first time in a long time because there was nothing else. **"I forced myself," she said.** "It disgusted me, and I felt guilty," she recounted. | ✓ | | ✓ | | | ✓ | ✓ | | | | ✓ | ✓ | | | | | | | |
| At the Rome Olympics, the historic event takes place during the marathon: Ethiopian Abebe Bikila becomes the first athlete from black Africa to become an Olympic champion. **What's more, he achieved this feat... barefoot!** He had indeed developed the habit of running barefoot back home in Ethiopia. | ✓ | | | ✓ | ✓ | ✓ | ✓ | | | | | | | ✓ | | ✓ | | ✓ | |

Table 1: Examples (translated from French) of sentences in context and reference labels for Tasks A (presence of an emotion), B (mode(s) of expression), C (type/complexity of the emotions(s)), and D (emotional category(ies). Tasks B, C, and D are multi-label tasks.

complementary human evaluation shows that the prediction errors made by the proposed model are generally in the same proportions as those made by humans. Finally, the paper discusses interactions between expression modes and emotional categories. While complexity analysis is the motivation of our work, the paper is restricted to Tasks A-D. Application to complexity analysis are left for future work.

Section 2 browses the literature on emotion identification in written texts, particularly in NLP. Sections 3, 4 and 5 detail the tasks addressed, the associated data, and the proposed model, respectively. Section 6 reports the experiments and results.

## 2 Framework and Related Work

This section provides a brief overview of the framework for emotion analysis in which the paper is situated and which justifies the choice of schema and data (annotated with this schema). It also positions our work among studies in NLP.

### 2.1 The Analysis of Emotions as a Complexity Factor of a Text

In psycholinguistics, the key role of characters' emotions on text comprehension is well-documented (e.g., Dijkstra et al., 1995; Dyer, 1983). Among recent works, two influencing factors have been highlighted in children's understanding of emotions, and thus of the texts themselves: the *type of emotion* expressed, basic or complex—the complex emotions (e.g., pride, shame) being more difficult to grasp as they require knowledge of social norms—(Davidson, 2006; Blanc and Quenette, 2017); as well as *the way emotions are expressed* (Creissen and Blanc, 2017)), directly *via* an emotional label, indirectly through the mention of an emotional behavior, or through the description of an emotional situation, the latter being the most difficult to understand. Of course, the notion of emotional category is also addressed in psycholinguistics, and it has been shown that some categories take longer to be mastered by children (e.g., Baron-Cohen et al., 2010).

On the NLP side, several works (see e.g., Bostan and Klinger, 2018; Acheampong et al., 2020; Öhman, 2020) highlight the great heterogeneity of emotion annotation schemas—and annotated corpora—, thus clearly demonstrating the difficulty of modeling emotions and, in the end, of analyzing them. This heterogeneity ranges from the notions (e.g., the number and types of emotional categories) and the type of data studied (journals, tweets, etc.) up to the annotation procedures (*crowdsourcing*, annotation by experts) and evaluation methods implemented (e.g., with or without agreement between annotators). Although some works strive to take into account broader sets of notions and linguistic cues to analyze emotions (e.g., Casel et al., 2021; Kim and Klinger, 2019), the most commonly used concept remains the notion of *emotional category*, often approached through a list of basic emotions introduced either by Ekman (1992) (anger, disgust, fear, joy, sadness, and surprise) or Plutchik (1980) (Ekman's categories, anticipation, and trust), with a focus on one way of expressing emotions: the emotional lexicon. As highlighted in (Klinger, 2023) and in (Troiano et al., 2023), a few very recent approaches in NLP aim to acquire a deeper understanding of the textual units that support the evocation of emotions outside of directly emotional lexical terms (e.g., "happy", "anger"). These approaches are then inspired by psychological and/or linguistic models of emotions. We adopt the same approach here because we aim to capture both direct and indirect modes of expression of emotions in texts. Like Troiano et al. (2023), we seek to assess to what extent computational models can capture emotions expressed indirectly (e.g., via the description of situations that are/ associated with emotions with regard to social norms and conventions). More specifically, our work adopts the framework proposed by Etienne et al. (2022), which proposes a detailed annotation schema of emotions for French. To our knowledge, this is the only work with the explicit objective of analyzing emotions in texts by addressing both direct and indirect modes of expression in French.

## 2.2 Automatic Identification of Emotions

In NLP, the analysis of emotions in texts is generally treated as a classification task. The previously mentioned heterogeneity of annotation schemas and annotated corpora is then reflected in the diversity of predicted classes, the granularity of elements to be classified, and the methods for developing and evaluating classifiers. The way results are presented thus also varies from one paper to another, making performance comparison more difficult.

The focus is often on the classification of basic emotions (Strapparava and Mihalcea, 2007; Mohammad, 2012; Abdaoui et al., 2017; Demszky et al., 2020; Öhman et al., 2020; Bianchi et al., 2021), although some works use a mix of basic and complex emotions (Balahur et al., 2012; Fraisse and Paroubek, 2015; Abdaoui et al., 2017; Mohammad et al., 2018; Liu et al., 2019; Demszky et al., 2020). Moreover, there is a long history of building and using emotional lexicons, and the diversity of linguistic markers of emotions (e.g., split syntactic structures, exclamation points) is not systematically taken into account, although it is mentioned in several works (Alm et al., 2005; Mohammad, 2012; Kim and Klinger, 2018; Demszky et al., 2020)) with even, in the case of Balahur et al. (2012) for example, the objective to detect implicit emotions. These works have the limitation of focusing each time only on one mode of expression, thus leaving aside the complementarities between modes. For their part, based on Scherer's model of emotional components process (2005), Casel et al. (2021) annotated and then predicted several components of emotions, such as physiological symptoms and motor expressions of emotions, or the cognitive evaluation of events. Although Casel et al. (2021) deal with a broader set of cues, these are not rigorously motivated linguistically. Therefore, relying on Etienne et al. (2022), the originality of our work lies in taking into account different modes of expression of emotions.

Historically, *Support Vector Machine* (SVM) models have been widely used to classify sentences (Aman and Szpakowicz, 2007; Mohammad, 2012)) or texts (Abdaoui et al., 2017; Balahur et al., 2012; Fraisse and Paroubek, 2015; Mohammad, 2012) according to the emotional category they express. Until the advent of embeddings, the inputs were mainly symbolic: bags of words or $n$-grams, features based on emotional resources such as WordNetAffect (Aman and Szpakowicz, 2007; Balahur et al., 2012; Strapparava and Mihalcea, 2007) or emotional lexicons (Strapparava and Mihalcea, 2007; Abdaoui et al., 2017; Kim and Klinger, 2018). Today, neural networks (Kim and Klinger, 2018) and Transformer architectures (Liu et al., 2019; Demszky et al., 2020; Öhman et al., 2020; Bianchi et al., 2021, 2022) obviously dominate the state of the art. For French, to our knowledge, the only one approach using Transformer models for emotion recognition that exists is (Cortal et al., 2023). But, as the authors point it out, they need to explore for future work more deeply emotion expression modes in order to improve their classifier. This is the point we are addressing as the modes of emotions are at the heart of our work.

## 3 Tasks

Built in the global perspective of enabling the analysis of emotions as a complexity factor, our work thus takes into account two key elements to address the complexity of an emotion: its category and its mode of expression. The goal is to propose a Transformer model for 4 classification tasks (noted A, B, C, and D) at the *sentence* level, as opposed to the text level (this can, for example, allow studying how the presence of emotions evolves along a text). Sentences can contain several emotions, as in Table 1. Therefore, the classifications are multi-label with no interdependency across labels within the same task.

### 3.1 Task A: Presence of Emotion

The first task aims to predict the presence of emotional information in a given sentence (binary prediction).

### 3.2 Task B: Mode of Expression

The mode of expression focuses on the linguistic means used to convey the presence of an emotion in a text. Following Etienne et al. (2022), 4 modes are considered: the **labeled emotions** directly indicated by a term from the emotional lexicon (e.g., *happy*, *scared*); the **behavioral emotions** which rely on the description of an emotional behavior, such as physiological manifestations (e.g., *crying*, *smiling*) or other behaviors (e.g., *slapping someone*); the **displayed emotions** which are expressed by very heterogeneous surface linguistic features of statements that mainly reflect the emotional state of the writer (e.g., interjections, short sentences); the **suggested emotions** which emanate from the description of a situation generally associated with an emotional feeling according to social norms and conventions (e.g., *seeing a good friend after a long period* suggests joy).

### 3.3 Task C: Type of Emotion

Task C aims to predict the presence of *basic* and *complex* emotion types (2 simultaneous binary predictions). To our knowledge, this notion has not yet been studied as such in automatic emotion analysis (although the emotional categories *basic* and *complex* have been used in NLP (*cf.* section 2.2)). This is probably due to the fact that the type of an expressed emotion is directly related to its emotional category. However, the type of emotion is in itself a marker of complexity, as we have seen.

### 3.4 Task D: Emotional Category

In accordance with Etienne et al. (2022), Task D is designed to label 11+1 emotional categories, namely the 6 basic emotions of Ekman (*anger*, *disgust*, *fear*, *joy*, *sadness*, and *surprise*) and 5 complex emotions (*admiration*, *embarrassment*, *guilt*, *jealousy*, and *pride*). A last category, named *other*, is used to capture markers that express any other emotion (e.g., hate, contempt, love, *etc.*).

| Subset | Texts | Sent. | Tokens | Emotional sent. |
|---|---|---|---|---|
| train | 1,129 | 19,553 | 360K | 3,952 |
| dev | 182 | 2,770 | 53K | 438 |
| test | 283 | 5,588 | 102K | 984 |
| Total | 1,594 | 27,911 | 515K | 5,374 |

Table 2: Statistics over the dataset.

## 4 Data

As detailed in Table 2, our proposed corpus consists of 1,594 French texts (28K sentences, 515K words) intended for children aged 6 to 14 years, divided into 3 types: mainly journalistic texts (91% of the sentences), encyclopedic articles (9%), and novels (1%). Annotations conducted by 6 experts associate emotional units (segments) in the texts with their mode of expression and emotional category, following the annotation schema and guide in (Etienne et al., 2022). Inter-annotator agreements are presented in Appendix A. These annotations are then merged from the segment level to the sentence level. Thus, a given sentence may cover several emotional units (1.54 unit per sentence on average at least one unit is present). The presence of emotions and the types of emotions have been derived from the mode of expression and emotional category labels. In the end, each sentence is associated with a vector of 19 booleans (again, see Table 1). The data are divided into training, development, and test sets (70/10/20% of the sentences, respectively), such that all sentences from a text are in the same subset, in order to avoid a training bias on the peculiarities of the texts (e.g., the name of a character).

Table 3 presents the proportion of labels within the corpus. Overall, the proportions are comparable from one subset to another. Several imbalances appear within the tasks. **(A)** Only 15-20% of sentences are emotional. **(B)** Modes of expression are quite evenly distributed, *displayed* being the least frequent (3% of sentences) and *suggested* the most common (6%). The sums of the percentages of each mode are higher than the percentages of the *emotional* label because certain emotions are conveyed by several modes and a sentence can also contain several emotional units whose respective modes differ. **(C)** The labels of emotion types are very unbalanced, with a clear dominance of basic emotions. The emotional category 'other' (task D) is not associated with any type of emotion, hence the fact that the sum of the percentages *basic* and *complex* is lower than that of emotional sentences. **(D)** The labels of emotional categories are unbalanced, with percentages always below 5% of sentences. The categories *anger, fear, joy, sadness, surprise*, and *other* are dominant, while others are very rare (*disgust*, *guilt*, and *jealousy*).

Finally, Table 4 presents the co-occurrences of each label for Tasks B, C, and D on the test set. Overall, when an emotion is present, it appears several modes (B) are usually used. This is less true for types (C) and categories (D). Still, some emotions are rarely alone, like *disgust*, *embarassment*, *guilt* or *pride*. Regarding categories, some associations seem more frequent than others, e.g., *joy+pride*, *fear+sadness*, *joy+pride*, and *joy+surprise*.

## 5 Proposed Model

All tasks are learned together, leading to a single proposed model. This model results from fine-tuning the base version of the pre-trained CamemBERT model (Martin et al., 2020). It is a BERT-type encoder model with 110 million parameters and 12 BERT layers. It was pre-trained on 138GB of French texts (Suárez et al., 2019). Although fine-tuning more recent and larger generative language models like Llama2 or Mistral would likely yield better results, the choice of a reasonably sized model is motivated by two reasons. Firstly, our goal is to demonstrate that, unlike several other tasks in NLP, fine-grained emotion characterization in texts cannot be achieved by leveraging large generic (i.e., non-specialized) language models via in-context learning (i.e., without fine-tuning). Secondly, our work aims for a lightweight solution, so that emotion characterization can be used as a processor for analyzing text complexity in a massive collection of texts from a public search engine. Thus, while fine-tuning larger models is part of our future work, this paper does not address it.

| Task | Labels | Sent. Prop. (%) train | dev | test |
|---|---|---|---|---|
| (A) Pres. of emotion | emotional | 20.2 | 15.8 | 17.6 |
| (B) Expression mode | behavioral | 4.6 | 3.6 | 4.3 |
| | labeled | 5.3 | 5.2 | 5.7 |
| | displayed | 3.6 | 2.3 | 3.5 |
| | suggested | 7.1 | 5.8 | 6.3 |
| (C) Emotion type | basic | 15.4 | 12.6 | 13.9 |
| | complex | 2.0 | 2.1 | 2.3 |
| (D) Emotional category | admiration | 0.6 | 1.1 | 1.0 |
| | anger | 4.6 | 3.2 | 3.4 |
| | disgust | 0.2 | 0.3 | 0.2 |
| | embarrass. | 0.6 | 0.6 | 0.6 |
| | fear | 3.8 | 3.3 | 3.8 |
| | guilt | 0.1 | 0.0 | 0.1 |
| | jealousy | 0.0 | 0.0 | 0.0 |
| | joy | 3.2 | 2.3 | 3.6 |
| | pride | 0.7 | 0.4 | 0.9 |
| | sadness | 2.5 | 2.0 | 2.5 |
| | surprise | 3.0 | 3.1 | 2.5 |
| | other | 5.0 | 3.2 | 3.7 |

Table 3: Distribution of labels

| (B) Expression mode(s) | + behavioral | + labeled | + displayed | + suggested | *no other* |
|---|---|---|---|---|---|
| behavioral | – | 49 | 23 | 59 | 130 |
| labeled | 49 | – | 28 | 76 | 189 |
| displayed | 23 | 28 | – | 61 | 97 |
| suggested | 59 | 76 | 61 | – | 179 |

| (C) Emotion type(s) | + basic | + complex | *no other* |
|---|---|---|---|
| basic | – | 71 | 708 |
| complex | 71 | – | 56 |

| (D) Emotion category(ies) | + admiration | + anger | + disgust | + embarrass. | + fear | + guilt | + jealousy | + joy | + pride | + sadness | + surprise | + other | *none other* |
|---|---|---|---|---|---|---|---|---|---|---|---|---|---|
| admiration | – | 1 | 0 | 0 | 0 | 0 | 0 | 21 | 14 | 4 | 15 | 3 | 23 |
| anger | 1 | – | 0 | 3 | 8 | 0 | 1 | 2 | 0 | 15 | 8 | 10 | 146 |
| disgust | 0 | 0 | – | 1 | 2 | 1 | 0 | 0 | 0 | 3 | 1 | 1 | 6 |
| embarass. | 0 | 3 | 1 | – | 6 | 2 | 0 | 1 | 0 | 7 | 1 | 5 | 13 |
| fear | 0 | 8 | 2 | 6 | – | 1 | 0 | 4 | 0 | 35 | 12 | 14 | 145 |
| guilt | 0 | 0 | 1 | 2 | 1 | – | 0 | 0 | 0 | 0 | 0 | 0 | 1 |
| jealousy | 0 | 1 | 0 | 0 | 0 | 0 | – | 0 | 0 | 0 | 0 | 0 | 0 |
| joy | 21 | 2 | 0 | 1 | 4 | 0 | 0 | – | 34 | 7 | 20 | 21 | 124 |
| pride | 14 | 0 | 0 | 0 | 0 | 0 | 0 | 34 | – | 1 | 11 | 5 | 11 |
| sadness | 4 | 15 | 3 | 7 | 35 | 0 | 0 | 7 | 1 | – | 4 | 12 | 64 |
| surprise | 15 | 8 | 1 | 1 | 12 | 0 | 0 | 20 | 11 | 4 | – | 5 | 92 |
| other | 3 | 10 | 1 | 5 | 14 | 0 | 0 | 21 | 5 | 12 | 5 | – | 119 |

Table 4: Co-occurrences of the labels in the test set of multi-label tasks B, C, and D.

We fine-tune the CamemBERT model by replacing its last token prediction layer with a binary classification layer of the size of the number of labels, using binary cross-entropy as the loss function. The fine-tuning involves all model weights, i.e., no layers are frozen. The final model is not directly learned from CamemBERT. An initial fine-tuning is conducted on Task A alone for 3 epochs (classification layer of size 1), then the final model is fine-tuned on all tasks starting from this intermediate model for an additional 6 epochs (the final classification layer is replaced by a fresh layer of size 19). The optimizer is Adam with a learning rate of $10^{-5}$ (no decay) and batches of 8 examples. The choice of the hyper-parameters was made based on prototyping experiments on the development set.

Other experiments were conducted on the development set[2], for example, on the choice of a window around sentences, class weighting or not, or the choice of initial fine-tuning only on Task A or not. Ultimately, the results presented are those of the best strategy obtained on the development set averaging results over 3 training runs with different random initializations. Notably, a weighting between classes is adopted so as not to overly favor the majority classes. The maximum weighting factor is capped at 50 to, conversely, not give too much importance to very rare classes. Finally, the model takes as input a triplet of sentences where the target sentence to be labeled is surrounded by its preceding and following sentence in the form before:{previous}</s>current: {target}</s>after:{next}</s>.

| Task | Model | Training variant | Macro R | Macro P | Macro F1 |
|---|---|---|---|---|---|
| (A) Presence of emotion | Naive | | 0.20 | 0.18 | 0.19 |
| | SVM | bag-of-tokens | 0.48 | 0.66 | 0.56 |
| | | embeddings | 0.50 | 0.67 | 0.57 |
| | XGBoost | bag-of-tokens | 0.22 | 0.70 | 0.34 |
| | | embeddings | 0.19 | 0.67 | 0.57 |
| | GPT3.5 | pos. ex. only | 0.62 | 0.44 | 0.52 |
| | | pos.+neg. ex. | 0.74 | 0.26 | 0.38 |
| | ours | all tasks | 0.76 | **0.74** | **0.75** |
| | | only A | **0.77** | 0.73 | **0.75** |
| (B) Expression mode | Naive | | 0.05 | 0.05 | 0.05 |
| | SVM | bag-of-tokens | 0.27 | 0.72 | 0.37 |
| | | embeddings | 0.20 | 0.67 | 0.29 |
| | XGBoost | bag-of-tokens | 0.22 | **0.73** | 0.31 |
| | | embeddings | 0.06 | 0.31 | 0.10 |
| | GPT3.5 | pos. ex. only | 0.51 | 0.10 | 0.15 |
| | | pos.+neg. ex. | 0.47 | 0.08 | 0.13 |
| | ours | all tasks | **0.63** | 0.67 | 0.64 |
| | | only A+B | **0.63** | 0.67 | **0.65** |
| (C) Emotion type | Naive | | 0.09 | 0.08 | 0.08 |
| | SVM | bag-of-tokens | 0.21 | 0.34 | 0.26 |
| | | embeddings | 0.21 | **0.83** | 0.27 |
| | XGBoost | bag-of-tokens | 0.12 | 0.66 | 0.20 |
| | | embeddings | 0.07 | 0.38 | 0.12 |
| | GPT3.5 | pos. ex. only | **0.76** | 0.12 | 0.20 |
| | | pos.+neg. ex. | 0.37 | 0.17 | 0.22 |
| | ours | all tasks | 0.56 | 0.66 | **0.60** |
| | | only A+C | 0.28 | 0.27 | 0.27 |
| (D) Emotional category | Naive | | 0.02 | 0.02 | 0.02 |
| | SVM | bag-of-tokens | 0.12 | 0.49 | 0.19 |
| | | embeddings | 0.12 | 0.48 | 0.18 |
| | XGBoost | bag-of-tokens | 0.19 | **0.57** | 0.27 |
| | | embeddings | 0.04 | 0.21 | 0.07 |
| | GPT3.5 | pos. ex. only | **0.70** | 0.11 | 0.17 |
| | | pos.+neg. ex. | 0.64 | 0.15 | 0.13 |
| | ours | all tasks | 0.40 | 0.46 | **0.42** |
| | | only A+B | 0.39 | 0.46 | 0.41 |

Table 5: Model performances (averages over 3 runs, all standard deviations are below 0.02).

## 6 Automatic and Human Evaluations

### 6.1 Comparison with Other Models

The proposed model is compared to three other types of models. **SVM** models were trained as they are a historical approach in the field. Two types of input features were used: (*i*) bag-of-tokens where tokens come from the CamemBERT tokenizer, restricted to those from the training set, resulting in input vectors of dimension 18,437; (*ii*) sentence embeddings of size 768 obtained with SentenceTransformer (Reimers and Gurevych, 2019) and CamemBERT (the pretrained model, not our fine-tuned model) as the token encoder[3]. **XGBoost** models were trained as it is a more recent, lightweight, and competitive technique for many classification tasks, especially with unbalanced data (Chen and Guestrin, 2016). The input features are the same as for the SVMs. Our approach is compared to **GPT-3.5**[4] (Ouyang et al., 2022). For a given input sample, GPT-3.5 is incrementally solicited to annotate it with binary labels (yes/no). Consecutively for each task and label, a natural language description of what is expected is provided to the model before asking for a response,

[2]Details are published in a research report, which cannot be cited here for anonymity reasons.

[3]https://huggingface.co/dangvantuan/sentence-camembert-base

[4]Version 0311, with a temperature of zero.

accompanied by examples from the training set for each label. Different prompts were tested exhibiting examples in a few-shot manner for each label. In one version, only 2-4 positive examples are used, whereas the other also reports negative ones (2-3). Details can be found in Appendix C. Unlike SVM, XGBoost, and our model, this approach does require any training. Finally, results for a **naive** approach are also reported to help measuring how far each model is from this lower bound. For each label, this naive approach randomly predicts the presence or absence of the label based on the Bernouilli law parametrized by the frequency of the label in the training set.

Table 5 summarizes the performances on the test set of the models for each task and compares them to our model. Models are evaluated through recall (R), precision (P), and F1 scores. Overall, it appears that our proposed model significantly outperforms SVMs, XGBoost, and GPT-3.5 in terms of F1 scores for all tasks, with values almost double those of the best-ranked model for tasks B, C, and D. It seems especially that all other models tend to favor either recall (GPT-3.5) or precision (SVM, XGBoost), while our model is balanced. Finally, the poor results of GPT-3.5 show that the task is difficult. This calls for either fine-tuning as we did, or more advanced inference techniques of large language models, e.g., by decomposing more the reasoning for each task using *-of-thought techniques or by exploring example selection methods.

Table 5 also reports the comparison with 4 variants of the model where Tasks B to D are trained separately on top of A. These results show that multi-task does not degrade the performance but it does not really improve them neither, except for Task C where guessing the category probably helps. This may lead one to consider that the interaction between mode and category is not very strong. Further discussions are exposed in Section 6.5.

## 6.2 Comparison with Related Work

In the absence of truly similar work to ours, this section reports additional results to give a better intuition of the performance of our model.

**Closest Comparable Works** Table 6 summarizes the performances of the three closest works we could find in the literature. They were chosen because they all predict labels at a granularity close to that of the sentence. (Öhman et al., 2020) allows a comparison with another Transformer model; (Fraisse and Paroubek, 2015) with another work in French; and (Kim and Klinger, 2018) with a method that works at the level of linguistic markers (as opposed to the phrasal or textual level). All focus solely on emotional categories. The results show that our model is competitive.

| Ref. | Lg | Labels | Model | Lexicon | Granularity | Macro-F1 |
|---|---|---|---|---|---|---|
| ours | Fr | anger, disg., joy, fear, surpr., sadn. | Transformer | none | sent. triplets | 0.52 |
| (Öhman et al., 2020) | En | same + trust, anticipation | Transformer | none | sent. | 0.54 |
| (Kim and Klinger, 2018) | En | same + trust, anticipation | symb. | NRC lexicon | sent. triplets | 0.31 |
| | | | MLP | none | sent. triplets | 0.31 |
| (Fraisse, Paroubek, 2015) | Fr | anger, fear, sadness | SVM | custom | paragr. | 0.31 |

Table 6: Comparison elements with close works.

| Task | Label | Approach | Macro-F1 |
|---|---|---|---|
| (A) Pres. of emotion | emotional | ours | **0.75** |
| | | TextBlob | 0.30 |
| | | Emotaix | 0.45 |
| (B) Expression mode | behavioral | ours | **0.63** |
| | | Emotaix | 0.04 |
| | labeled | ours | **0.81** |
| | | Emotaix | 0.56 |
| (D) Emot. categories (labeled mode only) | all | ours | **0.47** |
| | | Emotaix | 0.43 |
| Emotion polarity | positive | ours | **0.58** |
| | | TextBlob | 0.16 |
| | negative | ours | **0.68** |
| | | TextBlob | 0.17 |

Table 7: Comparison with tools available for French.

**Implementations Based on Existing Resources** In the absence of dedicated models for French, two resources are currently available in French if one wants to consider emotion identification in texts: TextBlob (`https://textblob.readthedocs.io/`), a sentiment analysis library that integrates a French lexicon where terms are associated with a negative and positive weight reflecting their polarity; Emotaix (Piolat and Bannour, 2009), another lexicon comprising associations (i)

| Source of label | Evaluator's opinion | Proportion (num. of labels) emot. cat. | expr. mode |
|---|---|---|---|
| human | Agree | 94.2% (163) | 96.0% (170) |
| | Disagree | 6.8% (10) | 4.0% (7) |
| model | Agree | 89.4% (144) | 97.1% (166) |
| | Disagree | 10.6% (17) | 2.9% (7) |
| human and model | Agree | 95.5% (105) | 97.7% (129) |
| | Disagree | 4.5% (5) | 2.3% (3) |
| human **but** **not** model | Agree | 92.1% (58) | 91.1% (41) |
| | Disagree | 7.9% (5) | 8.9% (4) |
| model **but** **not** human | Agree | 76.5% (39) | 90.2% (37) |
| | Disagree | 23.5% (12) | 9.8% (4) |

Table 8: Experts' agreement regarding predictions of the human annotator and/or our model.

of terms with emotional categories for the labeled mode only, and (ii) other terms with the behavioral mode (but this time without information on the emotional category). While it is expected that our transformer model outperforms there tools, the experiments allow us to determine the extent of the significant gap and on which tasks (including unseen tasks during training). Several tasks managed by our model were replicated *via* TextBlob and Emotaix. To account for the differences between these resources and our proposed model, Task B was limited to only the behavioral and labeled modes and Task D to the labeled mode. Moreover, our model was tested on a task of predicting emotional polarity on our test set since TextBlob is designed for this use. To predict polarity *via* our model, categories were predicted and empirically projected towards positive or negative polarity (e.g., *anger* is *negative*, *joy* is *positive*). As shown in Table 7, our model performs significantly better than TextBlob and Emotaix, including in the emotional polarity task for which it was not specifically designed. The only task where the competition remains is the prediction of categories when the mode is labeled, which is the easiest situation compared to considering all modes.

### 6.3 Human Evaluation

Given the difficulty of the tasks considered, it is appropriate to cross-reference the automatic evaluation with a human analysis, particularly to give an intuition of what the observed prediction errors represent. A perceptual validation experiment was thus conducted with three experts in text complexity and emotions. Each of them was informed of the tasks and the definitions of labels in psycholinguistics and linguistics. They were then each confronted with 150 sentences from the test set and their labels for emotional category and mode of expression. These labels came either from the human reference annotations or from the predictions of our model. For each label, the experts had to say whether they agreed or not with the proposed annotation. Of course, they were not aware of the origin of the labels.

| Task | Macro R | Macro P | Macro F1 | Labels | R | P | F1 |
|---|---|---|---|---|---|---|---|
| (A) Pres. of emot. | 0.76 | 0.74 | 0.75 | emotional | .76 | .74 | .75 |
| (B) Express. mode | 0.63 | 0.67 | 0.64 | behavioral | .60 | .65 | .63 |
| | | | | labeled | .81 | .80 | .81 |
| | | | | displayed | .67 | .73 | .70 |
| | | | | suggested | .43 | .48 | .45 |
| (C) Emot. type | 0.56 | 0.66 | 0.60 | basic | .70 | .73 | .72 |
| | | | | complex | .41 | .59 | .48 |
| (D) Emot. category | 0.40 | 0.46 | 0.42 | admiration | .28 | .46 | .35 |
| | | | | anger | .67 | .68 | .68 |
| | | | | disgust | .00 | .00 | .00 |
| | | | | embarass. | .36 | .60 | .45 |
| | | | | fear | .72 | .66 | .69 |
| | | | | guilt | .00 | .00 | .00 |
| | | | | jealousy | .00 | .00 | .00 |
| | | | | joy | .53 | .71 | .61 |
| | | | | pride | .33 | .62 | .43 |
| | | | | sadness | .43 | .50 | .46 |
| | | | | surprise | .70 | .74 | .72 |
| | | | | other | .75 | .59 | .66 |

Table 9: Detailed performances of our model.

Table 8 reports the experts' agreement rates with the proposed labels, depending on the source of the label.[5] Although the strongest agreement is when the human and model labels match (*human & model*), the agreement scores are generally very high, especially for the mode of expression. These results thus tend to show that, even when the model predicts differently from the reference, the prediction is generally considered relevant by human experts. This demonstrates that our model is able to generalize correctly and that the F1 scores from previous experiments underestimate the perceived quality of the model's predictions.

### 6.4 Results by Label

Table 9 presents the results of our classifier on all labels of all tasks from the test set. Additional observations can be made as follows. Regarding expression modes (B), labeled emotions are very

[5]We considered that the experts agree with a label when at least 2 out of 3 declared that they agreed with the label.

| | admiration | anger | disgust | embarrass. | fear | guilt | jealousy | joy | pride | sadness | surprise |
|---|---|---|---|---|---|---|---|---|---|---|---|
| behavioral | 14 | 48 | 12 | 16 | 15 | 7 | 0 | 19 | 8 | 14 | 3 |
| labeled | 38 | 12 | 17 | 36 | 41 | 47 | 0 | 25 | 12 | 29 | 23 |
| displayed | 15 | 11 | 17 | 16 | 4 | 20 | 33 | 16 | 17 | 11 | 52 |
| suggested | 33 | 29 | 55 | 32 | 41 | 27 | 67 | 41 | 62 | 47 | 22 |

(a) Frequencies (%) for each pair (mode, category)

| | admiration | anger | disgust | embarrass. | fear | guilt | jealousy | joy | pride | sadness | surprise |
|---|---|---|---|---|---|---|---|---|---|---|---|
| behavioral | .04 | .47 | – | .00 | .23 | .00 | .01 | .17 | – | .11 | .03 |
| labeled | .06 | .18 | .02 | .07 | .50 | .01 | .00 | .27 | .05 | .18 | .21 |
| displayed | .07 | .13 | .01 | .04 | .02 | – | – | .33 | .03 | .16 | .53 |
| suggested | .05 | .18 | .03 | .03 | .24 | .00 | – | .18 | .06 | .14 | .08 |

(b) F1 of each mode w.r.t. the reference category

| | admiration | anger | disgust | embarrass. | fear | guilt | jealousy | joy | pride | sadness | surprise |
|---|---|---|---|---|---|---|---|---|---|---|---|
| behavioral | .11 | .60 | – | .16 | .30 | .00 | .00 | .26 | – | .19 | .01 |
| labeled | .45 | .29 | .00 | .57 | .63 | .00 | .00 | .53 | .45 | .44 | .41 |
| displayed | .04 | .08 | .00 | .00 | .03 | – | – | .26 | .06 | .04 | .58 |
| suggested | .16 | .35 | .00 | .31 | .34 | .00 | – | .28 | .25 | .28 | .22 |

(c) F1 of each category w.r.t. the reference mode

Table 10: Interactions between mode and category: frequency of cooccurence in the reference (a) ; impact of each on the prediction of the other (b and c).

well recognized (F1 > 0.8), unlike suggested emotions (F1 < 0.5). This is not surprising as labeled emotions are the easiest to identify for a human annotator, while suggested emotions have the largest part of interpretation (as shown by inter-annotator agreements in Appendix A). Performance for emotion types (C) seems in turn linked to the results on emotional categories, since the *basic* label is, as intuition would suggest, better recognized than the *complex* label. Finally, regarding emotional categories (D), three of them are never predicted (*guilt*, *disgust*, and *jealousy*). These are the rarest labels in the training set, probably too rare for the model to learn to predict them. Indeed, the best-predicted emotional categories are the basic emotions, more frequent, namely the labels *surprise*, *fear*, and *anger* (see Table 3). However, while *surprise* is the best-predicted label of Task D, it is not the most represented in the training set. Conversely, *sadness* is not well recognized, even though it is one of the most frequent emotional categories. From our additional analyses, this seems to be explained by sometimes strong interactions between the notions of expression mode and emotional category.

### 6.5 Correlation Between Mode and Category

This final section assesses how specific modes impact the prediction of emotional categories, and *vice-versa*. As background information, Table 10.a reports the cooccurrence relative frequencies between modes and categories in the test set.

Table 10.b explores how the mode's predictability varies with the emotional category expressed. Strong associations between emotional categories and expression modes enhance mode recognition, but the suggested mode remains challenging across categories, highlighting its complexity for both our model and human annotators.

Then, Table 10.c indicates that F1 scores are generally higher when emotions are expressed through the labeled mode. However, *anger* and *surprise* deviate from this pattern, performing better in *behavioral* and *displayed* modes, respectively. The effectiveness of our model in recognizing emotions like behavioral *anger* and displayed *surprise* is influenced by their strong association with these modes in the training data. However, factors such as the rarity of the emotion in the training set (e.g., *disgust*) and the linguistic characteristics of the mode also play significant roles. For instance, *joy* and *fear* are better recognized when labeled, despite being frequently suggested, due to the inherent challenge in recognizing the suggested mode.

## 7 Conclusion and Perspectives

In this paper, we have addressed the task of detecting and classifying emotions in written texts, as opposed to conversational data. Due to the applicative perspective towards complexity analysis, we introduced a dataset of French texts and a model (`https://huggingface.co/TextToKids`) which, additionnally to the usual notion of emotion categories, takes into account their direct but also indirect modes of expression. The experiments show that this model performs well compared to other approaches, comparable works, and solutions from off-the-shelf resources. Human evaluation has shown that this level is almost equivalent to what humans can do.

In the future, intra-sentential predictions should be investigated, delimiting units and including other notions such as the experiencers. This would require fine-tuning generative models (as opposed to the discriminative model used in this paper). Then, a direct application of our model is the analysis of complexity as the predicted labels reflect markers of complexity. More broadly, our work could contribute to research in psychology to study the link between emotional language and the psychological state of the writer/speaker.

## 8 Limitations

The main limitation of the presented article is the choice to work at the sentence level, contextualized by their preceding and following sentences, which restricts the task and may not accurately reflect how a reader analyzes a text. As shown in (Etienne et al., 2022) and (Battistelli et al., 2022), emotional units can be linked to text segments further in the text due to causal relationships (a given situation leads to an emotional state, or an emotional state triggers an action). This can lead to group sentences together, ultimately allowing for a structuring of passages at the text level. The restriction to a window of three sentences does not allow the model to leverage this information. Another consequence of working at the sentence level is the loss of the notion of emotional unit. If two emotions are present in a sentence, the current annotations no longer indicate which segments of the sentence each emotion respectively pertains to. We plan to provide another version of our corpus, annotated at the unit level and without contextual restrictions.

## References


Amine Abdaoui, Jérôme Azé, Sandra Bringay, and Pascal Poncelet. 2017. Feel: a french expanded emotion lexicon. *Language Resources and Evaluation*, 51(3):833–855. Publisher: Springer.

Francisca Adoma Acheampong, Chen Wenyu, and Henry Nunoo-Mensah. 2020. Text-based emotion detection: Advances, challenges, and opportunities. *Engineering Reports*, 2(7):e12189. Publisher: Wiley Online Library.

Cecilia Ovesdotter Alm, Dan Roth, and Richard Sproat. 2005. Emotions from Text: Machine Learning for Text-based Emotion Prediction. In *Proceedings of the Human Language Technology Conference and Conference on Empirical Methods in Natural Language Processing (HLT-EMNLP)*, pages 579–586, Vancouver, British Columbia, Canada. Association for Computational Linguistics.

Saima Aman and Stan Szpakowicz. 2007. Identifying expressions of emotion in text. In *Proceedings of the International Conference on Text, Speech and Dialogue (TSD)*, pages 196–205. Springer.

Alexandra Balahur, Jesús M Hermida, and Andrés Montoyo. 2012. Detecting implicit expressions of emotion in text: A comparative analysis. *Decision support systems*, 53(4):742–753. Publisher: Elsevier.

Simon Baron-Cohen, Ofer Golan, Sally Wheelwright, and Yael Granader. 2010. Emotion Word Comprehension from 4 to 16 Years Old: A Developmental Survey. *Frontiers in Evolutionary Neuroscience*, 0. Publisher: Frontiers.

Delphine Battistelli, Aline Étienne, and Gwénolé Lecorvé. 2022. L'émotion à un niveau textuel: la fonction structurante des émotions observée à partir d'annotations. *Discours. Revue de linguistique, psycholinguistique et informatique. A journal of linguistics, psycholinguistics and computational linguistics*, (30).

Federico Bianchi, Debora Nozza, and Dirk Hovy. 2021. Feel-it: Emotion and sentiment classification for the italian language. In *Proceedings of the Workshop on Computational Approaches to Subjectivity, Sentiment and Social Media Analysis*, pages 76–83.

Federico Bianchi, Debora Nozza, and Dirk Hovy. 2022. XLM-EMO: Multilingual emotion prediction in social media text. In *Proceedings of the 12th Workshop on Computational Approaches to Subjectivity, Sentiment & Social Media Analysis*, pages 195–203, Dublin, Ireland. Association for Computational Linguistics.

Nathalie Blanc and Guy Quenette. 2017. La production d'inférences émotionnelles entre 8 et 10 ans : quelle méthodologie pour quels résultats ? *Enfance*, 4(4):503–511. Place: Paris Publisher: NecPlus.

Laura-Ana-Maria Bostan and Roman Klinger. 2018. An Analysis of Annotated Corpora for Emotion Classification in Text. In *Proceedings of the International Conference on Computational Linguistics (COLING)*, pages 2104–2119, Santa Fe, New Mexico, USA. Association for Computational Linguistics.

Carlos Busso, Murtaza Bulut, Chi-Chun Lee, Abe Kazemzadeh, Emily Mower, Samuel Kim, Jeannette N Chang, Sungbok Lee, and Shrikanth S Narayanan. 2008. Iemocap: Interactive emotional dyadic motion capture database. *Language resources and evaluation*, 42:335–359.

Felix Casel, Amelie Heindl, and Roman Klinger. 2021. Emotion recognition under consideration of the emotion component process model. In *Proceedings of the Conference on Natural Language Processing*, pages 49–61, Düsseldorf, Germany. KONVENS 2021 Organizers.

Sheng-Yeh Chen, Chao-Chun Hsu, Chuan-Chun Kuo, Lun-Wei Ku, et al. 2018. Emotionlines: An emotion corpus of multi-party conversations. *arXiv preprint arXiv:1802.08379*.

Tianqi Chen and Carlos Guestrin. 2016. Xgboost: A scalable tree boosting system. In *Proceedings of the ACM SIGKDD international conference on knowledge discovery and data mining*, pages 785–794.

Gustave Cortal, Alain Finkel, Patrick Paroubek, and Lina Ye. 2023. Emotion recognition based on psychological components in guided narratives for emotion regulation. In *Proceedings of the 7th Joint SIGHUM Workshop on Computational Linguistics for Cultural*

*Heritage, Social Sciences, Humanities and Literature*, pages 72–81, Dubrovnik, Croatia. Association for Computational Linguistics.

S. Creissen and N. Blanc. 2017. Quelle représentation des différentes facettes de la dimension émotionnelle d'une histoire entre l'âge de 6 et 10ans ? apports d'une étude multimédia. *Psychologie Française*, 62(3):263–277. Cognition et multimédia : les atouts du numérique en situation d'apprentissage.

Denise Davidson. 2006. The Role of Basic, Self-Conscious and Self-Conscious Evaluative Emotions in Children's Memory and Understanding of Emotion. *Motivation and Emotion*, 30(3):232–242.

Denise Davidson, Zupei Luo, and Matthew J. Burden. 2001. Children's recall of emotional behaviours, emotional labels, and nonemotional behaviours: Does emotion enhance memory? *Cognition and Emotion*, 15(1):1–26. Place: United Kingdom Publisher: Taylor & Francis.

Dorottya Demszky, Dana Movshovitz-Attias, Jeongwoo Ko, Alan S. Cowen, Gaurav Nemade, and Sujith Ravi. 2020. GoEmotions: A Dataset of Fine-Grained Emotions. *CoRR*, abs/2005.00547. ArXiv: 2005.00547.

Katinka Dijkstra, Rolf A Zwaan, Arthur C Graesser, and Joseph P Magliano. 1995. Character and reader emotions in literary texts. *Poetics*, 23(1-2):139–157. Publisher: Elsevier.

Michael G Dyer. 1983. The role of affect in narratives. *Cognitive science*, 7(3):211–242. Publisher: Wiley Online Library.

Katharina Ehret, Aleksandrs Berdicevskis, Christian Bentz, and Alice Blumenthal-Dramé. 2023. Measuring language complexity: challenges and opportunities. *Linguistics Vanguard*, 9(s1):1–8.

Paul Ekman. 1992. An argument for basic emotions. *Cognition and Emotion*, 6(3-4):169–200. Publisher: Routledge _eprint: https://doi.org/10.1080/02699939208411068.

Aline Etienne, Delphine Battistelli, and Gwénolé Lecorvé. 2022. A (Psycho-)Linguistically Motivated Scheme for Annotating and Exploring Emotions in a Genre-Diverse Corpus. In *Proceedings of the Conference on Language Resources and Evaluation (LREC)*, Marseille, France.

Amel Fraisse and Patrick Paroubek. 2015. Utiliser les interjections pour détecter les émotions. In *Actes de la conférence sur le Traitement Automatique des Langues Naturelles*, pages 279–290.

Evgeny Kim and Roman Klinger. 2018. Who feels what and why? annotation of a literature corpus with semantic roles of emotions. In *Proceedings of the International Conference on Computational Linguistics (COLING)*, pages 1345–1359.

Evgeny Kim and Roman Klinger. 2019. An Analysis of Emotion Communication Channels in Fan-Fiction: Towards Emotional Storytelling. In *Proceedings of the Workshop on Storytelling*, pages 56–64, Florence, Italy. Association for Computational Linguistics.

Roman Klinger. 2023. Where are we in event-centric emotion analysis? bridging emotion role labeling and appraisal-based approaches.

Chen Liu, Muhammad Osama, and Anderson de Andrade. 2019. DENS: A Dataset for Multi-class Emotion Analysis. *CoRR*, abs/1910.11769. ArXiv: 1910.11769.

Louis Martin, Benjamin Muller, Pedro Javier Ortiz Suárez, Yoann Dupont, Laurent Romary, Éric de la Clergerie, Djamé Seddah, and Benoît Sagot. 2020. CamemBERT: a Tasty French Language Model. In *Proceedings of the Annual Meeting of the Association for Computational Linguistics (ACL)*, pages 7203–7219, Online. Association for Computational Linguistics.

Saif Mohammad. 2012. #Emotional Tweets. In *Proceedings of the Joint Conference on Lexical and International Workshop on Semantic Evaluation (SemEval)*, pages 246–255, Montréal, Canada. Association for Computational Linguistics.

Saif Mohammad, Felipe Bravo-Marquez, Mohammad Salameh, and Svetlana Kiritchenko. 2018. SemEval-2018 Task 1: Affect in Tweets. In *Proceedings of the International Workshop on Semantic Evaluation (SemEval)*, pages 1–17, New Orleans, Louisiana. Association for Computational Linguistics.

Long Ouyang, Jeffrey Wu, Xu Jiang, Diogo Almeida, Carroll Wainwright, Pamela Mishkin, Chong Zhang, Sandhini Agarwal, Katarina Slama, Alex Ray, et al. 2022. Training language models to follow instructions with human feedback. *Proceedings of the Advances in Neural Information Processing Systems*, 35:27730–27744.

Annie Piolat and Rachid Bannour. 2009. An example of text analysis software (emotaix-tropes) use: The influence of anxiety on expressive writing. *Current psychology letters. Behaviour, brain & cognition*, 25(2, 2009).

Robert Plutchik. 1980. A general psychoevolutionary theory of emotion. In *Theories of emotion*, pages 3–33. Elsevier.

Soujanya Poria, Devamanyu Hazarika, Navonil Majumder, Gautam Naik, Erik Cambria, and Rada Mihalcea. 2018. Meld: A multimodal multi-party dataset for emotion recognition in conversations. *arXiv preprint arXiv:1810.02508*.

Soujanya Poria, Navonil Majumder, Rada Mihalcea, and Eduard Hovy. 2019. Emotion recognition in conversation: Research challenges, datasets, and recent advances. *IEEE Access*, 7:100943–100953.

Nils Reimers and Iryna Gurevych. 2019. Sentence-bert: Sentence embeddings using siamese bert-networks. In *Proceedings of the Conference on Empirical Methods in Natural Language Processing and the International Joint Conference on Natural Language Processing (EMNLP-IJCNLP)*, pages 3982–3992.

Klaus R Scherer. 2005. What are emotions? And how can they be measured? *Social science information*, 44(4):695–729. Publisher: Sage Publications Sage CA: Thousand Oaks, CA.

Carlo Strapparava and Rada Mihalcea. 2007. SemEval-2007 Task 14: Affective Text. In *Proceedings of the International Workshop on Semantic Evaluations (SemEval)*, pages 70–74, Prague, Czech Republic. Association for Computational Linguistics.

Pedro Javier Ortiz Suárez, Benoît Sagot, and Laurent Romary. 2019. Asynchronous pipeline for processing huge corpora on medium to low resource infrastructures. In *Proceedings of the Workshop on the Challenges in the Management of Large Corpora*. Leibniz-Institut für Deutsche Sprache.

E. Troiano, L. Oberländer, and R. Klinger. 2023. Dimensional modeling of emotions in text with appraisal theories: Corpus creation, annotation reliability, and prediction. *Computational Linguistics*, 49(1).

Emily Öhman. 2020. Emotion annotation: Rethinking emotion categorization. *Proceedings of the CEUR Workshop*, 2865:134–144. Publisher: CEUR-WS.

Emily Öhman, Marc Pàmies, Kaisla Kajava, and Jörg Tiedemann. 2020. XED: A Multilingual Dataset for Sentiment Analysis and Emotion Detection. In *Proceedings of the International Conference on Computational Linguistics (COLING)*, pages 6542–6552, Barcelona, Spain (Online). International Committee on Computational Linguistics.

## A Inter-Annotator Agreement

To maximize the number of annotations, each text has been annotated by one annotator. Then, the validity of the annotations has been evaluated by comparing the annotations of two productive annotators from the 6 ones in the whole campaign (referred to as A1 and A2) with another 7-th expert. The Cohen's Kappa for each label is given in 11. For a comparison, in (Kim and Klinger, 2018), *joy* is annotated with a Kappa value of 0.4.

## B Confusion matrices

Table 12 reports the confusion matrices for each task for our model.

These details first show that, inspite of the imbalance between emotional and non-emotional samples, the classification is not biased.

| Label | Label | A1 *vs.* A7 | A2 *vs.* A7 |
|---|---|---|---|
| (A) Presence of emotion | emotional | 0.65 | 0.68 |
| (B) Expression mode | behavioral | 0.65 | 0.75 |
| | labeled | 0.79 | 0.67 |
| | displayed | 0.61 | 0.74 |
| | suggested | 0.53 | 0.38 |
| (C) Emotion type | basic | 0.64 | 0.68 |
| | complex | 0.50 | 0.61 |
| (D) Emotion category | admiration | 0.36 | 0.70 |
| | anger | 0.73 | 0.69 |
| | disgust | 0.75 | 1.00 |
| | embarrass. | 0.53 | 0.50 |
| | fear | 0.65 | 0.63 |
| | guilt | 0.50 | – |
| | jealousy | 1.00 | – |
| | joy | 0.54 | 0.47 |
| | pride | 0.49 | 0.00 |
| | sadness | 0.55 | 0.28 |
| | surprise | 0.60 | 0.85 |

Table 11: Cohen's Kappa for each label between annotators A1 and A2, and an additional one, A7

Regarding the modes (B), most frequent errors relates to guessing a mode where there is none or the contrary. Then, *behavioral* and *suggested* modes are those with the highest number of false positives. This is probably due to the fact that these mode are less direct and require interpretation. Finally, the most frequent confusions between two modes are *labeled* guessed as *suggested*, and the reciprocal. This maybe means that the definition of a *suggested* emotion falls back in the end to a valence consideration of lexical items.

On the side of types (C), the biggest confusion is with the *none* case. Then, there is no specific bias towards *basic* or *complex*.

Finally, our model primarily predicts the classes of Task D where they are expected. Mainly, no prevalent confusion between classes emerges. When no emotional category is expected, the classes *other, anger, fear,* and *sadness* are the most predicted. These false positives do not clash with the *other* class, which is very heterogeneous, but are surprising for the other classes, which are normally better defined.

## C Prompts for GPT-3.5

GPT-3.5 was used in conversational mode. The prompts are thus an alternation of messages between the *user* and the *assistant*, preceded by a global message from the *system*. The user's messages cover all the labels from all tasks A to D, explaining the meaning of each label, while the assistant's responses are binary ("yes" / "no") to

| (A) | emo. | not emo. |
|---|---|---|
| emo. | 753 | 231 |
| not emo. | 258 | 4338 |

| (C) | basic | comp. | *none* |
|---|---|---|---|
| basic | 547 | 48 | 205 |
| comp. | 35 | 54 | 50 |
| *none* | 195 | 17 | 4536 |

| (B) | behav. | label. | displ. | sugg. | *none* |
|---|---|---|---|---|---|
| behav. | 142 | 45 | 19 | 63 | 48 |
| label. | 30 | 260 | 33 | 78 | 30 |
| displ. | 15 | 25 | 131 | 36 | 53 |
| sugg. | 42 | 79 | 44 | 145 | 132 |
| *none* | 60 | 39 | 38 | 88 | 4536 |

| (D) | adm. | ang. | disg. | emb. | fear | guilt | jal. | joy | pride | sad. | surp. | other | *none* |
|---|---|---|---|---|---|---|---|---|---|---|---|---|---|
| adm. | 16 | 0 | 0 | 0 | 0 | 0 | 0 | 7 | 7 | 1 | 10 | 5 | 23 |
| ang. | 1 | 125 | 0 | 5 | 10 | 0 | 0 | 3 | 0 | 6 | 6 | 12 | 41 |
| disg. | 0 | 0 | 0 | 2 | 3 | 0 | 0 | 1 | 0 | 6 | 0 | 4 | 1 |
| emb. | 0 | 2 | 0 | 12 | 2 | 0 | 0 | 0 | 0 | 6 | 4 | 6 | 9 |
| fear | 1 | 11 | 0 | 3 | 151 | 0 | 0 | 3 | 0 | 20 | 8 | 17 | 41 |
| guilt | 0 | 0 | 0 | 1 | 0 | 0 | 0 | 0 | 0 | 1 | 0 | 0 | 2 |
| jal. | 0 | 1 | 0 | 0 | 0 | 0 | 0 | 0 | 0 | 0 | 0 | 0 | 0 |
| joy | 9 | 2 | 0 | 1 | 4 | 0 | 0 | 109 | 15 | 6 | 20 | 26 | 52 |
| pride | 4 | 0 | 0 | 1 | 0 | 0 | 0 | 8 | 16 | 0 | 5 | 4 | 20 |
| sad. | 4 | 9 | 0 | 5 | 26 | 0 | 0 | 5 | 0 | 58 | 4 | 15 | 41 |
| surp. | 6 | 7 | 0 | 1 | 8 | 0 | 0 | 9 | 5 | 2 | 100 | 6 | 29 |
| other | 3 | 9 | 0 | 2 | 12 | 0 | 0 | 18 | 3 | 11 | 3 | 155 | 35 |
| *none* | 9 | 15 | 0 | 1 | 60 | 0 | 0 | 29 | 5 | 35 | 21 | 71 | 4340 |

(Rows: Reference; columns: Predictions.)

Table 12: Confusion matrices of our model for Tasks A, B, C, and D

indicate the presence or absence of the respective class. Two types of messages are considered for the user: either the explanations of each label are accompanied by positive examples, or they are accompanied by both positive and negative examples (i.e., counter-examples). Only Task A (presence or absence of emotional information) is an exception since it is always accompanied by counter-examples, regardless of the type of prompt. Sections C.2 and C.3 then show the details of the two types of prompts. We use version 0311 of GPT-3.5 for all experiments.

### C.1 Detailed results

Table 13 provides detailed results on the test set for each approach compared to our model. Overall, these results show that our model performs better and that the approach without counter-examples is better than the one with counter-examples. The main problem with GPT-3.5 seems to be that it predicts too many labels (high recall but low precision). However, it is worth noting that GPT-3.5 seems to perform better on rare classes because our model does not predict them.

### C.2 With positive examples only

```
System:
Tu joues le rôle d'un expert linguiste qui annote des phrases
en t'intéressant à leur dimension émotionnelle.
    L'annotation porte au niveau de la phrase et prend la forme de
questions successives. Pour comprendre le contexte, la phrase
à annoter est donnée avec sa phrase précédente et sa phrase
suivante, mais la réponse à chaque question doit uniquement
porter sur la seule phrase à annoter, et non sur la phrase
précédente ou suivante.
    - Phrase précédente: Nicolas Hulot n'appartient à aucun parti
politique.
- Phrase à annoter: Il a refusé trois fois le poste de ministre
de l'Ecologie avant d'accepter la proposition d'Emmanuel Macron.
- Phrase suivante: Mais ça ne s'est pas très bien passé.
    User:
Définition: une phrase est dite "émotionnelle" si elle exprime
explicitement ou implicitement une émotion, qu'elle soit
exprimée par le narrateur ou un personnage. Par exemple:
- émotionnelle: "Cette information a beaucoup énervé Marie."
- émotionnelle: "Andrée a sautillé partout en chantant."
- émotionnelle: "Oh, non... C'est vraiment dommage !"
- émotionnelle: "Ces deux amis se retrouvent après une longue
séparation."
- non émotionnelle: "Avant d'arriver devant une salle de classe,
les enseignants, eux aussi, sont sur les bancs de l'école."
- non émotionnelle: "De 2007 à 2012, il a été le Premier ministre
de l'ancien président Nicolas Sarkozy."
- non émotionnelle: "Récemment, une nouvelle autorisation a été
délivrée pour un deuxième test dans le courant de l'année 2019."
- non émotionnelle: "Avant de sortir, Billy prépare un dîner
orange : une soupe de potiron, des cuisses de canard à l'orange
avec une purée de carottes et une tarte à la citrouille."
    Question: La phrase à annoter est-elle **émotionnelle** ?
    Réponse (oui/non):
    Assistant:
<réponse du modèle>
    User:
Définition: La catégorie émotionnelle "colère" recouvre les
émotions suivantes: agacement, colère, contestation, désaccord
(si émotion suggérée), désapprobation, énervement, fureur/rage,
indignation, insatisfaction, irritation, mécontentement,
réprobation et révolte. Par exemple :
- "C'est notamment pour cette raison que des "gilets jaunes", les
personnes qui manifestent et bloquent des routes dans le pays
depuis plusieurs semaines, sont en colère."
- "- Ton commentaire est déplacé, jeune homme ! a-t-elle dit
d'un air pincé."
    Question: Si la phrase à annoter est émotionnelle, est-ce
que la catégorie émotionnelle **colère** est présente ?
    Réponse (oui/non):
    Assistant:
<réponse du modèle>
    User:
Définition: La catégorie émotionnelle "dégoût" recouvre les
émotions suivantes: dégoût, lassitude et répulsion. Par exemple
:
- "Beurk !"
- "Ça peut paraître dégoûtant, mais on peut manger des insectes."

    Question: Si la phrase à annoter est émotionnelle, est-ce
que la catégorie émotionnelle **dégoût** est présente ?
    Réponse (oui/non):
    Assistant:
<réponse du modèle>
    User:
Définition: La catégorie émotionnelle "joie" recouvre les
émotions suivantes: amusement, enthousiasme, exaltation, joie
et plaisir. Par exemple :
- "Pour fêter ses buts, il lui arrive souvent de danser."
- "- Je suis bien aise de vous voir, me dit le roi sur un ton
amical."
    Question: Si la phrase à annoter est émotionnelle, est-ce
que la catégorie émotionnelle **joie** est présente ?
    Réponse (oui/non):
    Assistant:
<réponse du modèle>
    User:
Définition: La catégorie émotionnelle "peur" recouvre les
émotions suivantes: angoisse, appréhension, effroi, horreur,
inquiétude, méfiance, peur, stress et timidité. Par exemple :
- "Le Front national, qui est d'extrême droite, faisait peur, à
cause des idées qu'il défendait."
- "Il y avait un grand silence dans la maison."
```

| Tasks | Modèle E | | | | GPT3.5 with positive examples only | | | | GPT3.5 with positive and negative examples | | | | Labels |
|---|---|---|---|---|---|---|---|---|---|---|---|---|---|
| | macro-F1 | R | P | F1 | macro-F1 | R | P | F1 | macro-F1 | R | P | F1 | |
| (A) | **0.75** | **0.76** | **0.74** | **0.75** | 0.52 | 0.62 | 0.44 | 0.52 | 0.38 | 0.74 | 0.26 | 0.38 | emotional |
| (B) | **0.64** | **0.60** | **0.65** | **0.63** | 0.15 | 0.22 | 0.15 | 0.18 | 0.13 | 0.42 | 0.07 | 0.12 | behavioral |
| | | **0.81** | **0.80** | **0.81** | | 0.40 | 0.10 | 0.15 | | 0.44 | 0.13 | 0.20 | labeled |
| | | 0.67 | **0.73** | **0.70** | | **0.90** | 0.07 | 0.12 | | 0.66 | 0.05 | 0.10 | displayed |
| | | 0.43 | **0.48** | **0.45** | | **0.53** | 0.09 | 0.15 | | 0.37 | 0.07 | 0.11 | suggested |
| (C) | **0.60** | 0.70 | **0.73** | **0.72** | 0.20 | **0.71** | 0.20 | 0.32 | 0.22 | 0.47 | 0.29 | 0.35 | basic |
| | | 0.41 | **0.59** | **0.48** | | **0.80** | 0.04 | 0.08 | | 0.26 | 0.05 | 0.09 | complex |
| (D) | **0.42** | 0.28 | **0.46** | **0.35** | 0.17 | **0.82** | 0.04 | 0.07 | 0.13 | 0.53 | 0.03 | 0.05 | admiration |
| | | **0.67** | **0.68** | **0.68** | | 0.66 | 0.23 | 0.35 | | 0.59 | 0.27 | 0.37 | anger |
| | | 0.00 | 0.00 | 0.00 | | **0.80** | 0.07 | 0.13 | | **0.80** | **0.13** | **0.23** | disgust |
| | | 0.36 | **0.60** | **0.45** | | 0.42 | 0.11 | 0.18 | | **0.76** | 0.02 | 0.05 | embarrassment |
| | | 0.72 | **0.66** | **0.69** | | 0.73 | 0.15 | 0.25 | | **0.74** | 0.10 | 0.18 | fear |
| | | 0.00 | 0.00 | 0.00 | | **1.00** | 0.22 | **0.36** | | **1.00** | 0.00 | 0.01 | guilt |
| | | 0.00 | 0.00 | 0.00 | | 0.00 | 0.00 | 0.00 | | 0.00 | 0.00 | 0.00 | jealousy |
| | | 0.53 | **0.71** | **0.61** | | **0.84** | 0.11 | 0.19 | | 0.68 | 0.15 | 0.24 | joy |
| | | 0.33 | **0.62** | **0.43** | | **0.96** | 0.02 | 0.05 | | 0.77 | 0.02 | 0.04 | pride |
| | | 0.43 | **0.50** | **0.46** | | **0.45** | 0.25 | 0.32 | | 0.40 | 0.11 | 0.17 | sadness |
| | | 0.70 | **0.74** | **0.72** | | **0.87** | 0.06 | 0.11 | | 0.79 | 0.05 | 0.09 | surprise |
| | | 0.75 | **0.59** | **0.66** | | **0.80** | 0.04 | 0.08 | | 0.61 | 0.04 | 0.07 | other |

Table 13: Detailed comparison between our model and the two approaches based on GPT3.5

Question: Si la phrase à annoter est émotionnelle, est-ce que la catégorie émotionnelle **peur** est présente ?
Réponse (oui/non):

**Assistant:**
<réponse du modèle>

**User:**
Définition: La catégorie émotionnelle "surprise" recouvre les émotions suivantes: étonnement, stupeur, surprise. Par exemple :
- "Finalement, ils ont été pris en charge... par les agriculteurs locaux, dans un camion benne !"
- "Tous, étonnés, se taisent."

Question: Si la phrase à annoter est émotionnelle, est-ce que la catégorie émotionnelle **surprise** est présente ?
Réponse (oui/non):

**Assistant:**
<réponse du modèle>

**User:**
Définition: La catégorie émotionnelle "tristesse" recouvre les émotions suivantes: blues, chagrin, déception, désespoir, peine, souffrance et tristesse. Par exemple :
- "Sa mère venait de mourir et son père était au front."
- "L'âne continuait à examiner la peinture d'un regard plutôt attristé."

Question: Si la phrase à annoter est émotionnelle, est-ce que la catégorie émotionnelle **tristesse** est présente ?
Réponse (oui/non):

**Assistant:**
<réponse du modèle>

**User:**
Définition: La catégorie émotionnelle "admiration" recouvre les émotions suivantes: admiration. Par exemple :
- "De nos jours, ce site exceptionnel permet de montrer toute la richesse de la civilisation romaine et la façon dont les villes et la société étaient organisées."
- "- Tes enfants sont vraiment merveilleux, ma chérie, dit-elle à sa fille."

Question: Si la phrase à annoter est émotionnelle, est-ce que la catégorie émotionnelle **admiration** est présente ?
Réponse (oui/non):

**Assistant:**
<réponse du modèle>

**User:**
Définition: La catégorie émotionnelle "culpabilité" recouvre les émotions suivantes: culpabilité. Par exemple :
- "Et je l'avais bien mérité."
- "Surtout, il ne faut pas se sentir coupable de ne pas avoir réagi."

Question: Si la phrase à annoter est émotionnelle, est-ce que la catégorie émotionnelle **culpabilité** est présente ?
Réponse (oui/non):

**Assistant:**
<réponse du modèle>

**User:**
Définition: La catégorie émotionnelle "embarras" recouvre les émotions suivantes: embarras, gêne, honte, humiliation et timidité. Par exemple :
- "Après cette humiliante défaite, Napoléon abdique une nouvelle fois, ce qui marque définitivement la fin de l'Empire et de sa période de retour appelée "les Cent jours"."
- "Légèrement décontenancée, la prof s'est raclé la gorge et commencé la lecture."

Question: Si la phrase à annoter est émotionnelle, est-ce que la catégorie émotionnelle **embarras** est présente ?
Réponse (oui/non):

**Assistant:**
<réponse du modèle>

**User:**
Définition: La catégorie émotionnelle "fierté" recouvre les émotions suivantes: fierté et orgueil. Par exemple :
- "Flavia entre dans la cour comme une conquérante, entourée de ses supporters."
- "Magawa peut être fier de lui, car il vient de recevoir une médaille d'or."

Question: Si la phrase à annoter est émotionnelle, est-ce que la catégorie émotionnelle **fierté** est présente ?
Réponse (oui/non):

**Assistant:**
<réponse du modèle>

**User:**
Définition: La catégorie émotionnelle "jalousie" recouvre les émotions suivantes: jalousie. Par exemple :
- "Mais quand Flavia découvre le jeune génie du piano, elle se sent comme écrasée."
- "On dirait presque qu'il fait partie de l'instrument."

Question: Si la phrase à annoter est émotionnelle, est-ce que la catégorie émotionnelle **jalousie** est présente ?
Réponse (oui/non):

**Assistant:**
<réponse du modèle>

**User:**
Définition: La catégorie émotionnelle "autre" recouvre les émotions suivantes: amour, courage, curiosité, désir, détermination, envie, espoir, haine, impuissance, mépris et soulagement. Par exemple :
- "Dans chaque camp, ils se sont mobilisés pour donner envie aux gens de voter comme eux."
- "Ils n'apprécient pas du tout l'attitude des dirigeants, notamment celle du président, "qu'ils jugent méprisant, déconnecté de la réalité, du quotidien", note le sociologue Alexis Spire."

Question: Si la phrase à annoter est émotionnelle, est-ce que la catégorie émotionnelle **autre** est présente ?
Réponse (oui/non):

**Assistant:**
<réponse du modèle>

**User:**
Définition: Les émotions suivantes sont dites "de base" : Colère, Dégoût, Joie, Peur, Surprise, Tristesse.
Question: Si la phrase à annoter est émotionnelle, contient-elle une **émotion de base** ?
Réponse (oui/non):
**Assistant:**
<réponse du modèle>
**User:**
Définition: Les émotions suivantes sont dites "complexes": Admiration, Culpabilité, Embarras, Fierté, Jalousie.
Question: Si la phrase à annoter est émotionnelle, contient-elle une **émotion complexe** ?
Réponse (oui/non):
**Assistant:**
<réponse du modèle>
**User:**
Définition: Une émotion est dite du mode "désigné" lorsqu'elle est exprimée par un terme du lexique émotionnel. Par exemple :
- "Pierre est heureux d'être bientôt à la retraite.", où la joie de Pierre est désignée par le terme "heureux".
- "Cette information a beaucoup énervé Marie.", où la colère de Marie est désignée par le terme "énervé".
Question: Si la phrase à annoter est émotionnelle, est-ce que le mode **désigné** est utilisé ?
Réponse (oui/non):
**Assistant:**
<réponse du modèle>
**User:**
Définition: Une émotion est dite du mode "comportemental" lorsqu'elle est exprimée par la description d'une manifestation physique (physiologique ou comportementale) de l'émotion. Par exemple :
- "Paul sanglote.", où la tristesse de Paul est exprimée par le comportement "sanglote".
- "Andrée a sautillé partout en chantant.", où la joie de Andrée est exprimée par le comportement "sautillé partout en chantant".
Question: Si la phrase à annoter est émotionnelle, est-ce que le mode **comportemental** est utilisé ?
Réponse (oui/non):
**Assistant:**
<réponse du modèle>
**User:**
Définition: Une émotion est dite du mode "montré" lorsqu'elle est exprimée par des caractéristiques linguistiques de l'énoncé qui traduisent l'état émotionnel dans lequel se trouvait l'énonciateur au moment de l'énonciation. Par exemple :
- "Oh, chouette ! Quelle bonne idée !", car la joie de l'énonciateur est traduite au sein de l'énoncé par les interjections "oh" et "chouette", les énoncés averbaux et les points d'exclamations.
- "Oh, non... C'est vraiment dommage !", car la tristesse de l'énonciateur est traduite au sein de l'énoncé par l'interjection "oh", l'énoncé averbal, les points de suspension et le point d'exclamation.
Question: Si la phrase à annoter est émotionnelle, est-ce que le mode **montré** est utilisé ?
Réponse (oui/non):
**Assistant:**
<réponse du modèle>
**User:**
Définition: Une émotion est dite du mode "suggéré" lorsqu'elle est exprimée par la description d'une situation associée de manière conventionnelle à un ressenti émotionnel. Par exemple :
- "Le père de Jeanne est mort hier à cause d'un cancer.", où la tristesse de Jeanne est suggérée par la description du décès, il y a peu de temps, de son père (une personne proche d'elle).
- "Ces deux amis se retrouvent après une longue séparation.", où la joie des deux amis est suggérée par la description de leurs retrouvailles après un temps long.
Question: Si la phrase à annoter est émotionnelle, est-ce que le mode **suggéré** est utilisé ?
Réponse (oui/non):

**Assistant:**

<réponse du modèle>

## C.3 With positive and negative examples

**System:**
Tu joues le rôle d'un expert linguiste qui annote des phrases d'après leurs dimensions émotionnelle.

Les différentes annotations sont toute binaires (absence ou présence d'une propriété). Elles vont porter sur la nature émotionnelle ou non des phrases et, si oui, le mode d'expression de la ou des émotions présentes (désignée, comportementale, montrée ou suggérée), la ou les catégories émotionnelles (joie, peur, colère, tristesse, etc.) et le ou les types d'émotion ("de base" ou "complexe"). Chaque propriété est décrite par une définition et des exemples.

L'annotation La phrase à annoter est entourée des balises <annotate>...</annotate>.

**User:**
Définition : une phrase est dite "émotionnelle" si elle exprime explicitement ou implicitement une émotion, qu'elle soit exprimée par le narrateur ou un personnage.

Question : La phrase à annoter est-elle **émotionnelle** ?

Exemples :

- <annotate>Avant de sortir, Billy prépare un dîner orange : une soupe de potiron, des cuisses de canard à l'orange avec une purée de carottes et une tarte à la citrouille.</annotate> -> non
- <annotate>Cette information a beaucoup énervé Marie.</annotate> -> oui
- <annotate>Andrée a sautillé partout en chantant.</annotate> -> oui
- <annotate>Récemment, une nouvelle autorisation a été délivrée pour un deuxième test dans le courant de l'année 2019.</annotate> -> non - <annotate>Oh, non... C'est vraiment dommage !</annotate> -> oui
- <annotate>De 2007 à 2012, il a été le Premier ministre de l'ancien président Nicolas Sarkozy.</annotate> -> non
- <annotate>Ces deux amis se retrouvent après une longue séparation. -> oui
- <annotate>Avant d'arriver devant une salle de classe, les enseignants, eux aussi, sont sur les bancs de l'école.</annotate> -> non

Annotation (oui/non) :
- Nicolas Hulot n'appartient à aucun parti politique. <annotate>Il a refusé trois fois le poste de ministre de l'Ecologie avant d'accepter la proposition d'Emmanuel Macron.</annotate> Mais ça ne s'est pas très bien passé. ->

**Assistant:**
réponse du modèle

**User:**
Définition : La catégorie émotionnelle "colère" recouvre les émotions suivantes: agacement, colère, contestation, désaccord (si émotion suggérée), désapprobation, énervement, fureur/rage, indignation, insatisfaction, irritation, mécontentement, réprobation et révolte.

Question : Si la phrase à annoter est émotionnelle, est-ce que la catégorie émotionnelle **colère** est présente ?

Exemples :
- <annotate>De 2007 à 2012, il a été le Premier ministre de l'ancien président Nicolas Sarkozy.</annotate> -> non
- <annotate>C'est notamment pour cette raison que des "gilets jaunes", les personnes qui manifestent et bloquent des routes dans le pays depuis plusieurs semaines, sont en colère.</annotate> -> oui.
- <annotate>Tous, étonnés, se taisent.</annotate> -> non.
- <annotate>- Ton commentaire est déplacé, jeune homme ! a-t-elle dit d'un air pincé.</annotate> -> oui.
- <annotate>Après cette humiliante défaite, Napoléon abdique une nouvelle fois, ce qui marque définitivement la fin de l'Empire et de sa période de retour appelée "les Cent jours".</annotate> -> non.

Annotation (oui/non) :
- Nicolas Hulot n'appartient à aucun parti politique. <annotate>Il a refusé trois fois le poste de ministre de l'Ecologie avant d'accepter la proposition d'Emmanuel Macron.</annotate> Mais ça ne s'est pas très bien passé. ->

**Assistant:**
réponse du modèle

**User:**
Définition : La catégorie émotionnelle "dégoût" recouvre les émotions suivantes: dégoût, lassitude et répulsion.

Question : Si la phrase à annoter est émotionnelle, est-ce que la catégorie émotionnelle **dégoût** est présente ?

Exemples :
- <annotate>Ça peut paraître dégoûtant, mais on peut manger des insectes.</annotate> -> oui.
- <annotate>Beurk !</annotate> -> oui.
- <annotate>Finalement, ils ont été pris en charge... par les agriculteurs locaux, dans un camion benne !</annotate> -> non.
- <annotate>Le Front national, qui est d'extrême droite, faisait peur, à cause des idées qu'il défendait.</annotate> -> non.
- <annotate>Avant d'arriver devant une salle de classe, les enseignants, eux aussi, sont sur les bancs de l'école.</annotate> -> non

Annotation (oui/non) :
- Nicolas Hulot n'appartient à aucun parti politique. <annotate>Il a refusé trois fois le poste de ministre de l'Ecologie avant d'accepter la proposition d'Emmanuel Macron.</annotate> Mais ça ne s'est pas très bien passé. ->

**Assistant:**
réponse du modèle

**User:**
Définition : La catégorie émotionnelle "joie" recouvre les émotions suivantes: amusement, enthousiasme, exaltation, joie et plaisir.

Question : Si la phrase à annoter est émotionnelle, est-ce que la catégorie émotionnelle **joie** est présente ?

Exemples :
- <annotate>Dans chaque camp, ils se sont mobilisés pour donner envie aux gens de voter comme eux.</annotate> -> non.
- <annotate>- Je suis bien aise de vous voir, me dit le roi sur un ton amical.</annotate> -> oui.
- <annotate>Beurk !</annotate> -> non.
- <annotate>Avant d'arriver devant une salle de classe, les enseignants, eux aussi, sont sur les bancs de l'école.</annotate> -> non
- <annotate>Pour fêter ses buts, il lui arrive souvent de danser.</annotate> -> oui.

Annotation (oui/non) :
- Nicolas Hulot n'appartient à aucun parti politique. <annotate>Il a refusé trois fois le poste de ministre de l'Ecologie avant d'accepter la proposition d'Emmanuel Macron.</annotate> Mais ça ne s'est pas très bien passé. ->

**Assistant:**
réponse du modèle

**User:**
Définition : La catégorie émotionnelle "peur" recouvre les émotions suivantes: angoisse, appréhension, effroi, horreur, inquiétude, méfiance, peur, stress et timidité.

Question : Si la phrase à annoter est émotionnelle, est-ce que la catégorie émotionnelle **peur** est présente ?

Exemples :
- <annotate>Le Front national, qui est d'extrême droite, faisait peur, à cause des idées qu'il défendait.</annotate> -> oui.
- <annotate>Dans chaque camp, ils se sont mobilisés pour donner envie aux gens de voter comme eux.</annotate> -> non.
- <annotate>Ça peut paraître dégoûtant, mais on peut manger des insectes.</annotate> -> non.
- <annotate>Récemment, une nouvelle autorisation a été délivrée pour un deuxième test dans le courant de l'année 2019.</annotate> -> non
- <annotate>Il y avait un grand silence dans la maison.</annotate> -> oui.

Annotation (oui/non) :
- Nicolas Hulot n'appartient à aucun parti politique. <annotate>Il a refusé trois fois le poste de ministre de l'Ecologie avant d'accepter la proposition d'Emmanuel Macron.</annotate> Mais ça ne s'est pas très bien passé. ->

**Assistant:**
réponse du modèle

**User:**
Définition : La catégorie émotionnelle "surprise" recouvre les émotions suivantes: étonnement, stupeur, surprise.

Question : Si la phrase à annoter est émotionnelle, est-ce que la catégorie émotionnelle **surprise** est présente ?

Exemples :
- <annotate>Finalement, ils ont été pris en charge... par les agriculteurs locaux, dans un camion benne !</annotate> -> oui.
- <annotate>Avant d'arriver devant une salle de classe, les enseignants, eux aussi, sont sur les bancs de l'école.</annotate> -> non
- <annotate>Mais quand Flavia découvre le jeune génie du piano, elle se sent comme écrasée.</annotate> -> non.
- <annotate>Beurk !</annotate> -> non.
- <annotate>Tous, étonnés, se taisent.</annotate> -> oui.

Annotation (oui/non) :
- Nicolas Hulot n'appartient à aucun parti politique. <annotate>Il a refusé trois fois le poste de ministre de l'Ecologie avant d'accepter la proposition d'Emmanuel Macron.</annotate> Mais ça ne s'est pas très bien passé. ->

**Assistant:**
réponse du modèle

**User:**
Définition : La catégorie émotionnelle "tristesse" recouvre les émotions suivantes: blues, chagrin, déception, désespoir, peine, souffrance et tristesse.

Question : Si la phrase à annoter est émotionnelle, est-ce que la catégorie émotionnelle **tristesse** est présente ?

Exemples :
- <annotate>Avant d'arriver devant une salle de classe, les enseignants, eux aussi, sont sur les bancs de l'école.</annotate> -> non
- <annotate>Le Front national, qui est d'extrême droite, faisait peur, à cause des idées qu'il défendait.</annotate> -> non.
- <annotate>Sa mère venait de mourir et son père était au front.</annotate> -> oui.
- <annotate>Légèrement décontenancée, la prof s'est raclé la gorge et commencé la lecture.</annotate> -> non.
- <annotate>L'âne continuait à examiner la peinture d'un regard plutôt attristé.</annotate> -> oui.

Annotation (oui/non) :
- Nicolas Hulot n'appartient à aucun parti politique. <annotate>Il a refusé trois fois le poste de ministre de l'Ecologie avant d'accepter la proposition d'Emmanuel Macron.</annotate> Mais ça ne s'est pas très bien passé. ->

**Assistant:**
réponse du modèle

**User:**
Définition : La catégorie émotionnelle "admiration" recouvre les émotions suivantes: admiration.

Question : Si la phrase à annoter est émotionnelle, est-ce que la catégorie émotionnelle **admiration** est présente ?

Exemples :
- <annotate>Tous, étonnés, se taisent.</annotate> -> non.
- <annotate>De nos jours, ce site exceptionnel permet de montrer toute la richesse de la civilisation romaine et la façon dont les villes et la société étaient organisées.</annotate> -> oui.
- <annotate>Magawa peut être fier de lui, car il vient de recevoir une médaille d'or.</annotate> -> non.
- <annotate>Avant de sortir, Billy prépare un dîner orange : une soupe de potiron, des cuisses de canard à l'orange avec une purée de carottes et une tarte à la citrouille.</annotate> -> non
- <annotate>- Tes enfants sont vraiment merveilleux, ma chérie, dit-elle à sa fille.</annotate> -> oui.

Annotation (oui/non) :
- Nicolas Hulot n'appartient à aucun parti politique. <annotate>Il a refusé trois fois le poste de ministre de l'Ecologie avant d'accepter la proposition d'Emmanuel Macron.</annotate> Mais ça ne s'est pas très bien passé. ->

**Assistant:**
réponse du modèle

**User:**
Définition : La catégorie émotionnelle "culpabilité" recouvre les émotions suivantes: culpabilité.

Question : Si la phrase à annoter est émotionnelle, est-ce que la catégorie émotionnelle **culpabilité** est présente ?

Exemples :
- <annotate>Et je l'avais bien mérité.</annotate> -> oui.
- <annotate>Tous, étonnés, se taisent.</annotate> -> non.
- <annotate>Surtout, il ne faut pas se sentir coupable de ne pas avoir réagi.</annotate> -> oui.
- <annotate>Tous, étonnés, se taisent.</annotate> -> non.
- <annotate>Avant d'arriver devant une salle de classe, les enseignants, eux aussi, sont sur les bancs de l'école.</annotate> -> non

Annotation (oui/non) :
- Nicolas Hulot n'appartient à aucun parti politique. <annotate>Il a refusé trois fois le poste de ministre de l'Ecologie avant d'accepter la proposition d'Emmanuel Macron.</annotate> Mais ça ne s'est pas très bien passé. ->

**Assistant:**
réponse du modèle

**User:**
Définition : La catégorie émotionnelle "embarras" recouvre les émotions suivantes: embarras, gêne, honte, humiliation et timidité.

Question : Si la phrase à annoter est émotionnelle, est-ce que la catégorie émotionnelle **embarras** est présente ?

Exemples :
- <annotate>Le Front national, qui est d'extrême droite, faisait peur, à cause des idées qu'il défendait.</annotate> -> non.
- <annotate>- Tes enfants sont vraiment merveilleux, ma chérie, dit-elle à sa fille.</annotate> -> non.
- <annotate>Avant d'arriver devant une salle de classe, les enseignants, eux aussi, sont sur les bancs de l'école.</annotate> -> non
- <annotate>Après cette humiliante défaite, Napoléon abdique une nouvelle fois, ce qui marque définitivement la fin de l'Empire et de sa période de retour appelée "les Cent jours".</annotate> -> oui.
- <annotate>Légèrement décontenancée, la prof s'est raclé la gorge et commencé la lecture.</annotate> -> oui.

Annotation (oui/non) :
- Nicolas Hulot n'appartient à aucun parti politique. <annotate>Il a refusé trois fois le poste de ministre de l'Ecologie avant d'accepter la proposition d'Emmanuel Macron.</annotate> Mais ça ne s'est pas très bien passé. ->

**Assistant:**
réponse du modèle

**User:**
Définition : La catégorie émotionnelle "fierté" recouvre les émotions suivantes: fierté et orgueil.

Question : Si la phrase à annoter est émotionnelle, est-ce que la catégorie émotionnelle **fierté** est présente ?

Exemples :
- <annotate>Avant de sortir, Billy prépare un dîner orange : une soupe de potiron, des cuisses de canard à l'orange avec une purée de carottes et une tarte à la citrouille.</annotate> -> non
- <annotate>On dirait presque qu'il fait partie de l'instrument.</annotate> -> non.
- <annotate>Magawa peut être fier de lui, car il vient de recevoir une médaille d'or.</annotate> -> oui.
- <annotate>Flavia entre dans la cour comme une conquérante, entourée de ses supporters.</annotate> -> oui.
- <annotate>Il y avait un grand silence dans la maison.</annotate> -> non.

Annotation (oui/non) :
- Nicolas Hulot n'appartient à aucun parti politique. <annotate>Il a refusé trois fois le poste de ministre de l'Ecologie avant d'accepter la proposition d'Emmanuel Macron.</annotate> Mais ça ne s'est pas très bien passé. ->

**Assistant:**
réponse du modèle

**User:**
Définition : La catégorie émotionnelle "jalousie" recouvre les émotions suivantes: jalousie.

Question : Si la phrase à annoter est émotionnelle, est-ce que la catégorie émotionnelle **jalousie** est présente ?

Exemples :
- <annotate>On dirait presque qu'il fait partie de l'instrument.</annotate> -> oui.
- <annotate>Et je l'avais bien mérité.</annotate> -> non.
- <annotate>Et je l'avais bien mérité.</annotate> -> non.
- <annotate>Mais quand Flavia découvre le jeune génie du piano, elle se sent comme écrasée.</annotate> -> oui.
- <annotate>Avant d'arriver devant une salle de classe, les enseignants, eux aussi, sont sur les bancs de l'école.</annotate> -> non

Annotation (oui/non) :
- Nicolas Hulot n'appartient à aucun parti politique. <annotate>Il a refusé trois fois le poste de ministre de l'Ecologie avant d'accepter la proposition d'Emmanuel Macron.</annotate> Mais ça ne s'est pas très bien passé. ->

**Assistant:**
réponse du modèle

**User:**
Définition : La catégorie émotionnelle "autre" recouvre les émotions suivantes: amour, courage, curiosité, désir, détermination, envie, espoir, haine, impuissance, mépris et soulagement.

Question : Si la phrase à annoter est émotionnelle, est-ce que la catégorie émotionnelle **autre** est présente ?

Exemples :
- <annotate>De nos jours, ce site exceptionnel permet de montrer toute la richesse de la civilisation romaine et la façon dont les villes et la société étaient organisées.</annotate> -> non.
- <annotate>L'âne continuait à examiner la peinture d'un regard plutôt attristé.</annotate> -> non.
- <annotate>Récemment, une nouvelle autorisation a été délivrée pour un deuxième test dans le courant de l'année 2019.</annotate> -> non
- <annotate>Ils n'apprécient pas du tout l'attitude des dirigeants, notamment celle du président, "qu'ils jugent méprisant, déconnecté de la réalité, du quotidien", note le sociologue Alexis Spire.</annotate> -> oui.
- <annotate>Dans chaque camp, ils se sont mobilisés pour donner envie aux gens de voter comme eux.</annotate> -> oui.

Annotation (oui/non) :
- Nicolas Hulot n'appartient à aucun parti politique. <annotate>Il a refusé trois fois le poste de ministre de l'Ecologie avant d'accepter la proposition d'Emmanuel Macron.</annotate> Mais ça ne s'est pas très bien passé. ->

**Assistant:**
réponse du modèle

**User:**
Définition : Les émotions suivantes sont dites "de base" : Colère, Dégoût, Joie, Peur, Surprise, Tristesse.

Question : Si la phrase à annoter est émotionnelle, contient-elle une **émotion de base** ?

Annotation (oui/non) :
- Nicolas Hulot n'appartient à aucun parti politique. <annotate>Il a refusé trois fois le poste de ministre de l'Ecologie avant d'accepter la proposition d'Emmanuel Macron.</annotate> Mais ça ne s'est pas très bien passé. ->

**Assistant:**
réponse du modèle

**User:**
Définition : Les émotions suivantes sont dites "complexes": Admiration, Culpabilité, Embarras, Fierté, Jalousie.

Question : Si la phrase à annoter est émotionnelle, contient-elle une **émotion complexe** ?

Annotation (oui/non) :
- Nicolas Hulot n'appartient à aucun parti politique. <annotate>Il a refusé trois fois le poste de ministre de l'Ecologie avant d'accepter la proposition d'Emmanuel Macron.</annotate> Mais ça ne s'est pas très bien passé. ->

**Assistant:**
réponse du modèle

**User:**
Définition : Une émotion est dite du mode "désigné" lorsqu'elle est exprimée par un terme du lexique émotionnel.

Question : Si la phrase à annoter est émotionnelle, est-ce que le mode **désigné** est utilisé ?

Exemples :
- <annotate>Pierre est heureux d'être bientôt à la retraite.</annotate> -> oui (car la joie de Pierre est désignée par le terme "heureux").
- <annotate>Oh, non... C'est vraiment dommage !</annotate> -> non.
- <annotate>Avant d'arriver devant une salle de classe, les enseignants, eux aussi, sont sur les bancs de l'école.</annotate> -> non
- <annotate>Oh, non... C'est vraiment dommage !</annotate> -> non.
- <annotate>Cette information a beaucoup énervé Marie.</annotate> -> oui (car la colère de Marie est désignée par le terme "énervé").

Annotation (oui/non) :
- Nicolas Hulot n'appartient à aucun parti politique. <annotate>Il a refusé trois fois le poste de ministre de l'Ecologie avant d'accepter la proposition d'Emmanuel Macron.</annotate> Mais ça ne s'est pas très bien passé. ->

**Assistant:**
réponse du modèle

**User:**
Définition : Une émotion est dite du mode "comportemental" lorsqu'elle est exprimée par la description d'une manifestation physique (physiologique ou comportementale) de l'émotion.

Question : Si la phrase à annoter est émotionnelle, est-ce que le mode **comportemental** est utilisé ?

Exemples :
- <annotate>Cette information a beaucoup énervé Marie.</annotate> -> non.
- <annotate>Paul sanglote.</annotate> -> oui (car la tristesse de Paul est exprimée par le comportement "sanglote").
- <annotate>Avant d'arriver devant une salle de classe, les enseignants, eux aussi, sont sur les bancs de l'école.</annotate> -> non
- <annotate>Le père de Jeanne est mort hier à cause d'un cancer.</annotate> -> non.
- <annotate>Andrée a sautillé partout en chantant.</annotate> -> oui (car la joie de Andrée est exprimée par le comportement "sautillé partout en chantant").

Annotation (oui/non) :
- Nicolas Hulot n'appartient à aucun parti politique. <annotate>Il a refusé trois fois le poste de ministre de l'Ecologie avant d'accepter la proposition d'Emmanuel Macron.</annotate> Mais ça ne s'est pas très bien passé. ->

**Assistant:**
réponse du modèle

**User:**
Définition : Une émotion est dite du mode "montré" lorsqu'elle est exprimée par des caractéristiques linguistiques de l'énoncé qui traduisent l'état émotionnel dans lequel se trouvait l'énonciateur au moment de l'énonciation.

Question : Si la phrase à annoter est émotionnelle, est-ce que le mode **montré** est utilisé ?

Exemples :
- <annotate>Andrée a sautillé partout en chantant.</annotate> -> non.
- <annotate>Paul sanglote.</annotate> -> non.
- <annotate>Oh, chouette ! Quelle bonne idée !</annotate> -> oui (car la joie de l'énonciateur est traduite au sein de l'énoncé par les interjections "oh" et "chouette", les énoncés averbaux et les points d'exclamations).
- <annotate>Oh, non... C'est vraiment dommage !</annotate> -> oui (car la tristesse de l'énonciateur est traduite au sein de l'énoncé par l'interjection "oh", l'énoncé averbal, les points de suspension et le point d'exclamation.)
- <annotate>Avant d'arriver devant une salle de classe, les enseignants, eux aussi, sont sur les bancs de l'école.</annotate> -> non

Annotation (oui/non) :
- Nicolas Hulot n'appartient à aucun parti politique. <annotate>Il a refusé trois fois le poste de ministre de l'Ecologie avant d'accepter la proposition d'Emmanuel Macron.</annotate> Mais ça ne s'est pas très bien passé. ->

**Assistant:**
réponse du modèle

**User:**
Définition : Une émotion est dite "suggérée" lorsqu'elle est exprimée par la description d'une situation associée de manière conventionnelle à un ressenti émotionnel.

Question : Si la phrase à annoter est émotionnelle, est-ce que le mode **suggéré** est utilisé ?

Exemples :
- <annotate>Oh, chouette ! Quelle bonne idée !</annotate> -> non.
- <annotate>Le père de Jeanne est mort hier à cause d'un cancer.</annotate> -> oui (car où la tristesse de Jeanne est suggérée par la description du décès, il y a peu de temps, de son père, une personne proche d'elle).
- <annotate>Ces deux amis se retrouvent après une longue séparation.</annotate> -> oui (car la joie des deux amis est suggérée par la description de leurs retrouvailles après un temps long).
- <annotate>De 2007 à 2012, il a été le Premier ministre de l'ancien président Nicolas Sarkozy.</annotate> -> non
- <annotate>Andrée a sautillé partout en chantant.</annotate> -> non.

Annotation (oui/non) :
- Nicolas Hulot n'appartient à aucun parti politique. <annotate>Il a refusé trois fois le poste de ministre de l'Ecologie avant d'accepter la proposition d'Emmanuel Macron.</annotate> Mais ça ne s'est pas très bien passé. ->

**Assistant:**

réponse du modèle

# Comparing Tools for Sentiment Analysis of Danish Literature from Hymns to Fairy Tales: Low-Resource Language and Domain Challenges

**Pascale Feldkamp**
Center for Humanities Computing
Aarhus University
pascale.moreira@cc.au.dk

**Jan Kostkan**
Center for Humanities Computing
Aarhus University
jan.kostkan@cas.au.dk

**Ea Lindhardt Overgaard**
School of Communication and Culture
Aarhus University
elt@cc.au.dk

**Mia Jacobsen**
Center for Humanities Computing
Aarhus University
miaj@cas.au.dk

**Yuri Bizzoni**
Center for Humanities Computing
Aarhus University
yuri.bizzoni@cc.au.dk

## Abstract

While Sentiment Analysis has become increasingly central in computational approaches to literary texts, the literary domain still poses important challenges for the detection of textual sentiment due to its highly complex use of language and devices – from subtle humor to poetic imagery. Furthermore, these challenges are only further amplified in low-resource language and domain settings. In this paper we investigate the application and efficacy of different Sentiment Analysis tools on Danish literary texts, using historical fairy tales and religious hymns as our datasets. The scarcity of linguistic resources for Danish and the historical context of the data further compounds the challenges for the tools. We compare human annotations to the continuous valence scores of both transformer- and dictionary-based Sentiment Analysis methods to assess their performance, seeking to understand how distinct methods handle the language of Danish prose and poetry.

## 1 Introduction and related works

Sentiment Analysis (SA) is a highly popular field in Computational Linguistics and NLP, as it attempts to interpret the sentimental and emotional aspects of texts, with applications that range from consumer review analysis (Tsao et al., 2018) to social media monitoring (Bollen et al., 2011; Asur and Huberman, 2010). It is, moreover, an increasingly central method for computational literary studies research as well (Rebora, 2023), where it has found popular applications to explore the narrative development (Zehe et al., 2016) or visualizing "sentiment arcs" of novels (i.e., the sequential highs and lows of valence throughout a narrative) (Jockers, 2014; Reagan et al., 2016). The sentiment arcs of novels – after applying a detrending technique to abstract from the noisy signal of raw valence scores – have also been used to assess, for example, the connection between narrative dynamics and reader appreciation (Bizzoni et al., 2023).

Still, the relation between sentiment arcs extracted with SA tools and actual reader experience remains understudied – both in their raw and detrended forms. Though recent studies of narrative sentiment arcs, like that of Elkins (2022), go some way in comparing various approaches to SA, they either do not contrast SA tools against a human gold standard at a granular level or have focused on single case studies (Bizzoni and Feldkamp, 2023).

Partially this is due to the very complexity of the literary domain. Literary texts often aim to evoke rather than explicitly communicate; operate at multiple narrative levels (Jakobson, 2010 (1981; Rosenblatt, 1982; Booth, 1983); make high use of ambiguity and poetic devices; offer several interpretations; and have been shown to rely on specific linguistic registers to evoke affective reactions (Bizzoni and Feldkamp, 2024).[1] For these reasons, SA tools might be more effective in other domains (Alantari et al., 2022; Elsahar and Gallé, 2019; Ohana et al., 2012; Bowers and Dombrowski, 2021) than the literary, although some studies have suggested that Transformer-based models might be able to bridge the gap and perform better on literary

[1]Naturally, these phenomena extend outside the literary domain as well (Rentoumi et al., 2009), for example, tweets using irony or figurative language likely effect diverging interpretations (Sandri et al., 2023; Stengel-Eskin et al., 2021).



*Proceedings of the 14th Workshop on Computational Approaches to Subjectivity, Sentiment, & Social Media Analysis*, pages 186–199
August 15, 2024 ©2024 Association for Computational Linguistics

or poetic material as well (Schmidt et al., 2021).

Beyond domain-specificity, an obvious obstacle to a wider use of SA for literature is the issue of multilinguality. The majority of research in SA – both in more general NLP and in the literary domain – has concentrated on well-resourced languages like English (Ribeiro et al., 2016). Once again, Transformer-based architectures able to generalize across multiple languages (Devlin et al., 2019) have helped reduce the gap, and multilingual transformers hold a significant promise for cross-lingual SA (Elkins, 2022), but language- and culture-related biases from English pretraining have been shown to impact the performance of transfer learning on low-resource languages (De Bruyne et al., 2022; Papadimitriou et al., 2023; Xu et al., 2022).

When it comes to Danish specifically, the main dictionary-based SA tools – Afinn, Sentida, and Danish Sentiment Lexicon (DSL) – have been shown to perform comparably across domains (Schneidermann and Pedersen, 2022), with Sentida in particular, showing a strong correlation with human judgments for both fiction and social media (Lauridsen et al., 2019). While such dictionaries appear to show a consistent performance for Danish SA, they are not widely tested at a fine-grained level, nor on historical Danish. Assessing the performance of models on historical Danish and Norwegian literary texts, Allaith et al. (2023) found that multilingual transformer models outperformed both fine-tuned models and classifiers based on lexical resources in the target language, which aligns with the findings of Schmidt et al. (2021) and Schmidt and Burghardt (2018) for historical German drama.

With the present study, we seek to examine two main issues: i) the challenge for SA models of understanding sentiment in *historical* literary texts – both prose (fairy tales) and poetry (religious hymns); ii) the challenge of applying SA models on fiction written in under-resourced languages like Danish. We evaluate how different SA tools – transformer-based and dictionary-based approaches – perform on the literary texts compared to a human gold standard.[2] In addition, we apply three English-based methods widely used for literary SA (Bowers and Dombrowski, 2021; Elkins and Chun, 2019; Bizzoni et al., 2023) on text that was Google-translated, as a point of comparison for the performance of Danish-based tools. Finally, we examine SHAP-scores of the best-performing transformer-based method to gauge differences between transformer- and dictionary-based methods.

## 2 Methodology

### 2.1 Datasets

We use two different datasets: (i) three literary fairy tales by Hans Christian Andersen and (ii) a collection of Danish religious hymns. We selected these datasets to provide a historical while rich and varied set of Danish literature, taking both narrative and poetic complexity as well as their cultural significance into consideration.[3]

The HCA dataset is larger than the hymns dataset by number of words (Table 1) – but not by number of annotations (fairy tales were annotated on a sentence- and hymns on a verse-basis). Both datasets are from within the period 1798–1873, which is additionally challenging for models predominantly based/pretrained on modern Danish.

| | Texts | V/S | Words | $\bar{x}$ V/S | Period |
|---|---|---|---|---|---|
| **HCA** | 3 | 791 | 18,910 | 263.7 | 1837-1847 |
| **Hymns** | 65 | 1,914 | 10,303 | 32.9 | 1798-1873 |

Table 1: The **HCA** and the **Hymns** datasets: The total number of verses or sentences (V/S) and words per dataset, and mean ($\bar{x}$) number of verses or sentences per text.

**Literary Fairy Tales** The HCA dataset includes three of Andersen's most known fairy tales: "The Little Mermaid" (1837), "The Ugly Duckling" (1844), and "The Shadow" (1847)(CCLM, 2003).[4] These texts are emblematic of Danish cultural heritage and literary tradition, known for a simple but involving narrative and memorable character representations. Andersen's fairy tales often contain multiple layers of meaning and sentiment, ranging from joy and wonder to sadness and introspection, while keeping an essential simplicity, both stylistically and in the narrative arc (Lundskær-Nielsen, 2014; Alm and Sproat, 2005), which makes them

[2]The annotated resource is available for further studies at: `https://github.com/centre-for-humanities-computing/Danish_literary_sentiment/`

[3]Andersen's production being arguably the most central in Danish literary heritage (Ringgaard and Thomsen, 2017), while hymns of N.F.S. Grundtvig (also included here) are less internationally known but equally significant in shaping the national cultural identity (Nielsen, 2020).

[4]Spelling has been modernized in these texts editions, though vocabulary has not been significantly changed.

an ideal case for testing sentiment analysis tools on literary Danish.

**Religious Hymns** To further create a literary challenge for tools, we used a hymns dataset, comprising 65 Danish religious hymns around the 19$^{th}$ century,[5] where each verse is coupled with its modernized Danish version.[6] The hymns are characterized by a more structured formality and an archaic and poetic language, especially in the original versions – for example, the use of the latinized "est" for "is" ("*er*"). The inclusion of both original and modernized texts allows us to observe whether language evolution might significantly affect Danish SA. Hymns are challenging for SA tools due to the poetic and figurative language, subtle emotional tones, as well as their cultural and religious contexts – especially Christian values and symbolic structures of meaning (Skovsted et al., 2019; Nielsen, 2020). Finally, while the prosaic fairy tales are divided into sentences, verses were chosen as the unit of analysis for the hymns, seeing that the verse constitutes the building block of poetry more than the sentence. A syntactically sound sentence might thus not be present in every verse, so verses may be syntactically simpler but semantically more challenging, which may further confound sentiment annotation (both human and automatic).

We selected Andersen's fairy tales and Danish hymns to challenge and evaluate sentiment analysis tools across two very different, but highly representative, types of literary texts. Andersen's tales have narratives and emotional depth, but use standard prose linguistic structures - so they will test the models' ability to handle complex emotional narratives. In contrast, the hymns rely on poetic expression and do not represent a story but rather a non-narrative message. They provide a test case for the models' sensitivity to subtler, less structured, sentiment evocation.

[5]From 1798 (n=35), 1857 (n=17) and 1873 (n=13). Note that the years refer to the publication date of three official church hymn collections.

[6]Two literary scholars modernized the original Danish prompting ChatGPT 3.5 (prompt: "Oversæt til moderne dansk retstavning", i.e. "translate to modern Danish spelling".), and subsequently validated each output verse against the original. The date for this was May 20, 2024.

## 2.2 English Translations

We obtained translations of sentences and verses via google-translate (not manually validated).[7] We used these translations in combination with two English dictionary-based systems and the RoBERTa base xlm multilingual (which we also apply to the original Danish) as a raw baseline for comparison to systems developed in and for Danish.

## 2.3 Human annotation

Human annotators (n=3) read H.C. Andersen's fairytales from beginning to end and scored *each sentence* on a 0 to 10 valence scale:[8] 0 signifying the lowest, and 10 the highest valence.[9] For the hymns, annotators (n=2) read and scored *each verse line* on the same scale. The valence score was intended to represent the sentiment expressed by the sentence and verse. The annotators were instructed to avoid rating how a sentence or verse made them feel and to try to report only on the sentiments actually embedded in the sentence, i.e., to think about the valence of the individual sentence and verse, without overthinking the story's/hymn's narrative to reduce contextual interpretation.

It is worth noting that humans rarely reach an agreement higher than 80% (or 0.80 Krippendorff's $\alpha$) on non-fiction texts for tasks like positive/neutral/negative discrete tagging (Wilson et al., 2005) or continuous scale polarity annotation (Batanović et al., 2020). In our case, detrending the annotators' scores (see Section 2.4.4) always improved the Inter Annotator Reliability (Table 2), which might be seen as a natural effect of smoothing time-series (removing outliers). An example of detrended arcs of the annotators' individual and mean scores – the latter of which is used to compare systems' scores – is visualized in Fig. 1.

## 2.4 Automatic annotation

We used several SA models for Danish, transformer- and dictionary-based, to score the texts for valence.

[7]We used the deep translator package in python to retrieve google-translated sentences: `https://pypi.org/project/deep-translator/` Translations were retrieved on May 20, 2024.

[8]Sentences were tokenized using the nltk tokenize package: `https://www.nltk.org/api/nltk.tokenize.html`

[9]Annotators were all native Danish speakers, two with a background in literary studies (MA, PhD) and one from cognitive science (MA). The two annotators of the hymns (MA and PhD of literature) had domain knowledge in 19$^{th}$ century Scandinavian literature and historical religious hymns.

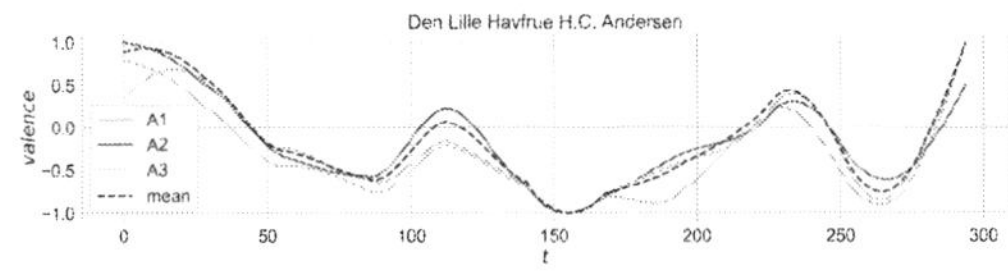


Figure 1: Sentiment arcs of **The Little Mermaid** after detrending annotators' values. The black line represents the mean annotator score.

#### 2.4.1 Dictionary- and rule-based methods

Dictionary-based methods (that are usually rule-based as well) – meaning tools that use a predefined dictionary to assign basic valence to words – remain popular especially in humanities research, due to their transparency and versatility. Moreover, they seem to perform well (Bizzoni and Feldkamp, 2023) – even on so-called "nonlinear" narratives (Richardson, 2000; Elkins and Chun, 2019) although they appear to do poorly on a word-basis (Reagan et al., 2017). Our chosen models were:
**Afinn**: valence dictionary without rules, extracted from twitter-data and various open sources.[10] The dictionary contains many inflections of the same lemma. Valence scores range from -5 to +5.
**Sentida**: a rule-based system inspired by the English VADER (observes negations, adverb modifiers, etc.).[11] Sentida combines the Afinn dictionary with the 10,000 most frequent Danish lemmas, that were manually annotated by the authors (Lauridsen et al., 2019). Upon inference, it relies on stemming to find matching dictionary items. Valence scores range from -5 to +5.
**Asent**: a rule-based system, using the Afinn dictionary by default, while adding rules (e.g. negations, modifiers, intensifiers, etc.).[12] Valence scores range from -1 to +1.

**Score normalization** For comparing models on raw scores, we maintained the different eays of scaling in each dictionary-based method. For detrending the time series, however, we normalized all scales – including the human annotation scale – to the range -1 to +1.[13]

#### 2.4.2 Transformer-based methods

More recent Transformer-based approaches have found application both in Danish and as multilingual models, and have shown both potential and pitfalls in SA for literary texts (Elkins, 2022). We chose to use all off-the-shelf models currently developed for Danish SA and a widely used multilingual model, RoBERTa xlm (Conneau et al., 2020):[14]
**Senda**: was developed specifically for Danish.[15] It was built on the Roberta architecture, pretrained on a large corpus of Danish texts.
**Alexandra institute** sentiment base:[16] is another example of a Danish-oriented transformer that has been fined-tuned for SA tasks. It is hosted by the Alexandra Institute.
**RoBERTa** base xlm multilingual:[17] was trained using the cross-lingual language training approach, that is supposed to enhance its ability of understanding and processing tens of different languages by transferring its learned skills – in other words, by using what it has learned from one language to help it in another language. Its ability to transfer learning across languages might potentially allow it to generalize more powerfully on sentiment analysis, but it could also hinder its ability to deal with language-specific expressions, especially in unusual domains.

**Score transformation** Note that we converted the categorical Transformer output to continuous SA scores by using the confidence score of labels as a proxy for sentiment intensity. If the model classifies a sentence as *positive* with a confidence of, for example, 0.89, we interpret it as a valence score of +0.89 for this sentence, and so on. Note that we converted scores of the *neutral* category to neutral (0), also seeing that most human scores fall into the vicinity of neutral (5 on the human 0-10 annotation scale).[18][19]

#### 2.4.3 English-based models

To compare Danish tools to English tools as a baseline, we used the Google translated sentences (see section 2.2), applying often used English-language

[10] `https://github.com/fnielsen/afinn`
[11] `https://github.com/Guscode/Sentida`
[12] `https://github.com/KennethEnevoldsen/asent`
[13] We used the MinMaxScaler-approach for normalization.

[14] We maintained all presets as the default when applying these models, so that the hyperparameters are as specified in the documentation of the individual model (see the model hyperlinks).
[15] `https://huggingface.co/larskjeldgaard/senda`
[16] `https://huggingface.co/alexandrainst/da-sentiment-base`
[17] `https://huggingface.co/cardiffnlp/twitter-xlm-roberta-base-sentiment`
[18] For the distribution of scores, see Appendix (Fig. 6a).
[19] Bizzoni and Feldkamp (2023) similarly used this method for converting discrete transformer output to continuous scores.

tools. We chose the two dictionary- and rule-based models **VADER** and **Syuzhet**, because of their popularity and use in literary SA studies (Allaith et al., 2023; Bizzoni et al., 2022b; Bizzoni and Feldkamp, 2023), and the same **RoBERTA** multilingual model as applied on the Danish texts (see above), due to observed good performance on literary prose in Bizzoni and Feldkamp (2023). All of these were applied to Google-translated sentences which had not been manually checked for accuracy.

#### 2.4.4 Arcs and Detrending

In the analysis of sentiment within literary texts, the consideration of narrative arcs has been central (Rebora, 2023), particularly for texts with a clear story progression like fairy tales, where studies have used detrending methods to gauge the role of sentiment dynamics for reader appreciation (Bizzoni et al., 2022a). However, for other types of literature such as hymns, which do not exhibit explicit story development, narrative arcs are not as apt as an analytical framework. For this reason, we consider both the raw and detrended sentiment arcs of the fairy tales in our dataset, but *do not detrend the hymns*. For the fairy tales, we examine whether detrending can improve the correlation between scores and human annotations. The detrended scores are derived through a polynomial fit of the original data, designed to smooth out the noise and highlight the overall narrative shape.[20] The detrending process allows observation of the underlying emotional trajectory of the story without the interference of short-term fluctuations, providing a clearer view of how sentiments evolve.

## 3 Results

### 3.1 Human annotation

We report a relatively high inter-rater reliability (IRR), with a correlation (Spearman's *rho*) between their scores of 0.726 for the hymns.[21] For the fairy tales we find an average correlation of 0.64 – non-detrended; detrended annotator scores have a correlation coefficient > 0.80 (Table 2). As mentioned, higher agreement for detrended values is an effect of smoothing values (removing outliers) and suggests that annotators agree on the overall shape of the narrative when abstracting from the granular level. IRR is high, especially in the case of hymns (considering the fragmentariness of the verses) and considering that humans often have low agreement for sentiment annotation, not least continuous-scale annotation.[22]

| | Spearman's *rho* ($\bar{x}$) | Krippendorff's $\alpha$ |
|---|---|---|
| **Mermaid** | 0.80 (0.94) | 0.85 (0.91) |
| **Duckling** | 0.47 (0.89) | 0.65 (0.90) |
| **Shadow** | 0.65 (0.80) | 0.76 (0.78) |
| **Hymns** | 0.73 (-) | 0.72 (-) |

Table 2: Inter Rater Reliability between annotators (n=3) in the fairy tales, using the mean Spearman correlation coefficient (p<0.01) – with Krippendorff's Alpha for reference. Correlation between the annotators' non-detrended values and detrended values (in parenthesis).

### 3.2 Sentiment Analysis on Andersen's Fairy Tales

The sentiment scoring of H.C. Andersen's fairy tales *The Ugly Duckling*, *The Little Mermaid* and *The Shadow* appears quite challenging for both dictionary- and transformer-based models. Considering raw (non-detrended) scores, the transformer-based models generally perform better than dictionary-based tools across all three stories (Table 3). Notably, *The Ugly Duckling* shows the highest Spearman correlation with RoBERTa (0.58) and *The Little Mermaid* with Asent (0.54) and Sentida (0.51). Human annotations of *The Shadow* also appear more aligned to RoBERTa again, achieving a correlation of 0.56. Still, it should be noted that RoBERTa does not perform consistently (i.e., in the case of *The Little Mermaid*) where dictionary-based Syuzhet on Danish-English Google translations are performing comparably and more consistently. Notably, the best and most consistently performing system appears to be the RoBERTa applied to Google translations.

When considering detrended scores improvement is evident across most models. Note that the correlation (and Krippendorrf's $\alpha$) also improves when human scores are detrended (Table 2). *The*

[20]We use Nonlinear Adaptive Filtering technique to detrend arcs. For more on this method, see Jianbo Gao et al. (2010) as well as the implementation on narrative fiction in Hu et al. (2021).

[21]We report the Spearman correlation coefficient here. As annotators operated within a continuous valence spectrum, divided into ten categories, we find that correlation measures more clearly reflect the values' direction and nuance (parallelity vs exactness), compared to categorical inter-annotator agreement measures. We provide Krippendorff's $\alpha$ for reference, where the level of measurement was considered interval.

[22]For a continuous sentiment annotation task similar to the one presented here – albeit on modern fiction – Bizzoni and Feldkamp (2023) report a Spearman correlation between annotators (n=2) of 0.624.

| | Afinn | Sentida | Asent | Alex.in. | Senda | RoB | VADER | Syuzhet | RoB |
|---|---|---|---|---|---|---|---|---|---|
| *Duckling* | 0.29 | 0.44 | 0.28 | 0.50 | 0.45 | **0.58** | 0.42 | 0.50 | 0.57 |
| *Mermaid* | 0.37 | 0.51 | **0.54** | 0.49 | 0.37 | 0.38 | 0.49 | 0.51 | 0.52 |
| *Shadow* | 0.38 | 0.34 | 0.39 | 0.43 | 0.28 | **0.56** | 0.51 | 0.47 | 0.63 |
| **Average** | 0.35 | 0.43 | 0.40 | 0.47 | 0.37 | **0.51** | 0.47 | 0.49 | 0.57 |
| *Duckling (D.)* | 0.41 | 0.18 | 0.42 | 0.65 | 0.55 | **0.67** | 0.32 | 0.46 | 0.62 |
| *Mermaid (D.)* | 0.70 | 0.73 | 0.72 | 0.71 | 0.01 | **0.75** | 0.81 | 0.63 | 0.71 |
| *Shadow (D.)* | 0.39 | 0.53 | 0.39 | 0.40 | 0.25 | **0.70** | 0.42 | 0.45 | 0.82 |
| **Average (D.)** | 0.50 | 0.48 | 0.51 | 0.59 | 0.27 | **0.71** | 0.52 | 0.51 | 0.72 |

Table 3: Spearman correlation between **raw** (above) / **detrended arcs** (below), i.e., between raw/detrended system scores and raw/detrended human mean scores. Dictionary and rule-based systems (left), transfomer-based systems (middle) and three English systems' scores on Google-translated sentences included as a baseline (right). Note that RoBERTa (RoB) on the right was used on translated sentences, and RoBERTa on the left on the original Danish sentences. Best performing Danish tools in bold, best baseline in green. Note that although correlations on detrended arcs seem high, on *The Little Mermaid*, all correlations (Spearman's *rho*) between annotators' detrended arcs have a Spearman correlation >0.93.

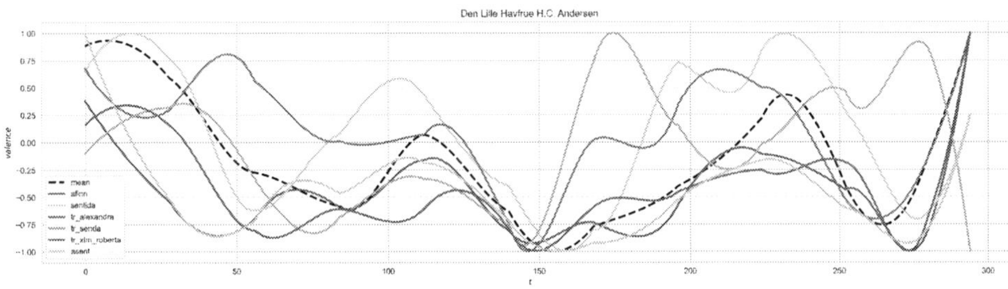


Figure 2: An example of visualized sentiment arcs of **The Little Mermaid**: Detrended arcs of systems and mean annotator score (black line). The x-axis represents the story progression in sentences.

*Little Mermaid* exhibits a particularly high correlation for detrended scores, with RoBERTa scoring 0.75 and Asent closely following at 0.72. While Asent's performance on *The Little Mermaid* is particularly surprising as its correlation with the raw arcs is close worse, we can see that transformers generally handle sentiment analysis for this task better than dictionary-based systems, both due to dictionary-based systems overemphasizing peaks in the sentiment arc (like Sentida in Fig. 2) or missing them (as Afinn, also Fig. 2). Transformers, however, appear to exhibit more extreme values, the distributions of their scores being less normal with a higher standard deviation than human and dictionary-based systems' scores (see the Appendix for the distribution of all scores).[23] In general, most models' performance improves when outlier effects are minimized.

[23]Note that the distribution of transformer scores may be an effect of using the confidence score for our transformation of their output labels (see section 2.4.4). Since the confidence scores of models tends to be relatively high (close to 0.9 in the range 0-1), using the confidence score for converting labels to values results in many high and low values.

### 3.3 Sentiment Analysis on Danish Religious Hymns

The analysis of Danish religious hymns presents a different pattern. Sentida consistently performs best among dictionary-based models in both original and modernized texts, achieving Spearman correlations of 0.49 and 0.53 respectively (Table 4). This suggests Sentida's rule-based approach, designed for short social media-like texts, captures the emotional tone in the hymns effectively.

Transformer-based models do not exhibit the significant advantage that they had in fairy tales. In the modernized hymns, RoBERTa shows a better correlation (0.46) than in the original (0.39), suggesting that modern language adaptations is more amenable to transformer processing, potentially due to the training data characteristics. But all transformer models perform worse than rule-based models. It is notable that the English systems, RoBERTa, VADER and Syuzhet, applied to Google translations, perform better than other systems. Syuzhet performs better than any other

| | Afinn | Sentida | Asent | Alex.in. | Senda | RoB | VADER | Syuzhet | RoB |
|---|---|---|---|---|---|---|---|---|---|
| **Hymns orig.** | 0.39 | **0.49** | 0.40 | 0.39 | 0.32 | 0.39 | - | - | - |
| **Hymns mod.** | 0.40 | **0.53** | 0.41 | 0.39 | 0.35 | 0.46 | - | - | - |
| **EN (baseline)** | - | - | - | - | - | - | 0.55 | 0.58 | 0.66 |

Table 4: Sentiment analysis of hymns: Spearman correlation between scores on the **original** (above) **modernized lines** (middle) and, for comparison, the three English system's scores of google-translated lines (below) to the human mean scores. Note that RoBERTa (RoB) on the right was used on translated sentences, and RoBERTa on the left on the original Danish sentences. Best performing Danish tools in bold, best baseline in green. Note that the Spearman's *rho* between the annotators of the hymns (n=2) is 0.726.

dictionary-based systems, possible due to it being developed for the literary domain.[24]

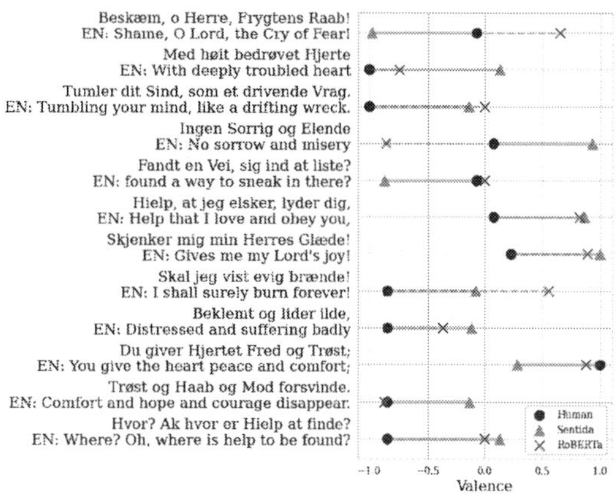


Figure 3: The 12 verses of the hymns with the highest absolute disagreement between human and Sentida score on original text (descending). RoBERTa scores are visualized for comparison. Validated English translation is supplied below the original Danish text.

An inspection of verses with the highest disagreement between human scores and scores of the best-performing Danish model (Sentida) of the original text suggests that disagreement results both from non-modern spelling and archaic vocabulary, but also from the genre and domain particularities of the hymns (Fig. 3). A clear example is the verse "beklemt og lider ilde": It contains both an overall archaic vocabulary and word-order, but models do not pick up on its negative tone. Even one archaic word in a verse appears to lead to errors for Sentida: In the line containing the archaic "hielp", humans rate the verse close to neutral, since the word suggests a wished-for state rather than an actuality, while models appear to weight the positive words in the verse highly, not observing the conditional. This is also the case for the first line, exhibiting the top disagreement, where the word "beskæm" (archaic) in combination with the poetic apostrophe ("o Lord") indicates the wish for God to "shame" in the sense of "reject" fear.

Apostrophes are not the only poetic feature that appears to confound model scores, generally, high-disagreement verses suggest that the genre and domain is a challenge to the models. For example, the last line in Fig. 3 employs repetition as well as the poetic exclamation "Ak", which may have prompted annotators to assign a very negative score, while models are blind sensitive to these genre- or domain-specific poetic devices. RoBERTa shows some similarities with Sentida, in this regard, with some overlap in which verses appear among the top disagreements with humans, like here the "Ak"-verse (for the top 12 verses with most disagreement of both models, see the Appendix).

### 3.4 Comparison

A comparison between the fairy tales and hymns reveals an essential reversal of fortune for the models taken into consideration. The fairy tales, which use language creatively in order to construe a relatively simple narrative, provide longer, richer sentences, and appear to allow transformers to leverage their ability to deal with complex syntactic and semantic interactions, leading to higher correlations especially in the detrended analyses. This aligns with what has been observed in several previous studies about the strength of transformers in handling varied and complex sentence structures and meanings (Li et al., 2023; Madusanka et al., 2023).

In contrast, the hymns are of poetic language, broken in short verses, often repetitive, figurative or allegoric, and heavily patterned. This kind of text seems to benefit less from the contextual capabilities of transformers. The short nature of

[24]Although domain-specific tools tend to rely on less data, the Syuzhet dictionary is relatively large: developed from 165,000 human-coded sentences from contemporary literary novels in the Nebraska Literary Lab (Jockers, 2015).

the verses, the weight of single words (compared to their weight in more complex interactions of narrative prose), and poetic devices, seems to allow dictionary and rule-based methods to shine, while they might be reducing the effectiveness of Transformer-based sentiment analysis: not only do the dictionary-based models' go up, but the Transformers' performance go down, compared to the correlation in the fairy tales.

The consistently high performance of Sentida across different types of texts suggests that some rule-based systems, especially those tailored or adapted to specific languages like Danish, can effectively capture sentiment even without the contextual depth provided by transformers, especially where historical language is being treated. Still, both the baseline models, VADER and Syuzhet applied to google-translated text, also show a good performance – and consistently so – outperform Danish models in the Hymns, while constituting a robust alternative for the fairy tales as well.

### 3.4.1 Comparing the two best-performing Danish models

As Sentida and RoBERTa were the best-performing systems, we computed the word-level SHAP-values from RoBERTa's output (applied to Danish) to compare them to the weights indexed in Sentida.[25] SHAP-values are used to understand models' predictions, gauging the importance of individual features in informing the predicted label (in the case of RoBERTa, the role of individual tokens in positive, neutral, or negative results)(Lundberg and Lee, 2017). The process involves calculating the contribution of each word by removing it and observing the change in the model's prediction. The impact of context (preceding/following words) is addressed by iterating this process over permutations of the words.[26]

As can be seen in Table 5, RoBERTa's word-level SHAP scores explain a higher proportion of the variance in Sentida scores for Andersen's fairy tales compared to Hymns, both for positive and negative sentiments.The model's ability to predict positive sentiment variance is slightly stronger in

|  | POS (H) | NEG (H) | POS (A) | NEG (A) |
|---|---|---|---|---|
| $R^2$ | 0.16 | 0.13 | 0.20 | 0.15 |

Table 5: The $R^2$ score of regression models on Sentida's scores of words and SHAP-score (viz. RoBERTa word-weights) for Hymns (H) and Andersen's fairy tales (A) – i.e., the $R^2$ score represents the percentage of the variance in Sentida scores that SHAP-scores explain, ranging between 0 (no explanation), to 1 (complete explanation of variance).

the fairy tales (0.20) than in the hymns (0.16). The same pattern holds for negative sentiment, though the difference is less pronounced (0.15 vs. 0.13)

The difference in $R^2$ between the two datasets suggests both vocabulary differences and that RoBERTa is actually acting "more like" Sentida on the data it performs best on (HCA). Andersen might use more frequent words and/or words that are simpler semantically and thus easier to agree upon across these two different systems. Moreover, as is also visualized in Fig. 4, more than half of the words in the fairy tales (55.6%) and close to half in the hymns (48.9%) are assigned a 0 score by Sentida, while RoBERTa tends to assign more words a positive or negative value (see the Appendix for a list of top-positive and negative words not recognized by Sentida).

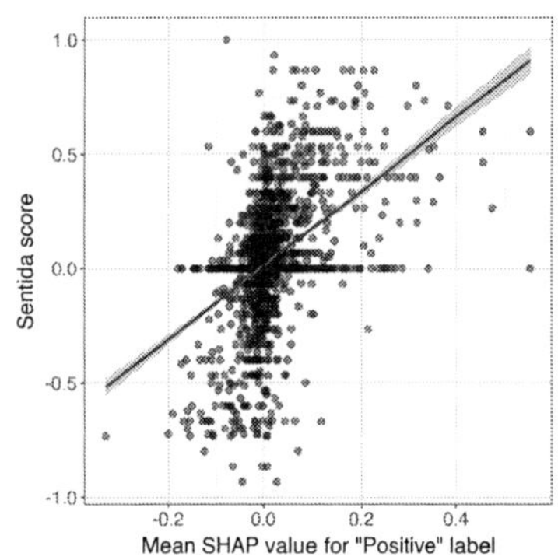


Figure 4: Visualization of the correlation – in the case of fairy tales (HCA) – between the Sentida score of words (y-axis) and their corresponding SHAP-score of the RoBERTa model (x-axis), here, the degree to which the word contributes to the model assigning the "positive" label.

Considering that Roberta (on Danish) underperforms with respect to Sentida on the hymns, which are evaluated at the verse level, discrepancies in their vocabularies can be illuminating. Given the reduced dimension of poetic verses, sentimental evaluation at that level has less to do with syn-

[25]Note that we used a custom tokenization: instead of using the RoBERTa tokenization, which usually splits one Danish word into multiple tokens, we consider one word (whitespace separated) as one token for the SHAP analysis.

[26]In our case, 10 random forward and backward permutations (20 in total), after which we average the differences between SHAP-values of permutated features and original features, as implemented in the SHAP Python package: PermutationExplainer

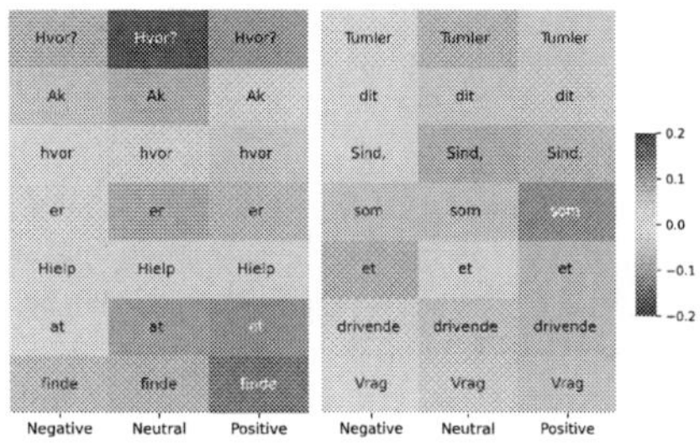


Figure 5: Two sentence examples (left, right). The heatmap shows how words contribute to the label (Negative, Neutral, Positive) assigned to sentences by RoBERTa, where weights are measured as SHAP-scores. Higher values (in red) signify how much a word contributes *toward* the label (on the x-axis) and the bluer the word, the more it contributes *away* from the label assigned. For example, 'finde' in the sentence on the left contributes toward the positive label. The sentences are ordered from top to bottom.

tax or larger discourse-structures, and much more to do with the interplay of individual words' nuances. The nature of the poetic language often adopted in the hymns, that tends to weigh on the contrast and association of terms, might also give a particularly important role to lexical semantics in the overall valence of each verse. It is not too far-fetched to imagine that the scores of Sentida, manually curated and directly assigned by annotators (n=3)(Lauridsen et al., 2019), are the real point of advantage of the model in these circumstances.

As salient examples, we also examined the SHAP-scores of two sentences, which both occur among sentences with top disagreement between human scores and the RoBERTa and Sentida model (see sentences in appendix). While humans rated a sentence like the leftmost of Fig. 5 very negatively (see Fig. 3), we find RoBERTa labelling it neutral, mostly due to the words 'finde' and 'Hvor?' pulling it in opposite directions. Notably, the model does seem to recognize a difference between 'Hvor' with and without the questionmark, and does recognize the poetic exclamation ('Ak') as somewhat negative, suggesting a sensitivity to the register. As suggested before, it appears not to process the 19$^{th}$ century spelling of 'hielp' (hjælp) adequately, which has close to a 0 SHAP-score for all labels. Similarly, for the rightmost sentence in Fig. 5, the negative poetic imagery which may make humans rate the sentence accordingly is not reflected in the SHAP-scores of words, notably with the negatively associated "vrag" (wreck) weighted toward netural.

## 4 Conclusion and Future Works

We have tested sentiment analysis tools on Danish literary prose and poetry, using a small collection of historical fairy tales by H.C. Andersen for prose and of traditional religious hymns for poetry. Our goal was to study the abilities and limitations of SA methodologies in handling a particularly low-resource setting: relatively low-resource language on low-resource domains. Employing both human annotators and a range of sentiment analysis models, we have shown that transformer-based models generally outperform dictionary-based systems in the analysis of fairy tales, especially when considering detrended scores – consistent with previous work (Bizzoni and Feldkamp, 2023; Allaith et al., 2023; Schmidt et al., 2021). These models seem to have a better ability to interpret the emotional and narrative structures of fairytales more effectively, and better mimic the human experience of reading narrative fiction. However, for the poetic hymns with short verses, the performance gap between transformers and dictionary-based models changes, and dictionary-based approaches, especially Sentida, show better performance. A combination of approaches may be explored in the future, as our comparison using SHAP-scores suggests that models capture different aspects of texts. Including more texts from different authors in the dataset may also give a more nuanced picture of SA in Danish, and it should be noted that the prose part of our corpus – a single author – may bias the results. Still, as Danish resources are consistently outperformed, both by the multilingual model or by the English baseline models applied to raw Google translations, we observe that there is a need for developing a Danish-based model for SA of literary texts across genres and periods.

In future, we would like to expand the dataset to include a broader range of genres and apply more models and model adaptions. Integrating comprehensive historical, semantic, and emotional lexica, may also improve the granularity and accuracy of sentiment predictions. Further refining detrending techniques may also be beneficial, particularly for texts where narrative context heavily influences sentiment interpretation. Finally, more extensive collaboration between linguists and literary scholars may help refine the algorithms used, embedding deeper literary and linguistic insights into the development of sentiment analysis tools for treating specific language use of the literary domain.

## Limitations

We want to underline that our results are based on a limited set of Danish literary historical texts and should be interpreted accordingly. It should also be noted that the prose part of our corpus – consisting of a single author (whereas hymns have several authors) – may bias our results. Moreover, the demographic of our dataset is reduced (in terms of gender, ethnicity, age, social class, etc.). While this work has aimed to test Danish resources for continuous sentiment analysis, there are various other English-based resources which may perform better than the ones selected here – especially more recent generative methods.

## References


Huwail J. Alantari, Imran S. Currim, Yiting Deng, and Sameer Singh. 2022. An empirical comparison of machine learning methods for text-based sentiment analysis of online consumer reviews. *International Journal of Research in Marketing*, 39(1):1–19.

Ali Allaith, Kirstine Degn, Alexander Conroy, Bolette Pedersen, Jens Bjerring-Hansen, and Daniel Hershcovich. 2023. Sentiment Classification of Historical Danish and Norwegian Literary Texts. In *Proceedings of the 24th Nordic Conference on Computational Linguistics (NoDaLiDa)*, pages 324–334, Tórshavn, Faroe Islands. University of Tartu Library.

Cecilia Ovesdotter Alm and Richard Sproat. 2005. Emotional Sequencing and Development in Fairy Tales. In *Affective Computing and Intelligent Interaction*, pages 668–674, Berlin, Heidelberg. Springer.

Sitaram Asur and Bernardo A. Huberman. 2010. Predicting the Future with Social Media. In *2010 IEEE/WIC/ACM International Conference on Web Intelligence and Intelligent Agent Technology*, volume 1, pages 492–499.

Vuk Batanović, Miloš Cvetanović, and Boško Nikolić. 2020. A versatile framework for resource-limited sentiment articulation, annotation, and analysis of short texts. *PLoS ONE*, 15(11).

Yuri Bizzoni and Pascale Feldkamp. 2023. Comparing transformer and dictionary-based sentiment models for literary texts: Hemingway as a case-study. In *Proceedings of the 3rd International Workshop on Natural Language Processing for Digital Humanities*, pages 219–226, Tokyo, Japan. Association for Computational Linguistics.

Yuri Bizzoni and Pascale Feldkamp. 2024. Below the sea (with the sharks): Probing textual features of implicit sentiment in a literary case-study. In *Proceedings of the Third Workshop on Understanding Implicit and Underspecified Language*, pages 54–61, Malta. Association for Computational Linguistics.

Yuri Bizzoni, Pascale Moreira, Mads Rosendahl Thomsen, and Kristoffer Nielbo. 2023. Sentimental matters - predicting literary quality by sentiment analysis and stylometric features. In *Proceedings of the 13th Workshop on Computational Approaches to Subjectivity, Sentiment, & Social Media Analysis*, pages 11–18, Toronto, Canada. Association for Computational Linguistics.

Yuri Bizzoni, Telma Peura, Kristoffer Nielbo, and Mads Thomsen. 2022a. Fractal sentiments and fairy tales-fractal scaling of narrative arcs as predictor of the perceived quality of Andersen's fairy tales. *Journal of Data Mining & Digital Humanities*, NLP4DH.

Yuri Bizzoni, Telma Peura, Kristoffer Nielbo, and Mads Thomsen. 2022b. Fractality of sentiment arcs for literary quality assessment: The case of nobel laureates. In *Proceedings of the 2nd International Workshop on Natural Language Processing for Digital Humanities*, pages 31–41, Taipei, Taiwan. Association for Computational Linguistics.

Johan Bollen, Huina Mao, and Xiaojun Zeng. 2011. Twitter mood predicts the stock market. *Journal of Computational Science*, 2(1):1–8.

Wayne C. Booth. 1983. *The Rhetoric of Fiction*, 2nd edition edition. University of Chicago Press, Chicago.

Katherine Bowers and Quinn Dombrowski. 2021. Katia and the Sentiment Snobs. Blog: Datasitter's Club.

Center for Children's Literature and Media CCLM. 2003. Danske børn og unge har stort kendskab til H.C. Andersen.

Alexis Conneau, Kartikay Khandelwal, Naman Goyal, Vishrav Chaudhary, Guillaume Wenzek, Francisco Guzmán, Edouard Grave, Myle Ott, Luke Zettlemoyer, and Veselin Stoyanov. 2020. Unsupervised cross-lingual representation learning at scale. In *Proceedings of the 58th Annual Meeting of the Association for Computational Linguistics*, pages 8440–8451, Online. Association for Computational Linguistics.

Luna De Bruyne, Pranaydeep Singh, Orphee De Clercq, Els Lefever, and Veronique Hoste. 2022. How language-dependent is emotion detection? evidence from multilingual BERT. In *Proceedings of the 2nd Workshop on Multi-lingual Representation Learning (MRL)*, pages 76–85, Abu Dhabi, United Arab Emirates (Hybrid). Association for Computational Linguistics.

Jacob Devlin, Ming-Wei Chang, Kenton Lee, and Kristina Toutanova. 2019. BERT: Pre-training of deep bidirectional transformers for language understanding. In *Proceedings of the 2019 Conference of the North American Chapter of the Association for Computational Linguistics: Human Language Technologies, Volume 1 (Long and Short Papers)*, pages 4171–4186, Minneapolis, Minnesota. Association for Computational Linguistics.

Katherine Elkins. 2022. *The Shapes of Stories: Sentiment Analysis for Narrative*. Cambridge University Press.

Katherine Elkins and Jon Chun. 2019. Can Sentiment Analysis Reveal Structure in a Plotless Novel? ArXiv:1910.01441 [cs].

Hady Elsahar and Matthias Gallé. 2019. To Annotate or Not? Predicting Performance Drop under Domain Shift. In *Proceedings of the 2019 Conference on Empirical Methods in Natural Language Processing and the 9th International Joint Conference on Natural Language Processing (EMNLP-IJCNLP)*, pages 2163–2173, Hong Kong, China. Association for Computational Linguistics.

Qiyue Hu, Bin Liu, Mads Rosendahl Thomsen, Jianbo Gao, and Kristoffer L Nielbo. 2021. Dynamic evolution of sentiments in *Never Let Me Go* : Insights from multifractal theory and its implications for literary analysis. *Digital Scholarship in the Humanities*, 36(2):322–332.

Roman Jakobson. 2010 (1981). Linguistics and poetics. In *Linguistics and Poetics*, pages 18–51. De Gruyter Mouton.

Jianbo Gao, H. Sultan, Jing Hu, and Wen-Wen Tung. 2010. Denoising Nonlinear Time Series by Adaptive Filtering and Wavelet Shrinkage: A Comparison. *IEEE Signal Processing Letters*, 17(3):237–240.

Matthew Jockers. 2014. A Novel Method for Detecting Plot. Matthew L. Jockers Blog.

Matthew L. Jockers. 2015. *Syuzhet: Extract Sentiment and Plot Arcs from Text.*

Gustav Aarup Lauridsen, Jacob Aarup Dalsgaard, and Lars Kjartan Bacher Svendsen. 2019. SENTIDA: A New Tool for Sentiment Analysis in Danish. *Journal of Language Works - Sprogvidenskabeligt Studentertidsskrift*, 4(1):38–53. Number: 1.

Bingzhi Li, Guillaume Wisniewski, and Benoît Crabbé. 2023. Assessing the Capacity of Transformer to Abstract Syntactic Representations: A Contrastive Analysis Based on Long-distance Agreement. *Transactions of the Association for Computational Linguistics*, 11:18–33. Place: Cambridge, MA Publisher: MIT Press.

Scott M Lundberg and Su-In Lee. 2017. A Unified Approach to Interpreting Model Predictions. In *Advances in Neural Information Processing Systems*, volume 30. Curran Associates, Inc.

Tom Lundskær-Nielsen. 2014. The Language of Hans Christian Andersen's Fairy Tales – Compared with Earlier Tales. *Scandinavistica Vilnensis*, 1(9):97–112. Number: 9.

Tharindu Madusanka, Riza Batista-navarro, and Ian Pratt-hartmann. 2023. Identifying the limits of transformers when performing model-checking with natural language. In *Proceedings of the 17th Conference of the European Chapter of the Association for Computational Linguistics*, pages 3539–3550, Dubrovnik, Croatia. Association for Computational Linguistics.

Marita A. Nielsen. 2020. Salmesprog. In *Dansk Sproghistorie Bind 4. Sprog i brug*. Aarhus University Press and Society for Danish Language and Literature (DSLDK).

Bruno Ohana, Sarah Jane Delany, and Brendan Tierney. 2012. A Case-Based Approach to Cross Domain Sentiment Classification. In *Case-Based Reasoning Research and Development*, Lecture Notes in Computer Science, pages 284–296, Berlin, Heidelberg. Springer.

Isabel Papadimitriou, Kezia Lopez, and Dan Jurafsky. 2023. Multilingual BERT has an accent: Evaluating English influences on fluency in multilingual models. In *Findings of the Association for Computational Linguistics: EACL 2023*, pages 1194–1200, Dubrovnik, Croatia. Association for Computational Linguistics.

Andrew J. Reagan, Christopher M. Danforth, Brian Tivnan, Jake Ryland Williams, and Peter Sheridan Dodds. 2017. Sentiment analysis methods for understanding large-scale texts: a case for using continuum-scored words and word shift graphs. *EPJ Data Science*, 6(1):1–21. Number: 1 Publisher: SpringerOpen.

Andrew J Reagan, Lewis Mitchell, Dilan Kiley, Christopher M Danforth, and Peter Sheridan Dodds. 2016. The Emotional Arcs of Stories Are Dominated by Six Basic Shapes. *EPJ Data Science*, 5(1):1–12.

Simone Rebora. 2023. Sentiment Analysis in Literary Studies. A Critical Survey. *Digital Humanities Quarterly*, 17(2).

Vassiliki Rentoumi, George Giannakopoulos, Vangelis Karkaletsis, and George A. Vouros. 2009. Sentiment Analysis of Figurative Language using a Word Sense Disambiguation Approach. In *Proceedings of the International Conference RANLP-2009*, pages 370–375, Borovets, Bulgaria. Association for Computational Linguistics.

Filipe N. Ribeiro, Matheus Araújo, Pollyanna Gonçalves, Marcos André Gonçalves, and Fabrício Benevenuto. 2016. SentiBench - a benchmark comparison of state-of-the-practice sentiment analysis methods. *EPJ Data Science*, 5(1):1–29.

Brian Richardson. 2000. Linearity and Its Discontents: Rethinking Narrative Form and Ideological Valence. *College English*, 62(6):685–695.

Dan Ringgaard and Mads Rosendahl Thomsen, editors. 2017. *Danish literature as world literature*. Literatures as world literature. Bloomsbury Academic, New York.

Louise M. Rosenblatt. 1982. The literary transaction: Evocation and response. *Theory Into Practice*, 21(4):268–277.

Marta Sandri, Elisa Leonardelli, Sara Tonelli, and Elisabetta Jezek. 2023. Why Don't You Do It Right? Analysing Annotators' Disagreement in Subjective Tasks. In *Proceedings of the 17th Conference of the European Chapter of the Association for Computational Linguistics*, pages 2428–2441, Dubrovnik, Croatia. Association for Computational Linguistics.

Thomas Schmidt and Manuel Burghardt. 2018. An Evaluation of Lexicon-based Sentiment Analysis Techniques for the Plays of Gotthold Ephraim Lessing. In *Proceedings of the Second Joint SIGHUM Workshop on Computational Linguistics for Cultural Heritage, Social Sciences, Humanities and Literature*, pages 139–149, Santa Fe, New Mexico. Association for Computational Linguistics.

Thomas Schmidt, Katrin Dennerlein, and Christian Wolff. 2021. Using Deep Learning for Emotion Analysis of 18th and 19th Century German Plays. *Fabrikation von Erkenntnis: Experimente in den Digital Humanities* -.

Nina Schneidermann and Bolette Pedersen. 2022. Evaluating a New Danish Sentiment Resource: the Danish Sentiment Lexicon, DSL. In *Proceedings of the 2nd Workshop on Sentiment Analysis and Linguistic Linked Data*, pages 19–24, Marseille, France. European Language Resources Association.

Morten Skovsted, Mads Djernes, Kirsten Nielsen, Martin Horsntrup, and Hanne J. Jakobsen. 2019. Hvad gør en ny salme til en god salme? *Salmedatabasen*.

Elias Stengel-Eskin, Jimena Guallar-Blasco, and Benjamin Van Durme. 2021. Human-model divergence in the handling of vagueness. In *Proceedings of the 1st Workshop on Understanding Implicit and Underspecified Language*, pages 43–57, Online. Association for Computational Linguistics.

Hsiu-Yuan Tsao, Ming-Yi Chen, Hao-Chiang Koong Lin, and Yu-Chun Ma. 2018. The asymmetric effect of review valence on numerical rating: A viewpoint from a sentiment analysis of users of TripAdvisor. *Online Information Review*, 43(2):283–300. Publisher: Emerald Publishing Limited.

Theresa Wilson, Janyce Wiebe, and Paul Hoffmann. 2005. Recognizing Contextual Polarity in Phrase-Level Sentiment Analysis. In *Proceedings of Human Language Technology Conference and Conference on Empirical Methods in Natural Language Processing*, pages 347–354, Vancouver, British Columbia, Canada. Association for Computational Linguistics.

Yuemei Xu, Han Cao, Wanze Du, and Wenqing Wang. 2022. A Survey of Cross-lingual Sentiment Analysis: Methodologies, Models and Evaluations. *Data Science and Engineering*, 7(3):279–299.

Albin Zehe, Martin Becker, Lena Hettinger, Andreas Hotho, Isabella Reger, and Fotis Jannidis. 2016. Prediction of Happy Endings in German Novels Based on Sentiment Information. In *Interactions between Data Mining and Natural Language Processing*, pages 9–16, Riva del Garda.

# A Appendix

| Verse | English translation | Human | RoB | Sentida |
|---|---|---|---|---|
| Beskæm, o Herre, Frygtens Raab! | *Shame, O Lord, the Cry of Fear!* | -0.08 | 0.65 | -0.98 |
| Med høit bedrøvet Hjerte | *With deeply troubled heart* | -1.00 | -0.74 | 0.13 |
| Tumler dit Sind, som et drivende Vrag. | *Tumbling, your mind, like a drifting wreck.* | -1.00 | 0.00 | -0.14 |
| Ingen Sorrig og Elende | *No sorrow and misery* | 0.08 | -0.86 | 0.93 |
| Fandt en Vei, sig ind at liste? | *Found a way to sneak in there?* | -0.08 | 0.00 | -0.87 |
| Hielp, at jeg elsker, lyder dig, | *Help that I love and obey you,* | 0.08 | 0.82 | 0.87 |
| Skjenker mig min Herres Glæde! | *Gives me my Lord's joy!* | 0.23 | 0.89 | 1.00 |
| Skal jeg vist evig brænde! | *I shall surely burn forever!* | -0.85 | 0.55 | -0.08 |
| Beklemt og lider ilde, | *Distressed and suffering badly* | -0.85 | -0.37 | -0.12 |
| Du giver Hjertet Fred og Trøst; | *You give the heart peace and comfort;* | 1.00 | 0.88 | 0.28 |
| Trøst og Haab og Mod forsvinde. | *Comfort and hope and courage disappear.* | -0.85 | -0.87 | -0.13 |
| Hvor? Ak hvor er Hielp at finde? | *Where? Oh, where is help to be found?* | -0.85 | 0.00 | 0.13 |
| Til Smerte, Spot og Spe! | *For pain, ridicule, and mockery!* | -1.00 | 0.00 | -0.55 |
| Tumler dit Sind, som et drivende Vrag. | *Tumbling, your mind, like a drifting wreck.* | -1.00 | 0.00 | -0.14 |
| Skjuler mig for Synd og Død, | *Hides me from sin and death,* | -0.08 | -0.93 | -0.49 |
| Af Pine, Kval og Plage | *Of torment, anguish, and suffering* | -0.85 | 0.00 | -0.38 |
| Fra Forkrænkelse og Død; | *From Violation and Death;* | -0.85 | 0.00 | -0.73 |
| Ei Trøst jeg fandt, ei Lindring kom | *No comfort I found, no relief came* | -0.85 | 0.00 | -0.30 |
| Hvor? Ak hvor er Hielp at finde? | *Where? Oh, where is help to be found?* | -0.85 | 0.00 | 0.13 |
| Paa Jorden er der Strid og Had, | *On Earth there is strife and hate,* | -0.85 | 0.00 | -0.37 |
| Mishaab og Strid har hver timelig Stund. | *Hopelessness and strife have each earthly hour.* | -0.85 | 0.00 | -0.29 |
| Ham det fryder, at Dødsstriden | *He delights that the struggle of death* | 0.08 | -0.92 | 0.47 |
| Gjør dit Guld Dig frydefuld? | *Does your gold make you joyful?* | -0.08 | -0.92 | 0.53 |
| Forkast da Barnet ei, som kommer | *Do not reject the child who comes* | -0.08 | -0.92 | -0.09 |

Table 6: The 12 verses of the **Hymns** that exhibit the highest absolute disagreement between the human mean vs Sentida (top 12 rows) and vs RoBERTa (RoB) scores (bottom 12). Highlighted rows recur in the top 12 disagreement-verses of both RoBERTa and Sentida. Note that human mean values tend to recur: due to two annotators for the hymns, only whole and half numbers within the 0-10 range are possible, so that normalized values reflect this.

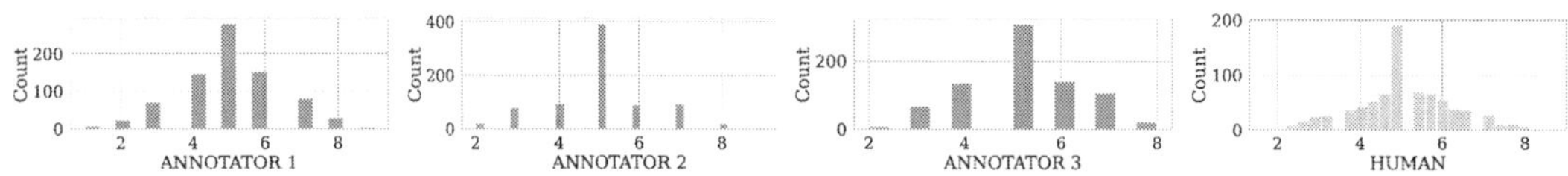


(a) Distribution of annotators' and the human mean scores.

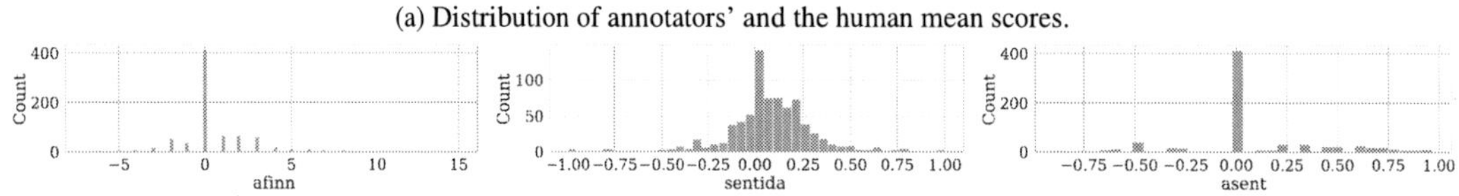


(b) Distribution of dictionary-based methods' scores.

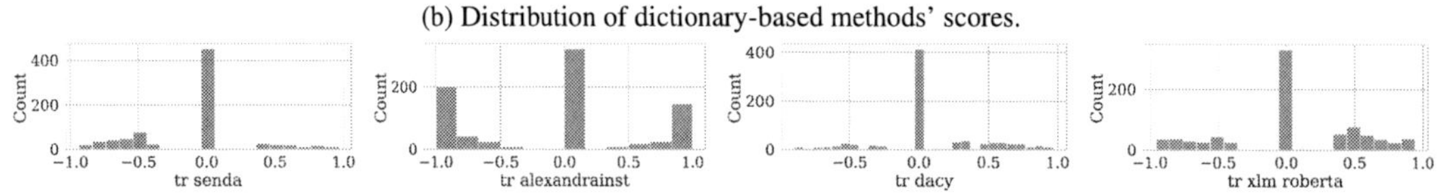


(c) Distribution of transformer-based methods' scores.

Figure 6: **HCA dataset**, distributions of scores per Sentiment Analysis method.

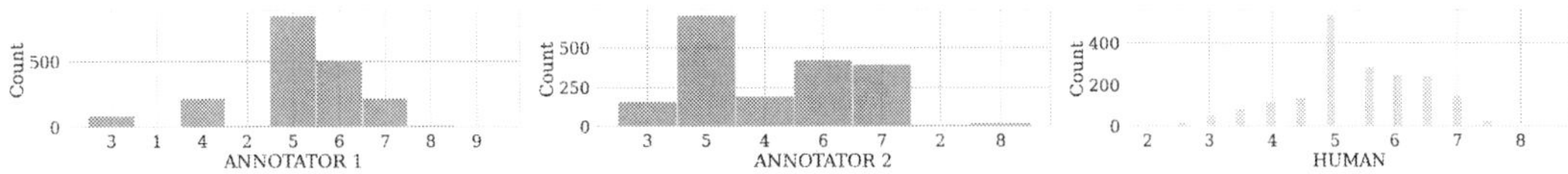


(a) Distribution of annotators' and the human mean scores.

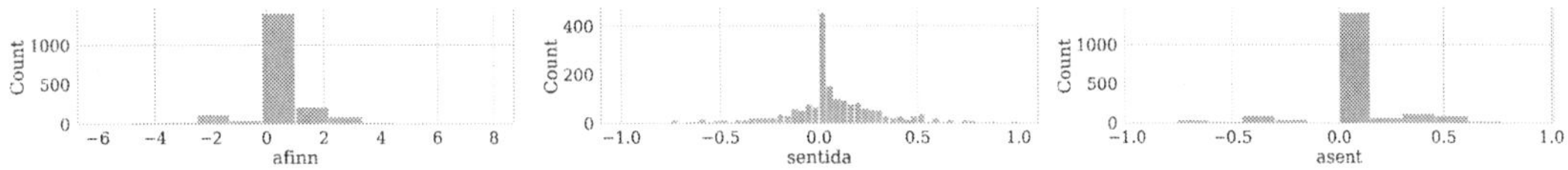


(b) Distribution of dictionary-based methods' scores.

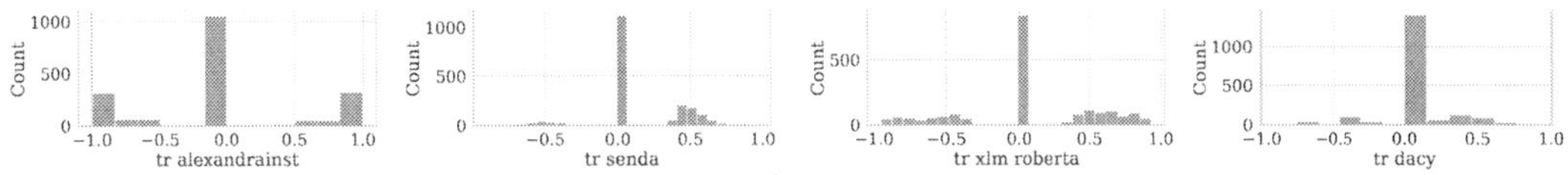


(c) Distribution of transformer-based methods' scores.

Figure 7: **Hymns dataset**, distributions of scores per Sentiment Analysis method.

| Word | English translation |
|---|---|
| mærkværdig | *odd* |
| fornemste | *most distinguished* |
| fineste | *nicest* |
| underligt | *curious/strange* |
| klogeste | *smartest* |
| herligt | *magnificent* |
| underlig | *curious/strange* |
| klogt | *smart* |
| pragt | *splendor* |
| morsomt | *funny* |
| nedrig | *lowly* |
| styg | *hideous* |
| skammede | *shamed* |
| nykker | *whims* |
| kostbart | *precious* |
| kalkunkylling | *turkey chicken* |
| fangst | *catch* |
| værre | *worse* |
| forvildet | *bewildered/lost* |
| grueligste | *most gruesome* |

Table 7: Top 10 positively (top) and negatively (bottom) weighed words of RoBERTa (as gauged via SHAP-scores) in the fairy tales that are not indexed in Sentida (the stem of some words, like "klog", are indexed in Sentida, yet it is unrecognized with the 't'-ending). Note that while most words appear to be reasonably justified for their positive/negative label, some artifacts appear (e.g. "kalkunkylling").

# Multi-Target User Stance Discovery on Reddit

**Benjamin Steel**
School of Computer Science
McGill University
Montreal, Canada
benjamin.steel@mail.mcgill.ca

**Derek Ruths**
School of Computer Science
McGill University
Montreal, Canada
derek.ruths@mcgill.ca

## Abstract

We consider how to credibly and reliably assess the opinions of individuals using their social media posts. To this end, this paper makes three contributions. First, we assemble a workflow and approach to applying modern natural language processing (NLP) methods to multi-target user stance detection in the wild. Second, we establish why the multi-target modeling of user stance is qualitatively more complicated than uni-target user-stance detection. Finally, we validate our method by showing how multi-dimensional measurement of user opinions not only reproduces known opinion polling results, but also enables the study of opinion dynamics at high levels of temporal and semantic resolution.

## 1 Introduction

People act in accordance with their opinions and beliefs (Bliuc et al., 2007). Therefore, efforts to understand and predict large scale human behaviour - from political opinion polls to consumer market studies - massively benefit from accurate maps of human opinions. There is ample evidence that social media is a valuable space in which to measure human opinions (Reveilhac et al., 2022). However, there are notable methodological gaps between the latest advances in natural language processing (NLP) on social media and the methods needed by practitioners (from analysts to social science researchers) who want opinion measurement that simply "works".

For practitioners, the ideal opinion measurement method has several properties: the ability to look at opinions of users on multiple topics at once, the ability to measure these at both high temporal and topical resolution, and to do this with minimal cost and time investment. In contrast, methodological research on this topic tends to focus on just one of these properties. For example, there is work that explores multiple topic measurement, but requires massive training datasets (Zhou et al., 2023). There are other studies that consider temporal and topical resolution, but do this only at the post, rather than user level (Li et al., 2021).

All this amounts to substantial progress in opinion measurement, but progress that is not directly useful to those who need to measure user opinions as the *starting point* of their studies.

We take the position that all the techniques to build such a practitioner-useful method actually exist - they need only be assembled. While this is happy news, we find that assembling these pieces together into a single, clear workflow is highly non-trivial and involves solving a highly non-trivial methodological issue. Namely, rendering the measurements taken of multiple user opinions comparable with one another. This becomes an issue because we may be much better at measuring opinion on one topic than on another. Nonetheless, we still want to ask questions about how these opinions interact with one another across user populations.

In this paper, we present a coherent workflow that assembles techniques from NLP at large into a recipe for the measurement of user stance in social media data at large scale. In the process, we show how to address the issue mentioned above, accurately assessing the opinions of a user on different topics with differing measurement error. We then validate our workflow by studying the multi-target opinions of users on parts of Reddit associated with Canada, showing that the resulting opinion data align with known trends, and that we can characterize previously unmeasured aspects of the online Canadian political discussion.

It is worth noting that this paper is not the final word on a practitioner-useful tool for multi-target opinion studies on social media. While our approach does assemble techniques into a clear, prescriptive workflow, manual tuning must still be done. Moreover, we have not provided a single software tool that automates the process. Both con-



*Proceedings of the 14th Workshop on Computational Approaches to Subjectivity, Sentiment, & Social Media Analysis*, pages 200–214
August 15, 2024 

ceptually and practically, our recipe is hardly "plug-and-play". Nonetheless, we consider this an important step towards rendering the many advancements in opinion measurement useful for practitioners. Further, we submit our work as a starting point and indication of the need for future research that takes seriously the question of how to streamline multi-target user opinion measurement on social media.

We release the source code for our work at github.com/bendavidsteel/user-stance-discovery.

## 2 Background

Our pipeline has three stages: finding stance targets via topic modelling, classifing text stance via stance detection, and finally, inferring user stance via user stance detection. We will therefore review the background of each of these fields.

### 2.1 Topics Discovery

We define topic discovery here as the process of going from a raw text corpus of documents, and producing topical clusters of those documents.

Topic discovery has improved over purely bag of words clustering methods (e.g. latent dirichlet allocation (Blei et al., 2003)) with the use of language encoders and hierarchical clustering (Grootendorst, 2022), which aids with topic fidelity and tunable discovery. Multiple topic modelling steps has been shown to be effective for exploring political issues in a polarized Turkey (Rashed et al., 2021), a method of interest to us in its ability to discover viewpoints within a specific topic.

Beyond this, we would specifically like to be able to discover topics with heavily divided discussion, and for this methods for polarized topic discovery have surfaced (Paschalides et al., 2021), but have so far only been validated on news articles, and require a seed topic, and as such we will not be using this method here.

### 2.2 Text Stance Detection

Defined here as detecting the stance of a piece of text (e.g. favor, against, or neutral) towards a stance target (e.g. something one might have an opinion on, i.e. gun control).

Zero-shot stance detection is improving but not yet on-par with few-shot methods (Allaway and McKeown, 2023), showing that small amounts of training data are worthwhile for improving accuracy. Decoder-only language models (LLMs) are showing their utility for stance detection (Cruickshank and Ng, 2023), including using chain-of-thought methods (Zhang et al., 2023a), showing the effectiveness of prompt-based methods over classification head methods. Other work has provided extra data to the models, whether contextual data from social media, (Li et al., 2023) or additional descriptions of the stance target (Zhu et al., 2022). Additionally, work has shown stance detection benefits from multi-target-stance training (Li et al., 2021).

All these methods indicate the utility of few-shot data, prompting decoder language models, and additional context for improving text stance detection.

### 2.3 User Stance Detection

Here defined as inferring the stance of a user (a person expressing their stance on a platform through text posts) towards one or many stance targets.

Similar methods have been created for user stance detection previously, but many rely on platform specific features, where user stance views can be distinguished by following relevant accounts, or using specific, recognisable hashtags (Darwish et al., 2020; Samih and Darwish, 2021; Abeysinghe, 2023; Introne, 2023; Zhu et al., 2020; Jiang et al., 2023b; Zhang et al., 2023b). This technique can improve accuracy over text only features, but limits the method to only contexts where users interact with influential, opinionated extra-linguistic features, excluding other datasets without these features, or where this data is unavailable. It also ties the performance of the system to the extent that a stance of interest has associated prominent, opinionated entities.

Almadan et al. compare user-stance and text-stance opinion polling methods on Twitter, showing that user-stance produces more meaningful features for gauging public opinion (Almadan et al., 2023), but they only look at stance on vaccination, and use a pre-trained stance classifier trained on thousands of tweets. Zhou et al. focused on user-stance prediction of Weibo users (Zhou et al., 2023), but pre-selected stance targets, used more than 50,000 thousand labelled tweets for training, and focus on prediction as opposed to measurement. Wang et al. explore topical stance detection on an online discussion forum (Wang and Chen, 2021), however, they use sentiment analysis as a proxy for stance, which is poorly correlated with stance (Almadan et al., 2023). They also use likes, dislikes, and comment sentiment, as semi-supervision signals, which is poorly motivated, which, combined with dictionary based sentiment classification methods, results in poor accuracy. Kim et al. look at user stance on Reddit (Kim et al., 2023), but only look at one stance target, and do not control for the accuracy of their classifier on different labels.

With this work in mind, we will focus on building a user stance detection method that can work without platform specific features, use on the order of $10^1$ training examples, and allows proper stance comparison by way of accounting for the accuracy of the classifiers used.

## 3 Pipeline Method

As currently practiced in the literature, user stance detection on a corpus of user-organized social media post data involves three stages (Almadan et al., 2023; Zhou et al., 2023; Wang and Chen, 2021):

1. **Stance target selection:** identifying the set of stance targets (i.e. something one might have an opinion on, e.g. gun control) on which we seek to measure each user's stance.
2. **Text stance inference on each stance target:** for each stance target, classifying each social media post in the corpus with a stance (e.g. favor, against, or neutral) on that target.
3. **User stance inference on each stance target:** for each user, aggregating the stance classifications for each of the user's posts to a user stance for that stance target.

Here we detail a pipeline that uses a host of already-existing methods to realize all three of these stages. Notably, because our aim is to measure the stance of each user on *multiple* targets at once, in Stage 3, we introduce a novel normalization approach to ensure that the user stance scores can be compared across targets.

### 3.1 Stance Target Selection

In this stage, our objective is to select the set of targets we will assess user stance towards. This is an intrinsically exploratory process. The practitioner will arrive at this step with an idea of the themes they want to study (e.g, "public health", "climate change", and "employment"). In this stage, we aim to distill these general themes into clearly defined stances that are both representative of the original intent and informed by the data available.

Our approach here uses an exploratory analysis of topics present within the data, focused by the themes we approach the study with.

We begin by running topic modelling on the post text (included titles and comments), to obtain a characterization of the most frequently discussed items in the corpus. To obtain these topics, we embed the texts with the sentence transformers model ‘all-MiniLM-L12-v2‘ (Reimers and Gurevych, 2019), reduced the dimensionality of the vector embeddings down to 5 dimensions using UMAP (McInnes et al., 2018), and clustered the reduced embeddings using HDBSCAN (McInnes and Healy, 2017), using the BERTopic library (Grootendorst, 2022).

At this point, we have topics, of which we manually select those we deem relevant to the original themes. For these selected topics, we seek to understand potential debates in order to find stance targets. We therefore take inspiration from Rashed et al. (2021), by further reducing the vector embeddings down to 2 dimensions, and re-clustering the data points, to find sub-topic discussion in each topic. These sub-topics provide a high-resolution picture of what themes are actually present in the data and in what relative abundance. Both presence and abundance are important to the selection of stance targets: it is impossible to measure user opinions about things that they have never mentioned.

The final step in this stage is for the practitioner to use the topic characterization, trends, statistics available to, combined with their own domain expertise, to define the stance targets for each topic themselves (i.e. choose the stance target *vaccine mandates* for a vaccines related topic).

### 3.2 Text Stance Detection

This stage focuses on inferring the stance of each post towards each of the stance targets selected in Stage 1. There are several steps involved here: (1) building training data, (2) training stance classifiers that work for each stance target, and (3) running the stance classifiers on the corpus posts.

**Building training data.** To train multiple stance detectors, we require training data for each in the form of annotated posts. Many stance detection systems can require thousands of training datapoints (Almadan et al., 2023; Zhou et al., 2023). From a practitioners perspective, it's important that we minimize the training dataset size to limit cost and coding time. As will be discussed, we chose a method where we found that coding 100 posts for each stance target, sampled from their respective topic, was sufficient: labelling them with their stance, with labels selected from ‘favor‘, ‘against‘, or ‘neutral‘. We used the definitions of stance from

Semeval-2016 (Mohammad et al., 2016). We used two annotators for each of these labelling tasks, ensuring that our annotations were sufficient quality by running an interannotator agreement statistic (Gwet, 2008). An adjudicator then chose the final gold stance label, by looking at the two annotator's labels.

**Training stance classifiers.** With labelled data in hand, we then train and test stance classifiers. There are multiple paradigms for building such classifiers. Thus in this stage, our aim is to design and build performant classifiers, through experimentation, for individual stance target-stance pairs (e.g., target-for, target-neutral, target-against) - these will be used later as part of an ensemble classifier to infer final post stances.

Due to the powerful zero-shot and few-shot abilities of auto-regressive LLMs, we used 'Starling-7B' as a base classifier model, a 7 billion parameter pre-trained auto-regressive LLM, tuned for helpfulness using reinforcement learning (Zhu et al., 2023). We experimented with others, including 'GPT-3.5-Turbo-Instruct' (OpenAI, 2023), 'Mistral-7B-Instruct-0.1' (Jiang et al., 2023a), and 'Zephyr 7B Beta' (Tunstall et al., 2023), but found that Starling-7B provided the highest accuracy, lowest cost, and its open weights access allowed fine-tuning.

As mentioned above, we seek to obtain the best possible classifiers for each combination of stance-target and stance, for use in our ensemble classifier. But we found that prompting a model for a binary of whether a text post is a specific stance or not performed worse than prompting the model for a choice out of all of the possible stances, see Appendix A.1.1 for experimental results. As such, we decided on a prompt that draws inspiration from prompts given to human annotators in previous stance detection tasks (Mohammad et al., 2016). The prompt (see Appendix A.1.2) includes a description of the stance target, which improved the accuracy of the classifier, and contextual posts, as these have both been shown to improve performance (Li et al., 2023; Zhu et al., 2022). These contextual inputs are provided alongside the stance target, and text post in question, and the model is prompted to select from the 3 stance classes as an output.

In order to further fine-tune the classifier, we needed a measure of classifier performance: we calculated the precision and recall measures for both the 'favor' and 'against' labels, and average these values, as is standard in stance detection (Mohammad et al., 2016). We used the F-beta score as our target metric (Baeza-Yates, 1999), using a beta value of 0.5, as we deemed that for this task precision is more important than recall. The reasoning for this is that if the model indicates someone has a clear opinion, we want to be sure that they do indeed have that opinion, so we need a high precision. Conversely, many expressed opinions are very subtle, and we deemed it acceptable to label as 'neutral' posts that don't clearly signal a favor or against stance.

We then improve the accuracy of our classification model with fine tuning. Initially, we experimented with chain-of-thought (CoT) methods (Zhang et al., 2023a), in-context learning (ICL) methods (Dong et al., 2022), and automated prompt-tuning methods (Li and Liang, 2021), using the DSPy library to speed up experimentation (Khattab et al., 2023). We found ICL and CoT methods were slow, and parameter-efficient fine-tuning (PEFT) methods using minimal training and validation sets resulted in the highest accuracy scores and the fastest inference speeds (Liu et al., 2022). We experimented with two variations: (1) PEFT the classifiers on all annotated stance examples, and (2) PEFT as (1), then copying that model and PEFT separate models on only the examples for a single stance target, which we dub 'two-step PEFT'. For both PEFT methods, we use 10 examples for training, and 10 for validation, with the remaining 80 from each stance target used as the test set.

The modeling work described thus far yields $N + 2$ viable classifiers, where $N$ is the number of stance targets: the original zero-shot prompt Starling classifier, the PEFT-tuned classifier on all stances, and then two-step PEFT classifiers (one for each of the $N$ stance targets). While one might expect that the two-step PEFT classifiers would perform best across the board, they did not. For some stance targets-label pairs, the zero-shot Starling or fine-tuned Starling classifiers performed better - which is consistent with the natural sensitivities of model training observed in other work.

To identify the best classifier for inferring the target-stance pair $(t, s)$, we evaluated the performance of each classifier on the relevant stance target (i.e., "does this post express stance $s$ on stance target $t$?") across the annotated data (on the held out test set). We refer to this classifier as $C_{(t,s)}$

and denote its cross-validation performance score as $0 \leq S_{(t,s)} \leq 1$. Note that for a given post $x$, $C_{(t,s)}(x)$ is either $Y$ (yes, it does express that stance $s$ on stance target $t$) or $N$ (it does not).

We conclude this stage, then, with $3N$ classifiers: $\{C_{(t,\texttt{for})}, C_{(t,\texttt{neutral})}, C_{(t,\texttt{against})}\}$, for each of the $N$ stance targets, $t$.

**Final stance classification.** To infer the stance of a post towards a specific stance target, we employ a simple adapted voting ensemble model: for a given post to classify and a given stance target, we run the post through each of the best classifiers for that stance target and each stance label ($\{C_{(t,\texttt{for})}, C_{(t,\texttt{neutral})}, C_{(t,\texttt{against})}\}$). We then select the final label, $l_t^x$, for that post by favoring the most accurate classifier that assigns its label to the post. In other words:

$B = \{s : s \in \{\texttt{for}, \texttt{against}\} \wedge C_{(t,s)} = Y\}$
if $|B| > 0$
  $l_t^x = \texttt{argmax}_{s \in B} S_{(t,s)}$
else
  $l_t^x = \texttt{neutral}$
endif

Notice that we only choose 'neutral' as the label if all other labels are not assigned. In effect, we exclude neutral predictions from explicitly weighing into the label selection, as 'neutral' always has the highest precision of any label (due to 'neutral' being the easiest label to predict).

We then used this simple ensemble method to combine model classifications into a final stance classification for each comment. For each stance target, we classify only the posts in the respective topic.

### 3.3 User Stance

In this stage, we aim to obtain a measure that represents each user's stance on each stance target. However, all we currently have is a stance classification for each of their posts. Our task then, is to devise a method for aggregating the comment stance classifications into a user stance mean, and for confidence estimations, a variance. Here, we discuss that aggregation process.

**Stance Aggregation.** The simplest method is to simply assign $-1$, 0, and 1 to the stance predictions 'against', 'neutral', and 'favor' respectively, and take the mean of these classifications as the user stance. This allows us to fairly compare the extent to which two users favor, or dis-favor, a stance. However, our classifiers not only have differing accuracy on each stance target, but they also have differing accuracy on each stance label ('favor', 'neutral' or 'against'). This means that if the classifier has higher recall at classifying text in favor of something than against it, users will seem more strongly in favor of the stance target than against it. We cannot fairly compare users favoring or dis-favoring a stance target, or compare the stance of two users on different stance targets, using this simple aggregation scheme. Even if we did not use an ensemble classifier, the differing performance of a model between labels means we need to compensate for this in any aggregation. We need to take into account the accuracy of the classifier that made the predictions.

With this in mind, we propose two methods for determining a user stance mean and variance from the predicted comment stances, using the classifier accuracy:

**Weighted Mean.** The simplest method is to use the weighted mean and variance of the comment stances, with weights for each comment stance being the precision of the classifier used for the comment stance prediction. We use precision as the weight, as for non-neutral predictions, this acts as a proxy for the probability that the prediction is correct. So for a set of $n$ classification outputs $x$ with associated classifier precision $w$:

$$\forall j \in \text{users}, \mu_j = \frac{\sum^n w_i x_i}{\sum^n w_i} \quad (1)$$

$$\sigma_j^2 = \left(\frac{n}{n-1}\right)\left(\frac{\sum^n w_i x_i^2}{\sum^n w_i} - \mu_w^2\right) \quad (2)$$

We can find the mean $\mu_j$ and variance $\sigma_j^2$ of a user's stance.

Through experimentation with a generative model of user stance, this method is fast, simple, and recovers the mean accurately, but gives a poor characterization of the variance, due to not factoring in the recall of the classifier. See Appendix A.2.2 for experimental results.

**Inferred Mean.** We therefore wanted another aggregator that could factor in the likelihood of misclassification from our classifiers. To do this we used a probabilistic generative model of the latent user stance generating the posts, which are then observed by our classifiers with error. We can then fit this model to our data, and infer the latent user stance. We will set this problem up as a maximum a posteriori probability (MAP) estimate, so that we can set a prior on our expectation of the user stance. This allows us to add an inductive bias that says: the more posts a user has, the more we'll be convinced of their stance. With a preference for fast optimization over our large dataset, we used stochastic variational inference (SVI) instead of the slower markov chain monte carlo (MCMC) inference.

We define the commenting distribution of a user as a normal distribution $\mathcal{N}(\mu, \sigma)$, where the latent continuous stance of a comment is sampled from this distribution, to represent that users produce a range of stances around their actual stance (e.g. someone favoring a target wouldn't necessarily always write content favoring their target with the same strength). Given this, the likelihood function for our latent comment stances given a user with a stance distribution is:

$$\begin{aligned} \forall j \in \text{users}, \mu_j &\sim \mathcal{N}(\mu_{loc}, \sigma_{loc}) \\ \sigma_j &\sim \log \mathcal{N}(\mu_{scale}, \sigma_{scale}) \end{aligned} \tag{3}$$

$$\forall i \in \text{posts}_j, s_i \sim \text{Normal}(\mu_j, \sigma_j) \tag{4}$$

Where $\mu_{loc}, \sigma_{loc}, \mu_{scale}, \sigma_{scale}$ are parameters to set, $u_j$ and $\sigma_j$ are the user stance variables to estimate, and $s_i$ is the latent continuous comment stance on a given stance target. As we are measuring the posts in a discrete fashion i.e. labels of 'for', 'against', or 'neutral', we need to discretize the latent continuous comment stance:

$$q_i = \begin{cases} against & \text{if } s_i < -\frac{1}{3} \\ neutral & \text{if } -\frac{1}{3} \leq s_i \leq \frac{1}{3} \\ for & \text{if } s_i > \frac{1}{3} \end{cases} \tag{5}$$

Where $q_i$ is the latent discretized comment stance.

At this point in the probabilistic model, we have discretized latent comment stances, but we need to fit this model to our stance predictions. So the output of our probabilistic model must be the observed comment stances, where we observe the discretized latent comment stance with the error of the classifier that observed them. We need a categorical distribution that can represent that classifier error. The closest thing we have to the true categorical distribution of the classifier error given a true comment stance, is the column of the confusion matrix for the true comment stance, obtained at test time. We can normalize this column to get an approximation of the classifier's categorical error distribution, as has been used in similar methods previously (Kerrigan et al., 2021).

$$\text{x}_i \sim \text{Categorical}(P(X|Q = q_i)) \tag{6}$$

Where $x_i$ is the observed comment stance.

With that, our probabilistic model of the likelihood function of our data generation process is complete. To optimize the model, we need to approximate the posterior of this process, with the variational distribution. To produce a variational distribution, we use the confusion matrix of the model to approximate the $P(Q|X = x_i)$ probability: the probability of the true latent comment stance, given the comment stance observations. We model the latent variables $\mu_j$ and $\sigma_j$ in the variational distribution as $Delta$ distributions, for MAP inference. Given this likelihood function, and the variational distribution, we can find the variables $\mu_j$ and $\sigma_j$ which most likely gave us our data by maximising the evidence lower bound (ELBO). See Appendix A.2.1 for training details.

With this method in hand, we can aggregate the comment stance predictions into our final user stance mean and variance, $\mu_j$ and $\sigma_j$. We evaluated this method using synthetic data, and found that while it apportioned probability mass more accurately for users with fewer data points and classifiers with error, this came at a cost of the mean of the inferred normal systematically underestimating the true user stance, due to the distributed probability mass. This makes the method suitable for downstream applications that can use this information well (i.e. probabilistic models), but less appropriate for applications which can only factor in the mean. See Appendix A.2.2 for experimental results and discussion of this evaluation.

## 4 Experiments

We validated the proposed method by looking at Canadian political opinion dynamics on Reddit. After detecting stances over the Reddit corpus collected using the proposed method, we evaluated the extent to which inferred user stances reproduce known opinion polling results and temporal opinion trends.

### 4.1 Data, stance-targets, and inference

**Data.** Using the Pushshift dataset, we collected all 2022 content from the 4 largest Canadian-centric subreddits: 'r/canada', 'r/vancouver', 'r/ontario', and 'r/toronto' (Baumgartner et al., 2020).

| Stance Target | Description | Fleiss' Kappa |
|---|---|---|
| Vaccine Mandates | Laws requiring personal use of COVID-19 vaccines | 0.53 |
| Renter Protections | Laws protecting the rights of people renting housing | 0.23 |
| NDP | The NDP Party of Canada | 0.59 |
| Liberals | The Liberal Party of Canada | 0.56 |
| Conservatives | The Conservative Party of Canada | 0.63 |
| Gun Control | Laws regulating the use of firearms | 0.55 |
| Drug Decriminalization | Policy decriminalizing illegal drugs | 0.46 |
| Liberal Immigration Policy | Laws favoring more immigration | 0.59 |
| Canadian Aid to Ukraine | Government financial and military aid to Ukraine | 0.623 |
| French Language Laws | Laws mandating the use of the French language | 0.547 |

Table 1: Our chosen stance targets, descriptions for each stance target for reader context, and the Fleiss' Kappa statistic for the interannotator agreement of the annotations from our annotators (Gwet, 2008).

| | Prec | Rec | F1 |
|---|---|---|---|
| 1. Zero Shot (Avg) | 0.42 | 0.61 | 0.45 |
| 2. Two-step PEFT (Avg) | 0.60 | 0.51 | 0.52 |
| 3. PEFT (Avg) | 0.59 | 0.52 | 0.53 |
| 4. Ensemble (Avg) | 0.74 | 0.64 | 0.65 |
| 5. Always Favor | 0.06 | 0.50 | 0.10 |
| 6. Annotator | 0.74 | 0.84 | 0.77 |
| 7. Twitter | 0.93 | 0.91 | 0.92 |
| 8. Reddit | - | - | 0.594 |

Table 2: Mean macro precision, recall, and F1 (excluding neutral label) of techniques used, including methods composing the ensemble (1-3), the ensemble (4), baselines (including human performance) (5-6), and prior work (7-8). Prior work is selected from previous comparable work, and included to contextualize the performance of our classifiers with contemporaneous work, but note these numbers are not for the same dataset. We report the F1 metric, as this is the one reported by prior work. Prior work: (Samih and Darwish, 2021) (Twitter), and (Kim et al., 2023) (Reddit)

**Stance target selection.** For topic modeling, we used a higher than recommended number of neighbours parameter for UMAP of 30, and a minimum cluster size of 0.1% of the dataset for HDBSCAN, to find larger topics that covered coarse-grained political issues. This left us with 80 clusters aligned with political issues, where 51% of texts were considered outliers from these clusters. The actual selection of the stance targets was, frankly, subjective - though we expect this would be the case in empirical opinion studies as well. In the end, we selected the stance targets shown in Table 1, where we also include a description of the stance target. The posts in the topics associated with these chosen stance targets represented 16% of the text in our dataset.

**Annotation and modeling.** We took 100 samples from topics linked to our selected stance targets and double-annotated them using the annotation procedure described in Section 3.2. We ran the Fleiss' Kappa interannotator agreement statistic on the annotations, and present them in Table 1.

We tried training our classifiers with a number of different methods, and we report the metrics from each of those methods in Table 2. Our two methods of parameter efficient fine-tuning worked out to produce the classifiers with the highest accuracy. We then used the highest accuracy individual classifiers for our ensemble method.

**Stance detection.** We ran the classifier on all the comments from each topic deemed close to our targets for all users who had at least 5 comments (as a rough proxy for ensuring we had enough classifications to obtain a reasonable stance signal). We then ran our user stance aggregation methods, to obtain user stance scores for each user on each stance target.

### 4.2 Investigations

There are many political behaviour investigations we can perform with the data available from this work, both to learn about views on political issues in Canadian politics, and validate the accuracy of our results. We therefore ask 3 initial research questions (RQs):

1. **RQ1: Can we find the political issue opinion correlation between sets of issues, and which are the strongest among them?** We

start by taking a static, big picture view of online opinions in Canadian politics.

2. **RQ2: What can we learn about polarization in Canadian political discussion from this data?** If there are correlations in political issue opinions, this indicates there is polarization (political sorting). Can we quantify that polarization, and the polarization of subsets of the data?
3. **RQ3: Do we observe fluctuations in political issue opinion over time, and do these line up with potentially explanatory events?** Political issues change over time, and with them, the opinions of the people. If we can observe this with confidence, it will provide a strong tool for viewing and understanding reactions to public policy.

#### 4.2.1 RQ1: Static user opinions trends

It is well-established that opinions on certain topics are correlated (Baldassarri and Gelman, 2008). This is the question we prepare to investigate here. In Figure 1, we see selected scatter plots of users' opinions on multiple stance targets (See Fig. 4 for all scatter plots and distributions). These trends in these scatter plots can be inspected to assess the correlations that may exist between different stance targets. We used the inferred mean method for the user stance data in this experiment.

We fit a weighted least squares models to each of the opinion comparisons (Seber and Lee, 2012), and include the resulting correlation, p-value, and $R^2$ value in Figure 1. Note many people have only posted opinionated ('favor' or 'against', not 'neutral') comments on one stance target or the other, and therefore we get a prominent 'cross' on the scatter, combined with an obvious cluster of users who are opinionated on both stances. In order to see the correlation of this opinionated cluster of users, we re-calculate the correlation without users who have not posted an opinionated comment. We report these correlations with the highest $R^2$ values in Table 3, where we see numerous strong correlations between stance targets.

Inferred stances reveal strong correlations in user stance between targets. Crucially, inter-target stance correlations line up with Canadian political party platforms - that is, users who support a political party are likely to aligned with the party's political platform (CBC, 2021). For example, we find strong opposite correlations between Liberals and Gun Control, and Conservatives and Gun Control.

| Target A | Target B | $\rho$ | $R^2$ |
|---|---|---|---|
| Vacc. Mandates | Gun Control. | 0.29 | 0.12 |
| Vacc. Mandates | Immigr. Pol. | 0.16 | 0.13 |
| Liberals | Gun Control | 0.29 | 0.15 |
| Liberals | Immigr. Pol. | 0.20 | 0.15 |
| Gun Control | Immigr. Pol. | 0.28 | 0.19 |

Table 3: User stance correlations issue pairs, including only correlations with $R^2 >= 0.1$ for brevity.

For many political issue pairings, users are polarized - that is, they are self-sorting into ideological camps (Baldassarri and Gelman, 2008). Curiously, some of the highest correlations and most predictive relationships between political issue stances were non-party stance targets, suggesting political issues are more polarizing than party allegiances.

#### 4.2.2 RQ2: Polarization.

We want to dive more into the topic of polarization, due to the evidence we see for it in the correlation data, and it's consequences for society (Klein, 2020). Using this static opinion data, we compute polarization measures for each subset of stance targets (Gubanov et al., 2021). Imagine a room of opinionated people - if they all know each others full spectrum of opinions, symmetric polarization gives the extent to which two separate groups of disagreeing people would form. However, if we were to only let them know a subset of each others opinions, then asymmetric polarization tells us which subsets of opinions produce the most and least divided rooms.

Using asymmetric polarization, we find that gun control and liberal immigration policy are among the most polarized stance targets, and that renter protections and Canadian aid to Ukraine are the least polarized stance targets. The measure tells us that 'r/canada' is the most polarized subreddit with a symmetric polarization measure of 0.11, and 'r/vancouver' is the least polarized subreddit with a measure of 0.04, indicating that national political discussion is more polarized than provincial political discussion.

#### 4.2.3 RQ3: Temporal trends

Our method provides annotations for timestamped social media data. As a result, we also obtain information about how user opinions change, en mass, over time. To the best of our knowledge, this level of population opinion polling is unmatched for political issues beyond party opinion and major topi-

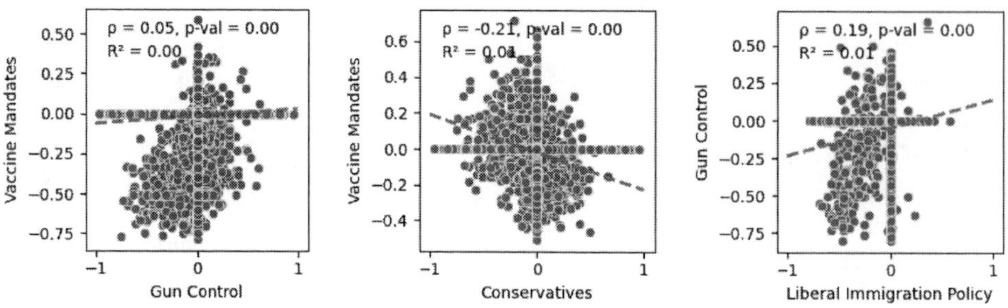


(a) Vaccine mandates and gun control user stance scatter plot.

(b) Vaccine mandates and conservatives user stance scatter plot.

(c) Gun control and liberal immigration policy user stance scatter plot.

Figure 1: Scatter plots compare user stances on two different stance targets. We fit a weighted least squares method to the data (using the inverse of the sum of the user stance variances as a weight), to find the correlation of the data.

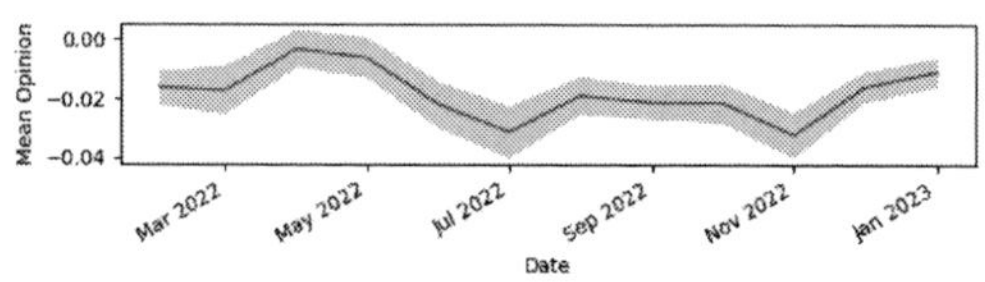


(a) Vaccine mandates opinion timeline.

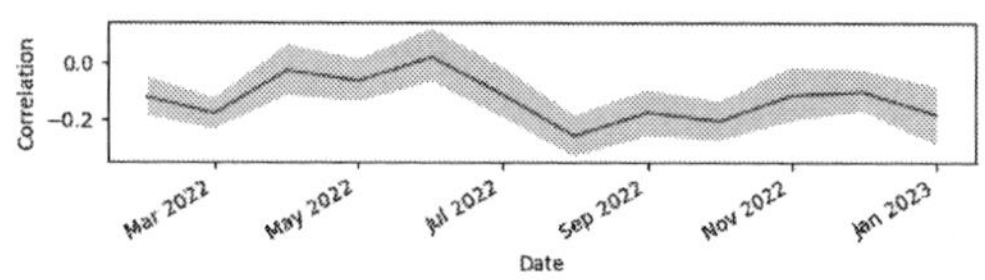


(b) Vaccine mandates and conservatives opinion correlation timeline.

Figure 2: Movement of stance opinion and correlation over 2022. The shaded bars indicate the confidence intervals of the moving statistic, as determined by the bootstrap method (Efron and Tibshirani, 1994).

cal issues (e.g. vaccine mandates).

To do this, we look at how the aggregated user opinions shift over each month of 2022. We constructed figures of the change in mean user opinion and correlation of user opinions on a month by month basis, complete with confidence intervals found via the bootstrap method (Efron, 1992). We include a sample of these in Figure 2.

These temporal opinion shifts reflect known inflection points in policy and public opinion. For example, looking at vaccine mandates opinion trends (Fig. 2a), the first data point we have is in April 2022, when the overall stance on vaccine mandates reaches a high, coinciding with polling suggesting that the public was less worried about COVID-19 (Coletto and Anderson, 2022). By July, the opinion for vaccine mandates drops as reports circulate about vaccine skepticism (Institute, 2022). The correlation between conservatives stance and vaccine mandates stance also drops, indicating conservatives become more likely to be against vaccine mandates (or vice versa), (Fig. 2b) following reports about vaccine hesitancy, and talk of ending vaccine mandates (Lavery, 2022; Boutilier, 2022).

## 5 Discussion

In this work, we aimed to provide a complete template method for moving from raw social media data and inferring user stances across multiple stance targets. While the method itself primarily assembles existing methods, it does so in systematic a way that, to our knowledge, have not been attempted before. Moreover, we have also contributed a novel approach to rendering a user's stance on multiple stance targets comparable. Applied to Reddit data, the user stance trends our method yields reflect known and notable behaviour.

**Future work** These findings collectively point to the utility of the method we proposed in this paper. But there is a great deal of work to be done to improve these methods. For the first part of our methodology, automated techniques that can select the most salient stance targets would reduce any potential bias in manually choosing them, and initial methods for this have started to appear (Paschalides et al., 2021). Our methodology could also be extended to non-text based platforms by means of large multimodal models (LMMs) (Liu et al., 2023). And finally, there is much analysis work possible with the user stance signals, where we could use more sophisticated modelling techniques to uncover more complex opinion dynamics.

## 6 Ethical Statement

The method described in this work has a strong privacy violating potential. Although all of the text used in this work is publicly available for anyone with an internet connection, rapid progression of derived features from social trace data makes informed consent impossible. Just as this method allows us to understand large scale human behaviour, it also makes it possible to track and predict individual user's stances. However, we believe these methods have strong democratic potential for better understanding population perspectives. Therefore we believe it is critical to always focus our analysis on this data in the aggregate, and use this data to understand large scale trends as opposed to investigating specific users.

## 7 Limitations

We would highlight that our template does not capture the only assembly of existing methods to achieve its aim. Our objective here is to provide *a* credible and reproducible way of measuring multi-target user stance, and we invite future work to improve and contribute other frameworks for this task.

A drawback of our method is the disconnection between topics and opinion dimensions. The first disadvantage of this is that choosing the stance target we examine in the topic of interest is done manually, and this opens this choice up to being either an opinion dimension which is either not heavily discussed and therefore not representative of the analysed discussion, or a misleading dimension of disagreement that is better associated with a larger, more delineated discussion. Future work should use an automated method to discover these stance targets (Paschalides et al., 2021).

Another, related, problem in this method is how we can understand the idea of a 'neutral' stance in each stance category. For some topics, many comments associated with that topic are discussing the stance target in question, such as comments associated with a gun topic discussing gun control. However, for other topics, like Canadian political parties, a smaller share of the comments in this topic are discussing the new democratic party (NDP), so the NDP get a disproportionately higher number of 'neutral' comments.

Finally there is more work to be done on the user stance aggregation process, namely to further validate the likelihood function and variational distribution that we used. We experimented with using a beta distribution to represent skew in the potential user stance, but had difficulties with limiting the distribution parameters to realistic user stance distributions, so more work can be done here.

## References


TM Abeysinghe. 2023. Utilizing multi-modal weak signals to improve user stance inference in social media.

Emily Allaway and Kathleen McKeown. 2023. Zero-shot stance detection: Paradigms and challenges. *Frontiers in Artificial Intelligence*, 5:1070429.

Ali Almadan, Mary Lou Maher, and Jason Windett. 2023. Stance detection for gauging public opinion: A statistical analysis of the difference between tweet-based and user-based stance in twitter. In *Future of Information and Communication Conference*, pages 358–374. Springer.

R Baeza-Yates. 1999. Modern information retrieval. *Addison Wesley google schola*, 2:127–136.

Delia Baldassarri and Andrew Gelman. 2008. Partisans without constraint: Political polarization and trends in american public opinion. *American Journal of Sociology*, 114(2):408–446.

Jason Baumgartner, Savvas Zannettou, Brian Keegan, Megan Squire, and Jeremy Blackburn. 2020. The pushshift reddit dataset. In *Proceedings of the international AAAI conference on web and social media*, volume 14, pages 830–839.

David M Blei, Andrew Y Ng, and Michael I Jordan. 2003. Latent dirichlet allocation. *Journal of machine Learning research*, 3(Jan):993–1022.

Ana-Maria Bliuc, Craig McGarty, Katherine Reynolds, and Daniela Muntele. 2007. Opinion-based group membership as a predictor of commitment to political action. *European journal of social psychology*, 37(1):19–32.

Alex Boutilier. 2022. 'this will be pierre poilievre's party': Conservatives reckon with a new direction. *Global News*.

CBC. 2021. How do the main parties compare on these issues? `https://newsinteractives.cbc.ca/elections/federal/2021/party-platforms/`. Accessed: 2024-05-17.

David Coletto and Bruce Anderson. 2022. Covid anxiety moderate to low: 6th wave hasn't caused a spike in fear. *Abacus Data*.

Iain J Cruickshank and Lynnette Hui Xian Ng. 2023. Use of large language models for stance classification. *arXiv preprint arXiv:2309.13734*.

Kareem Darwish, Peter Stefanov, Michaël Aupetit, and Preslav Nakov. 2020. Unsupervised user stance detection on twitter. In *Proceedings of the International AAAI Conference on Web and Social Media*, volume 14, pages 141–152.

Qingxiu Dong, Lei Li, Damai Dai, Ce Zheng, Zhiyong Wu, Baobao Chang, Xu Sun, Jingjing Xu, and Zhifang Sui. 2022. A survey for in-context learning. *arXiv preprint arXiv:2301.00234*.

Bradley Efron. 1992. Bootstrap methods: another look at the jackknife. In *Breakthroughs in statistics: Methodology and distribution*, pages 569–593. Springer.

Bradley Efron and Robert J Tibshirani. 1994. *An introduction to the bootstrap*. Chapman and Hall/CRC.

Maarten Grootendorst. 2022. Bertopic: Neural topic modeling with a class-based tf-idf procedure. *arXiv preprint arXiv:2203.05794*.

Dmitry A Gubanov, Ilya V Petrov, and Alexander G Chkhartishvili. 2021. Multidimensional model of opinion dynamics in social networks: polarization indices. *Automation and Remote Control*, 82:1802–1811.

Kilem Li Gwet. 2008. Computing inter-rater reliability and its variance in the presence of high agreement. *British Journal of Mathematical and Statistical Psychology*, 61(1):29–48.

Angus Reid Institute. 2022. Covid-19: Half want boosters asap, but two-in-five among vaccinated say they're not sold on another shot.

Joshua Introne. 2023. Measuring belief dynamics on twitter. In *Proceedings of the International AAAI Conference on Web and Social Media*, volume 17, pages 387–398.

Albert Q Jiang, Alexandre Sablayrolles, Arthur Mensch, Chris Bamford, Devendra Singh Chaplot, Diego de las Casas, Florian Bressand, Gianna Lengyel, Guillaume Lample, Lucile Saulnier, et al. 2023a. Mistral 7b. *arXiv preprint arXiv:2310.06825*.

Julie Jiang, Xiang Ren, and Emilio Ferrara. 2023b. Retweet-bert: political leaning detection using language features and information diffusion on social networks. In *Proceedings of the International AAAI Conference on Web and Social Media*, volume 17, pages 459–469.

Gavin Kerrigan, Padhraic Smyth, and Mark Steyvers. 2021. Combining human predictions with model probabilities via confusion matrices and calibration. *Advances in Neural Information Processing Systems*, 34:4421–4434.

Omar Khattab, Arnav Singhvi, Paridhi Maheshwari, Zhiyuan Zhang, Keshav Santhanam, Sri Vardhamanan, Saiful Haq, Ashutosh Sharma, Thomas T Joshi, Hanna Moazam, et al. 2023. Dspy: Compiling declarative language model calls into self-improving pipelines. *arXiv preprint arXiv:2310.03714*.

Rachel Kim, Veniamin Veselovsky, and Ashton Anderson. 2023. Capturing dynamics in online public discourse: A case study of universal basic income discussions on reddit. *arXiv preprint arXiv:2312.09611*.

Diederik P Kingma and Jimmy Ba. 2014. Adam: A method for stochastic optimization. *arXiv preprint arXiv:1412.6980*.

Ezra Klein. 2020. *Why we're polarized*. Simon and Schuster.

Irelyne Lavery. 2022. Poilievre popular among conservative voters, but not all canadians feel the same: poll. *Global News*.

Xiang Lisa Li and Percy Liang. 2021. Prefix-tuning: Optimizing continuous prompts for generation. *arXiv preprint arXiv:2101.00190*.

Yingjie Li, Chenye Zhao, and Cornelia Caragea. 2021. Improving stance detection with multi-dataset learning and knowledge distillation. In *Proceedings of the 2021 Conference on Empirical Methods in Natural Language Processing*, pages 6332–6345.

Yupeng Li, Haorui He, Shaonan Wang, Francis CM Lau, and Yunya Song. 2023. Improved target-specific stance detection on social media platforms by delving into conversation threads. *IEEE Transactions on Computational Social Systems*.

Haokun Liu, Derek Tam, Mohammed Muqeeth, Jay Mohta, Tenghao Huang, Mohit Bansal, and Colin A Raffel. 2022. Few-shot parameter-efficient fine-tuning is better and cheaper than in-context learning. *Advances in Neural Information Processing Systems*, 35:1950–1965.

Haotian Liu, Chunyuan Li, Yuheng Li, and Yong Jae Lee. 2023. Improved baselines with visual instruction tuning. *arXiv preprint arXiv:2310.03744*.

Leland McInnes and John Healy. 2017. Accelerated hierarchical density based clustering. In *2017 IEEE international conference on data mining workshops (ICDMW)*, pages 33–42. IEEE.

Leland McInnes, John Healy, and James Melville. 2018. Umap: Uniform manifold approximation and projection for dimension reduction. *arXiv preprint arXiv:1802.03426*.

Saif Mohammad, Svetlana Kiritchenko, Parinaz Sobhani, Xiaodan Zhu, and Colin Cherry. 2016. Semeval-2016 task 6: Detecting stance in tweets. In *Proceedings of the 10th international workshop on semantic evaluation (SemEval-2016)*, pages 31–41.

OpenAI. 2023. Gpt-3.5 turbo. `https://platform.openai.com/docs/models/gpt-3-5-turbo`. Accessed: 2024-05-16.

Demetris Paschalides, George Pallis, and Marios D Dikaiakos. 2021. Polar: a holistic framework for the modelling of polarization and identification of polarizing topics in news media. In *Proceedings of the 2021 IEEE/ACM International Conference on Advances in Social Networks Analysis and Mining*, pages 348–355.

Ammar Rashed, Mucahid Kutlu, Kareem Darwish, Tamer Elsayed, and Cansın Bayrak. 2021. Embeddings-based clustering for target specific stances: The case of a polarized turkey. In *Proceedings of the International AAAI Conference on web and social media*, volume 15, pages 537–548.

Nils Reimers and Iryna Gurevych. 2019. Sentence-bert: Sentence embeddings using siamese bert-networks. In *Proceedings of the 2019 Conference on Empirical Methods in Natural Language Processing*. Association for Computational Linguistics.

Maud Reveilhac, Stephanie Steinmetz, and Davide Morselli. 2022. A systematic literature review of how and whether social media data can complement traditional survey data to study public opinion. *Multimedia tools and applications*, 81(7):10107–10142.

Younes Samih and Kareem Darwish. 2021. A few topical tweets are enough for effective user stance detection. In *Proceedings of the 16th Conference of the European Chapter of the Association for Computational Linguistics: Main Volume*, pages 2637–2646.

George AF Seber and Alan J Lee. 2012. *Linear regression analysis*. John Wiley & Sons.

Lewis Tunstall, Edward Beeching, Nathan Lambert, Nazneen Rajani, Kashif Rasul, Younes Belkada, Shengyi Huang, Leandro von Werra, Clémentine Fourrier, Nathan Habib, et al. 2023. Zephyr: Direct distillation of lm alignment. *arXiv preprint arXiv:2310.16944*.

Jenq-Haur Wang and Kuan-Ting Chen. 2021. Aggregating user-centric and post-centric sentiments from social media for topical stance prediction. In *Proceedings of the 33rd Conference on Computational Linguistics and Speech Processing (ROCLING 2021)*, pages 226–235.

Bowen Zhang, Xianghua Fu, Daijun Ding, Hu Huang, Yangyang Li, and Liwen Jing. 2023a. Investigating chain-of-thought with chatgpt for stance detection on social media. *arXiv preprint arXiv:2304.03087*.

Hong Zhang, Haewoon Kwak, Wei Gao, and Jisun An. 2023b. Wearing masks implies refuting trump?: Towards target-specific user stance prediction across events in covid-19 and us election 2020. In *Proceedings of the 15th ACM Web Science Conference 2023*, pages 23–32.

Zijian Zhou, Shuoyu Hu, Kai Yang, and Haizhou Wang. 2023. Tksp: Long-term stance prediction for social media users by fusing time series features and event dynamic evolution knowledge. In *International Conference on Knowledge Science, Engineering and Management*, pages 406–421. Springer.

Banghua Zhu, Evan Frick, Tianhao Wu, Hanlin Zhu, and Jiantao Jiao. 2023. Starling-7b: Improving llm helpfulness harmlessness with rlaif.

Lixing Zhu, Yulan He, and Deyu Zhou. 2020. Neural opinion dynamics model for the prediction of user-level stance dynamics. *Information Processing & Management*, 57(2):102031.

Qinglin Zhu, Bin Liang, Jingyi Sun, Jiachen Du, Lanjun Zhou, and Ruifeng Xu. 2022. Enhancing zero-shot stance detection via targeted background knowledge. In *Proceedings of the 45th international ACM SIGIR conference on research and development in information retrieval*, pages 2070–2075.

# A Appendix

## A.1 Prompt

### A.1.1 Prompt Type

We experimented with two main prompt types:

- **All stances**: One question: is the stance favor, against, or neutral?
- **Ask each stance**: One prompt asking if the post favors the stance target, one prompt asking if the post is against the stance target.

See Table 4 for the best performing result from each prompt type. We see that the single question outperforms the 'ask for each stance' method.

| | Prec | Rec | F1 |
|---|---|---|---|
| All stances | 0.42 | 0.61 | 0.45 |
| Ask each stance | 0.40 | 0.31 | 0.29 |

Table 4: Best performing results from each prompt type. See

### A.1.2 Final Prompt

We used the following prompt for our stance classifier, that we arrived at after manual experimentation. Any curly brackets demarked variables not preceded by a $ are templated for the parameter used in that example:

> Predict the stance of the comment towards {target_opinion}. Here is an explanation of what we mean by {target_opinion}: {target_explanation} If the comment is directly or indirectly in favor of {target_opinion}, or opposing

or critizing something opposed to {target_opinion}, then the stance should be favor. If the comment is directly or indirectly against {target_opinion}, or opposing or critizing something in favor of {target_opinion}, then the stance should be against. If the comment is discussing something irrelevant to {target_opinion}, or if it is unclear what the stance is, then the stance should be neutral.

Post: The post being commented on, may be useful in determining what the comment is discussing.
Parent Comment: The parent comment being replied to, may be useful in determining the context of the comment.
Comment: The comment to determine the opinion of.
Stance: The stance of the comment is ${favor, neutral, or against}

Post: {post}
Parent Comment: {parent_comment}
Comment: {comment}
Stance: The stance of the comment is

After additional experimentation, we used different wordings for the stance targets listed in the paper above to improve accuracy, and wrote out stance target descriptions. These alternate wordings and descriptions can be seen in the project GitHub repository github.com/bendavidsteel/user-stance-discovery. We used the same stance target descriptions for our annotators.

### A.2 User Stance Estimation

#### A.2.1 Training

We used the Pyro library [1] to build and train the probabilistic model, using the clipped Adam optimizer (Kingma and Ba, 2014) for 1000 epochs, with an initial learning rate of 0.1 decaying to 0.001 over the training run.

#### A.2.2 Experiments

We used a simple generative model of a user to generate synthetic data to test the user stance inference with. The model has a latent user stance $\mu$ (represented as a scalar between -1 and 1), and user stance variance $\sigma^2$ (the variance of of comment stances, to model consistency of stance), to parameterize a user stance distribution. We can then draw $N$ comments from this normal distribution, model classifying them with error via a categorical distribution defined by a specific precision and recall (to simulate a classifier with error), to produce the final synthetic data. We show the results from the experiments we did in Figure 3.

We can see that for this generative model, though the weighted mean method recovers the true generative model user stance mean most accurately, it fails to apportion probability mass well when there are fewer data points, or the precision/recall is lower, resulting in inaccurate variances. The inferred mean method can more accurately apportion probability mass, but systematically underestimates the true user stance for classifiers with lower recall and precision. This is because probability mass is placed more around 0, the centre of the user stance domain, to account for possible neutral posts, and there is no probability mass placed beyond 1 or -1, as that is the limit of our discrete comment stances. The normal distribution therefore correspondingly moves towards 0. This could be improved by modelling the user stance as a beta distribution, as the skew can accommodate for the possible neutral posts. However, in tests, we found it difficult to constrain the beta distribution to reasonable user stance distributions. More work is necessary here.

### A.3 Static User Opinions

We include in Fig. 4 a general overview of static user stances on the stance targets we cover in this work.

[1]https://github.com/pyro-ppl/pyro

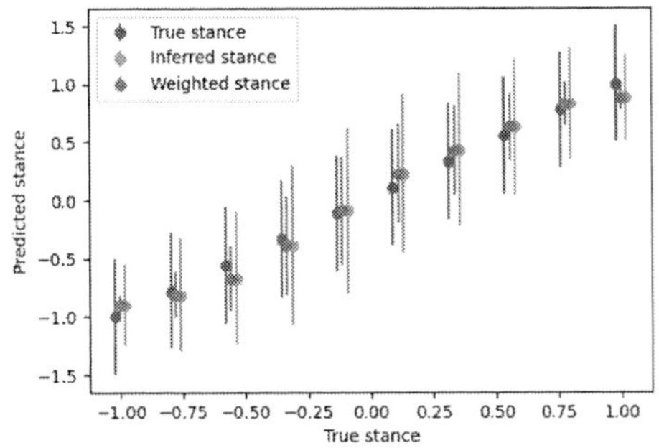


(a) Experiment with $N = 100$, $\sigma^2 = 0.5$, $Precision = 1.0$, and $Recall = 1.0$.

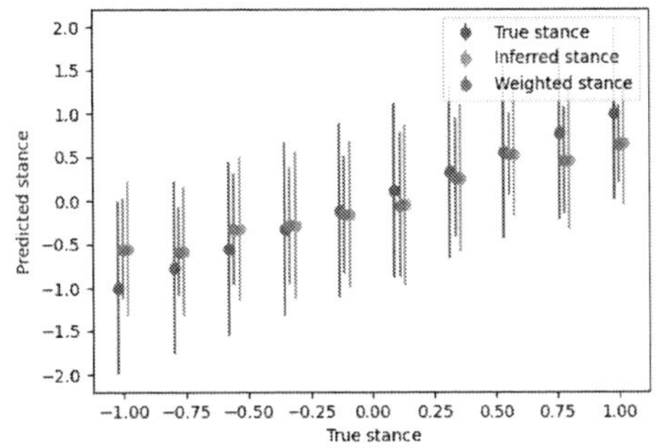


(b) Experiment with $N = 100$, $\sigma^2 = 1.0$, $Precision = 1.0$, and $Recall = 1.0$.

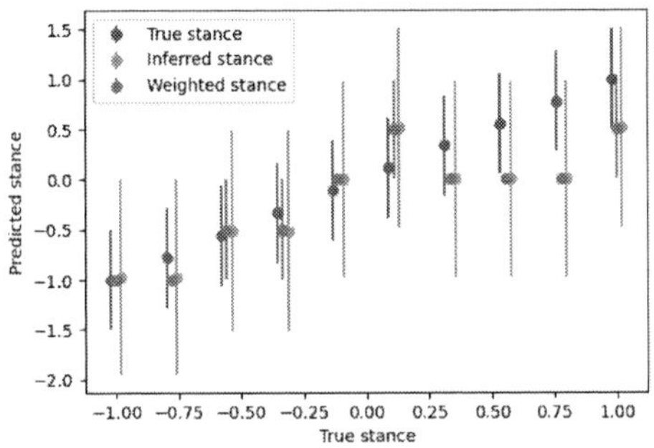


(c) Experiment with $N = 2$, $\sigma^2 = 0.5$, $Precision = 1.0$, and $Recall = 1.0$. Note that the weighted user stance method reports a variance of 0 due to the small number of data points all being in the same class, whereas the inference method reports a large variance, indicating there's still great uncertainty in the user stance.

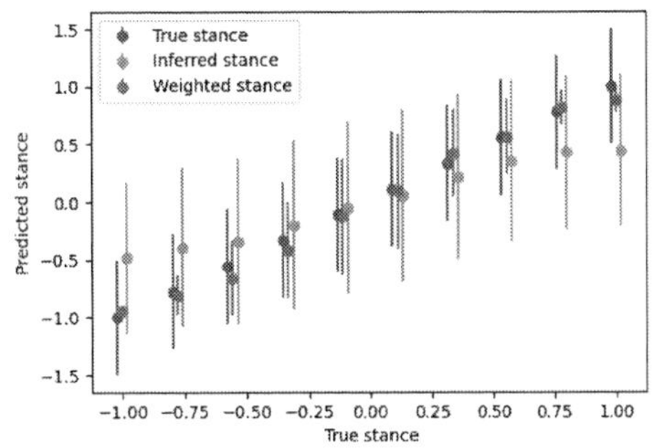


(d) Experiment with $N = 100$, $\sigma^2 = 0.5$, $Precision = 0.559$, and $Recall = 0.559$. Note that the inference method tends to systematically underestimate the true user stance, due to the high classifier error ensuring user stance probability mass is spread out.

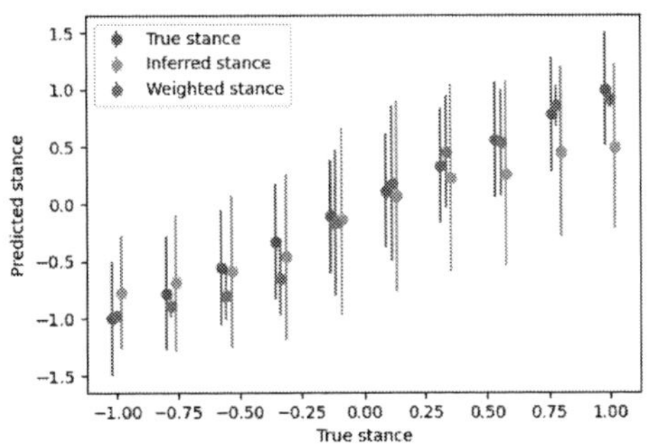


(e) Experiment with $N = 100$, $\sigma^2 = 0.5$, $Precision = 0.718$, and $Recall = 0.396$.

Figure 3: Results from validation of our weighted and inferred user stance methods in Section 3.3. For all experiments, we generate $N$ comments from 10 synthetic users with $\mu$ ranging from -1 to 1, and plot the predicted user stance against the true user stance. We vary the $\sigma^2$, $N$, precision and recall by experiment to test the methods in different situations.

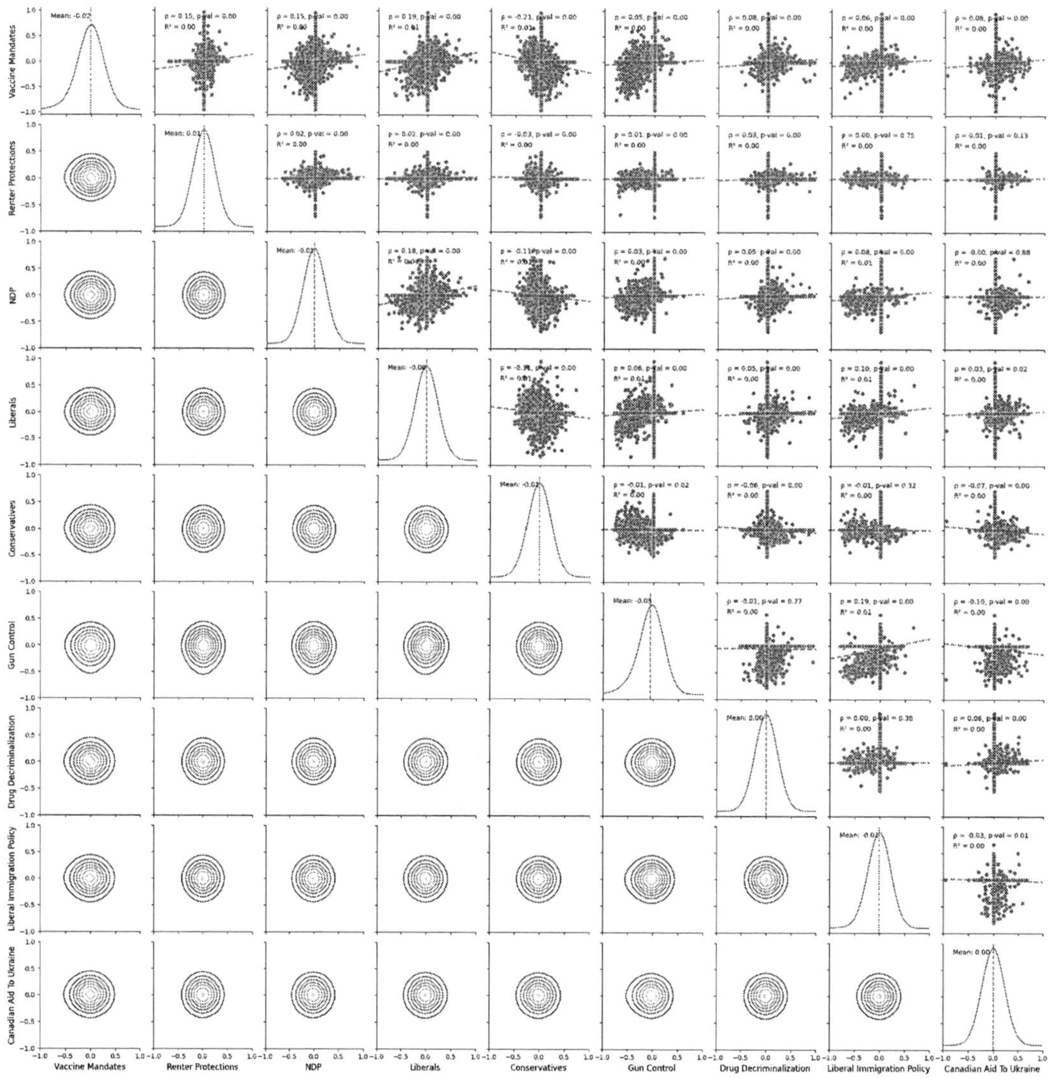


Figure 4: Plot exploring user stances for each stance target. The diagonal plot shows the inferred distribution of each stance target, determined by summing all of the normal distributions we determine through SVI. We include the mean of this distribution, as a dashed line. The below diagonal plots show the inferred distribution of paired stance dimensions, showing where users are likely to fit within a bi-dimensional stance space, determined by summing all inferred bivariate user stance normal distributions. The above diagonal plots show a scatter graph of user stances in each bivariate space, including a correlation determined by the weighted least squares method.

# Subjectivity Detection in English News using Large Language Models

**Mohammad Shokri**
Graduate Center
CUNY

**Vivek Sharma**
Graduate Center
CUNY

**Elena Filatova**
City Tech College
CUNY

**Shweta Jain**
John Jay College
CUNY

**Sarah Ita Levitan**
Hunter College
CUNY

## Abstract

Trust in media has reached a historical low as consumers increasingly doubt the credibility of the news they encounter. This growing skepticism is exacerbated by the prevalence of opinion-driven articles, which can influence readers' beliefs to align with the authors' viewpoints. In response to this trend, this study examines the expression of opinions in news by detecting subjective and objective language. We conduct an analysis of the subjectivity present in various news datasets and evaluate how different language models detect subjectivity and generalize to out-of-distribution data. We also investigate the use of in-context learning (ICL) within large language models (LLMs) and propose a straightforward prompting method that outperforms standard ICL and chain-of-thought (CoT) prompts.

## 1 Introduction

We live in a world dominated by information where we observe an unprecedented pace of news and opinion propagation. There is an increased demand for fact-checking, as inaccurate stories are disseminated constantly. Opinion pieces and news stories play an important role in shaping individuals' ideologies and beliefs. The rise of subjectivity in news reporting has become increasingly evident in recent years, particularly in online publications (Blake et al., 2019). In addition, fake news and misleading articles often rely heavily on subjective language Jeronimo et al. (2019).

According to estimates, only 41% of publishers categorize their articles by type (e.g., editorial, review, analysis), and among those that do, there is a lack of consistency (Harris, 2017). Opinions are usually conveyed through subjective language and detecting such language accurately is crucial for effective fact-checking. Subjective language includes utterances that communicate emotions, opinions, and beliefs. In addition, many NLP fields (e.g., sentiment analysis) benefit from successfully detecting subjectivity in text.

| Subj. Score | Example Sentence |
|---|---|
| 0.93 | No punishment could ever be enough for him. |
| 0.55 | While what happened to Arthur is rare, the NPSCC has raised concerns about the risks to children during lockdown. |
| 0.45 | But while countries from Latin America to Europe are now ordering batches of Sputnik, the rollout in Russia itself has been slow, as people prove deeply reluctant to be injected. |
| 0.04 | Jones was found guilty of fatally shooting Mr. Howell, as insurance executive, during a 1999 carjacking on his driveway. |

Table 1: Examples of sentences from News-2 with their subjectivity levels: higher subjectivity scores correspond to higher subjectivity level within text.

Most studies focus on identifying subjectivity within three scopes: Document-level, sentence-level, and aspect-level. While document-level and sentence-level tasks differ in the length of their textual input, aspect-based subjectivity analysis aims to identify opinions toward specific aspects in a particular sequence. In this study, we focus on detecting subjective clues in text within sentences. This aligns perfectly with our broader goal of analyzing news articles to identify potential techniques for manipulating readers' interpretations of reported events.

One of the main challenges for learning subjective language arises from the nature of the task. Subjectivity exists on a spectrum, where sentences at the extreme ends are easier to categorize, but as you move towards the center, it becomes increasingly challenging and reliant on personal interpretation to assign a single label due to the nuanced blend of perspectives (see Table 1). In most existing datasets, finding the ground truth on sentence subjectivity is done via majority voting among a group of annotators. However, this could lead to extremely noisy labels due to the low inter-



*Proceedings of the 14th Workshop on Computational Approaches to Subjectivity, Sentiment, & Social Media Analysis*, pages 215–226
August 15, 2024 ©2024 Association for Computational Linguistics

annotator agreement (Davani et al., 2022). Humans often disagree in their assessment of controversial topics due to a variety of reasons such as socio-demographic factors, political stance, environment, and culture (Luo et al., 2020).

Despite language models' strong performance on various benchmarks, they still lack human-level performance in semantics-related tasks. While fine-tuning a language model on a specific dataset/task could lead to a higher score for that particular dataset/task, it often does not generalize well outside of the training distribution.

Online news articles exhibit a range of writing styles, word choices, and sentence structures. This diversity creates a challenge for model robustness. As large pre-trained language models are trained on huge data collections from a wide range of text distributions, they perform relatively robustly when confronted with different datasets, making them a useful tool for our problem. In this work, we investigate how three different language models detect subjectivity in the news domain and where they fail. Our main research questions are:

**RQ1**. To what extent does fine-tuning a language model like BERT generalize to out-of-distribution data from the news domain?
**RQ2**. How well do pre-trained state-of-the-art large language models such as GPT-3.5, GPT-4, and Gemini detect subjectivity in news?
**RQ3**. How can we improve LLM performance using different prompting methods?

This work contributes empirical studies and insights about the efficacy of language models in detecting subjectivity in news and addressing generalization challenges. We propose and evaluate prompting methods to enhance the performance of LLMs at detecting subjectivity in news.

## 2 Related Work

**Subjectivity Analysis.** Various methodologies have been explored for subjectivity analysis. Early work on fine-grained subjectivity detection focused on developing subjectivity lexicons and developing hand-crafted rules to learn subjectivity clues and opinion-bearing terms in sentences (Yu and Hatzivassiloglou, 2003; Gordon et al., 2003; Riloff et al., 2005; Riloff and Wiebe, 2003; Kim and Hovy, 2005). These methods, while simple, often struggle with nuanced expressions and lack generalizability. As machine learning techniques matured, SVMs, Naive Bayes classifiers, and decision tree classifiers emerged as prominent choices. These models leverage features like n-grams, Part-of-speech tags, and syntactic structures for classification, demonstrating improved performance and flexibility (Harb et al., 2008; Goldberg and Zhu, 2006; Zhang et al., 2007). With the advent of deep learning, RNNs and LSTMs gained significant attention due to their capability to capture intricate contextual dependencies in textual data (Irsoy and Cardie, 2014). However, recent advancements in language models and transfer learning reshaped the field. Transfer learning, in particular, allows pre-training models on massive corpora to learn a general representation of words and expressions. Followed by fine-tuning, models can outperform all the previous feature-based and lexicon-based techniques.

**In-Context Learning.** In-context learning refers to a situation where a frozen language model performs a task by only conditioning on the prompt task. A study by McCann et al. (2018) is a foundational framework for the concept of in-context learning, where multiple NLP tasks are treated as a unified question-answering problem. In addition, the first GPT paper (Radford et al., 2018) paved the way with some tentative prompt-based experiments with the model. However, it was not until GPT-3 (Brown et al., 2020) that the full potential of in-context learning was realized. The seminal GPT-3 paper demonstrates the unprecedented capability of large-scale language models to perform various NLP tasks with minimal task-specific fine-tuning, relying solely on the context provided in the prompt. With the scaling of the model size and data size, large language models demonstrate in-context learning (Dong et al., 2022; Chowdhery et al., 2023). As in-context learning provides interpretable ways for communicating with LLMs, its performance is sensitive to many factors in the prompt, such as the order of examples, length of the examples, and the semantic similarity of the examples to the test set. (Dong et al., 2022; Wang et al., 2023; Zhao et al., 2021; Min et al., 2022). This work evaluates LLMs for subjectivity detection and explores prompting methods for improving generalizability.

## 3 Datasets

We use multiple datasets to ensure the generalizability of our approach outside of the training domain: MPQA, a classic dataset in the subjectivity domain Wiebe et al. (2005) and two recently introduced datasets consisting of subjective sentences in the news domain. One of the news datasets (News-1) is focused on political news (Antici et al., 2023); the second dataset (News-2) is focused on crime and COVID-19 Savinova and Del Prado (2023). This diversity in news topics provides a distribution shift within the news domain in our experiments.

**MPQA.** The MPQA (Multi-Perspective Question Answering) dataset Wiebe et al. (2005) is a significant dataset in sentiment analysis and opinion mining research. This dataset is designed to address the multifaceted nature of subjective language and offers a diverse collection of text segments annotated with sentiment polarity and subjectivity information. It comprises a variety of sources, including news articles, product reviews, discussion forums, and social media posts, and reflects the varied contexts in which subjective expressions manifest. To exclude variability across text genres, we only include the MPQA sentences from news articles in our experiments. We work with MPQA opinion corpus version three. After preprocessing steps and removing sentences with less than 5 words, we are left with 1,707 sentences, 954 subjective and 753 objective.

**News-1.** We use a recently introduced News dataset (Antici et al., 2023), a collection of subjective and objective sentences extracted from 8 different online political news outlets. This dataset focuses on controversial political topics such as civil rights, politics, law, and economics. We refer to this dataset as "News-1". It consists of 1049 sentences extracted from 23 news articles, out of which 638 are labeled objective and 411 are labeled subjective.

**News-2.** Our third dataset is collected by Savinova and Del Prado (2023). This dataset contains sentences from news articles and Facebook posts about "crime" and "COVID-19" published by four major UK news sources with a total size of 7,751 sentences. We filter out the Facebook posts since they are shorter and possibly not written by journalists. Hence, all our experiments throughout the paper are carried out using only news sentences with a total count of 2,973 sentences containing 1013 subjective sentences and 1960 objective sentences. An important characteristic of this dataset is that its labels are continuous numbers in the range $[0, 1]$, with 1 being the most subjective and 0 being the most objective. The annotators are instructed to evaluate the sentence subjectivity on a 7-point scale, and they set the mean as the final label. A portion of the dataset is manually labeled and the rest is labeled with the model trained on the manually-labeled set. We refer to this dataset as "News-2" in the rest of this paper. Several examples from the News-2 dataset are presented in Table 1.

## 4 Methods

### 4.1 Lexical Features

We first examine the linguistic features that are traditionally used for distinguishing subjective language from objective language. We select lexical features helpful to distinguish the subjective language in news articles from mere news reporting (Krüger et al., 2017) and add 9 lexical richness features (McCarthy and Jarvis, 2007) to form our linguistic features set for this study. The features from Krüger et al. (2017)'s study are claimed to be robust against change in topic and domain and we explore their effectiveness in this our study. We train a logistic regression model with these features to establish our baseline.

### 4.2 Fine-tuning

First, we study how fine-tuning a language model like BERT helps generalize to out-of-distribution data from the news domain. We fine-tune several popular language models to asses the adaptability of each for our datasets (Section 5.2). A problem often associated with fine-tuning is over-fitting: the model adapts to the training dataset and cannot generalize to out-of-distribution data. However, as the goal of our study is to design a system that can be used in real-time, it is expected to run on data from different distributions than the training data distribution. Hence, we analyze how well a model trained on each dataset generalizes to the other two datasets. We fine-tune a model on each of our datasets and test on the remaining pair as out-of-distribution data (OOD).

### 4.3 Re-formulating the task

Next, we examine the effect of re-formulating the problem as an entailment task (Section 5.3). As demonstrated by Wang et al. (2021), language models become better few-shot learners as they benefit from transforming the classification problem into a language entailment task. Therefore, we transformed the problem into a language entailment problem. We convert the sentences in all three of our datasets into pairs of hypotheses and premises and use a RoBERTa-large model for entailment classification. The RoBERTa model is already trained on the MNLI dataset (Williams et al., 2017), so it has learned whether a sentence (hypothesis) entails another sentence (premise). We additionally train it on a small set of the MPQA dataset which has high-quality labels to teach the model the specifics of our task.

### 4.4 In-Context Learning

In-context learning has become an increasingly popular paradigm for adapting large language models to different tasks (Brown et al., 2020; Kojima et al., 2022). To answer how well the pre-trained state-of-the-art large language models such as GPT-3.5, GPT-4, and Gemini detect subjectivity in the news domain, we examine three large pre-trained language models in both zero-shot and few-shot settings and study how different prompting strategies affect in-context learning performance. We work with Google's Gemini (Team et al., 2023), GPT-3.5-turbo (Brown et al., 2020), and GPT-4 (Bubeck et al., 2023). We access Gemini through Vertex AI API, GPT models through Openai API, and the RoBERTa model through Hugging Face Hub. As few-shot examples in the prompt teach the model the nuances of the task, models demonstrate high sensitivity to the training examples in the prompt. Mitigating this issue requires manual inspection for high-quality relevant examples. Hence, we address research question 3: how could we improve LLM performance using different prompting methods? We examine more general prompting strategies to explain the task and reasoning process to the model without relying on hand-picked examples.

## 5 Experiments

### 5.1 Baseline

As our baseline, we use a logistic regression model with 36 linguistic features. We train a logistic regression separately on each dataset and test it on the remaining two datasets. Table 2 presents macro average scores for the logistic regression model across the three datasets. We compute scores for (1) training and testing within the dataset; and (2) using one of the datasets for training and the other two datasets for testing. The Logistic Regression model trained on the MPQA dataset yields the highest score on out-of-distribution data (OOD), exhibiting the highest out-of-distribution generalization. Although the logistic regression model does not achieve high scores, it provides a great deal of interpretability and one can easily figure out what features contributed to the model's predictions. This could be done by analyzing the largest coefficients of the model or by using SHAP values (Lundberg and Lee, 2017) to explain every prediction and quantify the feature contributions.

| **Result for Dataset** | **Logistic Regression (Baseline)** | | |
|---|---|---|---|
| | trained on MPQA | trained on News-1 | trained on News-2 |
| MPQA | 0.54 | 0.30 | 0.34 |
| News-1 | 0.50 | 0.39 | 0.44 |
| News-2 | 0.42 | 0.48 | 0.65 |
| OOD Avg | **0.46** | 0.39 | 0.39 |
| | **BERT FT** | | |
| MPQA | 0.86 | 0.38 | 0.53 |
| News-1 | 0.62 | 0.79 | 0.65 |
| News-2 | 0.66 | 0.65 | 0.90 |
| OOD Avg | **0.64** | 0.51 | 0.59 |

Table 2: Classification results for the baseline (Logistic Regression) and BERT FT. For each column, OOD avg is the average of the two rows corresponding to out-of-distribution data.

### 5.2 Fine-Tuning

We fine-tune several pre-trained language models: BERT (Devlin et al., 2018), RoBERTa (Liu et al., 2019), and Llama-2 (Touvron et al., 2023) on each dataset separately to compare performance with zero-shot and few-shot learners. We tune the hyperparameters for each model using grid search and save the best model based on the validation set evaluation. As expected, fine-tuning achieves high F-1 scores for every dataset as the model fully adapts to the training dataset. These results are presented in Table 3. In addition, we run the best model for each dataset on the two other datasets to measure its OOD generalization. Although fine-tuning achieves high F-1 scores for every dataset, its performance drops significantly when tested on OOD data points. Therefore, with the current size and state of available datasets, fine-tuning does not offer a robust solution for classifying subjectivity. Table 2 shows that BERT trained on either of the news datasets has OOD generalization power comparable to the logistic regression model trained on MPQA.

### 5.3 Reformulating as Entailment

We use the RoBERTa-Large model trained on the MNLI dataset from the Hugging Face Hub. The

| Dataset | Baseline | BERT | Llama-2 | RoBERTa-L |
|---|---|---|---|---|
| MPQA | 0.54 | 0.86 | 0.77 | 0.82 |
| News-1 | 0.65 | 0.79 | 0.72 | 0.76 |
| News-2 | 0.39 | 0.90 | 0.69 | 0.87 |

Table 3: Fine-tuned models on each dataset. Baseline is a logistic regression model trained on lexical and syntactic features.

model has learned to classify a hypothesis sentence as entailing, contradicting, or neutral towards a premise sentence. We train the model on 20 sentences from the MPQA dataset to further adapt it for the task. For every sentence $S_1$ in the datasets, we add a premise sentence, $S_2$ = *"This sentence is Subjective"*. Every *entail* label is translated to subjective, and every *contradict* label is translated to objective. We feed the model $< S_1, S_2 >$ pairs from each dataset. The results are shown in Table 4.

| Dataset | Models | |
|---|---|---|
| | RoBERTa MNLI* | RoBERTa MNLI trained on MPQA |
| MPQA | 0.43 | 0.86 |
| News-1 | 0.38 | 0.66 |
| News-2 | 0.36 | 0.72 |

Table 4: RoBERTa-MNLI* model has been fine-tuned on 20 examples from MPQA dataset to learn the structure of the task, outputting only 'entail' or 'not entail' without considering 'neutral' for any sentence.

After training on the MPQA dataset, the RoBERTa model performs well on the News-1 and News-2 datasets. Its out-of-distribution (OOD) generalization outperforms the best BERT model fine-tuned on MPQA from Section 5.2 and the logistic regression models' OOD generalization. However, to evaluate its capabilities in a zero-shot setting, we train the model on 20 sentences from the MPQA dataset to further teach it our task. When tested on new data, it does not perform well.

### 5.4 Zero-Shot Inference

In this section, we describe our experiments with four large language models. In the Zero-shot setting, we prompt the language models to assess the subjectivity of the test sentences without giving them any examples (see Table 9). We use a temperature value of 0 for all our experiments with all three models. We also test the RoBERTa-MNLI model in the zero-shot setting, as explained above in Section 4.3.

As displayed in Table 5, the three large language

| Dataset | Zero-Shot Models | | | |
|---|---|---|---|---|
| | GPT-3.5 | GPT-4 | Gemini | RoBERTa MNLI |
| MPQA | 0.68 | **0.77** | 0.62 | - |
| News-1 | 0.68 | 0.62 | **0.71** | 0.38 |
| News-2 | **0.78** | 0.74 | 0.73 | 0.36 |
| **Average** | 0.71 | 0.71 | 0.69 | 0.39 |

Table 5: LLM's macro f1 score in zero-shot setting on each dataset. As RoBERTa-MNLI is fine-tuned on 20 sentences from MPQA, its score on MPQA test set is not considered under a Zero-shot test setting.

models vary in their performance across different datasets, but on average across all datasets, GPT-3.5 and GPT-4 score slightly higher than Gemini. Further, compared to the previous sections, the models show more robust performance across all datasets, reducing the gap between best and worst scores.

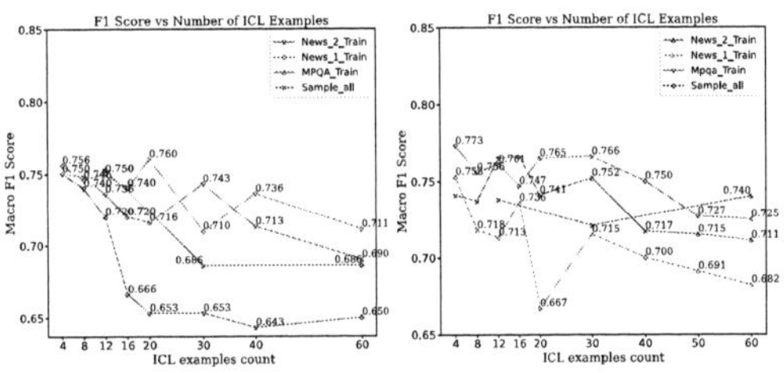


Figure 1: The left graph presents the scores with random seed set to 42; the right graph presents the scores with random seed set to 100.

### 5.5 Few-Shot In Context Learning

In Section 5.4, we showed that LLMs perform well and robustly in zero-shot settings without seeing any examples from the target text distribution. To answer RQ3, we investigate whether different sampling strategies for in-context learning examples can increase performance. We experiment with varying factors in the prompts and evaluate the impact of each factor on performance. The variants include the number of ICL examples in the prompt, the random seed for sampling sentences from the data, the subjective-to-objective ratio in ICL examples in the prompt, and the dataset from which we draw the ICL examples to account for in-distribution and OOD sentences. In Table 6, we report the average macro F1 scores over five experiments for each set of variants.

**Count of ICL Examples.** The first factor we study is the count of example sentences in the prompt. As previously proven in supervised machine learning, more labeled data could lead to better performance. However, this does not seem to be true with ICL examples (Min et al., 2022). We use a fixed random seed for sampling sentences from our datasets. We test the model with prompts containing {4, 8, 12, 16, 20, 30, 40, 50, 60} ICL examples. For each test, we add new sentences to the previously existing ones; for example, the 8-ICL examples prompt adds 4 new sentences to the 4-ICL examples prompt, and so on. Similar to Min et al. (2022)'s findings, we do not see any clear increasing trend in performance with a higher number of examples (Figure 1). Moreover, the best performance is achieved with fewer than 20 labeled examples. Figure 1 shows that the choice of random seed can substantially affect performance.

**Input Data Distribution.** An intuitive assumption is that using in-distribution-data in the prompt should help the model conditioning on the input reach better performance. However, unlike to Min et al. (2022), we observe that in many cases, sampling from OOD data outperforms a prompt with in-distribution training examples. This finding aligns with the rest of their findings, in that the model learns more information about the task and the input-output structure than the data itself. In addition, their work shows that assigning random labels to input sentences does not hurt performance, suggesting that the model does not learn substantial information about the data. Furthermore, we observe that sampling equally from all three datasets performs competitively in $k = 12$ ICL examples, however, we can not hypothesize more generally due to the limited number of experiments.

**Subjective to Objective Ratio.** To learn the effect of the majority labels on the performance, we set up several experiments where we changed the subjective-objective ratio in ICL examples. Unlike (Zhao et al., 2021) we do not observe a strong correlation between majority labels and the model's predictions. As shown in Figure 2, two out of three of our experiments suggest that increasing the subjective-objective ratio in training examples marginally hurts the performance.

### 5.6 Chain of Thought Prompting

Due to the instability and unpredictability of standard few-shot in context learning, we switch to *Chain of Thought* prompting (Wei et al., 2022) expecting higher performance and stability. Standard few-shot prompting has shown promising results in many tasks, except for the tasks that require reason-

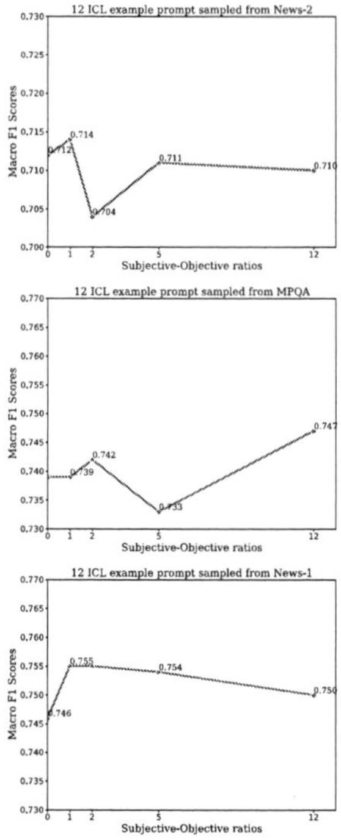


Figure 2: Changing the ratio of subjective to objective sentences in the 12-example prompt.

ing. With Chain of Thought (CoT) prompting, we break down the task into smaller steps, which the model is more likely to solve, hence teaching the model to reason about the task the same as how humans do. This method requires manual task-aware examples curated by experts in the prompt. However, it has been demonstrated Kojima et al. (2022) that one can bypass that step and require the model to think step by step and achieve competitive results with standard CoT prompts. This approach, called *Zero-shot Chain of Thought*, is task-agnostic and comparatively simple to implement. We extend this method by adding instructions for classifying our sentences in Figure 3. We do not provide any examples for the model but explain a general framework for classifying sentences as subjective or objective based on the annotation scheme done by Wiebe et al. (2005). We refer to this prompting method by *ZCoT-Inst* in the rest of this paper. Table 6 depicts our results for each prompting strategy. In all three models, ZCoT-Inst leads to best average performance across all datasets. We also observed that the biggest gain of standard CoT prompting happens for the MPQA dataset, which might be due to the reason that our chain of thought instructions aligns well with MPQA's annotation procedure.

a)

```
Classify the following sentence into subjective or objective.
Sentence: {}

Answer:
```

b)

```
Classify the following sentence into subjective or objective.

Sentence: {}

Answer: Let's think step by step!

First, find phrases that express opinions, personal views, or emotions.
Second, find how intensely each phrase expresses opinions, personal views,
or emotions.
Third, if there is one or more such phrases with an intensity medium or
higher, classify the sentence as subjective.
```

Figure 3: (a) Zero-Shot prompt (b) Zero-Shot CoT prompt with manual instructions.

The results in Table 6 indicate that the Chain of Thought prompting does not work well on GPT-3.5 as it scores higher with standard zero-shot prompts (see Table 5. This could be because reasoning abilities increase with model size. Comparing Table 5 and Table 6 shows that even though the highest score for News-1 and News-2 is achieved with zero-shot prompting, the highest score for MPQA is achieved with GPT-4 with ZCoT-Inst prompt. The highest average score across all three datasets is achieved by GPT-4 with ZCot-Inst prompt, which gains a 2.3% increase compared to the Zero-shot setting. This demonstrates the efficacy of our method and effectively addresses RQ3.

### 5.7 Ensemble Model

Next, we explore an ensemble of our three large language models. We feed every sentence to each of our models while prompting them to just output the final label. For each sentence, we get three predictions by the models and we use the majority vote as the final verdict. We test the ensemble model in a Zero-shot setting(all three models are given the same zero-shot prompt) and with a CoT prompt(all three models are given the same CoT prompt). In addition, we also run an ensemble model of the three prompting strategies (Zero-shot, ZCoT-Inst, and Zero-shot CoT) and we refer to it by all-prompts. All-prompts setting is an ensemble of 9 different predictions (3 prompt settings for each model) and we use the majority vote as the final verdict. Table 7 summarizes the results. The ensemble model with a Zero-shot prompt achieves the highest scores on News-1 and News-2 datasets among all the non-fine-tuned models in our experiments. The All-prompts setting achieves the highest average score of all our experiments. However, it is less practical than the other settings because it captures each model's predictions under three different prompting settings.

| Dataset | Prompting Methods | | |
|---|---|---|---|
| | Zero-Shot CoT | ZCoT-Inst | Standard CoT |
| MPQA | 0.70 | 0.69 | **0.76** |
| News-1 | 0.65 | **0.67** | 0.59 |
| News-2 | **0.73** | **0.73** | 0.68 |
| **Average** | 0.693 | **0.696** | 0.676 |

(a) GPT-3.5 average macro F-1 scores over 3 runs.

| Dataset | Prompting Methods | | |
|---|---|---|---|
| | Zero-Shot CoT | ZCoT-Inst | Standard CoT |
| MPQA | 0.76 | **0.80** | 0.75 |
| News-1 | 0.66 | **0.67** | 0.55 |
| News-2 | **0.77** | 0.73 | 0.66 |
| **Average** | 0.73 | **0.733** | 0.653 |

(b) GPT-4 average macro F-1 scores over 3 runs.

| Dataset | Prompting Methods | | |
|---|---|---|---|
| | Zero-Shot CoT | ZCoT-Inst | Standard CoT |
| MPQA | 0.67 | 0.73 | **0.76** |
| News-1 | 0.69 | **0.72** | 0.60 |
| News-2 | 0.73 | **0.74** | 0.70 |
| **Average** | 0.696 | **0.73** | 0.686 |

(c) Gemini average macro F-1 scores over 3 runs.

Table 6: Comparison of (a) GPT-3.5 and (b) GPT-4 and (c) Gemini average macro F-1 scores on different datasets.

| Dataset | Ensemble Model | | | |
|---|---|---|---|---|
| | Zero-Shot | Zero-Shot CoT | ZCoT-Inst | All-prompts |
| MPQA | 0.70 | 0.75 | 0.75 | **0.76** |
| News-2 | **0.80** | 0.75 | 0.76 | 0.78 |
| News-1 | **0.72** | 0.67 | **0.72** | 0.70 |
| **Average** | 0.74 | 0.723 | 0.743 | **0.746** |

Table 7: Ensemble model performance on three datasets.

## 6 Error Analysis

In this section, we analyze false negatives and false positives predicted by the best model from the previous section. As discussed in Section 5.6, *ZCoT-Inst* outperforms all the other prompting techniques across all models. Therefore, the analysis in this section is with regard to the models' prediction in that setting. We look at the predictions by the models for test sets in each dataset. There are 220 sentences in the MPQA test set, 219 sentences in the News-1 test set, and 298 sentences in the News-2 test set.

Table 8 summarizes the classification results of the models on each of our datasets. GPT-4 gener-

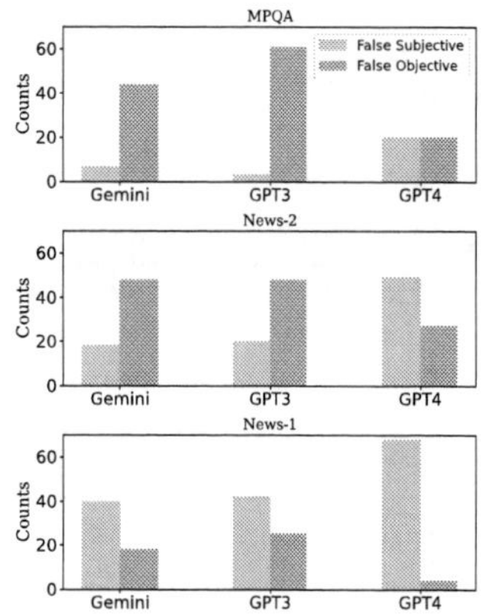


Figure 4: False objective and false subjective prediction counts by each model.

| Model | MPQA | | News-1 | | News-2 | |
|---|---|---|---|---|---|---|
| | Subjective | Objective | Subjective | Objective | Subjective | Objective |
| | P / R | P / R | P / R | P / R | P / R | P / R |
| **GPT-3.5** | 0.94 / 0.50 | 0.60 / 0.94 | 0.67 / 0.77 | 0.72 / 0.59 | 0.74 / 0.53 | 0.78 / 0.90 |
| **GPT-4** | 0.83 / 0.84 | 0.79 / 0.77 | 0.62 / 0.96 | 0.90 / 0.36 | 0.61 / 0.74 | 0.84 / 0.74 |
| **Gemini** | 0.93 / 0.51 | 0.60 / 0.94 | 0.70 / 0.83 | 0.78 / 0.60 | 0.76 / 0.54 | 0.78 / 0.91 |

Table 8: Precision (P) and Recall (R) for Different models and datasets.

ally has a higher recall for subjective class compared to the other models. Gemini and GPT-3.5 exhibit similar behavior across all three datasets with generally higher precision and lower recall in subjective class compared to GPT-4. These differences might justify the advantage of the ensemble model as compared to the individual models. Figure 4 demonstrates the counts of false subjective (sentences annotated as '*objective*'), and false objective (sentences annotated as '*subjective*'), instances across each model within every dataset.

**Sentiment.** We analyze the misclassified sentences and assess positive and negative sentiment patterns across datasets using the RoBERTa-based sentiment analysis model trained on tweets (Loureiro et al., 2022). We aim to inspect if the models struggle with sentences carrying strong sentiments (positive or negative), which intuitively should be easier to identify. First, we run the sentiment analysis model on every sentence in all three of our datasets, to understand their sentiment distribution. Figure 5 summarizes the information. In general, subjective sentences in all three datasets, range from high positive to high negative sentiment with more than half of the instances carrying neutral or negative sentiment. This is the case for objective sentences in both News-1 and News-2 datasets, whereas MPQA's objective sentences mostly contain neutral sentences which could speak for the distribution shift among the datasets.

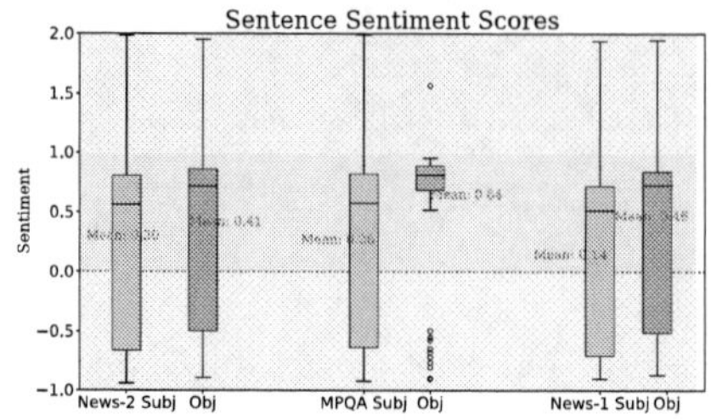


Figure 5: Sentiment scores across subjective and objective sentences in each dataset. [-1,0) in the y axis represents negative sentiment, [0-1] represents neutral sentiment, and(1,2] represents positive sentiment.

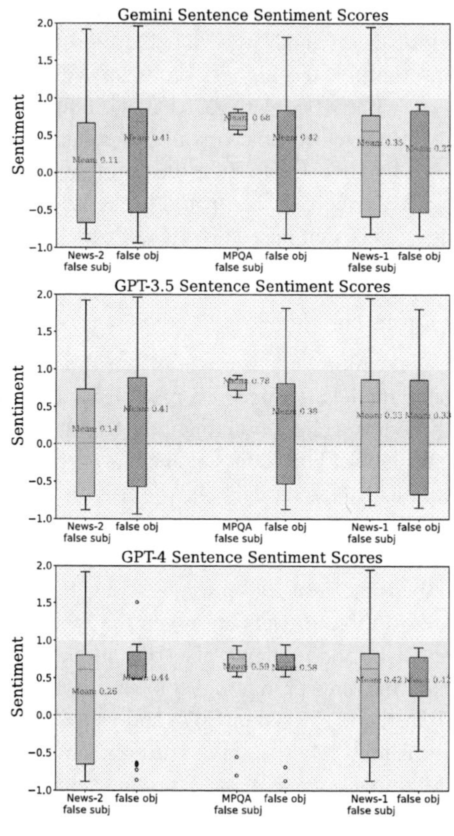


Figure 6: Different models sentiment score across false subjective and false objective sets.

Next, we proceed to examine the sentiment scores of false subjective and false objective sentences predicted by all three models. Similar to the previous analyses for general classification reports of the models, Gemini and GPT-3.5 exhibit very

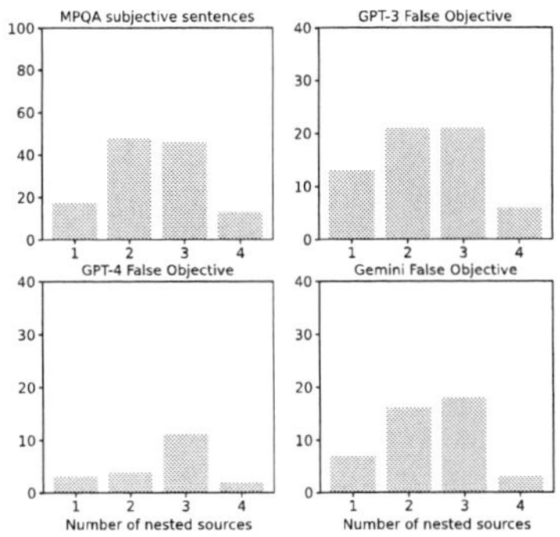


Figure 7: False objective instances in each model versus subjective sentences in MPQA dataset.co

similar behavior in their false predictions across all three datasets. Their false predictions only slightly differ in mean sentiment scores, whereas GPT-4's false predictions tend to have higher mean sentiment scores across all datasets. GPT-4's false subjective set seems to be shifted more towards neutral sentiment as its having higher scores for mean and median. However, GPT-4's false objective prediction sets are quite different than other models in terms of sentiment. In contrast to Gemini and GPT-3.5, it is noticeable that for all three datasets, GPT-4's false objective predictions mainly lay in the neutral zone of the sentiment graph. This might signal that a model can detect easier subjective signs, such as high-sentiment words, and fails to detect subjectivity in neutral sentences. Another reason could be due to the inductive bias of the prompt (Figure 3) that relies on the sentiment of extracted subjective terms.

**Opinion Holders.** According to our initial examination of false objective sentences, none of the instances have obvious, significant clues of subjectivity. Therefore, classifying these sentences correctly requires identifying nested opinion holders in them. We examine the misclassified sentences of each model on the MPQA dataset, as MPQA has fine-grained annotations for subjective terms and their nested sources (opinion holders) in every sentence. The source of a subjective frame is defined as the person or entity that is expressing the opinion. Consider the following example from Wiebe et al. (2005) work on annotating subjective texts:

> "China criticized the U.S. report's criticism of China's human rights record."

In the sentence above, the U.S. report's criticism is the target of China's criticism. Thus, the nested source for *criticism* is <writer, China, U.S. report>, as writer of the text is a default source of subjectivity in all written texts. Hence, the sentence above has 4 nested sources. Figure 7 summarizes our findings: both Gemini and GPT-3 fail in adhering to the original distribution of nested opinion holders. However, GPT-4 diverges from this trend, primarily failing in statements containing three nested opinion holders.

## 7 Conclusion

In this work, we investigate how language models learn and classify subjective language across three different datasets from the news domains. We examine how well different models generalize to out-of-distribution data. In addition, we analyze how LLMs detect subjective language with different prompts. Based on our experiments, we conclude that the standard in-context learning does not guarantee robust classification as it introduces a great deal of sensitivity to the examples provided in the prompt. In future work, we plan to investigate how different prompting techniques, such as explaining how to detect potentially subjective terms and analyzing sentiment intensity, can lead to better, more robust performance across different datasets.

## Limitations

There are several algorithms for domain adaptation when the source and target data distributions are known, such as sample re-weighting. There also exist algorithms for cases when the target distribution is unknown, usually referred to as domain-generalization. In our study we mainly focused on fine-tuning and did not explore domain generalization algorithms for our smaller models.

## Acknowledgement

We would like to express our sincere gratitude to the Rosen Center for Advanced Computing(RCAC), Purdue University Laboratory for the computational resources, Anvil. Their lab was supported by the National Science Foundation (NSF) under grant [2005632]. This work was supported by an unrestricted gift from Google through the Google CyberNYC Initiative.

## References


Francesco Antici, Andrea Galassi, Federico Ruggeri, Katerina Korre, Arianna Muti, Alessandra Bardi, Alice Fedotova, and Alberto Barrón-Cedeño. 2023. A corpus for sentence-level subjectivity detection on english news articles. *arXiv preprint arXiv:2305.18034*.

Jonathan S Blake et al. 2019. *News in a digital age: Comparing the presentation of news information over time and across media platforms*. Rand Corporation.

Tom Brown, Benjamin Mann, Nick Ryder, Melanie Subbiah, Jared D Kaplan, Prafulla Dhariwal, Arvind Neelakantan, Pranav Shyam, Girish Sastry, Amanda Askell, et al. 2020. Language models are few-shot learners. *Advances in neural information processing systems*, 33:1877–1901.

Sébastien Bubeck, Varun Chandrasekaran, Ronen Eldan, Johannes Gehrke, Eric Horvitz, Ece Kamar, Peter Lee, Yin Tat Lee, Yuanzhi Li, Scott Lundberg, et al. 2023. Sparks of artificial general intelligence: Early experiments with gpt-4. *arXiv preprint arXiv:2303.12712*.

Aakanksha Chowdhery, Sharan Narang, Jacob Devlin, Maarten Bosma, Gaurav Mishra, Adam Roberts, Paul Barham, Hyung Won Chung, Charles Sutton, Sebastian Gehrmann, et al. 2023. Palm: Scaling language modeling with pathways. *Journal of Machine Learning Research*, 24(240):1–113.

Aida Mostafazadeh Davani, Mark Díaz, and Vinodkumar Prabhakaran. 2022. Dealing with disagreements: Looking beyond the majority vote in subjective annotations. *Transactions of the Association for Computational Linguistics*, 10:92–110.

Jacob Devlin, Ming-Wei Chang, Kenton Lee, and Kristina Toutanova. 2018. Bert: Pre-training of deep bidirectional transformers for language understanding. *arXiv preprint arXiv:1810.04805*.

Qingxiu Dong, Lei Li, Damai Dai, Ce Zheng, Zhiyong Wu, Baobao Chang, Xu Sun, Jingjing Xu, and Zhifang Sui. 2022. A survey on in-context learning. *arXiv preprint arXiv:2301.00234*.

Andrew B Goldberg and Xiaojin Zhu. 2006. Seeing stars when there aren't many stars: Graph-based semi-supervised learning for sentiment categorization. In *Proceedings of TextGraphs: The first workshop on graph based methods for natural language processing*, pages 45–52.

Andrew Gordon, Abe Kazemzadeh, Anish Nair, and Milena Petrova. 2003. Recognizing expressions of commonsense psychology in english text. In *Proceedings of the 41st annual meeting of the association for computational linguistics*, pages 208–215.

Ali Harb, Michel Plantié, Gerard Dray, Mathieu Roche, François Trousset, and Pascal Poncelet. 2008. Web opinion mining: How to extract opinions from blogs? In *Proceedings of the 5th international conference on Soft computing as transdisciplinary science and technology*, pages 211–217.

Laurie Beth Harris. 2017. Helping readers tell the difference between news and opinion: 7 good questions with duke reporters' lab's rebecca iannucci.

Ozan Irsoy and Claire Cardie. 2014. Opinion mining with deep recurrent neural networks. In *Proceedings of the 2014 conference on empirical methods in natural language processing (EMNLP)*, pages 720–728.

Caio Libanio Melo Jeronimo, Leandro Balby Marinho, Claudio EC Campelo, Adriano Veloso, and Allan Sales da Costa Melo. 2019. Fake news classification based on subjective language. In *Proceedings of the 21st International Conference on Information Integration and Web-based Applications & Services*, pages 15–24.

Soo-Min Kim and Eduard Hovy. 2005. Automatic detection of opinion bearing words and sentences. In *Companion Volume to the Proceedings of Conference including Posters/Demos and tutorial abstracts*.

Takeshi Kojima, Shixiang Shane Gu, Machel Reid, Yutaka Matsuo, and Yusuke Iwasawa. 2022. Large language models are zero-shot reasoners. *Advances in neural information processing systems*, 35:22199–22213.

Katarina R Krüger, Anna Lukowiak, Jonathan Sonntag, Saskia Warzecha, and Manfred Stede. 2017. Classifying news versus opinions in newspapers: Linguistic features for domain independence. *Natural Language Engineering*, 23(5):687–707.

Yinhan Liu, Myle Ott, Naman Goyal, Jingfei Du, Mandar Joshi, Danqi Chen, Omer Levy, Mike Lewis, Luke Zettlemoyer, and Veselin Stoyanov. 2019. Roberta: A robustly optimized bert pretraining approach. *arXiv preprint arXiv:1907.11692*.

Daniel Loureiro, Francesco Barbieri, Leonardo Neves, Luis Espinosa Anke, and Jose Camacho-Collados. 2022. Timelms: Diachronic language models from twitter. *arXiv preprint arXiv:2202.03829*.

Scott M Lundberg and Su-In Lee. 2017. A unified approach to interpreting model predictions. *Advances in neural information processing systems*, 30.

Yiwei Luo, Dallas Card, and Dan Jurafsky. 2020. Detecting stance in media on global warming. *arXiv preprint arXiv:2010.15149*.

Bryan McCann, Nitish Shirish Keskar, Caiming Xiong, and Richard Socher. 2018. The natural language decathlon: Multitask learning as question answering. *arXiv preprint arXiv:1806.08730*.

Philip M McCarthy and Scott Jarvis. 2007. vocd: A theoretical and empirical evaluation. *Language Testing*, 24(4):459–488.

Sewon Min, Xinxi Lyu, Ari Holtzman, Mikel Artetxe, Mike Lewis, Hannaneh Hajishirzi, and Luke Zettlemoyer. 2022. Rethinking the role of demonstrations: What makes in-context learning work? *arXiv preprint arXiv:2202.12837*.

Alec Radford, Karthik Narasimhan, Tim Salimans, Ilya Sutskever, et al. 2018. Improving language understanding by generative pre-training.

Ellen Riloff and Janyce Wiebe. 2003. Learning extraction patterns for subjective expressions. In *Proceedings of the 2003 conference on Empirical methods in natural language processing*, pages 105–112.

Ellen Riloff, Janyce Wiebe, and William Phillips. 2005. Exploiting subjectivity classification to improve information extraction. In *AAAI*, pages 1106–1111.

Elena Savinova and Fermin Moscoso Del Prado. 2023. Analyzing subjectivity using a transformer-based regressor trained on naïve speakers' judgements. In *Proceedings of the 13th Workshop on Computational Approaches to Subjectivity, Sentiment, & Social Media Analysis*, pages 305–314.

Gemini Team, Rohan Anil, Sebastian Borgeaud, Yonghui Wu, Jean-Baptiste Alayrac, Jiahui Yu, Radu Soricut, Johan Schalkwyk, Andrew M Dai, Anja Hauth, et al. 2023. Gemini: a family of highly capable multimodal models. *arXiv preprint arXiv:2312.11805*.

Hugo Touvron, Louis Martin, Kevin Stone, Peter Albert, Amjad Almahairi, Yasmine Babaei, Nikolay Bashlykov, Soumya Batra, Prajjwal Bhargava, Shruti Bhosale, et al. 2023. Llama 2: Open foundation and fine-tuned chat models. *arXiv preprint arXiv:2307.09288*.

Sinong Wang, Han Fang, Madian Khabsa, Hanzi Mao, and Hao Ma. 2021. Entailment as few-shot learner. *arXiv preprint arXiv:2104.14690*.

Xinyi Wang, Wanrong Zhu, and William Yang Wang. 2023. Large language models are implicitly topic models: Explaining and finding good demonstrations for in-context learning. *arXiv preprint arXiv:2301.11916*, page 3.

Jason Wei, Xuezhi Wang, Dale Schuurmans, Maarten Bosma, Fei Xia, Ed Chi, Quoc V Le, Denny Zhou, et al. 2022. Chain-of-thought prompting elicits reasoning in large language models. *Advances in Neural Information Processing Systems*, 35:24824–24837.

Janyce Wiebe, Theresa Wilson, and Claire Cardie. 2005. Annotating expressions of opinions and emotions in language. *Language resources and evaluation*, 39:165–210.

Adina Williams, Nikita Nangia, and Samuel R Bowman. 2017. A broad-coverage challenge corpus for sentence understanding through inference. *arXiv preprint arXiv:1704.05426*.

Hong Yu and Vasileios Hatzivassiloglou. 2003. Towards answering opinion questions: Separating facts from opinions and identifying the polarity of opinion sentences. In *Proceedings of the 2003 conference on Empirical methods in natural language processing*, pages 129–136.

Wei Zhang, Clement Yu, and Weiyi Meng. 2007. Opinion retrieval from blogs. In *Proceedings of the sixteenth ACM conference on Conference on information and knowledge management*, pages 831–840.

Zihao Zhao, Eric Wallace, Shi Feng, Dan Klein, and Sameer Singh. 2021. Calibrate before use: Improving few-shot performance of language models. In *International Conference on Machine Learning*, pages 12697–12706. PMLR.

# A Additional Experimental Details

## A.1 Prompts

Here we provide more details about the prompts used in our experiments to make models predict the subjectivity of our test datasets. Table 9 presents all four prompts that we used in our experiments. As seen in the table, models prompted with standard CoT and Zero-shot CoT with instructions, generate longer answers required post-processing to extract the final label. To extract the final answer from the longer answers, we feed the answer to a Gemini model and prompt it to extract the final label from the answer.

| Prompt Name | Prompt Text |
|---|---|
| Zero-shot | Classify the following sentence into Subjective or Objective. Just output the label.<br>Sentence: { } Label: |
| Zero-shot CoT | Classify the following sentences into Subjective or Objective. Let's think step by step.<br>Sentence: { } Label: |
| ZCoT-Inst | Classify the following sentence into Subjective or Objective. output reasoning for each step.<br>Sentence: { }<br>Answer: Lets think step by step!<br>First, find phrases that might express opinions or personal views.<br>Second, find out how intense each phrase is expressing opinions or personal views.<br>Third, if there is one or more phrases with expression intensity medium or above, classify the sentence as Subjective. |
| Standard CoT | Classify the Sentence into Subjective or Objective.<br><br>Sentence: Meanwhile, some other countries, including Japan and Germany, already issued statements on Bush's new climate change policy in rather different tones.<br>Answer: First, the phrases that might express opinions or personal views are 'rather different'. The expression intensity of the phrase is medium. Since there is one or more phrases with expression intensity medium or above, classify the sentence as Subjective.<br>Sentence: { } Answer: |

Table 9: Different prompt used in our experiments. We only include one example for standard CoT for demonstration purposes, but our experiments are done with 6 examples in standard CoT prompt setting.

## A.2 Logistic Regression Features

Here we list the features used for training a logistic regression model as our baseline. The features were taken from the work by Krüger et al. (2017). The set of features are claimed to be robust for classifying opinion vs news report.

| Feature | Description |
|---|---|
| SentLength | sentence length measured in tokens (inverted) |
| TokenLength | Avg. token length measured in characters (inverted) |
| Negation | Norm. frequency of lemmatized negation words |
| NegationSuffix | Norm. frequency of negation suffix *n't* |
| Complexity | Norm. frequency of finite verbs per sentence |
| Questions | Ratio of question marks |
| Exclamations | Ratio of exclamation marks |
| Commas | Ratio of commas |
| Semicolons | Ratio of semicolons |
| Temporal Conn. | Ratio of temporal connectives |
| Causal Conn. | Ratio of causal connectives |
| Contrastive Conn. | Ratio of contrastive connectives |
| Expansive Conn. | Ratio of expansive connectives |
| Citations | Ratio of citations |
| CitationLength | Avg. number of tokens per citation |
| Past | Ratio of past tense outside quotes |
| Present | Ratio of present tense outside quotes |
| VoS | Ratio of lemmatised communication verbs outside quotes |
| Modals | Ratio of lemmatised modal verbs outside quotes |
| Future: Will | Ratio of verb 'will' outside quotes |
| 1st person | Norm. frequency of 1st person pronouns outside quotes |
| 2nd person | Norm. frequency of 2nd person pronouns outside quotes |
| 1st/2nd person | Norm. frequency of 1st and 2nd person pronouns outside quotes |
| Digits | Norm. frequency of digits |
| Interjections | Norm. frequency of interjections |
| Sentiment | Norm. text polarity outside quotes |
| Sentiment Adj | Norm. text polarity outside quotes in adjectives only |

Table 10: Features and Descriptions

We supplement the above list of features with 9 lexical richness features from *lexicalrichness* python library. These form the set of 36 features that we use to train a logistic regression model.

# Monitoring Depression Severity and Symptoms in User-Generated Content: An Annotation Scheme and Guidelines

**Falwah AlHamed**[1,2], **Rebecca Bendayan**[3], **Julia Ive**[4], and **Lucia Specia**[1]

[1]Department of Computing, Imperial College London, London, UK
[1]{f.alhamed20,l.specia}@imperial.ac.uk
[2]King Abdulaziz City for Science and Technology(KACST), Riyadh, Saudi Arabia
[3]King's College London, London, UK
[4]Queen Mary University of London, London, UK
[4]j.ive@qmul.ac.uk

## Abstract

Depression is a highly prevalent condition recognized by the World Health Organization as a leading contributor to global disability. Many people suffering from depression express their thoughts and feelings using social media, which thus becomes a source of data for research in this domain. However, existing annotation schemes tailored to studying depression symptoms in social media data remain limited. Reliable and valid annotation guidelines are crucial for accurately measuring mental health conditions for those studies. This paper addresses this gap by presenting a novel depression annotation scheme and guidelines for detecting depression symptoms and their severity in social media text. Our approach leverages validated depression questionnaires and incorporates the expertise of psychologists and psychiatrists during scheme refinement. The resulting annotation scheme achieves high inter-rater agreement, demonstrating its potential for suitable depression assessment in social media contexts.

## 1 Introduction

Within the domain of mental health, a multitude of disorders exists, each characterized by distinct symptoms that influence cognitive processes, emotional states, and behavioural patterns. This study directs its focus toward depression, a prevalent condition acknowledged by the World Health Organization (WHO) as a significant contributor to global disability (McManus et al., 2009). According to WHO estimates, approximately 264 million individuals worldwide suffer from the burdens of depression. Understanding the occurrence and severity of depression in online platforms can offer valuable insights for early detection, intervention, and support (Association, 2013). However, extracting meaningful information about depression from social media posts presents significant challenges due to the unstructured and nuanced nature of the content.

Labelling social media data for mental disorders like depression is a common practice in research, yet it presents notable challenges. Unlike clinical data, social media lacks validated indicators of sadness or formal diagnoses, necessitating the development of labelling techniques. Achieving consensus on and applying these labels proves challenging due to the subjective nature of mental health evaluation and the need for nuanced annotation schemes. However, existing schemes tailored to studying depression symptoms in social media data are limited. Ensuring the reliability and validity of such guidelines is important to accurately measure mental health issues in social media studies.

## 2 Related Work

The accurate annotation of user-generated content (UGC) is essential for developing reliable datasets to train machine learning models for various mental health applications (De Choudhury et al., 2013; Chancellor et al., 2021). Prior research has recognized the importance of creating annotation schemes specifically for labelling mental health data extracted from social media platforms(Benetka et al., 2020; Mowery et al., 2015; Straton et al., 2020). The first pilot study on annotation scheme for depression was conducted by Mowery et al. (2015) leveraging the DSM-5 criteria for item definition. However, their study employed a relatively small dataset for annotation, in which the dataset was collected only based on "depression" keywords in social media, which might have resulted in the inclusion of data from non-depressed users, potentially compromising the scheme's accuracy in reflecting true depression. Additionally, they reported low inter-annotator agreement, raising concerns regarding the scheme's applicability and reliability. Another study by (Yao et al., 2021) investigated the development of an annotation scheme for depression in online discussions



*Proceedings of the 14th Workshop on Computational Approaches to Subjectivity, Sentiment, & Social Media Analysis*, pages 227–233
August 15, 2024 

on the Chinese social media platform Sina Weibo. Their work focused specifically on Chinese forums and employed accuracy as the metric for inter-annotator agreement. It is important to note that accuracy can be inflated by chance agreement, potentially overestimating the scheme's reliability. These limitations necessitate further refinement of annotation schemes for depression to ensure their robustness and broad applicability. A recent study by Chancellor et al. (2021) addressed the challenge of annotating suicide risk and protective factors within online support forums. Their work yielded an annotation scheme and guidelines that achieved high inter-annotator agreement. Their approach emphasized incorporating the expertise of psychologists during guideline design. Additionally, they identified key considerations for developing robust annotation schemes, which informed the methodology employed in the present study.

## 3 Dataset

For the dataset, the study targeted platforms with a significant volume of textual content in English. The source of the data used in this experiment was introduced in (Alhamed et al., 2024). It consisted of tweets from users who self-disclosed being diagnosed with depression. The dataset underwent manual inspection to select only original tweets, excluding replicated tweets or narratives about others. Only users who specified the month and year of their diagnosis were included. Posts preceding and following the diagnosis date were extracted. The final dataset contains more than 1 million posts of people who self-reported being diagnoed with depression, with each post labelled as "before" or "after" depression diagnosis.

## 4 Depression Standardized Questionnaires

Depression is characterized by several symptoms, substantially impairing people's ability to function at work or school and to cope with daily life. At its most severe, depressive symptoms can be linked to suicidal ideation and are associated with a high risk for suicide. In the context of diagnostic and screening protocols for this illness, clinicians commonly administer standardized questionnaires to patients. These questionnaires consist of a series of questions about the patient's emotional state and daily activities over a designated timeframe. Based on the patient's responses, sometimes a score is generated to ascertain whether the patient exhibits symptoms of depression and to determine the severity level. To build the annotation scheme, we relied on three popular standardized questionnaires: the Patient Health Questionnaire (PHQ-9), the Beck Depression Inventory (BDI), and the Center for Epidemiologic Studies Depression Scale (CES-D). PHQ-9 is a validated depression screening tool developed by Kroenke et al. (2001). It comprises nine questions corresponding to the Diagnostic and Statistical Manual of Mental Disorders (DSM-IV) criteria for major depressive disorder. Individuals rate the frequency of experiencing depressive symptoms over the past two weeks on a scale from 0 to 3. Scores are summed to indicate the severity of depressive symptoms, with higher scores suggesting greater impairment. CES-D is a validated questionnaire developed by Radloff (1977) to measure the presence and severity of depressive symptoms in the general population. Consisting of 20 items covering various aspects of depressive symptomatology, such as depressed mood, feelings of guilt and worthlessness, sleep disturbance, and loss of appetite, the CES-D provides a reliable assessment of depression severity. BDI is a widely used and well-validated tool for measuring depressive symptomatology in adults (Beck et al., 1961). BDI is a self-report questionnaire consisting of 21 items, each addressing a specific cognitive or behavioural symptom of depression (Beck et al., 1996). Respondents rate the severity of each symptom on a 4-point Likert scale, resulting in a total score that reflects the level of depression present. These questionnaires are widely used in clinical practice and research due to their brevity, simplicity, and demonstrated reliability and validity in assessing depression severity across diverse populations.

Our scheme draws upon the foundations laid by these three validated questionnaires. We extracted symptoms from these questionnaires and we explored their usability and appropriateness to extract symptoms from social media. We did this by collecting feedback from a panel of experts of psychologists and psychiatrists. The aim is to evaluate which symptoms could be discerned from social media platforms.

## 5 Study Design

In this section, we provide an overview of the procedures and methodologies employed in the development of our annotation scheme. The main

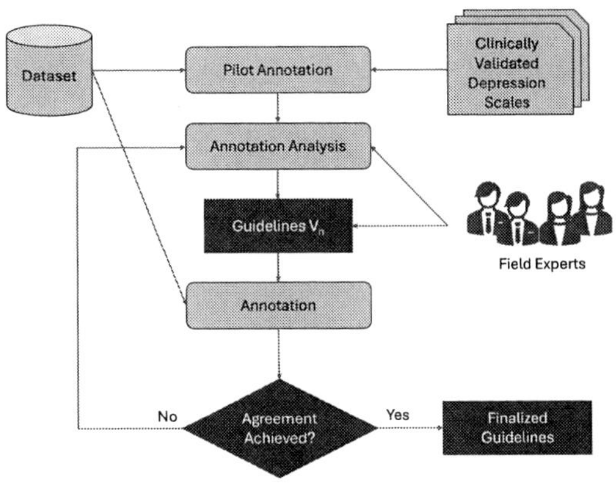


Figure 1: Annotation Process

goal of our work is to lay a foundation towards building a valid and reliable annotating scheme for depression that is able to: 1) indicate symptoms of depression from user-generated content in social media, 2) indicate the occurrence and severity of depression from user-generated content in social media. We used Labelstudio [1] as a labelling interface for all experiments in this work. Within Label Studio, we designed a custom labelling interface to meet the specific needs of our task, as none of the available templates offered a suitable match.

### 5.1 Annotators

The annotators for this task are five clinical psychologists, each possessing a minimum of three years of specialized experience in diagnosing depression and/or anxiety disorders. Their participation in this task is entirely voluntary, without any incentives, and motivated by a commitment to improve mental health research.

## 6 Scheme Development

In this section we are explaining in detail the procesudres and methods taken to develop the annotation scheme. First we looked into the most used questionnaires for diagnosing depression in clinical practice and in research. Then, we created a survey based on all symptoms occurred in these questionnaires. The survey was for psychologits/psychiatrsits to narrow down the symptoms and choose which of these symptoms can be detectd from texts posted on a social media platform. After that, the selected symptoms was categorized in a shorter list to facilitate the annotation procedure by annotators. each step is thoroughly described in the following sections.

[1]https://labelstud.io/

### 6.1 Annotating Depression Symptoms

Initially, we constructed a survey encompassing all symptoms identified in validated depression questionnaires, namely: PHQ-9, CES-D, and BDI. This survey was then distributed to psychologists and psychiatrists, who were tasked with identifying symptoms potentially detectable from textual content posted on social media platforms. Following this, the selected symptoms were refined and categorized into a concise list to streamline the annotation process for annotators. Each of these steps is detailed in the subsequent sections.

### 6.2 Psychologists/Psychiatrists Survey

To ascertain the ability of each symptom to indicate depression from textual descriptions, we engaged psychology experts in a survey. We conducted a survey containing all symptoms from all three questionnaires, which resulted in 50 symptoms. The survey then was distributed to 17 psychologists and psychiatrists. The aim was to select items from questionnaires that reflect symptoms of depression that can be manifested within users' text on social media platforms. The survey aimed to determine whether each symptom could independently signify depression or if it necessitated accompanying symptoms for diagnostic clarity, or whether the item by itself can be used to identify clinically significant depression. Based on the collective insights garnered from this survey, we refined the initial list to include only symptoms that could effectively identify depression either in isolation or when coupled with other symptoms, 40 symptoms resulted from this step.

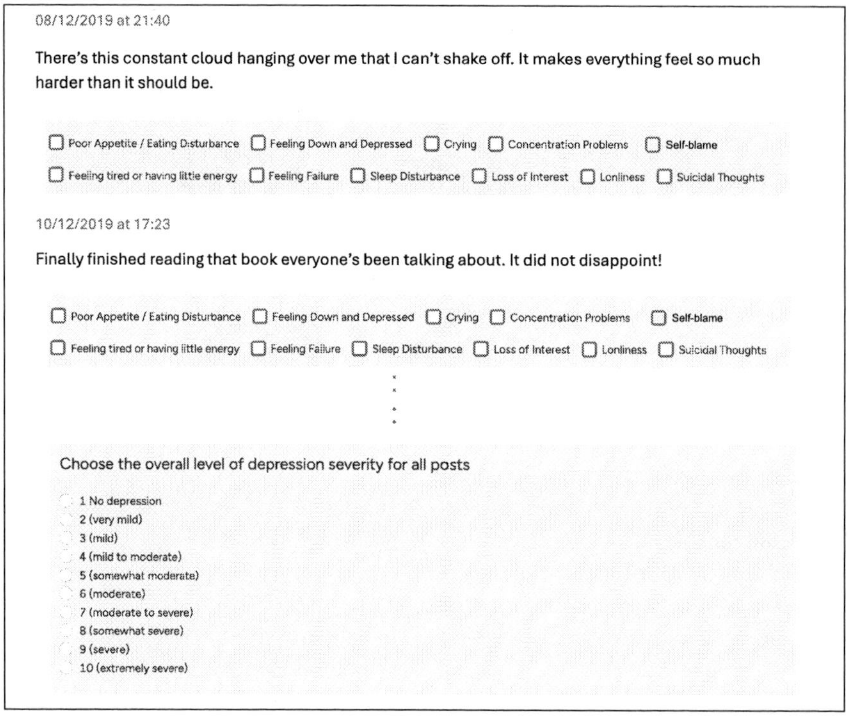


Figure 2: Example of annotating a chunk that contains multiple posts. Depression symptoms annotation task is post-level, while severity annotation task is chunk-level. Posts are generated using the OpenAI GPT-4 model, closely mimicking original posts to protect users' privacy.

### 6.3 Categorizing and Refining Annotation Items

We conducted a comprehensive analysis of depression symptoms derived from survey results which are 40 distinct symptoms. Considering the potential overlap of symptoms across the aforementioned questionnaires, and to streamline and condense the extensive list of symptoms, we proceeded to categorize them into a concise set of symptom categories (details can be found in Appendix A). This categorization process aimed to facilitate a more efficient and manageable list for the identification and assessment of depression symptoms. The final list consists of 11 symptom categories: poor appetite/eating disturbance, feeling down and depressed, crying, concentration problems, feeling tired or having little energy, feeling failure, sleep disturbance, loss of interest, self-blame and shame, loneliness, and suicidal thoughts.

### 6.4 Annotation Process

The annotation process employed a cyclical approach to ensure validity and annotator agreement. First, a pilot scheme was conducted utilizing established depression scales to develop an initial annotation framework. Subsequently, five independent annotators applied this framework to the data (450 posts). Following this initial annotation round, a collaborative analysis was undertaken. This analysis involved both the annotators (clinical psychologists) and field experts. The field experts included a clinical psychology consultant with expertise in annotation guideline development and a computer science specialist experienced in annotating mental health applications. Their feedback on the annotation process and scheme informed subsequent modifications. With these revisions incorporated, a second round of annotation was conducted utilizing the refined scheme. This iterative process of annotation, analysis, and refinement was repeated for a total of three rounds. This cyclical approach led to the establishment of final depression annotation guidelines and a scheme deemed to be valid by the field experts and achieved a satisfactory level of annotator agreement. The annotation process is illustrated in Figure 1.

### 6.5 Annotating Depression Severity

In the context of annotating depression severity in social media posts, experts in psychology have recommended incorporating a timeframe of one to two weeks to accurately measure the occurrence and severity of depressive symptoms. Aligning with the Center for Epidemiologic Studies Depression Scale (CES-D), we segmented tweets into 1-week intervals, herein referred to as "chunks." Each chunk represents tweets spanning a week, requiring annotators to review all tweets within the chunk to assess depression occurrence and severity. Initially, our depression severity scheme comprised four categories: **No depression** (indicating absence of depressive symptoms), **Mild depression** (denoting mild indications of depression), **Moderate depression** (suggesting moderate manifestations of depression), and **Severe depression** (representing severe symptoms or inclinations towards suicidal thoughts).

In a pilot study involving 45 chunks, annotators encountered challenges in accurately categorizing depression severity, particularly when it fell between two predefined categories, such as mild and moderate. Consequently, a suggestion emerged to enhance the granularity of the severity scale. To address this, we transitioned to a **10-point severity scale** (0 to 9 where 0 indicates no depression and 9 indicates extremely severe depression). This adaptation aims to provide a more nuanced framework, facilitating a finer alignment of observed symptoms with corresponding severity levels. An example of our final annotation scheme with example posts is shown in Figure 2. It is noteworthy that the adjustment of severity levels from 4 to 10 scale might lead to decreased inter-rater agreement. However, the primary aim is to enhance the reliability and precision of data annotation, thereby fostering more meaningful insights for psychologists and psychiatrists analyzing social media posts concerning depression severity.

## 7 Results

To assess the consistency of our annotations, we employed Cohen's kappa ($\kappa$), a well-established statistic for measuring inter-rater agreement for nominal data (Cohen, 1960). This metric accounts for agreement that may occur by chance, providing a more robust concordance measure than simple accuracy agreement. In our study, we achieved a pairwise kappa score of 0.67 for 45 chunks of tweets, encompassing a total of 450 individual posts annotated. This value falls within the range typically interpreted as indicating "substantial" agreement (Landis and Koch, 1977). The high level of agreement achieved through kappa analysis strengthens the reliability of our findings and underscores the consistency with which the annotation scheme was applied. We posit that the high inter-annotator agreement achieved in this work stems, at least in part, from the collaborative approach involving computer scientists and field experts with psychological and psychiatric backgrounds. This collaborative effort ensured that the annotation scheme and guidelines were grounded in both technical expertise and clinical knowledge. This work has the potential to significantly contribute to the field of digital health and social media. The proposed scheme and guidelines can serve as a robust baseline for collecting and labelling high-quality, gold-standard datasets. Machine learning models trained on such datasets could be developed to detect depression symptoms and assess their severity. If integrated with established mental health support systems, these models could potentially function as preventive tools by facilitating early intervention.

## 8 Conclusion

This work addressed the critical need for robust annotation schemes for detecting depression symptoms and severity in social media text. We presented an annotation scheme and corresponding guidelines informed by validated depression questionnaires (PHQ-9, CES-D, and BDI) and refined through collaboration with psychologists and psychiatrists. The resulting scheme demonstrates good inter-rater agreement (Cohen's kappa = 0.67), signifying its potential for reliable depression assessment in social media contexts. This scheme and its accompanying guidelines can serve as a valuable foundation for collecting and labelling high-quality, gold-standard datasets. Future research will leverage this scheme to create a labelled dataset and develop machine learning models capable of accurately detecting depression symptoms from social media data.

## Limitations

The annotation scheme is designed for screening purposes and is not intended for clinical diagnosis of depression. While tested on a specific dataset, further validation across diverse datasets, including different languages, is necessary to establish its applicability and reliability. Moreover, the scheme is specifically tailored to evaluate depression symptoms and severity, potentially limiting its application to other mental health conditions.

## Ethics Statement

This study has received ethics approval from the Science Engineering Technology Research Ethics Committee at Imperial College London (SETREC Reference: 21IC7222).

## References


Falwah Alhamed, Julia Ive, and Lucia Specia. 2024. Classifying social media users before and after depression diagnosis via their language usage: A dataset and study. In *Proceedings of the 2024 Joint International Conference on Computational Linguistics, Language Resources and Evaluation (LREC-COLING 2024)*, pages 3250–3260.

American Psychiatric Association. 2013. *Diagnostic and statistical manual of mental disorders : DSM-5*, 5th ed. edition. American Psychiatric Association Arlington, VA.

Aaron T Beck, Michael H Steer, and Gregory K Brown. 1996. *Manual for the Beck Depression Inventory-II*. Psychological Corporation.

Aaron T Beck, Charles H Ward, Morris Mendelsohn, John Mock, and James Erbaugh. 1961. An inventory for measuring depression. *Archives of General Psychiatry*, 4(6):561–571.

David Benetka, Alicia Moreno-Moral, Lorena Romero-Fombuena, and Juan Lopez-Gazpio. 2020. An annotation scheme for mental health discussions in social media. In *International Conference on Computational Linguistics (Proceedings of the Conference: Long Papers, 2020)*, pages 2617–2627. Association for Computational Linguistics.

Stevie Chancellor, Steven A Sumner, Corinne David-Ferdon, Tahirah Ahmad, and Munmun De Choudhury. 2021. Suicide Risk and Protective Factors in Online Support Forum Posts: Annotation Scheme Development and Validation Study. *JMIR Ment Health*, 8(11):e24471.

Jacob Cohen. 1960. A coefficient of agreement for nominal scales. *Educational and Psychological Measurement*, 20(1):37–46.

Munmun De Choudhury, Shanika M De Silva, K Wiemer-Hastings, and James W Pennbaker. 2013. Identifying depression using social media. In *The future of mental health: An international perspective*, pages 170–180.

Kurt Kroenke, Robert L Spitzer, and Janet B Williams. 2001. The phq-9: validity of a brief depression severity measure. *Journal of General Internal Medicine*, 16(9):606–613.

J Richard Landis and Gary G Koch. 1977. The measurement of observer agreement for categorical data. *Biometrics*, 33(1):159–174.

S. McManus, H. Meltzer, T. Brugha, P. E. Bebbington, and R. Jenkins. 2009. Adult psychiatric morbidity in england: results of a household survey.

Danielle L Mowery, Craig Bryan, and Mike Conway. 2015. Towards developing an annotation scheme for depressive disorder symptoms: A preliminary study using twitter data. In *Proceedings of the 2nd workshop on computational linguistics and clinical psychology: From linguistic signal to clinical reality*, pages 89–98.

Lenore S Radloff. 1977. The ces-d scale: A self-report depression scale for research in the general population. *Applied Psychological Measurement*, 1(3):385–401.

Nadiya Straton, Hyeju Jang, and Raymond Ng. 2020. Stigma annotation scheme and stigmatized language detection in health-care discussions on social media. In *Proceedings of the Twelfth Language Resources and Evaluation Conference*, pages 1178–1190, Marseille, France. European Language Resources Association.

Xiaoxu Yao, Guang Yu, Jingyun Tang, and Jialing Zhang. 2021. Extracting depressive symptoms and their associations from an online depression community. *Computers in Human Behavior*, 120:106734.


## A Symptoms Categories List

A list of symptoms and the corresponding symptom category is shown in Table 1.

| Symptom | Category |
|---|---|
| I did not feel like eating; my appetite was poor | Poor Appetite / Eating Disturbance |
| I was bothered by the problem: Poor appetite or overeating | |
| My appetite is much worse than before. | |
| I have lost/gained noticeable weight | |
| I felt that I could not shake off the blues even with help from my family or friends. | Feeling Down and Depressed |
| I felt depressed | |
| I felt sad | |
| I was bothered by the problem: feeling down, depressed, or hopeless | |
| I am sad all the time and I can't snap out of it. | |
| I had crying spells | Crying |
| I cry all the time | |
| I used to be able to cry, but over the last 2 weeks I can't cry even though I want to. | |
| I had trouble keeping my mind on what I was doing. | Concentration Problems |
| I was bothered by the problem: Trouble concentrating on things, such as reading the newspaper or watching tv | |
| I feel irritated all the time. | |
| I have greater difficulty in making decisions more than I used to | |
| I felt that everything I did was an effort. | Feeling tired or having little energy |
| I could not get "going" | |
| I was bothered by the problem: Feeling tired or having little energy | |
| I was bothered by the problem: Moving or speaking so slowly that other people could have noticed. Or the opposite being so fidgety or restless that I have been moving around | |
| I have to push myself very hard to do anything. or I can't do any work at all. | |
| I get tired from doing almost anything | |
| I thought my life had been a failure. | Feeling Failure |
| I was bothered by the problem: Feeling bad about myself, or that I am a failure or let myself or my family down | |
| I feel I have nothing to look forward to. | |
| As I look back on my life, all I can see is a lot of failures. | |
| My sleep was restless | Sleep Disturbance |
| I was bothered by the problem: Trouble falling or staying asleep, or sleeping too much | |
| I wake up several hours earlier than I used to and cannot get back to sleep. | |
| I was bothered by the problem: Little interest or pleasure in doing things | Loss of Interest |
| I don't get real satisfaction out of anything anymore. or I am dissatisfied or bored with everything. | |
| I have lost most of my interest in other people | |
| I have almost no interest in sex. | |
| I feel quite guilty most of the time. | Self-Blame and Shame |
| I expect to be punished. | |
| I am disgusted with myself. | |
| I blame myself all the time for my faults. | |
| I felt lonely | Loneliness |
| I was bothered by the problem: Thoughts that I would be better off dead, or of hurting myself | Suicidal Thoughts |
| I would like to kill myself. | |

Table 1: Shortened list of depression symptoms with the finalized categories.

# RideKE: Leveraging Low-Resource, User-Generated Twitter Content for Sentiment and Emotion Detection in Kenyan Code-Switched Dataset

**Naome A. Etori and Maria L. Gini**
Department of Computer Science and Engineering
University of Minnesota -Twin Cities
{etori001, gini} @umn.edu

## Abstract

Social media has become a crucial open-access platform for individuals to express opinions and share experiences. However, leveraging low-resource language data from Twitter is challenging due to scarce, poor-quality content and the major variations in language use, such as slang and code-switching. Identifying tweets in these languages can be difficult as Twitter primarily supports high-resource languages. We analyze Kenyan code-switched data and evaluate four state-of-the-art (SOTA) transformer-based pretrained models for sentiment and emotion classification, using supervised and semi-supervised methods. We detail the methodology behind data collection and annotation, and the challenges encountered during the data curation phase. Our results show that XLM-R outperforms other models; for sentiment analysis, XLM-R supervised model achieves the highest accuracy (69.2%) and F1 score (66.1%), XLM-R semi-supervised (67.2% accuracy, 64.1% F1 score). In emotion analysis, DistilBERT supervised leads in accuracy (59.8%) and F1 score (31%), mBERT semi-supervised (accuracy (59% and F1 score 26.5%). AfriBERTa models show the lowest accuracy and F1 scores. All models tend to predict neutral sentiment, with Afri-BERT showing the highest bias and unique sensitivity to empathy emotion. [1]

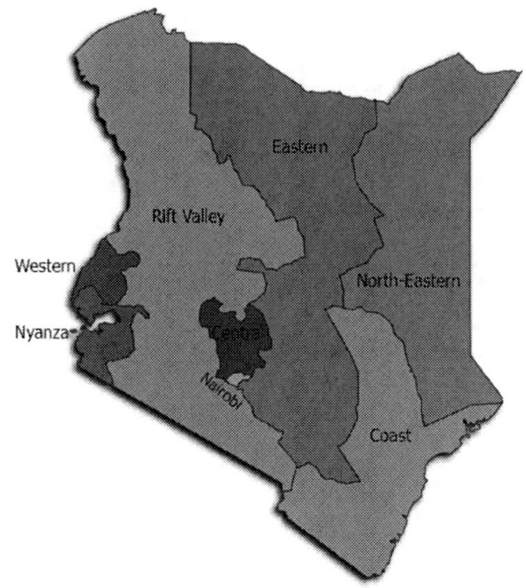


Figure 1: **Geographical representation of RideKE:** *diverse local accents collected in tweets, such as Rift Valley (e.g., Eldoret, Nakuru), Central (e.g., Nyeri, Kiambu), Nairobi (e.g., Kasarani, Kileleshwa), Western (e.g., Kakamega, Bungoma), Nyanza (e.g., Kisumu, Kisii), Eastern (e.g., Machakos, Embu) Coast (e.g., Mombasa, Malindi), and North-Eastern (e.g., Garissa, Mandera).*

## 1 Introduction

Kenya, reflecting Africa's extensive multilingual diversity, offers a unique insight into the continent's rich linguistic heritage, standing as a focal point of language contact, expansion, and diversity. It is home to many languages that bridge its vibrant storytelling, poetry, song, and literature and exemplifies Africa's linguistic wealth, albeit on a more localized scale. With over 40 languages grouped into Bantu, Nilotic, and Cushitic, Kenya's linguistic landscape is diverse and dynamic (Dwivedi, 2014; Carter-Black, 2007; Banks-Wallace, 2002).

Central to linguistic diversity is the co-official language status of English and Kiswahili, with the latter spoken by the majority and enjoying near-equal prominence with English. However, the linguistic equilibrium faces challenges from Sheng, a language that blends English, Kiswahili, and words from other ethnic languages that initially were used in Nairobi Eastlands slums. Sheng emerged as a sociolect among urban youth in the city's working-class neighborhoods and has since spread across various social and age groups. Hence, it is an inte-

[1]https://github.com/NEtori21/Ride_hailing_project



*Proceedings of the 14th Workshop on Computational Approaches to Subjectivity, Sentiment, & Social Media Analysis*, pages 234–249
August 15, 2024 ©2024 Association for Computational Linguistics

| Tweets | Sentiment | Emotion |
|---|---|---|
| Uber kenya did your App stop accepting cards for package deliveries? I have had two riders this morning cancel picking a package because they want me to pay cash. | Negative | Frustration |
| Thank you for the love and support and for the feedback as well. Tell all your friends to ride a littleCab. Buy Kenyan, build Kenya. | Positive | Love |
| Uber drivers are not employees of Uber Kenya Uber is only an app. The link between you as a rider and the driver. But yes they should look after them because the drivers keep them afloat. | Neutral | Neutral |
| A ride will be canceled for one reason or another and both parties should have the liberty to. Sometimes clients will cancel due to the proximity of the driver and other times because the driver is unreachable. | Neutral | Neutral |
| Hope everyone making the most of this awesome Uber kenya Jan offer! Spread the word! Loving it. #Uber kenya | Positive | Happy |
| Giving drivers right to refer the rider to another driver then that is totally not a good idea. Some drivers are connecting while he like really far from you, he wastes time, then after more than 5 mins refers another driver | Neutral | Happy |
| Greater experience for Uber riders with new product | Positive | Happy |
| I am reporting your driver for taking payment twice. I had ordered an Uber for a friend with payment with a card and then he tells the passenger to pay via Mpesa. | Negative | Frustration |
| I also stopped using Uber kenya after I was charged for cancelling a trip as per the drivers request. Little cab iko tu sawa. | Negative | Frustration |
| Crooked policies. Uber kenya. I think you need to sort out your service. | Negative | Angry |
| Honestly, Am disappointed with them. kucancel trips ndio wanajua lately. | Negative | Frustration |

Table 1: Sample Tweets with Sentiment and Emotion Labels.

gral part of Kenyan culture, influencing the traditional dominance of English and Kiswahili (Barasa, 2016; Momanyi, 2009; Mazrui, 1995).

In recent years, language diversity has also been mirrored in the urban transportation sector, primarily due to the growth of Ride-Hailing Services (RHS) such as Uber, Bolt, and Little Cab. These services have rapidly transformed from urban novelties to essential components of daily mobility for many Kenyans, connecting remote areas with vibrant urban cities. However, with the entry of global giants like Uber in 2015, followed by Bolt and the local contender Little Cab, this transformation is not just physical; it extends into digital and social media platforms such as Twitter.

Since many languages are spoken across Kenya, each population has its own dialect. Hence, code-switching is common in these new forms of communication, where speakers alternate between two or more languages in one conversation (Kanana Erastus and Kebeya, 2018; Santy et al., 2021; Angel et al., 2020; Thara and Poornachandran, 2018). Analyzing sentiment and emotions in code-switched language context is critical in the broad natural language processing (NLP) field, for example, creating systems that can predict emotional states from text to speech which can be applied in various use cases, such as measuring consumer satisfaction (Ren and Quan, 2012), natural disasters (Vo and Collier, 2013), marketing strategy (Zamani et al., 2016), e-learning (Ortigosa et al., 2014), e-commerce(Jabbar et al., 2019) and psychological states (Aytuğ, 2018). However, despite this linguistic richness, African languages remain significantly underrepresented in NLP research (Muhammad et al., 2023a). Although NLP research has made extensive progress and demonstrated broad utility over the past two decades, the focus on African languages has been limited. This disparity is often attributed to the scarcity of high-quality, annotated datasets for these languages.

Recently, researchers (Muhammad et al., 2023a)[2] have focused on addressing this challenge by introducing a comprehensive benchmark with over 110,000 tweets across 14 African languages, Swahili among them, and introduced the first Africentric SemEval Shared task (Muhammad et al., 2023b). Various studies have evaluated the performance of state-of-the-art (SOTA) transformer models on African languages, highlighting unique challenges and opportunities (Aryal et al., 2023).

However, research on social media NLP analysis for RHS datasets mainly targets high-resource languages. NLP for low-resource languages is constrained by factors like NLP research's geographical and language diversity (Joshi et al., 2020). Using pre-trained transformer models, we introduce RideKE, a sentiment and emotion analysis dataset for African-accented English code switched with Swahili and Sheng.

[2] https://github.com/afrisenti-semeval/afrisent-semeval-2023

| Code-switched Reference | English Translation |
|---|---|
| I recently interacted with one Uber driver who told me that **huko ni mbali, lazima uongeze pesa**. Different from the estimate on the app. He almost dropped me midway because I argued that it wasn't fair. **Hawa madere ni wazimu walai.** | I recently interacted with one Uber driver who told me that the place is far, you have to add money. Different from the estimate on the app. He almost dropped me midway because I argued that it wasn't fair. These drivers are crazy, really. |
| In Mombasa, they ask you how much the App has displayed as the cost, then tell you it's too low, madam **unaona utaongeza ngapi, hiyo pesa ni kidogo** | In Mombasa they ask you how much the app has displayed as the cost then tell you it's too low, madam how much extra?, That's little money |

Table 2: Example of code-switched sentences in Tweets

Our dataset contains over 29,000 tweets, each sentiment classified as either positive, negative, or neutral, and emotions classified as frustration, happy, angry, sad, empathy, fear, love, and surprise. The dataset represents one location, Kenya, as shown in Table 1. Our goal is to advance research in low-resource languages.

The experiments in this paper are designed to allow us to answer the following specific questions:

1. How do pretrained language models enhance the detection and representation of Kenyan low-resource languages and accents in modern NLP tools?
2. How does the performance of sentiment and emotion detection varies across different pretrained transformer-based models?
3. How effective are different transformer-based models in performing sentiment and emotion detection on the low-resource (RideKE) dataset using semi-supervised learning?

Our paper makes the following contributions as we address these questions:

- We use semi-supervised learning to classify sentiments and emotions. We compare four SOTA transformer-based models and provide a detailed model performance analysis.
- We contribute a partially curated human-annotated labeled public dataset with over 29,000 tweets from the RHS domain. This is Kenya's first-ever code-switched sentiment and emotion dataset in the RHS domain. It contributes resources to low-resource areas, which can be used for other analyses.

## 2 Literature Review

### 2.1 Sentiment Analysis on Social Media

Sentiment analysis (SA) emerged as a significant field early in the 2000s (Das and Chen, 2001; Nasukawa and Yi, 2003). SA (Dave et al., 2003; Pang et al., 2008) aims to determine the attitudes, opinions, or emotions expressed in text on specific topics or entities (Liu, 2022) and has become an increasingly popular research area. Due to higher user-generated content available on social media, understanding sentiment in text cannot be overstated (Naseem and Musial, 2019).

Diverse strategies to accurately interpret and classify user sentiments have been employed. For example, lexicon-based approaches, like SENTIWORDNET (Baccianella et al., 2010) and AFINN (Nielsen, 2011), used predefined word lists to classify text sentiment. While effective in some applications, these methods often struggled with context and nuance. Rule-based systems (Suttles and Ide, 2013) further enhanced this method by applying contextual rules to detect sentiment nuances, including handling negations (Taboada et al., 2011).

Advancements in Machine learning (ML) (Pang et al., 2002), such as supervised techniques trained on large amounts of labeled sentiment datasets, offer another powerful avenue for SA. Hence, the exploration of semi-supervised methods in SA could leverage unlabelled data to address the challenge of data annotation and labeling (Vo and Zhang, 2015; Hwang and Lee, 2021). Deep learning approaches such as Convolutional Neural Networks (CNN) (Chen, 2015) have significantly advanced SA capabilities. However, SA on social media poses unique challenges compared to more traditional domains due to the informal and conversational nature of the text (Medhat et al., 2014; Naseem and Musial, 2019).

### 2.2 Code-Switching on Low-resource

Code-switching, the practice of alternating between two or more languages or dialects within a conversation, is particularly prevalent in multilingual communities and has become increasingly visible on social media platforms (Poplack, 2000; Scotton, 1993; Danet and Herring, 2007). It presents unique challenges and opportunities for NLP (Barman et al., 2014). Most NLP research traditionally focuses on high-resource languages like English, leaving low-resource languages underrepresented (Strassel and Tracey, 2016; Adelani et al., 2021). This gap is more pronounced in African and code-switched languages due to linguistic variability (Adelani et al., 2021). Therefore, high-resource language techniques may underperform on low-resource language data (Lewis, 2014). The study in (Lee and Wang, 2015) emphasizes the importance of analyzing emotions in code-switching data. The use of Generative Pre-trained Transformers (GPT) to generate synthetic code-switched data has been proposed to address data scarcity (Terblanche et al., 2024). A recent survey (Winata et al., 2022) revealed that until October 2022, only a few papers from the ACL Anthology and ISCA Proceedings focused on code-switching research in African languages. For South African languages (Niesler et al., 2018; Niesler and De Wet, 2008) the first dataset was presented in 2018. Even though Swahili-English code-switching has been studied in a few papers (Piergallini et al., 2016; Otundo and Grice, 2022), no datasets are available.

### 2.3 Transformer-based Pretrained Models

Transformer-based architectures (Vaswani et al., 2017), such as BERT (Bidirectional Encoder Representations from Transformers) (Devlin et al., 2018), have gained popularity owing to their effectiveness in learning general representations using large unlabelled datasets (Matthew, 2018) that can further be fine-tuned for downstream tasks (Gururangan et al., 2020; Bhattacharjee et al., 2020). Hence, it has become the foundation for many NLP tasks (Bhattacharjee et al., 2020).

Pretrained language models are trained on large, diverse datasets (Raffel et al., 2020). For example, RoBERTa (Liu et al., 2019) was pretrained on over 160GB of uncompressed text, from BOOKCORPUS (Zhu et al., 2015) and CommonCrawl English dataset (Nagel, 2018). These models learn representations that perform well across various tasks, handling datasets of different sizes from diverse sources while remaining easily understandable (Wang et al., 2019). Examples of a few applications in low-resource include improving speech recognition accuracy (ASR) (Olatunji et al., 2023), machine translation (MT) (Wang et al., 2024) and

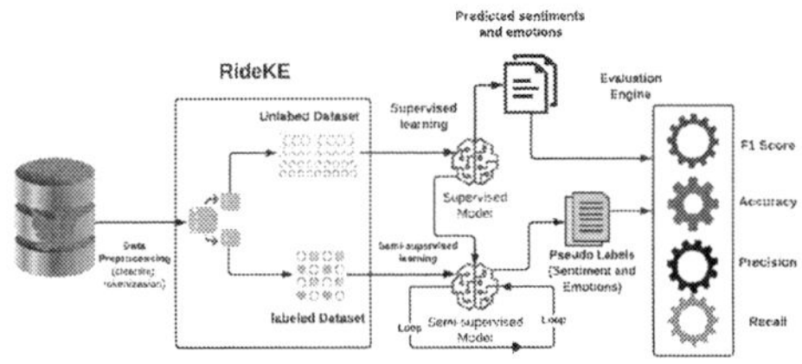


Figure 2: **Methodology:** *Overview of the RideKE sentiment and emotion analysis framework. Unlabeled and labeled datasets are preprocessed and used to train supervised and semi-supervised models for sentiment and emotion prediction. The semi-supervised learning loop generates pseudo labels for evaluation of performance.*

SA (Muhammad et al., 2023a).

## 3 Methods and Datasets

### 3.1 Overview of RideKE Dataset

RideKE dataset. as shown in Table 1 and 2, includes a blend of Kenyan-accented English, approx. (70%), with a minority mix of Swahili and Sheng (30%). The dataset includes a total of 29,623 entries across 12 distinct columns. See Table 13 in the Appendix.

### 3.2 Data Collection

We used a systematic scraping process using the snscrape python library [3] which allows for querying and retrieving tweets based on specified criteria. We targeted three keyword search terms—#UBER-Kenya, #BOLT-kenya, and #LITTLECAB, from January 2017 to April 2023, capturing not only the tweet texts but also other essential metadata such as user engagement metrics (likes, retweets, replies), user account details (followers, following, tweet counts), and relational markers (hashtags, user mentions). Initially, the data was in a dictionary format but it was later converted to DataFrame using pandas and preserved in a CSV format to ensure reproducibility.

#### 3.2.1 Geo-based data collection

The tweet's location metadata was crucial in determining the regional focus of our study. We referenced Kenya's location as shown in Table 3. To ensure uniformity, we used a simple yet effective keyword filtering normalization technique to address location inconsistencies as shown by the diverse representations of Nairobi in the dataset

[3] https://pypi.org/project/snscrape/1

shown in Table 3. To isolate the relevant tweets, we applied a filter on the `user_location` field to include only locations mentioning Kenya and discard entries with missing data and all those with no location. We assessed the frequency distribution of different locations using value count function.

| Location | Tweet Count |
|---|---|
| Kenya | 18974 |
| Nairobi, Kenya | 11960 |
| *Not specified* | 10868 |
| Nairobi | 4776 |
| Nairobi, Kenya | 620 |
| nairobery | 1 |
| Africa, Nairobi Kenya | 1 |
| Mt. Meru | 1 |
| 3rd Parklands | 1 |
| New Jersey | 1 |

Table 3: **Tweet Counts by location:** *We only included locations mentioning Kenya*

### 3.3 Language Detection

We used `langdetect` [4] Python library to detect languages within text. It revealed diverse languages, `English` being the most prevalent, then `Indonesian`, `Swahili` and others as shown in Table 10. For the Sheng language, native speakers manually detected the language. We only kept English (code-switched) for our analysis.

### 3.4 Data Preprocessing

Tweets often feature slang, abbreviations, and non-alphanumeric characters such as hashtags and emojis, contributing to the data's unstructured nature (Adebara and Abdul-Mageed, 2022). We implemented a refined text preprocessing pipeline to enhance data consistency and accurate analysis. The pipeline standardizes data by converting text to strings, trimming whitespace, lowering case, and expanding contractions to preserve semantic integrity. The text is then normalized by reducing repeated characters, removing punctuation, newlines, and tabs, and then tokenizing.

### 3.5 Data Annotation

Inspired by (Raffel et al., 2020) established guidelines, we created a set of annotation guidelines for emotion annotations to ensure a standardized and high-quality approach in our labeling efforts, as shown in Table 12. We added a 'frustration' label and used 'happy' instead of 'joy.' For the sentiment annotation, we adhered to the established annotation framework detailed by (Mohammad, 2016). However, human annotation is time-consuming and costly. We employed two Kenyan volunteer annotators fluent in English, Swahili, and Sheng. One holds a bachelor's degree in political science and the other in computer science. They received a small token of appreciation for their efforts. We ensured the annotator's comprehension of the task. Two annotators labeled the same dataset entries to enhance quality. Each labeled 1,554 tweets with sentiment labels (positive, negative, neutral) and emotion labels (sadness, happy, love, anger, fear, surprise, frustration, and neutral).

#### 3.5.1 Annotation Quality Control

We used Cohen's Kappa (Artstein, 2017)[5] as our primary metric for assessing the level of inter-annotator agreement between the two annotators. It is perfect for categorical items, such as sentiment and emotion labels. Cohen's Kappa provides a means to compute an inter-rater agreement score that accounts for the probability of random agreement:

$$\kappa = \frac{P_o - P_e}{1 - P_e} \tag{1}$$

where $P_o$ is the observed agreement, and $P_e$ is the expected agreement by chance.

To assign the final sentiment and emotion label to each tweet, we employed a majority voting method (Davani et al., 2022) to determine the final label of the tweet (Mohammad, 2022). Instances of complete disagreement among annotators were resolved by involving a lead annotator and applying a majority rule rather than omitting them from the dataset. We found a Cohen's Kappa coefficient of 0.60 for sentiment classification tasks. Cohen's Kappa score for the emotion annotations is approximately 0.67, which indicates a substantial level of agreement beyond chance and suggests a good degree of consistency in their annotations.

#### 3.5.2 Data Splits

The dataset was split into three sets (A, B, and C) as shown in the dataset division Table 4. We used ChatGPT (Brown et al., 2020) for automatic labeling to augment the training dataset and increase training labels since we had only two human annotators. Set A provided Ground truth labels for initial supervised training. Set B is the test dataset

[4] `https://pypi.org/project/langdetect/1`

[5] `https://github.com/zyocum/cohens_kappa`

that is manually annotated by human annotators. Set C represented the unlabelled dataset Used in a semi-supervised training loop, with empty rows and duplicates removed, labels standardized and encoded.

| Set | Description | Details |
|---|---|---|
| Set A | 553 human, 636 ChatGPT | Supervised Train |
| Set B | 2,000 human | Testing |
| Set C | 27,090 unlabelled | Semi-supervised |

Table 4: Dataset Division

### 3.6 Semi-supervised Learning Phase

Semi-supervised learning (SSL) offers a framework for utilizing large amounts of unlabelled data when obtaining labels is expensive (Chapelle et al., 2006; Learning, 2006) as applied to our case. Research shows SSL improves performance on different machine learning tasks such as text classification and machine translation (Najafi et al., 2019). SSL connects supervised and unsupervised learning by utilizing a small fraction of labelled data alongside a larger pool of unlabeled data to improve learning accuracy. SSL has been widely studied to show effectiveness for a wide range of low-resource applications, such as in text-to-speech synthesis (TTS) (Saeki et al., 2023), speech recognition (Du et al., 2023; Thomas et al., 2013), machine translation(Pham et al., 2023; Singh and Singh, 2022), POS-Taggers (Garrette et al., 2013), and sentiment classification (Gupta et al., 2018). Our work extends the application of SSL to sentiment and emotion classification tasks. We seek to mitigate this limitation by leveraging labeled and unlabeled data to train pretrained models. We used accuracy, precision, recall, and F1 scores to evaluate the models' performance.

## 4 Experiments

### 4.1 Models and Architecture

We evaluate four transformer-based models in our experiments: **DistilBERT** (Sanh et al., 2019), a smaller and faster version of BERT; **mBERT** (Devlin et al., 2018), a multilingual version of BERT trained on 104 languages; **XLM-RoBERTa** (Conneau et al., 2019), a multilingual model trained on 100 languages with improved performance; and **AfriBERTa large** (Ogueji et al., 2021), a model specifically designed for African languages to address the unique linguistic challenges in this region. Each model was trained on supervised and semi-supervised learning on sentiment and emotion classification tasks. The initial supervised training and subsequent semi-supervised fine-tuning were conducted separately for each model.

### 4.2 Experimental Setup

#### 4.2.1 Supervised Learning Phase

In supervised training, we utilized the human-annotated, well-curated labeled dataset. We used batches ranging from 16 to 64 depending on the model sizes, optimizing for computational efficiency. A combined categorical cross-entropy loss shown in Figure 3 function, with equal weighting for sentiment and emotion tasks, guided the model toward effective multitasking. We applied a dropout rate of 0.1 for each model to prevent overfitting and enhance generalization. We employed the Adam optimizer, with a learning rate $1e-5$ through 10 epochs of training and monitoring. Initially, the four transformer-based models were fine-tuned on a dataset with 1,189 labeled tweets. We then evaluated the model.

#### 4.2.2 Semi-supervised Learning Phase

Our goal in using SSL is to leverage the vast, unlabeled datasets to mitigate the high cost of human annotations. Following an initial supervised learning phase, each transformer-based model underwent a semi-supervised training loop. In this loop, the models dynamically labeled the unlabeled dataset based on their predictions, generating a pseudo-labeled dataset. We employed a dynamic threshold, set at the 75th percentile of the models' probability predictions across all classes for each batch, to ensure only high-confidence predictions were used for labeling. Samples with predictions below this threshold were excluded to minimize the inclusion of erroneous labels in the training data.

We extended the semi-supervised training loop over 4 epochs, a duration we empirically selected to refine the models' generalization capabilities without causing performance degradation due to overtraining, as indicated by either worsening or plateauing loss. We carefully chose the hyperparameters to ensure optimal training dynamics and model performance.

We set the learning rate at 1e-5 and dynamically adjusted it using a learning rate scheduler during training to optimize generalization and reduce overfitting. The batch size varied between 16 and 64, depending on the specific transformer model, to en-

| Model | Sentiment | | | | Emotions | | | |
|---|---|---|---|---|---|---|---|---|
| | Accuracy | Precision | Recall | F1-Score | Accuracy | Precision | Recall | F1-Score |
| DistilBERT supervised | 0.578 | 0.598 | 0.629 | 0.546 | 0.598 | 0.334 | 0.315 | 0.310 |
| DistilBERT semi-supervised | 0.553 | 0.585 | 0.598 | 0.516 | 0.544 | 0.264 | 0.266 | 0.252 |
| mBERT supervised | 0.638 | 0.621 | 0.663 | 0.596 | 0.592 | 0.253 | 0.298 | 0.265 |
| mBERT semi-supervised | 0.635 | 0.622 | 0.661 | 0.598 | 0.594 | 0.297 | 0.317 | 0.297 |
| XLM-R supervised | 0.692 | 0.665 | 0.723 | 0.661 | 0.658 | 0.343 | 0.267 | 0.258 |
| XLM-R semi-supervised | 0.672 | 0.644 | 0.702 | 0.641 | 0.620 | 0.334 | 0.248 | 0.230 |
| AfriBERTa large supervised | 0.398 | 0.500 | 0.479 | 0.358 | 0.604 | 0.163 | 0.191 | 0.157 |
| AfriBERTa semi-supervised | 0.413 | 0.534 | 0.491 | 0.366 | 0.556 | 0.145 | 0.177 | 0.142 |

Table 5: **Model Performance Evaluation on Sentiment and Emotion Analysis Tasks.** *Performance evaluation of supervised and semi-supervised training for sentiment and emotion analysis across models. Results represent averages over multiple runs.*

| Model | Negative | | | Neutral | | | Positive | | |
|---|---|---|---|---|---|---|---|---|---|
| | Precision | Recall | F1 | Precision | Recall | F1 | Precision | Recall | F1 |
| DistilBERT supervised | 0.920 | 0.385 | 0.543 | 0.284 | 0.635 | 0.392 | - | - | - |
| DistilBERT semi-supervised | 0.901 | 0.325 | 0.478 | 0.268 | 0.604 | 0.371 | - | - | - |
| mBERT supervised | 0.906 | 0.467 | 0.616 | 0.330 | 0.587 | 0.423 | - | - | - |
| mBERT semi-supervised | 0.873 | 0.443 | 0.588 | 0.363 | 0.628 | 0.460 | - | - | - |
| XLM-R supervised | 0.921 | 0.563 | 0.699 | 0.417 | 0.714 | 0.526 | - | - | - |
| XLM-R semi-supervised | 0.850 | 0.524 | 0.648 | 0.392 | 0.712 | 0.506 | 0.691 | 0.871 | 0.771 |
| AfriBERTa large supervised | 0.794 | 0.100 | 0.178 | 0.144 | 0.492 | 0.223 | - | - | - |
| AfriBERTa semi-supervised | 0.874 | 0.096 | 0.174 | 0.171 | 0.560 | 0.261 | 0.558 | 0.817 | 0.663 |

Table 6: **Model Performance Evaluation on Sentiment classification Tasks Labels.** *Performance evaluation for Negative, Neutral, and Positive sentiments across various models. A dash (-) indicates missing values, i.e., the models did not predict all positive sentiment instances. The results represent averages over multiple runs.*

sure computational efficiency. We used a combined loss function shown in Figure 3 for sentiment and emotion analysis and applied a dropout rate of 0.1 to prevent overfitting. We employed the Adam optimizer with a learning rate of 1e-5 and no weight decay.

## 5 Results and Discussions

### 5.1 Sentiment Analysis

Table 5 summarizes the performance of all models on sentiment analysis. XLM-R supervised achieves the highest overall performance with an accuracy of 62.5% and an F1-score of 66.7%. This is followed closely with semi-supervised XLM-R, which has an accuracy of 62.1% and an F1-score of 68.3%. However, DistilBERT supervised performance falls behind with an accuracy of 57.8% and an F1-score of 54.6%. On the other hand, mBERT models show consistency between supervised and semi-supervised training, maintaining average F1-scores of 59.8% and 59.6%, respectively. AfriBERTa models struggled, with the supervised learning achieving an F1-score of 35.8%, and overall poorest performance across all metrics.

The detailed performance metrics for negative, neutral, and positive sentiment classification are

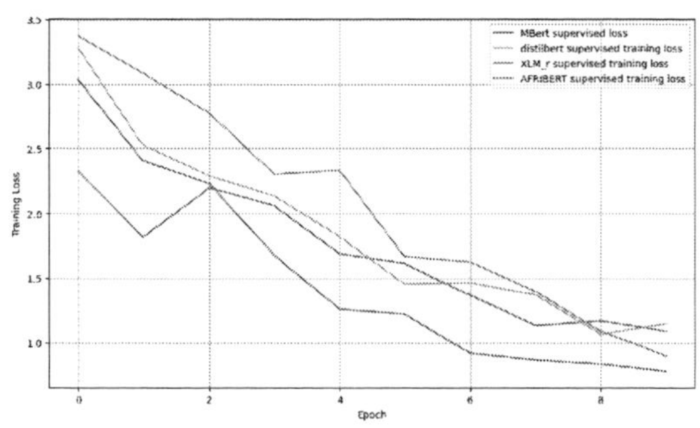


(a) Supervised Loss

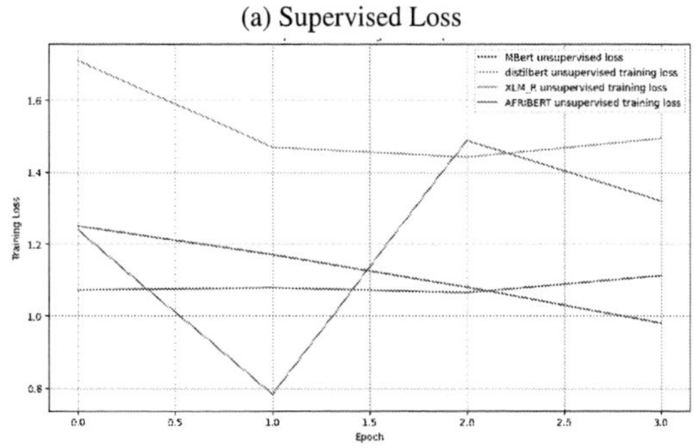


(b) Semi-supervised Loss

Figure 3: **Training loss** *(a) supervised and (b) semi-supervised learning.*

| Metrics | Neutral<br>Precision | Recall | F1-score | Frustration<br>Precision | Recall | F1-score | Happy<br>Precision | Recall | F1-score |
|---|---|---|---|---|---|---|---|---|---|
| Distilbert_supervised | 0.130 | 0.176 | 0.150 | 0.444 | 0.364 | 0.400 | 0.000 | 0.000 | 0.000 |
| Distilbert_semi_supervised | 0.141 | 0.121 | 0.131 | 0.132 | 0.227 | 0.167 | 0.000 | 0.000 | 0.000 |
| mBERT_supervised | 0.043 | 0.059 | 0.050 | 0.000 | 0.000 | 0.000 | 0.000 | 0.000 | 0.000 |
| mBERT_semi_supervised | 0.284 | 0.234 | 0.256 | 0.100 | 0.045 | 0.063 | 0.000 | 0.000 | 0.000 |
| XLM_R_supervised_training | 1.000 | 0.118 | 0.211 | 0.000 | 0.000 | 0.000 | 0.000 | 0.000 | 0.000 |
| XML_R_semi_supervised | 0.571 | 0.037 | 0.070 | 0.333 | 0.015 | 0.029 | 0.000 | 0.000 | 0.000 |
| AfriBERTa_large_supervised | 0.000 | 0.000 | 0.000 | 0.000 | 0.000 | 0.000 | 0.000 | 0.000 | 0.000 |
| AfriBERTa_semi_supervised | 0.000 | 0.000 | 0.000 | 0.000 | 0.000 | 0.000 | 0.000 | 0.000 | 0.000 |

Table 7: **Model Performance Evaluation on Emotion classification Tasks.** *Performance metrics of supervised and semi-supervised learning for (Neutral, Frustration, and Happy) emotion analysis across models. Showing poor performance of happy emotions.*

| Model | Anger<br>Precision | Recall | F1-Score | Love<br>Precision | Recall | F1-Score | Fear<br>Precision | Recall | F1-Score |
|---|---|---|---|---|---|---|---|---|---|
| Distilbert_supervised | 0.517 | 0.861 | 0.646 | 0.333 | 0.222 | 0.267 | 0.000 | 0.000 | 0.000 |
| Distilbert_semi_supervised | 0.445 | 0.833 | 0.580 | 0.357 | 0.212 | 0.266 | 0.000 | 0.000 | 0.000 |
| mBERT_supervised | 0.524 | 0.795 | 0.632 | 0.408 | 0.444 | 0.426 | 0.000 | 0.000 | 0.000 |
| mBERT_semi_supervised | 0.487 | 0.838 | 0.616 | 0.438 | 0.430 | 0.434 | 0.000 | 0.000 | 0.000 |
| XLM_R_supervised | 0.553 | 0.943 | 0.697 | 0.489 | 0.489 | 0.489 | 0.000 | 0.000 | 0.000 |
| XML_R_semi_supervised | 0.506 | 0.918 | 0.652 | 0.427 | 0.461 | 0.443 | 0.000 | 0.000 | 0.000 |
| AfriBERTa_large_supervised | 0.484 | 0.975 | 0.647 | 0.250 | 0.022 | 0.041 | 0.000 | 0.000 | 0.000 |
| AfriBERTa_semi_supervised | 0.417 | 0.920 | 0.574 | 0.182 | 0.012 | 0.023 | 0.000 | 0.000 | 0.000 |

Table 8: **Model Performance Evaluation on Emotion Classification Tasks.** *Performance metrics of supervised and semi-supervised training for (Anger, Love, and Fear) emotion analysis across models. The model performed poorly on Fear emotions.*

| Model | Sadness<br>Precision | Recall | F1-Score | Empathy<br>Precision | Recall | F1-Score | Surprise<br>Precision | Recall | F1-Score |
|---|---|---|---|---|---|---|---|---|---|
| Distilbert_supervised | 0.500 | 0.222 | 0.308 | 0.833 | 0.652 | 0.732 | 0.250 | 0.333 | 0.286 |
| Distilbert_semi_supervised | 0.100 | 0.083 | 0.091 | 0.844 | 0.580 | 0.688 | 0.360 | 0.337 | 0.348 |
| mBERT_supervised | 0.200 | 0.222 | 0.211 | 0.865 | 0.660 | 0.749 | 0.237 | 0.500 | 0.321 |
| mBERT_semi_supervised | 0.129 | 0.167 | 0.145 | 0.855 | 0.621 | 0.720 | 0.377 | 0.516 | 0.436 |
| XLM_R_supervised | 0.250 | 0.111 | 0.154 | 0.791 | 0.747 | 0.768 | 0.000 | 0.000 | 0.000 |
| XML_R_semi_supervised | 0.154 | 0.083 | 0.108 | 0.767 | 0.701 | 0.733 | 0.250 | 0.021 | 0.039 |
| AfriBERTa_large_supervised | 0.000 | 0.000 | 0.000 | 0.731 | 0.719 | 0.725 | 0.000 | 0.000 | 0.000 |
| AfriBERTa_semi_supervised | 0.000 | 0.000 | 0.000 | 0.706 | 0.659 | 0.682 | 0.000 | 0.000 | 0.000 |

Table 9: **Model Performance Evaluation on Emotion classification Tasks.** *Performance metrics of supervised and semi-supervised training methods for emotion (Sadness, Empathy, and Surprise) analysis across various models. Showing outstanding performance on Empathy emotions.*

presented in Table 6. For the negative sentiment, the supervised XLM-R achieves a high F1-score of 69.9%, unlike the semi-supervised AfriBERTa, which has the worst F1-score of 17.4%. In neutral sentiment classification, the supervised XLM-R again excels with an F1-score of 52.6%. For the positive sentiment, the semi-supervised XLM-R stands out with an exceptional F1-score of 77.1%, and the semi-supervised AfriBERTa shows robust performance with an F1-score of 66.3%.

## 5.2 Emotion Analysis

Table 5 summarizes the performance of all models on emotion analysis. The models generally show lower performance than sentiment analysis. The supervised DistilBERT achieves the highest F1-score of 31%, followed by mBERT semi-supervised, with an F1-score of 29.7%.

Table 7 shows performance for emotion classification across neutral, frustration, and happy. DistilBERT supervised leads in frustration with an F1-score of 40%. All models perform poorly on happy emotion classification. In Table 8, XLM-R supervised leads for anger and love emotions with F1-scores of 69.7% and 48.9%, respectively, but all models struggle with fear emotion. Table 9 shows low performance for sadness and surprise but outstanding performance for empathy with XLM-R supervised, leading with an F1-score of 76.8%.

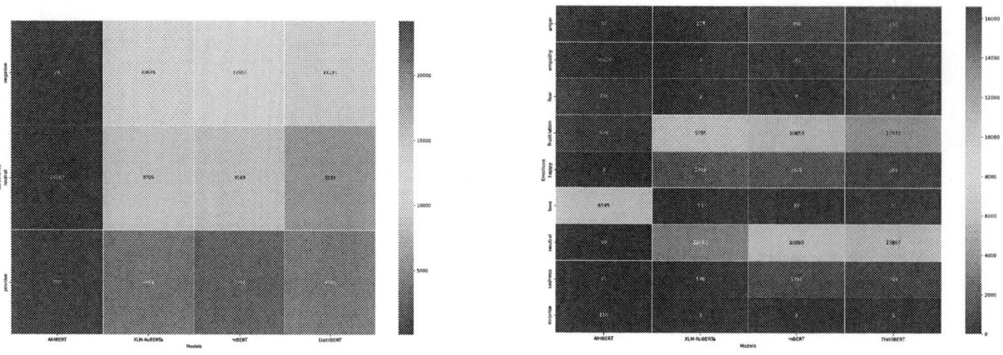

(a) Sentiment Prediction Comparison Across Models

(b) Emotion Prediction Comparison Across Models

Figure 4: *Heatmaps comparing sentiment and emotion predictions across different models. AfriBERT model most frequently predicts neutral sentiment and shows the highest sensitivity for empathy emotions.*

### 5.3 Pretrained Models performance

As shown in Figure 4, XLM-R, particularly in its supervised form, consistently outperforms other models across sentiment and emotion analysis tasks. mBERT also performs reliably well in sentiment analysis and some emotion classifications. DistilBERT, while efficient, has limitations in handling a range of emotions. AfriBERTa shows lower performance across most metrics than other models. Despite being tailored to African languages, AfriBERTa models do not perform as well in sentiment and even worse in emotion analysis.

### 5.4 Semi-Supervised Performance Analysis

The detailed analysis of SSL models reveals mixed outcomes, with clear performance enhancements in certain models and tasks, particularly in sentiment analysis. For example, mBERT's semi-supervised version slightly improved sentiment analysis with an F1-score of 59.8% compared to 59.6% for supervised version. In emotion analysis, mBERT's semi-supervised version outperformed its supervised counterpart with an F1-score of 29.7% versus 26.5%. The semi-supervised AfriBERTa achieved an F1-score of 36.6% in sentiment analysis, marginally higher than the supervised version's 35.8%, and scored 15.7% compared to 14.2% in emotion task.

## 6 Limitations

We acknowledge the subjective nature of sentiment and emotion analysis, which can be influenced by label bias, leading to inconsistencies in labeled data. We will publicly share our dataset to address this issue and facilitate further study on label bias and annotator disagreement. Secondly, the cost of obtaining labeled datasets, particularly from native speakers, can be challenging. Transformer models, SOTA for sentiment and emotion analysis, require large data and computational resources, which is still challenging in low-resource setting. Lastly, We recognize the ethical considerations of LLM use.

## 7 Conclusions and Future Work

We presented RideKE, a code-switched dataset from Twitter, with sentiment and emotion labels partially annotated for Kenyan-accented English mixed with Swahili and Sheng. Our semi-supervised learning shows mixed results, with clear performance enhancements in certain models and tasks, particularly in sentiment analysis, suggesting its potential to generally enhance model performance. We highlight the benefits of semi-supervised learning in improving model performance and reducing data annotation costs.

In the future, we aim to further enhance model performance by expanding the pool of human-labeled datasets, use other semi-supervised approaches, utilizing techniques like few-shot learning, and experimenting with different model architectures and hyperparameters tuning.


## Acknowledgments

We thank the volunteer annotators who dedicated their time and expertise to this project, which would not have succeeded without their commitment.

## References


Ife Adebara and Muhammad Abdul-Mageed. 2022. Towards afrocentric nlp for african languages: Where we are and where we can go. *arXiv preprint arXiv:2203.08351*.

David Ifeoluwa Adelani, Jade Abbott, Graham Neubig, Daniel D'souza, Julia Kreutzer, Constantine Lignos, Chester Palen-Michel, Happy Buzaaba, Shruti Rijhwani, Sebastian Ruder, et al. 2021. Masakhaner: Named entity recognition for african languages. *Transactions of the Association for Computational Linguistics*, 9:1116–1131.

Jason Angel, Segun Taofeek Aroyehun, Antonio Tamayo, and Alexander Gelbukh. 2020. NLP-CIC at SemEval-2020 task 9: Analysing sentiment in code-switching language using a simple deep-learning classifier. *arXiv preprint arXiv:2009.03397*.

Ron Artstein. 2017. Inter-annotator agreement. *Handbook of linguistic annotation*, pages 297–313.

Saurav K Aryal, Howard Prioleau, and Surakshya Aryal. 2023. Sentiment analysis across multiple african languages: A current benchmark. *arXiv preprint arXiv:2310.14120*.

ONAN Aytuğ. 2018. Sentiment analysis on twitter based on ensemble of psychological and linguistic feature sets. *Balkan Journal of Electrical and Computer Engineering*, 6(2):69–77.

Stefano Baccianella, Andrea Esuli, and Fabrizio Sebastiani. 2010. Sentiwordnet 3.0: An enhanced lexical resource for sentiment analysis and opinion mining. In *Proceedings of the Seventh International Conference on Language Resources and Evaluation (LREC'10)*, pages 2200–2204.

JoAnne Banks-Wallace. 2002. Talk that talk: Storytelling and analysis rooted in african american oral tradition. *Qualitative health research*, 12(3):410–426.

Sandra Barasa. 2016. Spoken code-switching in written form? manifestation of code-switching in computer mediated communication. *Journal of Language Contact*, 9(1):49–70.

Utsab Barman, Amitava Das, Joachim Wagner, and Jennifer Foster. 2014. Code mixing: A challenge for language identification in the language of social media. In *Proceedings of the First Workshop on Computational Approaches to Code Switching*, pages 13–23.

Kasturi Bhattacharjee, Miguel Ballesteros, Rishita Anubhai, Smaranda Muresan, Jie Ma, Faisal Ladhak, and Yaser Al-Onaizan. 2020. To BERT or not to BERT: Comparing task-specific and task-agnostic semi-supervised approaches for sequence tagging. *arXiv preprint arXiv:2010.14042*.

Tom Brown, Benjamin Mann, Nick Ryder, Melanie Subbiah, Jared D Kaplan, Prafulla Dhariwal, Arvind Neelakantan, Pranav Shyam, Girish Sastry, Amanda Askell, et al. 2020. Language models are few-shot learners. *Advances in Neural Information Processing Systems*, 33:1877–1901.

Jan Carter-Black. 2007. Teaching cultural competence: An innovative strategy grounded in the universality of storytelling as depicted in african and african american storytelling traditions. *Journal of Social Work Education*, 43(1):31–50.

Olivier Chapelle, Bernhard Schölkopf, and Alexander Zien. 2006. *Introduction to Semi-Supervised Learning*. MIT press.

Yahui Chen. 2015. Convolutional neural network for sentence classification. Master's thesis, University of Waterloo.

Alexis Conneau, Kartikay Khandelwal, Naman Goyal, Vishrav Chaudhary, Guillaume Wenzek, Francisco Guzmán, Edouard Grave, Myle Ott, Luke Zettlemoyer, and Veselin Stoyanov. 2019. Unsupervised cross-lingual representation learning at scale. *arXiv preprint arXiv:1911.02116*.

Brenda Danet and Susan C Herring. 2007. *The multilingual Internet: Language, culture, and communication online*. Oxford University Press.

Sanjiv Ranjan Das and Mike Y Chen. 2001. Yahoo! for amazon: Sentiment parsing from small talk on the web. *For Amazon: Sentiment Parsing from Small Talk on the Web (August 5, 2001). EFA*.

Aida Mostafazadeh Davani, Mark Díaz, and Vinodkumar Prabhakaran. 2022. Dealing with disagreements: Looking beyond the majority vote in subjective annotations. *Transactions of the Association for Computational Linguistics*, 10:92–110.

Kushal Dave, Steve Lawrence, and David M Pennock. 2003. Mining the peanut gallery: Opinion extraction and semantic classification of product reviews. In *Proceedings of the 12th International Conference on World Wide Web*, pages 519–528.

Jacob Devlin, Ming-Wei Chang, Kenton Lee, and Kristina Toutanova. 2018. Bert: Pre-training of deep bidirectional transformers for language understanding. *arXiv preprint arXiv:1810.04805*.

Ye-Qian Du, Jie Zhang, Xin Fang, Ming-Hui Wu, and Zhou-Wang Yang. 2023. A semi-supervised complementary joint training approach for low-resource speech recognition. *IEEE/ACM Transactions on Audio, Speech, and Language Processing*.

Amitabh Vikram Dwivedi. 2014. Linguistic realities in Kenya: A preliminary survey. *Ghana Journal of Linguistics*, 3(2):27–34.

Dan Garrette, Jason Mielens, and Jason Baldridge. 2013. Real-world semi-supervised learning of POS-taggers for low-resource languages. In *Proceedings of the 51st Annual Meeting of the Association for Computational Linguistics (Volume 1: Long Papers)*, pages 583–592.

Rahul Gupta, Saurabh Sahu, Carol Espy-Wilson, and Shrikanth Narayanan. 2018. Semi-supervised and transfer learning approaches for low resource sentiment classification. In *2018 IEEE international conference on acoustics, speech and signal processing (ICASSP)*, pages 5109–5113. IEEE.

Suchin Gururangan, Ana Marasović, Swabha Swayamdipta, Kyle Lo, Iz Beltagy, Doug Downey, and Noah A Smith. 2020. Don't stop pretraining: Adapt language models to domains and tasks. *arXiv preprint arXiv:2004.10964*.

Hohyun Hwang and Younghoon Lee. 2021. Semi-supervised learning based on auto-generated lexicon using XAI in sentiment analysis. In *Proceedings of the International Conference on Recent Advances in Natural Language Processing (RANLP 2021)*, pages 593–600.

Jahanzeb Jabbar, Iqra Urooj, Wu JunSheng, and Naqash Azeem. 2019. Real-time sentiment analysis on e-commerce application. In *2019 IEEE 16th international conference on networking, sensing and control (ICNSC)*, pages 391–396. IEEE.

Pratik Joshi, Sebastin Santy, Amar Budhiraja, Kalika Bali, and Monojit Choudhury. 2020. The state and fate of linguistic diversity and inclusion in the NLP world. *arXiv preprint arXiv:2004.09095*.

Fridah Kanana Erastus and Hilda Kebeya. 2018. Functions of urban and youth language in the new media: The case of Sheng in Kenya. *African youth languages: New media, performing arts and sociolinguistic development*, pages 15–52.

Semi-Supervised Learning. 2006. Semi-supervised learning. *CSZ2006. html*, 5.

Sophia Lee and Zhongqing Wang. 2015. Emotion in code-switching texts: Corpus construction and analysis. In *Proceedings of the Eighth SIGHAN workshop on chinese language processing*, pages 91–99.

M Paul Lewis. 2014. Ethnologue: Languages of the world. https://www.sil.org/about/endangered-languages/languages-of-the-world.

Bing Liu. 2022. *Sentiment Analysis and Opinion Mining*. Springer Nature.

Yinhan Liu, Myle Ott, Naman Goyal, Jingfei Du, Mandar Joshi, Danqi Chen, Omer Levy, Mike Lewis, Luke Zettlemoyer, and Veselin Stoyanov. 2019. Roberta: A robustly optimized bert pretraining approach. *arXiv preprint arXiv:1907.11692*.

E Matthew. 2018. Peters, mark neumann, mohit iyyer, matt gardner, christopher clark, kenton lee, luke zettlemoyer. deep contextualized word representations. In *Proc. of NAACL*, volume 5.

Alamin M Mazrui. 1995. Slang and code-switching: The case of Sheng in Kenya. *Afrikanistische Arbeitspapiere: Schriftenreihe des Kölner Instituts für Afrikanistik*, (42):168–179.

Walaa Medhat, Ahmed Hassan, and Hoda Korashy. 2014. Sentiment analysis algorithms and applications: A survey. *Ain Shams engineering journal*, 5(4):1093–1113.

Saif Mohammad. 2016. A practical guide to sentiment annotation: Challenges and solutions. In *Proceedings of the 7th Workshop on Computational Approaches to Subjectivity, Sentiment and Social Media Analysis*, pages 174–179.

Saif M Mohammad. 2022. Ethics sheet for automatic emotion recognition and sentiment analysis. *Computational Linguistics*, 48(2):239–278.

Clara Momanyi. 2009. The effects of'Sheng'in the teaching of Kiswahili in Kenyan schools. *Journal of Pan African Studies*.

Shamsuddeen Hassan Muhammad, Idris Abdulmumin, Abinew Ali Ayele, Nedjma Ousidhoum, David Ifeoluwa Adelani, Seid Muhie Yimam, Ibrahim Sa'id Ahmad, Meriem Beloucif, Saif Mohammad, Sebastian Ruder, et al. 2023a. Afrisenti: A twitter sentiment analysis benchmark for african languages. *arXiv preprint arXiv:2302.08956*.

Shamsuddeen Hassan Muhammad, Idris Abdulmumin, Seid Muhie Yimam, David Ifeoluwa Adelani, Ibrahim Sa'id Ahmad, Nedjma Ousidhoum, Abinew Ayele, Saif M Mohammad, and Meriem Beloucif. 2023b. Semeval-2023 task 12: sentiment analysis for african languages (afrisenti-semeval). *arXiv preprint arXiv:2304.06845*.

Sebastian Nagel. 2018. Common Crawl - Blog - Index to WARC Files and URLs in Columnar Format — commoncrawl.org. `https://commoncrawl.org/blog/index-to-warc-files-and-urls`. [Accessed 27-06-2024].

Amir Najafi, Shin-ichi Maeda, Masanori Koyama, and Takeru Miyato. 2019. Robustness to adversarial perturbations in learning from incomplete data. *Advances in Neural Information Processing Systems*, 32.

Usman Naseem and Katarzyna Musial. 2019. Dice: Deep intelligent contextual embedding for twitter sentiment analysis. In *2019 International Conference on Document Analysis and Recognition (ICDAR)*, pages 953–958. IEEE.

Tetsuya Nasukawa and Jeonghee Yi. 2003. Sentiment analysis: Capturing favorability using natural language processing. In *Proceedings of the 2nd International Conference on Knowledge Capture*, pages 70–77.

Finn Årup Nielsen. 2011. A new anew: Evaluation of a word list for sentiment analysis in microblogs. *arXiv preprint arXiv:1103.2903*.

Thomas Niesler and Febe De Wet. 2008. Accent identification in the presence of code-mixing. In *Odyssey*, page 27.

Thomas Niesler et al. 2018. A first south african corpus of multilingual code-switched soap opera speech. In *Proceedings of the Eleventh International Conference on Language Resources and Evaluation (LREC 2018)*.

Kelechi Ogueji, Yuxin Zhu, and Jimmy Lin. 2021. Small data? no problem! exploring the viability of pretrained multilingual language models for low-resourced languages. In *Proceedings of the 1st Workshop on Multilingual Representation Learning*, pages 116–126.

Tobi Olatunji, Tejumade Afonja, Aditya Yadavalli, Chris Chinenye Emezue, Sahib Singh, Bonaventure FP Dossou, Joanne Osuchukwu, Salomey Osei, Atnafu Lambebo Tonja, Naome Etori, et al. 2023. Afrispeech-200: Pan-african accented speech dataset for clinical and general domain asr. *Transactions of the Association for Computational Linguistics*, 11:1669–1685.

Alvaro Ortigosa, José M Martín, and Rosa M Carro. 2014. Sentiment analysis in facebook and its application to e-learning. *Computers in human behavior*, 31:527–541.

Billian Khalayi Otundo and Martine Grice. 2022. Intonation in advice-giving in kenyan english and kiswahili. *Proceedings of Speech Prosody 2022*, pages 150–154.

Bo Pang, Lillian Lee, and Shivakumar Vaithyanathan. 2002. Thumbs up? sentiment classification using machine learning techniques. *arXiv preprint cs/0205070*.

Bo Pang, Lillian Lee, et al. 2008. Opinion mining and sentiment analysis. *Foundations and Trends® in information retrieval*, 2(1–2):1–135.

Viet H Pham, Thang M Pham, Giang Nguyen, Long Nguyen, and Dien Dinh. 2023. Semi-supervised neural machine translation with consistency regularization for low-resource languages. *arXiv preprint arXiv:2304.00557*.

Mario Piergallini, Rouzbeh Shirvani, Gauri Shankar Gautam, and Mohamed Chouikha. 2016. Word-level language identification and predicting codeswitching points in swahili-english language data. In *Proceedings of the second workshop on computational approaches to code switching*, pages 21–29.

Shana Poplack. 2000. Toward a typology of codeswitching. *L. WEI (éd.), The bilingualism reader. London, New York: Routeledge*, pages 221–255.

Colin Raffel, Noam Shazeer, Adam Roberts, Katherine Lee, Sharan Narang, Michael Matena, Yanqi Zhou, Wei Li, and Peter J Liu. 2020. Exploring the limits of transfer learning with a unified text-to-text transformer. *Journal of Machine Learning Research*, 21(140):1–67.

Fuji Ren and Changqin Quan. 2012. Linguistic-based emotion analysis and recognition for measuring consumer satisfaction: an application of affective computing. *Information Technology and Management*, 13:321–332.

Takaaki Saeki, Heiga Zen, Zhehuai Chen, Nobuyuki Morioka, Gary Wang, Yu Zhang, Ankur Bapna, Andrew Rosenberg, and Bhuvana Ramabhadran. 2023. Virtuoso: Massive multilingual speech-text joint semi-supervised learning for text-to-speech. In *ICASSP 2023-2023 IEEE International Conference on Acoustics, Speech and Signal Processing (ICASSP)*, pages 1–5. IEEE.

Victor Sanh, Lysandre Debut, Julien Chaumond, and Thomas Wolf. 2019. Distilbert, a distilled version of bert: smaller, faster, cheaper and lighter. *arXiv preprint arXiv:1910.01108*.

Sebastin Santy, Anirudh Srinivasan, and Monojit Choudhury. 2021. BERTologiCoMix: How does code-mixing interact with multilingual BERT? In *Proceedings of the Second Workshop on Domain Adaptation for NLP*, pages 111–121.

Carol Myers Scotton. 1993. *Social motivations for codeswitching: Evidence from Africa*. Clarendon Press.

Salam Michael Singh and Thoudam Doren Singh. 2022. Low resource machine translation of English–Manipuri: A semi-supervised approach. *Expert Systems with Applications*, 209:118187.

Stephanie Strassel and Jennifer Tracey. 2016. Lorelei language packs: Data, tools, and resources for technology development in low resource languages. In *Proceedings of the Tenth International Conference on Language Resources and Evaluation (LREC'16)*, pages 3273–3280.

Jared Suttles and Nancy Ide. 2013. Distant supervision for emotion classification with discrete binary values. In *International Conference on Intelligent Text Processing and Computational Linguistics*, pages 121–136. Springer.

Maite Taboada, Julian Brooke, Milan Tofiloski, Kimberly Voll, and Manfred Stede. 2011. Lexicon-based methods for sentiment analysis. *Computational linguistics*, 37(2):267–307.

Michelle Terblanche, Kayode Olaleye, and Vukosi Marivate. 2024. Prompting towards alleviating code-switched data scarcity in under-resourced languages with gpt as a pivot. *arXiv preprint arXiv:2404.17216*.

S Thara and Prabaharan Poornachandran. 2018. Code-mixing: A brief survey. In *2018 International Conference on Advances in Computing, Communications and Informatics (ICACCI)*, pages 2382–2388. IEEE.

Samuel Thomas, Michael L Seltzer, Kenneth Church, and Hynek Hermansky. 2013. Deep neural network features and semi-supervised training for low resource speech recognition. In *2013 IEEE International Conference on Acoustics, Speech and Signal Processing*, pages 6704–6708. IEEE.

Ashish Vaswani, Noam Shazeer, Niki Parmar, Jakob Uszkoreit, Llion Jones, Aidan N Gomez, Łukasz Kaiser, and Illia Polosukhin. 2017. Attention is all you need. *Advances in neural information processing systems*, 30.

Bao-Khanh Ho Vo and NIGEL Collier. 2013. Twitter emotion analysis in earthquake situations. *Int. J. Comput. Linguistics Appl.*, 4(1):159–173.

Duy-Tin Vo and Yue Zhang. 2015. Target-dependent twitter sentiment classification with rich automatic features. In *Twenty-fourth International Joint Conference on Artificial Intelligence*.

Alex Wang, Yada Pruksachatkun, Nikita Nangia, Amanpreet Singh, Julian Michael, Felix Hill, Omer Levy, and Samuel Bowman. 2019. Superglue: A stickier benchmark for general-purpose language understanding systems. *Advances in Neural Information Processing systems*, 32.

Jiayi Wang, David Adelani, Sweta Agrawal, Marek Masiak, Ricardo Rei, Eleftheria Briakou, Marine Carpuat, Xuanli He, Sofia Bourhim, Andiswa Bukula, et al. 2024. Afrimte and africomet: Enhancing comet to embrace under-resourced african languages. In *Proceedings of the 2024 Conference of the North American Chapter of the Association for Computational Linguistics: Human Language Technologies (Volume 1: Long Papers)*, pages 5997–6023.

Genta Indra Winata, Alham Fikri Aji, Zheng-Xin Yong, and Thamar Solorio. 2022. The decades progress on code-switching research in nlp: A systematic survey on trends and challenges. *arXiv preprint arXiv:2212.09660*.

H Zamani, A Abas, and MKM Amin. 2016. Eye tracking application on emotion analysis for marketing strategy. *Journal of Telecommunication, Electronic and Computer Engineering (JTEC)*, 8(11):87–91.

Yukun Zhu, Ryan Kiros, Rich Zemel, Ruslan Salakhutdinov, Raquel Urtasun, Antonio Torralba, and Sanja Fidler. 2015. Aligning books and movies: Towards story-like visual explanations by watching movies and reading books. In *Proceedings of the IEEE international conference on computer vision*, pages 19–27.

# A Appendix

## A.1 Language Detection

| Language Code | Occurrences | Language |
|---|---|---|
| en | 29845 | English |
| id | 3288 | Indonesian |
| sw | 624 | Swahili |
| no | 192 | Norwegian |
| da | 119 | Danish |
| tr | 95 | Turkish |
| nl | 81 | Dutch |
| af | 73 | Afrikaans |
| de | 71 | German |
| ca | 55 | Catalan |
| so | 46 | Somali |
| sv | 34 | Swedish |
| et | 26 | Estonian |
| tl | 15 | Tagalog (Filipino) |
| hu | 14 | Hungarian |
| fr | 14 | French |
| es | 10 | Spanish |
| hr | 9 | Croatian |
| it | 8 | Italian |
| cy | 8 | Welsh |
| fi | 6 | Finnish |
| pl | 4 | Polish |
| sl | 3 | Slovenian |
| lt | 3 | Lithuanian |
| ro | 3 | Romanian |

Table 10: Count of language detection in the RideKE dataset

## A.2 Tweets Per Location

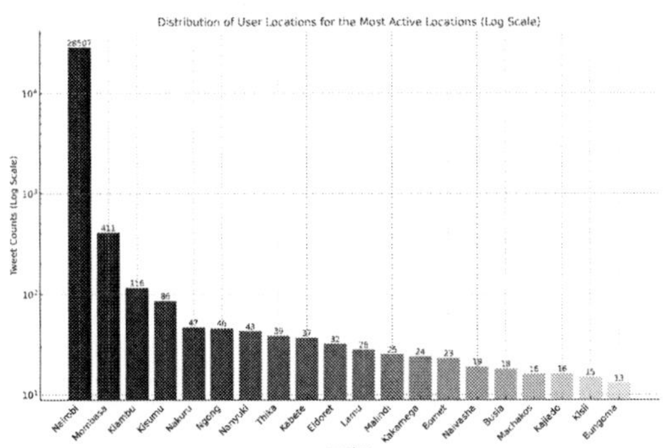


Figure 5: Number of tweets per location on a logarithmic scale. Nairobi appears to be the most active location per dataset.

## A.3 Sheng-to-English Sample Sentences

| Sheng | English Translation |
|---|---|
| dere anadai | Driver demands |
| kuna some people eating | people benefitting |
| ferry slay queens | Ferry divas |
| Mmemulikwaa oya | on the spotlight ! |
| Mhesh | honorable sir |
| wazungu's | white people |
| sikwembe ya Yesu | strong faith in Jesus |
| Hiyo pesa ni kadonye | That's little money |
| fare noma | Expensive fare |
| kuweka ngata | To fuel |

Table 11: Sheng to English Example Sentences

### A.4 Annotation Guidelines

<table>
<tr><th>Aspect</th><th>Details</th></tr>
<tr><td>Title</td><td>Annotation Guidelines for RHS Conversation on Twitter</td></tr>
<tr><td>Task</td><td>Annotating emotions in tweets related to RHS experiences</td></tr>
<tr><td>Annotation Process</td><td><ul><li>Emotion Definition: Annotators accurately identify and label the predominant emotion expressed in each tweet based on the emotional tone conveyed by the text.</li><li>Keyword Identification: Pay attention to keywords or phrases that suggest the presence of a particular emotion.</li><li>Context Matters: Consider the tweet's context, including any relevant hashtags, mentions, or user profiles, for a better understanding of the emotional context.</li><li>Tweet Length: Emotions can be expressed differently in short and long tweets.</li></ul></td></tr>
<tr><td>Emotion Labels Guidelines</td><td><ol><li>Anger: Label when the tweet expresses frustration, annoyance, resentment, or strong displeasure toward RHS, drivers, or related issues. Look for keywords and tone indicative of anger. Keywords: angry, furious, annoyed, upset. Example: "Terrible experience with Uber driver! He was rude and refused to follow the GPS directions #Angry".</li><li>Happy: Label when the tweet reflects joy, satisfaction, contentment, or delight regarding RHS experiences. Look for expressions of happiness, appreciation, or positive feedback. Keywords: happy, delighted, thrilled, satisfied. Example: "Just had the best ride ever with the friendliest driver! #HappyCustomer #GreatService"</li><li>Fear: Label when the tweet expresses anxiety, worry, concern, or fear about RHS safety, incidents, or perceived risks. Identify cues of fear or apprehension. Keywords: afraid, scared, worried, nervous. Example: "My ride is taking an unfamiliar route, and I'm getting worried. Is this safe? #Fear"</li><li>Suprise: Label when the tweet indicates astonishment, amazement, or unexpected reactions to RHS experiences.Keywords: surprised, shocked, amazed, unexpected. Example: "Wow, my driver gave me a free upgrade to a luxury car! #Surprised</li><li>Love: Label when the tweet reflects affection, appreciation, or strong positive emotions toward RHS, drivers, or related aspects. Look for expressions of love or admiration. Keywords: love, adore, appreciate, grateful. Example: "Wow, my driver gave me a free upgrade to a luxury car! #Surprised #Love"</li><li>Frustration: Label when the tweet expresses dissatisfaction, irritation, or being fed up with RHS issues. Identify cues of frustration and annoyance. Keyword: frustrated, annoyed, fed up, irritated. Example: "Been waiting for my ride for ages. This is so frustrating!#Frustrated #LateAgain"</li><li>Neutral: Label when the tweet does not exhibit any strong emotional sentiment or when the emotion is unclear or ambiguous. Use this label sparingly and only when other emotions are not evident. Example: "Just booked my ride for tomorrow morning. #RideHail #PlanningAhead</li></ol></td></tr>
<tr><td>Quality Control</td><td>Monitor inter-annotator agreement to ensure consistency among annotators. Resolve disagreements through discussion and clarification.</td></tr>
<tr><td>Privacy and Ethical Considerations</td><td>Respect user privacy and report any offensive content appropriately.</td></tr>
</table>

Table 12: Annotation guidelines for ride-hailing service conversation emotions on Twitter

## A.5 Sample dataset structure

| Keyword | Date | Tweets | reply count | retweet count | like count | verified | user followers | user following | user tweets | user location | country |
|---|---|---|---|---|---|---|---|---|---|---|---|
| #UBER-Kenya | 2023-04-10 | Did Nairobi ask you to double Nairobi fare price ? That's how Uber Kenya and bolt steal from us here. | 1 | 0 | 0 | 0 | 2104 | 981 | 23173 | Mombasa | Kenya |
| #UBER-Kenya | 2023-03-30 | Uber Kenya made an order that was cancelled by a restaurant but I've already paid. How do I follow up on my refund? | 1 | 0 | 0 | 0 | 946 | 975 | 4642 | Nairobi | Kenya |
| #UBER-Kenya | 2023-03-30 | Uber Kenya made an order that was cancelled by a restaurant but I've already paid. How do I follow up on my refund? | 1 | 0 | 0 | 0 | 946 | 975 | 4642 | Nairobi | Kenya |
| #UBER-Kenya | 2023-04-02 | Uber is losing the Kenyan market to Nairobi apps, customers are tired of being asked by drivers where in Nairobi they are going. Nairobi apps show Nairobi drivers where the customer is, where is going and price hence drivers will decide to accept or decline the request. | 2 | 0 | 0 | 0 | 46 | 297 | 817 | Nairobi | Kenya |
| #UBER-Kenya | 2023-03-27 | Uber Kenya how can your driver click not paid when he was paid? And Nairobi is proof of payment? | 2 | 0 | 0 | 0 | 5744 | 1338 | 208846 | Nairobi | Kenya |
| #BOLT-Kenya | 2023-04-06 | Hello, thanks for writing in. Kindly do reach out to us via kenyabolt.eu and a member of our team will respond and assist accordingly. | 0 | 0 | 0 | 1 | 15093 | 447 | 16966 | Nairobi | Kenya |
| #BOLT-Kenya | 2023-01-16 | Let's have an honest conversation here...this morning you lowered the base category to 8ksh per kilometer. We all know that fuel is still very high. What method did you use to reach this point, Did you involve drivers about the | 1 | 0 | 3 | 0 | 14 | 87 | 82 | Nairobi | Kenya |
| #BOLT-Kenya | 2022-11-19 | If you don't communicate. Let us as drivers do what we feel like doing. Because bolt Kenya is manner less. | 0 | 0 | 0 | 0 | 11 | 69 | 66 | Nairobi | Kenya |
| #BOLT-Kenya | 2019-10-27 | How come Bolt Kenya does not have an active customer service line for queries? | 0 | 0 | 0 | 0 | 23 | 180 | 35 | Nairobi | Kenya |
| #BOLT-Kenya | 2019-05-20 | Thanks to Boltkenya been arriving at my studio sessions and interviews on time and with comfort. You too can enjoy this service by simply downloading boltkenya and using my code FEMIONEBOLT to get kshs250 off | 0 | 0 | 3 | 0 | 40629 | 528 | 24042 | Nairobi | Kenya |
| #LITTLECAB | 2022-07-31 | Now #Littlecab will not allow me to cancel a ride I did not take until I pay. Exhausting! | 0 | 0 | 0 | 0 | 636 | 2222 | 4085 | Nairobi | Kenya |
| #LITTLECAB | 2022-07-31 | And they let me have their driver. The security officer at #Carnivorekenya says that they do not verify the drivers. What is the whole point of telling us to use #littlecab if you have no relationship with them. Just destroyed my whole experience attending a beautiful musical. | 1 | 0 | 0 | 0 | 636 | 2222 | 4085 | Nairobi | Kenya |
| #LITTLECAB | 2022-05-10 | Use #Littlecab. These other Apps are foreign and exploitive. | 0 | 0 | 1 | 0 | 480 | 987 | 4740 | Mombasa | Kenya |
| #LITTLECAB | 2020-12-23 | Why do we always encounter cabs from #LittleCab that arrive with different number plates from what is registered in your system? While I don't board them in principle for security concerns, it may one day be costly for a desperate client | 2 | 0 | 0 | 0 | 4712 | 3044 | 20683 | Nairobi | Kenya |

Table 13: Original sample of the tweets data structure

# POLygraph: Polish Fake News Dataset

**Daniel Dzienisiewicz, Filip Graliński, Piotr Jabłoński**
**Marek Kubis, Paweł Skórzewski, Piotr Wierzchoń**
Adam Mickiewicz University, Poznań
ul. Wieniawskiego 1, 61-712 Poznań, Poland
{dzienis,filip.gralinski,piotr.jablonski,
marek.kubis,pawel.skorzewski,piotr.wierzchon}@amu.edu.pl

## Abstract

This paper presents the POLygraph dataset, a unique resource for fake news detection in Polish. The dataset, created by an interdisciplinary team, is composed of two parts: the "fake-or-not" dataset with 11,360 pairs of news articles (identified by their URLs) and corresponding labels, and the "fake-they-say" dataset with 5,082 news articles (identified by their URLs) and tweets commenting on them. Unlike existing datasets, POLygraph encompasses a variety of approaches from source literature, providing a comprehensive resource for fake news detection. The data was collected through manual annotation by expert and non-expert annotators. The project also developed a software tool that uses advanced machine learning techniques to analyze the data and determine content authenticity. The tool and dataset are expected to benefit various entities, from public sector institutions to publishers and fact-checking organizations. Further dataset exploration will foster fake news detection and potentially stimulate the implementation of similar models in other languages. The paper focuses on the creation and composition of the dataset, so it does not include a detailed evaluation of the software tool for content authenticity analysis, which is planned at a later stage of the project.

## 1 Introduction

This paper describes a dataset created for a project aimed at detecting and analyzing fake news on the Polish web. Fake news poses a significant threat in real-world situations, eroding trust in institutions, manipulating public opinion, and fueling societal tensions. To address this challenge, our project employs a unique hybrid research approach, merging narratological, comparative, and sociological techniques with natural language processing and big data analytics. An interdisciplinary team of experts in various fields, including mathematics, computer science, philology, media studies, law, philosophy, folklore, and IT, collaborates on this endeavor. The project aims to develop a fake news detection software tool that uses a comprehensive database of sources, authors, and content, as well as advanced machine learning techniques and implicit trust ranking analyses to determine the authenticity of the content.

The dataset described in this paper consists of two parts. The first part, referred to as the "fake-or-not" dataset, contains 11,360 pairs of news articles (identified by URLs) and labels indicating whether the news is fake or not. The second part, known as the "fake-they-say" dataset, comprises 5,082 news articles (identified by URLs) and tweets commenting on them. Each tweet is accompanied by a label expressing the commentator's opinion about the article's truthfulness.

Our software tool and its underlying dataset are intended to serve various beneficiaries, including public sector entities like the Ministry of Internal Affairs and Administration, the Ministry of Defense, the Police, the Internal Security Agency, and the Internal Security Service for public safety purposes. It could also be helpful for publishers, the Warsaw Stock Exchange, the Financial Supervision Commission (to monitor potential manipulations affecting company valuations or the country's macroeconomic status), fact-checking organizations, and analytical firms.

## 2 Related Work

### 2.1 Tasks and Datasets

In today's digital age, the rapid dissemination of information has led to an intertwined web of factual narratives and misinformation. The challenge of distinguishing between the two has spurred extensive research in various domains. Tasks such as fact verification (Schuster et al., 2019; Lewis et al., 2020), fact-checking (Wang, 2017; Bhattarai et al., 2022), fact-based text editing (Iso et al.,



*Proceedings of the 14th Workshop on Computational Approaches to Subjectivity, Sentiment, & Social Media Analysis*, pages 250–263
August 15, 2024 ©2024 Association for Computational Linguistics

2020), and table-based fact verification (Chen et al., 2020; Eisenschlos et al., 2020) are crucial in this endeavor. The complexity is further heightened by the introduction of counterfactual elements, which encompass counterfactual detection (Yang et al., 2020), inference (Pawlowski et al., 2020; Poulos and Zeng, 2021), and explanation (Plumb et al., 2020; Ramon et al., 2020). Moreover, the classification of comments (Bornheim et al., 2021) based on their toxicity, engagement, and fact-claiming nature is an emerging area of interest.

The broader challenge of misinformation (Thorne and Vlachos, 2021; Bhattarai et al., 2022) encapsulates various facets, including fake news detection (Shu et al., 2017; Wang, 2017), deepfake detection (Rossler et al., 2019; Li et al., 2020b), and fake image detection (Afchar et al., 2018; Rossler et al., 2019). The political sphere, as evidenced by stance detection tasks (Hanselowski et al., 2018; Borges et al., 2019) related to the US 2020 Election (Kawintiranon and Singh, 2021), is particularly susceptible to these challenges. Complementary research areas such as hate speech detection (Davidson et al., 2017; Mathew et al., 2021), propaganda technique identification (Blaschke et al., 2020), aggression identification (Orăsan, 2018; Risch and Krestel, 2018), satire detection (Li et al., 2020a; Ionescu and Chifu, 2021), humor detection (Castro et al., 2016; Weller and Seppi, 2019), rumor detection (Kochkina et al., 2017; Zubiaga et al., 2018; Gorrell et al., 2019), and deception detection (Guo et al., 2023) further underscore the multifaceted nature of this challenge.

Several datasets and competitions, such as those hosted on Kaggle[1] and the ISOT Fake News Dataset (Ahmed et al., 2017, 2018), have been developed to foster advancements in this domain. RumourEval competition (Gorrell et al., 2019) provided a dataset of dubious posts and ensuing conversations in social media, annotated both for stance and veracity. The competition received many submissions that used state-of-the-art methodology to tackle the challenges involved in rumor verification. Another example is the FEVER (Fact Extraction and VERification) dataset (Thorne et al., 2018), consisting of 185,445 claims generated by altering sentences from Wikipedia and subsequently classified without knowledge of the sentence they were derived from as "supported", "refuted", or "not enough info".

[1]https://www.kaggle.com/c/fake-news

For a comprehensive approach, it is imperative to integrate diverse sources, including fact-checking websites, encyclopedias, urban legends, conspiracy theories, and Wikipedia entries on fake news. Archival resources, such as the urban legend archive curated by Graliński (2012), offer unique insights. Furthermore, domain-specific datasets, focusing on works of sci-fi authors like Lem, Pratchett, and Sapkowski, or niche forums like Wykop.pl[2] and Hyperreal[3], provide a rich tapestry of data for analysis. An example of such a dataset is BAN-PL (Kolos et al., 2024), collecting content from the Wykop.pl web service that contains offensive language, which makes an essential contribution to the automated detection of such language online, including hate speech and cyberbullying.

Our methodology for categorizing fake news and non-fake news is anchored in established guidelines, as outlined by resources like EUfactcheck[4]. Additionally, the emergence of fake news detectors, evident in browser plugins and extensions such as SurfSafe[5], Reality Defender[6], or Fake News Chrome Extension[7], presents promising avenues for real-time misinformation mitigation.

This research aims to introduce a comprehensive Polish fake news dataset to lay a robust foundation for future endeavors in the realm of misinformation detection and analysis within the Polish context.

### 2.2 Annotation Methodologies

The current fake news detection techniques can be classified into several groups. For instance, according to Wang et al. (2021), there are three categories of methods: propagation structure-based, user information-based, and news content-based. Propagation structure-based methods involve extracting features related to news dissemination in social media. User information-based methods focus on the users involved in the circulation of news, covering aspects such as users' gender, social media friends, followers, and location. On the other hand, news content-based methods concentrate solely on analyzing the content of the news rather than information about users and news dissemination.

[2]https://wykop.pl

[3]https://hyperreal.info

[4]https://eufactcheck.eu/wp-content/uploads/2020/02/EUfactcheck-manual-DEF2.pdf

[5]https://www.getsurfsafe.com/

[6]https://realitydefender.com

[7]https://tlkh.github.io/fake-news-chrome-extension

A mixed approach to fake news detection was proposed by Zhang and Ghorbani (2020), who identified four components considered particularly important in characterizing fake news: creator/disseminator, target, news content, and social context. Zhou and Zafarani (2020), on the other hand, divide fake news detection models into methods based on the analysis of the annotator's knowledge (knowledge-based fake news detection), the style in which the news is written (style-based fake news detection), the method of disseminating the news (propagation-based fake news detection), and assessing the credibility of news sources (source-based fake news detection).

## 3 Data Collection

The POLygraph: Polish Fake News Dataset was collected entirely from the Internet. The research team designed a mechanism using two methods: API data access and web scraping. For Twitter (nowadays X), we utilized the Twitter API[8], which provided a powerful set of tools for Academic Researchers[9] at the time. This allowed us to access archived data without putting additional strain on web services. The functions and methods provided in the API allowed us to search and filter the entire available content of Twitter freely, going all the way back to the first published tweet in 2006[10]. We downloaded tweets from 2021-01-01 to 2022-04-30 to match the timeframe of other data sources. Twitter API provided the ability to search the entire archive and download up to 10 million tweets. For websites, a custom scraper was employed to extract and save only the relevant content.

### 3.1 Sources, Contents, and Authors

The database of 5,000 sources was prepared by scraping a list of 1,300 starter websites. The scraper then visited at least 25 documents from each page and extracted subsequent links to external documents. Then, it repeated the process of searching and archiving documents. The XPath expression used to extract links from documents[11] provided the ability to retrieve all links whose `href` attribute does not start with `mailto:` or `tel:` and then return them as a list. In the next step, this list was iterated, and each address was passed to the parser, which added the address to the internal queue. The scraped pages were archived as HTML files with linked materials in a structure consistent with the command `wget -H -k -r -l 1 url`. The downloaded HTML files were automatically anonymized and then compressed into a ZIP archive, taking as the name documents a 128-bit hash function calculated based on the URL of the archived document.

### 3.2 Tagged Press Articles

The aim of this stage of data collection was to create a database of about 3,000 tagged press articles. For this purpose, we queried Twitter to search for tweets whose content would be related to commenting on the truthfulness of the information, particularly expressing the opinion that some content constitutes fake news. We expected that entries of this type would contain references to newspaper articles and other sites that would be interesting to annotate for potential false information. To obtain the URLs we were interested in, we used access to the Twitter API. We performed two variants of this search, differing in the query used and the time frame, resulting in two sets of entries:

- V2 dataset – a query focused on finding tweets where the author directly expresses their opinion on whether something is fake or not; uses phrases like "it wasn't fake" and "it was fake" in Polish and English[12] (1–29 April 2022; 574,545 obtained entries).
- V3 dataset – a query like in V2, but extended with terms for debunking or verifying information, e.g., "verified", "correction", "where is this info from"[13] (1 January 2010–31 July 2022; 3,580,901 obtained entries).

In total, we collected 4,155,446 tweets. Using a script to extract URLs from text, we obtained 339,259 URLs from this set.

[8] `https://developer.twitter.com/en/docs/twitter-api`

[9] `http://web.archive.org/web/20230212021429/https://developer.twitter.com/en/products/twitter-api/academic-research`

[10] `https://twitter.com/jack/status/20`

[11] `response.xpath("//body//a[not(starts-with(@href,'mailto:'))][not(starts-with(@href,'tel:'))]/@href").getall()`

[12] `(lang:pl (fejk OR fake OR fakenews OR "to nie był fake" OR "to był fake" OR "to nie był fejk" OR "to był fejk")) OR (lang:en (fejk OR "to nie był fake" OR "to był fake" OR "to nie był fejk" OR "to był fejk"))`

[13] `(lang:pl (fake OR fakenews OR "fake news" OR factcheck )) OR ("to byl fejk" OR "to byl fake" OR "to nie byl fejk" OR "to nie byl fake" OR fejk OR "fejk-njus" OR dementi OR zweryfikowane OR "zrodlo potwierdzone" OR sprostowanie OR sprostowane OR "skad to info" OR "skad ta informacja" OR "przepraszam za podanie")`

The list of URLs was processed with another script, which uses Mercury Parser[14], `html2text`[15], and BeautifulSoup[16] to extract text from the website located at the given URL. During the script execution, the following are rejected:

- pages for which Mercury Parser found no text,
- pages for which the HTML returned by Mercury Parser was empty,
- pages that failed to convert HTML to text with either `html2text` or BeautifulSoup,
- pages whose language, detected based on the text using the `langdetect5` library, was other than Polish,
- pages for which `langdetect5` was unable to detect the language,
- repeated pages.

As a result, we received 63,776 examples in the JSON format supported by the Doccano (Nakayama et al., 2018) annotation tool.

To give annotators access to a website preview, we created a spider (web crawler) that takes screenshots of the pages referenced by the URLs in the list and saves them to PNG files. The script uses the Scrapy[17] framework and the `splash`[18] library. Then, using another script, we filtered the obtained examples in JSON format, discarding those for which it was impossible to take a screenshot of the page. Ultimately, we received 7,242 examples in JSON format (for Doccano), divided into 19 packages of 400 examples each (the last package was incomplete). In this way, a collection of articles was prepared for detailed tagging. Each example in the collection was designated for annotation by at least three independent annotators. The annotation was carried out using the Doccano platform, as described in Section 4.1.

### 3.3 Tweets Expressing Opinions about Press Articles

The starting point for obtaining a database of tweets expressing opinions about press articles was the dataset of 4,155,466 tweets described in Section 3.2. The subsequent processing stage was to extract external URLs of websites in Polish from this set of tweets. We wanted the resulting list of URLs to be both representative and diverse. To achieve this, we only considered one entry from each author and discarded URLs obtained through URL shorteners because they were likely redirects to other URLs in the set. Of the 4,155,446 tweets we rejected:

- 3,249,033 tweets that did not refer to any external URL,
- 466,002 tweets in a language other than Polish,
- 197,208 tweets whose author was repeated,
- 63,885 tweets that contained more than one link to an external URL, and it was not possible to clearly indicate which of them they directly referred to,
- 46,665 tweets containing a URL that was most likely obtained using a shortener,
- 38,720 tweets containing the URL of a fact-checking website,
- 18,999 tweets containing an invalid URL.

74,934 examples left.

We wrote a Python spider called `tsv2pngs` using the Scrapy framework and the `splash` library. For each example from the source `data.tsv` file, the spider takes a screenshot of the tweet and a screenshot of the page the tweet refers to, combines them and saves the result as a PNG file. To access tweet content more easily, we used the Nitter service, which is a free, open-source front-end Twitter mirror. Before combining the screenshots, we scale them as needed to ensure the resulting PNG file is readable for annotators. Screenshots with aspect ratios (picture height to width ratio) greater than 8:1 are rejected. As a result, we obtained 22,206 PNG images of page screenshots. A script that transforms data from TSV to JSONL files allowed us to obtain 74,934 examples in JSONL format. An additional script utilizes the `urllib` library to filter out specific examples from the input file, including those without corresponding PNG screenshots, those with repeated website domains, and those that are part of a user-provided list. In our case, we supplied a list of examples annotated as part of

[14] https://hub.docker.com/r/wangqiru/mercury-parser-api
[15] https://github.com/Alir3z4/html2text
[16] https://www.crummy.com/software/BeautifulSoup
[17] https://scrapy.org
[18] https://splash.readthedocs.io

the pilot annotation. Ultimately, we ended up with 8,108 examples divided into three packages, which constituted data for three "fake-they-say" annotation tasks on the Doccano platform, described in Section 4.4.1.

## 4 Data Annotation

### 4.1 *Fake-or-not* Annotation Methodology

The starting point for creating a set of questions for annotators in the discussed POLygraph dataset was the annotation scheme used in research on fake news in Japanese media by Murayama et al. (2022). The cited researchers proposed an annotation scheme that includes seven types of information: 1) the factuality of the news, 2) the disseminator's intention, 3) the target of the news, 4) the sender's attitude towards the recipient, 5) purpose of the news, 6) degree of social harmfulness of the news, 7) the type of harm that the news can cause.

The above set of questions is multidimensional, as it allows for considering a more comprehensive range of information than just the factuality aspect of the news. However, our catalog of questions expands beyond the above data. Although it is dominated by a text-centric approach, the questions are also aimed, among others, at determining the annotator's attitude towards the content, which helps recognize their bias and emotions evoked by the text. The detailed list of all 19 questions used in this annotation and related statistics are presented in Appendix A.

The annotation was performed on the Doccano platform by a total of 161 annotators. The annotators in this task were experts and students of political sciences and journalism (see Section 9). All annotators underwent detailed training, including special case analysis. The total number of annotated news articles was 7,006, including 6,339 articles annotated by at least two independent annotators. The level of agreement between annotators was estimated by calculating Fleiss' kappa and varied depending on the question.

It is worth noting that our questionnaire contained many subjective and ambiguous questions because we wanted to investigate fake news in depth. Therefore, we do not expect perfect agreement among human annotators, especially when dealing with ambiguous or controversial cases. The nuanced nature of fake news detection further contributes to this expectation. The agreement scores reported by other studies on similar tasks take values around $0.3 \sim 0.4$. For instance, the RumourEval 2019 shared task achieved a Fleiss' kappa of 0.39 for veracity annotation and 0.35 for stance annotation (Gorrell et al., 2019). Thus, we believe that kappa scores within these limits would confirm the dataset's usefulness for the purpose for which it was built.

### 4.2 Gonito.net Platform

We used the Gonito.net (Graliński et al., 2016) platform with the GEval (Graliński et al., 2019) evaluation tool to store and manage training, validation and testing data and evaluate the models used in the project. Gonito.net is an open-source platform for comparing and evaluating machine learning models, enabling reproducibility of experiments. On the Gonito.net platform, individual machine-learning tasks are organized as so-called challenges. A challenge is a set of training, validation and test data stored in a Git repository, associated with a set of evaluation metrics. Solutions to individual challenges can be put on the platform (in the form of model prediction results on a test set), which are automatically assessed using the GEval tool according to metrics related to the challenge. We have prepared two challenges for the project: *fake-or-not* and *fake-they-say*.

### 4.3 *Fake-or-not* Challenge

The *fake-or-not* challenge is to create a model that will determine whether the article underneath it is fake news or not, based on the URL. The data for the challenge comes from three sources, detailed descriptions of which are provided below in the appropriate subsections: pilot annotation (Section 4.3.1), annotation tasks on the Doccano annotation platform (Section 4.3.2), and fact-checking websites (Section 4.3.3). Based on these three sources, a dataset (set A) was created containing 10,191 records – pairs: URL, label 1 (fake news) or `0` (not fake news). Set A was split in the proportions 9:2:5 into a training set (4,482 records), validation set (1,256) and test set (3,202). The split was made deterministically – based on the last hexadecimal digit of the MD5 hash function value for the URL. Additionally, set B was obtained from annotation tasks on the Doccano platform, containing 2,420 analogous records (pairs: URL, label `1/0`). Set B has been fully included in the training set. To sum up, we have a total of 6,902 records in the training set, 1,256 records in the validation set and 3,202 records in the test set. Out of all 11,360 records,

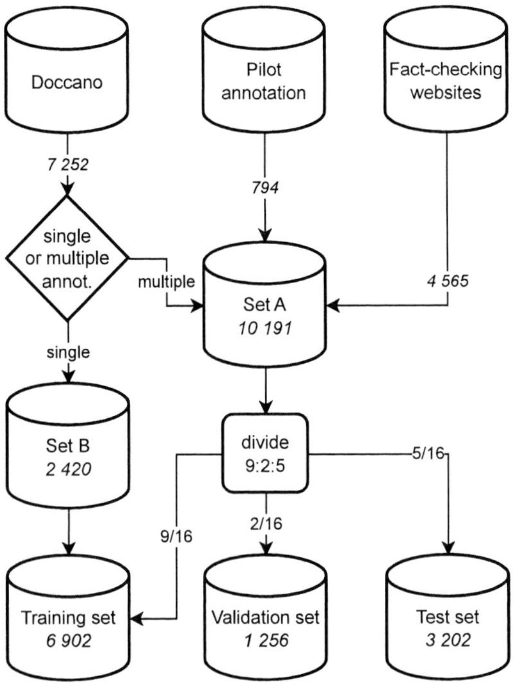


Figure 1: Data acquisition and processing workflow for *fake-or-not* challenge.

there were 4,350 records marked with label 1 and 7,116 records marked with label 0. The diagram in Figure 1 summarizes the whole process.

#### 4.3.1 Pilot Annotation Task

As part of the annotation pilot, we prepared a set of 998 URLs of press articles. The method of collecting data is described in Section 3. Each article was annotated by two independent annotators with one of three labels: "fake news", "truth", and "unknown". The inter-annotator agreement measured by Cohen's kappa was 0.421. Then, URLs marked as "fake news" or "truth" by at least one annotator and for which both annotators' annotations did not conflict were labeled 1 and 0, respectively. This way, we obtained 794 records (97 with label 1 and 697 with label 0), which were added to set A.

#### 4.3.2 Massive Annotation Task

Annotation of the tasks described in Section 4.1 consisted of answering 19 detailed questions about the text. We only used the answers to question 12 to prepare data for the fake-or-not challenge ("In your opinion, does the text contain false information?"). Annotated examples for which the annotator chose the answer "yes" or "no" were selected (the answer "not subject to assessment" was omitted). Replies

| Set | Label 1 | Label 0 | Total |
|---|---|---|---|
| A | 354 | 4,397 | 4,751 |
| B | 1,179 | 1,231 | 2,410 |
| Total | 1,533 | 5,628 | 7,161 |

Table 1: Label distribution

have been grouped by the related URLs. If the majority of the annotations for a given URL were "yes", then a record consisting of the URL and label 1 was added to the dataset, whereas if the majority of the annotations for the given URL were "no", a record consisting of the URL address and label 1. The URL was omitted in case of an equal number of "yes" and "no" annotations.

Additionally, the obtained records were divided into two sets, depending on how many majority annotations there were for a given URL. If only one annotator indicated the majority answer (this also means that no annotator indicated the minority answer), the record was put in set B. Otherwise, i.e., if at least two annotators indicated the majority answer, the record was put in set A. This way, we obtained 7,161 records, with 4,751 records in set A and 2,410 in set B. The label distribution is shown in Table 1.

#### 4.3.3 Data from Fact-checking Websites

Opinions from fact-checking websites (476 opinions from `fakehunter.pap.pl`, 2,125 opinions from `demagog.org.pl`, and 2,637 reviews from `afp.com`) were used as another source of data. If the opinion was expressed as "fake news", "false", "manipulation", etc., a record consisting of the appropriate URL address and label 1 was added to the dataset. If the opinion was expressed as "true", the appropriate record was tagged with 0. This way, we obtained 4,924 records (3,784 with label 1 and 1,140 with label 0), which were added to set A.

### 4.4 *Fake-they-say* Annotation

#### 4.4.1 Annotation Methodology

The "fake-they-say" annotation task was developed to assess the degree of the tweet author's belief in the (un)truthfulness of the information they commented on. The annotators received access to the content of 1) the tweet being rated, 2) the entire discussion regarding the news, and 3) the news itself. The task was to read the content of the comment on a specific piece of news and/or the entire accompanying discussion and then select one of the following six labels defining the tweet author's attitude towards the content of the article:

- *hard-claim-fake* (the author of the tweet claims that the news they are commenting on is false),
- *hard-claim-not-fake* (the author of the tweet claims that the news they are commenting on is true),
- *no-claim* (it is impossible to determine what the author of the tweet thinks, or the comment does not refer to the issue of (un)truthfulness of the news),
- *sarcasm* (the author of the tweet is ironizing, expressing themselves sarcastically),
- *soft-claim-fake* (the author of the tweet probably believes that the news they are commenting on is false),
- *soft-claim-not-fake* (the author of the tweet probably does not think the news they are commenting on is false).

The annotators in this task were experts and students of political sciences and journalism. All annotators underwent detailed training. There were 48 annotators, and they annotated 4,356 press articles in total, including 3,235 articles annotated by at least two independent annotators. The level of agreement between annotators was estimated by calculating Fleiss' kappa as $\kappa = 0.4343$.

#### 4.4.2 Challenge Description

The *fake-they-say* challenge is to create a model that, based on the tweet's text and the URL, will determine what the tweet's author thinks about the article located at the given URL. The data for the challenge comes from two sources (detailed descriptions provided below in the relevant subsections): pilot annotation and annotation tasks on the Doccano annotation platform. These two sources created a dataset containing 5,082 records, consisting of the following fields:

- label: one of the 6 labels described in Section 3.3 (*hard-claim-fake*, *hard-claim-not-fake*, *no-claim*, *sarcasm*, *soft-claim-fake*, *soft-claim-not-fake*),
- tweet text,
- tweet URL,
- URL address of the commented article,
- PNG image consisting of a screenshot of the tweet and a screenshot of the commented article.

The dataset was split in the proportions 13:1:2 into the training set (4,040 records), validation set (316 records) and test set (726 records). The split was made deterministically – based on the last hexadecimal digit of the MD5 hash function value for the URL. In total, we obtained 806 *hard-claim-fake* records, 102 *hard-claim-not-fake* records, 1,254 *no-claim* records, 44 *sarcasm* records, 421 *soft-claim-fake* records and 166 *soft-claim-not-fake* records.

#### 4.4.3 Pilot Annotation Data

As part of the annotation pilot, we prepared a collection of 1,000 tweets referring to various URL addresses. The method of collecting data is described in Section 3. Each tweet was annotated by 4 independent annotators with one of the 6 labels described in Section 3.3 (*hard-claim-fake*, *hard-claim-not-fake*, *no-claim*, *sarcasm*, *soft-claim-fake*, *soft-claim-not-fake*). Then, the annotations for each tweet were aggregated according to the following algorithm:

1. If all annotators have chosen the same label, assign that label.
2. Otherwise:
   - if any annotators have chosen the label **-claim-fake* and no annotators have chosen the label **-claim-not-fake*, assign the label *soft-claim-fake*,
   - if any annotators have chosen the label **-claim-not-fake* and no annotators have chosen the label **-claim-fake*, assign the label *soft-claim-not-fake*.
3. In other cases, assign the label *no-claim*.

This way, we obtained 1,000 records.

#### 4.4.4 Data from Annotation Tasks on the Doccano Platform

The method of collecting data for annotation tasks is described in Section 3. Annotation in these tasks consisted of selecting one of the 6 labels described in Section 3.3 (*hard-claim-fake*, *hard-claim-not-fake*, *no-claim*, *sarcasm*, *soft-claim-fake*, *soft-claim-not-fake*) based on the text of the tweet and the content of the website to which the tweet concerned. Then, the annotations for each tweet were aggregated according to the same algorithm as in the case of the pilot annotation. This way, we obtained 4,082 records.

## 5 Anonymization/Privatization

Privatization is an important step in the process of constructing any language resource that combines news and social media text. It requires thoughtful planning with regard to the categories of personal identifiable data that should or should not be anonymized. On the one hand, the names of public figures and coarse-grained descriptions of geographical locations of events are not considered private. Thus, they should not be anonymized in the corpus. On the other hand, the names of private citizens, their home addresses or any other personal identifiable information should be removed. To solve this problem, we developed a privatization tool that consists of three modules: 1) named entity recognizer, 2) alphanumeric expression classifier, and 3) privacy checker.

The named entity recognizer follows Transformer architecture (Vaswani et al., 2017) and utilizes a pre-trained language model (Devlin et al., 2019). It is based on the HerBERT model[19](Mroczkowski et al., 2021) with a token classification head attached. The alphanumeric expression classifier is responsible for detecting potentially private phrases with strict definitions that can be described using regular expressions. The categories of expressions identified by this module are summarised in Table 2. The privacy checker considers all expressions detected by the named entity recognizer and the alphanumeric expression classifier to be private by default. It makes public only the names that appear in an index of public figures built on the basis of DBpedia (Lehmann et al., 2015) entries that belong to the `<https://dbpedia.org/ontology/Person>` class in the DBpedia ontology, denoted by the Polish or English language code.

| Category | Description |
|---|---|
| url | uniform resource locator |
| email | e-mail address |
| cardnumber | credit/debit card number |
| zipcode | postal code |
| username | username in social media |
| nip | tax ID |
| passport | passport number |
| idcard | identity card number |
| crypto | crypto wallet address |
| macaddr | MAC address |
| accountnumber | bank account number |
| address | physical address |
| phone | phone number |

Table 2: Categories of data detected by the alphanumeric expression classifier.

| Set | fake-or-not | fake-they-say |
|---|---|---|
| Training set | 6,902 | 4,040 |
| Validation set | 1,256 | 316 |
| Test set | 3,202 | 726 |
| Total | 11,360 | 5,082 |

Table 3: The POLygraph dataset summary

## 6 Dataset Summary and Discussion

The POLygraph Polish fake news dataset consists of two parts: *fake-or-not* and *fake-they-say*, which are detailed in Sections 4.3 and 4.4.Together, they form a new dataset for detecting fake news in Polish. Unlike existing datasets, this dataset is not solely or predominantly based on a binary true-false classification but draws on various approaches proposed in source literature. The overview of the dataset is shown in Table 3.

This approach results in collecting a range of data typically utilized in news-content-based, knowledge-based, and user-information-based fake news detection methods. Although the POLygraph dataset has not yet been used in real-world scenarios, it was developed for a project aimed at verifying information sources and detecting fake news. Further exploration of the collected data by an interdisciplinary team of researchers will foster fake news detection and provide institutions and scholars with a more comprehensive range of data than previous fake news datasets. The envisioned use case involves building tools that detect false information and mark such information in search engines, potentially tested by monitoring social media messages over some time.

Additionally, adapting the POLygraph dataset for other languages should not pose a significant problem. The dataset itself is based on solutions proposed for other languages, often very different from one another, such as English and Japanese. This universality strengthens the argument that the

[19]https://huggingface.co/allegro/herbert-base-cased

core concept can be applied across various languages and cultural settings. Some proposed solutions might require modifications depending on the specific language, but the core strength remains – the applicability across diverse contexts. The presented annotation scheme will hopefully serve as a stimulus for implementing an analogous detection model for other languages.

## 7 Acknowledgments

This research was conducted as part of a project "From Urban Legend to Fake News. A Global Detector of Contemporary Falsehoods", funded by the Polish National Centre for Research and Development, grant number INFOSTRATEG-I/0045/2021.

## 8 Limitations

This study acknowledges the inherent challenges in building a comprehensive fake news detection system. The dataset, while extensive, might not capture every form of misinformation online, limiting the generalizability of the findings. Additionally, the use of human annotation introduces subjectivity, as annotators may have differing definitions of what "fake news" is. Including subjective and ambiguous questions to explore fake news in depth can lead to disagreements, especially in borderline cases. However, perfect agreement is not expected in such nuanced tasks – similar projects report agreement scores around $0.3 \sim 0.4$ (Gorrell et al., 2019), which is deemed acceptable here.

The complexity of fake news detection is reflected in the multidimensional annotation scheme employed. This paper focuses on data collection and annotation, with the evaluation of the dataset's efficacy in machine learning tasks planned for a future stage. Similarly, the description and evaluation of a potential fake news recognition tool using this dataset are beyond the scope of this article.

Furthermore, the study primarily focuses on the Polish language, limiting its direct applicability to other languages and cultures. The ever-evolving nature of fake news tactics also necessitates continuous updates to the dataset and any future detection tool to maintain effectiveness.

Despite these limitations, this study offers valuable insights into fake news detection and lays a robust foundation for future research in this area.

## 9 Ethics Statement

The human annotators were recruited from a pool of student volunteers who expressed interest in participating in the project. They were informed about the project's purpose, methods, and expected outcomes, and they gave their consent before starting the annotation task. They were given clear instructions and guidelines for the annotation task and received feedback and support whenever needed. They were free to withdraw from the project at any time without any negative consequences. The annotators did not receive payment for participating in the project, as they agreed to volunteer their time and effort for scientific research. The authors have the right to use the data presented in the paper, and they ensured that the data was anonymized and privatized to protect the privacy and confidentiality of the individuals and entities involved.

## References

Darius Afchar, Vincent Nozick, Junichi Yamagishi, and Isao Echizen. 2018. Mesonet: a compact facial video forgery detection network. In *2018 IEEE International Workshop on Information Forensics and Security (WIFS)*, pages 1–7.

Hadeer Ahmed, Issa Traore, and Sherif Saad. 2017. Detection of online fake news using n-gram analysis and machine learning techniques. In *Intelligent, Secure, and Dependable Systems in Distributed and Cloud Environments*, pages 127–138, Cham. Springer International Publishing.

Hadeer Ahmed, Issa Traore, and Sherif Saad. 2018. Detecting opinion spams and fake news using text classification. *Security and Privacy*, 1(1):e9.

Bimal Bhattarai, Ole-Christoffer Granmo, and Lei Jiao. 2022. Explainable tsetlin machine framework for fake news detection with credibility score assessment. In *Proceedings of the Thirteenth Language Resources and Evaluation Conference*, pages 4894–4903, Marseille, France. European Language Resources Association.

Verena Blaschke, Maxim Korniyenko, and Sam Tureski. 2020. CyberWallE at SemEval-2020 task 11: An analysis of feature engineering for ensemble models for propaganda detection. In *Proceedings of the Fourteenth Workshop on Semantic Evaluation*, pages 1469–1480, Barcelona (online). International Committee for Computational Linguistics.

Luís Borges, Bruno Martins, and Pável Calado. 2019. Combining similarity features and deep representation learning for stance detection in the context of checking fake news. *J. Data and Information Quality*, 11(3).

Tobias Bornheim, Niklas Grieger, and Stephan Bialonski. 2021. FHAC at GermEval 2021: Identifying German toxic, engaging, and fact-claiming comments with ensemble learning. In *Proceedings of the GermEval 2021 Shared Task on the Identification of Toxic, Engaging, and Fact-Claiming Comments*, pages 105–111, Duesseldorf, Germany. Association for Computational Linguistics.

Santiago Castro, Matías Cubero, Diego Garat, and Guillermo Moncecchi. 2016. Is this a joke? detecting humor in spanish tweets. In *Advances in Artificial Intelligence - IBERAMIA 2016*, pages 139–150, Cham. Springer International Publishing.

Wenhu Chen, Hongmin Wang, Jianshu Chen, Yunkai Zhang, Hong Wang, Shiyang Li, Xiyou Zhou, and William Yang Wang. 2020. Tabfact: A large-scale dataset for table-based fact verification. In *International Conference on Learning Representations*.

Thomas Davidson, Dana Warmsley, Michael Macy, and Ingmar Weber. 2017. Automated hate speech detection and the problem of offensive language. *Proceedings of the International AAAI Conference on Web and Social Media*, 11(1):512–515.

Jacob Devlin, Ming-Wei Chang, Kenton Lee, and Kristina Toutanova. 2019. BERT: Pre-training of deep bidirectional transformers for language understanding. In *Proceedings of the 2019 Conference of the North American Chapter of the Association for Computational Linguistics: Human Language Technologies, Volume 1 (Long and Short Papers)*, pages 4171–4186, Minneapolis, Minnesota. Association for Computational Linguistics.

Julian Eisenschlos, Syrine Krichene, and Thomas Müller. 2020. Understanding tables with intermediate pre-training. In *Findings of the Association for Computational Linguistics: EMNLP 2020*, pages 281–296, Online. Association for Computational Linguistics.

Genevieve Gorrell, Elena Kochkina, Maria Liakata, Ahmet Aker, Arkaitz Zubiaga, Kalina Bontcheva, and Leon Derczynski. 2019. SemEval-2019 task 7: RumourEval, determining rumour veracity and support for rumours. In *Proceedings of the 13th International Workshop on Semantic Evaluation*, pages 845–854, Minneapolis, Minnesota, USA. Association for Computational Linguistics.

Filip Graliński. 2012. *Znikająca nerka: mały leksykon współczesnych legend miejskich.* Media Rodzina.

Filip Graliński, Rafał Jaworski, Łukasz Borchmann, and Piotr Wierzchoń. 2016. Gonito.net – open platform for research competition, cooperation and reproducibility. In António Branco, Nicoletta Calzolari, and Khalid Choukri, editors, *Proceedings of the 4REAL Workshop: Workshop on Research Results Reproducibility and Resources Citation in Science and Technology of Language*, pages 13–20. European Language Resources Association (ELRA).

Filip Graliński, Anna Wróblewska, Tomasz Stanisławek, Kamil Grabowski, and Tomasz Górecki. 2019. GEval: Tool for debugging NLP datasets and models. In *Proceedings of the 2019 ACL Workshop BlackboxNLP: Analyzing and Interpreting Neural Networks for NLP*, pages 254–262, Florence, Italy. Association for Computational Linguistics.

Xiaobao Guo, Nithish Muthuchamy Selvaraj, Zitong Yu, Adams Wai-Kin Kong, Bingquan Shen, and Alex Kot. 2023. Audio-visual deception detection: Dolos dataset and parameter-efficient crossmodal learning. In *Proceedings of the IEEE/CVF International Conference on Computer Vision (ICCV)*, pages 22135–22145.

Andreas Hanselowski, Avinesh PVS, Benjamin Schiller, Felix Caspelherr, Debanjan Chaudhuri, Christian M. Meyer, and Iryna Gurevych. 2018. A retrospective analysis of the fake news challenge stance-detection task. In *Proceedings of the 27th International Conference on Computational Linguistics*, pages 1859–1874, Santa Fe, New Mexico, USA. Association for Computational Linguistics.

Radu Tudor Ionescu and Adrian Gabriel Chifu. 2021. Fresada: A french satire data set for cross-domain satire detection. In *2021 International Joint Conference on Neural Networks (IJCNN)*, pages 1–8.

Hayate Iso, Chao Qiao, and Hang Li. 2020. Fact-based Text Editing. In *Proceedings of the 58th Annual Meeting of the Association for Computational Linguistics*, pages 171–182, Online. Association for Computational Linguistics.

Kornraphop Kawintiranon and Lisa Singh. 2021. Knowledge enhanced masked language model for stance detection. In *Proceedings of the 2021 Conference of the North American Chapter of the Association for Computational Linguistics: Human Language Technologies*, pages 4725–4735, Online. Association for Computational Linguistics.

Elena Kochkina, Maria Liakata, and Isabelle Augenstein. 2017. Turing at SemEval-2017 task 8: Sequential approach to rumour stance classification with branch-LSTM. In *Proceedings of the 11th International Workshop on Semantic Evaluation (SemEval-2017)*, pages 475–480, Vancouver, Canada. Association for Computational Linguistics.

Anna Kolos, Inez Okulska, Kinga Głąbińska, Agnieszka Karlinska, Emilia Wisnios, Paweł Ellerik, and Andrzej Prałat. 2024. BAN-PL: A Polish dataset of banned harmful and offensive content from wykop.pl web service. In *Proceedings of the 2024 Joint International Conference on Computational Linguistics, Language Resources and Evaluation (LREC-COLING 2024)*, pages 2107–2118, Torino, Italia. ELRA and ICCL.

Jens Lehmann, Robert Isele, Max Jakob, Anja Jentzsch, Dimitris Kontokostas, Pablo N. Mendes, Sebastian Hellmann, Mohamed Morsey, Patrick van Kleef,

Sören Auer, and Christian Bizer. 2015. DBpedia - A large-scale, multilingual knowledge base extracted from wikipedia. *Semantic Web*, 6(2):167–195.

Patrick Lewis, Ethan Perez, Aleksandra Piktus, Fabio Petroni, Vladimir Karpukhin, Naman Goyal, Heinrich Küttler, Mike Lewis, Wen-tau Yih, Tim Rocktäschel, Sebastian Riedel, and Douwe Kiela. 2020. Retrieval-augmented generation for knowledge-intensive nlp tasks. In *Advances in Neural Information Processing Systems*, volume 33, pages 9459–9474. Curran Associates, Inc.

Lily Li, Or Levi, Pedram Hosseini, and David Broniatowski. 2020a. A multi-modal method for satire detection using textual and visual cues. In *Proceedings of the 3rd NLP4IF Workshop on NLP for Internet Freedom: Censorship, Disinformation, and Propaganda*, pages 33–38, Barcelona, Spain (Online). International Committee on Computational Linguistics (ICCL).

Yuezun Li, Xin Yang, Pu Sun, Honggang Qi, and Siwei Lyu. 2020b. Celeb-df: A large-scale challenging dataset for deepfake forensics. In *Proceedings of the IEEE/CVF Conference on Computer Vision and Pattern Recognition (CVPR)*.

Binny Mathew, Punyajoy Saha, Seid Muhie Yimam, Chris Biemann, Pawan Goyal, and Animesh Mukherjee. 2021. Hatexplain: A benchmark dataset for explainable hate speech detection. *Proceedings of the AAAI Conference on Artificial Intelligence*, 35(17):14867–14875.

Robert Mroczkowski, Piotr Rybak, Alina Wróblewska, and Ireneusz Gawlik. 2021. HerBERT: Efficiently pretrained transformer-based language model for Polish. In *Proceedings of the 8th Workshop on Balto-Slavic Natural Language Processing*, pages 1–10, Kiyv, Ukraine. Association for Computational Linguistics.

Taichi Murayama, Shohei Hisada, Makoto Uehara, Shoko Wakamiya, and Eiji Aramaki. 2022. Annotation-scheme reconstruction for "fake news" and Japanese fake news dataset. In *Proceedings of the Thirteenth Language Resources and Evaluation Conference*, pages 7226–7234, Marseille, France. European Language Resources Association.

Hiroki Nakayama, Takahiro Kubo, Junya Kamura, Yasufumi Taniguchi, and Xu Liang. 2018. doccano: Text annotation tool for human. Software available from https://github.com/doccano/doccano.

Constantin Orăsan. 2018. Aggressive language identification using word embeddings and sentiment features. In *Proceedings of the First Workshop on Trolling, Aggression and Cyberbullying (TRAC-2018)*, pages 113–119, Santa Fe, New Mexico, USA. Association for Computational Linguistics.

Nick Pawlowski, Daniel C. Castro, and Ben Glocker. 2020. Deep structural causal models for tractable counterfactual inference. In *Proceedings of the 34th International Conference on Neural Information Processing Systems*, NIPS '20, Red Hook, NY, USA. Curran Associates Inc.

Gregory Plumb, Jonathan Terhorst, Sriram Sankararaman, and Ameet Talwalkar. 2020. Explaining groups of points in low-dimensional representations. In *Proceedings of the 37th International Conference on Machine Learning*, volume 119 of *Proceedings of Machine Learning Research*, pages 7762–7771. PMLR.

Jason Poulos and Shuxi Zeng. 2021. RNN-Based Counterfactual Prediction, With an Application to Homestead Policy and Public Schooling. *Journal of the Royal Statistical Society Series C: Applied Statistics*, 70(4):1124–1139.

Yanou Ramon, David Martens, Foster Provost, and Theodoros Evgeniou. 2020. A comparison of instance-level counterfactual explanation algorithms for behavioral and textual data: Sedc, lime-c and shap-c. *Advances in Data Analysis and Classification*, 14(4):801–819.

Julian Risch and Ralf Krestel. 2018. Aggression identification using deep learning and data augmentation. In *Proceedings of the First Workshop on Trolling, Aggression and Cyberbullying (TRAC-2018)*, pages 150–158, Santa Fe, New Mexico, USA. Association for Computational Linguistics.

Andreas Rossler, Davide Cozzolino, Luisa Verdoliva, Christian Riess, Justus Thies, and Matthias Niessner. 2019. Faceforensics++: Learning to detect manipulated facial images. In *Proceedings of the IEEE/CVF International Conference on Computer Vision (ICCV)*.

Tal Schuster, Darsh Shah, Yun Jie Serene Yeo, Daniel Roberto Filizzola Ortiz, Enrico Santus, and Regina Barzilay. 2019. Towards debiasing fact verification models. In *Proceedings of the 2019 Conference on Empirical Methods in Natural Language Processing and the 9th International Joint Conference on Natural Language Processing (EMNLP-IJCNLP)*, pages 3419–3425, Hong Kong, China. Association for Computational Linguistics.

Kai Shu, Amy Sliva, Suhang Wang, Jiliang Tang, and Huan Liu. 2017. Fake news detection on social media: A data mining perspective. *SIGKDD Explor. Newsl.*, 19(1):22–36.

James Thorne and Andreas Vlachos. 2021. Evidence-based factual error correction. In *Proceedings of the 59th Annual Meeting of the Association for Computational Linguistics and the 11th International Joint Conference on Natural Language Processing (Volume 1: Long Papers)*, pages 3298–3309, Online. Association for Computational Linguistics.

James Thorne, Andreas Vlachos, Christos Christodoulopoulos, and Arpit Mittal. 2018. FEVER: a large-scale dataset for fact extraction and VERification. In *Proceedings of the 2018 Conference of the North American Chapter of the Association for Computational Linguistics: Human Language Technologies, Volume 1 (Long Papers)*, pages 809–819, New Orleans, Louisiana. Association for Computational Linguistics.

Ashish Vaswani, Noam Shazeer, Niki Parmar, Jakob Uszkoreit, Llion Jones, Aidan N. Gomez, Łukasz Kaiser, and Illia Polosukhin. 2017. Attention is all you need. In *Proceedings of the 31st International Conference on Neural Information Processing Systems*, NIPS'17, pages 6000–6010, Red Hook, NY, USA. Curran Associates Inc.

William Yang Wang. 2017. "liar, liar pants on fire": A new benchmark dataset for fake news detection. In *Proceedings of the 55th Annual Meeting of the Association for Computational Linguistics (Volume 2: Short Papers)*, pages 422–426, Vancouver, Canada. Association for Computational Linguistics.

Yuhang Wang, Li Wang, Yanjie Yang, and Tao Lian. 2021. Semseq4fd: Integrating global semantic relationship and local sequential order to enhance text representation for fake news detection. *Expert Systems with Applications*, 166:1–12.

Orion Weller and Kevin Seppi. 2019. Humor detection: A transformer gets the last laugh. In *Proceedings of the 2019 Conference on Empirical Methods in Natural Language Processing and the 9th International Joint Conference on Natural Language Processing (EMNLP-IJCNLP)*, pages 3621–3625, Hong Kong, China. Association for Computational Linguistics.

Xiaoyu Yang, Stephen Obadinma, Huasha Zhao, Qiong Zhang, Stan Matwin, and Xiaodan Zhu. 2020. SemEval-2020 task 5: Counterfactual recognition. In *Proceedings of the Fourteenth Workshop on Semantic Evaluation*, pages 322–335, Barcelona (online). International Committee for Computational Linguistics.

Xichen Zhang and Ali A. Ghorbani. 2020. An overview of online fake news: Characterization, detection, and discussion. *Information Processing and Management: an International Journal*, 57(2):1–26.

Xinyi Zhou and Reza Zafarani. 2020. A survey of fake news: fundamental theories, detection methods, and opportunities. *ACM Computing Surveys*, 53(5):1–40.

Arkaitz Zubiaga, Ahmet Aker, Kalina Bontcheva, Maria Liakata, and Rob Procter. 2018. Detection and resolution of rumours in social media: A survey. *ACM Comput. Surv.*, 51(2).

## A Appendix: Annotation Questions

Q1: Specify the type of text.

a) article on a news website
b) social media post
c) blog post
d) other

Q2: Define the subject matter of the text.

a) politics
b) society
c) medicine
d) military
e) economy
f) entertainment
g) education
h) science and technology
i) tourism
j) culture
k) sports
l) business
m) crime
n) safety
o) religion
p) other

Q3: What is your attitude to the text?

a) I agree with the text.
b) I do not agree with the text.
c) I have a neutral attitude to the text.

Q4: What emotions does the text evoke in you?

a) positive
b) negative
c) The text does not evoke emotions in me.

Q5: What content dominates in the text?

a) facts
b) opinions
c) both

Q6: Is the text persuasive?

a) yes
b) no
c) I don't know

Q7: What do you think is the purpose of the news?

a) information - the text is purely informative, it reports and describes events
b) disinformation - the author deliberately provides false information in order to obtain some benefits (e.g. political or financial)
c) propaganda - the text is persuasive and affects the emotions, attitudes, opinions and/or actions of the target audience for ideological, religious and other purposes

d) partisan promotion of political views - the text presents information in a biased way from the perspective of a specific political party or political ideology
e) entertainment (satire / parody) - the purpose of the text is to provide the target with entertainment and / or criticism of individuals or groups
f) other

Q8: Who do you think is the potential target of the news?

a) recipient of general news from news websites
b) recipient of entertainment
c) supporter of a specific political party
d) supporter of a specific socio-political ideology

Q9: Does the author/disseminator believe that the news they are writing about is true?

a) yes, the author openly expresses the belief that they agree with what they are disseminating
b) yes; however, the author expresses doubts about the veracity of the news
c) no, the author openly denies the veracity of the news
d) no comments are made by the author

Q10: Does the author refer to the sources of the cited information?

a) yes
b) no
c) sometimes / not always

Q11: What narrative style is the main basis of the news?

a) conflict (often specific to political events, centered around disagreement, division, difference or rivalry)
b) responsibility (assigning responsibility for the cause/effect of the presented problem to specific persons/institutions etc.)
c) morality (related to the moralizing tendencies of the media; it most often refers to condemnation or other forms of moral evaluation of the presented events)
d) human story (personalization which introduces emotional elements, the main character is most often the victim of a tragic event or crisis; greater importance is attached to the individual affected by the event than its global consequences)
e) consequences (related to a broader context and impact on various areas of social life)

Q12: In your opinion, does the text contain false information?

a) yes
b) no
c) not subject to assessment (the text contains only the author's opinion)

Q13: What kind of false information is contained in the text?

a) fake news - false information has been included in the article intentionally and it is possible to verify it (without referring to external sources!)
b) rumor - the author refers to unconfirmed information (e.g. rumors)
c) satire - the author cites false information that is humorous, ironic, mocking; it is not intended to mislead the reader
d) clickbait - the title attracts attention, but does not reflect the content of the news

Q14: Where is the false information located in the text?

a) in the title/headline
b) in one fragment
c) false information is repeated in several fragments of the text
d) in the image
e) the whole text is false

Q15: How much of the text must be read in order to realize that it contains false information?

a) headline / title
b) the title and part of the text
c) the entire text

Q16: If the news contains false information, do you think the author of the text knows that they are disseminating false information?

a) They know it.
b) They probably know it.
c) They don't know it.
d) They definitely don't know it.

Q17: Have you come across the false information contained in the text before?

a) Yes.
b) No.

Q18: How socially harmful is the false information contained in the text?

a) 0 (harmless)
b) 1 (slight harm, e.g. lack of understanding of certain events)
c) 2 (moderately harmless, e.g. causing confusion and anxiety)
d) 3 (moderately harmful, e.g. leading to conspiracy theories)
e) 4 (relatively harmful, e.g. damage to the reputation of people and institutions, prejudice against a nation, race etc.)
f) 5 (very harmful, e.g. health and life hazard)

Q19: What kind of threat may be posed by the false information?

a) lack of understanding of political and social events
b) damage to the reputation of persons and institutions, undermining trust in persons and institutions
c) prejudice against nation, race, state
d) confusion and fear of society
e) the emergence of conspiracy theories
f) risk to health and life
g) none

# Exploring Language Models to Analyze Market Demand Sentiments from News

**Abir Naskar, Manjira Sinha** and **Tirthankar Dasgupta**
TCS Research
India
(abir.naskar, sinha.manjira, dasgupta.tirthankar)@tcs.com

## Abstract

Obtaining demand trends for products is an essential aspect of supply chain planning. It helps in generating scenarios for simulation before actual demands start pouring in. Presently, experts obtain this number manually from different News sources. In this paper, we have presented methods that can automate the information acquisition process. We have presented a joint framework that performs information extraction and sentiment analysis to acquire demand related information from business text documents. The proposed system leverages a TwinBERT-based deep neural network model to first extract product information for which demand is associated and then identify the respective sentiment polarity. The articles are also subjected to causal analytics, that, together yield rich contextual information about reasons for rise or fall of demand of various products. The enriched information is targeted for the decision-makers, analysts and knowledge workers. We have exhaustively evaluated our proposed models with datasets curated and annotated for two different domains namely, *automobile* sector and *housing*. The proposed model outperforms the existing baseline systems.

## 1 Introduction

Demand forecasting is one of the fundamental aspects of business planning that drives a host of strategic and operational decisions taken by a company. It feeds into budgeting, financial planning, campaign management for sales and marketing divisions and capacity planning through scenario generation. Different stages of supply chain planning leverage information from different sources to predict probable demand for products or services across different regions. These include current sales data as well as insights about future demand gathered from a plethora of sources like social media, customer surveys or analyst reports, News etc. While analysis of relevant consumer generated content from social media has been found to have direct impact on demand of consumer goods in short term, for long term demand assessment human experts still rely on business News and analyst reports. Given the high volumes of business relevant content available for real-time demand assessment today, human curation and compilation of such information is gradually becoming impossible. Consequently text mining methods are envisaged to play a significant role in extracting and compiling the relevant information from a multitude of sources in an efficient and effective way.

In this paper, we have presented an information extraction model that exploits the transformer based neural network architectures to acquire demand related information from business text documents like News articles and reports. The task is to first identify demand related information from News and other business text sources and then resolve all associated aspects of it like product or service names, region, time, and rise or fall of demand along with reasons of the specific rise and fall, if mentioned in the text. Text elements indicative of positive sentiments in association to demand are indicative of rise in demand while negative sentiments associated with a demand indicates a fall in demand. Since business text can be written in very complex ways, hence extracting all these parameters correctly from text is a non-trivial task. For example, Table 1 example (1) contains interesting insight about positive and negative demand information for two different car models. In this paper, we present results related to the automobile and housing sector, and show how demand related insights for ten years are generated. Performance analysis of the proposed architecture is obtained using a gold-standard data set that has been manually annotated for computing the accuracy of the information extraction and enrichment processes.

News documents and analyst reports not only



*Proceedings of the 14th Workshop on Computational Approaches to Subjectivity, Sentiment, & Social Media Analysis*, pages 264–272
August 15, 2024 

| Text segments with causality marked | Subject-of-Demand: Polarity(['SDE','P'] |
|---|---|
| While demand for smaller model is soaring, sales of Some traditional vehicles have remained strong. | ['smaller models', 'NEG'] ['traditional vehicles','POS'] |
| The report found that out of A3 compact Q3 and Q5 SUVS of Audi, the demand for Q5 SUVs are significantly higher. | ['AUDI', 'POS'] ['Q5 SUV','POS'] |
| $\{$*Earnings of Hyundai Kia will likely drop*$\}_{effect}$ for the third quarter of the year $\{$*due to slump in local production*$\}_{cause}$. | ['Hyundai Kia', 'NEG'] |

Table 1: Examples of complex text segment with demand - the target is to extract all relevant information components

carry information related to future demands, they also carry expert insights on reasons for demand fluctuations. These articles can be mined for creating a knowledge base of demand impacting factors that can be used in a predictive solution for improved demand forecasting. A wide range of events has been found to impact demand in direct and indirect ways. Economic recession, pandemic, political unrest, legal battles are just few among a large class of events that have had provable impact on demands for a wide range of products and services in recent times.

We would like to emphasize that the framework does not implement any demand-forecasting model. Rather, the proposed framework gathers early demand signals and post-facto knowledge about demand alterations and presents these insights to a human decision maker, who can further use these to refine the outputs of a mathematical forecasting model. In this work we restrict ourselves to mining demand relation information from News and analysts reports only and do not consider social media inputs. But this being a reasonably well-explored area, we do provide a review of work done in this area. We have worked with large collections of News articles to extract demand related insights.

The rest of the paper is organised as follows: section 2 discusses about the problem definition. Section 3 presents our proposed TwinBERT architecture for subject of demand identification and polarity classification task. Section 4 presents the dataset used for training and testing the models followed by the experiment design and results in section 5. Section 6 discusses about the reason behind the rise and fall of demand and finally section 7 concludes the paper.

## 2 Mining demand related insights from business text

Table 1 shows few example texts that contains information about demand for automobiles across the globe. As we can see, it may contain demand related information at very granular level that includes demand estimates for specific regions along with time when those demand patterns are likely to be seen, or at very high level like "passenger vehicles". For example, the text segment, *"The report found that out of A3 compact Q3 and Q5 SUVS of Audi, the demand for Q5 SUVs are significantly higher."*, mentions about three product names namely, *A3*, *compact Q3* and *Q5 SUVS* of Audi. Out of this only demand of *Q5 SUV* has been mentioned in the text with a *positive* demand and the rest are *neutral.* Therefore it is important to correctly filter out the exact subject of demand entity along with its sentiment for which demand is associated. We define the Subject-of-Demand Entity (SDE) as: *An entity with whom information components exhibit a direct relation by virtue of being linked semantically.* For Example, in the text, *"With increased demand Mahindra is forced to enhance production capacity of Quantoas Nasik plant."*, "*Quanto*" is the SDE.

Apart from extracting the subject-of-demand and their corresponding polarities, it is also important to gather key insights about the reason behind the rise or fall of demand. Such insights can be identified from text documents by performing proper causal analysis of a given text input. For example, Table 1 example 3 illustrate a negative demand for *Hyundai KIA* with proper causal reasoning (*"slump in local production"*).

Based on the above factors, we define the following target tasks for this paper:

- Task-1: Given a text mentioning about a product demand, identify the relevant Subject-of-Demand entities (SDEs).
- Task-2: Given a text with identified SDEs, identify the sentiment polarities (*positive* for rise in demand and *negative* for fall in demand) corresponding to each SDE.

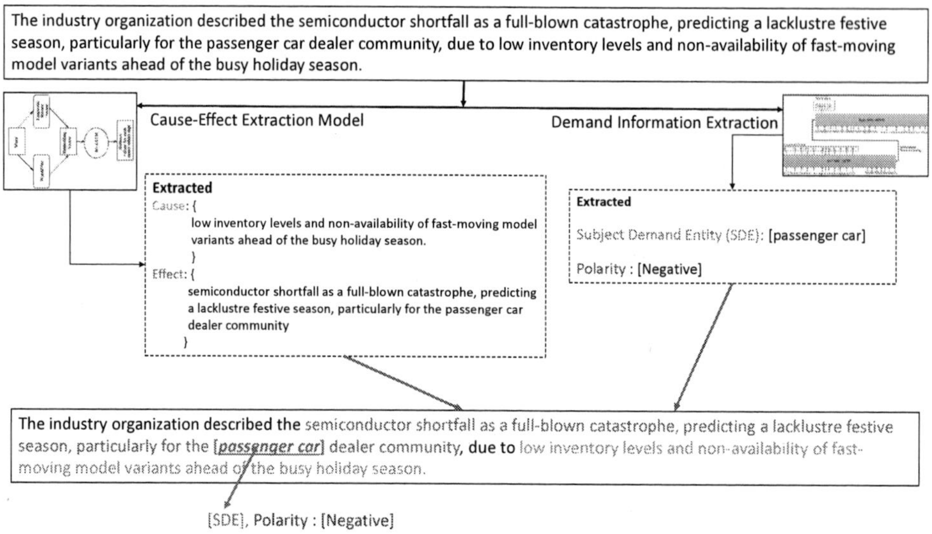


Figure 1: Working of the demand and causality extraction engine. The same text is passed to both the demand extraction as well as causality identification unit. The output label of both the models are merged together to get the final output.

- Task-3: Given a text with demand information, identify the specific causes of rise and fall of demand.

Accordingly, in this paper, we propose a joint training framework to extract both SDE as well as the sentiment corresponding to the extracted SDE from textual mentions. We use BERT (Devlin et al., 2018) as our backbone network and use a sequence labeling model to detect the start/end positions of SDE-sentiment pair(s) from a text segment.

Following the work of (Mao et al., 2021), we propose a TwinBERT architecture to represent the above extraction task using two machine reading comprehension (MRC) problems. MRC methods are known to be effective if a pre-trained BERT model is used. We decompose the SDE-polarity pair extraction task to two different sub-tasks of SDE detection ($BERT_1$)and sentiment identification ($BERT_2$).

Similarly, for causal inference, we have used the cause-effect extraction tool as presented in the literature (Dasgupta et al., 2018). The proposed model is based on linguistically informed BiLSTM architecture (LiBiLSTM) to extract cause and effect events from a given input text.

As illustrated in Figure 1, the same input text segment is passed to both the TwinBERT architecture as well as the cause-effect extraction architecture. The output of both the models are then combined together to get the respective *SDE, Polarity and causes-effect* relations. In the next section we will define in details the working of the TwinBERT model for SDE extraction and polarity classification task.

## 3 The proposed TwinBERT model for subject-of-demand extraction and polarity classification

As illustrated in Figure 2, our model consists of two parts. Both parts use a multi-layer bidirectional Transformer based language representation model (BERT) (Devlin et al., 2018) as their backbone models to encode the context information. The goal of the left part is to extract all SDEs from the given text. As we discussed earlier, we have used the sequence labeling task for this purpose. The goal of the right part is to extract the sentiment polarity with respect to a given specific SDE. This is done by applying a classification model that classifies a given text segment based on its [CLS] token. It is worth mentioning here that an input text may have multiple SDEs. Therefore, the right part of the model will take input separate text-SDE pairs corresponding to each SDE extracted by the left part.

To obtain the sequence classification and sequence labeling, the final layers of the the proposed left and right TwinBERT models have been

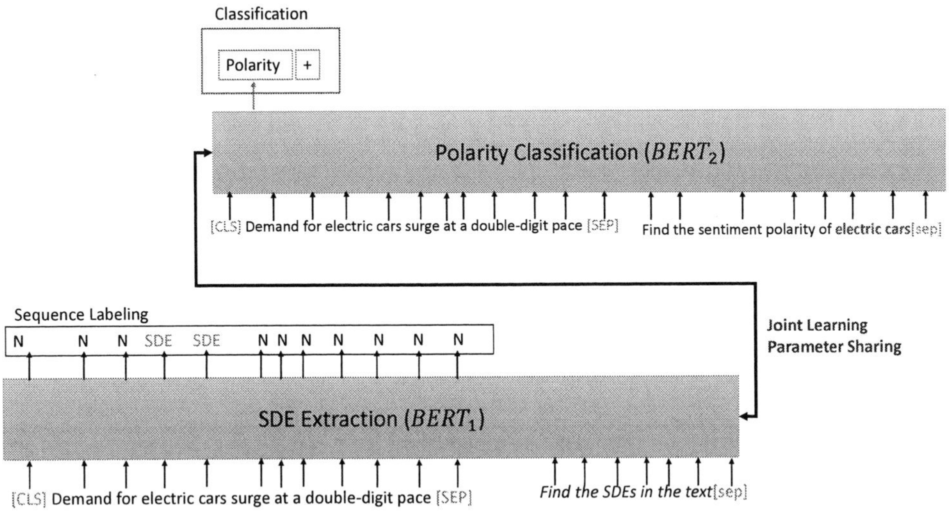


Figure 2: Overview of the Joint Training of Subject-of-Demand (SDE) Extraction and SDE Polarity Classification.

trained with two separate loss functions $L_1$ and $L_2$. Where, $L_1(\theta) = -\sum_{t=1}^{M}\sum_{k=1}^{K} \bar{y}_t^k log(y_t)$ and $L_2(\theta) = -\sum_{t=1}^{N}\sum_{j=1}^{J} \bar{q}_t^{i,j} log(q_t^i)$ $q_t$ is the vector representation of the predicted output of the model for the input word $w_t^i$. $K$ and $J$ are the number of class labels for each task (which is three in our case). The model is fine-tuned end-to-end via minimizing the cross-entropy loss.

We define the joint loss function using a linear combination of the loss functions of the two tasks as:

$$L_{joint}(\theta) = \lambda * L_1(\theta) + (1-\lambda) * I_{[y_{text}==1]} * L_2(\theta) \quad (1)$$

Where, $\lambda$ controls the contribution of losses of the individual tasks in the overall joint loss. $I_{[y_{text}==1]}$ is an indicator function which activates the loss only when the corresponding *SDE-Extractor* classification label is 1, since we do not want to backpropagate the *PolarityClassifier* loss when the corresponding *SDE-Extractor* output is 0 i.e if the *SDE-Extractor* does not return any SDE as output.

## 4 The dataset

We have curated around 74,150 news documents across the two target domains over the time period of ten years(2012 to 2021). From the given dataset we have extracted all the text segment containing words related to the concept "demand", using seed words like: *demand, requirement, need, market need, desire* etc. This gave us around 29000 text documents that contain demand related concepts. For example, text segment (1) below is mentioning about demand of automobile products where as text (2) is not related to any product demand.

1. *November saw demand for new cars, trucks and crossovers surge at a double-digit pace.*
2. *There have been numerous reports of police officers stopping such cars, and demanding that the driver produces his or her tax registration ID.*

Once, we filter out the product demand text, we present them for expert level annotations across each domains by six annotators. The annotation process undergoes the following tasks:

Task-1: Given a demand related textual mention, identify the respective subject-of-demand entities (SDE).

Task-2: If the text contains at least one SDE, then the task is to determine the sentiment polarity associated with the entity. The task here is to classify the sentiment as positive, negative or neutral. Some sample annotations are mentioned in Table 1. Finally, we have a gold standard data of 12200 text documents. Out of this, 7400 texts are from Automobile domain and the rest 4800 from Housing domain. Overall, around 43% positive demand samples, 37% negative demand samples and 20% neutral demand samples. We have used 70% of the overall data for training the classifier and rest 30% for testing purpose.

### 4.1 Conversion to *TwinBERT* compatible data format

As illustrated above, the original annotated dataset needs to be converted before it is fed into the *TwinBERT* Network. Both the *SDE-Extractor* and the *PolarityClassifier* use the input text as their contexts along with a specific query. The *SDE-Extractor* is constructed with the query, q1 = "Find the SDE terms in the text." While, the *PolarityClassifier* is constructed with the query q2 = "Find the sentiment polarity for the <SDE> in the text." This is illustrated in Figure 3.

## 5 Evaluation

In order to demonstrate the importance of the proposed neural network architecture for demand extraction, we make a comparative study of the performances of the model with respect to other standard neural network architecture. We have kept the same set of hyper-parameters for understanding the difference in their performance. The experiments were conducted using the following models: 1) Cascaded CNN-BiLSTM model: We use a standard CNN model coupled with a Bilstm layer for the extraction of SDEs and further classification of the aspect level polarities. We used the pre-trained Word2Vec embeddings to train the model. We run for training using a mini-batch size of 128 for each fold, and optimized using the Adam Optimizer. For the Bi-LSTM, 64 hidden units were used. For the CNN, layers for kernel sizes 2 to 6 were included in the network. 2) BERT model: We used the pre-trained BERT model as proposed by (Devlin et al., 2018) and fined tuned them over the proposed dataset. Here, two separate models are used to train the SDEs and their polarities. In all our experiments, 10-fold cross validation was used for the purpose of fair evaluation on the datasets. For each fold, 10 epochs were run for training using a mini-batch size of 12 for each fold, and optimized using the Adam Optimizer with learning rate of $2 * e^{-5}$.

**Evaluating the Subject-of-Demand Entity Extraction:** We quantify the performance of the demand classification score in terms of the precision, recall and F-measure values. For the SDE extraction task we perform the evaluation with respect to the different neural network models as discussed in the previous section. The extracted entities were then compared with the gold standard annotations. Table 2 depicts the evaluation results of the SDE extraction and polarity classification model for both Automobile and Housing domain data. For *Automobile domain*, we have achieved an F-measure of 0.81 with precision of 0.79 and recall of 0.83 respectively for Subject-of-Demand entities. Similarly, for the *Housing domain*, we have observed an F-Score of 0.79 with a precision of 0.77 and recall of 0.81.

**Evaluating the sentiment polarity of extracted SDEs classifier:** We quantify the performance of the polarity classification score in terms of the precision, recall and F-measure values. Table 2 depicts the evaluation results of the demand classification system for both *Automobile* and *Housing* domain data. We found that throughout all the target classes the performance of the TwinBERT network is significantly higher than the individual single task BERT as well as multi-task BERT based models. The proposed architecture significantly reduces the false negative score and achieves a high true positive score, thereby achieving a high precision and recall. During the analysis of the individual datasets we have observed that for the Automobile dataset, we have achieved an F1 score of 82% using the TwinBERT model. This is the highest accuracy that we have achieved between both the datasets. In around 20% of cases our system failed to classify the demand class correctly. For Housing domain, we achieved an accuracy of 71.2% with precision of 73%, recall of 79% and F-measure of 75.8%.

### 5.1 Comparison of Proposed Model Architecture With LLMs

In the era of large language models (LLMs), there is considerable potential to outperform numerous transformer designs. After conducting the experiments on the given dataset, we compared its output to that of LLAMA-2 13B (Touvron et al., 2023) and Mistral-7B (Jiang et al., 2023). First, we have evaluated the SDE detection ability of LLAMA-2 using zero-shot (Wang et al., 2019) and few-shot prompt techniques. Here, we have used the few-shot technique demonstrated by (Min et al., 2022) and given examples of sentences with and without SDEs as prompt.

Similarly, we have also fine-tuned the pre-trained Mistral-7B Model with the given dataset to compare LLM's ability to perform the domain-specific task of SDE detection and polarity classification with our proposed architecture. The Mistral-7B outperforms the LLAMA-2 34B despite having

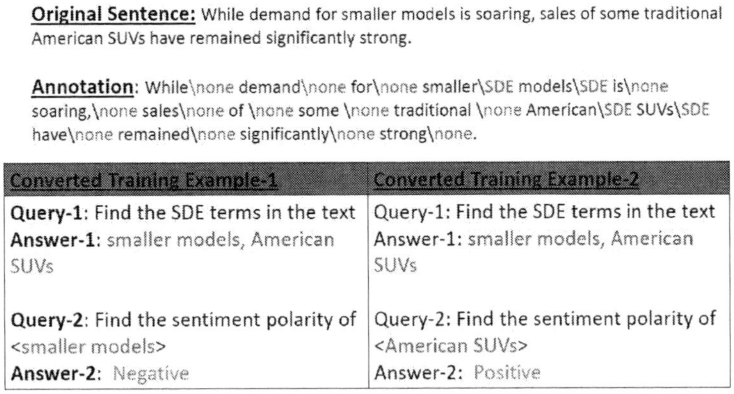


Figure 3: Illustration of the TwinBERT compatible data conversation

| Automobile Domain | | | | | | | | | | | | |
|---|---|---|---|---|---|---|---|---|---|---|---|---|
| | SDE Extraction | | | Positive | | | Negative | | | Neutral | | |
| **Models** | **P** | **R** | **F1** | **P** | **R** | **F1** | **P** | **R** | **F1** | **P** | **R** | **F1** |
| $BERT_{base}$ | 0.62 | 0.66 | 0.64 | 0.59 | 0.77 | 0.67 | 0.63 | 0.77 | 0.69 | 0.64 | 0.71 | 0.67 |
| LLAMA-2-13B | 0.68 | 0.76 | 0.72 | 0.69 | 0.67 | 0.68 | 0.63 | 0.71 | 0.65 | 0.76 | 0.71 | 0.74 |
| Mistral-7B | 0.79 | 0.77 | 0.78 | 0.77 | 0.72 | 0.75 | 0.72 | 0.78 | 0.75 | 0.76 | 0.78 | 0.77 |
| Proposed TwinBERT | 0.79 | 0.83 | 0.81 | 0.72 | 0.70 | 0.71 | 0.63 | 0.69 | 0.66 | 0.84 | 0.82 | 0.83 |
| Housing Domain | | | | | | | | | | | | |
| $BERT_{base}$ | 0.69 | 0.66 | 0.67 | 0.62 | 0.71 | 0.66 | 0.52 | 0.68 | 0.58 | 0.74 | 0.67 | 0.70 |
| LLAMA-2-13B | 0.57 | 0.72 | 0.64 | 0.52 | 0.68 | 0.59 | 0.66 | 0.68 | 0.67 | | | |
| Mistral-7B | 0.73 | 0.78 | 0.75 | 0.64 | 0.74 | 0.69 | 0.59 | 0.71 | 0.650 | 0.67 | 0.69 | 0.67 |
| Proposed TwinBERT | 0.77 | 0.81 | 0.79 | 0.67 | 0.77 | 0.72 | 0.62 | 0.68 | 0.65 | 0.64 | 0.69 | 0.66 |

Table 2: SDE extraction and polarity classification results for the automobile and housing domain.

only 7.3 billion parameters on various benchmarks (Jiang et al., 2023). Here, we have primarily used transfer learning, with additional modifications such as quantization and the integration of LoRA adapters (Dettmers et al., 2023) to fine-tune Mistral. The training process involves several key steps. Each data sample is augmented with a prompt indicating the task context and the statement to be evaluated for SDE extraction and polarity classification.

### 5.2 Outcome of fine-tuned Mistral-7B and LLAMA-2

Empirical evidence presented in Table-2 demonstrates that our TwinBERT architecture achieves superior performance compared to LLAMA-2 13B. As we can see, the performance of LLAMA-2 using the few-shot approach was notably limited. This limitation stemmed from the complexity of defining SDEs, which necessitates a comprehensive representation beyond the provided four examples as prompt. As evidenced in the presented table (Ref: Table 2), while LLAMA-2 achieved a high precision score, its recall and F1 scores were significantly lower, primarily due to its tendency to classify the majority of sentences as not-claims. Consequently, LLAMA-2 exhibited suboptimal classification performance, particularly in the zero-shot scenario. Conversely, although TwinBERT emerged as a superior classifier in Precision, Recall, and F1 scores, its superiority can be attributed to its adherence to the intricate definition of SDEs, thereby underscoring its effectiveness in classification tasks.

Here, we ran an experiment to compare the output of our proposed architecture with our fine-tuned Mistral Model. We gave the trained Mistral model 50% of the total data sample and asked it to extract the SDEs and its polarity sentences. However, the Large Language Model's hallucinatory property posed a challenge. Out of the 50% sentences, the trained Mistral Model provided a distinct classification for only 25% sentences, while the remaining 25% cases resulted in a rather confusing answer. Among those, it categorized correctly for 22% cases. Therefore, we concluded that while training the large language model on a specific domain can improve its SDE extraction capacity, the inherent property of the Large Language Model can still pose a challenge.

## 6 Analyzing the rise and fall of demand

Apart from classification and extraction of demand related events and entities it is useful to visualize these demand information and perform causal analysis to generate reports on the various product trends. We illustrate this considering examples from the automobile sector. Accordingly, we have crawled around 5000 automobile News articles from India and United States during the period of 2012 and 2020. Average document size ranges to 300 $\pm$ 80 words. We have applied our TwinBERT model to extract demand information such as product names, location and polarity (i.e positive and negative demand). Once the information is extracted, the different automobile model names are segregated and grouped together according to the categories. The mapping between the model names to the respective categories are done using the state-of-the-art automobile ontology auto.schema.org[1]. The automotive extension of schema.org [2] stores the most important real-world objects related to popular vehicles like cars, buses and two wheeler vehicles. While the extension allows for a fair description of all kinds of vehicles, it focuses predominantly on passenger automobiles from the retail market perspective.

Next, we pass the text segments of each articles to a causal analytics module that identifies causal events from text. For this, we have used the cause-effect extraction tool as presented in the literature (Dasgupta et al., 2018). The proposed model is based on linguistically informed BiLSTM architecture (LiBiLSTM) to extract cause and effect events from a given input text. For example, in the following text:

"In the passenger vehicle segment, showroom sales declined by 11% year on year to 243183 units as customers stayed away from the showrooms due to lack of improvement in availability of credit or finance options, higher cost of ownership and overall slowdown in the economy." The extracted cause and effect events are:

`CAUSE`: *lack of improvement in availability of credit or finance options, higher cost of ownership and overall slowdown in the economy.*

`EFFECT`: *showroom sales declined by 11%*

Figure 4 depicts the overall demand distribution of top 5 automobile types in India. During the period of 2012 to 2018 we observe a steady demand for almost all segment of vehicles. As expected, the highest demand are for two-wheeler vehicles as compared to all other types. We primarily observe two major spikes in the dataset. a) With respect to passenger vehicles we observe sudden spike in demand during 2015 particularly for fuel efficient cars and electric vehicles. b) A severe decline of demand is observed across all automobile segments during late 2018 till 2020. We try to perform an in-depth analysis of the reasons for such a rise and fall of demand. Our causal analysis during those period revealed that the sharp rises in demand during 2015 coincided with news reports of launch of hybrid, electric and fuel efficient cars of Nissan and Ford during that time period. On the other hand, major reasons for fall in demand can be attributed due to many factors including: *Overall price rise across automobile sector, Economic slowdown in India, High oil price, BS-IV implementation, and Unavailability of semiconductors.*

In Figure 5, we present the distribution of demand of the top five car models during 2012 to 2016 across the region of the Unites States of America and Canada. We observe that, while the demand for fuel-efficient vehicles increased initially, the demand trend of such cars have consistently been downwards after the initial two years. One of the primary reason behind such an event is the lowering of gasoline prices and increase in oil prices in those areas. Unsurprisingly, demand for diesel vehicles have remained consistently low in the entire region of the USA and Canada. We also observe a constant low demand for electric cars as compared to standard SUVs. Corresponding news documents indicate that the primary reason behind this is the high cost of rechargeable batteries, low gas price and limited mileage offered by electric cars. However, the demand for electric vehicles have consistently risen over the past seven years across geographic locations. Another notable observation is the exponential increase in demand for SUV cars and trucks throughout the given time period.

## 7 Related Works

Demand forecasting is an important aspects in the supply chain business. The demand forecasting models traditionally uses features like seasonality of goods, price points, previous experience etc. Beyer et al. (Beyer et al., 2005) explored

[1]https://schema.org/docs/automotive.html

[2]www.auto.schma.org

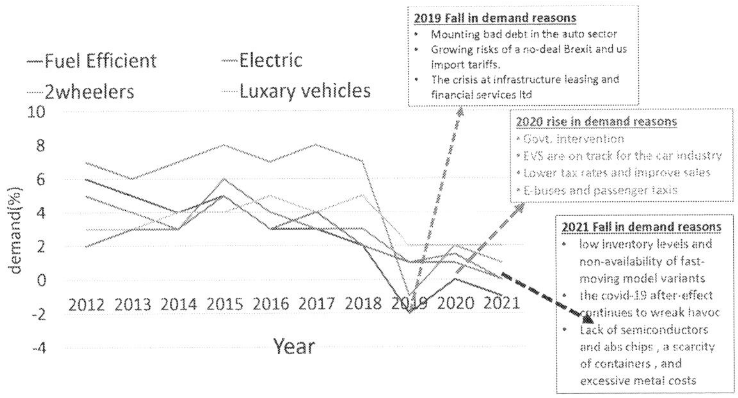


Figure 4: Demand trend analysis along with causal reasoning of automobiles in India.

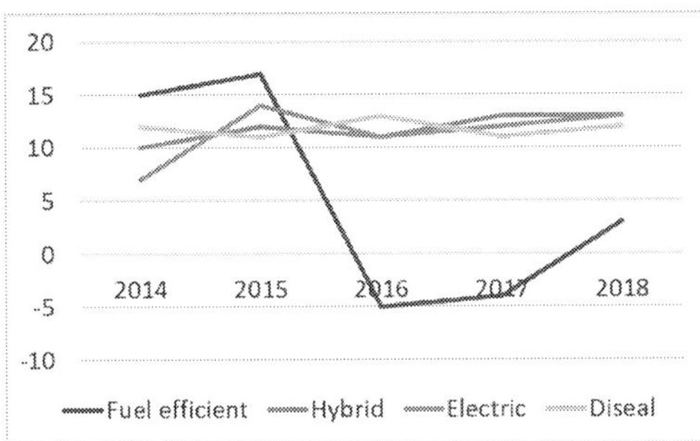


Figure 5: Demand trend analysis of top 4 car types over the past five years at USA.

the way to find demand profile of a new product which would be introduced in market using the demand profiles of similar products already in market. Berry et al. (Berry et al., 2004) examined the situation when the number of observations is associated with the number of products within a given market. It is necessary for manufacturers to give the retailers view about the demand potential of their new products. Desai et al. studied how a high-demand manufacturer can use advertising, slotting allowances, and wholesale prices to signal its high demand to retailers (Desai, 2000). Mark E. Ferguson explored statistical methods for estimating demand with constrained data and product substitutions (Ferguson, 2020). Abbasimehr et al. proposed multi-layer LSTM networks for predict the demand (Abbasimehr et al., 2020). Gunter et al. (Gunter et al., 2020) explored the Airbnb demand to New York City by employing spatial panel data at the listing level. Along with the traditional features two new features Item categorization using word2vec with clustering and session of the day based on the time was proposed by Dholakia et al. (Dholakia et al., 2020) to obtain an improved and intuitive demand forecasting model.

## 8 Conclusion

In this paper we have developed methods to mine product-specific demand information components from large volumes of text data. The work primarily focuses on analyzing text documents and extracts specific Subject-of-Demand Entities from text segments that mentions about demand of a product, determine the sentiment, in terms of rise and fall of demand, associated to the subject-of-demand and finally analyzes the reason for the rise and fall by performing causal analytics. Accordingly, we propose the use of a TwinBERT architecture for the entity extraction and sentiment classification task. We have evaluated our system using a manually annotated gold standard dataset belonging to two different domains. We have observed that our proposed model significantly outperforms the existing baseline models.

## Limitations

1. One of the limitation of the present work is that it fails to identify implicit demands.

2. An in-depth analysis of the performance of LLMs on demand mining is required.

3. Evaluation of the causal models are not explicitly discussed in the paper.

## References


Hossein Abbasimehr, Mostafa Shabani, and Mohsen Yousefi. 2020. An optimized model using lstm network for demand forecasting. *Computers & Industrial Engineering*, page 106435.

Steve Berry, Oliver B Linton, and Ariel Pakes. 2004. Limit theorems for estimating the parameters of differentiated product demand systems. *The Review of Economic Studies*, 71(3):613–654.

Dirk M Beyer, Fereydoon Safai, and Farid AitSalia. 2005. Profile-based product demand forecasting. US Patent 6,978,249.

Tirthankar Dasgupta, Rupsa Saha, Lipika Dey, and Abir Naskar. 2018. Automatic extraction of causal relations from text using linguistically informed deep neural networks. In *Proceedings of the 19th Annual SIGdial Meeting on Discourse and Dialogue*, pages 306–316, Melbourne, Australia. Association for Computational Linguistics.

Preyas S Desai. 2000. Multiple messages to retain retailers: Signaling new product demand. *Marketing Science*, 19(4):381–389.

Tim Dettmers, Artidoro Pagnoni, Ari Holtzman, and Luke Zettlemoyer. 2023. Qlora: Efficient finetuning of quantized llms. In *Advances in Neural Information Processing Systems*, volume 36, pages 10088–10115. Curran Associates, Inc.

Jacob Devlin, Ming-Wei Chang, Kenton Lee, and Kristina Toutanova. 2018. Bert: Pre-training of deep bidirectional transformers for language understanding. *arXiv preprint arXiv:1810.04805*.

Rishit Dholakia, Richa Randeria, Riya Dholakia, Hunsii Ashar, and Dipti Rana. 2020. Cognitive demand forecasting with novel features using word2vec and session of the day. In *Modern Approaches in Machine Learning and Cognitive Science: A Walkthrough*, pages 59–72. Springer.

Mark E Ferguson. 2020. Estimating demand with constrained data and product substitutions. In *Channel Strategies and Marketing Mix in a Connected World*, pages 1–27. Springer.

Ulrich Gunter, Irem Önder, and Bozana Zekan. 2020. Modeling airbnb demand to new york city while employing spatial panel data at the listing level. *Tourism Management*, 77:104000.

Albert Q. Jiang, Alexandre Sablayrolles, Arthur Mensch, Chris Bamford, Devendra Singh Chaplot, Diego de las Casas, Florian Bressand, Gianna Lengyel, Guillaume Lample, Lucile Saulnier, Lélio Renard Lavaud, Marie-Anne Lachaux, Pierre Stock, Teven Le Scao, Thibaut Lavril, Thomas Wang, Timothée Lacroix, and William El Sayed. 2023. Mistral 7b. *Preprint*, arXiv:2310.06825.

Yue Mao, Yi Shen, Chao Yu, and Longjun Cai. 2021. A joint training dual-mrc framework for aspect based sentiment analysis. *arXiv preprint arXiv:2101.00816*.

Sewon Min, Xinxi Lyu, Ari Holtzman, Mikel Artetxe, Mike Lewis, Hannaneh Hajishirzi, and Luke Zettlemoyer. 2022. Rethinking the role of demonstrations: What makes in-context learning work? *Preprint*, arXiv:2202.12837.

Hugo Touvron, Louis Martin, Kevin Stone, Peter Albert, Amjad Almahairi, Yasmine Babaei, Nikolay Bashlykov, Soumya Batra, Prajjwal Bhargava, Shruti Bhosale, et al. 2023. Llama 2: Open foundation and fine-tuned chat models. *arXiv preprint arXiv:2307.09288*.

Wei Wang, Vincent W Zheng, Han Yu, and Chunyan Miao. 2019. A survey of zero-shot learning: Settings, methods, and applications. *ACM Transactions on Intelligent Systems and Technology (TIST)*, 10(2):1–37.

# Impact of Decoding Methods on Human Alignment of Conversational LLMs

**Shaz Furniturewala[1,3*], Kokil Jaidka[2,3], Yashvardhan Sharma[1],**
[1]Birla Institute of Technology and Science, Pilani
[2]NUS Center for Trusted Internet and Community, National University of Singapore
[3]Department of Communications and New Media, National University of Singapore

## Abstract

To be included into chatbot systems, Large language models (LLMs) must be aligned with human conversational conventions. However, being trained mainly on web-scraped data gives existing LLMs a voice closer to informational text than actual human speech. In this paper, we examine the effect of decoding methods on the alignment between LLM-generated and human conversations, including Beam Search, Top K Sampling, and Nucleus Sampling. We present new measures of alignment in substance, style, and psychometric orientation, and experiment with two conversation datasets. Our results provide subtle insights: better alignment is attributed to fewer beams in Beam Search and lower values of P in Nucleus Sampling. We also find that task-oriented and open-ended datasets perform differently in terms of alignment, indicating the significance of taking into account the context of the interaction.

## 1 Introduction

As large language models (LLMs) continue to evolve, their integration into chatbot systems has increasingly focused on not just understanding but also on aligning with human conversational norms. Models are trained and finetuned to be 'perfect assistants' which has inadvertently given them a voice that is eager, overly enthusiastic, and marked by use of words and phrases that feature prominently in informational and instructional texts but not so much in true human conversations (Zhou et al., 2024). Therefore, LLM-human alignment is a crucial problem and has been studied across various contexts, such as coding, problem-solving, summarization, translation, and reasoning (for a review, see Shi et al., 2024). Among various techniques explored to improve this alignment, the perturbation of decoding parameters—such as Beam Search, Top K Sampling, and Nucleus Sampling—has shown promise. These decoding methods, encompassing both deterministic strategies like beam search and stochastic approaches such as temperature scaling, fundamentally influence how a model generates text. Preliminary studies suggest that while deterministic methods may better adhere to specific instructions, stochastic methods like P and K sampling could excel in scenarios involving unaligned models by introducing variability in responses (Shi et al., 2024). Despite their potential, the impact of these methods on the quality of chatbot outputs, particularly in mimicking human conversational patterns, has not been comprehensively analyzed.

Achieving a high degree of alignment between the outputs of these models and actual human interactions is crucial not only for maintaining the natural flow of dialogue but also for ensuring the relevance and contextuality of the responses provided by chatbots. Yet, current evaluation methods are limited in their ability to assess whether these systems successfully emulate the human-like attributes essential for nuanced interactions. For instance, most work focuses on automatic evaluation methods such as BLEU, ROUGE, and METEOR with some others using classifiers trained on human judgement (Yeh et al., 2021). While there has been some work in the creation of psychological metrics (Giorgi et al., 2023), it merely focuses on broad aspects of dialog like emotion and personality. A study of dialogue dynamics requires an understanding of the deeper subtleties of interpersonal engagement beyond content, such as style and psychological orientation. Unlike emotion, style and psychological orientation are nuanced and multifaceted aspects of communication that have not been studied as much and are harder to accurately measure and control.

This paper aims to bridge this gap by systematically investigating the effects of different decoding

*Work done during internship at NUS Center for Trusted Internet and Community



*Proceedings of the 14th Workshop on Computational Approaches to Subjectivity, Sentiment, & Social Media Analysis*, pages 273–279
August 15, 2024 ©2024 Association for Computational Linguistics

methods on the alignment between chatbot outputs and human-like responses. We hypothesize that adjusting these decoding parameters can significantly enhance the naturalistic appeal and user engagement of chatbot conversations. To test this hypothesis, we employ a novel methodological approach, analyzing the performance of conversational LLMs through a series of experiments involving real human conversations. Our work offers the following contributions:

- Two new parallel corpora of synthetic LLM-generated conversations, curated through turn-by-turn prompts with real-world dialogues sourced from two human-human datasets, collected across a variety of decoding methods.
- New metrics for measuring LLM alignment to human conversations in substance, style, and psychometric orientation.

Our findings aim to provide deeper insights into the practical applications of decoding methods and their potential to improve the human-likeness of chatbot interactions, thereby guiding future developments in chatbot design and deployment.

## 2 Empirical Evaluation

In this section we describe the datasets used for our experiments, the metrics employed to measure humane conversational traits, and the decoding methods used in the LLM's generation process. We created a turn-by-turn synthetic dataset of LLM generated conversations, adhering to a structured process across each conversation turn. Each conversation began with the opening turns of a conversation from one of the two datasets we considered—BOLT and CraiglistBargains—and we invited each LLM we considered to generate the next utterance by the speaker indicated. We then evaluated human-LLM conversation alignment along dimensions of Style, Psychometrics, and Semantic content. In this work we use Llama 3 (8B) and Llama 3 Instruct (8B) for our experiments. Further, we vary the decoding methods during generation utilising Beam Search, Top K Sampling, and Nucleus Sampling, to gain insights into their impact on the quality of generated conversations.

### 2.1 Datasets

**BOLT SMS/Chat Dataset** (Chen, Song et al., 2018), developed by the Linguistic Data Consortium consists of naturally occurring English conversations involving native speakers. The corpus contains 18,429 two-person conversations totaling 3,674,802 words across 375,967 messages. For the purposes of this work, 2640 conversations ranging from 5 to 125 turns were used.

**CraigslistBargains** (He et al., 2018) is a collection of 6682 human-human negotiation conversations between AMT agents. The agents are assigned the role of buyer and seller and are asked to negotiate the price of a real Craigslist listing. For this work, 5357 conversations ranging from 5 to 28 turns were used.

### 2.2 Measures

The following 6 metrics measure the stylistic, psychometric, and semantic similarity between the human and LLM generated texts. They are relative measures, using the original text as a reference in comparison with the LLM generated text. Each measure is computed at the utterance level and averaged across the entire conversation to arrive at a score.

#### 2.2.1 Stylistic

Style is a broad concept with various aspects. For the purposes of this paper we picked two aspects that are relevant to the datasets being used and are significantly impacted by the decoding parameters as seen in Figure 2.

**Politeness** We used the ConvoKit Library (Danescu-Niculescu-Mizil et al., 2013) to compute 21 characteristics representing facets of politeness, including deference, hedging, gratitude, factuality, among others. We then calculated the cross entropy score between each human and LLM generated utterance.

**Negotiation** Based on the work done by Niculae et al. (2015), we extracted 8 linguistic cues from each utterance including Claim, Premise, Contingency, Expansion, Temporal (Past and Future), Subject, and Comparison. We use these linguistic cues as a negotiation vector and compute the cross entropy score between the human and LLM generated utterance.

#### 2.2.2 Pyschometric

**Self Concept** We annotated 10,956 text messages from the BOLT dataset for the presence of three characteristics of self concept: Autonomy, Competence, and Relatedness. These annotations were done by Amazon Mechanical Turk workers on an interface we designed that provided positive and negative examples of each characteristic. We fine-tuned a classifier on this data and computed the cross entropy score between the predictions for the human and LLM generated utterances.

**Empathy** We finetune an empathy classifier on the dataset created by Buechel et al. (2018). It contains 1860 short texts annotated for empathic concern. This classifier predicts the presence of empathic concern in the human and LLM generated utterances and we compute the cross entropy score between them.

### 2.2.3 Semantic

**Verbosity** For each utterance, we measure verbosity as the absolute difference between the length of the human and LLM generated utterances.

**Semantic Similarity** We compute the semantic similarity between the human and LLM generated utterances using BERTScore (Zhang* et al., 2020).

## 2.3 Decoding Parameters

The standard generation setup uses the default temperature value of 1.0 and deterministic greedy decoding with no sampling. In the appendix we also display results on temperature perturbations.

**Beam Search** (Luong et al., 2015; Graves, 2012) Using this decoding strategy, we can allow the model to evaluate multiple hypotheses at a time and ultimately pick the sequence that has the highest overall probability. While it is computationally more expensive, it can generate sequences that begin with low probability tokens but have the overall highest probability. In this work we evaluate beam search with 2, 4, 6, and 8 beams.

**Top K Sampling** Introduced by Fan et al. (2018), this generation strategy filters out the K most probable next tokens and redistributes the probability mass among them. Then, based on their new probabilities, the next token is randomly chosen among them. In this work we evaluate Top-K Sampling with K = 30, 40, 50, 60, and 70.

**Nucleus Sampling (Top P)** (Holtzman et al., 2020) This sampling method filters the smallest number of tokens whose probability cumulatively exceeds P. In this manner, it dynamically changes the number of tokens being filtered based on the probability distribution. We evaluate Nucleus Sampling with P = 0.6, 0.7, 0.8, 0.9, 1.0.

| Beams | Change | P | Change | K | Change |
|---|---|---|---|---|---|
| 2 | **3.82%** | 0 | 2.35% | 1 | 1.64% |
| | | 0.5 | -1.80% | 20 | -3.21% |
| 4 | 1.37% | 0.6 | 1.85% | 30 | -5.02% |
| | | 0.7 | **2.50%** | 40 | -1.19% |
| 6 | -2.33% | 0.8 | -5.66% | 50 | -1.33% |
| | | 0.9 | -3.09% | 60 | -0.55% |
| 8 | 0.21% | 1 | -2.67% | 70 | **2.99%** |

Table 1: Average change in alignment across the six metrics for various values of the decoding methods.

## 3 Results

In this section we will analyse the results of the experiments described in Section 2. Initially, our analysis focuses on identifying how variants of different decoding parameters perform, then we examine turn-level results.

Table 1 displays the average change in alignment scores over the base decoding method for each decoding parameter perturbation. The change in comparison to base is measured as the decrease in the cross entropy score of the generated text with the ground truth. Thus, a higher percentage change represents a greater decrease in the cross entropy score indicated better alignment with the human responses. These scores are averaged across both datasets (BOLT, CraigslistBargains) and across both models (Llama 3, Llama 3 Instruct).

We notice that using 2 Beams outperforms the base greedy decoding strategy, however, further increasing the number of beams diminishes this increase in performance, indicating a potential local minimum (or a local maximum in alignment). Lower values of P (0.6-0.7) have the best performance while P=1.0 demonstrates a significant decrease in alignment compared to base (greedy) decoding. This indicates that some of the least likely tokens in the vocabulary contribute to the drop in alignment when included in the sequence. Finally, there no observable trend in the perturbations of Top K Sampling with all values of K performing, on average, similarly to the base method, i.e., greedy decoding.

In Figure 1, we plot the scores (scaled down and smoothened) divided by dataset and along with the number of turns in the conversation. This allows us to examine task-specific performance as a function of the length of the conversation. We see that as conversations get longer, the LLM is able to more accurately emulate these traits. Notably, this trend applies for negotiation on BOLT but not on CraigslistBargains where the performance quickly plateaus. For both datasets, Politeness, Self-Concept, Empathy, and Verbosity follow a similar trend of improving performance as the conversations get longer with beam search and nucleus sampling consistently outperforming Top K

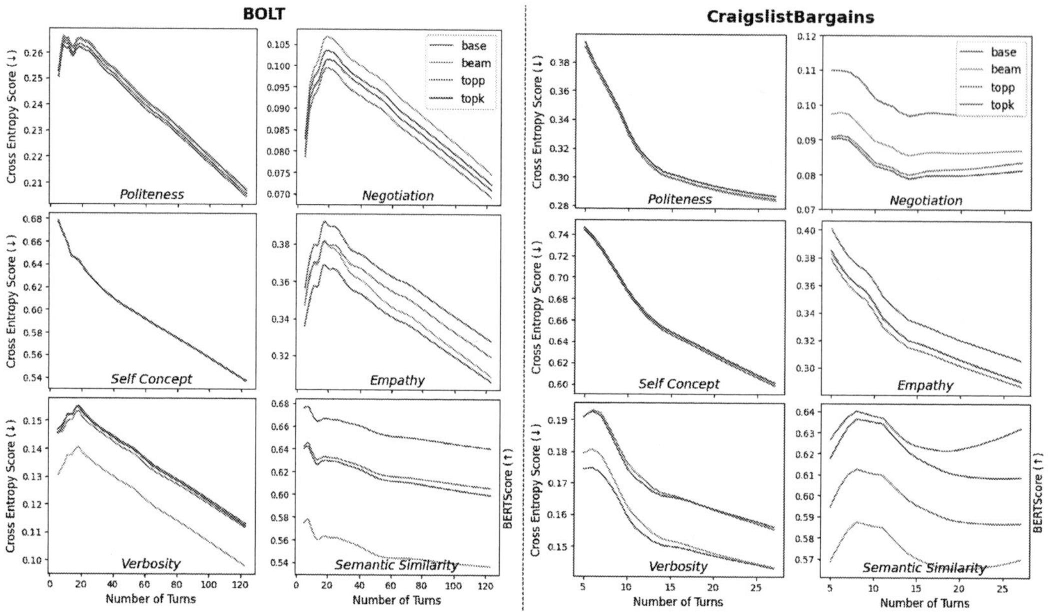


Figure 1: Turn-based scores for each decoding parameter, averaged across all perturbations and both models (Llama 2 and Llama 3).

sampling. This is consistent with our previous conclusions about these two decoding methods. In addition, it indicates that for these metrics, alignment is correlated with the amount of context provided.

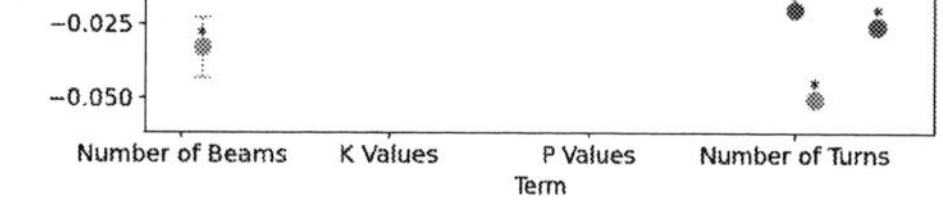


Figure 2: The parameters effecting significant positive and negative changes in style, psychometrics and semantics of LLM conversations. Calculated using multi-level models controlling for model and dataset differences.

To validate our insights and conclusions from these experiments, we compute the correlation coefficients of the decoding parameters with the measures. In Figure 2 we plot the coefficients of multilevel linear models for each of the six metrics calculated for the three decoding methods—Beam Search, Top K Sampling, Top P Sampling—and the number of turns or the length of a conversation. A positive coefficient indicates that a high value for that parameter predicts better alignment and a negative coefficient predicts worse alignment. Asterisks represent statistically significant associations ($p<0.001$). The first notable observation from the figure is that Top K sampling does not have any significant non-zero coefficients for any of the given metrics. Beam search only has non-zero coefficients with Negotation and Verbosity, having a positive coefficient for the former and negative one for the latter. Politeness, Negotiation, and Verbosity all have positive coefficients for P value and proportionally negative correlations for the number of turns.

## 4 Discussion and Conclusion

The broader context of the datasets appears to affect the quality of generated conversations, as BOLT, being a chit-chat dataset, does not require the same amount of negotiation as the task oriented CraigslistBargains and allows the LLM to adapt to these traits quickly. Similarly, the models show decreasing Semantic Similarity on BOLT compared to CraigslistBargains where performance stays consistently high across conversations. The goal-oriented task of CraigslistBargains tends to have highly probable responses in a specific direction for each input. On the contrary, BOLT is very open-ended with each dialog allowing the conversation to go in many different directions. A similar effect is seen in the quality metrics, where over the course of a long conversation, the lack of structure in the task is seen to lead to more deviations by the LLM in BOLT compared to CraigslistBargains, manifesting as the decreased alignment performance seen in the graph.

Our experiments suggest that lower P values improve instruction adherence, while top-K sampling, unlike nucleus sampling, has a smaller impact, as the fixed number of tokens being filtered each time results in much less control over the redistributed probability mass as compared to variable tokens with a fixed cumulative probability threshold. Thus, the best decoding method for human aligned conversational LLM output is likely a combination of **Low P Nucleus Sampling and Beam Search with a small number of beams.**

A larger number of beams incorporates more obscure, lower probability words into the sequence that leads to worse alignment, possibly through introducing linguistic artifacts such as obscure words and longer texts to the sequence that undo the potential advantages of having more beams.

## 5 Limitations

One particular limitation of our work is the usage of two specific aspects of style: Politeness and Negotiation. To ensure concise insights we limited the experiments to these two aspects since they pertain the most to the task specific dataset we used (CraigslistBargains). We believe the results observed for these two aspects should translate to other facets of style on other datasets and we hope to address this by expanding on these experiments in our future work.

## 6 Acknowledgements

This work is supported by the Ministry of Education, Singapore under its MOE AcRF TIER3 Grant (MOE-MOET32022-0001). The travel grant for this research is supported by the Department of Communication and New Media at the National University of Singapore.

## References

Sven Buechel, Anneke Buffone, Barry Slaff, Lyle Ungar, and João Sedoc. 2018. Modeling empathy and distress in reaction to news stories. In *Proceedings of the 2018 Conference on Empirical Methods in Natural Language Processing*, pages 4758–4765, Brussels, Belgium. Association for Computational Linguistics.

Chen, Song , Fore, Dana, Strassel, Stephanie, Lee, Haejoong, and Wright, Jonathan. 2018. Bolt english sms/chat.

Cristian Danescu-Niculescu-Mizil, Moritz Sudhof, Daniel Jurafsky, Jure Leskovec, and Christopher Potts. 2013. A computational approach to politeness with application to social factors. In *Annual Meeting of the Association for Computational Linguistics*.

Angela Fan, Mike Lewis, and Yann Dauphin. 2018. Hierarchical neural story generation. *Preprint*, arXiv:1805.04833.

Salvatore Giorgi, Shreya Havaldar, Farhan Ahmed, Zuhaib Akhtar, Shalaka Vaidya, Gary Pan, Lyle H. Ungar, H. Andrew Schwartz, and Joao Sedoc. 2023. Psychological metrics for dialog system evaluation. *Preprint*, arXiv:2305.14757.

Alex Graves. 2012. Sequence transduction with recurrent neural networks. *arXiv preprint arXiv:1211.3711*.

He He, Derek Chen, Anusha Balakrishnan, and Percy Liang. 2018. Decoupling strategy and generation in negotiation dialogues. In *Proceedings of the 2018 Conference on Empirical Methods in Natural Language Processing*, pages 2333–2343, Brussels, Belgium. Association for Computational Linguistics.

Ari Holtzman, Jan Buys, Li Du, Maxwell Forbes, and Yejin Choi. 2020. The curious case of neural text degeneration. *Preprint*, arXiv:1904.09751.

Thang Luong, Ilya Sutskever, Quoc Le, Oriol Vinyals, and Wojciech Zaremba. 2015. Addressing the rare word problem in neural machine translation. In *Proceedings of the 53rd Annual Meeting of the Association for Computational Linguistics and the 7th International Joint Conference on Natural Language Processing (Volume 1: Long Papers)*, pages 11–19, Beijing, China. Association for Computational Linguistics.

Vlad Niculae, Srijan Kumar, Jordan Boyd-Graber, and Cristian Danescu-Niculescu-Mizil. 2015. Linguistic harbingers of betrayal: A case study on an online strategy game. In *Proceedings of the 53rd Annual Meeting of the Association for Computational Linguistics and the 7th International Joint Conference on Natural Language Processing (Volume 1: Long Papers)*, pages 1650–1659, Beijing, China. Association for Computational Linguistics.

Chufan Shi, Haoran Yang, Deng Cai, Zhisong Zhang, Yifan Wang, Yujiu Yang, and Wai Lam. 2024. A thorough examination of decoding methods in the era of llms. *arXiv preprint arXiv:2402.06925*.

Yi-Ting Yeh, Maxine Eskenazi, and Shikib Mehri. 2021. A comprehensive assessment of dialog evaluation metrics. *Preprint*, arXiv:2106.03706.

Tianyi Zhang*, Varsha Kishore*, Felix Wu*, Kilian Q. Weinberger, and Yoav Artzi. 2020. Bertscore: Evaluating text generation with bert. In *International Conference on Learning Representations*.

Xuhui Zhou, Zhe Su, Tiwalayo Eisape, Hyunwoo Kim, and Maarten Sap. 2024. Is this the real life? is this just fantasy? the misleading success of simulating social interactions with llms. *arXiv preprint arXiv:2403.05020*.

# A Appendix

## A.1 Classifiers

For the metrics computing Empathy and Self Concept we trained classifiers on annotated data to predict the presence of these attributes in the text. Both classifiers were finetuned variants of Microsoft's DeBERTa V3 Large model with 304 M parameters. For empathy, this classifier was trained on the NewsEmpathy (Buechel et al., 2018) dataset containing 1860 instances of annotated text. The model was finetuned for 4 epochs, with a learning rate of 5e-6 and weight decay of 0.01. It achieved a validation F1 Score of 0.71. For Self Concept, the classifier was trained on a dataset we annotated. It consists of 10956 texts extracted from the BOLT dataset and annotated for the presence of Autonomy, Competence, and Relatedness. This model was trained for 1 epoch with a learning rate of 1e-5 and weight decay of 0.01. It achieved a validation macro F1 score of 0.83.

## A.2 Impact of Instruction Finetuning

Table 2 shows the complete results for both Llama 3 variants, with and without instruction finetuning. From the table we can see that the trends are identical among them. Fewer beams and lower P values show better human alignment for both models, with K values showing no consistent trend. However, notably, the model not instruction finetuned appears to show larger improvements in alignment when using decoding methods compared to the instruction finetuned variant. Llama 3 shows a 3.73% overall improvement over base when using P=0.5 compared to only 1.40% for Llama 3 Instruct.

## A.3 Justification for using cross entropy score

We compute the four stylistic and psychometric measures as the cross entropy scores between feature vectors of the generated text and the ground truth. These feature vectors are largely all n-dimensional one-hot encoded vectors. Much like multi-class classification tasks where minimizing cross entropy is equivalent to maximizing likelihood, lower cross-entropy for the feature vectors of these four measures indicates higher alignment with the ground truth human dialog.

| | Politeness | Negotiation | Self Concept | Empathy | Verbosity | Semantic Similarity |
|---|---|---|---|---|---|---|
| Llama 3 Instruct | 0.312 | 0.099 | 0.666 | 0.541 | 0.232 | 0.622 |
| | | | Number of Beams | | | |
| 2 | 0.311 | 0.093 | 0.666 | 0.546 | 0.221 | **0.639** |
| 4 | 0.314 | 0.087 | 0.667 | 0.544 | **0.216** | 0.628 |
| 6 | 0.312 | **0.073** | 0.667 | 0.548 | 0.227 | 0.619 |
| 8 | **0.310** | 0.104 | **0.666** | **0.530** | 0.231 | 0.629 |
| | | | P Value | | | |
| 0 | 0.315 | 0.104 | 0.667 | 0.558 | **0.203** | 0.640 |
| 0.5 | 0.315 | 0.101 | 0.667 | 0.544 | 0.213 | **0.646** |
| 0.6 | 0.313 | 0.111 | 0.667 | 0.568 | 0.207 | 0.606 |
| 0.7 | 0.315 | 0.108 | 0.666 | 0.543 | 0.214 | 0.620 |
| 0.8 | **0.312** | 0.104 | 0.666 | **0.516** | 0.229 | 0.612 |
| 0.9 | 0.313 | **0.095** | **0.665** | 0.538 | 0.218 | 0.604 |
| 1 | 0.313 | 0.096 | 0.666 | 0.570 | 0.220 | 0.644 |
| | | | K Value | | | |
| 1 | 0.315 | 0.103 | 0.667 | 0.558 | **0.203** | **0.640** |
| 20 | 0.313 | 0.120 | 0.668 | 0.534 | 0.214 | 0.615 |
| 30 | 0.307 | 0.110 | 0.666 | 0.538 | 0.221 | 0.620 |
| 40 | **0.306** | 0.108 | 0.667 | **0.504** | 0.225 | 0.622 |
| 50 | 0.309 | 0.106 | **0.665** | 0.536 | 0.240 | 0.635 |
| 60 | 0.312 | **0.088** | 0.666 | 0.560 | 0.212 | 0.627 |
| 70 | 0.312 | 0.103 | 0.666 | 0.545 | 0.224 | 0.629 |
| Llama 3 | 0.316 | 0.102 | 0.661 | 0.661 | 0.174 | 0.553 |
| | | | Number of Beams | | | |
| 2 | 0.315 | **0.082** | 0.642 | 0.666 | **0.141** | 0.465 |
| 4 | 0.314 | 0.104 | **0.636** | **0.654** | 0.141 | **0.496** |
| 6 | 0.314 | 0.111 | 0.668 | 0.667 | 0.198 | 0.477 |
| 8 | **0.310** | 0.088 | 0.667 | 0.668 | 0.197 | 0.472 |
| | | | P Value | | | |
| 0 | 0.313 | **0.073** | 0.666 | **0.621** | 0.200 | 0.481 |
| 0.5 | 0.316 | 0.087 | **0.643** | 0.662 | **0.147** | 0.499 |
| 0.6 | 0.314 | 0.076 | 0.666 | 0.682 | 0.216 | 0.507 |
| 0.7 | 0.312 | 0.095 | 0.667 | 0.647 | 0.207 | **0.534** |
| 0.8 | 0.319 | 0.097 | 0.667 | 0.675 | 0.228 | 0.498 |
| 0.9 | **0.310** | 0.078 | 0.665 | 0.667 | 0.205 | 0.462 |
| 1 | 0.315 | 0.103 | 0.668 | 0.663 | 0.185 | 0.487 |
| | | | K Value | | | |
| 1 | 0.313 | 0.082 | 0.666 | **0.624** | 0.202 | 0.481 |
| 20 | 0.315 | 0.115 | 0.664 | 0.668 | 0.183 | 0.440 |
| 30 | 0.317 | 0.106 | 0.669 | 0.669 | 0.214 | **0.499** |
| 40 | 0.322 | 0.091 | 0.612 | 0.674 | 0.216 | 0.446 |
| 50 | 0.314 | 0.090 | 0.668 | 0.647 | 0.197 | 0.494 |
| 60 | 0.313 | 0.106 | **0.598** | 0.657 | **0.183** | 0.467 |
| 70 | **0.312** | **0.065** | 0.612 | 0.646 | 0.201 | 0.477 |

Table 2: Scores for Llama 3 and Llama 3 Instruct on all six psychological metrics for various values of the decoding parameters.

# Loneliness Episodes: A Japanese Dataset for Loneliness Detection and Analysis

**Naoya Fujikawa** and **Quang Toan Nguyen** and **Kazuhiro Ito**
**Shoko Wakamiya** and **Eiji Aramaki**
Nara Institute of Science and Technology, Japan
fujikawa.naoya.fi8@is.naist.jp, nqt.quangtoan@gmail.com
{ito.kazuhiro.ih4, wakamiya, aramaki}@is.naist.jp

## Abstract

Loneliness, a significant public health concern, is closely connected to both physical and mental well-being. Hence, detection and intervention for individuals experiencing loneliness are crucial. Identifying loneliness in text is straightforward when it is explicitly stated but challenging when it is implicit. Detecting implicit loneliness requires a manually annotated dataset because whereas explicit loneliness can be detected using keywords, implicit loneliness cannot be. However, there are no freely available datasets with clear annotation guidelines for implicit loneliness. In this study, we construct a freely accessible Japanese loneliness dataset with annotation guidelines grounded in the psychological definition of loneliness. This dataset covers loneliness intensity and the contributing factors of loneliness. We train two models to classify whether loneliness is expressed and the intensity of loneliness. The model classifying loneliness versus non-loneliness achieves an F1-score of 0.833, but the model for identifying the intensity of loneliness has a low F1-score of 0.400, which is likely due to label imbalance and a shortage of a certain label in the dataset. We validate performance in another domain, specifically X (formerly Twitter), and observe a decrease. In addition, we propose improvement suggestions for domain adaptation.

## 1 Introduction

Loneliness has become a major global concern, affecting both mental and physical well-being. Previous research shows that loneliness constitutes a significant risk factor for both coronary heart disease and stroke (Valtorta et al., 2016). Another study shows that loneliness is a risk factor for morbidity and mortality (Luo et al., 2012). It also increases health-risk behaviors (Shankar et al., 2011). Hence, addressing the issue of loneliness is crucial.

The degree of negative impact varies depending on the intensity of loneliness. Beutel et al. (2017) indicate that the greater the intensity of loneliness, the higher the proportion of individuals experiencing depression and suicidal ideation. Furthermore, it is noteworthy that over half of individuals experiencing strong loneliness report depressive symptoms. Lee et al. (2019) demonstrate that people who feel more loneliness have lower resilience, optimism, and mental well-being. For these reasons, classifying the intensity of loneliness is as important for intervention as discovering individuals experiencing loneliness.

Identifying loneliness and intervening for these people are crucial. People who feel lonely tend to have less contact with supportive family and friends than those who do not, and they often use social media more frequently (Lampraki et al., 2022). Numerous previous studies have created corpora using keyword-based approaches on social media (Andy et al., 2022; Kiritchenko et al., 2020). These corpora only considered loneliness when it was explicitly mentioned, using specific keywords to label posts. This limits finding posts where loneliness is stated implicitly rather than explicitly, possibly leading to underreporting because users hesitate to share loneliness posts due to social stigma around admitting loneliness. An example of loneliness stated explicitly is "I feel lonely and isolated at work," where the explicit expressions "isolate" and "lonely" are included. In contrast, an example of loneliness stated implicitly is "I am being ignored by various people at school," where there is no direct expression, but loneliness can be inferred from "being ignored."

Prior work has created a dataset that could also encompass cases where loneliness was implicitly expressed. A recent study collected text and psychological characteristics (Nakai et al., 2023), but this text is not publicly available. On the contrary, a publicly available dataset has been pub-



*Proceedings of the 14th Workshop on Computational Approaches to Subjectivity, Sentiment, & Social Media Analysis*, pages 280–293
August 15, 2024 ©2024 Association for Computational Linguistics

lished (Jiang et al., 2022). However, their study has two limitations: the annotation process relies on subjectivity due to the absence of a clear definition of loneliness, and they did not differentiate by intensity.

This study aims to provide a publicly available Japanese loneliness dataset with clear annotation guidelines. We created annotation guidelines based on the psychological definition of loneliness and annotated a corpus that is publicly available. Moreover, we labeled whether loneliness is expressed, its intensity in detecting people suffering from severe loneliness, and the contributing factors.

To create the loneliness dataset, we used a Japanese short episode corpus[1], called LIFE STORY. This corpus is composed of episodes recalled from emotions collected through crowdsourcing. In line with previous work, creating datasets using social media would become difficult to utilize if API regulations change. Considering that the LIFE STORY corpus is freely available, it is advantageous for research from the perspective of reproducibility and ease of use.

Our contributions are as follows:

- We built a Japanese loneliness dataset[2] by annotating an episode corpus, which is created for the detection and analysis of loneliness (Section 3);
- We constructed classifiers to determine whether loneliness is expressed and to assess the intensity of loneliness using our dataset (Section 4);
- We indicated the feasibility of domain adaptation, employing posts from X (Section 5).

## 2 Related Work

### 2.1 Definition of Loneliness and Social Needs

Many definitions of loneliness have been proposed (Taylor, 2020; Sullivan, 1953; Ma et al., 2020). However, they all share three important common points (Peplau and Perlman, 1982). First, loneliness arises from inadequacies in an individual's social connections. Second, loneliness is subjective; it does not equate to objective social isolation. It is possible for an individual to be alone without experiencing loneliness, and conversely, one can feel lonely even when surrounded by a crowd. Third, loneliness is uncomfortable and distressing. The differences among various definitions of loneliness are due to the nature of social deficiency. One approach emphasizes social needs, and another approach emphasizes cognitive processes. The social needs approach suggests that individuals may experience loneliness without explicitly identifying themselves as lonely or consciously understanding the nature of their distress. In contrast, the cognitive approach focuses on the perceptions and self-reports of loneliness, paying attention to those who recognize themselves as lonely.

For interventions in loneliness, it is important to identify not only those who recognize their loneliness but also those who are emotionally distressed without recognizing it as loneliness. Therefore, when defining loneliness, we prioritize the social needs aspect. We introduced the definition of loneliness presented by Hawkley and Cacioppo (2010).

Social needs are conceptualized in various ways (Deci and Ryan, 2008; Lindenberg, 1996; Steverink et al., 2020). We have chosen the approach by Ormel et al. (1999), which is one of the most representative, and is composed of *Affection*, *Behavioral Confirmation*, and *Status*.

### 2.2 Loneliness Dataset

Research on constructing datasets related to implicit loneliness is limited (Nakai et al., 2023; Jiang et al., 2022). Nakai et al. (2023) tried to predict psychological states including loneliness from texts describing eating experiences collected using crowdsourcing with 877 individuals. They collected text data on meal experiences, satisfaction levels with meals, and psychological characteristics, then created a classifier using BERT. The loneliness scores they gathered are not about how lonely the texts express but about how lonely the writers usually feel; thus, loneliness related to the text is not assigned. Additionally, this dataset has not been made publicly available, which motivates this study to construct an openly available dataset.

Jiang et al. (2022) constructed a loneliness dataset from posts on Reddit. To create a corpus, they collected posts from two loneliness-related subreddits (r/loneliness, r/lonely) and two subreddits targeting young adults (r/youngadults, r/college). For each post in the corpus, three anno-

[1]https://sociocom.naist.jp/life-story-data/

[2]https://github.com/sociocom/Japanese-Loneliness-Dataset

tators determined whether it expressed loneliness. Posts judged as expressing loneliness were further annotated with duration, situation, interpersonal relationships, and interactions. However, the criteria for determining whether a post expresses loneliness are not clearly defined. In previous studies, the definition of loneliness for dataset construction has traditionally relied on the subjective judgment of annotators. In contrast, we attempted annotation based on a definition of loneliness that allows for objective interpretation. We believe that this initial attempt is crucial for detecting loneliness to prevent serious conditions such as depression and suicide.

## 3 A Japanese Dataset for Loneliness

### 3.1 Corpus

This study leverages a Japanese short episode corpus, called LIFE STORY[3], for constructing the Japanese dataset. The LIFE STORY corpus, which is freely available, has been continuously collected since 2017, offering age, gender, and open-ended Japanese episodes associated with seven primary emotions: sadness, anxiety, anger, disgust, trust, surprise, and joy.

We focused on sadness and anxiety as emotions related to loneliness (Cacioppo et al., 2010; Mullarkey et al., 2018; Meltzer et al., 2012). In a preliminary study, we evaluated 50 episodes of each emotion to determine if they expressed loneliness based on the criteria specified in the annotation guidelines (details in Section 3.2.2). For sad episodes, out of 50 episodes, one annotator classified 12 episodes as expressing loneliness, while the other annotator classified 16 episodes. For anxious episodes, one annotator classified 1 episode as expressing loneliness, and the other annotator classified 0 episodes. Due to the very low relationship observed between anxiety and loneliness in this sample, we chose to annotate only sad episodes when creating the corpus. We annotated sad episodes extracted from the LIFE STORY corpus. Examples translated from Japanese of such episodes include: "*I couldn't purchase the desired item at the auction*" and "*I had to decline my friend's invitations because I was short on money during Golden Week.*"

[3] https://sociocom.naist.jp/life-story-data/

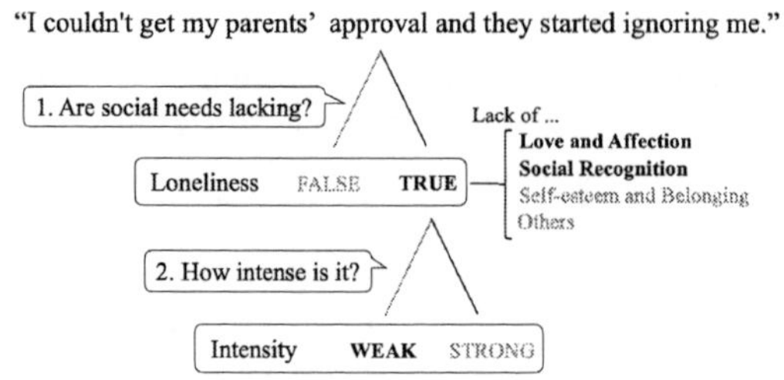


Figure 1: Overview of the annotation process. We annotated the episodes in the LIFE STORY corpus in the order of loneliness or non-loneliness, and the intensity of loneliness. We also classified unsatisfied social needs as loneliness factors within the step of loneliness or non-loneliness. This episode is labeled as *TRUE* due to a lack of *Love and Affection* and *Social Recognition*, and is labeled as weak in terms of the intensity of loneliness.

### 3.2 Label Definitions

#### 3.2.1 Overview

We annotated the episodes in the LIFE STORY corpus with the following two steps:

**Step 1** Loneliness or Non-Loneliness: We first labeled episodes to determine whether they express loneliness or not. Loneliness episodes were labeled as *TRUE*, while non-loneliness episodes were labeled as *FALSE*. Additionally, we also labeled unsatisfied social needs as loneliness factors. Social needs include *Love and Affection*, *Social Recognition*, and *Self-esteem and Belonging*.

**Step 2** Intensity of Loneliness: For loneliness episodes, we further categorized the intensity levels of such expressions. The intensity of loneliness is either *STRONG* or *WEAK*.

Figure 1 illustrates the hierarchical labeling structure. For example, consider the episode: "*I couldn't get my parents' approval and they started ignoring me.*" This is labeled as *TRUE* for step 1 and *WEAK* for step 2 based on the criteria (details in Sections 3.2.2 and 3.2.3). Loneliness factors are labeled as unsatisfied social needs for *Love and Affection* and *Social Recognition*.

#### 3.2.2 Loneliness or Non-Loneliness

This section details the annotation scheme used to identify loneliness episodes and categorize their loneliness factors. We adopted the definition of loneliness proposed by Hawkley and Cacioppo

(2010): *Loneliness is defined as a distressing feeling that accompanies the perception that one's social needs are not being met by the quantity or especially the quality of one's social relationships.*

Based on the definition, episodes in which any one of the social needs is not satisfied are judged to express loneliness. In other words, a single unsatisfied social need can lead to the judgment of loneliness. In psychology, it has been proposed that social needs are composed of *Affection*, *Behavioral Confirmation*, and *Status* (Ormel et al., 1999). For the purpose of this study, we have slightly adjusted these categories to better relate to loneliness and have classified them into three categories: *Love and Affection*, *Social Recognition*, and *Self-esteem and Belonging*. *Status* can be considered as a factor contributing to loneliness. However, when looking at the definitions, we can see that the definition of *Status* is actually derived from our definition of social needs rather than directly causing loneliness itself. Therefore, in this study we consider that the source of loneliness from *Status* arises from a lack of *Self-esteem and Belonging*, and *Social Recognition*. Below is a description of the social needs employed in this study:

**Love and Affection** This involves receiving affection from people one cares about (e.g., family, friends). It is derived from *Affection* (one of the social needs proposed by Ormel et al. (1999)), with the addition of "love" to enhance understanding. An example of a lack of *Love and Affection* is as follows: "*I had a disagreement with my parents and lost touch with them.*"

**Social Recognition** This involves receiving external validation and acceptance through one's behavior in a social environment. It is derived from *Behavioral Confirmation* (one of the social needs proposed by Ormel et al. (1999)), which is the sense of approval by others. It depends on external evaluations. An example of a lack of *Social Recognition* is as follows: "*Many of my friends at school are fashionable, but I don't have the money to buy a variety of clothes, so I can't be fashionable and join in the conversation.*"

**Self-esteem and Belonging** This involves the internal sense of being accepted and valued within a group or society. It is also rooted from *Behavioral Confirmation*. It depends on internal evaluations. An example of a lack of *Self-esteem and Belonging* is as follows: "*I feel out of place because I am the only one without a Ph.D.*"

Furthermore, we introduced an *Others* label to address situations where none of the specified unsatisfied social needs were identified, yet loneliness was perceived. The example is "*It's sad to spend every day feeling lonely and in a depressed state.*" If an episode does not lack any of the social needs, we assigned only a *FALSE* label for loneliness.

To ensure consistent labeling within the dataset, we added two criteria for episodes labeled as *FALSE*. First, episodes where loneliness arises from an external source rather than the writer themselves are classified as *FALSE*. The example is "*My wife said she doesn't fit in at work and feels lonely.*" Second, episodes lacking explicit vocabulary related to social connection are also labeled as *FALSE*. On this criterion, the example of *TRUE* is "*I have a disagreement with my parents and have lost touch with them*" because it involves both explicit social connection vocabulary ("parent" and "lost touch with") and expresses loneliness. In contrast, the example of *FALSE* is "*I had a dream about a sad event from the past, and the sadness came back to me when I remembered it*".

#### 3.2.3 Intensity of Loneliness

We also assigned the intensity of loneliness to episodes classified as *TRUE*, distinguishing between two levels: *STRONG* and *WEAK*. *STRONG* denotes situations in which loneliness markedly disrupts daily life or is explicitly accompanied by the expression of negative emotions. In contrast, all episodes that are not labeled *STRONG* are labeled *WEAK*. *STRONG* episodes include sentences such as "*I can't work since my parents passed away*" and "*I can't sleep at night because my beloved dog died.*" Conversely, *WEAK* episodes include sentences such as "*My family is busy with work and I'm lonely*" and "*I was sad when I had to transfer schools and say goodbye to my friends.*"

### 3.3 Dataset Construction

Two annotators independently labeled the data. We preprocessed the sad episodes excerpted from the LIFE STORY corpus (May and August 2023 surveys) by removing noises (# and * symbols, which are used in preprocessing the LIFE STORY corpus) and excluding texts shorter than or equal to 10 characters. We also converted text to lowercase, normalized Unicode using NFKC, and replaced numbers with 0. The magnitude of numbers can be important for understanding loneliness; however, NLP models often struggle to handle these numbers effectively. Therefore, numbers were not used as a feature in this model.

Each annotator labeled a total of 600 episodes including 200 common episodes for inter-annotator agreement calculation. In cases where annotators encountered difficulty determining loneliness or non-loneliness, they labeled it as *TRUE* to prioritize recall. Moreover, when faced with uncertainty regarding the intensity, annotators assigned a label of *WEAK* to prioritize the precision of *STRONG*.

Our dataset contains 800 annotated episodes, along with an additional 200 common episodes for inter-annotator agreement calculation. We randomly sampled 100 episodes each from these 200, ensuring an equal proportion of labels from both annotators. These were combined with the remaining 800 episodes for a total of 1,000 episodes. The breakdown of labels is as follows: there are 350 episodes labeled as *TRUE* and 650 episodes labeled as *FALSE*. Among those labeled as *TRUE*, 25 are classified as *STRONG* and 325 as *WEAK*. In the original Japanese dataset, the average length of the texts was 28.6 characters, with a standard deviation of 25.3 characters and a median of 21.0 characters.

### 3.4 Inter-Annotator Agreement

To calculate the agreement between annotators, we used the agreement rate and Cohen's $\kappa$ coefficient (Cohen, 1960). The agreement rates for the labels are notably high, with 0.935 (187 out of 200) for determining loneliness or non-loneliness, 0.905 for social needs (181 out of 200), 0.984 (62 out of 63) for intensity among episodes determined as *TRUE* by the two annotators, and 0.905 (181 out of 200) encompassing all labels (loneliness or non-loneliness, social needs, intensity). Moreover, Cohen's $\kappa$ coefficient also indicates substantial agreement, measuring at 0.857 for loneliness or non-loneliness and 0.849 for intensity among episodes determined as *TRUE* by the two annotators. This suggests that we have constructed a consistent dataset and that our definition is clear enough to understand, enabling researchers to easily expand the dataset.

We conducted a qualitative analysis to understand the limitations of the guidelines. Examples translated from Japanese where the annotations do not match are shown in Table 1. Note that original examples and their transliterations are listed in Appendix A. Examples (1)-(5) do not match in terms of loneliness. The social needs shown in the table are labeled by an annotator who classified them as *TRUE*. The cause of the disagreement in annotations would arise from differences in the emotions held by annotators when they encounter the same situation as the episode. For example, in example (3), the difference arises depending on whether annotators believe they are socially accepted when they cannot communicate. Similarly, in example (5), the difference arises depending on whether annotators lack self-esteem or a sense of belonging when their thoughts are not understood.

## 4 Experiments

### 4.1 Settings

To validate the applicability of our dataset, we created two classification models: $M_{lonely}$, which classifies loneliness or non-loneliness, and $M_{inten}$, which assesses the intensity of loneliness. To train the models, we split the data into 70% for training, 15% for validation, and 15% for testing while maintaining class balance. We used the Japanese pre-trained BERT model[4]. We inserted an affine layer into the final layer of the pre-trained BERT model for classification. We set the learning rate of the pre-trained layers to $5.0 \times 10^{-5}$, and the learning rate of the final layer to $1.0 \times 10^{-4}$. We used the Adam optimizer with 20 epochs. For early stopping criteria, if the maximum validation accuracy of $M_{lonely}$ and the maximum F1 score of $M_{inten}$ did not change continuously for three epochs, the learning process was finished.

### 4.2 Results

Table 2 shows the evaluation results of the models. $M_{lonely}$ achieves an accuracy of 0.880 and an F1-score of 0.833. $M_{inten}$ achieved an accuracy of 0.943 whereas exhibits a low F1-score of 0.400. This discrepancy will be due to the scarcity of *STRONG* labels and the imbalance of labels in the dataset. Specifically, there are only 25 episodes

[4] https://huggingface.co/tohoku-nlp/bert-base-japanese-whole-word-masking

| | Episode | Social needs |
|---|---|---|
| (1) | A friend I have known for a long time has become too weak to go out after undergoing a coronary artery bypass surgery. | *Love & Affection* |
| (2) | They make it sound as if I am spreading things that I am not saying.. | *Social Recognition* |
| (3) | It's sad to think that I cannot communicate due to the language barrier. | *Social Recognition* |
| (4) | I'm troubled that I'm not being understood even doing the right thing and fail at what I want to do. | *Self-esteem & Belonging* |
| (5) | It's sad that I'm not being appreciated enough. | *Self-esteem & Belonging* |

Table 1: Examples translated from Japanese of annotation disagreement. The social needs are labeled by an annotator who categorized them as *TRUE*. Discrepancies in annotations stem from variations in the emotions experienced by annotators when confronted with the same scenario as the episode.

| | Acc | F1 | Prec | Rec |
|---|---|---|---|---|
| $M_{lonely}$ | 0.880 | 0.833 | 0.804 | 0.865 |
| $M_{inten}$ | 0.943 | 0.400 | 1.00 | 0.250 |

Table 2: Evaluation metrics. $M_{lonely}$ achieves a high accuracy and F1-score. $M_{inten}$ achieved a high accuracy whereas exhibits a low F1-score.

labeled as *STRONG*. This shortage results in a deflated F1-score, despite achieving a precision of 1.0 for the *STRONG* class.

### 4.3 Discussion

We conducted an error analysis on the test data. Table 3 shows examples translated from Japanese of episodes, ground truth labels, and predicted labels by $M_{lonely}$. Note that original examples and their transliterations are seen in in Appendix A. Examples (6)-(10) represent correct predictions by $M_{lonely}$, whereas examples (11)-(15) represent incorrect ones. $M_{lonely}$ accurately classified the loneliness experienced when the relationship with the person who you loved drifts away, as exemplified in (6), as well as the loneliness resulting from the loss of family members or pets, as depicted in (7) and (8). However, $M_{lonely}$ tended to misclassify instances where *Social Recognition* or *Self-esteem and Belonging* were unsatisfied, as seen in (11) and (12). When annotators label episodes involving *Social Recognition* and *Self-esteem and Belonging*, there is often inconsistency, which is considered difficult for $M_{lonely}$ to predict. Furthermore, $M_{lonely}$ occasionally misclassified the episode where someone else, not the author themselves, felt lonely as *TRUE*, as observed in (13). Moreover, there were several episodes, such as (14) and (15), where *FALSE* was the ground truth label but could potentially be labeled as *TRUE* by annotators. Episodes like these are challenging to label even manually and are also difficult for machine learning models to predict.

Table 4 shows examples translated from Japanese of episodes, ground truth labels, and predicted labels by $M_{inten}$. Note that original examples and their transliterations are seen in Appendix A. Examples (16)-(20) represent correct predictions by $M_{inten}$, whereas examples (21)-(23) represent incorrect ones. $M_{inten}$ correctly classified the episode with a strong negative expression indicating a loss of trust in people as *STRONG*, as exemplified in (16), which is only episode classified as *STRONG*. $M_{inten}$ also correctly classified the episode mentioning only the death of a relative or a pet as *WEAK* in (17) and (18). In addition, $M_{inten}$ correctly classified episodes where there were no strong negative expressions and no interference with daily life as *WEAK* in (19) and (20). In contrast, $M_{inten}$ did not correctly classify some episodes with interference in daily life or strong negative expressions as *STRONG*, as seen in (21), (22), and (23). Annotators classify these episodes as *STRONG* using these words as clues, such as "sad every day" in (22) and "really sad" in (23), following the guidelines. $M_{inten}$ does not predict them as *STRONG* and is not learning in accordance with the guidelines. There are only 17 episodes of the label *STRONG* in the training data, which is insufficient for achieving consistent classification for $M_{inten}$.

## 5 Prediction of Social Media Posts

To assess the feasibility of domain application, we evaluated the created models using X data.

### 5.1 Social Media Posts

We collected posts from Japan from July 1 to 31, 2022 by using the X (formerly Twitter) API[5].

[5]https://developer.x.com/en/docs/twitter-api

| | Episode | Gold | Pred |
|---|---|---|---|
| (6) | It's sad that my daughter, who used to spend most of her holidays with her parents, has recently prioritized her boyfriend and go out more often. | T | T |
| (7) | My father died of cancer. | T | T |
| (8) | The loss of a beloved pet. | T | T |
| (9) | I'm sad because I lost the key to my motorcycle. | F | F |
| (10) | The team I support couldn't win the championship. | F | F |
| (11) | I didn't pass the part-time job interview. | T | F |
| (12) | I was sad because my boss did not appreciate my work. | T | F |
| (13) | My daughter might be getting divorced. | F | T |
| (14) | I experienced power harassment in workplace from a senior colleague in the same department this spring. | F | T |
| (15) | My thought is not understood. | F | T |

Table 3: Examples translated from Japanese of episodes, ground truth labels, and predicted labels by $M_{lonely}$. Examples (6)-(10) represent correct predictions by $M_{lonely}$, whereas examples (11)-(15) represent incorrect ones. T and F mean *TRUE* and *FALSE*, respectively.

| | Episode | Gold | Pred |
|---|---|---|---|
| (16) | I am a self employed business person. A contractor I have been working well with for 5 years defaulted on 1.25m yen in debt and did a moonlight flit. The lawyer I consulted told me to give up. I lost faith in humanity. | S | S |
| (17) | My parent passed away. | W | W |
| (18) | My pet has passed away. | W | W |
| (19) | I was not allowed to attend the dinner party with my husband and children. | W | W |
| (20) | The intimidation from the colleague and what I want to convey do not come across. | W | W |
| (21) | I am as saddened as my wife is by the passing of her mother. I will never forget the hospitality she extended to me the first time we stayed at her parents' house, though I believe she lived out her natural life at the age of 95. I feel like I lost my parent too. | S | W |
| (22) | I was harassed by the former company's president and felt sad every day. | S | W |
| (23) | I was really sad when my wife secretly borrowed money and ran away because she couldn't pay it back. | S | W |

Table 4: Examples translated from Japanese of episodes, ground truth labels, and predicted labels by $M_{inten}$. Examples (16)-(20) represent correct predictions by $M_{inten}$, whereas examples (21)-(23) represent incorrect ones. S and W mean *STRONG* and *WEAK*, respectively.

| | Episode | Gold | Pred |
|---|---|---|---|
| (24) | I can't meet the person I want to see due to various obstacles. | T | T |
| (25) | Jealous...death. | F | T |
| (26) | Good night. | F | T |

Table 5: Examples translated from Japanese of posts predicted as *TRUE* by $M_{lonely}$, along with their ground truth labels. T means *TRUE*, F means *FALSE*.

We preprocessed the collected posts by removing emojis, URLs, mentions, RT, tweets from users with 'bot' in their username, and duplicate posts, in addition to the preprocessing steps performed on the LIFE STORY corpus. The number of posts after preprocessing is 750,240. To align with the sad category of the annotated LIFE STORY corpus used to fine-tune our BERT models ($M_{lonely}$ and $M_{inten}$), we conducted emotion analysis on X posts by creating a new model using the LIFE STORY corpus with Naive Bayes (MultinomialNB [6] from scikit-learn) to extract posts expressing sadness. Through this process, we can better ensure that the sadness posts extracted from X, used as input, will be of the same nature as the data used for fine-tuning our models. We used the emotion categories of the corpus as ground truth labels and calculated the probabilities for classification into each emotion category. Note that for the preliminary experiment, we also constructed BERT trained on LIFE STORY corpus for emotion analysis. However, since the performance did not differ significantly from Naive Bayes, we used Naive Bayes due to its high interpretability. Subsequently, we extracted the posts classified as sad, which is 57,648 posts, and inputted them into $M_{lonely}$. We fed the posts classified as *TRUE* by $M_{lonely}$ into $M_{inten}$. Finally, 6,902 and 496 posts

[6] https://scikit-learn.org/stable/modules/generated/sklearn.naive_bayes.MultinomialNB.html

| | Episode | Gold | Pred |
|---|---|---|---|
| (27) | Please let me take a break from Twitter for a while. This morning, my mother passed away. Over the past two years, she was bedridden in a facility, going in and out of the hospital, and back to the facility repeatedly. I knew this moment would inevitably come, but it's still extremely painful. It was so hard not being able to see her for two years due to the pandemic. | S | S |
| (28) | I woke up and now I can't sleep. Prime Minister Suga's comment that former Prime Minister Abe was lonely resonates deeply in my heart, and it's too painful. I wonder if Mrs. Akie Abe is also lonely and spending sleepless nights. I'm worried about her. | W | S |

Table 6: Examples translated from Japanese of posts predicted as *STRONG* by $M_{inten}$, along with their ground truth labels. S means *STRONG*, W means *WEAK*.

were classified as *TRUE* and *STRONG*, respectively.

### 5.2 Results and Discussion

To evaluate the performance of the two models ($M_{lonely}$ and $M_{inten}$), we randomly sampled and manually annotated 300 posts: 150 posts classified as *TRUE* and 150 posts classified as *STRONG*. We calculated precision from these annotated posts. The reason for using precision as the evaluation metric instead of F1-score or accuracy is due to the inability to annotate on a large scale. To use F1-score or accuracy, posts need to be annotated before prediction. Due to the extremely low number of posts classified as *TRUE* and *STRONG* within the data from X, a large number of annotations are necessary to properly evaluate it. Therefore, this time annotations were made after predictions, on posts labeled by the model as *TRUE* and *STRONG* to calculate precision. Calculating accuracy and F1-score is planned for future work. The resulting precision for $M_{lonely}$ was 0.113, and for $M_{inten}$ it was 0.02, which is significantly lower compared to its performance on the LIFE STORY corpus. From those results, we can conclude that these models lacked the ability for domain adaptation for X posts. These inferior results can be attributed to the significant differences in syntax, vocabulary, and word usage between social media texts and the LIFE STORY episodes.

Table 5 lists examples translated from Japanese of posts predicted as *TRUE* by $M_{lonely}$, along with their ground truth labels. Note that original examples and their transliterations are listed in Appendix A. As seen in (24), $M_{lonely}$ can detect loneliness when someone wants to meet but cannot. However, $M_{lonely}$ often mistakenly predicts *TRUE* when influenced by expressions related to "death" because those words frequently occur in loneliness episodes in our dataset, as seen in (25). Many of the posts predicted as *TRUE* included greetings, as seen in (26). As LIFE STORY corpus does not contain greetings, it appears that the model cannot predict accurately when the text contains only greetings.

Table 6 shows examples translated from Japanese of posts predicted as *STRONG* by $M_{inten}$, along with their ground truth labels. Note that original examples and their transliterations are listed in Appendix A. As shown in (27), $M_{inten}$ correctly classified the posts expressing hardship over the loss of a mother with strong negative expressions as *STRONG*. Similar to the evaluation on the dataset, consistency in $M_{inten}$ was not observed.

## 6 Limitations

Based on the definition of loneliness, we classified whether the text expressed loneliness, but the emotions perceived by the readers and the writers may be different (Kajiwara et al., 2021; Ramos et al., 2022). Accordingly, we plan to collect texts and loneliness scores of their writers through crowdsourcing. In terms of completeness, we annotated episodes evoked by sadness; hence, loneliness that occurs alongside other emotions or loneliness that occurs independently of other emotions may not be captured. In addition, the loneliness dataset we created lacks a sufficient number of *STRONG* labels for learning. We plan to expand our dataset to secure an ample number of *STRONG* labels, thereby addressing the low recall issue in the model for classification of intensity. Regarding the guidelines, the disagreement among annotators often arises from the fact that different people perceive the same situation differently. This is evident in texts involving *Social Recognition* and *Self-esteem and Belonging*.

We created a BERT-based classifier, but using other models may result in higher performance. Considering the rapid development in recent years, it is also necessary to consider using generative models represented by GPT-4. The performance of our models decreased when predicting on X data, which is distinct from our dataset. Research has shown significant differences in syntax, vocabulary, and word usage between normal conversations and social media text, such as that found on X (Bryden et al., 2013). Social media platforms often feature unique language patterns influenced by their community structures. For example, X users may adopt specific terminologies, abbreviations, and stylistic choices that reflect the norms and culture of the online community they engage with. Therefore, our current model is not appropriate for predicting loneliness and its intensity in social media texts, and it is quite challenging to achieve good performance with such inconsistent data. To address this problem, Arefyev et al. (2021) proposed a technique for more efficient domain and task adaptation of pre-trained masked language models such as BERT before fine-tuning them on a specific task. This technique forces the model to predict words that are highly indicative of the target task classes (e.g., sentiment words for sentiment analysis), allowing it to learn better task-relevant representations during adaptation. We will use this method for domain adaptation in future work.

## 7 Conclusion

We present a freely available Japanese loneliness dataset[7], which is created by annotating a short episode corpus, with clear guidelines. Our annotation guidelines are based on the psychological definition of loneliness. Using this guideline for annotation, the results showed a Cohen's $\kappa$ coefficient of 0.857 for loneliness or non-loneliness and 0.849 for intensity among episodes determined as loneliness by two annotators, indicating consistency. We also construct classifiers to identify whether loneliness is expressed and to assess the intensity of loneliness using our dataset. The model classifying loneliness or non-loneliness achieved an F1-score of 0.833. However, the model identifying loneliness intensity had a low F1-score of 0.400, which is likely due to insufficient learning of a specific label and the imbalance of labels in the dataset. In addition, these models show low performance in a domain distinct from the texts used for training.

In the future, we plan to expand our dataset to alleviate data imbalance and address the shortage of a specific label, as well as to improve domain adaptation for social media. We also plan to create a classification model for social needs to identify factors contributing to loneliness, which will provide valuable insights for detection and intervention methods.

## Acknowledgments

This work was supported by JST-Mirai Program Grant Number JPMJMI21J2, Japan.

## References

Anietie Andy, Garrick Sherman, and Sharath Chandra Guntuku. 2022. Understanding the expression of loneliness on twitter across age groups and genders. *PLOS ONE*, 17(9):1–19.

Nikolay Arefyev, Dmitrii Kharchev, and Artem Shelmanov. 2021. NB-MLM: Efficient domain adaptation of masked language models for sentiment analysis. In *Proceedings of the 2021 Conference on Empirical Methods in Natural Language Processing*, pages 9114–9124, Online and Punta Cana, Dominican Republic. Association for Computational Linguistics.

Manfred E Beutel, Eva M Klein, Elmar Brähler, Iris Reiner, Claus Jünger, Matthias Michal, Jörg Wiltink, Philipp S Wild, Thomas Münzel, Karl J Lackner, et al. 2017. Loneliness in the general population: prevalence, determinants and relations to mental health. *BMC psychiatry*, 17(1):1–7.

John Bryden, Sebastian Funk, and Vincent Jansen. 2013. Word usage mirrors community structure in the online social network twitter. *EPJ Data Science*, 2.

John T. Cacioppo, Louise C. Hawkley, and Ronald A. Thisted. 2010. Perceived social isolation makes me sad: 5-year cross-lagged analyses of loneliness and depressive symptomatology in the chicago health, aging, and social relations study. *Psychology and aging*, 25 2:453–63.

Jacob Cohen. 1960. A coefficient of agreement for nominal scales. *Educational and Psychological Measurement*, 20:37 – 46.

Edward L Deci and Richard M Ryan. 2008. Self-determination theory: A macrotheory of human motivation, development, and health. *Canadian psychology/Psychologie canadienne*, 49(3):182.

Louise C Hawkley and John T Cacioppo. 2010. Loneliness matters: A theoretical and empirical review of consequences and mechanisms. *Annals of behavioral medicine*, 40(2):218–227.

[7]https://github.com/sociocom/Japanese-Loneliness-Dataset

Yueyi Jiang, Yunfan Jiang, Liu Leqi, and Piotr Winkielman. 2022. Many ways to be lonely: Fine-Grained characterization of loneliness and its potential changes in COVID-19. In *Proceedings of the International AAAI Conference on Web and Social Media*, volume 16, pages 405–416.

Tomoyuki Kajiwara, Chenhui Chu, Noriko Takemura, Yuta Nakashima, and Hajime Nagahara. 2021. WRIME: A new dataset for emotional intensity estimation with subjective and objective annotations. In *Proceedings of the 2021 Conference of the North American Chapter of the Association for Computational Linguistics: Human Language Technologies*, pages 2095–2104, Online. Association for Computational Linguistics.

Svetlana Kiritchenko, Will E Hipson, Robert J Coplan, and Saif M Mohammad. 2020. SOLO: A corpus of tweets for examining the state of being alone. *arXiv preprint arXiv:2006.03096*.

Charikleia Lampraki, Adar Hoffman, Angélique Roquet, and Daniela S Jopp. 2022. Loneliness during COVID-19: Development and influencing factors. *PLOS ONE*, 17(3):e0265900.

Ellen E. Lee, Colin Depp, Barton W. Palmer, Danielle Glorioso, Rebecca Daly, Jinyuan Liu, Xin M. Tu, Ho-Cheol Kim, Peri Tarr, Yasunori Yamada, and et al. 2019. High prevalence and adverse health effects of loneliness in community-dwelling adults across the lifespan: role of wisdom as a protective factor. *International Psychogeriatrics*, 31(10):1447–1462.

Siegwart Lindenberg. 1996. Continuities in the theory 10 of social production functions. *Verklarende sociologie: Opstellen voor Reinhard Wippler, Thesis Publishers, Amsterdam*, pages 169–184.

Ye Luo, Louise C. Hawkley, Linda J. Waite, and John T. Cacioppo. 2012. Loneliness, health, and mortality in old age: A national longitudinal study. *Social Science Medicine*, 74(6):907–914. Part Special Issue: Migration, 'illegality', and health: Mapping embodied vulnerability and debating health-related deservingness.

Ruimin Ma, Farhana Mann, Jingyi Wang, Brynmor Lloyd-Evans, James Terhune, Ahmed Al-Shihabi, and Sonia Johnson. 2020. The effectiveness of interventions for reducing subjective and objective social isolation among people with mental health problems: a systematic review. *Social Psychiatry and Psychiatric Epidemiology*, 55.

Howard Meltzer, Paul Bebbington, Michael Dennis, Rachel Jenkins, Sally McManus, and Traolach Brugha. 2012. Feelings of loneliness among adults with mental disorder. *Social psychiatry and psychiatric epidemiology*, 50.

Michael Mullarkey, Igor Marchetti, and Christopher Beevers. 2018. Using network analysis to identify central symptoms of adolescent depression. *Journal of Clinical Child Adolescent Psychology*, 48.

Kentaro Nakai, Ritsuko Iwai, and Takatsune Kumada. 2023. An examination of eating experiences in relation to psychological states, loneliness, and depression using bert. *New Frontiers in Artificial Intelligence*, pages 196–214.

Johan Ormel, Siegwart Lindenberg, Nardi Steverink, and Lois M Verbrugge. 1999. Subjective well-being and social production functions. *Social indicators research*, 46:61–90.

Letitia Anne Peplau and Daniel Perlman. 1982. *Loneliness: A Sourcebook of Current Theory, Research and Therapy*. Wiley Series on Personality Processes. Wiley.

Patrick John Ramos, Kiki Ferawati, Kongmeng Liew, Eiji Aramaki, and Shoko Wakamiya. 2022. Emotion analysis of writers and readers of Japanese tweets on vaccinations. In *Proceedings of the 12th Workshop on Computational Approaches to Subjectivity, Sentiment & Social Media Analysis*, pages 95–103, Dublin, Ireland. Association for Computational Linguistics.

Aparna Shankar, Anne Mcmunn, James Banks, and Andrew Steptoe. 2011. Loneliness, social isolation, and behavioral and biological health indicators in older adults. *Health psychology : official journal of the Division of Health Psychology, American Psychological Association*, 30:377–85.

Nardi Steverink, Siegwart Lindenberg, Tali Spiegel, and Anna P. Nieboer. 2020. The associations of different social needs with psychological strengths and subjective well-being: An empirical investigation based on social production function theory. *Journal of Happiness Studies*, 21(3):799–824.

Harry Stack Sullivan. 1953. *The Interpersonal Theory of Psychiatry*. Routledge.

Harry Taylor. 2020. Social isolation's influence on loneliness among older adults. *Clinical Social Work Journal*, 48.

Nicole K Valtorta, Mona Kanaan, Simon Gilbody, Sara Ronzi, and Barbara Hanratty. 2016. Loneliness and social isolation as risk factors for coronary heart disease and stroke: systematic review and meta-analysis of longitudinal observational studies. *Heart*, 102(13):1009–1016.

## A Appendix

| | Episode | Social needs |
|---|---|---|
| (1) | 長らく付き合いがあって、仲良くしていた友人が、冠動脈置換手術によって、弱ってしまって出かけられなくなった。<br>Nagaraku tsukiai ga atte, nakayoku shiteita yûjin ga, kandômyakushujutsu ni yotte, yowatte shimatte dekake rarenaku natta.<br>A friend I have known for a long time has become too weak to go out after undergoing a coronary artery bypass surgery. | *Love & Affection* |
| (2) | 私が言いふらしていないことをあたかも私が言っているようにされていること。<br>Watashi ga iifurashite inai koto wo atakamo watashi ga itteiru yôni sareteirukoto.<br>They make it sound as if I am spreading things that I am not saying. | *Social Recognition* |
| (3) | 言葉が通じないなと思うと悲しい。<br>Kotoba ga tûjinai na to omou to kanashii.<br>It's sad to think that I cannot communicate due to the language barrier. | *Social Recognition* |
| (4) | 正しいことをしても理解されていないことがあり、何とかしたいがなんともならない悩み。<br>Tadashii koto wo shite mo rikaisa reteinaikoto ga ari, nantoka shitai ga nantomo naranai nayami.<br>I'm troubled that I'm not being understood even when I'm doing the right thing. I want to do something about it but I can't. | *Self-esteem & Belonging* |
| (5) | 自分自身の評価があまり良くなくて悲しい。<br>Jibunjishin no hyôka ga amari yokuna kute kanashii.<br>It's sad that I'm not being appreciated enough. | *Self-esteem & Belonging* |

Table 7: Original examples of annotation disagreement and their transliterations. The social needs are labeled by an annotator who categorized them as *TRUE*. Discrepancies in annotations stem from variations in the emotions experienced by annotators when confronted with the same scenario as the episode. Note that The original text in example (2) has been corrected due to a typographical error (the particle ' が' was duplicated).

| | Episode | Gold | Pred |
|---|---|---|---|
| (6) | これまで親と休日を過ごすことが多かった娘が、最近は彼氏を優先するようになり、外出が増えたことが悲しい。<br>Koremade oya to kyûjitsu wo sugosu koto ga ôkatta musume ga, saikin wa kareshi wo yûsensuru yô ni nari, gaishutsu ga fueta koto ga kanashii.<br>It's sad that my daughter, who used to spend most of her holidays with her parents, has recently prioritized her boyfriend and go out more often. | T | T |
| (7) | 父ががんで亡くなったこと<br>Chichi ga gan de nakunatta koto.<br>My father died of cancer. | T | T |
| (8) | 可愛がっていたペットが亡くなったこと<br>Kawaigatte ita petto ga nakunatta koto.<br>The loss of a beloved pet. | T | T |
| (9) | バイクの鍵をなくしてしまって悲しい<br>Baiku no kagi wo nakushite shimatte kanashii.<br>I'm sad because I lost the key to my motorcycle. | F | F |
| (10) | 応援しているチームが優勝できなかったこと<br>Ôenshite iru tîmu ga yûshô dekinakatta koto.<br>The team I support couldn't win the championship. | F | F |
| (11) | パートの面接に受からなかった。<br>Pâto no mensetsu ni ukara nakatta.<br>I didn't pass the part-time job interview. | T | F |
| (12) | 職場で仕事の成果物が上司に理解されず悲しかった。<br>Shokuba de shigoto no seikabutsu ga jôshi ni rikaisare zu kanashi katta.<br>I was sad because my boss did not appreciate my work. | T | F |
| (13) | 娘が離婚するかも知れなくなった。<br>Musume ga rikonsuru kamo shirenaku natta.<br>My daughter might be getting divorced. | F | T |
| (14) | 今年春、職場で、同じ部の先輩からパワハラを受けた。<br>Kotoshi haru, shokuba de, onaji bu no sempai kara pawahara wo uketa.<br>I experienced power harassment in workplace from a senior colleague in the same department this spring. | F | T |
| (15) | 思いを分かってもらえない<br>Omoi wo wakatte moraenai.<br>My thought is not understood. | F | T |

Table 8: Original examples of episodes, their transliterations, ground truth labels, and predicted labels by $M_{lonely}$. Examples (6)-(10) represent correct predictions by $M_{lonely}$, whereas examples (11)-(15) represent incorrect ones. T means *TRUE*, F means *FALSE*.

| | Episode | Gold | Pred |
|---|---|---|---|
| (16) | 仕事上自営業をしており5年ぐらいの付き合いで仲良く仕事を貰ってた業者さんに125万円踏んだおされました。その業者は夜逃げしてしまい弁護士に相談したら勉強代だと思って諦めた方が良いと言われました。本当に人間不信になります。<br>Shigoto jô jieigyô wo shite ori 5 nen gurai no tsukiai de nakayoku shigoto wo moratte ita gyôsha san ni 125 manen fundaosare mashita. Sono gyôsha wa yonigeshite shimai bengoshi ni sôdan shitara benkyôdai da to omotte akirameta hô ga ii to iware mashita. Hontô ni ningenfushin ni narimasu.<br>I am a self employed business person. A contractor I have been working well with for 5 years defaulted on 1.25m yen in debt and did a moonlight flit. The lawyer I consulted told me to give up. I lost faith in humanity. | S | S |
| (17) | 親が亡くなったことです<br>Oya ga nakunatta koto desu.<br>My parent passed away. | W | W |
| (18) | ペットがしんでしまった。<br>Petto ga shinde shimatta.<br>My pet has passed away. | W | W |
| (19) | 夫と子供のお食事会に参加させてもらえなかった事<br>Otto to kodomo no oshokujikai ni sankasasete moraenakatta koto.<br>I was not allowed to attend the dinner party with my husband and children. | W | W |
| (20) | 職場の同僚からの恫喝や伝えたい事が伝わらない事<br>Shokuba no dôryô kara no dôkatsu ya tsutaetai koto ga tsutawaranai koto.<br>The intimidation from the colleague and what I want to convey do not come across. | W | W |
| (21) | 妻の母親が亡くなって妻同様に悲しみに暮れている。初めて妻の実家に泊まったときによくもてなしをしていただいたことが忘れられない。95歳で天寿を全うしたと思うが。これで私には親は居なくなってしまった。<br>Tsuma no hahaoya ga nakunatte tsuma dôyô ni kanashimi ni kureteiru. Hajimete tsuma no jikka ni tomatta toki ni yoku motenashi wo shite itadaita koto ga wasurerarenai. 95 sai de tenju wo mattoushita to omouga. Kore de watashi ni wa oya wa inakunatte shimatta.<br>I am as saddened as my wife is by the passing of her mother. I will never forget the hospitality she extended to me the first time we stayed at her parents' house, though I believe she lived out her natural life at the age of 95. I feel like I lost my parent too. | S | W |
| (22) | 前の会社の社長からパワハラを、受けて毎日悲しかった。<br>Mae no kaisha no shachô kara pawahara wo, ukete mainichi kanashi katta.<br>I was harassed by the former company's president and felt sad every day. | S | W |
| (23) | 妻が私に内緒で借金をし、支払えなくなって家出した時は本当に悲しかった。<br>Tsuma ga watashi ni naisho de shakkin wo shi, shiharaenaku natte iedeshita toki wa hontô ni kanashi katta.<br>I was really sad when my wife secretly borrowed money and ran away because she couldn't pay it back. | S | W |

Table 9: Original examples of episodes, their transliterations, ground truth labels, and predicted labels by $M_{inten}$. Examples (16)-(20) represent correct predictions by $M_{inten}$, whereas examples (21)-(23) represent incorrect ones. S means *STRONG*, W means *WEAK*.

| | Episode | Gold | Pred |
|---|---|---|---|
| (24) | 会いたい人に会えない。。。いろいろ障壁があって<br>Aitai hito ni aenai... Iroiro shôheki ga atte.<br>I can't meet the person I want to see due to various obstacles. | T | T |
| (25) | 羨ましい... 死亡。<br>Urayamashii...shibô.<br>Jealous...death. | F | T |
| (26) | おやすみなさいまし。<br>Oyasuminasai mashi.<br>Good night. | F | T |

Table 10: Original examples of posts and their transliterations predicted as *TRUE* by $M_{lonely}$, along with their ground truth labels. T means *TRUE*, F means *FALSE*.

|  | Episode | Gold | Pred |
|---|---|---|---|
| (27) | Twitter しばらく休ませて下さい。今朝、おふくろが他界しました。 ここ 2 年間施設で寝たきりで病院入退院、施設と何回も繰り返しでこの時は必ずは来るとは思って覚悟はしてたけど、かなり辛いです。コロナ禍で 2 年も会えなく辛すぎでした。<br>Twitter shibaraku yasumasete kudasai. Kesa, ofukuro ga takaishi mashita. Koko 2 nenkan shisetsu de netakiri de byôin nyûtaiin, shisetsu to nankai mo kurikaeshi de kono toki wa kanarazu wa kuru to wa omotte kakugo wa shiteta kedo, kanari tsurai desu. Koronaka de 2 nen mo aenaku tsura sugi deshita.<br>Please let me take a break from Twitter for a while. This morning, my mother passed away. Over the past two years, she was bedridden in a facility, going in and out of the hospital, and back to the facility repeatedly. I knew this moment would inevitably come, but it's still extremely painful. It was so hard not being able to see her for two years due to the pandemic. | S | S |
| (28) | 目が覚めて、寝れなくなってしまった。安倍さんは寂しがりやだったという菅さんのコメントが、胸に響いてつらすぎます。昭恵夫人も寂しくて、寝られない日々を送られているのだろうか。心配です。<br>Me ga samete, nerenaku natte shimatta. Abe san wa samishigariya datta to iu Suga san no komento ga, mune ni hibiite turasugi masu. Akie fujin mo samishikute, nerarenai hibi wo okurarete iruno darôka. Shimpai desu.<br>I woke up and now I can't sleep. Prime Minister Suga's comment that former Prime Minister Abe was lonely resonates deeply in my heart, and it's too painful. I wonder if Mrs. Akie Abe is also lonely and spending sleepless nights. I'm worried about her. | W | S |

Table 11: Original examples of posts and their transliterations predicted as *STRONG* by $M_{inten}$, along with their ground truth labels. S means *STRONG*, W means *WEAK*.

# Estimation of Happiness Changes through Longitudinal Analysis of Employees' Texts

**Junko Hayashi**[1], **Kazuhiro Ito**[1], **Masae Manabe**[2], **Yasushi Watanabe**[2], **Masataka Nakayama**[2], **Yukiko Uchida**[2], **Shoko Wakamiya**[1], and **Eiji Aramaki**[1]

[1]Nara Institute of Science and Technology, Nara, Japan
[2]Kyoto University, Kyoto, Japan
{hayashi.junko.hh5, ito.kazuhiro.ih4, wakamiya, aramaki}@is.naist.jp
{manabe.masae.4y, nakayama.masataka.4v, uchida.yukiko.6m}@kyoto-u.ac.jp
yasushi.watanabe.77@gmail.com

## Abstract

Measuring happiness as a determinant of well-being is increasingly recognized as crucial. While previous studies have utilized free-text descriptions to estimate happiness on a broad scale, limited research has focused on tracking individual fluctuations in happiness over time owing to the challenges associated with longitudinal data collection. This study addresses this issue by obtaining longitudinal data from two workplaces over two and six months respectively. Subsequently, the data is used to construct a happiness estimation model and assess individual happiness levels. Evaluation of the model performance using correlation coefficients shows variability in the correlation values among individuals. Notably, the model performs satisfactorily in estimating 9 of the 11 users' happiness scores, with a correlation coefficient of 0.4 or higher. To investigate the factors affecting the model performance, we examine the relationship between the model performance and variables such as sentence length, lexical diversity, and personality traits. Correlations are observed between these features and model performance.

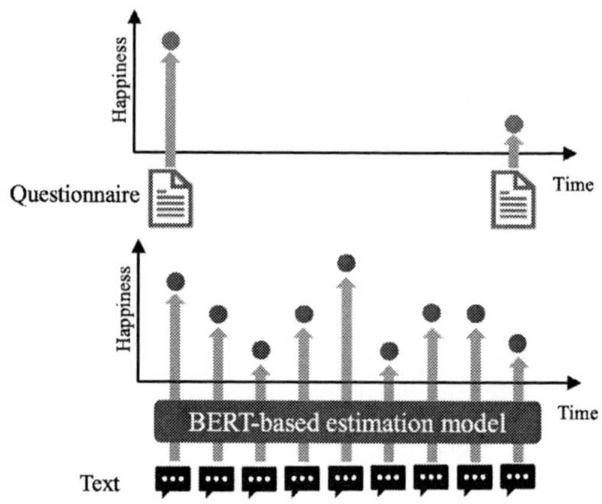


Figure 1: Overview of questionnaire-based survey methods (above) and BERT-based estimation model (below). To perform short-term surveys that cannot be easily conducted using questionnaires, this study estimates changes in happiness levels based on free-text responses.

## 1 Introduction

Well-being, happiness, and mental quality of life (referred to as "happiness" herein) are key factors affecting workplace performance (Diener and Biswas-Diener, 2002). Low happiness tends to cause issues such as decreased productivity (Shi et al., 2013) and increased turnover (Hurtz and Donovan, 2000). Hence, monitoring happiness is essential in order to make interventions, such as having them seek consultation at the appropriate time. Consequently, several studies regarding happiness measurement have been conducted. However, these studies primarily utilized questionnaire-based survey methods, which do not adequately examine short-term changes in individual happiness in the workplace. Thus, studies suffer from capturing short-term happiness, because most of the questionnaires, such as the Satisfaction with Life Scale (SWLS) (Diener et al., 1985), are not designed for daily assessment.

This study addresses the challenge of capturing short-term happiness. To achieve this, we leveraged free-text diaries, which can be reported daily and offers a more flexible alternative to traditional questionnaires. Previous studies have demonstrated the feasibility of estimating happiness from text data (Schwartz et al., 2015; Wu et al., 2017; Coşkun and Ozturan, 2018; Jaidka et al., 2020; Kjell et al., 2022; Song and Zhao, 2023). However, these studies primarily focused on estimating overall happiness levels at the mass level, instead of monitoring individual changes in happiness over time.

This study aims to capture longitudinal individual happiness in the workplace (see Figure 1). Thus, we obtained daily self-report texts with happiness scores from employees in their workplaces and then



*Proceedings of the 14th Workshop on Computational Approaches to Subjectivity, Sentiment, & Social Media Analysis*, pages 294–304
August 15, 2024 ©2024 Association for Computational Linguistics

constructed a model based on bidirectional encoder representations from a transformer (BERT) (Devlin et al., 2018) to estimate happiness from the text. To generalize the model, we constructed a model that estimates happiness using only one diary for a specific day.

The contribution of this study is two-fold:

- A new task is proposed that employs happiness estimation model in the workplace (Section 5.1).
- Suggestions are provided for mitigating performance issues using a happiness estimation model (Section 5.2).

The proposed model is considerably simpler than conventional questionnaires, thereby facilitating future psychological research.

## 2 Related work

We describe studies that solved the task of estimating happiness from text. Previous studies that constructed estimation models can be categorized into two approaches: one that utilizes datasets containing texts annotated by individuals other than the original authors, and another that employs datasets containing texts and happiness levels obtained from the same individuals.

First, we introduce an approach that uses a dataset in which happiness is assigned to a text by a person who is not the author of the text. There are studies that estimate happiness on a large scale from social media posts (Sametoğlu et al., 2023). These studies (Mitchell et al., 2013; Schwartz et al., 2015; Jaidka et al., 2020) use dictionaries such as Linguistic Inquiry and Word Count (LIWC)[1] and LabMT (Dodds et al., 2011).

Second, we introduce an approach employing datasets where both the texts and happiness levels are collected from the same individuals (Wu et al., 2017; Kjell et al., 2022; Song and Zhao, 2023). In this case, no specific annotators are involved and no particular criterion is set for happiness. However, the happiness levels of individuals exhibit commonalities, as shown in the texts. These studies used methods such as support vector machines and decision trees. In a study that estimated happiness using BERT with textual responses to life-satisfaction questions (Kjell et al., 2022), higher performances were obtained compared with other studies. Therefore, in this study, we used BERT as a training method to estimate happiness in the workplace.

[1] `https://www.liwc.app`

## 3 Materials

### 3.1 Data collection

We obtained two types of data: personality traits, which were obtained simultaneously prior to performing a survey; and daily reports, which were obtained throughout the experimental period, i.e., during the survey.

All participants completed a questionnaire at the beginning of the study period. Each item was answered based on a 5-point Likert scale. These scales are customized for investigating cooperativeness and autonomy in the workplace and have been proposed in the papers discussed for each item. We were the only researchers to verify the obtained data.

**Cooperativeness** The question pertaining to cooperativeness comprised 10 items, such as "I'm concerned about others' perception of me at the workplace." These questions refer to the following scale: (Hitokoto and Uchida, 2014). All the questions are listed in Table 4.

**Autonomy** Each question comprised 10 items, such as "I always try to form my own opinion within the company." Such questions are based on the scales reported by (Watanabe et al., 2023; Domae et al., 2024). All the questions are listed in Table 5.

Next, we obtained two items: daily report texts and self-reported happiness scores.

**Daily report text** The daily reports encompass free descriptions in Japanese detailing the participants' daily lives, with no character limits. Examples of these data are presented in Table 2.

**Self-reported happiness score** An 11-point scale ranging from 0 (extremely unhappy) to 10 (extremely happy) was used. This study focused on the cognitive aspects of workplace happiness. Questions pertaining to happiness were based on the Cantril ladder (Cantril, 1965), which assesses happiness via comparison to an 11-step ladder.

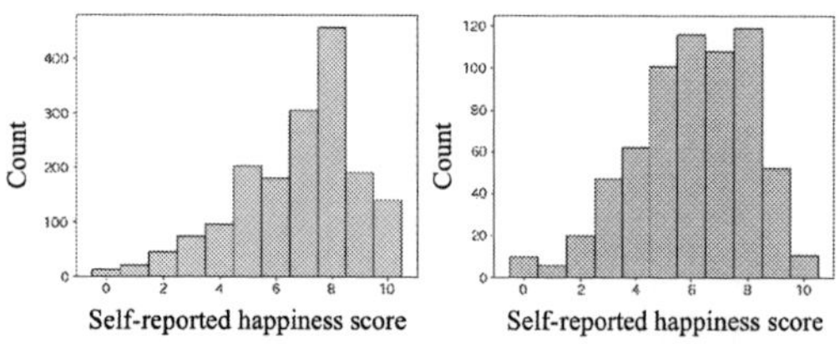

(a) Company A (b) Company B

Figure 2: Distribution of self-reported happiness scores based on data obtained.

We used the data of company A, which were used in a previous study to investigate the happiness levels of employees at the company(Ito et al., 2023). Furthermore, we obtained additional data from company B to evaluate the estimation model. The name of each company has been changed to preserve anonymity.

An original web browser-based application was used to obtain the daily reports. The instructions provided to the participants included: "The input timing is typically once or more per working day, thus reflecting the day's events at the end of the work day."

### 3.2 Data Statistics and Examples

Data were obtained from company A, which is a major advertising and marketing company in Japan. In this company, 94 members participated in the input of daily reports over two months (from September 1 to October 31, 2022). Consequently, 1,728 data points were obtained from company A (Table 1). Figure 2 (a) shows the distribution of the data obtained.

Additionally, data were obtained from company B, which is a major Japanese electronics manufacturer. In this company, 11 employees provided daily report texts over six months (from December 19, 2022, to May 18, 2023). Consequently, 652 data points were collected from company B (Table 1). Figure 2 (b) shows the distribution of the data obtained.

## 4 Experiments

### 4.1 Modeling

We constructed a model in which the input was the daily report text and the output was the estimated happiness score. The training data were obtained from company A. In this experiment, we built a bidirectional encoder representation from a transformer (BERT) (Devlin et al., 2018)-based estimation model. Specifically, we constructed a regression model of the AutoModel for Sequence Classification[2] using Tohoku University's pre-trained BERT[3]. The learning rate was set to 0.000002, the number of epochs to 20, and AdamW (Loshchilov and Hutter, 2017) was used as the optimizer. We did not conduct a detailed validation to select the best model from the existing models because our focus was on whether the task can be solved, not on achieving a high-performance model.

### 4.2 Evaluation metrics

The model constructed using company A's data was tested using company B's data. By testing models with data from a completely different population, we successfully verified the generality of the model under strict conditions. The purpose of this study is not so much to estimate the correct level of happiness as to assess whether changes in happiness are captured. For the evaluation index, we employed the Pearson correlation coefficient, which has been used in previous studies (Song and Zhao, 2023). Subsequently, the correlation coefficient between the estimated happiness score derived from the model (hereafter referred to as "estimated happiness score") and the self-reported happiness score by employees was computed.

### 4.3 User-based Happiness Estimation

For each user, we calculated the correlation coefficient between the self-reported and estimated happiness scores. We tested the performance of the model trained on company A's data in predicting the estimated level of happiness from the texts of individuals in company B. The eleven users in company B are U1 to U11, respectively. In this study, the model was applied to a completely different population.

## 5 Results

### 5.1 User-based happiness estimation

The correlation coefficients of the happiness estimation for each user in company B are shown in Table 3 and the time series is shown in Figure 3. The model performance is defined as the correlation coefficient between the self-reported and estimated happiness scores. In Table 3, we observed that the performance of the model in estimating the

[2]https://huggingface.co/docs/transformers/model_doc/auto

[3]https://github.com/cl-tohoku/bert-japanese

| | Users | Reports | Average number of characters | Collection period |
|---|---|---|---|---|
| Company A | 94 | 1,728 | 58.8 | 09/01/2022 ~ 10/31/2022 (2-months) |
| Company B | 11 | 652 | 72.2 | 12/19/2022 ~ 05/18/2023 (6-months) |

Table 1: Data Statistics

| | Daily report text (Translated from Japanese) | Self-reported HS |
|---|---|---|
| (1) | The most significant advantage of remote work is being able to nap. Although rather conspicuous, I would like to be able to nap in the office as well. | 7 |
| (2) | Rushing on Monday mornings. Addressing complaints is difficult. | 2 |
| (3) | Although I had much work to perform since morning, I participated in a fun drinking party! I enjoyed interacting with some people I have not met before! The delicious food at a standing bar and the tasty wine were a great start to the week! It was incredibly fun. | 10 |
| (4) | Insufficient time... I am exhausted... | 1 |
| (5) | I had new insights for marketing. Additionally, I am continuing with the accident response. | 5 |

Table 2: Examples of daily report text and self-reported happiness score (Self-reported HS). The data were confidential, so the text has been slightly modified. After translating the Japanese into English, parts of the diary have been deleted and expressions have been changed.

happiness of each user varied. The variations in the correlation coefficients reflect the efficacy of the estimation model in capturing fluctuations in happiness over time.

We discuss the results for the characteristic users. First, the correlation coefficient for U1 in Table 3 could not be calculated because the self-reported happiness score of U1 remained consistently at 8 (Figure 3, U1). For users who answered the same number in the questionnaire but not in the free-response form, different information can be obtained daily. Additionally, incorporating the behaviors of users who responded in such manner into the model may facilitate happiness estimation.

Next, one user indicated a negative correlation coefficient, although not significant (Figure 3, U3). We examined the daily report text of this user and discovered that the user frequently used the expression, "A nice day that..." in the daily report. This suggests that the performance of the estimation model may be affected by differences in the writing style of each user.

As shown in Figure 3, only one user (U5) answered 0 after April. Although the user initially provided diverse texts, after April, his entries were primarily zeros and the content became uniform. Some users could not easily provide accurate estimates after such environmental changes. Although the occurrence of events can complicate data acquisition, inadequate data may reflect an individual's happiness level.

| user | corr | | user | corr | |
|---|---|---|---|---|---|
| U1 | - | | U7 | 0.63 | ** |
| U2 | 0.64 | ** | U8 | 0.63 | ** |
| U3 | -0.05 | | U9 | 0.48 | ** |
| U4 | 0.59 | ** | U10 | 0.55 | ** |
| U5 | 0.40 | * | U11 | 0.59 | ** |
| U6 | 0.40 | * | | | |

Table 3: Correlation coefficients for each user. U1 to U11 represent the 11 users of company B. Significant positive correlations were observed across most users, except for U1 and U3. Because the self-reported happiness score of U1 was always 8, we could not calculate the correlation coefficient and p-value. $^{*}p < .005$ and $^{**}p < .001$.

Finally, we assessed the happiness estimation for all users. Inter-individual variations in the factors influencing happiness can affect prediction accuracy. Because the training and test datasets used in this study encompass various distinct user profiles, the determinants of happiness may vary considerably. This suggests that incorporating user personality traits and writing habits into the model may improve estimation performance.

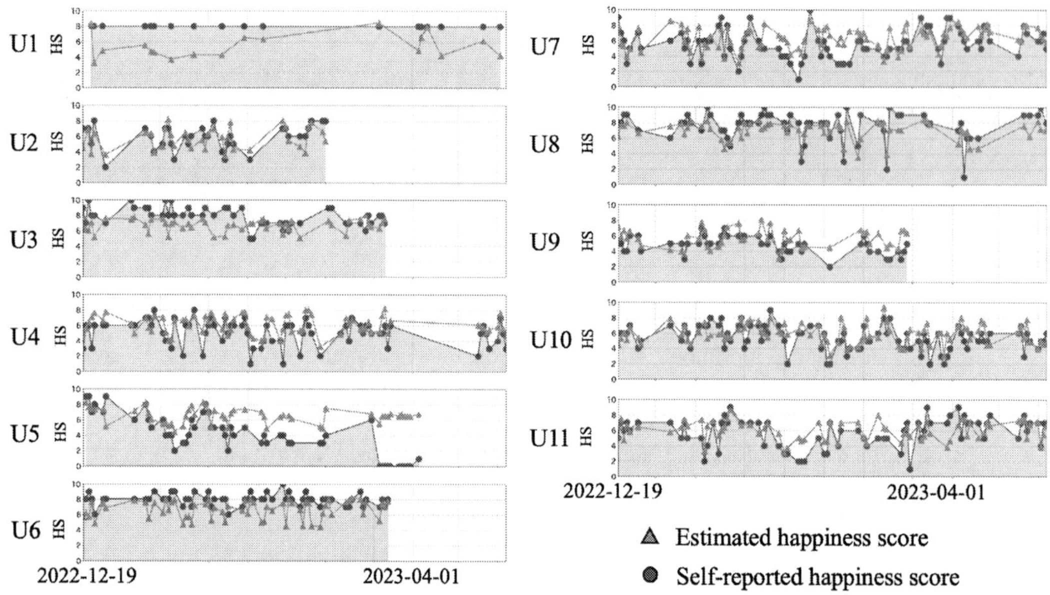


Figure 3: Estimation of happiness level of company B's user. Blank periods indicate that the individual did not complete the diary. Vertical axis represents happiness score (HS), whereas horizontal axis represents time. Background color in graphs highlight time series representing transition of self-reported happiness score.

### 5.2 Analysis

The performance of the model depends on the content of the user's daily report text. Considering user differences as intervening factors may increase the effectiveness of the happiness estimation models. Therefore, we explored the following features for users from U2 to U11, for which correlation coefficients could be computed.

**Average length of sentences** The model performance may have been influenced by the length of the diary entries. Previous studies showed that the length of sentences differs from author to author (Yule, 1939).

**Lexical diversity** The model performance may have been influenced by the lexical diversity. Research has demonstrated that lexical diversity differs among individuals (Gregori-Signes and Clavel-Arroitia, 2015).

**Personality** Differences in personality may cause differences in diaries. In this study, the following personality traits were collected during the experiment. This study examines items of **cooperativeness** and **autonomy**.

The results are visualized using box and scatter plots (Figure 4). In the scatter plots, the horizontal and vertical axes represent the model performance and feature, respectively. The box plot partitions the model performance into two sections: above- and below-median section.

Additionally, we obtained the correlation coefficients and p-values for each of the characteristics. The results showed a trend, although insignificant, which is likely due to the small sample size of 10 participants. Thus, the following discussion is limited to trends in the data, and we will attempt to obtain additional data to validate our analysis.

#### 5.2.1 Average length of sentences

Longer sentences in the diary contain more information. We examined the effect of the average sentence length per user on the model performance (Figure 4 (a)). The results showed that the group with a longer average sentence performed better in estimating happiness. The median values remained consistent across both groups in the box plots.

The results suggest that a longer user diary corresponds to the likelihood of the model performing better. Furthermore, the longer the diary sentences, the more likely they are to contain more information concerning happiness.

#### 5.2.2 Lexical diversity

We examined the relationship between the lexical diversity of each user's diary and the model performance. Lexical diversity is an evaluation

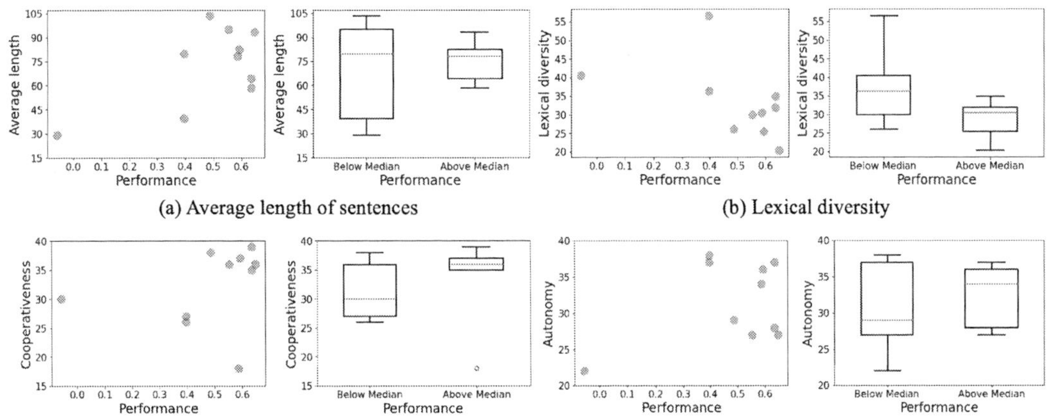


(a) Average length of sentences

(b) Lexical diversity

(c) Cooperativeness

(d) Autonomy

Figure 4: Scatter plot and box plot of factors and performance. Scatter plot and box plot of average length of sentences (a). Correlation coefficient was 0.63 ($p = 0.052$). Scatter plot and box plot of lexical diversity (b). Correlation coefficient was -0.51 ($p = 0.135$). Scatter plot and box plot of cooperativeness (c). Correlation coefficient was 0.28 ($p = 0.435$). Scatter plot and box plot of autonomy (d). Correlation coefficient was 0.38 ($p = 0.274$). In this figure, U1 is excluded due to the inability to calculate its model performance.

of whether a user writes different content in each diary. The diversity of each user's diary was evaluated using the Self-BLEU (Zhu et al., 2018) metric. Self-BLEU uses the BLEU score (Papineni et al., 2002) to evaluate the overall similarity between a group of three or more sentences. A high score indicates that the daily report texts are similar, whereas a low score indicates that the Daily report texts are diverse. In this experiment, we computed BLEU scores using SacreBLEU (Post, 2018).

The results showed that users with low self-BLEU scores performed better (Figure 4 (b)). This finding indicates that greater lexical diversity in the diaries is associated with improved happiness estimation. Moreover, this indicates that individual motivation may affect the model performance. Users who repeatedly inputted the same text from April onward (see Figure 3, U5) had the highest self-BLEU scores and low model performance. Given the diversity of the daily report text before April 1, the self-BLEU score was affected by the events after April. In April, the number of members changed and the number of employees increased. Self-BLEU scores are affected by events that complicate continuous daily reporting.

### 5.2.3 Cooperativeness

The relationship between cooperativeness and model performance was investigated. For cooperativeness, we used the total score of the answers to the 10 questions.

Four of the five users whose model performances were above the median were relatively highly cooperative within their group (Figure 4 (c)). Cooperative users are more likely to engage with others in the workplace while working. Increased interactions with many people suggest that there is more diversity in work and a greater likelihood of variation in diary content. Additionally, more cooperative users may have been more willing to participate in the experiment. Such users can employ strategies to enhance the content richness. However, users with the lowest cooperativeness were in the above-median model performance group, whereas users with the highest cooperativeness were in the below-median model performance group. Nonetheless, the trend suggests that the model performed well when the users were cooperative.

### 5.2.4 Autonomy

Next, we investigated the relationship between autonomy and model performance. We used the total score of the answers to the 10 autonomy questions.

U3, located at the bottom left of scatter plot in Figure 4 (d), has the lowest autonomy score and model performance. The lack of autonomy in creating new sentences each time may result in only similar sentences written, thus adversely affecting the model performance.

However, recognizing and accomplishing tasks contribute minimally to their annotation in journals.

As shown in the box plot, the users with the greatest and least autonomy belonged to the group of users exhibiting low performance. This suggests that autonomy does not affect happiness estimation as much as cooperativeness.

## 6 Conclusion and future works

In this study, we estimated happiness scores from diaries obtained longitudinally over six months using a transformer-based model. The analysis revealed a significant correlation between the estimated and self-reported happiness scores of 9 among 11 participants.

The findings of this study suggest three key avenues for future research and application.

First, happiness can be enhanced via targeted interventions. This study demonstrated the feasibility of estimating happiness levels in real time using free-text descriptions. Furthermore, when a shift in happiness occurs, free-text descriptions can provide insights into the underlying events or experiences.

Second, this study focused on estimating happiness scores from texts, as free texts contain abundant information beyond happiness. A nuanced examination of texts can provide insight into the determinants of happiness, the author's experiences, and the related emotions. Analyzing the characteristics of texts enables the measurement of happiness and various aspects that contribute to happiness, such as cooperativeness and autonomy.

Third, the efficacy of happiness estimation from texts is affected by individual traits, including writing style and personality. Understanding each user's diary patterns may enable a preliminary assessment of the happiness estimation performance of the model. This may determine whether another instruction is to be employed to predict the happiness of users with shorter or fewer diary entries more accurately. For example, setting requirements such as the minimum character count for diary entries can enhance the performance. The findings of this study emphasize the importance of considering individual user characteristics when estimating happiness from texts, which can provide a better assessment of happiness.

## Limitation

Using this task as a substitute for conventional questionnaires presents five major challenges.

First, cases exist where the relationship between a specific event and the happiness level is different for each individual. For example, the statement "Today is a holiday."may elicit happiness in some people but not in others. To understand the relationship between holidays and happiness, a significant amount of information, such as the author's beliefs, values, and current situation, is required, in addition to sufficient texts.

Second, the model is not generalized. The model used in this study is based on data obtained from experiments conducted by two companies. The participants of this study were from company A, which is an advertising and marketing business company, and company B, which is an electronics manufacturer. Because the vocabulary varies with the company characteristics, more data should be obtained from diverse industries and companies.

Third, the data acquisition was biased. Because both datasets were obtained simultaneously, the respondents were able to describe their happiness level and free texts consistently.

Fourth, this study was conducted using a limited sample size. The findings were validated based on data obtained from 10 participants. To enhance the robustness and applicability of these findings, more data should be obtained from larger cohorts of users.

Fifth, our experiments were restricted to the Japanese language.

## Acknowledgments

This research was supported by the Japan Science and Technology Agency, Japan Society for the Future, and JPMJMI21J2.

## References

Hadley Cantril. 1965. *The Pattern of Human Concerns*. Rutgers University Press.

Mustafa Coşkun and Meltem Ozturan. 2018. europehappinessmap: A framework for multi-lingual sentiment analysis via social media big data (a twitter case study). *Information*, 9(5):102.

Jacob Devlin, Ming-Wei Chang, Kenton Lee, and Kristina Toutanova. 2018. Bert: Pre-training of deep bidirectional transformers for language understanding. *arXiv preprint arXiv:1810.04805*.

Ed Diener and Robert Biswas-Diener. 2002. Will money increase subjective well-being? *Social Indicators Research*, 57(2):119–169.

Ed Diener, Robert A. Emmons, Randy J. Larsen, and Sharon Griffin. 1985. The satisfaction with life scale. *Journal of Personality Assessment*, 49(1):71–75.

Peter Sheridan Dodds, Kameron Decker Harris, Isabel M. Kloumann, Catherine A. Bliss, and Christopher M. Danforth. 2011. Temporal patterns of happiness and information in a global social network: Hedonometrics and twitter. *PLoS ONE*, 6(12):e26752.

Hiina Domae, Masataka Nakayama, Kosuke Takemura, Yasushi Watanabe, Matthias S. Gobel, and Yukiko Uchida. 2024. Antecedents and consequences of telework during the covid-19 pandemic: a natural experiment in japan. *Humanities and Social Sciences Communications*, 11(1).

Carmen Gregori-Signes and Begoña Clavel-Arroitia. 2015. Analysing lexical density and lexical diversity in university students' written discourse. *Procedia - Social and Behavioral Sciences*, 198:546–556.

Hidehumi Hitokoto and Yukiko Uchida. 2014. Interdependent happiness: Theoretical importance and measurement validity. *Journal of Happiness Studies*, 16(1):211–239.

Gregory M. Hurtz and John J. Donovan. 2000. Personality and job performance: The big five revisited. *Journal of Applied Psychology*, 85(6):869–879.

Kazuhiro Ito, Shoko Wakamiya, Masae Manabe, Yasushi Watanabe, Masataka Nakayama, Yukiko Uchida, and Eiji Aramaki. 2023. Mood sharedness: Well-being indicator on the team status, rather than individual factors. Preprint on webpage at `https://www.researchsquare.com/article/rs-3666850/v1`.

Kokil Jaidka, Salvatore Giorgi, H. Andrew Schwartz, Margaret L. Kern, Lyle H. Ungar, and Johannes C. Eichstaedt. 2020. Estimating geographic subjective well-being from twitter: A comparison of dictionary and data-driven language methods. *Proceedings of the National Academy of Sciences*, 117(19):10165–10171.

Oscar N. E. Kjell, Sverker Sikström, Katarina Kjell, and H. Andrew Schwartz. 2022. Natural language analyzed with ai-based transformers predict traditional subjective well-being measures approaching the theoretical upper limits in accuracy. *Scientific Reports*, 12(1).

Ilya Loshchilov and Frank Hutter. 2017. Decoupled weight decay regularization. *arXiv preprint*.

Lewis Mitchell, Morgan R. Frank, Kameron Decker Harris, Peter Sheridan Dodds, and Christopher M. Danforth. 2013. The geography of happiness: Connecting twitter sentiment and expression, demographics, and objective characteristics of place. *PLoS ONE*, 8(5):e64417.

Kishore Papineni, Salim Roukos, Todd Ward, and Wei-Jing Zhu. 2002. Bleu: a method for automatic evaluation of machine translation. In *Proceedings of the 40th Annual Meeting of the Association for Computational Linguistics*, pages 311–318, Philadelphia, Pennsylvania, USA. Association for Computational Linguistics.

Matt Post. 2018. A call for clarity in reporting BLEU scores. In *Proceedings of the Third Conference on Machine Translation: Research Papers*, pages 186–191, Belgium, Brussels. Association for Computational Linguistics.

S. Sametoğlu, D.H.M. Pelt, J.C. Eichstaedt, L.H. Ungar, and M. Bartels. 2023. The value of social media language for the assessment of wellbeing: A systematic review and meta-analysis. *The Journal of Positive Psychology*, 19(3):471–489.

H. Andrew Schwartz, Maarten Sap, Margaret L. Kern, Johannes C. Eichstaedt, Adam Kapelner, Megha Agrawal, Eduardo Blanco, Lukasz Dziurzynski, Gregory Park, David Stillwell, Michal Kosinski, Martin E.P. Seligman, and Lyle H. Ungar. 2015. Predicting individual well-being through the language of social media. In *Biocomputing 2016*. WORLD SCIENTIFIC.

Yuyan Shi, Lindsay E. Sears, Carter R. Coberley, and James E. Pope. 2013. Classification of individual well-being scores for the determination of adverse health and productivity outcomes in employee populations. *Population Health Management*, 16(2):90–98.

Mengyao Song and Nan Zhao. 2023. Predicting life satisfaction based on the emotion words in self-statement texts. *Frontiers in Psychiatry*.

Yasushi Watanabe, Kosuke Takemura, Masataka Nakayama, Matthias S Gobel, Hiina Domae, and Yukiko Uchida. 2023. Person-organization fit in japan: A longitudinal study of the effects of clan culture and interdependence on employee well-being. *Current Psychology*, 43(17):15445–15458.

Jiaqi Wu, Marilyn Walker, Pranav Anand, and Steve Whittaker. 2017. Linguistic reflexes of well-being and happiness in echo. In *Proceedings of the 8th Workshop on Computational Approaches to Subjectivity, Sentiment and Social Media Analysis*. Association for Computational Linguistics.

G. Udny Yule. 1939. On sentence-length as a statistical characteristic of style in prose: With application to two cases of disputed authorship. *Biometrika*, 30(3/4):363.

Yaoming Zhu, Sidi Lu, Lei Zheng, Jiaxian Guo, Weinan Zhang, Jun Wang, and Yong Yu. 2018. Texygen: A benchmarking platform for text generation models. In *The 41st International ACM SIGIR Conference on Research amp; Development in Information Retrieval*, SIGIR '18. ACM.

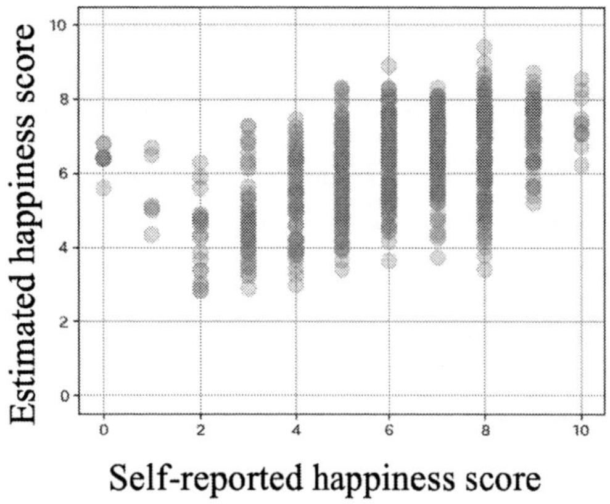


Figure 5: Results of workplace happiness estimation experiments. Vertical axes represent estimated and self-reported happiness scores, respectively. Correlation coefficient was 0.49 ($p < 0.001$).

# A Appendix

## A.1 Workplace-based Happiness Estimation

To estimate workplace happiness, the happiness level was estimated for each workplace and evaluated by determining the correlation coefficient. The correlation coefficient between the self-reported and estimated happiness scores was 0.49 (Figure 5).

| | Questionnaire (Translated from Japanese) |
|---|---|
| (1) | I am concerned about others' perception about me. |
| (2) | When interacting with people in my company, I am concerned about the relationships and statuses between me and them. |
| (3) | I think it is important to maintain harmony among my work colleagues. |
| (4) | Avoiding disagreements with others in the workplace. |
| (5) | When I disagree with someone in my company, I typically accept that person's opinion. |
| (6) | I respect people who have a sense of humility in the workplace. |
| (7) | I would sacrifice my own interests for the good of the company to which I belong. |
| (8) | I typically feel that my social interactions with others at the workplace are more important than my accomplishments. |
| (9) | I feel that my destiny is intertwined with the destiny of others' at the workplace. |
| (10) | I may change my attitude or behavior at the workplace depending on another person or the situation. |

Table 4: Questionnaire pertaining to cooperativeness. Each item was answered on a 5-point Likert scale ranging from 1 (not applicable at all) to 5 (extremely applicable). All questionnaires are in Japanese and have been translated into English.

| | Questionnaire (Translated from Japanese) |
|---|---|
| (1) | I always try to form my own opinion within the company. |
| (2) | I do not mind being the sole recipient of accolades at the workplace. |
| (3) | I think the best decisions at the workplace are those made by myself. |
| (4) | I typically make decisions on my own at the workplace. |
| (5) | I behave in the same manner regardless of my status in the company. |
| (6) | I do not mind if my thoughts or actions differ from those of others at the workplace. |
| (7) | I always speak up for myself at the workplace. |
| (8) | Being independent at the workplace is extremely important to me. |
| (9) | I enjoy being unique and different from others at the workplace. |
| (10) | My actions at the workplace are not governed by others' perceptions. |

Table 5: Questionnaire pertaining to autonomy. Each item was answered on a 5-point Likert scale ranging from 1 (not applicable at all) to 5 (extremely applicable). All questionnaires are in Japanese and have been translated into English.

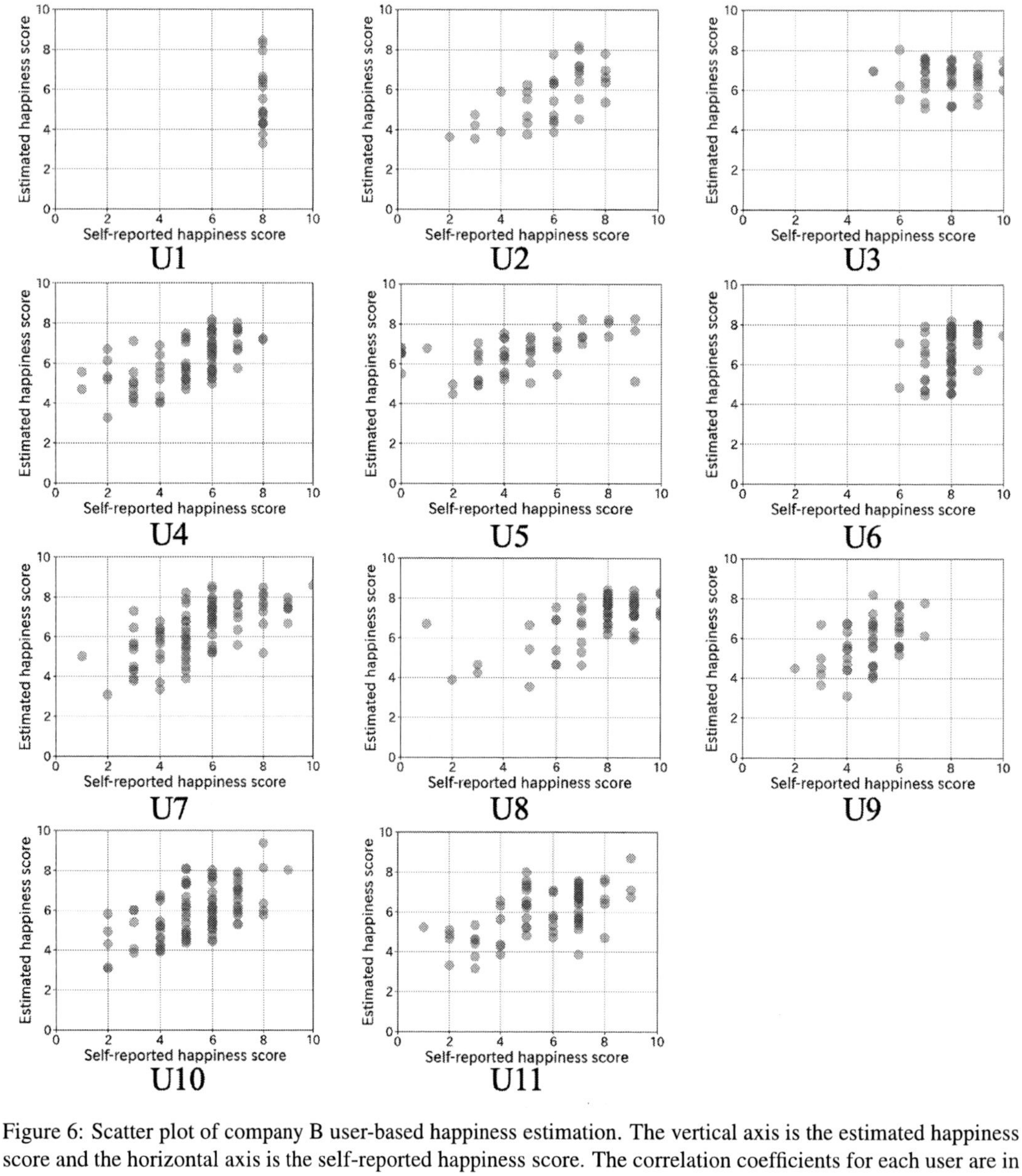


Figure 6: Scatter plot of company B user-based happiness estimation. The vertical axis is the estimated happiness score and the horizontal axis is the self-reported happiness score. The correlation coefficients for each user are in Table 3.

# Subjectivity Theory vs. Speaker Intuitions: Explaining the Results of a Subjectivity Regressor Trained on Native Speaker Judgements

**Elena Savinova** and **Jet Hoek**
Centre for Language Studies, Radboud University, Nijmegen, the Netherlands
elena.savinova@ru.nl, jet.hoek@ru.nl

## Abstract

In this paper, we address the issue of explainability in a transformer-based subjectivity regressor trained on native English speakers' judgements. The main goal of this work is to test how the regressor's predictions, and therefore native speakers' intuitions, relate to theoretical accounts of subjectivity. We approach this goal using two methods: a top-down manual selection of theoretically defined subjectivity features and a bottom-up extraction of top subjective and objective features using the LIME explanation method. The explainability of the subjectivity regressor is evaluated on a British news dataset containing sentences taken from social media news posts and from articles on the websites of the same news outlets. Both methods provide converging evidence that theoretically defined subjectivity features, such as emoji, evaluative adjectives, exclamations, questions, intensifiers, and first person pronouns, are prominent predictors of subjectivity scores. Thus, our findings show that the predictions of the regressor, and therefore native speakers' perceptions of subjectivity, align with subjectivity theory. However, an additional comparison of the effects of different subjectivity features in author text and the text of cited sources reveals that the distinction between author and source subjectivity might not be as salient for naïve speakers as it is in the theory.

## 1 Introduction

Subjectivity analysis is the task of identifying opinions, attitudes, evaluations and beliefs in texts. State-of-the-art approaches to detecting subjectivity at the sentence level (e.g., Huo and Iwaihara, 2020; Kasnesis et al., 2021; Pachov et al., 2023; Schlicht et al., 2023; Zhao et al., 2015) are based on machine learning classifiers and often approach the problem of subjectivity detection as a binary task. This is largely due to the fact that subjectivity detection is often used as a preparatory step for fact-checking pipelines or sentiment analysis. However, there are a few problems with such an approach. Firstly, theoretical accounts of subjectivity in linguistics suggest that it is a gradual rather than a binary concept, meaning that some utterances can be more subjective than others (Langacker, 1990; Traugott, 1995). Secondly, because this common approach treats subjectivity as a preparatory task for fact-checking or sentiment analysis, the problem of explainabilty of state-of-the-art subjectivity detection models seems to have been outside the focus of attention of scholars working on subjectivity detection tools. In an attempt to tackle the continuous nature of subjectivity, Savinova and Moscoso Del Prado (2023) created a transformer-based subjectivity regressor trained on native English speakers' judgements. The aim of the present contribution is to address the issue of explainability of this subjectivity regressor applying a combination of two approaches: 1) a top-down approach using manual selection of theoretically defined subjectivity features and 2) a bottom-up approach using an automatic local interpretable model-agnostic explanation method (LIME). By collecting evidence from these two approaches, we can gain insights into the features that our transformer-based regressor utilizes for subjectivity analysis, as well as understand how they align with subjectivity theory. Although early rule-based subjectivity detection algorithms (Riloff and Wiebe, 2003; Riloff et al., 2003; Wiebe and Riloff, 2005) relied on some of the theory-based features to distinguish between subjective and objective texts, it is unclear how important these features are for the state-of-the-art machine learning-based models of subjectivity analysis.

Another contribution of the present study lies in the comparison of subjectivity theory with native speakers' perceptions of subjectivity. State-of-the-art subjectivity detection models for English are mostly trained on the gold standard subjectivity



*Proceedings of the 14th Workshop on Computational Approaches to Subjectivity, Sentiment, & Social Media Analysis*, pages 305–315
August 15, 2024 

dataset (Pang and Lee, 2004) that was automatically annotated using the source of a text as a proxy for its subjectivity: the dataset contains 5,000 sentences taken from movie review snippets, automatically labeled as subjective, and 5,000 sentences taken from movie plot summaries, automatically labeled as objective. Although this division undoubtedly correlates with the subjectivity distinction, this automatic annotation is not very accurate and does not reflect native speakers' intuitions about subjectivity (Savinova and Moscoso Del Prado, 2023). Similarly, datasets with manual annotations of subjectivity following specific theoretical guidelines (e.g., Antici et al., 2023), and therefore subjectivity detection models trained on such datasets (Pachov et al., 2023; Schlicht et al., 2023), may not coincide with the way subjectivity is perceived by naïve language users. In the present paper, we are looking at the explainability of a subjectivity regressor that was trained on the subjectivity judgements by naïve native English speakers who did not follow any explicit annotation guidelines. Therefore, we can assume that our regressor reflects an average native speaker's understanding of subjectivity. By directly testing the predictive value of theoretically defined subjectivity features for the regressor's subjectivity scores and comparing LIME's explanations with these features, we can understand how subjectivity theory corresponds to native speakers' perceptions of subjectivity.

## 2 Methodology

### 2.1 Dataset and model

The dataset and the model that we work with are described in detail in Savinova and Moscoso Del Prado (2023). The dataset contains sentences from news posts on Facebook and news articles on the websites of four major British news outlets (BBC, Sky News, Daily Mail, Metro) on the topics of "crime" and "Covid-19". There are 4,778 sentences (72,236 words) taken from Facebook news posts and 2,973 sentences (65,058 words) taken from news articles on the websites.

For a subset of 398 sentences from this dataset, subjectivity annotations of 19 native English speakers were collected in such a way that every speaker received 100 randomly assigned sentences for annotation and every sentence was annotated by 4 or 5 speakers. The annotators had to rate subjectivity of the sentences on a 7-point scale. There were no explicit annotation guidelines except for brief definitions of *subjective* as meaning "expressing personal opinions, emotions, feelings and tastes, hopes and wishes, self-made conclusions (e.g., *This is awful*)", and *objective* meaning "reporting facts, events, conclusions supported by data (e.g., *The President had a meeting with the Prime minister*)". We ensured that the annotators rated subjectivity by including comprehension checks in the form of clearly objective (*London is the capital of the UK*) and clearly subjective (*This is very beautiful*) sentences that had to receive a score of 1 and 7, respectively, in order for a participant's data to be included. The mean correlation between each rater and the other raters was .64. After transforming the mean subjectivity scores into a [0-1] scale, we split this labeled subset into training, validation and test sets (298/50/50) and trained a RoBERTa-base model (Liu et al., 2019) fine-tuned on our unlabeled sentences to produce subjectivity scores per sentence. Model performance on the test set showed that it correlated highly with the average speaker judgements (.79). The model was then applied to annotate the whole dataset for subjectivity. The annotated dataset is available in open access.

### 2.2 Approach to Explainability

In order to explain the predictions of our model on the dataset and to elucidate how they relate to subjectivity theory, we employ two methods: a top-down approach and a bottom-up approach. With the top-down approach, we manually selected the most common subjectivity features identified in linguistic theories on subjectivity (in a social media context) and annotated our dataset for the presence of these features. We then built a linear regression with the presence of each feature as a predictor, controlling for sentence length, to check whether theoretically defined subjectivity features indeed correlate with higher subjectivity scores and to estimate the relative importance of each feature in contributing to the subjectivity score. This approach can provide insights on the alignment between the model scores, and therefore average speaker judgements about subjectivity, and theoretically defined subjectivity features.

In contrast to the top-down approach that starts with the theory, the bottom-up approach starts with the data and allows us to to look at the features that are important for the model's scores for each sentence. To perform such a bottom-up inspection, we chose to look at the local explainability of our model on each sentence in our dataset using LIME (Local Interpretable Model-agnostic Explanations) method (Ribeiro et al., 2016). This method is model-agnostic and provides a good approximation for interpretation of any model's local behaviour. For textual data, LIME treats words as features and creates perturbations of the text entry by excluding different words. A local explainable model is then trained on the dataset consisting of these perturbations and their corresponding scores given by the original black box model. This results in every word/feature receiving a weight score indicating its contribution to the original model's prediction. For our bottom-up approach, we applied LIME to every sentence in our dataset and extracted the words/features and their mean weights and frequency in order to look at the top subjective and objective features. Comparing these top features to theoretically defined features can shed light on the local importance of different subjective features in the explainability of our regressor and in native speakers' local reasoning.

### 2.3 Subjectivity features

In order to interpret the results of the model using a top-down approach, we selected a number of theoretically defined subjectivity features from the literature. An overview of the features with examples and corroborating literature is provided in the Appendix (Table A1). We annotated each sentence in our dataset for the presence of these features. For every feature, the number of elements corresponding to this feature in every sentence was extracted. As a preparatory step, the sentences were preprocessed (i.e., tokenized, lemmatized, POS-tagged) using the *en_core_web_sm* pipeline for English from the Spacy library (Honnibal et al., 2020). The subjective elements were identified by their lemmas.

**Emoji** were identified by adding *spacymoji* pipeline to the preprocessing step. **First and second person pronouns** consisted of a list of all possible pronoun forms. **Questions** and **exclamations** were identified by a question and an exclamation mark, respectively. The list of **modal adverbials and adjectives** (e.g., *possible*, *likely*, *indeed*) was taken from Biber and Finegan (1988) and Biber (2004). We selected only those elements that have a modal meaning (factive, non-factive, evidential, certainty, doubt and likelihood adverbials). **Modal verbs** (e.g., *can*, *could*, *should*) were taken from Biber (2004). **Evaluative adjectives and adverbs** (e.g., *adorable*, *terrified*, *incredibly*) were taken from several sources: 1) attitudinal stance adverbials and adjectives from Biber and Finegan (1988) and Biber (2004), 2) adjectives from the Spacy sentiment lexicon, which uses the TextBlob library (De Smedt and Daelemans, 2012), with a subjectivity score above .7, 3) adjectives from MPQA subjectivity lexicon (Wiebe et al. 2005) tagged as "strong subjectivity", which means that they should be subjective in most contexts (Wilson et al., 2005). Since subjectivity lexicons are compiled using corpus data, usually from a specific genre or text type, they may miss out on subjective adjectives when applied in a different context. Therefore, after compiling this list of items, we extracted all adjectives from our dataset that were not part of the list and manually added 72 adjectives we considered subjective, such as, for instance, *worrying*, *hellish*, and *vile*. **Focus particles** (e.g., *only*, *just*, *too*) were taken from König (1991). **Intensifiers** (e.g., *very*, *really*, *totally*) were taken from Zhiber and Korotina (2019). **Epistemic phrases** of the form 'I + cognitive verb' (e.g., *I think*, *I believe*) were taken from Wierzbicka (2006). They were identified by searching for "I" followed by one of the cognitive verbs in present tense with optional negation in between.

## 3 Explaining the model using manual feature selection

### 3.1 Procedure

To estimate whether our model's predictions, and therefore native speakers' intuitions, correspond to the theoretically defined features outlined above, we built a linear regression model in R (R Core Team, 2022) predicting the subjectivity score with subjectivity features as categorical factors (presence/absence of the feature). All factors were coded using treatment contrasts so that the effect of every feature is estimated when the other features are absent. To control for sentence length, we also included log-transformed word count as a predictor in the regression. Logarithmic transformation allowed us to account for the non-linear relationship between the word count and the subjectivity score. The results of the regression model can be found in Table 1 with estimates ranked from largest to smallest.

### 3.2 Results

The results show that all predictors were significant, suggesting that the theoretically defined subjectiv-

| Predictor | Estimate | Estimated means[1] | Std. error | $t$ | $p$ |
|---|---|---|---|---|---|
| Emoji | 0.29 | 0.40-0.69 | 0.01 | 23.28 | <.001 |
| First and second person pronouns | 0.18 | 0.38-0.57 | 0.01 | 31.36 | <.001 |
| Exclamations | 0.16 | 0.40-0.57 | 0.02 | 8.20 | <.001 |
| Questions | 0.14 | 0.40-0.54 | 0.01 | 12.29 | <.001 |
| Intensifiers | 0.14 | 0.40-0.54 | 0.01 | 12.03 | <.001 |
| Evaluative adjectives and adverbs | 0.12 | 0.38-0.50 | 0.005 | 25.83 | <.001 |
| Epistemic phrases | 0.11 | 0.40-0.51 | 0.02 | 5.28 | <.001 |
| Modal verbs | 0.10 | 0.39-0.49 | 0.01 | 18.98 | <.001 |
| Modal adverbials and adjectives | 0.05 | 0.40-0.45 | 0.01 | 6.43 | <.001 |
| Focus particles | 0.05 | 0.40-0.45 | 0.01 | 8.37 | <.001 |
| Word count | -0.09 | NA | 0.003 | -30.32 | <.001 |

[1] Estimated means of the model when the predictor is absent versus present, obtained using the *effects* package (Fox and Weisberg, 2018).

Table 1: Model output of features as subjectivity predictors, ordered by the estimates.

ity features correspond to the speakers' intuitions that our model was trained on. Comparison of the estimates suggests that the presence of emoji leads to the most substantial change in subjectivity score. Together with first and second person pronouns, exclamations, questions, intensifiers and epistemic phrases, these features bring the score over .5, assuming this threshold roughly indicates the transition from objective to subjective. The other features, in particular modal adverbials and focus particles, contribute to a minimal shift in subjectivity scores. Log-transformed word count turned out to be a significant predictor of subjectivity scores as well: Figure 1 shows that higher word count leads to lower subjectivity scores, which is most noticeable in the 1-15 word count range. This is understandable given social media data, since many one- and two-word posts on social media contain an evaluative adjective and/or an emoji (e.g., *Awful* 😩 ). It should be noted that the linear regression model explains 40% of the variance (adjusted $R^2$=.40), suggesting that the selected subjectivity features cannot fully explain the subjectivity regressor. This is not surprising: a sentence can be subjective even without explicit subjective elements (e.g., *The lights are on, so he is home*), which is why using rule-based subjectivity feature extraction will always result in an underestimation of the scores compared to the machine learning-based subjectivity detection. However, it could also be the case that the theory on subjectivity misses out on features that are deemed important to naïve speakers. Any such features could be identified by a bottom-up, theory-agnostic explainability approach.

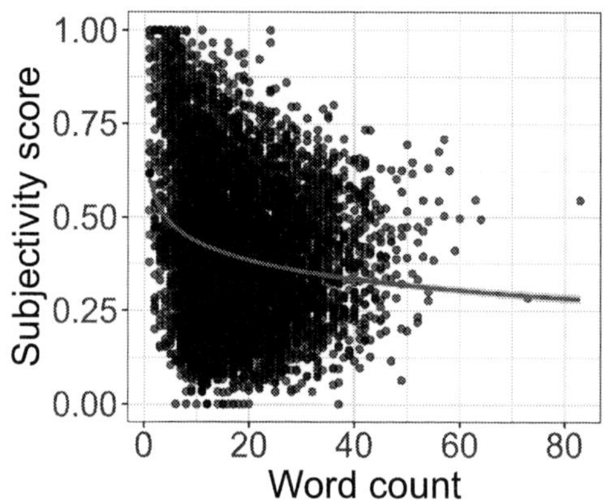


Figure 1: Effect of word count on subjectivity score.

## 4 Explaining the model using LIME

### 4.1 Procedure

As stated above, LIME can offer model-agnostic local approximations of model explanations based on textual features, i.e. words (Ribeiro et al., 2016). Although LIME has been used to explain sentiment analysis models (e.g., Chowdhury et al., 2021; Jain et al., 2023), its applicability to subjectivity analysis models appears to have been largely overlooked. It is important to note that LIME cannot provide an explanation of the internal working of the black box model, which goes beyond human-understandable features like words. However, since the black box, especially in the case of transformer models, cannot be understood as such, LIME provides a useful tool for interpreting what the black box model does locally on a level comprehensible to humans.

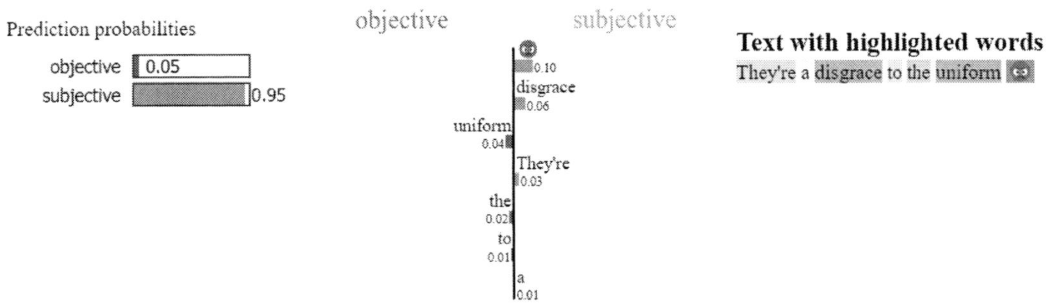


Figure 2: Example of LIME output for a sentence.

To explain our subjectivity regressor locally, we applied LIME to every sentence in our dataset and collected the weights associated with every feature in every sentence. We then computed the frequency of every feature in our dataset (case-insensitive), its mean weight in the dataset and the minimum and maximum weights. We modified the original LIME code, which uses a simple regular expression to tokenize the input and identify only words as potential textual features. Instead, we employed the TweetTokenizer from NLTK package (Bird et al., 2009), enabling the recognition of punctuation marks and emoji as potential features as well. Figure 2 provides an example of LIME output for one of the sentences from our dataset with weights per feature. As the output indicates, features that contribute to objectivity are associated with negative scores, while features that contribute to subjectivity are associated with positive scores.

### 4.2 Results

The complete list of 12,535 unique features resulting from application of LIME to our dataset is available in open access. To interpret the LIME output for our dataset, we decided to look at the top 200 subjective and objective features with the highest and lowest weights, respectively. For illustration, Table 2 shows the top 10 most subjective and objective features identified by LIME. Among the top objective features, the most prominent categories were numbers (*6400*), dates and times (*13:00*), proper nouns (*Churchill*) and concrete nouns (*candles*, *airbag*), links (*https://trib.al/7nvqdio*), verbs (*matches*, *redeployed*) and non-evaluative adjectives (*month-long*, *water-related*). In contrast, the top subjective features were dominated by emoji, evaluative adjectives (*unforgivable*, *reckless*, *stunning*) and evaluative nouns (*hypocrite*, *downfall*, *gamechanger*). It is notable that all types of emoji, not only the ones representing faces/emotions, were found to be very subjective according to LIME results.

Inspection of both subjective and objective features revealed a strong frequency bias: almost all of the top 200 features were encountered in our dataset only once. It is not surprising that these infrequent words received the most extreme scores, since their weights were based only on one example sentence. To compare the findings with the results of the top-down approach that includes theory-based subjectivity features, we eliminated the frequency bias by excluding features with a frequency of less than five. The remaining data consisted of 3,285 features, which is approximately a quarter of the original list. Table 3 shows top 10 subjective and objective features in this subset of the data. After selecting only those LIME features that are encountered at least 5 times in the dataset, we annotated them for the presence of the theoretical subjectivity features described in Section 2.3. Epistemic phrases were not used for annotation because they require multiword expressions. Subsequently, we checked which theoretical features appeared in the top 200 subjective and objective LIME features.

In line with our expectations, there were no theoretically defined subjectivity features among the top 200 objective LIME features. On the contrary, all theoretical subjectivity features were present among the top 200 subjective LIME features. The latter included the question and exclamation marks, 58 evaluative adjectives, 11 emoji, 10 modal verbs, 6 modal adverbials, 6 intensifiers, one personal pronoun (*I*) and one focus particle (*too*). The theoretically defined features thus accounted for around 48% of the top 200 subjective LIME features. The other subjective features identified by LIME mostly included emotionally laden nouns (*horror*, *shock*, *hope*) and verbs (*missed*, *enjoy*, *worry*). While

| Feature | Mean weight | Frequency | Feature | Mean weight | Frequency |
|---|---|---|---|---|---|
| -202012/01 | -0.32 | 1 | 🔽 | 0.30 | 2 |
| four-year-old | -0.28 | 1 | 🐧 | 0.30 | 1 |
| accounted | -0.28 | 1 | 🏊 | 0.30 | 1 |
| re-arrested | -0.27 | 1 | 😖 | 0.29 | 1 |
| Churchill | -0.27 | 1 | 😦 | 0.28 | 1 |
| murder-suicide | -0.27 | 1 | heartlessly | 0.27 | 1 |
| https://trib.al/7nvqdio | -0.26 | 1 | 😪 | 0.26 | 1 |
| mugshots | -0.25 | 1 | [illegible] | 0.24 | 2 |
| plea | -0.24 | 1 | 😧 | 0.24 | 1 |
| 120ft | -0.24 | 1 | 🙏 | 0.23 | 1 |

Table 2: Top 10 objective (left) and subjective (right) LIME features in the dataset.

| Feature | Mean weight | Frequency | Feature | Mean weight | Frequency |
|---|---|---|---|---|---|
| detect | -0.16 | 5 | 💔 | 0.19 | 20 |
| jailed | -0.16 | 104 | 🙌 | 0.19 | 10 |
| arrests | -0.15 | 12 | 💉 | 0.18 | 5 |
| fined | -0.14 | 8 | 🙏 | 0.16 | 7 |
| homicide | -0.14 | 5 | 😱 | 0.13 | 5 |
| two-year-old | -0.14 | 5 | terrifying | 0.11 | 6 |
| arrested | -0.13 | 121 | awful | 0.11 | 8 |
| 25,000 | -0.13 | 5 | shocking | 0.11 | 9 |
| eight-year-old | -0.13 | 5 | 👏 | 0.09 | 12 |
| anti-vaxxer | -0.12 | 11 | wonderful | 0.09 | 8 |

Table 3: Top 10 objective (left) and subjective (right) LIME features with frequency above 5 in the dataset.

these features were not included in our top-down analysis, they are in line with the general definition of subjectivity provided by the theory: a speaker conveying their judgement, opinion, or emotion. Interestingly, the top 200 subjective LIME features also included multiple negative words, such as *wasn't, didn't, none, no*. Some theoretical literature (e.g., Dancygier, 2012) suggests that negation can be considered a subjective viewpoint device because it evokes an alternative set-up and expresses the speaker's negative stance towards this set-up (for instance, *This is not funny* could be interpreted as expressing the speaker's negative attitude to the alternative *This is funny*). More work is needed to investigate the role of negative words in signalling subjectivity.

It is noteworthy that while for the LIME results, evaluative adjectives were clearly dominating the top subjective features list, in the manual approach, they seem to be of a lesser importance and do not bring the score over .50. We believe that this could have several reasons. Firstly, our list of evaluative adjectives in the top-down approach consisted of a large number of adjectives (1611), not all of which are *always* subjective. In contrast, the evaluative adjectives appearing in the top subjective LIME features seem to be those that are very subjective independent of the context. In other words, it appears that our top-down approach may lack accuracy with respect to evaluative adjectives. Secondly, the relatively low importance of evaluative adjectives in the top-down approach could be related to the fact that they often co-occur with stronger subjectivity indicators, such as, for instance, emoji or exclamation marks.

Interestingly, the top 200 subjective LIME features also contained three versions of quotation marks (", ', '), suggesting that the quotations of third party sources in news texts were treated as subjective. This goes against the strict approach to subjectivity where subjectivity of a third person cited source should not count, since it is being merely reported by the author (Sanders, 1994). Moreover, quoting sources, however subjective their comments are, has a place within the tradition of objective news reporting. In other words, while *This is terrible* is subjective, *He said: "This is terrible"* should be (more) objective. In an attempt to take a closer look at whether our model, and consequently native speakers, distinguish between author and source subjectivity, we conducted additional analyses that are reported in the next section.

## 5 Author vs. source subjectivity

In texts that cite other sources, such as news, two types of subjectivity can be distinguished: author subjectivity and the subjectivity of the reported sources (Banfield, 1982; Pit, 2003; Sanders, 1994). This distinction is unclear in the case of indirect reported speech, when it is unknown who exactly is responsible for the wording of the cited fragment (e.g., *Shepherd's mother said that medical staff treated her daughter well and did everything in their power to save her*). In contrast, in the case of direct speech it is always clear that the quoted part corresponds to the voice of the source; the sentence could therefore be considered objective since it is merely (objectively) reporting the subjectivity of the source. When collecting annotations for the subjectivity regressor, we did not explicitly instruct the raters about this distinction, since we do not know whether naïve speakers share the intuition that fragments with citations are objective.

In order to test whether this distinction is indeed important to naïve language users, we identified author and source fragments in every sentence in our dataset using quotation marks. We then counted the presence of subjectivity features in author and source text separately using the top-down approach with theoretically defined features. The dataset was then extended in such a way that the sentences containing both author and source subjectivity were split into two separate entries, and Origin of subjectivity (author vs. source) was added as a separate variable. We built another linear regression model specifying interactions of Origin with all subjectivity features except for emoji, which was entered as a main effect, since there was only one case of emoji used in the source text.

The results revealed four significant interactions with Origin: personal pronouns ($t$=-4.48, $p$<.001), questions ($t$=-2.40, $p$=.02), intensifiers ($t$=-3.11, $p$=.002) and epistemic phrases ($t$=-2.82, $p$=.005). The interaction plots (Figure 3) show that the effect of encountering these features in the author text leads to a bigger change in subjectivity score as compared to the source text. On the one hand, such an outcome would be predicted if speakers distinguish between author and source subjectivity: source subjectivity is reported and therefore should influence speakers' judgements less than author subjectivity. On the other hand, there were no significant interactions for the other subjectivity features. In addition, there was a main effect of Origin ($t$=22.51, $p$<.001), indicating that the source text was overall more subjective than the author text, which supports our findings from LIME where quotation marks appeared in the top subjectivity features. This suggests that subjective quotations of third person sources are still considered subjective by the model and native speakers. However, by not commenting on the author versus source distinction when collecting annotations, we may have implicitly prompted the participants to rate all kinds of subjectivity, regardless of whether it stemmed from the author or the source. Whether author versus source subjectivity is indeed a relevant distinction for naïve language users and whether the relevance differs between subjectivity features seems like a fruitful direction for future research.

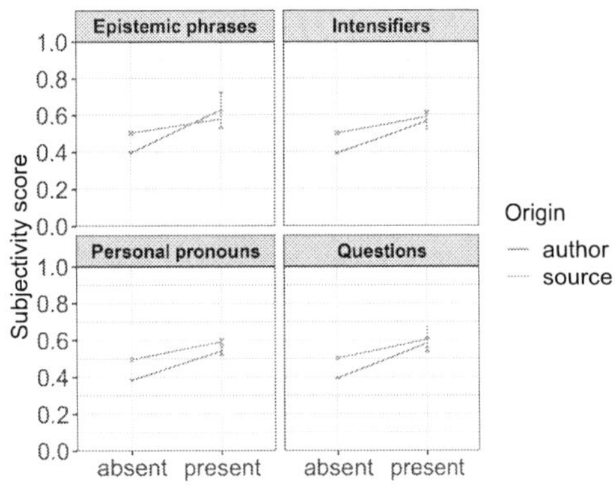


Figure 3: Interaction plots for model estimated marginal means, with confidence intervals.

It should be noted that in this more complex model, modal adverbials ($t$=.60, $p$=.55) and focus particles ($t$=1.39, $p$=.16) showed no significant effect on subjectivity scores. Upon closer inspection of our data, we found that certain evidential modal adverbials, such as *allegedly*, *reportedly*, *apparently*, were on average associated with rather low subjectivity scores (.25, .31, .33, respectively). These adverbials seem to be used in news discourse, and especially in crime news, to indicate the common agreement/existence of evidence about what is being introduced and, as such, are rather employed to underline objectivity and impartiality of the author. Among the focus particles, *merely* and *at least* were associated with rather low subjectivity scores (.24 and .26). A closer inspection revealed that these were used in the context of news in their rather factual non-focus meanings (e.g., *people who merely tested negative*; *at least 20 killed*). These qualitative observations underline that whether a specific feature is a subjectivity indicator can be dependent on the context.

## 6 Density of subjectivity features

A single utterance may contain multiple subjective elements (e.g., *Delivering smiles during a tough time!* contains both an evaluative adjective and an exclamation mark). The output of LIME and the linguistic theory on subjectivity suggest that, at least in some cases, more subjective features in the sentence should lead to increased subjectivity (for example, *This is really really bad* seems more subjective than *This is bad*). At the same time, it is also intuitively clear that adding an exclamation mark to the sentence that already has an emoji at the end will probably not make it much more subjective than it already is. This division of labour between subjectivity features in different contexts is clearly visible in the different weights that the LIME features get depending on the sentence that is being analyzed. To test the relationship between the number of subjective elements in a sentence and its subjectivity score, we built a generalized additive model (GAM) with smooth terms for the count of all subjective elements in the sentence (including multiple instances of one feature) and for word count as a control. The results of the model, which explained 39.5% of deviance, showed significance of both the smooth term for the word count ($p$<.001) and the smooth term for the number of subjective elements in a sentence ($p$<.001). The effect of the latter is visualized in Figure 4. The visualization shows a logarithmic curve, which illustrates that increasing the number of subjective features from 0 to 4 has a strong positive effect on the subjectivity score, while for any subsequent increase the effect levels off.

## 7 Conclusion

In this paper, we approached the problem of explainability of a transformer-based subjectivity regressor trained on native English speakers' judgements using two methods: a top-down manual selection of theoretically defined subjectivity features and a bottom-up extraction of top subjective and objective features using LIME explanation method. The explainability was tested on a news dataset containing sentences from social media news posts and articles on the websites of the corresponding news outlets. The results of the two methods provided a similar picture: most of the theory-based subjectivity features turned out to be important for our regressor's predictions. According to both methods, emoji, exclamations, questions, intensifiers and first person pronouns turned out to be prominent predictors of subjectivity scores. The results of the bottom-up approach also revealed the significance of evaluative adjectives, especially the ones that are highly subjective across contexts, as a top subjective feature. We also found that the more subjective elements are present in a sentence, the more subjective it becomes. Overall, our findings suggest that the features used by the subjectivity regressor in its judgements align with the subjectivity theory.

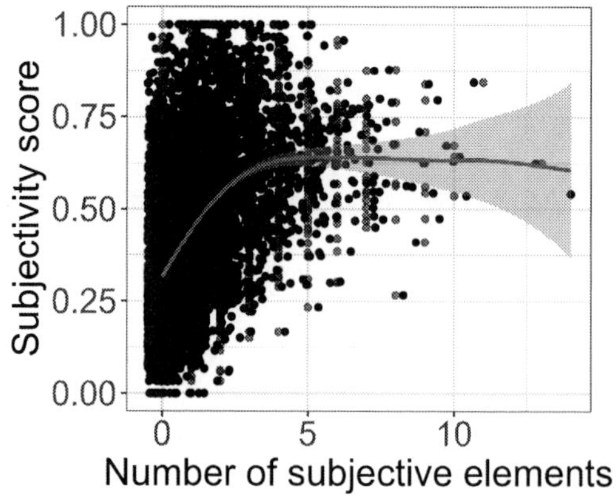

Figure 4: Results of GAM for the density of subjective elements.

Since the regressor was trained on native English speakers' intuitions and, therefore, represents an average speaker's perception of subjectivity, our findings mentioned above seem to indicate that the naïve speakers' perceptions correspond to the theoretical accounts of subjectivity in linguistics. At the same time, our regressor does not seem to distinguish between author and source subjectivity, contrary to what theory predicts. Future work could investigate what role this distinction plays in naïve speakers' perceptions of subjectivity.

## Limitations

The list of subjectivity features that we used in this work was not exhaustive. For instance, we did not include affective nouns and verbs (e.g, *enjoy*, *horror*, *love*) as subjective features in our top-down approach, but they did show up in the LIME output, which suggests that they belong to some of the most influential features for the subjectivity regressor and for native speakers' judgements. We also employed a rather coarse measure in our analysis of the density of subjectivity features. The effect of number of subjective elements might vary depending on the particular type of subjectivity feature or the specific combination of such features. In addition, subjectivity cannot be reduced to explicit subjective elements. In that sense, both the manual selection of features and the LIME method are limited in their explanation capacity since they can only take into account explicit subjective markers.

Our limitation in the approach to author vs. source subjectivity lies in the fact that we provided minimal instructions for annotators for the sake of obtaining their natural intuitions about subjectivity. This could have prompted participants to rate any kind of subjectivity. In addition, splitting the texts by sentence resulted in some quotations being fragmented and unrecognizable as cited text without context. Finally, our approach to annotation of Origin was not conceptually ideal, as it resulted in splitting some sentences into author and source parts and assigning the same score to them. Future work is needed to address the issue of author vs. source subjectivity in speakers' intuitions more comprehensively, potentially within context.

## Acknowledgements

We would like to thank Jetske Adams and Michael Voronov for their help with the LIME code. We would also like to thank Wilbert Spooren for his assistance in selecting theory-based subjectivity features and his help with editing the section on model explanation using manual feature selection.

## References

Francesco Antici, Andrea Galassi, Federico Ruggeri, Katerina Korre, Arianna Muti, Alessandra Bardi, Alice Fedotova, and Alberto Barrón-Cedeño. 2023. A corpus for sentence-level subjectivity detection on English news articles. *arXiv:2305.18034*.

Angeliki Athanasiadou. 2006. *Subjectification: Various paths to subjectivity*. Mouton de Gruyter.

Ann Banfield. 1982. *Unspeakable sentences: Narration and representation in the language of fiction*. Routledge.

Douglas Biber. 2004. Historical patterns for the grammatical marking of stance: A cross-register comparison. *Journal of historical pragmatics*, 5(1):107–136.

Douglas Biber and Edward Finegan. 1988. Adverbial stance types in English. *Discourse processes*, 11(1):1–34.

Douglas Biber and Edward Finegan. 1989. Drift and the evolution of English style: A history of three genres. *Language*, 65(3):487–517.

Douglas Biber and Edward Finegan. 2001. Diachronic relations among speech-based and written registers in English. In S. Conrad and D. Biber, editors, *Variation in English*, pages 66–83. Routledge.

Steven Bird, Edward Loper, and Ewan Klein. 2009. *Natural Language Processing with Python: Analyzing Text with the Natural Language Toolkit*. O'Reilly Media Inc., Sebastopol, CA.

Kounteyo Roy Chowdhury, Arpan Sil, and Sharvari Rahul Shukla. 2021. Explaining a black-box sentiment analysis model with local interpretable model diagnostics explanation (LIME). In *Advances in Computing and Data Sciences: 5th International Conference, ICACDS 2021*, pages 90–101. Springer.

Barbara Dancygier. 2012. Negation, stance verbs, and intersubjectivity. In B. Dancygier and E. Sweetser, editors, *Viewpoint in language: A multimodal perspective*, pages 69–93. Cambridge University Press.

Tom De Smedt and Walter Daelemans. 2012. Pattern for python. *Journal of Machine Learning Research*, 13(66):2063–2067.

John Fox and Sanford Weisberg. 2018. *An R companion to applied regression*. Sage.

Mario Haim, Michael Karlsson, Raul Ferrer-Conill, Aske Kammer, Dag Elgesem, and Helle Sjøvaag. 2021. You should read this study! It investigates scandinavian social media logics. *Digital Journalism*, 9(4):406–426.

Matthew Honnibal, Sofie Montani, Ines Van Landeghem, and Boyd Adriane. 2020. Spacy: Industrial-strength natural language processing in python.

Marianne Hundt and Christian Mair. 1999. "Agile" and "uptight" genres: The corpus-based approach to language change in progress. *International Journal of Corpus Linguistics*, 4(2):221–242.

Hairong Huo and Mizuho Iwaihara. 2020. Utilizing BERT pretrained models with various fine-tune methods for subjectivity detection. In *4th International Joint Conference, APWeb-WAIM 2020, Tianjin, China, September 18-20, 2020, Proceedings, Part II*, pages 270–284. Springer.

Rachna Jain, Ashish Kumar, Anand Nayyar, Kritika Dewan, Rishika Garg, Shatakshi Raman, and Sahil Ganguly. 2023. Explaining sentiment analysis results on social media texts through visualization. *Multimedia Tools and Applications*, 82(15):22613–22629.

Panagiotis Kasnesis, Lazaros Toumanidis, and Charalampos Z. Patrikakis. 2021. Combating fake news with transformers: A comparative analysis of stance detection and subjectivity analysis. *Information*, 12(10):409.

Christopher Kennedy. 2013. Two sources of subjectivity: Qualitative assessment and dimensional uncertainty. *Inquiry*, 56(2-3):258–277.

Ekkehard König. 1991. *The meaning of focus particles: A comparative perspective*. Routledge.

Ronald W Langacker. 1990. *Subjectification*. Walter de Gruyter.

Geoffrey N. Leech. 2009. *Change in contemporary English: A grammatical study*. Cambridge University Press.

Yinhan Liu, Myle Ott, Naman Goyal, Jingfei Du, Mandar Joshi, Danqi Chen, Omer Levy, Mike Lewis, Luke Zettlemoyer, and Veselin Stoyanov. 2019. RoBERTa: A robustly optimized BERT pretraining approach. *arXiv:1907.11692*.

Petra K. Novak, Jasmina Smailović, Borut Sluban, and Igor Mozetič. 2015. Sentiment of emojis. *PloS one*, 10(12):e0144296.

Georgi Pachov, Dimitar Dimitrov, Ivan Koychev, and Preslav Nakov. 2023. Gpachov at checkthat! 2023: A diverse multi-approach ensemble for subjectivity detection in news articles. In *Working Notes of the Conference and Labs of the Evaluation Forum (CLEF 2023)*, pages 404–412.

Bo Pang and Lillian Lee. 2004. A sentimental education: Sentiment analysis using subjectivity summarization based on minimum cuts. In *Proceedings of the 42nd Annual Meeting of the Association for Computational Linguistics (ACL-04)*, pages 271–278, Barcelona, Spain.

Michael Pearce. 2005. Informalization in UK party election broadcasts 1966-97. *Language and Literature*, 14(1):65–90.

Mirna Pit. 2003. *How to express yourself with a causal connective: Subjectivity and causal connectives in Dutch, German and French*. Rodopi.

R Core Team. 2022. *R: A Language and Environment for Statistical Computing*. R Foundation for Statistical Computing, Vienna, Austria.

Marco Tulio Ribeiro, Sameer Singh, and Carlos Guestrin. 2016. "Why should I trust you?": Explaining the predictions of any classifier. In *Proceedings of the 22nd ACM SIGKDD International Conference on Knowledge Discovery and Data Mining*, pages 1135–1144.

Ellen Riloff and Janyce Wiebe. 2003. Learning extraction patterns for subjective expressions. In *Proceedings of the 2003 conference on Empirical methods in natural language processing*, pages 105–112.

Ellen Riloff, Janyce Wiebe, and Theresa Wilson. 2003. Learning subjective nouns using extraction pattern bootstrapping. In *Proceedings of the seventh conference on Natural language learning at HLT-NAACL 2003*, pages 25–32.

José Sanders. 1994. *Perspective in narrative discourse*. Doctoral dissertation. Tilburg University, Tilburg.

Elena Savinova and Fermin Moscoso Del Prado. 2023. Analyzing subjectivity using a transformer-based regressor trained on naïve speakers' judgements. In *Proceedings of the 13th Workshop on Computational Approaches to Subjectivity, Sentiment, & Social Media Analysis*, pages 305–314, Toronto, Canada. Association for Computational Linguistics.

Ipek Baris Schlicht, Lynn Khellaf, and Defne Altiok. 2023. Dwreco at checkthat! 2023: Enhancing subjectivity detection through style-based data sampling. In *Working Notes of the Conference and Labs of the Evaluation Forum (CLEF 2023)*, pages 306–317.

Elizabeth Closs Traugott. 1995. Subjectification in grammaticalization. In D. Stein and S. Wright, editors, *Subjectivity and subjectivisation: Linguistic perspectives*, volume 1, pages 31–54. Cambridge University Press.

Kirsten Vis, José Sanders, and Wilbert Spooren. 2012. Diachronic changes in subjectivity and stance – a corpus linguistic study of Dutch news texts. *Discourse, Context & Media*, 1(2-3):95–102.

Kasper Welbers and Michaël Opgenhaffen. 2019. Presenting news on social media: Media logic in the communication style of newspapers on facebook. *Digital journalism*, 7(1):45–62.

Ingrid Westin and Christer Geisler. 2002. A multidimensional study of diachronic variation in British newspaper editorials. *ICAME Journal*, 26:133–152.

Janyce Wiebe. 1994. Tracking point of view in narrative. *Computational Linguistics*, 20(2):233–287.

Janyce Wiebe and Ellen Riloff. 2005. Creating subjective and objective sentence classifiers from unannotated texts. In *In Proceedings of the 6th International Conference on Computational Linguistics and Intelligent Text Processing (CICLing-05)*, pages 486–497. Springer.

Janyce Wiebe, Theresa Wilson, and Claire Cardie. 2005. Annotating expressions of opinions and emotions in language. *Language resources and evaluation*, 39(2-3):165–210.

Anna Wierzbicka. 2006. *English: Meaning and culture*. Oxford University Press.

Theresa Wilson, Janyce Wiebe, and Paul Hoffmann. 2005. Recognizing contextual polarity in phrase-level sentiment analysis. In *Proceedings of Human Language Technology Conference and Conference on Empirical Methods in Natural Language Processing*, pages 347–354, Vancouver, British Columbia, Canada. Association for Computational Linguistics.

Han Zhao, Zhengdong Lu, and Pascal Poupart. 2015. Self-adaptive hierarchical sentence model. In *Proceedings of the Twenty-Fourth International Joint Conference on Artificial Intelligence (IJCAI 2015)*, pages 4069–4076. AAAI Press.

Evgeniya Zhiber and Larisa Korotina. 2019. Intensifying adverbs in the English language. *Training, Language and Culture*, 3(3):70–88.


# A Appendix

| **Subjectivity feature** | **Supporting literature**[1] | **Examples** |
|---|---|---|
| Emoji | N, W&O | *Horrific news* 😱 |
| First and second person pronouns | B&F, H&M, P, V, W&G | *I, me, my, you, our, yourself* |
| Questions | B&F, V, W, W&G | *Will I be protected if I have a booster?* |
| Exclamations | H, L, V, W | *Watch live!* |
| Modal adverbials and adjectives | B, B&F, V, W | *sure, possibly, in fact, apparently* |
| Modal verbs | B, B&F, V, W, W&G | *can, could, should, seem to* |
| Evaluative adjectives and adverbs | A, Ke, B&F, W2 | *honestly, amazing, horrible, immense* |
| Focus particles | K, V | *only, just, already, exactly* |
| Intensifiers | B&F, V, W, W&G, Z&K | *very, really, extremely, so* |
| Epistemic phrases | B, Wie | *I think, I believe, I would say, I guess* |

[1] A = Athanasiadou (2006), B = Biber (2004), B&F = Biber and Finegan (1988, 1989, 2001), H = Haim et al. (2021), Hundt and Mair (1999), K = König (1991), Ke = Kennedy (2013), L = Leech (2009), N = Novak et al. (2015), P = Pearce (2005), V = Vis et al. (2012), W = Wiebe (1994), W2 = Wiebe et al. (2005); Wie = Wierzbicka (2006), W&G = Westin and Geisler (2002), W&O = Welbers and Opgenhaffen (2019), Z&K = Zhiber and Korotina (2019)

Table A1: List of subjectivity features used in the top-down approach, with the corresponding theoretical literature and examples.

# Comparing Pre-trained Human Language Models: Is it Better with Human Context as Groups, Individual Traits, or Both?

**Nikita Soni**[1], **Niranjan Balasubramanian**[1], **H. Andrew Schwartz**[1], and **Dirk Hovy**[2]
[1]Stony Brook University, [2]Bocconi University
{nisoni, niranjan, has}@cs.stonybrook.edu, dirk.hovy@unibocconi.it

## Abstract

Pre-trained language models consider the context of neighboring words and documents but lack any author context of the human generating the text. However, language depends on the author's states, traits, social, situational, and environmental attributes, collectively referred to as human context (Soni et al., 2024). Human-centered natural language processing requires incorporating human context into language models. Currently, two methods exist: pre-training with 1) group-wise attributes (e.g., *over-45-year-olds*) or 2) individual traits. Group attributes are simple but coarse — not all 45-year-olds write the same way — while individual traits allow for more personalized representations, but require more complex modeling and data. It is unclear which approach benefits what tasks. We compare pre-training models with human context via 1) group attributes, 2) individual users, and 3) a combined approach on five user- and document-level tasks. Our results show that there is no best approach, but that human-centered language modeling holds avenues for different methods.

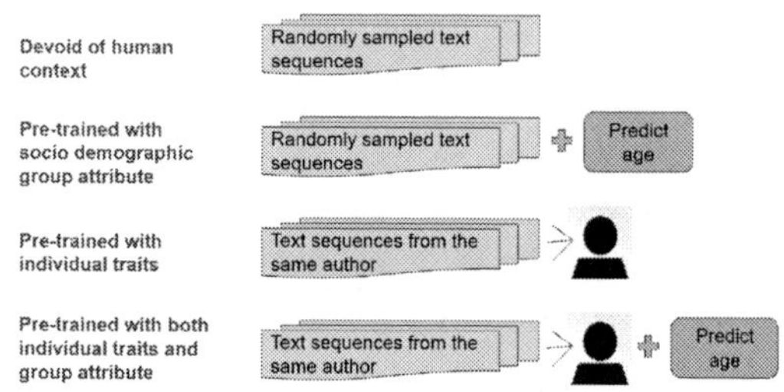


Figure 1: Pre-training a language model with no human context, with socio-demographic group attribute, with individual traits, and with both group and individual traits.

## 1 Introduction

Language is a fundamental form of human expression that varies between people. Pre-trained Language Models (PLMs) account for the textual context of neighboring words and documents but lack the human context of the author "generating" the language. However, language is highly dependent on the human context (Soni et al., 2024), i.e., an author's changing states (Fleeson, 2001; Mehl and Pennebaker, 2003), traits, social, situational, and environmental attributes. For example, a person's language differs when hiking (situation/environment) versus when feeling dejected (state) over a breakup (situation). It is essential to model the additional *human context* to better understand human language with PLMs (Soni et al., 2024). Two strands of human-centered Natural Language Processing (NLP) emerged to model the people behind the language. The first focuses on the *group context*, building on the sociolinguistic notion of specific socio-demographic attributes influencing the language of a particular group. These socio-demographic attributes include age, gender (Volkova et al., 2013; Hovy, 2015), location (Kulkarni et al., 2016; Garimella et al., 2017), personality (Schwartz et al., 2013; Lynn et al., 2017), and more. The second approach focuses on building personalized language models that target *individualistic contexts* (King and Cook, 2020; Delasalles et al., 2019), and latent attributes inferred from an individual's historical language (Matero et al., 2021; Soni et al., 2022) to better model the user.

While these two strands have advanced human-centered NLP, we still do not understand their relative strengths, complementarity, and impact on different tasks (Soni et al., 2024). People are not defined by their group memberships alone (Orlikowski et al., 2023), and individual traits might not be generalizable enough across groups. Further, cross-cultural psychology research (Hofstede and Bond, 1984) notes the importance of both individualism and collectivism and Soni et al. suggest a flexible interplay of these concepts when including human context in PLMs. We might expect models



*Proceedings of the 14th Workshop on Computational Approaches to Subjectivity, Sentiment, & Social Media Analysis*, pages 316–328
August 15, 2024 ©2024 Association for Computational Linguistics

informed by both group and individual features to perform better, but no data exists on this. In this work, we empirically evaluate these hypotheses and compare the effects of including different types of human context in PLMs (i.e., groups context (collectivism), individualistic aspects (individualism), and a combination of both) on specific tasks. We answer the following broader research questions:
***(RQ1)**: How can we incorporate group and individual human context into pre-training?*
***(RQ2)**: How does pre-training with different human contexts affect downstream performance for different tasks?*

Recent works trained PLMs with socio-demographic group context (Hung et al., 2023), and individual context (Soni et al., 2022). However, no empirical studies compare the impacts of different types of human contexts included in language modeling. We compare the downstream tasks' performance of models from these works with that of a new PLM trained with group and individual contexts. We test all systems on five downstream tasks from these works to ensure a variety of tasks and prediction properties at three levels: 1) user level, with historical language from authors (age estimation and personality assessment), 2) document-level, with historical language from some authors (stance detection), 3) document-level, without historical language from authors (topic detection and age category classification).

Note that because we focus on empirically comparing pre-training with different types of human context, we cannot compare to the larger language models like GPT4, which are not yet pre-trained/trainable with human context but are envisioned to become large human language models in the future (Soni et al., 2024). Recent studies have explored methodologies like user-adapters (Zhong et al., 2021) and user-centric prompting (Li et al., 2023) to include human context into the larger language models. In contrast, we focus specifically on comparing the impact of *pre-training* LMs with different human contexts, as Soni et al. (2024) argue that pre-training will allow for modeling a richer human context by explicitly handling the multi-level structure of documents connected to people, as opposed to specific and limited benefits of user-centric prompting and fine-tuning (Salemi et al., 2023; Choi et al., 2023).

PLMs pre-trained on individual *and* group features enhance performance on two user-level regression tasks that use multiple user documents: age estimation and personality assessment. In contrast, PLMs pre-trained on *individual* human context alone improve performance on document-level classification tasks like stance and topic detection. Our findings suggest user-level tasks focusing on individual people are best modeled as a mix of both group attributes and unique characteristics. However, document-level tasks that are more personal, like stance detection, are best addressed by modeling the individual context alone. Adding group attributes degrades performance.

By their very nature, models of this kind touch upon sensitive user information. For this reason, we adopt a responsible release strategy, making only the code for the comparisons publicly available, along with the exact splits of the TrustPilot and Stance datasets used[1]. We build on top of the publicly available code from Soni et al. (2022) and Hung et al. (2023). We acquired the models and data from the authors of the respective works in a secure manner. For more information about the models and data, see Sections 4 and 5. For a discussion of the ethical implications of the models and data, see the Ethical Considerations section.

**Contributions.** (1) We empirically compare three pre-training strategies for language models with human context: individual traits, group socio-demographic features, and a combination of both.
(2) We evaluate each pre-training strategy on five downstream tasks: two multi-document user-level regression (personality-openness evaluation and age estimation) and three single document-level classification tasks (stance detection, topic detection, and age category classification).
(3) We find that the two user-level regression tasks perform better with PLMs pre-trained with individual and group human contexts. Conversely, the three single document-level tasks perform better with PLMs pre-trained with individual context alone. Further, pre-training with group and individual contexts reduces performance for document-level tasks.

## 2 Related Work

**Socio-demographic and latent human factors.** Much work in human-centered NLP has focused on identifying and evaluating inclusion of human context in our models. Initial studies show benefits of grouping people by socio-demographic factors

[1] https://github.com/soni-n/HumanContextLanguageModels_Comparison

like age or gender (Volkova et al., 2013; Hovy, 2015) and geographical region (Bamman et al., 2014; Garimella et al., 2017) to capture the variation in language usage and meaning among different groups, and improving text classification tasks like sentiment analysis. Additionally, adapting to socio-demographic user factors (Lynn et al., 2017), social networks (Huang et al., 2014; Radfar et al., 2020), and social media attributes (Bamman and Smith, 2015) have been effective to enhance the performance in tasks like sarcasm detection, and toxic language detection. Some studies go beyond modeling explicit groups, to learn individual representations latently Jaech and Ostendorf (2018); Delasalles et al. (2019) or via historical language Matero et al. (2021).

**Pre-traing with human context.** With respect to pre-trained LMs, recent studies have used adapter-based methodology (Li et al., 2021; Zhong et al., 2021) to include individual human contexts for downstream tasks. More recently, large language models have used user-centric prompting (Li et al., 2023) to include human context and evaluate on personalized and social tasks, resulting in mediocre performance (Salemi et al., 2023; Choi et al., 2023). However, few studies have explored including human context within the pre-training regime of LMs. Hung et al. (2023) generalize the task-specific EMPATH-BERT (Guda et al., 2021) to create a PLM injected with demographic group information using a dynamic multi-task learning setup. Additionally, Soni et al. (2022) pre-train a LM with individual human context derived from user's historical language. Our study aims at comparing the impacts of pre-training LMs with individual, or group, or combined individual plus group human context.

## 3 Integrating Human Context in PLMs

For our comparison, we use three systems representing the three paradigms of pre-training with human context (Figure 1). We want to tease apart the contributions of different types of human context: 1) grouping people, 2) modeling individual users, and 3) modeling both group and individual human contexts. As noted earlier, we focus on recent approaches for pre-training language models with additional human context.

**Pre-training with group context.** We build on a model from Hung et al. (2023) that explores demographic adaptation in transformer-based PLMs. It is a bidirectional auto-encoder-based PLM injecting demographic knowledge in a multi-task learning setup where they train for masked language modeling (MLM) and classify the gender or age of an author. They use the Trustpilot dataset [2] of multilingual reviews with demographic labels (Hovy, 2015), and evaluate on multiple text classification tasks, including demographic attribute classification, sentiment analysis, and topic detection. For our comparison study, we use the US-English subset of the Trustpilot data for two tasks: topic detection (TD) across two age categories, and age attribute classification (AC) (more details in section 5). Additionally, we use a monolingual BERT pre-trained with age specialization on the Blogs authorship corpus (Schler et al., 2006). This choice allows us to eliminate a domain influence (i.e., Trustpilot reviews), given that the other PLMs under comparison lack this specialization.

**Pre-training with individual human context.** Soni et al. (2022) introduced human language modeling (HuLM) in PLMs, which is regular language modeling given an additional context of the individual generating the language. This additional context is a dynamic vector derived from the authors' historical texts motivated by the idea of capturing the changing human states expressed in language. It also adds coherence to texts generated by the same author. They introduce Human-aware Recurrent Transformer (HaRT), an autoregressive PLM to evaluate the effect of individual human context on language modeling and multiple user-level and document-level downstream tasks. We build on HaRT and use two user-level tasks, age estimation and personality (openness) assessment, and on a document-level task, stance detection, for our comparisons study.

**Pre-training with both group and individual human context.** We train a PLM to integrate both individual and group human context by introducing a multi-task learning setup into HaRT that incorporates group features. This approach facilitates training a PLM with both group and individual context. We evaluate the model on two multi-document user-level regression tasks: age estimation and personality assessment, and three single document-level classification tasks: stance detection, topic detection, and age group classification. Importantly, the only difference in this multi-task learning setup compared to HaRT is the

[2]https://www.trustpilot.com/

inclusion of a demographic attribute prediction during pre-training, similar to how Hung et al. (2023) adapted traditional PLMs for group context.

## 4 Models

### 4.1 Pre-training with individual human context

**HaRT.** Soni et al. (2022) use a 12-layered autoregressive GPT-2 based architecture with a modified self-attention computation at layer 2. This modification to the query vector now includes the individual human context via a dynamic user-state vector.

$$Q_i^{IN} = W_q^T[H_i^{(IN-1)}; U_{i-1}]$$

where $IN$ is the insert layer (layer 2), $Q_i$ is the query vector under computation, $H_i$ is the hidden states vector, and $U_{i-1}$ is the user-state vector derived from the previous block of language seen from the user. All the text from a user is processed in the same forward pass with recurrent processing of blocks of fixed-length (1024) tokens chunked after temporally ordering the social media posts by created time. The user state is recurrently updated using the hidden states from layer 11 and computed as follows:

$$U_i = tanh(W_U U_{i-1} + W_H H^{(E)})$$

where, $E$ is the extract layer (layer 11), $U_i$ is the updated user-state vector, $U_{i-1}$ is the user-state vector from the previous block, and $H^E$ is the hidden states vector from layer 11. This formulation of updating the user-state vector extends the previous user-state vector information with the current language block's information.

**HULM Pre-training Task.** HaRT is pre-trained for the human language modeling (HULM) task defined as predicting the next token given the previous tokens while conditioning on previous user state $U_{1:t-1}$ (Soni et al., 2022) .

$$Pr(\mathbf{W}_t|\mathbf{U}_{t-1}) = \prod_{i=1}^{n} Pr(w_{t,i}|w_{t,1:i-1}, \mathbf{U}_{1:t-1})$$

This is translated into a pre-training objective to maximize:

$$\prod_{a \in \text{Users}} \prod_{t=1}^{|\mathcal{B}_a|} \prod_{i=1}^{|B_t^{(a)}|} Pr(w_{t,i}|w_{t,1:i-1}, B_{1:t-1}^{(a)})$$

where, $w_{t,i}$ is the $i^{th}$ token in the $t^{th}$ block ($B_t^{(a)}$) for user $a$. The tokens from the previous blocks are represented using HaRT's recurrently updated user-state vector. Soni et al. use cross-entropy loss for the HULM objective.

### 4.2 Pre-training with group human context

**BERT$_{\text{DS}}$ and BERT$_{\text{age-MLM}}$.** Hung et al. (2023) explore socio-demographic adapted BERT models to inject group human context into PLMs. We use two models: one specialized for age (demographic attribute) under the multi-task learning setup, and the other adapted to the age corpora through standard masked language modeling. We denote these as BERT$_{\text{DS}}$ and BERT$_{\text{age-MLM}}$, respectively.

**Multi-Task Learning.** Hung et al. (2023) train for both domain adaptation using the masked language modeling ($L_{mlm}$) loss and for classifying demographic category using the binary cross-entropy loss ($L_{dem}$). Both losses must be combined to simultaneously learn multiple objectives. To account for the *homoscedastic uncertainty* (Kendall et al., 2018) of both losses, they adopt a dynamic multi-task learning (MTL) objective for training with group human context. Homoscedastic uncertainty is a task-dependent weighting to derive a multi-task loss function that can optimally learn the weights and balance the impact of multiple loss functions and their different scales. The tasks are dynamically weighted using the variance of the task-specific loss ($\sigma_t^2$) over training instances of the task $t \in \{mlm, dem\}$:

$$\tilde{L_t} = \frac{1}{2\sigma_t^2} L_t + \log \sigma_t$$

Hung et al. minimize the sum of both the uncertainty adjusted losses: $\tilde{L}_{mlm} + \tilde{L}_{dem}$.

### 4.3 Pre-training with both individual and group human context

**GRIT.** We train HaRT under a multi-task learning setup for both the individual context — through the HuLM pre-training task (see Section 4.1) — and the group features — via a regression task to predict a (continuous) socio-demographic attribute of the author. We call the model as **GR**oup and **I**ndividual HaR**T** (GRIT). The model uses the user-state vectors (see Section 4.1) to predict the socio-demographic attribute of the author:

$$Pr(attribute|\overline{\mathbf{U}})$$

We chunk a user's language history into blocks and process them in a single forward pass. Each block of text from a user results in a user-state vector. We use the average of the user-state vectors from each non-padded block of texts from an author to compute their final user-state representation. This representation is layer-normed and linearly transformed before making a continuous-valued prediction for the specific attribute.

We pre-train one model for the continuous attribute age ($\text{GRIT}_{\text{age}}$) and one for the continuous attribute personality type openness ($\text{GRIT}_{\text{ope}}$). The models train on a regression loss for the attribute prediction regression tasks using mean squared error loss ($L_{mse}$), and a classification loss for the HULM task using cross-entropy loss ($L_{ce}$). We must combine both losses to jointly learn the two objectives and account for the *homoscedastic uncertainty* (Kendall et al., 2018) of the losses. Since we combine a regression and a classification loss, we train the model to learn to balance the loss for a continuous and discrete output as derived in Kendall et al. (2018) and compute our joint objective as follows:

$$\frac{1}{\sigma_{ce}^2} L_{ce} + \frac{1}{2\sigma_{mse}^2} L_{mse} + \log \sigma_{ce} + \log \sigma_{mse}$$

where, $\sigma_{ce}^2$ and $\sigma_{mse}^2$ are the variances of the task-specific losses over the training instances of the respective tasks.

To add numerical stability, we adjust the loss calculation to use log of the variance:

$$\exp^{-\eta_{ce}} L_{ce} + \frac{1}{2}(\exp^{-\eta_{mse}} L_{mse} + \eta_{ce} + \eta_{mse})$$

where $\eta_x = \log \sigma_x^2$ for $x \in \{mse, ce\}$. We let $\sigma_{ce}$ and $\sigma_{mse}$ be learnable parameters for the model. In practice, we do not halve the $\eta_{ce}$ term in the above equation since we found it to perform better with our multi-task learning experiments.

**Pre-training Data and Training.** We use the same Facebook posts dataset (Park et al., 2015) and training, validation, and test splits as those used by Soni et al. (2022). For both $\text{GRIT}_{\text{age}}$ and $\text{GRIT}_{\text{ope}}$, we use the demographic and personality scores, respectively, obtained from consenting Facebook users (Kosinski et al., 2013). This data is identical to that used by HaRT for the age estimation and personality assessment tasks. During training, we use a learning rate of 5e-5 in the multi-tasking training setup, employing the homoscedastic loss computation method described earlier. Following the experimental settings for HaRT, each training instance is capped to 4 blocks of 1024 tokens each. We use a train batch size of 1 per device and an evaluation batch size of 20 per device, trained over 2 GPUs for 8 epochs. Further details can be found in Appendix A.1.

### 4.4 Fine-Tuning

We utilize the results of fine-tuned $\text{BERT}_{\text{DS}}$ and $\text{BERT}_{\text{age-MLM}}$ from Hung et al. (2023), as well as fine-tuned HaRT models from Soni et al. (2022) where available. We fine-tune both GRIT models for all downstream tasks, and HaRT for 2 document-level tasks. Additionally, we use the Optuna framework (Akiba et al., 2019) for hyperparameter search, closely following the experimental settings in Soni et al. (2022). Details can be found in Appendix A.2.

### 4.5 Transfer Learning

We experiment with fine-tuning $\text{GRIT}_{\text{age}}$ in a multi-task learning setup for both the HULM task and predicting personality (openness). Similarly, we fine-tune $\text{GRIT}_{\text{ope}}$ to predict age while also training for the HULM task. We observe that this form of transfer learning yields the best performance for the user-level regression tasks (refer to Section 6.1).

## 5 Experiments

Our study's goal is to compare the downstream performance of models pre-trained with human contexts in three forms: socio-demographic group factors, individual traits, and combined. To this end, we evaluate performances of the models defined in Section 4 on two multi-document user-level regression tasks: predicting age and a personality score (openness), and on three single document-level classification tasks: stance detection, topic detection, and age classification. We also compare against $\text{GPT-2}_{\text{HLC}}$ from Soni et al. (2022) as a PLM adapted to the social media domain but devoid of human context. All experiments were run using Optuna trials (Akiba et al., 2019) to search for the best hyperparameters and reduce the effects of randomness. More details are provided in Appendix A.2

### 5.1 User Level Regression Tasks

We consider two user-level social scientific tasks: age estimation, and personality (openness) assessment, which require predicting continuous outcomes (real-valued age, or openness score) for a user given multiple documents written by them. We use the same data splits as used by Soni et al. (2022) for our comparison study.

Since $GRIT_{age}$ is pre-trained using age estimation as one of the tasks, we use directly evaluate it on the held-out test set. This allows for direct comparison with HaRT fine-tuned for the age estimation task. Furthermore, we can potentially attribute performance differences to the training with combined group and individual context, as $GRIT_{age}$ incorporates the group feature into HaRT's architecture. Similarly, $GRIT_{ope}$ is evaluated on the held-out test set for personality assessment. Moreover, we evaluate $GRIT_{age}$ and $GRIT_{ope}$ for the tasks of personality assessment and age estimation, respectively, using the transfer learning mechanism described in Section 4.5. We report and compare pearson $r$ for age estimation and disattenuated pearson $r$ for personality assessment.

### 5.2 Document-Level Classification Tasks

We compare different models for stance detection vs. topic detection and age classification tasks. These tasks classify a single input document (tweet message or a review) that a user writes into label categories. For stance detection, we also utilize the historical messages of a user where available, as in Soni et al. (2022). However, we do not have the user information or any user historical language available for the other two tasks, so we evaluate solely based on the single document input.

All models process the input document(s) and feed the layer-normed last non-padded token representation to the classification layer to classify the document into label categories. Only GRIT and HaRT incorporate user information and the historical language available for the stance detection task. However, $GPT\text{-}2_{HLC}$, and both $BERT_{DS}$ and $BERT_{age\text{-}MLM}$ lack this hierarchical structure and can only use the input document without access to historical data for making predictions. We compare the results from Soni et al. (2022) and Hung et al. (2023) wherever applicable and fine-tune all the parameters of the respective pre-trained models and the classification heads for other task-model combinations using the standard cross-entropy loss.

**Stance Detection** Given a single annotated tweet, this task predicts a user's stance as in favor of, against, or neutral towards one of the five targets: atheism, climate change as a real concern, feminism, Hillary Clinton, and legalization of abortion. We fine-tune $GRIT_{age}$ and $GRIT_{ope}$ for each target separately, and use the results from Soni et al. (2022) for $GPT\text{-}2_{HLC}$ and HaRT. We report the average of weighted F1 scores[3] with three labels across all five targets. We use the train/dev/test split provided by Soni et al. (2022) over the SemEval 2016 dataset (Mohammad et al., 2016). HaRT and GRIT models maintain the temporal accuracy by using only the messages posted earlier than the labeled messages from the extended dataset (Lynn et al., 2019) as a user's historical language.

**Topic Detection** We use the US subset of the TrustPilot reviews dataset (Hovy, 2015) from two age groups: below 35 or above 45 [4]. Given a single review, the task is to predict the review topics from five categories: Flights, Online marketplace, Fitness & Nutrition, Electronics, and Hotels. To maintain consistency, we adopt the same train, development, and test set splits as Hung et al. (2023) to ensure a stratified demographically-conditioned label distribution. We fine-tune $GPT\text{-}2_{HLC}$, HaRT, $GRIT_{age}$, and $GRIT_{ope}$ using these data splits to predict the topic for a given review, and report macro-F1 scores[3]. We also compare to results from $BERT_{age\text{-}MLM}$ and $BERT_{DS}$ (Hung et al., 2023).

**Demographic Attribute Classification** We use the same subset of the TrustPilot dataset as for topic detection and the same train, development, and test splits from Hung et al. (2023). Given a single review, this task predicts the age group binary label (<35 years old or >45 years old). Age categories are equally represented in each set. We fine-tune $GPT\text{-}2_{HLC}$, HaRT, $GRIT_{age}$ and $GRIT_{ope}$ using the provided splits to predict if the review is written by someone below 35 years or above 45 years, and report macro-F1 scores[3]. We also compare to results from $BERT_{age\text{-}MLM}$ and $BERT_{DS}$ (Hung et al., 2023).

### 5.3 Human Language Modeling

To compare the effects of individual and group factors on language modeling performance, we evaluate on the test set from the pre-trained data splits. We report and compare perplexity scores from the pre-trained GPT-2 ($GPT\text{-}2_{frozen}$), $GPT\text{-}2_{HLC}$, HaRT, $GRIT_{age}$ and $GRIT_{ope}$ for the human language modeling task.

[3]We use this metric to maintain consistency with previous works under comparison (Soni et al., 2022; Hung et al., 2023).

[4]As suggested by Hovy (2015), this split of the age ranges results in roughly equally-sized data sets and is non-contiguous, avoiding fuzzy boundaries.

| Model | Human Context | *Age* ($r$) | *OPE* ($r_{dis}$) |
|---|---|---|---|
| GPT-2HLC | None | 0.839 | 0.521 |
| HaRT | Individual | 0.868 | 0.619 |
| GRITage | Ind + Grp | **0.890** | **0.658** |
| GRITope | Ind + Grp | 0.884 | 0.643 |

Table 1: Pearson $r$ for age, disattenuated Pearson $r$ for openness. Pre-training with individual plus group context show benefits in estimating age and assessing personality (openness). Bold = best in column. We find no statistical difference between GRITage and GRITope for the task of age estimation. All other results show statistical significance $p < 0.05$ using paired t-test.

## 6 Results and Discussion

We report results for all the tasks here, discussing their respective impacts from pre-training LMs with individual human context, group context, and both individual and group context.

### 6.1 Comparisons Study

**User-Level Regression Tasks.** Table 1 shows the results of the two user-level regression tasks. We find that GRIT models outperform others for both age estimation and personality assessment tasks. Additionally, upon comparing the transfer learning (Section 4.5) outcomes of GRITage for openness and GRITope for age to those of the HaRT and GPT-2HLC models, we consistently observe superior performance with the GRIT models, further substantiating their efficacy.

Note that while GPT-2HLC is a PLM that is adapted to the social-media domain, it lacks human context. HaRT incorporates individual human context in pre-training, and GRIT extends this by integrating both group and individual human contexts in pre-training (Figure 1). As shown in Table 1, there are gains observed from GPT-2HLC (no human context) to HaRT (individual human context), and further to GRIT (individual + group human context). This suggests that pre-training PLMs with individual and group human context can benefit multi-document user-level regression tasks, such as those we considered. Importantly, the only difference between HaRT and GRIT models lies in the integration of the demographic attribute prediction (group context). Both models are pre-trained and evaluated on precisely the same data, allowing performance differences to be attributed to the additional group context combined with individualistic human context.

**Document-Level Classification Tasks.** Table 2 shows the results for the 3 document-level classification tasks: stance detection, topic detection (TD) for 2 age groups (<35 and >45), and demographic attribute (age) group classification (AC). We see that task fine-tuned HaRT (individual human context) models perform better on all tasks.

HaRT models inherently include an additional context of the individual user and do not treat all inputs as if written by the same user. The considered stance detection task primarily relates to personal opinions and preferences, rather than group-level ones, making HaRT well-suited for incorporating such personalization due to its pre-training with individual human context. While a group context may also influence a person's stance to some extent, empirical observations show that the combination of individual and group contexts negatively impacts performance. Additionally, models pre-trained with group context (BERTDS) perform well in group-based tasks such as topic detection and age classification. However, models pre-trained on both individual and group human context (GRIT) do not appear to enhance results in group-based, and personal stance detection tasks resulting in slightly worse performance.

Further, it is important to note that the individual human context (HaRT) derived for some of the users using their historical tweets, where available, in the stance detection dataset provides a richer human context as we see greater gains in the performance of HaRT over GPT-2HLC. Conversely, when historical language is not available for certain datasets (topic detection and attribute classification), HaRT does not perform worse than GPT-2HLC and may even achieve marginal gains due to the inherent human context in the model. However, we leave the evaluation of the impact of historical language on human context for future work.

**Perplexity.** We also compare the language modeling capability of the various models. Table 3 reports perplexity on the held-out test set. The frozen GPT-2 performs poorly compared to the social media domain adapted GPT-2HLC, while HaRT model with individual human context perform the best. In contrast, GRIT models with both individual and group human context exhibit a slightly lower perplexity than HaRT. An individual's language is inherently personal, yet it can also be influenced by their group context to some extent, thereby affecting the perplexity results in language modeling

| Model | Human Context | *Stance* ($F1_{wtd}$) | *TD (<35)* ($F1_{mac}$) | *TD (>45)* ($F1_{mac}$) | *AC* ($F1_{mac}$) |
|---|---|---|---|---|---|
| GPT-2$_{HLC}$ | None | 68.60 | 69.77 | 65.43 | 63.93 |
| BERT$_{age\text{-}MLM}$ | Group | - | 68.40 | 64.60 | 61.90 |
| BERT$_{DS}$ | Group | - | 69.30 | 65.00 | 64.10 |
| HaRT | Individual | **71.10** | **69.84** | **65.65** | **64.33** |
| GRIT$_{age}$ | Ind + Grp | 70.82 | 69.21 | 64.52 | 62.56 |
| GRIT$_{ope}$ | Ind + Grp | 70.07 | 66.53 | 64.84 | 61.18 |

Table 2: Weighted F1 for stance detection, macro-F1 for topic detection (TD), and age classification (AC) on TrustPilot reviews. Pre-training with individual context appear to benefit all tasks. **Bold** = best in column; McNemar's test comparing classifiers does not show statistical significance between the best performing model (HaRT) and the best baseline with no individual context (GPT-2$_{HLC}$).

| Model | Human Context | Test (*ppl*) |
|---|---|---|
| GPT-2$_{frozen}$ | None | 114.82 |
| GPT-2$_{HLC}$ | None | 36.39 |
| HaRT | Individual | **28.24** |
| GRIT$_{age}$ | Ind + Grp | 31.77 |
| GRIT$_{ope}$ | Ind + Grp | 30.32 |

Table 3: Comparing perplexity on language modeling for models trained with individual and group contexts.

| Age bucket | #Users | *HaRT (Ind)* | *GRIT$_{age}$ (Ind+Grp)* | *GRIT$_{ope}$ (Ind+Grp)* |
|---|---|---|---|---|
| <18 | 1113 | 0.223 | **0.394** | 0.393 |
| 18-21 | 1387 | 0.230 | **0.278** | 0.276 |
| 21-30 | 1557 | 0.512 | **0.531** | 0.519 |
| 30-45 | 695 | 0.485 | **0.530** | 0.520 |
| 45+ | 248 | 0.106 | **0.205** | 0.180 |

Table 4: Pearson $r$ for age over five age buckets using different types of human contexts for error analysis. Bold indicates best in row. We find no statistical difference between GRIT$_{age}$ and GRIT$_{ope}$ for buckets 21-30 and 30-45. All other results show statistical significance $p < 0.05$ using paired t-test.

tasks. However, GRIT models pre-trained with both individual and group context yield slightly worse perplexity measures. Additionally, we observe similar trends in perplexity gains from GPT-2$_{HLC}$ (no human context) to HaRT (individual context) or GRIT (individual plus group context) as also demonstrated in Soni et al. (2022).

### 6.2 Error Analysis and Disparity

We conduct an error analysis based on a socio-demographic group attribute (age groups), specifically focusing on age and openness prediction tasks.

| Task\Model | *HaRT (Ind)* | *GRIT$_{age}$ (Ind+Grp)* | *GRIT$_{ope}$ (Ind+Grp)* |
|---|---|---|---|
| Age ($r$) | 0.215 | **0.181** | 0.185 |
| OPE ($r_{dis}$) | 0.075 | 0.090 | **0.072** |

Table 5: Mean error disparity for age estimation and openness personality assessment over five age buckets. Bold indicates best in column (lower is better).

We measure the performance of GRIT and HaRT in terms of error disparity (Shah et al., 2020) — a systematic difference in error based on demographics as exemplified by the "Wall Street Journal Effect" (Hovy and Søgaard, 2015). We analyze both the prediction outcomes and error disparity in age and openness prediction for both models: HaRT, which considers individual context, and GRIT, which incorporates both individual and group context.

First, we split the task test dataset into different buckets based on the age groups (specifically, <18, 18-21, 21-30, 30-45, and >45 years old) of the users in the test set, and then we compare the performance of our models across these buckets. Results from Table 4 indicate that pre-training with individual and group contexts together performs better for estimating age across all the age groups, which implies it makes fewer errors as a function of the socio-demographic attribute age. We see similar trends for assessing openness personality (see Appendix Tables 6 and 8), suggesting that the group attribute prediction may act as a regularizer for models pre-trained with both individual and group contexts, thus aiding the models to make fewer errors across all age buckets.

To further confirm, we compute the mean error disparity ($MED$) as the sum of the differences in the performance metric (Pearson correlation for age, and disattenuated Pearson correlation for openness) across each pair of age buckets, which is then averaged by the number of pairs (Shah et al., 2020). A lower averaged sum of differences implies fewer errors as a function of the age groups. Lower $MED$ scores for models pre-trained with individual and group context in Table 5 support our previous error analysis.

## 7 Conclusion

NLP benefits from modeling latent human context, such as socio-demographic group features or individual traits. A recent development has been to incorporate this additional human context into the pre-training regimen of LMs. However, humans exhibit varying degrees of group and individual characteristics. Understanding the impacts of pre-training with different types of human context will advance the integration of human context into our base LLMs (**?**). To assess the impacts, we compare three types of PLMs pre-trained with socio-demographic group attributes, individual human contexts, and combined group and individual traits, across five user- and document-level tasks. Our findings indicate that pre-training with both individual *and* group human context improves the two user-level regression tasks: age and personality prediction. Pre-training with individual human context enhances the performance of the three single-document classification tasks, including stance and topic detection. Interestingly, inclusion of both individual and group attributes results in reduced performance on the text classification tasks. Meanwhile, pre-training solely on group context aids in group-based document classification tasks, albeit suboptimally. These results represent a promising step towards modeling human context and offer valuable insights for the NLP community to investigate additional strategies for improving models with task-dependent human context during pre-training.

## Limitations

The purpose of our study is to compare the impacts of modeling socio-demographic group attributes and modeling individual user traits, and we use relevant models to represent each of the approaches. There are likely to be other ways to model these approaches and the models we use are only one of the ways. Additionally, these models in themselves have limitations like the blocks mechanism to process all the text from author induces compute requirements resulting in a capping of the number of blocks used for training. While it is also unclear how many blocks are sufficient to capture the human context, and if it is helpful to use the earliest language or the most recently used language in the capped number of blocks.
Secondly, some of the datasets (TrustPilot) used do not have appropriate user identification or historical language to create an individual human context. Lastly, as noted earlier, models and data that touch upon sensitive user information require an extremely responsible usage and limit researchers to make them publicly available.

## Ethical Considerations

Models that incorporate socio-demographic information need to be considered with special scrutiny. On the one hand, they have the potential to produce fairer and more inclusive results, because they can account for human language variation. On the other hand, they risk revealing identifying or sensitive information, which can lead to profiling and stereotyping. These may present opportunities for unintended malicious exploitations. For example, models that improve demographic groups prediction or psychological assessments could be used for targeting content for individuals without their awareness or consent. Such models may also risk release of private information of the research participant if trained on private data unchecked for exposing identifying information. For this reason, we take a conservative release strategy. While we support open research and reproducibility, data and privacy protection take precedence. Thus, we will only be releasing the code for our comparison study and the data that does not contain sensitive information i.e., stance detection datasets and TrustPilot datasets for topic detection and attribute classification. This is also in accordance with the DUA we have received from the authors of the papers/models that we employ in our work.
Our comparison study aims to guide and further speed the growing body of human-centered AI research. The models under comparison aim to enable applicability in the interdisciplinary studies of the human condition leading to helpful tools for psychological health. However, at this point these models are not intended for use in practice and should be evaluated for failures. All user-level tasks presented here were reviewed and approved or exempted by an academic institutional review board (IRB). Our studies are limited to US-English

due to comparability reasons. However, similar effects are likely to hold for other languages, and should be evaluated in future work.

## Acknowledgments

This research is supported in part by the Office of the Director of National Intelligence (ODNI), Intelligence Advanced Research Projects Activity (IARPA), via the HIATUS Program contract #2022-22072200005, and a grant from the CDC/NIOSH (U01 OH012476). The views and conclusions contained herein are those of the authors and should not be interpreted as necessarily representing the official policies, either expressed or implied, of ODNI, IARPA, any other government organization, or the U.S. Government. The U.S. Government is authorized to reproduce and distribute reprints for governmental purposes notwithstanding any copyright annotation therein.

## References

Takuya Akiba, Shotaro Sano, Toshihiko Yanase, Takeru Ohta, and Masanori Koyama. 2019. Optuna: A next-generation hyperparameter optimization framework. In *Proceedings of the 25th ACM SIGKDD international conference on knowledge discovery & data mining*, pages 2623–2631.

David Bamman, Chris Dyer, and Noah A. Smith. 2014. Distributed Representations of Geographically Situated Language. In *Proceedings of the 52nd Annual Meeting of the Association for Computational Linguistics (Volume 2: Short Papers)*, pages 828–834, Baltimore, Maryland. Association for Computational Linguistics.

David Bamman and Noah Smith. 2015. Contextualized Sarcasm Detection on Twitter. *Proceedings of the International AAAI Conference on Web and Social Media*, 9(1):574–577. Number: 1.

Minje Choi, Jiaxin Pei, Sagar Kumar, Chang Shu, and David Jurgens. 2023. Do LLMs understand social knowledge? evaluating the sociability of large language models with SocKET benchmark. In *Proceedings of the 2023 Conference on Empirical Methods in Natural Language Processing*, pages 11370–11403, Singapore. Association for Computational Linguistics.

Edouard Delasalles, Sylvain Lamprier, and Ludovic Denoyer. 2019. Learning Dynamic Author Representations with Temporal Language Models. *2019 IEEE International Conference on Data Mining (ICDM)*, pages 120–129. ArXiv: 1909.04985.

William Fleeson. 2001. Toward a structure-and process-integrated view of personality: Traits as density distributions of states. *Journal of personality and social psychology*, 80(6):1011.

Aparna Garimella, Carmen Banea, and Rada Mihalcea. 2017. Demographic-aware word associations. In *Proceedings of the 2017 Conference on Empirical Methods in Natural Language Processing*, pages 2285–2295, Copenhagen, Denmark. Association for Computational Linguistics.

Bhanu Prakash Reddy Guda, Aparna Garimella, and Niyati Chhaya. 2021. EmpathBERT: A BERT-based framework for demographic-aware empathy prediction. In *Proceedings of the 16th Conference of the European Chapter of the Association for Computational Linguistics: Main Volume*, pages 3072–3079, Online. Association for Computational Linguistics.

Geert Hofstede and Michael H Bond. 1984. Hofstede's culture dimensions: An independent validation using rokeach's value survey. *Journal of cross-cultural psychology*, 15(4):417–433.

Dirk Hovy. 2015. Demographic Factors Improve Classification Performance. In *Proceedings of the 53rd Annual Meeting of the Association for Computational Linguistics and the 7th International Joint Conference on Natural Language Processing (Volume 1: Long Papers)*, pages 752–762, Beijing, China. Association for Computational Linguistics.

Dirk Hovy and Anders Søgaard. 2015. Tagging Performance Correlates with Author Age. In *Proceedings of the 53rd Annual Meeting of the Association for Computational Linguistics and the 7th International Joint Conference on Natural Language Processing (Volume 2: Short Papers)*, pages 483–488, Beijing, China. Association for Computational Linguistics.

Yu-Yang Huang, Rui Yan, Tsung-Ting Kuo, and Shou-De Lin. 2014. Enriching cold start personalized language model using social network information. In *Proceedings of the 52nd Annual Meeting of the Association for Computational Linguistics (Volume 2: Short Papers)*, pages 611–617, Baltimore, Maryland. Association for Computational Linguistics.

Chia-Chien Hung, Anne Lauscher, Dirk Hovy, Simone Paolo Ponzetto, and Goran Glavaš. 2023. Can demographic factors improve text classification? revisiting demographic adaptation in the age of transformers. In *Findings of the Association for Computational Linguistics: EACL 2023*, pages 1565–1580, Dubrovnik, Croatia. Association for Computational Linguistics.

Aaron Jaech and Mari Ostendorf. 2018. Personalized language model for query auto-completion. In *Proceedings of the 56th Annual Meeting of the Association for Computational Linguistics (Volume 2: Short Papers)*, pages 700–705, Melbourne, Australia. Association for Computational Linguistics.

Alex Kendall, Yarin Gal, and Roberto Cipolla. 2018. Multi-task learning using uncertainty to weigh losses for scene geometry and semantics. In *Proceedings of the IEEE conference on computer vision and pattern recognition*, pages 7482–7491.

Milton King and Paul Cook. 2020. Evaluating approaches to personalizing language models. In *Proceedings of the Twelfth Language Resources and Evaluation Conference*, pages 2461–2469, Marseille, France. European Language Resources Association.

Michal Kosinski, David Stillwell, and Thore Graepel. 2013. Private traits and attributes are predictable from digital records of human behavior. *Proceedings of the National Academy of Sciences*, 110(15):5802–5805.

Vivek Kulkarni, Bryan Perozzi, and Steven Skiena. 2016. Freshman or Fresher? Quantifying the Geographic Variation of Language in Online Social Media. *Proceedings of the International AAAI Conference on Web and Social Media*, 10(1):615–618. Number: 1.

Cheng Li, Mingyang Zhang, Qiaozhu Mei, Weize Kong, and Michael Bendersky. 2023. Automatic prompt rewriting for personalized text generation. *arXiv preprint arXiv:2310.00152*.

Lei Li, Yongfeng Zhang, and Li Chen. 2021. Personalized transformer for explainable recommendation. In *Proceedings of the 59th Annual Meeting of the Association for Computational Linguistics and the 11th International Joint Conference on Natural Language Processing (Volume 1: Long Papers)*, pages 4947–4957.

Veronica Lynn, Salvatore Giorgi, Niranjan Balasubramanian, and H. Andrew Schwartz. 2019. Tweet Classification without the Tweet: An Empirical Examination of User versus Document Attributes. In *Proceedings of the Third Workshop on Natural Language Processing and Computational Social Science*, pages 18–28, Minneapolis, Minnesota. Association for Computational Linguistics.

Veronica Lynn, Youngseo Son, Vivek Kulkarni, Niranjan Balasubramanian, and H. Andrew Schwartz. 2017. Human Centered NLP with User-Factor Adaptation. In *Proceedings of the 2017 Conference on Empirical Methods in Natural Language Processing*, pages 1146–1155, Copenhagen, Denmark. Association for Computational Linguistics.

Matthew Matero, Nikita Soni, Niranjan Balasubramanian, and H. Andrew Schwartz. 2021. MeLT: Message-level transformer with masked document representations as pre-training for stance detection. In *Findings of the Association for Computational Linguistics: EMNLP 2021*, pages 2959–2966, Punta Cana, Dominican Republic. Association for Computational Linguistics.

Matthias R Mehl and James W Pennebaker. 2003. The sounds of social life: a psychometric analysis of students' daily social environments and natural conversations. *Journal of personality and social psychology*, 84(4):857.

Saif M. Mohammad, Svetlana Kiritchenko, Parinaz Sobhani, Xiaodan Zhu, and Colin Cherry. 2016. Semeval-2016 task 6: Detecting stance in tweets. In *Proceedings of the International Workshop on Semantic Evaluation*, SemEval '16, San Diego, California.

Matthias Orlikowski, Paul Röttger, Philipp Cimiano, and Dirk Hovy. 2023. The ecological fallacy in annotation: Modeling human label variation goes beyond sociodemographics. In *Proceedings of the 61st Annual Meeting of the Association for Computational Linguistics (Volume 2: Short Papers)*, pages 1017–1029, Toronto, Canada. Association for Computational Linguistics.

Gregory Park, H. Andrew Schwartz, Johannes C. Eichstaedt, Margaret L. Kern, Michal Kosinski, David J. Stillwell, Lyle H. Ungar, and Martin E. P. Seligman. 2015. Automatic personality assessment through social media language. *Journal of Personality and Social Psychology*, 108(6):934–952.

Bahar Radfar, Karthik Shivaram, and Aron Culotta. 2020. Characterizing Variation in Toxic Language by Social Context. *Proceedings of the International AAAI Conference on Web and Social Media*, 14:959–963.

Alireza Salemi, Sheshera Mysore, Michael Bendersky, and Hamed Zamani. 2023. Lamp: When large language models meet personalization. *arXiv preprint arXiv:2304.11406*.

Jonathan Schler, Moshe Koppel, Shlomo Argamon, and James W Pennebaker. 2006. Effects of age and gender on blogging. In *AAAI spring symposium: Computational approaches to analyzing weblogs*, volume 6, pages 199–205.

H. Andrew Schwartz, Johannes C. Eichstaedt, Margaret L. Kern, Lukasz Dziurzynski, Stephanie M. Ramones, Megha Agrawal, Achal Shah, Michal Kosinski, David Stillwell, Martin E. P. Seligman, and Lyle H. Ungar. 2013. Personality, Gender, and Age in the Language of Social Media: The Open-Vocabulary Approach. *PLOS ONE*, 8(9):e73791. Publisher: Public Library of Science.

Deven Santosh Shah, H Andrew Schwartz, and Dirk Hovy. 2020. Predictive biases in natural language processing models: A conceptual framework and overview. In *Proceedings of the 58th Annual Meeting of the Association for Computational Linguistics*, pages 5248–5264.

Nikita Soni, Matthew Matero, Niranjan Balasubramanian, and H. Andrew Schwartz. 2022. Human language modeling. In *Findings of the Association for Computational Linguistics: ACL 2022*, pages 622–636, Dublin, Ireland. Association for Computational Linguistics.

Nikita Soni, H. Schwartz, João Sedoc, and Niranjan Balasubramanian. 2024. Large human language models: A need and the challenges. In *Proceedings of the 2024 Conference of the North American Chapter of the Association for Computational Linguistics: Human Language Technologies (Volume 1: Long Papers)*, pages 8631–8646, Mexico City, Mexico. Association for Computational Linguistics.

Svitlana Volkova, Theresa Wilson, and David Yarowsky. 2013. Exploring Demographic Language Variations to Improve Multilingual Sentiment Analysis in Social Media. In *Proceedings of the 2013 Conference on Empirical Methods in Natural Language Processing*, pages 1815–1827, Seattle, Washington, USA. Association for Computational Linguistics.

Wanjun Zhong, Duyu Tang, Jiahai Wang, Jian Yin, and Nan Duan. 2021. UserAdapter: Few-Shot User Learning in Sentiment Analysis. In *Findings of the Association for Computational Linguistics: ACL-IJCNLP 2021*, pages 1484–1488, Online. Association for Computational Linguistics.

# A Appendix

## A.1 Pre-training GRIT

**Pre-training data.** We use a subset of the pre-training data for HaRT, consisting of the demographics and personality information. This subset contains the Facebook posts from Park et al. (2015) as used by Soni et al.. Our dataset is consistent with the inclusion criteria for HaRT to ensure moderate language history for each user: we include English posts from users with at least 50 total posts and at least 1000 words. This dataset consists of just over 63,000 unique users, which we split into a training dataset consisting of messages from 56,930 users, a development dataset that consists of messages from 1836 users that were not part of the training set, and a test set of messages from a separate set of 4438 users that are neither in training nor the development set. To evaluate the human attribute prediction in $\text{GRIT}_{ope}$, we use a subset of the test set consisting of messages from 1745 users to accommodate for questionnaire reliability. We use the Facebook posts for the HuLM task and the demographic and personality scores of consenting Facebook users (Kosinski et al., 2013) for the human attribute prediction task.

**Training.** We use HaRT's pre-trained weights as the base weights for GRIT and randomly initialize the newly introduced weights for human attribute prediction. GRIT is trained on our pre-training dataset using the 5e-5 learning rate after experimenting with a few learning rates, including that used for HaRT's pre-training. Following HaRT, and due to computing limitations, each training instance is capped to 8 blocks of 1024 tokens each,

| Age bucket | #Users | *HaRT (Ind)* | *$GRIT_{age}$ (Ind+Grp)* | *$GRIT_{ope}$ (Ind+Grp)* |
|---|---|---|---|---|
| <18 | 503 | 0.627 | **0.644** | 0.618 |
| 18-21 | 560 | 0.557 | **0.608** | 0.592 |
| 21-30 | 563 | 0.715 | **0.741** | 0.738 |
| 30-45 | 249 | 0.594 | **0.669** | 0.667 |
| 45+ | 68 | 0.567 | 0.546 | **0.599** |

Table 6: Disattenuated pearson $r$ for openness over five age buckets using different types of human contexts for error analysis. Bold indicates best in row.

| Age bucket | #Users | *HaRT (Ind)* | *$GRIT_{age}$ (Ind+Grp)* | *$GRIT_{ope}$ (Ind+Grp)* |
|---|---|---|---|---|
| <18 | 1113 | 4.07 | **2.52** | 2.82 |
| 18-21 | 1387 | 6.52 | 4.00 | **3.89** |
| 21-30 | 1557 | 17.82 | **12.64** | 13.11 |
| 30-45 | 695 | 48.59 | **39.79** | 40.43 |
| 45+ | 248 | **114.92** | 121.66 | 134.72 |

Table 7: Mean squared error for age over five age buckets using different types of human contexts for error analysis. Bold indicates best in row (lower error is better).

| Age bucket | #Users | *HaRT (Ind)* | *$GRIT_{age}$ (Ind+Grp)* | *$GRIT_{ope}$ (Ind+Grp)* |
|---|---|---|---|---|
| <18 | 503 | 0.423 | **0.410** | 0.429 |
| 18-21 | 560 | 0.496 | **0.487** | 0.506 |
| 21-30 | 563 | 0.429 | **0.380** | 0.381 |
| 30-45 | 249 | 0.578 | **0.489** | 0.489 |
| 45+ | 68 | 0.584 | 0.501 | **0.467** |

Table 8: Mean squared error for openness over five age buckets using different types of human contexts for error analysis. Bold indicates best in row (lower error is better).

with train batch size as 1 per device and evaluation batch size as 20 per device, trained over 2 GPUs for eight epochs. We explored multiple joint losses before resorting to the homoscedastic loss computation. Since HaRT caps to 4 train blocks for user-level downstream tasks, we also pre-train $GRIT_{age}$ and $GRIT_{ope}$ with four training blocks.

### A.2 Experimental Settings

We closely follow the experimental settings from Soni et al. (2022) and similarly use Optuna framework (Akiba et al., 2019) for hyperparameter search. We search for learning rates between 5e-6 and 5e-4, and between 1e-7 and 1e-5 for different tasks. We will make our best found hyperparameter values publicly available with our code and results in the github repository. All experiments are run on NVIDIA RTX A6000 GPUs of 48GB. Pre-training takes approx 14 hours for 1 epoch and fine-tuning takes approx 1-4 hours depending on the task.

# LLMs for Targeted Sentiment in News Headlines: Exploring the Descriptive–Prescriptive Dilemma

**Jana Juroš** **Laura Majer** **Jan Šnajder**
University of Zagreb Faculty of Electrical Engineering and Computing
TakeLab
{jana.juros, laura.majer, jan.snajder}@fer.hr

## Abstract

News headlines often evoke sentiment by intentionally portraying entities in particular ways, making targeted sentiment analysis (TSA) of headlines a worthwhile but difficult task. Due to its subjectivity, creating TSA datasets can involve various annotation paradigms, from *descriptive* to *prescriptive*, either encouraging or limiting subjectivity. LLMs are a good fit for TSA due to their broad linguistic and world knowledge and in-context learning abilities, yet their performance depends on prompt design. In this paper, we compare the accuracy of state-of-the-art LLMs and fine-tuned encoder models for TSA of news headlines using descriptive and prescriptive datasets across several languages. Exploring the descriptive–prescriptive continuum, we analyze how performance is affected by prompt prescriptiveness, ranging from plain zero-shot to elaborate few-shot prompts. Finally, we evaluate the ability of LLMs to quantify uncertainty via calibration error and comparison to human label variation. We find that LLMs outperform fine-tuned encoders on descriptive datasets, while calibration and F1-score generally improve with increased prescriptiveness, yet the optimal level varies.

## 1 Introduction

News framing impacts information perception, shapes public opinion, and guides discussions on key topics (Semetko and Valkenburg, 2000). News headlines – succinct and attention-grabbing introductions to full news stories – often evoke sentiment by portraying entities in specific ways. Targeted sentiment analysis (TSA) is the task of determining the polarity of sentiment expressed towards the target entity (Pei et al., 2019). While sentiment analysis is inherently challenging due to subjectivity, TSA introduces additional complexity by requiring the differentiation between targeted and overall sentiment.

For subjective tasks like TSA, the choice of data annotation paradigm is crucial. Rottger et al. (2022) identified two contrasting paradigms: *descriptive* and *prescriptive*. The descriptive paradigm encourages subjectivity and diverse interpretations, typically with brief guidelines. In contrast, the prescriptive paradigm discourages subjectivity by providing detailed interpretation guidelines.

Fine-tuned encoders such as BERT (Devlin et al., 2019) show strong TSA performance across various languages (Wu and Ong, 2021; Zhang et al., 2020; Mutlu and Özgür, 2022). However, using these models in different languages or domains requires new fine-tuning, and adapting them to low-resource languages necessitates pre-trained models and labeled data. In contrast, large language models (LLMs) offer a versatile approach to TSA across various domains by leveraging their broad linguistic and world knowledge, as well as in-context learning (Brown et al., 2020), without the need for annotated datasets or fine-tuning. However, LLMs performance is often inconsistent and contingent on prompt design (Mizrahi et al., 2024), making it challenging to identify optimal settings. Furthermore, it is unclear how specific TSA criteria, defined during annotation, can be transferred using zero- and few-shot prompting.

In this paper, we compare the zero- and few-shot performance of open and closed-source LLMs to fine-tuned encoder models on datasets annotated following the descriptive or prescriptive paradigm. We then explore the influence of prompt design on the performance of LLMs for the prescriptive TSA dataset of Croatian news headlines. Similar to crafting effective annotation guidelines, finding the appropriate *level of prescriptiveness* is essential in prompt design. The recent use of LLMs as data annotators (Wang et al., 2021; Pangakis et al., 2023; Alizadeh et al., 2023) further invites a direct comparison of annotation paradigms and prompt design: less prescriptive prompts give more interpretive freedom, while highly detailed prompts



*Proceedings of the 14th Workshop on Computational Approaches to Subjectivity, Sentiment, & Social Media Analysis*, pages 329–343
August 15, 2024 

constrain it. Building on this parallel, we evaluate the predictive accuracy of LLMs using prompts constructed from annotation guidelines with different levels of prescriptiveness, ranging from plain zero-shot to elaborate few-shot prompts matching annotation guidelines.

Another interesting connection between annotation and prompting is label variation. Regardless of whether subjectivity is encouraged, some human label variation is inevitable in subjective tasks and may be leveraged to improve model performance (Mostafazadeh Davani et al., 2022). Similarly, LLM inconsistency, typically viewed as a limitation, can diversify responses to emulate human label variation. Recent LLM uncertainty quantification methods (Rivera et al., 2024; Xiong et al., 2023; Tian et al., 2023) can be used for the same purpose. Building on this idea, we assess LLMs' capability to quantify predictive uncertainty in TSA of headlines using calibration error and compare label distribution with human label variation.

Our experiments mainly focus on a Croatian dataset labeled with TSA on news headlines accompanied by detailed, prescriptive annotation guidelines. Additionally, we evaluate zero-shot LLMs and BERT on English, Polish, and Spanish TSA datasets with less prescriptive guidelines. Our contributions include (1) comparing LLMs and BERT for TSA on news headlines in four languages, (2) evaluating the effect of prompt prescriptiveness on LLMs' predictive accuracy, and (3) assessing calibration error and label distribution across models based on prompt prescriptiveness. This study offers valuable insights into LLMs' zero- and few-shot potential for TSA of news headlines.

## 2 Related Work

Sentiment analysis of news headlines is an important task that has garnered significant attention in prior work (Agarwal et al., 2016; Joshi et al., 2016; Aslam et al., 2020; Nemes and Kiss, 2021; Rozado et al., 2022). In addition to overall sentiment, TSA is crucial for understanding how entities are portrayed in news articles. Cortis et al. (2017) apply TSA on financial headlines, where sentiment is less implicit and topically constrained. Dufraisse et al. (2023) and Steinberger et al. (2011) present multilingual datasets for TSA in news articles. Hamborg and Donnay (2021) present a dataset for TSA on English news articles reporting on political topics, while (Balahur et al., 2013) focus on quotes from news articles. Overcoming the need for a labeled dataset, LLMs present a possible solution for TSA due to their in-context learning (ICL) abilities and broad background. Huang et al. (2020) conducted an analysis to identify and mitigate the entity bias of LLMs trained for sentiment analysis on Wikipedia and news articles. Chumakov et al. (2023) leverage both few-shot learning and fine-tuning with GPT models on mixed-domain Russian and English datasets to model sentiment effectively without domain-specific data.

## 3 Datasets and Models

Our experiments utilize, to our knowledge, the only two available datasets for TSA in general news headlines, alongside one domain-specific dataset. These datasets cover four languages and employ different annotation styles.

**STONE.** The STONE dataset (Barić et al., 2023) offers overall sentiment and targeted sentiment along with extracted target entities for Croatian news headlines, using ternary labels (positive, neutral, negative). Each of the 2855 headlines has 6 labels assigned by 6 annotators, with inter-annotator agreement (IAA) of $\kappa = 0.416$ (moderate agreement). Annotators were instructed using prescriptive, detailed guidelines (obtained from the authors upon our request). If a headline contained multiple entities, the target entity was chosen randomly and disclosed to the annotators.

**SEN.** The SEN (Baraniak and Sydow, 2021) dataset includes 3819 English and Polish news headlines, each featuring targeted sentiment labels and corresponding target entities. It comprises a Polish part (SEN_pl), an English part (SEN_en_r) annotated by volunteer researchers, and an English part (SEN_en_amt) annotated using Amazon Mechanical Turk. The reported Fleiss' kappa IAA are $\kappa = .459$, $\kappa = .309$, and $\kappa = .303$, respectively. Unlike STONE, SEN lacks raw labels, providing only an aggregated gold label per headline (positive, neutral, and negative), and was annotated using vaguer annotator guidelines, adhering more to the descriptive paradigm.

**Spanish.** The Spanish dataset (ES) of Salgueiro et al. (2022) comprises 1976 headlines concerning the 2019 Argentinian Presidential Elections. Three annotators assigned ternary labels to each headline with masked targets, with IAA of $\alpha = .62$. The authors do not disclose annotation guidelines, which

| | STONE | ES | SEN en_amt | SEN en_r | SEN pl |
|---|---|---|---|---|---|
| GPT 3.5 | 61.3 | 64.2 | 66.1 | 61.5 | 60.0 |
| GPT 4 | 65.9 | **67.0** | **68.8** | 63.2 | **69.5** |
| Neural Chat | 59.8 | 63.0 | 66.3 | **63.8** | 58.1 |
| Llama 3 | 53.5 | 60.5 | 59.2 | 52.7 | 51.2 |
| Phi-3 | 43.5 | 61.7 | 58.3 | 52.7 | 47.3 |
| Gemma | 48.4 | 60.5 | 60.0 | 52.7 | 51.2 |
| BERT* | **74.9** | 66.7 | 63.6 | 56.2 | 61.9 |

Table 1: F1 scores across languages and datasets

suggests the straight-forward descriptive paradigm.

**Models.** We experiment with four open-source models: Neural Chat (NC) (7B), Llama 3 (8B), Phi-3 (3.8B), and Gemma (9B), pitted against two proprietary OpenAI models – GPT-4 Turbo (560B) and GPT-3.5 Turbo (175B) (OpenAI et al., 2023) (cf. Appendix A.3 for more details).

# 4 Experiments and Results

## 4.1 Predictive Accuracy

We first evaluate the LLMs' accuracy of TSA on headlines and compare them to top-performing BERT* models. We use the BERT models specifically pre-trained for each language – RoBERTa-base (Liu et al., 2019) for English, BERTić (Ljubešić and Lauc, 2021) for Croatian, BETO (Cañete et al., 2023) for Spanish and Polish-RoBERTa-base-v2 (Dadas et al., 2020) for Polish – and fine-tune each for TSA on the corresponding training set (cf. Appendix A.1 for dataset split sizes and A.2 for hyperparameters details). For LLMs, we use zero-shot prompting on the test set, using basic prompts outlining the task and the target classes (cf. Appendix B.1).

Table 1 presents the F1 scores on the test set portions of each dataset. On the descriptive datasets (SEN and ES), LLMs outperform BERT-based models. GPT-4 achieves the highest F1 score on the Polish SEN and the crowdsourced English SEN. Interestingly, on the English SEN annotated by researchers, NC outperforms both fine-tuned BERT models and GPT. However, on STONE– the prescriptively annotated dataset – BERTić surpasses all other models by a significant margin. We argue this performance difference might stem from using different annotation paradigms. The best-performing LLMs seem to grasp the descriptive paradigm well, performing TSA closest to annotators. On the other hand, the performance gap observed in LLMs on STONE may stem from the prompts' vagueness and lack of alignment with its prescriptiveness – a question we explore next.

| Level | Description |
|---|---|
| 1 | Concise, exploring the fundamental concepts of sentiment and targeted sentiment. |
| 2 | Includes a definition of targeted sentiment specifically within the framework of news headlines. |
| 3 | Provided with concise guidelines. |
| 4 | Comprehensive instructions provided as guidelines, excluding examples. |
| 5 | Comprehensive instructions presented as guidelines, including examples and brief explanations. |
| 6 | Comprehensive instructions provided exactly as they were presented to the annotators. |

Table 2: Short descriptions of prompt prescriptiveness levels (cf. Appendix B.3 for full prompts)

## 4.2 Level of Prompt Prescriptiveness

We utilize the STONE dataset and its annotator guidelines to create six prompts of increasing prescriptiveness level, with each subsequent level incorporating additional information from the guidelines. Table 2 outlines these six levels (cf. Appendix A for full prompts). Our goal is to assess the ability of LLMs to follow instructions as accurately as human annotators and to determine the most effective level of prompt prescriptiveness.

Table 3 shows the results. We observe variance in performance across all levels for all models. GPT-4 consistently outperforms other models across all levels, with GPT-4 and Neural Chat reaching their performance peaks at level 4 (detailed instructions formatted as guidelines without examples) and GPT 3.5 performing best at level 3 (concise guidelines). The performance drop seen at levels 5 and 6, the only ones with few-shot examples, may be due to the sensitivity regarding the selection and ordering of examples, a phenomenon observed in few-shot prompting (Lu et al., 2022; Chang and Jia, 2023). The increasing accuracy from levels 1 to 4 suggests that more prescriptive instructions positively impact LLM performance. Despite their overall lower performance, Llama 3, Gemma, and Phi-3 significantly improve at levels 5 and 6 (few-shot prompts). This difference in performance could be due to instruction tuning, which may have reduced sensitivity to few-shot configuration and improved context following.

## 4.3 Uncertainty Quantification

Given the inherent subjectivity of TSA and leveraging the stochastic nature of predictions generated

| Level | NC | GPT 3.5 | GPT 4 | Llama 3 | Gemma | Phi-3 |
|---|---|---|---|---|---|---|
| 1 | 59.8 | 60.1 | 65.9 | 53.5 | 48.4 | 43.5 |
| 2 | 61.2 | 58.3 | 64.3 | 50.9 | 48.8 | 40.6 |
| 3 | 61.5 | **65.7** | 69.9 | 52.9 | 55.8 | 44.2 |
| 4 | **63.1** | 64.0 | **70.2** | 51.9 | 53.1 | 43.6 |
| 5 | 60.5 | 63.0 | 66.8 | 60.6 | 59.3 | **49.4** |
| 6 | 62.5 | 64.5 | 68.2 | **61.9** | **59.4** | 46.3 |

Table 3: F1 scores for levels of prompt prescriptiveness

by LLMs, we explore how LLMs can model human label variation and whether this varies across levels of prompt prescriptiveness. Using STONE, we approach this question from two angles: (1) examining the relationship between LLMs' predictive and calibration accuracies and (2) investigating if the uncertainty of LLM predictions aligns with inter-annotator disagreement.

We use three uncertainty quantification methods: self-consistency sampling, distribution prompting, and verbal confidence assessment. *Self-consistency sampling* (SCS) (Xiong et al., 2023) leverages the inherent stochasticity of LLMs, influenced additionally by internal parameters such as temperature. For each headline, we prompt the same model six times and accumulate the responses to mimic the distribution of six annotator responses, setting the temperature to 0.7 for all models (cf. Appendix A.4 for details). The second method, which we refer to as *distribution prompting* (DP), prompts the model to explicitly predict how six annotators would label the targeted sentiment, directly resulting in a distribution of positive, neutral, and negative responses. Lastly, the *verbal confidence assessment* (VCA) method (Xiong et al., 2023) prompts the LLM to produce three predictions for each headline, representing each sentiment class, along with a confidence score ranging from 0 to 100. For the complete set of prompts used in each method, refer to Table 9 in Appendix B.2.

In addition to evaluating the model's prediction accuracy, we also consider model calibration. Calibration evaluates the alignment between a model's expressed confidence and its actual accuracy: ideally, predictions with a 70% confidence should be accurate 70% of the time. To analyze the calibration error, we consider only the labels with the highest confidence score for each headline and calculate the expected calibration error (ECE), computed as the average discrepancy between model confidence and observed accuracy. Model predictions are divided into $m$ quantile-scaled bins $B_i$, with $m$ set to 10 for this analysis. For each bin, we calculate both

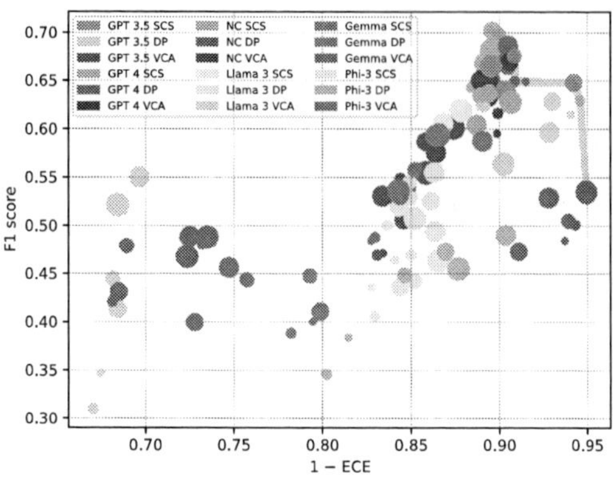


Figure 1: Comparison of F1 scores and calibration accuracy for various uncertainty quantification methods and across levels of prompt prescriptiveness (indicated by dot size). The gray lines indicate the Pareto front.

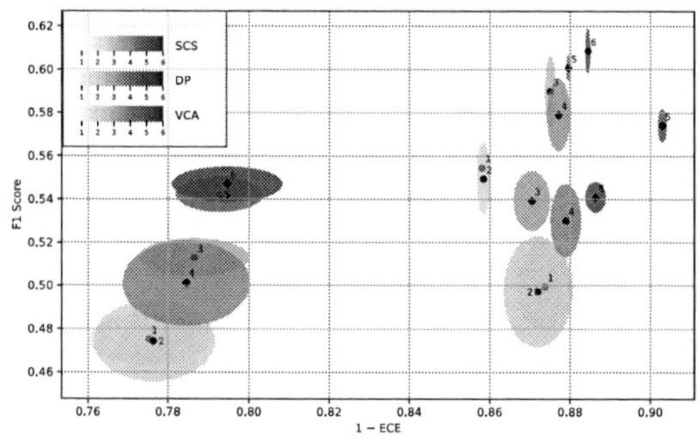


Figure 2: F1 scores and calibration accuracy averaged over all models across different uncertainty quantification methods and prescriptiveness levels (shaded ellipses indicate covariances)

the average accuracy $\text{acc}(B_i)$ and the average confidence $\text{conf}(B_i)$. The Expected Calibration Error (ECE) is then derived as the weighted sum of the absolute differences between these averages, with weights proportional to the bin size $n$:

$$\text{ECE} = \sum_{i=1}^{m} \frac{|B_i|}{n} \left| \text{acc}(B_i) - \text{conf}(B_i) \right|. \quad (1)$$

Figure 1 compares the predictive accuracy (F1 score) with calibration accuracy, defined as $1 - \text{ECE}$, evaluated for each model. Figure 2 provides an overview of both metrics averaged across all models (cf. Tables 6 and 7 in Appendix A.7 for comprehensive data across all models). GPT-4 stands out as the best model, with the highest F1 scores and sound calibration, stable across different levels of prescriptiveness and uncertainty quantification methods. In comparison, the other models'

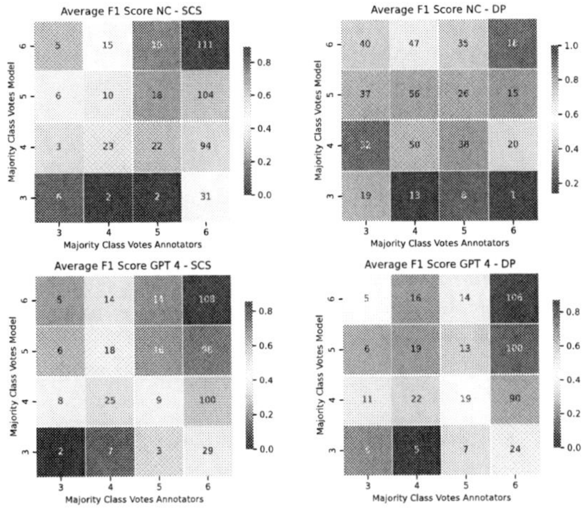

Figure 3: F1 score per majority vote bins for annotators (X) and model (Y) for SCS vs. DP for NC and GPT-4

performance is significantly affected by the uncertainty quantification method employed. Considering the averaged results, F1 scores are higher for SCS compared to DP and VCA, This aligns with expectations, as the models' predictions are evaluated solely against the gold labels. Average calibration accuracy is generally high (above 0.75) across models and uncertainty methods. Higher prescriptiveness levels show an increasing trend in predictive and calibration accuracy, with the optimal level varying by uncertainty method (Level 6 for SCS and VCA, and Level 5 for DP). This suggests that prescriptive annotation guidelines can enhance LLM performance for prescriptive datasets.

Besides quantifying uncertainty, SCS and DP can model human label variation, implicitly (SCS) or explicitly (DP). We compare these label distributions to human label variation. Figure 3 shows heatmaps of average F1 scores for the two best-performing open- and closed-source models, GPT-4 and NC. The axes represent the majority vote per instance by annotators and model. The highest F1 score is achieved when both the annotators' votes and the models' prediction are unanimous (6 votes). The lowest F1 scores are generally achieved for instances with less agreement within annotators or model votes. For GPT-4, DP performs similarly to SCS, whereas for NC, there is a significant performance drop and dispersion of model votes in bins, signaling the model is not grasping the concept. This suggests that SCS is a better choice for modeling label distribution across models.

# 5 Conclusion

Building on parallels with annotation paradigms for subjective tasks, we investigated the performance of LLM in-context learning for targeted sentiment analysis on news headlines. Our findings indicate that predictive accuracy increases with prompt prescriptiveness, though the optimal level varies by model, and only some models benefit from few-shot prompting. Calibration generally improves with prompt prescriptiveness, and self-consistency sampling aligns best with human label variation.

# Limitations and Risks

**Limitations.** We find several limitations in this work. Firstly, our choice of LLMs is restricted. This is primarily due to computing and budget constraints. We are aware that a more expansive collection of models is necessary for a more comprehensive overview of LLM performance, along with open-source models larger than 8B parameters. Additionally, we prompted both GPT models using batches of data, which impacted performance during initial tests, but did not warrant the high costs of repeating the prompt for each individual instance.

Secondly, the aspect of varying prescriptiveness in prompts was only evaluated on one dataset, STONE. To our knowledge, there are currently no publicly available datasets on TSA in news headlines annotated with detailed guidelines. Furthermore, since the dataset in focus is in Croatian, it is unclear whether a difference in performance is due to the difference in the ability for sentiment analysis or the general understanding of the language and its cultural and political background, both essential for the task.

Finally, while evaluating the effect of prompt prescriptiveness level, the six levels were chosen arbitrarily so that they resemble a logical step-up in detail level. This number and method of prompt generation can differ based on the task at hand and annotation guidelines.

**Risks.** The risks in our work are mostly connected with the risks associated with sentiment analysis. Automatically evaluating sentiment might promote exclusion towards certain entities. As we performed no masking of entities, internal model biases could affect the classification.

## References


Apoorv Agarwal, Vivek Sharma, Geeta Sikka, and Renu Dhir. 2016. Opinion mining of news headlines using SentiWordNet. In *2016 Symposium on Colossal Data Analysis and Networking (CDAN)*, pages 1–5.

Meysam Alizadeh, Maël Kubli, Zeynab Samei, Shirin Dehghani, Juan Diego Bermeo, Maria Korobeynikova, and Fabrizio Gilardi. 2023. Open-source large language models outperform crowd workers and approach chatgpt in text-annotation tasks.

Faheem Aslam, Tahir Mumtaz Awan, Jabir Hussain Syed, Aisha Kashif, and Mahwish Parveen. 2020. Sentiments and emotions evoked by news headlines of coronavirus disease (covid-19) outbreak. *Humanities and Social Sciences Communications*, 7(1).

Alexandra Balahur, Ralf Steinberger, Mijail Kabadjov, Vanni Zavarella, Erik van der Goot, Matina Halkia, Bruno Pouliquen, and Jenya Belyaeva. 2013. Sentiment Analysis in the News. ArXiv:1309.6202 [cs].

Katarzyna Baraniak and Marcin Sydow. 2021. A dataset for Sentiment analysis of Entities in News headlines (SEN). *Procedia Computer Science*, 192:3627–3636.

Ana Barić, Laura Majer, David Dukić, Marijana Grbeša-zenzerović, and Jan Snajder. 2023. Target Two Birds With One SToNe: Entity-Level Sentiment and Tone Analysis in Croatian News Headlines. In *Proceedings of the 9th Workshop on Slavic Natural Language Processing 2023 (SlavicNLP 2023)*, pages 78–85, Dubrovnik, Croatia. Association for Computational Linguistics.

Tom B. Brown, Benjamin Mann, Nick Ryder, Melanie Subbiah, Jared Kaplan, Prafulla Dhariwal, Arvind Neelakantan, Pranav Shyam, Girish Sastry, Amanda Askell, Sandhini Agarwal, Ariel Herbert-Voss, Gretchen Krueger, Tom Henighan, Rewon Child, Aditya Ramesh, Daniel M. Ziegler, Jeffrey Wu, Clemens Winter, Christopher Hesse, Mark Chen, Eric Sigler, Mateusz Litwin, Scott Gray, Benjamin Chess, Jack Clark, Christopher Berner, Sam McCandlish, Alec Radford, Ilya Sutskever, and Dario Amodei. 2020. Language models are few-shot learners.

José Cañete, Gabriel Chaperon, Rodrigo Fuentes, Jou-Hui Ho, Hojin Kang, and Jorge Pérez. 2023. Spanish Pre-trained BERT Model and Evaluation Data. ArXiv:2308.02976 [cs].

Ting-Yun Chang and Robin Jia. 2023. Data curation alone can stabilize in-context learning. In *Proceedings of the 61st Annual Meeting of the Association for Computational Linguistics (Volume 1: Long Papers)*, pages 8123–8144, Toronto, Canada. Association for Computational Linguistics.

Stanislav Chumakov, Anton Kovantsev, and Anatoliy Surikov. 2023. Generative approach to Aspect Based Sentiment Analysis with GPT Language Models. *Procedia Computer Science*, 229:284–293.

Keith Cortis, André Freitas, Tobias Daudert, Manuela Huerlimann, Manel Zarrouk, Siegfried Handschuh, and Brian Davis. 2017. SemEval-2017 Task 5: Fine-Grained Sentiment Analysis on Financial Microblogs and News. In *Proceedings of the 11th International Workshop on Semantic Evaluation (SemEval-2017)*, pages 519–535, Vancouver, Canada. Association for Computational Linguistics.

Sławomir Dadas, Michał Perełkiewicz, and Rafał Poświata. 2020. Pre-training polish transformer-based language models at scale. In *Artificial Intelligence and Soft Computing*, pages 301–314. Springer International Publishing.

Jacob Devlin, Ming-Wei Chang, Kenton Lee, and Kristina Toutanova. 2019. Bert: Pre-training of deep bidirectional transformers for language understanding.

Evan Dufraisse, Adrian Popescu, Julien Tourille, Armelle Brun, and Jerome Deshayes. 2023. MAD-TSC: A Multilingual Aligned News Dataset for Target-dependent Sentiment Classification. In *Proceedings of the 61st Annual Meeting of the Association for Computational Linguistics (Volume 1: Long Papers)*, pages 8286–8305, Toronto, Canada. Association for Computational Linguistics.

Felix Hamborg and Karsten Donnay. 2021. NewsMTSC: A Dataset for (Multi-)Target-dependent Sentiment Classification in Political News Articles. In *Proceedings of the 16th Conference of the European Chapter of the Association for Computational Linguistics: Main Volume*, pages 1663–1675, Online. Association for Computational Linguistics.

Po-Sen Huang, Huan Zhang, Ray Jiang, Robert Stanforth, Johannes Welbl, Jack Rae, Vishal Maini, Dani Yogatama, and Pushmeet Kohli. 2020. Reducing Sentiment Bias in Language Models via Counterfactual Evaluation. ArXiv:1911.03064 [cs].

Kalyani Joshi, Bharathi N, and Jyothi Rao. 2016. Stock trend prediction using news sentiment analysis. *International Journal of Computer Science and Information Technology*, 8:67–76.

Yinhan Liu, Myle Ott, Naman Goyal, Jingfei Du, Mandar Joshi, Danqi Chen, Omer Levy, Mike Lewis, Luke Zettlemoyer, and Veselin Stoyanov. 2019. Roberta: A robustly optimized bert pretraining approach.

Nikola Ljubešić and Davor Lauc. 2021. BERTi\'c – The Transformer Language Model for Bosnian, Croatian, Montenegrin and Serbian. ArXiv:2104.09243 [cs].

Yao Lu, Max Bartolo, Alastair Moore, Sebastian Riedel, and Pontus Stenetorp. 2022. Fantastically ordered prompts and where to find them: Overcoming few-shot prompt order sensitivity.

Moran Mizrahi, Guy Kaplan, Dan Malkin, Rotem Dror, Dafna Shahaf, and Gabriel Stanovsky. 2024. State of what art? a call for multi-prompt llm evaluation.

Aida Mostafazadeh Davani, Mark Díaz, and Vinodkumar Prabhakaran. 2022. Dealing with Disagreements: Looking Beyond the Majority Vote in Subjective Annotations. *Transactions of the Association for Computational Linguistics*, 10:92–110.

M. Melih Mutlu and Arzucan Özgür. 2022. A Dataset and BERT-based Models for Targeted Sentiment Analysis on Turkish Texts. ArXiv:2205.04185 [cs].

László Nemes and Attila Kiss. 2021. Prediction of stock values changes using sentiment analysis of stock news headlines. *Journal of Information and Telecommunication*, 5(3):375–394.

OpenAI, :, Josh Achiam, Steven Adler, Sandhini Agarwal, Lama Ahmad, Ilge Akkaya, Florencia Leoni Aleman, Diogo Almeida, Janko Altenschmidt, Sam Altman, Shyamal Anadkat, Red Avila, Igor Babuschkin, Suchir Balaji, Valerie Balcom, Paul Baltescu, Haiming Bao, Mo Bavarian, Jeff Belgum, Irwan Bello, ..., and Barret Zoph. 2023. Gpt-4 technical report.

Nicholas Pangakis, Samuel Wolken, and Neil Fasching. 2023. Automated annotation with generative AI requires validation. *CoRR*, abs/2306.00176.

Jiaxin Pei, Aixin Sun, and Chenliang Li. 2019. Targeted sentiment analysis: A data-driven categorization.

Matthew Renze and Erhan Guven. 2024. The Effect of Sampling Temperature on Problem Solving in Large Language Models. ArXiv:2402.05201 [cs].

Mauricio Rivera, Jean-François Godbout, Reihaneh Rabbany, and Kellin Pelrine. 2024. Combining Confidence Elicitation and Sample-based Methods for Uncertainty Quantification in Misinformation Mitigation. ArXiv:2401.08694 [cs].

Paul Rottger, Bertie Vidgen, Dirk Hovy, and Janet Pierrehumbert. 2022. Two contrasting data annotation paradigms for subjective NLP tasks. In *Proceedings of the 2022 Conference of the North American Chapter of the Association for Computational Linguistics: Human Language Technologies*, pages 175–190, Seattle, United States. Association for Computational Linguistics.

David Rozado, Ruth Hughes, and Jamin Halberstadt. 2022. Longitudinal analysis of sentiment and emotion in news media headlines using automated labelling with Transformer language models. *PLOS ONE*, 17(10):e0276367.

Tomás Alves Salgueiro, Emilio Recart Zapata, Damián Furman, Juan Manuel Pérez, and Pablo Nicolás Fernández Larrosa. 2022. A spanish dataset for targeted sentiment analysis of political headlines.

Holli Semetko and Patti Valkenburg. 2000. Framing european politics: A content analysis of press and television news. *Journal of Communication*, 50:93 – 109.

Josef Steinberger, Polina Lenkova, Mijail Kabadjov, Ralf Steinberger, and Erik van der Goot. 2011. Multilingual Entity-Centered Sentiment Analysis Evaluated by Parallel Corpora. In *Proceedings of the International Conference Recent Advances in Natural Language Processing 2011*, pages 770–775, Hissar, Bulgaria. Association for Computational Linguistics.

Katherine Tian, Eric Mitchell, Allan Zhou, Archit Sharma, Rafael Rafailov, Huaxiu Yao, Chelsea Finn, and Christopher D. Manning. 2023. Just Ask for Calibration: Strategies for Eliciting Calibrated Confidence Scores from Language Models Fine-Tuned with Human Feedback. ArXiv:2305.14975 [cs].

Shuohang Wang, Yang Liu, Yichong Xu, Chenguang Zhu, and Michael Zeng. 2021. Want to reduce labeling cost? GPT-3 can help. In *Findings of the Association for Computational Linguistics: EMNLP 2021*, pages 4195–4205, Punta Cana, Dominican Republic. Association for Computational Linguistics.

Zhengxuan Wu and Desmond C. Ong. 2021. Context-Guided BERT for Targeted Aspect-Based Sentiment Analysis. *Proceedings of the AAAI Conference on Artificial Intelligence*, 35(16):14094–14102.

Miao Xiong, Zhiyuan Hu, Xinyang Lu, Yifei Li, Jie Fu, Junxian He, and Bryan Hooi. 2023. Can LLMs Express Their Uncertainty? An Empirical Evaluation of Confidence Elicitation in LLMs. ArXiv:2306.13063 [cs].

Huibing Zhang, Junchao Dong, Liang Min, and Peng Bi. 2020. A BERT Fine-tuning Model for Targeted Sentiment Analysis of Chinese Online Course Reviews. *International Journal on Artificial Intelligence Tools*, 29(07n08):2040018.

# A Appendix

## A.1 Additional Information on Datasets

In Table 4 the dataset sizes alongside the respective class counts are shown. For the STONE dataset (Barić et al., 2023) and the Spanish dataset (ES) (Cañete et al., 2023), we used the split for train, validation, and test sets given by the respective authors. For the variations of the SEN dataset, we used a 60/20/20 split generated using the sci-kit learn library with a fixed random seed of 42.

## A.2 Optimization of BERT* Hyperparameters

For the BERT* models, we performed a grid search for hyperparameter optimization. We varied the learning rates, batch sizes, and number of epochs.

| | | STONE | ES | SEN | | |
|---|---|---|---|---|---|---|
| | | | | en_amt | en_r | pl |
| train | all | 1614 | 1371 | 806 | 662 | 688 |
| | pos | 463 | 548 | 163 | 102 | 162 |
| | neutr | 810 | 434 | 314 | 355 | 308 |
| | neg | 341 | 389 | 329 | 205 | 218 |
| valid | all | 231 | 459 | 269 | 220 | 230 |
| | pos | 59 | 173 | 50 | 30 | 55 |
| | neutr | 120 | 167 | 89 | 118 | 101 |
| | neg | 52 | 119 | 130 | 72 | 74 |
| test | all | 462 | 609 | 269 | 220 | 230 |
| | pos | 122 | 241 | 54 | 45 | 50 |
| | neutr | 231 | 166 | 106 | 115 | 99 |
| | neg | 109 | 202 | 109 | 60 | 81 |

Table 4: Dataset sizes and sentiment counts used in experiments.

| | STONE | ES | SEN | | |
|---|---|---|---|---|---|
| | | | en_amt | en_r | pl |
| learning rate | 1e-5 | 1e-5 | 2e-5 | 2e-5 | 3e-5 |
| batch size | 16 | 16 | 16 | 64 | 32 |
| num of epochs | 4 | 5 | 3 | 3 | 5 |

Table 5: Optimal hyperparameters determined for each dataset: for STONE, the results are obtained using the BERTić model; for ES, we used the BETO model; for SEN_en_amt and SEN_en_r, RoBERTa-base is utilized; and for SEN_pl, Polish-RoBERTa-base-v2 is employed.

The grid search covered the following hyperparameter values:

$$\text{learning rate} : \{5\text{e-}5, 3\text{e-}5, 2\text{e-}5, 1\text{e-}5, 5\text{e-}6\}$$
$$\text{batch size} : \{16, 32, 64, 128, 256\}$$
$$\text{number of epochs} : \{1, 2, 3, 4, 5\}$$

The optimal hyperparameters are summarized in Table 5.

### A.3 Additional Information on Models

In our experiments, we employed the following LLMs:

**Neural Chat** [1] (7B): A fine-tuned model based on Mistral[2] with good coverage of domain and language.

**Llama 3 instruct (8B)** [3] : Instruction-tuned models fine-tuned and optimized for dialogue/chat use cases that outperform many of the available open-source chat models on common benchmarks.

**Phi-3 Mini instruct** [4] (3.8B): Phi-3 Mini is a lightweight, state-of-the-art open model by Microsoft[5], trained with a focus on high-quality and reasoning dense properties.

**Gemma** [6] (8.5B): Gemma is a lightweight, state-of-the-art open model built by Google DeepMind.[7]

**GPT-4 Turbo** [8] (560B): Latest generation OpenAI[9] model in time of running our experiments. We used the `gpt-4-1106-preview` model.

**GPT-3.5 Turbo**[10] (175B): Released in 2023, faster and more affordable OpenAI model. We used the `gpt-3.5-turbo-0125` model.

### A.4 Setting the LLM Temperature Hyperparameter

Even though the optimal sampling temperature for problem-solving tasks is 0.0, as it maximizes reproducibility without compromising accuracy, LLMs showed relatively stable problem-solving performance across temperatures from 0.0 to 1.0, regardless of the LLM, prompt-engineering technique, or problem domain (Renze and Guven, 2024). For the purposes of uncertainty quantification and calibration assessment, we opted for a temperature of 0.7, maintaining stable performance while leveraging the stochastic properties of LLMs.

### A.5 Additional Information on GPU Usage

We utilized a total of 201 hours of GPU resources. Specifically, 14 hours were allocated for obtaining results for optimal models and hyperparameters for BERT-based models. Additionally, 38 hours were dedicated to GPT 3.5 Turbo, 76 hours to GPT 4 Turbo, 62 hours to Neural Chat inference, and 11 hours to Mistral. Neural Chat and Mistral were run locally, while the GPT models were executed using the OpenAI Platform [11].

### A.6 Additional Information on Used Toolkits

For tokenizing data to obtain results on BERT-based models, we utilized the PyTorch Transformers library[12].

### A.7 Complete results

In this section, we present the complete results for all levels of prescriptiveness detail across all methods of uncertainty quantification. In Table 6 F1 scores are provided for all models and levels, and in Table 7 ECE is given per level and model. Figure 1 shows it graphically.

[11] https://platform.openai.com/docs/introduction

| | NC | | | GPT 3.5 | | | GPT 4 | | | Llama 3 | | | Gemma | | | Phi-3 | | |
|---|---|---|---|---|---|---|---|---|---|---|---|---|---|---|---|---|---|---|
| | SCS | DP | VCA | SCS | DP | VCA | SCS | DP | VCA | SCS | DP | VCA | SCS | DP | VCA | SCS | DP | VCA |
| 1 | 60.3 | 48.4 | 52.4 | 60.9 | 61.5 | 47.1 | 66.0 | 64.9 | 59.5 | 53.4 | 46.4 | 34.7 | 48.4 | 40.0 | 42.7 | 43.6 | 38.4 | 48.6 |
| 2 | 62.0 | 50.1 | 54.9 | 61.4 | **62.9** | 46.9 | 64.4 | 64.9 | 61.6 | 50.1 | 46.9 | 30.9 | 48.8 | 38.8 | 42.1 | 40.6 | 34.6 | 48.1 |
| 3 | 63.5 | 50.5 | 53.9 | **67.6** | 62.5 | 53.9 | 69.9 | 66.4 | 63.2 | 52.9 | 54.5 | 44.4 | 55.8 | 44.7 | 47.9 | 44.2 | 44.9 | 44.4 |
| 4 | **63.7** | 47.3 | 58.7 | 64.8 | 62.8 | 50.6 | **70.2** | 66.9 | **66.9** | 51.9 | 52.6 | 41.3 | 53.1 | 41.1 | 43.1 | 43.6 | 47.2 | 39.9 |
| 5 | 60.4 | 52.9 | 57.6 | 63.9 | 59.6 | 53.1 | 66.8 | **68.6** | 65.0 | 60.6 | **55.5** | **55.0** | 59.3 | **58.7** | **48.9** | **49.4** | **48.9** | 45.6 |
| 6 | 62.8 | **53.5** | **60.1** | 66.5 | 56.3 | **55.4** | 68.2 | 64.7 | 64.9 | **61.9** | 50.7 | 52.1 | **59.4** | 53.5 | 46.7 | 46.3 | 45.5 | **48.8** |

Table 6: F1 scores for levels of detail in prompt and uncertainty quantification metrics.

| | NC | | | GPT 3.5 | | | GPT 4 | | | Llama 3 | | | Gemma | | | Phi-3 | | |
|---|---|---|---|---|---|---|---|---|---|---|---|---|---|---|---|---|---|---|
| | SCS | DP | VCA | SCS | DP | VCA | SCS | DP | VCA | SCS | DP | VCA | SCS | DP | VCA | SCS | DP | VCA |
| 1 | 13.1 | 6.3 | 15.9 | 11.3 | 6.0 | 16.6 | 11.1 | **8.5** | 10.1 | 15.3 | 15.9 | 32.5 | 17.2 | 20.5 | 31.8 | 17.2 | 18.5 | 27.9 |
| 2 | 12.1 | 5.7 | 15.6 | 10.9 | **5.4** | 16.9 | 11.6 | 9.1 | 10.1 | 16.4 | 15.0 | 32.9 | 17.0 | 21.8 | 31.9 | 17.0 | 19.8 | 26.8 |
| 3 | 11.1 | 6.1 | 15.3 | 9.2 | 10.9 | 15.1 | **10.1** | 9.5 | 10.5 | 15.1 | 15.1 | 31.8 | 14.8 | 20.7 | 31.1 | 14.8 | 15.4 | **24.3** |
| 4 | 10.6 | 8.9 | 14.2 | **5.8** | 7.0 | 15.4 | 10.4 | 9.7 | **9.4** | 15.7 | 13.9 | 31.6 | 15.6 | 20.1 | 31.5 | 15.6 | 13.1 | 27.2 |
| 5 | 11.3 | 7.2 | 13.6 | 9.7 | 7.2 | 16.6 | 10.8 | 9.5 | 11.1 | 13.2 | **13.7** | **30.3** | 13.6 | **11.0** | **27.5** | 13.6 | **9.6** | 25.3 |
| 6 | **9.4** | **5.1** | **12.6** | 10.5 | 9.8 | **14.2** | 10.5 | 10.6 | 10.7 | **12.2** | 14.8 | 31.6 | **13.4** | 15.7 | 27.7 | **13.4** | 12.3 | 26.5 |

Table 7: Expected calibration error (ECE) for levels of detail in prompt and uncertainty quantification metrics.

| | Prompt |
|---|---|
| **System** | You are a helpful assistant who performs targeted sentiment classification in Croatian news headlines. The available sentiment classes are positive, neutral, and negative. For each given headline, identify the targeted sentiment class towards the entity. |
| **User** | Classify targeted sentiment towards entity {*entity*} in the following news headline: {*headline*} |

Table 8: System and user prompt for zero-shot basic TSA on LLMs

# B Prompt Catalogue

## B.1 Prompts for Basic LLM Inference

Prompts for basic zero-shot TSA on LLMs are provided in Table 8. The system prompt establishes the task, and the user prompt provides the headline and target entity of the headline to be evaluated. The system prompt is aligned with Level 1 prescriptiveness in Table 10, and the user prompt corresponds to the Self-consistency Sampling (SCS) method of uncertainty quantification in Table 9.

## B.2 Uncertainty quantification methods

Table 9 provides the user prompts for all the uncertainty quantification methods.

## B.3 Prompts by Prescriptiveness Level

In this section, the complete prompts system and user prompts are given in tables 10, 11, 12, 13 and 14. The yellow highlight shows an expansion in text and information compared to the previous level.

| | Prompt |
|---|---|
| **SCS** | Classify targeted sentiment towards entity {*entity*} in the following news headline: {*headline*} |
| **DP** | Your task is to imagine you are representing 6 different people detecting the targeted sentiment in Croatian news headlines, each following the given guidelines. For a headline and an entity, you need to return detected targeted sentiment for each of the 6 voters.<br>Detect targeted sentiment for entity '*entity*' in headline: '*headline*'. Possible sentiment classes are positive, neutral and negative. Please return the answer in JSON format like:<br>["targeted sentiment 1":"class 1"<br>"targeted sentiment 2":"class 2"<br>"targeted sentiment 3":"class 3"<br>"targeted sentiment 4":"class 4"<br>"targeted sentiment 5":"class 5"<br>"targeted sentiment 6":"class 6"] |
| **VCA** | You are a helpful assistant who performs targeted sentiment classification in Croatian news headlines. Following the given guidelines, please return the confidence for detection of each class.<br>Detect targeted sentiment for entity {*entity*} in headline: {*headline*}. Possible sentiment classes are positive, neutral and negative. Please return the confidence for each class in format like:<br>["confidence positive class", "confidence neutral class" ,"confidence negative class"] |

Table 9: User prompt used for inference on the STONE dataset accross methods for uncertainty quantification.

| Level | Prompt |
|---|---|
| 1 | You are a helpful assistant who performs targeted sentiment classification in Croatian news headlines. The available sentiment classes are positive, neutral, and negative. For each given headline, identify the targeted sentiment class towards the entity. |
| 2 | You are a helpful assistant who performs targeted sentiment classification in Croatian news headlines. Targeted sentiment involves understanding the author's intention to evoke emotion towards a target entity, considering the deliberate choice in conveying news and recognizing that the same information can be presented in various ways, with the understanding that such intentional choices aid in detecting the targeted sentiment. The available sentiment classes are positive, neutral, and negative. For each given headline, identify the targeted sentiment class towards the entity. |
| 3 | You are a helpful assistant who performs targeted sentiment classification in Croatian news headlines. Targeted sentiment is the emotional stance the author aims to convey specifically towards a mentioned entity. It involves interpreting the intention behind the author's choice of language and tone when discussing the target entity. The sentiment is not only influenced by the conveyed information but also by the author's subjective evaluation and emotional coloring of the entity. Actions associated with the entity play a role in determining the sentiment, with negative actions implying a negative quality and, consequently, a negative sentiment. Distinguishing between negative actions and negative occurrences is crucial, as negative occurrences towards the entity don't color the entity. In headlines featuring a quote, the entity authoring the quote is attributed neutral sentiment as they are merely conveying an opinion. The overall goal of the author, whether it be praise or criticism, is considered in cases of headlines with a mix of positive and negative views. In summary, targeted sentiment is the nuanced emotional evaluation directed specifically at a particular entity within the context of news reporting. The available sentiment classes are positive, neutral, and negative. For each given headline, identify the targeted sentiment class towards the entity. |

Table 10: System prompts used for inference on the STONE dataset.

| Level | Prompt |
|---|---|
| 4 | You are a helpful assistant who performs targeted sentiment classification in Croatian news headlines.<br><br>Guidelines for Targeted Sentiment Annotation:<br><br>1. Detecting Sentiment through Author's Intent and News Presentation: Evaluate the intended sentiment towards an entity by analyzing the emotions the author aims to evoke and recognizing that news can be conveyed in multiple ways, with the chosen manner of conveyance serving a purpose and aiding in targeted sentiment detection.<br><br>2. Impact of Entity Actions: Acknowledge that entity actions influence sentiment, with negative actions implying negative quality. However, distinguish between negative actions undertaken by the entity and negative occurrences directed towards the entity that do not inherently portray the entity in a negative light.<br><br>3. Neutrality of Quoting Authors: In headlines featuring quotes, two types of entities are involved: the statement's author and the entities mentioned in the quote. If the target entities in the headline are the authors of the statement, the sentiment towards them typically leans towards neutrality because, in this scenario, they serve as conveyors of an opinion rather than direct subjects of sentiment.<br><br>4. Overall Authorial Goal: Consider the author's overall goal, whether it involves praise or criticism, especially in mixed-view headlines.<br><br>The available sentiment classes are positive, neutral, and negative. For each given headline, identify the targeted sentiment class towards the entity. |
| 5 | You are a helpful assistant who performs targeted sentiment classification in Croatian news headlines.<br><br>Guidelines for Targeted Sentiment Annotation:<br><br>1. Detecting Sentiment through Author's Intent and News Presentation:<br>Evaluate the intended sentiment towards an entity by analyzing the emotions the author aims to evoke and recognizing that news can be conveyed in multiple ways, with the chosen manner of conveyance serving a purpose and aiding in targeted sentiment detection.<br>Examples Illustrating Sentiment towards Entity Solin:<br><br>Headline: 'SRAMOTA USolinuse djeca nemaju gdje liječiti, roditelji očajni'<br>Targeted Sentiment: Negative<br>Explanation: The author criticizes Solin, suggesting a disgraceful situation where children lack medical care, portraying a negative sentiment.<br><br>Headline: 'U Solinu radi samo jedna pedijatrica, roditelji traže hitno rješenje'<br>Targeted Sentiment: Negative<br>Explanation: The negative sentiment persists as the author emphasizes the shortage of pediatricians in Solin, prompting urgent solutions according to parents.<br><br>Headline: 'U Solinu nastupio nedostatak liječničkog kadra'<br>Targeted Sentiment: Neutral<br>Explanation: The sentiment is neutral here as the author focuses on conveying information about the shortage of medical staff without explicitly criticizing the responsible institutions. |

Table 11: System prompts used for inference on the STONE dataset.

| Level | Prompt |
|---|---|
| | 2. Impact of Entity Actions:<br>Recognize that entity actions play a role in shaping sentiment, particularly with negative actions like murder and theft suggesting a negative quality. However, distinguish between negative actions where the entity is the perpetrator and negative occurrences where the entity is the recipient. Acknowledge that in the case of negative occurrences, the entity cannot be held responsible for the consequences but may be in a negative situation as a result, implying neutrality in the assessment.<br>Headlines with negative quality of entities linked to their actions:<br><br>a) Examples of linking entity quality to actions:<br>Headline: 'Bivša tehnološka direktorica Elizabeth Holmes osuđena na 11 godina zatvora'<br>Entity: Elizabeth Holmes<br>Targeted Sentiment: Negative<br>Explanation: Negative sentiment is assigned to Elizabeth Holmes based on her negative actions.<br><br>Headline: 'Zbog ubojstva srpskih civila sudit će se Đuri Brodarcu, bivšem Sanaderovom savjetniku'<br>Entity: Đuro Brodarac<br>Targeted Sentiment: Negative<br>Explanation: Negative sentiment is assigned to Đuro Brodarac due to his association with a serious crime.<br><br>b) Examples of negative occurences towards the entity.<br><br>Headline: 'Potres u Indoneziji: Poginulo najmanje 46 ljudi, ozlijeđenih oko 700'<br>Entity: Indonezija<br>Targeted Sentiment: Neutral<br>Explanation: Neutral sentiment is assigned to Indonesia as the entity is a recipient of a negative occurrence.<br><br>Headline: 'Horor u Mogadišuu: U terorističkom napadu na hotel 10 mrtvih, ozlijeđen i somalijski ministar'<br>Entity: Mogadišu<br>Targeted Sentiment: Neutral<br>Explanation: Similar to the previous example, neutral sentiment is assigned to Mogadishu as it is a recipient of a negative occurrence. |
| 5 | 3. Neutrality of Quoting Authors:<br>Define sentiment towards the entity by considering the author's stance in a statement, whether the author is the headline writer or the individual quoted. When conveying someone's sentiment in a quote, transfer that sentiment to the mentioned entity. In headlines quoting individuals, recognize two entity types: the statement's author and the entities mentioned in the quote. If the target entities in the headline are the authors of the statement, the sentiment is typically neutral since they serve as conveyors of an opinion.<br>Examples of Handling Quotes in Headlines:<br><br>Headline: 'Milanović: Žao mi je što sam podržao Bidena'<br>Entity: Milanović<br>Targeted Sentiment: Neutral<br>Entity: Biden<br>Targeted Sentiment: Negative<br>Explanation: Neutral sentiment is assigned to Milanović, who is conveying an opinion, while negative sentiment is assigned to Biden based on the conveyed sentiment.<br><br>Headline: 'Gotovac: Ako sam ja politički antitalent, onda je tom antitalentu išlo bolje nego Grbinu'<br>Entity: Gotovac<br>Targeted Sentiment: Positive<br>Entity: Grbin<br>Targeted Sentiment: Negative<br>Explanation: Positive sentiment is assigned to Gotovac, who comments on himself, while negative sentiment is assigned to Grbin based on the conveyed sentiment.<br><br>Headline: 'Anka Mrak Taritaš: Tužna sam i razočarana situacijom u Zagrebu. Tomašević ne bi dobio dobru ocjenu'<br>Entity: Anka Mrak Taritaš<br>Targeted Sentiment: Neutral<br>Entity: Tomašević<br>Targeted Sentiment: Negative<br>Explanation: Neutral sentiment is assigned to Anka Mrak Taritaš, the quoted individual, while negative sentiment is assigned to Tomašević based on the conveyed sentiment. |

Table 12: System prompts used for inference on the STONE dataset.

| Level | Prompt |
|---|---|
| 5 | 4. Overall Authorial Goal:<br>Consider the author's overall goal, whether it involves praise or criticism, especially in mixed-view headlines.<br>Example of a Combined Statement (Combination of Positive and Negative Views)<br><br>Headline: 'Vanna je definitivno promijenila stil naglavačke i dosadne kombinacije zamijenila onima koje prate trendove'<br>Entity: Vanna<br>Targeted Sentiment: Positive<br>Explanation: A positive sentiment is attributed to Vanna because the author's intention is to praise the improvement in her style, despite simultaneously criticizing her previous dressing style.<br><br>The available sentiment classes are positive, neutral, and negative. For each given headline, identify the targeted sentiment class towards the entity. |
| 6 | You are a helpful assistant who performs targeted sentiment classification in Croatian news headlines. Here are some guidelines for detecting targeted sentiment in news headlines:<br>To determine sentiment towards an entity, we consider the kind of emotion the statement's author intended to evoke regarding the target entity, that is, how the author intended to "color" that entity. To aid in discerning the intended sentiment towards the entity, one can consider the fact that the same piece of news can always be conveyed in multiple ways. The chosen manner of conveying a piece of news is selected with a purpose, and understanding that intention can be utilized for targeted sentiment detection.<br>An example of various ways of reporting the same news about entity Solin:<br><br>Headline: 'SRAMOTA USolinuse djeca nemaju gdje liječiti, roditelji očajni'<br>Targeted Sentiment: Negative<br>Explanation: Negative sentiment is attributed to Solin due to the author's intention to criticize the institution for the shortage of pediatricians.<br><br>Headline: 'U Solinu radi samo jedna pedijatrica, roditelji traže hitno rješenje'<br>Targeted Sentiment: Negative<br>Explanation: Similar negative sentiment is conveyed towards Solin by criticizing the shortage of medical staff.<br><br>Headline: 'U Solinu nastupio nedostatak liječničkog kadra'<br>Targeted Sentiment: Neutral<br>Explanation: Neutral sentiment is assigned as the author's intention is to convey information without criticizing the responsible institutions.<br><br>When detecting targeted sentiment, we can assign a quality to the target entity as an aid in determining sentiment, based on the emotion the statement's author associates with it. The quality of the entity is linked to the actions of that entity, which can be either negative or positive. Negative actions of the entity, such as murder, theft, and other illegal or socially unacceptable activities like insults, are attributed to the quality of that entity. Negative actions signify a negative quality of the entity, implying a negative sentiment. The same approach will be applied in cases of positive actions of the entity, indicating a positive sentiment towards the entity. It is necessary to distinguish between the negative actions of an entity and negative occurrences towards the entity. In the case of negative actions by the entity, the entity is the perpetrator and therefore responsible for that action. In the case of negative occurrences towards the entity, the entity is the recipient of the negative action and cannot be held responsible for the consequences of the action, although it may be in a negative situation as a result.<br><br>Examples of linking entity quality to actions:<br><br>Headline: 'Bivša tehnološka direktorica Elizabeth Holmes osuđena na 11 godina zatvora'<br>Entity: Elizabeth Holmes<br>Targeted Sentiment: Negative<br>Explanation: Negative sentiment is assigned to Elizabeth Holmes based on her negative actions. |

Table 13: System prompts used for inference on the STONE dataset.

| Level | Prompt |
|---|---|
| | Headline: 'Zbog ubojstva srpskih civila sudit će se Đuri Brodarcu, bivšem Sanaderovom savjetniku'<br>Entity: Đuro Brodarac<br>Targeted Sentiment: Negative<br>Explanation: Negative sentiment is assigned to Đuro Brodarac due to his association with a serious crime.<br><br>Examples of negative occurences towards the entity.<br><br>Headline: 'Potres u Indoneziji: Poginulo najmanje 46 ljudi, ozlijeđenih oko 700'<br>Entity: Indonezija<br>Targeted Sentiment: Neutral<br>Explanation: Neutral sentiment is assigned to Indonesia as the entity is a recipient of a negative occurrence.<br><br>Headline: 'Horor u Mogadišuu: U terorističkom napadu na hotel 10 mrtvih, ozlijeđen i somalijski ministar'<br>Entity: Mogadišu<br>Targeted Sentiment: Neutral<br>Explanation: Similar to the previous example, neutral sentiment is assigned to Mogadishu as it is a recipient of a negative occurrence.<br><br>We define sentiment towards the entity as the author's stance towards the target entity in a statement. The statement's author can be the person who wrote the article headline or the author whose quote is conveyed in the form of the article headline. When conveying someone's negative/positive sentiment in a quote or paraphrase, that sentiment is transferred to the entity. In headlines conveying someone's quote, there are two types of entities - the statement's author and the entities mentioned in the quote. If the target entities in the headline are the authors of the statement, the sentiment towards them will usually be neutral because, in this case, they are just conveyors of an opinion. An exception is the following example with entity Gotovac, where the statement's author comments on himself, and the expressed sentiment is then transferred to the author himself. |
| 6 | Examples of Handling Quotes in Headlines:<br><br>Headline: 'Milanović: Žao mi je što sam podržao Bidena'<br>Entity: Milanović<br>Targeted Sentiment: Neutral<br>Entity: Biden<br>Targeted Sentiment: Negative<br>Explanation: Neutral sentiment is assigned to Milanović, who is conveying an opinion, while negative sentiment is assigned to Biden based on the conveyed sentiment.<br><br>Headline: 'Gotovac: Ako sam ja politički antitalent, onda je tom antitalentu išlo bolje nego Grbinu'<br>Entity: Gotovac<br>Targeted Sentiment: Positive<br>Entity: Grbin<br>Targeted Sentiment: Negative<br>Explanation: Positive sentiment is assigned to Gotovac, who comments on himself, while negative sentiment is assigned to Grbin based on the conveyed sentiment.<br><br>Headline: 'Anka Mrak Taritaš: Tužna sam i razočarana situacijom u Zagrebu. Tomašević ne bi dobio dobru ocjenu'<br>Entity: Anka Mrak Taritaš<br>Targeted Sentiment: Neutral<br>Entity: Tomašević<br>Targeted Sentiment: Negative<br>Explanation: Neutral sentiment is assigned to Anka Mrak Taritaš, the quoted individual, while negative sentiment is assigned to Tomašević based on the conveyed sentiment. |

Table 14: System prompts used for inference on the STONE dataset.

| Level | Prompt |
|---|---|
| 6 | In the case of a headline containing a combination of positive and negative views towards the entity, the final goal of the author towards the entity is considered, i.e., whether the author aimed for praise or criticism.<br><br>Example of a Combined Statement (Combination of Positive and Negative Views):<br><br>Headline: 'Vanna je definitivno promijenila stil naglavačke i dosadne kombinacije zamijenila onima koje prate trendove'<br>Entity: Vanna<br>Targeted Sentiment: Positive<br>Explanation: Positive sentiment is assigned to Vanna as the author's intention is to praise the improvement in her style despite also criticizing her previous dressing choices.<br><br>The available sentiment classes are positive, neutral, and negative. For each given headline, identify the targeted sentiment class towards the entity. |

Table 15: System prompts used for inference on the STONE dataset.

# Context is Important in Depressive Language: A Study of the Interaction Between the Sentiments and Linguistic Markers in Reddit Discussions

**Neha Sharma** and **Kairit Sirts**
Institute of Computer Science, University of Tartu, Estonia
neha.sharma@ut.ee, sirts@ut.ee

## Abstract

Research exploring linguistic markers in individuals with depression has demonstrated that language usage can serve as an indicator of mental health. This study investigates the impact of discussion topic as context on linguistic markers and emotional expression in depression, using a Reddit dataset to explore interaction effects. Contrary to common findings, our sentiment analysis revealed a broader range of emotional intensity in depressed individuals, with both higher negative and positive sentiments than controls. This pattern was driven by posts containing no emotion words, revealing the limitations of the lexicon based approaches in capturing the full emotional context. We observed several interesting results demonstrating the importance of contextual analyses. For instance, the use of 1st person singular pronouns and words related to anger and sadness correlated with increased positive sentiments, whereas a higher rate of present-focused words was associated with more negative sentiments. Our findings highlight the importance of discussion contexts while interpreting the language used in depression, revealing that the emotional intensity and meaning of linguistic markers can vary based on the topic of discussion.

## 1 Introduction

Research on linguistic markers of depression aiming to identify people at risk (De Choudhury et al., 2013; Yates et al., 2017; Coppersmith et al., 2018; Chancellor and De Choudhury, 2020) have found that individuals with depression often use more first-person pronouns and negative emotion words and fewer positive emotion words than healthy controls (Trifu et al., 2017; Savekar et al., 2023; Rude et al., 2004; Chung and Pennebaker, 2007). Despite these consistent findings, their effects are relatively modest, with a recent meta-analysis showing small effect sizes (Pearson $r$ of 0.19 for the first-person pronouns, 0.12 for negative emotion words, and -0.21 for positive emotion words)(Tølbøll, 2019).

Thus far, research has concentrated on identifying the main effects, i.e., the overall significant differences between depression and control groups. Nevertheless, as can be expected, studies have shown that the linguistic markers of the same person can vary depending on the communication context (Mehl et al., 2012).

According to Beck's cognitive model of depression (Beck, 1979; Beck and Alford, 2009), schemas of depressive symptoms develop over time and, when active, shape an individual's perceptions, thoughts, and feelings, which influence the linguistic choices of that person when expressing their thoughts and feelings. It is entirely possible and even likely, especially in the case of mild to moderate depression, that the depressive schemas are variably activated in different contexts. Thus, the schema influence on thoughts and linguistic choices are not the same in every context. Therefore, identifying distinct linguistic markers of depression may greatly rely on the context and the activation of depressive schemas at the moment. In light of these considerations, a more fine-grained analysis focusing on interaction effects is indicated, considering in which linguistic contexts these differences occur more strongly and which linguistic features co-occur consistently.

Only a few studies have explored the contextual effect on language markers for depression. Bernard et al. (2016) found that higher depression levels correlate with increased use of first-person pronouns. However, they noted that the frequent use of negative emotion words is linked more to higher negative affect than to the depression level itself, suggesting that the prevalence of negative emotion words is not depression per se but rather a negative effect on the state, which is presumably more common in individuals with depression than in healthy controls.

Seabrook et al. (2018) and Teodorescu et al. (2023) studied the association between depression and the variability of emotion word rates over time, assuming that people might express different proportions of positive and negative emotion words over time. Both studies found that negative emotion



*Proceedings of the 14th Workshop on Computational Approaches to Subjectivity, Sentiment, & Social Media Analysis*, pages 344–361
August 15, 2024 

variability was positively associated with depression. That means, two people might express the same overall proportion of negative emotion words, but the higher variability over time (e.g., a higher rate of negative emotion words on one occasion and a lower rate on another occasion) predicted higher depressive symptomatology (Seabrook et al., 2018) or the diagnostic status (Teodorescu et al., 2023).

From the computational linguistics point of view, Ireland and Iserman (2018) studied the linguistic markers of anxiety in posts originating from anxiety-related and neutral sub-reddits and found that anxious individuals' word choices differed depending on the sub-reddit. However, we are unaware of any computational linguistics study that has researched the contextual aspects of linguistic markers of depression.

In this paper, we study the linguistic variation that relates contexts to differential affective tones. Our focus is specifically on understanding the features of the so-called "depressive language", i.e., the social science aspect, and not on predicting the diagnostic labels based on textual data, which has been the predominant goal in many previous studies (Guntuku et al., 2017). This approach will help us better understand the varied and context-dependent ways depression influences how people express themselves.

We start with the assumption that the affective quality expressed in texts varies between contexts and thus also necessitates for the authors making different linguistic choices. We operationalize affective tone as sentiment and contexts as different discussion topics, assuming that some topics activate the depressive schemas more than others. To study the interactions, we use simple linear regression analysis to understand which psycholinguistic features, extracted with the LIWC tool (Pennebaker et al., 2015), correlate with the differential affective tones between depressed and control users over different topics as context. For our study, we utilize a Reddit-based dataset containing posts from various subreddits of users with and without self-declared depression diagnosis for clinical and control groups, respectively.

Our study centers on the following key research question:

**RQ:** ***Which psycholinguistic features affect the sentiment differences observed between depression and control groups across various topics?***

To address this RQ effectively, we begin with a preliminary analysis to lay the groundwork for a deeper inquiry, i.e., ***Are there differences between depression and control groups regarding the topics discussed and sentiments expressed within our dataset?***

Based on prior research, we expected that individuals with depression will exhibit more negative sentiment and less positive sentiment (Rude et al., 2004; Savekar et al., 2023). Our analysis showed that the posts of people from the depression group showed more negative sentiment. However, contrary to our expectations, we found that the depression group also had more posts with positive sentiment. We then followed up with the analyses investigating the RQ. We found that although overall, the depression group used more negative emotion words than the control group, in the contextual analyses, the usage of anger- and sadness-related words were significantly related to the overall positive sentiment of the posts. A small-scale qualitative analysis suggested that posts containing mixed emotions (i.e., references to both positive and negative aspects) might play a role in this correlation. We conclude the paper with some further analyses investigating this direction.

## 2 Method

### 2.1 Data

| | Depression | Control | Total |
|---|---|---|---|
| #users | 1316 | 1316 | 2632 |
| Total #posts | 195.2K | 364.4K | 559.6K |
| Avg #posts per user (std) | 148 (78) | 277 (146) | 213 (133) |
| Avg #words per post (std) | 35 (38) | 25 (30) | 28 (33) |

Table 1: Statistics of the balanced depression dataset.

We used an existing Reddit-based data set comprising posts from users with self-reported mental health diagnoses (SMHD) (Cohan et al., 2018). Each diagnosed user is matched with nine control users on average. The data set covers nine mental health diagnoses, including depression. For this study, we used the depression part only involving 1316 users with the self-reported depression diagnosis. We randomly sampled an equivalent number of 1316 control users to create a balanced data set. Additionally, we filtered out all posts containing less than three or more than 200 words. Table 1 shows the statistics of the study dataset. More details about the underlying SMHD dataset can be found in Appendix A.

### 2.2 Sentiment Analysis

We evaluated two sentiment models for applicability to our dataset: a RoBERTa-based model, trained on Twitter (Barbieri et al., 2020), and the lexicon-based VADER (Hutto and Gilbert, 2014). On comparing both models on a set of manually annotated 200 posts randomly drawn from our dataset, we found that although VADER demonstrated slightly higher accuracy (0.69) than RoBERTa (0.66), it more often confused posts with positive and negative sentiments. Therefore, we chose the RoBERTa-based model for subsequent analyses. For more details of the comparative analysis, refer to the Appendix B.

### 2.3 Topic Modeling

BERTopic (Grootendorst, 2022) leverages the power of transformer-based language models to capture the contextual information and meaning of words in each document. We used the default topic model setting for our purpose, as according to the BERTopic documentation,[1] the default model works quite well for most use cases. More than 5000 topics were initially derived from the model, with about 50% of the data classified as outliers (documents not fitting any topic, labeled as -1). Utilizing the "reduced outlier" function, which leverages the c-TF-IDF strategy and cosine similarity, the proportion of outliers was reduced to 0.25%. Additionally, the "automatic topic reduction" function was applied to reduce the number of topics, resulting in 4187 topics.

### 2.4 LIWC Analysis

LIWC (Linguistic Inquiry and Word Count) is a lexicon-based tool that analyzes texts by mapping words to psycho-linguistic attributes, resulting in the proportion of words in various categories. These categories include Summary Variables, Linguistic Dimensions, Psychological Processes, and more, detailed in (Pennebaker et al., 2015) and Appendix D. Among the 110 LIWC attributes, we selected 63 attributes relevant to our research objectives that were not highly correlated to each other to avoid multicollinearity in the subsequent linear regression analysis. We assessed the correlations using Pearson's correlation coefficient with a threshold of 0.5. Appendix D shows the list of selected attributes.

#### 2.4.1 User-based LIWC Analysis

Because our data is a balanced and length-restricted subset of the SMHD depression dataset, we first analyze the difference in LIWC attributes between the depression and control groups and compare our results to those reported by Cohan et al. (2018). Similarly to the cited study, the group means are aggregated over users, i.e., for computing the feature values for a single user, all their posts were first concatenated. Similarly, we performed Welch's t-test (Welch, 1947) with adjusted p-value using Bonferroni correction. For effect size assessment, we calculated Cohen's d statistics (Cohen, 1987).

#### 2.4.2 Topic-Specific LIWC Analysis

In the main analysis of the paper, we wanted to understand which LIWC attributes affect the sentiments expressed in relation to various topics. Moreover, we wanted to capture the sentiment differences between depression and control groups. For that, we employed linear regression analysis with the features derived from LIWC attributes as independent variables and an overall sentiment polarity difference between groups as the dependent variable.

**The dependent variable,** i.e., the sentiment difference between depression and control groups per topic, is calculated as the net sentiment score difference denoted as $y = (pos - neg)_{\text{depression}} - (pos - neg)_{\text{control}}$ (see Table 2 for some examples), where pos and neg columns show the percentage of positive and negative sentiments per topic and group, respectively. For instance, in Topic 0 (Animals), for the depression group, 28.0% of posts are labeled as positive, whereas 26.0% have a negative sentiment. The net difference is 2%, showing that overall, the depression group has slightly more positive sentiment towards that topic. In contrast, for the control group, the net difference is $19.1\% - 23.9\% = -4.8\%$, showing that over-

| Topics | Depression | | Control | | Sent diff |
|---|---|---|---|---|---|
| | pos | neg | pos | neg | y |
| 0 Animals | 28.0 | 26.0 | 19.1 | 23.9 | 6.8 |
| 1 Relationships | 14.4 | 46.4 | 13.4 | 31.3 | -14.1 |
| 2 US elections | 20.2 | 18.5 | 16.8 | 73.4 | -5.0 |

Table 2: Dependent variable calculation.

[1] https://maartengr.github.io/BERTopic/index.html

all, the control group has more negative sentiment towards that topic. Subtracting these differences $y = 2 - (-4.8) = 6.8$ yields an outcome value capturing the overall difference between depression and control groups towards that topic. Positive difference refers to more positive sentiment in the depression group posts, while negative value means more positive sentiment in the control group posts. Values close to zero indicate the similarity of positive and negative sentiment proportions in both depression and control groups.

**Independent features** were computed in two steps. First, we calculated mean aggregated LIWC attribute scores for both groups topic-wise. For instance, consider Topic 0 (Animals) and the Analytic feature (see Table 3). For the depression group, the average score of that attribute for Topic 0 is 43.0, while for the control group it is 49.7. Subsequently, we calculated the difference between these scores, i.e., $f_{\text{Analytic}} = 43.0 - 49.7 = -6.7$. Positive feature values refer to higher proportion of the attribute value in the depression group, while negative feature values mean that control group had more of that attribute. Independent features were computed this way for all topics and 63 selected attributes, resulting in a size $4187 \times 63$ (topics $\times$ attributes) matrix. This dataset was used to fit the linear regression model using the ordinary least squares method.

| Topics | Analytic | | | Clout | | |
|---|---|---|---|---|---|---|
| | Dep | Ctr | $f_A$ | Dep | Ctr | $f_C$ |
| 0 Animals | 43.0 | 49.7 | -6.7 | 47.3 | 49.6 | -2.3 |
| 1 Relationships | 25.5 | 26.5 | -1.0 | 59.3 | 62.3 | -3.0 |
| 2 US elections | 48.8 | 57.2 | -8.4 | 32.4 | 34.2 | -1.8 |

Table 3: Independent feature calculation for the regression analysis (Dep = Depression group, Ctr = Control group, $f_A = f_{\text{Analytic}}$ ,$f_C = f_{\text{Clout}}$).

# 3 Results

## 3.1 User-based LIWC analysis

The analysis, shown in Table 4, revealed more significant differences and larger effect sizes between the groups than those reported by Cohan et al. (2018). This discrepancy may arise firstly because we only tested 63 pre-selected, uncorrelated attributes, which makes the adjusted p-value threshold higher than it would be with the full attribute set used by Cohan et al. (2018). Secondly, although

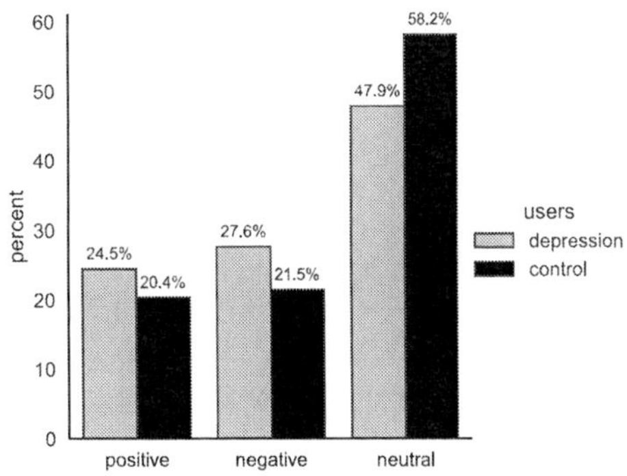


Figure 1: Sentiment distribution of both groups.

Cohan et al. (2018) does not report means and standard deviations, we expect the standard deviations to be smaller in our subset due to restrictions on the post length, which affects both the attribute significance and the magnitude of the effect sizes.

Most attributes that showed statistical significance in both studies (13 out of 14) had consistent effect sizes, except for the present focus. While Cohan et al. (2018) found a small positive effect size, indicating a higher proportion of present-focused words in the depression group, our subsample showed a negative effect size, aligning with studies suggesting that individuals with depression are generally less present-focused (Nolen-Hoeksema et al., 2008; Rodriguez et al., 2010). Thus, our random subsample appears to be representative of the whole depression part of the SMHD data.

## 3.2 Sentiment Analysis

As shown in Figure 1, the depression group exhibits more negative sentiments (6%) and, unexpectedly, more positive sentiments (4%) than the control group. This variation in sentiment distribution is statistically supported by the Chi-square test ($\chi^2(2) = 5503.79, p < 0.001$). This suggests that the users with depression not only express more negative emotionality but display an overall higher emotionality in their posts.

## 3.3 Topic Modeling

Topic modeling resulted in 4187 topics discussed by both groups, of which 13 low-frequency topics were unique to one group only. These topics and their posts were removed from the data, resulting in 4174 topics. We analyzed the frequency and sentiment distribution of these topics among the user groups. Despite the general common topic discussions, noticeable differences in topic preva-

| LIWC Attributes | Depression mean | Depression std | Control mean | Control std | p-value | Cohen's d this study | Cohen's d Cohan et al. (2018) |
|---|---|---|---|---|---|---|---|
| Word Count | 36.1 | 14.5 | 24.6 | 10.9 | *** | 0.90 | N/S |
| Analytic | 42.4 | 9.9 | 48.8 | 10.0 | *** | −0.63 | N/S |
| Clout | 37.5 | 10.8 | 40.6 | 9.7 | *** | −0.30 | -0.06 |
| Authentic | 56.0 | 9.7 | 49.6 | 9.7 | *** | 0.65 | 0.2 |
| 1st person singular | 6.1 | 1.8 | 4.7 | 1.8 | *** | 0.77 | 0.23 |
| 3rd person singular | 1.2 | 0.9 | 1.0 | 0.7 | *** | 0.29 | 0.09 |
| Impersonal pronouns | 5.8 | 0.9 | 5.5 | 1.2 | *** | 0.22 | 0.06 |
| Insight | 2.8 | 0.7 | 2.4 | 0.7 | *** | 0.49 | 0.09 |
| Causation | 1.7 | 0.4 | 1.6 | 0.5 | ** | 0.15 | N/S |
| Tentative | 3.1 | 0.7 | 2.9 | 0.8 | *** | 0.28 | 0.07 |
| Certitude | 0.9 | 0.3 | 0.8 | 0.3 | *** | 0.34 | N/S |
| Differentiation | 3.7 | 0.7 | 3.6 | 0.9 | *** | 0.19 | 0.08 |
| Negative emotion | 0.7 | 0.3 | 0.5 | 0.3 | *** | 0.65 | N/S |
| Anxiety | 0.1 | 0.1 | 0.1 | 0.1 | *** | 0.60 | 0.07 |
| Anger | 0.2 | 0.1 | 0.1 | 0.1 | ** | 0.16 | N/S |
| Sadness | 0.1 | 0.1 | 0.1 | 0.1 | *** | 0.44 | N/S |
| Swear words | 0.4 | 0.4 | 0.6 | 0.7 | *** | −0.24 | N/S |
| Social behavior | 3.7 | 0.9 | 3.5 | 0.9 | *** | 0.26 | N/S |
| Interpersonal | 0.3 | 0.2 | 0.3 | 0.2 | * | −0.15 | N/S |
| Communication | 1.7 | 0.6 | 1.5 | 0.6 | *** | 0.37 | N/S |
| Family | 0.4 | 0.4 | 0.2 | 0.3 | *** | 0.40 | 0.06 |
| Friends | 0.2 | 0.2 | 0.2 | 0.2 | *** | 0.25 | N/S |
| Female references | 0.8 | 0.7 | 0.5 | 0.6 | *** | 0.45 | 0.13 |
| Culture | 0.7 | 0.5 | 0.9 | 0.9 | *** | −0.35 | N/S |
| Lifestyle | 3.0 | 1.0 | 3.3 | 1.2 | *** | −0.27 | N/S |
| Illness | 0.2 | 0.2 | 0.1 | 0.1 | *** | 0.54 | N/S |
| Wellness | 0.1 | 0.1 | 0.1 | 0.1 | *** | 0.26 | N/S |
| Mental health | 0.1 | 0.1 | 0.02 | 0.07 | *** | 0.50 | N/S |
| Substances | 0.1 | 0.2 | 0.1 | 0.1 | *** | 0.21 | N/S |
| Want | 0.4 | 0.2 | 0.3 | 0.2 | *** | 0.29 | N/S |
| Fatigue | 0.04 | 0.05 | 0.03 | 0.07 | * | 0.15 | N/S |
| Reward | 0.1 | 0.1 | 0.2 | 0.2 | *** | −0.28 | N/S |
| Risk | 0.3 | 0.1 | 0.2 | 0.1 | *** | 0.25 | N/S |
| Perception | 8.3 | 1.2 | 8.5 | 1.6 | ** | −0.16 | N/S |
| Feeling | 0.5 | 0.3 | 0.4 | 0.3 | *** | 0.42 | N/S |
| Past focus | 3.6 | 1.0 | 3.2 | 1.0 | *** | 0.41 | 0.08 |
| Present focus | 3.9 | 0.8 | 4.1 | 1.0 | *** | −0.27 | 0.09 |
| Conversational | 1.0 | 0.6 | 1.3 | 0.9 | *** | −0.38 | N/S |

Table 4: Difference between psycholinguistic LIWC attributes between depression and control groups. Only statistically significant attributes are shown. Adjusted p-value thresholds for multiple comparisons is 0.00079 and denoted as * < 0.00079, ** < 0.00015, *** < 0.000015, equivalent to * < 0.05, ** < 0.01, *** < 0.001. The table includes effect sizes (Cohen's d) for both this study and Cohan et al. (2018), with 'N/S' indicating no statistical difference found in the latter study.

lence and sentiment patterns emerged between the depression and control groups. While the detailed examination of topic modeling outputs is not the central focus of our research, as its purpose is to segment the data into contexts for further analyses, the differences in topic distributions and sentiment distributions in topics between groups might be interesting in their own right. We provide some further analyses in Appendix C.

### 3.4 Topic-Specific LIWC Analysis

Using a linear regression model with 63 LIWC attributes as predictors, we assessed the sentiment differences outlined in Section 2.4.2. The model accounted for 26.6% of the variability in sentiment difference, $R^2 = 0.266, F(63, 4110) = 23.63, p < 0.001$, with 25 attributes being statistically significant ($p = 0.05$). Figure 2 illustrates the impact of the significant attributes on the sentiment difference outcome variable. Recall that positive attribute values refer to the depression group expressing more of that attribute in a topic. Thus, positive model weights indicate these features are associated with higher positive sentiment in the depression group posts across topics. Complete results are in Appendix E.

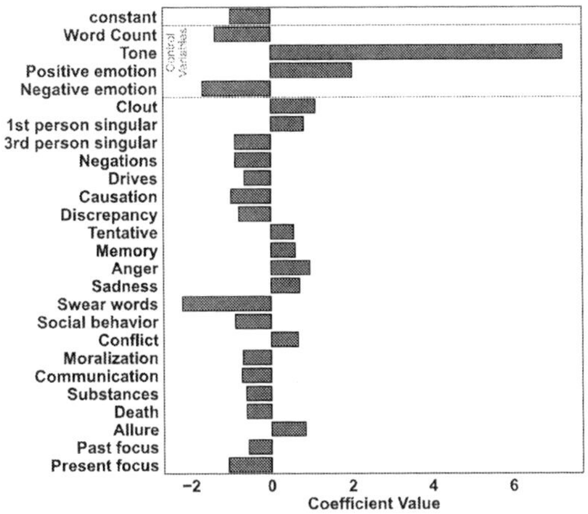


Figure 2: The linear regression model coefficients of the statistically significant features and their impact on the sentiment difference.

The bias term was significant, and its negative value shows that overall, the sentiment of the depression group tends to be more negative than that of the control group. Control variables such as word count, tone, and positive and negative emotions showed expected correlations with sentiment values. The average post length in our data was longer for the depression group compared to the control group (see Table 1). The negative coefficient shows that higher positive sentiment for the depression group is associated with shorter posts than the control group. The positive and negative emotion features are expected to be closely correlated to the positive and negative sentiment values. The coefficients of these features are in the expected direction. Finally, the tone feature, which includes both positive and negative tone, has the largest absolute coefficient and a positive weight, having the largest impact on the outcome variable.

A higher proportion of first-person singular pronouns is related to a higher positive sentiment, and a higher proportion of third-person singular pronouns is related to a higher negative sentiment. Time orientation features, such as past focus and present focus, have negative coefficients, meaning that a higher proportion of words in those categories are related to a higher negative sentiment. There are some features that, with their negative weight, are perhaps quite expectedly related to a higher negative sentiment: swear words, moralization, substances, and death. In contrast, more conflict-related words are associated with higher positive sentiment.

Finally, we highlight the two remaining emotion-related features: anger and sadness. These features have positive weights, correlating with more positive sentiment. In contrast to other findings mentioned above, these results are surprising, as anger and sadness as instances of negative emotions are expected to be more correlated with overall negative sentiment. In the next section, we will attempt to understand these findings.

## 4 Anger and Sadness

In the previous section, we found that the use of anger- and sadness-related words, typically seen as negative emotion words, correlates with positive sentiment. In order to get some idea of the observed phenomenon, we reviewed some of the posts with positive sentiments that contained anger- and sadness-related words. Examples 1–3 shown in Table 5 suggest that these posts express what might be called *mixed emotions*, i.e., containing a mixed usage of positive and negative emotion words. Building on this observation, we designed two analyses to study 1) if posts with mixed emotions could be responsible for overall higher positive sentiments observed for the depression group, and 2) if posts with mixed emotions might significantly contribute to the observed positive relationship between the anger- and sadness-related feature and positive sentiment.

**Mixed Emotions:** First, we need to operationalize what it means for a post to display mixed emotions. We define posts with mixed emotions as those that contain both positive and negative emotion words, i.e., the LIWC attribute of both positive and negative emotions is greater than zero. We aimed to examine the role of mixed emotion posts in our findings by comparing subsets of data both with and without mixed emotions. Given the possible combination of emotion words, we further categorized the data into four segments rather than with or without mixed emotions, which are: Mixed Emotions (both positive and negative emotion words, 3.6% of the total posts), Positive Emotions (only positive emotion words, 15.9%), Negative Emotions (only negative words, 8.7%), and Neutral Emotions (neither positive nor negative words, 71.8%).

**Sentiment Distribution:** First, we looked at the differences in sentiment proportions between depression and control groups in each of those data

| No | Topic | Post text | Sentiment | Attribute |
|---|---|---|---|---|
| 1 | Art | I truly admire and appreciate the art; it's impressive. Yet, it's also causing me a great deal of frustration. It's amazing, though. | Positive | Anger |
| 2 | Empathy | In times of sadness, we seek understanding and compassion. It's music that has the power to uplift our spirits. | Positive | Sadness |
| 3 | Albums | My all-time favorite musical work is the second symphony. It deeply saddens me. | Positive | Sadness |
| 4 | Animals | Whenever I'm feeling low, a walk with my dog always helps. He invariably does something silly or amusing during our walk, which never fails to lift my spirits. | Positive | 1st person pronoun |
| 5 | Gym | Previously, I relied on gym buddies, but their absence meant I stopped too. Now, I've taken control—working out alone, focusing on my diet, and tracking my progress. Sometimes friends join, but mostly, it's just me. This self-reliance has led to sustained success for the first time. My motivation and achievements are my own, though I welcome occasional companionship and encouragement. This self-empowered approach has transformed into my lifestyle, leaving no room for excuses, for myself or others. | Positive | 1st person pronoun |
| 6 | Family | My father left when I was a child, leaving me confused about his reasons. Over time, living with my mother helped me understand his choice, though being with her has been challenging. I wish he hadn't left on my birthday. Despite this, we've reconnected and improved our relationship. | Negative | Past focus |
| 7 | Emotions | Do you ever worry that just as life gets better, something bad will happen? This fear of sudden, negative changes when things are going well makes me hesitant to fully invest myself. How do you deal with this anxiety? | Negative | Present focus |

Table 5: Posts of depressed users with sentiment label and relative language attributes and associated topics. All posts have been rephrased to maintain the privacy of users.

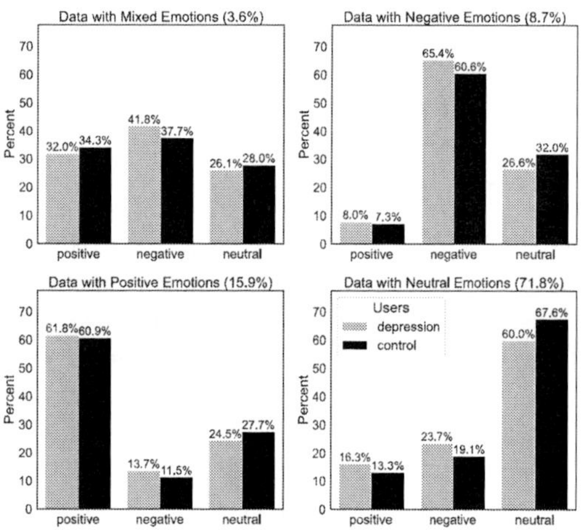


Figure 3: Sentiment distribution across data splits.

splits (shown in Figure 3). As expected, negative sentiments dominate in Negative Emotions split, positive sentiments in Positive Emotions split, and neutral sentiment in Neutral Emotions split. Mixed Emotions data shows an almost uniform distribution over sentiments. When looking at group differences in the positive sentiment, the proportion is similar in both groups in both the Mixed Emotions, Positive Emotions and Negative Emotions split, while in the Neutral Emotions group the depression group has more positive sentiment. Because the Neutral split is the biggest (72%), we conclude that this split, instead of the Mixed Emotions as we expected, drives the overall sentiment pattern observed in Figure 1. This analysis highlights an important limitation of lexicon-based systems, which struggle to grasp the overall context and sentiment in the absence of polarized emotional words. While the RoBERTa-based sentiment model is not perfect, it can capture emotional tone that is concealed from the lexicon-based LIWC system.

**Anger and Sadness in Mixed Emotions:** Next, we explored if mixed emotion posts might be related to positive correlations between anger and sadness features and the positive sentiment as found in Section 3.4. Figure 4 plots the median anger and sadness scores for the overall data, Mixed Emotions split and the Negative Emotions split.[2] Both anger and sadness scores were highest in the Negative Emotions split and lowest in the Mixed Emotions split across all sentiments. However, the overall pattern of median anger and sadness scores in Mixed Emotions split differs from other splits. In contrast to other slits, both the median anger and sadness scores are *highest* in

[2]Positive and Neutral Emotions splits are omitted as by definition they do not exhibit any negative emotion words.

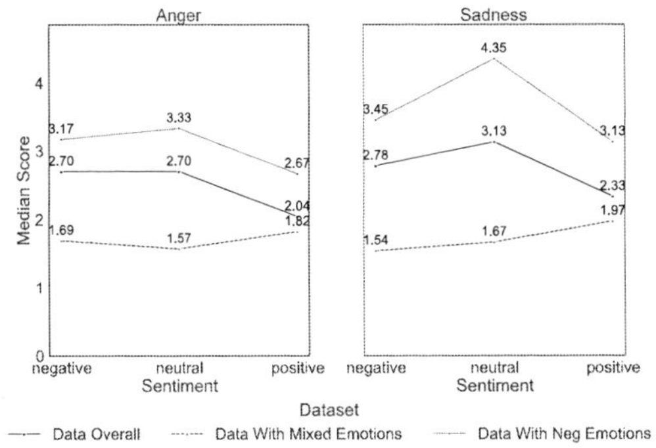


Figure 4: Median anger and sadness scores across data splits.

positive sentiment posts.

## 5 Discussion

This study aimed to investigate the relationship between (psycho)linguistic features and affective tone across contexts operationalized as topics in depressed and non-depressed reddit users. Overall sentiment analysis revealed that the depression group expressed more negative sentiment, aligning with prior studies (Liu et al., 2022), yet also more positive sentiment, which was unexpected. In further analyses that split the data into four subsections regarding the presence or absence of positive or negative emotion words, we found that the so-called neutral posts containing neither positive nor negative emotion words according to LIWC were driving this pattern. This finding highlighting the constraints of the lexicon-based systems, which fail to capture the full emotional context in absence of explicit emotional words.

A higher proportion of first-person singular pronouns was related to a higher positive sentiment, contrasting with previous research linking it to negative emotionality (Tackman et al., 2019; Bernard et al., 2016). However, another study Brockmeyer et al. (2015) found that for people with depression, the higher usage of first-person singular pronouns was related to texts elicited in the positive memory recall task but not in the negative memory recall task. Thus, although the majority of studies (Lyons et al., 2018; Rude et al., 2004; Stirman and Pennebaker, 2001; De Choudhury et al., 2013; Savekar et al., 2023; Trifu et al., 2017; Chung and Pennebaker, 2007) (including this one) have found the overall higher usage of first-person pronouns by individuals with depression, the interaction studies considering either affective, topical, or other contexts might show a different and more interesting picture, the analysis of which could be a topic of future studies. Examples 4 and 5 in Table 5 provide illustration; despite the self-referential nature of the language, the sentiments expressed in these posts are notably positive.

In the main effect LIWC analyses, the depression group displayed more past-focused language and less present-focused language, similar to previous works (Trifu et al., 2017; Smirnova et al., 2013; Imbault and Kuperman, 2018). At the same time, in linear regression analyses, both past-focused and present-focused features were negatively associated with the positive sentiment difference. As an illustration, in the Example 6 in Table 5, the user expresses negative affect in relation to past experiences. In contrast, in Example 7, the user conveys a current state of worry, leading to negative sentiments about present circumstances, demonstrating that in certain contexts, present focus might be an indication for depressive language.

Finally, we observed a significantly higher use of negative emotional words in the depression group, including anxiety-, anger- and sadness-related words, which is in line with previous studies (Trifu et al., 2017; Savekar et al., 2023; Rude et al., 2004; Chung and Pennebaker, 2007). In the linear regression analysis, although the association between the negative emotion words and the sentiment difference were, similarly to the main effect, negative, the correlations between the sentiment difference and the anger and sadness features were positive, i.e., the higher rate of anger and sadness words were related to more positive sentiment. Qualitative analysis of positive sentiment posts with non-zero anger or sadness scores revealed a pattern of mixed emotions, i.e., texts containing features of both positivity and negativity, such as starting by describing something negative, but ending in a positive note. When exploring the potential role of mixed emotions in this relation, we found that in contrast to other types of posts, the posts with mixed emotions have the highest anger and sadness scores in posts with positive sentiment. While this result does not provide definitive evidence for the role of mixed emotions in the observed positive correlations between anger and sadness features and positive sentiment, it shows that posts with mixed emotions behave differently from other posts containing negative emotion words and thus can play a different role in the depressive language.

## 6 Conclusion

In conclusion, our research highlights the important role of discussion context in shaping emotional expressions among individuals with (but also without) depression. Contrary to prior studies, we observed not only more negative sentiments but also more positive sentiments within the depression group—a pattern that was not captured by the LIWC, illustrating the limitations accurately interpreting emotions in the absence of explicit emotional words. Analyses also revealed notable interactions between linguistic markers—such as anger and sadness—and positive sentiments, suggesting a potentially important role of posts with mixed emotions. In summary, our findings support the notion that the research in linguistic markers of depression requires going beyond studying main effects and necessitates a contextual and multifaceted approach.

## Limitations

There are several limitations to consider in our study. Firstly, the validity of the sentiment analysis model cannot be ensured because although the model is trained on social media data (Twitter), our data comprises Reddit posts, which, even with the length restriction imposed on our subsample, are, on average, considerably longer than tweets. We assessed the model's performance by manually annotating a random subset of 200 posts and found that the disagreements stemmed mostly from the model's tendency to categorize positive and negative posts as neutral. Thus, it is likely that the amount of posts with positive and negative sentiments is somewhat underestimated.

Two key limitations concern the SMHD dataset utilized. Firstly, the dataset spans from 2006 to 2017. It is important to acknowledge that the presence and severity of depression may vary over time for individuals (Harrigian and Dredze, 2022). There is a possibility that some users labeled as depressed did not have depression during the entire timeline, and such temporal uncertainty may impact the interpretation of results. Second, the control group is auxiliary (Ernala et al., 2019), i.e., although the control group was selected from non-mental health-related sub-Reddits, there is no way to be sure if controls are actually controls or if there are users in the control group who might be on the spectrum with any mental health disorders.

The LIWC tool, despite its widespread use, faces limitations due to its lexicon-based approach particularly with contextual nuances. An example includes incorrectly assigning a high anger emotion score to a statement like "Rita Madder is freaking great" because of the word "Madder," despite no anger being expressed. Our findings further validate this limitation, as neutral emotion settings revealed a significant difference in positive sentiment distributions among groups, highlighting the inadequacy of lexicon-based systems in capturing the true sentiment context.

Additionally, our regression analysis explains only 26% of the variance of the sentiment difference, indicating that unaccounted factors might influence the observed patterns in language and sentiments. This limitation could partly stem from LIWC's challenges in capturing context. Moreover, our findings are derived from a dataset specifically concerning depression, limiting the generalizability of our conclusions to broader populations and contexts. Further research with diverse datasets is necessary to apply these results more universally.

## Ethical Considerations

In our study, we analyzed the language of the social media posts of both depressed and non-depressed users. We used the existing SMHD dataset (Cohan et al., 2018) that we obtained from its creators by signing a user agreement; we have adhered to the terms and conditions outlined in this agreement when conducting this study. In our work, we search for general patterns and do not make predictions or draw conclusions about any particular user in the dataset. Also, we believe that our findings are interesting for the social science sphere, however, we believe that they will not be directly useful for drawing conclusions about users posting in social media.

## Data and Code Availability Statement

In the interest of fostering transparency and reproducibility, the source code supporting the findings of this study is publicly available. The code repository, which includes the scripts and any additional documentation necessary for replicating the analyses and results presented in this paper, can be accessed at the following GitHub link.[3]. For access to the data itself, please contact the authors of Cohan et al. (2018).

[3]https://github.com/nehasharma666/Depression

## Acknowledgement

This research was supported by the Estonian Research Council Grant PSG721.

## References

Francesco Barbieri, Jose Camacho-Collados, Luis Espinosa Anke, and Leonardo Neves. 2020. TweetEval: Unified benchmark and comparative evaluation for tweet classification. In *Findings of the Association for Computational Linguistics: EMNLP 2020*, pages 1644–1650, Online. Association for Computational Linguistics.

Aaron T. Beck. 1979. *Cognitive therapy of depression*. Guilford press.

Aaron T. Beck and Brad A. Alford. 2009. *Depression: Causes and treatment*. University of Pennsylvania Press.

Jared D. Bernard, Jenna L. Baddeley, Benjamin F. Rodriguez, and Philip A. Burke. 2016. Depression, language, and affect: an examination of the influence of baseline depression and affect induction on language. *Journal of Language and Social Psychology*, 35(3):317–326.

Timo Brockmeyer, Johannes Zimmermann, Dominika Kulessa, Martin Hautzinger, Hinrich Bents, Hans-Christoph Friederich, Wolfgang Herzog, and Matthias Backenstrass. 2015. Me, myself, and I: self-referent word use as an indicator of self-focused attention in relation to depression and anxiety. *Frontiers in psychology*, 6:1564.

Stevie Chancellor and Munmun De Choudhury. 2020. Methods in predictive techniques for mental health status on social media: a critical review. *NPJ digital medicine*, 3(1):43.

Cindy Chung and James Pennebaker. 2007. The psychological functions of function words. In *Social communication*, pages 343–359. Psychology Press.

Arman Cohan, Bart Desmet, Andrew Yates, Luca Soldaini, Sean MacAvaney, and Nazli Goharian. 2018. SMHD: a Large-Scale Resource for Exploring Online Language Usage for Multiple Mental Health Conditions. In *Proceedings of the 27th International Conference on Computational Linguistics*, pages 1485–1497.

Jacob Cohen. 1987. Statistical power analysis for the behavioral sciences (revised edition). *Laurence Erlbaum Associates: Hillsdale, NJ, USA*.

Glen Coppersmith, Ryan Leary, Patrick Crutchley, and Alex Fine. 2018. Natural language processing of social media as screening for suicide risk. *Biomedical informatics insights*, 10.

Munmun De Choudhury, Michael Gamon, Scott Counts, and Eric Horvitz. 2013. Predicting depression via social media. In *Proceedings of the international AAAI conference on web and social media*, 1, pages 128–137.

Sindhu Kiranmai Ernala, Michael L. Birnbaum, Kristin A. Candan, Asra F. Rizvi, William A. Sterling, John M. Kane, and Munmun De Choudhury. 2019. Methodological gaps in predicting mental health states from social media: Triangulating diagnostic signals. In *Proceedings of the 2019 CHI conference on human factors in computing systems*, pages 1–16.

Maarten R. Grootendorst. 2022. BERTopic: Neural topic modeling with a class-based TF-IDF procedure. *ArXiv*, abs/2203.05794.

Sharath Chandra Guntuku, David B. Yaden, Margaret L. Kern, Lyle H. Ungar, and Johannes C. Eichstaedt. 2017. Detecting depression and mental illness on social media: an integrative review. *Current Opinion in Behavioral Sciences*, 18:43–49.

Keith Harrigian and Mark Dredze. 2022. Then and now: Quantifying the longitudinal validity of self-disclosed depression diagnoses. In *Proceedings of the Eighth Workshop on Computational Linguistics and Clinical Psychology*, pages 59–75.

Clayton Hutto and Eric Gilbert. 2014. Vader: A parsimonious rule-based model for sentiment analysis of social media text. In *Proceedings of the international AAAI conference on web and social media*, 1, pages 216–225.

Constance Imbault and Victor Kuperman. 2018. Emotional reactivity and perspective-taking in individuals with and without severe depressive symptoms. *Scientific reports*, 8(1):7634.

Molly Ireland and Micah Iserman. 2018. Within and between-person differences in language used across anxiety support and neutral reddit communities. In *Proceedings of the Fifth Workshop on Computational Linguistics and Clinical Psychology: From Keyboard to Clinic*, pages 182–193.

Tony Liu, Jonah Meyerhoff, Johannes C. Eichstaedt, Chris J. Karr, Susan M. Kaiser, Konrad P. Kording, David C. Mohr, and Lyle H. Ungar. 2022. The relationship between text message sentiment and self-reported depression. *Journal of affective disorders*, 302:7–14.

Minna Lyons, Nazli Deniz Aksayli, and Gayle Brewer. 2018. Mental distress and language use: Linguistic analysis of discussion forum posts. *Computers in Human Behavior*, 87:207–211.

Mattias R. Mehl, Megan L. Robbins, and Shannon E. Holleran. 2012. How taking a word for a word can be problematic: Context-dependent linguistic markers of extraversion and neuroticism. *Journal of Methods and Measurement in the Social Sciences*, 3(2):30–50.

Susan Nolen-Hoeksema, Blair E Wisco, and Sonja Lyubomirsky. 2008. Rethinking rumination. *Perspectives on psychological science*, 3(5):400–424.

James W. Pennebaker, Ryan L. Boyd, Kayla Jordan, and Kate Blackburn. 2015. The development and psychometric properties of LIWC2015. Technical report, the University of Texas in Austin.

Aubrey J. Rodriguez, Shannon E. Holleran, and Matthias R. Mehl. 2010. Reading between the lines: The lay assessment of subclinical depression from written self-descriptions. *Journal of personality*, 78(2):575–598.

Stephanie Rude, Eva-Maria Gortner, and James Pennebaker. 2004. Language use of depressed and depression-vulnerable college students. *Cognition & Emotion*, 18(8):1121–1133.

Anbu Savekar, Shashikanta Tarai, and Moksha Singh. 2023. Structural and functional markers of language signify the symptomatic effect of depression: A systematic literature review. *European Journal of Applied Linguistics*, 11(1):190–224.

Elizabeth M. Seabrook, Margaret L. Kern, Ben D. Fulcher, and Nikki S. Rickard. 2018. Predicting depression from language-based emotion dynamics: longitudinal analysis of facebook and twitter status updates. *Journal of medical Internet research*, 20(5):e168.

D. Smirnova, E. Sloeva, N. Kuvshinova, A. Krasnov, D. Romanov, and G. Nosachev. 2013. Language changes as an important psychopathological phenomenon of mild depression. *European Psychiatry*, 28:1.

Shannon Wiltsey Stirman and James W. Pennebaker. 2001. Word use in the poetry of suicidal and nonsuicidal poets. *Psychosomatic medicine*, 63(4):517–522.

Allison M. Tackman, David A. Sbarra, Angela L. Carey, M. Brent Donnellan, Andrea B. Horn, Nicholas S. Holtzman, To'Meisha S. Edwards, James W. Pennebaker, and Matthias R. Mehl. 2019. Depression, negative emotionality, and self-referential language: A multi-lab, multi-measure, and multi-language-task research synthesis. *Journal of personality and social psychology*, 116(5):817.

Daniela Teodorescu, Tiffany Cheng, Alona Fyshe, and Saif Mohammad. 2023. Language and mental health: Measures of emotion dynamics from text as linguistic biosocial markers. In *Proceedings of the 2023 Conference on Empirical Methods in Natural Language Processing*, pages 3117–3133.

Katrine Bønneland Tølbøll. 2019. Linguistic features in depression: a meta-analysis. *Journal of Language Works-Sprogvidenskabeligt Studentertidsskrift*, 4(2):39–59.

Raluca Nicoleta Trifu, Bogdan Nemeş, Carolina Bodea-Haţegan, and Doina Cozman. 2017. Linguistic indicators of language in major depressive disorder (MDD). An evidence based research. *Journal of Evidence-Based Psychotherapies*, 17(1).

Bernard L. Welch. 1947. The generalization of Student's problem when several different population variances are involved. *Biometrika*, 34(1-2):28–35.

Andrew Yates, Arman Cohan, and Nazli Goharian. 2017. Depression and self-harm risk assessment in online forums. In *Proceedings of the 2017 Conference on Empirical Methods in Natural Language Processing*, pages 2968–2978.

# Appendices

## A Dataset

SMHD is a collection of self-reported mental health diagnoses from Reddit, designed for academic and research purposes (Cohan et al., 2018). SMHD contains posts of Reddit users with nine mental health disorders along with matched control users from a period spanning from January 2006 to December 2017 including depression, ADHD, anxiety, bipolar, PTSD, autism, OCD, schizophrenia, and eating disorder.

The SMHD dataset includes posts from 20,406 clinical users who have claimed to have been diagnosed with a mental health condition and 335,952 control users who are unlikely to have one of the mental health conditions studied. The clinical users were identified based on the textual patterns of self-reported diagnosis (e.g., I was diagnosed with depression) and keywords related to diagnoses (language related to mental health such as the name of a condition, and general terms like diagnosis, mental illness, or suffering from, etc.). Control users were selected based on the criteria that they had not posted in any mental health related subreddits. Control users were selected from a group of potential candidates based on their similarity to clinical users, determined by their subreddit activity and number of posts. The criteria for selecting control users were rigorous: candidates were excluded if they did not meet the required subreddit overlap or minimum post count criteria or used any mental health-related terms in their posts.

After collecting all related user posts, the authors of Cohan et al. (2018) removed all mental health-related posts for clinical users to make the data of both user groups similar. In the dataset, each user is represented by a unique identification number, and their data includes the text of the posts made by that user. Table 6 shows the number of posts and tokens per diagnosis.

| Diagnosis | Posts | Tokens |
|---|---|---|
| depression | 1,272K | 57.4M |
| adhd | 872K | 40.5M |
| anxiety | 795K | 36.9M |
| bipolar | 575K | 26.2M |
| ptsd | 258K | 13.7M |
| autism | 248K | 11.6M |
| ocd | 203K | 9.4M |
| schizophrenia | 123K | 6.1M |
| eating | 53K | 2.5M |
| control | 115,669K | 3,031.6M |

Table 6: SMHD dataset statistics.

## B Sentiment Analysis

We evaluated two sentiment analysis models for applicability to our dataset: a transformer-based model, RoBERTa, trained on Twitter (Barbieri et al., 2020), and the VADER sentiment analysis model (Hutto and Gilbert, 2014). After manually annotating 200 posts for ground truth by the first author of this paper, we compared both models' predictions against these annotations.

The VADER model exhibited a slightly higher overall accuracy of 69% compared to the 66% achieved by the transformer-based model (see Table 7). At the same time, compared to the RoBERTa model, VADER shows much lower precision and recall for the positive class, considerably lower precision for the neutral class, and considerably lower recall for the negative class. When looking at the errors made by both models (see the confusion matrices in Figure 5), we saw that while the RoBERTa model tended to confuse the positive or negative posts as neutral, i.e., it tended to overpredict the neutral label, VADER more often confused positive and negative posts. The latter is the limitation of its lexicon-based approach due to its reliance on a static list of sentiment-laden words without considering the broader context in which they appear. Because for our study, we considered confusing negative posts as positive and vice versa as a more severe error than predicting neutral instead of either valence, we chose the RoBERTa model despite its somewhat lower accuracy.

## C Topic modeling

We explored the topics by looking 1) at the frequency of posts by user groups and 2) the sentiment distribution of each topic across user groups.

**Topic frequencies:** The frequency distribution of the top 50 most frequent topics is shown in Figure 6, which shows the proportion of posts for each topic, normalized by the total posts per group. These top 50 topics represent 11.3% of the depression posts and 11.2% of the control posts. See Figure 7 for more details about the topics and their word representations, as extracted from the BERTopic.

As shown in Figure 6, in our dataset, the depression group discusses topics that are related to, for example, animals, relationships, dieting, books, music albums, movies, grooming, LGBTQ themes, and emotions more compared to controls. Whereas the control group discusses topics related to Karambit/Gaming items, US elections, colors, ammunition, Reddit voting, cars, Online Gaming medals, football, rocket league/Online gaming items trade more compared to depression.

**Topic and Sentiment Interactions:** In addition to topics having different frequency distributions by groups, they also show different sentiment patterns. Figure 8 shows the sentiment distribution of both groups for the top 50 topics. For instance, regarding discussions related to animals, the depression group expressed more positive sentiments than the control group. On the other hand, for the relationship-related topic, the depression group expressed more negative sentiments. On the topic of US elections, although it is more frequent in the control group, the depression group expresses slightly more negative sentiments. In topics related to relationships, family, and LGBTQ, the depression and control users express a similar proportion of positive sentiment, while the depression users also express considerably more negative sentiment. In terms of the adult content-related topic, while the most prevalent sentiment is positive for both groups, the control group expresses considerably more positive sentiment and less negative sentiment than the depression group. At the same time, although most sentiments towards the topic related to animals are neutral, the depression group expresses more positive sentiments than the control group. There are several other topics where the depression group expresses the more positive sentiment; the ones with the most visible difference between the

| | Precision | | Recall | | F1 | |
|---|---|---|---|---|---|---|
| | Vader | RoBERTa | VADER | RoBERTa | VADER | RoBERTa |
| Positive | 0.64 | 0.71 | 0.68 | 0.75 | 0.66 | 0.73 |
| Negative | 0.81 | 0.53 | 0.50 | 0.79 | 0.62 | 0.64 |
| Neutral | 0.66 | 0.88 | 0.85 | 0.48 | 0.74 | 0.62 |
| Accuracy | | | | | 0.69 | 0.66 |
| Macro | 0.70 | 0.71 | 0.68 | 0.68 | 0.67 | 0.67 |
| Weighted | 0.71 | 0.72 | 0.69 | 0.66 | 0.68 | 0.66 |

Table 7: Classification Report for the VADER and RoBERTa sentiment models.

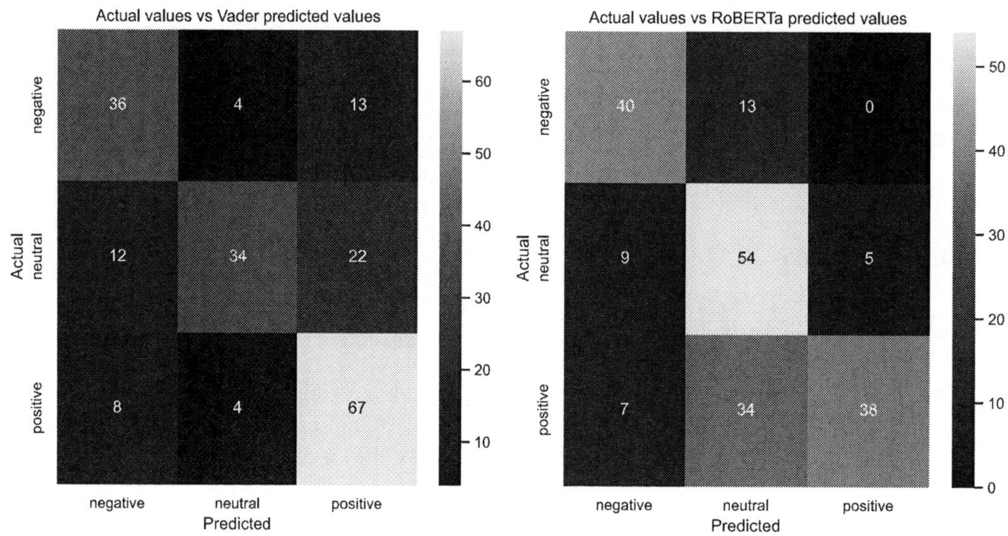


Figure 5: Confusion matrices of the VADER and RoBERTa predicted values compared to the manually annotated subset of 200 posts.

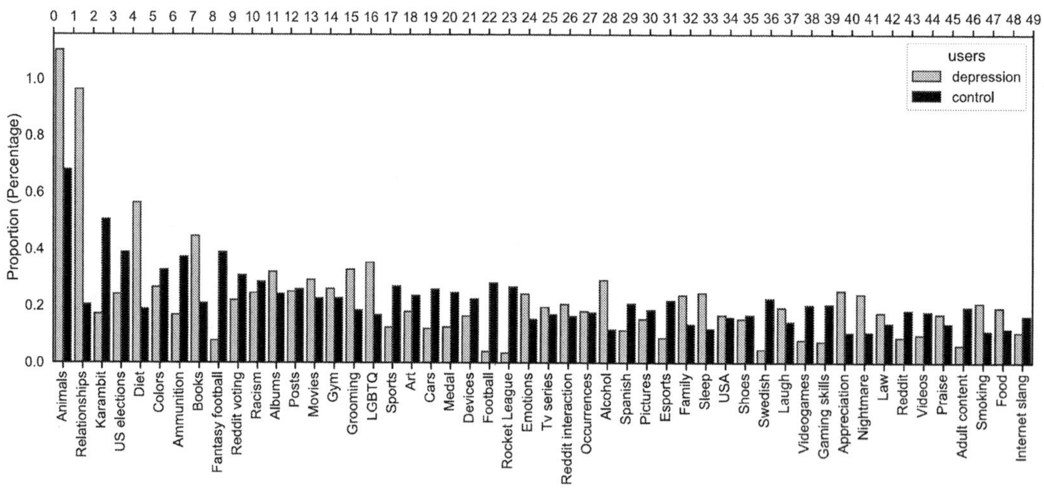


Figure 6: Frequency distribution of top 50 topics.

groups are related to grooming (topic 15), art (topic 18), TV series (topic 25), Reddit interactions (topic 26) and gaming skills (topic 39).

## D LIWC

Linguistic Inquiry and Word Count (LIWC-22) software, developed by Pennebaker et al. (2015) was used in our research.[4]

LIWC contains four summary variables: Analytic Thinking, Clout, Authenticity, and Emotional Tone. The Analytic Thinking variable indicates how people use words that suggest formal, logical, and hierarchical thinking patterns. Clout is an indicator that refers to the relative social status, confidence, or leadership-related language. Authenticity shows the degree to which a person is self-monitoring, i.e., spontaneous language use with no self-regulation and filters. Emotional Tone is an indicator of positive and negative emotional tone dimensions. The linguistic dimensions contain attributes representing the percentage of words in a given text containing pronouns, articles, verbs, etc. Psychological processes contain the attributes related to cognitive processes, affect (emotional state, emotional tone), and social processes (social behavior, social references). The extended dictionary contains attributes related to culture, lifestyle, physical health, time orientations, and conversational aspects. A full description of these attributes can be found in (Pennebaker et al., 2015). The selected 63 attributes and their description are in Table 8.

## E Linear regression results

Table 9 represents the impact of various linguistic and psychological attributes on the sentiment difference between the depression and control groups. Attributes associated with positive coefficients indicate a positive influence on sentiment in the depression group. In contrast, the negative coefficients suggest a negative influence on the depression group sentiment.

[4]We acknowledge that the use of LIWC is subject to a license, and we have obtained the necessary license for research purposes from the official LIWC website `https://www.liwc.app/`

| Id | Topic | Word Representation |
|---|---|---|
| 0 | Animals | cat, dog, dogs, cats, kitten, puppy, name, pet, names, kitty |
| 1 | Relationships | relationship, ex, her, she, feelings, relationships, cheating, dating, cheated, breakup |
| 2 | Karambit | keys, steam, karambit, float, mw, doppler, bayonet, ft, ch, fv |
| 3 | US elections | trump, bernie, hillary, vote, obama, election, donald, clinton, president, marchagainsttrump |
| 4 | Diet | weight, fat, calories, calorie, pounds, lbs, overweight, muscle, diet, skinny |
| 5 | Colors | color, colors, green, blue, purple, red, yellow, colour, black, colorblind |
| 6 | Ammunition | rifle, ammo, gun, barrel, rifles, recoil, mag, shotgun, scope, bolt |
| 7 | Books | books, book, kindle, read, reading, author, novel, series, novels, textbooks |
| 8 | Fantasy football | wr, rb, ppr, rbs, scoring, wrs, te, gordon, fournette, jordy |
| 9 | Reddit voting | upvote, downvote, downvoted, upvotes, downvotes, upvoted, downvoting, voted, vote, votes |
| 10 | Racism | asian, racist, white, racism, privilege, black, race, blacks, asians, whites |
| 11 | Albums | album, song, albums, songs, music, band, lyrics, listen, listened, listening |
| 12 | Posts | posted, comment, posting, history, comments, post, threads, thread, posts, deleted |
| 13 | Movies | movie, film, movies, filming, scene, films, watched, filmed, watch, critics |
| 14 | Gym | gym, squat, squats, deadlift, crossfit, lifting, workout, bench, weights, lift |
| 15 | Grooming | hair, beard, shave, shaving, haircut, razor, shaved, mustache, hairy, hairs |
| 16 | LGBTQ | gay, marriage, wife, divorce, marry, married, divorced, husband, straight, homo |
| 17 | Sports | lebron, football, nba, rugby, basketball, kobe, jordan, soccer, sport, cavs |
| 18 | Art | art, paint, artwork, illustration, deadline, www, painting, commissions, storyboarding, infographics |
| 19 | Cars | ninja, truck, wrx, bmw, car, subaru, cars, mustang, suv, vw |
| 20 | Medal | mmr, bronze, silver, rank, ranked, plat, diamond, challenger, ranking, gold |
| 21 | Devices | watches, watch, phones, damasko, htc, galaxy, samsung, phone, iphone, nokia |
| 22 | Football | liverpool, arsenal, rooney, chelsea, striker, manchester, goal, messi, united, suarez |
| 23 | Rocket League | crates, crimson, heatwave, loopers, offers, lime, cert, keys, painted, tw |
| 24 | Emotions | hear, glad, welcome, sorry, heard, problem, help, bro, happy, hope |
| 25 | Tv series | episode, episodes, show, season, seasons, watched, eps, watching, shows, aired |
| 26 | Reddit interaction | reply, read, response, reading, responding, answer, replied, thanks, detailed, comment |
| 27 | Occurrences | happen, happened, happening, happens, exact, happend, gonna, prolly, often, going |
| 28 | Alcohol | drinking, drunk, sober, drink, alcohol, hangover, alcoholic, drinks, drank, alcoholism |
| 29 | Spanish | que, de, el, la, en, por, para, lo, je, los |
| 30 | Pictures | imgur, pics, pic, photo, pictures, photos, picture, image, upload, images |
| 31 | Esports | tsm, clg, fnatic, na, lcs, teams, eu, skt, worlds, fnc |
| 32 | Family | dad, mom, grandpa, mother, daddy, father, son, mum, uncle, naugthy |
| 33 | Sleep | sleep, wake, asleep, awake, waking, bed, nap, woke, sleeping, insomnia |
| 34 | USA | nc, ohio, michigan, carolina, virginia, ucf, nj, county, lsu, kentucky |
| 35 | Shoes | shoes, shoe, boots, heels, feet, sneakers, toe, pair, toes, wear |
| 36 | Swedish | det, att, som, och, inte, jag, har, om, en, med |
| 37 | Laugh | laughed, laugh, laughing, chuckle, laughter, loud, giggles, amused, hard, made |
| 38 | Videogames | xbox, console, consoles, pc, sony, gaming, platform, exclusives, xbone, playstation |
| 39 | Gaming skills | levelled, invention, skill, levelling, level, achieved, mining, skills, inventioni, thieving |
| 40 | Appreciation | advice, appreciate, thank, thanks, appreciated, excellent, heeney, oversee, solid, jtr |
| 41 | Nightmare | dream, dreams, nightmares, lucid, dreaming, nightmare, dreamt, vivid, woke, dreamed |
| 42 | Law | lawyer, jury, justice, judge, guilty, court, sue, lawsuit, innocent, lawyers |
| 43 | Reddit | added, ready, adding, online, available, trade, rn, add, whenever, spritzee |
| 44 | Videos | video, videos, youtube, vid, vids, link, uploaded, channel, cutinhalf, upload |
| 45 | Praise | awesome, amazing, cool, thank, incredible, dope, thanks, wonderful, dude, brilliant |
| 46 | Adult content | kik, sexy, hot, body, ass, ahm, meeting, hmu, chat, alexandraoweny |
| 47 | Smoking | smoking, smoke, cigarettes, cigarette, smokers, smoker, nicotine, smoked, smokes, tobacco |
| 48 | Food | breakfast, dinner, hungry, eat, meal, food, eating, lunch, meals, eats |
| 49 | Internet slang | gt, lt, ftfy, gtfo, gts, lolzdudezorz, div, zoop, drumjunkie, checkerboard |

Figure 7: Top 50 topics and their word representations.

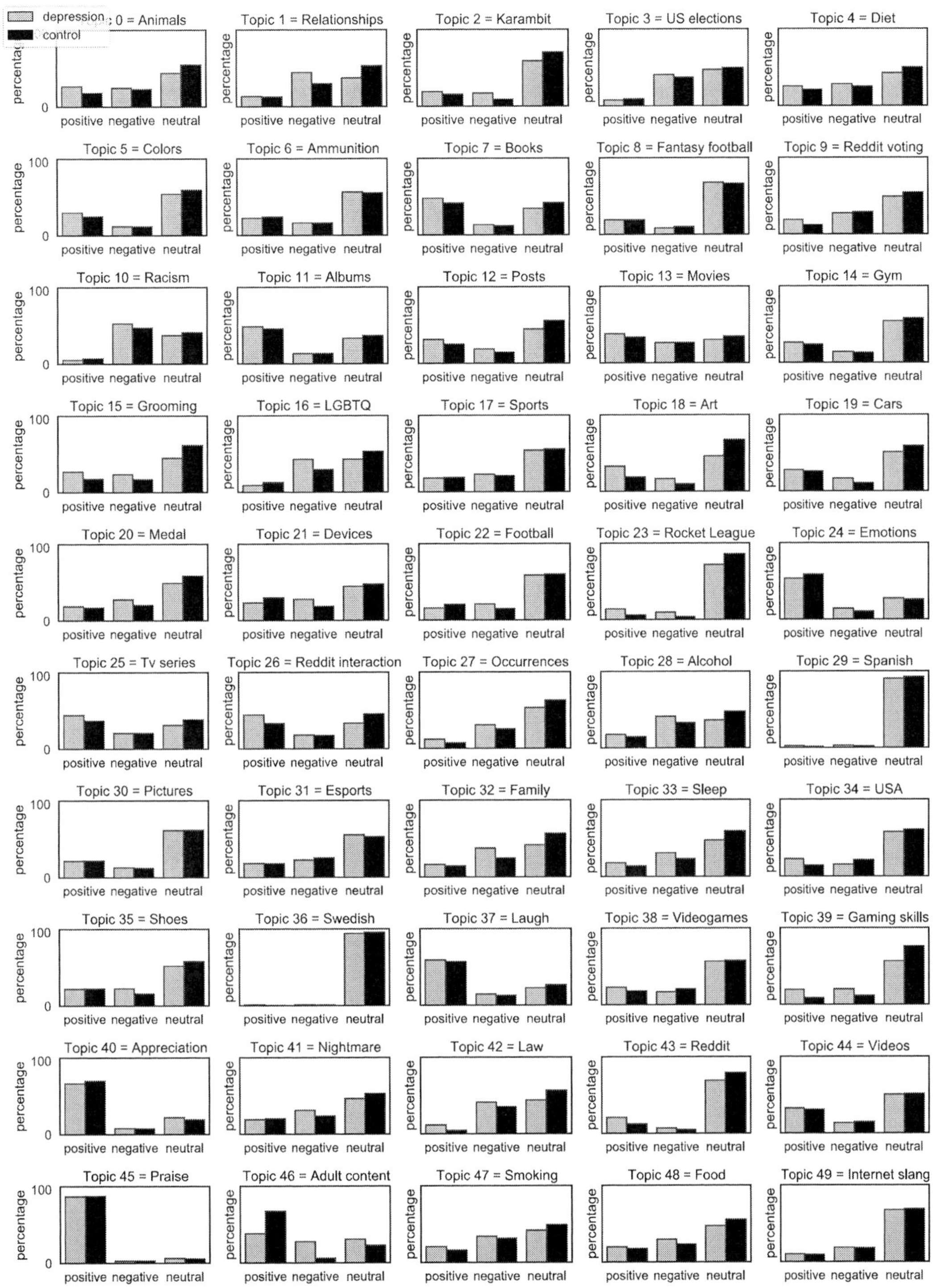


Figure 8: Top 50 topics and their sentiment distributions.

| Category | Description |
|---|---|
| *Summary Variables* | |
| Word Count | Total word count |
| Analytical thinking | Metric of logical, formal thinking |
| Clout | Language of leadership, status |
| Authentic | Perceived honesty, genuineness |
| Emotional tone | Degree of positive (negative) tone |
| *Linguistic Dimensions* | |
| pronouns | |
| 1st person singular | I, me, my, myself |
| 1st person plural | we, our, us, lets |
| 2nd person | you, your, u, yourself |
| 3rd person singular | he, she, her, his |
| 3rd person plural | they, their, them, themsel* |
| Impersonal pronouns | that, it, this, what |
| Auxiliary verbs | is, was, be, have |
| Negations | not, no, never, nothing |
| *Psychological Processes* | |
| Drives | we, our, work, us |
| *Cognition* | |
| All-or-none | all, no, never, always |
| *cognitive processes* | |
| Insight | know, how, think, feel |
| Causation | how, because, make, why |
| Discrepancy | would, can, want, could |
| Tentative | if, or, any, something |
| Certitude | really, actually, of course, real |
| Differentiation | but, not, if, or |
| Memory | remember, forget, remind, forgot |
| *Affect* | |
| *Emotion* | |
| Positive emotion | good, love, happy, hope |
| Negative emotion | bad, hate, hurt, tired |
| Anxiety | worry, fear, afraid, nervous |
| Anger | hate, mad, angry, frustr* |
| Sadness | :(, sad, disappoint*, cry |
| Swear words | shit, fuckin*, fuck, damn |
| *Social processes* | |
| Social behavior | said, love, say, care |
| Politeness | thank, please, thanks, good morning |
| Interpersonal | conflict fight, kill, killed, attack |
| Moralization | wrong, honor*, deserv*, judge |
| Communication | said, say, tell, thank* |
| *Social referents* | |
| Family | parent*, mother*, father*, baby |
| Friends | friend*, boyfriend*, girlfriend*, dude |
| Female references | she, her, girl, woman |
| Male references | he, his, him, man |
| *Expanded Dictionary* | |
| Culture | car, united states, govern*, phone |
| Lifestyle | work, home, school, working |
| Religion | god, hell, christmas*, church |
| *Physical* | |
| *Health* | |
| Illness | hospital*, cancer*, sick, pain |
| Wellness | healthy, gym*, supported, diet |
| Mental health | mental health, depressed, suicid*, trauma* |
| Substances | beer*, wine, drunk, cigar* |
| Sexual | sex, gay, pregnan*, dick |
| Food | food*, drink*, eat, dinner* |
| Death | death*, dead, die, kill |
| *States* | |
| Need | have to, need, had to, must |
| Want | want, hope, wanted, wish |
| Acquire | get, got, take, getting |
| Lack | don't have, didn't have, *less, hungry |
| Fulfilled | enough, full, complete, extra |
| Fatigue | tired, bored, don't care, boring |
| *Motives* | |
| Reward | opportun*, win, gain*, benefit* |
| Risk | secur*, protect*, pain, risk* |
| Curiosity | scien*, look* for, research*, wonder |
| Allure | have, like, out, know |
| *Perception* | in, out, up, there |
| quad Feeling | feel, hard, cool, felt |
| *Time orientation* | |
| Past focus | was, had, were, been |
| Present focus | is, are, I'm, can |
| Future focus | will, going to, have to, may |
| Conversational | yeah, oh, yes, okay |

Table 8: Selected LIWC attributes and their descriptions.

| Attribute | Coefficient | SE | t-value | p-value | 95% CI |
|---|---|---|---|---|---|
| constant | −0.9998 | 0.248 | −4.037 | <0.001 | −1.485 to −0.514 |
| *Summary Variables* | | | | | |
| Word Count | −1.3876 | 0.263 | −5.274 | <0.001 | −1.903 to −0.872 |
| Clout | 1.1090 | 0.485 | 2.285 | 0.022 | 0.158 to 2.060 |
| Emotional tone | 7.2384 | 0.287 | 25.198 | <0.001 | 6.675 to 7.802 |
| *Linguistic Dimensions* | | | | | |
| pronouns | | | | | |
| 1st person singular | 0.8189 | 0.377 | 2.175 | 0.030 | 0.081 to 1.557 |
| 3rd person singular | −0.8896 | 0.387 | −2.298 | 0.022 | −1.648 to −0.131 |
| Negations | −0.8863 | 0.304 | −2.916 | 0.004 | −1.482 to −0.290 |
| *Psychological Processes* | | | | | |
| Drives | −0.6603 | 0.298 | −2.216 | 0.027 | −1.245 to −0.076 |
| *Cognition* | | | | | |
| *cognitive processes* | | | | | |
| Causation | −0.9897 | 0.264 | −3.747 | <0.001 | −1.508 to −0.472 |
| Discrepancy | −0.7955 | 0.320 | −2.485 | 0.013 | −1.423 to −0.168 |
| Tentative | 0.5659 | 0.271 | 2.086 | 0.037 | 0.034 to 1.098 |
| Memory | 0.6089 | 0.251 | 2.422 | 0.015 | 0.116 to 1.102 |
| *Affect* | | | | | |
| *Emotion* | | | | | |
| Positive emotion | 2.0170 | 0.280 | 7.195 | <0.001 | 1.467 to 2.567 |
| Negative emotion | −1.7006 | 0.420 | −4.045 | <0.001 | −2.525 to −0.876 |
| Anger | 0.9660 | 0.342 | 2.828 | 0.005 | 0.296 to 1.636 |
| Sadness | 0.7130 | 0.296 | 2.408 | 0.016 | 0.132 to 1.294 |
| Swear words | −2.1978 | 0.272 | −8.086 | <0.001 | −2.731 to −1.665 |
| *Social processes* | | | | | |
| Social behavior | −0.8867 | 0.416 | −2.134 | 0.033 | −1.701 to −0.072 |
| Interpersonal | 0.6695 | 0.314 | 2.131 | 0.033 | 0.053 to 1.286 |
| Moralization | −0.6971 | 0.271 | −2.575 | 0.010 | −1.228 to −0.166 |
| Communication | −0.7260 | 0.348 | −2.086 | 0.037 | −1.408 to −0.044 |
| *Expanded Dictionary* | | | | | |
| *Physical* | | | | | |
| *Health* | | | | | |
| Substances | −0.6174 | 0.255 | −2.419 | 0.016 | −1.118 to −0.117 |
| Death | −0.6125 | 0.284 | −2.160 | 0.031 | −1.168 to −0.057 |
| *Motives* | | | | | |
| Allure | 0.8486 | 0.278 | 3.049 | 0.002 | 0.303 to 1.394 |
| *Time orientation* | | | | | |
| Past focus | −0.5674 | 0.286 | −1.981 | 0.048 | −1.129 to −0.006 |
| Present focus | −1.0653 | 0.320 | −3.334 | 0.001 | −1.692 to −0.439 |

Table 9: Linear regression analysis summary.

# To Aggregate or Not to Aggregate. That is the Question: A Case Study on Annotation Subjectivity in Span Prediction

**Kemal Kurniawan**[1] **Meladel Mistica**[1] **Timothy Baldwin**[1,2] **Jey Han Lau**[1]
[1]The University of Melbourne [2]MBZUAI
{kurniawan.k,misticam,laujh}@unimelb.edu.au
tb@ldwin.net

## Abstract

This paper explores the task of automatic prediction of text spans in a legal problem description that support a legal area label. We use a corpus of problem descriptions written by laypeople in English that is annotated by practising lawyers. Inherent subjectivity exists in our task because legal area categorisation is a complex task, and lawyers often have different views on a problem, especially in the face of legally-imprecise descriptions of issues. Experiments show that training on majority-voted spans outperforms training on disaggregated ones.[1]

| Area of law | Annotated description |
|---|---|
| ELDER LAW | I was admitted in a Public Hospital. I want the right to go home, NOT aged care! |
| GUARDIANSHIP AND ADMINISTRATION | I was admitted in a Public Hospital. I want the right to go home, NOT aged care! |

Table 1: Examples of a description annotated with spans for two different areas of law.

## 1 Introduction

Automatic categorisation of lay descriptions of problems into relevant legal areas is of critical importance for providers of free legal assistance (Mistica et al., 2021). In our case, we have access to a dataset where a legal problem description is annotated by multiple lawyers who first perform document-level annotation by choosing relevant legal areas,[2] and then, for each legal area chosen, the lawyers highlight text spans that support their decision. These spans not only help justify the selected areas of law but also improve the interpretability of their decision.

The categorisation of legal areas is a complex problem, and lawyers sometimes have different views on a problem, especially when the task is performed on legally-imprecise descriptions of the personal circumstances of an individual. Therefore, subjectivity is inherent in our task. This subjectivity leads to annotation disagreements, both at the document- and the span-level. While such disagreements are often seen as noise that needs to be eliminated in data annotation (Plank, 2022), here they are signal because they are produced by subject-matter experts.

In this paper, we explore the task of automatic span prediction using our expert-annotated dataset, as illustrated in Table 1. Given a problem description (which is a short document) and an area of law, the task aims to predict text spans in the description that support the area of law label. We describe the development of machine learning models for the task that are trained on a corpus containing legal problem descriptions written by laypeople in English. Across various evaluation scenarios, we find that aggregating training span annotations outperforms keeping them disaggregated.

## 2 Problem Statement

Given a text expressed as a sequence of $N$ words $\boldsymbol{x} = x_1 x_2 \ldots x_N$ and a label $l$, the goal is to predict a set of non-overlapping spans $S = \{(b_i, e_i)\}_{i=1}^{M}$ where $1 \leq b_i \leq e_i \leq N$ such that the text segments $\{x_{b_i} x_{b_i+1} \ldots x_{e_i}\}_{i=1}^{M}$ explain the reason for assigning $l$ to $\boldsymbol{x}$. In other words, $b_i$ and $e_i$ respectively denote the beginning and the end indices of the $i$-th span supporting the assignment of $l$ to $\boldsymbol{x}$. We cast the problem as sequence tagging by modelling the probability of $S$ given $\boldsymbol{x}$ and $l$ as

$$P(S \mid \boldsymbol{x}, l) \propto \exp f(\boldsymbol{x}, \boldsymbol{y}, l) \quad (1)$$

[1]Code is available at https://github.com/kmkurn/wassa2024.

[2]There are 32 possible legal areas including NEIGHBOURHOOD DISPUTES, ELDER LAW, and HOUSING AND RESIDENTIAL TENANCIES.



*Proceedings of the 14th Workshop on Computational Approaches to Subjectivity, Sentiment, & Social Media Analysis*, pages 362–368
August 15, 2024 

where $\boldsymbol{y} = y_1 y_2 \dots y_N$ is a sequence of $N$ tags representing the spans in $S$, each $y_i$ corresponds to $x_i$, and $f$ is a real-valued function that measures the relevance of $\boldsymbol{y}$ in supporting the assignment of $l$ to $\boldsymbol{x}$. To get $\boldsymbol{y}$ from $S$, we use an encoding where $y_i$ takes one of 5 possibilities depending on the position of $i$ in a span (Sekine et al., 1998):

1. singleton, if $\exists(b, e) \in S$ where $b = e = i$;
2. beginning, if $\exists(b, e) \in S$ where $b = i < e$;
3. end, if $\exists(b, e) \in S$ where $b < i = e$;
4. inside, if $\exists(b, e) \in S$ where $b < i < e$; and
5. outside, otherwise.

The span prediction problem is then equivalent to finding the highest scoring sequence

$$\boldsymbol{y}^\star = \arg\max_{\boldsymbol{y}} f(\boldsymbol{x}, \boldsymbol{y}, l).$$

The sequence $\boldsymbol{y}^\star$ is then decoded to get the final predicted spans.

## 3 Corpus

The corpus was collected by Justice Connect,[3] an Australian public benevolent institution[4] that connects laypeople seeking legal assistance with pro bono lawyers. On its website, Justice Connect allows help-seekers to describe their problem in free text format in English. After anonymising identifiable information, problem descriptions collected from July 2020 to early December 2023 were presented to a pool of lawyers to be annotated. Each annotator selected one or more out of the 32 areas of law that applied to the problem (thus it is a *multi-label* classification problem), representing the different law specialisations the case relates to. On average, a problem description is labelled with 3 areas of law. For each document-level area of law selected, the annotator then select spans of words[5] that support their decision. On average, each problem description is annotated by 5 lawyers. This whole annotation process was carried out by Justice Connect. In other words, we do not perform any additional annotation and simply use the annotated corpus.

Relating to the problem statement in Section 2, the description and the area of law form the inputs $\boldsymbol{x}$ and $l$ respectively, while the spans make up the output $S$. Together, the input and the output form a labelled example of the task. Following prior work on a similar corpus (Mistica et al., 2021), we employ 20-fold cross validation to create the training and the test sets and randomly take 10% of the training set to form the development set. Over the 20 folds we have a total of 35K unique problem description and legal area pairs, with a total of 3.8M words in the problem descriptions.

## 4 Method

### 4.1 Subjectivity-Aware Evaluation

Because of the inherent subjectivity of the labelling task, a test input (consisting of a problem description and an area of law) can have multiple valid span annotations whose boundaries may not match exactly. Specifically for a given problem description, the same area of law can be supported by different spans. Similarly, the same span can support different areas of law. To deal with this mismatched boundaries issue, we adopt both span- and word-level evaluation. To address the issue of multiple valid spans, we experiment with 2 types of gold spans: majority-voted and best-matched. With these strategies, we have a total of 4 combinations of evaluation setup.

#### 4.1.1 Span- and Word-Level Evaluation

In span-level evaluation, a predicted span is considered correct if it starts from and ends at the same positions as a gold span. In other words, their span boundaries must match exactly to be considered equal.

In contrast, word-level evaluation considers a word in a predicted span as correct if it is also a word in a gold span. Put simply, this evaluation gives a positive score to two overlapping spans whose boundaries do not match exactly.

We use precision, recall, and $F_1$ scores as evaluation metrics. We use the evaluation script[6] of CoNLL-2000 chunking shared task (Tjong Kim Sang and Buchholz, 2000) to perform both types of evaluation.[7]

#### 4.1.2 Majority-Voted and Best-Matched Gold Spans

We perform strict majority voting to get the majority-voted gold spans for evaluation. For example, if there are 2 annotators with the following span annotations:

[3] https://justiceconnect.org.au

[4] As defined by the Australian government: https://www.acnc.gov.au/charity/charities/4a24f21a-38af-e811-a95e-000d3ad24c60/profile

[5] The number of words must be at least three.

[6] Downloadable from https://www.cnts.ua.ac.be/conll2000/chunking/output.html.

[7] Word-level evaluation is achieved by passing -r as option.

1. *[I was fired from work] because of [my complaint against my boss] months ago,*
2. *I was [fired from work] because of my [complaint against my boss months ago]*

where square brackets denote a span, then the gold spans are *fired from work* and *complaint against my boss*. In other words, only words voted by more than 50% of the annotators are included. In particular, words voted by exactly 50% of the annotators are *not* included.

Another type of gold spans we experiment with is the best-matched spans. Given an input and its predicted spans, best-matched spans of that input are its span annotations against which the predicted spans result in the highest $F_1$ score when evaluated. These span annotations must come from a single annotator. For instance, if (a) there are 2 annotators with the same span annotations as before, (b) the predicted span is only *fired from work*, and (c) span-level $F_1$ is used, then the best-matched spans are the spans given by the second annotator. A similar approach has been used in automatic text summarisation (Lin, 2004).

### 4.2 Model

We parameterise the function $f$ in Equation (1) with a neural sequence tagger. The tagger uses a pretrained language model to provide contextual word representations and a bidirectional LSTM (Hochreiter and Schmidhuber, 1997) with a CRF output layer (Collobert et al., 2011) as the classifier similar to previous work (Lample et al., 2016). We use the implementation provided by the open-source NLP library FLAIR (Akbik et al., 2019).[8]

Following prior work on a similar corpus (Mistica et al., 2021), we use the base and uncased version of BERT (Devlin et al., 2019) as the pretrained language model. The problem description and the area of law are joined and given as a single text input to BERT. For example, if the problem description is *My landlord kicked me out without reason* and the area of law is HOUSING AND RESIDENTIAL TENANCIES then the input is *My landlord kicked me out without reason* <sep> HOUSING AND RESIDENTIAL TENANCIES where <sep> marks the end of the problem description. Both <sep> and succeeding input words corresponding to the area of law are excluded from evaluation.

[8] Version 0.13.

### 4.3 Training

We experiment with two approaches to dealing with subjectivity in model training. The first approach (MV) aggregates span annotations with majority voting similar to how the majority-voted gold spans are constructed (Section 4.1). This approach resolves subjectivity by only including spans on which the majority of annotators agree.

The second approach is repeated labelling (REL) which treats multiple annotations of the same input as separate labelled examples (Sheng et al., 2008). In other words, annotations in the training set are left as they are without any attempt to aggregate them. This approach embraces subjectivity by treating all annotations equally.

While REL may seem counterintuitive because the same input can be presented with different annotations, these annotations may have consistent patterns. Spans that are often (resp. rarely) annotated give a strong signal of the presence (resp. absence) of a true span. We expect that models can learn the correct spans from these signals.

For both approaches, the tagger is trained for 10 epochs to maximise the probability of the sequence of tags in the training set. Both learning rate and batch size are tuned on the development set. The word-level $F_1$ score against majority-voted spans is used as the hyperparameter tuning objective.

### 4.4 Comparisons

**Baseline** We employ a model that predicts spans randomly as a baseline (RANDOM) which reflects a model that does not perform any learning from data. The model tags each word in the input description with one out of 3 possibilities uniformly at random: start of a span, continuation of a span, or outside of any span. This sequence of tags is then decoded into a set of spans as the output.

**Expert performance** The majority-voted gold spans in Section 4.1 may not resemble spans produced by a real annotator. Therefore, even an expert annotator may not achieve perfect performance when evaluated against the majority-voted gold spans. We compute this expert performance to serve as a more realistic upper bound of model performance on our dataset. We estimate this performance by evaluating the performance of the best annotator of each test input, where best is defined as resulting in the highest $F_1$ score against the majority-voted gold spans. Note that this is different from the best-matched spans mentioned in

Section 4.1 because here the gold spans are fixed to the majority-voted spans while the predicted spans come from the best annotator. While there are limitations to this estimation (see Limitations), we argue that the estimate is still useful as a point of reference.

## 5 Results

Table 2 shows that both MV and REL perform substantially better than RANDOM in terms of $F_1$ scores for all 4 evaluation setups, indicating the potential of both methods. Comparing MV and REL across both types of gold spans, while the former is on par with the latter in word-level evaluation, MV outperforms REL substantially in span-level evaluation. This finding is consistent across precision and recall, and thus demonstrates that MV is overall superior to REL. However, the table also shows that RANDOM outperforms both MV and REL in terms of word-level recall across both types of gold spans, which points to an area for improvement.

While the performance numbers with majority-voted gold spans are lower than the best-matched counterparts, the patterns of model performance are consistent across both types of gold spans. This result suggest that both types of gold spans are equally acceptable for handling subjectivity in span annotations. However, using the majority-voted gold spans has the advantage of time efficiency because the gold spans do not need to be recomputed when evaluating different models.

For majority-voted spans, Table 2a shows that model performance is still far behind expert performance, suggesting that there is still plenty of room for improvement. Furthermore, the expert performance is moderately high in span-level evaluation and approaches perfect performance in the word-level counterpart. This finding demonstrates that the majority-voted spans are realistic as they show a high degree of similarity to span annotations given by experts.

### 5.1 Experiments with Other Pretrained Language Models

We also experiment with an improved version of BERT known as DeBERTaV3 (He et al., 2023). Key differences include a more complex model architecture, a simpler pretraining objective, and a larger amount of pretraining data. We use the base version of DeBERTaV3 which has the same number of layers, attention heads, and hidden units but four times the vocabulary size of the base version of BERT, as used in the previous experiment. We evaluate only against the majority-voted gold spans based on the previous findings. Due to time constraints, we use the hyperparameters (learning rate and batch size) tuned on the first fold (out of 20) for all the folds of the dataset.

Table 3 shows that both MV and REL outperform RANDOM substantially on both span- and word-level evaluations across all metrics except for word-level recall where RANDOM achieves the best score. This finding agrees with that of the BERT-based models. Looking at $F_1$ scores, the table shows that REL is on par with MV in span-level evaluation and marginally outperforms MV in the word-level counterpart. This finding contradicts the results for BERT-based models, suggesting the effectiveness of REL with improved language models.

Furthermore, the table shows that for span-level evaluation, REL outperforms MV in precision but performs worse than MV in recall. In contrast, for word-level evaluation, MV outperforms REL in precision but performs worse than REL in recall. These findings suggest that with stronger language models, the best method depends not only on whether span- or word-level evaluation is prioritised but also on whether precision or recall is more crucial. These patterns of performance again contradict those of the BERT-based models, suggesting that the choice of pretrained language models is important. We leave the analysis on the possible reasons behind these findings and the evaluation on best-matched gold spans for future work.

Lastly, comparing to Table 2a, we see that DeBERTa-based models outperform the BERT-based counterparts across the board. This finding is unsurprising because DeBERTa was developed as an improvement over BERT (He et al., 2021).

## 6 Related Work

Pruthi et al. (2020) have studied the span prediction problem under the name of evidence extraction. However, their model also performs classification jointly and is trained in a semi-supervised manner. More importantly, they did not consider subjectivity in the span annotations. In contrast, we focus only on predicting spans, supervised learning, and incorporating subjectivity in model training and evaluation.

Previous work has leveraged a similar dataset of

| Method | Span | | | Word | | |
|---|---|---|---|---|---|---|
| | P | R | $F_1$ | P | R | $F_1$ |
| RANDOM | 0.2 ± 0.0 | 4.1 ± 0.1 | 0.4 ± 0.0 | 17.1 ± 0.0 | **66.6 ± 0.0** | 27.2 ± 0.0 |
| MV | **17.9 ± 1.9** | **18.5 ± 0.3** | **18.2 ± 1.1** | **58.2 ± 0.4** | 48.7 ± 0.1 | **53.0 ± 0.1** |
| REL | 11.2 ± 1.4 | 12.6 ± 0.3 | 11.8 ± 0.9 | 57.5 ± 0.7 | 48.9 ± 1.2 | 52.8 ± 0.5 |
| Expert | 80.2 | 67.5 | 73.3 | 91.0 | 97.5 | 94.2 |

(a) Majority-voted gold spans

| Method | Span | | | Word | | |
|---|---|---|---|---|---|---|
| | P | R | $F_1$ | P | R | $F_1$ |
| RANDOM | 0.0 ± 0.0 | 1.2 ± 0.0 | 0.1 ± 0.0 | 31.0 ± 0.0 | **66.9 ± 0.0** | 42.4 ± 0.0 |
| MV | **20.9 ± 2.2** | **26.3 ± 0.4** | **23.3 ± 1.5** | 69.2 ± 0.5 | 48.6 ± 0.2 | 57.1 ± 0.1 |
| REL | 17.1 ± 2.2 | 24.1 ± 0.5 | 19.9 ± 1.7 | **69.6 ± 0.5** | 48.7 ± 1.2 | **57.3 ± 0.7** |

(b) Best-matched gold spans

Table 2: Span- and word-level precision, recall, and $F_1$ scores (in %) of the span prediction model against majority-voted and best-matched gold spans. Mean ($\pm$ std) across 3 runs are reported except for Expert.

| Method | Span | | | Word | | |
|---|---|---|---|---|---|---|
| | P | R | $F_1$ | P | R | $F_1$ |
| RANDOM | 0.2 ± 0.0 | 4.1 ± 0.1 | 0.4 ± 0.0 | 17.1 ± 0.0 | **66.6 ± 0.0** | 27.2 ± 0.0 |
| MV | 18.4 ± 1.6 | **19.7 ± 0.3** | **19.0 ± 1.0** | **61.3 ± 0.4** | 50.2 ± 0.3 | 55.2 ± 0.0 |
| REL | **23.7 ± 2.6** | 14.8 ± 0.1 | 18.2 ± 0.8 | 58.7 ± 0.3 | 53.0 ± 0.4 | **55.7 ± 0.2** |

Table 3: Span- and word-level precision, recall, and $F_1$ scores (in %) of the DeBERTaV3-based model against majority-voted gold spans. Mean ($\pm$ std) across 3 runs are reported. RANDOM performance is copied from Table 2a.

legal problem descriptions (Mistica et al., 2021). They focussed on the text classification aspect where areas of law are assigned to a problem description. Different from their work, ours treats the area of law as given and focusses on predicting the spans that support the assignment of the area of law.

Our work falls within the broader theme of human label variation (Plank, 2022). Previous work has mainly focussed on text classification tasks (Leonardelli et al., 2023; Fornaciari et al., 2021; Nie et al., 2020, *inter alia*). In contrast, we focus on spans, which are still understudied in this area. Our work is also related to data perspectivism.[9]

## 7 Conclusion

We explore the task of automatically predicting text spans in a legal problem description that support the labelling of an area of law. We develop neural sequence taggers that deal with the inherent subjectivity of the task. Experiments across various subjectivity-aware evaluation setups show that training on majority-voted annotations outperforms training on the disaggregated counterparts.

## Limitations

The dataset we use in this work cannot be released publicly, which is a major limitation of our work in terms of reproducibility. This is because the topics discussed are sensitive, and more importantly, the help-seekers have not given their consent to share their data. Nevertheless, we believe our work still offers valuable scientific knowledge on handling subjectivity, especially in span annotation tasks.

For the evaluation using majority-voted gold spans, we estimate the expert performance by determining the best annotator of each test input. However, the majority-voted gold spans are a function of the best annotator's spans. Thus, the estimated expert performance is dominated by test inputs that are annotated by fewer annotators. To mitigate this issue, a leave-one-annotator-out strategy can be employed, which we leave for future work.

The best-matched gold spans are likely to come from various annotators. Taken together, these spans may not reflect a realistic pattern of a single human annotator. A remedy is to evaluate against a

[9] `https://pdai.info/`

single best annotator. However, this approach is not straightforward in our case because an annotator may annotate only a subset of examples. We thus leave this approach for future work.

## Acknowledgements

We thank the anonymous reviewers for their constructive feedback on the paper. This research is supported by the Australian Research Council Linkage Project (project number: LP210200917) and funded by the Australian Government. This research is done in collaboration with Justice Connect, an Australian public benevolent institution.[10]

## References

Alan Akbik, Tanja Bergmann, Duncan Blythe, Kashif Rasul, Stefan Schweter, and Roland Vollgraf. 2019. FLAIR: An easy-to-use framework for state-of-the-art NLP. In *Proceedings of the 2019 Conference of the North American Chapter of the Association for Computational Linguistics (Demonstrations)*, pages 54–59.

Ronan Collobert, Jason Weston, Léon Bottou, Michael Karlen, Koray Kavukcuoglu, and Pavel Kuksa. 2011. Natural Language Processing (almost) from Scratch. *Journal of Machine Learning Research*, 12(Aug):2493–2537.

Jacob Devlin, Ming-Wei Chang, Kenton Lee, and Kristina Toutanova. 2019. BERT: Pre-training of Deep Bidirectional Transformers for Language Understanding. In *Proceedings of the 2019 Conference of the North American Chapter of the Association for Computational Linguistics: Human Language Technologies, Volume 1 (Long and Short Papers)*, pages 4171–4186.

Tommaso Fornaciari, Alexandra Uma, Silviu Paun, Barbara Plank, Dirk Hovy, and Massimo Poesio. 2021. Beyond Black & White: Leveraging Annotator Disagreement via Soft-Label Multi-Task Learning. In *Proceedings of the 2021 Conference of the North American Chapter of the Association for Computational Linguistics: Human Language Technologies*, pages 2591–2597.

Pengcheng He, Jianfeng Gao, and Weizhu Chen. 2023. DeBERTaV3: Improving DeBERTa using ELECTRA-style pre-training with gradient-disentangled embedding sharing. In *The Eleventh International Conference on Learning Representations*.

Pengcheng He, Xiaodong Liu, Jianfeng Gao, and Weizhu Chen. 2021. DeBERTa: Decoding-enhanced BERT with disentangled attention. In *9th International Conference on Learning Representations*.

[10]As defined by the Australian government: https://www.acnc.gov.au/charity/charities/4a24f21a-38af-e811-a95e-000d3ad24c60/profile

Sepp Hochreiter and Jürgen Schmidhuber. 1997. Long short-term memory. *Neural Computation*, 9(8):1735–1780.

Guillaume Lample, Miguel Ballesteros, Sandeep Subramanian, Kazuya Kawakami, and Chris Dyer. 2016. Neural architectures for named entity recognition. In *Proceedings of the 2016 Conference of the North American Chapter of the Association for Computational Linguistics: Human Language Technologies*, pages 260–270.

Elisa Leonardelli, Gavin Abercrombie, Dina Almanea, Valerio Basile, Tommaso Fornaciari, Barbara Plank, Verena Rieser, Alexandra Uma, and Massimo Poesio. 2023. SemEval-2023 Task 11: Learning with Disagreements (LeWiDi). In *Proceedings of the 17th International Workshop on Semantic Evaluation (SemEval-2023)*, pages 2304–2318.

Chin-Yew Lin. 2004. Rouge: A package for automatic evaluation of summaries. In *Text Summarization Branches out: Proceedings of the ACL-04 Workshop*, volume 8.

Meladel Mistica, Jey Han Lau, Brayden Merrifield, Kate Fazio, and Timothy Baldwin. 2021. Semi-automatic Triage of Requests for Free Legal Assistance. In *Proceedings of the Natural Legal Language Processing Workshop 2021*, pages 217–227.

Yixin Nie, Xiang Zhou, and Mohit Bansal. 2020. What can we learn from collective human opinions on natural language inference data? In *Proceedings of the 2020 Conference on Empirical Methods in Natural Language Processing (EMNLP)*, pages 9131–9143.

Barbara Plank. 2022. The "Problem" of Human Label Variation: On Ground Truth in Data, Modeling and Evaluation. In *Proceedings of the 2022 Conference on Empirical Methods in Natural Language Processing*, pages 10671–10682.

Danish Pruthi, Bhuwan Dhingra, Graham Neubig, and Zachary C. Lipton. 2020. Weakly- and Semi-supervised Evidence Extraction. In *Findings of the Association for Computational Linguistics: EMNLP 2020*, pages 3965–3970.

Satoshi Sekine, Ralph Grishman, and Hiroyuki Shinnou. 1998. A decision tree method for finding and classifying names in Japanese texts. In *Sixth Workshop on Very Large Corpora*.

Victor S. Sheng, Foster Provost, and Panagiotis G. Ipeirotis. 2008. Get another label? improving data quality and data mining using multiple, noisy labelers. In *Proceedings of the 14th ACM SIGKDD International Conference on Knowledge Discovery and Data Mining*, KDD '08, pages 614–622.

Erik F. Tjong Kim Sang and Sabine Buchholz. 2000. Introduction to the CoNLL-2000 Shared Task Chunking. In *Fourth Conference on Computational Natural Language Learning and the Second Learning Language in Logic Workshop*.

# Findings of WASSA 2024 Shared Task on Empathy and Personality Detection in Interactions

**Salvatore Giorgi**[1], **João Sedoc**[2], **Valentin Barriere**[3], **Shabnam Tafreshi**[4]
[1]National Institute on Drug Abuse, Baltimore, USA
[2]New York University, New York, USA
[3]Universidad de Chile – DCC | CENIA, Santiago, Chile
[4]inQbator AI at eviCore Healthcare, Evernorth Healthcare
sal.giorgi@gmail.com,jsedoc@stern.nyu.edu,
vbarriere@dcc.uchile.cl,stafresh@umd.edu

## Abstract

This paper presents the results of the WASSA 2024 shared task on predicting empathy, emotion, and personality in conversations and reactions to news articles. Participating teams were given access to a new, unpublished extension of the WASSA 2023 shared task dataset. This task is both multi-level and multi-modal: data is available at the person, essay, dialog, and dialog-turn levels and includes formal (news articles) and informal text (essays and dialogs), self-report data (personality and distress), and third-party annotations (empathy and emotion). The shared task included a new focus on conversations between humans and LLM-based virtual agents which occur immediately after reading and reacting to the news articles. Participants were encouraged to explore the multi-level and multi-modal nature of this data. Participation was encouraged in four tracks: (i) predicting the perceived empathy at the dialog level, (ii) predicting turn-level empathy, emotion polarity, and emotion intensity in conversations, (iii) predicting state empathy and distress scores, and (iv) predicting personality. In total, 14 teams participated in the shared task. We summarize the methods and resources used by the participating teams.

## 1 Introduction

Empathy, emotions, and similar affective states are fundamental human relationships, informing complex social interactions and cognition (Cassell, 2001; Picard, 2000). These states can be consciously and unconsciously expressed through facial expressions, writing, speech, body language, and mimicry (Shoumy et al., 2020) and have effects on cooperation (Manson et al., 2013), romantic relationships (Ireland et al., 2011), and therapist ratings (Lord et al., 2015). In the context of human-agent interactions, these phenomena are essential to make machines understand the world and have humans actively and genuinely engage with them.

Dialog systems have become increasingly conversant, due to advances in generative artificial intelligence. As such, it has been suggested that these systems could be applied across a wide range of human facing applications, such as mental and behavioral healthcare and substance use recovery (Demszky et al., 2023; Stade et al., 2024b,a; Giorgi et al., 2024). Along with this, automatic agents are being designed with human-like traits such as empathy (Rashkin et al., 2019), emotion (Zhou and Wang, 2018; Huber et al., 2018), and personas (Roller et al., 2021; Cheng et al., 2023). There are also attempts to align such systems with human preferences, opinions, beliefs, and culture (Santurkar et al., 2023; Scherrer et al., 2024; Havaldar et al., 2023). Despite this active attention, implementations of such systems have had limited success and standardized data sets in which empathy, and related complex emotional states, can be modeled are in short supply Omitaomu et al. (2022).

While studying affect-related phenomena in the context of automatic dialog agents and human-bot interactions has become ubiquitous, Lahnala et al. (2022) has noted that concepts such as empathy are traditionally poorly defined. This shared task attempts to address these issues by presenting participants with multiple, psychologically grounded definitions of empathy allowing participants to study multiple forms of empathy, varying measurements of empathy (e.g., self-report and other-report), and their interactions. This includes trait empathy (empathy which is stable over time and systematically differs across people), state empathy (empathy experienced at a specific place in time), perceived empathy (how one's conversational partner views their empathy), and conversational turn empathy (the level of empathy expressed at each stage of a conversation).

This paper presents the WASSA 2024 Empathy Shared Task on Empathy and Personality Detection in Interactions, which allows studying empathy,



*Proceedings of the 14th Workshop on Computational Approaches to Subjectivity, Sentiment, & Social Media Analysis*, pages 369–379
August 15, 2024 

personality, and perception in human-human and human-bot interactions. Past WASSA shared tasks were also held on emotion, empathy, distress, or personality detection in text essays (Tafreshi et al., 2021; Barriere et al., 2022, 2023). Thus, this year's task builds on past shared tasks, with data very similar to past years, plus a brand new type of data. We used a new dataset from (Omitaomu et al., 2022) containing reactions to news article data and annotations similar to (Buechel et al., 2018a) and (Tafreshi et al., 2021), including news articles that express harm to an entity (e.g., individual, group of people, nature).

The news articles are accompanied by essays where authors express their empathy and distress in response to the content. Each essay is self-reported empathy and distress. They are also enriched with additional information, such as the authors' personality traits, IRI, and demographic details, including age, gender, ethnicity, income, and education level. Similar to the WASSA 2023 shared task, we include subsequent conversations that the study participants had after writing their essays. Every turn in the conversation was third-party annotated for empathy, emotion, and emotional polarity. In this year's task, we introduced two new components, the first is that after each conversation, participants rated the empathy of their conversational partner. The second new component of the task is that we included conversations between people and a conversational AI system.

Given this dataset as input, the shared task consists of four tracks (see Section 4.1 for each tracks' respective definitions of empathy and emotion):

1. Empathy Prediction in Conversations (CONV-Dialog), which consists of predicting the perceived empathy at the dialog-level.
2. Empathy and Emotion Prediction in Conversations Turns (CONV-Turn), which consists in predicting the perceived empathy, emotion polarity, and emotion intensity at the speech-turn-level in a conversation.
3. Empathy Prediction (EMP), which consists of predicting both the empathic concern and the personal distress at the essay-level.
4. Personality Prediction (PER), which consists of predicting the personality (openness, conscientiousness, extraversion, agreeableness, and emotional stability; OCEAN) of the essay writer, knowing all his/her essays, dialogs, and the news articles from which they reacted.

## 2 Related Work

### 2.1 Empathy and Distress

Several studies have attempted to both predict empathy from text (Litvak et al., 2016), model empathy in counseling (Xiao et al., 2015, 2016), and build empathetic conversational agents (Rashkin et al., 2019; Gao et al., 2021). Hosseini and Caragea (2021) looks at members of online health communities seek or provide empathy. Other studies have used appraisal theory to study empathy in Reddit conversations (Zhou and Jurgens, 2020; Yang and Jurgens, 2024). Computational methods have also been used to distinguish between good and bad types of empathy (Yaden et al., 2023; Abdul-Mageed et al., 2017), where "bad empathy" involves taking on the feelings of others, which can lead to empathetic burnout, while "good empathy" (also called compassion) is a prosocial motivator without emotional contagion. Given the extensive work on this subject, there are several in depth review articles (Shetty et al., 2024; Lahnala et al., 2022).

### 2.2 Personality Prediction

Predicting personality from text (including social media data) has been rigorously validated via psychometric tests (e.g., convergent validity, divergent validity, and test-retest reliability; Park et al., 2015). Dialog agents are also being designed with personalities (Liu et al., 2022). Similarly, large Language Models are being used for personality classification (Ganesan et al., 2023; Peters and Matz, 2024; Yang et al.) and for studying the personality of the model's themselves (Safdari et al., 2023; Salecha et al., 2024; Miotto et al., 2022). Similar to empathy, there are several survey papers on personality prediction models, theories, and techniques (Vora et al., 2020; Beck and Jackson, 2022).

## 3 Data Collection and Annotation

The source of the data for the shared task is from Omitaomu et al. (2022). We extend this dataset with essay-level emotion annotations by the authors. Although the dataset is different from the data set of Buechel et al. (2018b) used in WASSA 2021 and 2022 shared task (Tafreshi et al., 2021; Barriere et al., 2022), it can be considered an extension. Table 1 shows the train, development, and test splits. We first briefly present how the original dataset was collected and annotated in subsection 3.1.

|  | Train | Dev | Test |
|---|---|---|---|
| People | 75 | 83 | 34 |
| Conversations | 500 | 33 | 67 |
| Essays | 1,000 | 66 | 83 |
| Speech-Turns | 11,166 | 990 | 2,316 |

Table 1: Corpus statistics detailing the number of annotations.

### 3.1 Initial Data Collection and Annotation

Here we provide a brief overview of the data collection process employed by Omitaomu et al. (2022). They recruited crowd workers from MTurk.com and utilized the Qualtrics survey platform and ParlAI for data collection. The data collection process began with an intake phase, during which crowd workers provided their demographic information and completed surveys for the Big Five (OCEAN) personality traits and the Interpersonal Reactivity Index (IRI; Davis, 1983). Next, pairs of crowd workers read news articles. Each pair read one article of the 100 articles. After reading the article, the crowd workers wrote an essay of 300 to 800 characters about the article they read and rated their empathy and distress levels using the Batson scale (Batson et al., 1987). Then, the pair of crowd workers engaged in online text conversation where they were instructed to talk about the article for a minimum of 10 turns per person in training and development sets and 15 turns per person in the test set.

After the conversations were collected, a new task was created to collect turn-level annotations for each conversation. The workers were asked to rate the empathy, emotional polarity, and emotional intensity of each turn. Three crowd workers annotated each turn and were given the context of the previous turns in the conversation.

## 4 Shared Task

We set up all four tracks in CodaLab[1]. We describe each task separately in Section 4.1 and then describe dataset, resources, and evaluation metrics in Section 4.2. Tracks 2, 3, and 4 are similar to the ones offered by WASSA 2022 and 2023 shared tasks.

[1] https://codalab.lisn.upsaclay.fr/competitions/18810

### 4.1 Tracks

**Track 1 - Empathy Prediction in Conversations (CONV-Dialog):** The formulation of this task is to predict, for each conversation, the perceived empathy at the dialog-level. As described in Sec 3, immediately after each conversation participants were asked to rate the empathy of their conversational partner towards the patient of harm on a 1 to 7 ordinal scale. The participants were asked to predict the rated value of the partner. In the case of a human-bot conversation, there was only one rating since the conversational AI system was not tasked to do this rating. This track was newly introduced as part of this year's shared task.

**Track 2 - Turn-level Empathy and Emotion in Conversations (CONV-Turn):** The formulation of this task is to predict, for each conversational turn, the emotion polarity and intensity as well as the third-party annotations of empathy. The targets are third-party assessment of emotional polarity (positive, negative, or neutral) and both emotional intensity and empathy coded on an ordinal scale from 1 to 5 with a not applicable option. This track was introduced in WASSA 2023, but the data in this year's task (2024) is new.

**Track 3 - State Empathy Prediction (EMP):** The formulation of this task is to predict, for each essay, Batson's empathic concern ("feeling for someone") and personal distress ("suffering with someone") scores (Batson et al., 1987). Teams are expected to develop models that predict the empathy score for each essay (self-report data from the essay writer). Both empathy and distress scores are real values between 1 and 7. Empathy score is an average of 7-point scale ratings, representing each of the following states (warm, tender, sympathetic, softhearted, moved, compassionate); distress score is an average of 7-point scale ratings, representing each of the following states (worried, upset, troubled, perturbed, grieved, disturbed, alarmed, distressed). These are state measures: measures that vary within people across time. For optional use, we made personality, demographic information, and emotion labels available for each essay. This track was previously done in WASSA 2023, 2022, and 2021, but this year's task uses new data.

**Track 4 - Personality Prediction (PER):** This task asked participants to predict personality scores for each essay. To code personality information, the Big 5 personality traits were provided, also known

| Team | Perceived Empathy |
|---|---|
| Fraunhofer SIT | **.193** |
| ConText | .191 |
| Chinchunmei | .172 |
| EmpatheticFIG | .012 |
| Baseline | .023 |

Table 2: Track 1 CONV-Dialog: Results of the teams participating in the EMP track (product moment correlations), order by descending effect size.

as the OCEAN model (Gosling et al., 2003b). In the OCEAN model, the theory identifies five factors (Openness to experience, Conscientiousness, Extraversion, Agreeableness, and Neuroticism[2]). Participants were asked to produce scores for each of the five factors. For each essay, the writer was asked to complete the Ten Item Personality Inventory (Gosling et al., 2003a), two items for each of the five factors. Thus, this is self-reported essay-level data. This task was previously done in WASSA 2022 and 2023, but the data in this year's task (2024) is new.

**Multi-task:** We gave the participants a unique id for each conversation so that the participants could use multi-task learning methods to tackle all the tasks simultaneously. Moreover, speakers in the train, dev, and test datasets were given unique ids so that teams could use several of the participant's essays or conversations in order to improve the results. This was proven to help in WASSA 2022 for the PER and IRI subtasks (Barriere et al., 2022).

### 4.2 Setup

**Dataset:** Participants were provided the dataset described in Section 3. Participants were allowed to add the development set to the training set and submit systems trained on both. The test set was made available to the participants at the beginning of the evaluation period.

**Resources and Systems Restrictions** Participants were allowed to use any lexical resources (e.g., emotion or empathy dictionaries) of their choice, additional training data, or off-the-shelf emotion or empathy models. We did not put any restrictions on this shared task. We proposed several baseline models for this article, which are described in Section 4.3.

[2]For the shared task, neuroticism has been reverse coded as emotional stability

| Team | Emotion Intensity | Emotion Polarity | Empathy | Avg |
|---|---|---|---|---|
| ConText | **.622** | .679 | .577 | **.626** |
| Chinchunmei | .607 | **.680** | .582 | .623 |
| EmpatheticFIG | .601 | .671 | .559 | .610 |
| Last-min-submission-team | .589 | .663 | .534 | .595 |
| hyy3 | .581 | .644 | .544 | .590 |
| Empathify | .584 | .638 | .541 | .588 |
| empaths | .473 | .422 | .534 | .477 |
| Fraunhofer SIT | .032 | -.018 | .034 | -.007 |
| Zhenmei | -.043 | -.020 | -.027 | -.030 |
| Baseline | .417 | .646 | **.694** | .586 |

Table 3: Track 2 CONV-Turn: Results of the teams participating in the CONV-Turn track (product moment correlations), order by average descending effect size.

**Systems Evaluation:** The organizers published an evaluation script that calculates product moment correlations for the predictions of the four tasks. The product moment correlation coefficient is the linear correlation between two variables, and it produces scores from -1 (perfectly inversely correlated) to 1 (perfectly correlated). A score of 0 indicates no correlation. The official competition metric for the empathy in conversations task (CONV-Dialog) is the product moment correlation for perceived empathy. The official competition metric for the empathy and emotion in conversation task (CONV-Turn) is the average of the three product moment correlations (emotion intensity, emotion polarity, and empathy). The official competition metric for the state empathy prediction task (EMP) is the average of the two product moment correlations (empathy and distress). The official competition metric for the personality task (PER) is the average of the product moment correlations of the five factors.

### 4.3 Baselines

**CONV-Dialog:** Similar to Omitaomu et al. (2022), we fine-tuned a RoBERTa (base) pretrained language model (Liu et al., 2019). The model was trained on the training set and used the development set for model validation. We trained one model for all dialog turns of the person being assessed. The model was trained using regression since this was on a 7 point scale. The training was for 30 epochs, and the model checkpoint with the best validation set product moment correlation was kept.

**CONV-Turn:** Following Omitaomu et al. (2022), we fine-tuned a RoBERTa (base) pretrained language model (Liu et al., 2019). The model was trained on the training set and used the development set for model validation. We trained one

| Team | Empathy | Distress | Avg. |
|---|---|---|---|
| RU | .523 | .383 | .453 |
| Chinchunmei | .474 | .311 | .393 |
| Fraunhofer SIT | .375 | .395 | .385 |
| 1024m | .361 | .327 | .344 |
| ConText | .390 | .252 | .321 |
| Empathify | .290 | .217 | .253 |
| Daisy | .345 | .082 | .213 |
| Baseline | **.629** | **.477** | **.553** |

Table 4: Track 3 EMP: Results of the teams participating in the EMP track (product moment correlations).

model for each of the turn-level label types. The training was for 30 epochs, and the model checkpoint with the best validation set product moment correlation was kept.

**EMP:** Like the CONV models, we fine-tuned a RoBERTa (base) pretrained language model (Liu et al., 2019). For training, we used both the training data of the essays and the WASSA22 and WASSA23 training data (Barriere et al., 2023, 2022). We created separate models for empathy and distress, and used the same checkpoint and stopping criteria as the CONV task models.

**PER:** Similar to the 2023 shared task, we used a Big 5 personality model developed by Park et al. (2015). This model was trained on Facebook status updates from 66,732 people who self-reported questionnaire-based Big Five personality traits. This model used ngrams and topics extracted from the Facebook status updates in an $\ell_2$ penalized Ridge regression. This model was then applied to all text generated by each person in the test set (i.e., essays and conversations), producing Big 5 estimates for each.

## 5 Results and Discussion

A total of 14 teams participated in this year's shared task, with 4, 9, 7, and 3 teams across the four tracks, respectively. The results for each task are summarized below.

### 5.1 Empathy Prediction (CONV-Dialog)

Table 2 shows the results for Track 1. Here participants were asked to predict (via a regression task) perceived empathy, as rated by conversational partners. A total of four teams participated in this track, and were evaluated via product moment correlation. The system with the highest test set correlation was *Fraunhofer SIT* ($r = .193$), though it should be noted that no team had a statistically significant correlation ($p < .05$).

### 5.2 Turn-level Empathy and Emotion Prediction (CONV-Turn)

Table 3 shows the results of Track 2. Participants were asked to predict third-party assessments emotion intensity, emotion polarity, and empathy for each turn in the dialogs. Teams were evaluated via the average product moment correlation across the three measures. Team *ConText* had the highest average correlation ($r = .626$), as well as the highest correlation for emotion intensity ($r = .622$). Team *Chinchunmei* had the highest correlations for emotion polarity ($r = .680$) and empathy ($r = .582$), and also had the second highest average correlation ($r = .623$). The RoBERTa-base baseline outperforms on Empathy, but underperformed across all other dimensions. All top correlations were statistically significant ($p < .05$).

### 5.3 State Empathy and Distress Predictions (EMP)

Table 4 shows the results for Track 3. A total of 7 teams participated in this track. Teams were ranked via the average product moment correlation across both empathy and distress. Team *RU* had the highest ranked system with an average correlation of $r = .453$. This team also had the highest empathy correlation ($r = .523$). Team *Fraunhofer SIT* had the highest distress correlation ($r = .395$). Our baseline RoBERTa-base model outperformed all other models likely due to the inclusion of the data from the prior years. All top correlations were statistically significant ($p < .05$).

### 5.4 Personality Predictions (PER)

Table 5 shows the results for Track 4. Three teams participated in this task. Team *amsqr* attained the highest average correation ($r = .300$). This team's results for the Agreeableness ($r = .540$) and Emotional Stability ($r = .757$) factors were the only significant correlations in the results ($p < .05$). Only one team that participated in this task submitted a system description paper. Thus, it is unclear how *amsqr* achieved their results.

### 5.5 Comparison with previous results

Table 6 shows the results of each track across previous shared tasks from 2021 (Tafreshi et al.,

| Team | Openness | Conscientiousness | Extraversion | Agreeableness | Emotional Stability | Avg. |
|---|---|---|---|---|---|---|
| amsqr | **.170** | **.303** | -.272 | **.540** | **.757** | **.300** |
| NU | -.103 | .102 | -.085 | .154 | .279 | .069 |
| 1024m | .059 | -.032 | -.128 | -.015 | -.009 | -.025 |
| Baseline | .042 | .207 | **.300** | .127 | -.012 | .133 |

Table 5: Track 4 PER: Results of the teams participating in the PER track (product moment correlations).

2021), 2022 (Barriere et al., 2022), and 2023 (Barriere et al., 2023). Note that the numbers reported for (Buechel et al., 2018b) are the average empathy and distress scores for their best system ($r = .404$ for empathy and $r = .444$ for distress). This system used 10-fold cross validation, rather than dedicated train, development, and test sets, and thus, these results are not comparable to those in this shared task. In WASSA 2023, which shared three out of four tracks, results for Track 2 (CONV-Turn) were higher in magnitude, with eight out of ten systems (including baseline) scoring above (highest average $r = .758$) the best team in this year's shared task (*ConText*). For Track 3 (EMP), this year's best scoring team (*RU*) outperformed all of the nine teams that participated in this track in 2023 (highest average $r = .418$). Finally, for Track 4 (PER) the highest performing team this year (*amsqr)* outperformed last year's teams (highest average $r = .252$).

## 6 Overview of Submitted Systems

Below we summarize the algorithms and resources used by the teams.

### 6.1 Machine Learning Architectures

The machine learning architectures used by the participating teams are summarized in Table 7. Similar to last year's shared task, most teams relied on BERT (Devlin et al., 2019) and related variants: RoBERTa (Liu et al., 2019), DeBERTa (He et al.), SieBERT (Hartmann et al., 2023), and similar variants finetuned for sentiment (Barbieri et al., 2020). These models were used out-of-the-box, and in custom architectures, such as those used to create history-dependent embedding. New this year are systems based on more modern large language models, such as Llama (Touvron et al., 2023) and GPT variants (e.g., ChatGPT and GPT-4o; Brown et al., 2020). Two systems utilized psychologically-grounded or theory-based features, where features were chosen based on their known relationships to emotion and empathy. Finally, other transformer-based models were used, though less often: T5 (Raffel et al., 2020) and Longformer (Beltagy et al., 2020).

| | CONV Dialog | CONV Turn | EMP | PER |
|---|---|---|---|---|
| Buechel et al. (2018b) | - | - | .242 | - |
| WASSA 2021 | - | - | **.545** | - |
| WASSA 2022 | - | - | .540 | .230 |
| WASSA 2023 | - | **.758** | .418 | .252 |
| This year (2024) | .193 | .626 | .453 | **.300** |

Table 6: Comparison of best performing scores across each track for previous years of the shared task. Reported average product moment correlation.

### 6.2 Resources

Two teams used a RoBERTa model finetuned on the GoEmotions data set (Demszky et al., 2020), which contains Reddit posts annotated for 27 emotions. One team analyzed their model using a SHAP (SHapley Additive exPlanations) analysis (Lundberg and Lee, 2017) in tandem with the GoEmotions-based emotions classifier, which highlighted which emotions were most associated with empathy and distress. Several teams used large language models for data augmentation. Llama and GPT-related models were used for paraphrasing and for predicting psychological indicators (e.g., perspective-taking, sympathy, and compassion) used downstream to predict turn-level empathy. Similarly, mT5 (Xue et al., 2021) was used to extract figurative language (metaphor, idiom, and hyperbole) labels for conversational turns. While not an external resource, one team used a built a knowledge graph from self reported demographics (age, gender, income, and education) and empathy (trait level; IRI). Finally, LIWC (Boyd et al., 2022) was used to understand what types of turn-level text were most associated emotional intensity, emotional polarity, and empathy.

| Alg. | # of teams | CONV Dialog | CONV Turn | EMP | PER |
|---|---|---|---|---|---|
| BERT-like | 9 | ✓ | ✓ | ✓ | ✓ |
| GPT-like | 3 | - | ✓ | ✓ | - |
| Llama-like | 3 | ✓ | ✓ | ✓ | - |
| Theory based | 2 | ✓ | ✓ | - | - |

Table 7: Algorithms used by the different teams. We listed all the techniques that teams reported in their system description papers. Note that not all participating teams submitted system papers.

## 7 Conclusion

In this paper, we presented the shared task on empathy and personality detection in essays and conversations in reactions to news articles, to which 14 teams participated and 12 submitted a paper. While this year saw an increase in large language models (i.e., GPT and Llama variants), though most teams still relied on BERT and RoBERTa variants. A small number of teams used task related resources, such as models finetuned on sentiment and emotion datasets. No external data sets were used, though generative AI systems were used for data augmentation. Two teams used empathy and emotion related features, such as figurative language and related psychologically-grounded indicators. One team used historical conversation context, when predicting turn-level labels. A single team used speaker self-report data, such as demographics (age, gender, race), socioeconomics (income and education), and trait-level empathy (IRI) alongside text-based features. Finally, no teams used used multi-task learning, leveraged the multi-modal or multi-level nature of the data, or made a distinction between bot and human data.

## Limitations

This shared task and the associated data are limited in several ways. First, despite the multi-modal aspects of the data, the number of words collect per person is limited (by both essay and conversation length). Thus, it may be more difficult to predict trait level measures (e.g., personality) than state or turn-level measures (e.g., emotion and empathy). This could explain the low performance in Track 4 PER. We note that past work on detecting personality from social media has used a minimum of 1000 words for accurate predictions (Lynn et al., 2020). Similarly, personality models are typically trained on larger personality questionnaires, such as the 20- or 100-item personality inventory (Park et al., 2015). The 10-item version could lead to noisier personality estimates which are more difficult to predict from text. Second, the person- and essay-level tasks both have small sample sizes, which could explain why none of the correlations in Track 1 were significant (i.e., the task was under powered). Finally, we only consider English language news articles and English conversations from crowd workers in the U.S., thus limiting the study of empathy to these cultures and languages/dialects.

## Ethics Statement

There are several ethical concerns one should consider when predicting affective measures. There is mounting evidence that emotion recognition systems are being use as part of mass surveillance systems by governments and private entities worldwide (Barkane, 2022). These systems are used in high stakes settings, such as law enforcement, and are known to discriminate and violate rights to privacy (Kieslich and Lünich, 2024). While there are many prosocial applications to embedding machines with emotions and empathy, such as mental health related chatbots, there are also several similar concerns. Such empathetic or emotional systems could increase trust with their end users through anthropromorphisms (Abercrombie et al., 2023), which could have several nefarious use cases (for example, spreading misinformation or political ads which elicit empathetic responses). Similarly, overly empathetic or agreeable systems could ignore or agree with unsafe or toxic input (Kim et al., 2022).

## Acknowledgements

V.B. has been funded by the grant National Center for Artificial Intelligence CENIA FB210017, Basal ANID.

## References

Muhammad Abdul-Mageed, Anneke Buffone, Hao Peng, Salvatore Giorgi, Johannes Eichstaedt, and Lyle Ungar. 2017. Recognizing pathogenic empathy in social media. In *Proceedings of the International AAAI Conference on Web and Social Media*, volume 11, pages 448–451.

Gavin Abercrombie, Amanda Cercas Curry, Tanvi Dinkar, Verena Rieser, and Zeerak Talat. 2023. Mirages. on anthropomorphism in dialogue systems. In *Proceedings of the 2023 Conference on Empirical Methods in Natural Language Processing*, pages 4776–4790.

Francesco Barbieri, Jose Camacho-Collados, Luis Espinosa Anke, and Leonardo Neves. 2020. Tweeteval: Unified benchmark and comparative evaluation for tweet classification. In *Findings of the Association for Computational Linguistics: EMNLP 2020*, pages 1644–1650.

Irena Barkane. 2022. Questioning the eu proposal for an artificial intelligence act: The need for prohibitions and a stricter approach to biometric surveillance 1. *Information Polity*, 27(2):147–162.

Valentin Barriere, João Sedoc, Shabnam Tafreshi, and Salvatore Giorgi. 2023. Findings of WASSA 2023 shared task on empathy, emotion and personality detection in conversation and reactions to news articles. In *Proceedings of the 13th Workshop on Computational Approaches to Subjectivity, Sentiment, & Social Media Analysis*, pages 511–525, Toronto, Canada. Association for Computational Linguistics.

Valentin Barriere, Shabnam Tafreshi, João Sedoc, and Sawsan Alqahtani. 2022. WASSA 2022 shared task: Predicting empathy, emotion and personality in reaction to news stories. In *Proceedings of the 12th Workshop on Computational Approaches to Subjectivity, Sentiment & Social Media Analysis*, pages 214–227, Dublin, Ireland. Association for Computational Linguistics.

C Daniel Batson, Jim Fultz, and Patricia A Schoenrade. 1987. Distress and empathy: Two qualitatively distinct vicarious emotions with different motivational consequences. *Journal of personality*, 55(1):19–39.

Emorie D Beck and Joshua J Jackson. 2022. A mega-analysis of personality prediction: Robustness and boundary conditions. *Journal of Personality and Social Psychology*, 122(3):523.

Iz Beltagy, Matthew E Peters, and Arman Cohan. 2020. Longformer: The long-document transformer. *arXiv preprint arXiv:2004.05150*.

Ryan L Boyd, Ashwini Ashokkumar, Sarah Seraj, and James W Pennebaker. 2022. The development and psychometric properties of liwc-22. *Austin, TX: University of Texas at Austin*, 10.

Tom Brown, Benjamin Mann, Nick Ryder, Melanie Subbiah, Jared D Kaplan, Prafulla Dhariwal, Arvind Neelakantan, Pranav Shyam, Girish Sastry, Amanda Askell, et al. 2020. Language models are few-shot learners. *Advances in neural information processing systems*, 33:1877–1901.

Sven Buechel, Anneke Buffone, Barry Slaff, Lyle Ungar, and João Sedoc. 2018a. Modeling empathy and distress in reaction to news stories. In *Proceedings of the 2018 Conference on Empirical Methods in Natural Language Processing*, pages 4758–4765, Brussels, Belgium. Association for Computational Linguistics.

Sven Buechel, Anneke Buffone, Barry Slaff, Lyle Ungar, and João Sedoc. 2018b. Modeling empathy and distress in reaction to news stories. In *Proceedings of the 2018 Conference on Empirical Methods in Natural Language Processing*, pages 4758–4765, Brussels, Belgium. Association for Computational Linguistics.

Justine Cassell. 2001. Embodied conversational agents: Representation and intelligence in user interfaces. *AI Magazine*, 22(4):67–83.

Myra Cheng, Tiziano Piccardi, and Diyi Yang. 2023. CoMPosT: Characterizing and evaluating caricature in LLM simulations. In *Proceedings of the 2023 Conference on Empirical Methods in Natural Language Processing*, pages 10853–10875, Singapore. Association for Computational Linguistics.

Mark H Davis. 1983. Measuring individual differences in empathy: Evidence for a multidimensional approach. *Journal of personality and social psychology*, 44(1):113.

Dorottya Demszky, Dana Movshovitz-Attias, Jeongwoo Ko, Alan Cowen, Gaurav Nemade, and Sujith Ravi. 2020. Goemotions: A dataset of fine-grained emotions. *arXiv preprint arXiv:2005.00547*.

Dorottya Demszky, Diyi Yang, David S Yeager, Christopher J Bryan, Margarett Clapper, Susannah Chandhok, Johannes C Eichstaedt, Cameron Hecht, Jeremy Jamieson, Meghann Johnson, et al. 2023. Using large language models in psychology. *Nature Reviews Psychology*, 2(11):688–701.

Jacob Devlin, Ming-Wei Chang, Kenton Lee, and Kristina Toutanova. 2019. Bert: Pre-training of deep bidirectional transformers for language understanding. In *Proceedings of the 2019 Conference of the North American Chapter of the Association for Computational Linguistics: Human Language Technologies, Volume 1 (Long and Short Papers)*, pages 4171–4186.

Adithya V Ganesan, Yash Kumar Lal, August Håkan Nilsson, and H. Andrew Schwartz. 2023. Systematic evaluation of gpt-3 for zero-shot personality estimation. In *Proceedings of the 13th Workshop on Computational Approaches to Subjectivity, Sentiment & Social Media Analysis*.

Jun Gao, Yuhan Liu, Haolin Deng, Wei Wang, Yu Cao, Jiachen Du, and Ruifeng Xu. 2021. Improving empathetic response generation by recognizing emotion cause in conversations. In *Findings of the association for computational linguistics: EMNLP 2021*, pages 807–819.

Salvatore Giorgi, Kelsey Isman, Tingting Liu, Zachary Fried, Brenda Curtis, et al. 2024. Evaluating generative ai responses to real-world drug-related questions. *Psychiatry Research*, page 116058.

Samuel D Gosling, Peter J Rentfrow, and William B Swann Jr. 2003a. A very brief measure of the big-five personality domains. *Journal of Research in personality*, 37(6):504–528.

Samuel D Gosling, Peter J Rentfrow, and Williams B Swann Jr. 2003b. A very brief measure of the big-five personality domains. *Journal of Research in Personality*, 37:504–528.

Jochen Hartmann, Mark Heitmann, Christian Siebert, and Christina Schamp. 2023. More than a feeling: Accuracy and application of sentiment analysis. *International Journal of Research in Marketing*, 40(1):75–87.

Shreya Havaldar, Bhumika Singhal, Sunny Rai, Langchen Liu, Sharath Chandra Guntuku, and Lyle Ungar. 2023. Multilingual language models are not multicultural: A case study in emotion. In *Proceedings of the 13th Workshop on Computational Approaches to Subjectivity, Sentiment, & Social Media Analysis*, pages 202–214.

Pengcheng He, Xiaodong Liu, Jianfeng Gao, and Weizhu Chen. Deberta: Decoding-enhanced bert with disentangled attention. In *International Conference on Learning Representations*.

Mahshid Hosseini and Cornelia Caragea. 2021. It takes two to empathize: One to seek and one to provide. In *Proceedings of the AAAI conference on artificial intelligence*, volume 35, pages 13018–13026.

Bernd Huber, Daniel McDuff, Chris Brockett, Michel Galley, and Bill Dolan. 2018. Emotional dialogue generation using image-grounded language models. In *Proceedings of the 2018 CHI Conference on Human Factors in Computing Systems*, page 277. ACM.

Molly E. Ireland, Richard B. Slatcher, Paul W. Eastwick, Lauren E. Scissors, Eli J. Finkel, and James W. Pennebaker. 2011. Language style matching predicts relationship initiation and stability. *Psychological Science*, 22(1):39–44. PMID: 21149854.

Kimon Kieslich and Marco Lünich. 2024. Regulating ai-based remote biometric identification. investigating the public demand for bans, audits, and public database registrations. In *The 2024 ACM Conference on Fairness, Accountability, and Transparency*, pages 173–185.

Hyunwoo Kim, Youngjae Yu, Liwei Jiang, Ximing Lu, Daniel Khashabi, Gunhee Kim, Yejin Choi, and Maarten Sap. 2022. ProsocialDialog: A prosocial backbone for conversational agents. In *Proceedings of the 2022 Conference on Empirical Methods in Natural Language Processing*, pages 4005–4029, Abu Dhabi, United Arab Emirates. Association for Computational Linguistics.

Allison Lahnala, Charles Welch, David Jurgens, and Lucie Flek. 2022. A critical reflection and forward perspective on empathy and natural language processing. In *Findings of the Association for Computational Linguistics: EMNLP 2022*, pages 2139–2158.

Marina Litvak, Jahna Otterbacher, Chee Siang Ang, and David Atkins. 2016. Social and linguistic behavior and its correlation to trait empathy. Association for Computational Linguistics.

Yifan Liu, Wei Wei, Jiayi Liu, Xianling Mao, Rui Fang, and Dangyang Chen. 2022. Improving personality consistency in conversation by persona extending. In *Proceedings of the 31st ACM International Conference on Information & Knowledge Management*, pages 1350–1359.

Yinhan Liu, Myle Ott, Naman Goyal, Jingfei Du, Mandar Joshi, Danqi Chen, Omer Levy, Mike Lewis, Luke Zettlemoyer, and Veselin Stoyanov. 2019. Roberta: A robustly optimized bert pretraining approach. *arXiv preprint arXiv:1907.11692*.

Sarah Peregrine Lord, Elisa Sheng, Zac E Imel, John Baer, and David C Atkins. 2015. More than reflections: Empathy in motivational interviewing includes language style synchrony between therapist and client. *Behavior therapy*, 46(3):296–303.

Scott M Lundberg and Su-In Lee. 2017. A unified approach to interpreting model predictions. *Advances in neural information processing systems*, 30.

Veronica Lynn, Niranjan Balasubramanian, and H Andrew Schwartz. 2020. Hierarchical modeling for user personality prediction: The role of message-level attention. In *Proceedings of the 58th annual meeting of the association for computational linguistics*, pages 5306–5316.

Joseph H Manson, Gregory A Bryant, Matthew M Gervais, and Michelle A Kline. 2013. Convergence of speech rate in conversation predicts cooperation. *Evolution and Human Behavior*, 34(6):419–426.

Marilù Miotto, Nicola Rossberg, and Bennett Kleinberg. 2022. Who is GPT-3? an exploration of personality, values and demographics. In *Proceedings of the Fifth Workshop on Natural Language Processing and Computational Social Science (NLP+CSS)*, pages 218–227, Abu Dhabi, UAE. Association for Computational Linguistics.

Damilola Omitaomu, Shabnam Tafreshi, Tingting Liu, Sven Buechel, Chris Callison-Burch, Johannes Eichstaedt, Lyle Ungar, and João Sedoc. 2022. Empathic conversations: A multi-level dataset of contextualized conversations. *arXiv preprint arXiv:2205.12698*.

Gregory Park, H Andrew Schwartz, Johannes C Eichstaedt, Margaret L Kern, Michal Kosinski, David J Stillwell, Lyle H Ungar, and Martin EP Seligman. 2015. Automatic personality assessment through social media language. *Journal of personality and social psychology*, 108(6):934.

Heinrich Peters and Sandra C Matz. 2024. Large language models can infer psychological dispositions of social media users. *PNAS nexus*, 3(6).

Rosalind W Picard. 2000. *Affective computing*. MIT press.

Colin Raffel, Noam Shazeer, Adam Roberts, Katherine Lee, Sharan Narang, Michael Matena, Yanqi Zhou, Wei Li, and Peter J Liu. 2020. Exploring the limits of transfer learning with a unified text-to-text transformer. *Journal of machine learning research*, 21(140):1–67.

Hannah Rashkin, Eric Michael Smith, Margaret Li, and Y-Lan Boureau. 2019. Towards empathetic open-domain conversation models: A new benchmark and dataset. In *Proceedings of the 57th Annual Meeting of the Association for Computational Linguistics*, pages 5370–5381.

Stephen Roller, Emily Dinan, Naman Goyal, Da Ju, Mary Williamson, Yinhan Liu, Jing Xu, Myle Ott, Eric Michael Smith, Y-Lan Boureau, et al. 2021. Recipes for building an open-domain chatbot. In *Proceedings of the 16th Conference of the European Chapter of the Association for Computational Linguistics: Main Volume*, pages 300–325.

Mustafa Safdari, Greg Serapio-García, Clément Crepy, Stephen Fitz, Peter Romero, Luning Sun, Marwa Abdulhai, Aleksandra Faust, and Maja Matarić. 2023. Personality traits in large language models. *arXiv preprint arXiv:2307.00184*.

Aadesh Salecha, Molly E. Ireland, Shashanka Subrahmanya, João Sedoc, Lyle H. Ungar, and Johannes C. Eichstaedt. 2024. Large language models show human-like social desirability biases in survey responses. *Preprint*, arXiv:2405.06058.

Shibani Santurkar, Esin Durmus, Faisal Ladhak, Cinoo Lee, Percy Liang, and Tatsunori Hashimoto. 2023. Whose opinions do language models reflect? In *International Conference on Machine Learning*, pages 29971–30004. PMLR.

Nino Scherrer, Claudia Shi, Amir Feder, and David Blei. 2024. Evaluating the moral beliefs encoded in llms. *Advances in Neural Information Processing Systems*, 36.

Vishal Anand Shetty, Shauna Durbin, Meghan S Weyrich, Airín Denise Martínez, Jing Qian, and David L Chin. 2024. A scoping review of empathy recognition in text using natural language processing. *Journal of the American Medical Informatics Association*, 31(3):762–775.

Nusrat J Shoumy, Li-Minn Ang, Kah Phooi Seng, DM Motiur Rahaman, and Tanveer Zia. 2020. Multimodal big data affective analytics: A comprehensive survey using text, audio, visual and physiological signals. *Journal of Network and Computer Applications*, 149:102447.

Elizabeth C Stade, johannes C Eichstaedt, Jane P Kim, and Shannon W Stirman. 2024a. Readiness for ai deployment and implementation (readi): A proposed framework for the evaluation of ai-mental health applications.

Elizabeth C Stade, Shannon Wiltsey Stirman, Lyle H Ungar, Cody L Boland, H Andrew Schwartz, David B Yaden, João Sedoc, Robert J DeRubeis, Robb Willer, and Johannes C Eichstaedt. 2024b. Large language models could change the future of behavioral healthcare: a proposal for responsible development and evaluation. *NPJ Mental Health Research*, 3(1):12.

Shabnam Tafreshi, Orphee De Clercq, Valentin Barriere, Sven Buechel, João Sedoc, and Alexandra Balahur. 2021. WASSA 2021 shared task: Predicting empathy and emotion in reaction to news stories. In *Proceedings of the Eleventh Workshop on Computational Approaches to Subjectivity, Sentiment and Social Media Analysis*, pages 92–104, Online. Association for Computational Linguistics.

Hugo Touvron, Thibaut Lavril, Gautier Izacard, Xavier Martinet, Marie-Anne Lachaux, Timothée Lacroix, Baptiste Rozière, Naman Goyal, Eric Hambro, Faisal Azhar, et al. 2023. Llama: Open and efficient foundation language models. *arXiv preprint arXiv:2302.13971*.

Hetal Vora, Mamta Bhamare, and Dr K Ashok Kumar. 2020. Personality prediction from social media text: An overview. *Int. J. Eng. Res*, 9(05):352–357.

Bo Xiao, Chewei Huang, Zac E Imel, David C Atkins, Panayiotis Georgiou, and Shrikanth S Narayanan. 2016. A technology prototype system for rating therapist empathy from audio recordings in addiction counseling. *PeerJ Computer Science*, 2:e59.

Bo Xiao, Zac E Imel, Panayiotis G Georgiou, David C Atkins, and Shrikanth S Narayanan. 2015. " rate my therapist": automated detection of empathy in drug and alcohol counseling via speech and language processing. *PloS one*, 10(12):e0143055.

Linting Xue, Noah Constant, Adam Roberts, Mihir Kale, Rami Al-Rfou, Aditya Siddhant, Aditya Barua, and Colin Raffel. 2021. mt5: A massively multilingual pre-trained text-to-text transformer. In *Proceedings of the 2021 Conference of the North American Chapter of the Association for Computational Linguistics: Human Language Technologies*, pages 483–498.

David B Yaden, Salvatore Giorgi, Matthew Jordan, Anneke Buffone, Johannes C Eichstaedt, H Andrew Schwartz, Lyle Ungar, and Paul Bloom. 2023. Characterizing empathy and compassion using computational linguistic analysis. *Emotion*.

Jiamin Yang and David Jurgens. 2024. Modeling empathetic alignment in conversation. In *Proceedings of the 2024 Conference of the North American Chapter of the Association for Computational Linguistics: Human Language Technologies (Volume 1: Long Papers)*, pages 3127–3148.

Tao Yang, Tianyuan Shi, Fanqi Wan, Xiaojun Quan, Qifan Wang, Bingzhe Wu, and Jiaxiang Wu. Psycot: Psychological questionnaire as powerful chain-of-thought for personality detection. In *The 2023 Conference on Empirical Methods in Natural Language Processing*.

Naitian Zhou and David Jurgens. 2020. Condolence and empathy in online communities. In *Proceedings of the 2020 Conference on Empirical Methods in Natural Language Processing (EMNLP)*, pages 609–626.

Xianda Zhou and William Yang Wang. 2018. MojiTalk: Generating emotional responses at scale. In *Proceedings of the 56th Annual Meeting of the Association for Computational Linguistics (Volume 1: Long Papers)*, pages 1128–1137, Melbourne, Australia. Association for Computational Linguistics.

# RU at WASSA 2024 Shared Task: Task-Aligned Prompt for Predicting Empathy and Distress

**Haein Kong**
Rutgers University
haein.kong@rutgers.edu

**Seonghyeon Moon**
Brookhaven National Laboratory
smoon@bnl.gov

## Abstract

This paper describes our approach for the WASSA 2024 Shared Task on Empathy Detection and Emotion Classification and Personality Detection in Interactions at ACL 2024. We focused on Track 3: Empathy Prediction (EMP) which aims to predict the empathy and distress of writers based on their essays. Recently, LLMs have been used to detect the psychological status of the writers based on the texts. Previous studies showed that the performance of LLMs can be improved by designing prompts properly. While diverse approaches have been made, we focus on the fact that LLMs can have different nuances for psychological constructs such as empathy or distress to the specific task. In addition, people can express their empathy or distress differently according to the context. Thus, we tried to enhance the prediction performance of LLMs by proposing a new prompting strategy: Task-Aligned Prompt (TAP). This prompt consists of aligned definitions for empathy and distress to the original paper and the contextual information about the dataset. Our proposed prompt was tested using ChatGPT and GPT4o with zero-shot and few-shot settings and the performance was compared to the plain prompts. The results showed that the TAP-ChatGPT-zero-shot achieved the highest average Pearson correlation of empathy and distress on the EMP track.

## 1 Introduction

This paper focuses on Track 3: Empathy Prediction (EMP) of the WASSA 2024 Shared Task 1 at ACL 2024 (Giorgi et al., 2024). This task aims to predict empathy and distress based on essays. Previous NLP research studied how empathy and distress are expressed in the text (Sedoc et al., 2019) and tried to predict the level of empathy and distress with computational methods (Buechel et al., 2018; Barriere et al., 2023). Predicting empathy and distress is an important task that can be applied to diverse contexts, including discerning empathetic conversation (Omitaomu et al., 2022).

Recently, researchers have started to use LLMs to detect psychological status based on text data. For example, Xu et al. (2024) tested multiple LLMs with different methods for the prediction tasks for stress, depression, and other mental states. LLMs have also been used in emotion classification (Nedilko and Chu, 2023) and cognitive distortion classification task (Chen et al., 2023). Lastly, Hasan et al. (2024) used LLMs to convert numerical data into meaningful text and rephrase the text for predicting empathy.

Previous studies have shown that prompt engineering can achieve promising results in predicting mental health. For example, Qin et al. (2023) used the Chain-of-Thought technique and clinically established diagnostic criteria (DSM) in prompt to predict depression on social media texts, showing the best performance across various settings. Chen et al. (2023) proposed Diagnose of Prompt based on cognitive psychology and showed the best performance in classifying cognitive distortions. These findings show that constructing the prompt can be an important factor affecting the prediction performance.

However, the definitions of psychological constructs of LLMs could not be the same as the task defined. For example, LLMs could have different nuances for empathy and distress compared to the original research (Buechel et al., 2018). Figure 1 shows the definitions of empathy and distress of ChatGPT (gpt-3.5-turbo) and from the original paper (Buechel et al., 2018). While they shared the general meanings of the two constructs, ChatGPT's responses don't have the detailed nuances defined in the original paper. If the LLMs have different notions for the target variables, the prediction performance could be worse compared to having aligned definitions of psychological constructs.

In addition, empathy and distress could be ex-



*Proceedings of the 14th Workshop on Computational Approaches to Subjectivity, Sentiment, & Social Media Analysis*, pages 380–384
August 15, 2024 ©2024 Association for Computational Linguistics

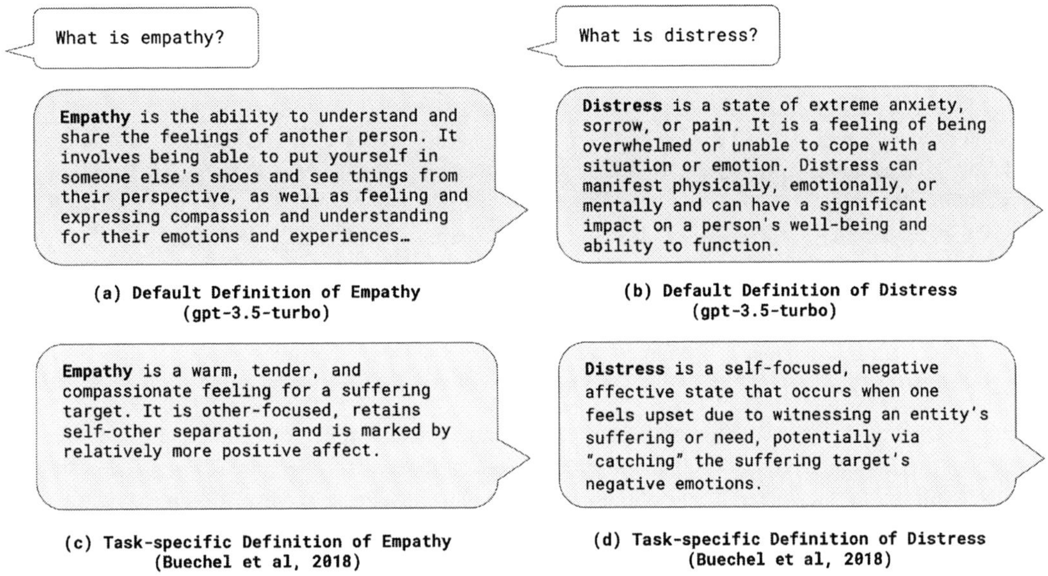


Figure 1: The Definitions of Empathy and Distress of ChatGPT and The Original Paper (Buechel et al., 2018)

pressed differently depending on the situation. This is due to the context-dependent nature of psychological constructs (Demszky et al., 2023). In other words, the way people express empathy could differ depending on who and how they communicate. Thus, it can be helpful to offer the detailed context of the dataset to LLMs.

To address the problems mentioned above, this study proposes a new prompt strategy, called Task-Aligned Prompt (TAP), for predicting empathy and distress. TAP consists of 1) definition alignment and 2) the context of the dataset. We tested the performance of our prompt compared to a plain prompt across zero-shot and few-shot settings with the models ChatGPT and GPT-4o. Our results show that the TAP-ChatGPT-zero-shot model achieved the best average Pearson correlation of empathy and distress on the development set. Our final submission ranked top 1 showing the best average Pearson correlation on the EMP track. This study shows the potential efficiency of LLMs in empathy and distress prediction and the strength of our approach.

## 2 Dataset

The dataset for Track 3 (EMP) consists of the level of empathy and distress of the writers, their essays, and the index of news articles (Buechel et al., 2018). The scores of both empathy and distress were measured with a 7-Likert scale using Batson's Empathic Concern – Personal Distress Scale (Batson et al., 1987). Thus, the level of empathy and distress range from 1 (not at all) to 7 (extremely).

Table 1 shows the number of instances for each dataset. The training set was only used in the few-shot prompting to give examples. The development dataset was used for both zero and few-shot promptings. The final evaluation was conducted on the test set.

| Dataset | Instances |
|---|---|
| Train | 1000 |
| Dev | 63 |
| Test | 83 |

Table 1: The Statistics of the Dataset

## 3 Methods

Our proposed Task-Aligned Prompt (TAP) aims to align LLMs for task-specific purposes. It mainly consists of 1) definition alignment and 2) dataset alignment. In the first stage, the prompts start with the definition of empathy and distress for each prediction task. The definitions of distress and empathy are retrieved from the previous paper that collected the dataset (Buechel et al., 2018) and the scales used to measure these states (Batson et al., 1987). In the second stage, the context of the text data was also retrieved from the original

| Model | Average Pearson Correlation | | Empathy Pearson Correlation | | Distress Pearson Correlation | |
|---|---|---|---|---|---|---|
| | Task-Aligned | Plain | Task-Aligned | Plain | Task-Aligned | Plain |
| ChatGPT zero-shot | **0.511** ↑ | 0.494 | $0.610_{0.010}$ | **$0.682_{0.011}$** | $0.413_{0.037}$ | $0.306_{0.004}$ |
| ChatGPT one-shot | 0.464 ↓ | 0.493 | $0.569_{0.015}$ | $0.639_{0.033}$ | $0.360_{0.085}$ | $0.347_{0.109}$ |
| ChatGPT three-shot | 0.468 ↑ | 0.465 | $0.571_{0.020}$ | $0.593_{0.016}$ | $0.365_{0.077}$ | $0.337_{0.055}$ |
| GPT-4o zero-shot | 0.482 ↑ | 0.436 | $0.520_{0.014}$ | $0.439_{0.008}$ | $0.445_{0.005}$ | $0.433_{0.005}$ |
| GPT-4o one-shot | 0.492 ↑ | 0.468 | $0.511_{0.016}$ | $0.512_{0.059}$ | **$0.474_{0.046}$** | $0.424_{0.056}$ |
| GPT-4o three-shot | 0.484 ↑ | 0.477 | $0.519_{0.051}$ | $0.493_{0.030}$ | $0.448_{0.032}$ | $0.461_{0.044}$ |

Table 2: The Experiment Results for The Development Set

paper (Buechel et al., 2018). These prompts were included in the system prompts. Then, the prompts for task explanation, the constraint for output, and the target text are included. These three components are used as a plain prompt in this study. The details of our prompts are described in the Appendix A.

This study tested the TAP with zero-shot and few-shot prompting strategies. The prompts for zero-shot and few-shot prompting are the same except the few-shot prompting includes several examples (1 or 3), which are a pair of text and an answer (the level of empathy or distress). The examples used for few-shot prompting were chosen randomly in the training set.

For the experiments, we used the two models, ChatGPT (gpt-3.5-turbo) and the latest released GPT-4o model (gpt-4o) from OpenAI API [1]. We set the temperature to 0 and top_p to 1 which are the common practice for greedy decoding (Gupta et al., 2023). However, there are still variations in the responses across different runs. Thus, we ran each prompt three times and reported the average Pearson correlations of those three attempts for the development set.

For the final evaluation, the TAP-ChatGPT-zero-shot model was used since it performed the best on the development set. We tried to submit the results once for the final evaluation. Thus, we ran the test dataset 3 times, averaged the predicted values of the three results, and submitted those values. Our submission achieved the best score on the EMP track.

## 4 Results

Table 2 shows the results of our experiments for the development set. It shows the average, empathy, and distress Pearson correlations for the plain and our proposed prompts for each model and strategy. The average Pearson correlation means the average of empathy and distress Pearson correlation. For each empathy and distress Pearson correlation, we reported the average values and the standard deviation of performances across 3 runs for all cases. The best performances for each Pearson correlation were highlighted.

The TAP-ChatGPT-zero-shot model performed the best, showing the highest average Pearson correlation ($r$ = .51). The Plain-ChatGPT-zero-shot model showed the best performance for the empathy Pearson correlation ($r$ = .49) while the TAP-GPT4o-one-shot model performs the best for the distress prediction ($r$ = 0.47). We marked the arrows next to TAP performances on the average Pearson correlation. The green arrow means the performance of our prompt is better than the plain prompt with the same models and strategies. Conversely, the red arrow means the plain prompt performed better than our prompt. We found that models with TAP outperformed every case except for one case.

Lastly, the TAP-ChatGPT-zero-shot model was used for the final evaluation. Table 3 shows the results of the top 3 teams in the EMP track. Our team, RU, ranked in the top 1 with an average Pearson coefficient of 0.453. Specifically, the Pearson coefficient for empathy and distress of our submission was 0.523 and 0.383 respectively.

| Rank | Team Name | Score |
|---|---|---|
| **1** | **RU (Ours)** | **0.453** |
| 2 | Chinchunmei | 0.393 |
| 3 | FraunhoferSIT | 0.385 |

Table 3: The Performances of The Top 3 Teams of EMP Track

[1] https://platform.openai.com/docs/models

## 5 Conclusion

This study showed the potential of LLMs in empathy and distress prediction tasks and our proposed prompt, Task-Aligned Prompt. Our experimental results showed that constructing prompts for LLMs to align the definitions of empathy and distress to the task and offering context of the dataset can benefit the prediction performance. Particularly, the TAP-ChatGPT-zero-shot model showed the best average Pearson correlation performance on the EMP track. These promising results strengthen the idea that the LLMs can be useful for predicting psychological states.

The limitation of our approach lies in its generalizability. Our approach may not be the most effective method for predicting empathy and distress across multiple datasets collected from diverse contexts and backgrounds. This is because our approach emphasizes aligning the detailed nuances and contexts to specific tasks.

Future research can continue to find an efficient prompting strategy for predicting empathy and distress. As mentioned above, researchers can study the one-size-fits-all prompts that can be applied to multiple datasets. In addition, improving the interpretability of LLMs prediction is also an important task in this field (Qin et al., 2023; Yang et al., 2024). While this study only focuses on predicting empathy and distress using LLMs, future studies can consider adding more layers to enhance the explainability and interpretability of LLMs.

## References


Valentin Barriere, João Sedoc, Shabnam Tafreshi, and Salvatore Giorgi. 2023. Findings of wassa 2023 shared task on empathy, emotion and personality detection in conversation and reactions to news articles. In *Proceedings of the 13th Workshop on Computational Approaches to Subjectivity, Sentiment, & Social Media Analysis*, pages 511–525.

C Daniel Batson, Jim Fultz, and Patricia A Schoenrade. 1987. Distress and empathy: Two qualitatively distinct vicarious emotions with different motivational consequences. *Journal of personality*, 55(1):19–39.

Sven Buechel, Anneke Buffone, Barry Slaff, Lyle Ungar, and João Sedoc. 2018. Modeling empathy and distress in reaction to news stories. *arXiv preprint arXiv:1808.10399*.

Zhiyu Chen, Yujie Lu, and William Yang Wang. 2023. Empowering psychotherapy with large language models: Cognitive distortion detection through diagnosis of thought prompting. *arXiv preprint arXiv:2310.07146*.

Dorottya Demszky, David Yang, David S. Yeager, and et al. 2023. Using large language models in psychology. *Nature Reviews Psychology*, 2:688–701.

Salvatore Giorgi, João Sedoc, Valentin Barriere, and Shabnam Tafreshi. 2024. Findings of wassa 2024 shared task on empathy and personality detection in interactions. In *Proceedings of the 14th Workshop on Computational Approaches to Subjectivity, Sentiment, & Social Media Analysis*.

Shashank Gupta, Vaishnavi Shrivastava, Ameet Deshpande, Ashwin Kalyan, Peter Clark, Ashish Sabharwal, and Tushar Khot. 2023. Bias runs deep: Implicit reasoning biases in persona-assigned llms. *arXiv preprint arXiv:2311.04892*.

Md Rakibul Hasan, Md Zakir Hossain, Tom Gedeon, and Shafin Rahman. 2024. Llm-gem: Large language model-guided prediction of people's empathy levels towards newspaper article. In *Findings of the Association for Computational Linguistics: EACL 2024*, pages 2215–2231.

Andrew Nedilko and Yi Chu. 2023. Team bias busters at wassa 2023 empathy, emotion and personality shared task: Emotion detection with generative pretrained transformers. In *Proceedings of the 13th Workshop on Computational Approaches to Subjectivity, Sentiment, & Social Media Analysis*, pages 569–573.

Damilola Omitaomu, Shabnam Tafreshi, Tingting Liu, Sven Buechel, Chris Callison-Burch, Johannes Eichstaedt, Lyle Ungar, and João Sedoc. 2022. Empathic conversations: A multi-level dataset of contextualized conversations. *Preprint*, arXiv:2205.12698.

Wei Qin, Zetong Chen, Lei Wang, Yunshi Lan, Weijieying Ren, and Richang Hong. 2023. Read, diagnose and chat: Towards explainable and interactive llms-augmented depression detection in social media. *arXiv preprint arXiv:2305.05138*.

João Sedoc, Sven Buechel, Yehonathan Nachmany, Anneke Buffone, and Lyle Ungar. 2019. Learning word ratings for empathy and distress from document-level user responses. *arXiv preprint arXiv:1912.01079*.

Xuhai Xu, Bingsheng Yao, Yuanzhe Dong, Saadia Gabriel, Hong Yu, James Hendler, Marzyeh Ghassemi, Anind K Dey, and Dakuo Wang. 2024. Mental-llm: Leveraging large language models for mental health prediction via online text data. *Proceedings of the ACM on Interactive, Mobile, Wearable and Ubiquitous Technologies*, 8(1):1–32.

Kailai Yang, Tianlin Zhang, Ziyan Kuang, Qianqian Xie, Jimin Huang, and Sophia Ananiadou. 2024. Mentallama: interpretable mental health analysis on social media with large language models. In *Proceedings of the ACM on Web Conference 2024*, pages 4489–4500.

## A Prompts

The details of our prompts are described in Table 4. Specifically, the prompts were made as follows:

- Task-Aligned Prompt = Definition (Empathy or Distress) + Dataset Context + Task + Output Constraint + Text
- Plain Prompt = Task + Output Constraint + Text

The definition and the context of the dataset were written in the system prompt. The rest of the components were written in the user prompt. For few-shot prompting, we gave a pair of text and response sets in the form of Text: [text], and Response: [response] in the Text section of the prompt.

| Name | Prompt |
|---|---|
| Definition (Empathy; system) | Empathy is a warm, tender, and compassionate feeling for a suffering target. It is other-focused, retains self-other separation, and is marked by relatively more positive affect. Empathy consists of warm, tender, sympathetic, softhearted, moved, and compassionate feelings. |
| Definition (Distress; system) | Distress is a self-focused, negative affective state that occurs when one feels upset due to witnessing an entity's suffering or need, potentially via "catching" the suffering target's negative emotions. Distress consists of worried, upset, troubled, perturbed, grieved, disturbed, alarmed, and distressed feelings. |
| Dataset context (system) | The following text is the reactions of people after reading news articles. They shared their feelings as they would with a friend in a private message or with a group of friends as a social media post. |
| Task | Evaluate the level of [empathy or distress] of the writer who wrote this text. |
| Output constraint | The answer should only contain a float value ranging from 1.0 (not at all) to 7.0 (extremely) using three decimal places. |
| Text | Text: [text] |

Table 4: Prompt Design

# Chinchunmei at WASSA 2024 Empathy and Personality Shared Task: Boosting LLM's Prediction with Role-play Augmentation and Contrastive Reasoning Calibration

**Tian Li**[1,2] **Nicolay Rusnachenko**[2] **Huizhi Liang**[2]
[1]Shumei AI Research Institute, Beijing, China
[2]Newcastle University, Newcastle Upon Tyne, England
{litianricardolee,rusnicolay}@gmail.com
Huizhi.Liang@newcastle.ac.uk

## Abstract

This paper presents the Chinchunmei team's contributions to the WASSA2024 Shared-Task 1: Empathy Detection and Emotion Classification. We participated in Tracks 1, 2, and 3 to predict empathetic scores based on dialogue, article, and essay content. We choose Llama3-8b-instruct as our base model. We developed three supervised fine-tuning schemes: standard prediction, role-play, and contrastive prediction, along with an innovative scoring calibration method called Contrastive Reasoning Calibration during inference. Pearson Correlation was used as the evaluation metric across all tracks. For Track 1, we achieved 0.43 on the devset and 0.17 on the testset. For Track 2 emotion, empathy, and polarity labels, we obtained 0.64, 0.66, and 0.79 on the devset and 0.61, 0.68, and 0.58 on the testset. For Track 3 empathy and distress labels, we got 0.64 and 0.56 on the devset and 0.33 and 0.35 on the testset.

## 1 Introduction

Empathy refers to the ability to understand and share the feelings or experiences of others. It involves identifying, comprehending, and sharing with others' emotions, thoughts, motivations, and personality traits (Bellet and Maloney, 1991; Hall et al., 2021). As one of the essential human qualities, empathy plays an essential role not only in various academic fields such as healthcare(Decety and Fotopoulou, 2015), neuroscience(Singer and Lamm, 2009), psychology, and philosophy (Yan and Tan, 2014) but also in everyday interactions. Since empathy expression depends on human reaction and its assessment often requires nuance analysis of various features—such as underlying meanings, references, and emotional release—identifying empathy in diverse scenarios has always been a hot research topic.

For the reasons above, WASSA 2024 (Giorgi et al., 2024; Barriere et al., 2023; Omitaomu et al., 2022) has once again hosted the Empathy Detection and Emotion Classification shared task. This year's contest introduces multi-level and multi-modal data, which comprises news articles, essays, and dialogs. It abandons simple classification labels in favor of a scoring system where different scores carry actual meaning. All tracks use Pearson Correlation as the evaluation metric. These factors collectively render this competition exceptionally challenging. In this competition, we participated in tracks 1, 2, and 3, all related to empathy detection.

During previous contests, most participants chose the encoder framework (Chen et al., 2022; Li et al., 2022b; Vasava et al., 2022; Li et al., 2022a; Meshgi et al., 2022). In this paper, to unify the diverse modalities and multiple labels across different tracks into a single model, we used the generative large language model (LLM) framework. However, as the training objective of LLM is the next token prediction, it can hardly carry on the discriminative training purpose. With limited samples and imbalanced label distributions, sometimes the model can only learn templated outputs rather than the logic behind the scoring. These issues are particularly severe in Track 1. To address these, we introduced various task templates to enrich the train set and incorporated the concepts of contrastive learning (Rethmeier and Augenstein, 2023; Sun et al., 2023; Li et al., 2023; Gao and Das, 2024) and contrastive chain-of-thought (Chu et al., 2023; Chia et al., 2023) to enhance the distinctiveness and reliability of the model's scoring. Additionally, our approach does not involve any external data. This further proves that the superiority of our solution stems from the technical approach itself and can be easily transferred to other similar tasks.

Our contributions are as follows:

- We introduced a role-playing template to enrich the training samples. By training the model to generate responses for a given role



*Proceedings of the 14th Workshop on Computational Approaches to Subjectivity, Sentiment, & Social Media Analysis*, pages 385–392
August 15, 2024 ©2024 Association for Computational Linguistics

- based on articles, preceding dialogue history, and the provided empathy, emotion intensity, and emotion polarity scores, we aimed to help the model capture the nuanced characteristics related to empathy in different expressions. Our experiments demonstrated significant improvements in Track 3 with this approach.
- We developed contrastive supervised fine-tune (C-SFT) and contrastive reasoning calibration (CRC) techniques for more reliable scoring generation. C-SFT not only enhances model performance but also mitigates data scarcity by creating contrastive pairs. CRC leverages chain-of-thought (COT) during inference to refine predictions, further enhancing the final performance. Our experiments showed notable improvements in both tracks 1 and 2 with these techniques.

## 2 Methodology

Our approach, illustrated in Fig 1, consists of two stages: the SFT stage and the inference stage. In the SFT stage, we enrich the training samples by introducing three templates: the standard prediction template, the role-play template, and the contrastive template. These are detailed in section 2.1.1, 2.1.2, and 2.1.3. In the inference stage, in addition to using the standard prediction template, we employ the contrastive template. This forces the model to compare scores of a specific label between two data points, thereby refining the prediction results. This is elaborated in section 2.2.1.

### 2.1 SFT Stage

#### 2.1.1 Standard Prediction Template

In this task, the LLM performs score predictions using the corresponding standard templates. According to the input length of Llama3-8b-instruct, we concatenate the article and task content together as input and train the model to predict all tracks' results. The template is shown in B.1.

#### 2.1.2 Role-play Template

Since parts of the data come from dialogues, performing the role-play fine-tuning based on dialogues enhances the model's perception between the roles and the empathic expression features, thereby strengthening the model's empathy detection result. Based on this assumption, we trained the model to generate the current text based on the dialogue history and the labels from Track 2. The template is shown in B.2.

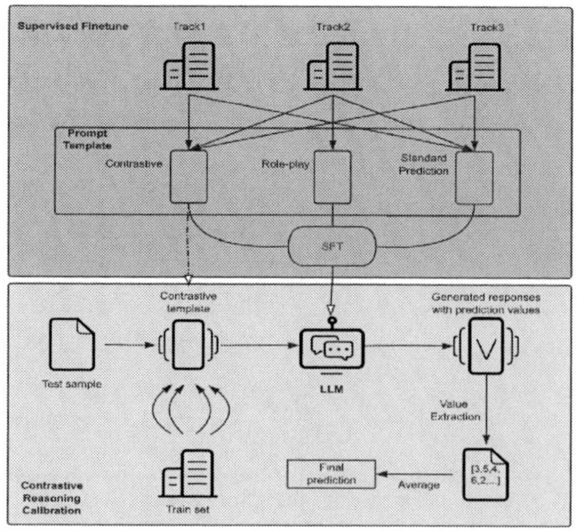


Figure 1: The overall flowchart of our method. It is divided into two stages: the red part represents the SFT stage, and the green part represents the inference stage.

#### 2.1.3 Contrastive Supervised Templates

One of the challenges of tracks 1, 2, and 3 is that their labels are comparable values rather than isolated labels. Treating it as a traditional classification task is inappropriate, as traditional classification tasks regard all misclassifications equally. Additionally, another challenge lies in data scarcity, as tracks 1 and 3 only have 1,000 training samples.

To address these two issues, we develop a novel C-SFT approach that uses contrastive pairs to fine-tune the LLM. This not only handles the magnitude discriminative training but also solves the data scarcity problem. By randomly sampling two pieces of data to form contrastive pairs, we can:

1. Enable the model to understand that label values are comparable rather than isolated by comparing the two samples' predictions.
2. Construct a vast amount of training samples through pairwise combinations.

However, this introduces three new issues. First, it doubles the input length. Second, if the two samples in a pair have identical scores, the discriminative training will fail. Third, an excessively large training set can be a burden for training. Therefore, we discard the article content and only sample 5000 pairs for each task and each label, prioritizing data with differing scores. Taking Track 1 as an example, we retain all pairs with score differences in the range $[2, +\inf]$, keep pairs with a score difference of 1 with a probability of 30%, and only retain pairs with identical scores with a probability of 0.1%. After sampling 9,000+ times, we obtain 5,000 contrastive pairs as training samples. Similar sampling strategies are adopted for tracks 2 and 3. The templates are list in B.3.

Furthermore, due to the presence of two speakers in a conversation, for Track 1 we also constructed contrastive pairs for these two speakers. Although this dataset is limited to fewer than 1000 pairs due to the number of dialogues, it further enriches the diversity of the training set. The template is also shown in B.3.

### 2.2 Inference Stage

#### 2.2.1 Contrastive Reasoning Calibration

After completing the SFT, we continue using the C-SFT templates for CRC prediction. Compared to standard prediction, predictions based on the C-SFT template are influenced by their contrastive samples. This is because before outputting the final prediction, the model first compares the two samples on a given label and then outputs the final results for both samples. This employs the COT feature, making the model's output more reliable. The algorithm is shown in Algorithm 1.

**Algorithm 1** Contrastive Reasoning Calibration

**Require:** Test sample $\mathbf{X} = \{x_1, x_2, ..., x_n\}$, train sample $\mathbf{S} = \{s_1, s_2, ..., s_m\}$, label value $\mathbf{V} = \{v_1, v_2, ..., v_o\}$, contrastive template $\mathbf{T}$
**Ensure:** Prediction $\mathbf{P} = \{p_1, p_2, ..., p_n\}$

$tempP = []$
**for** $x$ in $\mathbf{X}$ **do**
  **for** $v$ in $\mathbf{V}$ **do**
    Sample $i$ pieces of $s$ with label value $v$, $\hat{\mathbf{S}} = \{\hat{s}_1, \hat{s}_2, ..., \hat{s}_i\}$
    **for** $\hat{s}$ in $\hat{\mathbf{S}}$ **do**
      Randomly apply $(x, \hat{s})$ or $(\hat{s}, x)$ to $\mathbf{T}$
      Get results $(v_x, v_{\hat{s}})$ or $(v_{\hat{s}}, v_x)$
      $tempP \leftarrow v_x$
    **end for**
  **end for**
  $p_x = AVG(tempP)$
**end for**

We select contrastive data from the train set because the predictions on the training set are very accurate, making them ideal benchmarks for comparison. The choice of $i$ is constrained by our inference resources. For Track 1, $i$ is 4. For Track 2 and 3, $i$ is 1 to meet the competition deadline because of the limit of our computational resources. After the competition deadline, we continued experimenting with the $i$ set to 4 on the Track 2 dev set. The results are presented in the C

## 3 Experiment

This section introduces the train set statistics, the base model selection, and the fine-tuning settings.

### 3.1 Dataset-Sample Statistics

Tracks 1 and 2 use the same dialogue data. It includes 487 dialogues corresponding to 100 articles. Each dialogue involves two speakers, with a total of 75 participants. The text length per dialogue turn ranges from 1 to 701 characters. The turn number per dialogue ranges from 13 to 44. The overall dialogue length varies from 601 to 6701 characters.

For Track 2, as it involves predicting at each dialogue turn, the actual input can be in two modes: 1). Single turn mode, referred to as Track2-single-turn. 2). Multi-turn mode with context, referred to as Track2-multi-turn.

Track 3 samples consist of individual essays. The text length ranges from 300 to 800 characters.

The article data includes the title, source, object of suffering, and content. The content length ranges from 176 to 31,784 characters.

### 3.2 Dataset-Label Statistics

As for Track 1, this task includes only empathy scores ranging from 1 to 9. Over half of the scores are 7, indicating a highly imbalanced issue.

As for Track 2, this task includes three types of scores: emotion intensity, empathy, and emotion polarity. The emotion and empathy scores range from 0 to 5, all values being multiples of 1/3. The emotional polarity scores range from 0 to 2.6667, with a total of 10 distinct values.

As for Track 3, this task includes two types of scores: empathy and distress. Each score ranges from 0 to 7, all values being multiples of 1/7.

Since the labels contain floating-point numbers, to prevent negative impact on LLM encoding, we mapped all label values to an integer domain starting from 0. Even though the results are evaluated using Pearson correlation, this mapping does not negatively affect the performance evaluation.

### 3.3 Selection of Base Model

We compare the suitability of Llama2-7b-chat[1] and Llama3-8b-instruct[2] for all three tracks and finally choose the later one. This is because: 1). Llama3-8b-instruct has up to 8192 input length that can

[1]https://huggingface.co/meta-llama/Llama-2-7b-chat-hf

[2]https://huggingface.co/meta-llama/Meta-Llama-3-8B-Instruct

Table 1: The performance comparison of different SFT types combinations on devset

| Pearson | Track 1 | Track 2 single turn | | | | Track 2 multi turn | | | | Track 3 | | |
|---|---|---|---|---|---|---|---|---|---|---|---|---|
| Correlation | Empathy | Emotion | Empathy | Polarity | AVG | Emotion | Empathy | Polarity | AVG | Empathy | Distress | AVG |
| Baseline | -0.037 | **0.634** | 0.576 | **0.733** | **0.648** | **0.637** | 0.624 | 0.745 | 0.668 | 0.563 | 0.448 | 0.505 |
| +Role-play | 0.127 | 0.628 | 0.580 | 0.700 | 0.636 | 0.624 | 0.638 | 0.738 | 0.667 | **0.639** | **0.559** | **0.599** |
| +Role-play +C-SFT | **0.270** | 0.618 | **0.587** | **0.733** | 0.646 | 0.625 | **0.636** | **0.747** | **0.669** | 0.542 | 0.336 | 0.439 |

accept article content. 2). With the standard prediction template, Llama3-8b-instruct outperforms Llama2-7B-chat. Therefore, all subsequent results are based on the tuning of Llama3-8B-Instruct.

### 3.4 Training Configuration

Due to resource limits, all training processes use LoRA technique (Hu et al., 2021). The rank is 8, alpha is 16, and dropout is 0.

The epoch number is 3, and the learning rate (LR) is 2e-4. The LR scheduler employs the cosine strategy with 0.1 warmup ratio and 128 batch size.

## 4 Result and Analysis

### 4.1 Baseline

The baseline model is obtained by standard prediction fine-tuning. The devset results are in Table 1. Notably, the result of Track 1 is quite poor, probably due to the severe imbalance in sample labels.

### 4.2 Standard Prediction + Role Play

After incorporating the role-play template, tracks 1 and 3 on devset show significant improvement, proving the effectiveness of the role-play fine-tuning. However, according to Table 1, the Track 2 results fluctuate among all labels, making it difficult to distinguish any clear benefit. This is because the role-play and the Track2-multi-turn standard prediction are similar tasks, with the content and prediction swapped.

### 4.3 Standard Prediction + Role Play + Contrastive Tuning

According to Table 1, this approach further improves the devset results of Track 1 and Track2-multi-turn. However, for Track2-single-turn, there is a noticeable decline in emotion intensity. After analyzing the cases, we find that the dataset contains instances of similar data with different scores, causing confusion to the model and leading to tuning failures. We suspect that Track 2 labeling was based on the current and historical dialogue turns, resulting in similar texts with different labels. To save inference costs, we discard the Track2-single-turn in subsequent experiments.

Besides, the Track 3 devset results also declined. Our analysis suggests that this decline is due to Track 3's complex labeling system and its dependence on article content. Track 3 has up to 43 values for each label, greatly increasing the learning difficulty for the model. Moreover, skipping the article content may lost key semantic features. Thus, we submit our Track 3 testset results based on section 4.2 method and drop the Track 3 task in future experiments to reduce costs.

### 4.4 Contrastive Reasoning Calibration

To demonstrate that the success of our approach is not coincidental, we prepare an extra model using LR 8e-4 and apply the CRC method to both for comparison. The devset results in Table 2 show significant improvements across all labels for both models. This validates the effectiveness and robustness of our approach. Thus, for Track 1, we submit the testset results obtained from the model using LR 8e-4 with CRC. For Track 2, we submit the testset results from the model with LR 2e-4 using the same method.

Table 2: The performance comparison between standard prediction and CRC on devset

| Pearson | Track 1 | Track 2 multi turn | | | |
|---|---|---|---|---|---|
| Correlation | Empathy | Emotion | Empathy | Polarity | AVG |
| LR: 2e-5 | 0.270 | 0.625 | 0.636 | 0.747 | 0.669 |
| +CRC | 0.395 | 0.641 | **0.664** | **0.790** | **0.698** |
| LR: 8e-5 | 0.360 | 0.632 | 0.622 | 0.729 | 0.661 |
| +CRC | **0.434** | **0.662** | 0.645 | 0.773 | 0.693 |

## 5 Conclusion

Our experiments demonstrate the significant potential of the current LLM in empathy detection. Firstly, with a modest amount of SFT data preparation, we successfully created an 8B scale strong baseline LLM. Secondly, we improve it by introducing the Role-play and C-SFT tasks. Thirdly, we further enhance the performance using contrastive reasoning to refine scoring outputs. Finally, our solution secured third place in Track 1 and second place in both tracks 2 and 3. The testset results are shown in A. Since our techniques require no external data, they can be widely applied to similar classification or scoring tasks.

Regarding the performance decline for Track 3 after using C-SFT, we plan to conduct further investigations with long-context LLM to validate if the decline is due to the lack of article information.

## References


Valentin Barriere, João Sedoc, Shabnam Tafreshi, and Salvatore Giorgi. 2023. Findings of wassa 2023 shared task on empathy, emotion and personality detection in conversation and reactions to news articles. In *Proceedings of the 13th Workshop on Computational Approaches to Subjectivity, Sentiment, & Social Media Analysis*, pages 511–525.

Paul S Bellet and Michael J Maloney. 1991. The importance of empathy as an interviewing skill in medicine. *Jama*, 266(13):1831–1832.

Yue Chen, Yingnan Ju, and Sandra Kübler. 2022. IUCL at WASSA 2022 shared task: A text-only approach to empathy and emotion detection. In *Proceedings of the 12th Workshop on Computational Approaches to Subjectivity, Sentiment & Social Media Analysis*, pages 228–232, Dublin, Ireland. Association for Computational Linguistics.

Yew Ken Chia, Guizhen Chen, Luu Anh Tuan, Soujanya Poria, and Lidong Bing. 2023. Contrastive chain-of-thought prompting. *Preprint*, arXiv:2311.09277.

Zheng Chu, Jingchang Chen, Qianglong Chen, Weijiang Yu, Tao He, Haotian Wang, Weihua Peng, Ming Liu, Bing Qin, and Ting Liu. 2023. A survey of chain of thought reasoning: Advances, frontiers and future. *arXiv preprint arXiv:2309.15402*.

Jean Decety and Aikaterini Fotopoulou. 2015. Why empathy has a beneficial impact on others in medicine: unifying theories. *Frontiers in behavioral neuroscience*, 8:457.

Xiang Gao and Kamalika Das. 2024. Customizing language model responses with contrastive in-context learning. *arXiv preprint arXiv:2401.17390*.

Salvatore Giorgi, João Sedoc, Valentin Barriere, and Shabnam Tafreshi. 2024. Findings of wassa 2024 shared task on empathy and personality detection in interactions. In *Proceedings of the 14th Workshop on Computational Approaches to Subjectivity, Sentiment, & Social Media Analysis*.

Judith A Hall, Rachel Schwartz, and Fred Duong. 2021. How do laypeople define empathy? *The Journal of Social Psychology*, 161(1):5–24.

Edward J Hu, Yelong Shen, Phillip Wallis, Zeyuan Allen-Zhu, Yuanzhi Li, Shean Wang, Lu Wang, and Weizhu Chen. 2021. Lora: Low-rank adaptation of large language models. *arXiv preprint arXiv:2106.09685*.

Bin Li, Yixuan Weng, Qiya Song, Fuyan Ma, Bin Sun, and Shutao Li. 2022a. Prompt-based pre-trained model for personality and interpersonal reactivity prediction. In *Proceedings of the 12th Workshop on Computational Approaches to Subjectivity, Sentiment & Social Media Analysis*, pages 265–270, Dublin, Ireland. Association for Computational Linguistics.

Bin Li, Yixuan Weng, Qiya Song, Bin Sun, and Shutao Li. 2022b. Continuing pre-trained model with multiple training strategies for emotional classification. In *Proceedings of the 12th Workshop on Computational Approaches to Subjectivity, Sentiment & Social Media Analysis*, pages 233–238, Dublin, Ireland. Association for Computational Linguistics.

Zongxia Li, Paiheng Xu, Fuxiao Liu, and Hyemi Song. 2023. Towards understanding in-context learning with contrastive demonstrations and saliency maps. *arXiv preprint arXiv:2307.05052*.

Kourosh Meshgi, Maryam Sadat Mirzaei, and Satoshi Sekine. 2022. Uncertainty regularized multi-task learning. In *Proceedings of the 12th Workshop on Computational Approaches to Subjectivity, Sentiment & Social Media Analysis*, pages 78–88, Dublin, Ireland. Association for Computational Linguistics.

Damilola Omitaomu, Shabnam Tafreshi, Tingting Liu, Sven Buechel, Chris Callison-Burch, Johannes Eichstaedt, Lyle Ungar, and João Sedoc. 2022. Empathic conversations: A multi-level dataset of contextualized conversations. *Preprint*, arXiv:2205.12698.

Nils Rethmeier and Isabelle Augenstein. 2023. A primer on contrastive pretraining in language processing: Methods, lessons learned, and perspectives. *ACM Computing Surveys*, 55(10):1–17.

Tania Singer and Claus Lamm. 2009. The social neuroscience of empathy. *Annals of the new York Academy of Sciences*, 1156(1):81–96.

Weiwei Sun, Zhengliang Shi, Shen Gao, Pengjie Ren, Maarten de Rijke, and Zhaochun Ren. 2023. Contrastive learning reduces hallucination in conversations. In *Proceedings of the AAAI Conference on Artificial Intelligence*, volume 37, pages 13618–13626.

Himil Vasava, Pramegh Uikey, Gaurav Wasnik, and Raksha Sharma. 2022. Transformer-based architecture for empathy prediction and emotion classification. In *Proceedings of the 12th Workshop on Computational Approaches to Subjectivity, Sentiment & Social Media Analysis*, pages 261–264, Dublin, Ireland. Association for Computational Linguistics.

Lu Yan and Yong Tan. 2014. Feeling blue? go online: An empirical study of social support among patients. *Information Systems Research*, 25(4):690–709.

## A Test Results

Table 3 presents the final performance of our submitted test results. It is noteworthy that since the testset for Track 2 contains some missing data, some preprocessing is required to obtain the final results. The organizers' official approach involves removing all rows with missing data before calculating the evaluation metrics. However, since the missing data in Track 2's three labels are not consistent, an alternative method is to remove missing data separately for each label before calculating the evaluation metrics. These two approaches yielded different results. The results presented here use the official method.

## B Task Templates

### B.1 Standard Prediction Template

In the Standard prediction task, we used the following template for Track 1, 2, and 3:

```
<|start_header_id|>system<|end_header_id|>
You are a helpful assistant.<|eot_id|>

<|start_header_id|>user<|end_header_id|>
{taskDescription}

You must strictly follow the following template to generate
your the prediction:
Emotion intensity: {{ your prediction }}, empathy level:
{{ your prediction }}, emotion polarity: {{ your prediction }}.

Article title: {title}
Article source: {source}
Object of suffering: {objectOfSuffering}
Article content: {articleContent}

Speaker1: {content}
<|eot_id|>

<|start_header_id|>assistant<|end_header_id|>
Emotion intensity: {emotionValue}, empathy level:
{empathyValue}, emotion polarity: {emotionPolarity}.
<|eot_id|>
```

Figure 2: The template of Track 2's Standard Prediction

### B.2 Role-play Template

In the Role-play task, we used the conversation data from Track 2, the label results, and the following template to construct the training set:

### B.3 Contrastive templates

In contrastive SFT, we built two sets of contrast templates for Track 1.

For the comparison of two speakers in the same conversation, we used the template shown in Fig 4.

For the comparison of two people in different dialogues, we used the template in Fig 5.

```
<|start_header_id|>system<|end_header_id|>
You are a helpful assistant.<|eot_id|>

<|start_header_id|>user<|end_header_id|>
{taskDescription}

Meanwhile, the response should present the following
traits:
The emotion intensity is {emotionValue}, the empathy l
evel is {empathyValue}, the emotion polarity is {emotio
nPolarity}, and the self-disclosure status is {selfDisclos
ure}.

Article title: {title}
Article source: {source}
Object of suffering: {objectOfSuffering}
Article content: {articleContent}

Conversation history: {convHistory}
<|eot_id|>

<|start_header_id|>assistant<|end_header_id|>
{response}
<|eot_id|>
```

```
<|start_header_id|>system<|end_header_id|>
You are a helpful assistant.<|eot_id|>

<|start_header_id|>user<|end_header_id|>
This is a Perceived Empathy Level Comparison task.
You are asked to compare the perceived empathy lev
els of two speakers in a dialogue and predict the per
ceived empathy level for each person. In this dialogu
e, each turn is tagged with "Speaker1" or "Speaker2"
to indicate the speaker. In prediction, please use the
speaker tag to refer to the corresponding speaker's id
entity. You need to first provide the comparison result
 and then give the perceived empathy level for each
speaker. The empathy levels are divided into 9 levels.
All predictions must be within the range between 0 to
 8 and must be made using integers only.

Dialogue:
{content}
<|eot_id|>

<|start_header_id|>assistant<|end_header_id|>
Speaker1's perceived empathy level in this conversatio
n is [higher than/lower than/equal to] Speaker2's. Spe
aker1's perceived empathy level is {sp1pel}, and Spea
ker2's perceived empathy level is {sp2pel}.
<|eot_id|>
```

Figure 4: The contrastive template of Track1's two speakers within one dialogue

For Track2's single-turn situation, we create 3 templates for 3 labels. Taking Emotion Polarity as an example, the template is in Fig 6.

For Track2's multi-turn situation, we also create 3 templates for 3 labels. Taking Emotion Polarity as an example, the template is in Fig 7.

For Track3's Empathy/Distress prediction tasks, we used the templates shown in Fig 8 and 9.

For Track3's Empathy/Distress prediction tasks, we used the templates shown in Fig 8 and 9.

## C Post-competition experiments

Table 4, 5 show the result comparison of different $i$ on Track 2's devset and test set. It can be seen that increasing $i$ can further enhances the performance

Table 3: The results of our submission on test set

| Pearson Correlation | Track 1 Empathy | Track 2 Emotion | Empathy | Polarity | AVG | Track 3 Empathy | Distress | AVG |
|---|---|---|---|---|---|---|---|---|
| Our method | 0.172 | 0.607 | 0.582 | 0.680 | 0.623 | 0.474 | 0.311 | 0.393 |

```
<|start_header_id|>system<|end_header_id|>
You are a helpful assistant.<|eot_id|>

<|start_header_id|>user<|end_header_id|>

This is a Perceived Empathy Level Comparison task
across multiple dialogues. You are asked to compare the
perceived empathy levels of a speaker in two dialogues
and predict the perceived empathy levels of this speaker
in both dialogues. In both conversations, the speaker to
be predicted will be tagged as "Speaker1", while other
speakers will be tagged as "Speaker2". The two
dialogues will be tagged as "Conv1" and "Conv2". In
prediction, please use the corresponding conversation
tags to refer to each conversation. You only need to
compare and predict the perceived empathy levels of
Speaker1 in both conversations. There is no need to
annotate Speaker2. You should first provide the
comparison result, followed by the perceived empathy
levels of Speaker1 in both conversations. The perceived
empathy levels are divided into 9 levels. All annotations
are in the range between 0 to 8 and must be made using
integers only.

Conv1:
{conv1content}

Conv2:
{conv2content}
<|eot_id|>

<|start_header_id|>assistant<|end_header_id|>
Speaker1's perceived empathy level in Conv1 is [higher
than/lower than/equal to] Conv2. The perceived empathy
level in Conv1 is {conv1l}, and in Conv2 it is {conv2l}.
<|eot_id|>
```

Figure 5: The contrastive template of Track1's two speakers with two dialogues

```
<|start_header_id|>system<|end_header_id|>
You are a helpful assistant.<|eot_id|>

<|start_header_id|>user<|end_header_id|>
This is an Emotional Polarity Comparison task at the
sentence level. You are asked to compare the emotio
nal polarities of these two sentences and predict the
emotional polarities for each sentence. The two sente
nces are tagged as "Sent1" and "Sent2". In predictio
n, please use the corresponding sentence tag to refer
to each sentence. You should first provide the compa
rison result, then give the emotional polarity for each
sentence. The emotional polarity is divided into 10 lev
els. All annotations are in the range between 0 to 9 a
nd must be made using integers only.

Sent1:
{sent1}

Sent2:
{sent2}
<|eot_id|>

<|start_header_id|>assistant<|end_header_id|>
Sent1's emotional polarity is [higher than/lower than/e
qual to] Sent2. The emotional polarity of Sent1 is {s1
polarity}, and Sent2 is {s2polarity}.
<|eot_id|>
```

Figure 6: The contrastive template of Track2's single-turn Emotion Polarity

```
<|start_header_id|>system<|end_header_id|>
You are a helpful assistant.<|eot_id|>

<|start_header_id|>user<|end_header_id|>
This is an Emotional Polarity Comparison task at the
conversation-turn level. You are asked to compare the
emotional polarities of the last conversation turn of t
wo dialogues and predict the emotional polarities for
both. You need to focus on the last turn of the dialo
gue, which starts with the "Speaker1: " string at each
dialogue's last line. The two dialogues are tagged as
"Dia1" and "Dia2". In prediction, please use the corr
esponding dialogue tag to refer to each dialogue. You
should first provide the comparison result, then give
the perceived emotional polarity for each dialogue's la
st turn. The emotional polarity is divided into 10 level
s. All annotations are in the range between 0 to 9 an
d must be made using integers only.

Dia1:
{dia1}

Dia2:
{dia2}
<|eot_id|>

<|start_header_id|>assistant<|end_header_id|>
The emotional polarity of the Dia1's last turn is [highe
r than/lower than/equal to] than Dia2. The emotional p
olarity of Dia1's last turn is {s1polarity}, and Dia2's la
st turn is {s2polarity}.
<|eot_id|>
```

Figure 7: The contrastive template of Track2's multi-turn Emotion Polarity

```
<|start_header_id|>system<|end_header_id|>
You are a helpful assistant.<|eot_id|>

<|start_header_id|>user<|end_header_id|>
This is an Empathy Concern Level Comparison task a
t the essay level. You are asked to compare the emp
athy concern levels of two essays and predict the em
pathy concern levels for each essay. The two essays
will be tagged as "Essay1" and "Essay2". In predictio
n, please use the corresponding essay tag to refer to
each essay. You should first provide the comparison r
esult, then give the empathy concern level for each e
ssay. The empathy concern level is divided into 43 le
vels. All annotations are in the range between 0 to 42
and must be made using integers only.

Essay1:
{e1content}

Essay2:
{e2content}
<|eot_id|>

<|start_header_id|>assistant<|end_header_id|>
Essay1's empathy concern level is [higher than/lower t
han/equal to] Essay2's. Essay1's empathy concern lev
el is {e1value}, and Essay2's empathy concern level is
{e2value}.
<|eot_id|>
```

Figure 8: The contrastive template of Track3's Empathy

```
<|start_header_id|>system<|end_header_id|>
You are a helpful assistant.<|eot_id|>

<|start_header_id|>user<|end_header_id|>
This is an Personal Distress Level Comparison task at the
essay level. You are asked to compare the personal
distress levels of two essays and predict the personal
distress levels for each essay. The two essays will be
tagged as "Essay1" and "Essay2". In prediction, please
use the corresponding essay tag to refer to each essay.
You should first provide the comparison result, then give
the personal distress level for each essay. The personal
distress level is divided into 43 levels. All annotations are
in the range between 0 to 42 and must be made using
integers only.

Essay1:
{e1content}

Essay2:
{e2content}
<|eot_id|>

<|start_header_id|>assistant<|end_header_id|>
Essay1's personal distress level is [higher than/lower
than/equal to] Essay2's. Essay1's personal distress level
is {e1value}, and Essay2's personal distress level is
{e2value}.
<|eot_id|>
```

Figure 9: The contrastive template of Track3's Distress

of three label predictions.

Table 4: The performance comparison with different $i$ on Track 2 devset

| Pearson | Track 2 multi turn | | | |
|---|---|---|---|---|
| Correlation | Emotion | Empathy | Polarity | AVG |
| LR: 2e-5 | 0.625 | 0.636 | 0.747 | 0.669 |
| +CRC (i = 1) | 0.641 | 0.664 | **0.790** | 0.698 |
| +CRC (i = 4) | **0.650** | **0.672** | **0.790** | **0.704** |

Table 5: The performance comparison with different $i$ on Track 2 testset

| Pearson | Track 2 multi turn | | | |
|---|---|---|---|---|
| Correlation | Emotion | Empathy | Polarity | AVG |
| CRC (i = 1) | **0.607** | 0.582 | 0.680 | 0.623 |
| CRC (i = 4) | 0.606 | **0.586** | **0.685** | **0.626** |

## D Models

All models are released in our Huggingface team website[3]:

- **baseline model**: WASSA2024 EmpathyDetection Chinchunmei EXP300
- **baseline + role-play**: WASSA2024 EmpathyDetection Chinchunmei EXP302
- **baseline + role-play + C-SFT (LR 2e-5)**: WASSA2024 EmpathyDetection Chinchunmei EXP304
- **baseline + role-play + C-SFT (LR 8e-5)**: WASSA2024 EmpathyDetection Chinchunmei EXP305

[3]https://huggingface.co/collections/RicardoLee/chinchunmei-on-wassa2024-shared-task-1-66853bab4fd43e12c535efa8

# Empathify at WASSA 2024 Empathy and Personality Shared Task: Contextualizing Empathy with a BERT-Based Context-Aware Approach for Empathy Detection

Arda Numanoğlu[1], Süleyman Ateş[1], Nihan Kesim Çiçekli[1], Dilek Küçük[1]

[1]Middle East Technical University, Ankara, Turkey

{arda.numanoglu, ates.suleyman, cicekli, kucuk}@metu.edu.tr

## Abstract

Empathy detection from textual data is a complex task that requires an understanding of both the content and context of the text. This study presents a BERT-based context-aware approach to enhance empathy detection in conversations and essays. We participated in the WASSA 2024 Shared Task (Giorgi et al., 2024), focusing on two tracks: empathy and emotion prediction in conversations (CONV-turn) and empathy and distress prediction in essays (EMP). Our approach leverages contextual information by incorporating related articles and emotional characteristics as additional inputs, using BERT-based Siamese (parallel) architecture. Our experiments demonstrated that using article summaries as context significantly improves performance, with the parallel BERT approach outperforming the traditional method of concatenating inputs with the '[SEP]' token. These findings highlight the importance of context-awareness in empathy detection and pave the way for future improvements in the sensitivity and accuracy of such systems. Our system officially ranked 8th at both CONV-T and EMP tracks.

## 1 Introduction

The exploration of empathy detection from text presents a complex yet fascinating challenge that bridges the gap between human emotions and computational analysis. It is an area rich with potential for understanding how we connect and empathize through written communication. Empathy detection involves not only identifying the presence of empathy but also understanding its context, intensity, and the specific emotions it is associated with. The subjective nature of empathy amplifies the complexity of this task, considering the diversity of its expression in language and the contextual sensitivity required to accurately interpret it.

The WASSA 2024 Shared Task 1 focuses on empathy detection in different textual data with four different tracks for participants to compete in. We have participated in two of the four tracks, which are:

**Track 2:** Empathy and Emotion Prediction in Conversations (CONV-turn).

**Track 3:** Empathy and Distress Prediction in Essays (EMP).

Section 2 summarizes the related work. In section 3, we detail our system descriptions, including data preprocessing for each of the tracks. In section 4, we present our experimental results for our proposed system architectures, with useful comparisons. In section 5, we discuss our conclusions.

## 2 Related Work

Research in empathy detection and emotion classification has rapidly evolved with the introduction of sophisticated deep learning models. BERT (Bidirectional Encoder Representations from Transformers) (Devlin et al., 2018) is a pre-trained transformer model that has revolutionized natural language processing tasks. Guda et al. (2021) introduced a demographic-aware BERT-based model for empathy prediction, emphasizing the role of demographic information in enhancing accuracy. However, Wang et al. (2023) showed that demographic data does not always improve performance, as their text-only system excelled in empathy detection, indicating context-dependency. Chavan et al. (2023) improved BERT-based models' performance through ensembles for empathy and distress detection. Lu et al. (2023) highlighted the importance of window size in fine-tuning DeBERTa models for conversation-level empathy prediction, finding that optimizing window size is crucial for capturing empathetic content effectively.

In our work, we prioritize context-awareness by integrating contextual information into our model. This strategic integration allows for a more comprehensive analysis of textual nuances, significantly



*Proceedings of the 14th Workshop on Computational Approaches to Subjectivity, Sentiment, & Social Media Analysis*, pages 393–398
August 15, 2024 ©2024 Association for Computational Linguistics

enhancing our system's ability to accurately assess empathy across various text forms, including essays and dialogues. By analyzing both the input text and its context, our model achieves a higher Pearson correlation in detecting empathy and distress, especially in essay-level inputs.

## 3 System Description

In recent years, advancements in empathy detection at the essay level have not matched the progress seen in conversation-level detection (Barriere et al., 2023). We attribute this disparity to a few key challenges:

- the increased complexity associated with the larger number of words in essays.
- the potential reliance of the empathy concept on other aspects of the input.
- the relatively small size of available datasets.

We approach the problem from a different perspective. We begin by rethinking the concept of empathy itself. In our opinion, empathy should not be assessed solely based on the sentences, but also in relation to the context of those sentences. Since each essay-level and conversation-level input is written based on an article, we think it is beneficial to include those articles and the emotional characteristics of the sentences as context for the model. This enables the model to better conceptualize the empathetic nuances.

To develop an effective context-aware model for empathy detection, we initially included related articles along with the emotional characteristics of the input in our model configuration. However, systematic testing revealed that using just the related articles as context was more effective only at the essay level. Conversely, for conversational analysis, incorporating articles as context did not yield the desired results. We observed that most conversational turns consist of everyday dialogue, which does not share similar empathetic features with the articles. This discrepancy led the model to misunderstand the relationship between the context and the conversational turns. Therefore, we decided to use window-based turns as contextual input for the conversational turn analysis. This approach considers the immediate turn before and after each target turn, providing a more relevant context for predicting emotional intensity, emotional polarity, and empathy scores.

Detailed experiment results demonstrating the impact of these contextual elements on model performance are presented in the subsequent sections of this paper. Guided by these observations, we opted for the architectures illustrated in Figures 2 and 1, which are further detailed in the following sections.

### 3.1 Track 2: Empathy and Emotion Prediction in Conversations (CONV-turn)

The input for this track, which focuses on predicting emotional intensity, emotional polarity, and empathy in conversations, is the individual turn, with the context being the combination of turns determined by the window size. This allows the model to understand the immediate emotional and empathetic context within the conversation.

Inspired by the Siamese BERT Network architecture Reimers and Gurevych (2019), our model processes the input and the context in parallel. The input and the context are fed independently into identical BERT encoders as depicted in Figure 1. After pooling the outputs from the BERT encoder using the CLS token, the embeddings are concatenated and passed through fully connected layers (MLP) to predictions. The final output layer provides emotional intensity, emotional polarity and empathy scores.

### 3.2 Track 3: Empathy and Distress Prediction in Essays (EMP)

The architecture for empathy and distress prediction in essays integrates contextual information from the related article. This allows the model to capture nuanced expressions of empathy and distress.

Initially, we faced a challenge with articles being too long for the model's maximum input length, averaging 916 tokens. To address this, we used ChatGPT[1] to summarize the articles, reducing their length to 123 tokens while preserving essential context.

Our model includes input layers for both the essay text and the summarized article text, which are independently fed into identical BERT encoders. The outputs are pooled using the CLS token, concatenated, and passed through fully connected layers (MLP) to provide empathy and distress scores. The overall model architecture is detailed in Figure 2.

[1]We used ChatGPT version *gpt-3.5-turbo-1106* in our work.

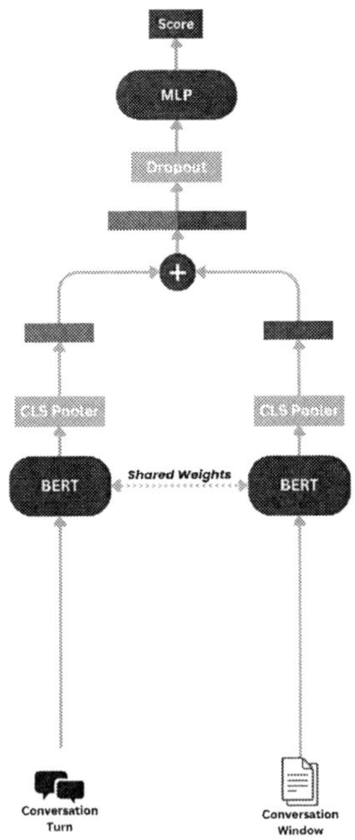


Figure 1: CONV-T Architecture

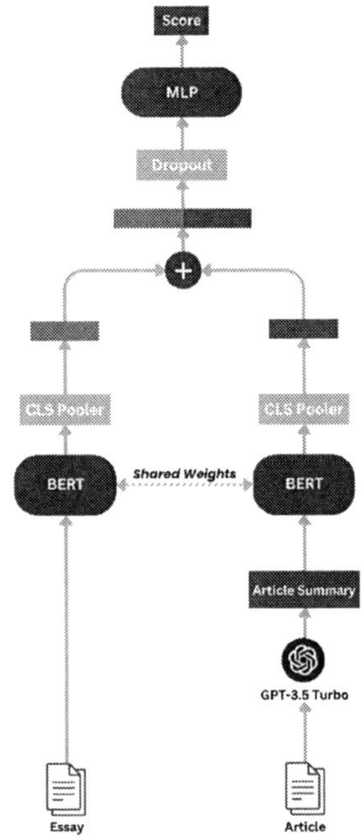


Figure 2: EMP Architecture

## 4 Experiments and Results

In this section, due to page limitations, we present the experimental setup and results of our study on essay-level empathy and distress detection using context-aware BERT-based models only. We aim to evaluate the effectiveness of our proposed architecture by examining the impact of layer manipulation and the type of context provided on the model's performance. We trained both models using a learning rate of 5e-4, an Adam epsilon of 1e-3, and a batch size of 16. Additionally, for the conversation-level model, we used a window size of 1.

### 4.1 Experimental Setup

BERT consists of 12 encoder layers. To determine the optimal configuration for empathy and distress detection, we tested three distinct model configurations regarding the BERT layers:

- **No layers frozen**: All layers of BERT model are trainable during the fine-tuning process.
- **Last two layers unfrozen**: Only the last two layers of the BERT model are trainable, while the remaining layers are kept frozen.
- **Last four layers unfrozen**: Similar to the previous configuration, but with the last four layers of the BERT model being trainable.

Additionally, we experimented with various types of context inputs to identify the most effective approach:

- **Emotion only**: The model receives only the emotional characteristics of the input text as context. We used a pretrained model from Hugging Face called roberta-base-go_emotions Lowe (2024) to extract the emotional labels of the sentences.
- **Article only**: The model receives the summarized article text as context, which provides relevant background information for the essay.
- **Combination of emotion and article**: Both emotional characteristics and summarized article text are provided as context.
- **No context**: The model receives no additional context, relying solely on the input text for empathy and distress detection.

These configurations were chosen to explore how different levels of fine-tuning and context types affect the model's ability to accurately detect empathy and distress.

We also conducted an experiment to measure the effectiveness of using two parallel BERT architectures similar to Siamese Networks and providing the input using the '[SEP]' token. This approach

| Model Configuration | No Context | Context as Emotion | Context as Article | Context as Article and Emotion |
|---|---|---|---|---|
| No layers frozen | 0.677 | 0.665 | **0.698** | 0.677 |
| Last two layers unfrozen | 0.607 | 0.615 | **0.663** | 0.634 |
| Last four layers unfrozen | 0.632 | 0.635 | 0.641 | **0.652** |

Table 1: The table shows the performance of different model configurations and context types in terms of Pearson correlations for empathy and distress detection.

| Input Configuration | Pearson Correlation |
|---|---|
| Parallel BERT (Independent Inputs) | **0.698** |
| Inputs separated with [SEP] Token | 0.671 |

Table 2: The table shows the Pearson correlation scores for essay-level empathy detection using Independent inputs and BERT with [SEP] token configurations.

| CONV-T Results | Pearson Correlation |
|---|---|
| Emotion Intensity | 0.743 |
| Emotional Polarity | 0.758 |
| Empathy | 0.706 |

Table 3: The table shows the Pearson correlation scores for CONV-T track.

aims to assess whether concatenating context and input text with '[SEP]' improves performance compared to processing them independently. All experiments use an evaluation dataset derived from WASSA2024's training data.

### 4.2 Results

Our findings are summarized in Table 1, which shows the performance of each configuration in terms of Pearson correlation for empathy and distress detection.

As depicted in Table 1, using the article alone as context yielded the best performance. This configuration outperformed the others, highlighting the significant impact of relevant textual context on the model's ability to accurately detect empathy and distress in essays. The results demonstrate that providing context as a separate input, rather than concatenating it with the primary text, significantly improves model performance.

Table 2 compares the performance of the parallel BERT architecture (independent input) with BERT using the '[SEP]' token to concatenate context and input text. The results indicate that the parallel BERT approach yields a higher Pearson correlation score, suggesting that processing context and input text independently is more effective than concatenating them with '[SEP]'.

### 4.3 Discussion

The experiments underscore the critical role of tailored model architecture and context selection in enhancing empathy and distress detection performance. Specifically, the use of article summaries as context proved to be the most effective, as illustrated in Table 1. This approach allows the model to better utilize its attention mechanism, enhancing its understanding of empathy.

Additionally, our results show that the performance improves as we increase the number of unfrozen layers, suggesting that deeper fine-tuning allows the model to better capture the nuances of empathy and distress. For completeness, we presented CONV-T results are in Table 3.

Comparing parallel BERT to BERT with the [SEP] token shows that processing context and input text independently improves performance. This suggests the model benefits from treating context and primary text as distinct inputs rather than concatenating them.

## 5 Conclusion

In this paper, we detailed the experimental setup and results, providing a comprehensive analysis of the impact of different configurations and context types on empathy and distress detection performance. Our findings illustrate that context-awareness is a key factor in accurately detecting empathy in textual data. By effectively leveraging contextual information through a separate input strategy, our model demonstrated improved performance over concatenating inputs with the '[SEP]' token. This research opens the door for further developments in enhancing the sensitivity and accuracy of empathy detection systems. Future work can explore additional dimensions of context and refine the methods of integrating context to further boost performance in real-world applications.

## Limitations

While our study demonstrates the potential of a context-aware BERT-based model for empathy and distress detection, several limitations must be acknowledged. First, the relatively small size and domain-specific nature of the available datasets constrain the generalizability of our findings to real-life applications, necessitating larger and more diverse datasets for validation. Additionally, our approach's reliance on the presence of context, such as article summaries for essay-level inputs, means that the model's performance is influenced by the availability and quality of this contextual information. In scenarios where context is absent, the model may face challenges in achieving similar levels of accuracy. Therefore, it is important to generalize the concept of context to enhance the model's applicability in diverse real-life situations. Developing methods to effectively incorporate and optimize contextual information will be crucial for future improvements and broader applicability.

## References


Valentin Barriere, João Sedoc, Shabnam Tafreshi, and Salvatore Giorgi. 2023. Findings of WASSA 2023 shared task on empathy, emotion and personality detection in conversation and reactions to news articles. In *Proceedings of the 13th Workshop on Computational Approaches to Subjectivity, Sentiment, & Social Media Analysis*, pages 511–525, Toronto, Canada. Association for Computational Linguistics.

Tanmay Chavan, Kshitij Deshpande, and Sheetal Sonawane. 2023. Empathy and distress detection using ensembles of transformer models. *Preprint*, arXiv:2312.02578.

Jacob Devlin, Ming-Wei Chang, Kenton Lee, and Kristina Toutanova. 2018. Bert: Pre-training of deep bidirectional transformers for language understanding. *arXiv preprint arXiv:1810.04805*.

Salvatore Giorgi, João Sedoc, Valentin Barriere, and Shabnam Tafreshi. 2024. Findings of wassa 2024 shared task on empathy and personality detection in interactions. In *Proceedings of the 14th Workshop on Computational Approaches to Subjectivity, Sentiment, & Social Media Analysis*.

Bhanu Prakash Reddy Guda, Aparna Garimella, and Niyati Chhaya. 2021. EmpathBERT: A BERT-based framework for demographic-aware empathy prediction. In *Proceedings of the 16th Conference of the European Chapter of the Association for Computational Linguistics: Main Volume*, pages 3072–3079, Online. Association for Computational Linguistics.

Sam Lowe. 2024. roberta-base-go_emotions. `https://huggingface.co/SamLowe/roberta-base-go_emotions`.

Xin Lu, Zhuojun Li, Yanpeng Tong, Yanyan Zhao, and Bing Qin. 2023. HIT-SCIR at WASSA 2023: Empathy and emotion analysis at the utterance-level and the essay-level. In *Proceedings of the 13th Workshop on Computational Approaches to Subjectivity, Sentiment, & Social Media Analysis*, pages 574–580, Toronto, Canada. Association for Computational Linguistics.

Damilola Omitaomu, Shabnam Tafreshi, Tingting Liu, Sven Buechel, Chris Callison-Burch, Johannes Eichstaedt, Lyle Ungar, and João Sedoc. 2022. Empathic conversations: A multi-level dataset of contextualized conversations. *Preprint*, arXiv:2205.12698.

Nils Reimers and Iryna Gurevych. 2019. Sentence-bert: Sentence embeddings using siamese bert-networks. *arXiv preprint arXiv:1908.10084*.

Yukun Wang, Jin Wang, and Xuejie Zhang. 2023. YNU-HPCC at WASSA-2023 shared task 1: Large-scale language model with LoRA fine-tuning for empathy detection and emotion classification. In *Proceedings of the 13th Workshop on Computational Approaches to Subjectivity, Sentiment, & Social Media Analysis*, pages 526–530, Toronto, Canada. Association for Computational Linguistics.

Table 4: Performance of the Empathify team on the CONV-T and EMP tracks on the WASSA2024 test set. Numbers represent Pearson correlation scores.

| Track | Empathy (r) | Emotion Polarity (r) | Emotion Intensity (r) | Empathy (r) | Distress (r) |
|---|---|---|---|---|---|
| CONV-T | 0.541 | 0.638 | 0.584 | - | - |
| EMP | - | - | - | 0.290 | 0.217 |

## A Appendix

We presented our WASSA2024 competition results in Table 4. Due to page limitations, we included our detailed results in the appendix. This table showcases the performance of the Empathify team on both the CONV-T and EMP tracks, based on the WASSA2024 test set. The numbers represent Pearson correlation scores (r values) for different emotion detection metrics. For the CONV-T track, we report the scores for Empathy, Emotion Polarity, and Emotion Intensity. For the EMP track, we provide the scores for Empathy and Distress.

# Zhenmei at WASSA-2024 Empathy and Personality Shared Track: Incorporating Pearson Correlation Coefficient as a Regularization Term for Enhanced Empathy and Emotion Prediction in Conversational Turns

**Liting Huang**
Guangzhou Xinhua College, China
huangliting2019@gmail.com

**Huizhi Liang**
University of Newcastle, UK
Huizhi.Liang@newcastle.ac.uk

## Abstract

In the realm of conversational empathy and emotion prediction, emotions are frequently categorized into multiple levels. This study seeks to enhance the performance of emotion prediction models by incorporating the Pearson correlation coefficient as a regularization term within the loss function. This regularization approach ensures closer alignment between predicted and actual emotion levels, mitigating extreme predictions and resulting in smoother and more consistent outputs. Such outputs are essential for capturing the subtle transitions between continuous emotion levels. Through experimental comparisons between models with and without Pearson regularization, our findings demonstrate that integrating the Pearson correlation coefficient significantly boosts model performance, yielding higher correlation scores and more accurate predictions. Our system officially ranked 9th at the Track 2: CONV-turn. The code for our model can be found at Link [1].

## 1 Introduction

Accurately predicting emotions is crucial for creating responsive and empathetic conversational systems. Emotions are typically classified into multiple levels, reflecting their nuanced and continuous nature. Many existing approaches focus on minimizing prediction errors but often overlook the linear relationship between predicted and actual emotion levels, resulting in extreme and unstable predictions (Acheampong et al., 2021; Zhou et al., 2024; Creanga and Dinu, 2024).

To address this, we propose enhancing emotion prediction models by incorporating the Pearson correlation coefficient as a regularization term in the loss function. The Pearson correlation measures the linear correlation between predicted and actual emotion levels. By including this metric, our approach aims to generate predictions that minimize absolute error while maintaining high correlation with actual emotions. Theoretical analysis confirms the differentiability and convergence of the proposed loss function, ensuring a stable and reliable optimization process.

Additionally, we introduce Consistent-Mixup data augmentation(CMDA) and boosting techniques to further improve model performance. CMDA creates new training samples by combining data from different classes, enhancing the model's ability to generalize. Boosting leverages the strengths of multiple models, such as BERT (Devlin et al., 2018), RoBERTa (Liu et al., 2019) and DeBERTa (He et al., 2020), by combining their predictions based on individual accuracies, thereby improving overall accuracy.

We conducted experiments to validate our approach, comparing models trained with and without Pearson regularization, and those enhanced with CMDA and boosting. Results show that incorporating the Pearson correlation coefficient significantly improves performance, yielding higher correlation scores and more accurate emotion predictions. Furthermore, combining CMDA and boosting techniques leads to even greater improvements in model effectiveness.

## 2 Related Work

Recent research has explored various fine-tuning strategies for Transformer-based models like BERT, RoBERTa, and DeBERTa to enhance downstream performance. Sun et al. (2019) demonstrated significant improvements with techniques such as layer-wise learning rate decay and data augmentation. Mosbach et al. (2020) provided insights into stable fine-tuning through learning rate schedules and early stopping. Additionally, Dong et al. (2019) proposed a unified pre-training framework for lan-

[1] https://github.com/gongziruo/Empathy-and-Emotion-Prediction-in-Conversations-Turns-CONV-turn



*Proceedings of the 14th Workshop on Computational Approaches to Subjectivity, Sentiment, & Social Media Analysis*, pages 399–403
August 15, 2024 ©2024 Association for Computational Linguistics

guage understanding and generation, while Gao et al. (2023) introduced progressive module training to incrementally fine-tune models, enhancing performance and stability.

In dialogue systems, Transformer models have been effectively applied to emotion prediction (Acheampong et al., 2021; Vazquez-Rodriguez et al., 2022). Tu et al. (2022) improved emotion recognition by leveraging context-aware embeddings and fine-tuning on emotion-labeled dialogue datasets. The WASSA 2023 shared task further explored empathy, emotion, and personality detection in conversations and reactions to news articles, highlighting the challenges and advancements in this domain (Barriere et al., 2023; Giorgi et al., 2024).

While Pearson correlation regularization remains underexplored, other methods like adversarial training (Liu et al., 2020) have been examined to enhance model robustness by adding input perturbations. These studies underscore the evolving fine-tuning methodologies for Transformer models, showcasing strategies such as layer-wise learning rate decay, context-aware embeddings, adversarial training, and progressive module training to enhance performance and stability in NLP tasks.

## 3 Methodology

### 3.1 Pearson Coefficient as Regularization Term

To incorporate the negative Pearson coefficient as a regularization term in the loss function, the total loss can be expressed as:

$$L_{\text{total}} = L_{\text{com}} + \lambda(1 - \rho(\hat{\mathbf{y}}, \mathbf{y})), \quad (1)$$

where $\lambda$ is the regularization coefficient, and $\rho(\hat{\mathbf{y}}, \mathbf{y})$ represents the Pearson correlation between predictions $\hat{\mathbf{y}}$ and true labels $\mathbf{y}$.

The combined loss $L_{\text{com}}$ is defined as:

$$L_{\text{com}} = aL_{\text{CE}} + \beta\left(-\frac{1}{N}\sum_{i=1}^{N}\sum_{j=1}^{C} P_{y_i j}\log(p_{ij})\right). \quad (2)$$

In this equation, $L_{\text{CE}}$ stands for Cross-Entropy Loss, a is the weight of $L_{\text{CE}}$, $P_{y_i j}$ indicates the penalty for misclassifying class $y_i$ as class $j$, $p_{ij}$ is the predicted probability for class $j$, $N$ is the number of samples, and $C$ represents the number of classes. Each value in the penalty matrix $\mathbf{P}$ is non-negative, with higher penalties assigned for misclassifications between labels that are numerically farther apart.

#### 3.1.1 Differentiability

The Pearson correlation coefficient between two variables $\hat{\mathbf{y}} = (\hat{y}_1, \ldots, \hat{y}_n)$ and $\mathbf{y} = (y_1, \ldots, y_n)$ is defined as:

$$\rho(\hat{\mathbf{y}}, \mathbf{y}) = \frac{\sum_{i=1}^{n}(\hat{y}_i - \bar{\hat{y}})(y_i - \bar{y})}{\sqrt{\sum_{i=1}^{n}(\hat{y}_i - \bar{\hat{y}})^2}\sqrt{\sum_{i=1}^{n}(y_i - \bar{y})^2}},$$

where $\bar{\hat{y}}$ and $\bar{y}$ are the sample means of $\hat{\mathbf{y}}$ and $\mathbf{y}$, respectively.

To derive the gradient of the Pearson correlation coefficient, we apply the quotient rule. Let $u = \sum_{i=1}^{n}(\hat{y}_i - \bar{x})(y_i - \bar{y})$ and $v = \sqrt{\sum_{i=1}^{n}(\hat{y}_i - \bar{\hat{y}})^2}\sqrt{\sum_{i=1}^{n}(y_i - \bar{y})^2}$. Then, the partial derivative of $\rho(\hat{\mathbf{y}}, \mathbf{y})$ with respect to $\hat{y}_i$ is given by:

$$\frac{\partial \rho(\hat{\mathbf{y}}, \mathbf{y})}{\partial \hat{y}_i} = \frac{v\frac{\partial u}{\partial \hat{y}_i} - u\frac{\partial v}{\partial \hat{y}_i}}{v^2}. \quad (3)$$

The partial derivatives of $u$ and $v$ with respect to $\hat{y}_i$ are:

$$\frac{\partial u}{\partial \hat{y}_i} = \frac{1}{n}(y_i - \bar{y}), \quad (4)$$

$$\frac{\partial v}{\partial \hat{y}_i} = \frac{\sigma_{\mathbf{y}}}{n\sigma_{\hat{\mathbf{y}}}}(\hat{y}_i - \bar{\hat{y}}), \quad (5)$$

where $\sigma_{\hat{\mathbf{y}}}$ and $\sigma_{\mathbf{y}}$ are the sample standard deviations of $\hat{\mathbf{y}}$ and $\mathbf{y}$, respectively.

Substituting these partial derivatives into the quotient rule and simplifying, we obtain the final expression for the partial derivative of the Pearson correlation coefficient with respect to $\hat{y}_i$:

$$\frac{\partial \rho(\hat{\mathbf{y}}, \mathbf{y})}{\partial \hat{y}_i} = \frac{1}{n\sigma_{\hat{\mathbf{y}}}\sigma_{\mathbf{y}}}\left((y_i - \bar{y}) - \rho(\hat{\mathbf{y}}, \mathbf{y}) \cdot (\hat{y}_i - \bar{\hat{y}})\right).$$

Similarly, the partial derivative with respect to $y_i$ is given by:

$$\frac{\partial \rho(\hat{\mathbf{y}}, \mathbf{y})}{\partial y_i} = \frac{1}{n\sigma_{\hat{\mathbf{y}}}\sigma_{\mathbf{y}}}\left((\hat{y}_i - \bar{\hat{y}}) - \rho(\hat{\mathbf{y}}, \mathbf{y}) \cdot (y_i - \bar{y})\right).$$

#### 3.1.2 Convergence Analysis

Consider the total loss function $L_{\text{total}}$ which includes the Pearson correlation coefficient as a regularization term, as shown in Equation (1).

The Pearson correlation coefficient $\rho(\hat{\mathbf{y}}, \mathbf{y})$ is a smooth function, composed of means, covariances, and standard deviations. Consequently, the regularization term $\lambda(1 - \rho(\hat{\mathbf{y}}, \mathbf{y}))$ is also smooth.

Since $\rho(\hat{\mathbf{y}}, \mathbf{y})$ is bounded within $[-1, 1]$, the regularization term is bounded as well:

$$0 \leq \lambda(1 - \rho(\hat{\mathbf{y}}, \mathbf{y})) \leq 2\lambda. \tag{6}$$

This boundedness ensures the regularization term does not overshadow the combined loss term $L_{\text{com}}$, allowing it to guide the optimization process effectively. Both $L_{\text{com}}$ and the regularization term are smooth and differentiable, making $L_{\text{total}}$ smooth and differentiable.

In gradient descent, a smooth and differentiable loss function typically ensures convergence to a local optimum with an appropriate learning rate.

The gradients of $L_{\text{total}}$ with respect to $\hat{\mathbf{y}}$ and $\mathbf{y}$ are:

$$\begin{aligned} \frac{\partial L_{\text{total}}}{\partial \hat{y}_i} &= \frac{\partial L_{\text{com}}}{\partial \hat{y}_i} - \frac{\lambda}{n\sigma_{\hat{\mathbf{y}}}\sigma_{\mathbf{y}}}\left((y_i - \bar{y})\right. \\ &\quad \left.- \rho(\hat{\mathbf{y}}, \mathbf{y}) \cdot (\hat{y}_i - \bar{\hat{y}})\right), \end{aligned} \tag{7}$$

$$\begin{aligned} \frac{\partial L_{\text{total}}}{\partial y_i} &= \frac{\partial L_{\text{com}}}{\partial y_i} - \frac{\lambda}{n\sigma_{\hat{\mathbf{y}}}\sigma_{\mathbf{y}}}\left((\hat{y}_i - \bar{\hat{y}})\right. \\ &\quad \left.- \rho(\hat{\mathbf{y}}, \mathbf{y}) \cdot (y_i - \bar{y})\right). \end{aligned} \tag{8}$$

The gradient descent update rules for $\hat{\mathbf{y}}$ and $\mathbf{y}$ are:

$$\hat{y}_i^{(t+1)} = \hat{y}_i^{(t)} - \eta \frac{\partial L_{\text{total}}}{\partial \hat{y}_i}, \tag{9}$$

$$y_i^{(t+1)} = y_i^{(t)} - \eta \frac{\partial L_{\text{total}}}{\partial y_i}, \tag{10}$$

where $\eta$ is the learning rate and $t$ denotes the iteration.

Given the smoothness and differentiability of the total loss function, and with an appropriate learning rate, the gradient descent algorithm is expected to converge to a local optimum, minimizing the total loss $L_{\text{total}}$.

In conclusion, the inclusion of the Pearson correlation coefficient as a regularization term maintains the smoothness and differentiability of $L_{\text{total}}$. This ensures the gradient descent algorithm converges to a local optimum, minimizing $L_{\text{total}}$.

### 3.2 Consistent-Mixup Data Augmentation

To enhance the robustness of emotion and empathy prediction models, we employed a Consistent-Mixup data augmentation (CMDA) technique. Traditional Mixup methods, which interpolate between pairs of inputs and their labels, can lead to inaccuracies in multi-label tasks like emotion and empathy prediction due to label complexity.

Our approach ensures that only samples with the same label are mixed, maintaining label consistency and preventing erroneous data. Given input sequences $x$ with labels $y$, the data augmentation process is:

$$\tilde{x} = \gamma x_i + (1 - \gamma)x_j, \tag{11}$$

where $y_i = y_j$ and $\gamma \sim \text{Beta}(\alpha, \alpha)$. The Beta distribution, denoted as $\text{Beta}(\alpha, \alpha)$, is a continuous probability distribution defined on the interval $[0, 1]$ and parameterized by two positive shape parameters $\alpha$. Setting both parameters to $\alpha$ ensures a symmetric distribution, which results in a balanced interpolation between inputs. This preserves the integrity of the labels, enhancing the quality of the augmented data and improving model performance and generalization.

| Data set | Model Type | Emotion | Emotional Polarity | Empathy |
|---|---|---|---|---|
| Dev | BERT (S) | 0.620 | 0.697 | 0.567 |
| | BERT (P) | 0.625 | 0.705 | 0.597 |
| | RoBERTa (S) | 0.637 | 0.705 | 0.592 |
| | RoBERTa (P) | 0.648 | 0.724 | 0.595 |
| | DeBERTa (S) | 0.620 | 0.720 | 0.599 |
| | DeBERTa (P) | 0.648 | 0.725 | 0.607 |
| | Boosting (S) | 0.653 | 0.744 | 0.616 |
| | Boosting (P) | **0.667** | 0.757 | 0.625 |
| | Boosting (PC) | 0.659 | **0.765** | **0.658** |
| Test | Boosting (PC) | **0.581** | **0.644** | **0.561** |

Table 1: Performance comparison of various models on Emotion, Emotional Polarity, and Empathy tasks on the development dataset (Dev) and test dataset (Test). (S) indicates the standard model, (P) indicates the model with added Pearson loss, and (PC) represents the model with Pearson loss and CMDA. The test results are reported for the Boosting (PC) model.

### 3.3 Experimental Setup

To validate the effectiveness of incorporating the Pearson correlation coefficient as a regularization term in emotion prediction models, we conducted a series of experiments using several state-of-the-art language models: BERT, RoBERTa, and DeBERTa. These models were chosen for their robust performance in various natural language understanding tasks. Additionally, we applied CMDA and boosting techniques to combine these models, aiming to enhance performance by leveraging their complementary strengths.

### 3.4 Datasets and Data Preprocessing

We used the Track 2 (CONV-turn) dataset, which contains 11,166 training items, 990 develop items, and around 2,300 test items, each with a dialogue text and three corresponding labels: emotional intensity, emotional polarity, and empathy. The length of each dialogue text ranges from 2 characters to 128 characters. The values of emotional intensity and empathy range from 0-5, and the values of emotional polarity range from 0-3. The data is preprocessed by identifying redundant columns and merging the redundant column contents into the correct columns to ensure that the final data is aligned with the corresponding features, and no data is lost in this process(Omitaomu et al., 2022).

### 3.5 Models and Training

Baseline Models: We implemented baseline versions of BERT, RoBERTa, and DeBERTa without Pearson regularization. These models were trained using the loss function ($L_{com}$).

Enhanced Models: For the enhanced versions, we added the Pearson correlation coefficient as a regularization term to the loss function. For a given predicted sentiment level $\hat{y}$ and actual sentiment level $y$ is defined as:

$$\text{Loss} = L_{\text{com}}(\hat{y}, y) - \lambda \cdot (1 - \text{Pearson}(\hat{y}, y)),$$

where $\lambda$ is a hyperparameter that controls the weight of the Pearson regularization term.

Training process: All models were trained using the Adam optimizer with a learning rate of $1e^{-5}$. To enhance the models, we incorporated data augmentation. Specifically, we employed CMDA ensuring the mixed labels remained consistent. Additionally, we adopted a boosting strategy by training three different models(BERT, RoBERTa, DeBERTa) and aggregating their outputs using a weighted average method to form the final prediction. This ensemble approach aimed to leverage the strengths of each individual model and improve overall performance.

### 3.6 Experimental Results

The evaluation metric used in this study is the Pearson Correlation Coefficient, which evaluates the linear correlation between the predicted and actual sentiment levels, reflecting the consistency of the predictions.

The study evaluates sentiment prediction models using the Pearson Correlation Coefficient to measure the linear correlation between predicted and actual sentiment levels. Table 1 shows that using Pearson correlation as a regularizer significantly enhances performance across all tested configurations. Enhanced models (BERT, RoBERTa, and DeBERTa with Pearson regularization) consistently outperform their baselines in Emotion, Emotional Polarity, and Empathy tasks.

Furthermore, Boosting models demonstrate additional improvements. The Boosting (Standard) model, which combines the results of the individual standard models using weighted averages, shows better performance than the individual models. The Boosting (Pearson) model, which similarly combines the Pearson-regularized models, achieves even higher scores. The best performance is from the Boosting (Pearson, CMDA) model, with top scores in Emotional Polarity (0.765) and Empathy (0.658). The Boosting (Pearson) model excels in Emotion (0.667), underscoring the benefits of Pearson correlation regularization.

The test set results also highlight the robustness of the models. The Boosting (Pearson, CMDA) model achieved scores of 0.581, 0.644, and 0.561 in Emotion, Emotional Polarity, and Empathy respectively. It is important to note that these scores are significantly higher than the official results of -0.027, -0.020, and -0.043 respectively. The discrepancy arose because an early version of the model was submitted by mistake, leading to the lower scores. The updated results presented here reflect the true performance of the final, optimized models.

## 4 Conclusion

We proposed an enhanced approach for emotion prediction by incorporating the Pearson correlation coefficient as a regularization term in the loss function, ensuring closer alignment between predicted and actual emotion levels. This method, along with CMDA and boosting techniques, significantly improved model performance, yielding higher correlation scores and more accurate predictions. Our findings underscore the potential of correlation-based regularization and advanced training techniques in enhancing Transformer-based models for emotion prediction tasks.

## Limitations

Due to time constraints, we submitted an earlier version of our results, leading to a lower score of -0.03 on TRACK CONV-turn. Here, we present the best results to accurately represent our system's performance, as shown in table 1. Relying solely on the Pearson correlation coefficient may not fully demonstrate our approach's effectiveness. A 1-3% increase in the Pearson coefficient, though modest, shows consistent improvement. For a more comprehensive evaluation, we will include other metrics, such as the F1 score, in future work. These additional metrics will further validate our approach.

## References


Francisca Adoma Acheampong, Henry Nunoo-Mensah, and Wenyu Chen. 2021. Transformer models for text-based emotion detection: a review of bert-based approaches. *Artificial Intelligence Review*, 54(8):5789–5829.

Valentin Barriere, João Sedoc, Shabnam Tafreshi, and Salvatore Giorgi. 2023. Findings of wassa 2023 shared task on empathy, emotion and personality detection in conversation and reactions to news articles. In *Proceedings of the 13th Workshop on Computational Approaches to Subjectivity, Sentiment, & Social Media Analysis*, pages 511–525.

Claudiu Creanga and Liviu P Dinu. 2024. Transformer based neural networks for emotion recognition in conversations. *arXiv preprint arXiv:2405.11222*.

Jacob Devlin, Ming-Wei Chang, Kenton Lee, and Kristina Toutanova. 2018. Bert: Pre-training of deep bidirectional transformers for language understanding. *arXiv preprint arXiv:1810.04805*.

Li Dong, Nan Yang, Wenhui Wang, Furu Wei, Xiaodong Liu, Yu Wang, Jianfeng Gao, Ming Zhou, and Hsiao-Wuen Hon. 2019. Unified language model pre-training for natural language understanding and generation. *Advances in neural information processing systems*, 32.

Qiankun Gao, Chen Zhao, Yifan Sun, Teng Xi, Gang Zhang, Bernard Ghanem, and Jian Zhang. 2023. A unified continual learning framework with general parameter-efficient tuning. In *Proceedings of the IEEE/CVF International Conference on Computer Vision*, pages 11483–11493.

Salvatore Giorgi, João Sedoc, Valentin Barriere, and Shabnam Tafreshi. 2024. Findings of wassa 2024 shared task on empathy and personality detection in interactions. In *Proceedings of the 14th Workshop on Computational Approaches to Subjectivity, Sentiment, & Social Media Analysis*.

Pengcheng He, Xiaodong Liu, Jianfeng Gao, and Weizhu Chen. 2020. Deberta: Decoding-enhanced bert with disentangled attention. *arXiv preprint arXiv:2006.03654*.

Xiaodong Liu, Hao Cheng, Pengcheng He, Weizhu Chen, Yu Wang, Hoifung Poon, and Jianfeng Gao. 2020. Adversarial training for large neural language models. *arXiv preprint arXiv:2004.08994*.

Yinhan Liu, Myle Ott, Naman Goyal, Jingfei Du, Mandar Joshi, Danqi Chen, Omer Levy, Mike Lewis, Luke Zettlemoyer, and Veselin Stoyanov. 2019. Roberta: A robustly optimized bert pretraining approach. *arXiv preprint arXiv:1907.11692*.

Marius Mosbach, Maksym Andriushchenko, and Dietrich Klakow. 2020. On the stability of fine-tuning bert: Misconceptions, explanations, and strong baselines. *arXiv preprint arXiv:2006.04884*.

Damilola Omitaomu, Shabnam Tafreshi, Tingting Liu, Sven Buechel, Chris Callison-Burch, Johannes Eichstaedt, Lyle Ungar, and João Sedoc. 2022. Empathic conversations: A multi-level dataset of contextualized conversations. *Preprint*, arXiv:2205.12698.

Chi Sun, Xipeng Qiu, Yige Xu, and Xuanjing Huang. 2019. How to fine-tune bert for text classification? In *Chinese computational linguistics: 18th China national conference, CCL 2019, Kunming, China, October 18–20, 2019, proceedings 18*, pages 194–206. Springer.

Geng Tu, Jintao Wen, Cheng Liu, Dazhi Jiang, and Erik Cambria. 2022. Context-and sentiment-aware networks for emotion recognition in conversation. *IEEE Transactions on Artificial Intelligence*, 3(5):699–708.

Juan Vazquez-Rodriguez, Grégoire Lefebvre, Julien Cumin, and James L Crowley. 2022. Transformer-based self-supervised learning for emotion recognition. In *2022 26th International Conference on Pattern Recognition (ICPR)*, pages 2605–2612. IEEE.

Weiwei Zhou, Jiada Lu, Chenkun Ling, Weifeng Wang, and Shaowei Liu. 2024. Boosting continuous emotion recognition with self-pretraining using masked autoencoders, temporal convolutional networks, and transformers. *arXiv preprint arXiv:2403.11440*.

# Empaths at WASSA 2024 Empathy and Personality Shared Task: Turn-Level Empathy Prediction Using Psychological Indicators

**Shaz Furniturewala[1*], Kokil Jaidka[2],**
[1]Birla Institute of Technology and Science, Pilani,
[2]NUS Center for Trusted Internet and Community, National University of Singapore,

## Abstract

For the WASSA 2024 Empathy and Personality Prediction Shared Task, we propose a novel turn-level empathy detection method that decomposes empathy into six psychological indicators: Emotional Language, Perspective-Taking, Sympathy and Compassion, Extroversion, Openness, and Agreeableness. A pipeline of text enrichment using a Large Language Model (LLM) followed by DeBERTA fine-tuning demonstrates a significant improvement in the Pearson Correlation Coefficient and F1 scores for empathy detection, highlighting the effectiveness of our approach. Our system officially ranked 7th at the CONV-turn track.

## 1 Introduction

Empathy, a critical construct in human social interaction, involves perceiving, understanding, and resonating with the emotional states and perspectives of others. This construct is essential in domains such as mental health support, customer service, and human-computer interaction (Paiva et al., 2014). Empathy comprises both cognitive and affective dimensions (Batson, 2009; Singer and Lamm, 2009), with the cognitive dimension involving the intellectual understanding of another's psychological state and the affective dimension involving the emotional experience of another's feelings.

Empathy detection in natural language processing (NLP) focuses on identifying and quantifying empathetic expressions in text. Accurate empathy detection can enhance the performance of automated systems in responding to human emotions appropriately (Shum et al., 2018). Applications include therapeutic conversational agents, customer service bots, and social robotics. Traditional empathy detection methods rely on lexical and syntactic analysis (Provence and Forcehimes, 2024), using features such as sentiment polarity, emotion lexicons, and dialogue acts. These methods often fail to capture the nuanced and context-dependent nature of empathy, rooted in deeper psychological constructs. Effective empathy detection requires a sophisticated analytical framework to interpret underlying psychological indicators.

Our study employs GPT-4o (OpenAI et al., 2024) to evaluate six psychological indicators for each utterance in our dataset. GPT-4o's advanced language understanding and generation capabilities allow it to assess and articulate the presence of these indicators, providing ratings and explanatory sentences. These enriched inputs are used to train a DeBERTa classifier (He et al., 2021), known for its superior performance in NLP tasks due to its enhanced attention mechanisms and optimized representation learning. Our empirical analysis demonstrates that incorporating the psychological indicators significantly enhances the performance of the empathy detection models, as evidenced by improvements in Pearson correlation, F1 scores, and accuracy metrics.

By integrating psychological indicators and leveraging advanced NLP models, our work offers a new pipeline for multi-task learning that relies on the cognitive underpinnings of human behavior. This contributes to developing more contextually aware and empathetic conversational agents, improving human-computer interaction, and enabling more emotionally intelligent automated systems.

## 2 Related Work

Simple approaches to empathy detection have employed rule-based systems and manually crafted features, leveraging predefined empathy-related keywords and patterns to identify empathetic ex-

*Work done during internship at NUS Center for Trusted Internet and Community



*Proceedings of the 14th Workshop on Computational Approaches to Subjectivity, Sentiment, & Social Media Analysis*, pages 404–411
August 15, 2024 ©2024 Association for Computational Linguistics

| Speaker | Utterance | Empathy |
|---|---|---|
| Person 1 | What did you think about this article | 0.6667 |
| Person 2 | It's definitely really sad to read, considering everything they're all going through. What did you think? | 4.3333 |
| Person 1 | I think it's super sad... they seem to never catch a break, always struggling. | 4.6667 |
| Person 2 | I can't imagine just living in an area that is constantly being ravaged by hurricanes or earthquakes. I take my location for granted. | 4.6667 |

Table 1: A snippet of the dataset.

pressions (Provence and Forcehimes, 2024). With the advent of machine learning, statistical models such as support vector machines (SVMs) and random forests were utilized, which leveraged a broader set of features, including syntactic structures, word embeddings, and discourse markers (Chen et al., 2020; Mathur et al., 2021). However, these approaches are limited by their reliance on predefined patterns and surface-level features, which may not generalize well across different contexts and fail to capture the complexity and contextual nature of empathetic language.

Recent advancements in deep learning have further propelled the field, with neural network architectures such as recurrent neural networks (RNNs) (Tavabi et al., 2019), LSTMs (Tan et al., 2019), and transformers (Guda et al., 2021) demonstrating significant improvements in capturing the contextual dependencies and semantic richness of empathetic language. Transformer-based models, particularly BERT (Devlin et al., 2019) and its variants, have shown remarkable performance in various NLP tasks, including empathy detection. These models are expected to provide a more nuanced understanding of empathetic expressions by leveraging self-attention mechanisms that model long-range dependencies and contextual relationships within the text. Nevertheless, these models would still need sufficient context to interpret empathetic behavior and, by themselves, do not offer a way to consider the specific psychological constructs that underpin empathetic behavior.

To address this gap, our approach for empathy detection focused on first enriching the data with more psychological indicators and then improving upon the design of the current best-performing model. Our objective was to focus on the psychological indicators underpinning empathy, leveraging our prior work in modeling cognitive appraisals of happiness (Liu and Jaidka, 2023) and purchase behavior (Yeo and Jaidka, 2023; Yeo et al., Accepted) by translating a text classification paradigm into a multi-task classification problem. Our prior work successfully demonstrated the effectiveness of using psychological constructs to enhance predictive models, providing a foundation for our current approach. We believed that applying a similar framework to empathy detection would yield robust and interpretable models capable of capturing the nuanced and multifaceted nature of empathetic expressions in language.

## 3 Method

We decomposed the concept of "Empathy" into theory-inspired fundamental components of empathetic behavior (Batson, 2009; Singer and Lamm, 2009), focusing on six distinct psychological indicators:

- Emotional Language: Represented by the use of emotion-laden words (e.g., "sad," "happy," "worried") and descriptions of feelings or emotions, both personal and those of others.
- Perspective-Taking: Indicated by statements that show an understanding of another person's point of view.
- Sympathy and Compassion: Demonstrated by expressions of concern for another person's well-being.
- Extroversion: Reflected by signs of sociability, such as mentions of interactions with others, excitement about social events, or enjoyment of group activities.
- Openness: Indicated by signs of creativity, intellectual curiosity, or unconventional thinking, such as discussing diverse topics, exploring different perspectives, or expressing interest in novel ideas.
- Agreeableness: Shown by kindness, altruism, or cooperation in the text, for example, ex-

pressions of concern for others' well-being, willingness to help, or avoiding conflict.

By enriching our data with information about these indicators, we aimed to provide a more comprehensive and interpretable framework for empathy detection. However, the challenge remains in accurately operationalizing these psychological constructs and ensuring that models can reliably differentiate and interpret these indicators within varied contexts and expressions of empathy. To do so, we closely relied on how these concepts are defined, worded, and measured in surveys to human participants.

### 3.1 Dataset

We use the dataset created by (Omitaomu et al., 2022) and provided as part of the WASSA 2024 Shared Task 2 (Giorgi et al., 2024; Barriere et al., 2023), which is an empathetic conversation dataset consisting of conversations in response to news articles. It consists of 500 conversations between AMT workers reacting to 100 articles about negative events from (Buechel et al., 2018). Each conversation is greater than 15 turns. This conversation data has been third-person annotated at the turn-level on a range of 0-5 for the level of empathy displayed in the text. Scores in the dataset, however, are also fractional, presumably due to averaging among reviewers. For training, we round the scores to the nearest integer; however, while computing the Pearson Correlation Coefficient, we use the original scores. We divide the 11059 utterances into a training set of 8294 and a test set of 2765. Table 1 contains a snippet of the Dataset. The results demonstrated in this paper are unofficial, based on the test dataset we created using a subset of the training data. The official result is also provided in Section 4.

### 3.2 Enrichment

For each utterance in the dataset, we used GPT-4o to detect the level of the psychological indicators described previously, rating them as Low, Medium, or High. Additionally, GPT-4o provided a sentence explaining the rating, highlighting words or phrases contributing to a high or low rating. Table 4 in Appendix A presents the generated ratings and explanations for a sample utterance from the dataset. The prompt used to generate them is also provided in Fig 1 in Appendix A. These ratings and explanations were used as additional context and concatenated to the original utterance. Subsequently, a DeBERTa V3 classifier was trained on this new set of inputs.

### 3.3 Models and baselines

We tested two classification models: DeBERTa-v3-Large finetuned and GPT-4o for zero-shot classification. For each model, we tested its performance on just the utterance and the utterance combined with additional context provided by the six psychological indicators. For the DeBERTa classifier, we concatenated the rating and explanation for each indicator to the original utterance, separated by [SEP] tokens. For GPT-4o, we crafted an instructional prompt, providing all the information in bullet points.

## 4 Results and Discussion

In Table 3, we demonstrate the Pearson Correlation Coefficient of the psychological indicator scores with the annotated empathy ratings. We converted the levels predicted by GPT-4o (Low, Medium, High) to integers (-1, 0, 1) and computed the coefficients of each feature with the empathy ratings. Emotional Language exhibited the highest positive correlation (0.481*), underscoring the significance of emotion-laden words in conveying empathy. Sympathy and Compassion also showed a strong positive correlation (0.437*), validating the role of compassionate expressions in empathetic communication. Perspective-Taking had a moderate positive correlation (0.186*), suggesting that understanding another person's point of view contributes to empathy but is less influential than direct emotional expressions. Interestingly, Extroversion had a negative correlation (-0.152*), implying that sociability may not align with empathetic responses in these conversations. Openness showed a very weak correlation (0.010), indicating minimal impact on empathy perception, while Agreeableness had a modest positive correlation (0.120*), reflecting a mild association with empathetic responses through expressions of kindness and cooperation. Table 2 reports the performance of the four classification methods in terms of their Pearson Correlation Coefficient, Accuracy, and F1 Score at empathy detection. While the coefficient is computed with the fractional empathy labels, the accuracy and F1 score are computed after rounding those labels to the nearest integer. This rounding is done because 6-label classification (0 to 5 in increments

| Model | Input | Pearson R | F1 (Rounded) | Accuracy (Rounded) |
|---|---|---|---|---|
| GPT-4o | Utterance Only | 0.38 | 0.24 | 0.29 |
| GPT-4o | Utterance + Indicators | 0.41 | 0.20 | 0.26 |
| DeBERTa | Utterance Only | 0.65 | 0.32 | 0.52 |
| DeBERTa | Utterance + Indicators | **0.68** | **0.35** | **0.55** |

Table 2: The Pearson Correlation Coefficient and F1 scores for each of the four classification methods.

| **Psych. Indicator** | **Pearson R** |
|---|---|
| Emotional Language | 0.481* |
| Perspective-Taking | 0.186* |
| Sympathy and Compassion | 0.437* |
| Extroversion | -0.152* |
| Openness | 0.010 |
| Agreableness | 0.120* |

Table 3: The Pearson Correlation Coefficient of the GPT-4o scores (converted to integers) for each psychological indicator with the annotated Empathy Rating.

of 1) is much simpler than 16-label classification (0 to 5 in increments of 0.33). Further, we found that the rounded labels have a correlation coefficient of 0.96 with the original labels, demonstrating minimal knowledge loss. There is a large gulf between the performance of GPT-4o and the trained DeBERTa classifier for both input formats, reiterating the necessity of relying on attention mechanisms for interpreting implicit concepts like empathy from dialogic data.

The results demonstrate the efficacy of incorporating psychological indicators into empathy detection models. The baseline DeBERTa model trained on utterances alone achieved a Pearson correlation of 0.65, an F1 score of 0.32, and an accuracy of 0.52. When augmented with the additional context from the six psychological indicators, the model's performance improved, achieving a Pearson correlation of 0.68, an F1 score of 0.35, and an accuracy of 0.55. This indicates that the enriched input provides more comprehensive information, allowing the model to understand and predict empathy levels.

In contrast, the zero-shot classification using GPT-4o showed more modest improvements. The model's Pearson correlation increased from 0.38 to 0.41 when augmented with the psychological indicators, although the F1 score and accuracy slightly decreased. This suggests that while the additional context benefits GPT-4o, the model may require further fine-tuning to leverage the enriched input fully.

It is to be noted that these results are on the test set generated as a subset of the provided training data. We were unable to conduct these experiments on the official test data as the labels for that were not available to us. The Pearson correlation coefficient for the Utterance + Indicators DeBERTa classifier on the official test dataset is 0.534.

## 5 Discussion and Conclusion

Our method for empathy detection relied on enriching the available data with more psychological indicators that could help support the ultimate Empathy label. We show that our approach boosts performance and provides interpretable AI insights, which can be crucial for applications requiring transparency and trust.

The significant improvement observed with the DeBERTa model underscores the importance of considering psychological components in empathy detection. However, it is the role and performance of GPT-4o, the leading LLM, that provides the most interesting insights. On the one hand, the nuanced explanations provided by GPT-4o offer valuable context that enhances the model's ability to detect empathy. On the other hand, its relatively poor performance in empathy prediction indicates that LLMs cannot yet effectively extract and understand all the underlying information in a dialogic exchange, even in a few-shot manner, highlighting the need for further exploration of reasoning-based approaches.

## 6 Limitations

We acknowledge one particular limitation of our work. The reliance on GPT-4o for both enriching the data and attempting to label it may lead to concept drift, where the interpretation of the labels relies heavily on prompt sensitivity and adherence, and ultimately digresses from the original definition. To address this, our future work will involve obtaining additional expert annotations and conducting a thorough inspection of GPT-4o's reasoning. This will ensure that our data enrichment is valid, nuanced, and accurately reflects human intent.

## References


Valentin Barriere, João Sedoc, Shabnam Tafreshi, and Salvatore Giorgi. 2023. Findings of wassa 2023 shared task on empathy, emotion and personality detection in conversation and reactions to news articles. In *Proceedings of the 13th Workshop on Computational Approaches to Subjectivity, Sentiment, & Social Media Analysis*, pages 511–525.

C. Batson. 2009. These things called empathy: Eight related but distinct phenomena. *The Social Neuroscience of Empathy*.

Sven Buechel, Anneke Buffone, Barry Slaff, Lyle Ungar, and João Sedoc. 2018. Modeling empathy and distress in reaction to news stories. *Preprint*, arXiv:1808.10399.

Zhuohao Chen, James Gibson, Ming-Chang Chiu, Qiaohong Hu, Tara K Knight, Daniella Meeker, James A Tulsky, Kathryn I Pollak, and Shrikanth Narayanan. 2020. Automated empathy detection for oncology encounters. In *2020 IEEE International Conference on Healthcare Informatics (ICHI)*, pages 1–8. IEEE.

Jacob Devlin, Ming-Wei Chang, Kenton Lee, and Kristina Toutanova. 2019. Bert: Pre-training of deep bidirectional transformers for language understanding. *Preprint*, arXiv:1810.04805.

Salvatore Giorgi, João Sedoc, Valentin Barriere, and Shabnam Tafreshi. 2024. Findings of wassa 2024 shared task on empathy and personality detection in interactions. In *Proceedings of the 14th Workshop on Computational Approaches to Subjectivity, Sentiment, & Social Media Analysis*.

Bhanu Prakash Reddy Guda, Aparna Garimella, and Niyati Chhaya. 2021. Empathbert: A bert-based framework for demographic-aware empathy prediction. *arXiv preprint arXiv:2102.00272*.

Pengcheng He, Xiaodong Liu, Jianfeng Gao, and Weizhu Chen. 2021. Deberta: Decoding-enhanced bert with disentangled attention. *Preprint*, arXiv:2006.03654.

Xuan Liu and Kokil Jaidka. 2023. I am psyam: Modeling happiness with cognitive appraisal dimensions. In *Findings of the Association for Computational Linguistics: ACL 2023*, pages 1192–1210.

Leena Mathur, Micol Spitale, Hao Xi, Jieyun Li, and Maja J Matarić. 2021. Modeling user empathy elicited by a robot storyteller. In *2021 9th International Conference on Affective Computing and Intelligent Interaction (ACII)*, pages 1–8. IEEE.

Damilola Omitaomu, Shabnam Tafreshi, Tingting Liu, Sven Buechel, Chris Callison-Burch, Johannes Eichstaedt, Lyle Ungar, and João Sedoc. 2022. Empathic conversations: A multi-level dataset of contextualized conversations. *Preprint*, arXiv:2205.12698.

OpenAI, Josh Achiam, Steven Adler, Sandhini Agarwal, Lama Ahmad, Ilge Akkaya, Florencia Leoni Aleman, Diogo Almeida, Janko Altenschmidt, Sam Altman, Shyamal Anadkat, Red Avila, Igor Babuschkin, Suchir Balaji, Valerie Balcom, Paul Baltescu, Haiming Bao, Mohammad Bavarian, Jeff Belgum, Irwan Bello, Jake Berdine, Gabriel Bernadett-Shapiro, Christopher Berner, Lenny Bogdonoff, Oleg Boiko, Madelaine Boyd, Anna-Luisa Brakman, Greg Brockman, Tim Brooks, Miles Brundage, Kevin Button, Trevor Cai, Rosie Campbell, Andrew Cann, Brittany Carey, Chelsea Carlson, Rory Carmichael, Brooke Chan, Che Chang, Fotis Chantzis, Derek Chen, Sully Chen, Ruby Chen, Jason Chen, Mark Chen, Ben Chess, Chester Cho, Casey Chu, Hyung Won Chung, Dave Cummings, Jeremiah Currier, Yunxing Dai, Cory Decareaux, Thomas Degry, Noah Deutsch, Damien Deville, Arka Dhar, David Dohan, Steve Dowling, Sheila Dunning, Adrien Ecoffet, Atty Eleti, Tyna Eloundou, David Farhi, Liam Fedus, Niko Felix, Simón Posada Fishman, Juston Forte, Isabella Fulford, Leo Gao, Elie Georges, Christian Gibson, Vik Goel, Tarun Gogineni, Gabriel Goh, Rapha Gontijo-Lopes, Jonathan Gordon, Morgan Grafstein, Scott Gray, Ryan Greene, Joshua Gross, Shixiang Shane Gu, Yufei Guo, Chris Hallacy, Jesse Han, Jeff Harris, Yuchen He, Mike Heaton, Johannes Heidecke, Chris Hesse, Alan Hickey, Wade Hickey, Peter Hoeschele, Brandon Houghton, Kenny Hsu, Shengli Hu, Xin Hu, Joost Huizinga, Shantanu Jain, Shawn Jain, Joanne Jang, Angela Jiang, Roger Jiang, Haozhun Jin, Denny Jin, Shino Jomoto, Billie Jonn, Heewoo Jun, Tomer Kaftan, Łukasz Kaiser, Ali Kamali, Ingmar Kanitscheider, Nitish Shirish Keskar, Tabarak Khan, Logan Kilpatrick, Jong Wook Kim, Christina Kim, Yongjik Kim, Jan Hendrik Kirchner, Jamie Kiros, Matt Knight, Daniel Kokotajlo, Łukasz Kondraciuk, Andrew Kondrich, Aris Konstantinidis, Kyle Kosic, Gretchen Krueger, Vishal Kuo, Michael Lampe, Ikai Lan, Teddy Lee, Jan Leike, Jade Leung, Daniel Levy, Chak Ming Li, Rachel Lim, Molly Lin, Stephanie Lin, Mateusz Litwin, Theresa Lopez, Ryan Lowe, Patricia Lue, Anna Makanju, Kim Malfacini, Sam Manning, Todor Markov, Yaniv Markovski, Bianca Martin, Katie Mayer, Andrew Mayne, Bob McGrew, Scott Mayer McKinney, Christine McLeavey, Paul McMillan, Jake McNeil, David Medina, Aalok Mehta, Jacob Menick, Luke Metz, Andrey Mishchenko, Pamela Mishkin, Vinnie Monaco, Evan Morikawa, Daniel Mossing, Tong Mu, Mira Murati, Oleg Murk, David Mély, Ashvin Nair, Reiichiro Nakano, Rajeev Nayak, Arvind Neelakantan, Richard Ngo, Hyeonwoo Noh, Long Ouyang, Cullen O'Keefe, Jakub Pachocki, Alex

Paino, Joe Palermo, Ashley Pantuliano, Giambattista Parascandolo, Joel Parish, Emy Parparita, Alex Passos, Mikhail Pavlov, Andrew Peng, Adam Perelman, Filipe de Avila Belbute Peres, Michael Petrov, Henrique Ponde de Oliveira Pinto, Michael, Pokorny, Michelle Pokrass, Vitchyr H. Pong, Tolly Powell, Alethea Power, Boris Power, Elizabeth Proehl, Raul Puri, Alec Radford, Jack Rae, Aditya Ramesh, Cameron Raymond, Francis Real, Kendra Rimbach, Carl Ross, Bob Rotsted, Henri Roussez, Nick Ryder, Mario Saltarelli, Ted Sanders, Shibani Santurkar, Girish Sastry, Heather Schmidt, David Schnurr, John Schulman, Daniel Selsam, Kyla Sheppard, Toki Sherbakov, Jessica Shieh, Sarah Shoker, Pranav Shyam, Szymon Sidor, Eric Sigler, Maddie Simens, Jordan Sitkin, Katarina Slama, Ian Sohl, Benjamin Sokolowsky, Yang Song, Natalie Staudacher, Felipe Petroski Such, Natalie Summers, Ilya Sutskever, Jie Tang, Nikolas Tezak, Madeleine B. Thompson, Phil Tillet, Amin Tootoonchian, Elizabeth Tseng, Preston Tuggle, Nick Turley, Jerry Tworek, Juan Felipe Cerón Uribe, Andrea Vallone, Arun Vijayvergiya, Chelsea Voss, Carroll Wainwright, Justin Jay Wang, Alvin Wang, Ben Wang, Jonathan Ward, Jason Wei, CJ Weinmann, Akila Welihinda, Peter Welinder, Jiayi Weng, Lilian Weng, Matt Wiethoff, Dave Willner, Clemens Winter, Samuel Wolrich, Hannah Wong, Lauren Workman, Sherwin Wu, Jeff Wu, Michael Wu, Kai Xiao, Tao Xu, Sarah Yoo, Kevin Yu, Qiming Yuan, Wojciech Zaremba, Rowan Zellers, Chong Zhang, Marvin Zhang, Shengjia Zhao, Tianhao Zheng, Juntang Zhuang, William Zhuk, and Barret Zoph. 2024. Gpt-4 technical report. *Preprint*, arXiv:2303.08774.

Ana Paiva, Iolanda Leite, and Tiago Ramos Ribeiro. 2014. Emotion modelling for social robots.

Scott Provence and Alyssa Forcehimes. 2024. Algorithms for empathy: Using machine learning to categorize common empathetic traits across professional and peer-based conversations. *Cureus*, 16.

Heung-Yeung Shum, Xiaodong He, and Di Li. 2018. From eliza to xiaoice: Challenges and opportunities with social chatbots. *Preprint*, arXiv:1801.01957.

Tania Singer and Claus Lamm. 2009. The social neuroscience of empathy. *Annals of the New York Academy of Sciences*, 1156.

Zhi-Xuan Tan, Arushi Goel, Thanh-Son Nguyen, and Desmond C Ong. 2019. A multimodal lstm for predicting listener empathic responses over time. In *2019 14th IEEE International Conference on Automatic Face & Gesture Recognition (FG 2019)*, pages 1–4. IEEE.

Leili Tavabi, Kalin Stefanov, Setareh Nasihati Gilani, David Traum, and Mohammad Soleymani. 2019. Multimodal learning for identifying opportunities for empathetic responses. In *2019 International Conference on Multimodal Interaction*, pages 95–104.

Gerard Yeo, Shaz Furniturewala, and Kokil Jaidka. Accepted. Beyond text: Leveraging multi-task learning and cognitive appraisal theory for post-purchase intention analysis. In *Findings of the Association for Computational Linguistics: ACL (2024)*.

Gerard Yeo and Kokil Jaidka. 2023. The peace-reviews dataset: Modeling cognitive appraisals in emotion text analysis. In *Findings of the Association for Computational Linguistics: EMNLP 2023*, pages 2822–2840.

## A Appendix

Table 4 contains an instance of the dataset and the ratings and explanations provided by GPT-4o on the six psychological indicators.

Figure 1 displays the prompt used to generate the ratings and explanations from GPT-4o.

I will provide you with a text. You have to rate the text as LOW, MEDIUM, or HIGH for each of the following five psychological dimensions and explain your score in a single sentence.
Psychological Dimensions:
- Emotional Language: HIGH emotional language contains emotion-laden words (e.g., "sad," "happy," "worried") and descriptions of feelings or emotions, both their own and those of others. LOW emotional lanugage would NOT have this.
- Perspective-Taking: HIGH perspective taking statements indicate an understanding of another person's point of view. LOW perspective taking statements DO NOT.
- Sympathy and Compassion: HIGH sympathy and compassion is represented by statements showing concern for another person's well-being. LOW sympathy and compassion is represented by statements that DO NOT.
- Extroversion: HIGH extroversion is indicated by signs of sociability, such as mentioning interactions with others, excitement about social events, or enjoyment of group activities.
- Openness: HIGH extroversion is indicated by signs of creativity, intellectual curiosity, or unconventional thinking. This might include discussing diverse topics, exploring different perspectives, or expressing interest in novel ideas. LOW openness would not include these.
- Agreeableness: HIGH agreeableness is indicated by kindness, altruism, or cooperation in the text. For example, expressions of concern for others' well-being, willingness to help, or avoiding conflict. LOW agreeableness is not indicated by these.
Report the result in JSON format with the text, the ratings, and the single sentence explanation for each of the five psychological dimensions. The JSON string should have the keys 'Text', 'Scores', 'Explanations'.
Be very strict while giving ratings and don't give HIGH ratings unnecessarily. Also, highlight factors that contributed both positively and negatively to your rating in the single sentence explanation.
Here is the text: [TEXT]

Figure 1: Prompt given to GPT-4o.

| | |
|---|---|
| Utterance | You've nailed it. Bringing children into the mix definitely amplifies the desire for privacy and protection. It's all about creating a safe and stable environment for them. |
| Emotional Language | **Medium**. The text contains words like 'desire' and implies concern for children's well-being, but lacks varied emotion-laden language. |
| Perspective-Taking | **High**. It acknowledges the point of view of someone concerned about privacy and protection for children, representing strong perspective-taking. |
| Sympathy and Compassion | **High**. The concern for creating a safe and stable environment for children shows significant sympathy and compassion towards their well-being. |
| Extroversion | **Low**. There is no mention of social interactions, excitement about social events, or enjoyment of group activities, indicating low extroversion. |
| Openness | **Low**. The text does not display signs of creativity, intellectual curiosity, or unconventional thinking, which reflect low openness. |
| Agreeableness | **Medium**. It shows some concern for others but does not explicitly demonstrate strong kindness, altruism, or cooperative behavior. |

Table 4: Ratings and explanations provided by GPT-4o for a sample utterance from the dataset.

# NU at WASSA 2024 Empathy and Personality Shared Task: Enhancing Personality Predictions with Knowledge Graphs; A Graphical Neural Network and LightGBM Ensemble Approach

**Emmanuel Osei-Brefo**
University of Newcastle, UK
emmanuel.osei-brefo@newcastle.ac.uk

**Huizhi Liang**
University of Newcastle, UK
Huizhi.Liang@newcastle.ac.uk

## Abstract

This paper proposes a novel ensemble approach that combines Graph Neural Networks (GNNs) and LightGBM to enhance personality prediction based on the personality Big 5 model. By integrating BERT embeddings from user essays with knowledge graph-derived embeddings, our method accurately captures rich semantic and relational information. Additionally, a special loss function that combines Mean Squared Error (MSE), Pearson correlation loss, and contrastive loss to improve model performance is introduced. The proposed ensemble model, made of Graph Convolutional Networks (GCNs), Graph Attention Networks (GATs), and LightGBM, demonstrates superior performance over other models, with significant improvements in prediction accuracy for the Big Five personality traits achieved. Our system officially ranked $2^{nd}$ at the Track 4: PER track.

## 1 Introduction

Personality prediction is a complex task that benefits from understanding both the semantic content of text and the relationships between entities. Traditional machine learning models often fail to capture this relational information. To address this, we propose a novel ensemble approach integrating BERT embeddings, knowledge graph features, Graph Convolutional Networks (GCNs), Graph Attention Networks (GATs), and LightGBM. In this paper, we describe our participation in WASSA 2024 Shared Track 4: Personality Prediction (PER). This year's Track 4, as outlined by (Giorgi et al., 2024), is similar to last year's Shared Track 4 in terms of predicting the Big Five personality traits (OCEAN). However, unlike the 2023 session, where each essay writer was asked to complete the Ten Item Personality Inventory (Barriere et al., 2023), this year's session does not require this step. Our method aims to enhance prediction accuracy by leveraging both semantic and relational data. In recent years, psychologists have developed a number of personality-testing questions (Zhang et al., 2022).

The Big Five model, comprising Openness, Conscientiousness, Extraversion, Agreeableness, and Neuroticism (OCEAN), is widely used for personality assessment (Barriere et al., 2023). Recent studies have shown the effectiveness of incorporating deep learning techniques in personality prediction (Mehta et al., 2020; Digman, 1990). Knowledge graphs (KGs) represent entities and their relationships, providing valuable contextual information (Peng et al., 2023). GNNs, particularly GCNs and GATs, can effectively process graph-structured data by capturing the structural relations between nodes (Zhang Si, 2019).

**Graph Neural Networks (GNNs):** Graph Neural Networks (GNNs) are employed in various domains such as social analysis, fraud detection (Akoglu et al., 2015), natural language processing, and computer vision due to their ability to capture structural relations between data, providing more insights compared to isolated data analysis (Zhang Si, 2019). Graph Convolutional Networks (GCNs) enhance this by aggregating information from neighboring nodes, enabling comprehensive extraction of interdependent data. BERT has been extensively used in several tasks to generate token or sentence representations enriched with prior knowledge (Osei-Brefo and Liang, 2022). Our main contributions for participating in the WASSA 2024 Shared Track 4: Personality Prediction (PER) are as follows:

- Integrating BERT embeddings with knowledge graph features.
- Development of an ensemble model that combines GCN, GAT, and LightGBM.



*Proceedings of the 14th Workshop on Computational Approaches to Subjectivity, Sentiment, & Social Media Analysis*, pages 412–419
August 15, 2024 ©2024 Association for Computational Linguistics

- Introduction of a novel loss function that combines Mean square error loss, Pearson correlation loss, and contrastive loss.

## 2 Related Work

Previous studies have explored the correlation between personality traits and empathy perception, highlighting the importance of agreeableness and conscientiousness in predicting empathy (Omitaomu et al., 2022; Melchers MC, 2016; Giorgi et al., 2024). Techniques such as text generation adversarial networks and multitask detection models have been employed to enhance personality prediction (Sun et al., 2018; Tu et al., 2022). Recent advancements include the use of dynamic deep graph convolutional networks and the integration of psychological language dictionaries with Transformer language models for improved personality detection (Yang et al., 2023; Kerz et al., 2022). Our approach builds on these methods by combining BERT embeddings, knowledge graphs, GCN, GAT, and LightGBM in a novel ensemble model.

## 3 Methodology

Figure 1 depicts the architecture of our proposed personality traits prediction system. As can be seen in figure 1, our methodology encompasses several key steps, which are:

- **BERT Pre-training**: A BERT pre-training is utilised to accurately represent the personality features extracted from the sentences in an individual's essays.
- **Knowledge Graph Integration**: These sentence representations are then combined with vector representations derived from knowledge graphs, which include demographic features and the Interpersonal Reactivity Index (IRI).
- **Graph Structure Processing**: During the graph structure data processing, we leverage the comprehensive mapping and syntactic analysis capabilities of multi-layer neural networks, specifically Graph Convolutional Networks (GCN) and Graph Attention Networks (GTA), in conjunction with LightGBM.
- **Personality Trait Modelling and Prediction**: This integrated approach allows the joint modelling and prediction of the individual's personality traits with high accuracy.

### 3.1 Feature Extraction

The feature extraction method employed combines BERT embeddings with knowledge graph embeddings to capture both semantic and relational information. The process involved is captured in Algorithm 1 presented in Appendix B.

### 3.2 Graphical Neural Network

In the OCEAN prediction task, a Graph Convolutional Networks (GCNs) and Graph Attention Networks (GATs) which are two advanced graph neural network models, were employed in conjunction with LightGBM to predict OCEAN traits.
LightGBM, a gradient boosting framework, is used to complement the graph neural networks. It excels in handling large-scale data and provides efficient training with lower memory usage.

### 3.3 Mathematical Formulation for GCN and GAT

For a graph $G = (V, E)$ with node features $X$:

**GCN Layer:**

$$H^{(l+1)} = \sigma\left(\tilde{D}^{-1/2}\tilde{A}\tilde{D}^{-1/2}H^{(l)}W^{(l)}\right)$$

Where $\tilde{A} = A + I$ is the adjacency matrix with added self-loops, $\tilde{D}$ is the degree matrix, $W^{(l)}$ are the trainable weights, and $\sigma$ is an activation function.
The adjacency matrix (Zheng et al., 2023) represents the connections between nodes in the graph. Each element in the matrix indicates whether a pair of nodes is connected, and the addition of self-loops ensures that each node is connected to itself. This is critical for the GCN since it allows the model to consider each node's own features in addition to its neighbors' features during convolution.
The adjacency matrix produced is shown in Figure 2 in the Appendix A.

**GAT Layer:**

$$H_i^{(l+1)} = \sigma\left(\sum_{j\in\mathcal{N}(i)} \alpha_{ij} W H_j^{(l)}\right)$$

where $\alpha_{ij}$ are the attention coefficients computed as:

$$\alpha_{ij} = \frac{\exp(\text{LeakyReLU}(\mathbf{a}^T[WH_i^{(l)}||WH_j^{(l)}]))}{\sum_{k\in\mathcal{N}(i)}\exp(\text{LeakyReLU}(\mathbf{a}^T[WH_i^{(l)}||WH_k^{(l)}]))}$$

with $\mathbf{a}$ as the attention mechanism's weight vector.

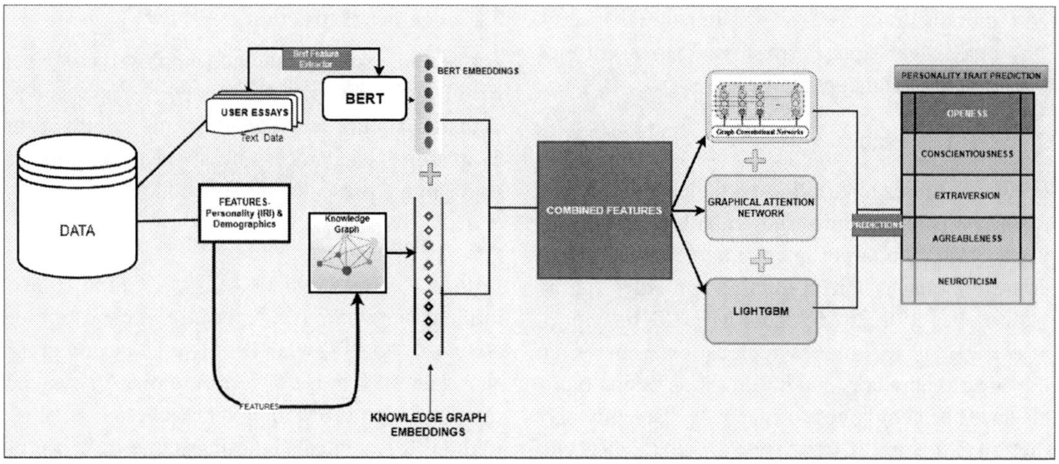


Figure 1: System Architecture of our proposed personality traits prediction system

### 3.4 Ensemble Prediction

The ensemble model combines predictions from GCN, GAT, and LightGBM using weighted average. The procedure involved is shown in Algorithm 4 in the Appendix B.

#### 3.4.1 Proposed Loss Functions

The loss function used in our methodology is designed to enhance the learning process by incorporating Mean Squared Error (MSE) loss, Pearson correlation loss, and contrastive learning loss. Each component serves a specific purpose:

- **MSE Loss:** It focuses on reducing the prediction error by minimizing the difference between predicted and actual values.
- **Pearson Loss:** Acts as a regularizer to ensure a strong correlation between predictions and targets, enhancing the alignment of predicted and actual OCEAN scores.
- **Contrastive Loss:** It adds an additional layer of learning by emphasizing the relationships between pairs of examples, which is crucial for capturing subtle differences in text and the combined effects of various features.

This multi-faceted approach improves the overall learning process by balancing error minimization, correlation enhancement, and relationship learning. The proposed loss functions are detailed below:

**Mean Squared Error (MSE) Loss:**

$$\ell_m = \frac{1}{N}\sum_{i=1}^{N}(y_i - \hat{y}_i)^2$$

**Contrastive Loss:**

$$\ell_c = \frac{1}{N}\sum_{i=1}^{N}(1-y_i)\cdot D_i^2 + y_i \cdot \max(0, m - D_i)^2$$

where $D_i$ is the Euclidean distance between a pair of samples, $y_i$ is the binary label indicating if the samples are similar, and $m$ is the margin.

**Pearson Loss:** The Pearson correlation coefficient between predictions $\hat{y}$ and targets $y$ is given by:

$$\rho = \frac{\sum_{i=1}^{N}(\hat{y}_i - \bar{\hat{y}})(y_i - \bar{y})}{\sqrt{\sum_{i=1}^{N}(\hat{y}_i - \bar{\hat{y}})^2}\sqrt{\sum_{i=1}^{N}(y_i - \bar{y})^2}}$$

The Pearson loss $\ell_\rho$ is then given by:

$$\ell_\rho = 1 - \rho$$

**Total Loss:**

$$\ell_T = \frac{1}{2}\ell_m + \lambda_{\text{reg}} \cdot \ell_\rho + \lambda_{\text{c}} \cdot \ell_c$$

where $N$ is the number of pairs, $\ell_m$ is the Mean Squared Error loss, $\ell_c$ is the Contrastive loss, and $\ell_\rho$ is the Pearson loss. The parameters $\lambda_{\text{reg}}$ and $\lambda_{\text{c}}$ are the regularization weights for the Pearson loss and Contrastive loss, respectively.

## 4 Experiments

### 4.1 Data Collection and Preprocessing

The dataset used in this study was the Track 4 dataset provided by the organizers, which was subsequently merged with the Task 3 dataset. This merging process involved integrating the essays of each individual from Task 4, resulting in a comprehensive dataset. The final training and development data included features such as:

- **Essays:** Detailed personal essays written by the participants.
- **Demographic Information:** Gender, education, race, age, and income.
- **IRI Features:** Scores from the Interpersonal Reactivity Index.
- **OCEAN Traits:** Target scores for the OCEAN personality traits.

This enriched dataset provided a robust foundation for our feature extraction and model training processes.

### 4.2 Feature Extraction

- **BERT Embeddings:** We utilized the BERT model to generate embeddings from user essays. These embeddings captured the contextual information and semantic nuances of the text, offering a rich representation of the user's language usage.
- **Knowledge Graph (KG) Construction:** For each user, a knowledge graph was constructed by extracting entities and relationships from their essays using spaCy. These entities and relationships were then represented in a directed graph using NetworkX.
- **KG Embeddings:** The Node2Vec algorithm was employed to generate embeddings for the nodes within the knowledge graph, capturing both structural and relational information.
- **Combined Feature Vector:** The BERT embeddings were combined with the node embeddings from the knowledge graph to form a comprehensive feature vector for each user.

### 4.3 Models Used

The models used are the Graph Convolutional Network (GCN) to capture the local neighborhood structure within the feature graph, the Graph Attention Network (GAT) that introduced attention mechanisms to allow the model to weigh the importance of different neighboring nodes, and the LightGBM model, which complemented the two graph models by providing robust predictions based on the extracted features. These three models leveraged the strengths of each other to improve overall prediction accuracy as an ensemble strategy. The configuration of hyper-parameters for the proposed model is shown in Table 1.

| Hyper-parameters | Description | size |
|---|---|---|
| batch size | size of mini-batch used | 32 |
| Learning Rate | Used for Adam Optimisation | $1 \times 10^{-4}$ |
| Optimiser used | Type of optimiser used | Adam optimisation |
| Number of iterations | Number of epochs used | 500 |

Table 1: Hyper-parameters used for the the Ensemble model

### 4.4 Model Evaluation

The performance of our models was evaluated using the Pearson correlation coefficient for each OCEAN trait and the average Pearson correlation across all traits. This evaluation metric was chosen because it measures the linear correlation between predicted and actual values, providing insight into the model's predictive accuracy.

### 4.5 Results and Discussion

The ensemble model is evaluated using the Pearson correlation coefficient. A significant improvement in prediction accuracy for the Big Five personality traits compared to baseline models was observed for the test data represented as Ensemble(b) model (unofficial test results) in Table 3. Tables 2 and 3 show the comparative performance of different models on the OCEAN traits for the validation set obtained from using 20% of the training dataset and all the samples of the test data provided by the organisers respectively. The ensemble model outperformed the baseline models, demonstrating the effectiveness of combining GNNs and LightGBM. Figures 3, 4 and 5 in Appendix C show the Loss and Pearson correlations plots per epoch for the GCN, GTA and Ensemble models, respectively. The integration of knowledge graph features and BERT embeddings proves to be particularly beneficial.

| Model | $\overline{\rho}$ | O | C | E | A | N |
|---|---|---|---|---|---|---|
| LSTM | 0.032 | 0.182 | 0.085 | 0.134 | -0.258 | 0.0148 |
| MLP | 0.066 | 0.254 | -0.336 | 0.517 | -0.249 | 0.144 |
| LLM(GPT 3.5) | 0.162 | 0.227 | 0.185 | 0.149 | 0.049 | 0.200 |
| Ensemble | **0.482** | **0.579** | **0.27** | **0.662** | **0.302** | **0.600** |

Table 2: Performance comparison of models on OCEAN traits for the validation Dataset, which is 20% of the training data provide by organisers, where $\overline{\rho}$ represents the average Pearson

| Model | $\overline{\rho}$ | O | C | E | A | N |
|---|---|---|---|---|---|---|
| LSTM | 0.077 | 0.088 | 0.296 | -0.406 | 0.206 | 0.199 |
| MLP | -0.051 | -0.178 | -0.111 | -0.103 | 0.185 | -0.047 |
| LLM(GPT 3.5) | 0.095 | 0.153 | -0.069 | 0.265 | 0.176 | -0.05 |
| Ensemble(a) | 0.069 | -0.103 | 0.102 | -0.085 | 0.154 | 0.279 |
| Ensemble(b) | **0.302** | **0.089** | **0.322** | **0.263** | **0.380** | **0.457** |

Table 3: Performance comparison of models on OCEAN traits for the test Dataset: Where Ensemble(a) represents the official pearson results released by the competition organisers and Ensemble(b) is the unofficial results obtained after further improvements to the models during post-competition phase. The LLM represents Open AI's GPT 3.5 turbo model

The main difference in the performance between Ensemble(a) model and Ensemble(b) model is the setting of hyper-parameters. We tuned the hyper-parameters of Ensemble(b) model during the post-submission stage, where different combinations of custom loss functions and optimal weights for the Ensemble models were explored. We selected the best setting of hyper-parameters for Ensemble(b) model.

In the context of personality detection, GCNs effectively captured the relationships and contextual information between nodes by leveraging the graph's topological structure and node characteristics. This capability significantly aided in the prediction of personality traits. The use of a fixed-weight matrix for convolution in GCNs ensured simplicity and scalability.

Additionally, the integration of GCN, GATs and LightGBM enhanced this approach by incorporating attention mechanisms. These mechanisms allowed the model to weigh the importance of different neighbors when aggregating information. The ensemble approach's success underscores the importance of combining different model strengths to achieve better prediction accuracy. The sensitivity analysis (detailed in Appendix D) further demonstrated the impact of different combinations of MSE, Pearson, and contrastive losses on the model's performance, highlighting the optimal weights for each component.

## 5 Conclusion and Future Work

This paper has proposed an ensemble approach to leverage BERT embeddings and knowledge graph embeddings for GNNs and LightGBM that significantly enhances personality prediction. The introduction of a specialised loss function that combines MSE, Pearson correlation loss, and contrastive losses was crucial for balancing error minimization, correlation enhancement, and the learning of relationships. Future work will involve the refinement of these methods with additional data sources to improve their performance.

## Limitations

The process of extracting meaningful features from text using BERT and constructing knowledge graphs requires substantial computational resources. Additionally, the quality of the extracted features can vary depending on the preprocessing and entity extraction methods used, potentially impacting the model's performance.

## References


Leman Akoglu, Hanghang Tong, and Danai Koutra. 2015. Graph based anomaly detection and description: a survey. *Data mining and knowledge discovery*, 29:626–688.

Valentin Barriere, Jo ao Sedoc, Shabnam Tafreshi, and Salvatore Giorgi. 2023. Findings of wassa 2023 shared task on empathy, emotion and personality detection in conversation and reactions to news articles. In *Proceedings of the 13th Workshop on Computational Approaches to Subjectivity, Sentiment, I& Social Media Analysis*, pages 511–525.

John M Digman. 1990. Personality structure: Emergence of the five-factor model. *Annual review of psychology*, 41(1):417–440.

Salvatore Giorgi, Joao Sedoc, Valentin Barriere, and Shabnam Tafreshi. 2024. Findings of wassa 2024 shared task on empathy and personality detection in interactions. In *Proceedings of the 14th Workshop on Computational Approaches to Subjectivity, Sentiment, I& Social Media Analysis*.

Elma Kerz, Yu Qiao, Sourabh Zanwar, and Daniel Wiechmann. 2022. Pushing on personality detection from verbal behavior: A transformer meets text contours of psycholinguistic features. *arXiv preprint arXiv:2204.04629*.

Yash Mehta, Samin Fatehi, Amirmohammad Kazameini, Clemens Stachl, Erik Cambria, and Sauleh Eetemadi. 2020. Bottom-up and top-down: Predicting personality with psycholinguistic and language model features. In *2020 IEEE international conference on data mining (ICDM)*, pages 1184–1189. IEEE.

Haas BW Reuter M Bischoff L Montag C Melchers MC, Li M. 2016. Similar personality patterns are associated with empathy in four different countries. *Front Psychol.*

Damilola Omitaomu, Shabnam Tafreshi, Tingting Liu, Sven Buechel, Chris Callison-Burch, Johannes C.

Eichstaedt, Lyle Ungar, and João Sedoc. 2022. Empathic conversations: A multi-level dataset of contextualized conversations. *ArXiv*, abs/2205.12698.

Emmanuel Osei-Brefo and Huizhi Liang. 2022. UoR-NCL at SemEval-2022 task 6: Using ensemble loss with BERT for intended sarcasm detection. In *Proceedings of the 16th International Workshop on Semantic Evaluation (SemEval-2022)*, pages 871–876, Seattle, United States. Association for Computational Linguistics.

Ciyuan Peng, Feng Xia, Mehdi Naseriparsa, and Francesco Osborne. 2023. Knowledge graphs: Opportunities and challenges. *Preprint*, arXiv:2303.13948.

Xiangguo Sun, Bo Liu, Jiuxin Cao, Junzhou Luo, and Xiaojun Shen. 2018. Who am i? personality detection based on deep learning for texts. In *2018 IEEE international conference on communications (ICC)*, pages 1–6. IEEE.

Geng Tu, Jintao Wen, Hao Liu, Sentao Chen, Lin Zheng, and Dazhi Jiang. 2022. Exploration meets exploitation: Multitask learning for emotion recognition based on discrete and dimensional models. *Knowledge-Based Systems*, 235:107598.

Tao Yang, Jinghao Deng, Xiaojun Quan, and Qifan Wang. 2023. Orders are unwanted: dynamic deep graph convolutional network for personality detection. In *Proceedings of the AAAI Conference on Artificial Intelligence*, volume 37, pages 13896–13904.

Shunxiang Zhang, Hanqing Xu, Guangli Zhu, Xiang Chen, and KuanChing Li. 2022. A data processing method based on sequence labeling and syntactic analysis for extracting new sentiment words from product reviews. *Soft Computing*, pages 1–14.

Xu Jiejun Maciejewski Ross Zhang Si, Tong Hanghang. 2019. Graph convolutional networks: a comprehensive review. *Computational Social Networks*.

Ruiling Zheng, Peifeng Su, and Xian'an Jin. 2023. Arithmetic-geometric matrix of graphs and its applications. *Applied Mathematics and Computation*, 442:127764.

## A The Adjacency Matrix

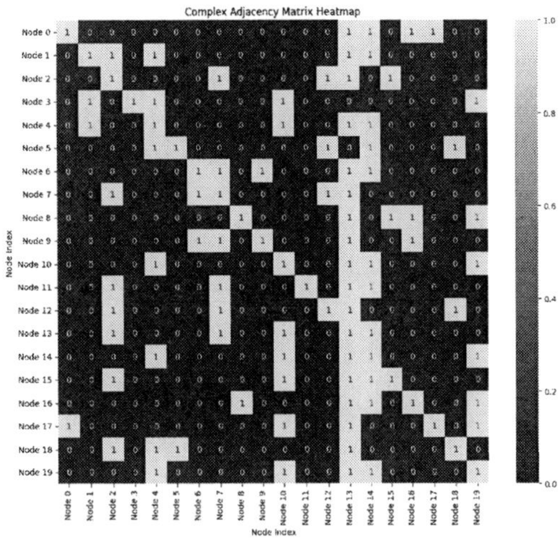


Figure 2: The Adjacency Matrix for the combined features used

## B Algorithms

**Algorithm 1** BERT Embedding Extraction

**Input:** Text data $T$
Initialize BERT tokenizer and model
**for** each text $t$ in $T$ **do**
    Tokenize $t$ using the BERT tokenizer
    Pass the tokenized text through the BERT model
    Extract the embeddings from the last hidden layer
**end for**
**return** embeddings $E$
**Output:** BERT embeddings $E$

**Algorithm 2** Knowledge Graph Construction and Embedding

**Input:** Text data $T$, additional features $F$
**for** each text $t$ in $T$ **do**
    Construct a knowledge graph $G$ from $t$ and $F$
    Generate node embeddings using Node2Vec
    Aggregate node embeddings to form a fixed-size graph embedding
**end for**
**return** embeddings $K$
**Output:** Knowledge graph embeddings $K$

**Algorithm 3** Ensemble Learning: Training GCN, GAT, and LightGBM

```
Input: Training data D, validation data V
Initialize GCN and GAT models
for each epoch do
    Train GCN on D and validate on V
    Train GAT on D and validate on V
    Compute training and validation losses
end for
Save the best performing GCN and GAT models
Initialize LightGBM models for each OCEAN trait
for each trait do
    Train the LightGBM model on D
    Validate the model on V
    Save the best performing LightGBM model
end for
return trained GCN, GAT, and LightGBM models
Output: Trained GCN, GAT, and LightGBM models
```

**Algorithm 4** Ensemble Prediction

```
Input: Models M, test data T
for each model m in M do
    Generate predictions on T
end for
Average the predictions from all models
return ensemble predictions P
Output: Ensemble predictions P
```

## C Loss and Pearson Plots

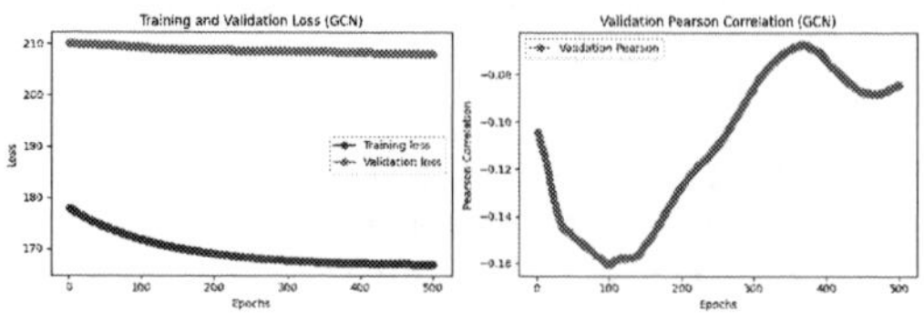


Figure 3: Loss and Pearson plots for GCN per epoch

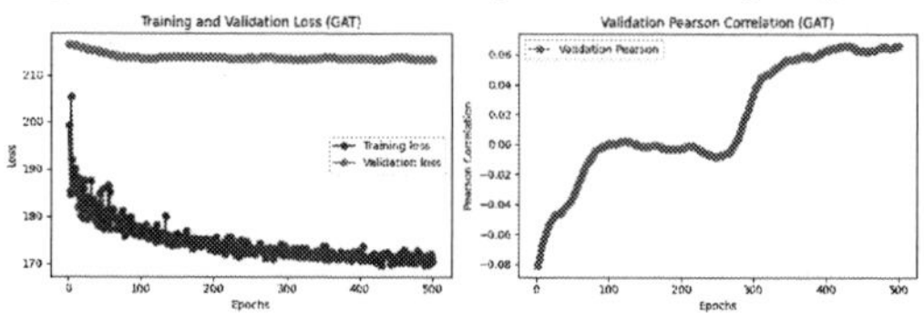


Figure 4: Loss and Pearson plots for GTA per epoch

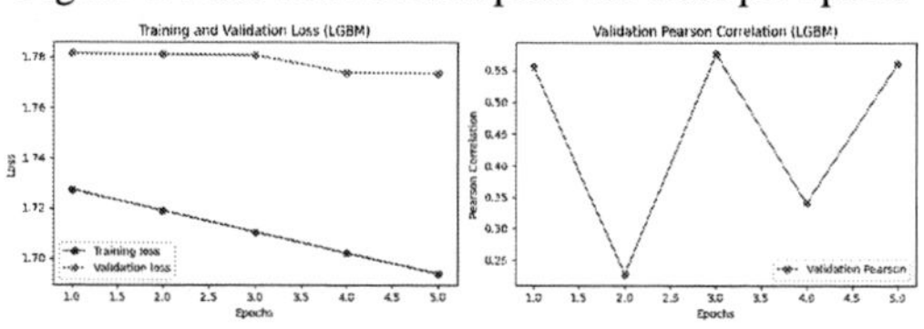


Figure 5: Loss and Pearson plots for the Ensemble GNN+LightGBM per epoch

## D Sensitivity Analysis of Loss components

| LOSSES | % Weights | | | Pearson Corr, $\rho$ | | | | | |
|---|---|---|---|---|---|---|---|---|---|
| | $\ell_m$ | $\ell_p$ | $\ell_c$ | O | C | E | A | N | $\overline{\rho}$ |
| $\ell_m$ | 1 | 0 | 0 | 0.522 | 0.431 | 0.654 | 0.213 | 0.475 | 0.459 |
| $\ell_m$ + $\ell_p$ | 0.5 | 0.5 | 0 | 0.542 | 0.237 | 0.630 | 0.274 | 0.558 | 0.482 |
| $\ell_m$+ $\ell_c$ | 0.5 | 0 | 0.5 | 0.548 | 0.265 | 0.614 | 0.314 | 0.601 | 0.468 |
| $\ell_m$ + $\ell_p$ + $\ell_c$ | 0.5* | 0.4* | 0.1* | 0.579 | 0.269 | 0.662 | 0.302 | 0.598 | **0.482** |
| | 0.5 | 0.3 | 0.2 | 0.567 | 0.242 | 0.627 | 0.273 | 0.604 | 0.462 |
| | 0.5 | 0.2 | 0.3 | 0.544 | 0.257 | 0.605 | 0.291 | 0.518 | 0.443 |
| | 0.5 | 0.1 | 0.4 | 0.545 | 0.254 | 0.648 | 0.319 | 0.540 | 0.461 |

Table 4: Sensitivity analysis to find the effect of each loss component: with optimal combination of 50% of MSE, 40% OF Pearson Loss and 10% of Constrastive loss

# Daisy at WASSA 2024 Empathy and Personality Shared Task: A Quick Exploration on Emotional Pattern of Empathy and Distress

**Rendi Chevi**
MBZUAI
rendi.chevi@mbzuai.ac.ae

**Alham Fikri Aji**
MBZUAI
alham.fikri@mbzuai.ac.ae

## Abstract

When we encountered upsetting or tragic situations involving other people, we might feel certain emotions that are congruent, though not necessarily identical, to what that person might went through. These kind of *vicarious* emotions are what defined empathy and distress, they can be seen as a form of emotional response to other people in need. In this paper, we describe our participation in WASSA 2024 Shared Task 3 in predicting writer's level of empathy and distress from their personal essays. We approach this task by assuming one's level of empathy and distress can be revealed from the emotional patterns within their essay. By extracting the emotional patterns from essays via an emotion classifier, we regress the empathy and distress levels from these patterns. Through correlation and model explainability analysis, we found that there are similar set of emotions, such as *sadness* or *disappointment*, and distinct set of emotions, such as *anger* or *approval*, that might describe the writer's level of empathy and distress. We hope that our approach and findings could serve as a basis for future work that try to model and explain empathy and distress from emotional patterns.

## 1 Introduction

Some of us, in some situation, have the ability to infer other people's psychologically real, internal state (Zaki and Ochsner, 2012), such as their emotions or intentions. This ability can result in us experiencing "vicarious emotions", which are emotions that we feel when something happen to someone else (Wondra and Ellsworth, 2015).

**Empathy and Distress as Emotions.** Empathy and distress can be seen as a form of vicarious emotions, specifically elicited in response to perceiving other people in need (Batson et al., 1987). One of the main differentiator between the two is in the type of emotional response people tend to express when being empathic or distressed. Empathy tend to be more associated with feeling *compassionate*, *tender*, or *warm* (Batson et al., 1981, 1987), while distress tend to be more associated with feeling *alarmed*, *worried*, or *troubled* (Batson et al., 1987).

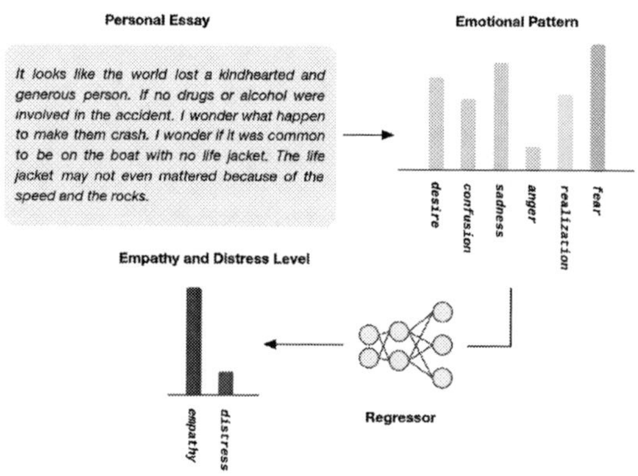


Figure 1: Overview of our approach. We extract emotional patterns from personal essay via an emotion classifier, and see whether we could regress and analyze the level of empathy and distress from these emotional patterns.

One could measure people's level of empathy and distress toward certain stimuli with emotional response-based scale following (Batson et al., 1987). This measure has also been used in (Buechel et al., 2018; Omitaomu et al., 2022), which is the basis of WASSA Shared Task dataset in the past years (Giorgi et al., 2024; Barriere et al., 2023).

**Our Contributions.** In our participation for WASSA 2024 *Shared Task 3: Empathy Prediction*, we intend to explore the task of predicting the writer's level of empathy and distress with almost exclusively leveraging the emotional pattern conveyed in their personal essay.

We are interested to see whether people's emotional response related to empathy and distress are reflected within their personal essay. If so, we



*Proceedings of the 14th Workshop on Computational Approaches to Subjectivity, Sentiment, & Social Media Analysis*, pages 420–424
August 15, 2024 ©2024 Association for Computational Linguistics

might be able to analyze a set of similar or distinct emotional pattern attributed to empathy and distress. Then predict the latter from the former. Our main contributions in this paper are summarized as follows:

- We extracted the emotional pattern conveyed in personal essays via an emotion classifier. We found that there are similar and distinct set of emotions correlated with empathy and distress.
- We experimented to fit a regressor to predict the level of empathy and distress from emotional patterns. Though it performed decently on the evaluation set, it still can't generalize well to the test set.
- We analyzed the regressor using SHAP (SHapley Additive exPlanations) analysis (Lundberg and Lee, 2017). We found that there are similar and distinct set of emotions impacting the regressor's predictions.
- Lastly, we outline the limitations from this quick and early exploration, which we hope would serve as a basis for future work to model and explain empathy and distress from emotional patterns.

## 2 System Description

### 2.1 Preliminaries

Let's first define our dataset comprising tuples of $\{x_i, e_i, d_i\}_{i=1:n}$, where $x_i$ is a personal essay, and $e_i$ and $d_i$ are the essay writer's level of empathy and distress (Batson et al., 1987), on a 7-point scale (1 = Not-at-all, 7 = Extremely).

As we would also like to incorporate emotional patterns conveyed in $x_i$, we define a set of emotion labels conveyed in $x_i$ as $\mathbf{v}_i = \{v_i^j\}_{j=1:m}$. This can include a set of primary emotions (e.g. *sadness*, *joy*) (Ekman, 1992; Plutchik, 1984) or more complex ones (e.g. *bittersweetness*, *grief*) (Plutchik, 1984; Cowen et al., 2019; Demszky et al., 2020). Since this information is unavailable and out-of-scope of the WASSA 2024 dataset, we would have to extract it on our own.

### 2.2 Extracting Emotional Pattern from Personal Essay

To extract emotional patterns from each essay $x_i$, we utilize an open-source multi-label emotion classifier [1], based on RoBERTa-Base (Liu et al., 2019) finetuned on GoEmotion dataset (Demszky et al., 2020). Model trained on this dataset is suitable as a proxy for identifying the writer's emotions, as the annotators of GoEmotion were asked to identify emotions expressed by the writer. It also provides emotion labels based on semantic space taxonomy (Cowen et al., 2019) with 27 emotions and 1 neutral labels, which offers a more fine-grained and diverse emotion classification.

To account for varying tones and emotions within a personal essay, we segment the essay into several overlapping chunks, predict emotions for each segment with the emotion classifier, and then average the predictions to obtain the final emotional pattern for that particular essay.

### 2.3 Predicting Empathy and Distress from Emotional Pattern

After we obtain the emotional pattern $\mathbf{v}_i$ for each $x_i$, we fit a regression model to learn the mapping between the $\mathbf{v}_i$ and $\{e_i, d_i\}$. We are experimenting with 2 regressors: (1) Support Vector Regression (SVR), and (2) neural network-based regressor of 5 layers of perceptron with leaky ReLU activation in each subsequent layer. Both regressors takes in $\mathbf{v}_i$ and outputting $\{e_i, d_i\}$.

## 3 Results and Analysis

### 3.1 Correlation between Emotions, Empathy, and Distress

Before we get into predicting empathy and distress from emotional pattern, we are interested to see whether there is a notable linear correlation between the extracted emotional pattern, $\mathbf{v}_i$, and the level of empathy and distress, $\{e_i, d_i\}$.

Figure 2 shows the Pearson correlation the extracted emotional pattern from essays and the writer's level of empathy and distress. We can see that there are a set of similar and distinct emotions correlated with empathy and distress. For instance, both empathy and distress seem to be positively correlated with *caring*, *desire*, and *optimism*. But, we can also see that empathy is negatively correlated with *anger* while distress is the opposite. Distress seems to be negatively correlated with *grief*, while empathy is the opposite.

Though we can see some notable set of emotions correlated with empathy and distress, the correlations are independently weak. But, we can't fully expect there would be a single, independent emotion that linearly correlates with empathy and

[1] https://huggingface.co/SamLowe/roberta-base-go_emotions

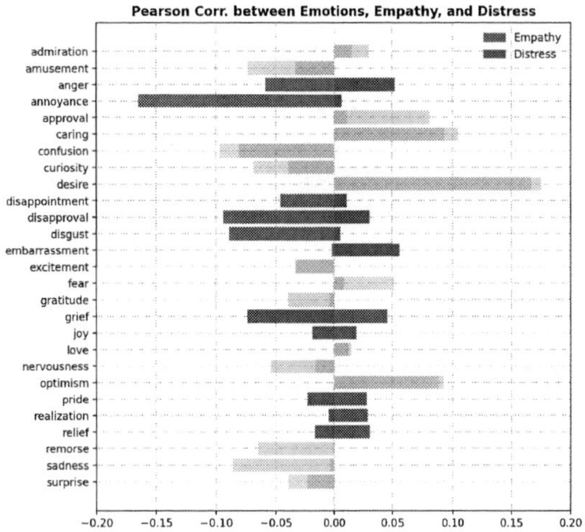


Figure 2: Pearson correlation between extracted emotional patterns from essays and empathy and distress. Emotions in opaque are ones that oppositely correlate with empathy and distress, while the transparent ones are correlated in the same direction.

distress. Even in (Batson et al., 1987), these vicarious emotions are associated and measured with multiple emotional adjectives. In the next section, we would report our result from fitting a regressor that learns a more complex, non-linear mapping between the extracted emotional patterns and empathy and distress.

## 3.2 Empathy and Distress Predictions from Emotional Patterns

Table 1 shows the results on empathy and distress prediction from emotional pattern, using the regressor described in Section 2.3. In predicting empathy from emotional pattern, we can see that the model performs decently across the unseen evaluation set, but had a notable performance drop in the test set which indicate overfitting. When predicting distress, though the regressor performs reasonably well in the evaluation set, it can't seem to generalize well into the test set.

**Performance Drop in Test Set.** It should be noted that we haven't done extensive efforts to improve the regressor's performance through regularization, hyperparameters tuning, or other methods, which might alleviate the overfitting in the test set.

We also hypothesized that maybe to approach this emotional pattern-based empathy-distress task, we should be taking other variables such as the stimuli and the writer's person factors (e.g. sociodemographics or trait empathy information) into account.

| | | Pearson Corr. ↑ | | |
|---|---|---|---|---|
| Model | | Train Set | Eval Set | Test Set |
| SVR | Empathy | 0.657 | 0.446 | 0.296 |
| | Distress | 0.625 | 0.416 | 0.165 |
| | Avg. | 0.641 | 0.431 | 0.231 |
| MLP | Empathy | 0.523 | 0.484 | 0.344 |
| | Distress | 0.488 | 0.515 | 0.082 |
| | Avg. | 0.506 | 0.499 | 0.213 |

Table 1: Empathy and distress prediction results from the regressors across dataset split.

As right now, we assume that all emotional patterns was elicited by the same stimuli and we don't consider how each person based on their person factors might have differences in the way they express empathy or distress from emotional sense.

## 3.3 Emotional Importance when Predicting Empathy and Distress

To further analyze the set of emotions that the regressor consider when predicting the value of empathy and distress, we conducted SHAP (Lundberg and Lee, 2017) analysis into the model. We conduct the analysis on the SVM regressor, as it is the one which has better trade-off in the empathy and distress prediction.

**What Emotions are Impacting the Regressor's Prediction?** Figure 3 and 4 shows the top-10 emotions that are impacting the model prediction the most. Each point represent an unseen sample from our evaluation and test dataset, its color tells the emotion level, and its position tells how much of that emotion pushes the model's prediction to the left (less empathic or distressed) or to the right (more emphatic or distressed).

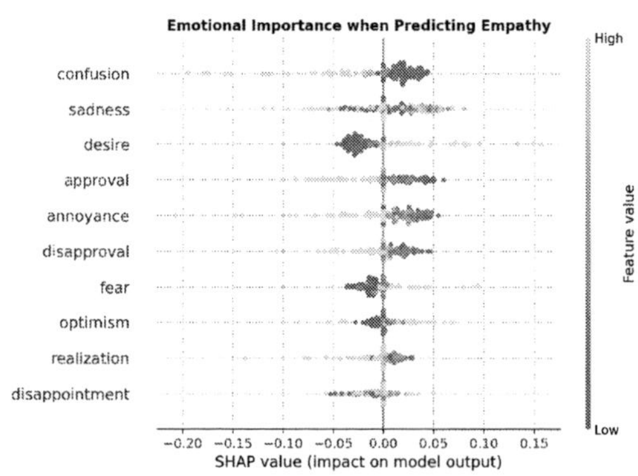


Figure 3: Emotional importance plot of the regressor predicting empathy.

In the empathy prediction, higher level of predicted empathy seems to be characterized by the lower the level of *confusion*, *approval*, *annoyance*, and *disapproval* and the higher level of *desire*, *fear*, and *optimism*. Interestingly, higher level of predicted distress could also be explained by similar level of emotions such as *desire*, *confusion*, and *fear*. But, the higher prediction of distress is also distinctly marked by *anger*, *curiosity*, *realization*, and surprisingly *caring*.

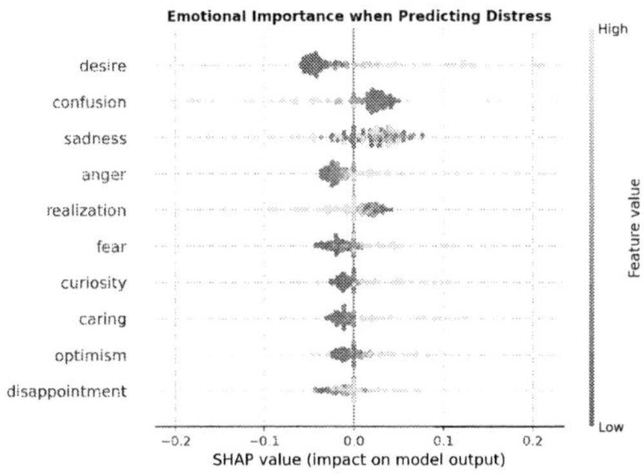


Figure 4: Emotional importance plot of the regressor predicting distress.

Another interesting observation is that, the level of *sadness* and *disappointment* doesn't seem to polarize the model prediction. Regardless of its level, the presence of *sadness* and *disappointment* tend to increase the predicted level of empathy and distress. Which makes sense, as the stimuli in the dataset are all involving upsetting and tragic news, where intuitively, people tend to vicariously share an expression of *sadness* and *disappointment* towards it.

## 4 Conclusion

In this paper, we describe our participation in the WASSA 2024 Shared Task 3 on predicting empathy and distress from personal essay. We approach this task by assuming that one's level of empathy and distress can be revealed from the emotional patterns expressed within their essay. Through extracting the emotional pattern in each personal essay, we directly fit a regressor into the emotional pattern and empathy-distress pairs. Our analysis shows that there are a set of similar and distinct emotions in the dataset and model's prediction that could describe empathy and distress. We hope that our approach and findings would serve as a basis for future work in modeling and explaining empathy and distress from emotional patterns.

## Limitation and Future Work

This paper presents our quick and early exploration on the analysis and explanation of written expression of empathy and distress. That being said, we shouldn't yet be drawing any definitive conclusion at this stage, and there are notable limitations which are subjects for future works and ethical considerations. Those limitations are (not limited to): (1) **Emotion Classifier:** Modeling the perceiver-dependent or subjectivity of emotions are still an open problem, and using an emotion classifier that hasn't taken this into account may not reflect the writer's emotions in the essays and would lead to an inaccurate analysis and conclusion. Additionally, we should probably consider an emotion classifier (or regressor) that takes emotion ordinality and intensity into account, as the empathy and distress variables themselves are labeled ordinally. (2) **Regressor Performance:** Here, we haven't experimented to improve the performance of the regressors through hyperparameters tuning, regularization, or other methods, which may explain the problem of overfitting and generalizability in the test set. (3) **Explainability Analysis:** As we try to explain what emotions drive the model's prediction, our explanation would very much be model-dependent, improving the previous limitations is necessary to ensure we conduct a meaningful and definitive analysis.

## Ethics Statement

It is important to acknowledge that not all people perceive and experience emotions the same, and not all people are able to adequately translate their emotions through essays or other kinds of modalities. We should not directly generalize any insights or findings derived from this study regarding people emotions, empathy, distress, and other psychological processes.

## References


Valentin Barriere, João Sedoc, Shabnam Tafreshi, and Salvatore Giorgi. 2023. Findings of wassa 2023 shared task on empathy, emotion and personality detection in conversation and reactions to news articles. In *Proceedings of the 13th Workshop on Computational Approaches to Subjectivity, Sentiment, & Social Media Analysis*, pages 511–525.

C Daniel Batson, Bruce D Duncan, Paula Ackerman, Terese Buckley, and Kimberly Birch. 1981. Is empathic emotion a source of altruistic motivation? *Journal of personality and Social Psychology*, 40(2):290.

C Daniel Batson, Jim Fultz, and Patricia A Schoenrade. 1987. Distress and empathy: Two qualitatively distinct vicarious emotions with different motivational consequences. *Journal of personality*, 55(1):19–39.

Sven Buechel, Anneke Buffone, Barry Slaff, Lyle Ungar, and João Sedoc. 2018. Modeling empathy and distress in reaction to news stories. In *Proceedings of the 2018 Conference on Empirical Methods in Natural Language Processing*, pages 4758–4765, Brussels, Belgium. Association for Computational Linguistics.

Alan Cowen, Disa Sauter, Jessica L Tracy, and Dacher Keltner. 2019. Mapping the passions: Toward a high-dimensional taxonomy of emotional experience and expression. *Psychological Science in the Public Interest*, 20(1):69–90.

Dorottya Demszky, Dana Movshovitz-Attias, Jeongwoo Ko, Alan Cowen, Gaurav Nemade, and Sujith Ravi. 2020. Goemotions: A dataset of fine-grained emotions. *arXiv preprint arXiv:2005.00547*.

Paul Ekman. 1992. An argument for basic emotions. *Cognition & emotion*, 6(3-4):169–200.

Salvatore Giorgi, João Sedoc, Valentin Barriere, and Shabnam Tafreshi. 2024. Findings of wassa 2024 shared task on empathy and personality detection in interactions. In *Proceedings of the 14th Workshop on Computational Approaches to Subjectivity, Sentiment, & Social Media Analysis*.

Yinhan Liu, Myle Ott, Naman Goyal, Jingfei Du, Mandar Joshi, Danqi Chen, Omer Levy, Mike Lewis, Luke Zettlemoyer, and Veselin Stoyanov. 2019. Roberta: A robustly optimized bert pretraining approach. *arXiv preprint arXiv:1907.11692*.

Scott M Lundberg and Su-In Lee. 2017. A unified approach to interpreting model predictions. In I. Guyon, U. V. Luxburg, S. Bengio, H. Wallach, R. Fergus, S. Vishwanathan, and R. Garnett, editors, *Advances in Neural Information Processing Systems 30*, pages 4765–4774. Curran Associates, Inc.

Damilola Omitaomu, Shabnam Tafreshi, Tingting Liu, Sven Buechel, Chris Callison-Burch, Johannes Eichstaedt, Lyle Ungar, and João Sedoc. 2022. Empathic conversations: A multi-level dataset of contextualized conversations. *Preprint*, arXiv:2205.12698.

Robert Plutchik. 1984. Emotions: A general psychoevolutionary theory. *Approaches to emotion*, 1984(197-219):2–4.

Joshua D Wondra and Phoebe C Ellsworth. 2015. An appraisal theory of empathy and other vicarious emotional experiences. *Psychological review*, 122(3):411.

Jamil Zaki and Kevin N Ochsner. 2012. The neuroscience of empathy: progress, pitfalls and promise. *Nature neuroscience*, 15(5):675–680.

# Last-min-submission at WASSA 2024 Empathy and Personality Shared Task: Enhancing Emotional Intelligence with Prompts

**Svetlana Churina**
Department of Communications and New Media & Centre for Trusted Internet and Community
National University of Singapore
Singapore
churinas@nus.edu.sg

**Preetika Verma & Suchismita Tripathy**
Birla Institute of Technology and Science, Pilani
India
f20190088@pilani.bits-pilani.ac.in
f20190554@pilani.bits-pilani.ac.in

## Abstract

This paper describes the system for the last-min-submission team in WASSA-2024 Shared Task 1: Empathy Detection and Emotion Classification. This task aims at developing models which can predict the empathy, emotion, and emotional polarity.

This system achieved relatively good results on the competition's official leaderboard. The code of this system is available here.

## 1 Introduction

Empathy is a warm, tender, and compassionate feeling directed toward a suffering target. It is a crucial aspect of human interaction, playing a significant role in promoting optimal well-being and fostering social connections.

The Workshop on Computational Approaches to Subjectivity, Sentiment, and Social Media Analysis (WASSA) has organized a 'Shared Task on Empathy Detection, Emotion Classification, and Personality Detection in Interactions.' The aim of this task is to develop models capable of predicting empathy, emotion, personality, and inter-personal index. The provided dataset includes essays written in reaction to news articles where harm has occurred to a person, group, or entity. Additionally, the dataset contains conversations between two users, showcasing their empathetic reactions to the same articles. Each speech turn in these conversations has been annotated with perceived empathy, emotion polarity, and emotion intensity.

Moreover, the dataset offers personality information, including the widely used Big Five (OCEAN) personality traits and the Interpersonal Reactivity Index. Previous research has found that women tend to exhibit higher empathy scores and that there is a negative association between age and empathy. Consequently, demographic information is also provided in the dataset.

The WASSA shared task 2024 (Giorgi et al., 2024) is divided into four tracks:

- Track 1: Empathy Prediction in Conversations (CONV-dialog)
- Track 2: Empathy and Emotion Prediction in Conversation Turns (CONV-turn)
- Track 3: Empathy Prediction (EMP)
- Track 4: Personality Prediction (PER)

We are participating in Track 2. This was newly introduced in WASSA 2023 (Barriere et al., 2023). It involves predicting the perceived empathy, emotion polarity, and emotion intensity at the speech-turn level in a conversation. This task requires a nuanced understanding of the conversational context and the ability to accurately assess the emotional content and empathetic responses within each turn.

The remainder of the paper is structured as follows: Section 2 includes system description, Section 3 talks about experimental results and Section 4 provides conclusion.

## 2 System Description

### 2.1 Feature extraction

The dataset (Omitaomu et al., 2022) for Track 2 has been provided with manual annotations regarding Emotion, Emotional Polarity, Empathy, and Self-Disclosure. It has been found that empathetic text is rich in pronouns, emotional, understanding, seeing, and feeling words (Shi et al., 2021). In this context, we extracted additional features of the text to gain a better understanding of empathy.

LIWC (Linguistic Inquiry and Word Count) quantifies language use by measuring the proportion of words in various categories in a given piece of text. These categories include linguistic categories (such as prepositions and pronouns), psychological processes (such as emotion, cognition,



*Proceedings of the 14th Workshop on Computational Approaches to Subjectivity, Sentiment, & Social Media Analysis*, pages 425–429
August 15, 2024 ©2024 Association for Computational Linguistics

and social), specific topics (such as words related to time, leisure, and money), and punctuation (such as commas and question marks). Using LIWC, we extracted semantic features such as pronoun usage, words related to sadness, politeness, and more. The most relevant features with their correlations can be found in Table 1. We can see, that empathy is strongly correlated with negative politeness (feature politeness HASNEGATIVE) as well as compassion.

| *Predictors* | *Corr* |
|---|---|
| **Empathy** | |
| compassion | 0.47 |
| feature politeness HASNEGATIVE | 0.37 |
| allsubj | 0.28 |
| inflammatory | 0.26 |
| NEGEMO | 0.236 |
| reasoning | 0.232 |
| SAD | 0.2 |
| feature politeness 1st person start | 0.19 |
| SOCIAL | -0.3 |
| turn id | -0.31 |
| YOU | -0.27 |
| TIME | -0.249 |
| likely to reject | -0.289 |
| **Emotion** | |
| compassion | 0.446 |
| feature politeness HASNEGATIVE | 0.434 |
| allsubj | 0.335 |
| toxicity | 0.343 |
| inflammatory | 0.32 |
| NEGEMO | 0.245 |
| SOCIAL | -0.290 |
| TIME | -0.248 |
| YOU | -0.246 |
| likely to reject | -0.22 |
| **Emotion Polarity** | |
| feature politeness HASNEGATIVE | 0.475 |
| toxicity | 0.34 |
| inflammatory | 0.294 |
| NEGEMO | 0.268 |
| SAD | 0.195 |
| respect | -0.37 |
| POSEMO | -0.349 |
| turn id | -0.337 |
| YOU | -0.238 |

Table 1: Table of extracted features with their orrelations

We found no significant correlation between the demographic features provided in Track 4 and the target scores. Therefore, we are not considering those features further.

### 2.2 GPT-3.5 turbo finetuning

We used zeroshot prompting with GPT-3.5 turbo (Brown et al., 2020) finetuned on the training dataset. The finetuning was done using OpenAI API for 3 epochs with default temperature. The data was structured as system prompt, prompt and completion trios as follows:

**Role:** System, **Content:** "You are given a conversation between two people, along with some additional sentiment analysis scores of the last dialog of the conversation."
**Role:** User, **Content:** <Prompt>
**Role:** Assistant, **Content:** <Expected response, with scores for Emotion, Emotion Polarity and Empathy>

We did not provide a validation dataset separately for finetuning, and instead combined the train and dev finetuning datasets we generated for final results generation on the test dataset.

### 2.3 Prompting details

The results of fine-tuning the GPT model heavily depend on the quality and structure of the prompts. For optimal performance, prompts should be carefully crafted and thoroughly tested. In our work, we explored the following approaches to determine the most effective method for our task:

- **Simple Instruction**: The prompt instructs the model to provide scores for 'empathy,' 'emotion,' and 'emotional polarity,' followed by the text to classify.
- **Simple Instruction with Text First**: This prompt is similar to the simple instruction prompt, but the text to classify is provided first, followed by the instruction.
- **Detailed Instruction**: The prompt describes the task goal in detail, explaining what each score means and providing the range of the scores.
- **Simple Instruction with Examples**: After the simple instructions, the prompt includes three samples, providing examples of text with different polarities of scores.

- **Detailed Instruction with Examples**: This is similar to the above, but uses detailed instructions instead of simple ones.

Each prediction is expected to be done on one dialog, as per the dataset. However, we noticed that often, the sentiment analysis for a dialog works better when the previous few dialogs or utterances are also provided to set up context. Using this, we set up prompts providing 2, 5, 10 previous dialogs (of the same conversation) along with each dialog for which the model is expected to predict the required scores.

- This prompt structure was used to generate finetuning data for the provided training dataset, excluding dialogs that did not have the required number of previous dialogs at all.
- Similar prompts were generated for the dev and test datasets. For dialogs that did not have 2, 5 or 10 previous dialogs, we provided as many previous dialogs as available).

We noticed that models finetuned with 2 previous dialogs had too little context for accurate analysis, and models with 10 previous dialogs seemed to get confused/distracted with the extra information provided. 5 previous dialogs (i.e. a total of 6 dialogs per prompt) was ideal, providing just enough information to predict scores.

Using prompts structured with upto 5 previous dialogs, providing the conversation snippet before the instruction, in addition to asking the model to predict all 3 scores in one go (i.e. emption, emotion polarity and empathy), we also tried modifying the instruction to ask the model to only predict one score at an time. Hence, we finetuned 3 specialised models that predict emotion, polarity and empathy separately. Contrary to what we expected however, these models had lower accuracy than the combined model which predicts all 3 scores at once.

Since text features have been extracted and showed improvement for simple models, we created a prompt variation that includes upto 5 previous dialogs, self-disclosure and features that showed a high correlation with the target scores:

- **Features before the conversation snippet**: Before giving the conversation snippet, the features (i.e. LIWC features and self-disclosure as obtained from the dataset) are provided along with explanatory feature names.
- **Features after the conversation snippet**: After giving the conversation snippet, the features (i.e. LIWC features and self-disclosure as obtained from the dataset) are provided along with explanatory feature names. Providing the conversation snippet first seems to help the model better understand the additional information we provided.

Adding LIWC extracted features was decreasing the performance of the model, so we excluded these from our final system.

### 2.4 Datasets used for finetuning

To augment our training data, we sought additional datasets containing emotion, empathy, or emotional polarity scores. One such dataset is the Emotional Reactions Dataset (Sharma et al., 2020), which provides empathy levels for response posts in the context of seeker posts. This dataset categorizes empathy into three levels: 0 (no empathy) to 2 (high empathy).

Due to the differing scoring systems between this dataset and our original dataset, we normalized the empathy scores to match the range of our required data. Despite this adjustment, fine-tuning our best-performing GPT model with the additional data resulted in a significant drop in performance, with scores decreasing from approximately 0.7 to around 0.3. This decline may be attributed to the differing scoring systems, which could have led to a mismatch in empathy levels after normalization.

## 3 Experimental Results

### 3.1 Classical ML approaches

We derived embedding vectors of size 1536 from the **text-embedding-3-small** model using the Embeddings endpoint provided by OpenAI. We creates two sets of embedding inputs, providing the complete utterance history as additional input for second. These were used to train various classical ML models such as Random Forest, RNN, LSTM, and Bi-LSTM. We observed that providing the utterance history increased the average score for all models. The results are present in table 2.

### 3.2 Adapter-based Finetuning

We fine-tuned an XXL version of the DeBERTAV2 (He et al., 2021) model with 1.5B parameters loaded from a pretrained checkpoint *deberta-v2-xxlarge* on Huggingface. LoRA (Hu et al., 2022)

| Model | Emotional polarity | Emotion | Empathy | Average |
|---|---|---|---|---|
| RNN (without utterance) | 0.6895 | 0.5672 | 0.5608 | 0.6058 |
| RNN (with utterance) | 0.7021 | 0.5745 | 0.5754 | 0.6173 |
| LSTM (without utterance) | 0.7157 | 0.5814 | 0.5780 | 0.6250 |
| LSTM (with utterance) | 0.6959 | 0.5954 | 0.6026 | 0.6313 |
| Bi-LSTM (without utterance) | 0.7101 | 0.5875 | 0.5657 | 0.6211 |
| Bi-LSTM (with utterance) | 0.7085 | 0.5881 | 0.5966 | 0.6311 |
| Random Forest (without utterance) | 0.5588 | 0.4374 | 0.5075 | 0.5012 |
| Random Forest (with utterance) | 0.5686 | 0.4574 | 0.5113 | 0.5125 |

Table 2: Pearson coefficients for different models using GPT embeddings

adapters were used to fine-tune the model for 5 epochs without adding the utterance history. The results are present in table 3.

| Model | Emotion | Polarity | Empathy | Average |
|---|---|---|---|---|
| DeBERTAV2 with LoRA | 0.5976 | 0.7312 | 0.6383 | 0.6557 |

Table 3: Pearson coefficients for finetuning DeBERTAV2 with LoRA

### 3.3 Finetuning GPT

Fine-tuning GPT-3.5-turbo using OpenAI API gave better results than the previous approaches.We experimented with different styles of prompting and controlled the number of previous dialogues while providing the utterance history.

#### 3.3.1 Controlling length of utterances

Utterance history comprises the previous dialogues spoken in the conversation. The conversations had variable sizes. We chose previous *n* turns and found that **n=5** produces the best results. Table 4 has the results for this experiment.

#### 3.3.2 Prompting

We tried out four different ways of prompting described in Table 5. Adding fewshot examples decreased the average scores. For our final model, we used zeroshot prompting with detailed instructions described in Table 6 in the Appendix.

| Utterance length | Emotion | Polarity | Empathy | Average |
|---|---|---|---|---|
| Previous 2 | 0.6356 | 0.7918 | 0.6611 | 0.6962 |
| Previous 10 | 0.6519 | 0.7791 | 0.6248 | 0.6853 |
| Previous 5 | 0.6467 | 0.8031 | 0.6653 | 0.7050 |
| All | 0.6215 | 0.7136 | 0.6293 | 0.6548 |

Table 4: Pearson coefficients for different finetuning GPT with different values of utterance lengths

| Prompting style | Emotion | Polarity | Empathy | Average |
|---|---|---|---|---|
| Simple instruction | 0.6443 | 0.7866 | 0.6538 | 0.6949 |
| Detailed instruction | 0.6627 | 0.7880 | 0.6655 | 0.7054 |
| Simple instruction + few shot examples | 0.6436 | 0.7845 | 0.6732 | 0.7004 |
| Detailed instruction + few shot examples | 0.6446 | 0.7913 | 0.6593 | 0.6984 |

Table 5: Pearson coefficients for different finetuning GPT with fewshot examples and different prompts

## 4 Conclusion

Empathy and emotion are complex and challenging to predict, largely due to their nuanced nature. Although research in this area is growing, it is still not as extensive as in other domains, leaving significant room for exploration. The limitation of available annotated data further restricts these possibilities. Our experiments indicated that, while adding extra textual features might theoretically enhance empathy detection, LLMs did not significantly improve the scores. However, we found that providing detailed instructions to LLMs increased clarity and resulted in slight improvements. Additionally, we observed that effective empathy and emotion detection requires understanding the background and previous context of the dialogue, underscoring the importance of context in these tasks.

## Acknowledgments

This work is supported by the Ministry of Education, Singapore under its MOE AcRF TIER3 Grant (MOE-MOET32022-0001). The travel grant for this research is supported by the Department of Communication and New Media at the National University of Singapore.

## References


Valentin Barriere, Jo ao Sedoc, Shabnam Tafreshi, and Salvatore Giorgi. 2023. Findings of wassa 2023 shared task on empathy, emotion and personality detection in conversation and reactions to news articles. In *Proceedings of the 13th Workshop on Computational Approaches to Subjectivity, Sentiment, Social Media Analysis*, pages 511–525.

Tom Brown, Benjamin Mann, Nick Ryder, Melanie Subbiah, Jared D Kaplan, Prafulla Dhariwal, Arvind Neelakantan, Pranav Shyam, Girish Sastry, Amanda Askell, Sandhini Agarwal, Ariel Herbert-Voss, Gretchen Krueger, Tom Henighan, Rewon Child, Aditya Ramesh, Daniel Ziegler, Jeffrey Wu, Clemens Winter, Chris Hesse, Mark Chen, Eric Sigler, Mateusz Litwin, Scott Gray, Benjamin Chess, Jack Clark, Christopher Berner, Sam McCandlish, Alec Radford, Ilya Sutskever, and Dario Amodei. 2020. Language models are few-shot learners. In *Advances in Neural Information Processing Systems*, volume 33, pages 1877–1901. Curran Associates, Inc.

Salvatore Giorgi, Jo ao Sedoc, Valentin Barriere, and Shabnam Tafreshi. 2024. Findings of wassa 2024 shared task on empathy and personality detection in interactions. In *Proceedings of the 14th Workshop on Computational Approaches to Subjectivity, Sentiment, Social Media Analysis*.

Pengcheng He, Xiaodong Liu, Jianfeng Gao, and Weizhu Chen. 2021. {DEBERTA}: {DECODING}-{enhanced} {bert} {with} {disentangled} {attention}. In *International Conference on Learning Representations*.

Edward J Hu, yelong shen, Phillip Wallis, Zeyuan Allen-Zhu, Yuanzhi Li, Shean Wang, Lu Wang, and Weizhu Chen. 2022. LoRA: Low-rank adaptation of large language models. In *International Conference on Learning Representations*.

Damilola Omitaomu, Shabnam Tafreshi, Tingting Liu, Sven Buechel, Chris Callison-Burch, Johannes Eichstaedt, Lyle Ungar, and João Sedoc. 2022. Empathic conversations: A multi-level dataset of contextualized conversations. *Preprint*, arXiv:2205.12698.

Ashish Sharma, Adam Miner, David Atkins, and Tim Althoff. 2020. A computational approach to understanding empathy expressed in text-based mental health support. In *Proceedings of the 2020 Conference on Empirical Methods in Natural Language Processing (EMNLP)*, pages 5263–5276, Online. Association for Computational Linguistics.

Shuju Shi, Yinglun Sun, Jose Zavala, Jeffrey Moore, and Roxana Girju. 2021. Modeling clinical empathy in narrative essays. In *2021 IEEE 15th International Conference on Semantic Computing (ICSC)*, pages 215–220.


# A Appendix

## A.1 Prompt Engineering for GPT-3.5

| Type | Prompt |
|---|---|
| Simple instruction (without features) | Analyze the last dialogue of the conversation and calculate its Emotion, Emotional Polarity, and Empathy scores. You are given a conversation between two people (P1 and P2). <Conversation> |
| Detailed instruction (without features) | Below is a dialogue between two people regarding a news article. They express their emotions and empathy through the conversation. The Emotion Score is considered to be a measure of how strongly the speaker is feeling the emotions they express (e.g., happy, anxious, sad, angry). The Emotional Polarity Score is considered to be a numerical value rating the type of emotion the speaker is experiencing. It ranges between 1 (positive), 2 (neutral), and 3 (negative). The Empathy Score is considered to be a measure of whether the speaker is taking on the feelings of the suffering victim. If they are, it evaluates how much the speaker seems to put themselves in the shoes of the suffering victim. The value is a numerical score between 1 (not at all) and 5 (extremely). Analyze the last dialogue of the conversation and calculate its Emotion, Emotional Polarity, and Empathy scores. You are given a conversation between two people (P1 and P2). <Conversation> |

Table 6: Prompts used on the finetuned GPT models

# hyy33 at WASSA 2024 Empathy and Personality Shared Task: Using the CombinedLoss and FGM for Enhancing BERT-based Models in Emotion and Empathy Prediction from Conversation Turns

**Huiyu Yang, Liting Huang, Tian Li, Nicolay Rusnachenko, Huizhi Liang***
Newcastle University, Newcastle Upon Tyne, England
{huiyu.yang33, huangliting2019, litianricardolee, rusnicolay}@gmail.com,
huizhi.liang@newcastle.ac.uk

## Abstract

This paper presents our participation to the WASSA 2024 Shared Task on Empathy Detection and Emotion Classification and Personality Detection in Interactions. We focus on Track 2: Empathy and Emotion Prediction in Conversations Turns (CONV-turn), which consists of predicting the perceived empathy, emotion polarity and emotion intensity at turn level in a conversation. In the method, we conduct BERT and DeBERTa based finetuning, implement the CombinedLoss which consists of a structured contrastive loss and Pearson loss, adopt adversarial training using Fast Gradient Method (FGM). This method achieved Pearson correlation of 0.581 for *Emotion*, 0.644 for *Emotional Polarity* and 0.544 for *Empathy* on the test set, with the average value of 0.590 which ranked 4th among all teams. After submission to WASSA 2024 competition, we further introduced the segmented mix-up for data augmentation, boosting for ensemble and regression experiments, which yield even better results: 0.6521 for *Emotion*, 0.7376 for *Emotional Polarity*, 0.6326 for *Empathy* in Pearson correlation on the development set. The implementation and fine-tuned models are publicly-available at `https://github.com/hyy-33/hyy33-WASSA-2024-Track-2`.

## 1 Introduction

Emotion detection and empathy analysis are important and inevitable topics in the processing of human interactions, which show great potential in various application scenarios (Nandwani and Verma, 2021; Sharma et al., 2020). To provide more insights into this topic, WASSA organizes workshop on related topics each year (Barriere et al., 2023). This year, WASSA 2024 focuses on Shared Task on Empathy Detection and Emotion Classification and Personality Detection in Interactions (Giorgi et al., 2024).

In this paper, we propose a solution towards Track 2: Empathy and Emotion Prediction in Conversations Turns (CONV-turn). In this task, participants are given conversations between two users that read the same essay, which contains reaction to news articles where there is harm to a person or group (Omitaomu et al., 2022). Each of their conversation turn (text content) has been annotated in perceived empathy, emotion polarity, and emotion intensity. Other meta information such as *article_id*, *conversation_id*, *turn_id* and *speaker_id* are also provided. A sample from the dataset is demonstrated in Figure 1.

| A Training Sample from Track 2 |
|---|
| **Text:**<br>I can't imagine just living in an area that is constantly being ravaged by hurricanes or earthquakes. I take my location for granted. |
| **Label:**<br>Emotion: 3<br>EmotionalPolarity: 2<br>Empathy: 4.6667<br>SelfDisclosure: 3.3333 |
| **Other meta information:**<br>id: 3, article_id: 35, conversation_id: 1,<br>turn_id: 3, speaker: "Person 2",<br>person_id_1: "p019", person_id_2: "p012" |

Figure 1: A Data Sample from Track 2

This task aims at developing appropriate methods to predict the perceived empathy, emotion polarity, and emotion intensity at the speech-turn-level during human conversation. In previous works, BERT (Devlin et al., 2019) is frequently used for emotion classification (Luo and Wang, 2019; Kannan and Kothamasu, 2022), its variations such as RoBERTa (Liu et al., 2019) and DeBERTa (He et al., 2020) also play important roles in empathy prediction and sentiment analysis (Vasava et al., 2022; Lu et al., 2023). Based on fine-tuned encoders, different strategies are further introduced

*The corresponding author.



*Proceedings of the 14th Workshop on Computational Approaches to Subjectivity, Sentiment, & Social Media Analysis*, pages 430–434
August 15, 2024 ©2024 Association for Computational Linguistics

to build more robust and reliable models, including adversarial training (Chen and Ji, 2022; Chang et al., 2023), data augmentation (Kwon and Lee, 2023) and ensemble strategy (Plaza-del Arco et al., 2022).

Our goal is to predict the interior emotion and empathy state of the user according to turn-level information from human-to-human conversations. To achieve this goal, we adopt BERT-based models including BERT (Devlin et al., 2019) and its variation of DeBERTa (He et al., 2020). Then, they are fine-tuned using task-oriented data from Track 2 with adversarial training using Fast Gradient Method (FGM). Also, we design a novel CombinedLoss, which consist of a structured contrastive loss and a Pearson loss. Then, after the submission to WASSA 2024 competition, data augmentation using the segmented mix-up strategy, ensemble with boosting method and regression experiments are further conducted.

## 2 Methodology

This section introduces the methodolgy of our proposed system for Track 2 in WASSA 2024. As in Figure 2, the proposed model includes: the fine-

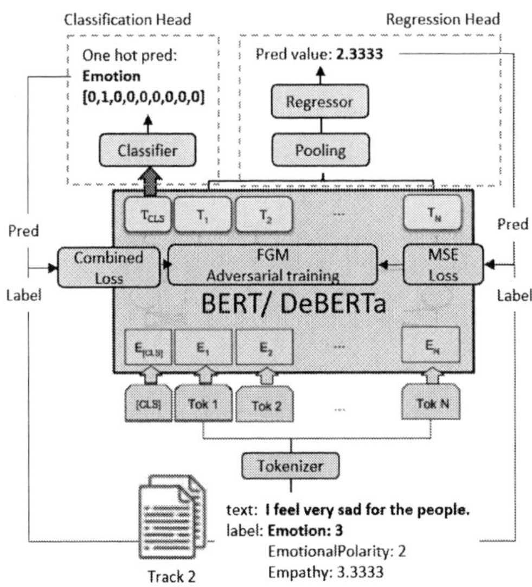


Figure 2: The proposed model

tuned BERT or DeBERTa, the CombinedLoss and the downstream head for classification (or regression). Also, augmentation and ensemble are implemented in corresponding parts.

### 2.1 Fine-tuned BERT and DeBERTa

In this paper, we conduct task-oriented fine-tuning for Track2 based on BERT (Devlin et al., 2019) and its variation of DeBERTa (He et al., 2020). For the base models, *bert-base-uncased* and *deberta-base* are introduced as the pretrained language models. Then, fine-tuning is conducted on the training set of Track 2, so that the encoders could adapt from general language modelling to our specific prediction task by adjusting the parameters.

### 2.2 The CombinedLoss

Different from commonly-used loss functions, our work proposes the CombinedLoss, which could be expressed as:

$$L_{\text{total}} = L_{\text{loss}} + \lambda(1 - Corr_{Pear}(\hat{\mathbf{y}}, \mathbf{y})), \quad (1)$$

where $L_{\text{loss}}$ is the structured contrastive loss for classification, $\lambda$ is the regularization coefficient, and $Corr_{Pear}(\hat{\mathbf{y}}, \mathbf{y})$ is the Pearson correlation coefficient (Cohen et al., 2009) between the prediction of $\hat{\mathbf{y}}$ and the ground truth label of $\mathbf{y}$.

Since emotions are classified into multiple levels in the dataset (Omitaomu et al., 2022), the Pearson correlation coefficient is used as a regularization term in the loss function. By using the negative Pearson coefficient, this loss function aims to capture the subtle scale between emotion levels.

### 2.3 Adversarial Training with FGM

To improve the robustness and the generalization ability of the proposed model, adversarial training is introduced as follows:

$$Obj = \min_{\theta} E(x, y) \left[\max L(f_\theta(x + \delta), y)\right], \quad (2)$$

in which $x$ is the input sample, $\delta$ is the added perturbation for adversarial training, $f_\theta$ is neural network function with $\theta$ as parameters. By maximizing $L(f_\theta(x + \delta))$, the most disturbing perturbation are introduced to the model, then the model is optimized to minimize the training error, which helps it to be robust to potential perturbations.

In this work, Fast Gradient Method (FGM) (Andriushchenko and Flammarion, 2020) is implemented as adversarial training strategy, which computes the most disturbing perturbation through scaling the gradient as below.

$$\delta = \epsilon \cdot \frac{g}{||g||_2} \quad (3)$$

$$g = \nabla_x L(x, y, \theta) \quad (4)$$

### 2.4 Augmentation: the Segmented Mix-up

To improve the generalization ability of models, mix-up is often used as a method for data augmentation. In this work, a segmented mix-up is proposed, which mixes inputs and labels within specific label ranges. This segmentation is essential because simple mix-up (Gong et al., 2022) between highly negative and highly positive samples could not generate meaningful intermediate samples.

For each dimension, e.g. *Emotion*, samples are divided into two segments: the lower segment with labels smaller or equal to the middle label, and the upper one with labels larger than the middle label. Each sample $(x_i, y_i)$ is paired with a partner sample $(x_j, y_j)$ from the same label segment, with $x_i$ and $x_j$ denote the tokenized sentences, and $y_i$ and $y_j$ represent their labels. The mix-up coefficient $\mu$ is sampled from a Beta distribution: $\mu \sim \text{Beta}(\alpha, \alpha)$, where $\alpha$ controls the mix-up strength. The generated inputs and labels are computed as:

$$\tilde{x}_i = \mu x_i + (1 - \mu) x_j, \tag{5}$$

$$\tilde{y}_i = \mu y_i + (1 - \mu) y_j, \tag{6}$$

### 2.5 Ensemble with Boosting

To build a more accurate and robust system, boosting is implemented as an ensemble strategy (Bühlmann, 2012), which combines fine-tuned BERT and DeBERTa models. In order to enhance the overall performance, weights are assigned according to the accuracy of each model on the development set. Through this, it is ensured that the model with the most reliable prediction has the greatest impact on the final output.

## 3 Experiments and Results

In this section, extensive experiments were conducted on the fine-tuned BERT and DeBERTa. Also, ablation study is performed to test the performance of different parts in the proposed model.

### 3.1 Datasets

The dataset of Track 2 includes a training set of 11,166 samples, a development set of 990 samples and a test set of 2,061 valid samples (Omitaomu et al., 2022). Each sample consists of the text content of a single dialogue turn and the corresponding label of *Emotion*, *Emotional Polarity* and *Empathy*, as well as some meta information of the speakers and the conversation. A data sample is shown in Figure 1.

| Model | Loss | FGM | Emo | EmoP | Emp | Avg |
|---|---|---|---|---|---|---|
| BERT | Cross-entropy | No | 0.5867 | 0.6824 | 0.5703 | 0.6131 |
| BERT | CombinedLoss | No | 0.5921 | 0.6836 | 0.5803 | 0.6187 |
| BERT | CombinedLoss | Yes | **0.6142** | **0.6899** | **0.5852** | **0.6298** |
| DeBERTa | Cross-entropy | No | 0.6255 | 0.7281 | 0.5918 | 0.6485 |
| DeBERTa | CombinedLoss | No | 0.6348 | 0.7364 | 0.6042 | 0.6585 |
| DeBERTa | CombinedLoss | Yes | **0.6399** | **0.7366** | **0.6064** | **0.6610** |

Table 1: Pearson correlation of fine-tuned models with CombinedLoss and FGM on the development set

### 3.2 Evaluation Metrics

To test the performance of the proposed solution, the official evaluation metric for Track 2 is the Pearson correlation (Cohen et al., 2009). Given sequences of prediction $\hat{y}$ and ground truth $y$, their Pearson correlation coefficient can be calculated as:

$$Corr_P(\hat{y}, y) = \frac{\sum_{i=1}^{n} \left( \frac{(\hat{y}_i - \bar{\hat{y}})}{\sigma_{\hat{y}}} \frac{(y_i - \bar{y})}{\sigma_y} \right)}{n}, \tag{7}$$

in which $E(\hat{y})$ and $E(y)$ stand for the expectations of $\hat{y}$ and $y$, $\sigma_{\hat{y}}$ and $\sigma_y$ stand for the standard deviations of $\hat{y}$ and $y$.

### 3.3 Implementation Details

**Baselines.** To compare the performance of proposed models, BERT (Devlin et al., 2019) and its variation DeBERTa (He et al., 2021) are introduced. For BERT, *bert-base-uncased* is used, with 12 encoder layers and 110M parameters. For DeBERTa, *deberta-base* is adopted with 390M parameters.

**Hyper-parameters.** For tokenization, input sentences are tokenized with *BertTokenizer* and *DebertaTokenizer* with the maximum length of 128. For optimization, AdamW optimizer is adopted with learning rate of $1 \times 10^{-6}$ and exponential decay with $\gamma = 0.99$ after grid search, the batch size is 400 for fine-tuning BERT and 200 for fine-tuning DeBERTa. For the segmented mix-up, $\alpha = 0.2$ is used. Other details could be found in our implementation.

**Labels and Categories.** The experiments are conducted on different downstream tasks of classification and regression. Because the original labels not only contain integer values but also include float values, such as 0.3333, 0.6667 in the training set and 0.5, 1.5 in the development set, we manually divided 9 categories for *Emotion*, 5 categories for *Emotional Polarity* and 11 categories for *Empathy* in classification (details could be found in our code of implementation). In regression experiments, we directly use original labels as target values.

| Model | Ensemble | Augment | Emo | EmoP | Emp | Avg |
|---|---|---|---|---|---|---|
| BERT | Boosting | No | 0.6521 | 0.7045 | 0.6069 | 0.6545 |
| DeBERTa | Boosting | No | 0.6470 | 0.7215 | 0.6112 | 0.6599 |
| BERT, DeBERTa | Boosting | No | 0.6485 | 0.7253 | 0.6140 | 0.6626 |
| BERT, DeBERTa | Boosting | Mix-up | **0.6521** | **0.7334** | **0.6326** | **0.6727** |

Table 2: Pearson correlation of fine-tuned models with ensemble and augmentation on the development set

| Model | Task | Emo | EmoP | Emp | Avg |
|---|---|---|---|---|---|
| DeBERTa | Classification | 0.6399 | 0.7366 | 0.6064 | 0.6610 |
| DeBERTa | Regression | **0.6409** | **0.7376** | **0.6105** | **0.6630** |

Table 3: Pearson correlation of fine-tuned DeBERTa (with CombinedLoss and FGM) in different downstream tasks on the development set

### 3.4 Results and Analysis

This section presents the results of Pearson correlation based on the experiments of the proposed models on the development set, and conducts analysis for the results.

**Fine-tuned BERT and DeBERTa.** It can be observed from Table 1 that the average results of fine-tuned DeBERTa is better than fine-tuned BERT, which shows the stronger ability of DeBERTa-based solution. And by implementing the CombinedLoss, both models demonstrate performance gain in *Emotion*, *Emotional Polarity* and *Empathy* prediction. Also, adding adversarial training using Fast Gradient Method (FGM) brings better overall performance, proving its contribution to the robustness and generalization ability of models. Our submission to WASSA 2024 competition is based on this fine-tuned DeBERTa with CombinedLoss and Fast Gradient Method (FGM).

**Ensemble and Augmentation.** The results of Table 2 show the combined boosting yields the best overall result, which confirms the effectiveness of our boosting strategy by assigning weights to models according to their accuracy. An interesting finding is that ensembling fine-tuned DeBERTas not always achieves the highest score in single dimension, this may due to the reason that single DeBERTa already achieves its upper limit, combining them only decreases the possible lower bound, while on the other hand, single BERT may has unstable scoring performance, thus the ensemble of BERTs leads to high reliablity and better results. Also, augmentation brings further improvement, indicating our segmented mix-up strategy successfully generates meaningful intermediate samples, which contribute to the fine-tuning process.

**Classification and Regression.** Table 3 presents the results of the fine-tuned DeBERTa (with CombinedLoss and FGM) in different downsteam tasks. The labelling details for classification and regression could be found in Section 3.3. From the results, it is shown that the fined-tuned DeBERTa achieved slightly better performance in regression task, which provides future research direction for us.

## 4 Conclusions

This paper presents our solution for Track 2 in WASSA 2024, which focused on the prediction of *Emotion*, *Emotional Polarity* and *Empathy* using turn-level information from user conversations. The submitted solution is built using fine-tuned DeBERTa with our proposed CombinedLoss and adversarial training startegy using Fast Gradient Method (FGM), which achieved Pearson correlation of 0.581 for *Emotion*, 0.644 for *Emotional Polarity* and 0.544 for *Empathy* on the test set, with the average value of 0.590 which ranked 4th among all teams. After the submission to WASSA 2024 competition, ensemble strategy using boosting method and data augmentation with the segmented mix-up are implemented, which further improve the performance of our model and yield better results: 0.6521 for *Emotion*, 0.7376 for *Emotional Polarity*, 0.6326 for *Empathy* in Pearson correlation on the development set. In the future, we plan to introduce larger datasets for model retraining at earlier stage (e.g. the Masked Language Model) for better domain adaptation, and consider introducing conversational context and speaker personality for better model construction. Also, the performance of such models in downstream regression tasks will be further investigated.

## Limitations

The limitations of the proposed work included: 1) The training set was relatively small with less than 12000 samples. Fine-tuning the models on larger datasets might improve the performance. 2) The labels in the training set and the development set was mis-matched. For instance, the development set contained *Emotion* labels of 0.5, 1.5 and 2.5, which were not presented in the training set. If the test set had similar patterns, then, the inconsistent labels between training and testing could cause degradation of the fine-tuned models.

## References


Maksym Andriushchenko and Nicolas Flammarion. 2020. Understanding and improving fast adversarial training. *Advances in Neural Information Processing Systems*, 33:16048–16059.

Valentin Barriere, João Sedoc, Shabnam Tafreshi, and Salvatore Giorgi. 2023. Findings of wassa 2023 shared task on empathy, emotion and personality detection in conversation and reactions to news articles. In *Proceedings of the 13th Workshop on Computational Approaches to Subjectivity, Sentiment, & Social Media Analysis*, pages 511–525.

Peter Bühlmann. 2012. Bagging, boosting and ensemble methods. *Handbook of computational statistics: Concepts and methods*, pages 985–1022.

Yu Chang, Yuxi Chen, and Yanru Zhang. 2023. nicenlp at semeval-2023 task 10: Dual model alternate pseudo-labeling improves your predictions. In *Proceedings of the 17th International Workshop on Semantic Evaluation (SemEval-2023)*, pages 307–311.

Hanjie Chen and Yangfeng Ji. 2022. Adversarial training for improving model robustness? look at both prediction and interpretation. In *Proceedings of the AAAI Conference on Artificial Intelligence*, volume 36, pages 10463–10472.

Israel Cohen, Yiteng Huang, Jingdong Chen, Jacob Benesty, Jacob Benesty, Jingdong Chen, Yiteng Huang, and Israel Cohen. 2009. Pearson correlation coefficient. *Noise reduction in speech processing*, pages 1–4.

Jacob Devlin, Ming-Wei Chang, Kenton Lee, and Kristina Toutanova. 2019. BERT: Pre-training of deep bidirectional transformers for language understanding. In *Proceedings of the 2019 Conference of the North American Chapter of the Association for Computational Linguistics: Human Language Technologies, Volume 1 (Long and Short Papers)*, pages 4171–4186, Minneapolis, Minnesota. Association for Computational Linguistics.

Salvatore Giorgi, João Sedoc, Valentin Barriere, and Shabnam Tafreshi. 2024. Findings of wassa 2024 shared task on empathy and personality detection in interactions. In *Proceedings of the 14th Workshop on Computational Approaches to Subjectivity, Sentiment, & Social Media Analysis*.

Xiaokang Gong, Wenhao Ying, Shan Zhong, and Shengrong Gong. 2022. Text sentiment analysis based on transformer and augmentation. *Frontiers in Psychology*, 13:906061.

Pengcheng He, Xiaodong Liu, Jianfeng Gao, and Weizhu Chen. 2020. Deberta: Decoding-enhanced bert with disentangled attention. *arXiv preprint arXiv:2006.03654*.

Pengcheng He, Xiaodong Liu, Jianfeng Gao, and Weizhu Chen. 2021. Deberta: Decoding-enhanced bert with disentangled attention.

Eswariah Kannan and Lakshmi Anusha Kothamasu. 2022. Fine-tuning bert based approach for multi-class sentiment analysis on twitter emotion data. *Ingénierie des Systèmes d'Information*, 27(1).

Soonki Kwon and Younghoon Lee. 2023. Explainability-based mix-up approach for text data augmentation. *ACM transactions on knowledge discovery from data*, 17(1):1–14.

Yinhan Liu, Myle Ott, Naman Goyal, Jingfei Du, Mandar Joshi, Danqi Chen, Omer Levy, Mike Lewis, Luke Zettlemoyer, and Veselin Stoyanov. 2019. Roberta: A robustly optimized bert pretraining approach. *arXiv preprint arXiv:1907.11692*.

Xin Lu, Zhuojun Li, Yanpeng Tong, Yanyan Zhao, and Bing Qin. 2023. Hit-scir at wassa 2023: Empathy and emotion analysis at the utterance-level and the essay-level. In *Proceedings of the 13th Workshop on Computational Approaches to Subjectivity, Sentiment, & Social Media Analysis*, pages 574–580.

Linkai Luo and Yue Wang. 2019. Emotionx-hsu: Adopting pre-trained bert for emotion classification. *arXiv preprint arXiv:1907.09669*.

Pansy Nandwani and Rupali Verma. 2021. A review on sentiment analysis and emotion detection from text. *Social network analysis and mining*, 11(1):81.

Damilola Omitaomu, Shabnam Tafreshi, Tingting Liu, Sven Buechel, Chris Callison-Burch, Johannes Eichstaedt, Lyle Ungar, and João Sedoc. 2022. Empathic conversations: A multi-level dataset of contextualized conversations.

Flor Miriam Plaza-del Arco, María-Teresa Martín-Valdivia, and Roman Klinger. 2022. Natural language inference prompts for zero-shot emotion classification in text across corpora. *arXiv preprint arXiv:2209.06701*.

Ashish Sharma, Adam S Miner, David C Atkins, and Tim Althoff. 2020. A computational approach to understanding empathy expressed in text-based mental health support. *arXiv preprint arXiv:2009.08441*.

Himil Vasava, Pramegh Uikey, Gaurav Wasnik, and Raksha Sharma. 2022. Transformer-based architecture for empathy prediction and emotion classification. In *Proceedings of the 12th Workshop on Computational Approaches to Subjectivity, Sentiment & Social Media Analysis*, pages 261–264.

# Fraunhofer SIT at WASSA 2024 Empathy and Personality Shared Task: Use of Sentiment Transformers and Data Augmentation With Fuzzy Labels to Predict Emotional Reactions in Conversations and Essays

**Raphael Antonius Frick** and **Martin Steinebach**
Fraunhofer SIT | ATHENE Center
Rheinstraße 75, Darmstadt, Germany
{raphael.frick, martin.steinebach}@sit.fraunhofer.de

## Abstract

Predicting emotions and emotional reactions during conversations and within texts poses challenges, even for advanced AI systems. The second iteration of the WASSA Empathy and Personality Shared Task focuses on creating innovative models that can anticipate emotional responses to news articles containing harmful content across four tasks. In this paper, we introduce our Fraunhofer SIT team's solutions for the three tasks: Task 1 (CONVD), Task 2 (CONVT), and Task 3 (EMP). It involves combining LLM-driven data augmentation with fuzzy labels and fine-tuning RoBERTa models pre-trained on sentiment classification tasks to solve the regression problems. In the competition, our solutions achieved 1st place in Track 1 (CONV-dialog), 8th in Track 2 (CONV-turn), and 3rd place in Track 3 (EMP).

## 1 Introduction

Consuming news articles and user-generated content online can evoke diverse emotions in individuals. Detecting empathic reactions to such content, often influenced by a reader's personality, remains a formidable challenge, even for advanced artificial intelligence (AI) systems.

The second iteration of the *Workshop on Computational Approaches to Subjectivity, Sentiment & Social Media Analysis* (Giorgi et al., 2024) shared task focuses on creating AI models capable of predicting empathy, emotion, and personality. For this, akin to the approach taken by Omitaomu et al., participants were assigned the task of reading news articles that contained harmful content related to individuals, groups, animals, or objects. Subsequently, they were required to express their reactions in essays and engage in discussions.

For the second iteration of the shared task, a new dataset was introduced. This dataset includes written essays along with associated Batson empathic concern and personal distress scores, as well as the Big Five personality traits (OCEAN) for each reader. Unlike the previous version (Barriere et al., 2023), the new dataset also incorporates conversations between two users who read the same article. Each speech turn in these conversations has been annotated for perceived empathy, emotion polarity, and intensity. Additionally, the dataset provides news articles referenced in the conversations and essays, along with person-level demographic information (age, gender, ethnicity, income, and education level).

The shared task was divided into four subtasks:

- **Task 1: Empathy Prediction in Conversations (CONVD):** Predicting perceived empathy at the dialog level.
- **Task 2: Empathy and Emotion Prediction in Conversation Turns (CONVT):** Predicting perceived empathy, emotion polarity, and intensity at the speech-turn level in a conversation.
- **Task 3: Empathy Prediction (EMP):** Predicting both empathy concern and personal distress at the essay level.
- **Task 4: Personality Prediction (PER):** Predicting the personality traits (openness, conscientiousness, extraversion, agreeableness, and emotional stability) of essay writers based on their essays, dialogs, and the news articles they reacted to.

Our team (Fraunhofer SIT) participated in Tasks 1, 2, and 3. In this paper, we present our solution that combines LLM-driven data augmentation with fuzzy target labels and fine-tuned sentiment transformer models. During the competition, our solution achieved 1st place in Task 1, 8th in Task 2, and 3rd place in Task 3, demonstrating strong performance across empathy classification tasks.



*Proceedings of the 14th Workshop on Computational Approaches to Subjectivity, Sentiment, & Social Media Analysis*, pages 435–440
August 15, 2024 

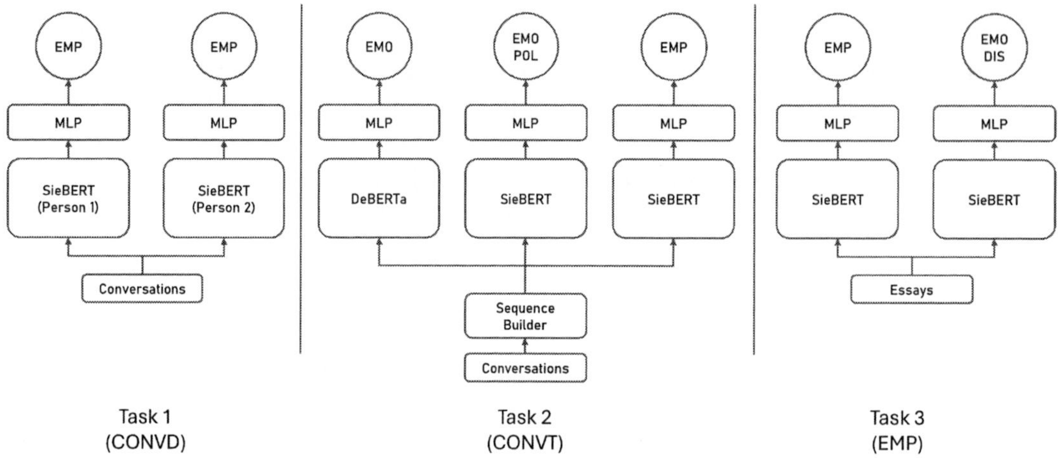


Figure 1: Proposed architectures for each subtask

## 2 Data Augmentation with Fuzzy Target Labels

Obtaining labeled training data for classification and regression tasks presents challenges. Experts skilled at assigning accurate labels are necessary and, regarding the shared task, enough participants are required willing to engage in discussions and contribute essays about their emotional reactions. Consequently, pre-training language models like BERT (Devlin et al., 2019) on task-specific data is often impractical and can impact fine-tuning applicability. To address this issue, we employed data augmentation in this shared task to generate new samples from the limited existing data. In particular, we focussed on *paraphrasing* and *back-translation* operations.

To maintain independence from external APIs, we performed augmentations using a local instance of *LLama V3 8B-Instruct* [1] (AI@Meta, 2024). For paraphrasing, we used *You are a paraphraser chatbot who just returns the paraphrased input sentences and nothing else!* as a system prompt instructing the model to return paraphrased sentences. For back-translation, *You are a translation chatbot who just returns the translated input sentences into {language} and nothing else! In cases, where translation is not possible, return the original input sentence.* was used to translate the sentences first into *German* and then back to *English*.

Despite being trained on multilingual texts, the translation capabilities of the small model introduce translation errors (Table 1). In this paper, we take advantage of the slight mistranslations to provide new data samples with similar meanings. However, while both operations, paraphrasing and back-translation, rephrase the sentences, either by changing the word order in the sentence and by applying synonym substitution, errors result in minor changes regarding the semantics. As such, it cannot be ensured that the labels associated with the original data sample are still correct. Therefore, we chose to add noise to the labels of the augmented data samples in the range of $[-0.2, 0.2]$ to the labels of Task 3 and noise in the range of $[-0.1, 0.1]$ to the labels of the augmented samples of Task 2. No noise was added to the data of Task 1, as they were provided as hard labels. We chose this particular value for various reasons. First, higher noise led to lower performance on the validation set, whereas too weak noise led to the models overfitting on the content of the data sample text. The results on the Mean-Squared Error (MSE) is displayed in Table 2.

## 3 System Descriptions

In this section, we present the architectures used to predict the target labels of each respective subtask. An overview is displayed in Figure 1.

### 3.1 Task 1: Empathy Prediction in Conversations

In a scenario where two people engage in dialogues about a read article, the goal was to predict their empathy levels. These empathy scores were represented as integer labels ranging from 1 to 9. Although classification models are typically used for

[1] LLama 3 8B Instruct

| Type | Sentence | Emotion | Emotional Polarity | Empathy |
|---|---|---|---|---|
| Original (OG) | take care! goodbye | 1.3333 | 0.3333 | 0.6667 |
| Paraphrase | Farewell! May you be well. | 1.2657 | 0.2986 | 0.6209 |
| BT: OG - GER | Bleib gesund! Auf Wiedersehen! | 1.3278 | 0.4124 | 0.6475 |
| BT: OG - GER - ENG | Stay healthy! Goodbye! | 1.3302 | 0.3110 | 0.7119 |
| Paraphrased BT | Wishing you well! Farewell! | 1.2915 | 0.3305 | 0.7476 |

Table 1: Example of LLM-based data augmentation on an utterance of the CONVT dataset

| | Empathy | Distress |
|---|---|---|
| No Augmentation | 2.9321 | 3.3328 |
| Augmentation | 2.9275 | 2.9101 |
| Fuzzy Augmentation | **2.9193** | **2.3299** |

Table 2: Influence of data augmentation on the validation loss (MSE) of the Task 2 (EMP) dataset

| | Perceived Empathy | |
|---|---|---|
| | r | p |
| Fraunhofer SIT | **0.193** | 0.127 |
| ConText | 0.191 | 0.130 |
| Chinchunmei | 0.172 | 0.173 |
| EmpatheticFIG | 0.012 | 0.923 |

Table 3: Results on the test set of the CONVD dataset (Task 1). Scores represent Pearson Correlation Coefficients

such predictions, we chose to frame this as a regression problem due to label imbalance in the dataset.

Additionally, we hypothesized a strong correlation between empathy estimation and sentiment. As a result, we conducted experiments by fine-tuning various models:

- **DeBERTa V3 Large:** DeBERTa V3 Large (He et al., 2021)[2] is a model trained on generic data, which improves upon BERT (Devlin et al., 2019) and RoBERTa (Liu et al., 2019) using disentangled attention and enhanced mask decoder and its previous iterations regarding efficiency.
- **SieBERT:** Unlike DeBERTa, SieBERT (Hartmann et al., 2023)[3] (based on a RoBERTa model) was fine-tuned on multiple sentiment estimation datasets. These 15 datasets cover various domains, including reviews and tweets. In experiments, SieBERT significantly outperformed previous related work on a synthetic benchmark dataset.
- **Twitter RoBERTa Base Sentiment:** Furthermore, we experimented with a Twitter RoBERTa Base Sentiment model (Barbieri et al., 2020)[4]. This model, as the name suggests, is built upon the RoBERTa architecture and was specifically trained using Twitter data.

To specify which person's empathy within the conversations should be predicted, a dedicated model was trained. Experiments involving additional tokens to indicate the target label for output did not yield favorable results and were therefore omitted.

To select the best-performing model, we trained multiple instances with different seeds. We used a low learning rate of $1.5e-06$ to align with the fine-tuning purpose. The optimizer employed was *AdamW* (Loshchilov and Hutter, 2019), and the learning rate was dynamically adjusted during training. The model was trained with a batch size of 16 and evaluated on 64 samples per batch. At every 15th step, performance was assessed on the validation set, and early stopping was implemented to mitigate overfitting.

Based on the 500 conversations from the training set and augmented data (including paraphrased, back-translated, and paraphrased back-translated examples), we compared the models' performance. The SieBERT-based model (Avg MSE: 2.205) outperformed the DeBERTa model (Avg MSE: 2.233) and Twitter RoBERTa Sentiment model (Avg MSE: 2.239) on the development set and was chosen for the final submission.

On the test set, the model achieved a Pearson Correlation Coefficient of 0.193, securing the top position in the competition (see Table 3). However, the high $p$ value suggests that the computed $r$ value lacks significance. This highlights the ongoing challenge of accurately estimating empathy at the dialogue level.

[2]DeBERTa V3 Large
[3]SieBERT
[4]Twitter RoBERTa Base Sentiment

| | Average | Empathy | | Emotion Polarity | | Emotion Intensity | |
|---|---|---|---|---|---|---|---|
| | r | r | p | r | p | r | p |
| ConText | **0.626** | 0.577 | 0.000 | 0.679 | 0.000 | **0.622** | 0.000 |
| Chinchunmei | 0.623 | **0.582** | 0.000 | **0.680** | 0.000 | 0.607 | 0.000 |
| EmpatheticFIG | 0.610 | 0.559 | 0.000 | 0.671 | 0.000 | 0.601 | 0.000 |
| Last_min_submission_team | 0.595 | 0.534 | 0.000 | 0.663 | 0.000 | 0.589 | 0.000 |
| hyy3 | 0.590 | 0.544 | 0.000 | 0.644 | 0.000 | 0.581 | 0.000 |
| Empathify | 0.588 | 0.541 | 0.000 | 0.638 | 0.000 | 0.584 | 0.000 |
| empaths | 0.477 | 0.534 | 0.000 | 0.422 | 0.000 | 0.473 | 0.000 |
| FraunhoferSIT | -0.007 | 0.034 | 0.125 | -0.018 | 0.409 | 0.032 | 0.141 |
| Zhenmei | -0.030 | -0.027 | 0.223 | -0.020 | 0.356 | -0.043 | 0.051 |

Table 4: Results on the test set of the CONV-T dataset (Task 2). Scores represent Pearson Correlation Coefficients

| | Average | Empathy | | Distress | |
|---|---|---|---|---|---|
| | r | r | p | r | p |
| RU | **0.453** | **0.523** | 0.000 | 0.383 | 0.000 |
| Chinchunmei | 0.393 | 0.474 | 0.000 | 0.311 | 0.004 |
| FraunhoferSIT | 0.385 | 0.375 | 0.000 | **0.395** | 0.000 |
| 1024m | 0.344 | 0.361 | 0.001 | 0.327 | 0.003 |
| ConText | 0.321 | 0.390 | 0.000 | 0.252 | 0.210 |
| Empathify | 0.253 | 0.290 | 0.008 | 0.217 | 0.049 |
| Daisy | 0.213 | 0.345 | 0.001 | 0.082 | 0.461 |

Table 5: Results on the test set of the EMP dataset (Task 3). Scores represent Pearson Correlation Coefficients

### 3.2 Task 2: Empathy and Emotion Prediction in Conversations Turns

The second task involved predicting emotional intensity, polarity, and empathy for each turn in a conversation. The training set comprised $11,166$ turns across 500 conversations provided alongside the shared task.

Recognizing that conversation history significantly influences emotional states at specific turns, the utterances were not classified individually. Instead, they were considered along with previous utterances within the conversation. To focus on utterances impacting the current emotional state, a context window of size 5 was used to create sequences of turns.

The models were trained similarly to those in Task 1, with the addition of introducing noise into augmented samples in the range of $[-0.1, 0.1]$. In experiments, the DeBERTa model excelled in classifying emotion on the validation set (Pearson Correlation Coefficient: 0.313), while fine-tuned SieBERT models performed best for emotional polarity (Pearson Correlation Coefficient: 0.3057) and empathy classification (Pearson Correlation Coefficient: 0.282).

During the evaluation on the test set, it was revealed, that the model was unable to provide correct classifications (Table 4). One reason for this might be, that the model was unable to learn significant information based on the short context windows, as indicated by the low validation scores. Future directions may incorporate combining larger context windows as well as the combination of information on turn and dialog level.

### 3.3 Task 3: Empathy Prediction

Our participation in the last task focused on estimating empathy and emotional distress related to a read article. Participants wrote essays expressing their feelings after reading the article. The training set included 1000 essays, while 66 essays were reserved for the development set.

During training, we fed the essays and their augmentations into individual models. Unlike the previous task, we introduced higher label noise ($[-0.2, 0.2]$). In addition, the batch size during training was raised to 48.

On the development set, the SieBERT models performed the best, with the Pearson Correlation Coefficient for the empathy being 0.6871 and for the emotional distress 0.684. In comparison, the best scores obtained by the DeBERTa model for the empathy estimation was 0.525 and for the emotional distress 0.5602. Using a sentiment transformer pretrained on Twitter data did improve the performance. The best performing Twitter RoBERTa Base Sentiment classifier achieved a Person Correlation Coefficient score of 0.6316 for the empathy estimations and a score of 0.6517 for the emotional distress detection. This shows not only the effectiveness of the sentiment transformers in solving these tasks, but also that the models perform better when trained on sentiment datasets consisting of data from different domains.

In the competition, our proposed system ranked third overall. While it excelled in predicting emotional distress compared to other systems, it fell short in classifying empathy, where it ranked fourth.

## 4 Conclusion and Future Work

In this paper, we presented the solutions developed by our team Fraunhofer SIT for the 2024 shared task of the *Workshop on Computational Approaches to Subjectivity, Sentiment & Social Media Analysis*. Our experiments revealed that models fine-tuned for sentiment estimation tasks often outperformed larger language models, such as DeBERTa, which were trained on more generic data. Data augmentation improved classification accuracy, and introducing noisy labels further refined performance. While our solutions achieved 1st place in Task 1, 8th in Task 2, and 3rd place in Task 3, the Pearson Correlation Coefficients indicate the need for additional research to achieve more stable results.

## 5 Limitations

Experiments have shown that solving the empathy and emotion estimation tasks poses various challenges. In the particular case of Track 1 (CONV-dialog), the performance of proposed the model according to the Pearson Correlation Coefficients is low despite the first place in the competition. One reason for this is that many of the models used were unable to predict meaningful labels during training. Instead, target labels that deviated from the mean were often incorrectly predicted. The transition from a regression to a classification problem did not solve the problem. This indicates that the imbalance of the labels often has a significant impact on the performance of the models.

Furthermore, the performance of the models depends on the seeds used. Training the models with different seeds leads to different results. However, taking advantage of data augmentation always led to an increase in performance.

Although the fine-tuned sentiment transformers based on SieBERT often performed best, the Twitter RoBERTa base sentiment models did not. This suggests that texts in tweets are stylistically too different from those in essays and even dialogs. Therefore, it is recommended to use sentiment transformers trained on general texts or texts from different data sources and domains.

## Acknowledgments

This work was supported by the German Federal Ministry of Education and Research (BMBF) and the Hessian Ministry of Higher Education, Research, Science and the Arts within their joint support of "ATHENE – CRISIS" and "ATHENE CHARM".

## References

AI@Meta. 2024. Llama 3 model card.

Francesco Barbieri, Jose Camacho-Collados, Luis Espinosa Anke, and Leonardo Neves. 2020. TweetEval: Unified benchmark and comparative evaluation for tweet classification. In *Findings of the Association for Computational Linguistics: EMNLP 2020*, pages 1644–1650, Online. Association for Computational Linguistics.

Valentin Barriere, João Sedoc, Shabnam Tafreshi, and Salvatore Giorgi. 2023. Findings of wassa 2023 shared task on empathy, emotion and personality detection in conversation and reactions to news articles. In *Proceedings of the 13th Workshop on Computational Approaches to Subjectivity, Sentiment, & Social Media Analysis*, pages 511–525.

Jacob Devlin, Ming-Wei Chang, Kenton Lee, and Kristina Toutanova. 2019. BERT: pre-training of deep bidirectional transformers for language understanding. In *Proceedings of the 2019 Conference of the North American Chapter of the Association for Computational Linguistics: Human Language Technologies, NAACL-HLT 2019, Minneapolis, MN, USA, June 2-7, 2019, Volume 1 (Long and Short Papers)*, pages 4171–4186. Association for Computational Linguistics.

Salvatore Giorgi, João Sedoc, Valentin Barriere, and Shabnam Tafreshi. 2024. Findings of wassa 2024 shared task on empathy and personality detection in interactions. In *Proceedings of the 14th Workshop on Computational Approaches to Subjectivity, Sentiment, & Social Media Analysis*.

Jochen Hartmann, Mark Heitmann, Christian Siebert, and Christina Schamp. 2023. More than a feeling: Accuracy and application of sentiment analysis. *International Journal of Research in Marketing*, 40(1):75–87.

Pengcheng He, Jianfeng Gao, and Weizhu Chen. 2021. Debertav3: Improving deberta using electra-style pre-training with gradient-disentangled embedding sharing. *Preprint*, arXiv:2111.09543.

Yinhan Liu, Myle Ott, Naman Goyal, Jingfei Du, Mandar Joshi, Danqi Chen, Omer Levy, Mike Lewis, Luke Zettlemoyer, and Veselin Stoyanov. 2019. Roberta: A robustly optimized BERT pretraining approach. *CoRR*, abs/1907.11692.

Ilya Loshchilov and Frank Hutter. 2019. Decoupled weight decay regularization. *Preprint*, arXiv:1711.05101.

Damilola Omitaomu, Shabnam Tafreshi, Tingting Liu, Sven Buechel, Chris Callison-Burch, Johannes Eichstaedt, Lyle Ungar, and João Sedoc. 2022. Empathic conversations: A multi-level dataset of contextualized conversations. *Preprint*, arXiv:2205.12698.

# EmpatheticFIG at WASSA 2024 Empathy and Personality Shared Task: Predicting Empathy and Emotion in Conversations with Figurative Language

**Gyeongeun Lee** * **Zhu Wang*** **Sathya N. Ravi** **Natalie Parde**
Department of Computer Science
University of Illinois at Chicago
{glee87, zwang260, sathya, parde}@uic.edu

## Abstract

Recent research highlights the importance of figurative language as a tool for amplifying emotional impact. In this paper, we dive deeper into this phenomenon and outline our methods for *Track 1, Empathy Prediction in Conversations* (CONV-dialog) and *Track 2, Empathy and Emotion Prediction in Conversation Turns* (CONV-turn) of the WASSA 2024 shared task. We leveraged transformer-based large language models augmented with figurative language prompts, specifically idioms, metaphors and hyperbole, that were selected and trained for each track to optimize system performance. For Track 1, we observed that a fine-tuned BERT with metaphor and hyperbole features outperformed other models on the development set. For Track 2, DeBERTa, with different combinations of figurative language prompts, performed well for different prediction tasks. Our method provides a novel framework for understanding how figurative language influences emotional perception in conversational contexts. Our system officially ranked 4th in the 1st track and 3rd in the 2nd track.

## 1 Introduction

The computational study of empathy[1] is crucial to enabling and advancing the development of innovative and resourceful tools for social good in various settings, ranging from online conversations to clinical therapy (Eysenbach et al., 2004; Elliott et al., 2018). At a broader level, recognizing emotional needs and appropriately responding to them are essential for successful interactions, making this an important step in chatbot development. However, despite the recent surge in interest in automated empathy detection (Barriere et al., 2023; Lee and Parde, 2024; Giorgi et al., 2024; Lee et al., 2024), research focusing on empathetic dialogue involving back-and-forth conversations (such as that by Rashkin et al. (2018)) still remains scarce. The Workshop on Computational Approaches to Subjectivity, Sentiment and Social Media Analysis (WASSA) 2023 (Barriere et al., 2023) and 2024 (Giorgi et al., 2024) provides the opportunity to explore this domain further with the *Empathic Conversations* dataset (Omitaomu et al., 2022).

Analyzing linguistic features is crucial in understanding how language is used to convey empathy and emotion in dialogue. Figurative language (non-literal language; see § 2.3.2 for more information), and particularly metaphor, has been shown to enhance the performance of emotion prediction models (Dankers et al., 2019), hold more emotional charge than literal language (Citron and Goldberg, 2014), and strengthen expressions (Mohammad et al., 2016; Li et al., 2023). From our own recent work, we found that figurative language prompts improved empathy detection performance when using the domain-specialized *AcnEmpathize* dataset (Lee et al., 2024). Therefore, we hypothesized that identifying the use of figurative language in *Empathic Conversations* could likewise provide deeper insight into the study of empathy and emotion. We thus propose methods to encode figurative language prompts into large language models (LLMs) for emotion and empathy prediction in conversations.

In this shared task, we participated in two of the four tracks:

- **Track 1**: *Empathy Prediction in Conversations* (CONV-dialog), focusing on predicting perceived empathy at the dialogue level.
- **Track 2**: *Empathy and Emotion Prediction in Conversation Turns* (CONV-turn), focused on predicting perceived empathy, emotion polarity, and emotion intensity at the speech-turn level in a conversation.

*Equal contribution

[1]We follow Davis et al. (1980)'s definition of *empathy* as the ability to understand and respond to the experiences and feelings of others.



*Proceedings of the 14th Workshop on Computational Approaches to Subjectivity, Sentiment, & Social Media Analysis*, pages 441–447
August 15, 2024 ©2024 Association for Computational Linguistics

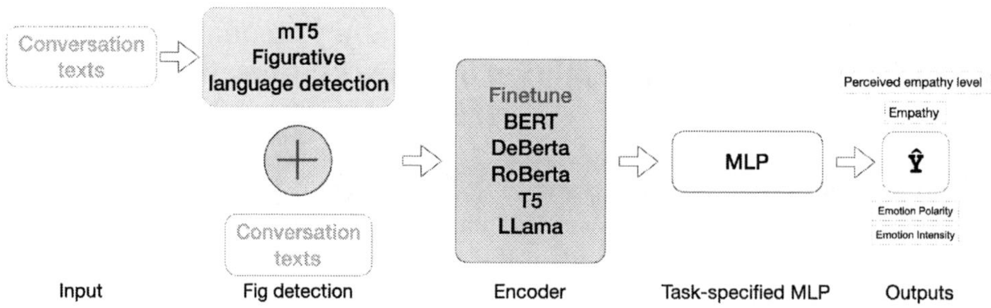


Figure 1: EmpatheticFIG architecture. We combined figurative language prompts with conversation text and passed the combined input through various text encoders. We applied different pre-trained LLMs, such as BERT and DeBERTa. Then, we used task-specific MLPs to obtain the outputs.

In both tracks, we implemented transformer-based models with additional figurative language prompts. We applied combinations of figurative language prompts that yielded the best performance on the development sets. In Track 1, we used metaphor and hyperbole features with BERT (Devlin et al., 2018). In Track 2, we used idiom and hyperbole features together for empathy prediction, hyperbole for emotional polarity, and metaphor for emotion intensity with DeBERTa (He et al., 2021).

## 2 System Description

### 2.1 Track 1: Empathy Prediction in Conversations (CONV-dialog)

The goal of this track was to predict the perceived empathy of one person towards another based on their conversation. For each conversation ID, we were given the speaker ID of Speaker 1 and their perceived empathy from the other person, Speaker 2. We extracted all texts from Speaker 2 in each conversation and combined them to predict the empathy level perceived by Speaker 1, implementing this as a multi-class classification problem.

### 2.2 Track 2: Empathy and Emotion Prediction in Conversation Turns (CONV-turn)

In this track, we used the text of each speaker in each conversation to predict turn-level annotated emotion, emotional polarity, and empathy. Since the target labels were provided for each turn, preprocessing the text was unnecessary. We encoded the conversations and figurative language prompts at the turn level, subsequently passing them through the task-specific multilayer perception (MLP) layer to obtain the output scores.

### 2.3 EmpatheticFIG

We propose EmpatheticFIG, a framework that incorporates figurative language prompts for empathy and emotion prediction in conversations. It draws inspiration from our earlier work (Lee et al., 2024) and that of others emphasizing the importance of metaphor to emotional expression (Citron and Goldberg, 2014; Mohammad et al., 2016; Dankers et al., 2019; Li et al., 2023). The main architecture is illustrated in Figure 1.

We used mT5 (Xue et al., 2021) to extract figurative language prompts (described further in §2.3.2) and appended these features to the conversation texts. These combined inputs were then processed by pre-trained LLMs, including BERT (Devlin et al., 2018), DeBerta (He et al., 2021), RoBERTa (Liu et al., 2019), T5 (Raffel et al., 2020), and Llama (Touvron et al., 2023). Finally, we applied task-specified MLP layers for Track 1 and for different tasks in Track 2 to generate outputs.

#### 2.3.1 Models and Hyperparameters

We conducted extensive experiments using different LLMs and hyperparameter settings. In Track 1, the backbone models were BERT-base, DeBerta-v3-base, RoBERTa-base, and Llama-3-8b. In Track 2, we fine-tuned BERT, DeBerta, RoBERTa, and T5-small. We fine-tuned BERT, DeBerta, RoBERTa, and T5 on conversation texts with figurative language prompts for both tracks. When using Llama, we utilized Parameter-Efficient Fine-Tuning (Hu et al., 2021, PEFT) to adapt the model weights for perceived empathy level prediction for Track 1.

For both tracks, we searched for the optimal hyperparameters from the following sets: learning rates ranging from {3e-4, 1e-4, 5e-5, 1e-5, 5e-6}, batch sizes from 2 to 64 depending on the model, and training epochs ranging from {1, 3, 5, 10, 30,

Table 1: The combined total number of texts containing each type of figurative language in the training and development datasets in Track 1 (CONV-dialog) and Track 2 (CONV-turn). Each text may include multiple types of figurative language.

| | Track 1 | Track 2 |
|---|---|---|
| # Texts | 1,037 | 12,080 |
| # Idiom | 552 (53%) | 6,378 (53%) |
| # Metaphor | 267 (26%) | 1,472 (12%) |
| # Hyperbole | 120 (12%) | 1,795 (15%) |
| Total Figurative | 939 (91%) | 9,645 (80%) |

50}. The AdamW (Loshchilov and Hutter, 2017) optimizer was used with a weight decay of 0.01.

### 2.3.2 Figurative Language Prompts

Since empathy is primarily conveyed through language, we focused our investigation on the performance benefits of incorporating automatically extracted linguistic constructs (figurative language phenomena) from the text to assist in predicting empathy and emotion labels. Figurative language is non-literal language (Paul, 1970) that serves to compare, exaggerate, and add nuanced meaning; oftentimes, it is used as a vehicle to simplify complicated or abstract ideas.

We applied the multi-figurative language detection method from Lai et al. (2023) to identify metaphor, idiom, and hyperbole (three distinct types of figurative language, explained later in this section) in *Empathic Conversations*. Lai et al. (2023)'s approach requires the use of a pre-trained LLM; we specifically employed mT5 (Xue et al., 2020) using predefined prompts of the format:

```
Which figure of speech does this
text contain?  (A) Literal  (B)
[Task] | Text: [Text]
```

We filled `[Task]` using `metaphor`, `idiom`, and `hyperbole`, respectively. Using this approach, we then one-hot encoded the labels for each detected type of figurative language if at least one type was present in the text. Finally, we appended a description to the original conversation text that reads, *The text contains <label>.*, where "label" represents the type of figurative language. Again, note that each text may contain more than one type of figurative language (which were appended separated by commas).

In Table 1, we summarize the distributions of figurative language types in the combined training and development datasets for Track 1 and Track 2. We find that the datasets for both are rich in figurative language—in total, figurative language is present in approximately 91% and 80% of the samples, respectively. Below, we briefly define and provide examples for each type of figurative language identified.

Table 2: Track 1 development set results. The best combinations of figurative language prompts for each model are shown here. "-" denotes models without figurative language prompts. Bold indicates the highest Pearson correlation coefficient (Pearson $r$).

| Model | Fig. Features | Pearson $r$ |
|---|---|---|
| RoBERTa | - | 0.164 |
| DeBERTa | - | 0.158 |
| Llama | - | 0.0713 |
| BERT | - | 0.185 |
| RoBERTa | metaphor | 0.198 |
| DeBERTa | all | 0.185 |
| Llama | - | 0.0713 |
| **BERT** | **metaphor, hyperbole** | **0.242** |

**Metaphor.** Metaphoric expressions frame conventional ideas in more accessible terms by assigning new meanings (Lakoff and Johnson, 1980). For example, the phrase "fight these natural disasters" from *Empathetic Conversations* personifies natural calamities as adversaries one must battle.

**Idiom.** Idiomatic expressions tie abstract ideas or meanings to more concrete anchors and often involve cultural context (Nunberg et al., 1994). For example, the phrase "pull through the hard times" from *Empathetic Conversations* uses idiomatic language to convey the act of enduring and surviving difficult times.

**Hyperbole.** Hyperbolic expressions are often used to exaggerate a statement or phenomenon (Claridge, 2010), as in "thousands of years of human progress." This phrase from the shared task dataset likely emphasizes the significance of human progress over a long period, rather than literally referring to exactly thousands of years.

## 3 Results and Discussions

To investigate the role of figurative language in empathy and emotion prediction in conversations, we implemented EmpatheticFIG for Track 1 and Track 2. We conducted experiments using different combinations of figurative language prompts and generally found that many models with idiom features performed worse, perhaps due to the high prevalence of idioms in the dataset. We present

Table 3: Track 2 development set results. The performance of the baseline models is displayed in rows 1-4, with DeBERTa as the top-performing baseline model. We also present the results of different combinations of figurative language prompts using DeBERTa in rows 5-11. Bold text indicates the best Pearson $r$ for each task. Different figurative language prompts improved different types of emotion and empathy predictions.

| Model | Empathy | Emotion Polarity | Emotion Intensity |
|---|---|---|---|
| T5-small (Raffel et al., 2020) | 0.556 | 0.63 | 0.658 |
| BERT (Devlin et al., 2018) | 0.619 | 0.735 | 0.653 |
| RoBERTa (Liu et al., 2019) | 0.626 | 0.739 | 0.658 |
| DeBERTa (He et al., 2021) | 0.633 | 0.759 | 0.66 |
| DeBERTa + idiom | 0.632 | 0.745 | 0.655 |
| DeBERTa + metaphor | 0.632 | 0.751 | **0.666** |
| DeBERTa + hyperbole | 0.633 | **0.765** | 0.659 |
| DeBERTa + idiom + metaphor | 0.62 | 0.745 | 0.644 |
| DeBERTa + metaphor + hyperbole | 0.6311 | 0.75 | 0.66 |
| DeBERTa + idiom + hyperbole | **0.661** | 0.748 | 0.622 |
| DeBERTa + all | 0.656 | 0.761 | 0.635 |

the experimental results on the development and test sets for Track 1 and Track 2 in Tables 2 and 3, respectively. To assess the impact of figurative language prompts, we also conducted ablation experiments using various combinations of figurative language types. Moreover, we evaluated the performance of these features across different LLMs. We discuss the results for Tracks 1 and 2 in more detail in §3.1 and §3.2, respectively.

### 3.1 Results for Track 1 (CONV-dialog)

Table 2 presents the development set results for Track 1, showcasing the averaged Pearson correlation values from three runs for each setting. Models incorporating figurative language prompts consistently outperformed the baseline models, suggesting that these features positively impact perceived empathy level predictions. Metaphors generally improved the performance for perceived empathy level prediction and seemed to enhance the ability of language models to capture the nuanced emotional cues in empathetic conversations.

We applied the settings that yielded the best performance on the development set to the test set, specifically using BERT with metaphor and hyperbole features, a learning rate of 5e-5, a batch size of 8, and an epoch length of 3. However, we observed a drop in performance on the test set (see results in Appendix A.1), potentially due to class imbalance and overfitting. We leave further investigations of test set performance for future work.

### 3.2 Results for Track 2 (CONV-turn)

We present the results for each task in Track 2 in Table 3. DeBERTa was the best performing model among all the baseline models. We observed that task performance varied depending on the specific figurative language prompts used on the development set. DeBERTa with idiom and hyperbole features notably improved empathy predictions. DeBERTa with hyperbole achieved the highest performance on emotion polarity predictions, while DeBERTa with metaphor slightly enhanced predictions for emotion intensity.

We found that different figurative language prompts provided varying levels of information and impact on different task predictions. For example, hyperbole contributed to improved emotion polarity, while idioms and hyperbole enhanced performance in empathy prediction for turn-level conversations. In contrast, metaphor had less impact on empathy and emotion predictions at the turn level (Track 2) compared to its impact at the dialogue level in Track 1. The test set performance (see Appendix A.2) also shows consistent results.

## 4 Conclusion

Our team, EmpatheticFIG, participated in Track 1 (Empathy Prediction in Conversations) and Track 2 (Empathy and Emotion Prediction in Conversation Turns) of the WASSA 2024 shared task. Our system architecture involved fine-tuning various LLMs, such as BERT and DeBERTa, with one or more combinations of figurative language types—idioms, metaphors, and hyperbole. The results showed that incorporating figurative language prompts was beneficial for predicting empathy and emotion in conversations. Our method provides unique insights into adapting figurative language prompts into LLMs.

## 5 Limitations and Future Work

We could experiment with larger, more complex models and perform extensive hyperparameter tuning. Additionally, we could verify the detection of figurative language expressions in the dataset and conduct a deeper analysis of their usage to better understand the reasons behind the performance. Furthermore, we could explore more types of figurative language beyond those we have already investigated.

## Acknowledgments

We thank the anonymous reviewers for their feedback, and the WASSA 2024 shared task organizers for running this task. This work was partially supported by the National Science Foundation under Grant No. 2125411. Any opinions, findings, and conclusions or recommendations are those of the authors and do not necessarily reflect the views of the National Science Foundation.

## References

Valentin Barriere, João Sedoc, Shabnam Tafreshi, and Salvatore Giorgi. 2023. Findings of wassa 2023 shared task on empathy, emotion and personality detection in conversation and reactions to news articles. In *Proceedings of the 13th Workshop on Computational Approaches to Subjectivity, Sentiment, & Social Media Analysis*, pages 511–525.

Francesca MM Citron and Adele E Goldberg. 2014. Metaphorical sentences are more emotionally engaging than their literal counterparts. *Journal of cognitive neuroscience*, 26(11):2585–2595.

Claudia Claridge. 2010. *Hyperbole in English: A corpus-based study of exaggeration*. Cambridge University Press.

Verna Dankers, Marek Rei, Martha Lewis, and Ekaterina Shutova. 2019. Modelling the interplay of metaphor and emotion through multitask learning. In *Proceedings of the 2019 Conference on Empirical Methods in Natural Language Processing and the 9th International Joint Conference on Natural Language Processing (EMNLP-IJCNLP)*, pages 2218–2229.

Mark H Davis et al. 1980. A multidimensional approach to individual differences in empathy. *JSAS: catalog of selected documents in psychology*, 10.

Jacob Devlin, Ming-Wei Chang, Kenton Lee, and Kristina Toutanova. 2018. Bert: Pre-training of deep bidirectional transformers for language understanding. *arXiv preprint arXiv:1810.04805*.

Robert Elliott, Arthur C Bohart, Jeanne C Watson, and David Murphy. 2018. Therapist empathy and client outcome: An updated meta-analysis. *Psychotherapy*, 55(4):399.

Gunther Eysenbach, John Powell, Marina Englesakis, Carlos Rizo, and Anita Stern. 2004. Health related virtual communities and electronic support groups: systematic review of the effects of online peer to peer interactions. *Bmj*, 328(7449):1166.

Salvatore Giorgi, João Sedoc, Valentin Barriere, and Shabnam Tafreshi. 2024. Findings of wassa 2024 shared task on empathy and personality detection in interactions. In *Proceedings of the 14th Workshop on Computational Approaches to Subjectivity, Sentiment, & Social Media Analysis*.

Pengcheng He, Jianfeng Gao, and Weizhu Chen. 2021. Debertav3: Improving deberta using electra-style pretraining with gradient-disentangled embedding sharing. *arXiv preprint arXiv:2111.09543*.

Edward J Hu, Yelong Shen, Phillip Wallis, Zeyuan Allen-Zhu, Yuanzhi Li, Shean Wang, Lu Wang, and Weizhu Chen. 2021. Lora: Low-rank adaptation of large language models. *arXiv preprint arXiv:2106.09685*.

Huiyuan Lai, Antonio Toral, and Malvina Nissim. 2023. Multilingual multi-figurative language detection. *arXiv preprint arXiv:2306.00121*.

George Lakoff and Mark Johnson. 1980. Metaphors we live by. *University of Chicago, Chicago, IL*.

Gyeongeun Lee and Natalie Parde. 2024. AcnEmpathize: A dataset for understanding empathy in dermatology conversations. In *Proceedings of the 2024 Joint International Conference on Computational Linguistics, Language Resources and Evaluation (LREC-COLING 2024)*, pages 143–153, Torino, Italia. ELRA and ICCL.

Gyeongeun Lee, Christina Wong, Meghan Guo, and Natalie Parde. 2024. Pouring your heart out: Investigating the role of figurative language in online expressions of empathy. In *Proceedings of the 262nd Annual Meeting of the Association for Computational Linguistics (ACL 2024)*, page Accepted, Bangkok, Thailand. Association for Computational Linguistics.

Yucheng Li, Frank Guerin, and Chenghua Lin. 2023. The secret of metaphor on expressing stronger emotion. *arXiv preprint arXiv:2301.13042*.

Yinhan Liu, Myle Ott, Naman Goyal, Jingfei Du, Mandar Joshi, Danqi Chen, Omer Levy, Mike Lewis, Luke Zettlemoyer, and Veselin Stoyanov. 2019. Roberta: A robustly optimized bert pretraining approach. *arXiv preprint arXiv:1907.11692*.

Ilya Loshchilov and Frank Hutter. 2017. Decoupled weight decay regularization. *arXiv preprint arXiv:1711.05101*.

Saif Mohammad, Ekaterina Shutova, and Peter Turney. 2016. Metaphor as a medium for emotion: An empirical study. In *Proceedings of the fifth joint conference on lexical and computational semantics*, pages 23–33.

Geoffrey Nunberg, Ivan A Sag, and Thomas Wasow. 1994. Idioms. *Language*, 70(3):491–538.

Damilola Omitaomu, Shabnam Tafreshi, Tingting Liu, Sven Buechel, Chris Callison-Burch, Johannes Eichstaedt, Lyle Ungar, and João Sedoc. 2022. Empathic conversations: A multi-level dataset of contextualized conversations. *Preprint*, arXiv:2205.12698.

Anthony M Paul. 1970. Figurative language. *Philosophy & Rhetoric*, pages 225–248.

Colin Raffel, Noam Shazeer, Adam Roberts, Katherine Lee, Sharan Narang, Michael Matena, Yanqi Zhou, Wei Li, and Peter J Liu. 2020. Exploring the limits of transfer learning with a unified text-to-text transformer. *Journal of machine learning research*, 21(140):1–67.

Hannah Rashkin, Eric Michael Smith, Margaret Li, and Y-Lan Boureau. 2018. Towards empathetic open-domain conversation models: A new benchmark and dataset. *arXiv preprint arXiv:1811.00207*.

Hugo Touvron, Thibaut Lavril, Gautier Izacard, Xavier Martinet, Marie-Anne Lachaux, Timothée Lacroix, Baptiste Rozière, Naman Goyal, Eric Hambro, Faisal Azhar, et al. 2023. Llama: Open and efficient foundation language models. *arXiv preprint arXiv:2302.13971*.

Linting Xue, Noah Constant, Adam Roberts, Mihir Kale, Rami Al-Rfou, Aditya Siddhant, Aditya Barua, and Colin Raffel. 2020. mt5: A massively multilingual pre-trained text-to-text transformer. *arXiv preprint arXiv:2010.11934*.

Linting Xue, Noah Constant, Adam Roberts, Mihir Kale, Rami Al-Rfou, Aditya Siddhant, Aditya Barua, and Colin Raffel. 2021. mT5: A massively multilingual pre-trained text-to-text transformer. In *Proceedings of the 2021 Conference of the North American Chapter of the Association for Computational Linguistics: Human Language Technologies*, pages 483–498, Online. Association for Computational Linguistics.

# A Appendix

## A.1 Test results for Track 1

We illustrate our test results for Track 1, noting a significant performance drop on the test set. The performance on the dev set was unstable and sensitive to hyperparameters. We will leave the investigation of the test set settings and improving the robustness of our system, EmpatheticFIG, for future work.

Table 4: Track 1 test set results.

| | **Perceived Empathy** | |
|---|---|---|
| | r | p |
| FraunhoferSIT | 0.193 | 0.127 |
| ConText | 0.191 | 0.130 |
| Chinchunmei | 0.172 | 0.173 |
| EmpatheticFIG | 0.012 | 0.923 |

## A.2 Test results for Track 2

The performance of our model on the test set in Track 2 showed similar pattern to our performance on the development set. Our model performed best in predicting emotion polarity, empathy, and emotion intensity (in this order) and achieved an average Pearson $r$ of 0.610.

Table 5: Track 2 test set results.

| | Average | Empathy | | Emotion Polarity | | Emotion Intensity | |
|---|---|---|---|---|---|---|---|
| | r | r | p | r | p | r | p |
| ConText | 0.626 | 0.577 | 0.000 | 0.679 | 0.000 | 0.622 | 0.000 |
| Chinchunmei | 0.623 | 0.582 | 0.000 | 0.680 | 0.000 | 0.607 | 0.000 |
| EmpatheticFIG | 0.610 | 0.559 | 0.000 | 0.671 | 0.000 | 0.601 | 0.000 |
| Last_min_submission_team | 0.595 | 0.534 | 0.000 | 0.663 | 0.000 | 0.589 | 0.000 |
| hyy3 | 0.590 | 0.544 | 0.000 | 0.644 | 0.000 | 0.581 | 0.000 |
| Empathify | 0.588 | 0.541 | 0.000 | 0.638 | 0.000 | 0.584 | 0.000 |
| empaths | 0.477 | 0.534 | 0.000 | 0.422 | 0.000 | 0.473 | 0.000 |
| FraunhoferSIT | -0.007 | 0.034 | 0.125 | -0.018 | 0.409 | 0.032 | 0.141 |
| Zhenmei | -0.030 | -0.027 | 0.223 | -0.020 | 0.356 | -0.043 | 0.051 |

# ConText at WASSA 2024 Empathy and Personality Shared Task: History-Dependent Embedding Utterance Representations for Empathy and Emotion Prediction in Conversations

**Patrícia Pereira**[1,2], **Helena Moniz**[1,3] **and João Paulo Carvalho**[1,2]
[1] INESC-ID, Lisbon
[2] Instituto Superior Técnico, University of Lisbon
[3] Faculdade de Letras, University of Lisbon
patriciaspereira@tecnico.ulisboa.pt

## Abstract

Empathy and emotion prediction are key components in the development of effective and empathetic agents, amongst several other applications. The WASSA shared task on empathy and emotion prediction in interactions presents an opportunity to benchmark approaches to these tasks. Appropriately selecting and representing the historical context is crucial in the modelling of empathy and emotion in conversations. In our submissions, we model empathy, emotion polarity and emotion intensity of each utterance in a conversation by feeding the utterance to be classified together with its conversational context, i.e., a certain number of previous conversational turns, as input to an encoder Pre-trained Language Model, to which we append a regression head for prediction. We also model perceived counterparty empathy of each interlocutor by feeding all utterances from the conversation and a token identifying the interlocutor for which we are predicting the empathy. Our system officially ranked $1^{st}$ at the CONV-turn track and $2^{nd}$ at the CONV-dialog track.

## 1 Introduction

Empathy and emotion prediction are crucial components in the development of effective and empathetic agents. There is a considerable effort to put forward modules that efficiently recognize empathy and emotion, in both users and agents from conversations and text pertaining to the most varied domains, since this knowledge can be leveraged in opinion mining, marketing, customer support, therapeutic practices, amongst other scenarios.

The WASSA shared task on empathy and emotion prediction in interactions (Barriere et al., 2023; Giorgi et al., 2024) presents an opportunity to benchmark approaches to these tasks.

In conversation pertaining tasks, knowledge of the relevant history of the conversation, i.e., the relevant previous conversational turns, is extremely useful in identifying interlocutor traits (Poria et al., 2019; Pereira et al., 2022).

The usual approach to model this history has been to produce history independent representations of each utterance and subsequently perform joint modeling of those representations. State-of-the art approaches start by resorting to embedding representations from language models and employ gated, graph neural network or a combination of both architectures to perform joint modelling of these embedding representations at a later step (Li et al., 2021; Shen et al., 2021). However, it is our contention that the Transformer, the backbone of these language models, is better at preserving the history information since it has a shorter path of information flow than the RNNs typically used for joint modelling. Following Pereira et al. (2023), we produce history-dependent embedding representations of each utterance, by feeding not only the utterance but also its relevant previous utterances, that pertain to the task, to the language model. We thus discard the need to deal with joint modelling after obtaining the embeddings since these constitute already an efficient representation of such history.

The results on the test set of our submissions on conversation pertaining tracks demonstrate the efficacy of our approach, both in selecting the appropriate conversational turns to be fed to the language model and in the way we feed these utterances. Our approach earned us the first place in the modelling of empathy, emotion polarity and emotion intensity of each utterance in a conversation and second place in the modelling of counterparty empathy, with a result very slightly below the top ranking submission.

## 2 System Descriptions

### 2.1 Task Descriptions

Given dyadic conversations, the tasks consist in:



*Proceedings of the 14th Workshop on Computational Approaches to Subjectivity, Sentiment, & Social Media Analysis*, pages 448–453
August 15, 2024 ©2024 Association for Computational Linguistics

- **Track CONV-turn:** Modelling empathy, emotion polarity and emotion intensity of each utterance in a conversation. Each utterance in a conversation was annotated with these 3 traits, on a scale or real numbers from 0 to 5.
- **Track CONV-dialog:** Modelling perceived counterparty empathy of each interlocutor in a conversation. Each interlocutor of a dyadic conversation rated the perceived counterparty empathy, on a scale of integers from 1 to 7.

### 2.2 History-Dependent Embedding Representations

Embeddings from Pre-trained Language Models (PLMs) are the most commonly used state-of-the-art approaches in these tasks. RoBERTa (Liu et al., 2019) is a PLM suceeding from BERT (Devlin et al., 2019), pre-trained to perform language modeling to learn deep contextual embeddings, i.e., vectors representing the semantics of each word or sequence of words. DeBERTa (He et al., 2020) differentiates from the previous PLMs by introducing disentangled attention and an enhanced mask decoder. Longformer (Beltagy et al., 2020) was conceived for tackling long texts, using modified attention mechanisms, acting on both local and global scale.

We now describe how we obtain embedding representations with the PLM. These processes are depicted in Figure 1. For each track we leverage different representations:

- **Track CONV-turn:** we feed as input to the PLM the utterance we intend to classify, $u_i$, concatenated with its conversational context corresponding to a number $c$ of previous utterances in the conversation, $(u_{i-1}, u_{i-2}, ..., u_{i-c})$. Concretely, we feed $u_i$ to the model, preceded by the [CLS] token and suceded by the [SEP] token, followed by the previous turns $u_{i-1}$ up to $u_{i-c}$, separated by the [SEP] token. An utterance consists in a sequence of $w_{it}$ tokens representing its $T_i$ words:

$$u_i = (w_{i1}, w_{i2}, ..., w_{iT_i}) \tag{1}$$

The motivation behind feeding previous context turns lies within the fact that empathy and emotion are deeply context-dependent. Similar to human judgement in which these traits are better evaluated given the conversational context, the language model also benefits from this knowledge.

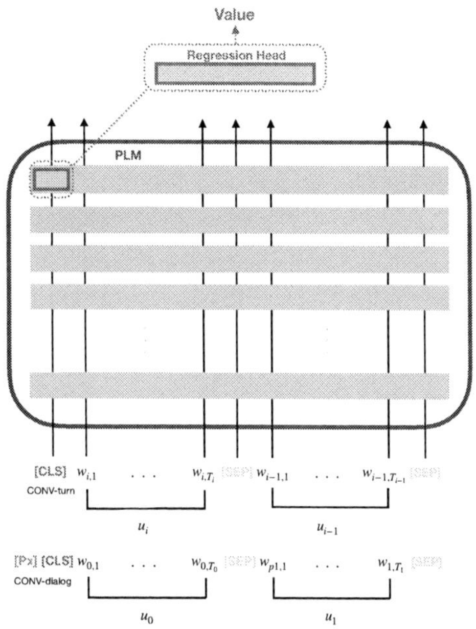


Figure 1: Model architecture. Utterances are given as input to the PLM, of which the [CLS] token of the last layer is fed to the regression head that predicts the trait value. First input line corresponds to Track CONV-turn and second to Track CONV-dialog.

- **Track CONV-dialog:** we use the same backbone architecture but instead of feeding a certain number of previous utterances of the conversation, we feed all the utterances and by the order of which they were written. We also add as input in the beginning a token corresponding to the interlocutor for which we are predicting the trait.

  Since we are predicting an interlocutor trait from a dialog, it is our contention that feeding all that dialog utterances provides the language model with the most complete information and that adding a token identifying the interlocutor for which we are predicting the trait makes the model establish a distinction between the interlocutors, which is necessary since the same dialog is used twice to predict both interlocutors' trait.

From the obtained embeddings we can extract a suitable representation for the sentence. Choosing all tokens from all layers would yield an extremely memory demanding classification layer and may not yield the best model performance. Thus we choose the first embedding from the last layer L, the [CLS], as in Equation 2:

$$pooled_i = PLM_{L,[CLS]}(input_i) \qquad (2)$$

The regression module that follows the PLM is a linear fully connected layer, applying a linear transformation to the pooled encoder output data, changing the dimension of this data from the PLM hidden size to 1:

$$value_i = pooled_i W^T + b \qquad (3)$$

We then minimize the Mean Squared Error (MSE) loss between the predicted value and the gold label:

$$loss = MSE(value_i, goldlabel_i) \qquad (4)$$

## 3 Experimental Setup

### 3.1 Training Details

The models used are RoBERTa, DeBERTa and Longformer, all in both base and large versions from the Transformers library by Hugging Face (Wolf et al., 2020). The Adam (Kingma and Ba, 2014) optimizer is used with an initial learning rate of 1e-5 and 5e-5, for the encoder and the regression head, respectively with a layer-wise decay rate of 0.95 after each training epoch for the encoder. The encoder is frozen for the first epoch. The batch size is set to 4. Gradient clipping is set to 1.0. As stopping criteria, early stopping is used to terminate training if there is no decrease after 5 consecutive epochs on the validation set over MSE, for a maximum of 40 epochs. The checkpoint used for obtaining the results on the test set is the one that achieves the lowest MSE on the validation set. When running training to determine which backbone model for each trait or number of context-turns on the CONV-turn track for each trait should be used for training the final model, we use the provided validation set as test set and perform a 90:10 split of the provided training set into training and validation sets.

Our code is publicly available[1].

[1] https://github.com/patricia-pereira/wassa-sharedtask

### 3.2 Dataset

The shared task dataset consists in empathic reactions to news stories and associated conversations, containing dyadic conversations in reaction to news articles where there is harm to a person, group, or other (Omitaomu et al., 2022). These conversations are turn-level annotated in perceived empathy, emotion polarity, and emotion intensity, and dialogue-level annotated in terms of perceived counterparty empathy.

Given a conversation, the data is processed and fed to the model to train as depicted in Table 1:

**Conversation:**
P1: its a shame with the drought
P2: It's terrible what is happening to the world today!
P1: I know so much distruction
P2: Do you think it is human caused?
**Emotion Intensity:** 1.3333
**Emotion Polarity:** 1
**Empathy:** 1
P1: maybe probably thoug
P2: I wonder what will be done to fix the destruction.
P1: probably nothing humans don't really care
**Perceived Empathy of P1 rated by P2:** 1
**Track CONV-turn (Emotion Intensity)**
**Input:** [CLS] Do you think it is human caused? [SEP]
I know so much distruction [SEP]
It's terrible what is happening to the world today! [SEP]
**Output:** 1.3333
**Track CONV-dialog (Person 1)**
**Input:** [P1][CLS] its a shame with the drought [SEP]
It's terrible what is happening to the world today! [SEP]
I know so much distruction [SEP]
Do you think it is human caused? [SEP]
maybe probably thoug [SEP]
I wonder what will be done to fix the destruction. [SEP]
probably nothing humans don't really care [SEP]
**Output:** 1

Table 1: Example of raw data and how it is given as input/output pairs to train the model

## 4 Results and Analysis

### 4.1 Track CONV-turn

We now report the results of our approach for Track CONV-turn on the validation set. For representative purposes we only report the backbone model that yielded the best results, RoBERTa-large.

| $c$ | Polarity | Intensity | Empathy |
|---|---|---|---|
| 0 | 0.7292 | 0.6242 | 0.6262 |
| 1 | 0.7812 | 0.6490 | 0.6688 |
| 2 | 0.7869 | **0.6700** | 0.6828 |
| 3 | 0.7841 | 0.6615 | 0.6815 |
| 4 | 0.7828 | 0.6627 | **0.6895** |
| 5 | 0.7912 | 0.6672 | 0.6774 |
| 6 | **0.7928** | 0.6586 | 0.6727 |

Table 2: Submission results for track CONV-turn on the validation set. Evolution of the Pearson correlation score with the number of appended context turns.

The lowest performance in all traits is the one obtained without introducing any context turns, highlighting the importance of considering context. The general tendency is for the performance to increase with the progressive increase of the number of context turns, up to a performance peak which is trait specific, and then for it to decrease. For the purpose of the shared task only one random seed was used to generate results, but we use 5 random seeds in our previous work (Pereira et al., 2023) to validate this tendency. The peak of performance is obtained with 6 context turns for Emotion Polarity, 2 turns for Emotion Intensity and 4 turns for Empathy.

We now report the results of our approach for Track CONV-turn on the test set and compare it with the results of other teams.

| Team | Avg | Polarity | Intensity | Empathy |
|---|---|---|---|---|
| Ours | 0.626 | 0.679 | 0.622 | 0.577 |
| $2^{nd}$ | 0.623 | 0.680 | 0.607 | 0.582 |
| $3^{rd}$ | 0.610 | 0.671 | 0.601 | 0.559 |
| $4^{th}$ | 0.595 | 0.663 | 0.589 | 0.534 |
| $5^{th}$ | 0.590 | 0.644 | 0.581 | 0.544 |
| $6^{th}$ | 0.588 | 0.638 | 0.584 | 0.541 |
| $7^{th}$ | 0.477 | 0.422 | 0.473 | 0.534 |
| $8^{th}$ | -0.007 | -0.018 | 0.032 | 0.034 |
| $9^{th}$ | -0.030 | -0.020 | -0.043 | -0.027 |

Table 3: Submission results for track CONV-turn on the test set. Our model uses RoBERTa-large with the number of context turns which yielded the best results for each trait on the validation set.

Our team ranked first place amongst nine teams, with an average Pearson score of 0.626. Some teams scored Pearson scores very close to ours while some teams scored Pearson scores much lower and even negative. This may indicate a very diverse set of approaches resulting in different scores.

### 4.2 Track CONV-dialog

Regarding results for the track CONV-dialog on the validation set, the backbone model which yielded the best result, a Pearson correlation score of 0.3416, was RoBERTa-base. This model has a max token length of 512 and we truncate the input to respect that limit. As we feed all the conversation to the model, which usually exceeds 512 tokens, it could be expected that a backbone model such as the Longformer which has a max token length of 4016 would yield better results. These results could indicate that it is not necessary to feed all the conversation to evaluate perceived counterparty empathy.

We now report the results of our approach for Track CONV-dialog on the test set and compare it with the results of other teams.

| Team | Empathy |
|---|---|
| $1^{st}$ | 0.193 |
| Ours | 0.191 |
| $3^{rd}$ | 0.172 |
| $4^{th}$ | 0.012 |

Table 4: Submission results for track CONV-dialog on the test set. Our model uses RoBERTa-base.

We achieved a Pearson score of 0.191, just 0.002 below the top ranking submission, placing our team second in the ranking.

The result on the test set was notably lower than the result on the validation set. This can be due to the different distributions of the sets but also due to the fact that with this small dataset, the provided validation set and the validation set for choosing the model when performing the 90:10 split on the provided training set are not large enough to be representative.

## 5 Discussion

When comparing results of both tracks we observe that the result on the CONV-dialog track is significantly lower than the result on the CONV-turn track. This might be due to the fact that there are more mature approaches for emotion and empathy prediction in conversational turns, especially pertaining to the field of Emotion Recognition in Conversations (Pereira et al., 2022), while there are less approaches and datasets for the task of predicting perceived counterparty empathy from entire conversations.

## 6 Conclusion and Future Work

We presented an efficient approach for representing the selected historical conversational context for modelling of empathy and emotion in conversations. It consisted in feeding the appropriate conversational turns as input to a PLM and resorting to a simple regression head, contrasting with approaches that feed each turn to a PLM and then perform joint modelling of the turns with more complex modules. We modelled empathy, emotion polarity and emotion intensity of each utterance in a conversation by feeding the utterance to be classified together with its conversational context and modelled perceived counterparty empathy of each interlocutor by feeding all utterances from the conversation and a token identifying the interlocutor for which we were predicting the empathy. The official results of our submissions demonstrate the efficacy of our approach, both in selecting the appropriate conversational turns to be fed to the language model and in the way we feed these utterances.

Concerning future work directions, for the task of perceived counterparty empathy, since best results were obtained with RoBERTa that only takes 512 tokens, it would be interesting to explore feeding the final 512 tokens of the conversation instead of the initial, or a different window of tokens.

## 7 Limitations

While our approach to modelling perceived counterparty empathy seems very promising when validated with the shared task dataset, given our position in the leaderboard, it still attains a modest Pearson correlation score. Furthermore, confronting with other approaches on other datasets is necessary to claim its generalization ability and suggested superiority.

## Acknowledgments

This work was supported by Fundação para a Ciência e a Tecnologia (FCT), through Portuguese national funds, Ref. UIDB/50021/2020, DOI: 10.54499/UIDB/50021/2020 and Ref. UI/BD/154561/2022 and the Portuguese Recovery and Resilience Plan, through project C645008882-00000055 (Responsible.AI).

## References

Valentin Barriere, João Sedoc, Shabnam Tafreshi, and Salvatore Giorgi. 2023. Findings of wassa 2023 shared task on empathy, emotion and personality detection in conversation and reactions to news articles. In *Proceedings of the 13th Workshop on Computational Approaches to Subjectivity, Sentiment, & Social Media Analysis*, pages 511–525.

Iz Beltagy, Matthew E Peters, and Arman Cohan. 2020. Longformer: The long-document transformer. *arXiv preprint arXiv:2004.05150.*

Jacob Devlin, Ming-Wei Chang, Kenton Lee, and Kristina Toutanova. 2019. BERT: Pre-training of deep bidirectional transformers for language understanding. In *Proceedings of the 2019 Conference of the North American Chapter of the Association for Computational Linguistics: Human Language Technologies, Volume 1 (Long and Short Papers)*, pages 4171–4186, Minneapolis, Minnesota. Association for Computational Linguistics.

Salvatore Giorgi, João Sedoc, Valentin Barriere, and Shabnam Tafreshi. 2024. Findings of wassa 2024 shared task on empathy and personality detection in interactions. In *Proceedings of the 14th Workshop on Computational Approaches to Subjectivity, Sentiment, & Social Media Analysis.*

Pengcheng He, Xiaodong Liu, Jianfeng Gao, and Weizhu Chen. 2020. Deberta: Decoding-enhanced bert with disentangled attention. *arXiv preprint arXiv:2006.03654.*

Diederik P Kingma and Jimmy Ba. 2014. Adam: A method for stochastic optimization. *arXiv preprint arXiv:1412.6980.*

Jiangnan Li, Zheng Lin, Peng Fu, and Weiping Wang. 2021. Past, present, and future: Conversational emotion recognition through structural modeling of psychological knowledge. In *Findings of the Association for Computational Linguistics: EMNLP 2021*, pages 1204–1214, Punta Cana, Dominican Republic. Association for Computational Linguistics.

Yinhan Liu, Myle Ott, Naman Goyal, Jingfei Du, Mandar Joshi, Danqi Chen, Omer Levy, Mike Lewis, Luke Zettlemoyer, and Veselin Stoyanov. 2019. Roberta: A robustly optimized bert pretraining approach. *arXiv preprint arXiv:1907.11692.*

Damilola Omitaomu, Shabnam Tafreshi, Tingting Liu, Sven Buechel, Chris Callison-Burch, Johannes Eichstaedt, Lyle Ungar, and João Sedoc. 2022. Empathic conversations: A multi-level dataset of contextualized conversations. *arXiv preprint arXiv:2205.12698.*

Patrícia Pereira, Helena Moniz, and Joao Paulo Carvalho. 2022. Deep emotion recognition in textual conversations: A survey. *arXiv preprint arXiv:2211.09172.*

Patrícia Pereira, Helena Moniz, Isabel Dias, and Joao Paulo Carvalho. 2023. Context-dependent embedding utterance representations for emotion recognition in conversations. In *Proceedings of the 13th Workshop on Computational Approaches to Subjectivity, Sentiment, & Social Media Analysis*, pages 228–236, Toronto, Canada. Association for Computational Linguistics.

Soujanya Poria, Navonil Majumder, Rada Mihalcea, and Eduard Hovy. 2019. Emotion recognition in conversation: Research challenges, datasets, and recent advances. *IEEE Access*, 7:100943–100953.

Weizhou Shen, Siyue Wu, Yunyi Yang, and Xiaojun Quan. 2021. Directed acyclic graph network for conversational emotion recognition. In *Proceedings of the 59th Annual Meeting of the Association for Computational Linguistics and the 11th International Joint Conference on Natural Language Processing (Volume 1: Long Papers)*, pages 1551–1560, Online. Association for Computational Linguistics.

Thomas Wolf, Lysandre Debut, Victor Sanh, Julien Chaumond, Clement Delangue, Anthony Moi, Pierric Cistac, Tim Rault, Remi Louf, Morgan Funtowicz, Joe Davison, Sam Shleifer, Patrick von Platen, Clara Ma, Yacine Jernite, Julien Plu, Canwen Xu, Teven Le Scao, Sylvain Gugger, Mariama Drame, Quentin Lhoest, and Alexander Rush. 2020. Transformers: State-of-the-art natural language processing. In *Proceedings of the 2020 Conference on Empirical Methods in Natural Language Processing: System Demonstrations*, pages 38–45, Online. Association for Computational Linguistics.

# Findings of the WASSA 2024 EXALT Shared Task on Explainability for Cross-Lingual Emotion in Tweets

**Aaron Maladry, Pranaydeep Singh and Els Lefever**
LT3, Ghent University, Belgium
{aaron.maladry,pranaydeep.singh,els.lefever}@ugent.be

## Abstract

This paper presents a detailed description and results of the first shared task on explainability for cross-lingual emotion in tweets. Given a tweet in one of the five target languages (Dutch, Russian, Spanish, English, and French), systems should predict the correct emotion label (Task 1), as well as the words triggering the predicted emotion label (Task 2). The tweets were collected based on a list of stop words to prevent topical or emotional bias and were subsequently manually annotated. For both tasks, only a training corpus for English was provided, obliging participating systems to design cross-lingual approaches. Our shared task received submissions from 14 teams for the emotion detection task and from 6 teams for the trigger word detection task. The highest macro F1-scores obtained for both tasks are respectively 0.629 and 0.616, demonstrating that cross-lingual emotion detection is still a challenging task.

Emotion detection is a well-studied task in the field of NLP and has already been addressed in previous SemEval shared tasks (Mohammad et al., 2018; Chatterjee et al., 2019). In this shared task, however, we wanted to go one step further and offer a manually annotated multilingual benchmark data set, where not only emotions are labeled, but also the words triggering these emotions. To this end, we aim to investigate to what extent emotion information is transferable across languages, by offering training data in English, and evaluation data for 5 different target languages, namely Dutch, Russian, Spanish, English, and French. In addition, predicting trigger words should be a first step to endorsing emotion detection systems with a means to explain why a specific emotion has been predicted. With an ever-rising flurry of black-box models, we aim to foster research that moves towards the interpretability and explainability of systems.

As there is no real consensus on a standard emotion labeling framework, we opted to apply the label set of Debruyne et al. (2019), which is justified both theoretically and practically. Frequency and cluster analysis of tweet annotations resulted in a label set containing 5 emotions: *Love, Joy, Anger, Fear* and *Sadness*. This label set certainly shows a resemblance to Ekman's basic emotions, but due to the applied data-driven approach, the label set is more grounded in the task of emotion detection in social-media text. As we did not crawl our data based on emojis (as opposed to Debruyne et al.), we also added a *neutral* emotion label to the emotion label set.

## 1 Dataset Construction

We present a fully annotated dataset of multilingual tweets that were gathered using the Twitter API. The dataset includes a variety of 5 European languages, including Dutch, Russian, Spanish, English and French. For each of these languages, we collected the tweets based on a list of stop words that originate from either Spacy (Honnibal and Montani, 2017) or NLTK (Bird et al., 2009) depending on the availability for the language. The stopwords were subsequently manually filtered by native speakers to remove any incorrect entries or content words. The selected tweets do not target a specific time frame, although we did exclude the COVID-19 years 2019-2021 to avoid a topical bias. With the use of stop words, the collected data is less likely to be affected by specific topical or emotional biases that can be inherited from search terms. After collecting a significant batch of about 200,000 tweets (excluding retweets), we randomly selected subsets to annotate for each language.

For the emotion labeling process, the annotators were provided with detailed annotation guidelines (Singh et al., 2023). The first level of annotations describes only the primary emotion expressed by the text, for which we assume the perspective



*Proceedings of the 14th Workshop on Computational Approaches to Subjectivity, Sentiment, & Social Media Analysis*, pages 454–463
August 15, 2024 

of the reader and answer the question "Which emotion do you think the writer intends to convey?". This means we only employ a single emotion label. As mentioned before, the emotion labels we use here are Love, Joy, Fear, Sadness, Anger and Neutral. These labels were the outcome of a broad study (De Bruyne et al., 2019), where annotations for 25 specific emotion labels were clustered into 5 broader categories, to which we added the neutral class. In the annotation guidelines, we provided all labels that are grouped under this broader emotion class as helper labels. The label "anger", for instance, groups the fine-grained emotion labels "disgust", "frustration", "rage" and "resentment". Inspecting these fine-grained labels can help the annotator to confidently choose the coarse-grained emotion label ("anger"). All annotators indicated they found this helpful when deciding between two similar positive emotions, such as "love" and "joy". As the collected tweets are gathered in a manner that aims to collect as generic data as possible, this also resulted in a lot of noise. Many tweets rely on specific contextual information, and as a result, some tweets cannot be interpreted and annotated reliably. Moreover, many tweets are obvious "spam" tweets, posted by automated bots. For these tweets, we introduced a "discard" label as an addition to the emotion label set. The tweets labeled with this discard label, which is around 30% of the annotated data, are excluded from the shared task to guard the quality of the annotations. Figure 1 illustrates the annotation of the emotion labels per tweet.

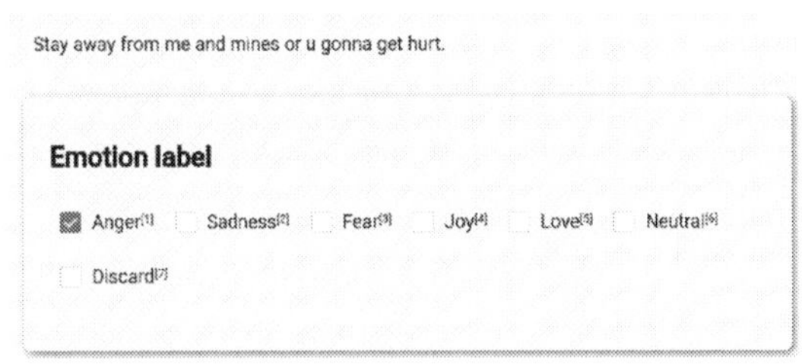


Figure 1: Sub-task 1: Annotation of Emotion label

To gauge the inter-annotator agreement for our labeling scheme, we tested the annotation scheme for Dutch, which is the native language of our 5 annotators. On a subset of 50 samples, we calculated Fleiss' Kappa (Fleiss, 1971), resulting in a moderate agreement score of 0.62, which can be considered satisfactory given the subjective nature of this task. Moreover, this agreement study includes the tweets that were annotated with the "discard" label. For the shared task train and test data, we remove these discards and therefore expect higher agreement on the actual emotion labels.

In addition to these primary emotion labels, the annotators were also instructed to identify the words that evoke that emotion. As these are the words that "trigger" the emotion, we refer to them as **trigger words** (Schroth et al., 2005). As a guideline to aid in identifying these trigger words, we instructed the annotators to imagine the text without one or more of the words. If the emotion changes or disappears when the words are removed or replaced, it points to the vitality of these words in identifying the emotion. Emojis, emoticons, and punctuation (such as ... and ! or ???) can also be indicated as a trigger. Detailed information on how these trigger words have been labeled can be found in the annotation guidelines (Singh et al., 2023). Figure 2 shows an example of the trigger words selected for a specific tweet.

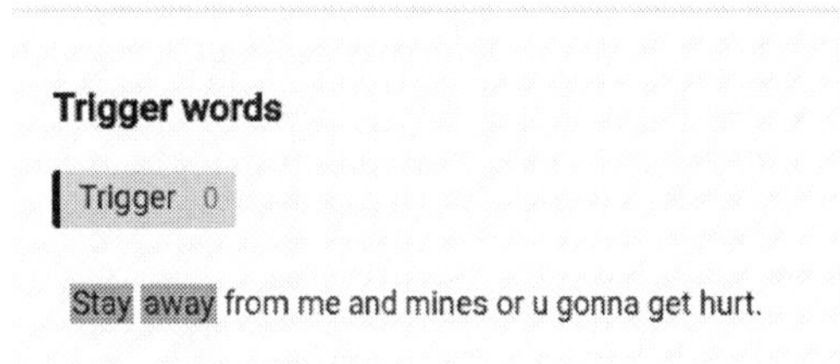


Figure 2: Sub-task 2: Annotation of trigger words.

We conceptualize trigger word detection as a binary token classification task, and calculate evaluation metrics in a pairwise manner, taking each annotator as the gold standard. For agreement on span detection tasks, Mathet et al. (2015) propose a gamma metric for unified class- and span agreement. More specifically, we employed soft gamma, which allows multiple-span annotations of an annotator to be matched with a single continuous span of another annotator. This makes sense for this task because it does not matter whether the important words are annotated as a continuous span or split into multiple shorter spans as long as they still correspond to the larger span. Using this metric, we calculated the agreement for each sentence and then averaged it to attain a corpus-level agreement score. This results in a soft gamma score of 0.4383, indicating that this task is quite subjective but still shows fair agreement (with a 0 gamma score representing random agreement and a 1 indicating complete agreement). Whilst this metric is created for span agreement in particular, there are a few arguments against its use for our trigger word detection task. Firstly, averaging across all sentences somewhat defeats the purpose of using a chance-corrected agreement metric because the agreement is only calculated on a sentence level and not on a corpus level. Secondly, it would be possible to calculate this agreement on the corpus level by concatenating the sentences, but in that case, longer sentences would have a higher impact on the score than shorter sentences, which is not a desired effect. To circumvent these limitations, we decided to evaluate the agreement between annotators based on Hamming distance and Mean Average Precision. *Hamming distance* is an edit distance metric that counts the words with wrongly assigned labels relative to the number of tokens in a sentence. In addition, we use *Mean Average Precision*, a popular metric for the evaluation of feature importance attribution techniques (Atanasova et al., 2020). Table 1 shows the agreement of trigger word annotations on the Dutch and English sets. The scores for Hamming distance are very small, which indicates that the span annotations are overall rather similar and that no annotators use significantly more trigger words than others. At the same time, the modest MAP scores indicate that the exact words that are essential for one annotator, may not be as essential for the others.

| | Hamming | MAP |
|---|---|---|
| Dutch Pairwise | 0.04 | 0.13 |
| English Pairwise | 0.03 | 0.18 |

Table 1: Trigger word annotation agreement

## 2 Tasks and Evaluation

Based on the manually annotated data set, we present the following two sub-tasks.

### 2.1 Cross-lingual Emotion Detection Task

The first task is to predict the correct emotion label for each tweet from 6 possible classes: *Love, Joy, Anger, Fear, Sadness, Neutral* in five target languages. More concretely, we present the participants with a train set of 5000 English tweets, a multi-lingual development set of 500 tweets and a multi-lingual test set of 2500.[1] The participants are free to use additional training resources, though they should be restricted to English only to evaluate the efficacy of the cross-lingual setup. Evaluation of this classification task is performed through macro-averaged precision, recall, and F1-score metrics, with the systems ranked based on their F1-score.

### 2.2 Prediction of the text span triggering the predicted emotion label

For the second task, we propose trigger word detection, a task that is focused on explaining which words are used to express the emotion. For the trigger word detection task, we discarded tweets that did not contain any trigger words, which leaves us with a train set of 3000 English tweets, a multilingual development set of 300 samples, and a multi-lingual test set of 832 samples. To evaluate the scores of the systems of our participants, we considered two evaluation methods. Firstly, we can evaluate trigger word detection as a binary token classification task. We propose using macro-averaged token F1-score for this purpose to overcome the label imbalance (with most tokens not being trigger words). In addition, as we anticipate the use of post-hoc explainability algorithms, we expect some of the authors to generate numerical importance tokens instead of binary indicators for each word. To evaluate these numerical importances, we employ Accumulated Precise Importance attribution, or API-score (Maladry et al., 2024). This is a sentence-level metric that sums up the (normalized) numerical importance of each trigger word token (based on human annotations). To illustrate, the API score for Example 1 equals 95% (33 + 18 + 19 + 25), with only 5% of the total importance being attributed to a non-trigger word.

**Example 1**

| | *sad* | *about* | *my* | *rejected* | *paper* | *:(* |
|---|---|---|---|---|---|---|
| *HUM.* | *1* | *0* | *0* | *1* | *1* | *1* |
| *IMP.* | *.33* | *0* | *.05* | *.18* | *.19* | *.25* |

## 3 Applied Methodologies

### 3.1 Baseline

Our baseline model for cross-lingual emotion detection employs an XLM-RoBERTa model finetuned on the English training data. As the ideal system setup makes use of a single model and can provide ad-hoc explainable predicts, we continued from the same fine-tuned emotion detection model for trigger word detection and applied the Layer

[1] All data is publicly available after registration through `https://huggingface.co/datasets/pranaydeeps/EXALT-v1`.

Integrated Gradients (Sundararajan et al., 2017) algorithm with transformers-interpret[2] to generate sub-token importance.[3] After matching these sub-token importance attributions back to the original words and normalizing them, we achieved the predictions for our numerical trigger word detection task. We converted all word-level importances to binary vectors based on the numerical values. All words with an importance value above 10% (compared to the total importance attributions in the sentence) were considered trigger words based on an exploratory study on a validation set. This conversion is illustrated in Example 2.[4]

**Example 2**

| | *sad* | *about* | *my* | *rejected* | *paper* | *:(* |
|---|---|---|---|---|---|---|
| *HUM.* | *1* | *0* | *0* | *1* | *1* | *1* |
| *IMP.* | *.33* | *0* | *.05* | *.18* | *.19* | *.25* |
| *x=10%* | *1* | *0* | *0* | *1* | *1* | *1* |

### 3.2 Participating Teams

As shown in Table 2, most participants to our shared task used fine-tuned large generative models like GPT4 and GPT3.5 (OpenAI et al., 2024), Gemma (Team et al., 2024), LLaMa-3 (AI@Meta, 2024), etc.

Besides the data we provided for the shared task, many participants also used external resources, such as earlier shared tasks for emotion detection (Mohammad et al., 2018; Chatterjee et al., 2019), and data augmentation methods. These augmentation methods often include translation to the target languages. Backtranslation was also a frequently employed method to augment the data.

For the trigger word detection tasks most teams started with a fine-tuned token classification system to calculate the numerical scores for the numerical trigger word detection task. In contrast, some systems started from a classification model and employed the same importance attributions techniques used by the baseline model. Although many parameters, thresholds, and different feature importance algorithms can be experimented with, the participants did not explore this extensively.

Some of the more distinct approaches for the shared task employed multi-agent workflows (Cheng et al., 2024a) and label projection with trigger word switching (Šmíd et al., 2024).

## 4 Results

### 4.1 Emotion Detection

As shown in Table 3, all 14 submitting teams outperformed the baseline score of 0.4476 macro-F1 for the emotion detection sub-task. Team 1024m (Kadiyala, 2024) had the best-performing system by quite a big margin with a macro-F1 of 0.6295 on the test set. The team utilized an ensemble of Gemma (Team et al., 2024), Claude-Opus[5], Llama-3 (AI@Meta, 2024), Mistral-v2-7B (Jiang et al., 2023) and applied majority voting for the final prediction. The second-best system, Team BCSZ (Cheng et al., 2024a), also employed an ensemble of generative models with the addition of different varieties of Agentic Workflows where an additional decision-making LM is deployed to make the final prediction based on the output of the individual LMs. Team DKE-Research (Wang et al., 2024) submitted the best-performing system without using large generative LMs directly or indirectly, with a macro-F1 of 0.5661. The team utilized knowledge distillation by training a monolingual English teacher model for emotion and transferring the knowledge to a multilingual model.

### 4.2 Binary Trigger Word detection

For the second sub-task of Binary Trigger Word Detection, again all 6 submitting teams comprehensively beat the baseline of sub-token importance using Layer Integrated Gradients. Team CT-cloud (Zhang et al., 2024) had the best-performing system (0.6158) by a small margin of 0.0063 macro-F1. The team applied token classification at the sub-word level, using the highest confidence among the sub-words as the confidence of each word. Most teams used similar post-hoc explainability approaches, while some utilized multi-task learning techniques. Team NYCU-NLP (Lin et al., 2024) used an ensemble of two large generative LMs (Starling-7B (2023) and Llama3-8B (2024)) with instruction fine-tuning.

### 4.3 Numerical Trigger Word Detection

The leader board of the Numerical Trigger Word Detection sub-task was identical to the Binary Triggers sub-task with one exception. Team UWB (Šmíd et al., 2024), which had the 3rd best

[2] `https://github.com/cdpierse/transformers-interpret`

[3] The code (and models) used for the baselines is publicly available through `https://github.com/pranaydeeps/WASSA24_EXALT/tree/main/starters_kit`.

[4] This example originates from Maladry et al. (2024), where x signifies the chosen threshold for converting a numerical attribution to a binary indicator.

[5] https://www.anthropic.com/claude

| Team Name | Emotion Rank | Binary Triggers Rank | Numerical Triggers Rank | Large Generative Language Models | Fine-tuning | Translation | Augmentation | Joint Modelling |
|---|---|---|---|---|---|---|---|---|
| 1024m | 1 | - | - | ✓ | ✓ | ✗ | ✗ | ✗ |
| BCSZ | 2 | 6 | 6 | ✓ | ✓ | ✗ | ✗ | ✗ |
| Treehouse | 3 | - | - | ✓ | ✗ | ✗ | ✓ | ✗ |
| NYCU-NLP | 4 | 5 | 5 | ✓ | ✓ | ✗ | ✗ | ✓ |
| HITSZ-HLT | 6 | 2 | 3 | ✗ | ✓ | ✓ | ✗ | ✓ |
| UWB | 7 | 3 | 1 | ✓ | ✓ | ✓ | ✗ | ✗ |
| wu_tlaxe | 8 | - | - | ✓ | ✓ | ✓ | ✗ | ✗ |
| DKE-Research | 9 | - | - | ✗ | ✓ | ✓ | ✗ | ✗ |
| NLPNewcomer | 10 | 4 | 4 | ✗ | ✓ | ✗ | ✗ | ✓ |
| CTcloud | 11 | 1 | 2 | ✗ | ✓ | ✗ | ✓ | ✗ |
| PCICUNAM | 12 | - | - | ✗ | ✓ | ✓ | ✗ | ✗ |
| LLiiMas | 13 | - | - | ✗ | ✓ | ✓ | ✗ | ✗ |
| EXALT-Baseline | 15 | 7 | 7 | ✗ | ✓ | ✗ | ✗ | ✗ |

Table 2: An overview of the methodologies used by the teams for the shared task and their overall rankings on the respective leaderboards of each sub-task.

| Team | Emotion_F1 |
|---|---|
| 1024m (Kadiyala, 2024) | 0.6295 |
| BCSZ (Cheng et al., 2024a) | 0.6046 |
| Treehouse (Cheng et al., 2024b) | 0.6015 |
| NYCU-NLP (Lin et al., 2024) | 0.5951 |
| CTYUN-AI | 0.5911 |
| HITSZ-HLT (Xiong et al., 2024) | 0.591 |
| UWB (Šmíd et al., 2024) | 0.591 |
| wu_tlaxe (Davenport et al., 2024) | 0.573 |
| DKE-Research (Wang et al., 2024) | 0.5661 |
| NLPNewcomer | 0.5444 |
| CTcloud (Zhang et al., 2024) | 0.5428 |
| PCICUNAM (Vázquez-Osorio et al., 2024) | 0.5183 |
| LLiiMas (Vázquez-Osorio and Gómez-Adorno, 2024) | 0.5067 |
| EXALT-Baseline | 0.4476 |

Table 3: Leader board based on macro-averaged F1-scores for Emotion Detection

| Team | Token F1 |
|---|---|
| CTcloud (Zhang et al., 2024) | 0.6158 |
| HITSZ-HLT (Xiong et al., 2024) | 0.6095 |
| UWB (Šmíd et al., 2024) | 0.5919 |
| NLPNewcomer | 0.5785 |
| NYCU-NLP (Lin et al., 2024) | 0.5636 |
| BCSZ (Cheng et al., 2024a) | 0.4778 |
| EXALT-Baseline | 0.2349 |

Table 4: Leader board based on macro-averaged token F1-score for trigger word detection.

| Team | API-score |
|---|---|
| UWB (Šmíd et al., 2024) | 0.7052 |
| CTcloud (Zhang et al., 2024) | 0.6972 |
| HITSZ-HLT (Xiong et al., 2024) | 0.6961 |
| NLP_Newcomer | 0.658 |
| NYCU-NLP (Lin et al., 2024) | 0.6442 |
| BCSZ (Cheng et al., 2024a) | 0.4548 |
| EXALT-Baseline | 0.216 |

Table 5: Leader board based on Accumulated Precise Importance for trigger word detection.

system for the binary task, achieved 1st place for the numerical triggers based on the API (Accumulated Precise Importance) metric. The methodology involved translating the English data into the target languages to generate additional training data while using special symbols for the trigger words to transfer them to the target language. They also utilize trigger-word switching, i.e., swapping trigger words between an English sentence and a translated sentence in one of the target languages. These simple yet ingenious ideas led to the best-performing system with an API-score of 0.7052.

## 5 Discussion

For this shared task, all teams experimented with widely varying methods for system fine-tuning and prompting large generative LMs (see Table 2), and these approaches have also resulted in some of the best systems for the first sub-task. The top 8 teams have directly or indirectly (Team HITSZ-HLT has indirectly used ChatGPT for augmenting their data) employed generative LMs. It is, however, surprising to see limited experimentation with approaches tailored for cross-lingual tasks such as MAD-X (Pfeiffer et al., 2020) or BLOOMZ (Muennighoff et al., 2023).

Figures 3 and 4 also visualize some interesting findings for individual emotion labels in the test set, as well as for each target language. *Neutral* and *Anger* seem to be the easiest emotions to label, while *Fear* is often the hardest. This can be attributed to the class imbalance as *Fear* had the least samples in the train and test sets by a significant margin. For the languages, surprisingly, English is not the best-performing target language. All systems performed best on the Spanish test set, while

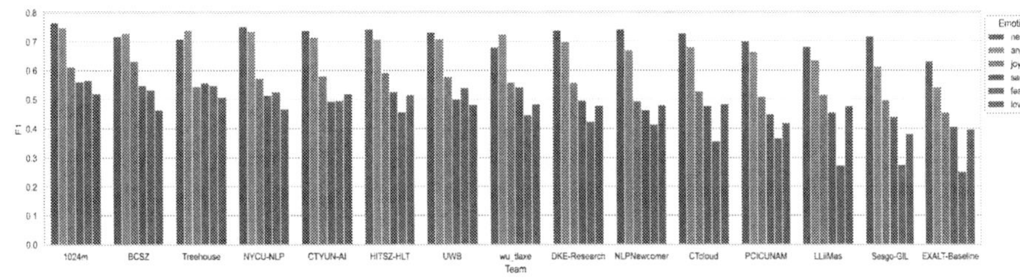


Figure 3: Scores per emotion label

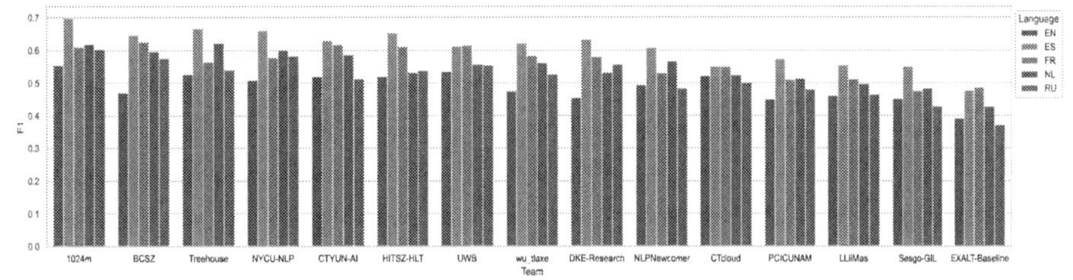


Figure 4: Scores per language

English and Russian were often the hardest. For detailed scores per emotion and per language for each system, please refer to Table 6.

It is also worthwhile to note that none of the teams experimented with alternate methodologies for sub-word attributions which is considered one of the cornerstones of explainability for LLMs or other ad-hoc explainability ideas. One of the more unique approaches for trigger word detection was the trigger word switching for data augmentation, applied by Team UWB, which relies on specifically translating (some or all) trigger words to the target languages. A few teams (NYCU-NLP, HITSZ-HLT, NLPNewcomer) employed joint multi-task approaches for the 3 sub-tasks. While these approaches are somewhere between post-hoc and ad-hoc interpretability, and therefore more interpretable than most of the post-hoc approaches proposed, they did not result in the top-performing system for the trigger-word detection sub-tasks.

## 6 Conclusion & Future work

In this shared task, we were able to fully work out our annotation scheme and streamline the annotation process for labeling emotion and trigger words for emotion. Thanks to our participants, we could investigate the cross-lingual transfer from English to a variety of European languages. Whilst cross-lingual transfer remains a relevant research topic, transferring to some languages is easier than others. As shown by related work, the difficulty of language transfer can be affected by different factors, such as the relatedness of the source and target language (de Vries et al., 2022) and whether or not the two languages share the same script (Zubillaga et al., 2024). The quantity of available resources for both languages, but especially the target language is highly relevant. This leaves us with three particular challenges: language relatedness, the availability of a shared script, and the availability of language resources. In the current run of the task, this was kept in check by selecting only European languages that (1) have sufficient resources, (2) are closely related and (3) share the same Latin script. Therefore, one of our goals for future runs of the shared task would be to expand the evaluation pool to languages that are strongly impacted by these difficulties.

In addition, whilst the approaches for cross-lingual explainability for emotion detection work quite well, one of the downsides remains that they are restricted to post-hoc explainability, often employing a separate system that is trained specifically for the explanation but is not explainable intrinsically. For that reason, we suggest future work to investigate the development of inherently (ad-hoc) explainable approaches.

| Team | EN | ES | FR | NL | RU | neutral | joy | sadness | anger | fear | love |
|---|---|---|---|---|---|---|---|---|---|---|---|
| 1024m | 0.55 | 0.70 | 0.61 | 0.62 | 0.60 | 0.77 | 0.61 | 0.56 | 0.75 | 0.57 | 0.52 |
| BCSZ | 0.47 | 0.65 | 0.63 | 0.60 | 0.58 | 0.72 | 0.63 | 0.55 | 0.73 | 0.53 | 0.47 |
| Treehouse | 0.53 | 0.67 | 0.56 | 0.62 | 0.54 | 0.71 | 0.55 | 0.56 | 0.74 | 0.55 | 0.51 |
| NYCU-NLP | 0.51 | 0.66 | 0.58 | 0.60 | 0.58 | 0.75 | 0.57 | 0.51 | 0.74 | 0.53 | 0.47 |
| CTYUN-AI | 0.52 | 0.63 | 0.62 | 0.59 | 0.51 | 0.74 | 0.58 | 0.49 | 0.72 | 0.50 | 0.52 |
| HITSZ-HLT | 0.52 | 0.65 | 0.61 | 0.53 | 0.54 | 0.74 | 0.59 | 0.53 | 0.71 | 0.46 | 0.52 |
| UWB | 0.53 | 0.61 | 0.62 | 0.56 | 0.55 | 0.73 | 0.58 | 0.50 | 0.71 | 0.54 | 0.48 |
| wu_tlaxe | 0.48 | 0.62 | 0.58 | 0.56 | 0.53 | 0.68 | 0.56 | 0.54 | 0.73 | 0.45 | 0.48 |
| DKE-Research | 0.45 | 0.63 | 0.58 | 0.53 | 0.56 | 0.74 | 0.56 | 0.50 | 0.70 | 0.42 | 0.48 |
| NLPNewcomer | 0.49 | 0.61 | 0.53 | 0.57 | 0.48 | 0.74 | 0.49 | 0.46 | 0.67 | 0.41 | 0.48 |
| CTcloud | 0.52 | 0.55 | 0.55 | 0.52 | 0.50 | 0.73 | 0.53 | 0.48 | 0.68 | 0.36 | 0.48 |
| PCICUNAM | 0.45 | 0.57 | 0.51 | 0.51 | 0.48 | 0.70 | 0.51 | 0.45 | 0.66 | 0.37 | 0.42 |
| LLiiMas | 0.46 | 0.55 | 0.51 | 0.50 | 0.46 | 0.68 | 0.52 | 0.46 | 0.64 | 0.27 | 0.48 |
| Sesgo-GIL | 0.45 | 0.55 | 0.48 | 0.48 | 0.43 | 0.72 | 0.50 | 0.44 | 0.61 | 0.27 | 0.38 |
| EXALT-Baseline | 0.39 | 0.48 | 0.49 | 0.43 | 0.37 | 0.63 | 0.46 | 0.41 | 0.54 | 0.25 | 0.40 |

Table 6: F1-scores for Emotion detection with fine-grained analysis for individual languages and emotion labels.

## Limitations

Emotion detection and explaining which part of a text is expressing the emotion are both highly subjective tasks. This is also reflected by the IAA scores included in this study. In our work, we are limited to single-annotator labels and were not able to provide multiple perspectives because that would significantly increase the annotation workload. Furthermore, we would need to find more annotators for all languages, which was not practically feasible. In addition, our annotation scheme does not allow multi-label classification, meaning that texts that contain multiple emotions were either labeled by their primary, most present, emotion or had to be discarded when there was a mix. For future work, we believe it would be interesting to take a closer look at the tweets that were discarded in this study to distinguish multi-emotion tweets from tweets that could not be understood without context. Furthermore, our study is still limited to European languages, which are relatively closely related. We expect that transferring models for emotion detection to unrelated or more distantly related languages is significantly harder and poses an interesting avenue for future research.

## Acknowledgments

Our special thanks go out to the student workers who performed the emotion annotation work for this shared task: Cas Van Raemdonck, Febe Coussée, Fran Meulebrouck, Jef Naert, Robbe Verwerft, and Wout Boven. This work was supported by Ghent University under grant BOF.24Y.2021.0019.01 .

## References

AI@Meta. 2024. Llama 3 model card.

Pepa Atanasova, Jakob Grue Simonsen, Christina Lioma, and Isabelle Augenstein. 2020. A diagnostic study of explainability techniques for text classification. In *Proceedings of the 2020 Conference on Empirical Methods in Natural Language Processing (EMNLP)*, pages 3256–3274, Online. Association for Computational Linguistics.

Steven Bird, Ewan Klein, and Edward Loper. 2009. *Natural language processing with Python: analyzing text with the natural language toolkit.* " O'Reilly Media, Inc.".

Ankush Chatterjee, Kedhar Nath Narahari, Meghana Joshi, and Puneet Agrawal. 2019. SemEval-2019 task 3: EmoContext contextual emotion detection in text. In *Proceedings of the 13th International Workshop on Semantic Evaluation*, pages 39–48, Minneapolis, Minnesota, USA. Association for Computational Linguistics.

Long Cheng, Qihao Shao, Chrisitine Zhao, Sheng Bi, and Gina-Anne Levow. 2024a. Teii: Think, explain, interact and iterate with large language models to solve cross-lingual emotion detection. In *Proceedings of the 14th Workshop of on Computational Approaches to Subjectivity, Sentiment & Social Media Analysis@ACL 2024*, Bangkok, Thailand.

Yao-Fei Cheng, Jeongyeob Hong, Andrew Wang, Anita Silva, and Gina-Anne Levow. 2024b. Treehouse at wassa 2024 shared task2: Explainability for cross-lingual emotion in tweets. In *Proceedings of the 14th Workshop of on Computational Approaches to Subjectivity, Sentiment & Social Media Analysis@ACL 2024*, Bangkok, Thailand.

Jon Davenport, Keren Ruditsky, Anna Batra, and Yulha Lhawa. 2024. Wu_tlaxe at wassa 2024 explainability for cross-lingual emotion in tweets shared task 1: Emotion through translation using twhin-bert and gpt. In *Proceedings of the 14th Workshop of on Computational Approaches to Subjectivity, Sentiment & Social Media Analysis@ACL 2024*, Bangkok, Thailand.

Luna De Bruyne, Orphée De Clercq, and Veronique Hoste. 2019. Towards an empirically grounded framework for emotion analysis. In *Proceedings of HUSO 2019, the fifth international conference on human and social analytics*, pages 11–16. IARIA, International Academy, Research, and Industry Association.

Wietse de Vries, Martijn Wieling, and Malvina Nissim. 2022. Make the best of cross-lingual transfer: Evidence from POS tagging with over 100 languages. In *Proceedings of the 60th Annual Meeting of the Association for Computational Linguistics (Volume 1: Long Papers)*, pages 7676–7685, Dublin, Ireland. Association for Computational Linguistics.

Joseph L Fleiss. 1971. Measuring nominal scale agreement among many raters. *Psychological bulletin*, 76(5):378.

Matthew Honnibal and Ines Montani. 2017. spaCy 2: Natural language understanding with Bloom embeddings, convolutional neural networks and incremental parsing. To appear.

Albert Q. Jiang, Alexandre Sablayrolles, Arthur Mensch, Chris Bamford, Devendra Singh Chaplot, Diego de las Casas, Florian Bressand, Gianna Lengyel, Guillaume Lample, Lucile Saulnier, Lélio Renard Lavaud, Marie-Anne Lachaux, Pierre Stock, Teven Le Scao, Thibaut Lavril, Thomas Wang, Timothée Lacroix, and William El Sayed. 2023. Mistral 7b. *Preprint*, arXiv:2310.06825.

Ram Mohan Rao Kadiyala. 2024. Large language models for cross-lingual emotion detection. In *Proceedings of the 14th Workshop of on Computational Approaches to Subjectivity, Sentiment & Social Media Analysis@ACL 2024*, Bangkok, Thailand.

Tzu-mi Lin, Zhe-Yu Xu, Jian-Yu Zhou, and Lung-Hao Lee. 2024. Assembling large language models for cross-lingual emotion and trigger detection. In *Proceedings of the 14th Workshop of on Computational Approaches to Subjectivity, Sentiment & Social Media Analysis@ACL 2024*, Bangkok, Thailand.

Aaron Maladry, Alessandra Teresa Cignarella, Els Lefever, Cynthia van Hee, and Veronique Hoste. 2024. Human and system perspectives on the expression of irony: An analysis of likelihood labels and rationales. In *Proceedings of the 2024 Joint International Conference on Computational Linguistics, Language Resources and Evaluation (LREC-COLING 2024)*, pages 8372–8382, Torino, Italia. ELRA and ICCL.

Yann Mathet, Antoine Widlöcher, and Jean-Philippe Métivier. 2015. The unified and holistic method gamma ($\gamma$) for inter-annotator agreement measure and alignment. *Computational Linguistics*, 41(3):437–479.

Saif Mohammad, Felipe Bravo-Marquez, Mohammad Salameh, and Svetlana Kiritchenko. 2018. SemEval-2018 task 1: Affect in tweets. In *Proceedings of the 12th International Workshop on Semantic Evaluation*, pages 1–17, New Orleans, Louisiana. Association for Computational Linguistics.

Niklas Muennighoff, Thomas Wang, Lintang Sutawika, Adam Roberts, Stella Biderman, Teven Le Scao, M Saiful Bari, Sheng Shen, Zheng-Xin Yong, Hailey Schoelkopf, Xiangru Tang, Dragomir Radev, Alham Fikri Aji, Khalid Almubarak, Samuel Albanie, Zaid Alyafeai, Albert Webson, Edward Raff, and Colin Raffel. 2023. Crosslingual generalization through multitask finetuning. *Preprint*, arXiv:2211.01786.

OpenAI, Josh Achiam, Steven Adler, Sandhini Agarwal, Lama Ahmad, Ilge Akkaya, Florencia Leoni Aleman, Diogo Almeida, Janko Altenschmidt, Sam Altman, Shyamal Anadkat, Red Avila, Igor Babuschkin, Suchir Balaji, Valerie Balcom, Paul Baltescu, Haiming Bao, Mohammad Bavarian, Jeff Belgum, Irwan Bello, Jake Berdine, Gabriel Bernadett-Shapiro, Christopher Berner, Lenny Bogdonoff, Oleg Boiko, Madelaine Boyd, Anna-Luisa Brakman, Greg Brockman, Tim Brooks, Miles Brundage, Kevin Button, Trevor Cai, Rosie Campbell, Andrew Cann, Brittany Carey, Chelsea Carlson, Rory Carmichael, Brooke Chan, Che Chang, Fotis Chantzis, Derek Chen, Sully Chen, Ruby Chen, Jason Chen, Mark Chen, Ben Chess, Chester Cho, Casey Chu, Hyung Won Chung, Dave Cummings, Jeremiah Currier, Yunxing Dai, Cory Decareaux, Thomas Degry, Noah Deutsch, Damien Deville, Arka Dhar, David Dohan, Steve Dowling, Sheila Dunning, Adrien Ecoffet, Atty Eleti, Tyna Eloundou, David Farhi, Liam Fedus, Niko Felix, Simón Posada Fishman, Juston Forte, Isabella Fulford, Leo Gao, Elie Georges, Christian Gibson, Vik Goel, Tarun Gogineni, Gabriel Goh, Rapha Gontijo-Lopes, Jonathan Gordon, Morgan Grafstein, Scott Gray, Ryan Greene, Joshua Gross, Shixiang Shane Gu, Yufei Guo, Chris Hallacy, Jesse Han, Jeff Harris, Yuchen He, Mike Heaton, Johannes Heidecke, Chris Hesse, Alan Hickey, Wade Hickey, Peter Hoeschele, Brandon Houghton, Kenny Hsu, Shengli Hu, Xin Hu, Joost Huizinga, Shantanu Jain, Shawn Jain, Joanne Jang, Angela Jiang, Roger Jiang, Haozhun Jin, Denny Jin, Shino Jomoto, Billie Jonn, Heewoo Jun, Tomer Kaftan, Łukasz Kaiser, Ali Kamali, Ingmar Kanitscheider, Nitish Shirish Keskar, Tabarak Khan, Logan Kilpatrick, Jong Wook Kim, Christina Kim, Yongjik Kim, Jan Hendrik Kirchner, Jamie Kiros, Matt Knight, Daniel Kokotajlo, Łukasz Kondraciuk, Andrew Kondrich, Aris Konstantinidis, Kyle Kosic, Gretchen Krueger, Vishal Kuo, Michael Lampe, Ikai Lan, Teddy Lee, Jan Leike, Jade Leung, Daniel Levy, Chak Ming Li, Rachel Lim, Molly Lin, Stephanie Lin, Mateusz Litwin, Theresa Lopez, Ryan Lowe, Patricia Lue, Anna Makanju, Kim Malfacini, Sam Manning, Todor Markov, Yaniv Markovski, Bianca Martin, Katie Mayer, Andrew Mayne, Bob McGrew, Scott Mayer McKinney, Christine McLeavey, Paul McMillan, Jake McNeil, David Medina, Aalok Mehta, Jacob Menick, Luke Metz, Andrey Mishchenko, Pamela Mishkin, Vinnie Monaco, Evan Morikawa, Daniel Mossing, Tong Mu, Mira Murati, Oleg Murk, David

Mély, Ashvin Nair, Reiichiro Nakano, Rajeev Nayak, Arvind Neelakantan, Richard Ngo, Hyeonwoo Noh, Long Ouyang, Cullen O'Keefe, Jakub Pachocki, Alex Paino, Joe Palermo, Ashley Pantuliano, Giambattista Parascandolo, Joel Parish, Emy Parparita, Alex Passos, Mikhail Pavlov, Andrew Peng, Adam Perelman, Filipe de Avila Belbute Peres, Michael Petrov, Henrique Ponde de Oliveira Pinto, Michael, Pokorny, Michelle Pokrass, Vitchyr H. Pong, Tolly Powell, Alethea Power, Boris Power, Elizabeth Proehl, Raul Puri, Alec Radford, Jack Rae, Aditya Ramesh, Cameron Raymond, Francis Real, Kendra Rimbach, Carl Ross, Bob Rotsted, Henri Roussez, Nick Ryder, Mario Saltarelli, Ted Sanders, Shibani Santurkar, Girish Sastry, Heather Schmidt, David Schnurr, John Schulman, Daniel Selsam, Kyla Sheppard, Toki Sherbakov, Jessica Shieh, Sarah Shoker, Pranav Shyam, Szymon Sidor, Eric Sigler, Maddie Simens, Jordan Sitkin, Katarina Slama, Ian Sohl, Benjamin Sokolowsky, Yang Song, Natalie Staudacher, Felipe Petroski Such, Natalie Summers, Ilya Sutskever, Jie Tang, Nikolas Tezak, Madeleine B. Thompson, Phil Tillet, Amin Tootoonchian, Elizabeth Tseng, Preston Tuggle, Nick Turley, Jerry Tworek, Juan Felipe Cerón Uribe, Andrea Vallone, Arun Vijayvergiya, Chelsea Voss, Carroll Wainwright, Justin Jay Wang, Alvin Wang, Ben Wang, Jonathan Ward, Jason Wei, CJ Weinmann, Akila Welihinda, Peter Welinder, Jiayi Weng, Lilian Weng, Matt Wiethoff, Dave Willner, Clemens Winter, Samuel Wolrich, Hannah Wong, Lauren Workman, Sherwin Wu, Jeff Wu, Michael Wu, Kai Xiao, Tao Xu, Sarah Yoo, Kevin Yu, Qiming Yuan, Wojciech Zaremba, Rowan Zellers, Chong Zhang, Marvin Zhang, Shengjia Zhao, Tianhao Zheng, Juntang Zhuang, William Zhuk, and Barret Zoph. 2024. Gpt-4 technical report. *Preprint*, arXiv:2303.08774.

Jonas Pfeiffer, Ivan Vulić, Iryna Gurevych, and Sebastian Ruder. 2020. MAD-X: An Adapter-Based Framework for Multi-Task Cross-Lingual Transfer. In *Proceedings of the 2020 Conference on Empirical Methods in Natural Language Processing (EMNLP)*, pages 7654–7673, Online. Association for Computational Linguistics.

Holly A Schroth, Jon Bain-Chekal, and David F Caldwell. 2005. Sticks and stones may break bones and words can hurt me: Words and phrases that trigger emotions in negotiations and their effects. *International Journal of Conflict Management*, 16(2):102–127.

Pranaydeep Singh, Aaron Maladry, and Els Lefever. 2023. Annotation Guidelines for Labeling Emotion in Multilingual Tweets: Version 1.0 - LT3 technical report – LT3 23-12.

Mukund Sundararajan, Ankur Taly, and Qiqi Yan. 2017. Axiomatic attribution for deep networks. In *International conference on machine learning*, pages 3319–3328. PMLR.

Gemma Team, Thomas Mesnard, Cassidy Hardin, Robert Dadashi, Surya Bhupatiraju, Shreya Pathak, Laurent Sifre, Morgane Rivière, Mihir Sanjay Kale, Juliette Love, Pouya Tafti, Léonard Hussenot, Pier Giuseppe Sessa, Aakanksha Chowdhery, Adam Roberts, Aditya Barua, Alex Botev, Alex Castro-Ros, Ambrose Slone, Amélie Héliou, Andrea Tacchetti, Anna Bulanova, Antonia Paterson, Beth Tsai, Bobak Shahriari, Charline Le Lan, Christopher A. Choquette-Choo, Clément Crepy, Daniel Cer, Daphne Ippolito, David Reid, Elena Buchatskaya, Eric Ni, Eric Noland, Geng Yan, George Tucker, George-Christian Muraru, Grigory Rozhdestvenskiy, Henryk Michalewski, Ian Tenney, Ivan Grishchenko, Jacob Austin, James Keeling, Jane Labanowski, Jean-Baptiste Lespiau, Jeff Stanway, Jenny Brennan, Jeremy Chen, Johan Ferret, Justin Chiu, Justin Mao-Jones, Katherine Lee, Kathy Yu, Katie Millican, Lars Lowe Sjoesund, Lisa Lee, Lucas Dixon, Machel Reid, Maciej Mikuła, Mateo Wirth, Michael Sharman, Nikolai Chinaev, Nithum Thain, Olivier Bachem, Oscar Chang, Oscar Wahltinez, Paige Bailey, Paul Michel, Petko Yotov, Rahma Chaabouni, Ramona Comanescu, Reena Jana, Rohan Anil, Ross McIlroy, Ruibo Liu, Ryan Mullins, Samuel L Smith, Sebastian Borgeaud, Sertan Girgin, Sholto Douglas, Shree Pandya, Siamak Shakeri, Soham De, Ted Klimenko, Tom Hennigan, Vlad Feinberg, Wojciech Stokowiec, Yu hui Chen, Zafarali Ahmed, Zhitao Gong, Tris Warkentin, Ludovic Peran, Minh Giang, Clément Farabet, Oriol Vinyals, Jeff Dean, Koray Kavukcuoglu, Demis Hassabis, Zoubin Ghahramani, Douglas Eck, Joelle Barral, Fernando Pereira, Eli Collins, Armand Joulin, Noah Fiedel, Evan Senter, Alek Andreev, and Kathleen Kenealy. 2024. Gemma: Open models based on gemini research and technology. *Preprint*, arXiv:2403.08295.

Jesus Vázquez-Osorio, Gerardo Eugenio Sierra-Martínez, Helena Gómez-Adorno, and Gemma Bel-Enguix. 2024. Pcicunam at wassa 2024: Cross-lingual emotion detection task with hierarchical classification and weighted loss functions. In *Proceedings of the 14th Workshop of on Computational Approaches to Subjectivity, Sentiment & Social Media Analysis@ACL 2024*, Bangkok, Thailand.

Pedro Vázquez-Osorio and Helena Gómez-Adorno. 2024. Lliimas at smm4h: Zero-shot cross-lingual emotion detection in multilingual tweets. In *Proceedings of the 14th Workshop of on Computational Approaches to Subjectivity, Sentiment & Social Media Analysis@ACL 2024*, Bangkok, Thailand.

Yuqi Wang, Zimu Wang, Nijia Han, Wei Wang, Qi Chen, Haiyang ZHang, Yushan Pan, and Anh Nguyen. 2024. Knowledge distillation from monolingual to multilingual models for intelligent and interpretable multilingual emotion detection. In *Proceedings of the 14th Workshop of on Computational Approaches to Subjectivity, Sentiment & Social Media Analysis@ACL 2024*, Bangkok, Thailand.

Feng Xiong, Jun Wang, Geng Tu, and Ruifeng Xu. 2024. Hitsz-hlt at wassa-2024 shared task 2: Language-agnostic multi-task learning for explainability of cross-lingual emotion detection. In *Proceedings of the 14th Workshop of on Computational Approaches to Subjectivity, Sentiment & Social Media Analysis@ACL 2024*, Bangkok, Thailand.

Jinghui Zhang, Yuan Zhao, Siqin Zhang, Ruijing Zhao, and Siyu Bao. 2024. Enhancing cross-lingual emotion detection with data augmentation and token-label mapping. In *Proceedings of the 14th Workshop of on Computational Approaches to Subjectivity, Sentiment & Social Media Analysis@ACL 2024*, Bangkok, Thailand.

Banghua Zhu, Evan Frick, Tianhao Wu, Hanlin Zhu, and Jiantao Jiao. 2023. Starling-7b: Improving llm helpfulness  harmlessness with rlaif.

Mikel Zubillaga, Oscar Sainz, Ainara Estarrona, Oier Lopez de Lacalle, and Eneko Agirre. 2024. Event extraction in basque: Typologically motivated cross-lingual transfer-learning analysis. *Preprint*, arXiv:2404.06392.

Jakub Šmíd, Pavel Pribá, and Pavel Král. 2024. Uwb at wassa-2024 shared task 2: Cross-lingual emotion detection. In *Proceedings of the 14th Workshop of on Computational Approaches to Subjectivity, Sentiment & Social Media Analysis@ACL 2024*, Bangkok, Thailand.

# Cross-lingual Emotion Detection through Large Language Models

**Ram Mohan Rao Kadiyala**
University of Maryland, College Park
rkadiyal@terpmail.umd.edu

## Abstract

This paper presents a detailed system description of our entry which finished 1st with a large lead at WASSA 2024 Task 2, focused on cross-lingual emotion detection. We utilized a combination of large language models (LLMs) and their ensembles to effectively understand and categorize emotions across different languages. Our approach not only outperformed other submissions with a large margin, but also demonstrated the strength of integrating multiple models to enhance performance. Additionally, We conducted a thorough comparison of the benefits and limitations of each model used. An error analysis is included along with suggested areas for future improvement. This paper aims to offer a clear and comprehensive understanding of advanced techniques in emotion detection, making it accessible even to those new to the field.

## 1 Introduction

Emotion detection in texts across different languages is a challenging yet crucial task, especially in the context of global digital communication. The ability to accurately identify emotions in text, regardless of the language, can significantly enhance interactions in various domains such as customer service, social media monitoring, and mental health assessments. This paper introduces our approach to cross-lingual emotion detection, which was recently recognized as the top submission in WASSA 2024 Task 2 (Maladry et al., 2024). Our system leveraged the capabilities of several open source and proprietary Large Language Models (LLMs), including GPT-4 (OpenAI, 2024) and Claude-Opus (Anthropic, 2024) in a zero-shot configuration, as well as LLAMA-3-8B (Touvron et al., 2023), Gemma-7B (GemmaTeam, 2024), and Mistral-v2-7B (Jiang et al., 2023), which were fine-tuned. To assess the robustness and efficiency of these models, we conducted tests in both 4-bit and 16-bit precision. This varied precision testing helps in understanding the trade-offs between computational efficiency and model performance. Additionally, we compared the performance of our models against the top submission's (Patkar et al., 2023) approach on a similar monolingual task from the previous years' shared task. Furthermore, we experimented with enhancing model performance by incorporating additional training data from previous editions of the shared task, specifically WASSA 2023 (Barriere et al., 2023) and WASSA 2022 (Barriere et al., 2022) emotion classification task datasets.

## 2 Dataset

The dataset consisted of texts belonging to one the 5 languages - Dutch, English, French, Russian and Spanish annotated as one of the 6 classes - Anger, Fear, Love, Joy, Neutral and Sadness. The distribution of languages and each class in each of the datasets can be seen in Table 1 and Table 2.

| Class ↓ | Train | Dev | Test |
|---|---|---|---|
| **Anger** | 1028 | 129 | 614 |
| **Fear** | 143 | 14 | 77 |
| **Joy** | 1293 | 102 | 433 |
| **Love** | 579 | 40 | 190 |
| **Neutral** | 1397 | 157 | 916 |
| **Sadness** | 560 | 58 | 270 |
| **Total** | 5000 | 500 | 2500 |

Table 1: Class distribution in each dataset split

| Class ↓ | Train | Dev | Test |
|---|---|---|---|
| **English** | 5000 | 100 | 500 |
| **French** | - | 100 | 500 |
| **Dutch** | - | 100 | 500 |
| **Russian** | - | 100 | 500 |
| **Spanish** | - | 100 | 500 |
| **Total** | 5000 | 500 | 2500 |

Table 2: Language distribution in each dataset split



*Proceedings of the 14th Workshop on Computational Approaches to Subjectivity, Sentiment, & Social Media Analysis*, pages 464–469
August 15, 2024 ©2024 Association for Computational Linguistics

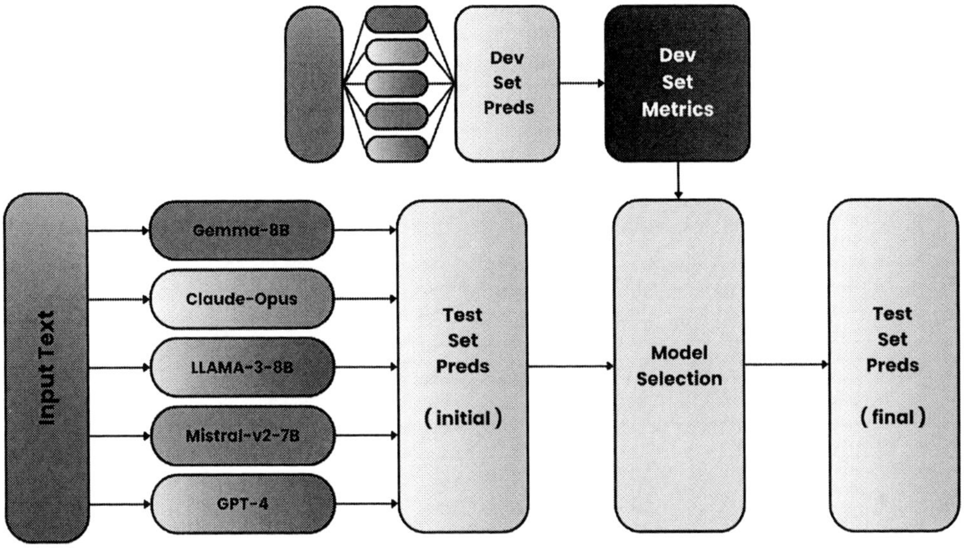


Figure 1: System Overview : Ensembles of LLMs

## 3 System Description

The non-proprietary LLMs were fine-tuned over just the training dataset over 5 epochs with a learning rate of 0.0002 and weight decay of 0.01. The proprietary systems were tested with various prompt over the development set and the best performing prompt was used to make predictions over the test set. Additionally the previous year's benchmark was also tested alongside by replacing RoBERTa (Liu et al., 2019) with XLM-RoBERTa (Conneau et al., 2020). Additionally other ensembles like majority vote, model selection based on features were also tested. The Code and Models are available over the GitHub repository[1] and Huggingface[2] [3] [4]. The primary metric was weighted F1 score, additionally Precision and Recall have also been observed.

### 3.1 Results Comparison

The results using each of the models on the development set by fine-tuning over 3 epochs on the training set can be seen in Table 3. Other approaches like data augmentation using previous years' emotion detection datasets, translating dev and test sets to English before making predictions did not improve the metrics. No pre-processing steps have been used. The metrics on the Test set can be seen in Table 4.

| Model ↓ | Description | F1 |
|---|---|---|
| GPT-4 | Zero-shot | **0.5616** |
| Claude-Opus | Zero-shot | 0.5581 |
| LLaMa-3-8B | Fine-tuned 3 epochs | 0.5474 |
| Mistral-v2-7B | Fine-tuned 3 epochs | 0.5466 |
| Gemma-8B | Fine-tuned 3 epochs | 0.5300 |
| Xlm-R | 10 epochs + SWA | 0.5392 |

Table 3: Performance of each model on Dev set

### 3.2 Error Analysis

Each of the models had its own advantages and drawbacks likely due to the differences in the pre-training data used by each of the models. The performance of each of the models was observed separately on each of the languages over the development set, this can be seen in Table 5. It can be seen that certain models performed better on some of the languages. This led to the conclusion that selecting an appropriate model based on language of the text to be classified might yield better results.

[1]Code Used : https://github.com/1024-m/ACL-2024-WASSA-EXALT

[2]The finetuned LLAMA Model : https://huggingface.co/1024m/EXALT-1A-LLAMA3-5A-16bit

[3]The fine-tuned Mistral Model : https://huggingface.co/1024m/EXALT-1A-MISTRAL-5A-16bit

[4]The finetuned GEMMA Model : https://huggingface.co/1024m/EXALT-1A-GEMMA-5A-16bit

| Model ↓ | Description | F1 score |
|---|---|---|
| llama-3-8b | fine-tuned , 5 epochs | 0.5931 |
| llama-3-8b | fine-tuned , test data translated , 5 epochs | 0.5701 |
| gemma-8b | fine-tuned , 5 epochs | 0.5450 |
| mistral-v2-7b | fine-tuned , 5 epochs | 0.5915 |
| gpt-4 | few-shot : one sample of each class | 0.5918 |
| claude-opus | zero-shot | 0.5257 |
| ensemble | model selection based on weighted-f1 scores , 5 epochs each | 0.5810 |
| ensemble | model selection based on macro-f1 scores , 5 epochs each | 0.5977 |
| ensemble | model selection based on micro-f1 scores , 5 epochs each | 0.5725 |
| ensemble | majority vote or model selection based on macro-f1 , 5 epochs each | **0.6295** |

Table 4: Performance of each models / approaches on Test set

| Language | Metric | GPT-4 | GEMMA | Claude-Opus | Mistral-v2 | LLAMA-3 |
|---|---|---|---|---|---|---|
| English | Micro F1 | 0.610 | 0.650 | 0.580 | **0.680** | 0.610 |
| English | Macro F1 | 0.443 | **0.594** | 0.470 | 0.590 | 0.481 |
| English | Weighted F1 | 0.582 | 0.655 | 0.563 | **0.671** | 0.587 |
| Russian | Micro F1 | **0.620** | 0.550 | 0.570 | 0.590 | 0.610 |
| Russian | Macro F1 | **0.506** | 0.425 | 0.454 | 0.434 | 0.457 |
| Russian | Weighted F1 | **0.633** | 0.574 | 0.584 | 0.603 | 0.627 |
| Spanish | Micro F1 | 0.670 | 0.700 | 0.630 | 0.740 | **0.770** |
| Spanish | Macro F1 | 0.521 | 0.552 | 0.597 | 0.659 | **0.687** |
| Spanish | Weighted F1 | 0.676 | 0.725 | 0.666 | 0.751 | **0.779** |
| French | Micro F1 | 0.590 | 0.610 | 0.610 | **0.630** | **0.630** |
| French | Macro F1 | 0.509 | 0.533 | 0.499 | **0.549** | 0.522 |
| French | Weighted F1 | 0.579 | **0.607** | 0.596 | 0.596 | 0.589 |
| Dutch | Micro F1 | **0.670** | 0.550 | 0.650 | 0.620 | 0.660 |
| Dutch | Macro F1 | **0.540** | 0.394 | **0.540** | 0.413 | 0.533 |
| Dutch | Weighted F1 | **0.657** | 0.576 | 0.636 | 0.610 | 0.642 |

Table 5: Performance of each model on Dev set : by each Language and Metric

### 3.3 Our System

Several approaches of using ensembles based on majority voting, model selection based on macro F1, micro F1 and the weighted F1 scores were tested. The best performing system uses a majority voting criteria from the 5 models used. In cases where consensus is not achieved i.e no clear majority, the output of the model with highest weighted F1 score was chosen as the final label.

### 3.4 Possible Extensions

As seen in Table 5, each of the models had their own advantages and disadvantages with varying performances on each language. It is likely that adding more models into the system and features like text length or utilizing different models for binary classification of whether the given text belongs to a class. This can be seen in Table 6 displaying varying effectiveness of each model in predicting each emotion. A viable approach would be predicting each emotion as a binary task and then using other methods in cases where none or more than one class ends up as true. The fine-tuned LLMs were loaded in 4bit precision and later fine tuned using LoRA (Hu et al., 2021) and tested in both 4bit precision and 16bit precision versions. The drop in performance in 4bit overall was minimal, however in many cases the predictions in 4bit ended up as correct while 16bit were incorrect. Another viable approach is to pick the top 2 likely class labels for each of the texts' predictions and using other methods to classify more effectively.

## 4 Conclusion

It can be seen from Table 4 that ensemble models have achieved a significantly better result over di-

| Class ↓ | GPT-4 | GEMMA-8B | Claude-Opus | Mistral-v2-7B | LLAMA-3-8B |
|---|---|---|---|---|---|
| Anger | **0.75** | 0.69 | 0.71 | 0.72 | 0.74 |
| Fear | 0.26 | 0.27 | **0.42** | 0.30 | 0.40 |
| Joy | 0.62 | 0.59 | 0.61 | **0.67** | 0.65 |
| Love | 0.40 | 0.44 | 0.33 | **0.46** | 0.34 |
| Neutral | 0.69 | 0.73 | 0.67 | 0.74 | **0.75** |
| Sadness | 0.42 | **0.47** | 0.45 | 0.39 | 0.40 |

Table 6: Performance of each model class wise : class F1 scores on Dev set

rect approaches. However not all approaches have been tested due to limit on number of submissions. As seen in Table 5, It can also be observed that from Table 6 that a similar trend was observed in using different models for each emotion detection too might aid in improving the performance further. As seen in Table 4 and Table 3, further training is likely to improve the results as the dev set results of fine-tuned models were lower that the proprietary models when trained on 3 epochs, but when the same models were further tuned over 2 more epochs, they performed better than proprietary models. Most of the errors when using proprietary models were with the neutral class texts being classified incorrectly or other classes being classified as being neutral. While the fine-tuned models were able to learn to be able to distinguish texts as neutral or some other class in a better way as seen in Table 6. The classes with lesser data samples as shown in Table 1 had significantly worse compared to other classes as seen in Table 6. Techniques like Stochastic weight averaging (SWA) (Izmailov et al., 2019) in this case only led to a minor improvement and techniques like augmentation using other datasets did not improve performance. It is likely that adding sufficient data for all classes can make the current proposed system better as enough correlation can be seen in training data amount from Table 1 and average performance of the discussed models on each of the classes from Table 6. The current proposed approach can be extended to other languages by testing performance on a small sample of that language to decide the extent of reliability of each model in making predictions over texts of that language. In case of using proprietary models the same prompt used for all texts, it is worth testing different prompts for texts of each language due to varying features of each language where one class might to higher number of false positives than other in a different language. Approaches like removal of stop words did not improve the performance. While using ensembles, texts completely in one language performed better that the texts where a portion of the text is in English and rest in a different language. These texts led to higher frequency of errors. The performance of proprietary models was a bit better on these kind of texts compared to the rest of the models tested probably due to larger model size and more code-mixed data in training. Other information like the specific prompts used on each of the LLMs, Prompt format for the fine-tuned LLMs used and other relevant plots are available in section 4.

## Limitations

Due to computational resource limitations, the models used (non-proprietary) were loaded in 4bit precision before being fine-tuned. It is likely that with higher precision usage of the models can yield better results. The models used (non-proprietary) were of the 7B or 8B variants. It is likely that larger variants may yield better results. The approaches might not be extendable to all languages as not all languages' data were covered in the pre-training data of the LLMs used in the current proposed system. Due to time limitations, not all LLMs were tested, especially some of the other proprietary LLMs which might perform better in one of languages in consideration.

## References


Anthropic. 2024. Claude-opus technical report.

Valentin Barriere, João Sedoc, Shabnam Tafreshi, and Salvatore Giorgi. 2023. Findings of WASSA 2023 shared task on empathy, emotion and personality detection in conversation and reactions to news articles. In *Proceedings of the 13th Workshop on Computational Approaches to Subjectivity, Sentiment, & Social Media Analysis*, pages 511–525, Toronto, Canada. Association for Computational Linguistics.

Valentin Barriere, Shabnam Tafreshi, João Sedoc, and Sawsan Alqahtani. 2022. WASSA 2022 shared task:

Predicting empathy, emotion and personality in reaction to news stories. In *Proceedings of the 12th Workshop on Computational Approaches to Subjectivity, Sentiment & Social Media Analysis*, pages 214–227, Dublin, Ireland. Association for Computational Linguistics.

Ankush Chatterjee, Kedhar Nath Narahari, Meghana Joshi, and Puneet Agrawal. 2019. SemEval-2019 task 3: EmoContext contextual emotion detection in text. In *Proceedings of the 13th International Workshop on Semantic Evaluation*, pages 39–48, Minneapolis, Minnesota, USA. Association for Computational Linguistics.

Alexis Conneau, Kartikay Khandelwal, Naman Goyal, Vishrav Chaudhary, Guillaume Wenzek, Francisco Guzmán, Edouard Grave, Myle Ott, Luke Zettlemoyer, and Veselin Stoyanov. 2020. Unsupervised cross-lingual representation learning at scale.

GemmaTeam. 2024. Gemma: Open models based on gemini research and technology.

Edward J. Hu, Yelong Shen, Phillip Wallis, Zeyuan Allen-Zhu, Yuanzhi Li, Shean Wang, Lu Wang, and Weizhu Chen. 2021. Lora: Low-rank adaptation of large language models.

Pavel Izmailov, Dmitrii Podoprikhin, Timur Garipov, Dmitry Vetrov, and Andrew Gordon Wilson. 2019. Averaging weights leads to wider optima and better generalization.

Albert Q. Jiang, Alexandre Sablayrolles, Arthur Mensch, Chris Bamford, Devendra Singh Chaplot, Diego de las Casas, Florian Bressand, Gianna Lengyel, Guillaume Lample, Lucile Saulnier, Lélio Renard Lavaud, Marie-Anne Lachaux, Pierre Stock, Teven Le Scao, Thibaut Lavril, Thomas Wang, Timothée Lacroix, and William El Sayed. 2023. Mistral 7b.

Yinhan Liu, Myle Ott, Naman Goyal, Jingfei Du, Mandar Joshi, Danqi Chen, Omer Levy, Mike Lewis, Luke Zettlemoyer, and Veselin Stoyanov. 2019. Roberta: A robustly optimized bert pretraining approach.

Aaron Maladry, Pranaydeep Singh, and Els Lefever. 2024. Findings of the wassa 2024 exalt shared task on explainability for cross-lingual emotion in tweets. In *Proceedings of the 14th Workshop of on Computational Approaches to Subjectivity, Sentiment Social Media Analysis@ACL 2024*, Bangkok, Thailand.

Saif Mohammad, Felipe Bravo-Marquez, Mohammad Salameh, and Svetlana Kiritchenko. 2018. SemEval-2018 task 1: Affect in tweets. In *Proceedings of the 12th International Workshop on Semantic Evaluation*, pages 1–17, New Orleans, Louisiana. Association for Computational Linguistics.

OpenAI. 2024. Gpt-4 technical report.

Aditya Patkar, Suraj Chandrashekhar, and Ram Mohan Rao Kadiyala. 2023. AdityaPatkar at WASSA 2023 empathy, emotion, and personality shared task: RoBERTa-based emotion classification of essays, improving performance on imbalanced data. In *Proceedings of the 13th Workshop on Computational Approaches to Subjectivity, Sentiment, & Social Media Analysis*, Toronto, Canada. Association for Computational Linguistics.

Hugo Touvron, Thibaut Lavril, Gautier Izacard, Xavier Martinet, Marie-Anne Lachaux, Timothée Lacroix, Baptiste Rozière, Naman Goyal, Eric Hambro, Faisal Azhar, Aurelien Rodriguez, Armand Joulin, Edouard Grave, and Guillaume Lample. 2023. Llama: Open and efficient foundation language models.

## A Text Transalation

Several translation models and approaches have been translated, with google-translate and using LLMs for translating being the better suited approaches. However the texts were returned without translation in code-mixed text cases is some instances. Despite the higher cost using LLMs worked perfectly in detecting the main language and also to test by translating all texts to English.

## B Prompts Used

The prompts used in the system and other analysis tasks were as follows :

- *Language Detection of texts* : "Classify given texts as English,Dutch,French,Spanish,Russian. Respond only with one word based on which language the text is in."
- *Translation completely to English* : "Translate the text to English. Respond with the same text if already in English completely."
- *Classification of Emotion (Proprietary)* : "Classify given texts as Neutral, Joy, Anger, Love, Sadness, Fear. Respond only with one word based on which would be closest classification of user emotion from the text."
- *Classification of Emotion (fine-tuned)* : "Given the input text , classify it based on what emotion is being exibited among the following : Joy/Neutral/Anger/Love/Sadness/Fear. Respond with only one emotion only among the options given. Respond with only one word and nothing else."

- *Binary Classification of each class separately* : "Is the text indicating `Class-name` ? Respond only with one word (YES / NO) based on input text."

## C Hyperparameters Used

Among the hyperparameter space explored for each approach, the best results were obtained with the following values. Rest of the parameters were unspecified during training and hence the default values have been used.

| | Transformers | LLMs |
|---|---|---|
| No.of Epochs | 10 | 5 |
| Learning rate | 2e-5 | 2e-4 |
| Weight Decay | 0.05 | 0.01 |

Table 7: Hyperparameters used in training the models used for fine-tuned transformers and LLMs

## D System Replication Instructions

The system can be replicated using the hyperparameters mentioned in Table 7 with seed value of 1024. The models used are available on huggingface in various configurations i.e LoRA adapters, 16bit and 4bit precision models.

LLAMA-3-8B model trained with additional data from previous years workshop datasets :

1024m/EXALT-1A-LLAMA3-5C-Lora
1024m/EXALT-1A-LLAMA3-5C-16bit
1024m/EXALT-1A-LLAMA3-5C-4bit

LLAMA-3-8B model trained with datasets translated to English using GPT-4 :

1024m/EXALT-1A-LLAMA3-5B-Lora
1024m/EXALT-1A-LLAMA3-5B-16bit
1024m/EXALT-1A-LLAMA3-5B-4bit

LLAMA-3-8B model used in the system (main) :

1024m/EXALT-1A-LLAMA3-5A-Lora
1024m/EXALT-1A-LLAMA3-5A-16bit
1024m/EXALT-1A-LLAMA3-5A-4bit

GEMMA-8B model used in the system (main) :

1024m/EXALT-1A-GEMMA-5A-Lora
1024m/EXALT-1A-GEMMA-5A-16bit
1024m/EXALT-1A-GEMMA-5A-4bit

Mistral-7B model used in the system (main) :

1024m/EXALT-1A-MISTRAL-5A-Lora
1024m/EXALT-1A-MISTRAL-5A-16bit
1024m/EXALT-1A-MISTRAL-5A-4bit

# Knowledge Distillation from Monolingual to Multilingual Models for Intelligent and Interpretable Multilingual Emotion Detection

**Yuqi Wang[1,2], Zimu Wang[1,2], Nijia Han[1], Wei Wang[1,†], Qi Chen[1], Haiyang Zhang[1], Yushan Pan[1], Anh Nguyen[2]**

[1]Xi'an Jiaotong Liverpool University [2]University of Liverpool

{yuqi.wang17,zimu.wang19,nijia.han23}@student.xjtlu.edu.cn

{wei.wang03,qi.chen02,haiyang.zhang,yushan.pan}@xjtlu.edu.cn

anh.nguyen@liverpool.ac.uk

## Abstract

Emotion detection from text is a crucial task in understanding natural language with wide-ranging applications. Existing approaches for multilingual emotion detection from text face challenges with data scarcity across many languages and a lack of interpretability. We propose a novel method that leverages both monolingual and multilingual pre-trained language models to improve performance and interpretability. Our approach involves 1) training a high-performing English monolingual model in parallel with a multilingual model and 2) using knowledge distillation to transfer the emotion detection capabilities from the monolingual teacher to the multilingual student model. Experiments on a multilingual dataset demonstrate significant performance gains for refined multilingual models like XLM-RoBERTa and E5 after distillation. Furthermore, our approach enhances interpretability by enabling better identification of emotion-trigger words. Our work presents a promising direction for building accurate, robust and explainable multilingual emotion detection systems.

## 1 Introduction

Emotion detection, a sub-category of sentiment analysis, is the process of computationally identifying, extracting and categorising the emotion expressed in text. This granular analysis of affective states, including joy, sadness, fear, and anger, represents a crucial task in natural language understanding (NLU) that has garnered substantial research attention for several decades due to its wide range of applications. The growth of social media platforms, such as Facebook and Twitter, has led to an increasing trend of individuals sharing their emotions, thoughts and experiences through short snippets of text in posts, tweets, comments and captions. Consequently, a vast volume of user-generated data enriched with emotional content has been generated, highlighting the immense value of automating the detection and analysis of underlying emotions.

Despite the significant progress made in emotion detection from text, there remain two key challenges that hinder the widespread applicability and trustworthiness of these systems: 1) the majority of existing work focused on developing models for high-resource languages like English, where large task-specific datasets for emotion detection, such as CANCEREMO (Sosea and Caragea, 2020) and EmoNet (Abdul-Mageed and Ungar, 2017), are readily available for training and fine-tuning. On the other hand, there is not enough training data for many minority languages, such as French and Dutch. This data scarcity poses a significant obstacle in building accurate and robust emotion detection models that can cater to the linguistic and cultural diversity present across different communities; 2) while current models excel at overall emotion classification, they often lack the ability to provide explanations or insights into the specific linguistic cues that triggered the detected emotions. Many previous studies have primarily concentrated on maximising the overall accuracy metrics (Wang et al., 2021; Wang and Gan, 2023), overlooking the importance of interpretability and rationale extraction.

Recent advances in multilingual pre-trained language models (multilingual PLM) present a promising direction. These models, such as mBERT (Devlin et al., 2019), XLM-RoBERTa (Conneau et al., 2020), and mDeberta (He et al., 2021), are pre-trained on large volumes of unlabeled text from multiple languages in an unsupervised manner, allowing them to capture rich cross-lingual representations that can be effectively transferred to downstream tasks like emotion detection. They play a crucial role in enabling cross-lingual trans-

[†]Corresponding author.



*Proceedings of the 14th Workshop on Computational Approaches to Subjectivity, Sentiment, & Social Media Analysis*, pages 470–475
August 15, 2024 

fer and facilitating joint training across different languages (Ruder et al., 2019). Furthermore, the transformer-based architecture with self-attention mechanisms can potentially provide interpretability benefits (Chefer et al., 2021), allowing us to analyse the important trigger words that contribute to the predictions. However, the task-specific performance of a fine-tuned multilingual PLM on the multilingual data may not be as comparable to that of separately trained monolingual language models evaluated on the data from their respective languages (Lothritz et al., 2021; Wu and Dredze, 2020). To address the above-mentioned issue, in this work, we propose a novel approach that combines the strengths of both monolingual and multilingual models for improved emotion detection performance and interpretability across diverse languages.

## 2 Methodology

### 2.1 Parallel Model Adaptation for Emotion Detection

Our proposed approach involves two separate training pipelines leveraging both monolingual and multilingual PLMs. In the first pipeline, we finetune a state-of-the-art English monolingual model (such as RoBERTa (Liu et al., 2019)), denoted as $\theta_{\text{en}}$, on the provided English emotion detection training set, enabling the model to capture the linguistic meanings and emotion cues that are specific to the English language; in parallel, we fine-tune a multilingual PLM like XLM-RoBERTa (Conneau et al., 2020), denoted as $\theta_{\text{mul}}$, on the same English set. The multilingual PLM, pre-trained on a large corpus of data from various languages, can leverage its cross-lingual representations to learn task-specific patterns from the data in a given language (Liu et al., 2020). By training these two models separately on the same English dataset, we can obtain a high-performance English monolingual model tailored for emotion detection, as well as a multilingual model that has adapted its cross-lingual representations to the task of emotion detection while still retaining its ability to generalise across languages.

### 2.2 Knowledge Distillation from the Monolingual Model

To further refine and improve the performance of the multilingual model, we propose a knowledge distillation strategy that utilises the high-performing monolingual English model as a teacher. The refinement scheme for the fine-tuned multilingual model is shown in Figure 1. Since the unlabelled data from development set is in various languages, we first translate all the non-English instances into English using neural machine translation systems based on Marian (Junczys-Dowmunt et al., 2018), i.e. $T : X \to X'$, where $X = \{x_i, x_2, ..., x_{|X|}\}$, standing for the original development set that contains multilingual texts and $X' = \{x'_i, x'_2, ..., x'_{|X'|}\}$, representing the translated English version. We then obtain predictions from both the monolingual model on the translated data $X'$, and the multilingual model on the original data $X$.

To transfer the ability of the monolingual model to the multilingual model, we compute the Kullback-Leibler (KL) divergence, a non-symmetric loss function, as the consistency loss between their output distribution $P$ and $Q$ on each instance. Importantly, we focus on minimising the consistency loss only when the quality of translated data in $X'$ is suspected to be of good quality, which ensures that we prioritise knowledge transfer from the teacher model on instances where the translation is sufficiently reliable. To achieve this, we introduce a normalised weight $\bar{w}_i$ for each translated instance $x'_i$ and compute the loss with these weights included, i.e.

$$\begin{aligned}\mathcal{L} &= \bar{w} * \mathrm{KL}(P\|Q)\\ &= \sum_{i=1}^{|X|} \bar{w}_i \left[ \sum_{j=1}^{k} p(y_j|x'_i, \theta_{en}) \log \frac{p(y_j|x'_i, \theta_{en})}{p(y_j|x_i, \theta_{xlm})} \right]\end{aligned} \tag{1}$$

where $p(y_j|x'_i, \theta_{en})$ and $p(y_j|x_i, \theta_{xlm})$ represent the output probabilities for the $j$-th category of the monolingual model on the $i$-th translated English instance and the multilingual model on the $i$-th original instance, respectively. $k$ is the number of categories for the emotion detection task.

### 2.3 Translation Quality Weighting

To compute the weight, which reflects the suspected translation quality, we first obtain the predictions of the same multilingual model on both the original data $x_i$ and translated data $x'_i$. We then calculate the disagreement between these two prediction using the mean squared error (MSE), a

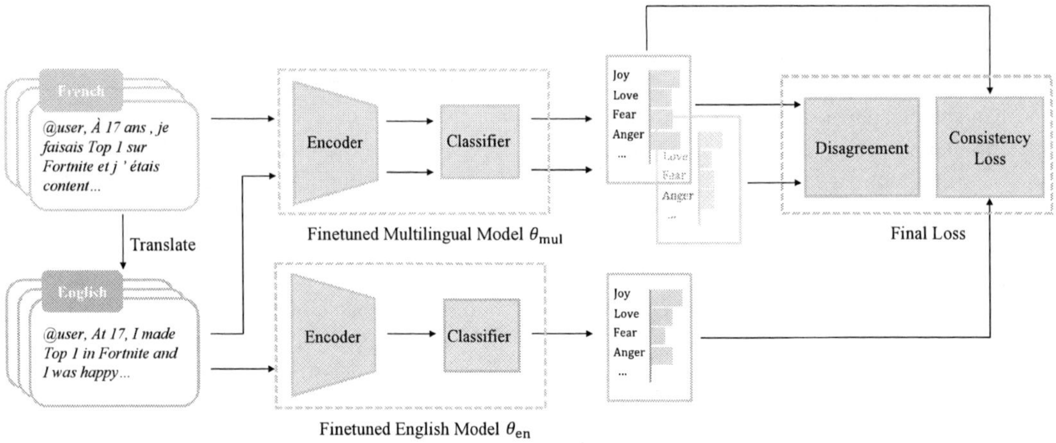


Figure 1: Our proposed refinement scheme for the fine-tuned multilingual model.

symmetric function, i.e.

$$w_i = \sum_{j=1}^{k} \left[ p^2\left(y_j|x_i', \theta_{\text{xlm}}\right) - p^2\left(y_j|x_i, \theta_{\text{xlm}}\right) \right] \tag{2}$$

A high MSE value between the predictions of the multilingual on $x$ and $x'$ suggests that the translation quality is likely poor, as the understanding of the model for the original instance and translated instance significantly disagrees, indicating the potential translation flaws or errors, conversely, a low MSE value illustrates the consistency between the original and translated versions, implying a higher translation quality. Therefore, when the disagreement is high, such a translated sample should contribute less to the final loss. To account for this, we normalise the weight as follows:

$$\bar{w_i} = 1 - \frac{w_i - \min(w)}{\max(w) - \min(w)} \tag{3}$$

## 3 Experimental Results

### 3.1 Datasets and Shared-task

We utilised the dataset on explainable cross-lingual emotion detection in tweets (EXALT)[1]. This dataset includes annotations for both word triggers and the overall expressed emotion for each instance. The training set is available in English only, while the development set and test set involve five different languages: English, French, Dutch, Russian and Spanish. More details about the shared task can be found in (Maladry et al., 2024).

[1]https://lt3.ugent.be/exalt/

### 3.2 Baseline

We conducted experiments involving generative models, discriminative models and feature extractors. For the generative models, we employed BLOOM (Le Scao et al., 2023) and BLOOMZ (Muennighoff et al., 2023) with 7.1 billion parameters. Both BLOOM and BLOOMZ are pre-trained on multilingual corpora, and BLOOMZ was further fine-tuned using prompted multitask learning.

For discriminative models, we utilised RoBERTa with the translated samples and XLM-RoBERTa. Additionally, we considered two recent feature exactors, BGE-M3 (Chen et al., 2024), and E5 (Wang et al., 2024), which were pre-trained on the massive multilingual text-pair to extract the cross-lingual features and construct the text embedding for multiple languages. To perform the classification task, we added a fully connected layer as the classifier and applied the average pooling to the text embedding to generate the predictions. The implementation details can be found in the Appendix .1.

### 3.3 Main Results

We reported the main results of the emotion detection task in Table 1. Based on the overall result, we can see that despite having a larger number of parameters, which generally indicates greater model capacity, generative models such as BLOOM and BLOOMZ did not perform as well as the large discriminative models. This implies that larger models do not necessarily lead to better performance in tasks that require detailed understanding and classification of emotions.

Another noteworthy observation is the signifi-

| Models | Development | | | Testing | | |
|---|---|---|---|---|---|---|
| | F1 | Precision | Recall | F1 | Precision | Recall |
| **Generators** | | | | | | |
| BLOOM-7b1 | 49.98 | 55.58 | 48.10 | 49.40 | 51.74 | 47.97 |
| BLOOMZ-7b1 | 47.82 | 52.44 | 46.18 | 49.69 | 51.65 | 48.54 |
| **Discriminators** | | | | | | |
| XLM-RoBERTa (base)* | 43.29 | 43.35 | 44.47 | 44.76 | 44.52 | 46.31 |
| XLM-RoBERTa (large) | 50.09 | 49.78 | 50.66 | 53.24 | 52.77 | 54.59 |
| RoBERTa (large) w. transl. | 52.21 | 51.57 | 54.02 | - | - | - |
| **Feature Extractors** | | | | | | |
| E5 | 49.60 | 50.09 | 49.67 | 54.28 | 54.05 | 55.26 |
| BGE-M3 | 49.67 | 49.23 | 50.60 | 51.51 | 52.40 | 51.37 |
| **Our Approach** | | | | | | |
| RoBERTa (large) + XLM-RoBERTa (large) | 55.53 | **58.80** | 54.07 | 54.54 | 57.28 | 53.39 |
| RoBERTa (large) + E5 | 54.94 | 56.39 | 54.42 | 55.98 | 56.26 | **56.36** |
| RoBERTa (large) + BGE-M3 | 53.49 | 54.63 | 53.12 | 51.75 | 50.73 | 53.55 |
| Ensemble | **56.01** | 56.58 | **55.79** | **56.61** | **58.30** | 55.73 |

Table 1: Main results on the development set and testing set for the emotion detection task. * The results are provided by the organiser.

cant performance improvements achieved by the multilingual PLMs after knowledge distillation from the monolingual RoBERTa model. On the development set, all evaluated multilingual models, including XLM-RoBERTa, E5, and BGE-M3, showed significant gains, with an average improvement of 4.87% in terms of the F1 score. The consistent improvements across all multilingual models suggest that the knowledge distillation strategy was effective in transferring the specialised emotion detection capabilities of the monolingual model to the multilingual model. However, the results on the test set were more varied. While XLM-RoBERTa and E5 still demonstrated obvious improvements, the BGE-M3 model only showed a minor increase of 0.24% in performance. This suggests that while the multi-functional pre-training strategy enables BGE-M3 to handle inputs of different granularities, it may have resulted in representations that are less aligned with specific emotion detection tasks and hinder the ability to deal with a large proportion of instances with linguistic phenomena in the test set.

### 3.4 Explainability of Transformers

To gain insights into the explainability of our models and their ability to identify emotion triggers, we evaluated their zero-shot performance on the binary trigger detection task. Without any explicit training on the fine-tuned emotion detection models, we directly reported the token-level F1 score and mean average precision (MAP) on this task, as presented in Table 2.

Notably, we observed that the trigger detection performances of each model on the development and test sets were basically consistent with their emotion detection performance. Both the refined XLM-RoBERTa and E5 models showed better trigger detection capabilities compared to their original versions. However, the performance of the BGE-M3 model on trigger detection became slightly worse than its original version, which can potentially account for the relatively poor performance gains observed on the emotion detection task on the test set.

| Models | Development | | Testing | |
|---|---|---|---|---|
| | F1 | MAP | F1 | MAP |
| XLM-R. | 33.60 | 25.11 | 30.77 | 24.23 |
| E5 | 33.03 | 24.62 | 30.46 | 23.78 |
| BGE-M3 | 33.60 | 24.68 | 29.84 | 23.22 |
| R. + XLM-R. (↑) | 33.73 | 25.46 | 31.25 | 24.34 |
| R. + E5 (↑) | 33.85 | 25.02 | 31.61 | 24.64 |
| R. + BGE-M3 (↓) | 32.97 | 24.49 | 29.35 | 23.03 |

Table 2: Zero-shot performance on binary trigger detection task as explainable results.

## 4 Conclusion and Future Work

In this work, we proposed a novel approach that combines the strength of monolingual and multilingual PLM for improved emotion detection performance. Our method involves training a high-performing English monolingual model in parallel with a multilingual model on the same English emotion detection training set. We then employ a knowledge distillation strategy to transfer the specialised emotion detection capabilities from the monolingual teacher model to refine the multilingual student model. Future work could explore more sophisticated knowledge distillation techniques, as well as employ more accurate and effective translation methods (Na et al., 2024).

## Limitations

There are several potential limitations in our work: 1) while a weighting scheme is proposed to account for the translation errors, the quality of the translation system can still significantly impact the knowledge distillation process; 2) the computational complexity involved in training multiple models and performing additional inference steps for weighting and distillation may pose practical limitations.

## Acknowledgements

We would like to acknowledge the financial support provided by the Postgraduate Research Scholarship (PGRS) (contract number PGRS-20-06-013) at Xi'an Jiaotong-Liverpool University. Additionally, this research has received partial funding from the Jiangsu Science and Technology Programme (contract number BK20221260) and the Research Development Fund (contract number RDF-22-01-132) at Xi'an Jiaotong-Liverpool University.

## References

Muhammad Abdul-Mageed and Lyle Ungar. 2017. Emonet: Fine-grained emotion detection with gated recurrent neural networks. In *Proceedings of the 55th annual meeting of the association for computational linguistics (volume 1: Long papers)*, pages 718–728.

Hila Chefer, Shir Gur, and Lior Wolf. 2021. Transformer interpretability beyond attention visualization. In *Proceedings of the IEEE/CVF conference on computer vision and pattern recognition*, pages 782–791.

Jianlv Chen, Shitao Xiao, Peitian Zhang, Kun Luo, Defu Lian, and Zheng Liu. 2024. Bge m3-embedding: Multi-lingual, multi-functionality, multi-granularity text embeddings through self-knowledge distillation. *arXiv preprint arXiv:2402.03216*.

Alexis Conneau, Kartikay Khandelwal, Naman Goyal, Vishrav Chaudhary, Guillaume Wenzek, Francisco Guzmán, Edouard Grave, Myle Ott, Luke Zettlemoyer, and Veselin Stoyanov. 2020. Unsupervised cross-lingual representation learning at scale. In *Proceedings of the 58th Annual Meeting of the Association for Computational Linguistics*. Association for Computational Linguistics.

Tim Dettmers, Artidoro Pagnoni, Ari Holtzman, and Luke Zettlemoyer. 2024. Qlora: Efficient finetuning of quantized llms. *Advances in Neural Information Processing Systems*, 36.

Jacob Devlin, Ming-Wei Chang, Kenton Lee, and Kristina Toutanova. 2019. Bert: Pre-training of deep bidirectional transformers for language understanding. In *Proceedings of the 2019 Conference of the North American Chapter of the Association for Computational Linguistics: Human Language Technologies, Volume 1 (Long and Short Papers)*, pages 4171–4186.

Pengcheng He, Jianfeng Gao, and Weizhu Chen. 2021. Debertav3: Improving deberta using electra-style pretraining with gradient-disentangled embedding sharing. *Preprint*, arXiv:2111.09543.

Marcin Junczys-Dowmunt, Roman Grundkiewicz, Tomasz Dwojak, Hieu Hoang, Kenneth Heafield, Tom Neckermann, Frank Seide, Ulrich Germann, Alham Fikri Aji, Nikolay Bogoychev, André F. T. Martins, and Alexandra Birch. 2018. Marian: Fast neural machine translation in C++. In *Proceedings of ACL 2018, System Demonstrations*, pages 116–121, Melbourne, Australia. Association for Computational Linguistics.

Teven Le Scao, Angela Fan, Christopher Akiki, Ellie Pavlick, Suzana Ilić, Daniel Hesslow, Roman Castagné, Alexandra Sasha Luccioni, François Yvon, Matthias Gallé, et al. 2023. Bloom: A 176b-parameter open-access multilingual language model.

Yinhan Liu, Jiatao Gu, Naman Goyal, Xian Li, Sergey Edunov, Marjan Ghazvininejad, Mike Lewis, and Luke Zettlemoyer. 2020. Multilingual denoising pretraining for neural machine translation. *Transactions of the Association for Computational Linguistics*, 8:726–742.

Yinhan Liu, Myle Ott, Naman Goyal, Jingfei Du, Mandar Joshi, Danqi Chen, Omer Levy, Mike Lewis, Luke Zettlemoyer, and Veselin Stoyanov. 2019. Roberta: A robustly optimized bert pretraining approach. *arXiv preprint arXiv:1907.11692*.

Cedric Lothritz, Kevin Allix, Bertrand Lebichot, Lisa Veiber, Tegawendé F Bissyandé, and Jacques Klein. 2021. Comparing multilingual and multiple monolingual models for intent classification and slot filling. In *International Conference on Applications of Natural Language to Information Systems*, pages 367–375. Springer.

Aaron Maladry, Pranaydeep Singh, and Els Lefever. 2024. Findings of the wassa 2024 exalt shared task on explainability for cross-lingual emotion in tweets. In *Proceedings of the 14th Workshop of on Computational Approaches to Subjectivity, Sentiment & Social Media Analysis@ACL 2024*, Bangkok, Thailand.

Niklas Muennighoff, Thomas Wang, Lintang Sutawika, Adam Roberts, Stella Biderman, Teven Le Scao, M Saiful Bari, Sheng Shen, Zheng Xin Yong, Hailey

Schoelkopf, et al. 2023. Crosslingual generalization through multitask finetuning. In *Proceedings of the 61st Annual Meeting of the Association for Computational Linguistics (Volume 1: Long Papers)*, pages 15991–16111.

Hongbin Na, Zimu Wang, Mieradilijiang Maimaiti, Tong Chen, Wei Wang, Tao Shen, and Ling Chen. 2024. Rethinking human-like translation strategy: Integrating drift-diffusion model with large language models for machine translation. *arXiv preprint arXiv:2402.10699*.

Sebastian Ruder, Anders Søgaard, and Ivan Vulić. 2019. Unsupervised cross-lingual representation learning. In *Proceedings of the 57th Annual Meeting of the Association for Computational Linguistics: Tutorial Abstracts*, pages 31–38.

Tiberiu Sosea and Cornelia Caragea. 2020. Canceremo: A dataset for fine-grained emotion detection. In *Proceedings of the 2020 Conference on Empirical Methods in Natural Language Processing (EMNLP)*, pages 8892–8904.

Rohan Taori, Ishaan Gulrajani, Tianyi Zhang, Yann Dubois, Xuechen Li, Carlos Guestrin, Percy Liang, and Tatsunori B Hashimoto. 2023. Alpaca: A strong, replicable instruction-following model. *Stanford Center for Research on Foundation Models. https://crfm. stanford. edu/2023/03/13/alpaca. html*, 3(6):7.

Liang Wang, Nan Yang, Xiaolong Huang, Linjun Yang, Rangan Majumder, and Furu Wei. 2024. Multilingual e5 text embeddings: A technical report. *arXiv preprint arXiv:2402.05672*.

Yuqi Wang, Qi Chen, and Wei Wang. 2021. Multi-task bert for aspect-based sentiment analysis. In *2021 IEEE international conference on smart computing (SMARTCOMP)*, pages 383–385. IEEE.

Zimu Wang and Hong-Seng Gan. 2023. Multi-level adversarial training for stock sentiment prediction. In *2023 IEEE 3rd International Conference on Computer Communication and Artificial Intelligence (CCAI)*, pages 127–134. IEEE.

Shijie Wu and Mark Dredze. 2020. Are all languages created equal in multilingual bert? *ACL 2020*, page 120.

## Appendix

### .1 Experimental Details

We downloaded all pre-trained models from the Hugging Face repository[2]. The translation system was implemented using machine translation models from the Helsinki-NLP group[3] and a standalone language identification tool (LANGID)[4]. Hardware acceleration was achieved using 2 NVIDIA 3090 GPUs.

For fine-tuning generative models with the provided training data, we employed a parameter-efficient approach using 4-bit quantized low-rank adaptation (QLoRA) (Dettmers et al., 2024). The learning rate was set to $5 \times 10^{-5}$, and we used the Alpaca (Taori et al., 2023) template. We showed the prompt for the emotion detection task in Table 3. The batch size was set to 2 per GPU, and the gradient accumulation steps were set to 2. For fine-tuning discriminative models and feature extractors, we utilised the Adam optimiser with parameters $\beta_1 = 0.9$ and $\beta_2 = 0.99$. The learning rate was set to $5 \times 10^{-6}$, and the batch size was set to 16 per GPU.

| *Below is an instruction that describes a task. Write a response that appropriately completes the request.*<br>*### Instruction:*<br>*Please use one word to describe the sentiment expressed in the given tweet.*<br>*Tweet:* `[Tweet]`<br>*### Response:* |
|---|

Table 3: Prompt used for generative model.

For all models, the epoch count was set to 20. Early stopping was implemented to mitigate the risk of overfitting. In order to achieve this, we further split the provided English data into a training set and a "validation set" with a ratio of 90:10. The best checkpoint on the "validation set" was saved.

In the refinement process, the learning rates for XLM-RoBERTa, E5, and BGE-M3 were set to $1 \times 10^{-7}$, $5 \times 10^{-7}$, and $7 \times 10^{-7}$, respectively, which were chosen from the "validation set" split from the original training set, so no labelled data in languages other than English was used.

For the binary trigger detection, we computed the cosine similarity between the last hidden state of the $< s >$ token and each token from the transformer. We chose a threshold for each model based on the result of the above-mentioned "validation set".

[2]https://huggingface.co/

[3]https://github.com/Helsinki-NLP/Opus-MT

[4]https://pypi.org/project/langid/

# HITSZ-HLT at WASSA-2024 Shared Task 2: Language-agnostic Multi-task Learning for Explainability of Cross-lingual Emotion Detection

**Feng Xiong**[1,3] **Jun Wang**[1,3] **Geng Tu**[1,3] **Ruifeng Xu**[1,2,3*]
[1]Harbin Institute of Technology, Shenzhen, China
[2]Peng Cheng Laboratory, Shenzhen, China
[3]Guangdong Provincial Key Laboratory of Novel Security Intelligence Technologies
23s151006@stu.hit.edu.cn, xuruifeng@hit.edu.cn

## Abstract

This paper describes the system developed by the HITSZ-HLT team for WASSA-2024 Shared Task 2, which addresses two closely linked subtasks: Cross-lingual Emotion Detection and Binary Trigger Word Detection in tweets. The main goal of Shared Task 2 is to simultaneously identify the emotions expressed and detect the trigger words across multiple languages. To achieve this, we introduce a **L**anguage-**a**gnostic **M**ulti **T**ask **L**earning (LaMTL) framework that integrates emotion prediction and emotion trigger word detection tasks. By fostering synergistic interactions between task-specific and task-agnostic representations, the LaMTL aims to mutually enhance emotional cues, ultimately improving the performance of both tasks. Additionally, we leverage large-scale language models to translate the training dataset into multiple languages, thereby fostering the formation of language-agnostic representations within the model, significantly enhancing the model's ability to transfer and perform well across multilingual data. Experimental results demonstrate the effectiveness of our framework across both tasks, with a particular highlight on its success in achieving second place in sub-task 2.

## 1 Introduction

Sentiment Analysis is an important task in Natural Language Processing (NLP), aiming to identify and assess the sentiment polarity in texts (Cambria, 2016). With the rapid development of social media and the Internet, sentiment analysis has become increasingly important in various fields such as customer service (Zvarevashe and Olugbara, 2018) and finance (Xing et al., 2020). Despite notable strides in sentiment analysis research (Jiang et al., 2023; Tu et al., 2023; Zhang et al., 2023; Hartmann et al., 2023; Zhong et al., 2023), challenges persist, particularly concerning foreign language texts where annotated data may be scarce.

Cross-lingual Sentiment Analysis (CLSA) (Liu, 2012) mitigates these challenges by utilizing resources from one or more source languages to assist in sentiment analysis for low-resource languages (Esuli et al., 2020). This approach addresses the lack of annotated corpora for many non-English languages, making it a crucial research area in NLP. The fundamental strategy entails the transfer and adaptation of knowledge across various linguistic contexts (Zhao et al., 2024). Building on the foundational principles of CLSA, our study further explores how these methodologies can be practically implemented to enhance model performance across diverse linguistic settings.

The main challenge in Shared Task 2 (Maladry et al., 2024) involves two key aspects: (1) Enhancing the model's capability to transfer knowledge to languages not present in the training data. (2) Developing strategies to effectively utilize complementarities between dual tasks given the limited availability of annotated data. To address the aforementioned challenges, we have developed a **L**anguage-**a**gnostic **M**ulti **T**ask **L**earning (LaMTL) framework that effectively navigates cross-lingual obstacles while simultaneously bridging shared emotional cues across dual tasks.

Specifically, we utilize ChatGPT[1] as a sophisticated tool for translation. By refining prompts, we translate the original tweets into Dutch, Russian, Spanish, and French, striving to maintain the original style as accurately as possible. By aligning the representations of identical tweets across different languages (Feng et al., 2022), we aim to develop a language-agnostic representation. Due to the complementary relationship between emotions and trigger words within tweets, we have designed a novel multi-task framework that includes both task-agnostic and task-specific encoders. The task-agnostic encoder captures task-invariant fea-

*Corresponding author.

[1]https://chat.openai.com/



*Proceedings of the 14th Workshop on Computational Approaches to Subjectivity, Sentiment, & Social Media Analysis*, pages 476–482
August 15, 2024 

tures, facilitating the identification of underlying commonalities and related characteristics across tasks, while the task-specific encoder learns features unique to each task. To ensure comprehensive training, we incorporated multiple loss functions, including reconstruction loss and task prediction loss. This approach aims to improve the accuracy and robustness of multi-task learning by leveraging both shared and task-specific features, ultimately enhancing the framework's performance on various tasks.

Additionally, we conducted a rigorous evaluation of our approach utilizing the EXALT dataset[2], which substantiated its effectiveness. This comprehensive validation process led to our achievement of an esteemed second place in a highly competitive arena, as documented on the official leaderboard[3].

## 2 Related Evaluation Tasks

In recent years, CLSA has gained widespread attention. In 2013, NLP&CC organized a cross-language evaluation by releasing annotated English data from Amazon user reviews and unannotated Chinese reviews. This initiative facilitated the development of methods for cross-lingual sentiment analysis. SemEval-2017 Task 4 (Rosenthal et al., 2017) focused on multilingual sentiment analysis of Twitter posts. This task utilized product ratings from platforms such as Amazon, TripAdvisor, and Yelp, and included five subtasks for both Arabic and English. SemEval-2020 Task 9 (Patwa et al., 2020) concentrated on sentiment analysis of code-mixed tweets in Hinglish and Spanglish, providing annotated corpora and attracting 89 submissions. The top models achieved F1 scores of 75.0% for Hinglish and 80.6% for Spanglish. SemEval-2022 Task 10 (Barnes et al., 2022) introduced the first shared task on Structured Sentiment Analysis. Participants were required to predict sentiment graphs composed of a holder, target, expression, and polarity across seven datasets in five languages.

## 3 Methodology

In this section, we offer a comprehensive introduction to each component of the proposed LaMTL framework, illustrated in Fig. 1.

[2]https://huggingface.co/datasets/pranaydeeps/EXALT-v1
[3]https://lt3.ugent.be/exalt

### 3.1 Feature Extraction

We first employ ChatGPT to translate each English tweet $\mathbf{x}_i^e$ from the training dataset $\mathbf{D}$ into $\mathbf{x}_i^\psi$, where $\psi \in \{d, r, s, f\}$ corresponds to Dutch, Russian, Spanish, and French, respectively. Subsequently, we utilize a multilingual pretrained model as the foundational encoder to extract feature representations from the tweets across various languages.

Specifically, for a tweet $\mathbf{x}_i = \{s_1, s_2, \ldots, s_{\mathcal{N}_i}\}$, where $\mathcal{N}_i$ denotes the number of words of $\mathbf{x}_i$, the corresponding sequence of tokens resulting from the application of subword tokenization techniques such as WordPiece and Byte Pair Encoding (BPE) is denoted by $\{w_1, w_2, \ldots, w_{\widehat{\mathcal{N}_i}}\}$. $\widehat{\mathcal{N}_i}$ signifies the number of tokens corresponding to $\mathbf{x}_i$. The output of the last layer is denoted as $\mathbf{h}^e \in \mathbb{R}^{\widehat{\mathcal{N}_i} \times d_h}$ and $\mathbf{h}^\psi \in \mathbb{R}^{\widehat{\mathcal{N}_i^\psi} \times d_h}$. For each word $s_j$, its representation $\mathbf{h}_j \in \mathbb{R}^{d_h}$ is obtained by averaging the representations of its corresponding tokens.

### 3.2 Cross-Lingual Semantic Alignment

The Cross-Lingual Semantic Alignment (SA) Module aims to align semantic representations across language barriers. To achieve this, we employ the Mean Squared Error (MSE) as a reconstruction loss function. This function aims to minimize the semantic distance between translated non-English tweets and their English counterparts. It promotes the convergence of the feature vectors $\mathbf{h}^\psi$ of the translated tweets toward the feature vectors $\mathbf{h}^e$ of the original English tweets, ensuring consistent semantic representation across languages. The reconstruction loss $L_{rec}$ can be represented as,

$$L_{rec} = \sum_{\psi} \mathrm{MSE}(\widehat{\mathbf{h}^e}, \widehat{\mathbf{h}^\psi}), \tag{1}$$

where $\widehat{\mathbf{h}^e}$ and $\widehat{\mathbf{h}^\psi}$ denote the [CLS] representation or the average of all tokens for $\mathbf{h}^e$ and $\mathbf{h}^\psi$.

### 3.3 Multi-Task Fusion

To effectively encapsulate the pertinent emotional cues in diverse tasks, we developed the Multi-Task Fusion (MTF) Module. This module integrates a task-invariant encoder alongside two task-specific encoders, each comprising a stacked structure of $L$ transformer encoder layers. In MTF, each tweet $\mathbf{x}_i$ is processed by three distinct encoders. The first encoder, $\mathbf{E}_s$, is task-invariant and designed to learn a generalized representation across multiple tasks by positioning the learned features within a common subspace. The other two encoders, $\mathbf{E}_e$ and $\mathbf{E}_t$,

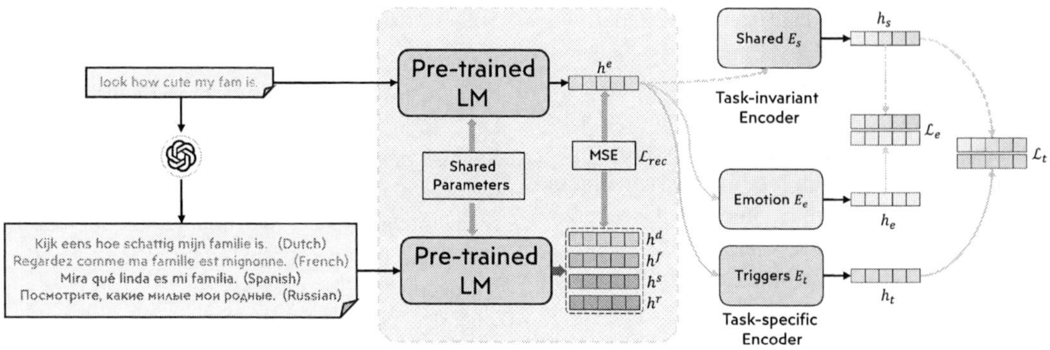


Figure 1: The proposed LaMTL framework. The graphical symbols directly correspond to the equations presented within the paper.

are task-specific. $\mathbf{E}_e$ is dedicated to emotion detection, focusing on the subtle emotional nuances embedded within the tweets. In contrast, $\mathbf{E}_t$ specializes in emotion trigger detection, identifying key triggers that indicate the presence or absence of specific emotional conditions. The process can be represented as:

$$\mathbf{h}_s = \mathbf{E}_s(\mathbf{h}^e, \Theta_s), \tag{2}$$

$$\mathbf{h}_\eta = \mathbf{E}_\eta(\mathbf{h}^e, \Theta_\eta), \eta \in \{e, t\}. \tag{3}$$

The encoder $\mathbf{E}_s$ shares parameters $\Theta_s$ across the two tasks, while $\mathbf{E}_\eta$ utilizes distinct parameters $\Theta_\eta$ for each task.

Finally, we concatenate the task-invariant representations $\mathbf{h}_s$ with the task-specific representation $\mathbf{h}_\eta$ and use a Multi-Layer Perceptron (MLP) with softmax for classification. Formally,

$$\mathcal{H}_\eta = \mathbf{h}_s \oplus \mathbf{h}_\eta, \tag{4}$$

$$\mathcal{P}_\eta = \mathrm{softmax}(\mathrm{MLP}_\eta(\mathcal{H}_\eta)), \tag{5}$$

$$\hat{\mathbf{y}}_\eta = \mathrm{argmax}(\mathcal{P}_\eta), \tag{6}$$

where $\oplus$ denotes the concatenation operation. Notably, we utilize $\hat{\mathbf{y}}_\eta$ as the prediction results for the task $\eta$.

### 3.4 Model Training

We utilize cross-entropy loss for the classification of the Cross-lingual Emotion Detection and Binary Trigger Word Detection tasks, denoted as $\mathcal{L}_e$ and $\mathcal{L}_t$, respectively. The computation process can be described as follows:

$$\mathcal{L}_\eta = -\frac{1}{N_\eta} \sum_{j=1}^{N_\eta} \sum_{k=1}^{C_\eta} \mathbf{y}_{\eta,[j][k]} \log(\mathcal{P}_{\eta,[j][k]}), \tag{7}$$

where $N$ denotes the number of samples, $C$ represents the number of classes for task $\eta$, $\mathcal{P}_{\eta,[j][k]}$ denotes the probability distribution for instance $j$ over class $k$, and $\mathbf{y}_{\eta,[j][k]}$ is a binary indicator that equals 1 if class $k$ is the correct classification for instance $j$ in task $\eta$, and 0 otherwise. Specifically, $C$ is set to 6 for task $\eta = e$ and to 2 for task $\eta = t$. For samples in the dataset containing two types of labels, we compute $\mathcal{L}_e$ and $\mathcal{L}_t$. For samples with only one type of label, we compute the loss specific to the corresponding task. To facilitate better-mixed learning, we apply a shuffling strategy to the dataset.

By combining the reconstruction loss and task-specific loss, our final loss function can be expressed as,

$$\mathcal{L} = \mathcal{L}_e + \mathcal{L}_t + \lambda_{rec}\mathcal{L}_{rec} + \lambda||\Theta||_2^2, \tag{8}$$

where $L_e$ and $L_t$ denote the classification loss for Cross-lingual Emotion Detection and Binary Trigger Word Detection, while $\lambda$ represents the L2 regularization weight, and $\Theta$ signifies the set of all trainable parameters.

## 4 Experiments

### 4.1 Baselines

To demonstrate the efficacy of our approach, we fine-tuned multilingual pre-trained models using the official codebase[4], including Multilingual-BERT (Devlin et al., 2019), LaBSE (Feng et al., 2022), and Multilingual-E5-Large (Wang et al., 2024). Furthermore, due to the robust multilingual capabilities of LLM, we conducted experiments using various configurations. Specifically,

[4]https://github.com/pranaydeeps/WASSA24_EXALT

| Methods | Emotion | Binary Triggers |
|---|---|---|
| EXALT-Baseline ♠ | 44.76 | 23.49 |
| Multilingual-BERT♣ | 34.40 | 23.57 |
| LaBSE♣ | 48.41 | 32.49 |
| Multilingual-E5-large ♣ | 51.70 | 25.68 |
| LLaMA2 + LoRAMoE ◇ | 49.03 | 57.05 |
| LLaMA3 + LoRA ◇ | <u>54.40</u> | <u>57.62</u> |
| GPT4 (Zero-shot)◇ | 52.57 | - |
| LaMTL‡ | **56.88** | **60.95** |

Table 1: Comparison of F1 score (%) conducted for the EXALT datasets. The results are presented such that the highest performance is denoted in bold, and the second highest performance is underlined. ♠ indicates results obtained from Codalab, ♣ indicates our re-implemented using the official codebase, ◇ indicates the results of our implementation on the validation set, and ‡ indicates the results of our implementation on the test set.

| Methods | Emotion | Binary Triggers |
|---|---|---|
| LaMTL‡ | **56.88** | **60.95** |
| w/o SA‡ | 54.85 | 58.47 |
| w/o MTF‡ | 54.90 | 59.84 |

Table 2: F1 score (%) for Ablation results.

we fine-tuned LLaMA-2 (Touvron et al., 2023) in conjunction with LoRAMoE (Dou et al., 2024) and LLaMA-3 (AI@Meta, 2024) with LoRA (Hu et al., 2022). Additionally, we performed zero-shot emotion detection experiments on GPT-4 (Achiam et al., 2023), and the designed prompt template can be found in Appendix A.

In ablation studies, 'w/o SA' denotes the removal of the SA module, and 'w/o MTF' indicates the removal of the MTF module.

### 4.2 Experimental Settings

In our experimental settings, we utilize a learning rate of 1e-4 with the AdamW optimizer to optimize the model parameters. We configured gradient accumulation to 4 and batch size to 8. In this study, we employ XLM-RoBERTa-Large (Conneau et al., 2020) as the backbone model. We configured the encoder in the MTF module as a single-layer transformer encoder. Additionally, the $\lambda_{rec}$ parameter was strategically set to 0.05. The word embedding dimension $d_h$ is 1024, and the maximum sequence length is 512. All experiments were conducted on a single RTX 4090 GPU, using BF16 precision to optimize both speed and computational efficiency.

| Team | Binary Triggers |
|---|---|
| CTcloud | **61.58** |
| HITSZ-HLT | <u>60.95</u> |
| UWB | 59.19 |
| NLP_Newcomer | 57.85 |
| NYCU-NLP | 56.36 |

Table 3: Top-5 F1 score (%) for Binary Trigger Word Detection. The results are presented such that the highest performance is denoted in bold, and the second highest performance is underlined.

### 4.3 Evaluation Metrics

We use the official metrics for evaluation. For the Cross-lingual Emotion Detection task, we use the Macro-averaged F1 score as the evaluation metric. For the Binary Trigger Word Detection task, we utilize the Token F1 score as the evaluation metric.

### 4.4 Experimental Results and Analysis

**Comparative Results:** Table 1 presents a comparative analysis of our LaMTL model against various cross-lingual baseline models and LLMs. Our LaMTL model consistently outperforms the baselines across both sub-tasks, demonstrating superior performance. In addition, LLMs also exhibit remarkable performance and will be a primary focus of our future research.

**Ablation Studies:** We conducted ablation experiments for our framework. According to the results shown in Table 2, the LaMTL model achieved F1 scores of 56.88% on the Emotion task and 60.95% on the Binary Triggers task. Removing the Cross-lingual Semantic Alignment (SA) module resulted in F1 score decreases of 2.03 and 2.48 percentage points for the Emotion and Binary Triggers tasks, respectively, indicating the importance of cross-linguistic feature semantic alignment, especially for the Binary Triggers Word Detection task. Similarly, removing the Multi-Task Fusion (MTF) module led to F1 score decreases of 1.98 and 1.11 percentage points for the Emotion and Binary Triggers tasks, respectively.

**Leaderboard Results:** Table 3 presents the performance of the top five teams in Binary Trigger Word Detection task. Our method achieves second place on the leaderboard.

## 5 Conclusions

In this paper, we propose a language-agnostic multitask learning approach to address the challenge of interpretability in cross-lingual sentiment analysis.

Firstly, we designed a reconstruction loss to mitigate cross-lingual discrepancies. Secondly, we implemented a multi-task learning framework to share sentiment cues between two tasks, thereby enhancing performance in both tasks. Through these methods, our model effectively enhances cross-lingual capabilities and facilitates the sharing of emotional cues between multiple tasks, thereby achieving competitive performance.

## 6 Limitations

Although our LaMTL framework has demonstrated significant efficacy in cross-lingual sentiment detection and binary trigger word detection, there are several limitations that need to be addressed in future work. The use of large-scale language models for translation introduces potential biases and inaccuracies, especially for less common or informal texts in tweets. These translation inconsistencies can affect the quality of language-agnostic representations. While our framework has achieved commendable results, real-world applications might present additional challenges, such as subtle nuances specific to certain domains and the evolving use of language, which were not extensively explored in this study. Addressing these limitations in future research is crucial for enhancing the applicability and performance of cross-lingual sentiment analysis models.

## Acknowledgments

This work was partially supported by the National Natural Science Foundation of China (62176076), the Natural Science Foundation of Guangdong (2023A1515012922), the Shenzhen Foundational Research Funding (JCYJ20220818102415032), and the Guangdong Provincial Key Laboratory of Novel Security Intelligence Technologies (2022B1212010005).

## References

Josh Achiam, Steven Adler, Sandhini Agarwal, Lama Ahmad, Ilge Akkaya, Florencia Leoni Aleman, Diogo Almeida, Janko Altenschmidt, Sam Altman, Shyamal Anadkat, et al. 2023. Gpt-4 technical report. *arXiv preprint arXiv:2303.08774*.

AI@Meta. 2024. Llama 3 model card.

Jeremy Barnes, Laura Oberlaender, Enrica Troiano, Andrey Kutuzov, Jan Buchmann, Rodrigo Agerri, Lilja Øvrelid, and Erik Velldal. 2022. SemEval 2022 task 10: Structured sentiment analysis. In *Proceedings of the 16th International Workshop on Semantic Evaluation (SemEval-2022)*, pages 1280–1295, Seattle, United States. Association for Computational Linguistics.

Erik Cambria. 2016. Affective computing and sentiment analysis. *IEEE Intelligent Systems*, 31(2):102–107.

Alexis Conneau, Kartikay Khandelwal, Naman Goyal, Vishrav Chaudhary, Guillaume Wenzek, Francisco Guzmán, Edouard Grave, Myle Ott, Luke Zettlemoyer, and Veselin Stoyanov. 2020. Unsupervised cross-lingual representation learning at scale. In *Proceedings of the 58th Annual Meeting of the Association for Computational Linguistics*, pages 8440–8451, Online. Association for Computational Linguistics.

Jacob Devlin, Ming-Wei Chang, Kenton Lee, and Kristina Toutanova. 2019. BERT: Pre-training of deep bidirectional transformers for language understanding. In *Proceedings of the 2019 Conference of the North American Chapter of the Association for Computational Linguistics: Human Language Technologies, Volume 1 (Long and Short Papers)*, pages 4171–4186, Minneapolis, Minnesota. Association for Computational Linguistics.

Shihan Dou, Enyu Zhou, Yan Liu, Songyang Gao, Jun Zhao, Wei Shen, Yuhao Zhou, Zhiheng Xi, Xiao Wang, Xiaoran Fan, Shiliang Pu, Jiang Zhu, Rui Zheng, Tao Gui, Qi Zhang, and Xuanjing Huang. 2024. Loramoe: Alleviate world knowledge forgetting in large language models via moe-style plugin.

Andrea Esuli, Alejandro Moreo, and Fabrizio Sebastiani. 2020. Cross-lingual sentiment quantification. *IEEE Intelligent Systems*, 35(3):106–114.

Fangxiaoyu Feng, Yinfei Yang, Daniel Cer, Naveen Arivazhagan, and Wei Wang. 2022. Language-agnostic BERT sentence embedding. In *Proceedings of the 60th Annual Meeting of the Association for Computational Linguistics (Volume 1: Long Papers)*, pages 878–891, Dublin, Ireland. Association for Computational Linguistics.

Jochen Hartmann, Mark Heitmann, Christian Siebert, and Christina Schamp. 2023. More than a feeling: Accuracy and application of sentiment analysis. *International Journal of Research in Marketing*, 40(1):75–87.

Edward J Hu, Yelong Shen, Phillip Wallis, Zeyuan Allen-Zhu, Yuanzhi Li, Shean Wang, Lu Wang, and Weizhu Chen. 2022. LoRA: Low-rank adaptation of large language models. In *International Conference on Learning Representations*.

Dazhi Jiang, Runguo Wei, Jintao Wen, Geng Tu, and Erik Cambria. 2023. Automl-emo: Automatic knowledge selection using congruent effect for emotion identification in conversations. *IEEE Transactions on Affective Computing*, 14(03):1845–1856.

Bing Liu. 2012. *Sentiment Analysis and Opinion Mining*. Synthesis Lectures on Human Language Technologies. Springer Cham.

Aaron Maladry, Pranaydeep Singh, and Els Lefever. 2024. Findings of the wassa 2024 exalt shared task on explainability for cross-lingual emotion in tweets. In *Proceedings of the 14th Workshop of on Computational Approaches to Subjectivity, Sentiment & Social Media Analysis@ACL 2024*, Bangkok, Thailand.

Parth Patwa, Gustavo Aguilar, Sudipta Kar, Suraj Pandey, Srinivas PYKL, Björn Gambäck, Tanmoy Chakraborty, Thamar Solorio, and Amitava Das. 2020. SemEval-2020 task 9: Overview of sentiment analysis of code-mixed tweets. In *Proceedings of the Fourteenth Workshop on Semantic Evaluation*, pages 774–790, Barcelona (online). International Committee for Computational Linguistics.

Sara Rosenthal, Noura Farra, and Preslav Nakov. 2017. SemEval-2017 task 4: Sentiment analysis in Twitter. In *Proceedings of the 11th International Workshop on Semantic Evaluation (SemEval-2017)*, pages 502–518, Vancouver, Canada. Association for Computational Linguistics.

Hugo Touvron, Louis Martin, Kevin Stone, Peter Albert, Amjad Almahairi, Yasmine Babaei, Nikolay Bashlykov, Soumya Batra, Prajjwal Bhargava, Shruti Bhosale, et al. 2023. Llama 2: Open foundation and fine-tuned chat models. *arXiv preprint arXiv:2307.09288*.

Geng Tu, Bin Liang, Ruibin Mao, Min Yang, and Ruifeng Xu. 2023. Context or knowledge is not always necessary: A contrastive learning framework for emotion recognition in conversations. In *Findings of the Association for Computational Linguistics: ACL 2023*, pages 14054–14067.

Liang Wang, Nan Yang, Xiaolong Huang, Linjun Yang, Rangan Majumder, and Furu Wei. 2024. Multilingual e5 text embeddings: A technical report. *arXiv preprint arXiv:2402.05672*.

Frank Xing, Lorenzo Malandri, Yue Zhang, and Erik Cambria. 2020. Financial sentiment analysis: An investigation into common mistakes and silver bullets. In *Proceedings of the 28th International Conference on Computational Linguistics*, pages 978–987, Barcelona, Spain (Online). International Committee on Computational Linguistics.

Wenxuan Zhang, Xin Li, Yang Deng, Lidong Bing, and Wai Lam. 2023. A survey on aspect-based sentiment analysis: Tasks, methods, and challenges. *IEEE Transactions on Knowledge and Data Engineering*, 35(11):11019–11038.

Chuanjun Zhao, Meiling Wu, Xinyi Yang, Wenyue Zhang, Shaoxia Zhang, Suge Wang, and Deyu Li. 2024. A systematic review of cross-lingual sentiment analysis: Tasks, strategies, and prospects. *ACM Computing Surveys*, 56(7).

Qihuang Zhong, Liang Ding, Juhua Liu, Bo Du, Hua Jin, and Dacheng Tao. 2023. Knowledge graph augmented network towards multiview representation learning for aspect-based sentiment analysis. *IEEE Transactions on Knowledge and Data Engineering*, 35(10):10098–10111.

Kudakwashe Zvarevashe and Oludayo O. Olugbara. 2018. A framework for sentiment analysis with opinion mining of hotel reviews. In *2018 Conference on Information Communications Technology and Society (ICTAS)*, pages 1–4.

## A Prompt Template for Emotion Detection

To employ GPT-4 for Cross-lingual Emotion Detection tasks, we have designed an effective prompt template, as illustrated in Figure 2.

```
Assuming the role of a tweet analyst, please analyze a tweet now.
Tweet: {}
Requirement:
Emotion: Identify the primary emotion from the following options:
["Anger", "Fear", "Joy", "Love", "Neutral", "Sadness"].
Explanation: provide an explanation in English for the identified emotion.
Please format your response in JSON as shown below:
{{
"Emotion": "<insert identified emotion here>",
"Explanation": "<provide explanation for the identified emotion here>"
}}
```

Figure 2: The designed prompt template for GPT-4.

# UWB at WASSA-2024 Shared Task 2: Cross-lingual Emotion Detection

**Jakub Šmíd[*], Pavel Přibáň[*], Pavel Král[*,†]**

University of West Bohemia, Faculty of Applied Sciences,
[*]Department of Computer Science and Engineering,
[†]NTIS – New Technologies for the Information Society
Univerzitní 2732/8, 301 00 Pilsen, Czech Republic
{jaksmid, pribanp, pkral}@kiv.zcu.cz
`https://nlp.kiv.zcu.cz`

## Abstract

This paper presents our system built for the WASSA-2024 Cross-lingual Emotion Detection Shared Task. The task consists of two subtasks: first, to assess an emotion label from six possible classes for a given tweet in one of five languages, and second, to predict words triggering the detected emotions in binary and numerical formats. Our proposed approach revolves around fine-tuning quantized large language models, specifically Orca 2, with low-rank adapters (LoRA) and multilingual Transformer-based models, such as XLM-R and mT5. We enhance performance through machine translation for both subtasks and trigger word switching for the second subtask. The system achieves excellent performance, ranking 1st in numerical trigger words detection, 3rd in binary trigger words detection, and 7th in emotion detection.

## 1 Introduction

Analyzing emotions in text, including emotion detection and other related tasks, is a well-studied area in natural language processing (NLP). This field has been extensively explored in various SemEval (Mohammad et al., 2018; Chatterjee et al., 2019) and WASSA (Klinger et al., 2018) competitions. The goal of WASSA-2024 Shared Task 2 (Maladry et al., 2024) is to predict specific emotions and identify the words that trigger these emotions. Additionally, this study investigates how emotional information can be transferred across five languages. While the training data is provided in English, the evaluation data includes English, Dutch, Russian, Spanish, and French.

Specifically, the task consists of two subtasks:

1) Cross-lingual emotion detection: Predicting emotion from six possible classes (*Love*, *Joy*, *Fear*, *Anger*, *Sadness*, *Neutral*) in five target languages.

2) Classifying words that express emotions: Identifying words that trigger emotions, with the output format being either binary (assigning a binary value to each token in the text) or numeric (assigning a numeric value to each token in the text).

Figure 1 shows an example from the dataset for both subtasks. For detailed label descriptions, see the annotation guidelines (Singh, Pranaydeep and Maladry, Aaron and Lefever, Els, 2023).

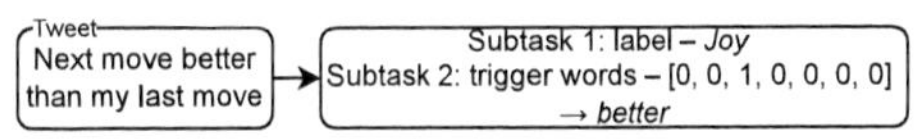


Figure 1: Example tweet with labels for both subtasks.

The first subtask can be considered a sentence-level classification task, while the second can be treated as a token-level classification task. Both subtasks can also be viewed as text-generation tasks (Raffel et al., 2023). Learning the representation of a given text is essential for solving these problems. Neural networks, including convolutional neural networks (CNNs) (Kim, 2014) and recurrent neural networks (RNNs) (Zaremba et al., 2015), alongside their variations, have been employed for this purpose. However, while these models are effective, they primarily rely on static word embeddings to capture semantic meanings. Consequently, they may struggle with more complex linguistic features such as anaphora and long-term dependencies.

Recent NLP research has shifted towards Transformer-based pre-trained language models (PLMs), such as BERT (Devlin et al., 2019) and T5 (Raffel et al., 2023). These models undergo initial pre-training on extensive datasets to grasp language representation intricacies. Subsequently, they can be fine-tuned on labelled data, capitalizing on the knowledge acquired during pre-training. For cross-lingual tasks, multilingual pre-trained models such as mT5 (Xue et al., 2021) and XLM-RoBERTa (XLM-R) (Conneau et al., 2020) have emerged as standard choices (Hu et al., 2020).



*Proceedings of the 14th Workshop on Computational Approaches to Subjectivity, Sentiment, & Social Media Analysis*, pages 483–489
August 15, 2024 ©2024 Association for Computational Linguistics

Recently, open-source large language models (LLMs), such as LLaMA 2 (Touvron et al., 2023) and Orca 2 (Mitra et al., 2023), have made significant progress across various NLP tasks. These models show remarkable performance in many zero- and few-shot tasks. Nevertheless, they are primarily pre-trained on English, which often necessitates additional fine-tuning to optimize their performance for other languages (Zhang et al., 2023). However, fine-tuning LLMs on non-specialized consumer GPUs presents challenges due to their large number of parameters. Techniques like QLoRA (Dettmers et al., 2023) address this issue by employing a quantized 4-bit frozen backbone LLM with a small set of learnable LoRA weights (Hu et al., 2021).

This paper proposes improving cross-lingual emotion detection by combining a quantized Orca 2 LLM, fine-tuned with LoRA, and machine translation. Additionally, we leverage fine-tuned Transformer-based multilingual language models, such as XLM-R and mT5, for trigger word detection. By incorporating alignment-free translation and trigger word switching, we aim to enhance performance further.[1]

## 2 System Description

We conduct experiments using the dataset provided by Maladry et al. (2024), which contains tweets in five different languages.

### 2.1 Problem Formulation

For both subtasks, the input is a sentence $x = \{x_i\}_{i=1}^{L}$ containing $L$ tokens. We denote the parameters of the models as $\Theta$, which includes task-specific parameters $\mathbf{W}$ and b. Given the sentence-label pairs $(x^S, y^S)$ in the source language $S$, the aim is to predict labels $y^T$ for the sentence $x^T$ in the target language $T$.

We formulate the emotion detection subtask as a text-generation problem, which can be modelled, for example, with decoder-only Transformer-based models. The decoder-only model calculates the probability of generating the next token $y_t$ at each step $t$ based on previous outputs $y_1, \ldots, y_{t-1}$ as

$$P_{\Theta}(y_t|y_1, \ldots, y_{t-1}) = \mathbf{Dec}(y_1, \ldots, y_{t-1}), \quad (1)$$

where $\mathbf{Dec}$ is the decoder function.

[1]The code is publicly available at `https://github.com/biba10/UWBWASSA2024SharedTask2`.

We formulate the second subtask as a token-level classification problem. Given the feature representations $\mathbf{h} = \{\mathbf{h}\}_{i=1}^{L}$ for each token in the sentence obtained by the model, we apply a linear layer on top to get the label distribution for each token $x_i$ as

$$P_{\Theta}(y_i|x_i) = \text{softmax}(\mathbf{W}\mathbf{h}_i + \mathbf{b}), \quad (2)$$

where $y \in \mathcal{Y} = \{0, 1\}$. We select the class with the highest probability. To obtain the numerical values, we extract the logits for class 1, which represents *"is a trigger word"* class, and apply the softmax function to these logits to get numbers between 0 and 1. We consider only the first token of each word for both binary and numerical values.

### 2.2 Label Projection

Following related work in cross-lingual classification (Hassan et al., 2022; Zhang et al., 2021), we translate the English training set into all non-English target languages using the Google API[2]. This approach significantly expands the training data. The process for the emotion detection task is straightforward: we translate the data and retain the original labels.

Creating translated data for the second subtask is more challenging because the translated text may not perfectly align with the original English text, resulting in different token counts between the two. Previous approaches (Mayhew et al., 2017; Fei et al., 2020) often rely on word alignment tools like fastAlign (Dyer et al., 2013) to map token-label pairs from the source sentence to the targeted one. We adopt an alignment-free label projection proposed by Zhang et al. (2021) to create pseudo-labelled data in the target languages.

First, we mark each trigger word in a sentence with predefined special symbols, such as "[]" or "{}", before translating it. We use distinct symbols for a sentence containing multiple trigger words. After translation, we extract the trigger words from the translated sentence using the special symbols. The translation system may occasionally overlook these special symbols, leading to their omission. In such cases, we discard the sentences. This process, illustrated in Figure 2, yields pseudo-labelled sentences in the target language.

Furthermore, we create additional datasets for the second subtask by combining data from different languages, as shown in the lower part of Figure 2. Given an English source sentence $x^S$ and its

[2]`https://translate.google.com/`

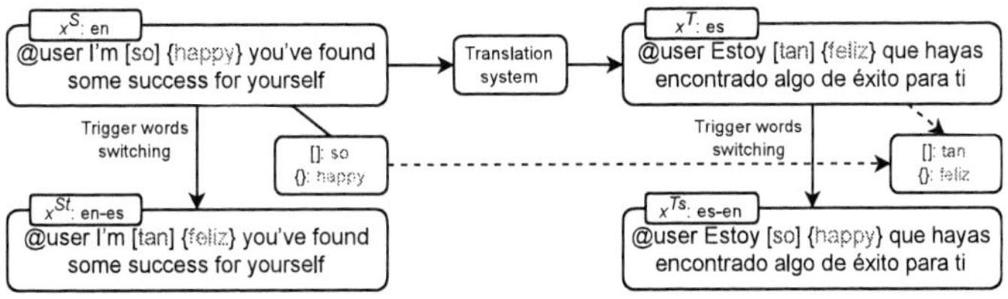


Figure 2: Example of label projection method with trigger words switching (lower part) for English and Spanish language pair.

translation $x^T$, we switch the trigger words to construct two new bilingual sentences: the first, $x^{St}$, originates from $x^S$ with trigger words expressed in the target language; the second, $x^{Ts}$, originates from $x^T$ with trigger words in the source language.

We denote the original English dataset as $D_S$, the translated dataset into all four non-English languages as $D_T$, the English source dataset with trigger words in other languages as $D_{St}$, and the translated dataset with trigger words in English as $D_{Ts}$.

## 2.3 LoRA

Fine-tuning LLMs like Orca 2 requires significant computational resources due to the model's extensive parameter count. To address this challenge, Dettmers et al. (2023) propose to use low-rank adapters (LoRA) (Hu et al., 2021) on top of a quantized backbone model. This method employs a small set of trainable parameters called adapters while keeping the original model frozen, thus reducing memory requirements.

For a pre-trained weight matrix $\mathbf{W}_0$, LoRA represents it with a low-rank decomposition as

$$\mathbf{W}_0 + \Delta\mathbf{W} = \mathbf{W}_0 + \mathbf{BA}, \tag{3}$$

where $\mathbf{B}$ and $\mathbf{A}$ are matrices with much lower dimensions than $\mathbf{W}_0$. During fine-tuning, $\mathbf{W}_0$ is frozen while the weights of $\mathbf{A}$ and $\mathbf{B}$ matrices are updated. Figure 3 shows the concept of LoRA.

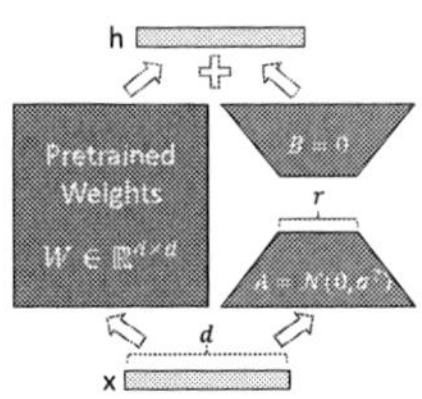


Figure 3: The illustrative depiction of parameter-saving LoRA fine-tuning proposed by Hu et al. (2021).

## 2.4 Models

We fine-tune the large versions of XLM-R (Conneau et al., 2020) and mT5 (Xue et al., 2021), as well as the 13B version of Orca 2 (Mitra et al., 2023), using the HuggingFace Transformers library[3] (Wolf et al., 2020). The Orca 2 model is used for the first subtask, while the XLM-R model and the encoder part of the mT5 model are employed for the second subtask.

## 2.5 Experimental Setup

For the initial hyperparameter selection, we sample 10% of the English training dataset as validation data for all experiments, following other cross-lingual work (Hu et al., 2019; Zhang et al., 2021) that simulate true unsupervised settings. This 10% is also excluded from the translation process that creates additional datasets. We use the original validation data in five languages to further reduce the number of models.

For both subtasks, we always fine-tune the models on the original English dataset $D_S$ (excluding the 10% of data used for validation) and explore the impact of incorporating additional data. Specifically, for the first subtask, we experiment with adding the translated dataset $D_T$. For the second subtask, we explore the following options: adding the translated dataset $D_T$, datasets with switched trigger words ($D_{St}$ and $D_{Ts}$), or both.

Figure 4 shows the prompt used for fine-tuning the Orca 2 model, where we train the model to output the specific emotion class in a textual format.

> Predict one emotion label for the given text. The possible labels are: "Love", "Joy", "Anger", "Fear", "Sadness", "Neutral".
> Answer in one following format: "Label: <emotion_label>"

Figure 4: Prompt for the emotion detection task.

### 2.5.1 Hyperparameters

We employ the AdamW optimizer (Loshchilov and Hutter, 2019) with a batch size 16 for all models.

[3] https://github.com/huggingface/transformers

For Orca 2, we use QLoRA for fine-tuning with 4-bit quantization, setting LoRA $r = 64$ and $\alpha = 16$, a learning rate 2e-4 with linear decay, and applying LoRA adapters on all linear Transformer block layers. We fine-tune the model for up to 5 epochs. For other models, we fine-tune them for up to 30 epochs and search for the learning rate from {2e-6, 2e-5, 5e-5, 2e-4} using a constant scheduler. All experiments are conducted on an NVIDIA A40 with 48 GB GPU memory.

### 2.5.2 Evaluation Metrics

The main metric for the emotion detection subtask is the macro-averaged F1 score. The primary metric for the binary trigger word detection subtask is the token-level F1 score, calculated on a token level and averaged across instances. A new metric called accumulated precise importance attribution is used for the numerical trigger word detection subtasks. After normalization (ignoring negative values and ensuring the attributions for each sentence add up to 1), this metric sums up the attributions for each trigger word (i.e., the tokens with a label 1).

## 3 Results

This section presents the results.

### 3.1 Emotion Detection

Table 1 shows the results of the emotion detection subtask. The results indicate that the Orca 2 largely benefits from the additional data translated into target languages, improving the results by over 3% on test data and by more than 7% on the validation set. The best model achieves a test score of 59.10, ranking seventh in the competition.

| Dataset | Dev | Test | Rank |
|---|---|---|---|
| $D_S$ | 50.12 | 55.73 | |
| $D_S + D_T$ | 57.74 | **59.10** | 7. |
| Baseline | | 44.76 | |
| Best | | 62.95 | |

Table 1: F1 macro scores on the emotion detection task with the Orca 2 model compared to baseline and best results (Maladry et al., 2024). **Bold** indicates the officially announced results and their competition rank.

Figure 5 and Figure 6 show the confusion matrices for the Orca 2 model fine-tuned on English data only and both English and translated data, respectively. The model fine-tuned on translated data demonstrates significantly better performance for the *Fear* (0.52 vs 0.29) and *Joy* (0.66 vs 0.55) classes while maintaining similar performance for other classes compared to the model fine-tuned only on English data.

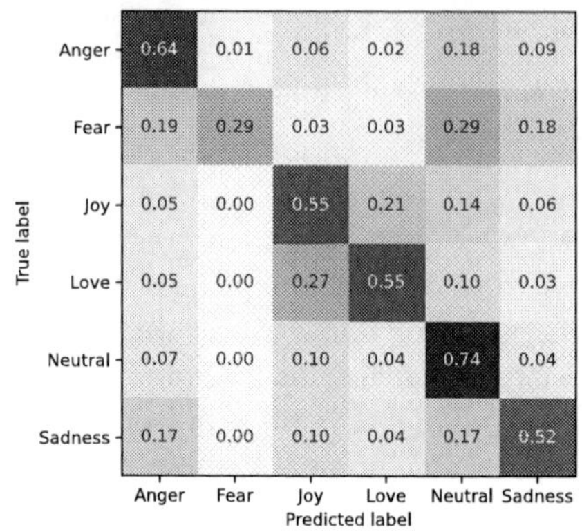


Figure 5: Confusion matrix on test data for the Orca 2 model fine-tuned on English data only.

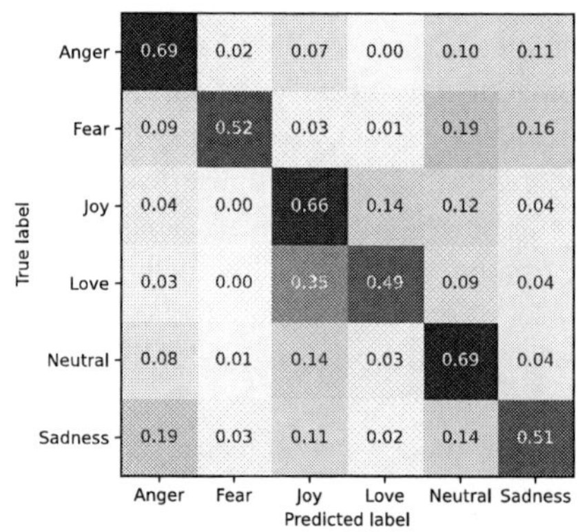


Figure 6: Confusion matrix on test data for the Orca 2 model fine-tuned on English and translated data.

Misclassified labels tend to cluster by sentiment. For instance, the *Love* label is frequently misclassified as *Joy*. The *Neutral*, *Anger*, and *Joy* classes appear to be the easiest to predict, likely due to their higher representation in the training and test data, as shown in Table 2.

| Label | Train | Dev | Test |
|---|---|---|---|
| Anger | 1,028 | 129 | 614 |
| Fear | 143 | 14 | 77 |
| Joy | 1,293 | 102 | 433 |
| Love | 579 | 40 | 190 |
| Neutral | 1,397 | 157 | 916 |
| Sadness | 560 | 58 | 270 |

Table 2: Label distribution for the emotion detection.

### 3.2 Trigger Words Detection

Table 3 presents the results of the trigger words detection subtask, evaluating the performance for binary and numerical outputs using various training combinations. For binary classification, XLM-R achieves the highest test score (59.19) when trained on the full combination of datasets ($D_S + D_T + D_{St} + D_{Ts}$), ranking third in the competition. Conversely, mT5 excels in numerical value prediction with a top test score of 70.52 under the same training conditions, securing first place. In most cases, the mT5 model's overall performance on numerical triggers is substantially worse than the performance of XLM-R. However, the results improve significantly when all dataset combinations are used.

Determining the best dataset combination and model is challenging due to the similar results achieved across many cases. Variability from random seeds during fine-tuning can obscure slight performance differences, which may not truly indicate superiority but rather random fluctuations. Nonetheless, our best test set results are obtained by training on a combination of the original, translated, and trigger words switched datasets. Combining all datasets for numerical trigger word detection using the mT5 model significantly improves the second-best settings by 8%.

| Model | Dataset | Binary | | | Numerical | | |
|---|---|---|---|---|---|---|---|
| | | Dev | Test | Rank | Dev | Test | Rank |
| XLM-R | $D_S$ | 61.85 | 58.59 | | 70.07 | 70.06 | |
| | $D_S + D_T$ | 60.82 | 56.69 | | 71.52 | 66.20 | |
| | $D_S + D_{St} + D_{Ts}$ | 57.97 | 53.18 | | 73.14 | 70.16 | |
| | $D_S + D_T + D_{St} + D_{Ts}$ | 60.46 | **59.19** | 3. | 70.05 | 70.02 | |
| mT5 | $D_S$ | 59.99 | 58.12 | | 60.11 | 60.00 | |
| | $D_S + D_T$ | 62.12 | 58.06 | | 63.14 | 62.06 | |
| | $D_S + D_{St} + D_{Ts}$ | 53.32 | 48.61 | | 66.18 | 62.86 | |
| | $D_S + D_T + D_{St} + D_{Ts}$ | 59.22 | 56.79 | | 70.92 | **70.52** | 1. |
| Baseline | | | 23.49 | | | 21.60 | |
| Best | | | 61.58 | | | 70.52 | |

Table 3: Token-level F1 score for binary trigger words detection and accumulate precise importance for numerical trigger words detection compared to baseline and best results (Maladry et al., 2024). **Bold** indicates the officially announced results and their competition rank.

### 3.3 Discussion

Overall, the Orca 2 benefits more from the translated data than the XLM-R and mT5 models, likely because the Orca 2 is pre-trained mostly on English data. In contrast, the other two models are multilingual. The translated data adds more knowledge to a model pre-trained mainly on English data than those already exposed to multiple languages. In addition, trigger word detection tasks may be more prone to translation errors, which could diminish the benefits of translated data for these tasks. However, the mT5 model shows marginal improvements from the translated and trigger words switched datasets for the numerical trigger words detection, improving the results by 8% and achieving the best result overall in the competition.

## 4 Conclusion

This paper describes our system for the WASSA-2024 Cross-lingual Emotion Detection Shared Task. We propose fine-tuning a quantized large language model with low-rank adapters combined with machine translation for the emotion detection subtask and fine-tuning multilingual Transformer-based models enhanced with machine translation and trigger word switching for the trigger words detection subtask. We show that additional translated data improves the performance. Our system achieves excellent results and ranks first in numerical trigger word detection, third in binary trigger word detection, and seventh in emotion detection.


## Acknowledgements

This work has been partly supported by the OP JAC project DigiTech no. CZ.02.01.01/00/23_021/0008402 and by the Grant No. SGS-2022-016 Advanced methods of data processing and analysis. Computational resources were provided by the e-INFRA CZ project (ID:90254), supported by the Ministry of Education, Youth and Sports of the Czech Republic.


## Limitations

The method relies on machine translation, thus its effectiveness depends on translation quality. In addition, we solve each subtask independently. Future research could address solving both subtasks simultaneously, potentially leading to a more robust model that better explains its decisions.

## Ethics Statement

We ensure fair and honest analysis while conducting our work ethically and without harming anybody. However, we acknowledge that the language models used in this paper may introduce unintended biases related to race or gender due to pre-training on large corpora.

## References


Ankush Chatterjee, Kedhar Nath Narahari, Meghana Joshi, and Puneet Agrawal. 2019. SemEval-2019 task 3: EmoContext contextual emotion detection in text. In *Proceedings of the 13th International Workshop on Semantic Evaluation*, pages 39–48, Minneapolis, Minnesota, USA. Association for Computational Linguistics.

Alexis Conneau, Kartikay Khandelwal, Naman Goyal, Vishrav Chaudhary, Guillaume Wenzek, Francisco Guzmán, Edouard Grave, Myle Ott, Luke Zettlemoyer, and Veselin Stoyanov. 2020. Unsupervised cross-lingual representation learning at scale. In *Proceedings of the 58th Annual Meeting of the Association for Computational Linguistics*, pages 8440–8451, Online. Association for Computational Linguistics.

Tim Dettmers, Artidoro Pagnoni, Ari Holtzman, and Luke Zettlemoyer. 2023. Qlora: Efficient finetuning of quantized llms. *Preprint*, arXiv:2305.14314.

Jacob Devlin, Ming-Wei Chang, Kenton Lee, and Kristina Toutanova. 2019. BERT: Pre-training of deep bidirectional transformers for language understanding. In *Proceedings of the 2019 Conference of the North American Chapter of the Association for Computational Linguistics: Human Language Technologies, Volume 1 (Long and Short Papers)*, pages 4171–4186, Minneapolis, Minnesota. Association for Computational Linguistics.

Chris Dyer, Victor Chahuneau, and Noah A. Smith. 2013. A simple, fast, and effective reparameterization of IBM model 2. In *Proceedings of the 2013 Conference of the North American Chapter of the Association for Computational Linguistics: Human Language Technologies*, pages 644–648, Atlanta, Georgia. Association for Computational Linguistics.

Hao Fei, Meishan Zhang, and Donghong Ji. 2020. Cross-lingual semantic role labeling with high-quality translated training corpus. In *Proceedings of the 58th Annual Meeting of the Association for Computational Linguistics*, pages 7014–7026, Online. Association for Computational Linguistics.

Sabit Hassan, Shaden Shaar, and Kareem Darwish. 2022. Cross-lingual emotion detection. In *Proceedings of the Thirteenth Language Resources and Evaluation Conference*, pages 6948–6958, Marseille, France. European Language Resources Association.

Edward J. Hu, Yelong Shen, Phillip Wallis, Zeyuan Allen-Zhu, Yuanzhi Li, Shean Wang, Lu Wang, and Weizhu Chen. 2021. Lora: Low-rank adaptation of large language models. *Preprint*, arXiv:2106.09685.

Junjie Hu, Sebastian Ruder, Aditya Siddhant, Graham Neubig, Orhan Firat, and Melvin Johnson. 2020. XTREME: A massively multilingual multitask benchmark for evaluating cross-lingual generalisation. In *Proceedings of the 37th International Conference on Machine Learning*, volume 119 of *Proceedings of Machine Learning Research*, pages 4411–4421. PMLR.

Minghao Hu, Yuxing Peng, Zhen Huang, Dongsheng Li, and Yiwei Lv. 2019. Open-domain targeted sentiment analysis via span-based extraction and classification. In *Proceedings of the 57th Annual Meeting of the Association for Computational Linguistics*, pages 537–546, Florence, Italy. Association for Computational Linguistics.

Yoon Kim. 2014. Convolutional neural networks for sentence classification. In *Proceedings of the 2014 Conference on Empirical Methods in Natural Language Processing (EMNLP)*, pages 1746–1751, Doha, Qatar. Association for Computational Linguistics.

Roman Klinger, Orphée De Clercq, Saif Mohammad, and Alexandra Balahur. 2018. IEST: WASSA-2018 implicit emotions shared task. In *Proceedings of the 9th Workshop on Computational Approaches to Subjectivity, Sentiment and Social Media Analysis*, pages 31–42, Brussels, Belgium. Association for Computational Linguistics.

Ilya Loshchilov and Frank Hutter. 2019. Decoupled weight decay regularization. *Preprint*, arXiv:1711.05101.

Aaron Maladry, Pranaydeep Singh, and Els Lefever. 2024. Findings of the wassa 2024 exalt shared task on explainability for cross-lingual emotion in tweets. In *Proceedings of the 14th Workshop of on Computational Approaches to Subjectivity, Sentiment & Social Media Analysis@ACL 2024*, Bangkok, Thailand.

Stephen Mayhew, Chen-Tse Tsai, and Dan Roth. 2017. Cheap translation for cross-lingual named entity recognition. In *Proceedings of the 2017 Conference on Empirical Methods in Natural Language Processing*, pages 2536–2545, Copenhagen, Denmark. Association for Computational Linguistics.

Arindam Mitra, Luciano Del Corro, Shweti Mahajan, Andres Codas, Clarisse Simoes, Sahaj Agarwal, Xuxi Chen, Anastasia Razdaibiedina, Erik Jones, Kriti Aggarwal, Hamid Palangi, Guoqing Zheng, Corby Rosset, Hamed Khanpour, and Ahmed Awadallah. 2023. Orca 2: Teaching small language models how to reason. *Preprint*, arXiv:2311.11045.

Saif Mohammad, Felipe Bravo-Marquez, Mohammad Salameh, and Svetlana Kiritchenko. 2018. SemEval-2018 task 1: Affect in tweets. In *Proceedings of the 12th International Workshop on Semantic Evaluation*, pages 1–17, New Orleans, Louisiana. Association for Computational Linguistics.

Colin Raffel, Noam Shazeer, Adam Roberts, Katherine Lee, Sharan Narang, Michael Matena, Yanqi Zhou, Wei Li, and Peter J. Liu. 2023. Exploring the limits of transfer learning with a unified text-to-text transformer. *Preprint*, arXiv:1910.10683.

Singh, Pranaydeep and Maladry, Aaron and Lefever, Els. 2023. Annotation guidelines for labeling emotion in multilingual tweets.

Hugo Touvron, Louis Martin, Kevin Stone, Peter Albert, Amjad Almahairi, Yasmine Babaei, Nikolay Bashlykov, Soumya Batra, Prajjwal Bhargava, Shruti Bhosale, Dan Bikel, Lukas Blecher, Cristian Canton Ferrer, Moya Chen, Guillem Cucurull, David Esiobu, Jude Fernandes, Jeremy Fu, Wenyin Fu, Brian Fuller, Cynthia Gao, Vedanuj Goswami, Naman Goyal, Anthony Hartshorn, Saghar Hosseini, Rui Hou, Hakan Inan, Marcin Kardas, Viktor Kerkez, Madian Khabsa, Isabel Kloumann, Artem Korenev, Punit Singh Koura, Marie-Anne Lachaux, Thibaut Lavril, Jenya Lee, Diana Liskovich, Yinghai Lu, Yuning Mao, Xavier Martinet, Todor Mihaylov, Pushkar Mishra, Igor Molybog, Yixin Nie, Andrew Poulton, Jeremy Reizenstein, Rashi Rungta, Kalyan Saladi, Alan Schelten, Ruan Silva, Eric Michael Smith, Ranjan Subramanian, Xiaoqing Ellen Tan, Binh Tang, Ross Taylor, Adina Williams, Jian Xiang Kuan, Puxin Xu, Zheng Yan, Iliyan Zarov, Yuchen Zhang, Angela Fan, Melanie Kambadur, Sharan Narang, Aurelien Rodriguez, Robert Stojnic, Sergey Edunov, and Thomas Scialom. 2023. Llama 2: Open foundation and fine-tuned chat models. *Preprint*, arXiv:2307.09288.

Thomas Wolf, Lysandre Debut, Victor Sanh, Julien Chaumond, Clement Delangue, Anthony Moi, Pierric Cistac, Tim Rault, Remi Louf, Morgan Funtowicz, Joe Davison, Sam Shleifer, Patrick von Platen, Clara Ma, Yacine Jernite, Julien Plu, Canwen Xu, Teven Le Scao, Sylvain Gugger, Mariama Drame, Quentin Lhoest, and Alexander Rush. 2020. Transformers: State-of-the-art natural language processing. In *Proceedings of the 2020 Conference on Empirical Methods in Natural Language Processing: System Demonstrations*, pages 38–45, Online. Association for Computational Linguistics.

Linting Xue, Noah Constant, Adam Roberts, Mihir Kale, Rami Al-Rfou, Aditya Siddhant, Aditya Barua, and Colin Raffel. 2021. mT5: A massively multilingual pre-trained text-to-text transformer. In *Proceedings of the 2021 Conference of the North American Chapter of the Association for Computational Linguistics: Human Language Technologies*, pages 483–498, Online. Association for Computational Linguistics.

Wojciech Zaremba, Ilya Sutskever, and Oriol Vinyals. 2015. Recurrent neural network regularization. *Preprint*, arXiv:1409.2329.

Wenxuan Zhang, Ruidan He, Haiyun Peng, Lidong Bing, and Wai Lam. 2021. Cross-lingual aspect-based sentiment analysis with aspect term code-switching. In *Proceedings of the 2021 Conference on Empirical Methods in Natural Language Processing*, pages 9220–9230, Online and Punta Cana, Dominican Republic. Association for Computational Linguistics.

Xiang Zhang, Senyu Li, Bradley Hauer, Ning Shi, and Grzegorz Kondrak. 2023. Don't trust ChatGPT when your question is not in English: A study of multilingual abilities and types of LLMs. In *Proceedings of the 2023 Conference on Empirical Methods in Natural Language Processing*, pages 7915–7927, Singapore. Association for Computational Linguistics.

# PCICUNAM at WASSA 2024: Cross-lingual Emotion Detection Task with Hierarchical Classification and Weighted Loss Functions

**Jesus Vázquez-Osorio [1,2], Gerardo Sierra[1,3],**
**Helena Gómez-Adorno[1,4], Gemma Bel-Enguix[1,3]**

[1]Universidad Nacional Autónoma de México,
[2]Posgrado en Ciencia e Ingeniería de la Computación, [3]Instituto de Ingeniería,
[4]Instituto de Investigaciones en Matemáticas Aplicadas y en Sistemas
**Correspondence:** jesusvo5599@comunidad.unam.mx, gsierram@iingen.unam.mx,
helena.gomez@iimas.unam.mx, gbele@iingen.unam.mx

## Abstract

This paper addresses the shared task of multilingual emotion detection in tweets, presented at the Workshop on Computational Approaches to Subjectivity, Sentiment, and Social Media Analysis (WASSA) co-located with the ACL 2024 conference. The task involves predicting emotions from six classes in tweets from five different languages using only English for model training. Our approach focuses on addressing class imbalance through data augmentation, hierarchical classification, and the application of focal loss and weighted cross-entropy loss functions. These methods enhance our transformer-based model's ability to transfer emotion detection capabilities across languages, resulting in improved performance despite the constraints of limited computational resources.

## 1 Introduction

This paper presents the team's proposal to solve the shared task 1 of multilingual classification of 6 emotions in tweets from 5 different languages using only English for model training. The presentation for this shared task was made for the Workshop on Computational Approaches to Subjectivity, Sentiment Social Media Analysis (WASSA) that will be co-located with the Annual Meeting of the Association of Computational Linguistics (ACL) 2024 in Bangkok, Thailand (Maladry et al., 2024).

To address the task, the team focused on 3 methodologies for its resolution; the methodologies were mainly based on solving the imbalance of classes in the data. According to several works (Al-Azzawi et al., 2023), the increase of data, especially of the classes with fewer examples in the datasets, improves the result when performing the classification task with data not belonging to the training dataset, that is, the generalization of data in the models is improved. There are different methodologies for data augmentation in text classification tasks. As mentioned in (Shaikh et al., 2021; Edwards et al., 2023), and taking advantage of the latest advances in text generation, the use of generative language models is a great method for this data augmentation task.

In addition to data augmentation, a hierarchical ranking was also applied in the classification task in order to test the performance of the model with this methodology since, as shown in (Jr. and Freitas, 2011; Wang et al., 2022), this technique can result in great benefits in tasks with unbalanced data.

Finally, two loss functions, the focal loss and the cross-entropy weighted loss, introduced by (Lin et al., 2017) were also used, which allows focusing the training on difficult examples by reducing the contribution of well-classified examples, which is crucial to handling class imbalance.

## 2 Task Description

The task of emotion detection in tweets is a challenge in the field of Natural Language Processing (NLP) that explores the transfer of emotional information between languages. The sub-task 1 of the shared task of cross-lingual emotion detection task involves predicting emotions from six classes: Love, Joy, Anger, Fear, Sadness, and Neutral from tweets in five different languages Dutch, Russian, Spanish, English, and French.

A dataset of 5,000 pre-labeled English tweets is provided for training and 500 for validation, along with a test set of 2,500 tweets in the different target languages for evaluation. Participants may use additional English training resources to assess the effectiveness of the cross-language transfer approach but no other language different from English resources.

## 3 Methodology

First, during the training stage, only the 5,000 training tweets with their respective pre-labeled



*Proceedings of the 14th Workshop on Computational Approaches to Subjectivity, Sentiment, & Social Media Analysis*, pages 490–494
August 15, 2024 ©2024 Association for Computational Linguistics

class were available, along with 500 validation data in different target languages without labels. In this stage, an exploratory analysis of the training data was carried out, in which the class imbalance in the training data was found. The target languages were detected in the validation data using the Python `langdetect` [1] library. In addition, using the `googletrans` [2] library, the texts were translated into English, and the emojis were converted into text with the `emoji` [3] library and the instances '*@user*' and '*http*' were removed from the tweets to make the predictions. Appendix B shows some examples of this text preprocessing.

### 3.1 Transformer Model Selection

Subsequently, using only the training data, different transformer models from the Hugging Face `Transformers` [4] library for zero-shot learning text classification were tested to predict the emotion of each tweet and obtain the classification report. Based on the results of these evaluations, the model with the highest macro *F1-score* in the training data test was selected to perform fine-tuning with the data.

### 3.2 Optimal Hyperparameter Search

Once the model to be used for this task was defined, the tokenizer of the pre-trained model was used to analyze the token length of the training tweets to define the token length to be used throughout the experiments. Next, a search for the best hyperparameters was conducted to fine-tune the model with the provided data. This hyperparameter search was performed using grid search, where the model was trained for one epoch with the training data split into 80% for training and 20% for validation, and different values for the hyperparameters '*weight decay*' and '*learning rate*' were proposed.

### 3.3 Strategies To Final Model

As mentioned, 3 techniques were used to handle class imbalance, which are described below:

#### 3.3.1 Data Augmentation With Paraphrasing

With the training data, the '*humarin/chatgpt_paraphraser_on_T5_base*' model from Hugging Face, (Vladimir Vorobev, 2023), which was fine-tuned from the model T5-base from Google (Raffel et al., 2020) for text paraphrasing, was used. The data were augmented such that texts from the underrepresented classes, in this case, Love, Sadness and Fear, were duplicated to train the chosen classification model with these augmented data.

The training dataset is read, and texts labeled as Love, Sadness and Fear are extracted. Each of these texts is then tokenized and paraphrased using the pre-trained model. The paraphrased texts are added to a new dataframe along with their labels. This new dataframe is concatenated with the original dataset to create the augmented dataset. Appendix C shows some examples of the paraphrasing of texts using the above-mentioned model.

#### 3.3.2 Hierarchical Ranking

Considering that there are 3 classes with the highest representation (Neutral, Joy, and Anger), and 3 with significantly lower representation in the training data (Love, Sadness, and Fear), the classification was trained with the chosen model in 2 stages. First, the model was trained to predict tweets among 4 classes: Neutral, Joy, Anger, and Other. Then, the same model was trained to predict among 3 classes: Love, Sadness, and Fear. The operation of this proposed technique involves performing the first classification (4 classes) and subsequently using the tweets classified as 'Other' as input for the second classifier (3 classes). This approach aims to prioritize the classification of the more represented classes.

#### 3.3.3 Loss Functions

Considering the loss functions of (Lin et al., 2017), the chosen transformer model was trained by adapting these functions according to the class imbalance, as they assign different weights to the classes based on their representation. This increases the importance of the difficult-to-classify examples by adding smoothness to the class labels to demonstrate generalization with other data.

Once the training phase was completed, the labels for the validation data were released to continue evaluating models; additionally, the test data was released, which was also subjected to the translation process using the same methodology as the validation data to test the final models.

## 4 Results

Figure 1 shows the result of the analysis of the classes in the training set, it is evident that the rep-

[1] `https://pypi.org/project/langdetect/`
[2] `https://pypi.org/project/googletrans/`
[3] `https://pypi.org/project/emoji/`
[4] `https://pypi.org/project/transformers/`

resentation of the Love, Sadness and Fear classes is significantly lower.

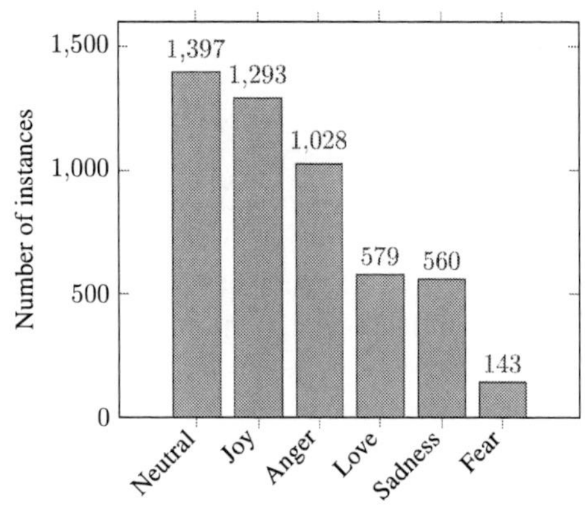


Figure 1: Class balance in training data provided.

Figure 2 presents the class distribution after data augmentation with model for text paraphrasing.

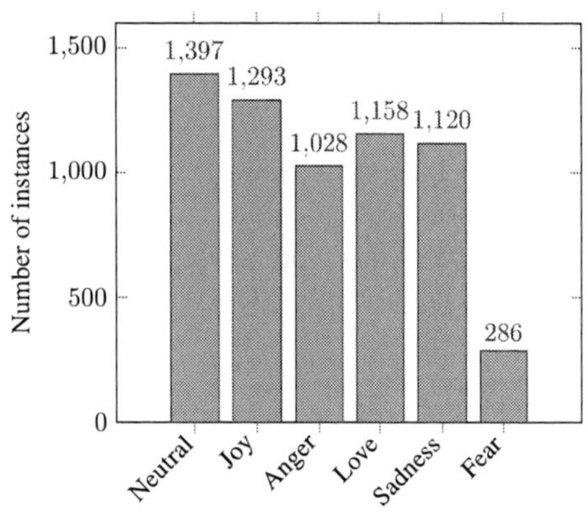


Figure 2: Class balance with data augmentation by paraphrasing data of the underrepresented classes.

For the selection of the transformer model, we present the highest results of the tested models in Table 1 (Sileod, 2022; AI, 2021). As mentioned, the model with the best performance evaluated with *F1-score* was selected, this is a fine-tuned model based on the *DeBERTa-v3-large* (He et al., 2021) from Microsoft, the model selected and used along all the experiments is '*MoritzLaurer/DeBERTa-v3-large-mnli-fever-anli-ling-wanli*' (Laurer et al., 2022) which was fine-tuned by us with the competition data.

In the grid search, the values from the Figure 3 were used for each hyperparameter in the table; within the search for the optimal pair of values for this task, *learning rate*=$5e-6$ and *weight decay*=$0.01$ emerged as the best options among the possible values.

| Model | F1-score |
|---|---|
| sileod/deberta-v3-base-tasksource-nli | .39 |
| facebook/bart-large-mnli | .40 |
| MoritzLaurer/DeBERTa-v3-large-mnli-fever-anli-ling-wanli | **.45** |

Table 1: Top three model performance without fine-tuning on training data.

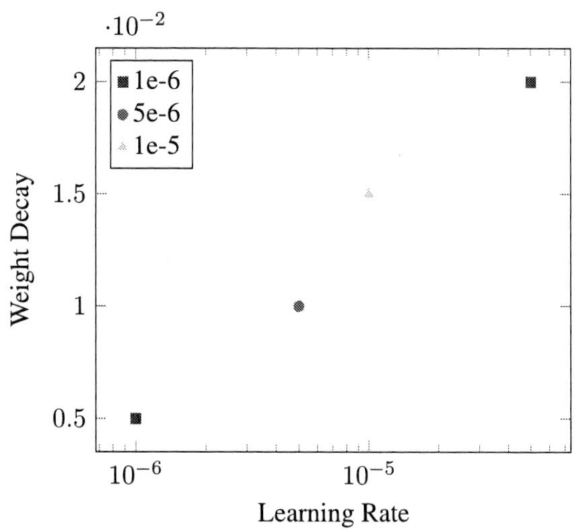


Figure 3: Values of the proposed hyperparameters to find the optimal pair.

For the fine-tuning of the model with the different strategies, different experiments were performed, not only 1 out of 1. Table 2 shows the best results obtained and the specifications of each one of them for the training phase.

For the evaluation phase we had the opportunity to present to the CodaLab [5] platform ten different predictions to get the performance of our models, in addition to testing the models in Table 2, based on the results of the training stage, for the evaluation stage the model with the loss function strategy was retrained with the same training data a few times to have different models trained and then used to rank the test data and present the predictions. Table 3 shows our top five prediction performances on the test data, which were obtained from the retraining of the model with the loss function strategy.

With the best result of 0.5183 we managed to beat the baseline provided by the organizers (0.4476). As for the participants, with this result

[5] https://codalab.lisn.upsaclay.fr/competitions/17730

| Strategy | Epochs | *Original Val. Data** | *Preprocessed Val. Data*** |
|---|---|---|---|
| Without any strategy | 10 | 0.4664 | 0.4669 |
| Data augmentation | 9 | 0.4716 | 0.4761 |
| Hierarchical ranking | 10 | 0.4935 | 0.4939 |
| Loss functions | 10 | **0.5013** | **0.5063** |

Table 2: Best results of the macro *F1-score* metric training stage for each strategy. *As provided. **Translated tweets, emojis converted to text and removing '*@user*' and '*http*' instances from tweets.

| Epoch | *F1-score* |
|---|---|
| 13 | 0.5022 |
| 17 | 0.5137 |
| 19 | 0.5168 |
| 15 | **0.5183** |
| 15 | 0.5099 |

Table 3: Best results of the macro *F1-score* metric evaluation stage.

we placed in the top 15.

## 5 Limitations and Future Work

The development of this task was carried out using limited computational resources (See A). For the training and evaluation of the models, the free resources of `Google Colab` [6] environment were used, supplemented with our own computational capacity. This restriction posed additional challenges, such as the need to optimize the use of available computing time and efficiently manage memory and processing resources. Despite these limitations, we were able to implement and experiment with advanced emotion classification models, demonstrating the feasibility of conducting significant NLP research with accessible and limited resources.

It is important to acknowledge that the hierarchical ranking approach may introduce cascading errors from the first classification stage to the second. This potential issue arises because any misclassification in the first stage (4 classes) can lead to incorrect input for the second stage (3 classes), thereby propagating errors. While this experiment did not include an in-depth study to evaluate the impact of these cascading errors, future work could focus on implementing and testing strategies to mitigate such issues. Possible solutions include using confidence thresholds to filter uncertain predictions, incorporating feedback loops for error correction, or employing ensemble methods to enhance the robustness of the hierarchical classification.

Unfortunately, due to time and resource constraints, we were unable to conduct an ablation study on the three techniques proposed in this paper. An ablation study would be valuable to isolate and compare the individual contributions of each technique to the overall performance. Future research should aim to conduct such a study to better understand the effectiveness of each technique when used separately and in conjunction with others. This would provide a clearer picture of the strengths and weaknesses of each approach and help optimize the overall classification performance.

## 6 Conclusion

In this work, we tackled the challenge of cross-lingual emotion detection in tweets using a transformer-based model trained only on English data. To overcome the class imbalance inherent in the dataset, we employed strategies such as data augmentation through paraphrasing, hierarchical classification, and the use of focal loss and weighted cross-entropy loss functions.

Despite utilizing limited computational resources, including free Google Colab environments and our own hardware, our approach demonstrated the feasibility of achieving competitive results in multilingual emotion detection tasks.

| Environment | Google Colab |
|---|---|
| GPU | T4 GPU |
| GPU RAM | 15 GB |
| System RAM | 12.7 GB |
| CUDA Version | 12.1 |
| Transformers Library Version | 4.40.2 |

Table 4: Software and hardware environment.

## 7 Acknowledgments

This work was carried out as part of PAPIIT project IT100822, IN104424 and the project CF2023-

[6]`https://colab.research.google.com/`

G64, which is funded by '*Consejo Nacional de Humanidades, Ciencias y Tecnologías* (CONAHCYT)'. We also extend our gratitude to our colleagues and mentors for their invaluable guidance and assistance throughout this project.

## References

Facebook AI. 2021. Bart large for mnli.

Sana Sabah Al-Azzawi, György Kovács, Filip Nilsson, Tosin Adewumi, and Marcus Liwicki. 2023. Nlp-ltu at semeval-2023 task 10: The impact of data augmentation and semi-supervised learning techniques on text classification performance on an imbalanced dataset. *arXiv*.

Aleksandra Edwards, Asahi Ushio, Hélène de Ribaupierre, Jose Camacho-Collados, and Alun Preece. 2023. Guiding generative language models for data augmentation in few-shot text classification. *arXiv preprint arXiv:2111.09064v2*.

Pengcheng He, Xiaodong Liu, Jianfeng Gao, and Weizhu Chen. 2021. Deberta: Decoding-enhanced bert with disentangled attention. In *International Conference on Learning Representations*.

Carlos N. Silla Jr. and Alex A. Freitas. 2011. A survey of hierarchical classification across different application domains. *Data Mining and Knowledge Discovery*, 22:31–72.

Moritz Laurer, Wouter van Atteveldt, Andreu Casas, and Kasper Welbers. 2022. Less annotating more clasifying - addressing the data scarcity issue of supervised machine learning with deep transfer learning and bert-nli.

Tsung-Yi Lin, Priya Goyal, Ross Girshick, Kaiming He, and Piotr Dollár. 2017. Focal loss for dense object detection. *Facebook AI Research (FAIR)*.

Aaron Maladry, Pranaydeep Singh, and Els Lefever. 2024. Findings of the wassa 2024 exalt shared task on explainability for cross-lingual emotion in tweets. In *Proceedings of the 14th Workshop of on Computational Approaches to Subjectivity, Sentiment Social Media Analysis@ACL 2024*.

Colin Raffel, Noam Shazeer, Adam Roberts, Katherine Lee, Sharan Narang, Michael Matena, Yanqi Zhou, Wei Li, and Peter J. Liu. 2020. Exploring the limits of transfer learning with a unified text-to-text transformer. *Journal of Machine Learning Research*, 21(140):1–67.

Sarang Shaikh, Sher Muhammad Daudpota, Ali Shariq Imran, and Zenun Kastrati. 2021. Towards improved classification accuracy on highly imbalanced text dataset using deep neural language models. *Applied Sciences*, 11(869).

Sileod. 2022. Deberta v3 base for tasksource nl.

Maxim Kuznetsov Vladimir Vorobev. 2023. A paraphrasing model based on chatgpt paraphrases.

Zihan Wang, Peiyi Wang, Lianzhe Huang, Xin Sun, and Houfeng Wang. 2022. Incorporating hierarchy into text encoder: a contrastive learning approach for hierarchical text classification. *arXiv preprint arXiv:2203.03825*.

## A Description of the computer resources used in the development of the task.

Table 4 shows the hardware and software environment with which all experiments were run.

## B Examples of text translation.

**Original Text:** Wat een mega baas die @user Op HET moment het doen . Absurd goed dit . rtl7darts wkdarts

**Translated Text:** What a mega boss who @USER is doing it at the moment.Absurd well this. rtl7darts wkdarts

**Original Text:** bref je vais finir les 4 pages de mon livre on se retrouve quand je serais desséchée http

**Translated Text:** In short I will finish the 4 pages of my book we meet when I am dried up http

**Original Text:** Quien le mete papas fritas a los sándwiches de miga ? digo así somos amigos

**Translated Text:** Who puts french fries to crumb sandwiches?I say so we are friends.

## C Examples of text paraphrasing.

**Original Text:** Mood of the day : worrying about online friends while being afraid of taking the risk of getting too close or too caring so not speaking while regretting to do so .

**Paraphrased Text:** The mood today is focused on stifling online friendships and the fear of losing too much control or attachment to others, leading to a lack of conversation and regret.

**Original Text:** @user But the fact your so hurt by the fact your idol has a boyfriend actually is homophobic much.

**Paraphrased Text:**The fact that your idol's partner is a homophobe is so hurtful to you.

**Original Text:** Gotta Move Back Home PanicIn4Words.

**Paraphrased Text:** I'm in a panic mode during the PanicIn4Words event, and it's time to move back home.

# TEII: Think, Explain, Interact and Iterate with Large Language Models to Solve Cross-lingual Emotion Detection

**Long Cheng***, **Qihao Shao***, **Christine Zhao**, **Sheng Bi**, **Gina-Anne Levow**†
Department of Linguistics
University of Washington
{lcheng97, qihaos, czhao028, shengbi, levow}@uw.edu

## Abstract

Cross-lingual emotion detection allows us to analyze global trends, public opinion, and social phenomena at scale. We participated in the Explainability of Cross-lingual Emotion Detection (EXALT) shared task, achieving an F1-score of 0.6046 on the evaluation set for the emotion detection sub-task. Our system outperformed the baseline by more than 0.16 F1-score absolute, and ranked second amongst competing systems. We conducted experiments using fine-tuning, zero-shot learning, and few-shot learning for Large Language Model (LLM)-based models as well as embedding-based BiLSTM and KNN for non-LLM-based techniques. Additionally, we introduced two novel methods: the Multi-Iteration Agentic Workflow and the Multi-Binary-Classifier Agentic Workflow. We found that LLM-based approaches provided good performance on multilingual emotion detection. Furthermore, ensembles combining all our experimented models yielded higher F1-scores than any single approach alone.

## 1 Introduction

In this study, we focused on tackling the cross-lingual emotion detection task for Tweets, which is a sub-task in EXALT@WASSA 2024 (Maladry et al., 2024). This task is interesting for its global application in understanding emotions across languages. It is also challenging due to linguistic diversity and cultural differences in emotional expression. To tackle the multilingual challenge, we conducted experiments using multilingual LLM-based models as well as classical machine learning models that used multilingual embeddings. An innovation developed within these experiments is the creation of an Agentic Workflow approach that leverages the strengths of multiple LLMs for the emotion detection task. All code will be released on GitHub[1].

## 2 Related Work

Previously, research like that of Hassan et al. (2022) explored classification using classical models such as BERT and SVMs, trained with various linguistic features. More recently, Thakkar et al. (2024) investigated sentiment recognition in tweets using both multimodal and multilingual approaches.

ChatDev by Qian et al. (2023), Gorilla by Patil et al. (2023), HuggingGPT by Shen et al. (2023), and the Reflexion framework by Shinn et al. (2023) highlighted the potential of multi-LLM-agent collaboration, termed Agentic Workflow, in solving complex tasks and its application to tool use, code generation, and similar activities. A related approach is AutoGen (Wu et al., 2023), where natural language and computer code are integrated to tackle complex tasks that are challenging for a single prompt or one LLM. We believe this broad methodology can be applied to the emotion detection task in a multilingual setting. In this work, we introduce Agentic Workflow using a multi-agent approach to enhance the performance of individual LLMs in detecting emotions in tweets.

## 3 System Description

We explored three broad classes of models for the EXALT cross-lingual emotion recognition tasks. One approach trained several KNN models and a BiLSTM model with multilingual embeddings to encode EXALT's cross-linguistic Tweet data directly (detailed in Appendix A). Another group of experiments employed LLM-based models weakly or not directly trained for EXALT, through prompting. For the third class of approaches, we developed two Agentic Workflow methods, using multiple agents: Multi-Iteration Agentic Workflow and Multi-Binary-Classifier Agentic Workflow. Finally,

*These authors contributed equally to this work.
†Corresponding author

[1]https://github.com/cl-victor1/EXALT_2024



*Proceedings of the 14th Workshop on Computational Approaches to Subjectivity, Sentiment, & Social Media Analysis*, pages 495–504
August 15, 2024 ©2024 Association for Computational Linguistics

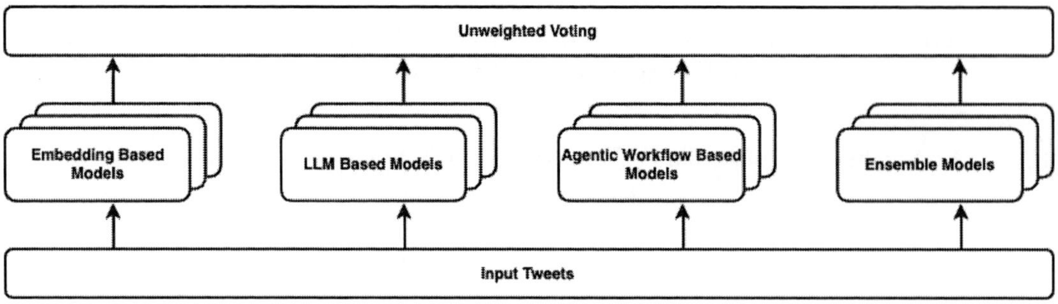


Figure 1: System architecture of the final ensemble model that combines both individual models and other ensemble models with fewer individual models.

we applied ensemble methods to aggregate across approaches. The system architecture we used for the final evaluation is illustrated in Figure 1.

### 3.1 Prompt Based Classification with LLMs

With the advancement of LLMs, formulating natural language processing problems into text completion problems via prompting has shown promising results. We explored fine-tuning OpenAI's GPT3.5, a zero-shot setting using OpenAI's GPT4[2] and Anthropic's Claude3[3], and a few-shot setting using OpenAI's GPT4. Additionally, leveraging the Chain-of-Thought (Wei et al., 2023) approach, we designed two more methods built upon the zero-shot model by explicitly asking for explanation from LLMs in their outputs. All detailed prompts that we used for different models can be found in Appendix C.

**Fine-tuning GPT3.5 (FineTuneGPT)** We partitioned the training dataset into a training dataset and a validation dataset, comprising 4000 and 1000 instances respectively, and used the datasets to create a fine-tuned GPT3.5 model. For inference, the system prompt remained consistent with that utilized during the fine-tuning process.

**Zero-Shot (ZeroShot)** Under the zero-shot setting, we set the system prompt to align with our task goal and then directly asked LLMs to output a label among the six emotion labels given a certain tweet.

**Zero-Shot with Explanation (ZSE) and Correction (ZSEC)** Building upon the zero-shot setting, we asked LLMs to provide an explanation before assigning emotion labels during inference (ZSE). Taking the Chain-of-Thought idea one step further, we introduced a second LLM in the same inference process, and used the output label from the first LLM as part of the input to the second LLM (ZSEC). More specifically, we asked the first LLM to explain and output the emotion label, and then we asked the second LLM to check whether it agreed with the label output by the first LLM. If the second LLM agreed with the first LLM, it would output the same label; otherwise, it would output an alternative label. In either case, the second LLM would also provide explanation before outputting the emotion label. With this approach, we take the output from the second LLM as the final output.

**Few-Shot (FewShot)** We set the system prompt similar to that of the zero-shot setting and provided a few example tweets with their associated emotion labels before asking LLMs to output a label for a certain tweet. We employed both random sampling and embedding-based KNN (with $k = 6$) to pick example tweets from the training dataset.

### 3.2 Agentic Workflow (AWF)

Drawing inspiration again from the concept of Chain-of-Thought (Wei et al., 2023) and the multi-agent conversation framework outlined in (Wu et al., 2023), we developed two Agentic Workflow methods to enhance the performance of LLMs.

**Multi-Iteration Agentic Workflow (MIAWF)** This approach involves using one or more LLM agents to adjudicate between the outputs of prior models. First, we identify the two top-performing models (agent 1 and agent 2) based on their respective F1-scores on dev data. Following this selection, an additional LLM is introduced as Agent 3. We prompted agent 3 to assess the outputs of Agents 1 and 2 and select the optimal label. In this manner, the classification decision is reduced to binary

[2] gpt-4-turbo-2024-04-09 and gpt-4o-2024-05-13
[3] claude-3-opus-20240229

from multi-class, and leverages the output of strong models.

After obtaining the results for agent 3, another LLM could be introduced as agent 4. The system prompt for agent 4 would remain the same as that for agent 3. However, this time, the source models for agent 4 are agent 3 and the better of agent 1 and agent 2. It is observed that agent 4 often outperforms agent 3 slightly on the dev set. In theory, this iteration could be repeated multiple times, but as the source models gradually become more similar to each other, the performance improvement may diminish. One iteration of MIAWF is presented in Figure 2.

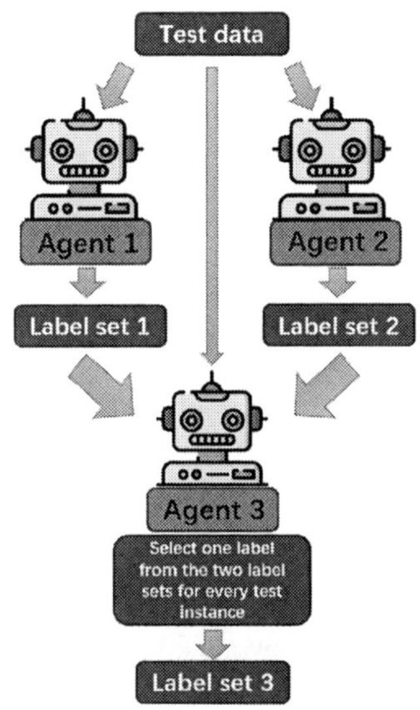


Figure 2: One iteration of Multi-Iteration Agentic Workflow. (This figure has been designed using images from Flaticon.com)

**Multi-Binary-Classifier Agentic Workflow (MB-CAWF)** This approach is inspired by both the idea of ensemble learning and the previous Agentic Workflow approach. First of all, we hypothesized that LLMs would have better performance on binary classification than on multi-class classification. Since there were six different emotions in Task 1, we made five binary classifiers, one for each of the emotions except for the emotion "Neutral". Secondly, we observed that LLMs had performed well in selecting the preferred output above. We thus extended the Agentic Workflow further and combined it with the binary classifiers.

Multi-Binary-Classifier Agentic workflow works as follows for inference on each instance:

1. Ask the LLM whether the tweet has each of the non-neutral emotions (Binary Classifiers).

2. If only one of the emotions is predicted positive, use that emotion as the predicted emotion.

3. If multiple emotions are predicted positive, ask the LLM to pick one among the positive ones as the predicted emotion.

4. If there is no emotion detected (all emotions predicted negative), tell the LLM that others think the tweet is of "Neutral" emotion and ask it to double check that classification. If so, output "Neutral" as the predicted emotion; otherwise, pick one among the other five emotions as the predicted emotion.

With this approach, we expect that both precision and recall are going to be improved, especially for non-neutral emotions.

### 3.3 Ensembles

Due to noticeable variations in outputs from our base models, primarily LLMs, we hypothesized that consolidating predictions through an ensemble mechanism would yield beneficial results. Consequently, during the development phase, we evaluated each model architecture at various hyperparameters to choose the highest dev-set F1-score version to include in our ensembles. Comparative analyses of these methods are provided in Table 2 in Appendix B. Since the unweighted voting ensemble demonstrated the best performance on the dev set, we opted to use it for the official runs, leveraging our established models. The ensembles using this straightforward unweighted voting approach, combining embedding-based, prompting, and Agentic Workflow models, outperformed all individual models.

### 3.4 LLM Selection

In our experiments during the model development phase, we observed that, in general, GPT4 performed better on the dev dataset than Claude3 did. Claude3 tended to be too insensitive to non-neutral emotions despite having higher precision on them. Based on this observation, we decided to use GPT4 as the main LLM for our models in the final evaluation on the test dataset while keeping using Claude3 as the second LLM that performed double check on the "Neutral" emotion in the Zero-Shot with Explanation and Correction model.

## 4 Results

In terms of individual models, the Zero-Shot (gpt4o) with Explanation and Correction model (ZSEC-gpt4o) achieved the best performance, achieving an F1-score of 0.5726. Other models, such as ZSEC-gpt4turbo and Multi-Binary-Classifier Agentic Workflow (MBCAWF), also perform competitively, with F1-scores exceeding 0.55. The overall system performance further improved through the use of Agentic Workflow and ensemble methods. Notably, the Ensemble-19 model achieves the highest F1-score of 0.6046 on the test dataset, outperforming the EXALT baseline by approximately 0.17 F1-score, ranking second. Results for all submitted single models, Agentic Workflow models, and ensembles for the emotion detection task are presented in Table 1, with baseline results provided by the EXALT organizers.

Emotion prediction often differs substantially across emotion labels, and that variation is reflected in our systems as well. Per-emotion F1-scores achieved by our top-performing model, Ensemble-19, illustrate a difference of up to 0.26 F-score, between the highest scoring emotions ( 0.73 for "Anger" and 0.72 for "Neutral") and the lowest scoring emotions - only 0.47 for "Love" and 0.53 for "Fear". This discrepancy underscores the uneven performance of classification across emotion categories and the continuing challenges of this task. The per-emotion F1-scores achieved by Ensemble-19 are shown in Appendix F.

| Models | F1-score | Precision | Recall |
|---|---|---|---|
| EXALT Baseline | 0.43 | 0.43 | 0.44 |
| ZSEC-gpt4turbo | 0.55 | 0.55 | 0.58 |
| ZSEC-gpt4o | 0.57 | 0.56 | 0.60 |
| MBCAWF | 0.56 | 0.56 | 0.59 |
| MIAWF-3[4] | 0.59 | 0.59 | 0.61 |
| MIAWF-5[5] | 0.60 | 0.59 | 0.62 |
| Ensemble-9[6] | 0.59 | 0.59 | 0.61 |
| Ensemble-8[7] | 0.60 | 0.60 | 0.62 |
| Ensemble-17[8] | 0.60 | 0.60 | 0.62 |
| Ensemble-19[9] | **0.60** | **0.60** | **0.62** |

Table 1: F1-score, precision and recall on the test dataset including the EXALT baseline results.

## 5 Discussion

There are a few findings that we would like to share. First of all, the effectiveness of explanation and correction over simpler prompting which was found on the dev dataset was replicated on the test dataset. These improvements are detailed in the experiments in Appendix G. Secondly, our manual error analysis (Appendix D) highlighted the subjective nature of the emotion recognition task. Humans may disagree, and the explanation provided by the models may also be reasonable, even in some cases where they do not match the gold standard. Thirdly, the justification provided by LLMs could potentially aid the explainability of the outputs. Inspection of automatically generated explanations often showed partial translations, which could be helpful in the cross-lingual setting (Appendix E).

Additionally, the tweet data employed in this study are drawn from six high-resource languages. Consequently, it is uncertain whether the models would produce comparable results for lower-resource languages. Further exploration is needed by applying the same methodology to tweets in diverse low-resource languages.

## 6 Conclusion

In this study, we have highlighted the potential of the Agentic Workflow method to enhance emotion detection performance of LLMs on multilingual tweets. Moreover, explicitly prompting LLMs to provide explanations for their decisions not only improves decision-making accuracy but also can aid human comprehension of their decisions. We firmly believe that explainability plays a crucial role in real-world applications by providing insight into the operations of these complex systems.

At the same time, we should be cautious about the risk associated with using LLMs in subjective tasks, since they may be incorrect but appear confident. Looking ahead, we envision exploring the application of Agentic Workflows across a broader spectrum of fields within sentiment analysis and the wider NLP domain.

[4]built on ZSEC-gpt4o and Ensemble-9

[5]built on MIAWF-4 (which is built on MIAWF-3 and Ensemble-8) and Ensemble-8

[6]Ensemble of 9 models (see Table 3 in Appendix B)

[7]Ensemble of 8 models (see Table 3 in Appendix B)

[8]Ensemble of 17 models (see Table 3 in Appendix B)

[9]Ensemble of 19 models (see Table 3 in Appendix B)

## 7 Limitations

The OpenAI and Anthropic models used in this work are closed-source and may continue undergoing reinforcement learning from human feedback (RLHF). Given this situation and the inherent non-deterministic nature of LLMs, reproducing the exact inference results may be challenging. A second issue of using LLMs was that occasionally outputs would be nonsensical, making manual post-processing almost unavoidable. In such case, we simply replaced the problematic outputs, of which the format was not "explanation + emotion label", with "Neutral" labels. Thirdly, due to cost and time constraints, we were unable to perform formal significance tests. Therefore, the results and findings presented in this paper are based on empirical observations from the experiments we conducted. Finally, the model latency of LLMs was quite high for inference on each instance, especially when the raw output contained more text. During the evaluation phase, we broke down the test dataset into multiple parts and parallelized the inference to speed up the process.

## References


Christian Amadi, Juliet Odii, Ofoegbu Christopher, and Chidimma Okpalla. 2023. Emotion detection using a bidirectional long-short term memory (bilstm) neural network. *International Journal of Current Pharmaceutical Review and Research*, Vol 4, no 11:1718–1732.

Sabit Hassan, Shaden Shaar, and Kareem Darwish. 2022. Cross-lingual emotion detection. In *Proceedings of the Thirteenth Language Resources and Evaluation Conference*, pages 6948–6958, Marseille, France. European Language Resources Association.

Aaron Maladry, Pranaydeep Singh, and Els Lefever. 2024. Findings of the wassa 2024 exalt shared task on explainability for cross-lingual emotion in tweets. In *Proceedings of the 14th Workshop of on Computational Approaches to Subjectivity, Sentiment & Social Media Analysis@ACL 2024*, Bangkok, Thailand.

Shishir G. Patil, Tianjun Zhang, Xin Wang, and Joseph E. Gonzalez. 2023. Gorilla: Large language model connected with massive apis. *Preprint*, arXiv:2305.15334.

Chen Qian, Xin Cong, Wei Liu, Cheng Yang, Weize Chen, Yusheng Su, Yufan Dang, Jiahao Li, Juyuan Xu, Dahai Li, Zhiyuan Liu, and Maosong Sun. 2023. Communicative agents for software development. *Preprint*, arXiv:2307.07924.

Yongliang Shen, Kaitao Song, Xu Tan, Dongsheng Li, Weiming Lu, and Yueting Zhuang. 2023. Hugginggpt: Solving ai tasks with chatgpt and its friends in hugging face. *Preprint*, arXiv:2303.17580.

Noah Shinn, Federico Cassano, Edward Berman, Ashwin Gopinath, Karthik Narasimhan, and Shunyu Yao. 2023. Reflexion: Language agents with verbal reinforcement learning. *Preprint*, arXiv:2303.11366.

Gaurish Thakkar, Sherzod Hakimov, and Marko Tadić. 2024. M2SA: Multimodal and multilingual model for sentiment analysis of tweets. In *Proceedings of the 2024 Joint International Conference on Computational Linguistics, Language Resources and Evaluation (LREC-COLING 2024)*, pages 10833–10845, Torino, Italia. ELRA and ICCL.

Jason Wei, Xuezhi Wang, Dale Schuurmans, Maarten Bosma, Brian Ichter, Fei Xia, Ed Chi, Quoc Le, and Denny Zhou. 2023. Chain-of-thought prompting elicits reasoning in large language models. *Preprint*, arXiv:2201.11903.

Qingyun Wu, Gagan Bansal, Jieyu Zhang, Yiran Wu, Beibin Li, Erkang Zhu, Li Jiang, Xiaoyun Zhang, Shaokun Zhang, Jiale Liu, Ahmed Hassan Awadallah, Ryen W White, Doug Burger, and Chi Wang. 2023. Autogen: Enabling next-gen llm applications via multi-agent conversation. *Preprint*, arXiv:2308.08155.

Wenbiao Yin and Lin Shang. 2022. Efficient nearest neighbor emotion classification with BERT-whitening. In *Proceedings of the 2022 Conference on Empirical Methods in Natural Language Processing*, pages 4738–4745, Abu Dhabi, United Arab Emirates. Association for Computational Linguistics.

Qimin Zhou and Hao Wu. 2018. NLP at IEST 2018: BiLSTM-attention and LSTM-attention via soft voting in emotion classification. In *Proceedings of the 9th Workshop on Computational Approaches to Subjectivity, Sentiment and Social Media Analysis*, pages 189–194, Brussels, Belgium. Association for Computational Linguistics.


## A Embedding-based Models

### A.1 K-Nearest Neighbors (KNN)

We explored KNN in the emotion detection subtask chosing high-dimensional sentence embeddings as our classification input for our categorical emotion label output. We were motivated by the findings in Yin and Shang (2022) which, although only calculated on English datasets, yielded high-efficiency, high-performing results even when only KNN was used for emotion classification. In our study, we compared KNN performance on OpenAI & TwHIN-BERT embeddings and found TwHIN-BERT outperformed OpenAI in dev-set F-1 score.

#### A.1.1 OpenAI KNN Parameters

We ran experiments on the dev dataset with different $k$ values (from 1 to 10) and with different embedding sizes for both OpenAI embedding models. The setting with best F1 score on the dev dataset was $k = 6$ with embedding size 256 using `text-embedding-3-large` model provided by OpenAI.

#### A.1.2 BERT KNN Parameters

TwHIN-BERT was selected because of its ability to project sentences cross-linguistically onto the same embedding space, fine-tuned on Tweet data. We selected the $k$ (in between 1 and 20) for BERT-KNN using 5-fold cross-validation F1 score on the training data and validation F1 score on the dev set. We were able to identify $k = 3$ as offering the best performance on both the training and dev set.

### A.2 Bidirectional LSTM (BiLSTM)

Bidirectional Long Short-Term Memory (BiLSTM) has been shown to be capable of capturing the long-range contextual information needed for emotion classification of short messages (Amadi et al., 2023). BiLSTM with attention, when applied to a similar implicit emotion classification task for WASSA2018 (Zhou and Wu, 2018), yielded competitive performance across emotion classes. Our BiLSTM took as input batches of 280 x 1024 length vectors, where 280 was the BERT tokenizer's padded max sequence length for a sentence and 1024 was the length of each token's TwHIN-BERT embeddings. Then, after feeding the input through a BiLSTM with 256 total hidden cells, we applied an attention layer over all 280 tokens to produce the emotion label for a sentence. The model used an Adam Optimizer coupled with a sparse categorical cross-entropy loss function during training on 90% of the training data. The remaining 10% was set aside as validation data and model training stopped after 3 epochs of no validation data loss improvement. The final model's attention layer was then used to produce Numerical Trigger scores for Task 3 as a metric to assess how much individual tokens contributed to a sentence's emotion. Words that had been split into multiple tokens were recombined before outputting these numerical trigger scores.

## B Information of Different Ensembles

The information are detailed in Table 2 and Table 3.

| Ensemble Types | F1-score | Precision | Recall |
|---|---|---|---|
| Unweighted voting | 0.61 | 0.63 | 0.60 |
| Weighted voting (weighted according to F1-score) | 0.60 | 0.61 | 0.60 |
| Agentic Workflow (GPT4) | 0.49 | 0.51 | 0.52 |
| Agentic Workflow (Claude3) | 0.50 | 0.51 | 0.51 |

Table 2: F1-score, precision and recall for all ensemble types on the dev dataset.

| Ensembles | Base Models |
|---|---|
| Ensemble-8 | MIAWF-3, BERT-KNN, ZSEC-gpt4o, FewShot, FineTuneGPT, ZeroShot, OpenAI-KNN, MBCAWF |
| Ensemble-9 | MIAWF-2, BERT-KNN, ZSEC-gpt4o, FewShot, FineTuneGPT, ZeroShot, OpenAI-KNN, MBCAWF, Explain_turbo |
| Ensemble-17 | 5 MIAWF models (with different source models), 5 ZSEC models (with the same prompts), BERT-KNN, FewShot, FineTuneGPT, ZeroShot, OpenAI-KNN, MBCAWF, BiLSTM |
| Ensemble-19 | 5 MIAWF models (with different source models), 5 ZSEC models (with the same prompts), BERT-KNN, FewShot, FineTuneGPT, ZeroShot, OpenAI-KNN, MBCAWF, BiLSTM, Ensemble-8, Ensemble-17 |

Table 3: Composition of all submitted ensembles on the test dataset.

## C Prompts

### C.1 Fine-tuning GPT3.5

**System:** As a supportive assistant specialized in tweet classification, you're tasked with determining the emotion conveyed in a given tweet. Utilizing your intuitive understanding, analyze the sentiment of the provided tweet. Your response should be just one word, choosing one emotion from these 6 emotions: Love, Joy, Anger, Fear, Sadness, Neutral.

### C.2 Zero-Shot and Few-Shot

**System:** You are a helpful assistant designed to output classification results.
**User:** Suppose there are six emotions: Love, Joy, Anger, Fear, Sadness, Neutral. Use your instinct, what is the emotion of the following tweet: '{tweet_text}'. Your response must be just one label from the six labels. Please do not output anything else.
**Assistant (only needed for few-shot):** {label}

### C.3 Zero-Shot with Explanation

**System:** You are an expert who takes an input tweet and outputs an emotion classification label among the following emotion labels: Love, Joy, Anger, Fear, Sadness, Neutral. Your output should start with the explanation and end with the emotion label. Explanation and emotion label should be separated by ||. Do not output newlines.
**System (only needed for correction):** You are an expert in checking emotion in tweets. There are six emotions 'Love, Joy, Anger, Fear, Sadness, Neutral'. You will be presented with a tweet that others think is '{emotion}'. Output '{emotion}' if you agree with that; otherwise, output one emotion label from other emotions that describes the emotion of the tweet the best. Your output should start with the explanation and end with the emotion label. Explanation and emotion should be separated by ||. Do not output newlines.
**User:** What is the emotion label of this tweet '{tweet}'?

### C.4 Multi-Iteration Agentic Workflow

**System:** As an expert specialized in tweet classification, you're presented with a tweet and two emotion labels: "{emotion1}" and "{emotion2}". Drawing upon your intuitive understanding, assess the emotion of the tweet provided. Your response should be either "{emotion1}" or "{emotion2}". If the two emotion labels are identical, return either one of them.

### C.5 Multi-Binary-Classifier Agentic Workflow

**System (Binary Classifier):** You are an expert in detecting '{emotion}' emotion in tweets. You will be presented with a tweet. Output 'yes' if you detect '{emotion}' emotion in the tweet; otherwise, output 'no'. Your response should only contain 'yes' or 'no'. No other output is allowed.
**System (Neutral Emotion Check):** You are an expert in checking emotion in tweets. You will be presented with a tweet that others think is 'Neutral'. Output 'Neutral' if you agree with that; otherwise, output one emotion from {emotions} that describes the emotion of the tweet the best. In the latter case, your response should only contain one of {emotions} and no other output is allowed.
**System (Agentic Workflow):** You are an expert in choosing emotions for tweets. You will be presented with a tweet. Pick one emotion from {emotions} that describes the emotion of the tweet the best. Your response should only contain one of emotions. No other output is allowed.

## D Empirical Error Analysis for Zero-Shot with Explanation

There are a lot of tweets of which the LLM got the labels incorrect while providing reasonable explanation to justify its own predictions. We are sharing a few of them here from both dev dataset and test dataset. From these samples shared, it is natural for us to think that the LLM predicted the labels of the tweets correctly after reading the explanation.

### D.1 Samples from Dev Dataset

**Tweet 1:** @user His performances at Hull don't lie , he's a good player . I remember reading somewhere that he went to Slav multiple times to say he's being played out of position and was told "you'll play where I play you"

**Gold Label for Tweet 1:** Joy

**Predicted Label for Tweet 1:** Neutral

**Explanation for Tweet 1:** The tweet reflects a tone of support and mild frustration directed towards the way a player was managed, mentioning how the player's good performances are evident and recalling an instance where the player was dismissed by the manager when raising concerns about their position. The overall sentiment seems to express a level of criticism towards the manager while recognizing the player's talent. There's a hint of negativity due to the mismanagement, yet it's overridden by acknowledgment of the player's ability.

**Tweet 2:** @user Fair enough . No 6 - 0 loss is ever acceptable .

**Gold Label for Tweet 2:** Sadness

**Predicted Label for Tweet 2:** Anger

**Explanation for Tweet 2:** The tweet expresses dissatisfaction and a negative sentiment as it highlights that a 6-0 loss is never acceptable. The phrase "Fair enough" might initially seem accommodating, but it's followed by a statement of strong disapproval. This compels us to classify the emotion of the tweet as Anger.

**Tweet 3:** yeah my ass is going wherever jasons going lmao

**Gold Label for Tweet 3:** Neutral

**Predicted Label for Tweet 3:** Joy

**Explanation for Tweet 3:** The tweet 'yeah my ass is going wherever jasons going lmao' expresses amusement and lightheartedness, likely in a joking or playful context due to the use of "lmao" (laughing my ass off). This shows joy.

**Tweet 4:** Finna drop another track

**Gold Label for Tweet 4:** Neutral

**Predicted Label for Tweet 4:** Joy

**Explanation for Tweet 4:** The tweet 'Finna drop another track' suggests excitement and anticipation about sharing new music. The conveyed emotion is positive, reflecting happiness or pride associated with creation or expression in music. Therefore, the appropriate emotion label is Joy.

**Tweet 5:** @user Just from reading the article it would seem sessions and Page will Be indicted soon if the Ruskies don't get them first

**Gold Label for Tweet 5:** Sadness

**Predicted Label for Tweet 5:** Fear

**Explanation for Tweet 5:** The tweet suggests a negative anticipation, possibly with a hint of fear or concern, regarding potential indictments and external threats. The mention of "indicted soon" and "Ruskies don't get them first" conveys a worrying and slightly fearful tone, with an element of political tension. Therefore, the most fitting emotion classification is Fear.

### D.2 Samples from Test Dataset

**Tweet 1:** @user Yea he found it hilarious afterwards

**Gold Label for Tweet 1:** Neutral

**Predicted Label for Tweet 1:** Joy

**Explanation for Tweet 1:** The tweet describes someone finding something hilarious, which indicates happiness and amusement.

**Tweet 2:** Aplem is doing a $ 50 and $ 20 Visa Card giveaway ! Check it out and dont miss your chance to get one ! http

**Gold Label for Tweet 2:** Neutral

**Predicted Label for Tweet 2:** Joy

**Explanation for Tweet 2:** The tweet expresses excitement and anticipation about a giveaway, which are indicators of a positive and joyous emotion.

**Tweet 3:** @user Me too . Namely women .

**Gold Label for Tweet 3:** Joy

**Predicted Label for Tweet 3:** Neutral

**Explanation for Tweet 3:** The tweet seems neutral and lacks emotional context. It is a mere statement without any indication of strong feelings.

**Tweet 4:** Debate over whether that should have been a penalty , but the bottom line is Fernanmendi bundled into Agutip - you cannot do that .

**Gold Label for Tweet 4:** Anger

**Predicted Label for Tweet 4:** Neutral

**Explanation for Tweet 4:** The tweet discusses a controversial situation in a sports event and the rules associated with it but does not express any overtly strong emotional response.

**Tweet 5:** back at it again http

**Gold Label for Tweet 5:** Joy

**Predicted Label for Tweet 5:** Neutral

**Explanation for Tweet 5:** The tweet "back at it again http" doesn't provide enough context or explicit emotional content. It appears to be a neutral statement about returning to an activity.

## E Zero-Shot with Explanation on Non-English Data

The following samples include tweets in different languages from both the dev dataset and test dataset and our model predicted the emotions labels for these tweets correctly. With the explanation, we were somewhat able to see why different labels were assigned without knowing the languages of the tweets. Note that we identified the languages of the sample tweets using Google Translate for the samples presented below.

### E.1 Samples from Dev Dataset

**Tweet 1 (Spanish):** Los tipos siguen sin traer la suya al país ! ¿Explícame como esperan que esto se calme si todos sabemos que ustedes no confían en ustedes ?

**Gold Label for Tweet 1:** Anger

**Predicted Label for Tweet 1:** Anger

**Explanation for Tweet 1:** The tweet expresses frustration and dissatisfaction with some people not bringing something important to the country and questioning their reliability, indicating a sense of distrust and annoyance. This feeling aligns with feelings of anger.

**Tweet 2 (French):** Après faut pas trop leur en demander , c ' est pas les plus futés qu ' il y a là dedans http

**Gold Label for Tweet 2:** Anger

**Predicted Label for Tweet 2:** Anger

**Explanation for Tweet 2:** The tweet "Après faut pas trop leur en demander, c'est pas les plus futés qu'il y a là dedans" implies a dismissal or a derogatory comment about the intelligence of others, suggesting a lack of respect or slight frustration. This conveys a sense of disdain or irritation towards the subjects being discussed, which aligns with the emotion of anger.

**Tweet 3 (Dutch):** Weersverwachting : Vandaag wordt het in Overlangel Zwaar bewolkt , lichte regen , min . 4 graden en niet warmer dan 1 . . .

**Gold Label for Tweet 3:** Neutral

**Predicted Label for Tweet 3:** Neutral

**Explanation for Tweet 3:** The tweet is a simple weather forecast stating the conditions as heavily cloudy with light rain and mentions temperatures. It has a factual tone without any personal feelings or emotions. Therefore, the emotion label for this tweet is Neutral.

**Tweet 4 (Russian):** Уважаемые коллеги , пришла ко мне моя знакомая , случай которой я описывала . . . http http

**Gold Label for Tweet 4:** Neutral

**Predicted Label for Tweet 4:** Neutral

**Explanation for Tweet 4:** The tweet provides minimal context or emotional indicators, primarily functioning as a statement of fact about a colleague visiting and mentioning a previous situation. The contents lack any clear emotional language or sentiment. Therefore, it is classified as neutral.

### E.2 Samples from Test Dataset

**Tweet 1 (Spanish):** Te quiero pa ' mi

**Gold Label for Tweet 1:** Love

**Predicted Label for Tweet 1:** Love

**Explanation for Tweet 1:** The phrase "Te quiero pa' mi" translates to "I want you for myself" in English and expresses a desire to be with someone, often imbued with affectionate and loving intent.

**Tweet 2 (French):** un boom dans le monde du jeu vidéo ? http

**Gold Label for Tweet 2:** Neutral

**Predicted Label for Tweet 2:** Neutral

**Explanation for Tweet 2:** The tweet asks a question about a significant event in the world of video gaming and includes a link, suggesting curiosity or interest but not clearly expressing any strong emotion.

**Tweet 3 (Dutch):** Zelfkennisbieb is uit haar functie ontheven . Drie dagen ontspanning . Daarna weer # inzicht opdoen . Kom jij dan lenen ? http

**Gold Label for Tweet 3:** Neutral

**Predicted Label for Tweet 3:** Neutral

**Explanation for Tweet 3:** The tweet mentions self-awareness being relieved from duty, followed by three days of relaxation and then gaining insight again. The overall tone is neutral and informative without strong emotional expressions.

**Tweet 4 (Russian):** 14 . Выгляжу лучше , чем когда - либо , довольна собой .

**Gold Label for Tweet 4:** Joy

**Predicted Label for Tweet 4:** Joy

**Explanation for Tweet 4:** The tweet translates to "14. I look better than ever, pleased with myself." which expresses self-satisfaction and happiness.

## F Per-emotion F1-scores Achieved by Ensemble-19

| Emotion Labels | F1-score | Precision | Recall | Support |
|---|---|---|---|---|
| Love | 0.47 | 0.55 | 0.41 | 190 |
| Joy | 0.63 | 0.55 | 0.74 | 433 |
| Anger | 0.73 | 0.76 | 0.70 | 614 |
| Fear | 0.53 | 0.44 | 0.68 | 77 |
| Sadness | 0.55 | 0.56 | 0.54 | 270 |
| Neutral | 0.72 | 0.76 | 0.68 | 916 |

Table 4: Per-emotion F1-scores of the Ensemble-19 model.

## G Effectiveness of Explanation and Correction

Note that during the evaluation phase, we only ran ZeroShot (gpt-4-turbo), ZSE (gpt-4o) and ZSEC (gpt-4o), of which the results are shown in Table 5. For ZeroShot (gpt-4o), we ran it after the gold labels were released for the test dataset. We noticed that there was a nonnegligible improvement on the evaluation metrics with ZeroShot (gpt-4o) comparing to ZeroShot (gpt-4-turbo). It remains uncertain to us whether the gpt-4o model has been updated since the evaluation phase, because due to cost and time constraints, we were unable to re-run the ZSE (gpt-4o) and ZSEC (gpt-4o) models again after the gold labels were released for the test dataset.

| **Models** | **F1-score** | **Precision** | **Recall** | **Accuracy** |
|---|---|---|---|---|
| ZeroShot (gpt-4-turbo) | 0.5459 | 0.5539 | 0.5682 | 0.6028 |
| ZeroShot (gpt-4o) | **0.5732** | **0.5685** | 0.5813 | 0.6164 |
| ZSE (gpt-4o) | 0.5723 | 0.5664 | 0.589 | 0.6232 |
| ZSEC (gpt-4o) | 0.5726 | 0.5631 | **0.5953** | **0.624** |

Table 5: Precision, Recall, F1-scores and Accuracy on the test dataset for ZeroShot, ZSE and ZSEC (correction on "Neutral").

# NYCU-NLP at EXALT 2024: Assembling Large Language Models for Cross-Lingual Emotion and Trigger Detection

**Tzu-Mi Lin, Zhe-Yu Xu, Jian-Yu Zhou, and Lung-Hao Lee***
Institute of Artificial Intelligence Innovation
National Yang Ming Chiao Tung University
No. 1001, Daxue Rd., East Dist., Hsinchu City 300093, Taiwan
*lhlee@nycu.edu.tw

**Abstract**

This study describes the model design of the NYCU-NLP system for the EXALT shared task at the WASSA 2024 workshop. We instruction-tune several large language models and then assemble various model combinations as our main system architecture for cross-lingual emotion and trigger detection in tweets. Experimental results showed that our best performing submission is an assembly of the Starling (7B) and Llama 3 (8B) models. Our submission was ranked sixth of 17 participating systems for the emotion detection subtask, and fifth of 7 systems for the binary trigger detection subtask.

## 1 Introduction

Emotion detection is a well-studied NLP task that aims to automatically identify affective information from texts. The EXALT task organized within the WASSA-2024 workshop focuses on the explainability of cross-lingual emotion detection in tweets. In the emotion detection subtask, the participating system should predict for each tweet an emotion label from 6 possible classes: Love, Joy, Anger, Fear, Sadness, and Neutral. To investigate transferable emotion information across languages, training data is provided in English and evaluation data consists of five different target languages: Dutch, Russian, Spanish, French and English. In the binary trigger detection subtask, participating systems should further identify which words or emoticons can be used to express the emotion.

This paper describes the **NYCU-NLP** (**N**ational **Y**ang **M**ing **C**hiao **T**ung **U**niversity, **N**atural **L**anguage **P**rocessing Lab) system for the EXALT shared task (Maladry et al., 2024). Our solution explores the use of instruction-tuned LLMs, including Mistral (7B) (Jiang et al., 2023), Starling (7B) (Zhu, 2023) and Llama 3 (8B) (Meta AI, 2024). We then assemble various model combinations as our main system architecture. Experimentally, our best performing submission was an assembly of Starling (7B) and Llama 3 (8B), which was ranked sixth of 17 participating systems for the emotion detection subtask and fifth of 7 systems for the binary trigger detection subtask.

The rest of this paper is organized as follows. Section 2 reviews recently related studies on emotion detection. Section 3 describes the NYCU-NLP system for the EXALT shared task. Section 4 presents the results and performance comparisons. Conclusions are finally drawn in Section 5.

## 2 Related Work

Transformer-based language models have been widely applied to emotion detection. An ensemble of the BERT and ELECTRA models was used to detect emotions (Kane et al., 2022). A knowledge-enriched transformer was designed for emotion detection in textual conversations (Zhong et al., 2019). A topic-driven transformer was proposed to detect emotions within dialogues (Zhu et al., 2021). Two hierarchical transformers were trained to use context-/speaker-sensitive information for emotion detection in conversations (Li et al., 2020). Sentiment-enhanced RoBERTa transformers were used to predict emotion and empathy intensities (Lin et al., 2023). Empirical evaluations also showed that transformer-based models such as BERT and XLNet outperformed conventional neural networks for sentiment intensity prediction (Lee et al., 2022). A transformer-based fusion model was developed to integrate semantic



*Proceedings of the 14th Workshop on Computational Approaches to Subjectivity, Sentiment, & Social Media Analysis*, pages 505–510
August 15, 2024 

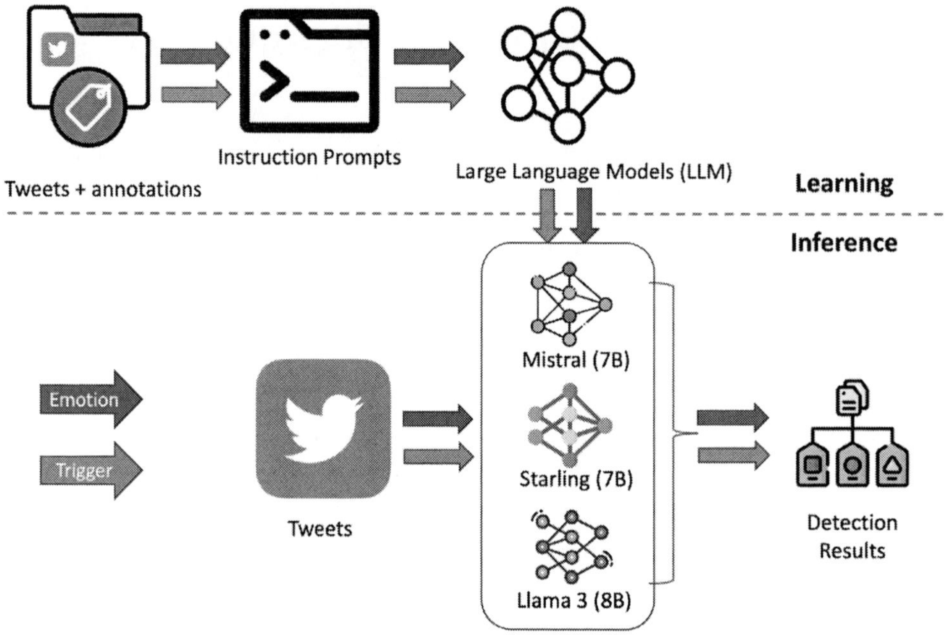


Figure 1: Our NYCU-NLP system architecture for the EXALT shared task.

representations at different degrees of linguistic granularity for emotional intensity prediction (Deng et al., 2023).

Recently, Large Language Models (LLM) have been used for emotion detection. Fine-tuned GPT-3 models with prompt engineering for zero-shot or few shot learning with ChatGPT and GPT-4 models were evaluated for emotion detection (Nedilko and Chu, 2023). Prompt engineering techniques were applied to a GPT model for emotion detection in a code-switching setting (Nedilko, 2023). Multiple features generated by ChatGPT were integrated for emotion recognition in conversations (Tu et al., 2023). The LLM-GEm system was designed to use GPT 3.5 for empathy prediction (Hasan et al., 2024). The abilities of CPT-4, Llama2-Chat-13B and Aplaca-13B to identify emotion triggers were evaluated, analyzing the importance of trigger words for emotion prediction (Singh et al., 2024). Given the results obtained by most such approaches, we are motivated to explore the application of LLMs to the emotion and trigger detection tasks.

## 3 The NYCU-NLP System

Figure 1 shows our NYCU-NLP system architecture for the EXALT shared task. We first instruction-tune LLMs and then assemble fine-tuned LLMs for cross-lingual emotion and binary trigger detection in tweets.

### 3.1 Large Language Models

The following LLMs are used to explore the effectiveness of our system architecture.

(1) Mistral (7B) (Jiang et al. 2023)

Mistral-7B is an open source LLM under the Apache 2.0 license which leverages Group-Query Attention (CQA) for faster inference and uses Sliding Window Attention (SWA) to handle longer sequences at smaller cost. Mistral-7B claims it outperforms Llama 2 (13B) across all evaluated benchmarks.

(2) Starling (7B) (Zhu et al., 2023)

Starling-7B is an open LLM trained by Reinforcement Learning from AI Feedback (RLAIF). A new ranking dataset, called Nectar, was used for the proposed new reward training and policy tuning pipeline. Starling-7B was mainly evaluated based on MT-Bench and AlpacaEval, which are GPT-4-based comparisons.

(3) Llama 3 (8B) (Meta AI, 2024)

Llama 3 is Meta's next generation release of the well-known Llama model. We use a pretrained and instruction-fine-tuned Llama 3 model with 8B parameters.

**System Prompt:** Emotion

"You are a master of sentiment analysis. Classify the input sentences into six emotion categories: 'Love', 'Joy', 'Anger', 'Fear', 'Sadness', and 'Neutral'. The answer MUST be one of the categories mentioned above."

**User Prompt:**

{tweet} // e.g., (I thank God for everything 😊 😊)

**Assistant Prompt:**

{emotion} // e.g., Joy

---

**System Prompt:** Trigger

"You are a master of sentiment analysis. Use '#' to identify which words and emoticons can trigger one of the following emotion categories: 'Love', 'Joy', 'Anger', 'Fear', and 'Sadness'.

**User Prompt:**

{tweet} // e.g., (I thank God for everything 😊 😊)

**Assistant Prompt:**

{trigger} // e.g., (I #thank# God for everything #😊## 😊#)

Figure 2: Prompts used for instruction fine-tuning.

### 3.2 Instruction Fine-tuning

We continually fine-tune these three publicly released LLM models. Figure 2 shows the prompts used for instruction fine-tuning (Wei et al., 2022). The system is configured as a master of sentiment analysis for both tasks. For the emotion detection subtask, we ask the LLM to classify the given sentence into six defined emotion categories. For the binary trigger detection subtask, we used the "#" symbol to emphasize words and emoticons that can be used to trigger the emotion.

We also use the Low-Rank Adaption (LoRA) technique (Hu et al., 2021), which freezes the pre-trained LLM weights and injects trainable rank decomposition matrices into each layer of the transformer architecture, greatly facilitating the instruction-tuning process for downstream tasks.

### 3.3 Assembly Mechanism

During the inference phase, we use a voting-based assembly mechanism, which each LLM conducting an independent detection for each testing instance, effectively integrating fine-tuned LLMs to determine the system output by a majority of votes.

For the emotion detection subtask, if a testing instance does not have a major category prediction, we use the 'neutral' emotion category as an alternative option.

For cases without a majority of prediction results in the binary trigger detection subtask, if a word or emoticon is identified by any one of our used models, we directly regard it as a trigger for our system output.

## 4 Performance Evaluation

### 4.1 Data

The datasets were mainly provided by task organizers, including the training data in English, along with development and test data for each of the five target languages. For the emotion detection subtask, there are respectively 5000, 3000 and 2500 instances in the training, development and test sets, and we used these datasets without augmentation. For the binary trigger subtask, we had respectively 3000, 300 and 832 instances for each provided dataset.

### 4.2 Settings

All pretrained models were downloaded from HuggingFace[1]. We continuously fine-tuned the LLM models using the training datasets only. All experiments were conducted on a server with two Nvidia V100 GPUs (Total 64GB memory). The hyperparameter values for our model implementation were manually optimized on the given development set as follows: epochs 20; batch size 2; optimizer AdamW; learning rate 1e-4; LoRA r 16; LoRA alpha 32; LoRA drop 0.1 and max token length of 20.

### 4.3 Results

Table 1 shows the submission results on the development set. Among three independent LLMs, Llama 3 (8B) outperformed the others in the terms of F1-scores on both subtasks. Assemble LLMs usually outperformed independent LLMs, except the Mistral may reduce performance. The best performance was achieved by an assembly of Starling (7B) and Llama 3 (8B), so we use this LLM setting either individually or in combination as our final submission for official ranking.

Table 2 shows the submission results on the test set. Independent Llama 3 (8B) outperformed independent Starling (7B) for all evaluation metrics.

[1] https://huggingface.co/mistralai/Mistral-7B-Instruct-v0.2
https://huggingface.co/Nexusflow/Starling-LM-7B-beta
https://huggingface.co/meta-llama/Meta-Llama-3-8B-Instruct

| LLMs (#para) | Emotion Detection | | | Binary Trigger Detection | | | |
|---|---|---|---|---|---|---|---|
| | Prec. | Recall | F1 | Token Prec. | Token Recall | Token F1 | MAP |
| Mistral (7B) | 0.5491 | 0.5114 | 0.5202 | 0.4239 | 0.4094 | 0.3768 | 0.3697 |
| Starling (7B) | 0.5677 | 0.4909 | 0.5127 | 0.6321 | 0.5430 | 0.5442 | 0.5219 |
| Llama 3 (8B) | 0.5394 | 0.5713 | 0.5784 | **0.6857** | 0.5641 | 0.5701 | 0.5438 |
| Mistral + Starling | 0.5771 | 0.5590 | 0.5641 | 0.6316 | 0.4906 | 0.5126 | 0.5058 |
| Mistral + Llama 3 | 0.5894 | 0.5728 | 0.5793 | 0.6774 | 0.5461 | 0.5605 | 0.5398 |
| Starling + Llama 3 | **0.6383** | **0.5778** | **0.5982** | 0.6277 | **0.6597** | **0.5836** | 0.5156 |
| Mistral + Starling + Llama 3 | 0.6376 | 0.5617 | 0.5866 | 0.6849 | 0.5798 | 0.5770 | **0.5466** |

Table 1: Submission results on the development set.

| LLMs (#para) | Emotion Detection | | | Binary Trigger Detection | | | |
|---|---|---|---|---|---|---|---|
| | Prec. | Recall | F1 | Token Prec. | Token Recall | Token F1 | MAP |
| Starling (7B) | 0.5636 | 0.5416 | 0.5496 | 0.5946 | 0.4454 | 0.4673 | 0.4649 |
| Llama 3 (8B) | 0.5872 | **0.5806** | 0.5815 | **0.6601** | 0.4859 | 0.5179 | 0.5103 |
| Starling + Llama 3 | **0.6200** | 0.5788 | **0.5951** | 0.6442 | **0.5901** | **0.5636** | **0.5162** |

Table 2: Submission results on the test set.

The assembly of Starling and Llama 3 obtained the best F1 score of 0.5951 for the emotion detection subtask, ranking the sixth of 17 participating systems. In addition, this assembly achieved the best token F1 of 0.5636 for the binary trigger detection subtask, ranking the fifth among all 7 participating systems.

### 4.4 Discussion

We did not use prompt engineering techniques to configure other prompts due to limited computational resources. Therefore, prompts used for instruction fine-tuning needed to be improved for performance enhancements.

In addition, since the LLMs were pre-trained using multi-lingual data, we do not use any machine translation techniques in the tasks.

## 5 Conclusions

This study describes the NYCU-NLP system for the EXALT shared task at the WASSA 2024 workshop, including model design and performance evaluation. We instruction-fine-tuned the LLMs to effectively detect cross-lingual emotions and triggers. Experimental results indicate that our best submission is an assembly of Starling (7B) and Llama 3 (8B) models, achieving a F1 score of 0.5961 for the emotion detection subtask (ranking sixth out of seventeen) and a token F1 of 0.5636 for the binary trigger detection subtask (ranking fifth out of seven).

This pilot study is our first exploration in the cross-lingual emotion and trigger detection task. In future, we will exploit other advanced LLMs to further improve performance.

## Acknowledgments

This study is partially supported by the National Science and Technology Council, Taiwan, under the grant NSTC 111-2628-E-A49-029-MY3. This work was also financially supported by the Co-creation Platform of the Industry Academia Innovation School, NYCU.

## Limitations

This work does not propose a new model to address this shared task. Due to computational resource limitations, experiments were conducted with basic settings without other advanced explorations to enhance system performance.

## References


Meta AI (2024). Llama 3 (April 18 version) [Large language model]. https://ai.meta.com/blog/meta-llama-3/

Yu-Chih Deng, Yih-Ru Wang, Sin-Horng Chen, and Lung-Hao Lee. 2023. Towards transformer fusions for Chinese sentiment intensity prediction in valence-arousal dimensions. *IEEE Access*, 11:109974-109982. https://doi.org/10.1109/ACCESS.2023.3322436

Md Rakibul Hasan, Md Zakir Hossain, Tom Gedeon, and Shafin Rahman. 2024. LLM-GEm: Large language model-guided prediction of people's empathy levels towards newspaper article. In *Findings of the Association for Computational Linguistics: EACL 2024*. Association for Computational Linguistics, pages 2214-2231.

Edward J. Hu, Yelong Shen, Phillip Wallis, Zeyuan Allen-Zhu, Yuanzhi Li, Shean Wang, Lu Wang, and Weizhu Chen. 2021. LoRA: Low-rank adaptation of large language models. *arXiv preprint, arXiv:2106.09685v2*. https://doi.org/10.48550/arXiv.2106.09685

Albert Q. Jiang, Alexandre Sablayrolles, Arthur Mensch, Chris Bamford, Devendra Singh Chaplot, Diego de las Casas, Florian Bressand, Gianna Lengyel, Guillaume Lample, Lucile Saulnier, Lelio Renard Lavaud, Marie-Anne Lachaux, Pierre Stock, Teven Le Scao, Thibaut Lavril, Thomas Wang, Timothee, Lacroix, and William El Sayed. 2023. Mistral 7B. *arXiv: 2310.06825v1*. https://doi.org/10.48550/arXiv.2310.06825

Aditya Kane, Shantanu Patankar, Sahil Khose, and Neeraja Kirtane, 2022. Transformer based ensemble for emotion detection. In *Proceedings of the 12th Workshop on Computational Approaches to Subjectivity, Sentiment, & Social Media Analysis*. Association for Computational Linguistics, pages 250-254. https://doi.org/10.18653/v1/2022.wassa-1.25

Lung-Hao Lee, Jian-Hong Li, ad Liang-Chih Yu. 2022. Chinese EmoBank: Building valence-arousal resources for dimensional sentiment analysis. *ACM Transactions on Asian and Low-Resource Language Information Processing*, 21(4): Article 65, 1-18. https://doi.org/10.1145/3489141

Jingye Li, Donghong Ji, Fei Li, Meishan Zhang, and Yijiang Liu. 2020. HiTrans: A transformer-based context- and speaker-sensitive model for emotion detection in conversations. In *Proceedings of the 28th International Conference on Computational Linguistics*. International Committee on Computational Linguistics, pages 4190-4200. https://doi.org/10.18653/v1/2020.coling-main.370

Tzu-Mi Lin, Jung-Ying Chang, and Lung-Hao Lee. 2023. NCUEE-NLP at WASSA 2023 Empathy, Emotion, and Personality Shared Task: Perceived intensity prediction using sentiment-enhanced RoBERTa transformers. In *Proceedings of the 13th Workshop on Computational Approaches to Subjectivity, Sentiment, & Social Media Analysis*. Association for Computational Linguistics, pages 548-552. https://doi.org/10.18653/v1/2023.wassa-1.49

Andrew Nedilko. 2023. Generative pretrained transformers for emotion detection in a code-switching setting. In *Proceedings of the 13th Workshop on Computational Approaches to Subjectivity, Sentiment, & Social Media Analysis*. Association for Computational Linguistics, pages 616-620. https://doi.org/10.18653/v1/2023.wassa-1.61

Andrew Nedilko, and Yi Chu. 2023. Team Bias Busters at WASSA 2023 Empathy, Emotion, and Personality shared task: emotion detection with generative pretrained transformers. n *Proceedings of the 13th Workshop on Computational Approaches to Subjectivity, Sentiment, & Social Media Analysis*. Association for Computational Linguistics, pages 569-573. https://doi.org/10.18653/v1/2023.wassa-1.53

Smriti Singh, Cornelia Caragea, and Junyi Jessy Li. 2024. Language models (mostly) do not consider emotion triggers when predicting emotion. In *Proceedings of the 2024 Conference of the North American Chapter of the Association for Computational Linguistics: Human Language Technologies (Volume 2: Short Papers)*. Association for Computational Linguistics, pages 603-614.

Geng Tu, Bin Liang, Bing Qin, Kam-Fai Wong, and Ruifeng Xu. 2023. An empirical study on multiple knowledge from ChatGPT for emotion recognition in conversations. In *Findings of the Association for Computational Linguistics: EMNLP 2023*. Association for Computational Linguistics, pages 12160-12173. https://doi.org/10.18653/v1/2023.findings-emnlp.813

Jason Wei, Maarten Bosma, Vincent Y. Zhao, Kelvin Guu, Adams Wei Yu, Brian Lester, Nan Du, Andrew M. Dai, and Quoc V. Le. 2022. Finetuned language models are zero-shot learners. In *Proceedings of the 10th International Conference on Learning Representations*. arXiv:2109.01652v5. https://doi.org/10.48550/arXiv.2109.01652

Banghua Zhu, Evan Frick, Tianhao Wu, Hanlin Zhu, and Jiantao Jiao. 2023. Strling-7B: Increasing LLM helpfulness & harmlessness with RLAIF. https://starling.cs.berkeley.edu/

Peixiang Zhong, Di Wang, Chunyan Miao. 2019. Knowledge-enriched Transformer for emotion detection in textual conversations. In *Proceedings of the 2019 Conference on Empirical Methods in Natural Language Processing and the 9th International Joint Conference on Natural Language Processing.* Association for Computational Linguistics, pages 165-176. https://doi.org/10.18653/v1/D19-1016

Lixing Zhu, Gabriele Pergola, Lin Gui, Deyu Zhou, and Yulan He. 2021. Topic-driven and knowledge-aware transformer for dialogue emotion detection. In *Proceedings of the 59th Annual Meeting of the Association for Computational Linguistics and the 11th International Joint Conference on Natural Language Processing (Volume 1: Long Papers)*. Association for Computational Linguistics, pages 1571-1582. https://doi.org/10.18653/v1/2021.acl-long.125

# Effectiveness of Scalable Monolingual Data and Trigger Words Prompting on Cross-Lingual Emotion Detection Task

**Yao-Fei Cheng***, **Jeongyeob Hong***, **Andrew Wang***, **Anita Silva***, **Gina-Anne Levow**
Department of Linguistics
University of Washington
{nlp5566,yeob,andrewzw,silvaa5,levow}@uw.edu

## Abstract

This paper introduces our submitted systems for WASSA 2024 Shared Task 2: Cross-Lingual Emotion Detection. We implemented a BERT-based classifier and an in-context learning-based system. Our best-performing model, using English Chain of Thought prompts with trigger words, reached 3rd overall with an F1 score of 0.6015. Following the motivation of the shared task, we further analyzed the scalability and transferability of the monolingual English dataset on cross-lingual tasks. Our analysis demonstrates the importance of data quality over quantity. We also found that augmented multilingual data does not necessarily perform better than English monolingual data in cross-lingual tasks. We open-sourced the augmented data and source code of our system for future research.[1]

## 1 Introduction

Recognizing the affect of tweets presents a crucial challenge as they encapsulate the semantic and emotional dialogue of individuals spanning diverse cultures and languages through a short, informal, and noisy medium. The unique constraint of limited length allows users to communicate through abbreviations, slang, and emojis. Such lexical idiosyncrasies, compounded by fragmented language and cultural references, further exacerbate the challenge for traditional natural language processing (NLP) models to interpret emotional content in tweets.

Previous studies have explored various approaches to sentiment and emotion classification (Mohammad, 2016). The SemEval-2018 Task 1 (Mohammad et al., 2018) presented an array of tasks for recognizing the affect of tweets, focusing on building monolingual English, Arabic, and Spanish systems. The vast majority of prior research on affect recognition models has been conducted on monolingual English data, but an increasing number of studies are now focused on the use of cross-lingual models to improve emotion classification (De Bruyne, 2023). WASSA 2024 Shared Task 2 follows the trend of multilingual emotion classification with an emphasis on model explainability and interpretability (Maladry et al., 2024). With the advent of large language models (LLM) accessible through closed API calls, explaining the rationale of LLM prediction is increasingly important.

In our participation in the WASSA 2024 Shared Task 2, we present key observations in data selection and monolingual vs. multilingual approaches through our comparison of our BERT-based models to LLM prompting methods. Our findings indicate that pre-training with in-domain data yields better performance than within-task data. Additionally, monolingual data (back-translated) outperforms multilingual data. We also introduce our balanced dataset for fine-tuning and make it open-source for future research[2].

## 2 System Overview

### 2.1 BERT-based classifier

We summarize our system in Figure 1, and detailed hyper-parameters can be found in Table 5. The system consists of 1) data augmentation, 2) preprocessing, 3) creating our Treehouse LM by continued pre-training the pre-trained TwHIN-BERT-Large (Zhang et al., 2022) language model with augmented data, and 4) fine-tuning the Treehouse LM with in-domain tweets for the downstream task.

#### 2.1.1 Data Augmentation

We observed a significant label imbalance for the provided official English training set (Official Train), as seen in Figure 3. To boost the robustness of our system, we used the English SemEval 2018

[1]* Equal contribution.

[2]https://github.com/freddy5566/cross-lingual-emotion-detection



*Proceedings of the 14th Workshop on Computational Approaches to Subjectivity, Sentiment, & Social Media Analysis*, pages 511–522
August 15, 2024 ©2024 Association for Computational Linguistics

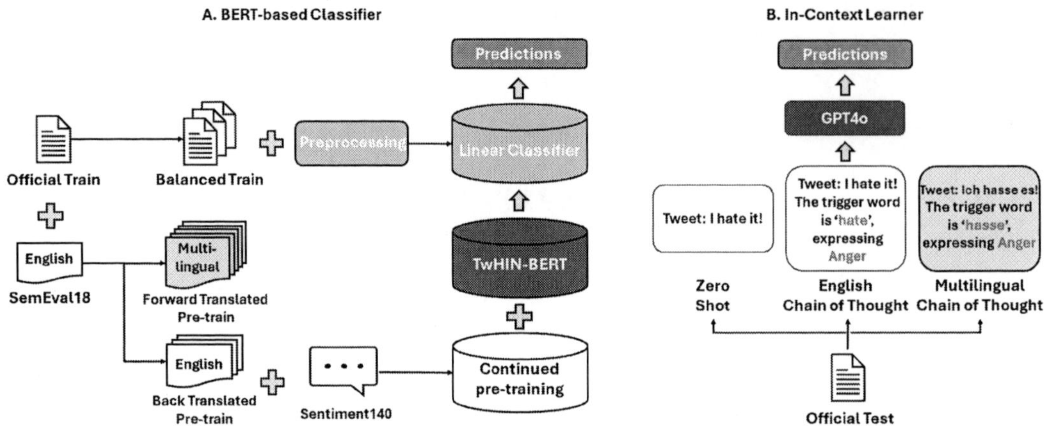


Figure 1: The left figure (A) shows the workflow of the BERT-based classifier, indicating the sources of augmented data for fine-tuning and continued pre-training. After continued pre-training, the model is fine-tuned to produce predictions. The right figure (B) illustrates our prompt-based system, which uses official test data and adds Chain of Thought examples, sending it directly to GPT4o for predictions.

Task1 dataset (Mohammad et al., 2018), and Sentiment140 (Go et al., 2009) to create an augmented training set for both fine-tuning and continued pre-training.

To build a balanced train set (Balanced Train) for fine-tuning, we filtered the English SemEval 2018 Task 1 dataset for entries that were labeled with one of the five underrepresented labels: Joy, Anger, Love, Sadness, or Fear. Then, we randomly selected the samples, reaching $6,970$ entries.

To build the augmented train set for continued pre-training (Back Translated Pre-train), we started with translating Arabic and Spanish samples in the SemEval 2018 Task 1 dataset into English. Combined with the Official Train dataset, the dataset reached a size of $27,458$. It was further back-translated with four target languages: Spanish, Russian, French, and Dutch, yielding a set of $132,290$ entries after removing instances from Official Train to prevent data contamination. All translations are conducted through Google Translation API.

Furthermore, we combined our Back Translated Pre-train dataset with the Sentiment140 dataset[3], a tweet dataset with 1.6 million instances. We experimented with the various combinations of the two datasets to show the scalability and transferability of the monolingual English dataset in cross-lingual emotion recognition. Table 1 summarizes the data used in the system.

To further compare the effect of language variety in training data, we also created a multilingual training set for fine-tuning and continued pre-training. Details are provided in the Appendix A.2. The multilingual dataset was used only for paper-writing purposes and was thus not used during the competition.

| Data | # of Sentences |
|---|---|
| Official Train | 5,000 |
| Balanced Train | 6,970 |
| Back Translated Pre-train | 132,290 |
| + Half Sentiment140 | 1,000,000 |
| + Full Sentiment140 | 1,737,290 |
| Sentiment140 | 1,600,000 |

Table 1: Data Distribution

#### 2.1.2 Pre-processing

Through experimentation, we found that certain pre-processing methods, such as lowercasing, autocorrection, and slang replacement, degraded performance. The impact of removing hashtags, numbers, and punctuation varied, as these elements can both convey important emotional context and introduce noise.

The optimal pre-processing methods we identified were: converting Unicode symbols to ASCII, removing mentions and links, eliminating repetitive characters, and converting over-segmented character sequences back into words. These choices

[3]https://www.kaggle.com/discussions/product-feedback/176309

| | Base | Zeroshot | EngCoT | MulCoT | TwHIN | $130k$ | $1M$ | $1.7M$ | Fwd |
|---|---|---|---|---|---|---|---|---|---|
| F1 | 0.4476 | 0.5872 | **0.6015** | 0.5966 | 0.5010 | 0.5220 | 0.5164 | 0.5171 | 0.5163 |
| Precision | 0.4452 | 0.5993 | **0.6039** | 0.5879 | 0.4944 | 0.5204 | 0.5284 | 0.5100 | 0.5225 |
| Recall | 0.4631 | 0.5798 | 0.6085 | **0.6125** | 0.5205 | 0.5311 | 0.5117 | 0.5314 | 0.5247 |

Table 2: EngCoT and MulCoT denote the English and multilingual prompts-based ICL methods, respectively. TwHIN column presents results without additional continued pre-training. $130k$, $1M$, and $1.7M$ each represent the size of the dataset used in continued pre-training. Fwd refers to the model trained with multilingual data.

indicate that TwHIN-BERT, trained on extensive Twitter data, effectively handles the inherent noise in tweets and that excessive pre-processing can overcorrect testing data and degrade its ability to capture semantic representations.

#### 2.1.3 Continued pre-training

Following the findings in Gururangan et al. (2020) of domain and task-adaptive continued pre-training, we continue to pre-train BERT-based LMs (Devlin et al., 2019; Liu et al., 2019; Nguyen et al., 2020; Conneau et al., 2020; Zhang et al., 2022) to further adapt the general Twitter domain to the specific Twitter domain of EXALT data with the augmented data introduced in Section 2.1.1.

#### 2.1.4 Fine-tuning

We fine-tuned the continued pre-trained LM for downstream emotion classification with the Balanced Train data. We add one linear classifier on top of the pre-trained LM that takes the CLS token $x$ as the input and applies a linear projection $T : \mathbb{R}^d \rightarrow \mathbb{R}^n$, where $d$ is the dimension of CLS token embedding and $n$ is the number of classes. The final distribution can be obtained by applying the softmax function $\sigma(T(x))$.

### 2.2 In-context Learner

Brown et al., 2020 found that large language models can learn the contextual information from raw text, indicating that they can be used for downstream tasks without fine-tuning on additional labeled data, a technique called in-context learning (ICL). In this section, we describe our method for building an ICL-based system.

#### 2.2.1 Chain of Thought with trigger words

Chain-of-Thought (CoT) is a method that introduces intermediate steps that decompose the reasoning process to the LLMs, enabling them to significantly improve their performance (Wei et al., 2022). To ensure the explainability of affect recognition, we designed English CoT prompts (EngCoT) that explain the classification process by identifying the trigger word. As shown in Figure 1, the given prompt points out that "hate" is the trigger word for the tweet "I hate it." We provided an explanation for the Neutral label where no clear trigger word exists based on the annotation guidelines (Singh, Pranaydeep and Maladry, Aaron and Lefever, Els, 2023). Example trigger words and tweets are selected from the trigger word detection dataset from subtask 2 of EXALT Shared Task.

Our system uses GPT4o, which performed best in comparison to other models. See A.6.2 for the details. Similar to the BERT-based classifier, we further analyzed system performance with multilingual CoT prompts (MulCoT). The experiment details and full prompts used in our system are provided in Appendix A.6.

## 3 Results

Table 2 summarizes our system results. The overall best-performing model was GPT4o with English Chain of Thought instructions (EngCoT). This system also reached 3rd place overall in the leaderboard. However, the best recall was achieved through multilingual CoT (MulCoT).

Regarding BERT-based classifiers, continued pre-training TwHIN-BERT with 130k back-translated data outperformed 1M and 1.7M models. A detailed ablation study can be found in Appendix A.3.

## 4 Discussion

### 4.1 Scalability of continued pre-training

We examine whether data quantity or quality is more important in pre-training. As suggested in (Sun et al., 2019), continued pre-training with in-domain or within-task data can provide a certain level of improvement to the downstream task. We used Back Translated Pre-train as the in-domain data because of the similarity of data distribution with fine-tuning data. We used Sentiment140 as the within-task pre-training data because it fits in the sentiment classification task to conduct this examination.

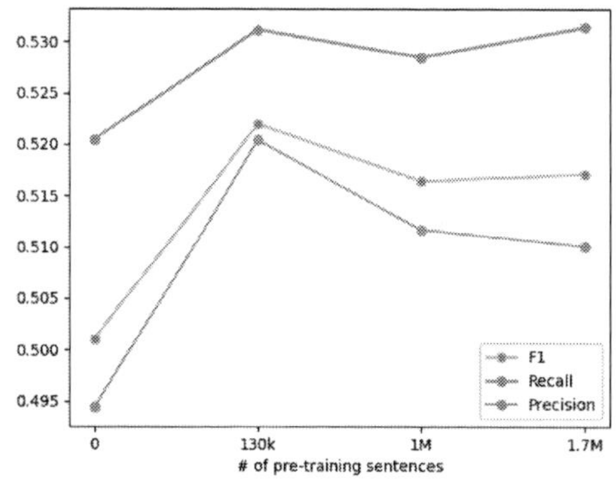


Figure 2: The impact of the scale of pre-training data.

As we can see in Figure 2, all models with continued pre-training perform better than those with no pre-training. Among them, pre-training with in-domain data achieved the best performance. On the other hand, the performance of models (1M and 1.7M) trained with within-task data slightly trails that of the model (130k) trained with in-domain data despite the huge difference in the amount of training data in the pre-training stage. This result suggests that the similarity of data distribution between pre-training and fine-tuning is key to yielding the best performance.

### 4.2 Multilingual vs. Monolingual

#### 4.2.1 BERT-based classifier

| | F1 | Recall | Precision |
|---|---|---|---|
| Balanced Train (7k) | 0.5010 | 0.5204 | 0.4943 |
| Subsampled (7k) | 0.4663 | 0.4908 | 0.4657 |
| All (25k) | **0.5163** | **0.5225** | **0.5247** |
| + Multi. PT (130k) | 0.5061 | 0.5125 | 0.5107 |

Table 3: The results on multilingual training data trained with TwHIN-Bert-Large. PT represents seed models with continued pre-training. Subsampled indicates Balanced Translated Train, and All indicates Forward Translated Train.

To investigate the effectiveness of multilingual data, we compared the multilingual model (please refer to Appendix A.2 for a detailed description) and back-translated English-only monolingual model.

The results, shown in Table 3, show our English back-translated model "Balanced Train" performing better than the multilingual model "Subsampled" under the same amount of training data. However, the multilingual model "All" outperforms "Balanced Train". We hypothesize that performance gain in "All" comes from the amount of training data. Furthermore, our experiments demonstrate that, unlike monolingual continued pre-training, multilingual continued pre-training can be harmful. The root causes still need further study.

#### 4.2.2 Prompting-based methods

Similar to our findings with the BERT-based classifier, the use of multilingual CoT did not outperform monolingual English CoT prompts. Further analysis of the output labels from EngCoT and MulCoT showed that both methods improve the F1 scores by enhancing Recall at the expense of Precision (Table 11 and 12). Compared to EngCoT, MulCoT resulted in a notable drop in Precision. This trend is consistent, as on average, over five runs, EngCoT achieved results of 0.5923, 0.5972, and 0.5997 in F1, Recall, and Precision, respectively. In comparison, MulCoT resulted in 0.5893, 0.6046, and 0.5863. The reason for such difference remains unanswered, but we present our additional experiments on prompts in Section A.6.3 for future research.

## 5 Conclusion

This paper describes our proposed systems for Shared Task 2 of WASSA 2024. Through the analysis of BERT-based classifiers and in-context learning-based systems, we highlight the importance of high-quality data and the effectiveness of CoT using trigger words. In our continued pre-training experiments, we discovered that aligning the data distribution between continued pre-training data and fine-tuning data is crucial. Without this alignment, the size of the dataset does not significantly impact information transferring into cross-lingual settings. While it may seem intuitive to use multilingual data for cross-lingual tasks, our findings revealed that this approach did not enhance performance in both systems. Further research is needed to understand the underlying mechanisms of in-context learning and its impact on performance.

## 6 Limitations

The main limitations of our work relate to these points: a) Our augmented data is highly dependent on the quality of Google Translation API. Furthermore, it is not a deterministic output; b) We did not perform an extensive hyper-parameter search in continued pre-training, which might improve classifiers' performance. c) We presented outputs from closed-source models, where access is limited through paywall APIs. d) The outputs from GPT-4 are not deterministic and are vulnerable to changes in prompts. e) Considering the similarity between sentiment classification and emotion detection, we treated the sentiment 140 data as within-task data. However, those two tasks are related, not identical; therefore, results could be affected by such differences.

## References


Tom B. Brown, Benjamin Mann, Nick Ryder, Melanie Subbiah, Jared Kaplan, Prafulla Dhariwal, Arvind Neelakantan, Pranav Shyam, Girish Sastry, Amanda Askell, Sandhini Agarwal, Ariel Herbert-Voss, Gretchen Krueger, T. J. Henighan, Rewon Child, Aditya Ramesh, Daniel M. Ziegler, Jeff Wu, Clemens Winter, Christopher Hesse, Mark Chen, Eric Sigler, Mateusz Litwin, Scott Gray, Benjamin Chess, Jack Clark, Christopher Berner, Sam McCandlish, Alec Radford, Ilya Sutskever, and Dario Amodei. 2020. Language models are few-shot learners.

Alexis Conneau, Kartikay Khandelwal, Naman Goyal, Vishrav Chaudhary, Guillaume Wenzek, Francisco Guzmán, Edouard Grave, Myle Ott, Luke Zettlemoyer, and Veselin Stoyanov. 2020. Unsupervised cross-lingual representation learning at scale. In *Proceedings of the 58th Annual Meeting of the Association for Computational Linguistics*.

Luna De Bruyne. 2023. The paradox of multilingual emotion detection. In *Proceedings of the 13th Workshop on Computational Approaches to Subjectivity, Sentiment, & Social Media Analysis*.

Jacob Devlin, Ming-Wei Chang, Kenton Lee, and Kristina Toutanova. 2019. BERT: Pre-training of deep bidirectional transformers for language understanding. In *Proceedings of the 57th Annual Meeting of the Association for Computational Linguistics*.

Alec Go, Richa Bhayani, and Lei Huang. 2009. Twitter sentiment classification using distant supervision. *CS224N project report, Stanford*, 1(12):2009.

Suchin Gururangan, Ana Marasović, Swabha Swayamdipta, Kyle Lo, Iz Beltagy, Doug Downey, and Noah A. Smith. 2020. Don't stop pretraining: Adapt language models to domains and tasks. In *Proceedings of the 58th Annual Meeting of the Association for Computational Linguistics*.

Yinhan Liu, Myle Ott, Naman Goyal, Jingfei Du, Mandar Joshi, Danqi Chen, Omer Levy, Mike Lewis, Luke Zettlemoyer, and Veselin Stoyanov. 2019. RoBERTa: A robustly optimized BERT pretraining approach. *arXiv preprint arXiv:1907.11692*.

Aaron Maladry, Pranaydeep Singh, and Els Lefever. 2024. Findings of the wassa 2024 exalt shared task on explainability for cross-lingual emotion in tweets. In *Proceedings of the 14th Workshop of on Computational Approaches to Subjectivity, Sentiment Social Media Analysis@ACL 2024*.

Sewon Min, Xinxi Lyu, Ari Holtzman, Mikel Artetxe, Mike Lewis, Hannaneh Hajishirzi, and Luke Zettlemoyer. 2022. Rethinking the role of demonstrations: What makes in-context learning work? In *Proceedings of the 2022 Conference on Empirical Methods in Natural Language Processing (EMNLP)*.

Saif Mohammad, Felipe Bravo-Marquez, Mohammad Salameh, and Svetlana Kiritchenko. 2018. SemEval-2018 task 1: Affect in tweets. In *Proceedings of the 12th International Workshop on Semantic Evaluation*.

Saif M. Mohammad. 2016. Sentiment analysis: Detecting valence, emotions, and other affectual states from text. In Herbert L. Meiselman, editor, *Emotion Measurement*, pages 201–237. Woodhead Publishing.

Dat Quoc Nguyen, Thanh Vu, and Anh Tuan Nguyen. 2020. BERTweet: A pre-trained language model for english tweets. In *Proceedings of the 2020 Conference on Empirical Methods in Natural Language Processing (EMNLP)*.

Singh, Pranaydeep and Maladry, Aaron and Lefever, Els. 2023. Annotation guidelines for labeling emotion in multilingual tweets.

Chi Sun, Xipeng Qiu, Yige Xu, and Xuanjing Huang. 2019. How to fine-tune BERT for text classification? In *Proceedings of the 57th Annual Meeting of the Association for Computational Linguistics*.

Boshi Wang, Sewon Min, Xiang Deng, Jiaming Shen, You Wu, Luke Zettlemoyer, and Huan Sun. 2023. Towards understanding chain-of-thought prompting: An empirical study of what matters. In *Proceedings of the 61th Annual Meeting of the Association for Computational Linguistics*.

Albert Webson and Ellie Pavlick. 2022. Do prompt-based models really understand the meaning of their prompts? In *Proceedings of the 2022 Conference of the North American Chapter of the Association for Computational Linguistics: Human Language Technologies*.

Jason Wei, Xuezhi Wang, Dale Schuurmans, Maarten Bosma, Brian Ichter, Fei Xia, Ed Chi, Quoc Le, and

Denny Zhou. 2022. Chain-of-thought prompting elicits reasoning in large language models. In *Proceedings of 36th Conference on Neural Information Processing Systems.*

Xinyang Zhang, Yury Malkov, Omar Florez, Serim Park, Brian McWilliams, Jiawei Han, and Ahmed El-Kishky. 2022. TwHIN-BERT: A Socially-Enriched Pre-trained Language Model for Multilingual Tweet Representations at Twitter. *arXiv preprint arXiv:2209.07562.*

# A Appendix

## A.1 Data

Figure 3 shows the label distribution in Official and Balanced Train.

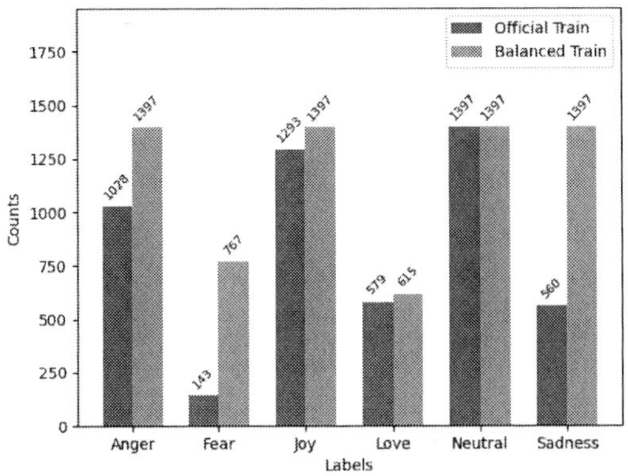


Figure 3: Comparison of Official train set with enhanced train set.

## A.2 Multilingual Training Data

| Data | # of Sentences |
|---|---:|
| Official Train | 5,000 |
| Balanced Train | 6,970 |
| Back Translated Pre-train | 132,290 |
| Forward Translated Train | 25,000 |
| Balanced Translated Train | 6,923 |
| Forward Translated Pre-train | 134,745 |

Table 4: Data Distribution

This section explains the process of building multilingual training data for fine-tuning and continued pre-training. Likewise, we translated the Official Train into four other languages and combined it with the Official Train, resulting in $25,000$ entries for the multilingual training set (Forward Translated Train). To have a fair comparison with Balanced Train, we also subsample 6,923 entries with a similar label distribution to Balanced Translated Train.

For the multilingual continued pre-training dataset (Forward Translated Pre-train), we combined $27,458$ English data, created by translating Arabic and Spanish SemEval data in English, and translated it into French, Dutch, Spanish, and Russian. After removing identical entries, the Forward Translated Pre-train contains $134,745$ entries. Table 4 summarizes the data.

## A.3 Classifiers

In this section, we conducted a detailed ablation study on BERT-based classifiers. We examined five strong pre-trained LMs (Devlin et al., 2019; Liu et al., 2019; Nguyen et al., 2020; Conneau et al., 2020; Zhang et al., 2022) with different conditions. The detailed hyper-parameters are summarized in Table 5.

| Hyper-parameter | Pre-training | Fine-tuning |
|---|---|---|
| Max sequence length | 128 | 512 |
| Precision | FP16 | FP16 |
| Total batch size | 128 | 64 |
| Learning rate | 1e-4 | 2e-6 |
| # of epoch | 10 | 20 |
| Weight decay | 0.1 | 0.1 |

Table 5: The hyper-parameters for pre-training and fine-tuning.

### A.3.1 Which pre-trained LM as the seed model?

Our results are summarized in Table 6. We found TwHIN-BERT performed best regardless of whether it was pre-processed or not and whether the test set was translated into English. Therefore, we use TwHIN-BERT as our seed model in the rest of the experiments.

### A.3.2 Pre-processing

Surprisingly, models without pre-processing generally perform better than those with pre-processing. We hypothesize that this is because TwHIN-BERT is capable of capturing and representing the deep lexical and semantic properties of tweets, having been trained on complete Twitter data. Although noisy, various lexical features of tweets are strong indicators of emotional context, unique tokens such as emoticons and emojis can be challenging for the model to tokenize and represent accurately. Therefore, a promising area for future research is to explore methods for converting these tokens into meaningful words or alternative representations.

## A.4 English dev/test

Another obvious trend is translating dev and test sets into English, dramatically improving performance. Despite some pre-trained models being trained in the multilingual datasets, the English-translated pairs still perform better. For example, XLM-Roberta with and without

| Model | Multilingual pre-trained | Pre-processing | Translated | F1 | Recall | Precision |
|---|---|---|---|---|---|---|
| TwHIN-BERT | ✓ | ✗ | ✗ | 0.3507 | 0.3585 | 0.3742 |
| Bert | ✗ | ✗ | ✗ | 0.2292 | 0.2461 | 0.3497 |
| BERTweet | ✗ | ✗ | ✗ | 0.2334 | 0.2493 | 0.3013 |
| Roberta | ✗ | ✗ | ✗ | 0.2334 | 0.2493 | 0.3013 |
| XLM-Roberta | ✓ | ✗ | ✗ | 0.2324 | 0.2466 | 0.2705 |
| TwHIN-BERT | ✓ | ✓ | ✗ | 0.2181 | 0.2319 | 0.3789 |
| Bert | ✗ | ✓ | ✗ | 0.2181 | 0.2319 | 0.3789 |
| BERTweet | ✗ | ✓ | ✗ | 0.2311 | 0.2450 | 0.3000 |
| Roberta | ✗ | ✓ | ✗ | 0.2311 | 0.2450 | 0.3000 |
| XLM-Roberta | ✓ | ✓ | ✗ | 0.2311 | 0.2450 | 0.3000 |
| TwHIN-BERT | ✓ | ✗ | ✓ | **0.4581** | **0.4735** | **0.4460** |
| Bert | ✗ | ✗ | ✓ | 0.4284 | 0.4345 | 0.4311 |
| BERTweet | ✗ | ✗ | ✓ | 0.3053 | 0.3123 | 0.3221 |
| Roberta | ✗ | ✗ | ✓ | 0.3053 | 0.3123 | 0.3221 |
| XLM-Roberta | ✓ | ✗ | ✓ | 0.3068 | 0.3079 | 0.3296 |
| TwHIN-BERT | ✓ | ✓ | ✓ | 0.4503 | 0.4696 | 0.4392 |
| Bert | ✗ | ✓ | ✓ | 0.4113 | 0.4175 | 0.4143 |
| BERTweet | ✗ | ✓ | ✓ | 0.3217 | 0.3331 | 0.3224 |
| Roberta | ✗ | ✓ | ✓ | 0.3217 | 0.3331 | 0.3224 |
| XLM-Roberta | ✓ | ✓ | ✓ | 0.3200 | 0.3268 | 0.3257 |

Table 6: The ablation study on pre-processing and translation. Translated indicated dev and test data translated into English via Google Translation API.

English translation, (0.3200/0.3268/0.3257) vs. (0.2311/0.2450/0.3000) for F1, Recall, and Precision, respectively. This is very intuitive because the training tweets are all in English. Therefore, models can only perform well on English tweet emotion classification.

### A.5 Data-augmentation

Our results on data augmentation are shown in Table 7. As we can see, it achieved performance gain in almost every pre-trained model. Notably, this data augmentation only works well on BERT and TwHIN-BERT. It is harmful for BERTweet and Roberta pairs and almost zero-gain for XLM-Roberta.

### A.6 In-Context Learning

#### A.6.1 Experiment Detail

We tested multiple OpenAI's GPT models using their APIs. Our system uses the latest model, GPT4o, which uses a different tokenizer that achieves better multilingual performance. Although ensuring deterministic output is challenging due to the GPU-based calculations of LLMs, we minimized the variables by setting the temperature, frequency penalty, and presence penalty as zero. Furthermore, we penalized undesirable output tokens and boosted the probability of desired labels. By setting log probability and max token number as one, we ensured our models to return label only.

#### A.6.2 Model Selection

We tested multiple GPT base models to find the best-performing one. On the dev dataset, Zeroshot GPT-4o outperformed both Zeroshot GPT-4 and Zeroshot GPT-3.5, achieving an F1 score of 0.5645, compared to 0.5616 and 0.4847, respectively. Therefore, we selected GPT-4o as our main model. Table 8 summarizes the results of various models and prompting methods.

#### A.6.3 Vulnerability of prompting

It is noteworthy that the effect of our Trigger Word CoT differs by model type. In Table 8, both GPT-4o and GPT-3.5 show a similar trend of increasing F1 scores with EngCoT and MulCoT. Compared to Zeroshot, EngCoT improved by approximately 0.2 to 0.4, and MulCoT gained roughly 0.5 to 0.7. However, as shown in Table 2, such gains were not transferable to the test data. Additionally, GPT-4 suffered from additional CoT steps, with the F1 score decreasing by approximately 0.5. This

| Model | Multilingual pre-trained | F1 | Recall | Precision |
|---|---|---|---|---|
| TwHIN-Bert | ✓ | **0.5010** | **0.5204** | **0.4943** |
| Bert | ✗ | 0.4964 | 0.5057 | 0.4907 |
| BERTweet | ✗ | 0.3130 | 0.3236 | 0.3393 |
| Roberta | ✗ | 0.3130 | 0.3236 | 0.3393 |
| XLM-Roberta | ✓ | 0.3247 | 0.3259 | 0.3345 |

Table 7: The results on English back-translated.

| | F1 | Recall | Precision |
|---|---|---|---|
| Zeroshot GPT-4o | 0.5645 | 0.5510 | 0.5881 |
| EngCoT GPT-4o | 0.5847 | 0.5885 | 0.5956 |
| MulCoT GPT-4o | **0.6101** | **0.6106** | **0.6155** |
| Zeroshot GPT-4 | 0.5616 | 0.5713 | 0.5709 |
| Fewshot GPT-4 | 0.5465 | 0.5509 | 0.5660 |
| EngCoT GPT-4 | 0.5115 | 0.5130 | 0.5413 |
| MulCoT GPT-4 | 0.5489 | 0.5498 | 0.5702 |
| Zeroshot GPT-3.5 | 0.4963 | 0.5225 | 0.5053 |
| FewShot GPT-3.5 | 0.4951 | 0.5176 | 0.5217 |
| EngCoT GPT-3.5 | 0.5305 | 0.5433 | 0.5564 |
| MulCoT GPT-3.5 | 0.5614 | 0.5822 | 0.5581 |

Table 8: The overall results of GPT results with varying models and prompting methods. Note that scores are not the 5-run average.

demonstrates that the effect of CoT and prompting methods depends on the model type, as well as the content and distribution of the dataset.

| | F1 | Recall | Precision |
|---|---|---|---|
| EngCoT GPT-3.5 (8) | 0.5305 | 0.5433 | 0.5564 |
| - 2 Neutral (6) | 0.4434 | 0.4155 | 0.5870 |
| + 2 Emotion (10) | 0.5062 | 0.5133 | 0.5494 |

Table 9: Results of GPT3.5 with varying number of CoT examples

Additionally, we conducted a simple ablation study on the number of CoT examples using GPT-3.5, which benefited the most from CoT with the dev data. Following the annotation guidelines, the current CoT steps consist of 8 examples: 5 emotion categories and 3 cases of the Neutral label. When we reduced the number of cases to 6 by removing two random Neutral examples, the F1 score dropped from 0.5305 to 0.4434. Adding two additional emotion-label examples decreased the F1 score to 0.5062.

This ablation study suggests that the number of CoT examples affects the results. However, as mentioned earlier, our findings are specific to the model types and dataset, making it difficult to generalize that 8 steps are the best. Furthermore, there is no strong evidence that our instructions significantly impacted the results, as several studies suggest that the quality and content of instructions do not matter much in ICL (Min et al., 2022; Webson and Pavlick, 2022; Wang et al., 2023).

#### A.6.4 Error Analysis

This section provides a label-wise analysis of the test data. Due to time and financial constraints, we were not able to perform a detailed ablation study and experiments on the test data.

| F1 | ZeroShot | Δ EngCoT | Δ MulCoT |
|---|---|---|---|
| **Anger** | 0.7342 | +0.0056 | +0.0024 |
| **Fear** | 0.5125 | **+0.0361** | **+0.0230** |
| **Joy** | 0.5376 | +0.0079 | +0.0028 |
| **Love** | 0.4972 | **+0.0107** | **+0.0215** |
| **Neutral** | 0.6901 | **+0.0194** | **+0.0160** |
| **Sadness** | 0.5516 | +0.0061 | -0.0094 |
| **Macro Avg** | 0.5872 | +0.0143 | +0.0094 |

Table 10: Label-wise F1 scores for ZeroShot, EngCoT, and MulCoT models.

As mentioned in Section 4.2.2, the majority of changes in F1 occur in the Fear, Love, and Neutral labels. Table 11 and Table 12 show that CoT improves the F1 scores of these labels by increasing Recall at the expense of Precision. Given that CoT improves Recall, the performance gain on Fear, the most underrepresented label in the dataset, seems intuitive. Similarly, Love, the second most scarce label, potentially benefits from the robustness provided by CoT. The changes in the Neutral label suggest that the model might be following the reasoning steps detailed in our CoT examples, where we emphasize the lack of keywords in the Neutral examples. However, there is no clear evidence supporting this hypothesis. Therefore, further research is needed to understand the effect of CoT reasoning steps.

| Recall | ZeroShot | Δ EngCoT | Δ MulCoT |
|---|---|---|---|
| **Anger** | 0.7378 | -0.0407 | -0.0228 |
| **Fear** | 0.5325 | +0.0909 | +0.1039 |
| **Joy** | 0.4873 | -0.0092 | +0.0069 |
| **Love** | 0.4684 | +0.0421 | +0.0790 |
| **Neutral** | 0.7380 | +0.0393 | -0.0153 |
| **Sadness** | 0.5148 | +0.0222 | +0.0445 |
| **Macro Avg** | 0.5798 | +0.0241 | +0.0327 |

Table 11: Label-wise recall for ZeroShot, EngCoT, and MulCoT models.

| Precision | ZeroShot | Δ EngCoT | Δ MulCoT |
|---|---|---|---|
| **Anger** | 0.7306 | +0.0576 | +0.0289 |
| **Fear** | 0.4940 | -0.0042 | -0.0317 |
| **Joy** | 0.5994 | +0.0356 | -0.0033 |
| **Love** | 0.5298 | -0.0246 | -0.0369 |
| **Neutral** | 0.6481 | +0.0045 | +0.0422 |
| **Sadness** | 0.5940 | -0.0140 | -0.0679 |
| **Macro Avg** | 0.5993 | +0.0092 | -0.0114 |

Table 12: Label-wise precision for ZeroShot, EngCoT, and MulCoT models.

#### A.6.5 Prompts

This section provides a list of prompts used in the ICL experiments and descriptions.

CoT examples are made up of 8 examples: 5 Emotion labels and 3 different cases of Neutral labels. For non-Neutral labels, we randomly selected tweets with token sizes between 5 and 10. We excluded lengthy tweets ( > 10) as it increases the cost and context window of prompts. On the other hand, shorter tweets ( < 5) do not provide enough context information. Therefore, we randomly selected from the given range of tweets. We also included tweets with emojis in the CoT examples as emojis also serve as trigger words in the given dataset. Similarly, we randomly selected from three different scenarios of Neutral labels: bot-like, opinionated, and fact-stating tweets.

| |
|---|
| **Role:** system<br>**Content:** Classify given tweets in the following 6 labels: Joy, Anger, Sadness, Love, Fear, and Neutral. Your answer should be a label. |
| **Role:** user<br>**Content:** @user Yea he found it hilarious afterwards |

Table 13: Base Prompts Examples.

| |
|---|
| **System:** Classify given tweets in the following 6 labels: Joy, Anger, Sadness, Love, Fear, and Neutral. Your answer should be a label. |
| **User:** Tweet: @user Job well done ! ! ! 200<br>The trigger word is 'Job well', indicating positive emotion. Also, it is not toward a specific person, more like an enthusiastic and energetic reaction.<br>**Assistant:** Joy<br>**User:** Tweet: My hair is so flat I hate it<br>The trigger word is 'hate it', indicating negative and furious emotion.<br>**Assistant:** Anger<br>**User:** Tweet: Our house looks so sad without the Christmas lights<br>The trigger words are 'so sad' and a sad emoji at the end, indicating sorrow.<br>**Assistant:** Sadness<br>**User:** Tweet: Thank you to whoever wonder traded me a shiny dialga<br>The trigger words are 'thank you', indicating positive emotion. Also, it is toward a specific person, 'me'.<br>**Assistant:** Love<br>**User:** Tweet: Gotta Move Back Home #PanicIn4Words<br>The trigger word is 'Panic' in PanicIn4Words, indicating being scared.<br>**Assistant:** Fear<br>**User:** Tweet: # NowOnAir @user Ft . @user - Nobody Knows . Listen live on http<br>There is no clear trigger word. This is also a tweet from bots.<br>**Assistant:** Neutral<br>**User:** Tweet: @user I always do this and I don't care at the morning afterwards .<br>There is no clear triggering word. Therefore, this is simply stating an opinion without any indication of emotion.'<br>**Assistant:** Neutral<br>**User:** Tweet: @user Hi Prashant , We dont have exact dates / timelines , but were working to roll it out to all eligible devices globally as quickly as possible . Stay tuned ! - Tim<br>There is no clear trigger word. This is simply stating a fact.<br>**Assistant:** Neutral |
| **User:** Give me all four of those hours . Cut nothing . http |

Table 14: Chain of thought example with English instructions.

| **System:** Classify given tweets in the following 6 labels: Joy, Anger, Sadness, Love, Fear, and Neutral. Your answer should be a label. |
|---|
| **User:** Tweet: @user Job well done ! ! ! 200<br>The trigger word is 'Job well', indicating positive emotion. Also, it is not toward a specific person, more like an enthusiastic and energetic reaction.<br>**Assistant:** Joy<br>**User:** Tweet: Meine Haare sind so platt, dass ich es hasse<br>The trigger word are 'es hasse', indicating a negative and furious emotion.<br>**Assistant:** Anger<br>**User:** Tweet: Notre maison a l'air si triste sans les lumières de Noël<br>The trigger words are 'si triste' and a sad emoji, indicating sorrow.<br>**Assistant:** Sadness<br>**User:** Tweet: Bedankt aan degene die zich afvraagt of hij mij een glimmende dialga heeft geruild<br>The trigger word is 'Bedankt', indicating a positive emotion directed towards a specific person.<br>**Assistant:** Love<br>**User:** Tweet: Tengo que regresar a casa #PánicoEn4Palabras<br>The trigger word is 'Pánico' in PanicIn4Words, indicating being scared.<br>**Assistant:** Fear<br>**User:** Tweet: # NowOnAir @user Ft . @user - Nobody Knows . Listen live on http<br>There is no clear trigger word. This is also a tweet from bots.<br>**Assistant:** Neutral<br>**User:** Tweet: @user I always do this and I don't care at the morning afterwards ..<br>There is no clear triggering word. Therefore, this is simply stating an opinion without any indication of emotion.'<br>**Assistant:** Neutral<br>**User:** Tweet: @user Hi Prashant , We dont have exact dates / timelines , but were working to roll it out to all eligible devices globally as quickly as possible . Stay tuned ! - Tim<br>There is no clear trigger word. This is simply stating a fact.<br>**Assistant:** Neutral |
| **User:** Give me all four of those hours . Cut nothing . http |

Table 15: Chain of thought example with multilingual instructions.

# WU_TLAXE at WASSA 2024 Explainability for Cross-Lingual Emotion in Tweets Shared Task 1: Emotion through Translation using TwHIN-BERT and GPT

**Jon Davenport**[1], **Keren Ruditsky**[1], **Anna Batra**[1],
**Yulha Lhawa**[1], **Gina-Anne Levow**[1],
[1]Computational Linguistics, University of Washington,
{jmeld,krudit,batraa,yulha,levow}@uw.edu
**Correspondence:** jmdeld@uw.edu

## Abstract

This paper describes our task 1 submission for the WASSA 2024 shared task on *Explainability for Cross-lingual Emotion in Tweets*. Our task is to predict the correct emotion label (Anger, Sadness, Fear, Joy, Love, and Neutral) for a dataset of English, Dutch, French, Spanish, and Russian tweets, while training exclusively on English emotion labeled data, to reveal what kind of emotion detection information is transferable cross-language (Maladry et al., 2024). To that end, we used an ensemble of models with a GPT-4 decider. Our ensemble consisted of a few-shot GPT-4 prompt system and a TwHIN-BERT system fine-tuned on the EXALT and additional English data. We ranked 8th place under the name WU_TLAXE with an F1 Macro score of 0.573 on the test set. We also experimented with an English-only TwHIN-BERT model by translating the other languages into English for inference, which proved to be worse than the other models.

## 1 Introduction

Cross-lingual emotion analysis is vital to identifying emotions across diverse languages and addressing challenges such as linguistic diversity and cultural differences. Our approach utilizes transfer learning and cross-lingual word embeddings (Xu et al., 2022) as introduced in models like TwHIN-BERT (Zhang et al., 2022) to handle these variations.

Research highlights the effectiveness of transformer-based models like GPT and BERT in capturing contextual nuances for accurate emotion recognition (Acheampong et al., 2021). Studies also show the potential of large language models like GPT and RoBERTa to enhance user interactions (Venkatakrishnan et al., 2023). Our experiments used an ensemble approach, featuring a GPT-4 decider, a few-shot GPT-4 prompt system, and a fine-tuned TwHIN-BERT system, trained on the EXALT data supplemented with additional English data to optimize cross-language emotion detection. We additionally experimented with an English-only TwHIN-BERT model.

## 2 System Description

Figure 1, our best performing system submitted to CodaLab, proved to be an ensemble model with GPT-4 as the decider. The decider generates a label based on each tweet's text, and two predicted labels, each provided by a different system. The systems that provided these competing predictions for the decider were on the one hand, a TwHIN-BERT (Zhang et al., 2022) fine-tuned model, and on the other hand, the results of a few-shot GPT-4 prompt system. The fine-tuned TwHIN model was trained on a processed dataset based on the provided training data and a supplemental English, emotion-labeled dataset from a past shared task, SemEval 2018 (Mohammad et al., 2018). Since our goal was to develop a multilingual system, we used NLLB machine translation (Costa-jussà et al., 2022) to generate parallel corpora for each of the test languages (Spanish, French, Dutch, Russian). Then we balanced our dataset by downsampling classes with over 10,000 examples, and up-sampling classes with fewer than 10,000 examples.

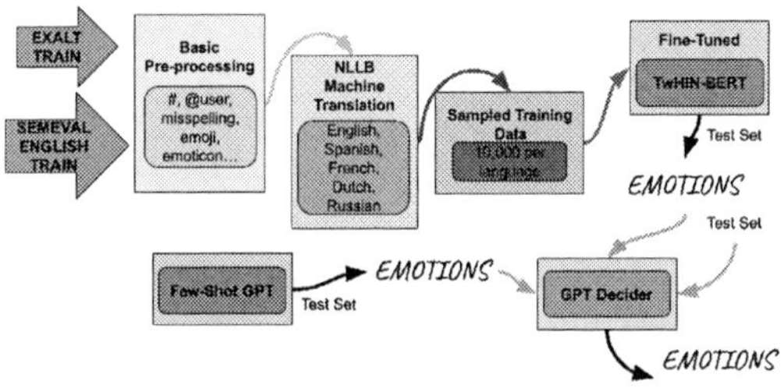


Figure 1: The GPT Ensemble architecture

We also experimented with an English-only



*Proceedings of the 14th Workshop on Computational Approaches to Subjectivity, Sentiment, & Social Media Analysis*, pages 523–527
August 15, 2024 ©2024 Association for Computational Linguistics

TwHIN-BERT model which uses NLLB to translate the other languages to English for inference, along with sampling of the data.

### 2.1 Few-Shot GPT-4

Few shot GPT-4 involved a simple system instruction prompt and a training set example for each language and each label. Chain of thought was not employed, as the goal was to evaluate GPT's performance in an information-rich prompt environment. We ran few shot GPT-4 on a computer cluster, using an API request. An example prompt is shown below.

```
{"role": "system", "content":
"You are a sentiment analysis
system assistant  designed to
classify the sentiment of each
tweet into one of the following
categories: Joy, Sadness, Love,
Anger, Neutral, Fear."},

{"role": "user", "content":
"J'ai téléchargé mon premier
article pour Gardez l'il
ouvert pour d'autres recettes
nutrition gainz delicious
biggestfan"},

{"role": "assistant",
"content":"Joy"}
```

### 2.2 Multilingual TwHIN-BERT

#### 2.2.1 Dataset

The initial dataset consisted of the EXALT training data and relevant English samples from the SemEval 2018 task. We augmented that data by using NLLB to translate each English tweet to each target language (Spanish, Dutch, French, Russian). We then balanced the dataset such that each label had 10,000 samples, and split the balanced dataset into train (0.9) and development (0.1) subsets.

#### 2.2.2 Approach

We fine-tuned the large version of TwHIN-BERT with our custom, multilingual dataset. We chose to use TwHIN-BERT because it has been pre-trained on tweets. We added a 6 label linear layer classification head to TwHIN-BERT, a dropout layer of 0.1, which then takes TwHIN-BERT's final layer's 1,024 dimension embedding and outputs a probability distribution over the label classes. For training, we set patience to two epochs and the learning rate at 2e-6, which resulted in 10 epochs of training, and used cross-entropy loss as our loss function. We fine-tuned TwHIN-BERT on a computer cluster with a L40 GPU.

### 2.3 GPT-4 Decider Ensemble

Our best performing multi-lingual model was a few-shot, ensemble model. We fed GPT-4 a system prompt that included instructions and several examples of an ensemble system decider. In each example the system is provided with the tweet's text, the label predicted by our multi-lingual fine-tuned TwHIN-BERT model, and the label predicted by our few-shot GPT query. An example prompt is shown below.

```
{"role": "system", "content":
"You are a sentiment analysis
ensemble classifier system
designed to classify the
sentiment of each tweet into
one of the following categories:
Joy, Sadness, Love, Anger,
Neutral, Fear. You will be given
a tweet and two labels provided
by other models, and you must
classify the sentiment based on
both the tweet and the other
model predictions."},

{"role": "user", "content":
"Label 1: Joy,  Label 2: Love,
Text: 15 year old tori-youve
been great. Bit of a twat but
youve been alright. Cant wait
to see the back end of you
tho ."},

{"role": "assistant",
"content":"Love"}
```

### 2.4 English-Only TwHIN-BERT

#### 2.4.1 Dataset

We developed an English only dataset based on the EXALT training data and sampling valid tweets from the SemEval 2018 competition. This yields a much smaller dataset, which we then balanced in two different ways. We down-sampled to the least-represented emotion class ("Fear", count 616), and we also up-sampled to the most-represented emotion ("Joy", 2,933), and trained a model on each dataset. In order to run this model on the training data, we developed a language-detection system, using spaCy, and then translated each (non-English) instance to English using NLLB. This resulted in an English-only version of the EXALT test set.

### 2.4.2 Approach

Throughout the competition, we were curious about how an English-only model would compare to a multi-lingual correlate. To test this, we experimented with an English only fine-tuned TwHIN-BERT. We fine-tuned the model in the same way as described with the Multilingual TwHIN-BERT (section 2.2).

## 3 Results

Table 1: Macro Test Results

| Model | F1 | Prec. | Recall |
|---|---|---|---|
| Few-Shot GPT-4 | 0.558 | 0.590 | 0.551 |
| TwHIN-BERT ml | 0.511 | 0.504 | 0.534 |
| GPT-4 Decider | 0.573 | 0.575 | 0.586 |
| TwHIN-BERT en | 0.440 | 0.447 | 0.495 |
| Baseline | 0.4476 | - | - |

The results in Table 1 show that the ensemble system with a GPT-4 decider achieved the highest performance with an F1 score of 0.573. Individually, the Few-Shot GPT-4 and TwHIN-BERT ml models scored lower, with F1 scores of 0.558 and 0.511 respectively. Thus, the ensemble method effectively enhanced the overall accuracy of emotion detection. These models also performed better than the EXALT organizer's baseline provided, which used inference on XLM-RoBERTa-base.

Our TwHIN-BERT en results, on the other hand, demonstrate that the English-only model performed worse than the rest, at 0.440. The TwHIN-BERT en, in fact, also performed slightly worse the organizer's baseline.

## 4 Discussion

As shown in the results section, the GPT-4 ensemble outperforms TwHIN-BERT and GPT-4 alone with respect to both F1 and recall. Few-shot GPT-4 had the highest precision and second highest recall and F1 scores followed by TwHIN-BERT. Focusing first on the three models attempted prior to the submission deadline, confusion matrices for all three models on the evaluation data are shown in Figures 2, 3, and 4. Compared to TWHIN-BERT, GPT-4 had higher accuracy in predicting Neutral (0.79 vs 0.57) and Fear (0.56 vs 0.39) labels, while TwHIN-BERT had better accuracy predicting Love (0.36 vs 0.49) and Sadness (0.45 vs 0.58) labels. Having access to decisions from both the previous models perhaps explains why the GPT-4 Decider model had the best performance with the highest accuracy across all labels aside from Sadness and Love (where TwHIN-BERT had the best results), and Neutral (where GPT-4 had the best results).

Improvement in the classification of Neutral labels appears to be the main contributor to the superior performance of the models making use of GPT-4 (GPT-4, GPT-4 Decider). However, the confusion matrices for the output of these two models also show relatively high rates of miss-classifying non-Neutral tweets as Neutral, suggesting that the GPT-4 models show a general over-reliance on the Neutral label. Given that there were more Neutral tweets in the evaluation data ('Neutral': 916, 'Joy': 433, 'Anger': 614, 'Sadness': 270, 'Fear': 77, 'Love': 190) compared to any other category, this also may account for the boost in performance seen by the GPT-4 models compared to TwHIN-BERT.

Across all three models, at least for the more common labels such as Joy and Anger, miss-classifications tended to cluster roughly by sentiment. For example, incorrect classifications of the Joy label were most often given to tweets labeled as Love or Neutral, and incorrect classifications of the Anger label were most often given to tweets labeled as Sadness or Fear. This suggests that even incorrect classifications often at least contained a similar sentiment (negative vs positive) to the actual label.

Moving on to the TwHIN-BERT model, the TwHIN-BERT en model performed far worse than all others on the test and development sets. The model was trained on an down-sampled dataset (TwHIN-BERT en), saw far fewer examples during fine-tuning than our multi-lingual model, and its performance suffered, proving to be our worst performing model.

A confusion matrix for the TwHIN-BERT en model is given below in Figure 5. TwHIN-BERT en manifests a bias towards predicting "Neutral" labels, despite training on a balanced dataset (each label had 616 samples). Consequently, it is possible that translation dilutes the intensity or polarity of some affect indicators. Perhaps more unexpected, is the same model's apparent tendency towards predicting "Sadness," and apparent aversion to predicting "Fear". We have fewer hypotheses for the

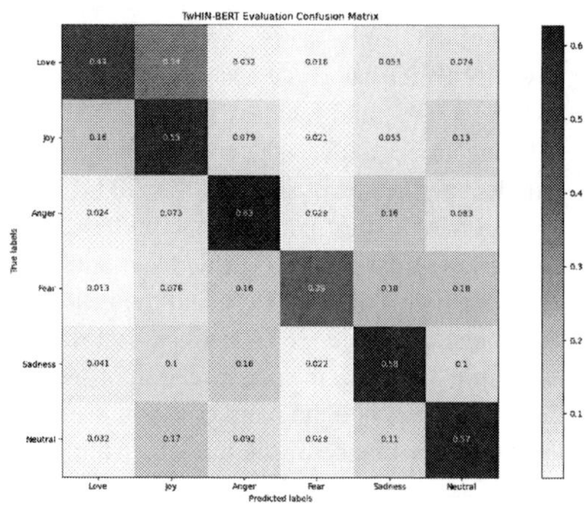


Figure 2: TwHIN-BERT ml Confusion Matrix

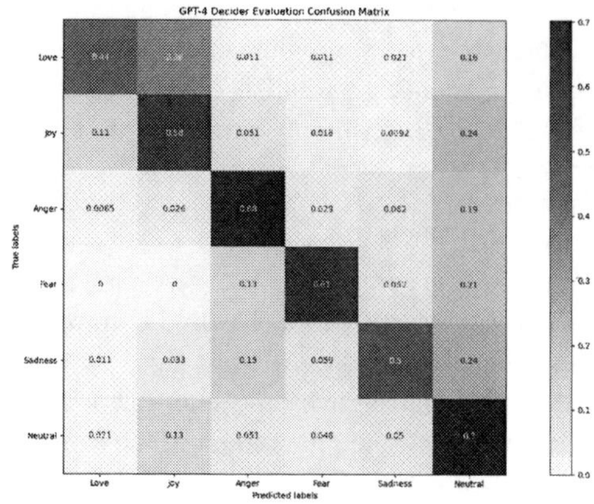


Figure 4: GPT-4 Decider Confusion Matrix

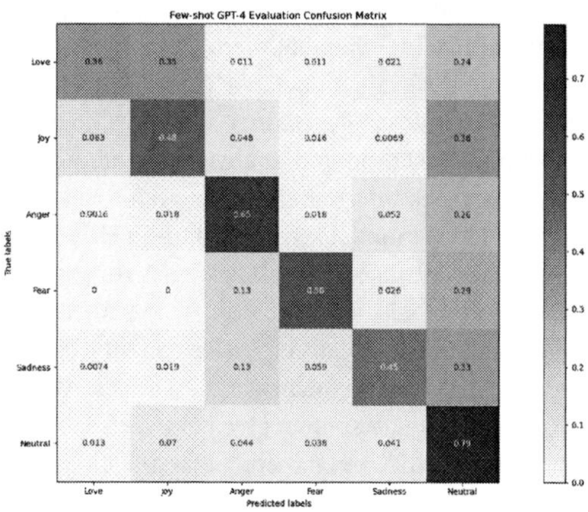


Figure 3: Few-shot GPT-4 Confusion Matrix

potential source of bias in these instances. Perhaps perceived "Fear" indicators are particularly challenging to translate, and perceived "Sadness" indicators are over-represented.

## 5 Conclusion

Novel, GPT-4 based models seem to out-perform straight-forward fine-tuning of the BERT based TwHIN-BERT even in few-shot contexts. The performance difference between the English-only and multi-lingual fine-tuned models surprised us. These results indicate that better future results might lie in prompt-based approaches to large language models. To that end, we foresee a wide range of experimentation in that domain, from chain of thought, to translation, multi-language prompting, and ensemble methods.

## 6 Limitations

We wanted to explore how fine-tuning a large language model like Llama-3 might perform, especially in comparison to few-shot GPT-4. Unfortunately, we could not acquire access to a GPU sufficient for that task in time. It seems possible, however, that ensemble and prompting techniques could prove more efficient or even superior to fine-tuning based approaches. We found late in our system building that continued pre-training on the test dataset domain, prior to fine-tuning, likely improves performance (Gururangan et al., 2020), and ideally we would like to test this approach as well.

Labeling emotions based off of short text, such as tweets, is highly subjective and it can be difficult to be consistent. This is a limitation of the shared task dataset and also extends to our model which is trained on this biased data.

One other notable limitation of our current systems is the reliance on translated datasets and data augmentation techniques that might not fully capture the nuanced expression of emotions across different languages and cultures. Translation errors and the inherent challenges of cross-lingual data can lead to misrepresentations of sentiment, affecting the models ability to accurately classify emotions in languages not originally included in the training set. This limitation highlights the need for better translation and data processing approaches that can more accurately reflect the true emotional content of different languages and cultural contexts.

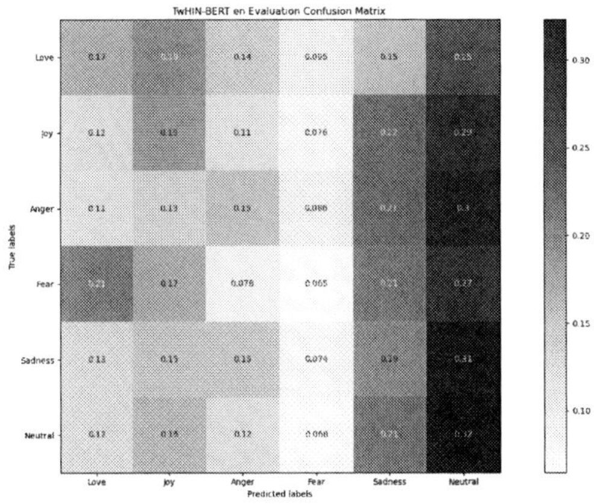


Figure 5: TwHIN-BERT en Confusion Matrix

## References


Francisca Adoma Acheampong, Henry Nunoo-Mensah, and Wenyu Chen. 2021. Transformer models for text-based emotion detection: a review of bert-based approaches. *Artificial Intelligence Review*, 54:5789–5829.

Marta R. Costa-jussà, James Cross, Onur Çelebi, Maha Elbayad, Kenneth Heafield, Kevin Heffernan, Elahe Kalbassi, Janice Lam, Daniel Licht, Jean Maillard, Anna Sun, Skyler Wang, Guillaume Wenzek, Al Youngblood, Bapi Akula, Loic Barrault, Gabriel Mejia Gonzalez, Prangthip Hansanti, John Hoffman, Semarley Jarrett, Kaushik Ram Sadagopan, Dirk Rowe, Shannon Spruit, Chau Tran, Pierre Andrews, Necip Fazil Ayan, Shruti Bhosale, Sergey Edunov, Angela Fan, Cynthia Gao, Vedanuj Goswami, Francisco Guzmán, Philipp Koehn, Alexandre Mourachko, Christophe Ropers, Safiyyah Saleem, Holger Schwenk, and Jeff Wang. 2022. No language left behind: Scaling human-centered machine translation. *Preprint*, arXiv:2207.04672.

Suchin Gururangan, Ana Marasovi, Swabha Swayamdipta, Kyle Lo, Iz Beltagy, Doug Downey, and Noah A. Smith. 2020. Don't stop pretraining: Adapt language models to domains and tasks. *Preprint*, arXiv:2004.10964.

Aaron Maladry, Pranaydeep Singh, and Els Lefever. 2024. Findings of the wassa 2024 exalt shared task on explainability for cross-lingual emotion in tweets. In *Proceedings of the 14th Workshop of on Computational Approaches to Subjectivity, Sentiment Social Media Analysis@ACL 2024*.

Saif Mohammad, Felipe Bravo-Marquez, Mohammad Salameh, and Svetlana Kiritchenko. 2018. SemEval-2018 task 1: Affect in tweets. In *Proceedings of the 12th International Workshop on Semantic Evaluation*, pages 1–17, New Orleans, Louisiana. Association for Computational Linguistics.

R. Venkatakrishnan, M. Goodarzi, and M. A. Canbaz. 2023. Exploring large language models' emotion detection abilities: Use cases from the middle east. In *2023 IEEE Conference on Artificial Intelligence (CAI)*, pages 241–244, Santa Clara, CA, USA. IEEE.

Yue Xu, Hua Cao, and Wei Du. 2022. A survey of cross-lingual sentiment analysis: Methodologies, models and evaluations. *Data Science and Engineering*, 7:279–299.

Xinyang Zhang, Yury Malkov, Omar Florez, Serim Park, Brian McWilliams, Jiawei Han, and Ahmed El-Kishky. 2022. Twhin-bert: A socially-enriched pre-trained language model for multilingual tweet representations. *arXiv preprint arXiv:2209.07562*.

# Enhancing Cross-Lingual Emotion Detection with Data Augmentation and Token-Label Mapping

**Jinghui Zhang**[1] and **Yuan Zhao** [1] and **Siqin Zhang**[1] and **Ruijing Zhao**[1] and **Siyu Bao**[1]
[1]China Telecom Cloud Technology Co., Ltd
{zhangjh33,zhaoyuan1,zhangsq20,zhaorj1, baosy}@chinatelecom.cn

## Abstract

Cross-lingual emotion detection faces challenges such as imbalanced label distribution, data scarcity, cultural and linguistic differences, figurative language, and the opaqueness of pretrained language models. This paper presents our approach to the EXALT shared task at WASSA 2024, focusing on emotion transferability across languages and trigger word identification. We employ data augmentation techniques, including back-translation and synonym replacement, to address data scarcity and imbalance issues in the emotion detection subtask. For the emotion trigger identification subtask, we utilize token and label mapping to capture emotional information at the subword level. Our system achieves competitive performance, ranking 13th, 1st, and 2nd in the Emotion Detection, Binary Trigger Word Detection, and Numerical Trigger Word Detection tasks.

## 1 Introduction

Emotion detection in text has attracted significant attention in recent years due to its diverse applications (Nandwani and Verma, 2021). The growing presence of multilingual and code-mixed content on social media has emphasized the need for cross-lingual emotion detection systems (Balahur and Turchi, 2014; Dashtipour et al., 2016).

However, developing accurate and interpretable cross-lingual emotion detection models presents several challenges, including the limited availability of labeled data in many languages (Xue et al., 2020), cultural and linguistic variations in emotion expression (Hareli et al., 2015), the use of figurative language and sarcasm in social media (Bouazizi and Ohtsuki, 2019; Reyes et al., 2012), and the lack of transparency in large pre-trained language models (PLMs) (Hase and Bansal, 2020; Feder et al., 2021).

To tackle these challenges and foster research on interpretable cross-lingual emotion detection, the EXALT shared task[1] was organized at WASSA 2024. EXALT focuses on the transferability of emotion information across languages and the identification of emotion triggers, encouraging the development of interpretable and explainable emotion detection systems.

This paper presents our approach to the EXALT shared task. The XLM-RoBERTa-XL (Goyal et al., 2021) model with encoder-only architecture is selected to better capture the emotion information contained in the context. For the emotion detection sub-task, we employ data augmentation techniques, such as back-translation and synonym replacement, to address the imbalanced and insufficient training data. For the emotion trigger identification subtask, we utilize token and label mapping to align subword-level predictions with word-level labels.

## 2 Related Work

### 2.1 Emotion Detection

Emotion detection aims to identify the emotional states expressed in text, such as joy, sadness, anger, and fear (Acheampong et al., 2020). Compared to sentiment analysis, which focuses on the overall polarity of text (positive, negative, or neutral), emotion detection provides a more fine-grained understanding of the affective information conveyed in text.

Traditional approaches to emotion detection relied on rule-based methods and machine learning algorithms, such as Naïve Bayes, Support Vector Machines (SVM), and decision trees (Alswaidan and Menai, 2020).Recently, deep learning models, including Convolutional Neural Networks (CNNs), Recurrent Neural Networks (RNNs), and Transformers, have achieved state-of-the-art performance on emotion detection tasks by learning rich feature representations from text (Birjali et al., 2021). However, the success of these models relies

[1]https://lt3.ugent.be/exalt/



*Proceedings of the 14th Workshop on Computational Approaches to Subjectivity, Sentiment, & Social Media Analysis*, pages 528–533
August 15, 2024 ©2024 Association for Computational Linguistics

heavily on large annotated datasets, which are time-consuming and expensive to collect, especially for low-resource languages and domains. Researchers are exploring techniques such as transfer learning (Hazarika et al., 2021), few-shot learning, and data augmentation to address this challenge and improve emotion detection performance in low-resource settings.

### 2.2 Data Augmentation

Data augmentation techniques have been widely adopted to address the issue of data scarcity in various natural language processing tasks, aiming to generate synthetic training data and improve model performance (Pellicer et al., 2023). These methods operate at different levels of granularity, such as word-level, phrase-level, and document-level.

At the word level, techniques like EDA (Wei and Zou, 2019) generate new examples by manipulating words or embeddings. Phrase-level augmentation, e.g., PPDB Augmenter (Ganitkevitch et al., 2013; Pavlick et al., 2015), uses paraphrase databases to replace phrases with semantic equivalents, adding linguistic diversity. Document-level techniques include back-translation (Mallinson et al., 2017), paraphrasing with models like T5 (Raffel et al., 2020) and BART (Lewis et al., 2019; Dopierre et al., 2021), and text generation using language models such as Llama (Touvron et al., 2023) and GPT-4 (Achiam et al., 2023).

### 2.3 Cross-lingual Transfer Learning

Cross-lingual transfer learning has emerged as a promising approach to overcome the data scarcity issue in low-resource languages. Methods such as machine translation (Demirtas and Pechenizkiy, 2013) and multilingual PLMs (Lewis et al., 2019; Xue et al., 2020) have been used to transfer knowledge from high-resource to low-resource languages.

However, these methods often fail to capture language-specific nuances in emotion expression and may suffer from translation errors. Adversarial training (Chen et al., 2018) and contrastive learning (Lin et al., 2023) have been proposed to learn language-invariant representations, but they often require parallel data or emotion lexicons.

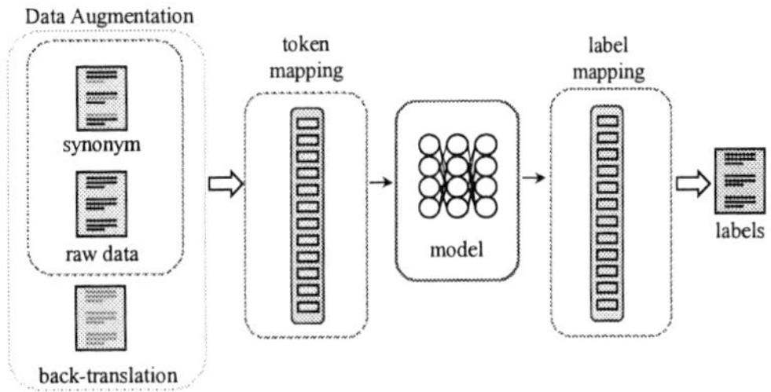


Figure 1: The overview of our work. The yellow and green dashed boxes represent the methods used in Task 1 and Tasks 2/3, respectively.

### 2.4 Interpretability in Natural Language Processing

Interpretability has gained significant attention in natural language processing, particularly with the increasing complexity of deep learning models (Danilevsky et al., 2020). Various approaches have been proposed to provide explanations for model predictions, such as attention mechanisms (Bibal et al., 2022), saliency maps (Wallace et al., 2020), and post-hoc explanations (Madsen et al., 2022).

However, most existing methods focus on providing explanations at the input feature level and may not offer fine-grained interpretability at the token level. In the context of emotion detection, identifying the specific words or phrases that trigger the predicted emotions is crucial for understanding the model's behavior.

## 3 Methods

This section illustrates our approach and main work, as shown in Figure 1. We focus on describing our data augmentation and token and label mapping methods. The details of the shared task can be found in this work (Maladry et al., 2024).

Briefly, Task 1 is sequence-classification task, where there are 6 possible emotion classes in the datasets. Task 2 and 3 are token-classification tasks that are focused on explaining which words are used to express the emotion. The training dataset contains only English data, while the test dataset contains five languages, i.e. Dutch, Russian, Spanish, English, and French.

### 3.1 Data Augmentation

The dataset for Task 1 includes 5,000 training samples, 500 development samples, and 2,500 test samples. For Tasks 2 and 3, the dataset consists of 3,000 training samples, 300 development samples, and 832 test samples.

| Label | Raw | Back-translation | Synonym |
|---|---|---|---|
| Anger | 1,028 | 192 | 1,028 |
| Fear | 143 | 576 | 143 |
| Joy | 1,293 | 239 | 1,290 |
| Love | 579 | 144 | 578 |
| Neutral | 1,397 | 259 | 1,396 |
| Sadness | 560 | 658 | 560 |

Table 1: Statistics of the labels distribution on the training set for Task 1.

The original data presents the characteristics of imbalanced label distribution, as shown in Table 1. For example, the proportion of Fear class is less than 3%. In order to mitigate this characteristic and enhance the diversity of the data to improve the generalisation of the model, we apply two data augmentation methods as detailed as follows. Other data augmentation methods would break sentence syntax, such as random deletion, or change emotion information, such as text generation with PLMs, and are therefore not considered in this work.

**Back-translation**: The original training samples are translated into other languages, in this case Dutch, French, Spanish and Russian, and then back into English to generate new instances. We adopted a stratified sampling approach to mitigate the imbalance in label distribution. Notably, back-translation may alter the position of trigger words, causing misalignment with their corresponding labels.

**Synonym replacement**: Words are randomly selected in the original samples and then replaced with their synonyms. In this paper, we implemented synonym replacement using the NLTK WordNet corpus (Loper and Bird, 2002). Notably, synonym replacement may alter the number of words, which lead to misalignment of the augmented data with the original labels.

We use DeepL to complete the back-translation. In Task 1, 2,068 new instances are added via back-translation, while 4,995 instances are added via synonym replacement. The details are shown in Table 1. In Task 2 and 3, 2,291 instances are added through synonym replacement.

### 3.2 Token and Label Mapping

The mapping between each subword and its corresponding input word is recorded when the tokenizer processes the input data. The label of the subword is assigned to be the same as the label of its corresponding word. During prediction, the label of each word is set to the maximum value among the predictions of all its corresponding subwords. Figure 2 illustrates the configuration of token and label mapping.

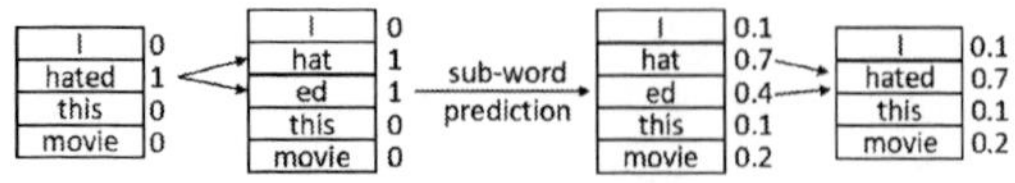


Figure 2: Configuration of token and label mapping.

By applying labels at the subword level, the emotional information of the text is captured more fine-grained. During the prediction phase, taking the maximum value of the subword predictions as the label of the corresponding word effectively integrates the emotional information at the subword level. Moreover, this method is easy to implement and compatible with various PLMs.

For Task 3, we map the output of the classifier layer of the fine-tuned language model to word-level numerical results. For Task 2, we compute the softmax of the classifier layer output, then map it into word-level numerical probabilities and finally convert it to a binary result using a threshold.

We have shared the main scripts of this paper on Github[2] for other researchers.

## 4 Experiments

We conducted experiments on NPU training machines, equipped with 8 Ascend 910B 64G NPUs, to compare the performance of multiple PLMs and investigate the impact of hyperparameter settings, data augmentation strategies on cross-lingual emotion detection.

### 4.1 Comparison of Pre-trained Language Models

Although many current PLMs adopt the decoder-only architecture, this architecture has limited support for natural language understanding tasks. In our tasks, we consider the information in the subsequent text to be equally important as the preceding text. Therefore, we compared multiple encoder-only models pre-trained on Dutch, Russian, Spanish, English, and French corpora to better understand the contextual content and cross-lingual emotion information.

We fine-tuned these models on the original data without data augmentation and tried different parameter freezing strategies. Figure 3 demonstrates that that larger models achieved better cross-lingual

[2] https://github.com/QQJellyy/CTcloud-EXALT-WASSA2024

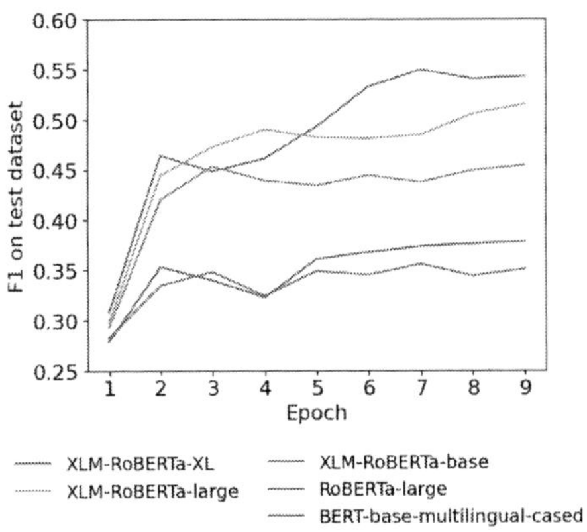


Figure 3: F1 on test dataset of each PLM for Task 1. All parameters of each PLM are fine-tuned using a learning rate of 4e-5 and a batch size of 128.

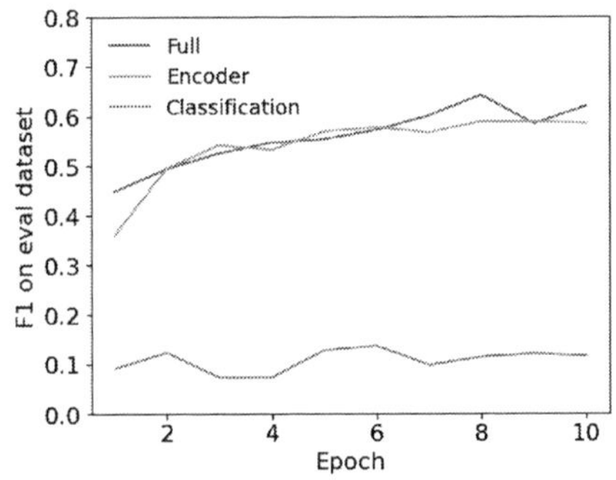


Figure 4: F1 of XLM-RoBERTa-large on eval dataset of each parameter freezing strategies for Task 1. Full, Encoder and Classification represent parameters of all layers, parameters of encoder layers and parameters of output layer are trainable, respectively.

emotion detection ability. In the meanwhile, Figure 4 suggests that the PLMs lack emotion detection capabilities, as the results by training only on the classification layer are significantly lower than the other training strategies.

Training on the English dataset significantly improves emotion detection abilities on five languages, indicating that emotion information has been effectively transferred across languages. We explain this phenomenon with a task analogy theory, e.g., 'Queen = King + (Woman-Man)' (Ethayarajh et al., 2018), where cross-lingual capabilities are inherent in PLMs, and emotion detection capability is attained through fine-tuning. The fine-tuned models integrate these capabilities and exhibit cross-lingual emotion detection abilities.

## 4.2 Hyperparameter Optimisation

We conduct hyperparameter optimisation on XLM-RoBERTa-large and employ an orthogonal approach to optimize each hyperparameter. As shown in Table 2, a learning rate of 4e-5 achieves the best classification results for Task 1. Learning rates that are too large or too small can be less effective. Similarly, we find that a batch size of 64 yields the best detection results.

| Rank | Learning Rate | F1 |
|---|---|---|
| 1 | 2e-6 | 0.3221 |
| 2 | 5e-6 | 0.4676 |
| 3 | 1e-5 | 0.4821 |
| 4 | 2e-5 | 0.5284 |
| 5 | 3e-5 | 0.5318 |
| 6 | 4e-5 | **0.5705** |
| 7 | 5e-5 | 0.4676 |

Table 2: F1 of XLM-RoBERTa-large on eval dataset for Task 1 after being fine-tuned without augmented dataset for 10 epochs. The batch size is 128.

| Task | Augmentation | F1 |
|---|---|---|
| Task1 | Null | 0.5242 |
| Task1 | Synonym | 0.5420 |
| Task1 | Translation | 0.5393 |
| Task1 | Synonym + Translation | **0.5432** |
| Task2 | Null | 0.6042 |
| Task2 | Synonym | **0.6158** |
| Task3 | Null | 0.6833 |
| Task3 | Synonym | **0.6972** |

Table 3: F1 of XLM-RoBERTa-XL on test dataset with different data augmentation. All parameters of each scenario are fine-tuned using a learning rate of 4e-5 and a batch size of 64.

For Task 1, we train the XLM-RoBERTa-XL model on the augmented data using the optimal hyperparameters described above. For Tasks 2 and 3, we use the same hyperparameters and further train the model saved from Task 1. When making predictions, we use the default value of 0.1 as the threshold for identifying trigger words.

## 4.3 Data Augmentation

Table 3 demonstrates that both synonym replacement and back-translation improve the model's performance. Synonym replacement enriches the training corpus, while back-translation implicitly introduces information about the target test language without altering the language of the training data.

## 5 Conclusion

In this paper, we address the label imbalance issue and enhanced data diversity in the training data by employing data augmentation techniques, including back-translation and synonym replacement. The augmented data is used to fine-tune the XLM-RoBERTa-XL model, achieving competitive results in all three tasks: 13th, 1st, and 2nd places in Task 1, Task 2, and Task 3, respectively. These results demonstrate the effectiveness of our methods for the transferability of emotion information across languages and the identification of emotion triggers.

The reason why we choose XLM-RoBERTa-XL model is that the encoder architecture is able to capture the context of the data, making it well-suited for token-level tasks. Furthermore, we select PLMs that have been trained on five languages to ensure that the models have the transferability of emotion information across languages, potentially contributing to the improved performance of our proposed system.

## 6 Limitations

In this paper, we assume that different models behave similarly, e.g., the optimal hyperparameters of XLM-RoBERTa-XL and XLM-RoBERTa-large are similar. However, this may not be the case in practice.

We use the default value of 0.1 as the threshold for identifying the trigger word in Task 2 and apply two data augmentation techniques, i.e. back-translation and synonym replacement. In the future, we can explore the impact of different classification threshold on model performance and try other data augmentation methods. Moreover, we can also go deep into model enhancing techniques on cross-lingual emotion detection task, such as task analogy and model fusion.

## References


Francisca Adoma Acheampong, Chen Wenyu, and Henry Nunoo-Mensah. 2020. Text-based emotion detection: Advances, challenges, and opportunities. *Engineering Reports*, 2(7):e12189.

Josh Achiam, Steven Adler, Sandhini Agarwal, Lama Ahmad, Ilge Akkaya, Florencia Leoni Aleman, Diogo Almeida, Janko Altenschmidt, Sam Altman, Shyamal Anadkat, et al. 2023. Gpt-4 technical report. *arXiv preprint arXiv:2303.08774*.

Nourah Alswaidan and Mohamed El Bachir Menai. 2020. A survey of state-of-the-art approaches for emotion recognition in text. *Knowledge and Information Systems*, 62(8):2937–2987.

Alexandra Balahur and Marco Turchi. 2014. Comparative experiments using supervised learning and machine translation for multilingual sentiment analysis. *Computer Speech & Language*, 28(1):56–75.

Adrien Bibal, Rémi Cardon, David Alfter, Rodrigo Wilkens, Xiaoou Wang, Thomas François, and Patrick Watrin. 2022. Is attention explanation? an introduction to the debate. In *Proceedings of the 60th Annual Meeting of the Association for Computational Linguistics (Volume 1: Long Papers)*, pages 3889–3900.

Marouane Birjali, Mohammed Kasri, and Abderrahim Beni-Hssane. 2021. A comprehensive survey on sentiment analysis: Approaches, challenges and trends. *Knowledge-Based Systems*, 226:107134.

Mondher Bouazizi and Tomoaki Ohtsuki. 2019. Multi-class sentiment analysis on twitter: Classification performance and challenges. *Big Data Mining and Analytics*, 2(3):181–194.

Xilun Chen, Yu Sun, Ben Athiwaratkun, Claire Cardie, and Kilian Weinberger. 2018. Adversarial deep averaging networks for cross-lingual sentiment classification. *Transactions of the Association for Computational Linguistics*, 6:557–570.

Marina Danilevsky, Kun Qian, Ranit Aharonov, Yannis Katsis, Ban Kawas, and Prithviraj Sen. 2020. A survey of the state of explainable ai for natural language processing. *arXiv preprint arXiv:2010.00711*.

Kia Dashtipour, Soujanya Poria, Amir Hussain, Erik Cambria, Ahmad YA Hawalah, Alexander Gelbukh, and Qiang Zhou. 2016. Multilingual sentiment analysis: state of the art and independent comparison of techniques. *Cognitive computation*, 8:757–771.

Erkin Demirtas and Mykola Pechenizkiy. 2013. Cross-lingual polarity detection with machine translation. In *Proceedings of the Second International Workshop on Issues of Sentiment Discovery and Opinion Mining*, pages 1–8.

Thomas Dopierre, Christophe Gravier, and Wilfried Logerais. 2021. Protaugment: Intent detection meta-learning through unsupervised diverse paraphrasing. In *Proceedings of the 59th Annual Meeting of the Association for Computational Linguistics and the 11th International Joint Conference on Natural Language Processing (Volume 1: Long Papers)*, pages 2454–2466. Association for Computational Linguistics.

Kawin Ethayarajh, David Duvenaud, and Graeme Hirst. 2018. Towards understanding linear word analogies. *arXiv preprint arXiv:1810.04882*.

Amir Feder, Nadav Oved, Uri Shalit, and Roi Reichart. 2021. Causalm: Causal model explanation through counterfactual language models. *Computational Linguistics*, 47(2):333–386.

Juri Ganitkevitch, Benjamin Van Durme, and Chris Callison-Burch. 2013. Ppdb: The paraphrase database. In *Proceedings of the 2013 conference of the north american chapter of the association for computational linguistics: Human language technologies*, pages 758–764.

Naman Goyal, Jingfei Du, Myle Ott, Giri Anantharaman, and Alexis Conneau. 2021. Larger-scale transformers for multilingual masked language modeling. *arXiv preprint arXiv:2105.00572*.

Shlomo Hareli, Konstantinos Kafetsios, and Ursula Hess. 2015. A cross-cultural study on emotion expression and the learning of social norms. *Frontiers in psychology*, 6:152022.

Peter Hase and Mohit Bansal. 2020. Evaluating explainable ai: Which algorithmic explanations help users predict model behavior? *arXiv preprint arXiv:2005.01831*.

Devamanyu Hazarika, Soujanya Poria, Roger Zimmermann, and Rada Mihalcea. 2021. Conversational transfer learning for emotion recognition. *Information Fusion*, 65:1–12.

Mike Lewis, Yinhan Liu, Naman Goyal, Marjan Ghazvininejad, Abdelrahman Mohamed, Omer Levy, Ves Stoyanov, and Luke Zettlemoyer. 2019. Bart: Denoising sequence-to-sequence pre-training for natural language generation, translation, and comprehension. *arXiv preprint arXiv:1910.13461*.

Nankai Lin, Yingwen Fu, Xiaotian Lin, Dong Zhou, Aimin Yang, and Shengyi Jiang. 2023. Cl-xabsa: Contrastive learning for cross-lingual aspect-based sentiment analysis. *IEEE/ACM Transactions on Audio, Speech, and Language Processing*.

Edward Loper and Steven Bird. 2002. Nltk: The natural language toolkit. *arXiv preprint cs/0205028*.

Andreas Madsen, Siva Reddy, and Sarath Chandar. 2022. Post-hoc interpretability for neural nlp: A survey. *ACM Computing Surveys*, 55(8):1–42.

Aaron Maladry, Pranaydeep Singh, and Els Lefever. 2024. Findings of the wassa 2024 exalt shared task on explainability for cross-lingual emotion in tweets. In *Proceedings of the 14th Workshop of on Computational Approaches to Subjectivity, Sentiment & Social Media Analysis@ACL 2024*, Bangkok, Thailand.

Jonathan Mallinson, Rico Sennrich, and Mirella Lapata. 2017. Paraphrasing revisited with neural machine translation. In *Proceedings of the 15th Conference of the European Chapter of the Association for Computational Linguistics: Volume 1, Long Papers*, pages 881–893.

Pansy Nandwani and Rupali Verma. 2021. A review on sentiment analysis and emotion detection from text. *Social network analysis and mining*, 11(1):81.

Ellie Pavlick, Pushpendre Rastogi, Juri Ganitkevitch, Benjamin Van Durme, and Chris Callison-Burch. 2015. Ppdb 2.0: Better paraphrase ranking, fine-grained entailment relations, word embeddings, and style classification. In *Proceedings of the 53rd Annual Meeting of the Association for Computational Linguistics and the 7th International Joint Conference on Natural Language Processing (Volume 2: Short Papers)*, pages 425–430.

Lucas Francisco Amaral Orosco Pellicer, Taynan Maier Ferreira, and Anna Helena Reali Costa. 2023. Data augmentation techniques in natural language processing. *Applied Soft Computing*, 132:109803.

Colin Raffel, Noam Shazeer, Adam Roberts, Katherine Lee, Sharan Narang, Michael Matena, Yanqi Zhou, Wei Li, and Peter J Liu. 2020. Exploring the limits of transfer learning with a unified text-to-text transformer. *Journal of machine learning research*, 21(140):1–67.

Antonio Reyes, Paolo Rosso, and Davide Buscaldi. 2012. From humor recognition to irony detection: The figurative language of social media. *Data & Knowledge Engineering*, 74:1–12.

Hugo Touvron, Thibaut Lavril, Gautier Izacard, Xavier Martinet, Marie-Anne Lachaux, Timothée Lacroix, Baptiste Rozière, Naman Goyal, Eric Hambro, Faisal Azhar, et al. 2023. Llama: Open and efficient foundation language models. *arXiv preprint arXiv:2302.13971*.

Eric Wallace, Matt Gardner, and Sameer Singh. 2020. Interpreting predictions of nlp models. In *Proceedings of the 2020 Conference on Empirical Methods in Natural Language Processing: Tutorial Abstracts*, pages 20–23.

Jason Wei and Kai Zou. 2019. Eda: Easy data augmentation techniques for boosting performance on text classification tasks. *arXiv preprint arXiv:1901.11196*.

Linting Xue, Noah Constant, Adam Roberts, Mihir Kale, Rami Al-Rfou, Aditya Siddhant, Aditya Barua, and Colin Raffel. 2020. mt5: A massively multilingual pre-trained text-to-text transformer. *arXiv preprint arXiv:2010.11934*.

# Author Index